HARPER COLLINS
SPANISH
DICTIONARY

SPANISH
DICTIONARY

Collins

ISBN 0-06-085173-2

The HarperCollins website address is
www.harpercollins.com

The HarperCollins UK website address is
www.fireandwater.com

Collins
An Imprint of HarperCollinsPublishers
10 East 53rd Street, New York, New York 10022-5299

first published 1990
second edition 2000

First Harper Resource printing: 2000

Typeset by Morton Word Processing Ltd, Scarborough
Printed in the United States of America

This book is part of the Collins Reference Library.

ÍNDICE

CONTENTS

INTRODUCCIÓN

Estamos muy satisfechos de que hayas decidido comprar el Diccionario de Inglés Collins y esperamos que lo disfrutes y que te sirva de gran ayuda ya sea en el colegio, en el trabajo, en tus vacaciones o en casa.

Esta introducción pretende darte algunas indicaciones para ayudarte a sacar el mayor provecho de este diccionario; no sólo de su extenso vocabulario, sino de toda la información que te proporciona cada entrada. Esta te ayudará a leer y comprender — y también a comunicarte y a expresarte — en inglés moderno.

El Diccionario de Inglés Collins comienza con una lista de abreviaturas utilizadas en el texto y con una ilustración de los sonidos representados por los símbolos fonéticos. Al final del diccionario encontrarás una tabla de los verbos irregulares del inglés, y para terminar, una sección sobre el uso de los números y de las expresiones de tiempo.

EL MANEJO DE TU DICCIONARIO COLLINS

La amplia información que te ofrece este diccionario aparece presentada en distintas tipografías, con caracteres de diversos tamaños y con distintos símbolos, abreviaturas y paréntesis. Los apartados siguientes explican las reglas y símbolos utilizados.

Entradas

Las palabras que consultas en el diccionario — las "entradas" — aparecen ordenadas alfabéticamente y en **caracteres gruesos** para una identificación más rápida. Las dos palabras que ocupan el margen superior de cada página indican la primera y la última entrada de la página en cuestión.

La información sobre el uso o la forma de determinadas entradas aparece entre paréntesis, detrás de la transcripción fonética, y generalmente en forma abreviada y en cursiva (p.ej.: (*fam*), (*COM*)).

En algunos casos se ha considerado oportuno agrupar palabras de una misma familia (**nación, nacionalismo; accept, acceptance**) bajo una misma entrada, en caracteres gruesos de tamaño algo más pequeño que los de la entrada principal.
Las expresiones de uso corriente en las que aparece una entrada se dan en negrita (p.ej.: **to be in a hurry**).

Símbolos fonéticos

La transcripción fonética de cada entrada (que indica su pronunciación) aparece entre corchetes, inmediatamente después de la entrada (p.ej.: **knead** [ni:d]). En la página xiii encontrarás una lista de los símbolos fonéticos utilizados en este diccionario.

Traducciones

Las traducciones de las entradas aparecen en caracteres normales, y en los casos en los que existen significados o usos diferentes, éstos aparecen separados mediante un punto y coma. A menudo encontrarás también otras palabras en cursiva y entre paréntesis antes de las traducciones. Estas sugieren contextos en los que la entrada podría aparecer (p.ej.: **rough** (*voice*) o (*weather*)) o proporcionan sinónimos (p.ej.: **rough** (*violent*)).

Palabras clave

Particular relevancia reciben ciertas palabras inglesas y españolas que han sido consideradas palabras "clave" en cada lengua. Estas pueden, por ejemplo, ser de utilización muy corriente o tener distintos usos (**de, haber; get, that**). La combinación de rombos ♦ y números te permitirá distinguir las diferentes categorías gramaticales y los diferentes significados. Las indicaciones en cursiva y entre paréntesis proporcionan además importante información adicional.

Información gramatical

Las categorías gramaticales aparecen en forma abreviada y en cursiva después de la transcripción fonética de cada entrada (*vt, adv, conj*).

También se indican la forma femenina y los plurales irregulares de los sustantivos del inglés (**child, ~ren**).

INTRODUCTION

We are delighted you have decided to buy the Collins Spanish Dictionary and hope you will enjoy and benefit from using it at school, at home, on holiday or at work.

This introduction gives you a few tips on how to get the most out of your dictionary — not simply from its comprehensive wordlist but also from the information provided in each entry. This will help you to read and understand modern Spanish, as well as communicate and express yourself in the language.

The Collins Spanish Dictionary begins by listing the abbreviations used in the text and illustrating the sounds shown by the phonetic symbols. You will find Spanish verb tables at the back, followed by a final section on numbers and time expressions.

USING YOUR COLLINS DICTIONARY

A wealth of information is presented in the dictionary, using various typefaces, sizes of type, symbols, abbreviations and brackets. The conventions and symbols used are explained in the following sections.

Headwords

The words you look up in a dictionary — "headwords" — are listed alphabetically. They are printed in **bold type** for rapid identification. The two headwords appearing at the top of each page indicate the first and last word dealt with on the page in question.

Information about the usage or form of certain headwords is given in brackets after the phonetic spelling. This usually appears in abbreviated form and in italics (e.g. (*fam*), (*COMM*)).

Where appropriate, words related to headwords are grouped in the same entry (**nación, nacionalismo; accept, acceptance**) in a slightly smaller bold type than the headword.

Common expressions in which the headword appears are shown in a different bold roman type (e.g. **hacer calor**).

Phonetic spellings

The phonetic spelling of each headword (indicating its pronunciation) is given in square brackets immediately after the headword (e.g. **dónde** ['donde]). A list of these symbols is given on page xiii.

Translations

Headword translations are given in ordinary type and, where more than one meaning or usage exists, these are separated by a semi-colon. You will often find other words in italics in brackets before the translations. These offer suggested contexts in which the headword might appear (e.g.

grande (*de tamaño*) or provide synonyms (e.g. **grande** (*alto*) *o* (*distinguido*)).

"Key" words

Special status is given to certain Spanish and English words which are considered as "key" words in each language. They may, for example, occur very frequently or have several types of usage (e.g. **de, haber**). A combination of lozenges ♦ and numbers helps you to distinguish different parts of speech and different meanings. Further helpful information is provided in brackets and in italics.

Grammatical information

Parts of speech are given in abbreviated form in italics after the phonetic spellings of headwords (e.g. *vt, adv, conj*).

Genders of Spanish nouns are indicated as follows: *nm* for a masculine and *nf* for a feminine noun. Feminine and irregular plural forms of nouns are also shown (**irlandés, esa; luz,** (*pl* **luces**)).

ABREVIATURAS

ABBREVIATIONS

abreviatura	ab(b)r	abbreviation
adjetivo, locución adjetiva	adj	adjective, adjectival phrase
administración	ADMIN	administration
adverbio, locución adverbial	adv	adverb, adverbial phrase
agricultura	AGR	agriculture
América Latina	AM	Latin America
anatomía	ANAT	anatomy
arquitectura	ARQ, ARCH	architecture
el automóvil	AUT(O)	the motor car and motoring
aviación, viajes aéreos	AVIAT	flying, air travel
biología	BIO(L)	biology
botánica, flores	BOT	botany
inglés británico	BRIT	British English
química	CHEM	chemistry
comercio, finanzas, banca	COM(M)	commerce, finance, banking
informática	COMPUT	computers
conjunción	conj	conjunction
construcción	CONSTR	building
compuesto	cpd	compound element
cocina	CULIN	cookery
economía	ECON	economics
electricidad, electrónica	ELEC	electricity, electronics
enseñanza, sistema escolar y universitario	ESCOL	schooling, schools and universities
España	Esp	Spain
especialmente	esp	especially
exclamación, interjección	excl	exclamation, interjection
femenino	f	feminine
lengua familiar (! vulgar)	fam (!)	colloquial usage (! particularly offensive)
ferrocarril	FERRO	railways
uso figurado	fig	figurative use
fotografía	FOTO	photography
(verbo inglés) del cual la partícula es inseparable	fus	(phrasal verb) where the particle is inseparable
generalmente	gen	generally
geografía, geología	GEO	geography, geology
geometría	GEOM	geometry
uso familiar (! vulgar)	inf (!)	colloquial usage (! particularly offensive)
infinitivo	infin	infinitive
informática	INFORM	computers
invariable	inv	invariable
irregular	irreg	irregular
lo jurídico	JUR	law
América Latina	LAM	Latin America
gramática, lingüística	LING	grammar, linguistics
masculino	m	masculine

ABREVIATURAS

ABBREVIATIONS

matemáticas	MATH	mathematics
masculino/femenino	m/f	masculine/feminine
medicina	MED	medicine
lo militar, ejército	MIL	military matters
música	MUS	music
sustantivo, nombre	n	noun
navegación, náutica	NAUT	sailing, navigation
sustantivo numérico	num	numeral noun
complemento	obj	(grammatical) object
	o.s.	oneself
peyorativo	pey, pej	derogatory, pejorative
fotografía	PHOT	photography
fisiología	PHYSIOL	physiology
plural	pl	plural
política	POL	politics
participio de pasado	pp	past participle
preposición	prep	preposition
pronombre	pron	pronoun
psicología, psiquiatría	PSICO, PSYCH	psychology, psychiatry
tiempo pasado	pt	past tense
química	QUÍM	chemistry
ferrocarril	RAIL	railways
religión	REL	religion
	sb	somebody
enseñanza, sistema escolar y universitario	SCH	schooling, schools and universities
singular	sg	singular
España	SP	Spain
	sth	something
sujeto	su(b)j	(grammatical) subject
subjuntivo	subjun	subjunctive
tauromaquia	TAUR	bullfighting
también	tb	also
técnica, tecnología	TEC(H)	technical term, technology
telecomunicaciones	TELEC, TEL	telecommunications
imprenta, tipografía	TIP, TYP	typography, printing
televisión	TV	television
universidad	UNIV	university
inglés norteamericano	US	American English
verbo	vb	verb
verbo intransitivo	vi	intransitive verb
verbo pronominal	vr	reflexive verb
verbo transitivo	vt	transitive verb
zoología	ZOOL	zoology
marca registrada	®	registered trademark
indica un equivalente cultural	≈	introduces a cultural equivalent

SPANISH PRONUNCIATION

Consonants

c	|k|	caja	c before a, o or u is pronounced as in cat
ce, ci	|θe, θi|	cero cielo	c before e or i is pronounced as in thin
ch	|tʃ|	chiste	ch is pronounced as ch in chair
d	|d, ð|	danés ciudad	at the beginning of a phrase or after l or n, d is pronounced as in English. In any other position it is pronounced like th in the
g	|g, ɣ|	gafas paga	g before a, o or u is pronounced as in gap, if at the beginning of a phrase or after n. In other positions the sound is softened
ge, gi	|xe, xi|	gente girar	g before e or i is pronounced similar to ch in Scottish loch
h		haber	h is always silent in Spanish
j	|x|	jugar	j is pronounced similar to ch in Scottish loch
ll	|ʎ|	talle	ll is pronounced like the lli in million
ñ	|ɲ|	niño	ñ is pronounced like the ni in onion
q	|k|	que	q is pronounced as k in king
r, rr	|r, rr|	quitar garra	r is always pronounced in Spanish, unlike the silent r in dancer. rr is trilled, like a Scottish r
s	|s|	quizás isla	s is usually pronounced as in pass, but before b, d, g, l, m or n it is pronounced as in rose
v	|b, ß|	vía dividir	v is pronounced something like b. At the beginning of a phrase or after m or n it is pronounced as b in boy. In any other position the sound is softened
z	|θ|	tenaz	z is pronounced as th in thin

b, f, k, l, m, n, p, t and x are pronounced as in English.

Vowels

a	[a]	p*a*ta	not as long as *a* in f*a*r. When followed by a consonant in the same syllable (i.e. in a closed syllable), as in am*a*nte, the *a* is short, as in b*a*t
e	[e]	m*e*	like *e* in th*ey*. In a closed syllable, as in g*e*nte, the *e* is short as in p*e*t
i	[i]	p*i*no	as in m*ea*n or mach*i*ne
o	[o]	l*o*	as in l*o*cal. In a closed syllable, as in c*o*ntrol, the *o* is short as in c*o*t
u	[u]	l*u*nes	as in r*u*le. It is silent after *q*, and in *gue, gui*, unless marked *güe, güi* e.g. antig*ü*edad

Diphthongs

ai, ay	[ai]	b*ai*le	as *i* in r*i*de
au	[au]	*au*to	as *ou* in sh*ou*t
ei, ey	[ei]	bu*ey*	as *ey* in gr*ey*
eu	[eu]	d*eu*da	both elements pronounced independently [e]/[u]
oi, oy	[oi]	h*oy*	as *oy* in t*oy*

Stress

The rules of stress in Spanish are as follows:

(a) when a word ends in a vowel or in *n* or *s*, the second last syllable is stressed: pat*a*ta, pat*a*tas, c*o*me, c*o*men

(b) when a word ends in a consonant other than *n* or *s*, the stress falls on the last syllable: par*e*d, habl*a*r

(c) when the rules set out in a and b are not applied, an acute accent appears over the stressed vowel: com*ú*n, geograf*í*a, ingl*é*s

In the phonetic transcription, the symbol |'| precedes the syllable on which the stress falls.

PRONUNCIACIÓN INGLESA

Vocales y diptongos

	Ejemplo inglés	*Ejemplo español/explicación*
ɑ:	f**a**ther	Entre *a* de p**a**dre y *o* de n**o**che
ʌ	b**u**t, c**o**me	*a* muy breve
æ	m**a**n, c**a**t	Se mantienen los labios en la posición de *e* en pena y luego se pronuncia el sonido *a*
ə	f**a**ther, **a**go	Sonido indistinto parecido a una *e* u *o* casi mudas
ə:	b**i**rd, h**ea**rd	Entre *e* abierta, y *o* cerrada, sonido alargado
ɛ	g**e**t, b**e**d	como en p**e**rro
ɪ	**i**t, b**i**g	Más breve que en s**i**
i:	t**ea**, s**ee**	Como en f**i**no
ɔ	h**o**t, w**a**sh	Como en t**o**rre
ɔ:	s**aw**, **a**ll	Como en p**o**r
u	p**u**t, b**oo**k	Sonido breve, más cerrado que b**u**rro
u:	t**oo**, y**ou**	Sonido largo, como en **u**no
aɪ	fl**y**, h**igh**	Como en fr**ai**le
au	h**ow**, h**ou**se	Como en p**au**sa
ɛə	th**ere**, b**ear**	Casi como en v**ea**, pero el sonido *a* se mezcla con el indistinto |ə|
eɪ	d**ay**, ob**ey**	*e* cerrada seguida por una *i* débil
ɪə	h**ere**, h**ear**	Como en man**í**a, mezclándose el sonido *a* con el indistinto |ə|
əu	g**o**, n**o**te	|ə| seguido por una breve *u*
ɔɪ	b**oy**, **oi**l	Como en v**oy**
uə	p**oor**, s**ure**	*u* bastante larga más el sonido indistinto |ə|

Consonantes

	Ejemplo inglés	*Ejemplo español/explicación*
d	men*d*ed	Como en con*d*e, an*d*ar
g	*g*o, *g*et, bi*g*	Como en *g*rande, *g*ol
dʒ	*g*in, *j*udge	Como en la *ll* andaluza y en *G*eneralitat (catalán)
ŋ	si*ng*	Como en ví*n*culo
h	*h*ouse, *h*e	Como la jota hispanoamericana
j	*y*oung, *y*es	Como en *y*a
k	*c*ome, mo*ck*	Como en *c*aña, Es*c*ocia
r	*r*ed, t*r*ead	Se pronuncia con la punta de la lengua hacia atrás y sin hacerla vibrar
s	*s*and, ye*s*	Como en ca*s*a, *s*esión
z	ro*s*e, *z*ebra	Como en de*s*de, mi*s*mo
ʃ	*sh*e, ma*ch*ine	Como en *ch*ambre (francés), ro*x*o (portugués)
tʃ	*ch*in, ri*ch*	Como en *ch*ocolate
v	*v*alley	Como en f, pero se retiran los dientes superiores vibrándolos contra el labio inferior
w	*w*ater, *wh*ich	Como en la *u* de h*u*evo, p*u*ede
ʒ	vi*s*ion	Como en *j*ournal (francés)
θ	*th*ink, my*th*	Como en re*c*eta, *z*apato
ð	*th*is, *th*e	Como en la *d* de habla*d*o, verda*d*

b, p, f, m, n, l, t iguales que en español

El signo * indica que la r final escrita apenas se pronuncia en inglés británico cuando la palabra siguiente empieza con vocal.

El signo ['] indica la sílaba acentuada.

ESPAÑOL – INGLÉS
SPANISH – ENGLISH

A, a

a |a| (*a* + *el* = *al*) *prep* **1** (*dirección*) to; **fueron ~ Madrid/Grecia** they went to Madrid/Greece; **me voy ~ casa** I'm going home
2 (*distancia*): **está ~ 15 km de aquí** it's 15 km from here
3 (*posición*): **estar ~ la mesa** to be at table; **al lado de** next to, beside; *ver tb* **puerta**
4 (*tiempo*): **~ las 10/~ medianoche** at 10/midnight; **~ la mañana siguiente** the following morning; **~ los pocos días** after a few days; **estamos ~ 9 de julio** it's the ninth of July; **~ los 24 años** at the age of 24; **al año/~ la semana** (*AM*) a year/week later
5 (*manera*): **~ la francesa** the French way; **~ caballo** on horseback; **~ oscuras** in the dark
6 (*medio, instrumento*): **~ lápiz** in pencil; **~ mano** by hand; **cocina ~ gas** gas stove
7 (*razón*): **~ 30 ptas el kilo** at 30 pesetas a kilo; **~ más de 50 km/h** at more than 50 km per hour
8 (*dativo*): **se lo di ~ él** I gave it to him; **vi al policía** I saw the policeman; **se lo compré ~ él** I bought it from him
9 (*tras ciertos verbos*): **voy ~ verle** I'm going to see him; **empezó ~ trabajar** he started working *o* to work
10 (+ *infin*): **al verle, le reconocí inmediatamente** when I saw him I recognized him at once; **el camino ~ recorrer** the distance we (*etc*) have to travel; **¡~ callar!** keep quiet!; **¡~ comer!** let's eat!

abad, esa [a'ßað, 'ðesa] *nm/f* abbot/abbess; **~ía** *nf* abbey
abajo [a'ßaxo] *adv* (*situación*) (down) below, underneath; (*en edificio*) downstairs; (*dirección*) down, downwards; **el piso de ~** the downstairs flat; **la parte de ~** the lower part; **¡~ el gobierno!** down with the government!; **cuesta/río ~** downhill; downstream; **de arriba ~** from top to bottom; **el ~ firmante** the undersigned; **más ~** lower *o* further down
abalanzarse [aßalan'θarse] *vr*: **~ sobre** *o* **contra** to throw o.s. at
abandonado, a [aßando'naðo, a] *adj* derelict; (*desatendido*) abandoned; (*desierto*) deserted; (*descuidado*) neglected

abandonar [aßando'nar] *vt* to leave; (*persona*) to abandon, desert; (*cosa*) to abandon, leave behind; (*descuidar*) to neglect; (*renunciar a*) to give up; (*INFORM*) to quit; **~se** *vr*: **~se a** to abandon o.s. to;
abandono *nm* (*acto*) desertion; abandonment; (*estado*) abandon, neglect; (*renuncia*) withdrawal, retirement; **ganar por abandono** to win by default
abanicar [aßani'kar] *vt* to fan; **abanico** *nm* fan; (*NAUT*) derrick
abaratar [aßara'tar] *vt* to lower the price of; **~se** *vr* to go *o* come down in price
abarcar [aßar'kar] *vt* to include, embrace; (*AM*) to monopolize
abarrotado, a [aßarro'taðo, a] *adj* packed
abarrotar [aßarro'tar] *vt* (*local, estadio, teatro*) to fill, pack
abarrotero, a [aßarro'tero, a] (*AM*) *nm/f* grocer; **abarrotes** *nmpl* (*AM*) groceries, provisions
abastecer [aßaste'θer] *vt*: **~ (de)** to supply (with); **abastecimiento** *nm* supply
abasto [a'ßasto] *nm* supply; **no dar ~ a** to be unable to cope with
abatido, a [aßa'tiðo, a] *adj* dejected, downcast
abatimiento [aßati'mjento] *nm* (*depresión*) dejection, depression
abatir [aßa'tir] *vt* (*muro*) to demolish; (*pájaro*) to shoot *o* bring down; (*fig*) to depress; **~se** *vr* to get depressed; **~se sobre** to swoop *o* pounce on
abdicación [aßðika'θjon] *nf* abdication
abdicar [aßði'kar] *vi* to abdicate
abdomen [aß'ðomen] *nm* abdomen; **abdominales** *nmpl* (*tb: ejercicios abdominales*) sit-ups
abecedario [aßeθe'ðarjo] *nm* alphabet
abedul [aße'ðul] *nm* birch
abeja [a'ßexa] *nf* bee
abejorro [aße'xorro] *nm* bumblebee
abertura [aßer'tura] *nf* = **apertura**
abeto [a'ßeto] *nm* fir
abierto, a [a'ßjerto, a] *pp de* **abrir** ♦ *adj* open; (*AM*) generous
abigarrado, a [aßiya'rraðo, a] *adj* multi-coloured
abismal [aßis'mal] *adj* (*fig*) vast, enormous
abismar [aßis'mar] *vt* to humble, cast down;

~se vr to sink; **~se en** (fig) to be plunged into

abismo [a'ßismo] nm abyss

abjurar [aßxu'rar] vi: **~ de** to abjure, forswear

ablandar [aßlan'dar] vt to soften; **~se** vr to get softer

abnegación [aßneɣa'θjon] nf self-denial

abnegado, a [aßne'ɣaðo, a] adj self-sacrificing

abocado, a [aßo'kaðo, a] adj: **verse ~ al desastre** to be heading for disaster

abochornar [aßotʃor'nar] vt to embarrass

abofetear [aßofete'ar] vt to slap (in the face)

abogado, a [aßo'ɣaðo, a] nm/f lawyer; (notario) solicitor; (en tribunal) barrister (BRIT), attorney (US); **~ defensor** defence lawyer o attorney (US)

abogar [aßo'ɣar] vi: **~ por** to plead for; (fig) to advocate

abolengo [aßo'lengo] nm ancestry, lineage

abolición [aßoli'θjon] nf abolition

abolir [aßo'lir] vt to abolish; (cancelar) to cancel

abolladura [aßoʎa'ðura] nf dent

abollar [aßo'ʎar] vt to dent

abominable [aßomi'naßle] adj abominable

abonado, a [aßo'naðo, a] adj (deuda) paid(-up) ♦ nm/f subscriber

abonar [aßo'nar] vt (deuda) to settle; (terreno) to fertilize; (idea) to endorse; **~se** vr to subscribe; **abono** nm payment; fertilizer; subscription

abordar [aßor'ðar] vt (barco) to board; (asunto) to broach

aborigen [aßo'rixen] nm/f aborigine

aborrecer [aßorre'θer] vt to hate, loathe

abortar [aßor'tar] vi (malparir) to have a miscarriage; (deliberadamente) to have an abortion; nm miscarriage; abortion

abotonar [aßoto'nar] vt to button (up), do up

abovedado, a [aßoße'ðaðo, a] adj vaulted, domed

abrasar [aßra'sar] vt to burn (up); (AGR) to dry up, parch

abrazar [aßra'θar] vt to embrace, hug

abrazo [a'ßraθo] nm embrace, hug; **un ~** (en carta) with best wishes

abrebotellas [aßreßo'teʎas] nm inv bottle opener

abrecartas [aßre'kartas] nm inv letter opener

abrelatas [aßre'latas] nm inv tin (BRIT) o can opener

abreviar [aßre'ßjar] vt to abbreviate; (texto) to abridge; (plazo) to reduce; **abreviatura** nf abbreviation

abridor [aßri'ðor] nm bottle opener; (de latas) tin o can opener

abrigar [aßri'ɣar] vt (proteger) to shelter; (suj: ropa) to keep warm; (fig) to cherish

abrigo [a'ßriɣo] nm (prenda) coat, overcoat; (lugar protegido) shelter

abril [a'ßril] nm April

abrillantar [aßriʎan'tar] vt to polish

abrir [a'ßrir] vt to open (up) ♦ vi to open; **~se** vr to open (up); (extenderse) to open out; (cielo) to clear; **~se paso** to find o force a way through

abrochar [aßro'tʃar] vt (con botones) to button (up); (zapato, con broche) to do up

abrumar [aßru'mar] vt to overwhelm; (sobrecargar) to weigh down

abrupto, a [a'ßrupto, a] adj abrupt; (empinado) steep

absceso [aßs'θeso] nm abscess

absentismo [aßsen'tismo] nm absenteeism

absolución [aßsolu'θjon] nf (REL) absolution; (JUR) acquittal

absoluto, a [aßso'luto, a] adj absolute; **en ~** adv not at all

absolver [aßsol'ßer] vt to absolve; (JUR) to pardon; (: acusado) to acquit

absorbente [aßsor'ßente] adj absorbent; (interesante) absorbing

absorber [aßsor'ßer] vt to absorb; (embeber) to soak up

absorción [aßsor'θjon] nf absorption; (COM) takeover

absorto, a [aß'sorto, a] pp de **absorber** ♦ adj absorbed, engrossed

abstemio, a [aßs'temjo, a] adj teetotal

abstención [aßsten'θjon] nf abstention

abstenerse [aßste'nerse] vr: **~ (de)** to abstain o refrain (from)

abstinencia [aßsti'nenθja] nf abstinence; (ayuno) fasting

abstracción [aßstrak'θjon] nf abstraction

abstracto, a [aß'strakto, a] adj abstract

abstraer [aßstra'er] vt to abstract; **~se** vr to be o become absorbed

abstraído, a [aßstra'iðo, a] adj absent-minded

absuelto [aß'swelto] pp de **absolver**

absurdo, a [aß'surðo, a] adj absurd

abuchear [aßutʃe'ar] vt to boo

abuelo, a [a'ßwelo, a] nm/f grandfather/ mother; **~s** nmpl grandparents

abulia [a'ßulja] nf apathy

abultado, a [aßul'taðo, a] adj bulky

abultar [aßul'tar] vi to be bulky

abundancia [aßun'danθja] nf: **una ~ de** plenty of; **abundante** adj abundant, plentiful

abundar [aßun'dar] vi to abound, be plentiful

aburguesarse [aßurɣe'sarse] vr to become middle-class

aburrido, a [aßu'rriðo, a] adj (hastiado) bored; (que aburre) boring; **aburrimiento**

nm boredom, tedium

aburrir |aβu'rrir| *vt* to bore; **~se** *vr* to be bored, get bored

abusar |aβu'sar| *vi* to go too far; ~ **de** to abuse

abusivo, a |aβu'siβo, a| *adj (precio)* exorbitant

abuso |a'βuso| *nm* abuse

abyecto, a |aβ'jekto, a| *adj* wretched, abject

acá |a'ka| *adv (lugar)* here; **¿de cuándo ~?** since when?

acabado, a |aka'βaðo, a| *adj* finished, complete; *(perfecto)* perfect; *(agotado)* worn out; *(fig)* masterly ♦ *nm* finish

acabar |aka'βar| *vt (llevar a su fin)* to finish, complete; *(consumir)* to use up; *(rematar)* to finish off ♦ *vi* to finish, end; **~se** *vr* to finish, stop; *(terminarse)* to be over; *(agotarse)* to run out; ~ **con** to put an end to; ~ **de llegar** to have just arrived; ~ **por hacer** to end (up) by doing; **¡se acabó!** it's all over!; *(¡basta!)* that's enough!

acabóse |aka'βose| *nm:* **esto es el ~** this is the last straw

academia |aka'ðemja| *nf* academy; **académico, a** *adj* academic

acaecer |akae'θer| *vi* to happen, occur

acallar |aka'ʎar| *vt (persona)* to silence; *(protestas, rumores)* to suppress

acalorado, a |akalo'raðo, a| *adj (discusión)* heated

acalorarse |akalo'rarse| *vr (fig)* to get heated

acampar |akam'par| *vi* to camp

acantilado |akanti'laðo| *nm* cliff

acaparar |akapa'rar| *vt* to monopolize; *(acumular)* to hoard

acariciar |akari'θjar| *vt* to caress; *(esperanza)* to cherish

acarrear |akarre'ar| *vt* to transport; *(fig)* to cause, result in

acaso |a'kaso| *adv* perhaps, maybe; **(por) si ~** (just) in case

acatamiento |akata'mjento| *nm* respect; *(ley)* observance

acatar |aka'tar| *vt* to respect; *(ley)* obey

acatarrarse |akata'rrarse| *vr* to catch a cold

acaudalado, a |akauða'laðo, a| *adj* well-off

acaudillar |akauði'ʎar| *vt* to lead, command

acceder |akθe'ðer| *vi:* ~ **a** *(petición etc)* to agree to; *(tener acceso a)* to have access to; *(INFORM)* to access

accesible |akθe'siβle| *adj* accessible

acceso |ak'θeso| *nm* access, entry; *(camino)* access, approach; *(MED)* attack, fit

accesorio, a |akθe'sorjo, a| *adj, nm* accessory

accidentado, a |akθiðen'taðo, a| *adj* uneven; *(montañoso)* hilly; *(azaroso)* eventful

♦ *nm/f* accident victim

accidental |akθiðen'tal| *adj* accidental; **accidentarse** *vr* to have an accident

accidente |akθi'ðente| *nm* accident; **~s** *nmpl (de terreno)* unevenness *sg*

acción |ak'θjon| *nf* action; *(acto)* action, act; *(COM)* share; *(JUR)* action, lawsuit; **accionar** *vt* to work, operate; *(INFORM)* to drive

accionista |akθjo'nista| *nm/f* shareholder, stockholder

acebo |a'θeβo| *nm* holly; *(árbol)* holly tree

acechar |aθe'tʃar| *vt* to spy on; *(aguardar)* to lie in wait for; **acecho** *nm:* **estar al acecho (de)** to lie in wait (for)

aceitar |aθei'tar| *vt* to oil, lubricate

aceite |a'θeite| *nm* oil; *(de oliva)* olive oil; **~ra** *nf* oilcan; **aceitoso, a** *adj* oily

aceituna |aθei'tuna| *nf* olive

acelerador |aθelera'ðor| *nm* accelerator

acelerar |aθele'rar| *vt* to accelerate

acelga |a'θelɣa| *nf* chard, beet

acento |a'θento| *nm* accent; *(acentuación)* stress

acentuar |aθen'twar| *vt* to accent; to stress; *(fig)* to accentuate

acepción |aθep'θjon| *nf* meaning

aceptable |aθep'taβle| *adj* acceptable

aceptación |aθepta'θjon| *nf* acceptance; *(aprobación)* approval

aceptar |aθep'tar| *vt* to accept; *(aprobar)* to approve

acequia |a'θekja| *nf* irrigation ditch

acera |a'θera| *nf* pavement *(BRIT)*, sidewalk *(US)*

acerca |a'θerka|: ~ **de** *prep* about, concerning

acercar |aθer'kar| *vt* to bring o move nearer; **~se** *vr* to approach, come near

acerico |aθe'riko| *nm* pincushion

acero |a'θero| *nm* steel

acérrimo, a |a'θerrimo, a| *adj (partidario)* staunch; *(enemigo)* bitter

acertado, a |aθer'taðo, a| *adj* correct; *(apropiado)* apt; *(sensato)* sensible

acertar |aθer'tar| *vt (blanco)* to hit; *(solución)* to get right; *(adivinar)* to guess ♦ *vi* to get it right, be right; ~ **a** to manage to; ~ **con** to happen o hit on

acertijo |aθer'tixo| *nm* riddle, puzzle

achacar |atʃa'kar| *vt* to attribute

achacoso, a |atʃa'koso, a| *adj* sickly

achantar |atʃan'tar| *vt (fam)* to scare, frighten; **~se** *vr* to back down

achaque *etc* |a'tʃake| *vb ver* **achacar** ♦ *nm* ailment

achicar |atʃi'kar| *vt* to reduce; *(NAUT)* to bale out

achicharrar |atʃitʃa'rrar| *vt* to scorch, burn

achicoria |atʃi'korja| *nf* chicory

aciago, a |a'θjaɣo, a| *adj* ill-fated, fateful

acicalar [aθika'lar] vt to polish; (*persona*) to dress up; **~se** vr to get dressed up

acicate [aθi'kate] nm spur

acidez [aθi'ðeθ] nf acidity

ácido, a ['aθiðo, a] adj sour, acid ♦ nm acid

acierto etc [a'θjerto] vb ver **acertar** ♦ nm success; (*buen paso*) wise move; (*solución*) solution; (*habilidad*) skill, ability

aclamación [aklama'θjon] nf acclamation; (*aplausos*) applause

aclamar [akla'mar] vt to acclaim; (*aplaudir*) to applaud

aclaración [aklara'θjon] nf clarification, explanation

aclarar [akla'rar] vt to clarify, explain; (*ropa*) to rinse ♦ vi to clear up; **~se** vr (*explicarse*) to understand; **~se la garganta** to clear one's throat

aclaratorio, a [aklara'torjo, a] adj explanatory

aclimatación [aklimata'θjon] nf acclimatization

aclimatar [aklima'tar] vt to acclimatize; **~se** vr to become acclimatized

acné [ak'ne] nm acne

acobardar [akoβar'ðar] vt to intimidate

acodarse [ako'ðarse] vr: **~ en** to lean on

acogedor, a [akoxe'ðor, a] adj welcoming; (*hospitalario*) hospitable

acoger [ako'xer] vt to welcome; (*abrigar*) to shelter; **~se** vr to take refuge

acogida [ako'xiða] nf reception; refuge

acometer [akome'ter] vt to attack; (*emprender*) to undertake; **acometida** nf attack, assault

acomodado, a [akomo'ðaðo, a] adj (*persona*) well-to-do

acomodador, a [akomoða'ðor, a] nm/f usher(ette)

acomodar [akomo'ðar] vt to adjust; (*alojar*) to accommodate; **~se** vr to conform; (*instalarse*) to install o.s.; (*adaptarse*): **~se (a)** to adapt (to)

acompañar [akompa'ɲar] vt to accompany; (*documentos*) to enclose

acondicionar [akondiθjo'nar] vt to arrange, prepare; (*pelo*) to condition

acongojar [akongo'xar] vt to distress, grieve

aconsejar [akonse'xar] vt to advise, counsel; **~se** vr: **~se con** to consult

acontecer [akonte'θer] vi to happen, occur; **acontecimiento** nm event

acopio [a'kopjo] nm store, stock

acoplamiento [akopla'mjento] nm coupling, joint; **acoplar** vt to fit; (*ELEC*) to connect; (*vagones*) to couple

acorazado, a [akora'θaðo, a] adj armour-plated, armoured ♦ nm battleship

acordar [akor'ðar] vt (*resolver*) to agree, resolve; (*recordar*) to remind; **~se** vr to agree; **~se (de algo)** to remember (sth); **acorde** adj (*MUS*) harmonious; **acorde con** (*medidas etc*) in keeping with ♦ nm chord

acordeón [akorðe'on] nm accordion

acordonado, a [akorðo'naðo, a] adj (*calle*) cordoned-off

acorralar [akorra'lar] vt to round up, corral

acortar [akor'tar] vt to shorten; (*duración*) to cut short; (*cantidad*) to reduce; **~se** vr to become shorter

acosar [ako'sar] vt to pursue relentlessly; (*fig*) to hound, pester; **acoso** nm harassment; **acoso sexual** sexual harassment

acostar [akos'tar] vt (*en cama*) to put to bed; (*en suelo*) to lay down; **~se** vr to go to bed; to lie down; **~se con uno** to sleep with sb

acostumbrado, a [akostum'braðo, a] adj usual; **~ a** used to

acostumbrar [akostum'brar] vt: **~ a uno a algo** to get sb used to sth ♦ vi: **~ (a) hacer** to be in the habit of doing; **~se** vr: **~se a** to get used to

acotación [akota'θjon] nf marginal note; (*GEO*) elevation mark; (*de límite*) boundary mark; (*TEATRO*) stage direction

ácrata ['akrata] adj, nm/f anarchist

acre ['akre] adj (*olor*) acrid; (*fig*) biting ♦ nm acre

acrecentar [akreθen'tar] vt to increase, augment

acreditar [akreði'tar] vt (*garantizar*) to vouch for, guarantee; (*autorizar*) to authorize; (*dar prueba de*) to prove; (*COM: abonar*) to credit; (*embajador*) to accredit; **~se** vr to become famous

acreedor, a [akree'ðor, a] adj: **~ de** worthy of ♦ nm/f creditor

acribillar [akriβi'ʎar] vt: **~ a balazos** to riddle with bullets

acróbata [a'kroβata] nm/f acrobat

acta ['akta] nf certificate; (*de comisión*) minutes pl, record; **~ de nacimiento/de matrimonio** birth/marriage certificate; **~ notarial** affidavit

actitud [akti'tuð] nf attitude; (*postura*) posture

activar [akti'βar] vt to activate; (*acelerar*) to speed up

actividad [aktiβi'ðað] nf activity

activo, a [ak'tiβo, a] adj active; (*vivo*) lively ♦ nm (*COM*) assets pl

acto ['akto] nm act, action; (*ceremonia*) ceremony; (*TEATRO*) act; **en el ~** immediately

actor [ak'tor] nm actor; (*JUR*) plaintiff ♦ adj: **parte ~a** prosecution

actriz [ak'triθ] nf actress

actuación [aktwa'θjon] nf action; (*comportamiento*) conduct, behaviour; (*JUR*) proceedings *pl*; (*desempeño*) performance

actual [ak'twal] *adj* present(-day), current;
~**idad** *nf* present; ~**idades** *nfpl* (*noticias*) news
sg; **en la** ~**idad** at present; (*hoy día*)
nowadays

actualizar [aktwali'θar] *vt* to update,
modernize

actualmente [aktwal'mente] *adv* at present;
(*hoy día*) nowadays

actuar [ak'twar] *vi* (*obrar*) to work, operate;
(*actor*) to act, perform ♦ *vt* to work, operate;
~ **de** to act as

acuarela [akwa'rela] *nf* watercolour

acuario [a'kwarjo] *nm* aquarium;
(ASTROLOGÍA): **A~** Aquarius

acuartelar [akwarte'lar] *vt* (MIL) to confine
to barracks

acuático, a [a'kwatiko, a] *adj* aquatic

acuchillar [akutʃi'ʎar] *vt* (TEC) to plane
(down), smooth

aciante [aku'θjante] *adj* urgent

acuciar [aku'θjar] *vt* to urge on

acudir [aku'ðir] *vi* (*asistir*) to attend; (*ir*) to
go; ~ **a** (*fig*) to turn to; ~ **en ayuda de** to go
to the aid of

acuerdo *etc* [a'kwerðo] *vb ver* **acordar** ♦ *nm*
agreement; ¡**de** ~! agreed!; **de** ~ **con**
(*persona*) in agreement with; (*acción*,
documento) in accordance with; **estar de** ~ to
be agreed, agree

acumular [akumu'lar] *vt* to accumulate,
collect

acuñar [aku'ɲar] *vt* (*moneda*) to mint; (*frase*)
to coin

acupuntura [akupun'tura] *nf* acupuncture

acurrucarse [akurru'karse] *vr* to crouch;
(*ovillarse*) to curl up

acusación [akusa'θjon] *nf* accusation

acusar [aku'sar] *vt* to accuse; (*revelar*) to
reveal; (*denunciar*) to denounce

acuse [a'kuse] *nm*: ~ **de recibo**
acknowledgement of receipt

acústica [a'kustika] *nf* acoustics *pl*

acústico, a [a'kustiko, a] *adj* acoustic

adaptación [aðapta'θjon] *nf* adaptation

adaptador [aðapta'ðor] *nm* (ELEC) adapter

adaptar [aðap'tar] *vt* to adapt; (*acomodar*) to
fit

adecuado, a [aðe'kwaðo, a] *adj* (*apto*)
suitable; (*oportuno*) appropriate

adecuar [aðe'kwar] *vt* to adapt; to make
suitable

a. de J.C. *abr* (= *antes de Jesucristo*) B.C.

adelantado, a [aðelan'taðo, a] *adj*
advanced; (*reloj*) fast; **pagar por** ~ to pay in
advance

adelantamiento [aðelanta'mjento] *nm*
(AUTO) overtaking

adelantar [aðelan'tar] *vt* to move forward;

(*avanzar*) to advance; (*acelerar*) to speed up;
(AUTO) to overtake ♦ *vi* to go forward,
advance; ~**se** *vr* to go forward, advance

adelante [aðe'lante] *adv* forward(s), ahead
♦ *excl* come in!; **de hoy en** ~ from now on;
más ~ later on; (*más allá*) further on

adelanto [aðe'lanto] *nm* advance; (*mejora*)
improvement; (*progreso*) progress

adelgazar [aðelɣa'θar] *vt* to thin (down)
♦ *vi* to get thin; (*con régimen*) to slim down,
lose weight

ademán [aðe'man] *nm* gesture; **ademanes**
nmpl manners; **en** ~ **de** as if to

además [aðe'mas] *adv* besides; (*por otra
parte*) moreover; (*también*) also; ~ **de**
besides, in addition to

adentrarse [aðen'trarse] *vr*: ~ **en** to go into,
get inside; (*penetrar*) to penetrate (into)

adentro [a'ðentro] *adv* inside, in; **mar** ~ out
at sea; **tierra** ~ inland

adepto, a [a'ðepto, a] *nm/f* supporter

aderezar [aðere'θar] *vt* (*ensalada*) to dress;
(*comida*) to season; **aderezo** *nm* dressing;
seasoning

adeudar [aðeu'ðar] *vt* to owe; ~**se** *vr* to run
into debt

adherirse [aðe'rirse] *vr*: ~ **a** to adhere to;
(*partido*) to join

adhesión [aðe'sjon] *nf* adhesion; (*fig*)
adherence

adicción [aðik'θjon] *nf* addiction

adición [aði'θjon] *nf* addition

adicto, a [a'ðikto, a] *adj*: ~ **a** addicted to;
(*dedicado*) devoted to ♦ *nm/f* supporter,
follower; (*toxicómano etc*) addict

adiestrar [aðjes'trar] *vt* to train, teach;
(*conducir*) to guide, lead; ~**se** *vr* to practise;
(*enseñarse*) to train o.s.

adinerado, a [aðine'raðo, a] *adj* wealthy

adiós [a'ðjos] *excl* (*para despedirse*) goodbye!,
cheerio!; (*al pasar*) hello!

aditivo [aði'tiβo] *nm* additive

adivinanza [aðiβi'nanθa] *nf* riddle

adivinar [aðiβi'nar] *vt* to prophesy;
(*conjeturar*) to guess; **adivino, a** *nm/f*
fortune-teller

adj *abr* (= *adjunto*) encl.

adjetivo [aðxe'tiβo] *nm* adjective

adjudicación [aðxuðika'θjon] *nf* award;
adjudication

adjudicar [aðxuði'kar] *vt* to award; ~**se** *vr*:
~**se algo** to appropriate sth

adjuntar [aðxun'tar] *vt* to attach, enclose;
adjunto, a *adj* attached, enclosed ♦ *nm/f*
assistant

administración [aðministra'θjon] *nf*
administration; (*dirección*) management;
administrador, a *nm/f* administrator;
manager(ess)

administrar |aðminis'trar| vt to administer;
administrativo, a adj administrative

admirable |aðmi'raßle| adj admirable

admiración |aðmira'θjon| nf admiration;
(asombro) wonder; (LING) exclamation mark

admirar |aðmi'rar| vt to admire; (extrañar) to
surprise; ~se vr to be surprised

admisible |aðmi'sißle| adj admissible

admisión |aðmi'sjon| nf admission;
(reconocimiento) acceptance

admitir |aðmi'tir| vt to admit; (aceptar) to
accept

admonición |aðmoni'θjon| nf warning

adobar |aðo'ßar| vt (CULIN) to season

adobe |a'ðoße| nm adobe, sun-dried brick

adoctrinar |aðoktri'nar| vt: ~ en to
indoctrinate with

adolecer |aðole'θer| vi: ~ de to suffer from

adolescente |aðoles'θente| nm/f adolescent,
teenager

adonde |a'ðonðe| conj (to) where

adónde |a'ðonðe| adv = dónde

adopción |aðop'θjon| nf adoption

adoptar |aðop'tar| vt to adopt

adoptivo, a |aðop'tißo, a| adj (padres)
adoptive; (hijo) adopted

adoquín |aðo'kin| nm paving stone

adorar |aðo'rar| vt to adore

adormecer |aðorme'θer| vt to put to sleep;
~se vr to become sleepy; (dormirse) to fall
asleep

adornar |aðor'nar| vt to adorn

adorno |a'ðorno| nm ornament; (decoración)
decoration

adosado, a |aðo'saðo, a| adj: **casa adosada**
semi-detached house

adquiero etc vb ver **adquirir**

adquirir |aðki'rir| vt to acquire, obtain

adquisición |aðkisi'θjon| nf acquisition

adrede |a'ðreðe| adv on purpose

adscribir |aðskri'ßir| vt to appoint

adscrito pp de **adscribir**

aduana |a'ðwana| nf customs pl

aduanero, a |aðwa'nero, a| adj customs cpd
♦ nm/f customs officer

aducir |aðu'θir| vt to adduce; (dar como
prueba) to offer as proof

adueñarse |aðwe'ɲarse| vr: ~ de to take
possession of

adulación |aðula'θjon| nf flattery

adular |aðu'lar| vt to flatter

adulterar |aðulte'rar| vt to adulterate

adulterio |aðul'terjo| nm adultery

adúltero, a |a'ðultero, a| adj adulterous
♦ nm/f adulterer/adulteress

adulto, a |a'ðulto, a| adj, nm/f adult

adusto, a |a'ðusto, a| adj stern; (austero)
austere

advenedizo, a |aðßene'ðiθo, a| nm/f

upstart

advenimiento |aðßeni'mjento| nm arrival;
(al trono) accession

adverbio |að'ßerßjo| nm adverb

adversario, a |aðßer'sarjo, a| nm/f adversary

adversidad |aðßersi'ðað| nf adversity;
(contratiempo) setback

adverso, a |að'ßerso, a| adj adverse

advertencia |aðßer'tenθja| nf warning;
(prefacio) preface, foreword

advertir |aðßer'tir| vt to notice; (avisar): ~ a
uno de to warn sb about o of

Adviento |að'ßjento| nm Advent

advierto etc vb ver **advertir**

adyacente |aðja'θente| adj adjacent

aéreo, a |a'ereo, a| adj aerial

aerobic |ae'roßik| nm aerobics sg

aerodeslizador |aeroðesliθa'ðor| nm
hovercraft

aeromozo, a |aero'moθo, a| (AM) nm/f air
steward(ess)

aeronáutica |aero'nautika| nf aeronautics sg

aeronave |aero'naße| nm spaceship

aeroplano |aero'plano| nm aeroplane

aeropuerto |aero'pwerto| nm airport

aerosol |aero'sol| nm aerosol

afabilidad |afaßili'ðað| nf friendliness;
afable adj affable

afamado, a |afa'maðo, a| adj famous

afán |a'fan| nm hard work; (deseo) desire

afanar |afa'nar| vt to harass; (fam) to pinch;
~se vr: ~se por hacer to strive to do

afear |afe'ar| vt to disfigure

afección |afek'θjon| nf (MED) disease

afectación |afekta'θjon| nf affectation;
afectado, a adj affected

afectar |afek'tar| vt to affect

afectísimo, a |afek'tisimo, a| adj
affectionate; **suyo** ~ yours truly

afectivo, a |afek'tißo, a| adj (problema etc)
emotional

afecto |a'fekto| nm affection; **tenerle** ~ **a uno**
to be fond of sb

afectuoso, a |afek'twoso, a| adj affectionate

afeitar |afei'tar| vt to shave; ~se vr to shave

afeminado, a |afemi'naðo, a| adj effeminate

Afganistán |afɣanis'tan| nm Afghanistan

afianzamiento |afjanθa'mjento| nm
strengthening; security

afianzar |afjan'θar| vt to strengthen; to
secure; ~se vr to become established

afiche |a'fitʃe| (AM) nm poster

afición |afi'θjon| nf fondness, liking; **la** ~ the
fans pl; **pinto por** ~ I paint as a hobby;
aficionado, a adj keen, enthusiastic; (no
profesional) amateur ♦ nm/f enthusiast, fan;
amateur; **ser aficionado a algo** to be very
keen on o fond of sth

aficionar |afiθjo'nar| vt: ~ **a uno a algo** to

make sb like sth; **~se** vr: **~se a algo** to grow
fond of sth

afilado, a [afi'laðo, a] adj sharp

afilar [afi'lar] vt to sharpen

afiliarse [afi'ljarse] vr to affiliate

afín [a'fin] adj (parecido) similar; (conexo)
related

afinar [afi'nar] vt (TEC) to refine; (MUS) to
tune ♦ vi (tocar) to play in tune; (cantar) to
sing in tune

afincarse [afin'karse] vr to settle

afinidad [afini'ðað] nf affinity; (parentesco)
relationship; **por ~** by marriage

afirmación [afirma'θjon] nf affirmation

afirmar [afir'mar] vt to affirm, state;
afirmativo, a adj affirmative

aflicción [aflik'θjon] nf affliction; (dolor) grief

afligir [afli'xir] vt to afflict; (apenar) to
distress; **~se** vr to grieve

aflojar [aflo'xar] vt to slacken; (desatar) to
loosen, undo; (relajar) to relax ♦ vi to drop;
(bajar) to go down; **~se** vr to relax

aflorar [aflo'rar] vi to come to the surface,
emerge

afluente [aflu'ente] adj flowing ♦ nm
tributary

afluir [aflu'ir] vi to flow

afmo, a abr (= afectísimo(a) suyo(a)) Yours

afónico, a [a'foniko, a] adj: **estar ~** to have a
sore throat; to have lost one's voice

aforo [a'foro] nm (de teatro etc) capacity

afortunado, a [afortu'naðo, a] adj
fortunate, lucky

afrancesado, a [afranθe'saðo, a] adj
francophile; (pey) Frenchified

afrenta [a'frenta] nf affront, insult; (deshonra)
dishonour, shame

África ['afrika] nf Africa; **africano, a** adj,
nm/f African

afrontar [afron'tar] vt to confront; (poner
cara a cara) to bring face to face

afuera [a'fwera] adv out, outside; **~s** nfpl
outskirts

agachar [aɣa'tʃar] vt to bend, bow; **~se** vr to
stoop, bend

agalla [a'ɣaʎa] nf (ZOOL) gill; **tener ~s** (fam)
to have guts

agarradera [aɣarra'ðera] (esp AM) nf handle

agarrado, a [aɣa'rraðo, a] adj mean, stingy

agarrar [aɣa'rrar] vt to grasp, grab; (AM) to
take, catch; (recoger) to pick up ♦ vi (planta)
to take root; **~se** vr to hold on (tightly)

agarrotar [aɣarro'tar] vt (persona) to
squeeze tightly; (reo) to garrotte; **~se** vr
(motor) to seize up; (MED) to stiffen

agasajar [aɣasa'xar] vt to treat well, fête

agazaparse [aɣaθa'parse] vr to crouch down

agencia [a'xenθja] nf agency; **~ inmobiliaria**
estate (BRIT) o real estate (US) agent's

(office); **~ de viajes** travel agency

agenciarse [axen'θjarse] vr to obtain,
procure

agenda [a'xenda] nf diary

agente [a'xente] nm/f agent; (de policía)
policeman/policewoman; **~ inmobiliario**
estate agent (BRIT), realtor (US); **~ de seguros**
insurance agent

ágil ['axil] adj agile, nimble; **agilidad** nf
agility, nimbleness

agilizar [axili'θar] vt (trámites) to speed up

agitación [axita'θjon] nf (de mano etc)
shaking, waving; (de líquido etc) stirring; (fig)
agitation

agitado, a [axi'taðo, a] adj hectic; (viaje)
bumpy

agitar [axi'tar] vt to wave, shake; (líquido) to
stir; (fig) to stir up, excite; **~se** vr to get
excited; (inquietarse) to get worried o upset

aglomeración [aɣlomera'θjon] nf: **~ de
tráfico/gente** traffic jam/mass of people

aglomerar [aɣlome'rar] vt to crowd
together; **~se** vr to crowd together

agnóstico, a [aɣ'nostiko, a] adj, nm/f
agnostic

agobiar [aɣo'βjar] vt to weigh down;
(oprimir) to oppress; (cargar) to burden

agolparse [aɣol'parse] vr to crowd together

agonía [aɣo'nia] nf death throes pl; (fig)
agony, anguish

agonizante [aɣoni'θante] adj dying

agonizar [aɣoni'θar] vi to be dying

agosto [a'ɣosto] nm August

agotado, a [aɣo'taðo, a] adj (persona)
exhausted; (libros) out of print; (acabado)
finished; (COM) sold out

agotador, a [aɣota'ðor, a] adj exhausting

agotamiento [aɣota'mjento] nm exhaustion

agotar [aɣo'tar] vt to exhaust; (consumir) to
drain; (recursos) to use up, deplete; **~se** vr to
be exhausted; (acabarse) to run out; (libro)
to go out of print

agraciado, a [aɣra'θjaðo, a] adj (atractivo)
attractive; (en sorteo etc) lucky

agradable [aɣra'ðaβle] adj pleasant, nice

agradar [aɣra'ðar] vt: **él me agrada** I like him

agradecer [aɣraðe'θer] vt to thank; (favor
etc) to be grateful for; **agradecido, a** adj
grateful; **¡muy agradecido!** thanks a lot!;
agradecimiento nm thanks pl; gratitude

agradezco etc vb ver **agradecer**

agrado [a'ɣraðo] nm: **ser de tu** etc **~** to be to
your etc liking

agrandar [aɣran'dar] vt to enlarge; (fig) to
exaggerate; **~se** vr to get bigger

agrario, a [a'ɣrarjo, a] adj agrarian, land cpd;
(política) agricultural, farming

agravante [aɣra'βante] adj aggravating
♦ nm: **con el ~ de que ...** with the further

difficulty that ...

agravar [aɣraˈβar] vt (*pesar sobre*) to make heavier; (*irritar*) to aggravate; **~se** vr to worsen, get worse

agraviar [aɣraˈβjar] vt to offend; (*ser injusto con*) to wrong; **~se** vr to take offence; **agravio** nm offence; wrong; (*JUR*) grievance

agredir [aɣreˈðir] vt to attack

agregado, a [aɣreˈɣaðo, a] nm/f: **A~** ≈ teacher (*who is not head of department*) ♦ nm aggregate; (*persona*) attaché

agregar [aɣreˈɣar] vt to gather; (*añadir*) to add; (*persona*) to appoint

agresión [aɣreˈsjon] nf aggression

agresivo, a [aɣreˈsiβo, a] adj aggressive

agriar [aˈɣrjar] vt to (turn) sour; **~se** vr to turn sour

agrícola [aˈɣrikola] adj farming cpd, agricultural

agricultor, a [aɣrikulˈtor, a] nm/f farmer

agricultura [aɣrikulˈtura] nf agriculture, farming

agridulce [aɣriˈðulθe] adj bittersweet; (*CULIN*) sweet and sour

agrietarse [aɣrjeˈtarse] vr to crack; (*piel*) to chap

agrimensor, a [aɣrimenˈsor, a] nm/f surveyor

agrio, a [ˈaɣrjo, a] adj bitter

agrupación [aɣrupaˈθjon] nf group; (*acto*) grouping

agrupar [aɣruˈpar] vt to group

agua [ˈaɣwa] nf water; (*NAUT*) wake; (*ARQ*) slope of a roof; **~s** nfpl (*de piedra*) water sg, sparkle sg; (*MED*) water sg, urine sg; (*NAUT*) waters; **~s abajo/arriba** downstream/upstream; **~ bendita/destilada/potable** holy/distilled/drinking water; **~ caliente** hot water; **~ corriente** running water; **~ de colonia** eau de cologne; **~ mineral (con/sin gas)** (carbonated/uncarbonated) mineral water; **~ oxigenada** hydrogen peroxide; **~s jurisdiccionales** territorial waters

aguacate [aɣwaˈkate] nm avocado (pear)

aguacero [aɣwaˈθero] nm (heavy) shower, downpour

aguado, a [aˈɣwaðo, a] adj watery, watered down

aguafiestas [aɣwaˈfjestas] nm/f inv spoilsport, killjoy

aguanieve [aɣwaˈnjeβe] nf sleet

aguantar [aɣwanˈtar] vt to bear, put up with; (*sostener*) to hold up ♦ vi to last; **~se** vr to restrain o.s.; **aguante** nm (*paciencia*) patience; (*resistencia*) endurance

aguar [aˈɣwar] vt to water down

aguardar [aɣwarˈðar] vt to wait for

aguardiente [aɣwarˈðjente] nm brandy, liquor

aguarrás [aɣwaˈrras] nm turpentine

agudeza [aɣuˈðeθa] nf sharpness; (*ingenio*) wit

agudizar [aɣuðiˈθar] vt (*crisis*) to make worse; **~se** vr to get worse

agudo, a [aˈɣuðo, a] adj sharp; (*voz*) high-pitched, piercing; (*dolor, enfermedad*) acute

agüero [aˈɣwero] nm: **buen/mal ~** good/bad omen

aguijón [aɣiˈxon] nm sting; (*fig*) spur

águila [ˈaɣila] nf eagle; (*fig*) genius

aguileño, a [aɣiˈleɲo, a] adj (*nariz*) aquiline; (*rostro*) sharp-featured

aguinaldo [aɣiˈnaldo] nm Christmas box

aguja [aˈɣuxa] nf needle; (*de reloj*) hand; (*ARQ*) spire; (*TEC*) firing-pin; **~s** nfpl (*ZOOL*) ribs; (*FERRO*) points

agujerear [aɣuxereˈar] vt to make holes in

agujero [aɣuˈxero] nm hole

agujetas [aɣuˈxetas] nfpl stitch sg; (*rigidez*) stiffness sg

aguzar [aɣuˈθar] vt to sharpen; (*fig*) to incite

ahí [aˈi] adv there; **de ~ que** so that, with the result that; **~ llega** here he comes; **por ~ that** way; (*allá*) over there; **200 o por ~** 200 or so

ahijado, a [aiˈxaðo, a] nm/f godson/daughter

ahínco [aˈinko] nm earnestness

ahogar [aoˈɣar] vt to drown; (*asfixiar*) to suffocate, smother; (*fuego*) to put out; **~se** vr (*en el agua*) to drown; (*por asfixia*) to suffocate

ahogo [aˈoɣo] nm breathlessness; (*fig*) financial difficulty

ahondar [aonˈdar] vt to deepen, make deeper; (*fig*) to study thoroughly ♦ vi: **~ en** to study thoroughly

ahora [aˈora] adv now; (*hace poco*) a moment ago, just now; (*dentro de poco*) in a moment; **~ voy** I'm coming; **~ mismo** right now; **~ bien** now then; **por ~** for the present

ahorcar [aorˈkar] vt to hang

ahorita [aoˈrita] (*fam: esp AM*) adv right now

ahorrar [aoˈrrar] vt (*dinero*) to save; (*esfuerzos*) to save, avoid; **ahorro** nm (*acto*) saving; **ahorros** nmpl (*dinero*) savings

ahuecar [aweˈkar] vt to hollow (out); (*voz*) to deepen; **~se** vr to give o.s. airs

ahumar [auˈmar] vt to smoke, cure; (*llenar de humo*) to fill with smoke ♦ vi to smoke; **~se** vr to fill with smoke

ahuyentar [aujenˈtar] vt to drive off, frighten off; (*fig*) to dispel

airado, a [aiˈraðo, a] adj angry

airar [aiˈrar] vt to anger; **~se** vr to get angry

aire [ˈaire] nm air; (*viento*) wind; (*corriente*) draught; (*MUS*) tune; **~s** nmpl: **darse ~s** to give o.s. airs; **al ~ libre** in the open air; **~ acondicionado** air conditioning; **airearse** vr (*persona*) to go out for a breath of fresh air;

airoso, a adj windy; draughty; (fig) graceful

aislado, a [ais'laðo, a] adj isolated; (incomunicado) cut-off; (ELEC) insulated

aislar [ais'lar] vt to isolate; (ELEC) to insulate

ajardinado, a [axarði'naðo, a] adj landscaped

ajedrez [axe'ðreθ] nm chess

ajeno, a [a'xeno, a] adj (que pertenece a otro) somebody else's; ~ a foreign to

ajetreado, a [axetre'aðo, a] adj busy

ajetreo [axe'treo] nm bustle

ají [a'xi] (AM) nm chil(l)i, red pepper; (salsa) chil(l)i sauce

ajillo [a'xiʎo] nm: **gambas al ~** garlic prawns

ajo ['axo] nm garlic

ajuar [a'xwar] nm household furnishings pl; (de novia) trousseau; (de niño) layette

ajustado, a [axus'taðo, a] adj (tornillo) tight; (cálculo) right; (ropa) tight(-fitting); (resultado) close

ajustar [axus'tar] vt (adaptar) to adjust; (encajar) to fit; (TEC) to engage; (IMPRENTA) to make up; (apretar) to tighten; (concertar) to agree (on); (reconciliar) to reconcile; (cuentas, deudas) to settle ♦ vi to fit; **~se** vr: **~se a** (precio etc) to be in keeping with, fit in with; **~ las cuentas a uno** to get even with sb

ajuste [a'xuste] nm adjustment; (COSTURA) fitting; (acuerdo) compromise; (de cuenta) settlement

al [al] (= a + el) ver a

ala ['ala] nf wing; (de sombrero) brim; (futbolista) winger; **~ delta** nf hang-glider

alabanza [ala'βanθa] nf praise

alabar [ala'βar] vt to praise

alacena [ala'θena] nf kitchen cupboard (BRIT), kitchen closet (US)

alacrán [ala'kran] nm scorpion

alambique [alam'bike] nm still

alambrada [alam'braða] nf wire fence; (red) wire netting

alambrado [alam'braðo] nm = **alambrada**

alambre [a'lambre] nm wire; **~ de púas** barbed wire

alameda [ala'meða] nf (plantío) poplar grove; (lugar de paseo) avenue, boulevard

álamo ['alamo] nm poplar; **~ temblón** aspen

alarde [a'larðe] nm show, display; **hacer ~ de** to boast of

alargador [alarɣa'ðor] nm (ELEC) extension lead

alargar [alar'ɣar] vt to lengthen, extend; (paso) to hasten; (brazo) to stretch out; (cuerda) to pay out; (conversación) to spin out; **~se** vr to get longer

alarido [ala'riðo] nm shriek

alarma [a'larma] nf alarm

alarmar vt to alarm; **~se** to get alarmed; **alarmante** [alar'mante] adj alarming

alba ['alβa] nf dawn

albacea [alβa'θea] nm/f executor/executrix

albahaca [al'βaka] nf basil

Albania [al'βanja] nf Albania

albañil [alβa'ɲil] nm bricklayer; (cantero) mason

albarán [alβa'ran] nm (COM) delivery note, invoice

albaricoque [alβari'koke] nm apricot

albedrío [alβe'ðrio] nm: **libre ~** free will

alberca [al'βerka] nf reservoir; (AM) swimming pool

albergar [alβer'var] vt to shelter

albergue etc [al'βerve] vb ver **albergar** ♦ nm shelter, refuge; **~ juvenil** youth hostel

albóndiga [al'βondiva] nf meatball

albornoz [alβor'noθ] nm (de los árabes) burnous; (para el baño) bathrobe

alborotar [alβoro'tar] vi to make a row ♦ vt to agitate, stir up; **~se** vr to get excited; (mar) to get rough; **alboroto** nm row, uproar

alborozar [alβoro'θar] vt to gladden; **~se** vr to rejoice

alborozo [alβo'roθo] nm joy

álbum ['alβum] (pl **~s, ~es**) nm album; **~ de recortes** scrapbook

alcachofa [alka'tʃofa] nf artichoke

alcalde, esa [al'kalde, esa] nm/f mayor(ess)

alcaldía [alkal'dia] nf mayoralty; (lugar) mayor's office

alcance etc [al'kanθe] vb ver **alcanzar** ♦ nm reach; (COM) adverse balance

alcantarilla [alkanta'riʎa] nf (de aguas cloacales) sewer; (en la calle) gutter

alcanzar [alkan'θar] vt (algo: con la mano, el pie) to reach; (alguien: en el camino etc) to catch up (with); (autobús) to catch; (suj: bala) to hit, strike ♦ vi (ser suficiente) to be enough; **~ a hacer** to manage to do

alcaparra [alka'parra] nf caper

alcayata [alka'jata] nf hook

alcázar [al'kaθar] nm fortress; (NAUT) quarter-deck

alcoba [al'koβa] nf bedroom

alcohol [al'kol] nm alcohol; **~ metílico** methylated spirits pl (BRIT), wood alcohol (US); **alcohólico, a** adj, nm/f alcoholic

alcoholímetro [alko'limetro] nm Breathalyser ® (BRIT), drunkometer (US)

alcoholismo [alko'lismo] nm alcoholism

alcornoque [alkor'noke] nm cork tree; (fam) idiot

alcurnia [al'kurnja] nf lineage

aldaba [al'daβa] nf (door) knocker

aldea [al'dea] nf village; **~no, a** adj village cpd ♦ nm/f villager

aleación [alea'θjon] nf alloy

aleatorio, a [alea'torjo, a] adj random

aleccionar [alekθjo'nar] vt to instruct; (adiestrar) to train

alegación [aleɣa'θjon] nf allegation

alegar [ale'ɣar] vt to claim; (JUR) to plead ♦ vi (AM) to argue

alegato [ale'ɣato] nm (JUR) allegation; (AM) argument

alegoría [aleɣo'ria] nf allegory

alegrar [ale'ɣrar] vt (causar alegría) to cheer (up); (fuego) to poke; (fiesta) to liven up; ~se vr (fam) to get merry o tight; ~se de to be glad about

alegre [a'leɣre] adj happy, cheerful; (fam) merry, tight; (chiste) risqué, blue; **alegría** nf happiness; merriment

alejamiento [alexa'mjento] nm removal; (distancia) remoteness

alejar [ale'xar] vt to remove; (fig) to estrange; ~se vr to move away

alemán, ana [ale'man, ana] adj, nm/f German ♦ nm (LING) German

Alemania [ale'manja] nf: ~ Occidental/ Oriental West/East Germany

alentador, a [alenta'ðor, a] adj encouraging

alentar [alen'tar] vt to encourage

alergia [a'lerxja] nf allergy

alero [a'lero] nm (de tejado) eaves pl; (de carruaje) mudguard

alerta [a'lerta] adj, nm alert

aleta [a'leta] nf (de pez) fin; (de ave) wing; (de foca, DEPORTE) flipper; (AUTO) mudguard

aletargar [aletar'ɣar] vt to make drowsy; (entumecer) to make numb; ~se vr to grow drowsy; to become numb

aletear [alete'ar] vi to flutter

alevín [ale'ßin] nm fry, young fish

alevosía [aleßo'sia] nf treachery

alfabeto [alfa'ßeto] nm alphabet

alfalfa [al'falfa] nf alfalfa, lucerne

alfarería [alfare'ria] nf pottery; (tienda) pottery shop; **alfarero, a** nm/f potter

alféizar [al'feiθar] nm window-sill

alférez [al'fereθ] nm (MIL) second lieutenant; (NAUT) ensign

alfil [al'fil] nm (AJEDREZ) bishop

alfiler [alfi'ler] nm pin; (broche) clip

alfiletero [alfile'tero] nm needlecase

alfombra [al'fombra] nf carpet; (más pequeña) rug; **alfombrar** vt to carpet; **alfombrilla** nf rug, mat; (INFORM) mouse mat o pad

alforja [al'forxa] nf saddlebag

algarabía [alɣara'ßia] (fam) nf gibberish; (griterío) hullabaloo

algas ['alɣas] nfpl seaweed

álgebra ['alxeßra] nf algebra

álgido, a ['alxiðo, a] adj (momento etc) crucial, decisive

algo ['alɣo] pron something; anything ♦ adv somewhat, rather; ¿~ **más?** anything else?; (en tienda) is that all?; por ~ **será** there must be some reason for it

algodón [alɣo'ðon] nm cotton; (planta) cotton plant; ~ **de azúcar** candy floss (BRIT), cotton candy (US); ~ **hidrófilo** cotton wool (BRIT), absorbent cotton (US)

algodonero, a [alɣoðo'nero, a] adj cotton cpd ♦ nm/f cotton grower ♦ nm cotton plant

alguacil [alɣwa'θil] nm bailiff; (TAUR) mounted official

alguien ['alɣjen] pron someone, somebody; (en frases interrogativas) anyone, anybody

alguno, a [al'ɣuno, a] adj (delante de nm: algún) some; (después de n): **no tiene talento** ~ he has no talent, he doesn't have any talent ♦ pron (alguien) someone, somebody; **algún que otro libro** some book o other; **algún día iré** I'll go one o some day; **sin interés** ~ without the slightest interest; ~ **que otro** an occasional one; ~s **piensan** some (people) think

alhaja [a'laxa] nf jewel; (tesoro) precious object, treasure

alhelí [ale'li] nm wallflower, stock

aliado, a [a'ljaðo, a] adj allied

alianza [a'ljanθa] nf alliance; (anillo) wedding ring

aliar [a'ljar] vt to ally; ~se vr to form an alliance

alias ['aljas] adv alias

alicates [ali'kates] nmpl pliers; ~ **de uñas** nail clippers

aliciente [ali'θjente] nm incentive; (atracción) attraction

alienación [aljena'θjon] nf alienation

aliento [a'ljento] nm breath; (respiración) breathing; **sin** ~ breathless

aligerar [alixe'rar] vt to lighten; (reducir) to shorten; (aliviar) to alleviate; (mitigar) to ease; (paso) to quicken

alijo [a'lixo] nm consignment

alimaña [ali'mana] nf pest

alimentación [alimenta'θjon] nf (comida) food; (acción) feeding; (tienda) grocer's (shop); **alimentador** nm: **alimentador de papel** sheet-feeder

alimentar [alimen'tar] vt to feed; (nutrir) to nourish; ~se vr to feed

alimenticio, a [alimen'tiθjo, a] adj food cpd; (nutritivo) nourishing, nutritious

alimento [ali'mento] nm food; (nutrición) nourishment

alineación [alinea'θjon] nf alignment; (DEPORTE) line-up

alinear [aline'ar] vt to align; ~se vr (DEPORTE) to line up; ~se en to fall in with

aliñar [ali'nar] vt (CULIN) to season; **aliño** nm (CULIN) dressing

alioli [ali'oli] *nm* garlic mayonnaise

alisar [ali'sar] *vt* to smooth

aliso [a'liso] *nm* alder

alistarse [alis'tarse] *vr* to enlist; (*inscribirse*) to enrol

aliviar [ali'βjar] *vt* (*carga*) to lighten; (*persona*) to relieve; (*dolor*) to relieve, alleviate

alivio [a'liβjo] *nm* alleviation, relief

aljibe [al'xiβe] *nm* cistern

allá [a'ʎa] *adv* (*lugar*) there; (*por ahí*) over there; (*tiempo*) then; **~ abajo** down there; **más ~** further on; **más ~ de** beyond; **¡~ tú!** that's your problem!

allanamiento [aʎana'mjento] *nm*: **~ de morada** burglary

allanar [aʎa'nar] *vt* to flatten, level (out); (*igualar*) to smooth (out); (*fig*) to subdue; (*JUR*) to burgle, break into

allegado, a [aʎe'ɣaðo, a] *adj* near, close
♦ *nm/f* relation

allí [a'ʎi] *adv* there; **~ mismo** right there; **por ~** over there; (*por ese camino*) that way

alma ['alma] *nf* soul; (*persona*) person

almacén [alma'θen] *nm* (*depósito*) warehouse, store; (*MIL*) magazine; (*AM*) shop; (*grandes*) **almacenes** *nmpl* department store *sg*; **almacenaje** *nm* storage

almacenar [almaθe'nar] *vt* to store, put in storage; (*proveerse*) to stock up with; **almacenero** *nm* (*AM*) shopkeeper

almanaque [alma'nake] *nm* almanac

almeja [al'mexa] *nf* clam

almendra [al'mendra] *nf* almond; **almendro** *nm* almond tree

almíbar [al'miβar] *nm* syrup

almidón [almi'ðon] *nm* starch; **almidonar** *vt* to starch

almirante [almi'rante] *nm* admiral

almirez [almi'reθ] *nm* mortar

almizcle [al'miθkle] *nm* musk

almohada [almo'aða] *nf* pillow; (*funda*) pillowcase; **almohadilla** *nf* cushion; (*TEC*) pad; (*AM*) pincushion

almohadón [almoa'ðon] *nm* large pillow; bolster

almorranas [almo'rranas] *nfpl* piles, haemorrhoids

almorzar [almor'θar] *vt*: **~ una tortilla** to have an omelette for lunch ♦ *vi* to (have) lunch

almuerzo *etc* [al'mwerθo] *vb ver* **almorzar**
♦ *nm* lunch

alocado, a [alo'kaðo, a] *adj* crazy

alojamiento [aloxa'mjento] *nm* lodging(s) (*pl*); (*viviendas*) housing

alojar [alo'xar] *vt* to lodge; **~se** *vr* to lodge, stay

alondra [a'londra] *nf* lark, skylark

alpargata [alpar'vata] *nf* rope-soled sandal, espadrille

Alpes ['alpes] *nmpl*: **los ~** the Alps

alpinismo [alpi'nismo] *nm* mountaineering, climbing; **alpinista** *nm/f* mountaineer, climber

alpiste [al'piste] *nm* birdseed

alquilar [alki'lar] *vt* (*suj: propietario: inmuebles*) to let, rent (out); (: *coche*) to hire out; (: *TV*) to rent (out); (*suj: alquilador: inmuebles, TV*) to rent; (: *coche*) to hire; **"se alquila casa"** "house to let (*BRIT*) o for rent (*US*)"

alquiler [alki'ler] *nm* renting; letting; hiring; (*arriendo*) rent; hire charge; **~ de automóviles** car hire; **de ~** for hire

alquimia [al'kimja] *nf* alchemy

alquitrán [alki'tran] *nm* tar

alrededor [alreðe'ðor] *adv* around, about; **~ de** around, about; **mirar a su ~** to look (round) about one; **~es** *nmpl* surroundings

alta ['alta] *nf* (*certificate of*) discharge; **dar de ~** to discharge

altanería [altane'ria] *nf* haughtiness, arrogance; **altanero, a** *adj* arrogant, haughty

altar [al'tar] *nm* altar

altavoz [alta'βoθ] *nm* loudspeaker; (*amplificador*) amplifier

alteración [altera'θjon] *nf* alteration; (*alboroto*) disturbance

alterar [alte'rar] *vt* to alter; to disturb; **~se** *vr* (*persona*) to get upset

altercado [alter'kaðo] *nm* argument

alternar [alter'nar] *vt* to alternate ♦ *vi* to alternate; (*turnar*) to take turns; **~se** *vr* to alternate; to take turns; **~ con** to mix with; **alternativa** *nf* alternative; (*elección*) choice; **alternativo, a** *adj* alternative; (*alterno*) alternating; **alterno, a** *adj* alternate; (*ELEC*) alternating

Alteza [al'teθa] *nf* (*tratamiento*) Highness

altibajos [alti'βaxos] *nmpl* ups and downs

altiplanicie [altipla'niθje] *nf* high plateau

altiplano [alti'plano] *nm* = **altiplanicie**

altisonante [altiso'nante] *adj* high-flown, high-sounding

altitud [alti'tuð] *nf* height; (*AVIAT, GEO*) altitude

altivez [alti'βeθ] *nf* haughtiness, arrogance; **altivo, a** *adj* haughty, arrogant

alto, a ['alto, a] *adj* high; (*persona*) tall; (*sonido*) high, sharp; (*noble*) high, lofty ♦ *nm* halt; (*MUS*) alto; (*GEO*) hill; (*AM*) pile ♦ *adv* (*de sitio*) high; (*de sonido*) loud, loudly ♦ *excl* halt!; **la pared tiene 2 metros de ~** the wall is 2 metres high; **en alta mar** on the high seas; **en voz alta** in a loud voice; **las altas horas de la noche** the small o wee hours; **en lo ~ de** at the top of; **pasar por ~** to overlook

altoparlante [altopar'lante] (*AM*) *nm* loudspeaker

altruismo [altru'ismo] *nm* altruism

altura [al'tura] *nf* height; (*NAUT*) depth; (*GEO*) latitude; **la pared tiene 1.80 de ~** the wall is 1 metre 80cm high; **a estas ~s** at this stage; **a estas ~s del año** at this time of the year

alubia [a'lußja] *nf* bean

alucinación [aluθina'θjon] *nf* hallucination

alucinar [aluθi'nar] *vi* to hallucinate ♦ *vt* to deceive; (*fascinar*) to fascinate

alud [a'luð] *nm* avalanche; (*fig*) flood

aludir [alu'ðir] *vi*: **~ a** to allude to; **darse por aludido** to take the hint

alumbrado [alum'braðo] *nm* lighting; **alumbramiento** *nm* lighting; (*MED*) childbirth, delivery

alumbrar [alum'brar] *vt* to light (up) ♦ *vi* (*MED*) to give birth

aluminio [alu'minjo] *nm* aluminium (*BRIT*), aluminum (*US*)

alumno, a [a'lumno, a] *nm/f* pupil, student

alunizar [aluni'θar] *vi* to land on the moon

alusión [alu'sjon] *nf* allusion

alusivo, a [alu'sißo, a] *adj* allusive

aluvión [alu'ßjon] *nm* alluvium; (*fig*) flood

alverja [al'ßerxa] (*AM*) *nf* pea

alza ['alθa] *nf* rise; (*MIL*) sight

alzada [al'θaða] *nf* (*de caballos*) height; (*JUR*) appeal

alzamiento [alθa'mjento] *nm* (*rebelión*) rising

alzar [al'θar] *vt* to lift (up); (*precio, muro*) to raise; (*cuello de abrigo*) to turn up; (*AGR*) to gather in; (*IMPRENTA*) to gather; **~se** *vr* to get up, rise; (*rebelarse*) to revolt; (*COM*) to go fraudulently bankrupt; (*JUR*) to appeal

ama ['ama] *nf* lady of the house; (*dueña*) owner; (*institutriz*) governess; (*madre adoptiva*) foster mother; **~ de casa** housewife; **~ de llaves** housekeeper

amabilidad [amaßili'ðað] *nf* kindness; (*simpatía*) niceness; **amable** *adj* kind; nice; **es usted muy amable** that's very kind of you

amaestrado, a [amaes'traðo, a] *adj* (*animal: en circo etc*) performing

amaestrar [amaes'trar] *vt* to train

amago [a'mayo] *nm* threat; (*gesto*) threatening gesture; (*MED*) symptom

amainar [amai'nar] *vi* (*viento*) to die down

amalgama [amal'yama] *nf* amalgam; **amalgamar** *vt* to amalgamate; (*combinar*) to combine, mix

amamantar [amaman'tar] *vt* to suckle, nurse

amanecer [amane'θer] *vi* to dawn ♦ *nm* dawn; **~ afiebrado** to wake up with a fever

amanerado, a [amane'raðo, a] *adj* affected

amansar [aman'sar] *vt* to tame; (*persona*) to subdue; **~se** *vr* (*persona*) to calm down

amante [a'mante] *adj*: **~ de** fond of ♦ *nm/f* lover

amapola [ama'pola] *nf* poppy

amar [a'mar] *vt* to love

amargado, a [amar'xaðo, a] *adj* bitter

amargar [amar'xar] *vt* to make bitter; (*fig*) to embitter; **~se** *vr* to become embittered

amargo, a [a'marxo, a] *adj* bitter; **amargura** *nf* bitterness

amarillento, a [amari'ʎento, a] *adj* yellowish; (*tez*) sallow; **amarillo, a** *adj, nm* yellow

amarrar [ama'rrar] *vt* to moor; (*sujetar*) to tie up

amarras [a'marras] *nfpl*: **soltar ~** to set sail

amasar [ama'sar] *vt* (*masa*) to knead; (*mezclar*) to mix, prepare; (*confeccionar*) to concoct; **amasijo** *nm* kneading; mixing; (*fig*) hotchpotch

amateur ['amatur] *nm/f* amateur

amazona [ama'θona] *nf* horsewoman; **A~s** *nm*: **el A~s** the Amazon

ambages [am'baxes] *nmpl*: **sin ~** in plain language

ámbar ['ambar] *nm* amber

ambición [ambi'θjon] *nf* ambition; **ambicionar** *vt* to aspire to; **ambicioso, a** *adj* ambitious

ambidextro, a [ambi'ðekstro, a] *adj* ambidextrous

ambientación [ambjenta'θjon] *nf* (*CINE, TEATRO etc*) setting; (*RADIO*) sound effects

ambiente [am'bjente] *nm* (*tb fig*) atmosphere; (*medio*) environment

ambigüedad [ambixwe'ðað] *nf* ambiguity; **ambiguo, a** *adj* ambiguous

ámbito ['ambito] *nm* (*campo*) field; (*fig*) scope

ambos, as ['ambos, as] *adj pl, pron pl* both

ambulancia [ambu'lanθja] *nf* ambulance

ambulante [ambu'lante] *adj* travelling *cpd*, itinerant

ambulatorio [ambula'torio] *nm* state health-service clinic

amedrentar [ameðren'tar] *vt* to scare

amén [a'men] *excl* amen; **~ de** besides

amenaza [ame'naθa] *nf* threat

amenazar [amena'θar] *vt* to threaten ♦ *vi*: **~ con hacer** to threaten to do

amenidad [ameni'ðað] *nf* pleasantness

ameno, a [a'meno, a] *adj* pleasant

América [a'merika] *nf* America; **~ del Norte/del Sur** North/South America; **~ Central/Latina** Central/Latin America; **americana** *nf* coat, jacket; *ver tb* **americano**; **americano, a** *adj, nm/f* American

amerizar [ameri'θar] *vi* (*avión*) to land (on

the sea)

ametralladora [ametraʎa'ðora] nf machine gun

amianto [a'mjanto] nm asbestos

amigable [ami'ɣaβle] adj friendly

amígdala [a'miɣðala] nf tonsil; **amigdalitis** nf tonsillitis

amigo, a [a'miɣo, a] adj friendly ♦ nm/f friend; (amante) lover; **ser ~ de algo** to be fond of sth; **ser muy ~s** to be close friends

amilanar [amila'nar] vt to scare; **~se** vr to get scared

aminorar [amino'rar] vt to diminish; (reducir) to reduce; **~ la marcha** to slow down

amistad [amis'tað] nf friendship; **~es** nfpl (amigos) friends; **amistoso, a** adj friendly

amnesia [am'nesja] nf amnesia

amnistía [amnis'tia] nf amnesty

amo ['amo] nm owner; (jefe) boss

amodorrarse [amoðo'rrarse] vr to get sleepy

amoldar [amol'dar] vt to mould; (adaptar) to adapt

amonestación [amonesta'θjon] nf warning; **amonestaciones** nfpl (REL) marriage banns

amonestar [amones'tar] vt to warn; (REL) to publish the banns of

amontonar [amonto'nar] vt to collect, pile up; **~se** vr to crowd together; (acumularse) to pile up

amor [a'mor] nm love; (amante) lover; **hacer el ~** to make love; **~ propio** self-respect

amoratado, a [amora'taðo, a] adj purple

amordazar [amorða'θar] vt to muzzle; (fig) to gag

amorfo, a [a'morfo, a] adj amorphous, shapeless

amoroso, a [amo'roso, a] adj affectionate, loving

amortajar [amorta'xar] vt to shroud

amortiguador [amortigwa'ðor] nm shock absorber; (parachoques) bumper; **~es** nmpl (AUTO) suspension sg

amortiguar [amorti'ɣwar] vt to deaden; (ruido) to muffle; (color) to soften

amortización [amortiθa'θjon] nf (de deuda) repayment; (de bono) redemption

amotinar [amoti'nar] vt to stir up, incite (to riot); **~se** vr to mutiny

amparar [ampa'rar] vt to protect; **~se** vr to seek protection; (de la lluvia etc) to shelter; **amparo** nm help, protection; **al amparo de** under the protection of

amperio [am'perjo] nm ampère, amp

ampliación [amplja'θjon] nf enlargement; (extensión) extension

ampliar [am'pljar] vt to enlarge; to extend

amplificación [amplifika'θjon] nf enlargement; **amplificador** nm amplifier

amplificar [amplifi'kar] vt to amplify

amplio, a ['ampljo, a] adj spacious; (de falda etc) full; (extenso) extensive; (ancho) wide; **amplitud** nf spaciousness; extent; (fig) amplitude

ampolla [am'poʎa] nf blister; (MED) ampoule

ampuloso, a [ampu'loso, a] adj bombastic, pompous

amputar [ampu'tar] vt to cut off, amputate

amueblar [amwe'ßlar] vt to furnish

amurallar [amura'ʎar] vt to wall up o in

anacronismo [anakro'nismo] nm anachronism

anales [a'nales] nmpl annals

analfabetismo [analfaße'tismo] nm illiteracy; **analfabeto, a** adj, nm/f illiterate

analgésico [anal'xesiko] nm painkiller, analgesic

análisis [a'nalisis] nm inv analysis

analista [ana'lista] nm/f (gen) analyst

analizar [anali'θar] vt to analyse

analogía [analo'xia] nf analogy

analógico, a [ana'loxiko, a] adj (INFORM) analog; (reloj) analogue (BRIT), analog (US)

análogo, a [a'naloxo, a] adj analogous, similar

ananá(s) [ana'na(s)] (AM) nm pineapple

anaquel [ana'kel] nm shelf

anarquía [anar'kia] nf anarchy; **anarquismo** nm anarchism; **anarquista** nm/f anarchist

anatomía [anato'mia] nf anatomy

anca ['anka] nf rump, haunch; **~s** nfpl (fam) behind sg

ancho, a ['antʃo, a] adj wide; (faldu) full; (fig) liberal ♦ nm width; (FERRO) gauge; **ponerse ~** to get conceited; **estar a sus anchas** to be at one's ease

anchoa [an'tʃoa] nf anchovy

anchura [an'tʃura] nf width; (extensión) wideness

anciano, a [an'θjano, a] adj old, aged ♦ nm/f old man/woman; elder

ancla ['ankla] nf anchor; **~dero** nm anchorage; **anclar** vi to (drop) anchor

andadura [anda'ðura] nf gait; (de caballo) pace

Andalucía [andalu'θia] nf Andalusia; **andaluz, a** adj, nm/f Andalusian

andamiaje [anda'mjaxe] nm = andamio

andamio [an'damjo] nm scaffold(ing)

andar [an'dar] vt to go, cover, travel ♦ vi to go, walk, travel; (funcionar) to go, work; (estar) to be ♦ nm walk, gait, pace; **~se** vr to go away; **~ a pie/a caballo/en bicicleta** to go on foot/on horseback/by bicycle; **~ haciendo algo** to be doing sth; **¡anda!** (sorpresa) go on!; **anda por o en los 40** he's about 40

andén [an'den] nm (FERRO) platform; (NAUT) quayside; (AM: de la calle) pavement (BRIT), sidewalk (US)

Andes ['andes] nmpl: **los ~** the Andes

Andorra [an'dorra] nf Andorra

andrajo [an'draxo] nm rag; **~so, a** adj ragged

anduve etc [an'duße] vb ver **andar**

anécdota [a'nekðota] nf anecdote, story

anegar [ane'var] vt to flood; (ahogar) to drown; **~se** vr to drown; (hundirse) to sink

anejo, a [a'nexo, a] adj, nm = **anexo**

anemia [a'nemja] nf anaemia

anestesia [anes'tesja] nf (sustancia) anaesthetic; (proceso) anaesthesia

anexar [anek'sar] vt to annex; (documento) to attach; **anexión** nf annexation; **anexionamiento** nm annexation; **anexo, a** adj attached ♦ nm annexe

anfibio, a [an'fißjo, a] adj amphibious ♦ nm amphibian

anfiteatro [anfite'atro] nm amphitheatre; (TEATRO) dress circle

anfitrión, ona [anfi'trjon, ona] nm/f host(ess)

ángel ['anxel] nm angel; **~ de la guarda** guardian angel; **tener ~** to be charming; **angelical** adj, **angélico, a** adj angelic(al)

angina [an'xina] nf (MED) inflammation of the throat; **~ de pecho** angina; **tener ~s** to have tonsillitis

anglicano, a [angli'kano, a] adj, nm/f Anglican

anglosajón, ona [anglosa'xon, ona] adj Anglo-Saxon

angosto, a [an'gosto, a] adj narrow

anguila [an'gila] nf eel

angula [an'gula] nf elver, baby eel

ángulo ['angulo] nm angle; (esquina) corner; (curva) bend

angustia [an'gustja] nf anguish; **angustiar** vt to distress, grieve

anhelar [ane'lar] vt to be eager for; (desear) to long for, desire ♦ vi to pant, gasp; **anhelo** nm eagerness; desire

anidar [ani'ðar] vi to nest

anillo [a'niʎo] nm ring; **~ de boda** wedding ring

animación [anima'θjon] nf liveliness; (vitalidad) life; (actividad) activity; bustle

animado, a [ani'maðo, a] adj lively; (vivaz) animated; **animador, a** nm/f (TV) host(ess), compère; (DEPORTE) cheerleader

animadversión [animaðßer'sjon] nf ill-will, antagonism

animal [ani'mal] adj animal; (fig) stupid ♦ nm animal; (fig) fool; (bestia) brute

animar [ani'mar] vt (BIO) to animate, give life to; (fig) to liven up, brighten up, cheer up; (estimular) to stimulate; **~se** vr to cheer up; to feel encouraged; (decidirse) to make up

one's mind

ánimo ['animo] nm (alma) soul; (mente) mind; (valentía) courage ♦ excl cheer up!

animoso, a [ani'moso, a] adj brave; (vivo) lively

aniquilar [aniki'lar] vt to annihilate, destroy

anís [a'nis] nm aniseed; (licor) anisette

aniversario [anißer'sarjo] nm anniversary

anoche [a'notʃe] adv last night; **antes de ~** the night before last

anochecer [anotʃe'θer] vi to get dark ♦ nm nightfall, dark; **al ~** at nightfall

anodino, a [ano'ðino, a] adj dull, anodyne

anomalía [anoma'lia] nf anomaly

anonadado, a [anona'ðaðo, a] adj: **estar/ quedar/sentirse ~** to be overwhelmed o amazed

anonimato [anoni'mato] nm anonymity

anónimo, a [a'nonimo, a] adj anonymous; (COM) limited ♦ nm (carta) anonymous letter; (: maliciosa) poison-pen letter

anormal [anor'mal] adj abnormal

anotación [anota'θjon] nf note; annotation

anotar [ano'tar] vt to note down; (comentar) to annotate

anquilosamiento [ankilosa'mjento] nm (fig) paralysis; stagnation

anquilosarse [ankilo'sarse] vr (fig: persona) to get out of touch; (método, costumbres) to go out of date

ansia ['ansja] nf anxiety; (añoranza) yearning; **ansiar** vt to long for

ansiedad [ansje'ðað] nf anxiety

ansioso, a [an'sjoso, a] adj anxious; (anhelante) eager; **~ de** o **por algo** greedy for sth

antagónico, a [anta'xoniko, a] adj antagonistic; (opuesto) contrasting; **antagonista** nm/f antagonist

antaño [an'taɲo] adv long ago, formerly

Antártico [an'tartiko] nm: **el ~** the Antarctic

ante ['ante] prep before, in the presence of; (problema etc) faced with ♦ nm (piel) suede; **~ todo** above all

anteanoche [antea'notʃe] adv the night before last

anteayer [antea'jer] adv the day before yesterday

antebrazo [ante'ßraθo] nm forearm

antecedente [anteθe'ðente] adj previous ♦ nm antecedent; **~s** nmpl (JUR): **~s penales** criminal record; (procedencia) background

anteceder [anteθe'ðer] vt to precede, go before

antecesor, a [anteθe'sor, a] nm/f predecessor

antedicho, a [ante'ðitʃo, a] adj afore-mentioned

antelación [antela'θjon] nf: **con ~** in

advance

antemano [ante'mano]: **de ~** *adv* beforehand, in advance

antena [an'tena] *nf* antenna; (*de televisión etc*) aerial; **~ parabólica** satellite dish

anteojo [ante'oxo] *nm* eyeglass; **~s** *nmpl* (AM) glasses, spectacles

antepasados [antepa'saðos] *nmpl* ancestors

anteponer [antepo'ner] *vt* to place in front; (*fig*) to prefer

anteproyecto [antepro'jekto] *nm* preliminary sketch; (*fig*) blueprint

anterior [ante'rjor] *adj* preceding, previous; **~idad** *nf*: **con ~idad** a prior to, before

antes ['antes] *adv* (*con prioridad*) before ♦ *prep*: **~ de** before ♦ *conj*: **~ de ir/de que te vayas** before going/before you go; **~ bien** (but) rather; **dos días ~** two days before o previously; **no quiso venir ~** she didn't want to come any earlier; **tomo el avión ~ que el barco** I take the plane rather than the boat; **~ que yo** before me; **lo ~ posible** as soon as possible; **cuanto ~ mejor** the sooner the better

antiaéreo, a [antia'ereo, a] *adj* anti-aircraft

antibalas [anti'ßalas] *adj inv*: **chaleco ~** bullet-proof jacket

antibiótico [anti'ßjotiko] *nm* antibiotic

anticiclón [antiθi'klon] *nm* anticyclone

anticipación [antiθipa'θjon] *nf* anticipation; **con 10 minutos de ~** 10 minutes early

anticipado, a [antiθi'paðo, a] *adj* (*pago*) advance; **por ~** in advance

anticipar [antiθi'par] *vt* to anticipate; (*adelantar*) to bring forward; (COM) to advance; **~se** *vr*: **~se a su época** to be ahead of one's time

anticipo [anti'θipo] *nm* (COM) advance

anticonceptivo, a [antikonθep'tißo, a] *adj, nm* contraceptive

anticongelante [antikonxe'lante] *nm* antifreeze

anticuado, a [anti'kwaðo, a] *adj* out-of-date, old-fashioned; (*desusado*) obsolete

anticuario [anti'kwarjo] *nm* antique dealer

anticuerpo [anti'kwerpo] *nm* (MED) antibody

antidepresivo [antiðepre'sißo] *nm* antidepressant

antídoto [an'tiðoto] *nm* antidote

antiestético, a [anties'tetiko, a] *adj* unsightly

antifaz [anti'faθ] *nm* mask; (*velo*) veil

antigualla [anti'ɣwaʎa] *nf* antique; (*reliquia*) relic

antiguamente [antiɣwa'mente] *adv* formerly; (*hace mucho tiempo*) long ago

antigüedad [antiɣwe'ðað] *nf* antiquity; (*artículo*) antique; (*rango*) seniority

antiguo, a [an'tiɣwo, a] *adj* old, ancient; (*que fue*) former

Antillas [an'tiʎas] *nfpl*: **las ~** the West Indies

antílope [an'tilope] *nm* antelope

antinatural [antinatu'ral] *adj* unnatural

antipatía [antipa'tia] *nf* antipathy, dislike; **antipático, a** *adj* disagreeable, unpleasant

antirrobo [anti'rroßo] *adj inv* (*alarma etc*) anti-theft

antisemita [antise'mita] *adj* anti-Semitic ♦ *nm/f* anti-Semite

antiséptico, a [anti'septiko, a] *adj* antiseptic ♦ *nm* antiseptic

antítesis [an'titesis] *nf inv* antithesis

antojadizo, a [antoxa'ðiθo, a] *adj* capricious

antojarse [anto'xarse] *vr* (*desear*): **se me antoja comprarlo** I have a mind to buy it; (*pensar*): **se me antoja que** I have a feeling that

antojo [an'toxo] *nm* caprice, whim; (*rosa*) birthmark; (*lunar*) mole

antología [antolo'xia] *nf* anthology

antorcha [an'tortʃa] *nf* torch

antro ['antro] *nm* cavern

antropófago, a [antro'pofaxo, a] *adj, nm/f* cannibal

antropología [antropolo'xia] *nf* anthropology

anual [a'nwal] *adj* annual

anuario [a'nwarjo] *nm* yearbook

anudar [anu'ðar] *vt* to knot, tie; (*unir*) to join; **~se** *vr* to get tied up

anulación [anula'θjon] *nf* annulment; (*cancelación*) cancellation

anular [anu'lar] *vt* (*contrato*) to annul, cancel; (*ley*) to revoke, repeal; (*suscripción*) to cancel ♦ *nm* ring finger

Anunciación [anunθja'θjon] *nf* (REL) Annunciation

anunciante [anun'θjante] *nm/f* (COM) advertiser

anunciar [anun'θjar] *vt* to announce; (*proclamar*) to proclaim; (COM) to advertise

anuncio [a'nunθjo] *nm* announcement; (*señal*) sign; (COM) advertisement; (*cartel*) poster

anzuelo [an'θwelo] *nm* hook; (*para pescar*) fish hook

añadidura [aɲaði'ðura] *nf* addition, extra; **por ~** besides, in addition

añadir [aɲa'ðir] *vt* to add

añejo, a [a'ɲexo, a] *adj* old; (*vino*) mellow

añicos [a'ɲikos] *nmpl*: **hacer ~** to smash, shatter

añil [a'ɲil] *nm* (BOT, *color*) indigo

año ['aɲo] *nm* year; **¡Feliz A~ Nuevo!** Happy New Year!; **tener 15 ~s** to be 15 (years old); **los ~s 90** the nineties; **~ bisiesto/escolar** leap/school year; **el ~ que viene** next year

añoranza [aɲo'ranθa] nf nostalgia; (anhelo) longing

apabullar [apaβu'ʎar] vt (tb fig) to crush, squash

apacentar [apaθen'tar] vt to pasture, graze

apacible [apa'θiβle] adj gentle, mild

apaciguar [apaθi'ɣwar] vt to pacify, calm (down)

apadrinar [apaðri'nar] vt to sponsor, support; (REL) to be godfather to

apagado, a [apa'ɣaðo, a] adj (volcán) extinct; (color) dull; (voz) quiet; (sonido) muted, muffled; (persona: apático) listless; **estar ~** (fuego, luz) to be out; (RADIO, TV etc) to be off

apagar [apa'ɣar] vt to put out; (ELEC, RADIO, TV) to turn off; (sonido) to silence, muffle; (sed) to quench

apagón [apa'ɣon] nm blackout; power cut

apalabrar [apala'βrar] vt to agree to; (contratar) to engage

apalear [apale'ar] vt to beat, thrash

apañar [apa'ɲar] vt to pick up; (asir) to take hold of, grasp; (reparar) to mend, patch up; **~se** vr to manage, get along

aparador [apara'ðor] nm sideboard; (AM: escaparate) shop window

aparato [apa'rato] nm apparatus; (máquina) machine; (doméstico) appliance; (boato) ostentation; **~ de facsímil** facsimile (machine), fax; **~ digestivo** (ANAT) digestive system; **~so, a** adj showy, ostentatious

aparcamiento [aparka'mjento] nm car park (BRIT), parking lot (US)

aparcar [apar'kar] vt, vi to park

aparear [apare'ar] vt (objetos) to pair, match; (animales) to mate; **~se** vr to make a pair; to mate

aparecer [apare'θer] vi to appear; **~se** vr to appear

aparejado, a [apare'xaðo, a] adj fit, suitable; **llevar o traer ~** to involve; **aparejador, a** nm/f (ARQ) master builder

aparejo [apa'rexo] nm harness; rigging; (de poleas) block and tackle

aparentar [aparen'tar] vt (edad) to look; (fingir): **~ tristeza** to pretend to be sad

aparente [apa'rente] adj apparent; (adecuado) suitable

aparezco etc vb ver **aparecer**

aparición [apari'θjon] nf appearance; (de libro) publication; (espectro) apparition

apariencia [apa'rjenθja] nf (outward) appearance; **en ~** outwardly, seemingly

apartado, a [apar'taðo, a] adj separate; (lejano) remote ♦ nm (tipográfico) paragraph; **~ (de correos)** post office box

apartamento [aparta'mento] nm apartment, flat (BRIT)

apartamiento [aparta'mjento] nm separation; (aislamiento) remoteness, isolation; (AM) apartment, flat (BRIT)

apartar [apar'tar] vt to separate; (quitar) to remove; **~se** vr to separate, part; (irse) to move away; to keep away

aparte [a'parte] adv separately; (además) besides ♦ nm aside; (tipográfico) new paragraph

aparthotel [aparto'tel] nm serviced apartments

apasionado, a [apasjo'naðo, a] adj passionate

apasionar [apasjo'nar] vt to excite; **le apasiona el fútbol** she's crazy about football; **~se** vr to get excited

apatía [apa'tia] nf apathy

apático, a [a'patiko, a] adj apathetic

Apdo abr (= Apartado (de Correos)) PO Box

apeadero [apea'ðero] nm halt, stop, stopping place

apearse [ape'arse] vr (jinete) to dismount; (bajarse) to get down o out; (AUTO, FERRO) to get off o out

apechugar [apetʃu'ɣar] vr: **~ con algo** to face up to sth

apedrear [apeðre'ar] vt to stone

apegarse [ape'ɣarse] vr: **~ a** to become attached to; **apego** nm attachment, devotion

apelación [apela'θjon] nf appeal

apelar [ape'lar] vi to appeal; **~ a** (fig) to resort to

apellidar [apeʎi'ðar] vt to call, name; **~se** vr: **se apellida Pérez** her (sur)name's Pérez

apellido [ape'ʎiðo] nm surname

apelmazarse [apelma'θarse] vr (masa, arroz) to go hard; (prenda de tana) to shrink

apenar [ape'nar] vt to grieve, trouble; (AM: avergonzar) to embarrass; **~se** vr to grieve; (AM) to be embarrassed

apenas [a'penas] adv scarcely, hardly ♦ conj as soon as, no sooner

apéndice [a'pendiθe] nm appendix; **apendicitis** nf appendicitis

aperitivo [aperi'tiβo] nm (bebida) aperitif; (comida) appetizer

apero [a'pero] nm (AGR) implement; **~s** nmpl farm equipment sg

apertura [aper'tura] nf opening; (POL) liberalization

apesadumbrar [apesaðum'brar] vt to grieve, sadden; **~se** vr to distress o.s.

apestar [apes'tar] vt to infect ♦ vi: **~ (a)** to stink (of)

apetecer [apete'θer] vt: **¿te apetece un café?** do you fancy a (cup of) coffee?; **apetecible** adj desirable; (comida) appetizing

apetito [ape'tito] nm appetite; **~so, a** adj

appetizing; (*fig*) tempting

apiadarse [apja'ðarse] *vr*: ~ **de** to take pity on

ápice ['apiθe] *nm* whit, iota

apilar [api'lar] *vt* to pile o heap up; ~**se** *vr* to pile up

apiñarse [api'ɲarse] *vr* to crowd o press together

apio ['apjo] *nm* celery

apisonadora [apisona'ðora] *nf* steamroller

aplacar [apla'kar] *vt* to placate; ~**se** *vr* to calm down

aplanar [apla'nar] *vt* to smooth, level; (*allanar*) to roll flat, flatten

aplastante [aplas'tante] *adj* overwhelming; (*lógica*) compelling

aplastar [aplas'tar] *vt* to squash (flat); (*fig*) to crush

aplatanarse [aplata'narse] *vr* to get lethargic

aplaudir [aplau'ðir] *vt* to applaud

aplauso [a'plauso] *nm* applause; (*fig*) approval, acclaim

aplazamiento [aplaθa'mjento] *nm* postponement

aplazar [apla'θar] *vt* to postpone, defer

aplicación [aplika'θjon] *nf* application; (*esfuerzo*) effort

aplicado, a [apli'kaðo, a] *adj* diligent, hard-working

aplicar [apli'kar] *vt* (*ejecutar*) to apply; ~**se** *vr* to apply o.s.

aplique *etc* [a'plike] *vb ver* **aplicar** ♦ *nm* wall light

aplomo [a'plomo] *nm* aplomb, self-assurance

apocado, a [apo'kaðo, a] *adj* timid

apodar [apo'ðar] *vt* to nickname

apoderado [apoðe'raðo] *nm* agent, representative

apoderarse [apoðe'rarse] *vr*: ~ **de** to take possession of

apodo [a'poðo] *nm* nickname

apogeo [apo'xeo] *nm* peak, summit

apolillarse [apoli'ʎarse] *vr* to get moth-eaten

apología [apolo'xia] *nf* eulogy; (*defensa*) defence

apoltronarse [apoltro'narse] *vr* to get lazy

apoplejía [apople'xia] *nf* apoplexy, stroke

apoquinar [apoki'nar] (*fam*) *vt* to fork out, cough up

aporrear [aporre'ar] *vt* to beat (up)

aportar [apor'tar] *vt* to contribute ♦ *vi* to reach port; ~**se** *vr* (*AM: llegar*) to arrive, come

aposento [apo'sento] *nm* lodging; (*habitación*) room

aposta [a'posta] *adv* deliberately, on purpose

apostar [apos'tar] *vt* to bet, stake; (*tropas etc*) to station, post ♦ *vi* to bet

apóstol [a'postol] *nm* apostle

apóstrofo [a'postrofo] *nm* apostrophe

apoyar [apo'jar] *vt* to lean, rest; (*fig*) to support, back; ~**se** *vr*: ~**se en** to lean on; **apoyo** *nm* (*gen*) support; backing, help

apreciable [apre'θjaβle] *adj* considerable; (*fig*) esteemed

apreciar [apre'θjar] *vt* to evaluate, assess; (*COM*) to appreciate, value; (*persona*) to respect; (*tamaño*) to gauge, assess; (*detalles*) to notice

aprecio [a'preθjo] *nm* valuation, estimate; (*fig*) appreciation

aprehender [apreen'der] *vt* to apprehend, detain

apremiante [apre'mjante] *adj* urgent, pressing

apremiar [apre'mjar] *vt* to compel, force ♦ *vi* to be urgent, press; **apremio** *nm* urgency

aprender [apren'der] *vt, vi* to learn

aprendiz, a [apren'diθ, a] *nm/f* apprentice; (*principiante*) learner; ~ **de conductor** learner driver; ~**aje** *nm* apprenticeship

aprensión [apren'sjon] *nm* apprehension, fear; **aprensivo, a** *adj* apprehensive

apresar [apre'sar] *vt* to seize; (*capturar*) to capture

aprestar [apres'tar] *vt* to prepare, get ready; (*TEC*) to prime, size; ~**se** *vr* to get ready

apresurado, a [apresu'raðo, a] *adj* hurried, hasty; **apresuramiento** *nm* hurry, haste

apresurar [apresu'rar] *vt* to hurry, accelerate; ~**se** *vr* to hurry, make haste

apretado, a [apre'taðo, a] *adj* tight; (*escritura*) cramped

apretar [apre'tar] *vt* to squeeze; (*TEC*) to tighten; (*presionar*) to press together, pack ♦ *vi* to be too tight

apretón [apre'ton] *nm* squeeze; ~ **de manos** handshake

aprieto [a'prjeto] *nm* squeeze; (*dificultad*) difficulty; **estar en un** ~ to be in a fix

aprisa [a'prisa] *adv* quickly, hurriedly

aprisionar [aprisjo'nar] *vt* to imprison

aprobación [aproβa'θjon] *nf* approval

aprobar [apro'βar] *vt* to approve (of); (*examen, materia*) to pass ♦ *vi* to pass

apropiación [apropja'θjon] *nf* appropriation

apropiado, a [apro'pjaðo, a] *adj* appropriate

apropiarse [apro'pjarse] *vr*: ~ **de** to appropriate

aprovechado, a [aproβe'tʃaðo, a] *adj* industrious, hard-working; (*económico*) thrifty; (*pey*) unscrupulous; **aprovechamiento** *nm* use; exploitation

aprovechar [aproβe'tʃar] *vt* to use; (*explotar*) to exploit; (*experiencia*) to profit from; (*oferta, oportunidad*) to take advantage of ♦ *vi* to progress, improve; ~**se** *vr*: ~**se de** to make use of; to take advantage of; ¡**que aproveche!** enjoy your meal!

aproximación [aproksima'θjon] nf
approximation; (de lotería) consolation prize;
aproximado, a adj approximate

aproximar [aproksi'mar] vt to bring nearer;
~se vr to come near, approach

apruebo etc vb ver **aprobar**

aptitud [apti'tuð] nf aptitude

apto, a ['apto, a] adj suitable

apuesta [a'pwesta] nf bet, wager

apuesto, a [a'pwesto, a] adj neat, elegant

apuntador [apunta'ðor] nm prompter

apuntalar [apunta'lar] vt to prop up

apuntar [apun'tar] vt (con arma) to aim at;
(con dedo) to point at o to; (anotar) to note
(down); (TEATRO) to prompt; **~se** vr (DEPORTE:
tanto, victoria) to score; (ESCOL) to enrol

apunte [a'punte] nm note

apuñalar [apuɲa'lar] vt to stab

apurado, a [apu'raðo, a] adj needy; (difícil)
difficult; (peligroso) dangerous; (AM) hurried,
rushed

apurar [apu'rar] vt (agotar) to drain;
(recursos) to use up; (molestar) to annoy; **~se**
vr (preocuparse) to worry; (darse prisa) to
hurry

apuro [a'puro] nm (aprieto) fix, jam; (escasez)
want, hardship; (vergüenza) embarrassment;
(AM) haste, urgency

aquejado, a [ake'xaðo, a] adj: **~ de** (MED)
afflicted by

aquél, aquélla [a'kel, a'keʎa] (pl **aquéllos,
as**) pron that (one); (pl) those (ones)

aquel, aquella [a'kel, a'keʎa] (pl **aquellos,
as**) adj that; (pl) those

aquello [a'keʎo] pron that, that business

aquí [a'ki] adv (lugar) here; (tiempo) now;
~ arriba up here; **~ mismo** right here; **~ yace**
here lies; **de ~ a siete días** a week from now

aquietar [akje'tar] vt to quieten (down),
calm (down)

ara ['ara] nf: **en ~s de** for the sake of

árabe ['araße] adj, nm/f Arab ♦ nm (LING)
Arabic

Arabia [a'raßja] nf: **~ Saudí o Saudita** Saudi
Arabia

arado [a'raðo] nm plough

Aragón [ara'xon] nm Aragon; **aragonés,
esa** adj, nm/f Aragonese

arancel [aran'θel] nm tariff, duty; **~ de
aduanas** customs (duty)

arandela [aran'dela] nf (TEC) washer

araña [a'raɲa] nf (ZOOL) spider; (lámpara)
chandelier

arañar [ara'ɲar] vt to scratch

arañazo [ara'ɲaθo] nm scratch

arar [a'rar] vt to plough, till

arbitraje [arßi'traxe] nm arbitration

arbitrar [arßi'trar] vt to arbitrate in; (DEPORTE)
to referee ♦ vi to arbitrate

arbitrariedad [arßitrarje'ðað] nf
arbitrariness; (acto) arbitrary act; **arbitrario,
a** adj arbitrary

arbitrio [ar'ßitrjo] nm free will; (JUR)
adjudication, decision

árbitro ['arßitro] nm arbitrator; (DEPORTE)
referee; (TENIS) umpire

árbol ['arßol] nm (BOT) tree; (NAUT) mast;
(TEC) axle, shaft; **arbolado, a** adj wooded;
(camino etc) tree-lined ♦ nm woodland

arboleda [arßo'leða] nf grove, plantation

arbusto [ar'ßusto] nm bush, shrub

arca ['arka] nf chest, box

arcada [ar'kaða] nf arcade; (de puente) arch,
span; **~s** nfpl (náuseas) retching sg

arcaico, a [ar'kaiko, a] adj archaic

arce [ar'θe] nm maple tree

arcén [ar'θen] nm (de autopista) hard
shoulder; (de carretera) verge

archipiélago [artʃi'pjelaxo] nm archipelago

archivador [artʃißa'ðor] nm filing cabinet

archivar [artʃi'ßar] vt to file (away); **archivo**
nm file, archive(s) (pl)

arcilla [ar'θiʎa] nf clay

arco ['arko] nm arch; (MAT) arc; (MIL, MUS)
bow; **~ iris** rainbow

arder [ar'ðer] vi to burn; **estar que arde**
(persona) to fume

ardid [ar'ðið] nm ploy, trick

ardiente [ar'ðjente] adj burning, ardent

ardilla [ar'ðiʎa] nf squirrel

ardor [ar'ðor] nm (calor) heat; (fig) ardour;
~ de estómago heartburn

arduo, a ['arðwo, a] adj arduous

área ['area] nf area; (DEPORTE) penalty area

arena [a'rena] nf sand; (de una lucha) arena;
~ movedizas quicksand sg

arenal [are'nal] nm (arena movediza)
quicksand

arengar [aren'gar] vt to harangue

arenisca [are'niska] nf sandstone; (cascajo)
grit

arenoso, a [are'noso, a] adj sandy

arenque [a'renke] nm herring

argamasa [arva'masa] nf mortar, plaster

Argel [ar'xel] n Algiers; **Argelia** nf Algeria;
argelino, a adj, nm/f Algerian

Argentina [arxen'tina] nf: **(la) ~** Argentina

argentino, a [arxen'tino, a] adj Argentinian;
(de plata) silvery ♦ nm/f Argentinian

argolla [ar'voʎa] nf (large) ring

argot [ar'vo] (pl **~s**) nm slang

argucia [ar'vuθja] nf subtlety, sophistry

argüir [ar'vwir] vt to deduce; (discutir) to
argue; (indicar) to indicate, imply; (censurar)
to reproach ♦ vi to argue

argumentación [arvumenta'θjon] nf (line
of) argument

argumentar [arvumen'tar] vt, vi to argue

argumento |arɣu'mento| nm argument; (razonamiento) reasoning; (de novela etc) plot; (CINE, TV) storyline

aria ['arja] nf aria

aridez |ari'ðeθ| nf aridity, dryness

árido, a |'ariðo, a| adj arid, dry; ~s nmpl (COM) dry goods

Aries ['arjes] nm Aries

ario, a |'arjo, a| adj Aryan

arisco, a |a'risko, a| adj surly; (insociable) unsociable

aristócrata |aris'tokrata| nm/f aristocrat

aritmética |arit'metika| nf arithmetic

arma |'arma| nf arm; ~s nfpl arms; ~ **blanca** blade, knife; (espada) sword; ~ **de fuego** firearm; ~s **cortas** small arms

armada |ar'maða| nf armada; (flota) fleet

armadillo |arma'ðiʎo| nm armadillo

armado, a |ar'maðo, a| adj armed; (TEC) reinforced

armador |arma'ðor| nm (NAUT) shipowner

armadura |arma'ðura| nf (MIL) armour; (TEC) framework; (ZOOL) skeleton; (FÍSICA) armature

armamento |arma'mento| nm armament; (NAUT) fitting-out

armar |ar'mar| vt (soldado) to arm; (máquina) to assemble; (navío) to fit out; ~la, ~ **un lío** to start a row, kick up a fuss

armario |ar'marjo| nm wardrobe; (de cocina, baño) cupboard

armatoste |arma'toste| nm (mueble) monstrosity; (máquina) contraption

armazón |arma'θon| nf o m body, chassis; (de mueble etc) frame; (ARQ) skeleton

armería |arme'ria| nf gunsmith's

armiño |ar'miɲo| nm stoat; (piel) ermine

armisticio |armis'tiθjo| nm armistice

armonía |armo'nia| nf harmony

armónica |ar'monika| nf harmonica

armonioso, a |armo'njoso, a| adj harmonious

armonizar |armoni'θar| vt to harmonize; (diferencias) to reconcile ♦ vi: ~ **con** (fig) to be in keeping with; (colores) to tone in with, blend

arnés |ar'nes| nm armour; **arneses** nmpl (de caballo etc) harness sg

aro |'aro| nm ring; (tejo) quoit; (AM: pendiente) earring

aroma |a'roma| nm aroma, scent

aromático, a |aro'matiko, a| adj aromatic

arpa |'arpa| nf harp

arpía |ar'pia| nf shrew

arpillera |arpi'ʎera| nf sacking, sackcloth

arpón |ar'pon| nm harpoon

arquear |arke'ar| vt to arch, bend; ~se vr to arch, bend

arqueología |arkeolo'xia| nf archaeology; **arqueólogo, a** nm/f archaeologist

arquero |ar'kero| nm archer, bowman

arquetipo |arke'tipo| nm archetype

arquitecto |arki'tekto| nm architect; **arquitectura** nf architecture

arrabal |arra'ßal| nm suburb; (AM) slum; ~es nmpl (afueras) outskirts

arraigado, a |arrai'xaðo, a| adj deep-rooted; (fig) established

arraigar |arrai'xar| vt to establish ♦ vi to take root; ~se vr to take root; (persona) to settle

arrancar |arran'kar| vt (sacar) to extract, pull out; (arrebatar) to snatch (away); (INFORM) to boot; (fig) to extract ♦ vi (AUTO, máquina) to start; (ponerse en marcha) to get going; ~ **de** to stem from

arranque etc |a'rranke| vb ver **arrancar** ♦ nm sudden start; (AUTO) start; (fig) fit, outburst

arrasar |arra'sar| vt (aplanar) to level, flatten; (destruir) to demolish

arrastrado, a |arras'traðo, a| adj poor, wretched; (AM) servile

arrastrar |arras'trar| vt to drag (along); (fig) to drag down, degrade; (suj: agua, viento) to carry away ♦ vi to drag, trail on the ground; ~se vr to crawl; (fig) to grovel; **llevar algo arrastrado** to drag sth along

arrastre |a'rrastre| nm drag, dragging

arre |'arre| excl gee up!

arrear |arre'ar| vt to drive on, urge on ♦ vi to hurry along

arrebatado, a |arreßa'taðo, a| adj rash, impetuous; (repentino) sudden, hasty

arrebatar |arreßa'tar| vt to snatch (away), seize; (fig) to captivate; ~se vr to get carried away, get excited

arrebato |arre'ßato| nm fit of rage, fury; (éxtasis) rapture

arrecife |arre'θife| nm (tb: ~ **de coral**) reef

arredrarse |arre'ðrarse| vr: ~ (ante algo) to be intimidated (by sth)

arreglado, a |arre'xlaðo, a| adj (ordenado) neat, orderly; (moderado) moderate, reasonable

arreglar |arre'xlar| vt (poner orden) to tidy up; (algo roto) to fix, repair; (problema) to solve; ~se vr to reach an understanding; **arreglárselas** (fam) to get by, manage

arreglo |a'rrexlo| nm settlement; (orden) order; (acuerdo) agreement; (MUS) arrangement, setting

arrellanarse |arreʎa'narse| vr: ~ **en** to sit back in/on

arremangar |arreman'gar| vt to roll up, turn up; ~se vr to roll up one's sleeves

arremeter |arreme'ter| vi: ~ **contra** to attack, rush at

arrendamiento |arrenda'mjento| nm letting; (alquilar) hiring; (contrato) lease; (alquiler) rent; **arrendar** vt to let, lease; to rent; **arrendatario, a** nm/f tenant

arreos [a'rreos] nmpl (de caballo) harness sg, trappings

arrepentimiento [arrepenti'mjento] nm regret, repentance

arrepentirse [arrepen'tirse] vr to repent; ~ **de** to regret

arrestar [arres'tar] vt to arrest; (encarcelar) to imprison; **arresto** nm arrest; (MIL) detention; (audacia) boldness, daring; **arresto domiciliario** house arrest

arriar [a'rrjar] vt (velas) to haul down; (bandera) to lower, strike; (cable) to pay out

---

PALABRA CLAVE

arriba [a'rriβa] adv **1** (posición) above; **desde ~** from above; **~ de todo** at the very top, right on top; **Juan está ~** Juan is upstairs; **lo ~ mencionado** the aforementioned

2 (dirección): **calle ~** up the street

3: **de ~ abajo** from top to bottom; **mirar a uno de ~ abajo** to look sb up and down

4: **para ~**: **de 5000 pesetas para ~** from 5000 pesetas up(wards)

♦ adj: **de ~**: **el piso de ~** the upstairs flat (BRIT) o apartment; **la parte de ~** the top o upper part

♦ prep: **~ de** (AM) above; **~ de 200 dólares** more than 200 dollars

♦ excl: **¡~!** up!; **¡manos ~!** hands up!; **¡~ España!** long live Spain!

---

arribar [arri'βar] vi to put into port; (llegar) to arrive

arribista [arri'βista] nm/f parvenu(e), upstart

arriendo etc [a'rrjendo] vb ver **arrendar** ♦ nm = **arrendamiento**

arriero [a'rrjero] nm muleteer

arriesgado, a [arrjes'ɣaðo, a] adj (peligroso) risky; (audaz) bold, daring

arriesgar [arrjes'ɣar] vt to risk; (poner en peligro) to endanger; **~se** vr to take a risk

arrimar [arri'mar] vt (acercar) to bring close; (poner de lado) to set aside; **~se** vr to come close o closer; **~se a** to lean on

arrinconar [arrinko'nar] vt (colocar) to put in a corner; (enemigo) to corner; (fig) to put on one side; (abandonar) to push aside

arrodillarse [arroði'ʎarse] vr to kneel (down)

arrogancia [arro'ɣanθja] nf arrogance; **arrogante** adj arrogant

arrojar [arro'xar] vt to throw, hurl; (humo) to emit, give out; (COM) to yield, produce; **~se** vr to throw o hurl o.s.

arrojo [a'rroxo] nm daring

arrollador, a [arroʎa'ðor, a] adj overwhelming

arrollar [arro'ʎar] vt (AUTO etc) to run over,

knock down; (DEPORTE) to crush

arropar [arro'par] vt to cover, wrap up; **~se** vr to wrap o.s. up

arroyo [a'rrojo] nm stream; (de la calle) gutter

arroz [a'rroθ] nm rice; **~ con leche** rice pudding

arruga [a'rruɣa] nf (de cara) wrinkle; (de vestido) crease

arrugar [arru'ɣar] vt to wrinkle; to crease; **~se** vr to get creased

arruinar [arrwi'nar] vt to ruin, wreck; **~se** vr to be ruined, go bankrupt

arrullar [arru'ʎar] vi to coo ♦ vt to lull to sleep

arsenal [arse'nal] nm naval dockyard; (MIL) arsenal

arsénico [ar'seniko] nm arsenic

arte ['arte] (gen m en sg y siempre f en pl) nm art; (maña) skill, guile; **~s** nfpl (bellas ~s) arts

artefacto [arte'fakto] nm appliance

arteria [ar'terja] nf artery

artesanía [artesa'nia] nf craftsmanship; (artículos) handicrafts pl; **artesano, a** nm/f artisan, craftsman/woman

ártico, a ['artiko, a] adj Arctic ♦ nm: **el Á~** the Arctic

articulación [artikula'θjon] nf articulation; (MED, TEC) joint; **articulado, a** adj articulated; jointed

articular [artiku'lar] vt to articulate; to join together

artículo [ar'tikulo] nm article; (cosa) thing, article; **~s** nmpl (COM) goods

artífice [ar'tifiθe] nm/f (fig) architect

artificial [artifi'θjal] adj artificial

artificio [arti'fiθjo] nm art, skill; (astucia) cunning

artillería [artiʎe'ria] nf artillery

artillero [arti'ʎero] nm artilleryman, gunner

artilugio [arti'luxjo] nm gadget

artimaña [arti'maɲa] nf trap, snare; (astucia) cunning

artista [ar'tista] nm/f (pintor) artist, painter; (TEATRO) artist, artiste; **~ de cine** film actor/actress; **artístico, a** adj artistic

artritis [ar'tritis] nf arthritis

arveja [ar'βexa] (AM) nf pea

arzobispo [arθo'βispo] nm archbishop

as [as] nm ace

asa ['asa] nf handle; (fig) lever

asado [a'saðo] nm roast (meat); (AM: barbacoa) barbecue

asador [asa'ðor] nm spit

asadura [asa'ðura] nf entrails pl, offal

asalariado, a [asala'rjaðo, a] adj paid, salaried ♦ nm/f wage earner

asaltante [asal'tante] nm/f attacker

asaltar [asal'tar] vt to attack, assault; (fig) to

assail; **asalto** *nm* attack, assault; (*DEPORTE*) round

asamblea [asam'blea] *nf* assembly; (*reunión*) meeting

asar [a'sar] *vt* to roast

asbesto [as'βesto] *nm* asbestos

ascendencia [asθen'denθja] *nf* ancestry; (*AM*) ascendancy; **de ~ francesa** of French origin

ascender [asθen'der] *vi* (*subir*) to ascend, rise; (*ser promovido*) to gain promotion ♦ *vt* to promote; **~ a** to amount to; **ascendiente** *nm* influence ♦ *nm/f* ancestor

ascensión [asθen'sjon] *nf* ascent; (*REL*): **la A~** the Ascension

ascenso [as'θenso] *nm* ascent; (*promoción*) promotion

ascensor [asθen'sor] *nm* lift (*BRIT*), elevator (*US*)

ascético, a [as'θetiko, a] *adj* ascetic

asco ['asko] *nm*: **¡qué ~!** how revolting *o* disgusting!; **el ajo me da ~** I hate *o* loathe garlic; **estar hecho un ~** to be filthy

ascua ['askwa] *nf* ember; **estar en ~s** to be on tenterhooks

aseado, a [ase'aðo, a] *adj* clean; (*arreglado*) tidy; (*pulcro*) smart

asear [ase'ar] *vt* to clean, wash; to tidy (up)

asediar [ase'ðjar] *vt* (*MIL*) to besiege, lay siege to; (*fig*) to chase, pester; **asedio** *nm* siege; (*COM*) run

asegurado, a [aseɣu'raðo, a] *adj* insured

asegurador, a *nm/f* insurer

asegurar [aseɣu'rar] *vt* (*consolidar*) to secure, fasten; (*dar garantía de*) to guarantee; (*preservar*) to safeguard; (*afirmar, dar por cierto*) to assure, affirm; (*tranquilizar*) to reassure; (*tomar un seguro*) to insure; **~se** *vr* to assure o.s., make sure

asemejarse [aseme'xarse] *vr* to be alike; **~ a** to be like, resemble

asentado, a [asen'taðo, a] *adj* established, settled

asentar [asen'tar] *vt* (*sentar*) to seat, sit down; (*poner*) to place, establish; (*alisar*) to level, smooth down *o* out; (*anotar*) to note down ♦ *vi* to be suitable, suit

asentir [asen'tir] *vi* to assent, agree; **~ con la cabeza** to nod (one's head)

aseo [a'seo] *nm* cleanliness; **~s** *nmpl* (*servicios*) toilet *sg* (*BRIT*), cloakroom *sg* (*BRIT*), restroom *sg* (*US*)

aséptico, a [a'septiko, a] *adj* germ-free, free from infection

asequible [ase'kiβle] *adj* (*precio*) reasonable; (*meta*) attainable; (*persona*) approachable

aserradero [aserra'ðero] *nm* sawmill; **aserrar** *vt* to saw

asesinar [asesi'nar] *vt* to murder; (*POL*) to

assassinate; **asesinato** *nm* murder; assassination

asesino, a [ase'sino, a] *nm/f* murderer, killer; (*POL*) assassin

asesor, a [ase'sor, a] *nm/f* adviser, consultant

asesorar [aseso'rar] *vt* (*JUR*) to advise, give legal advice to; (*COM*) to act as consultant to; **~se** *vr*: **~se con** *o* **de** to take advice from, consult; **asesoría** *nf* (*cargo*) consultancy; (*oficina*) consultant's office

asestar [ases'tar] *vt* (*golpe*) to deal, strike

asfalto [as'falto] *nm* asphalt

asfixia [as'fiksja] *nf* asphyxia, suffocation

asfixiar [asfik'sjar] *vt* to asphyxiate, suffocate; **~se** *vr* to be asphyxiated, suffocate

asgo *etc vb ver* **asir**

así [a'si] *adv* (*de esta manera*) in this way, like this, thus; (*aunque*) although; (*tan pronto como*) as soon as; **~ que** so; **~ como** as well as; **~ y todo** even so; **¿no es ~?** isn't it?, didn't you? *etc*; **~ de grande** this big

Asia ['asja] *nf* Asia; **asiático, a** *adj, nm/f* Asian, Asiatic

asidero [asi'ðero] *nm* handle

asiduidad [asiðwi'ðað] *nf* assiduousness; **asiduo, a** *adj* assiduous; (*frecuente*) frequent ♦ *nm/f* regular (customer)

asiento [a'sjento] *nm* (*mueble*) seat, chair; (*de coche, en tribunal etc*) seat; (*localidad*) seat, place; (*fundamento*) site; **~ delantero/trasero** front/back seat

asignación [asiɣna'θjon] *nf* (*atribución*) assignment; (*reparto*) allocation; (*sueldo*) salary; **~ (semanal)** pocket money

asignar [asiɣ'nar] *vt* to assign, allocate

asignatura [asiɣna'tura] *nf* subject; course

asilado, a [asi'laðo, a] *nm/f* inmate; (*POL*) refugee

asilo [a'silo] *nm* (*refugio*) asylum, refuge; (*establecimiento*) home, institution; **~ político** political asylum

asimilación [asimila'θjon] *nf* assimilation

asimilar [asimi'lar] *vt* to assimilate

asimismo [asi'mismo] *adv* in the same way, likewise

asir [a'sir] *vt* to seize, grasp

asistencia [asis'tenθja] *nf* audience; (*MED*) attendance; (*ayuda*) assistance; **asistente** *nm/f* assistant; **los asistentes** those present; **asistente social** social worker

asistido, a [asis'tiðo, a] *adj*: **~ por ordenador** computer-assisted

asistir [asis'tir] *vt* to assist, help ♦ *vi*: **~ a** to attend, be present at

asma ['asma] *nf* asthma

asno ['asno] *nm* donkey; (*fig*) ass

asociación [asoθja'θjon] *nf* association; (*COM*) partnership; **asociado, a** *adj* associate ♦ *nm/f* associate; (*COM*) partner

asociar [aso'θjar] vt to associate
asolar [aso'lar] vt to destroy
asomar [aso'mar] vt to show, stick out ♦ vi to appear; **~se** vr to appear, show up; **~ la cabeza por la ventana** to put one's head out of the window
asombrar [asom'brar] vt to amaze, astonish; **~se** vr (*sorprenderse*) to be amazed; (*asustarse*) to get a fright; **asombro** nm amazement, astonishment; (*susto*) fright; **asombroso, a** adj astonishing, amazing
asomo [a'somo] nm hint, sign
aspa ['aspa] nf (*cruz*) cross; (*de molino*) sail; **en ~** X-shaped
aspaviento [aspa'ßjento] nm exaggerated display of feeling; (*fam*) fuss
aspecto [as'pekto] nm (*apariencia*) look, appearance; (*fig*) aspect
aspereza [aspe're θa] nf roughness; (*agrura*) sourness; (*de carácter*) surliness; **áspero, a** adj rough; bitter, sour; harsh
aspersión [asper'sjon] nf sprinkling
aspiración [aspira'θjon] nf breath, inhalation; (*MUS*) short pause; **aspiraciones** nfpl (*ambiciones*) aspirations
aspirador [aspira'ðor] nm = **aspiradora**
aspiradora [aspira'ðora] nf vacuum cleaner, Hoover ®
aspirante [aspi'rante] nm/f (*candidato*) candidate; (*DEPORTE*) contender
aspirar [aspi'rar] vt to breathe in ♦ vi: **~ a** to aspire to
aspirina [aspi'rina] nf aspirin
asquear [aske'ar] vt to sicken ♦ vi to be sickening; **~se** vr to feel disgusted; **asqueroso, a** adj disgusting, sickening
asta ['asta] nf lance; (*arpón*) spear; (*mango*) shaft, handle; (*ZOOL*) horn; **a media ~** at half mast
asterisco [aste'risko] nm asterisk
astilla [as'tiʎa] nf splinter; (*pedacito*) chip; **~s** nfpl (*leña*) firewood sg
astillero [asti'ʎero] nm shipyard
astringente [astrin'xente] adj, nm astringent
astro ['astro] nm star
astrología [astrolo'xia] nf astrology; **astrólogo, a** nm/f astrologer
astronauta [astro'nauta] nm/f astronaut
astronave [astro'naße] nm spaceship
astronomía [astrono'mia] nf astronomy; **astrónomo, a** nm/f astronomer
astucia [as'tuθja] nf astuteness; (*ardid*) clever trick
asturiano, a [astu'rjano, a] adj, nm/f Asturian
astuto, a [as'tuto, a] adj astute; (*taimado*) cunning
asumir [asu'mir] vt to assume
asunción [asun'θjon] nf assumption; (*REL*):

A~ Assumption
asunto [a'sunto] nm (*tema*) matter, subject; (*negocio*) business
asustar [asus'tar] vt to frighten; **~se** vr to be (o become) frightened
atacar [ata'kar] vt to attack
atadura [ata'ðura] nf bond, tie
atajar [ata'xar] vt (*enfermedad, mal*) to stop ♦ vi (*persona*) to take a short cut
atajo [a'taxo] nm short cut
atañer [ata'ɲer] vi: **~ a** to concern
ataque etc [a'take] vb ver **atacar** ♦ nm attack; **~ cardíaco** heart attack
atar [a'tar] vt to tie, tie up
atardecer [atarðe'θer] vi to get dark ♦ nm evening; (*crepúsculo*) dusk
atareado, a [atare'aðo, a] adj busy
atascar [atas'kar] vt to clog up; (*obstruir*) to jam; (*fig*) to hinder; **~se** vr to stall; (*cañería*) to get blocked up; **atasco** nm obstruction; (*AUTO*) traffic jam
ataúd [ata'uð] nm coffin
ataviar [ata'ßjar] vt to deck, array; **~se** vr to dress up
atavío [ata'ßio] nm attire, dress; **~s** nmpl finery sg
atemorizar [atemori'θar] vt to frighten, scare; **~se** vr to get scared
Atenas [a'tenas] n Athens
atención [aten'θjon] nf attention; (*bondad*) kindness ♦ excl (be) careful!, look out!
atender [aten'der] vt to attend to, look after ♦ vi to pay attention
atenerse [ate'nerse] vr: **~ a** to abide by, adhere to
atentado [aten'taðo] nm crime, illegal act; (*asalto*) assault; **~ contra la vida de uno** attempt on sb's life
atentamente [atenta'mente] adv: **Le saluda ~** Yours faithfully
atentar [aten'tar] vi: **~ a o contra** to commit an outrage against
atento, a [a'tento, a] adj attentive, observant; (*cortés*) polite, thoughtful
atenuante [ate'nwante] adj extenuating
atenuar [ate'nwar] vt (*disminuir*) to lessen, minimize
ateo, a [a'teo, a] adj atheistic ♦ nm/f atheist
aterciopelado, a [aterθjope'laðo, a] adj velvety
aterido, a [ate'riðo, a] adj: **~ de frío** frozen stiff
aterrador, a [aterra'ðor, a] adj frightening
aterrar [ate'rrar] vt to frighten; to terrify
aterrizaje [aterri'θaxe] nm landing
aterrizar [aterri'θar] vi to land
aterrorizar [aterrori'θar] vt to terrify
atesorar [ateso'rar] vt to hoard
atestado, a [ates'taðo, a] adj packed ♦ nm

(*JUR*) affidavit

atestar [ates'tar] *vt* to pack, stuff; (*JUR*) to attest, testify to

atestiguar [atesti'ɣwar] *vt* to testify to, bear witness to

atiborrar [atiβo'rrar] *vt* to fill, stuff; **~se** *vr* to stuff o.s.

ático ['atiko] *nm* attic; **~ de lujo** penthouse (flat, *BRIT*) o apartment)

atinado, a [ati'naðo, a] *adj* (*sensato*) wise; (*correcto*) right, correct

atinar [ati'nar] *vi* (*al disparar*): **~ al blanco** to hit the target; (*fig*) to be right

atisbar [atis'βar] *vt* to spy on; (*echar una ojeada*) to peep at

atizar [ati'θar] *vt* to poke; (*horno etc*) to stoke; (*fig*) to stir up, rouse

atlántico, a [at'lantiko, a] *adj* Atlantic ♦ *nm*: **el (océano) A~** the Atlantic (Ocean)

atlas ['atlas] *nm* atlas

atleta [at'leta] *nm* athlete; **atlético, a** *adj* athletic; **atletismo** *nm* athletics *sg*

atmósfera [at'mosfera] *nf* atmosphere

atolladero [atoʎa'ðero] *nm* (*fig*) jam, fix

atolondramiento [atolondra'mjento] *nm* bewilderment; (*insensatez*) silliness

atómico, a [a'tomiko, a] *adj* atomic

atomizador [atomiθa'ðor] *nm* atomizer; (*de perfume*) spray

átomo ['atomo] *nm* atom

atónito, a [a'tonito, a] *adj* astonished, amazed

atontado, a [aton'taðo, a] *adj* stunned; (*bobo*) silly, daft

atontar [aton'tar] *vt* to stun; **~se** *vr* to become confused

atormentar [atormen'tar] *vt* to torture; (*molestar*) to torment; (*acosar*) to plague, harass

atornillar [atorni'ʎar] *vt* to screw on o down

atosigar [atosi'ɣar] *vt* to harass, pester

atracador, a [atraka'ðor, a] *nm/f* robber

atracar [atra'kar] *vt* (*NAUT*) to moor; (*robar*) to hold up, rob, ♦ *vi* to moor; **~se** *vr*: **~se (de)** to stuff o.s. (with)

atracción [atrak'θjon] *nf* attraction

atraco [a'trako] *nm* holdup, robbery

atracón [atra'kon] *nm*: **darse** o **pegarse un ~ (de)** (*fam*) to stuff o.s. (with)

atractivo, a [atrak'tiβo, a] *adj* attractive ♦ *nm* appeal

atraer [atra'er] *vt* to attract

atragantarse [atraɣan'tarse] *vr*: **~ (con)** to choke (on); **se me ha atragantado el chico l** can't stand the boy

atrancar [atran'kar] *vt* (*puerta*) to bar, bolt

atrapar [atra'par] *vt* to trap; (*resfriado etc*) to catch

atrás [a'tras] *adv* (*movimiento*) back(wards);

(*lugar*) behind; (*tiempo*) previously; **ir hacia ~** to go back(wards); to go to the rear; **estar ~** to be behind o at the back

atrasado, a [atra'saðo, a] *adj* slow; (*pago*) overdue, late; (*país*) backward

atrasar [atra'sar] *vi* to be slow; **~se** *vr* to remain behind; (*tren*) to be o run late; **atraso** *nm* slowness; lateness, delay; (*de país*) backwardness; **atrasos** *nmpl* (*COM*) arrears

atravesar [atraβe'sar] *vt* (*cruzar*) to cross (over); (*traspasar*) to pierce; to go through; (*poner al través*) to lay o put across; **~se** *vr* to come in between; (*intervenir*) to interfere

atravieso *etc vb ver* **atravesar**

atrayente [atra'jente] *adj* attractive

atreverse [atre'βerse] *vr* to dare; (*insolentarse*) to be insolent; **atrevido, a** *adj* daring; insolent; **atrevimiento** *nm* daring; insolence

atribución [atriβu'θjon] *nf*: **atribuciones** (*POL*) powers; (*ADMIN*) responsibilities

atribuir [atriβu'ir] *vt* to attribute; (*funciones*) to confer

atribular [atriβu'lar] *vt* to afflict, distress

atributo [atri'βuto] *nm* attribute

atril [a'tril] *nm* (*para libro*) lectern; (*MUS*) music stand

atrocidad [atroθi'ðað] *nf* atrocity, outrage

atropellar [atrope'ʎar] *vt* (*derribar*) to knock over o down; (*empujar*) to push (aside); (*AUTO*) to run over, run down; (*agraviar*) to insult; **~se** *vr* to act hastily; **atropello** *nm* (*AUTO*) accident; (*empujón*) push; (*agravio*) wrong; (*atrocidad*) outrage

atroz [a'troθ] *adj* atrocious, awful

ATS *nmf abr* (= *Ayudante Técnico Sanitario*) nurse

atto, a *abr* = **atento**

atuendo [a'twendo] *nm* attire

atún [a'tun] *nm* tuna

aturdir [atur'ðir] *vt* to stun; (*de ruido*) to deafen; (*fig*) to dumbfound, bewilder

atusar [atu'sar] *vt* to smooth (down)

audacia [au'ðaθja] *nf* boldness, audacity; **audaz** *adj* bold, audacious

audible [au'ðiβle] *adj* audible

audición [auði'θjon] *nf* hearing; (*TEATRO*) audition

audiencia [au'ðjenθja] *nf* audience; **A~** (*JUR*) High Court

audífono [au'ðifono] *nm* (*para sordos*) hearing aid

auditor [auði'tor] *nm* (*JUR*) judge advocate; (*COM*) auditor

auditorio [auði'torjo] *nm* audience; (*sala*) auditorium

auge ['auxe] *nm* boom; (*clímax*) climax

augurar [auɣu'rar] *vt* to predict; (*presagiar*)

to portend

augurio [au'ɣurjo] *nm* omen

aula ['aula] *nf* classroom; (*en universidad etc*) lecture room

aullar [au'ʎar] *vi* to howl, yell

aullido [au'ʎiðo] *nm* howl, yell

aumentar [aumen'tar] *vt* to increase; (*precios*) to put up; (*producción*) to step up; (*con microscopio, anteojos*) to magnify ♦ *vi* to increase, be on the increase; **~se** *vr* to increase, be on the increase; **aumento** *nm* increase; rise

aun [a'un] *adv* even; **~ así** even so; **~ más** even o yet more

aún [a'un] *adv*: **~ está aquí** he's still here; **~ no lo sabemos** we don't know yet; **¿no ha venido ~?** hasn't she come yet?

aunque [a'unke] *conj* though, although, even though

aúpa [a'upa] *excl* come on!

aureola [aure'ola] *nf* halo

auricular [auriku'lar] *nm* (*TEL*) earpiece, receiver; **~es** *nmpl* (*para escuchar música etc*) headphones

aurora [au'rora] *nf* dawn

auscultar [auskul'tar] *vt* (*MED: pecho*) to listen to, sound

ausencia [au'senθja] *nf* absence

ausentarse [ausen'tarse] *vr* to go away; (*por poco tiempo*) to go out

ausente [au'sente] *adj* absent

auspicios [aus'piθjos] *nmpl* auspices

austeridad [austeri'ðað] *nf* austerity; **austero, a** *adj* austere

austral [aus'tral] *adj* southern ♦ *nm* monetary unit of Argentina

Australia [aus'tralja] *nf* Australia; **australiano, a** *adj, nm/f* Australian

Austria ['austrja] *nf* Austria; **austríaco, a** *adj, nm/f* Austrian

auténtico, a [au'tentiko, a] *adj* authentic

auto ['auto] *nm* (*JUR*) edict, decree; (: *orden*) writ; (*AUTO*) car; **~s** *nmpl* (*JUR*) proceedings; (: *acta*) court record *sg*

autoadhesivo [autoaðe'siβo] *adj* self-adhesive; (*sobre*) self-sealing

autobiografía [autoβjoɣra'fia] *nf* autobiography

autobronceador [autoβronθea'ðor] *adj* self-tanning

autobús [auto'βus] *nm* bus

autocar [auto'kar] *nm* coach (*BRIT*), (passenger) bus (*US*)

autóctono, a [au'toktono, a] *adj* native, indigenous

autodefensa [autoðe'fensa] *nf* self-defence

autodeterminación [autoðetermina'θjon] *nf* self-determination

autodidacta [autoði'ðakta] *adj* self-taught

autoescuela [autoes'kwela] *nf* driving school

autógrafo [au'toɣrafo] *nm* autograph

autómata [au'tomata] *nm* automaton

automático, a [auto'matiko, a] *adj* automatic ♦ *nm* press stud

automotor, triz [automo'tor, 'triθ] *adj* self-propelled ♦ *nm* diesel train

automóvil [auto'moβil] *nm* (*motor*) car (*BRIT*), automobile (*US*); **automovilismo** *nm* (*actividad*) motoring; (*DEPORTE*) motor racing; **automovilista** *nm/f* motorist, driver; **automovilístico, a** *adj* (*industria*) motor *cpd*

autonomía [autono'mia] *nf* autonomy; **autónomo, a** (*ESP*), **autonómico, a** (*ESP*) *adj* (*POL*) autonomous

autopista [auto'pista] *nf* motorway (*BRIT*), freeway (*US*); **~ de peaje** toll road (*BRIT*), turnpike road (*US*)

autopsia [au'topsja] *nf* autopsy, postmortem

autor, a [au'tor, a] *nm/f* author

autoridad [autori'ðað] *nf* authority; **autoritario, a** *adj* authoritarian

autorización [autoriθa'θjon] *nf* authorization; **autorizado, a** *adj* authorized; (*aprobado*) approved

autorizar [autori'θar] *vt* to authorize; (*aprobar*) to approve

autorretrato [autorre'trato] *nm* self-portrait

autoservicio [autoser'βiθjo] *nm* (*tienda*) self-service shop (*BRIT*) o store (*US*); (*restaurante*) self-service restaurant

autostop [auto'stop] *nm* hitch-hiking; **hacer ~** to hitch-hike; **~ista** *nm/f* hitch-hiker

autosuficiencia [autosufi'θjenθja] *nf* self-sufficiency

autovía [auto'βia] *nf* ≈ A-road (*BRIT*), dual carriageway (*BRIT*), ≈ state highway (*US*)

auxiliar [auksi'ljar] *vt* to help ♦ *nm/f* assistant, helper; **auxilio** *nm* assistance, help; **primeros auxilios** first aid *sg*

Av *abr* (= *Avenida*) Av(e).

aval [a'βal] *nm* guarantee; (*persona*) guarantor

avalancha [aβa'lantʃa] *nf* avalanche

avance [a'βanθe] *nm* advance; (*pago*) advance payment; (*CINE*) trailer

avanzar [aβan'θar] *vt, vi* to advance

avaricia [aβa'riθja] *nf* avarice, greed; **avaricioso, a** *adj* avaricious, greedy

avaro, a [a'βaro, a] *adj* miserly, mean ♦ *nm/f* miser

avasallar [aβasa'ʎar] *vt* to subdue, subjugate

Avda *abr* (= *Avenida*) Av(e).

AVE ['aβe] *nm abr* (= *Alta Velocidad Española*) ≈ bullet train

ave ['aβe] *nf* bird; **~ de rapiña** bird of prey

avecinarse [aβeθi'narse] *vr* (*tormenta, fig*)

to be on the way

avellana [aβeˈʎana] nf hazelnut; **avellano** nm hazel tree

avemaría [aβemaˈria] nm Hail Mary, Ave Maria

avena [aˈβena] nf oats pl

avenida [aβeˈniða] nf (calle) avenue

avenir [aβeˈnir] vt to reconcile; **~se** vr to come to an agreement, reach a compromise

aventajado, a [aβentaˈxaðo, a] adj outstanding

aventajar [aβentaˈxar] vt (sobrepasar) to surpass, outstrip

aventura [aβenˈtura] nf adventure; **aventurado, a** adj risky; **aventurero, a** adj adventurous

avergonzar [aβerɣonˈθar] vt to shame; (desconcertar) to embarrass; **~se** vr to be ashamed; to be embarrassed

avería [aβeˈria] nf (TEC) breakdown, fault

averiado, a [aβeˈrjaðo, a] adj broken down; "**~**" "out of order"

averiguación [aβeriɣwaˈθjon] nf investigation; (descubrimiento) ascertainment

averiguar [aβeriˈɣwar] vt to investigate; (descubrir) to find out, ascertain

aversión [aβerˈsjon] nf aversion, dislike

avestruz [aβesˈtruθ] nm ostrich

aviación [aβjaˈθjon] nf aviation; (fuerzas aéreas) air force

aviador, a [aβjaˈðor, a] nm/f aviator, airman/woman

avicultura [aβikulˈtura] nf poultry farming

avidez [aβiˈðeθ] nf avidity, eagerness; **ávido, a** adj avid, eager

avinagrado, a [aβinaˈɣraðo, a] adj sour, acid

avión [aˈβjon] nm aeroplane; (ave) martin; **~ de reacción** jet (plane)

avioneta [aβjoˈneta] nf light aircraft

avisar [aβiˈsar] vt (advertir) to warn, notify; (informar) to tell; (aconsejar) to advise, counsel; **aviso** nm warning; (noticia) notice

avispa [aˈβispa] nf wasp

avispado, a [aβisˈpaðo, a] adj sharp, clever

avispero [aβisˈpero] nm wasp's nest

avispón [aβisˈpon] nm hornet

avistar [aβisˈtar] vt to sight, spot

avituallar [aβitwaˈʎar] vt to supply with food

avivar [aβiˈβar] vt to strengthen, intensify; **~se** vr to revive, acquire new life

axila [akˈsila] nf armpit

axioma [akˈsjoma] nm axiom

ay [ai] excl (dolor) ow!, ouch!; (aflicción) oh!, oh dear!; **¡~ de mí!** poor me!

aya [ˈaja] nf governess; (niñera) nanny

ayer [aˈjer] adv, nm yesterday; **antes de ~** the day before yesterday

ayote [aˈjote] (AM) nm pumpkin

ayuda [aˈjuða] nf help, assistance ♦ nm page; **ayudante, a** nm/f assistant, helper; (ESCOL) assistant; (MIL) adjutant

ayudar [ajuˈðar] vt to help, assist

ayunar [ajuˈnar] vi to fast; **ayunas** nfpl: **estar en ayunas** to be fasting; **ayuno** nm fast; fasting

ayuntamiento [ajuntaˈmjento] nm (consejo) town (o city) council; (edificio) town (o city) hall

azabache [aθaˈβatʃe] nm jet

azada [aˈθaða] nf hoe

azafata [aθaˈfata] nf air stewardess

azafrán [aθaˈfran] nm saffron

azahar [aθaˈar] nm orange/lemon blossom

azar [aˈθar] nm (casualidad) chance, fate; (desgracia) misfortune, accident; **por ~** by chance; **al ~** at random

azoramiento [aθoraˈmjento] nm alarm; (confusión) confusion

azorar [aθoˈrar] vt to alarm; **~se** vr to get alarmed

Azores [aˈθores] nfpl: **las ~** the Azores

azotar [aθoˈtar] vt to whip, beat; (pegar) to spank; **azote** nm (látigo) whip; (latigazo) lash, stroke; (en las nalgas) spank; (calamidad) calamity

azotea [aθoˈtea] nf (flat) roof

azteca [aθˈteka] adj, nm/f Aztec

azúcar [aˈθukar] nm sugar; **azucarado, a** adj sugary, sweet

azucarero, a [aθukaˈrero, a] adj sugar cpd ♦ nm sugar bowl

azucena [aθuˈθena] nf white lily

azufre [aˈθufre] nm sulphur

azul [aˈθul] adj, nm blue; **~ marino** navy blue

azulejo [aθuˈlexo] nm tile

azuzar [aθuˈθar] vt to incite, egg on

B, b

B.A. abr (= Buenos Aires) B.A.

baba [ˈbaβa] nf spittle, saliva; **babear** vi to drool, slaver

babero [baˈβero] nm bib

babor [baˈβor] nm port (side)

baboso, a [baˈβoso, a] (AM: fam) adj silly

baca [ˈbaka] nf (AUTO) luggage o roof rack

bacalao [bakaˈlao] nm cod(fish)

bache [ˈbatʃe] nm pothole, rut; (fig) bad patch

bachillerato [batʃiʎeˈrato] nm higher secondary school course

bacteria [bakˈterja] nf bacterium, germ

báculo [ˈbakulo] nm stick, staff

bagaje [baˈɣaxe] nm baggage, luggage

Bahama [baˈama]: **las (Islas) ~** nfpl the Bahamas

bahía [ba'ia] *nf* bay

bailar [bai'lar] *vt, vi* to dance; **~ín, ina** *nm/f* (ballet) dancer; **baile** *nm* dance; (*formal*) ball

baja ['baxa] *nf* drop, fall; (*MIL*) casualty; **dar de ~** (*soldado*) to discharge; (*empleado*) to dismiss

bajada [ba'xaða] *nf* descent; (*camino*) slope; (*de aguas*) ebb

bajar [ba'xar] *vi* to go down, come down; (*temperatura, precios*) to drop, fall ♦ *vt* (*cabeza*) to bow; (*escalera*) to go down, come down; (*precio, voz*) to lower; (*llevar abajo*) to take down; **~se** *vr* (*de coche*) to get out; (*de autobús, tren*) to get off; **~ de** (*coche*) to get out of; (*autobús, tren*) to get off

bajeza [ba'xeθa] *nf* baseness *no pl*; (*una ~*) vile deed

bajío [ba'xio] *nm* (*AM*) lowlands *pl*

bajo, a ['baxo, a] *adj* (*mueble, número, precio*) low; (*piso*) ground; (*de estatura*) small, short; (*color*) pale; (*sonido*) faint, soft, low; (*voz: en tono*) deep; (*metal*) base; (*humilde*) low, humble ♦ *adv* (*hablar*) softly, quietly; (*volar*) low ♦ *prep* under, underneath ♦ *nm* (*MUS*) bass; **~ la lluvia** in the rain

bajón [ba'xon] *nm* fall, drop

bakalao [baka'lao] (*fam*) *nm* rave (music)

bala ['bala] *nf* bullet

balance [ba'lanθe] *nm* (*COM*) balance; (*: libro*) balance sheet; (*: cuenta general*) stocktaking

balancear [balanθe'ar] *vt* to balance ♦ *vi* to swing (to and fro); (*vacilar*) to hesitate; **~se** *vr* to swing (to and fro); to hesitate; **balanceo** *nm* swinging

balanza [ba'lanθa] *nf* scales *pl*, balance; (*ASTROLOGÍA*): **B~ Libra**; **~ comercial** balance of trade; **~ de pagos** balance of payments

balar [ba'lar] *vi* to bleat

balaustrada [balaus'traða] *nf* balustrade; (*pasamanos*) banisters *pl*

balazo [ba'laθo] *nm* (*golpe*) shot; (*herida*) bullet wound

balbucear [balβuθe'ar] *vi, vt* to stammer, stutter; **balbuceo** *nm* stammering, stuttering

balbucir [balβu'θir] *vi, vt* to stammer, stutter

balcón [bal'kon] *nm* balcony

balde ['balde] *nm* bucket, pail; **de ~** (for) free, for nothing; **en ~** in vain

baldío, a [bal'dio, a] *adj* uncultivated; (*terreno*) waste ♦ *nm* waste land

baldosa [bal'dosa] *nf* (*azulejo*) floor tile; (*grande*) flagstone; **baldosín** *nm* (small) tile

Baleares [bale'ares] *nfpl*: **las (Islas) ~** the Balearic Islands

balido [ba'liðo] *nm* bleat, bleating

baliza [ba'liθa] *nf* (*AVIAT*) beacon; (*NAUT*) buoy

ballena [ba'ʎena] *nf* whale

ballesta [ba'ʎesta] *nf* crossbow; (*AUTO*) spring

ballet [ba'le] (*pl* **~s**) *nm* ballet

balneario, a [balne'arjo, a] *adj*: **estación balnearia** (*AM*) (bathing) resort ♦ *nm* spa, health resort

balón [ba'lon] *nm* ball

baloncesto [balon'θesto] *nm* basketball

balonmano [balon'mano] *nm* handball

balonvolea [balombo'lea] *nm* volleyball

balsa ['balsa] *nf* raft; (*BOT*) balsa wood

bálsamo ['balsamo] *nm* balsam, balm

baluarte [ba'lwarte] *nm* bastion, bulwark

bambolear [bambole'ar] *vi* to swing, sway; (*silla*) to wobble; **~se** *vr* to swing, sway; to wobble; **bamboleo** *nm* swinging, swaying, wobbling

bambú [bam'bu] *nm* bamboo

banana [ba'nana] (*AM*) *nf* banana; **banano** (*AM*) *nm* banana tree

banca ['banka] *nf* (*COM*) banking

bancario, a [ban'karjo, a] *adj* banking *cpd*, bank *cpd*

bancarrota [banka'rrota] *nf* bankruptcy; **hacer ~** to go bankrupt

banco ['banko] *nm* bench; (*ESCOL*) desk; (*COM*) bank; (*GEO*) stratum; **~ de crédito/de ahorros** credit/savings bank; **~ de arena** sandbank; **~ de datos** databank

banda ['banda] *nf* band; (*pandilla*) gang; (*NAUT*) side, edge; **la B~ Oriental** Uruguay; **~ sonora** soundtrack

bandada [ban'daða] *nf* (*de pájaros*) flock; (*de peces*) shoal

bandazo [ban'daθo] *nm*: **dar ~s** to sway from side to side

bandeja [ban'dexa] *nf* tray

bandera [ban'dera] *nf* flag

banderilla [bande'riʎa] *nf* banderilla

banderín [bande'rin] *nm* pennant, small flag

bandido [ban'diðo] *nm* bandit

bando ['bando] *nm* (*edicto*) edict, proclamation; (*facción*) faction; **los ~s** (*REL*) the banns

bandolera [bando'lera] *nf*: **llevar en ~** to wear across one's chest

bandolero [bando'lero] *nm* bandit, brigand

banquero [ban'kero] *nm* banker

banqueta [ban'keta] *nf* stool; (*AM: en la calle*) pavement (*BRIT*), sidewalk (*US*)

banquete [ban'kete] *nm* banquet; (*para convidados*) formal dinner

banquillo [ban'kiʎo] *nm* (*JUR*) dock, prisoner's bench; (*banco*) bench; (*para los pies*) footstool

bañador [bana'ðor] *nm* swimming costume (*BRIT*), bathing suit (*US*)

bañar [ba'nar] *vt* to bath, bathe; (*objeto*) to

dip; (*de barniz*) to coat; **~se** *vr* (*en el mar*) to
bathe, swim; (*en la bañera*) to have a bath
bañera [ba'ɲera] *nf* bath(tub)
bañero, a [ba'ɲero, a] (*AM*) *nm/f* lifeguard
bañista [ba'ɲista] *nm/f* bather
baño ['baɲo] *nm* (*en bañera*) bath; (*en río*)
dip, swim; (*cuarto*) bathroom; (*bañera*)
bath(tub); (*capa*) coating
baqueta [ba'keta] *nf* (*MUS*) drumstick
bar [bar] *nm* bar
barahúnda [bara'unda] *nf* uproar, hubbub
baraja [ba'raxa] *nf* pack (of cards); **barajar**
vt (*naipes*) to shuffle; (*fig*) to jumble up
baranda [ba'randa] *nf* = **barandilla**
barandilla [baran'diʎa] *nf* rail, railing
baratija [bara'tixa] *nf* trinket
baratillo [bara'tiʎo] *nm* (*tienda*) junkshop;
(*subasta*) bargain sale; (*conjunto de cosas*)
secondhand goods *pl*
barato, a [ba'rato, a] *adj* cheap ♦ *adv* cheap,
cheaply
baraúnda [bara'unda] *nf* = **barahúnda**
barba ['barßa] *nf* (*mentón*) chin; (*pelo*) beard
barbacoa [barßa'koa] *nf* (*parrilla*) barbecue;
(*carne*) barbecued meat
barbaridad [barßari'ðað] *nf* barbarity; (*acto*)
barbarism; (*atrocidad*) outrage; **una ~** (*fam*)
loads; **¡qué ~!** (*fam*) how awful!
barbarie [bar'ßarje] *nf* barbarism, savagery;
(*crueldad*) barbarity
barbarismo [barßa'rismo] *nm* = **barbarie**
bárbaro, a ['barßaro, a] *adj* barbarous, cruel;
(*grosero*) rough, uncouth ♦ *nm/f* barbarian
♦ *adv*: **lo pasamos ~** (*fam*) we had a great
time; **¡qué ~!** (*fam*) how marvellous!; **un éxito
~** (*fam*) a terrific success; **es un tipo ~** (*fam*)
he's a great bloke
barbecho [bar'ßetʃo] *nm* fallow land
barbero [bar'ßero] *nm* barber, hairdresser
barbilla [bar'ßiʎa] *nf* chin, tip of the chin
barbo ['barßo] *nm* barbel; **~ de mar** red
mullet
barbotear [barßote'ar] *vt, vi* to mutter,
mumble
barbudo, a [bar'ßuðo, a] *adj* bearded
barca ['barka] *nf* (small) boat; **~ pesquera**
fishing boat; **~ de pasaje** ferry; **~za** *nf* barge;
~za de desembarco landing craft
Barcelona [barθe'lona] *n* Barcelona
barcelonés, esa [barθelo'nes, esa] *adj* of o
from Barcelona
barco ['barko] *nm* boat; (*grande*) ship; **~ de
carga** cargo boat; **~ de vela** sailing ship
baremo [ba'remo] *nm* (*MAT, fig*) scale
barítono [ba'ritono] *nm* baritone
barman ['barman] *nm* barman
Barna *n* = **Barcelona**
barniz [bar'niθ] *nm* varnish; (*en la loza*)
glaze; (*fig*) veneer; **~ar** *vt* to varnish; (*loza*)

to glaze
barómetro [ba'rometro] *nm* barometer
barquero [bar'kero] *nm* boatman
barquillo [bar'kiʎo] *nm* cone, cornet
barra ['barra] *nf* bar, rod; (*de un bar, café*)
bar; (*de pan*) French stick; (*palanca*) lever;
~ de carmín o **de labios** lipstick; **~ libre** free
bar
barraca [ba'rraka] *nf* hut, cabin
barranco [ba'rranko] *nm* ravine; (*fig*)
difficulty
barrena [ba'rrena] *nf* drill; **barrenar** *vt* to
drill (through), bore; **barreno** *nm* large drill
barrer [ba'rrer] *vt* to sweep; (*quitar*) to sweep
away
barrera [ba'rrera] *nf* barrier
barriada [ba'rrjaða] *nf* quarter, district
barricada [barri'kaða] *nf* barricade
barrida [ba'rriða] *nf* sweep, sweeping
barrido [ba'rriðo] *nm* = **barrida**
barriga [ba'rrixa] *nf* belly; (*panza*) paunch;
barrigón, ona *adj* potbellied; **barrigudo, a**
adj potbellied
barril [ba'rril] *nm* barrel, cask
barrio ['barrjo] *nm* (*vecindad*) area,
neighborhood (*US*); (*en las afueras*) suburb;
~ chino red-light district
barro ['barro] *nm* (*lodo*) mud; (*objetos*)
earthenware; (*MED*) pimple
barroco, a [ba'rroko, a] *adj, nm* baroque
barrote [ba'rrote] *nm* (*de ventana*) bar
barruntar [barrun'tar] *vt* (*conjeturar*) to
guess; (*presentir*) to suspect; **barrunto** *nm*
guess; suspicion
bartola [bar'tola]: **a la ~** *adv*: **tirarse a la ~** to
take it easy, be lazy
bártulos ['bartulos] *nmpl* things, belongings
barullo [ba'ruʎo] *nm* row, uproar
basar [ba'sar] *vt* to base; **~se** *vr*: **~se en** to be
based on
báscula ['baskula] *nf* (*platform*) scales
base ['base] *nf* base; **a ~ de** on the basis of;
(*mediante*) by means of; **~ de datos** (*INFORM*)
database
básico, a ['basiko, a] *adj* basic
basílica [ba'silika] *nf* basilica

```
PALABRA CLAVE
```

bastante [bas'tante] *adj* **1** (*suficiente*)
enough; **~ dinero** enough o sufficient money;
~s libros enough books
2 (*valor intensivo*): **~ gente** quite a lot of
people; **tener ~ calor** to be rather hot
♦ *adv*: **~ bueno/malo** quite good/rather bad;
~ rico pretty rich; **(lo) ~ inteligente (como)
para hacer algo** clever enough o sufficiently
clever to do sth

bastar [bas'tar] *vi* to be enough o sufficient;

~se vr to be self-sufficient; **~ para** to be enough to; **¡basta!** (that's) enough!

bastardilla [bastar'ðiʎa] nf italics

bastardo, a [bas'tarðo, a] adj, nm/f bastard

bastidor [basti'ðor] nm frame; (de coche) chassis; (TEATRO) wing; **entre ~es** (fig) behind the scenes

basto, a ['basto, a] adj coarse, rough; **~s** nmpl (NAIPES) ≈ clubs

bastón [bas'ton] nm stick, staff; (para pasear) walking stick

bastoncillo [baston'θiʎo] nm cotton bud

basura [ba'sura] nf rubbish (BRIT), garbage (US)

basurero [basu'rero] nm (hombre) dustman (BRIT), garbage man (US); (lugar) dump; (cubo) (rubbish) bin (BRIT), trash can (US)

bata ['bata] nf (gen) dressing gown; (cubretodo) smock, overall; (MED, TEC etc) lab(oratory) coat

batalla [ba'taʎa] nf battle; **de ~** (fig) for everyday use

batallar [bata'ʎar] vi to fight

batallón [bata'ʎon] nm battalion

batata [ba'tata] nf sweet potato

batería [bate'ria] nf battery; (MUS) drums; **~ de cocina** kitchen utensils

batido, a [ba'tiðo, a] adj (camino) beaten, well-trodden ♦ nm (CULIN): **~ (de leche)** milk shake

batidora [bati'ðora] nf beater, mixer; **~ eléctrica** food mixer, blender

batir [ba'tir] vt to beat, strike; (vencer) to beat, defeat; (revolver) to beat, mix; **~se** vr to fight; **~ palmas** to clap, applaud

batuta [ba'tuta] nf baton; **llevar la ~** (fig) to be the boss, be in charge

baúl [ba'ul] nm trunk; (AUTO) boot (BRIT), trunk (US)

bautismo [bau'tismo] nm baptism, christening

bautizar [bauti'θar] vt to baptize, christen; (fam: diluir) to water down; **bautizo** nm baptism, christening

baya ['baja] nf berry

bayeta [ba'jeta] nf floorcloth

bayoneta [bajo'neta] nf bayonet

baza ['baθa] nf trick; **meter ~** to butt in

bazar [ba'θar] nm bazaar

bazofia [ba'θofja] nf trash

BCE nm abr (= Banco Central Europeo) ECB

beato, a [be'ato, a] adj blessed; (piadoso) pious

bebé [be'ße] (pl **~s**) nm baby

bebedor, a [beße'ðor, a] adj hard-drinking

beber [be'ßer] vt, vi to drink

bebida [be'ßiða] nf drink; **bebido, a** adj drunk

beca ['beka] nf grant, scholarship

becario, a [be'karjo, a] nm/f scholarship holder, grant holder

bedel [be'ðel] nm (ESCOL) janitor; (UNIV) porter

béisbol ['beisßol] nm (DEPORTE) baseball

belén [be'len] nm (de navidad) nativity scene, crib; **B~** Bethlehem

belga ['belɣa] adj, nm/f Belgian

Bélgica ['belxika] nf Belgium

bélico, a ['beliko, a] adj (actitud) warlike; **belicoso, a** adj (guerrero) warlike; (agresivo) aggressive, bellicose

beligerante [belixe'rante] adj belligerent

belleza [be'ʎeθa] nf beauty

bello, a ['beʎo, a] adj beautiful, lovely; **Bellas Artes** Fine Art

bellota [be'ʎota] nf acorn

bemol [be'mol] nm (MUS) flat; **esto tiene ~es** (fam) this is a tough one

bencina [ben'θina] nf (AM) (gasolina) petrol (BRIT), gasoline (US)

bendecir [bende'θir] vt to bless

bendición [bendi'θjon] nf blessing

bendito, a [ben'dito, a] pp de **bendecir** ♦ adj holy; (afortunado) lucky; (feliz) happy; (sencillo) simple ♦ nm/f simple soul

beneficencia [benefi'θenθja] nf charity

beneficiar [benefi'θjar] vt to benefit, be of benefit to; **~se** vr to benefit, profit; **~io, a** nm/f beneficiary

beneficio [bene'fiθjo] nm (bien) benefit, advantage; (ganancia) profit, gain; **~so, a** adj beneficial

benéfico, a [be'nefiko, a] adj charitable

beneplácito [bene'plaθito] nm approval, consent

benevolencia [beneßo'lenθja] nf benevolence, kindness; **benévolo, a** adj benevolent, kind

benigno, a [be'niɣno, a] adj kind; (suave) mild; (MED: tumor) benign, non-malignant

berberecho [berße'retʃo] nm (ZOOL, CULIN) cockle

berenjena [beren'xena] nf aubergine (BRIT), eggplant (US)

Berlín [ber'lin] n Berlin; **berlinés, esa** adj of o from Berlin ♦ nm/f Berliner

bermudas [ber'muðas] nfpl Bermuda shorts

berrear [berre'ar] vi to bellow, low

berrido [be'rriðo] nm bellow(ing)

berrinche [be'rrintʃe] (fam) nm temper, tantrum

berro ['berro] nm watercress

berza ['berθa] nf cabbage

besamel [besa'mel] nf (CULIN) white sauce, bechamel sauce

besar [be'sar] vt to kiss; (fig: tocar) to graze; **~se** vr to kiss (one another); **beso** nm kiss

bestia ['bestja] nf beast, animal; (fig) idiot;

~ **de carga** beast of burden
bestial [bes'tjal] *adj* bestial; (*fam*) terrific;
~**idad** *nf* bestiality; (*fam*) stupidity
besugo [be'suɣo] *nm* sea bream; (*fam*) idiot
besuquear [besuke'ar] *vt* to cover with
kisses; ~**se** *vr* to kiss and cuddle
betún [be'tun] *nm* shoe polish; (*QUÍM*)
bitumen
biberón [biβe'ron] *nm* feeding bottle
Biblia ['biβlja] *nf* Bible
bibliografía [biβljoɣra'fia] *nf* bibliography
biblioteca [biβljo'teka] *nf* library; (*mueble*)
bookshelves; ~ **de consulta** reference library;
~**rio, a** *nm/f* librarian
bicarbonato [bikarβo'nato] *nm* bicarbonate
bicho ['bitʃo] *nm* (*animal*) small animal;
(*sabandija*) bug, insect; (*TAUR*) bull
bici ['biθi] (*fam*) *nf* bike
bicicleta [biθi'kleta] *nf* bicycle, cycle; **ir en** ~
to cycle
bidé [bi'ðe] (*pl* ~**s**) *nm* bidet
bidón [bi'ðon] *nm* (*de aceite*) drum; (*de
gasolina*) can

PALABRA CLAVE

bien [bjen] *nm* **1** (*bienestar*) good; **te lo digo
por tu** ~ I'm telling you for your own good; **el**
~ **y el mal** good and evil
2 (*posesión*): ~**es** goods; ~**es de consumo**
consumer goods; ~**es inmuebles** *o* **raíces/~es
muebles** real estate *sg*/personal property *sg*
♦ *adv* **1** (*de manera satisfactoria, correcta etc*)
well; **trabaja/come** ~ she works/eats well;
contestó ~ he answered correctly; **me siento**
~ I feel fine; **no me siento** ~ I don't feel very
well; **se está** ~ **aquí** it's nice here
2 (*frases*): **hiciste** ~ **en llamarme** you were
right to call me
3 (*valor intensivo*) very; **un cuarto** ~ **caliente**
a nice warm room; ~ **se ve que** ... it's quite
clear that ...
4: **estar** ~: **estoy muy** ~ **aquí** I feel very happy
here; **está** ~ **que vengan** it's all right for them
to come; **¡está** ~**!** lo **haré** oh all right, I'll do it
5 (*de buena gana*): **yo** ~ **que iría pero** ... I'd
gladly go but ...
♦ *excl* **¡~!** (*aprobación*) O.K.!; **¡muy** ~**!** well
done!
♦ *adj inv* (*matiz despectivo*): **niño** ~ rich kid;
gente ~ posh people
♦ *conj* **1**: ~ ... ~: ~ **en coche** ~ **en tren** either
by car or by train
2: **no** ~ (*esp AM*): **no** ~ **llegue te llamaré** as
soon as I arrive I'll call you
3: **si** ~ even though; *ver tb* **más**

---

bienal [bje'nal] *adj* biennial
bienaventurado, a [bjenaßentu'raðo, a]
adj (*feliz*) happy, fortunate

bienestar [bjenes'tar] *nm* well-being, welfare
bienhechor, a [bjene'tʃor, a] *adj* beneficent
♦ *nm/f* benefactor/benefactress
bienvenida [bjembe'niða] *nf* welcome; **dar
la** ~ **a uno** to welcome sb
bienvenido [bjembe'niðo] *excl* welcome!
bife ['bife] (*AM*) *nm* steak
bifurcación [bifurka'θjon] *nf* fork
bifurcarse [bifur'karse] *vr* (*camino, carretera,
río*) to fork
bigamia [bi'xamja] *nf* bigamy; **bígamo, a**
adj bigamous ♦ *nm/f* bigamist
bigote [bi'xote] *nm* moustache; **bigotudo, a**
adj with a big moustache
bikini [bi'kini] *nm* bikini; (*CULIN*) toasted ham
and cheese sandwich
bilbaíno, a [bilßa'ino, a] *adj* from o of Bilbao
bilingüe [bi'lingwe] *adj* bilingual
billar [bi'ʎar] *nm* billiards *sg*; (*lugar*) billiard
hall; (*mini-casino*) amusement arcade;
~ **americano** pool
billete [bi'ʎete] *nm* ticket; (*de banco*)
(bank)note; (*US*), (*carta*) note;
~ **sencillo**, ~ **de ida solamente** single (*BRIT*) o
one-way (*US*) ticket; ~ **de ida y vuelta** return
(*BRIT*) o round-trip (*US*) ticket; ~ **de 20 libras**
£20 note
billetera [biʎe'tera] *nf* wallet
billetero [biʎe'tero] *nm* = **billetera**
billón [bi'ʎon] *nm* billion
bimensual [bimen'swal] *adj* twice monthly
bimotor [bimo'tor] *adj* twin-engined ♦ *nm*
twin-engined plane
bingo ['bingo] *nm* bingo
biodegradable [bioðeɣra'ðaßle] *adj*
biodegradable
biografía [bjoɣra'fia] *nf* biography;
biógrafo, a *nm/f* biographer
biología [bjolo'xia] *nf* biology; **biológico, a**
adj biological; (*cultivo, producto*) organic;
biólogo, a *nm/f* biologist
biombo ['bjombo] *nm* (folding) screen
biopsia [bi'opsja] *nf* biopsy
biquini [bi'kini] *nm* bikini
birlar [bir'lar] (*fam*) *vt* to pinch
Birmania [bir'manja] *nf* Burma
birria ['birrja] *nf*: **ser una** ~ (*película, libro*) to
be rubbish
bis [bis] *excl* encore! ♦ *adv*: **viven en el 27** ~
they live at 27a
bisabuelo, a [bisa'ßwelo, a] *nm/f* great-
grandfather/mother
bisagra [bi'saɣra] *nf* hinge
bisiesto [bi'sjesto] *adj*: **año** ~ leap year
bisnieto, a [bis'njeto, a] *nm/f* great-
grandson/daughter
bisonte [bi'sonte] *nm* bison
bisté [bis'te] *nm* = **bistec**
bistec [bis'tek] *nm* steak

bisturí [bistu'ri] *nm* scalpel
bisutería [bisute'ria] *nf* imitation *o* costume jewellery
bit [bit] *nm* (*INFORM*) bit
bizco, a ['biθko, a] *adj* cross-eyed
bizcocho [biθ'kotʃo] *nm* (*CULIN*) sponge cake
bizquear [biθke'ar] *vi* to squint
blanca ['blanka] *nf* (*MUS*) minim; **estar sin ~** to be broke; *ver tb* **blanco**
blanco, a ['blanko, a] *adj* white ♦ *nm/f* white man/woman, white ♦ *nm* (*color*) white; (*en texto*) blank; (*MIL, fig*) target; **en ~** blank; **noche en ~** sleepless night
blancura [blan'kura] *nf* whiteness
blandir [blan'dir] *vt* to brandish
blando, a ['blando, a] *adj* soft; (*tierno*) tender, gentle; (*carácter*) mild; (*fam*) cowardly; **blandura** *nf* softness; tenderness; mildness
blanquear [blanke'ar] *vt* to whiten; (*fachada*) to whitewash; (*paño*) to bleach ♦ *vi* to turn white; **blanquecino, a** *adj* whitish
blasfemar [blasfe'mar] *vi* to blaspheme, curse; **blasfemia** *nf* blasphemy
blasón [bla'son] *nm* coat of arms
bledo ['bleðo] *nm*: **me importa un ~** I couldn't care less
blindado, a [blin'daðo, a] *adj* (*MIL*) armour-plated; (*antibala*) bullet-proof; **coche** (*ESP*) *o* **carro** (*AM*) **~** armoured car
blindaje [blin'daxe] *nm* armour, armour-plating
bloc [blok] (*pl* **~s**) *nm* writing pad
bloque ['bloke] *nm* block; (*POL*) bloc; **~ de cilindros** cylinder block
bloquear [bloke'ar] *vt* to blockade; **bloqueo** *nm* blockade; (*COM*) freezing, blocking
blusa ['blusa] *nf* blouse
boato [bo'ato] *nm* show, ostentation
bobada [bo'βaða] *nf* foolish action; foolish statement; **decir ~s** to talk nonsense
bobería [boβe'ria] *nf* = **bobada**
bobina [bo'βina] *nf* (*TEC*) bobbin; (*FOTO*) spool; (*ELEC*) coil
bobo, a ['boβo, a] *adj* (*tonto*) daft, silly; (*cándido*) naïve ♦ *nm/f* fool, idiot ♦ *nm* (*TEATRO*) clown, funny man
boca ['boka] *nf* mouth; (*de crustáceo*) pincer; (*de cañón*) muzzle; (*entrada*) mouth, entrance; **~s** *nfpl* (*de río*) mouth *sg*; **~ abajo/arriba** face down/up; **se me hace agua la ~** my mouth is watering
bocacalle [boka'kaʎe] *nf* (entrance to a) street; **la primera ~** the first turning *o* street
bocadillo [boka'ðiʎo] *nm* sandwich
bocado [bo'kaðo] *nm* mouthful, bite; (*de caballo*) bridle; **~ de Adán** Adam's apple
bocajarro [boka'xarro]: **a ~** *adv* (*disparar*, *preguntar*) point-blank
bocanada [boka'naða] *nf* (*de vino*) mouthful, swallow; (*de aire*) gust, puff
bocata [bo'kata] (*fam*) *nm* sandwich
bocazas [bo'kaθas] (*fam*) *nm inv* bigmouth
boceto [bo'θeto] *nm* sketch, outline
bochorno [bo'tʃorno] *nm* (*vergüenza*) embarrassment; (*calor*): **hace ~** it's very muggy; **~so, a** *adj* muggy; embarrassing
bocina [bo'θina] *nf* (*MUS*) trumpet; (*AUTO*) horn; (*para hablar*) megaphone
boda ['boða] *nf* (*tb*: **~s**) wedding, marriage; (*fiesta*) wedding reception; **~s de plata/de oro** silver/golden wedding
bodega [bo'ðexa] *nf* (*de vino*) (wine) cellar; (*depósito*) storeroom; (*de barco*) hold
bodegón [boðe'xon] *nm* (*ARTE*) still life
bofe ['bofe] *nm* (*tb*: **~s: de res**) lights
bofetada [bofe'taða] *nf* slap (in the face)
bofetón [bofe'ton] *nm* = **bofetada**
boga ['boxa] *nf*: **en ~** (*fig*) in vogue
bogar [bo'xar] *vi* (*remar*) to row; (*navegar*) to sail
bogavante [boxa'ßante] *nm* lobster
Bogotá [boxo'ta] *n* Bogota
bohemio, a [bo'emjo, a] *adj, nm/f* Bohemian
boicot [boi'kot] (*pl* **~s**) *nm* boycott; **~ear** *vt* to boycott; **~eo** *nm* boycott
boina ['boina] *nf* beret
bola ['bola] *nf* ball; (*canica*) marble; (*NAIPES*) (grand) slam; (*betún*) shoe polish; (*mentira*) tale, story; **~s** (*AM*) *nfpl* bolas *sg*; **~ de billar** billiard ball; **~ de nieve** snowball
bolchevique [boltʃe'ßike] *adj, nm/f* Bolshevik
boleadoras [bolea'ðoras] (*AM*) *nfpl* bolas *sg*
bolera [bo'lera] *nf* skittle *o* bowling alley
boleta [bo'leta] (*AM*) *nf* (*billete*) ticket; (*permiso*) pass, permit
boletería [bolete'ria] (*AM*) *nf* ticket office
boletín [bole'tin] *nm* bulletin; (*periódico*) journal, review; **~ de noticias** news bulletin
boleto [bo'leto] *nm* ticket
boli ['boli] (*fam*) *nm* skittle; (*píldora*) Biro ®, pen
bolígrafo [bo'lixrafo] *nm* ball-point pen, Biro ®
bolívar [bo'lißar] *nm* monetary unit of Venezuela
Bolivia [bo'lißja] *nf* Bolivia; **boliviano, a** *adj, nm/f* Bolivian
bollería [boʎe'ria] *nf* cakes *pl* and pastries *pl*
bollo ['boʎo] *nm* (*pan*) roll; (*bulto*) bump, lump; (*abolladura*) dent
bolo ['bolo] *nm* skittle; (*píldora*) (large) pill; (*juego de*) **~s** *nmpl* skittles *sg*
bolsa ['bolsa] *nf* bag; (*AM*) pocket; (*ANAT*) cavity, sac; (*COM*) stock exchange; (*MINERÍA*) pocket; **de ~** pocket *cpd*; **~ de agua caliente** hot water bottle; **~ de aire** air pocket; **~ de**

papel paper bag; **~ de plástico** plastic bag
bolsillo [bol'siʎo] nm pocket; (cartera) purse; **de ~** pocket(-size)
bolsista [bol'sista] nm/f stockbroker
bolso ['bolso] nm (bolsa) bag; (de mujer) handbag
bomba ['bomba] nf (MIL) bomb; (TEC) pump ♦ (fam) adj: **noticia ~** bombshell ♦ (fam) adv: **pasarlo ~** to have a great time; **~ atómica/de humo/de efecto retardado** atomic/smoke/time bomb
bombardear [bombarðe'ar] vt to bombard; (MIL) to bomb; **bombardeo** nm bombardment; bombing
bombardero [bombar'ðero] nm bomber
bombear [bombe'ar] vt (agua) to pump (out o up); **~se** vr to warp
bombero [bom'bero] nm fireman
bombilla [bom'biʎa] nf (ESP) (light) bulb
bombín [bom'bin] nm bowler hat
bombo ['bombo] nm (MUS) bass drum; (TEC) drum
bombón [bom'bon] nm chocolate
bombona [bom'bona] nf (de butano, oxígeno) cylinder
bonachón, ona [bona'tʃon, ona] adj good-natured, easy-going
bonanza [bo'nanθa] nf (NAUT) fair weather; (fig) bonanza; (MINERÍA) rich pocket o vein
bondad [bon'daθ] nf goodness, kindness; **tenga la ~ de** (please) be good enough to; **~oso, a** adj good, kind
bonificación [bonifika'θjon] nf bonus
bonito, a [bo'nito, a] adj pretty; (agradable) nice ♦ nm (atún) tuna (fish)
bono ['bono] nm voucher; (FIN) bond
bonobús [bono'ßus] (ESP) nm bus pass
bonoloto [bono'loto] nf state-run weekly lottery
boquerón [boke'ron] nm (pez) (kind of) anchovy; (agujero) large hole
boquete [bo'kete] nm gap, hole
boquiabierto, a [bokia'ßjerto, a] adj: **quedar ~** to be amazed o flabbergasted
boquilla [bo'kiʎa] nf (para riego) nozzle; (para cigarro) cigarette holder; (MUS) mouthpiece
borbotón [borßo'ton] nm: **salir a borbotones** to gush out
borda ['borða] nf (NAUT) (ship's) rail; **tirar algo/caerse por la ~** to throw sth/fall overboard
bordado [bor'ðaðo] nm embroidery
bordar [bor'ðar] vt to embroider
borde ['borðe] nm edge, border; (de camino etc) side; (en la costura) hem; **al ~ de** (fig) on the verge o brink of; **ser ~** (ESP: fam) to be rude; **~ar** vt to border
bordillo [bor'ðiʎo] nm kerb (BRIT), curb (US)

bordo ['borðo] nm (NAUT) side; **a ~** on board
borinqueño, a [borin'keɲo, a] adj, nm/f Puerto Rican
borla ['borla] nf (adorno) tassel
borrachera [borra'tʃera] nf (ebriedad) drunkenness; (orgía) spree, binge
borracho, a [bo'rratʃo, a] adj drunk ♦ nm/f (habitual) drunkard, drunk; (temporal) drunk, drunk man/woman
borrador [borra'ðor] nm (escritura) first draft, rough sketch; (goma) rubber (BRIT), eraser
borrar [bo'rrar] vt to erase, rub out
borrasca [bo'rraska] nf storm
borrico, a [bo'rriko, a] nm/f donkey/she-donkey; (fig) stupid man/woman
borrón [bo'rron] nm (mancha) stain
borroso, a [bo'rroso, a] adj vague, unclear; (escritura) illegible
bosque ['boske] nm wood; (grande) forest
bosquejar [boske'xar] vt to sketch; **bosquejo** nm sketch
bostezar [boste'θar] vi to yawn; **bostezo** nm yawn
bota ['bota] nf (calzado) boot; (para vino) leather wine bottle; **~s de agua, ~s de goma** Wellingtons
botánica [bo'tanika] nf (ciencia) botany; ver tb **botánico**
botánico, a [bo'taniko, a] adj botanical ♦ nm/f botanist
botar [bo'tar] vt to throw, hurl; (NAUT) to launch; (AM) to throw out ♦ vi to bounce
bote ['bote] nm (salto) bounce; (golpe) thrust; (vasija) tin, can, (embarcación) boat; **de ~ en ~** packed, jammed full; **~ de la basura** (AM) dustbin (BRIT), trashcan (US); **~ salvavidas** lifeboat
botella [bo'teʎa] nf bottle; **botellín** nm small bottle
botica [bo'tika] nf chemist's (shop) (BRIT), pharmacy; **~rio, a** nm/f chemist (BRIT), pharmacist
botijo [bo'tixo] nm (earthenware) jug
botín [bo'tin] nm (calzado) half boot; (polaina) spat; (MIL) booty
botiquín [boti'kin] nm (armario) medicine cabinet; (portátil) first-aid kit
botón [bo'ton] nm button; (BOT) bud; **~ de oro** buttercup
botones [bo'tones] nm inv bellboy (BRIT), bellhop (US)
bóveda ['boßeða] nf (ARQ) vault
boxeador [boksea'ðor] nm boxer
boxear [bokse'ar] vi to box
boxeo [bok'seo] nm boxing
boya ['boja] nf (NAUT) buoy; (de caña) float
boyante [bo'jante] adj prosperous
bozal [bo'θal] nm (de caballo) halter; (de perro) muzzle

bracear [braθe'ar] vi (*agitar los brazos*) to wave one's arms

bracero [bra'θero] nm labourer; (*en el campo*) farmhand

bragas ['braɣas] nfpl (*de mujer*) panties, knickers (BRIT)

bragueta [bra'ɣeta] nf fly, flies pl

braille [breil] nm braille

bramar [bra'mar] vi to bellow, roar; **bramido** nm bellow, roar

brasa ['brasa] nf live o hot coal

brasero [bra'sero] nm brazier

Brasil [bra'sil] nm: (**el**) ~ Brazil; **brasileño, a** adj, nm/f Brazilian

bravata [bra'ßata] nf boast

braveza [bra'ßeθa] nf (*valor*) bravery; (*ferocidad*) ferocity

bravío, a [bra'ßio, a] adj wild; (*feroz*) fierce

bravo, a ['braßo, a] adj (*valiente*) brave; (*feroz*) ferocious; (*salvaje*) wild; (*mar etc*) rough, stormy ♦ excl bravo!; **bravura** nf bravery; ferocity

braza ['braθa] nf fathom; **nadar a la ~** to swim (the) breast-stroke

brazada [bra'θaða] nf stroke

brazado [bra'θaðo] nm armful

brazalete [braθa'lete] nm (*pulsera*) bracelet; (*banda*) armband

brazo ['braθo] nm arm; (ZOOL) foreleg; (BOT) limb, branch; **luchar a ~ partido** to fight hand-to-hand; **ir cogidos del ~** to walk arm in arm

brea ['brea] nf pitch, tar

brebaje [bre'ßaxe] nm potion

brecha ['bretʃa] nf (*hoyo, vacío*) gap, opening; (MIL, *fig*) breach

brega ['breɣa] nf (*lucha*) struggle; (*trabajo*) hard work

breva ['breßa] nf early fig

breve ['breße] adj short, brief ♦ nf (MUS) breve; **~dad** nf brevity, shortness

brezo ['breθo] nm heather

bribón, ona [bri'ßon, ona] adj idle, lazy ♦ nm/f (*pícaro*) rascal, rogue

bricolaje [briko'laxe] nm do-it-yourself, DIY

brida ['briða] nf bridle, rein; (TEC) clamp; **a toda ~** at top speed

bridge [britʃ] nm bridge

brigada [bri'ßaða] nf (*unidad*) brigade; (*trabajadores*) squad, gang ♦ nm ≈ staff-sergeant, sergeant-major

brillante [bri'ʎante] adj brilliant ♦ nm diamond

brillar [bri'ʎar] vi (*tb fig*) to shine; (*joyas*) to sparkle

brillo ['briʎo] nm shine; (*brillantez*) brilliance; (*fig*) splendour; **sacar ~ a** to polish

brincar [brin'kar] vi to skip about, hop about, jump about; **está que brinca** he's hopping mad

brinco ['brinko] nm jump, leap

brindar [brin'dar] vi: ~ **a** o **por** to drink (a toast) to ♦ vt to offer, present

brindis ['brindis] nm inv toast

brío ['brio] nm spirit, dash; **brioso, a** adj spirited, dashing

brisa ['brisa] nf breeze

británico, a [bri'taniko, a] adj British ♦ nm/f Briton, British person

brizna ['briθna] nf (*de hierba, paja*) blade; (*de tabaco*) leaf

broca ['broka] nf (TEC) drill, bit

brocal [bro'kal] nm rim

brocha ['brotʃa] nf (*large*) paintbrush; **~ de afeitar** shaving brush

broche ['brotʃe] nm brooch

broma ['broma] nf joke; **en ~** in fun, as a joke; **~ pesada** practical joke; **bromear** vi to joke

bromista [bro'mista] adj fond of joking ♦ nm/f joker, wag

bronca ['bronka] nf row; **echar una ~ a uno** to tick sb off

bronce ['bronθe] nm bronze; **~ado, a** adj bronze; (*por el sol*) tanned ♦ nm (sun)tan; (TEC) bronzing

bronceador [bronθea'ðor] nm suntan lotion

broncearse [bronθe'arse] vr to get a suntan

bronco, a ['bronko, a] adj (*manera*) rude, surly; (*voz*) harsh

bronquio ['bronkjo] nm (ANAT) bronchial tube

bronquitis [bron'kitis] nf inv bronchitis

brotar [bro'tar] vi (BOT) to sprout; (*aguas*) to gush (forth); (MED) to break out

brote ['brote] nm (BOT) shoot; (MED, *fig*) outbreak

bruces ['bruθes]: **de ~** adv: **caer** o **dar de ~ to** fall headlong, fall flat

bruja ['bruxa] nf witch; **brujería** nf witchcraft

brujo ['bruxo] nm wizard, magician

brújula ['bruxula] nf compass

bruma ['bruma] nf mist; **brumoso, a** adj misty

bruñir [bru'ɲir] vt to polish

brusco, a ['brusko, a] adj (*súbito*) sudden; (*áspero*) brusque

Bruselas [bru'selas] n Brussels

brutal [bru'tal] adj brutal

brutalidad [brutali'ðað] nf brutality

bruto, a ['bruto, a] adj (*idiota*) stupid; (*bestial*) brutish; (*peso*) gross; **en ~** raw, unworked

Bs.As. abr (= *Buenos Aires*) B.A.

bucal [bu'kal] adj oral; **por vía ~** orally

bucear [buθe'ar] vi to dive ♦ vt to explore; **buceo** nm diving

bucle ['bukle] nm curl

budismo [bu'ðismo] *nm* Buddhism
buen [bwen] *adj m ver* **bueno**
buenamente [bwena'mente] *adv*
(*fácilmente*) easily; (*voluntariamente*) willingly
buenaventura [bwenaßen'tura] *nf* (*suerte*)
good luck; (*adivinación*) fortune

PALABRA CLAVE
---

bueno, a ['bweno, a] *adj* (*antes de nmsg*:
buen) **1** (*excelente etc*) good; **es un libro ~, es
un buen libro** it's a good book; **hace ~, hace
buen tiempo** the weather is fine, it is fine; **el
~ de Paco** good old Paco; **fue muy ~ conmigo**
he was very nice *o* kind to me
2 (*apropiado*): **ser ~ para** to be good for;
creo que vamos por buen camino I think
we're on the right track
3 (*irónico*): **le di un buen rapapolvo** I gave
him a good *o* real ticking off; **¡buen
conductor estás hecho!** some *o* a fine driver
you are!; **¡estaría ~ que ...!** a fine thing it
would be if ...!
4 (*atractivo, sabroso*): **está ~ este bizcocho**
this sponge is delicious; **Carmen está muy
buena** Carmen is gorgeous
5 (*saludos*): **¡buen día!, ¡~s días!** (good)
morning!; **¡buenas (tardes)!** (good)
afternoon!; (*más tarde*) (good) evening!;
¡buenas noches! good night!
6 (*otras locuciones*): **estar de buenas** to be in
a good mood; **por las buenas o por las malas**
by hook or by crook; **de buenas a primeras** all
of a sudden
♦ *excl*: **¡~!** all right!; **~, ¿y qué?** well, so what?

Buenos Aires *nm* Buenos Aires
buey [bwei] *nm* ox
búfalo ['bufalo] *nm* buffalo
bufanda [bu'fanda] *nf* scarf
bufar [bu'far] *vi* to snort
bufete [bu'fete] *nm* (*despacho de abogado*)
lawyer's office
buffer ['bufer] *nm* (*INFORM*) buffer
bufón [bu'fon] *nm* clown
buhardilla [buar'ðiʎa] *nf* attic
búho ['buo] *nm* owl; (*fig*) hermit, recluse
buhonero [buo'nero] *nm* pedlar
buitre ['bwitre] *nm* vulture
bujía [bu'xia] *nf* (*vela*) candle; (*ELEC*) candle
(power); (*AUTO*) spark plug
bula ['bula] *nf* (*papal*) bull
bulbo ['bulßo] *nm* bulb
bulevar [bule'ßar] *nm* boulevard
Bulgaria [bul'varja] *nf* Bulgaria; **búlgaro,
a** *adj, nm/f* Bulgarian
bulla ['buʎa] *nf* (*ruido*) uproar; (*de gente*)
crowd
bullicio [bu'ʎiθjo] *nm* (*ruido*) uproar;
(*movimiento*) bustle

bullir [bu'ʎir] *vi* (*hervir*) to boil; (*burbujear*) to
bubble
bulto ['bulto] *nm* (*paquete*) package; (*fardo*)
bundle; (*tamaño*) size, bulkiness; (*MED*)
swelling, lump; (*silueta*) vague shape
buñuelo [bu'ɲwelo] *nm* ≈ doughnut (*BRIT*),
≈ donut (*US*); (*fruta de sartén*) fritter
BUP [bup] *nm abr* (*ESP*: = *Bachillerato
Unificado Polivalente*) secondary education and
leaving certificate for 14–17 age group
buque ['buke] *nm* ship, vessel
burbuja [bur'ßuxa] *nf* bubble; **burbujear** *vi*
to bubble
burdel [bur'ðel] *nm* brothel
burdo, a ['burðo, a] *adj* coarse, rough
burgués, esa [bur'ɣes, esa] *adj* middle-class,
bourgeois; **burguesía** *nf* middle class,
bourgeoisie
burla ['burla] *nf* (*mofa*) gibe; (*broma*) joke;
(*engaño*) trick
burladero [burla'ðero] *nm* (*bullfighter's*)
refuge
burlar [bur'lar] *vt* (*engañar*) to deceive ♦ *vi* to
joke; **~se** *vr* to joke; **~se de** to make fun of
burlesco, a [bur'lesko, a] *adj* burlesque
burlón, ona [bur'lon, ona] *adj* mocking
burocracia [buro'kraθja] *nf* civil service
burócrata [bu'rokrata] *nm/f* civil servant
burrada [bu'rraða] *nf*: **decir/soltar ~s** to talk
nonsense; **hacer ~s** to act stupid; **una ~**
(*mucho*) a (hell of a) lot
burro, a ['burro, a] *nm/f* donkey/she-donkey;
(*fig*) ass, idiot
bursátil [bur'satil] *adj* stock-exchange *cpd*
bus [bus] *nm* bus
busca ['buska] *nf* search, hunt ♦ *nm* (*TEL*)
bleeper; **en ~ de** in search of
buscar [bus'kar] *vt* to look for, search for,
seek ♦ *vi* to look, search, seek; **se busca
secretaria** secretary wanted
busque *etc vb ver* **buscar**
búsqueda ['buskeða] *nf* = **busca** *nf*
busto ['busto] *nm* (*ANAT, ARTE*) bust
butaca [bu'taka] *nf* armchair; (*de cine, teatro*)
stall, seat
butano [bu'tano] *nm* butane (gas)
buzo ['buθo] *nm* diver
buzón [bu'θon] *nm* (*en puerta*) letter box;
(*en la calle*) pillar box

C, c

C. *abr* (= *centígrado*) C; (= *compañía*) Co.
c. *abr* (= *capítulo*) ch.
C/ *abr* (= *calle*) St
c.a. *abr* (= *corriente alterna*) AC
cabal [ka'ßal] *adj* (*exacto*) exact; (*correcto*)
right, proper; (*acabado*) finished, complete;

~es *nmpl:* estar en sus ~es to be in one's right mind

cábalas ['kaβalas] *nfpl:* hacer ~ to guess

cabalgar [kaβal'var] *vt, vi* to ride

cabalgata [kaβal'vata] *nf* procession

caballa [ka'βaʎa] *nf* mackerel

caballeresco, a [kaβaʎe'resko, a] *adj* noble, chivalrous

caballería [kaβaʎe'ria] *nf* mount; (*MIL*) cavalry

caballeriza [kaβaʎe'riθa] *nf* stable; **caballerizo** *nm* groom, stableman

caballero [kaβa'ʎero] *nm* gentleman; (*de la orden de caballería*) knight; (*trato directo*) sir

caballerosidad [kaβaʎerosi'ðað] *nf* chivalry

caballete [kaβa'ʎete] *nm* (*ARTE*) easel; (*TEC*) trestle

caballito [kaβa'ʎito] *nm* (*caballo pequeño*) small horse, pony; ~s *nmpl* (*en verbena*) roundabout, merry-go-round

caballo [ka'βaʎo] *nm* horse; (*AJEDREZ*) knight; (*NAIPES*) queen; **ir en** ~ to ride; ~ **de vapor** o **de fuerza** horsepower; ~ **de carreras** racehorse

cabaña [ka'βaɲa] *nf* (*casita*) hut, cabin

cabaré [kaβa're] (*pl* ~s) *nm* cabaret

cabaret [kaβa're] (*pl* ~s) *nm* cabaret

cabecear [kaβeθe'ar] *vt, vi* to nod

cabecera [kaβe'θera] *nf* head; (*IMPRENTA*) headline

cabecilla [kaβe'θiʎa] *nm* ringleader

cabellera [kaβe'ʎera] *nf* (head of) hair; (*de cometa*) tail

cabello [ka'βeʎo] *nm* (*tb:* ~s) hair

caber [ka'βer] *vi* (*entrar*) to fit, go; **caben 3 más** there's room for 3 more

cabestrillo [kaβes'triʎo] *nm* sling

cabestro [ka'βestro] *nm* halter

cabeza [ka'βeθa] *nf* head; (*POL*) chief, leader; ~ **rapada** skinhead; ~**da** *nf* (*golpe*) butt; **dar** ~**das** to nod off; **cabezón, ona** *adj* (*vino*) heady; (*fam: persona*) pig-headed

cabida [ka'βiða] *nf* space

cabildo [ka'βildo] *nm* (*de iglesia*) chapter; (*POL*) town council

cabina [ka'βina] *nf* cabin; (*de camión*) cab; ~ **telefónica** telephone box (*BRIT*) o booth

cabizbajo, a [kaβiθ'βaxo, a] *adj* crestfallen, dejected

cable ['kaβle] *nm* cable

cabo ['kaβo] *nm* (*de objeto*) end, extremity; (*MIL*) corporal; (*NAUT*) rope, cable; (*GEO*) cape; **al** ~ **de 3 días** after 3 days

cabra ['kaβra] *nf* goat

cabré *etc vb ver* **caber**

cabrear [kaβre'ar] (*fam*) *vt* to bug; ~**se** *vr* (*enfadarse*) to fly off the handle

cabrío, a [ka'βrio, a] *adj* goatish; **macho** ~ (he-)goat, billy goat

cabriola [ka'βrjola] *nf* caper

cabritilla [kaβri'tiʎa] *nf* kid, kidskin

cabrito [ka'βrito] *nm* kid

cabrón [ka'βron] *nm* cuckold; (*fam!*) bastard (!)

caca ['kaka] (*fam*) *nf* pooh

cacahuete [kaka'wete] (*ESP*) *nm* peanut

cacao [ka'kao] *nm* cocoa; (*BOT*) cacao

cacarear [kakare'ar] *vi* (*persona*) to boast; (*gallina*) to crow

cacería [kaθe'ria] *nf* hunt

cacerola [kaθe'rola] *nf* pan, saucepan

cachalote [katʃa'lote] *nm* (*ZOOL*) sperm whale

cacharro [ka'tʃarro] *nm* earthenware pot; ~s *nmpl* pots and pans

cachear [katʃe'ar] *vt* to search, frisk

cachemir [katʃe'mir] *nm* cashmere

cacheo [ka'tʃeo] *nm* searching, frisking

cachete [ka'tʃete] *nm* (*ANAT*) cheek; (*bofetada*) slap (in the face)

cachiporra [katʃi'porra] *nf* truncheon

cachivache [katʃi'βatʃe] *nm* (*trasto*) piece of junk; ~s *nmpl* junk *sg*

cacho ['katʃo] *nm* (small) bit; (*AM: cuerno*) horn

cachondeo [katʃon'deo] (*fam*) *nm* farce, joke

cachondo, a [ka'tʃondo, a] *adj* (*ZOOL*) on heat; (*fam: sexualmente*) randy; (: *gracioso*) funny

cachorro, a [ka'tʃorro, a] *nm/f* (*perro*) pup, puppy; (*león*) cub

cacique [ka'θike] *nm* chief, local ruler; (*POL*) local party boss; **caciquismo** *nm* system of control by the local boss

caco ['kako] *nm* pickpocket

cacto ['kakto] *nm* cactus

cactus ['kaktus] *nm inv* cactus

cada ['kaða] *adj inv* each; (*antes de número*) every; ~ **día** each day, every day; ~ **dos días** every other day; ~ **uno/a** each one, every one; ~ **vez más/menos** more and more/less and less; **uno de** ~ **diez** one out of every ten

cadalso [ka'ðalso] *nm* scaffold

cadáver [ka'ðaβer] *nm* (dead) body, corpse

cadena [ka'ðena] *nf* chain; (*TV*) channel; **trabajo en** ~ assembly line work; ~ **perpetua** (*JUR*) life imprisonment

cadencia [ka'ðenθja] *nf* rhythm

cadera [ka'ðera] *nf* hip

cadete [ka'ðete] *nm* cadet

caducar [kaðu'kar] *vi* to expire; **caduco, a** *adj* expired; (*persona*) very old

caer [ka'er] *vi* to fall (down); ~**se** *vr* to fall (down); **me cae bien/mal** I get on well with him/I can't stand him; ~ **en la cuenta** to realize; **su cumpleaños cae en viernes** her birthday falls on a Friday

café [ka'fe] (*pl* ~s) *nm* (*bebida, planta*) coffee;

(*lugar*) café ♦ *adj* (*color*) brown; ~ **con leche** white coffee; ~ **solo** black coffee

cafetera [kafe'tera] *nf* coffee pot

cafetería [kafete'ria] *nf* (*gen*) café

cafetero, a [kafe'tero, a] *adj* coffee *cpd*; **ser muy ~** to be a coffee addict

cagar [ka'ɣar] (*fam!*) *vt* to bungle, mess up ♦ *vi* to have a shit (*!*)

caída [ka'iða] *nf* fall; (*declive*) slope; (*disminución*) fall, drop

caído, a [ka'iðo, a] *adj* drooping

caiga *etc vb ver* **caer**

caimán [kai'man] *nm* alligator

caja ['kaxa] *nf* box; (*para reloj*) case; (*de ascensor*) shaft; (*COM*) cashbox; (*donde se hacen los pagos*) cashdesk; (: *en supermercado*) checkout, till; ~ **de ahorros** savings bank; ~ **de cambios** gearbox; ~ **fuerte**, ~ **de caudales** safe, strongbox

cajero, a [ka'xero, a] *nm/f* cashier; ~ **automático** cash dispenser

cajetilla [kaxe'tiʎa] *nf* (*de cigarrillos*) packet

cajón [ka'xon] *nm* big box; (*de mueble*) drawer

cal [kal] *nf* lime

cala ['kala] *nf* (*GEO*) cove, inlet; (*de barco*) hold

calabacín [kalaβa'θin] *nm* (*BOT*) baby marrow; (: *más pequeño*) courgette (*BRIT*), zucchini (*US*)

calabaza [kala'βaθa] *nf* (*BOT*) pumpkin

calabozo [kala'βoθo] *nm* (*cárcel*) prison; (*celda*) cell

calada [ka'laða] *nf* (*de cigarrillo*) puff

calado, a [ka'laðo, a] *adj* (*prenda*) lace *cpd* ♦ *nm* (*NAUT*) draught

calamar [kala'mar] *nm* squid *no pl*

calambre [ka'lambre] *nm* (*tb*: ~**s**) cramp

calamidad [kalami'ðað] *nf* calamity, disaster

calar [ka'lar] *vt* to soak, drench; (*penetrar*) to pierce, penetrate; (*comprender*) to see through; (*vela*) to lower; ~**se** *vr* (*AUTO*) to stall; ~**se las gafas** to stick one's glasses on

calavera [kala'βera] *nf* skull

calcar [kal'kar] *vt* (*reproducir*) to trace; (*imitar*) to copy

calcetín [kalθe'tin] *nm* sock

calcinar [kalθi'nar] *vt* to burn, blacken

calcio ['kalθjo] *nm* calcium

calcomanía [kalkoma'nia] *nf* transfer

calculador, a [kalkula'ðor, a] *adj* (*persona*) calculating

calculadora [kalkula'ðora] *nf* calculator

calcular [kalku'lar] *vt* (*MAT*) to calculate, compute; ~ **que ...** to reckon that ...; **cálculo** *nm* calculation

caldear [kalde'ar] *vt* to warm (up), heat (up)

caldera [kal'dera] *nf* boiler

calderilla [kalde'riʎa] *nf* (*moneda*) small

change

caldero [kal'dero] *nm* small boiler

caldo ['kaldo] *nm* stock; (*consomé*) consommé

calefacción [kalefak'θjon] *nf* heating; ~ **central** central heating

calendario [kalen'darjo] *nm* calendar

calentador [kalenta'ðor] *nm* heater

calentamiento [kalenta'mjento] *nm* (*DEPORTE*) warm-up

calentar [kalen'tar] *vt* to heat (up); ~**se** *vr* to heat up, warm up; (*fig: discusión etc*) to get heated

calentura [kalen'tura] *nf* (*MED*) fever, (high) temperature

calibrar [kali'ßrar] *vt* to gauge, measure; **calibre** *nm* (*de cañón*) calibre, bore; (*diámetro*) diameter; (*fig*) calibre

calidad [kali'ðað] *nf* quality; **de ~** quality *cpd*; **en ~ de** in the capacity of, as

cálido, a ['kaliðo, a] *adj* hot; (*fig*) warm

caliente *etc vb ver* **calentar** ♦ *adj* hot; (*fig*) fiery; (*disputa*) heated; (*fam: cachondo*) randy

calificación [kalifika'θjon] *nf* qualification; (*de alumno*) grade, mark

calificar [kalifi'kar] *vt* to qualify; (*alumno*) to grade, mark; ~ **de** to describe as

calima [ka'lima] *nf* (*cerca del mar*) mist

cáliz ['kaliθ] *nm* chalice

caliza [ka'liθa] *nf* limestone

calizo, a [ka'liθo, a] *adj* lime *cpd*

callado, a [ka'ʎaðo, a] *adj* quiet

callar [ka'ʎar] *vt* (*asunto delicado*) to keep quiet about, say nothing about; (*persona, opinión*) to silence ♦ *vi* to keep quiet, be silent; ~**se** *vr* to keep quiet, be silent; ¡**cállate!** be quiet!, shut up!

calle ['kaʎe] *nf* street; (*DEPORTE*) lane; ~ **arriba/abajo** up/down the street; ~ **de un solo sentido** one-way street

calleja [ka'ʎexa] *nf* alley, narrow street; **callejear** *vi* to wander (about) the streets; **callejero, a** *adj* street *cpd* ♦ *nm* street map; **callejón** *nm* alley, passage; **callejón sin salida** cul-de-sac; **callejuela** *nf* side-street, alley

callista [ka'ʎista] *nm/f* chiropodist

callo ['kaʎo] *nm* callus; (*en el pie*) corn; ~**s** *nmpl* (*CULIN*) tripe *sg*

calma ['kalma] *nf* calm

calmante [kal'mante] *nm* sedative, tranquillizer

calmar [kal'mar] *vt* to calm, calm down ♦ *vi* (*tempestad*) to abate; (*mente etc*) to become calm

calmoso, a [kal'moso, a] *adj* calm, quiet

calor [ka'lor] *nm* heat; (*agradable*) warmth; **hace ~** it's hot; **tener ~** to be hot

caloría [kalo'ria] *nf* calorie

calumnia [ka'lumnja] *nf* calumny, slander; **calumnioso, a** *adj* slanderous

caluroso, a [kalu'roso, a] *adj* hot; (*sin exceso*) warm; (*fig*) enthusiastic

calva ['kalβa] *nf* bald patch; (*en bosque*) clearing

calvario [kal'βarjo] *nm* stations *pl* of the cross

calvicie [kal'βiθje] *nf* baldness

calvo, a ['kalβo, a] *adj* bald; (*terreno*) bare, barren; (*tejido*) threadbare

calza ['kalθa] *nf* wedge, chock

calzada [kal'θaða] *nf* roadway, highway

calzado, a [kal'θaðo, a] *adj* shod ♦ *nm* footwear

calzador [kalθa'ðor] *nm* shoehorn

calzar [kal'θar] *vt* (*zapatos etc*) to wear; (*un mueble*) to put a wedge under; **~se** *vr*: **~se los zapatos** to put on one's shoes; **¿qué (número) calza?** what size do you take?

calzón [kal'θon] *nm* (*tb: calzones nmpl*) shorts; (*AM: de hombre*) (under)pants; (*: de mujer*) panties

calzoncillos [kalθon'θiλos] *nmpl* underpants

cama ['kama] *nf* bed; **~ individual/de matrimonio** single/double bed

camafeo [kama'feo] *nm* cameo

camaleón [kamale'on] *nm* chameleon

cámara ['kamara] *nf* chamber; (*habitación*) room; (*sala*) hall; (*CINE*) cine camera; (*fotográfica*) camera; **~ de aire** inner tube; **~ de comercio** chamber of commerce; **~ frigorífica** cold-storage room

camarada [kama'raða] *nm* comrade, companion

camarera [kama'rera] *nf* (*en restaurante*) waitress; (*en casa, hotel*) maid

camarero [kama'rero] *nm* waiter

camarilla [kama'riλa] *nf* clique

camarón [kama'ron] *nm* shrimp

camarote [kama'rote] *nm* cabin

cambiable [kam'bjaβle] *adj* (*variable*) changeable, variable; (*intercambiable*) interchangeable

cambiante [kam'bjante] *adj* variable

cambiar [kam'bjar] *vt* to change; (*dinero*) to exchange ♦ *vi* to change; **~se** *vr* (*mudarse*) to move; (*de ropa*) to change; **~ de idea** to change one's mind; **~ de ropa** to change (one's clothes)

cambio ['kambjo] *nm* change; (*trueque*) exchange; (*COM*) rate of exchange; (*oficina*) bureau de change; (*dinero menudo*) small change; **en ~** on the other hand; (*en lugar de*) instead; **~ de divisas** foreign exchange; **~ de velocidades** gear lever

camelar [kame'lar] *vt* to sweet-talk

camello [ka'meλo] *nm* camel; (*fam: traficante*) pusher

camerino [kame'rino] *nm* dressing room

camilla [ka'miλa] *nf* (*MED*) stretcher

caminante [kami'nante] *nm/f* traveller

caminar [kami'nar] *vi* (*marchar*) to walk, go ♦ *vt* (*recorrer*) to cover, travel

caminata [kami'nata] *nf* long walk; (*por el campo*) hike

camino [ka'mino] *nm* way, road; (*sendero*) track; **a medio ~** halfway (there); **en el ~** on the way, en route; **~ de** on the way to; **~ particular** private road

camión [ka'mjon] *nm* lorry (*BRIT*), truck (*US*); **~ cisterna** tanker; **camionero, a** *nm/f* lorry o truck driver

camioneta [kamjo'neta] *nf* van, light truck

camisa [ka'misa] *nf* shirt; (*BOT*) skin; **~ de fuerza** straitjacket; **camisería** *nf* outfitter's (shop)

camiseta [kami'seta] *nf* (*prenda*) tee-shirt; (*: ropa interior*) vest; (*de deportista*) top

camisón [kami'son] *nm* nightdress, nightgown

camorra [ka'morra] *nf*: **buscar ~** to look for trouble

campamento [kampa'mento] *nm* camp

campana [kam'pana] *nf* bell; **~ de cristal** bell jar; **~da** *nf* peal; **~rio** *nm* belfry

campanilla [kampa'niλa] *nf* small bell

campaña [kam'paɲa] *nf* (*MIL, POL*) campaign

campechano, a [kampe'tʃano, a] *adj* (*franco*) open

campeón, ona [kampe'on, ona] *nm/f* champion; **campeonato** *nm* championship

campesino, a [kampe'sino, a] *adj* country *cpd*, rural; (*gente*) peasant *cpd* ♦ *nm/f* countryman/woman; (*agricultor*) farmer

campestre [kam'pestre] *adj* country *cpd*, rural

camping ['kampin] (*pl ~s*) *nm* camping; (*lugar*) campsite; **ir de o hacer ~** to go camping

campo ['kampo] *nm* (*fuera de la ciudad*) country, countryside; (*AGR, ELEC*) field; (*de fútbol*) pitch; (*de golf*) course; (*MIL*) camp; **~ de batalla** battlefield; **~ de deportes** sports ground, playing field

camposanto [kampo'santo] *nm* cemetery

camuflaje [kamu'flaxe] *nm* camouflage

cana ['kana] *nf* white o grey hair; **tener ~s** to be going grey

Canadá [kana'ða] *nm* Canada; **canadiense** *adj, nm/f* Canadian ♦ *nf* fur-lined jacket

canal [ka'nal] *nm* canal; (*GEO*) channel, strait; (*de televisión*) channel; (*de tejado*) gutter; **~ de Panamá** Panama Canal; **~izar** *vt* to channel

canalla [ka'naλa] *nf* rabble, mob ♦ *nm* swine

canalón [kana'lon] *nm* (*conducto vertical*) drainpipe; (*del tejado*) gutter

canapé [kana'pe] (*pl ~s*) *nm* sofa, settee;

(*CULIN*) canapé

Canarias [ka'narjas] *nfpl*: (**las Islas**) ~ the Canary Islands, the Canaries

canario, a [ka'narjo, a] *adj, nm/f* (native) of the Canary Isles ♦ *nm* (*ZOOL*) canary

canasta [ka'nasta] *nf* (round) basket; **canastilla** *nf* small basket; (*de niño*) layette

canasto [ka'nasto] *nm* large basket

cancela [kan'θela] *nf* gate

cancelación [kanθela'θjon] *nf* cancellation

cancelar [kanθe'lar] *vt* to cancel; (*una deuda*) to write off

cáncer ['kanθer] *nm* (*MED*) cancer; (*ASTROLOGÍA*): **C~** Cancer

cancha ['kantʃa] *nf* (*de baloncesto, tenis etc*) court; (*AM: de fútbol*) pitch

canciller [kanθi'ʎer] *nm* chancellor

canción [kan'θjon] *nf* song; ~ **de cuna** lullaby; **cancionero** *nm* song book

candado [kan'daðo] *nm* padlock

candente [kan'dente] *adj* red-hot; (*fig: tema*) burning

candidato, a [kandi'ðato, a] *nm/f* candidate

candidez [kandi'ðeθ] *nf* (*sencillez*) simplicity; (*simpleza*) naiveté; **cándido, a** *adj* simple; naive

candil [kan'dil] *nm* oil lamp; **~ejas** *nfpl* (*TEATRO*) footlights

candor [kan'dor] *nm* (*sinceridad*) frankness; (*inocencia*) innocence

canela [ka'nela] *nf* cinnamon

canelones [kane'lones] *nmpl* cannelloni

cangrejo [kan'grexo] *nm* crab

canguro [kan'guro] *nm* kangaroo; **hacer de** ~ to babysit

caníbal [ka'niβal] *adj, nm/f* cannibal

canica [ka'nika] *nf* marble

canijo, a [ka'nixo, a] *adj* frail, sickly

canino, a [ka'nino, a] *adj* canine ♦ *nm* canine (tooth)

canjear [kanxe'ar] *vt* to exchange

cano, a ['kano, a] *adj* grey-haired, white-haired

canoa [ka'noa] *nf* canoe

canon ['kanon] *nm* canon; (*pensión*) rent; (*COM*) tax

canónigo [ka'nonixo] *nm* canon

canonizar [kanoni'θar] *vt* to canonize

canoso, a [ka'noso, a] *adj* grey-haired

cansado, a [kan'saðo, a] *adj* tired, weary; (*tedioso*) tedious, boring

cansancio [kan'sanθjo] *nm* tiredness, fatigue

cansar [kan'sar] *vt* (*fatigar*) to tire, tire out; (*aburrir*) to bore; (*fastidiar*) to bother; **~se** *vr* to tire, get tired; (*aburrirse*) to get bored

cantábrico, a [kan'taβriko, a] *adj* Cantabrian; **mar C~** Bay of Biscay

cantante [kan'tante] *adj* singing ♦ *nm/f* singer

cantar [kan'tar] *vt* to sing ♦ *vi* to sing; (*insecto*) to chirp ♦ *nm* (*acción*) singing; (*canción*) song; (*poema*) poem

cántara ['kantara] *nf* large pitcher

cántaro ['kantaro] *nm* pitcher, jug; **llover a** ~**s** to rain cats and dogs

cante ['kante] *nm*: ~ **jondo** flamenco singing

cantera [kan'tera] *nf* quarry

cantidad [kanti'ðað] *nf* quantity, amount

cantimplora [kantim'plora] *nf* (*frasco*) water bottle, canteen

cantina [kan'tina] *nf* canteen; (*de estación*) buffet

canto ['kanto] *nm* singing; (*canción*) song; (*borde*) edge, rim; (*de un cuchillo*) back; ~ **rodado** boulder

cantor, a [kan'tor, a] *nm/f* singer

canturrear [kanturre'ar] *vi* to sing softly

canuto [ka'nuto] *nm* (*tubo*) small tube; (*fam: droga*) joint

caña ['kaɲa] *nf* (*BOT: tallo*) stem, stalk; (*carrizo*) reed; (*vaso*) tumbler; (*de cerveza*) glass of beer; (*ANAT*) shinbone; ~ **de azúcar** sugar cane; ~ **de pescar** fishing rod

cañada [ka'ɲaða] *nf* (*entre dos montañas*) gully, ravine; (*camino*) cattle track

cáñamo ['kaɲamo] *nm* hemp

cañería [kaɲe'ria] *nf* (*tubo*) pipe

caño ['kaɲo] *nm* (*tubo*) tube, pipe; (*de albañal*) sewer; (*MUS*) pipe; (*de fuente*) jet

cañón [ka'ɲon] *nm* (*MIL*) cannon; (*de fusil*) barrel; (*GEO*) canyon, gorge

caoba [ka'oβa] *nf* mahogany

caos ['kaos] *nm* chaos

cap. *abr* (= *capítulo*) ch.

capa ['kapa] *nf* cloak, cape; (*GEO*) layer, stratum; **so** ~ **de** under the pretext of; ~ **de ozono** ozone layer

capacidad [kapaθi'ðað] *nf* (*medida*) capacity; (*aptitud*) capacity, ability

capacitar [kapaθi'tar] *vt*: ~ **a algn para (hacer)** to enable sb to (do)

capar [ka'par] *vt* to castrate, geld

caparazón [kapara'θon] *nm* shell

capataz [kapa'taθ] *nm* foreman

capaz [ka'paθ] *adj* able, capable; (*amplio*) capacious, roomy

capcioso, a [kap'θjoso, a] *adj* wily, deceitful

capellán [kape'ʎan] *nm* chaplain; (*sacerdote*) priest

caperuza [kape'ruθa] *nf* hood

capicúa [kapi'kua] *adj inv* (*número, fecha*) reversible

capilla [ka'piʎa] *nf* chapel

capital [kapi'tal] *adj* capital ♦ *nm* (*COM*) capital ♦ *nf* (*ciudad*) capital; ~ **social** share o authorized capital

capitalismo [kapita'lismo] *nm* capitalism; **capitalista** *adj, nm/f* capitalist

capitán [kapi'tan] nm captain

capitanear [kapitane'ar] vt to captain

capitulación [kapitula'θjon] nf (rendición) capitulation, surrender; (acuerdo) agreement, pact; **capitulaciones (matrimoniales)** nfpl marriage contract sg

capitular [kapitu'lar] vi to make an agreement

capítulo [ka'pitulo] nm chapter

capó [ka'po] nm (AUTO) bonnet

capón [ka'pon] nm (gallo) capon

capota [ka'pota] nf (de mujer) bonnet; (AUTO) hood (BRIT), top (US)

capote [ka'pote] nm (abrigo: de militar) greatcoat; (: de torero) cloak

capricho [ka'pritʃo] nm whim, caprice; **~so, a** adj capricious

Capricornio [kapri'kornjo] nm Capricorn

cápsula ['kapsula] nf capsule

captar [kap'tar] vt (comprender) to understand; (RADIO) to pick up; (atención, apoyo) to attract

captura [kap'tura] nf capture; (JUR) arrest; **capturar** vt to capture; to arrest

capucha [ka'putʃa] nf hood, cowl

capullo [ka'puʎo] nm (BOT) bud; (ZOOL) cocoon; (fam) idiot

caqui ['kaki] nm khaki

cara ['kara] nf (ANAT, de moneda) face; (de disco) side; (descaro) boldness; **~ a** facing; **de ~** opposite, facing; **dar la ~** to face the consequences; **¿~ o cruz?** heads or tails?; **¡qué ~ (más dura)!** what a nerve!

carabina [kara'ßina] nf carbine, rifle; (persona) chaperone

Caracas [ka'rakas] n Caracas

caracol [kara'kol] nm (ZOOL) snail; (concha) (sea) shell

carácter [ka'rakter] (pl caracteres) nm character; **tener buen/mal ~** to be good natured/bad tempered

característica [karakte'ristika] nf characteristic

característico, a [karakte'ristiko, a] adj characteristic

caracterizar [karakteri'θar] vt to characterize, typify

caradura [kara'ðura] nm/f: **es un ~** he's got a nerve

carajillo [kara'xiʎo] nm coffee with a dash of brandy

carajo [ka'raxo] (fam!) nm: **¡~!** shit! (!)

caramba [ka'ramba] excl good gracious!

carámbano [ka'rambano] nm icicle

caramelo [kara'melo] nm (dulce) sweet; (azúcar fundida) caramel

caravana [kara'ßana] nf caravan; (fig) group; (AUTO) tailback

carbón [kar'ßon] nm coal; **papel ~** carbon

paper; **carboncillo** nm (ARTE) charcoal; **carbonero, a** nm/f coal merchant; **carbonilla** [-'niʎa] nf coal dust

carbonizar [karßoni'θar] vt to carbonize; (quemar) to char

carbono [kar'ßono] nm carbon

carburador [karßura'ðor] nm carburettor

carburante [karßu'rante] nm (para motor) fuel

carcajada [karka'xaða] nf (loud) laugh, guffaw

cárcel ['karθel] nf prison, jail; (TEC) clamp; **carcelero, a** adj prison cpd ♦ nm/f warder

carcoma [kar'koma] nf woodworm

carcomer [karko'mer] vt to bore into, eat into; (fig) to undermine; **~se** vr to become worm-eaten; (fig) to decay

cardar [kar'ðar] vt (pelo) to backcomb

cardenal [karðe'nal] nm (REL) cardinal; (MED) bruise

cardíaco, a [kar'ðiako, a] adj cardiac, heart cpd

cardinal [karði'nal] adj cardinal

cardo ['karðo] nm thistle

carearse [kare'arse] vr to come face to face

carecer [kare'θer] vi: **~ de** to lack, be in need of

carencia [ka'renθja] nf lack; (escasez) shortage; (MED) deficiency

carente [ka'rente] adj: **~ de** lacking in, devoid of

carestía [kares'tia] nf (escasez) scarcity, shortage; (COM) high cost

careta [ka'reta] nf mask

carga ['karʝa] nf (peso, ELEC) load; (de barco) cargo, freight; (MIL) charge; (responsabilidad) duty, obligation

cargado, a [kar'ʝaðo, a] adj loaded; (ELEC) live; (café, té) strong; (cielo) overcast

cargamento [karʝa'mento] nm (acción) loading; (mercancías) load, cargo

cargar [kar'ʝar] vt (barco, arma) to load; (ELEC) to charge; (COM: algo en cuenta) to charge; (INFORM) to load ♦ vi (MIL) to load; (AUTO) to load (up); **~ con** to pick up, carry away; (peso, fig) to shoulder, bear; **~se** (fam) vr (estropear) to break; (matar) to bump off

cargo ['karʝo] nm (puesto) post, office; (responsabilidad) duty, obligation; (JUR) charge; **hacerse ~ de** to take charge of o responsibility for

carguero [kar'ʝero] nm freighter, cargo boat; (avión) freight plane

Caribe [ka'rißе] nm: **el ~** the Caribbean; **del ~** Caribbean

caribeño, a [kari'ßeɲo, a] adj Caribbean

caricatura [karika'tura] nf caricature

caricia [ka'riθja] nf caress

caridad [kari'ðað] nf charity

caries ['karjes] nf inv tooth decay
cariño [ka'riɲo] nm affection, love; (caricia) caress; (en carta) love ...; **tener ~ a** to be fond of; **~so, a** adj affectionate
carisma [ka'risma] nm charisma
caritativo, a [karita'tiβo, a] adj charitable
cariz [ka'riθ] nm: **tener o tomar buen/mal ~** to look good/bad
carmesí [karme'si] adj, nm crimson
carmín [kar'min] nm lipstick
carnal [kar'nal] adj carnal; **primo ~** first cousin
carnaval [karna'βal] nm carnival
carne ['karne] nf flesh; (CULIN) meat; **~ de cerdo/cordero/ternera/vaca** pork/lamb/veal/beef; **~ de gallina** (fig): **se me pone la ~ de gallina sólo verlo** I get the creeps just seeing it
carné [kar'ne] (pl **~s**) nm: **~ de conducir** driving licence (BRIT), driver's license (US); **~ de identidad** identity card
carnero [kar'nero] nm sheep, ram; (carne) mutton
carnet [kar'ne] (pl **~s**) nm = **carné**
carnicería [karniθe'ria] nf butcher's (shop); (fig: matanza) carnage, slaughter
carnicero, a [karni'θero, a] adj carnivorous ♦ nm/f (tb fig) butcher; (carnívoro) carnivore
carnívoro, a [kar'niβoro, a] adj carnivorous
carnoso, a [kar'noso, a] adj beefy, fat
caro, a ['karo, a] adj dear; (COM) dear, expensive ♦ adv dear, dearly
carpa ['karpa] nf (pez) carp; (de circo) big top; (AM: de camping) tent
carpeta [kar'peta] nf folder, file
carpintería [karpinte'ria] nf carpentry, joinery; **carpintero** nm carpenter
carraspear [karraspe'ar] vi to clear one's throat
carraspera [karras'pera] nf hoarseness
carrera [ka'rrera] nf (acción) run(ning); (espacio recorrido) run; (competición) race; (trayecto) course; (profesión) career; (ESCOL) course
carreta [ka'rreta] nf wagon, cart
carrete [ka'rrete] nm reel, spool; (TEC) coil
carretera [karre'tera] nf (main) road, highway; **~ de circunvalación** ring road; **~ nacional** ≈ A road (BRIT), ≈ state highway (US)
carretilla [karre'tiʎa] nf trolley; (AGR) (wheel)barrow
carril [ka'rril] nm furrow; (de autopista) lane; (FERRO) rail
carrillo [ka'rriʎo] nm (ANAT) cheek; (TEC) pulley
carrito [ka'rrito] nm trolley
carro ['karro] nm cart, wagon; (MIL) tank; (AM: coche) car
carrocería [karroθe'ria] nf bodywork,

coachwork
carroña [ka'rroɲa] nf carrion no pl
carroza [ka'rroθa] nf (carruaje) coach
carrusel [karru'sel] nm merry-go-round, roundabout
carta ['karta] nf letter; (CULIN) menu; (naipe) card; (mapa) map; (JUR) document; **~ de ajuste** (TV) test card; **~ de crédito** credit card; **~ certificada** registered letter; **~ marítima** chart; **~ verde** (AUTO) green card
cartabón [karta'βon] nm set square
cartel [kar'tel] nm (anuncio) poster, placard; (ESCOL) wall chart; (COM) cartel; **~era** nf hoarding, billboard; (en periódico etc) entertainments guide; **"en ~era"** "showing"
cartera [kar'tera] nf (de bolsillo) wallet; (de colegial, cobrador) satchel; (de señora) handbag; (para documentos) briefcase; (COM) portfolio; **ocupa la ~ de Agricultura** she is Minister of Agriculture
carterista [karte'rista] nm/f pickpocket
cartero [kar'tero] nm postman
cartilla [kar'tiʎa] nf primer, first reading book; **~ de ahorros** savings book
cartón [kar'ton] nm cardboard; **~ piedra** papier-mâché
cartucho [kar'tutʃo] nm (MIL) cartridge
cartulina [kartu'lina] nf card
casa ['kasa] nf house; (hogar) home; (COM) firm, company; **en ~** at home; **~ consistorial** town hall; **~ de huéspedes** boarding house; **~ de socorro** first aid post
casado, a [ka'saðo, a] adj married ♦ nm/f married man/woman
casamiento [kasa'mjento] nm marriage, wedding
casar [ka'sar] vt to marry; (JUR) to quash, annul; **~se** vr to marry, get married
cascabel [kaska'βel] nm (small) bell
cascada [kas'kaða] nf waterfall
cascanueces [kaska'nweθes] nm inv nutcrackers pl
cascar [kas'kar] vt to crack, split, break (open); **~se** vr to crack, split, break (open)
cáscara ['kaskara] nf (de huevo, fruta seca) shell; (de fruta) skin; (de limón) peel
casco ['kasko] nm (de bombero, soldado) helmet; (NAUT: de barco) hull; (ZOOL: de caballo) hoof; (botella) empty bottle; (de ciudad): **el ~ antiguo** the old part; **el ~ urbano** the town centre; **los ~s azules** the UN peace-keeping force, the blue berets
cascote [kas'kote] nm rubble
caserío [kase'rio] nm hamlet; (casa) country house
casero, a [ka'sero, a] adj (pan etc) home-made ♦ nm/f (propietario) landlord/lady; **ser muy ~** to be home-loving; **"comida casera"** "home cooking"

caseta [ka'seta] nf hut; (*para bañista*) cubicle; (*de feria*) stall

casete [ka'sete] nm o f cassette

casi ['kasi] adv almost, nearly; ~ **nada** hardly anything; ~ **nunca** hardly ever, almost never; ~ **te caes** you almost fell

casilla [ka'siʎa] nf (*casita*) hut, cabin; (*AJEDREZ*) square; (*para cartas*) pigeonhole; **casillero** nm (*para cartas*) pigeonholes pl

casino [ka'sino] nm club; (*de juego*) casino

caso ['kaso] nm case; **en ~ de ...** in case of ...; **en ~ de que ...** in case ...; **el ~ es que** the fact is that; **en ese ~** in that case; **hacer ~ a** to pay attention to; **hacer o venir al ~** to be relevant

caspa ['kaspa] nf dandruff

cassette [ka'sete] nm o f = **casete**

casta ['kasta] nf caste; (*raza*) breed; (*linaje*) lineage

castaña [kas'taɲa] nf chestnut

castañetear [kastaɲete'ar] vi (*dientes*) to chatter

castaño, a [kas'taɲo, a] adj chestnut (-coloured), brown ♦ nm chestnut tree

castañuelas [kasta'ɲwelas] nfpl castanets

castellano, a [kaste'ʎano, a] adj, nm/f Castilian ♦ nm (*LING*) Castilian, Spanish

castidad [kasti'ðað] nf chastity, purity

castigar [kasti'ɣar] vt to punish; (*DEPORTE*) to penalize; **castigo** nm punishment; (*DEPORTE*) penalty

Castilla [kas'tiʎa] nf Castille

castillo [kas'tiʎo] nm castle

castizo, a [kas'tiθo, a] adj (*LING*) pure

casto, a ['kasto, a] adj chaste, pure

castor [kas'tor] nm beaver

castrar [kas'trar] vt to castrate

castrense [kas'trense] adj (*disciplina, vida*) military

casual [ka'swal] adj chance, accidental; ~**idad** nf chance, accident; (*combinación de circunstancias*) coincidence; ¡**qué ~idad!** what a coincidence!

cataclismo [kata'klismo] nm cataclysm

catador, a [kata'ðor, a] nm/f wine taster

catalán, ana [kata'lan, ana] adj, nm/f Catalan ♦ nm (*LING*) Catalan

catalizador [kataliθa'ðor] nm catalyst; (*AUT*) catalytic convertor

catalogar [katalo'ɣar] vt to catalogue; ~ **a algn (de)** (*fig*) to categorize sb (as)

catálogo [ka'taloɣo] nm catalogue

Cataluña [kata'luɲa] nf Catalonia

catar [ka'tar] vt to taste, sample

catarata [kata'rata] nf (*GEO*) waterfall; (*MED*) cataract

catarro [ka'tarro] nm catarrh; (*constipado*) cold

catástrofe [ka'tastrofe] nf catastrophe

catear [kate'ar] (*fam*) vt (*examen, alumno*) to fail

cátedra ['kateðra] nf (*UNIV*) chair, professorship

catedral [kate'ðral] nf cathedral

catedrático, a [kate'ðratiko, a] nm/f professor

categoría [kateɣo'ria] nf category; (*rango*) rank, standing; (*calidad*) quality; **de ~** (*hotel*) top-class

categórico, a [kate'ɣoriko, a] adj categorical

cateto, a ['kateto, a] (*pey*) nm/f peasant

catolicismo [katoli'θismo] nm Catholicism

católico, a [ka'toliko, a] adj, nm/f Catholic

catorce [ka'torθe] num fourteen

cauce ['kauθe] nm (*de río*) riverbed; (*fig*) channel

caucho ['kautʃo] nm rubber; (*AM: llanta*) tyre

caución [kau'θjon] nf bail; **caucionar** vt (*JUR*) to bail, go bail for

caudal [kau'ðal] nm (*de río*) volume, flow; (*fortuna*) wealth; (*abundancia*) abundance; ~**oso, a** adj (*río*) large

caudillo [kau'ðiʎo] nm leader, chief

causa ['kausa] nf cause; (*razón*) reason; (*JUR*) lawsuit, case; **a ~ de** because of

causar [kau'sar] vt to cause

cautela [kau'tela] nf caution, cautiousness; **cauteloso, a** adj cautious, wary

cautivar [kauti'ßar] vt to capture; (*atraer*) to captivate

cautiverio [kauti'ßerjo] nm captivity

cautividad [kautißi'ðað] nf = **cautiverio**

cautivo, a [kau'tißo, a] adj, nm/f captive

cauto, a ['kauto, a] adj cautious, careful

cava ['kaßa] nm champagne-type wine

cavar [ka'ßar] vt to dig

caverna [ka'ßerna] nf cave, cavern

cavidad [kaßi'ðað] nf cavity

cavilar [kaßi'lar] vt to ponder

cayado [ka'jaðo] nm (*de pastor*) crook; (*de obispo*) crozier

cayendo etc vb ver **caer**

caza ['kaθa] nf (*acción: gen*) hunting; (: *con fusil*) shooting; (*una ~*) hunt, chase; (*animales*) game ♦ nm (*AVIAT*) fighter

cazador, a [kaθa'ðor, a] nm/f hunter; **cazadora** nf jacket

cazar [ka'θar] vt to hunt; (*perseguir*) to chase; (*prender*) to catch

cazo ['kaθo] nm saucepan

cazuela [ka'θwela] nf (*vasija*) pan; (*guisado*) casserole

CD abbr (= *compact disc*) CD

CD-ROM abbr m CD-ROM

CE nf abr (= *Comunidad Europea*) EC

cebada [θe'ßaða] nf barley

cebar [θe'ßar] vt (*animal*) to fatten (up); (*anzuelo*) to bait; (*MIL, TEC*) to prime

cebo ['θeßo] nm (*para animales*) feed, food;

(*para peces, fig*) bait; (*de arma*) charge

cebolla [θe'βoʎa] nf onion; **cebolleta** nf spring onion; **cebollín** nm spring onion

cebra ['θeβra] nf zebra

cecear [θeθe'ar] vi to lisp; **ceceo** nm lisp

ceder [θe'ðer] vt to hand over, give up, part with ♦ vi (*renunciar*) to give in, yield; (*disminuir*) to diminish, decline; (*romperse*) to give way

cedro ['θeðro] nm cedar

cédula ['θeðula] nf certificate, document

cegar [θe'ɣar] vt to blind; (*tubería etc*) to block up, stop up ♦ vi to go blind; **~se** vr: **~se (de)** to be blinded (by)

ceguera [θe'ɣera] nf blindness

CEI abbr (= *Confederación de Estados Independientes*) CIS

ceja ['θexa] nf eyebrow

cejar [θe'xar] vi (*fig*) to back down

celador, a [θela'ðor, a] nm/f (*de edificio*) watchman; (*de museo etc*) attendant

celda ['θelda] nf cell

celebración [θeleβra'θjon] nf celebration

celebrar [θele'βrar] vt to celebrate; (*alabar*) to praise ♦ vi to be glad; **~se** vr to occur, take place

célebre ['θelebre] adj famous

celebridad [θeleβri'ðað] nf fame; (*persona*) celebrity

celeste [θe'leste] adj (*azul*) sky-blue

celestial [θeles'tjal] adj celestial, heavenly

celibato [θeli'βato] nm celibacy

célibe ['θeliβe] adj, nm/f celibate

celo¹ ['θelo] nm zeal; (*REL*) fervour; (*ZOOL*): **en ~** on heat; **~s** nmpl jealousy sg; **tener ~s** to be jealous

celo² ® ['θelo] nm Sellotape ®

celofán [θelo'fan] nm cellophane

celoso, a [θe'loso, a] adj jealous; (*trabajador*) zealous

celta ['θelta] adj Celtic ♦ nm/f Celt

célula ['θelula] nf cell; **~ solar** solar cell

celulitis [θelu'litis] nf cellulite

celuloide [θelu'loiðe] nm celluloid

cementerio [θemen'terjo] nm cemetery, graveyard

cemento [θe'mento] nm cement; (*hormigón*) concrete; (*AM: cola*) glue

cena ['θena] nf evening meal, dinner

cenagal [θena'ɣal] nm bog, quagmire

cenar [θe'nar] vt to have for dinner ♦ vi to have dinner

cenicero [θeni'θero] nm ashtray

cenit [θe'nit] nm zenith

ceniza [θe'niθa] nf ash, ashes pl

censo ['θenso] nm census; **~ electoral** electoral roll

censura [θen'sura] nf (*POL*) censorship

censurar [θensu'rar] vt (*idea*) to censure;

(*cortar: película*) to censor

centella [θen'teʎa] nf spark

centellear [θenteʎe'ar] vi (*metal*) to gleam; (*estrella*) to twinkle; (*fig*) to sparkle

centenar [θente'nar] nm hundred

centenario, a [θente'narjo, a] adj centenary; hundred-year-old ♦ nm centenary

centeno [θen'teno] nm (*BOT*) rye

centésimo, a [θen'tesimo, a] adj hundredth

centígrado [θen'tiɣraðo] adj centigrade

centímetro [θen'timetro] nm centimetre (*BRIT*), centimeter (*US*)

céntimo ['θentimo] nm cent

centinela [θenti'nela] nm sentry, guard

centollo [θen'toʎo] nm spider crab

central [θen'tral] adj central ♦ nf head office; (*TEC*) plant; (*TEL*) exchange; **~ eléctrica** power station; **~ nuclear** nuclear power station; **~ telefónica** telephone exchange

centralita [θentra'lita] nf switchboard

centralizar [θentrali'θar] vt to centralize

centrar [θen'trar] vt to centre

céntrico, a ['θentriko, a] adj central

centrifugar [θentrifu'ɣar] vt to spin-dry

centrista [θen'trista] adj centre cpd

centro ['θentro] nm centre; **~ comercial** shopping centre; **~ juvenil** youth club; **~ de llamadas** call centre

centroamericano, a [θentroameri'kano, a] adj, nm/f Central American

ceñido, a [θe'ɲiðo, a] adj (*chaqueta, pantalón*) tight(-fitting)

ceñir [θe'ɲir] vt (*rodear*) to encircle, surround; (*ajustar*) to fit (tightly)

ceño ['θeɲo] nm frown, scowl; **fruncir el ~** to frown, knit one's brow

CEOE nf abr (*ESP*: = *Confederación Española de Organizaciones Empresariales*) ≈ CBI (*BRIT*), employers' organization

cepillar [θepi'ʎar] vt to brush; (*madera*) to plane (down)

cepillo [θe'piʎo] nm brush; (*para madera*) plane; **~ de dientes** toothbrush

cera ['θera] nf wax

cerámica [θe'ramika] nf pottery; (*arte*) ceramics

cerca ['θerka] nf fence ♦ adv near, nearby, close; **~ de** near, close to

cercanías [θerka'nias] nfpl (*afueras*) outskirts, suburbs

cercano, a [θer'kano, a] adj close, near

cercar [θer'kar] vt to fence in; (*rodear*) to surround

cerciorar [θerθjo'rar] vt (*asegurar*) to assure; **~se** vr (*asegurarse*) to make sure

cerco ['θerko] nm (*AGR*) enclosure; (*AM*) fence; (*MIL*) siege

cerdo, a ['θerðo, a] nm/f pig/sow

cereal [θere'al] nm cereal; **~es** nmpl cereals,

grain sg

cerebro [θe'reßro] nm brain; (fig) brains pl

ceremonia [θere'monja] nf ceremony; **ceremonial** adj, nm ceremonial; **ceremonioso, a** adj ceremonious

cereza [θe'reθa] nf cherry

cerilla [θe'riλa] nf (fósforo) match

cernerse [θer'nerse] vr to hover

cero [θero] nm nothing, zero

cerrado, a [θe'rraðo, a] adj closed, shut; (con llave) locked; (tiempo) cloudy, overcast; (curva) sharp; (acento) thick, broad

cerradura [θerra'ðura] nf (acción) closing; (mecanismo) lock

cerrajero [θerra'xero] nm locksmith

cerrar [θe'rrar] vt to close, shut; (paso, carretera) to close; (grifo) to turn off; (cuenta, negocio) to close, shut; (la noche) to come down; **~se** vr to close, shut; **~ con llave** to lock; **~ un trato** to strike a bargain

cerro [θerro] nm hill

cerrojo [θe'rroxo] nm (herramienta) bolt; (de puerta) latch

certamen [θer'tamen] nm competition, contest

certero, a [θer'tero, a] adj (gen) accurate

certeza [θer'teθa] nf certainty

certidumbre [θerti'ðumßre] nf = **certeza**

certificado [θertifi'kaðo] nm certificate

certificar [θertifi'kar] vt (asegurar, atestar) to certify

cervatillo [θerßa'tiλo] nm fawn

cervecería [θerßeθe'ria] nf (fábrica) brewery; (bar) public house, pub

cerveza [θer'ßeθa] nf beer

cesante [θe'sante] adj redundant

cesar [θe'sar] vi to cease, stop ♦ vt (funcionario) to remove from office

cesárea [θe'sarea] nf (MED) Caesarean operation o section

cese [θese] nm (de trabajo) dismissal; (de pago) suspension

césped [θespeð] nm grass, lawn

cesta [θesta] nf basket

cesto [θesto] nm (large) basket, hamper

cetro [θetro] nm sceptre

cfr abr (= confróntese) cf.

chabacano, a [tʃaßa'kano, a] adj vulgar, coarse

chabola [tʃa'ßola] nf shack; **barrio de ~s** shanty town sg

chacal [tʃa'kal] nm jackal

chacha ['tʃatʃa] (fam) nf maid

cháchara ['tʃatʃara] nf chatter; **estar de ~** to chatter away

chacra ['tʃakra] (AM) nf smallholding

chafar [tʃa'far] vt (aplastar) to crush; (plan etc) to ruin

chal [tʃal] nm shawl

chalado, a [tʃa'lado, a] (fam) adj crazy

chalé [tʃa'le] (pl ~s) nm villa; ≈ detached house

chaleco [tʃa'leko] nm waistcoat, vest (US); **~ salvavidas** life jacket

chalet [tʃa'le] (pl ~s) nm = **chalé**

champán [tʃam'pan] nm champagne

champaña [tʃam'paɲa] nm = **champán**

champiñón [tʃampi'ɲon] nm mushroom

champú [tʃam'pu] (pl **champúes, champús**) nm shampoo

chamuscar [tʃamus'kar] vt to scorch, sear, singe

chance ['tʃanθe] (AM) nm chance

chancho, a ['tʃantʃo, a] (AM) nm/f pig

chanchullo [tʃan'tʃuλo] (fam) nm fiddle

chandal [tʃan'dal] nm tracksuit

chantaje [tʃan'taxe] nm blackmail

chapa ['tʃapa] nf (de metal) plate, sheet; (de madera) board, panel; (AM: AUTO) number (BRIT) o license (US) plate; **~do, a** adj: **~do en oro** gold-plated

chaparrón [tʃapa'rron] nm downpour, cloudburst

chapotear [tʃapote'ar] vi to splash about

chapurrear [tʃapurre'ar] vt (idioma) to speak badly

chapuza [tʃa'puθa] nf botched job

chapuzón [tʃapu'θon] nm: **darse un ~** to go for a dip

chaqueta [tʃa'keta] nf jacket

chaquetón [tʃake'ton] nm long jacket

charca ['tʃarka] nf pond, pool

charco ['tʃarko] nm pool, puddle

charcutería [tʃarkute'ria] nf (tienda) shop selling chiefly pork meat products; (productos) cooked pork meats pl

charla ['tʃarla] nf talk, chat; (conferencia) lecture

charlar [tʃar'lar] vi to talk, chat

charlatán, ana [tʃarla'tan, ana] nm/f (hablador) chatterbox; (estafador) trickster

charol [tʃa'rol] nm varnish; (cuero) patent leather

chascarrillo [tʃaska'rriλo] (fam) nm funny story

chasco ['tʃasko] nm (desengaño) disappointment

chasis ['tʃasis] nm inv chassis

chasquear [tʃaske'ar] vt (látigo) to crack; (lengua) to click; **chasquido** nm crack; click

chatarra [tʃa'tarra] nf scrap (metal)

chato, a ['tʃato, a] adj flat; (nariz) snub

chaval, a [tʃa'ßal, a] nm/f kid, lad/lass

checo, a ['tʃeko, a] adj, nm/f Czech ♦ nm (LING) Czech

checo(e)slovaco, a [tʃeko(e)slo'ßako, a] adj, nm/f Czech, Czechoslovak

Checo(e)slovaquia [tʃeko(e)sloˈβakja] *nf* Czechoslovakia

cheque [ˈtʃeke] *nm* cheque (*BRIT*), check (*US*); **~ de viajero** traveller's cheque (*BRIT*), traveler's check (*US*)

chequeo [tʃeˈkeo] *nm* (*MED*) check-up; (*AUTO*) service

chequera [tʃeˈkera] (*AM*) *nf* chequebook (*BRIT*), checkbook (*US*)

chicano, a [tʃiˈkano, a] *adj, nm/f* chicano

chícharo [ˈtʃitʃaro] (*AM*) *nm* pea

chichón [tʃiˈtʃon] *nm* bump, lump

chicle [ˈtʃikle] *nm* chewing gum

chico, a [ˈtʃiko, a] *adj* small, little ♦ *nm/f* (*niño*) child; (*muchacho*) boy/girl

chiflado, a [tʃiˈflaðo, a] *adj* crazy

chiflar [tʃiˈflar] *vt* to hiss, boo

Chile [ˈtʃile] *nm* Chile; **chileno, a** *adj, nm/f* Chilean

chile [ˈtʃile] *nm* chilli pepper

chillar [tʃiˈʎar] *vi* (*persona*) to yell, scream; (*animal salvaje*) to howl; (*cerdo*) to squeal

chillido [tʃiˈʎiðo] *nm* (*de persona*) scream; (*de animal*) howl

chillón, ona [tʃiˈʎon, ona] *adj* (*niño*) noisy; (*color*) loud, gaudy

chimenea [tʃimeˈnea] *nf* chimney; (*hogar*) fireplace

China [ˈtʃina] *nf*: (**la**) **~** China

chinche [ˈtʃintʃe] *nf* (*insecto*) (bed)bug; (*TEC*) drawing pin (*BRIT*), thumbtack (*US*) ♦ *nm/f* nuisance, pest

chincheta [tʃinˈtʃeta] *nf* drawing pin (*BRIT*), thumbtack (*US*)

chino, a [ˈtʃino, a] *adj, nm/f* Chinese ♦ *nm* (*LING*) Chinese

chipirón [tʃipiˈron] *nm* (*ZOOL, CULIN*) squid

Chipre [ˈtʃipre] *nf* Cyprus; **chipriota** *adj, nm/f* Cypriot

chiquillo, a [tʃiˈkiʎo, a] *nm/f* (*fam*) kid

chirimoya [tʃiriˈmoja] *nf* custard apple

chiringuito [tʃirinˈɣito] *nm* small open-air bar

chiripa [tʃiˈripa] *nf* fluke

chirriar [tʃiˈrrjar] *vi* to creak, squeak

chirrido [tʃiˈrriðo] *nm* creak(ing), squeak(ing)

chis [tʃis] *excl* sh!

chisme [ˈtʃisme] *nm* (*habladurías*) piece of gossip; (*fam: objeto*) thingummyjig

chismoso, a [tʃisˈmoso, a] *adj* gossiping ♦ *nm/f* gossip

chispa [ˈtʃispa] *nf* spark; (*fig*) sparkle; (*ingenio*) wit; (*fam*) drunkenness

chispear [tʃispeˈar] *vi* (*lloviznar*) to drizzle

chisporrotear [tʃisporroteˈar] *vi* (*fuego*) to throw out sparks; (*leña*) to crackle; (*aceite*) to hiss, splutter

chiste [ˈtʃiste] *nm* joke, funny story

chistoso, a [tʃisˈtoso, a] *adj* funny, amusing

chivo, a [ˈtʃiβo, a] *nm/f* (billy-/nanny-) goat; **~ expiatorio** scapegoat

chocante [tʃoˈkante] *adj* startling; (*extraño*) odd; (*ofensivo*) shocking

chocar [tʃoˈkar] *vi* (*coches etc*) to collide, crash ♦ *vt* to shock; (*sorprender*) to startle; **~ con** to collide with; (*fig*) to run into, run up against; **¡chócala!** (*fam*) put it there!

chochear [tʃotʃeˈar] *vi* to dodder, be senile

chocho, a [ˈtʃotʃo, a] *adj* doddering, senile; (*fig*) soft, doting

chocolate [tʃokoˈlate] *adj, nm* chocolate; **chocolatina** *nf* chocolate

chofer [tʃoˈfer] *nm* = **chófer**

chófer [ˈtʃofer] *nm* driver

chollo [ˈtʃoʎo] (*fam*) *nm* bargain, snip

choque *etc* [ˈtʃoke] *vb ver* **chocar** ♦ *nm* (*impacto*) impact; (*golpe*) jolt; (*AUTO*) crash; (*fig*) conflict; **~ frontal** head-on collision

chorizo [tʃoˈriθo] *nm* hard pork sausage, (type of) salami

chorrada [tʃoˈrraða] (*fam*) *nf*: **¡es una ~!** that's crap! (*!*); **decir ~s** to talk crap (*!*)

chorrear [tʃorreˈar] *vi* to gush (out), spout (out); (*gotear*) to drip, trickle

chorro [ˈtʃorro] *nm* jet; (*fig*) stream

choza [ˈtʃoθa] *nf* hut, shack

chubasco [tʃuˈβasko] *nm* squall

chubasquero [tʃuβasˈkero] *nm* lightweight raincoat

chuchería [tʃutʃeˈria] *nf* trinket

chuleta [tʃuˈleta] *nf* chop, cutlet

chulo [ˈtʃulo] *nm* (*de prostituta*) pimp

chupar [tʃuˈpar] *vt* to suck; (*absorber*) to absorb; **~se** *vr* to grow thin

chupete [tʃuˈpete] *nm* dummy (*BRIT*), pacifier (*US*)

chupito [tʃuˈpito] (*fam*) *nm* shot

churro [ˈtʃurro] *nm* (type of) fritter

chusma [ˈtʃusma] *nf* rabble, mob

chutar [tʃuˈtar] *vi* to shoot (at goal)

Cía *abr* (= *compañía*) Co.

cianuro [θjaˈnuro] *nm* cyanide

cibercafé [θiβerkaˈfe] *nm* cybercafé

cicatriz [θikaˈtriθ] *nf* scar; **~arse** *vr* to heal (up), form a scar

ciclismo [θiˈklismo] *nm* cycling

ciclista [θiˈklista] *adj* cycle *cpd* ♦ *nm/f* cyclist

ciclo [ˈθiklo] *nm* cycle; **~turismo** *nm*: **hacer ~turismo** to go on a cycling holiday

ciclón [θiˈklon] *nm* cyclone

ciego, a [ˈθjeɣo, a] *adj* blind ♦ *nm/f* blind man/woman

cielo [ˈθjelo] *nm* sky; (*REL*) heaven; **¡~s!** good heavens!

ciempiés [θjemˈpjes] *nm inv* centipede

cien [θjen] *num ver* **ciento**

ciénaga [ˈθjenaɣa] *nf* marsh, swamp

ciencia [ˈθjenθja] nf science; **~s** nfpl (ESCOL)
science sg; **~-ficción** nf science fiction
cieno [ˈθjeno] nm mud, mire
científico, a [θjenˈtifiko, a] adj scientific
♦ nm/f scientist
ciento [ˈθjento] (tb: **cien**) num hundred;
pagar al 10 por ~ to pay at 10 per cent
cierre etc [ˈθjerre] vb ver **cerrar** ♦ nm closing,
shutting; (con llave) locking; **~ de cremallera**
zip (fastener)
cierro etc vb ver **cerrar**
cierto, a [ˈθjerto, a] adj sure, certain; (un tal)
a certain; (correcto) right, correct; **~ hombre**
a certain man; **ciertas personas** certain o
some people; **sí, es ~** yes, that's correct
ciervo [ˈθjerβo] nm deer; (macho) stag
cierzo [ˈθjerθo] nm north wind
cifra [ˈθifra] nf number; (secreta) code
cifrar [θiˈfrar] vt to code, write in code
cigala [θiˈɣala] nf Norway lobster
cigarra [θiˈɣarra] nf cicada
cigarrillo [θiɣaˈrriʎo] nm cigarette
cigarro [θiˈɣarro] nm cigarette; (puro) cigar
cigüeña [θiˈɣweɲa] nf stork
cilíndrico, a [θiˈlindriko, a] adj cylindrical
cilindro [θiˈlindro] nm cylinder
cima [ˈθima] nf (de montaña) top, peak; (de
árbol) top; (fig) height
cimbrearse [θimbreˈarse] vr to sway
cimentar [θimenˈtar] vt to lay the
foundations of; (fig: fundar) to found
cimiento [θiˈmjento] nm foundation
cinc [θink] nm zinc
cincel [θinˈθel] nm chisel; **~ar** vt to chisel
cinco [ˈθinko] num five
cincuenta [θinˈkwenta] num fifty
cine [ˈθine] nm cinema
cineasta [θineˈasta] nm/f film director
cinematográfico, a [θinematoˈɣrafiko, a]
adj cine-, film cpd
cínico, a [ˈθiniko, a] adj cynical ♦ nm/f cynic
cinismo [θiˈnismo] nm cynicism
cinta [ˈθinta] nf band, strip; (de tela) ribbon;
(película) reel; (de máquina de escribir)
ribbon; **~ adhesiva** sticky tape; **~ de vídeo**
videotape; **~ magnetofónica** tape; **~ métrica**
tape measure
cintura [θinˈtura] nf waist
cinturón [θintuˈron] nm belt; **~ de seguridad**
safety belt
ciprés [θiˈpres] nm cypress (tree)
circo [ˈθirko] nm circus
circuito [θirˈkwito] nm circuit
circulación [θirkulaˈθjon] nf circulation;
(AUTO) traffic
circular [θirkuˈlar] adj, nf circular ♦ vi, vt to
circulate ♦ vi (AUTO) to drive; **"circule por la
derecha"** "keep (to the) right"
círculo [ˈθirkulo] nm circle; **~ vicioso** vicious

circle
circuncidar [θirkunθiˈdar] vt to circumcise
circundar [θirkunˈdar] vt to surround
circunferencia [θirkunfeˈrenθja] nf
circumference
circunscribir [θirkunskriˈβir] vt to
circumscribe; **~se** vr to be limited
circunscripción [θirkunskripˈθjon] nf (POL)
constituency
circunspecto, a [θirkunsˈpekto, a] adj
circumspect, cautious
circunstancia [θirkunsˈtanθja] nf
circumstance
cirio [ˈθirjo] nm (wax) candle
ciruela [θiˈrwela] nf plum; **~ pasa** prune
cirugía [θiruˈxia] nf surgery; **~ estética** o
plástica plastic surgery
cirujano [θiruˈxano] nm surgeon
cisne [ˈθisne] nm swan
cisterna [θisˈterna] nf cistern, tank
cita [ˈθita] nf appointment, meeting; (de
novios) date; (referencia) quotation
citación [θitaˈθjon] nf (JUR) summons sg
citar [θiˈtar] vt (gen) to make an appointment
with; (JUR) to summons; (un autor, texto) to
quote; **~se** vr: **se citaron en el cine** they
arranged to meet at the cinema
cítricos [ˈθitrikos] nmpl citrus fruit(s)
ciudad [θjuˈðað] nf town; (más grande) city;
~anía nf citizenship; **~ano, a** nm/f citizen
cívico, a [ˈθiβiko, a] adj civic
civil [θiˈβil] adj civil ♦ nm (guardia) policeman
civilización [θiβiliθaˈθjon] nf civilization
civilizar [θiβiliˈθar] vt to civilize
civismo [θiˈβismo] nm public spirit
cizaña [θiˈθaɲa] nf (fig) discord
cl. abr (= centilitro) cl.
clamar [klaˈmar] vt to clamour for, cry out for
♦ vi to cry out, clamour
clamor [klaˈmor] nm clamour, protest
clandestino, a [klandesˈtino, a] adj
clandestine; (POL) underground
clara [ˈklara] nf (de huevo) egg white
claraboya [klaraˈβoja] nf skylight
clarear [klareˈar] vi (el día) to dawn; (el cielo)
to clear up, brighten up; **~se** vr to be
transparent
clarete [klaˈrete] nm rosé (wine)
claridad [klariˈðað] nf (del día) brightness;
(de estilo) clarity
clarificar [klarifiˈkar] vt to clarify
clarinete [klariˈnete] nm clarinet
clarividencia [klariβiˈðenθja] nf
clairvoyance; (fig) far-sightedness
claro, a [ˈklaro, a] adj clear; (luminoso)
bright; (color) light; (evidente) clear, evident;
(poco espeso) thin ♦ nm (en bosque) clearing
♦ adv clearly ♦ excl (tb: **~ que sí**) of course!
clase [ˈklase] nf class; **~ alta/media/obrera**

upper/middle/working class; **~s particulares** private lessons, private tuition sg

clásico, a |'klasiko, a] adj classical

clasificación |klasifika'θjon] nf classification; (DEPORTE) league (table)

clasificar |klasifi'kar| vt to classify

claudicar |klauði'kar| vi to give in

claustro |'klaustro] nm cloister

cláusula |'klausula] nf clause

clausura |klau'sura| nf closing, closure; **clausurar** vt (congreso etc) to bring to a close

clavar |kla'ßar| vt (clavo) to hammer in; (cuchillo) to stick, thrust

clave |'klaße] nf key; (MUS) clef

clavel |kla'ßel| nm carnation

clavícula |kla'ßikula] nf collar bone

clavija |kla'ßixa| nf peg, dowel, pin; (ELEC) plug

clavo |'klaßo] nm (de metal) nail; (BOT) clove

claxon |'klakson| (pl ~s) nm horn

clemencia |kle'menθja] nf mercy, clemency

cleptómano, a |klep'tomano, a| nm/f kleptomaniac

clérigo |'klerixo] nm priest

clero |'klero] nm clergy

cliché |kli'tʃe| nm cliché; (FOTO) negative

cliente, a |'kljente, a] nm/f client, customer

clientela |kljen'tela] nf clientele, customers pl

clima |'klima] nm climate

climatizado, a |klimati'θaðo, a] adj air-conditioned

clímax |'klimaks] nm inv climax

clínica |'klinika] nf clinic; (particular) private hospital

clip |klip| (pl ~s) nm paper clip

clítoris |'klitoris] nm inv (ANAT) clitoris

cloaca |klo'aka] nf sewer

cloro |'kloro] nm chlorine

club |klub| (pl ~s o ~es) nm club; **~ de jóvenes** youth club

cm abr (= centímetro, centímetros) cm

C.N.T. (ESP) abr = Confederación Nacional de Trabajo

coacción |koak'θjon] nf coercion, compulsion; **coaccionar** vt to coerce

coagular |koaɣu'lar] vt (leche, sangre) to clot; **~se** vr to clot; **coágulo** nm clot

coalición |koali'θjon] nf coalition

coartada |koar'taða] nf alibi

coartar |koar'tar] vt to limit, restrict

coba |'koßa] nf: **dar ~ a uno** to soft-soap sb

cobarde |ko'ßarðe] adj cowardly ♦ nm coward; **cobardía** nf cowardice

cobaya |ko'ßaja] nf guinea pig

cobertizo |koßer'tiθo] nm shelter

cobertura |koßer'tura] nf cover

cobija |ko'ßixa] (AM) nf blanket

cobijar |koßi'xar] vt (cubrir) to cover;

(proteger) to shelter; **cobijo** nm shelter

cobra |'koßra] nf cobra

cobrador, a |koßra'ðor, a] nm/f (de autobús) conductor/conductress; (de impuestos, gas) collector

cobrar |ko'ßrar] vt (cheque) to cash; (sueldo) to collect, draw; (objeto) to recover; (precio) to charge; (deuda) to collect ♦ vi to be paid; **cóbrese al entregar** cash on delivery

cobre |'koßre] nm copper; **~s** nmpl (MUS) brass instruments

cobro |'koßro] nm (de cheque) cashing; **presentar al ~** to cash

cocaína |koka'ina] nf cocaine

cocción |kok'θjon] nf (CULIN) cooking; (en agua) boiling

cocear |koθe'ar] vi to kick

cocer |ko'θer| vt, vi to cook; (en agua) to boil; (en horno) to bake

coche |'kotʃe] nm (AUTO) car (BRIT), automobile (US); (de tren, de caballos) coach, carriage; (para niños) pram (BRIT), baby carriage (US); **ir en ~** to drive; **~ celular** Black Maria, prison van; **~ de bomberos** fire engine; **~ fúnebre** hearse; **coche-cama** (pl **coches-cama**) nm (FERRO) sleeping car, sleeper

cochera |ko'tʃera] nf garage; (de autobuses, trenes) depot

coche restaurante (pl **coches restaurante**) nm (FERRO) dining car, diner

cochinillo |kotʃi'niʎo] nm (CULIN) suckling pig, sucking pig

cochino, a |ko'tʃino, a] adj filthy, dirty ♦ nm/f pig

cocido |ko'θiðo] nm stew

cocina |ko'θina] nf kitchen; (aparato) cooker, stove; (acto) cookery; **~ eléctrica/de gas** electric/gas cooker; **~ francesa** French cuisine; **cocinar** vt, vi to cook

cocinero, a |koθi'nero, a] nm/f cook

coco |'koko] nm coconut

cocodrilo |koko'ðrilo] nm crocodile

cocotero |koko'tero] nm coconut palm

cóctel |'koktel] nm cocktail

codazo |ko'ðaθo] nm: **dar un ~ a uno** to nudge sb

codicia |ko'ðiθja] nf greed; **codiciar** vt to covet; **codicioso, a** adj covetous

código |'koðixo] nm code; **~ de barras** bar code; **~ civil** common law; **~ de (la) circulación** highway code; **~ postal** postcode

codillo |ko'ðiʎo] nm (ZOOL) knee; (TEC) elbow (joint)

codo |'koðo] nm (ANAT, de tubo) elbow; (ZOOL) knee

codorniz |koðor'niθ] nf quail

coerción |koer'θjon] nf coercion

coetáneo, a |koe'taneo, a] adj, nm/f contemporary

coexistir |koe(k)sis'tir| *vi* to coexist
cofradía |kofra'ðia| *nf* brotherhood, fraternity
cofre |'kofre| *nm* (*de joyas*) case; (*de dinero*) chest
coger |ko'xer| (*ESP*) *vt* to take (hold of); (*objeto caído*) to pick up; (*frutas*) to pick, harvest; (*resfriado, ladrón, pelota*) to catch ♦ *vi*: ~ **por el buen camino** to take the right road; **~se** *vr* (*el dedo*) to catch; **~se a algo** to get hold of sth
cogollo |ko'ɣoʎo| *nm* (*de lechuga*) heart
cogote |ko'ɣote| *nm* back o nape of the neck
cohabitar |koaβi'tar| *vi* to live together, cohabit
cohecho |ko'etʃo| *nm* (*acción*) bribery; (*soborno*) bribe
coherente |koe'rente| *adj* coherent
cohesión |koe'sjon| *nm* cohesion
cohete |ko'ete| *nm* rocket
cohibido, a |koi'βiðo, a| *adj* (*PSICO*) inhibited; (*tímido*) shy
cohibir |koi'βir| *vt* to restrain, restrict
coincidencia |koinθi'ðenθja| *nf* coincidence
coincidir |koinθi'ðir| *vi* (*en idea*) to coincide, agree; (*en lugar*) to coincide
coito |'koito| *nm* intercourse, coitus
coja *etc vb ver* **coger**
cojear |koxe'ar| *vi* (*persona*) to limp, hobble; (*mueble*) to wobble, rock
cojera |ko'xera| *nf* limp
cojín |ko'xin| *nm* cushion; **cojinete** *nm* (*TEC*) ball bearing
cojo, a *etc* |'koxo, a| *vb ver* **coger** ♦ *adj* (*que no puede andar*) lame, crippled; (*mueble*) wobbly ♦ *nm/f* lame person, cripple
cojón |ko'xon| (*fam*) *nm*: ¡**cojones**! shit! (*!*); **cojonudo, a** (*fam*) *adj* great, fantastic
col |kol| *nf* cabbage; **~es de Bruselas** Brussels sprouts
cola |'kola| *nf* tail; (*de gente*) queue; (*lugar*) end, last place; (*para pegar*) glue, gum; **hacer ~** to queue (up)
colaborador, a |kolaβora'ðor, a| *nm/f* collaborator
colaborar |kolaβo'rar| *vi* to collaborate
colada |ko'laða| *nf*: **hacer la ~** to do the washing
colador |kola'ðor| *nm* (*de líquidos*) strainer; (*para verduras etc*) colander
colapso |ko'lapso| *nm* collapse; **~ nervioso** nervous breakdown
colar |ko'lar| *vt* (*líquido*) to strain off; (*metal*) to cast ♦ *vi* to ooze, seep (through); **~se** *vr* to jump the queue; **~se en** to get into without paying; (*fiesta*) to gatecrash
colcha |'koltʃa| *nf* bedspread
colchón |kol'tʃon| *nm* mattress; **~ inflable** o **neumático** air bed, air mattress
colchoneta |koltʃo'neta| *nf* (*en gimnasio*)

mat; (*de playa*) air bed
colección |kolek'θjon| *nf* collection; **coleccionar** *vt* to collect; **coleccionista** *nm/f* collector
colecta |ko'lekta| *nf* collection
colectivo, a |kolek'tiβo, a| *adj* collective, joint ♦ *nm* (*AM*) (small) bus
colega |ko'lexa| *nm/f* colleague
colegial, a |kole'xjal, a| *nm/f* schoolboy/girl
colegio |ko'lexjo| *nm* college; (*escuela*) school; (*de abogados etc*) association; **~ electoral** polling station; **~ mayor** hall of residence
colegir |kole'xir| *vt* to infer, conclude
cólera |'kolera| *nf* (*ira*) anger; (*MED*) cholera; **colérico, a** |ko'leriko, a| *adj* irascible, bad-tempered
colesterol |koleste'rol| *nm* cholesterol
coleta |ko'leta| *nf* pigtail
colgante |kol'xante| *adj* hanging ♦ *nm* (*joya*) pendant
colgar |kol'xar| *vt* to hang (up); (*ropa*) to hang out ♦ *vi* to hang; (*TELEC*) to hang up
cólico |'koliko| *nm* colic
coliflor |koli'flor| *nf* cauliflower
colilla |ko'liʎa| *nf* cigarette end, butt
colina |ko'lina| *nf* hill
colisión |koli'sjon| *nf* collision; **~ de frente** head-on crash
collar |ko'ʎar| *nm* necklace; (*de perro*) collar
colmar |kol'mar| *vt* to fill to the brim; (*fig*) to fulfil, realize
colmena |kol'mena| *nf* beehive
colmillo |kol'miʎo| *nm* (*diente*) eye tooth; (*de elefante*) tusk; (*de perro*) fang
colmo |'kolmo| *nm*: ¡**es el ~**! it's the limit!
colocación |koloka'θjon| *nf* (*acto*) placing; (*empleo*) job, position
colocar |kolo'kar| *vt* to place, put, position; (*dinero*) to invest; (*poner en empleo*) to find a job for; **~se** *vr* to get a job
Colombia |ko'lombja| *nf* Colombia; **colombiano, a** *adj*, *nm/f* Colombian
colonia |ko'lonja| *nf* colony; (*de casas*) housing estate; (*agua de ~*) cologne
colonización |koloniθa'θjon| *nf* colonization; **colonizador, a** |koloniθa'ðor, a| *adj* colonizing ♦ *nm/f* colonist, settler
colonizar |koloni'θar| *vt* to colonize
coloquio |ko'lokjo| *nm* conversation; (*congreso*) conference
color |ko'lor| *nm* colour
colorado, a |kolo'raðo, a| *adj* (*rojo*) red; (*LAM: chiste*) rude
colorante |kolo'rante| *nm* colouring
colorear |kolore'ar| *vt* to colour
colorete |kolo'rete| *nm* blusher
colorido |kolo'riðo| *nm* colouring
columna |ko'lumna| *nf* column; (*pilar*) pillar;

(*apoyo*) support

columpiar |kolum'pjar| *vt* to swing; ~**se** *vr* to swing; **columpio** *nm* swing

coma ['koma] *nf* comma ♦ *nm* (*MED*) coma

comadre |ko'maðre| *nf* (*madrina*) godmother; (*chismosa*) gossip; **comadrona** *nf* midwife

comandancia [koman'danθja] *nf* command

comandante [koman'dante] *nm* commandant

comarca [ko'marka] *nf* region

comba ['komba] *nf* (*curva*) curve; (*cuerda*) skipping rope; **saltar a la** ~ to skip

combar [kom'bar] *vt* to bend, curve

combate [kom'bate] *nm* fight; **combatiente** *nm* combatant

combatir [komba'tir] *vt* to fight, combat

combinación [kombina'θjon] *nf* combination; (*QUÍM*) compound; (*prenda*) slip

combinar [kombi'nar] *vt* to combine

combustible [kombus'tiβle] *nm* fuel

combustión [kombus'tjon] *nf* combustion

comedia [ko'meðja] *nf* comedy; (*TEATRO*) play, drama

comediante [kome'ðjante] *nm/f* (*comic*) actor/actress

comedido, a [kome'ðiðo, a] *adj* moderate

comedor, a [kome'ðor, a] *nm* (*habitación*) dining room; (*cantina*) canteen

comensal [komen'sal] *nm/f* fellow guest (*o* diner)

comentar [komen'tar] *vt* to comment on

comentario [komen'tarjo] *nm* comment, remark; (*literario*) commentary; ~**s** *nmpl* (*chismes*) gossip *sg*

comentarista [komenta'rista] *nm/f* commentator

comenzar [komen'θar] *vt, vi* to begin, start; ~ **a hacer algo** to begin *o* start doing sth

comer [ko'mer] *vt* to eat; (*DAMAS, AJEDREZ*) to take, capture ♦ *vi* to eat; (*almorzar*) to have lunch; ~**se** *vr* to eat up

comercial [komer'θjal] *adj* commercial; (*relativo al negocio*) business *cpd*; **comercializar** *vt* (*producto*) to market; (*pey*) to commercialize

comerciante [komer'θjante] *nm/f* trader, merchant

comerciar [komer'θjar] *vi* to trade, do business

comercio [ko'merθjo] *nm* commerce, trade; (*negocio*) business; (*fig*) dealings *pl*; ~ **electrónico** e-commerce

comestible [komes'tiβle] *adj* eatable, edible; ~**s** *nmpl* food *sg*, foodstuffs

cometa [ko'meta] *nm* comet ♦ *nf* kite

cometer [kome'ter] *vt* to commit

cometido [kome'tiðo] *nm* task, assignment

comezón [kome'θon] *nf* itch, itching

cómic ['komik] *nm* comic

comicios [ko'miθjos] *nmpl* elections

cómico, a ['komiko, a] *adj* comic(al) ♦ *nm/f* comedian

comida [ko'miða] *nf* (*alimento*) food; (*almuerzo, cena*) meal; (*de mediodía*) lunch

comidilla [komi'ðiʎa] *nf*: **ser la** ~ **de la ciudad** to be the talk of the town

comienzo *etc* [ko'mjenθo] *vb ver* **comenzar** ♦ *nm* beginning, start

comillas [ko'miʎas] *nfpl* quotation marks

comilona [komi'lona] (*fam*) *nf* blow-out

comino [ko'mino] *nm*: **(no) me importa un** ~ I don't give a damn

comisaría [komisa'ria] *nf* (*de policía*) police station; (*MIL*) commissariat

comisario [komi'sarjo] *nm* (*MIL etc*) commissary; (*POL*) commissar

comisión [komi'sjon] *nf* commission

comité [komi'te] (*pl* ~**s**) *nm* committee

comitiva [komi'tiβa] *nf* retinue

como ['komo] *adv* as; (*tal* ~) like; (*aproximadamente*) about, approximately ♦ *conj* (*ya que, puesto que*) as, since; ¡~ **no!** of course!; ~ **no lo haga hoy** unless he does it today; ~ **si** as if; **es tan alto** ~ **ancho** it is as high as it is wide

cómo ['komo] *adv* how?, why? ♦ *excl* what?, I beg your pardon? ♦ *nm*: **el** ~ **y el porqué** the whys and wherefores

cómoda ['komoða] *nf* chest of drawers

comodidad [komoði'ðað] *nf* comfort; **venga a su** ~ come at your convenience

comodín [komo'ðin] *nm* joker

cómodo, a ['komoðo, a] *adj* comfortable; (*práctico, de fácil uso*) convenient

compact disc *nm* compact disk player

compacto, a [kom'pakto, a] *adj* compact

compadecer [kompaðe'θer] *vt* to pity, be sorry for; ~**se** *vr*: ~**se de** to pity, be *o* feel sorry for

compadre [kom'paðre] *nm* (*padrino*) godfather; (*amigo*) friend, pal

compañero, a [kompa'ɲero, a] *nm/f* companion; (*novio*) boy/girlfriend; ~ **de clase** classmate

compañía [kompa'ɲia] *nf* company

comparación [kompara'θjon] *nf* comparison; **en** ~ **con** in comparison with

comparar [kompa'rar] *vt* to compare

comparecer [kompare'θer] *vi* to appear (in court)

comparsa [kom'parsa] *nm/f* (*TEATRO*) extra

compartimiento [komparti'mjento] *nm* (*FERRO*) compartment

compartir [kompar'tir] *vt* to share; (*dinero, comida etc*) to divide (up), share (out)

compás [kom'pas] *nm* (*MUS*) beat, rhythm;

(MAT) compasses pl; (NAUT etc) compass

compasión [kompa'sjon] nf compassion, pity

compasivo, a [kompa'sißo, a] adj compassionate

compatibilidad [kompatißili'ðað] nf compatibility

compatible [kompa'tißle] adj compatible

compatriota [kompa'trjota] nm/f compatriot, fellow countryman/woman

compendiar [kompen'djar] vt to summarize; **compendio** nm summary

compenetrarse [kompene'trarse] vr to be in tune

compensación [kompensa'θjon] nf compensation

compensar [kompen'sar] vt to compensate

competencia [kompe'tenθja] nf (incumbencia) domain, field; (JUR, habilidad) competence; (rivalidad) competition

competente [kompe'tente] adj competent

competición [kompeti'θjon] nf competition

competir [kompe'tir] vi to compete

compilar [kompi'lar] vt to compile

complacencia [kompla'θenθja] nf (placer) pleasure; (tolerancia excesiva) complacency

complacer [kompla'θer] vt to please; **~se** vr to be pleased

complaciente [kompla'θjente] adj kind, obliging, helpful

complejo, a [kom'plexo, a] adj, nm complex

complementario, a [komplemen'tarjo, a] adj complementary

completar [komple'tar] vt to complete

completo, a [kom'pleto, a] adj complete; (perfecto) perfect; (lleno) full ♦ nm full complement

complicado, a [kompli'kaðo, a] adj complicated; **estar ~ en** to be mixed up in

cómplice ['kompliθe] nm/f accomplice

complot [kom'plo(t)] (pl ~s) nm plot

componer [kompo'ner] vt (MUS, LITERATURA, IMPRENTA) to compose; (algo roto) to mend, repair; (arreglar) to arrange; **~se** vr: **~se de** to consist of; **componérselas para hacer algo** to manage to do sth

comportamiento [komporta'mjento] nm behaviour, conduct

comportarse [kompor'tarse] vr to behave

composición [komposi'θjon] nf composition

compositor, a [komposi'tor, a] nm/f composer

compostura [kompos'tura] nf (actitud) composure

compra ['kompra] nf purchase; **ir de ~s** to go shopping; **comprador, a** nm/f buyer, purchaser

comprar [kom'prar] vt to buy, purchase

comprender [kompren'der] vt to understand; (incluir) to comprise, include

comprensión [kompren'sjon] nf understanding; **comprensivo, a** adj (actitud) understanding

compresa [kom'presa] nf: **~ higiénica** sanitary towel (BRIT) o napkin (US)

comprimido, a [kompri'miðo, a] adj compressed ♦ nm (MED) pill, tablet

comprimir [kompri'mir] vt to compress

comprobante [kompro'ßante] nm proof; (COM) voucher; **~ de recibo** receipt

comprobar [kompro'ßar] vt to check; (probar) to prove; (TEC) to check, test

comprometer [komprome'ter] vt to compromise; (poner en peligro) to endanger; **~se** vr (involucrarse) to get involved

compromiso [kompro'miso] nm (obligación) obligation; (cometido) commitment; (convenio) agreement; (apuro) awkward situation

compuesto, a [kom'pwesto, a] adj: **~ de** composed of, made up of ♦ nm compound

computador [komputa'ðor] nm computer; **~ central** mainframe computer; **~ personal** personal computer

computadora [komputa'ðora] nf = **computador**

cómputo ['komputo] nm calculation

comulgar [komul'gar] vi to receive communion

común [ko'mun] adj common ♦ nm: **el ~** the community

comunicación [komunika'θjon] nf communication; (informe) report

comunicado [komuni'kaðo] nm announcement; **~ de prensa** press release

comunicar [komuni'kar] vt, vi to communicate; **~se** vr to communicate; **está comunicando** (TEL) the line's engaged (BRIT) o busy (US); **comunicativo, a** adj communicative

comunidad [komuni'ðað] nf community; **~ autónoma** (POL) autonomous region; **C~ Económica Europea** European Economic Community

comunión [komu'njon] nf communion

comunismo [komu'nismo] nm communism; **comunista** adj, nm/f communist

---

PALABRA CLAVE

con [kon] prep **1** (medio, compañía) with; **comer ~ cuchara** to eat with a spoon; **pasear ~ uno** to go for a walk with sb
2 (a pesar de): **~ todo, merece nuestros respetos** all the same, he deserves our respect
3 (para ~): **es muy bueno para ~ los niños** he's very good with (the) children

4 (+ *infin*): **~ llegar tan tarde se quedó sin comer** by arriving so late he missed out on eating

♦ *conj*: **~ que: será suficiente ~ que le escribas** it will be sufficient if you write to her

conato [ko'nato] *nm* attempt; **~ de robo** attempted robbery

concebir [konθe'βir] *vt, vi* to conceive

conceder [konθe'ðer] *vt* to concede

concejal, a [konθe'xal, a] *nm/f* town councillor

concentración [konθentra'θjon] *nf* concentration

concentrar [konθen'trar] *vt* to concentrate; **~se** *vr* to concentrate

concepción [konθep'θjon] *nf* conception

concepto [kon'θepto] *nm* concept

concernir [konθer'nir] *vi* to concern; **en lo que concierne a ...** as far as ... is concerned; **en lo que a mí concierne** as far as I'm concerned

concertar [konθer'tar] *vt* (*MUS*) to harmonize; (*acordar: precio*) to agree; (: *tratado*) to conclude; (*trato*) to arrange, fix up; (*combinar: esfuerzos*) to coordinate ♦ *vi* to harmonize, be in tune

concesión [konθe'sjon] *nf* concession

concesionario [konθesjo'narjo] *nm* (licensed) dealer, agent

concha ['kontʃa] *nf* shell

conciencia [kon'θjenθja] *nf* conscience; **tener/tomar ~ de** to be/become aware of; **tener la ~ limpia/tranquila** to have a clear conscience

concienciar [konθjen'θjar] *vt* to make aware; **~se** *vr* to become aware

concienzudo, a [konθjen'θuðo, a] *adj* conscientious

concierto *etc* [kon'θjerto] *vb ver* **concertar** ♦ *nm* concert; (*obra*) concerto

conciliar [konθi'ljar] *vt* to reconcile

concilio [kon'θiljo] *nm* council

conciso, a [kon'θiso, a] *adj* concise

concluir [konklu'ir] *vt, vi* to conclude; **~se** *vr* to conclude

conclusión [konklu'sjon] *nf* conclusion

concluyente [konklu'jente] *adj* (*prueba, información*) conclusive

concordar [konkor'ðar] *vt* to reconcile ♦ *vi* to agree, tally

concordia [kon'korðja] *nf* harmony

concretar [konkre'tar] *vt* to make concrete, make more specific; **~se** *vr* to become more definite

concreto, a [kon'kreto, a] *adj, nm* (*AM*) concrete; **en ~** (*en resumen*) to sum up; (*específicamente*) specifically; **no hay nada en ~** there's nothing definite

concurrencia [konku'rrenθja] *nf* turnout

concurrido, a [konku'rriðo, a] *adj* (*calle*) busy; (*local, reunión*) crowded

concurrir [konku'rrir] *vi* (*juntarse: ríos*) to meet, come together; (: *personas*) to gather, meet

concursante [konkur'sante] *nm/f* competitor

concurso [kon'kurso] *nm* (*de público*) crowd; (*ESCOL, DEPORTE, competencia*) competition; (*ayuda*) help, cooperation

condal [kon'dal] *adj*: **la Ciudad C~** Barcelona

conde ['konde] *nm* count

condecoración [kondekora'θjon] *nf* (*MIL*) medal

condecorar [kondeko'rar] *vt* (*MIL*) to decorate

condena [kon'dena] *nf* sentence

condenación [kondena'θjon] *nf* condemnation; (*REL*) damnation

condenar [konde'nar] *vt* to condemn; (*JUR*) to convict; **~se** *vr* (*REL*) to be damned

condensar [konden'sar] *vt* to condense

condesa [kon'desa] *nf* countess

condición [kondi'θjon] *nf* condition; **condicional** *adj* conditional

condicionar [kondiθjo'nar] *vt* (*acondicionar*) to condition; **~ algo a** to make sth conditional on

condimento [kondi'mento] *nm* seasoning

condolerse [kondo'lerse] *vr* to sympathize

condón [kon'don] *nm* condom

conducir [kondu'θir] *vt* to take, convey; (*AUTO*) to drive ♦ *vi* to drive; (*fig*) to lead; **~se** *vr* to behave

conducta [kon'dukta] *nf* conduct, behaviour

conducto [kon'dukto] *nm* pipe, tube; (*fig*) channel

conductor, a [konduk'tor, a] *adj* leading, guiding ♦ *nm* (*FÍSICA*) conductor; (*de vehículo*) driver

conduje *etc vb ver* **conducir**

conduzco *etc vb ver* **conducir**

conectado, a [konek'taðo, a] *adj* (*INFORM*) on-line

conectar [konek'tar] *vt* to connect (up); (*enchufar*) plug in

conejillo [kone'xiλo] *nm*: **~ de Indias** (*ZOOL*) guinea pig

conejo [ko'nexo] *nm* rabbit

conexión [konek'sjon] *nf* connection

confección [konfe(k)'θjon] *nf* preparation; (*industria*) clothing industry

confeccionar [konfekθjo'nar] *vt* to make (up)

confederación [konfeðera'θjon] *nf* confederation

conferencia [konfe'renθja] *nf* conference; (*lección*) lecture; (*TEL*) call

conferir |konfe'rir| vt to award
confesar |konfe'sar| vt to confess, admit
confesión |konfe'sjon| nf confession
confesionario |konfesjo'narjo| nm
confessional
confeti |kon'feti| nm confetti
confiado, a |kon'fjaðo, a| adj (crédulo)
trusting; (seguro) confident
confianza |kon'fjanθa| nf trust; (seguridad)
confidence; (familiaridad) intimacy, familiarity
confiar |kon'fjar| vt to entrust ♦ vi to trust
confidencia |konfi'ðenθja| nf confidence
confidencial |konfiðen'θjal| adj confidential
confidente |konfi'ðente| nm/f confidant/e;
(policial) informer
configurar |konfiɣu'rar| vt to shape, form
confín |kon'fin| nm limit; **confines** nmpl
confines, limits
confinar |konfi'nar| vi to confine; (desterrar)
to banish
confirmar |konfir'mar| vt to confirm
confiscar |konfis'kar| vt to confiscate
confite |kon'fite| nm sweet (BRIT), candy (US)
confitería |konfite'ria| nf (tienda)
confectioner's (shop)
confitura |konfi'tura| nf jam
conflictivo, a |konflik'tiβo, a| adj (asunto,
propuesta) controversial; (país, situación)
troubled
conflicto |kon'flikto| nm conflict; (fig) clash
confluir |kon'flwir| vi (ríos) to meet; (gente)
to gather
conformar |konfor'mar| vt to shape, fashion
♦ vi to agree; **~se** vr to conform; (resignarse)
to resign o.s.
conforme |kon'forme| adj (correspondiente):
~ con in line with; (de acuerdo): **estar ~s (con
algo)** to be in agreement (with sth) ♦ adv as
♦ excl agreed! ♦ prep: ~ a in accordance
with; **quedarse ~ (con algo)** to be satisfied
(with sth)
conformidad |konformi'ðað| nf (semejanza)
similarity; (acuerdo) agreement;
conformista adj, nm/f conformist
confortable |konfor'taβle| adj comfortable
confortar |konfor'tar| vt to comfort
confrontar |konfron'tar| vt to confront; (dos
personas) to bring face to face; (cotejar) to
compare
confundir |konfun'dir| vt (equivocar) to
mistake, confuse; (turbar) to confuse; **~se** vr
(turbarse) to get confused; (equivocarse) to
make a mistake; (mezclarse) to mix
confusión |konfu'sjon| nf confusion
confuso, a |kon'fuso, a| adj confused
congelado, a |konxe'laðo, a| adj frozen; **~s**
nmpl frozen food(s); **congelador** nm
(aparato) freezer, deep freeze
congelar |konxe'lar| vt to freeze; **~se** vr

(sangre, grasa) to congeal
congeniar |konxe'njar| vi to get on (BRIT) o
along (US) well
congestión |konxes'tjon| nf congestion
congestionar |konxestjo'nar| vt to congest
congoja |kon'goxa| nf distress, grief
congraciarse |kongra'θjarse| vr to ingratiate
o.s.
congratular |kongratu'lar| vt to
congratulate
congregación |kongreɣa'θjon| nf
congregation
congregar |kongre'ɣar| vt to gather
together; **~se** vr to gather together
congresista |kongre'sista| nm/f delegate,
congressman/woman
congreso |kon'greso| nm congress
congrio |'kongrjo| nm conger eel
conjetura |konxe'tura| nf guess; **conjeturar**
vt to guess
conjugar |konxu'ɣar| vt to combine, fit
together; (LING) to conjugate
conjunción |konxun'θjon| nf conjunction
conjunto, a |kon'xunto, a| adj joint, united
♦ nm whole; (MUS) band; **en ~** as a whole
conjurar |konxu'rar| vt (REL) to exorcise;
(fig) to ward off ♦ vi to plot
conmemoración |konmemora'θjon| nf
commemoration
conmemorar |konmemo'rar| vt to
commemorate
conmigo |kon'miɣo| pron with me
conmoción |konmo'θjon| nf shock; (fig)
upheaval; ~ **cerebral** (MED) concussion
conmovedor, a |konmoβe'ðor, a| adj
touching, moving; (emocionante) exciting
conmover |konmo'βer| vt to shake, disturb;
(fig) to move
conmutador |konmuta'ðor| nm switch;
(AM: TEL: centralita) switchboard; (: central)
telephone exchange
cono |'kono| nm cone
conocedor, a |konoθe'ðor, a| adj expert,
knowledgeable ♦ nm/f expert
conocer |kono'θer| vt to know; (por primera
vez) to meet, get to know; (entender) to
know about; (reconocer) to recognize; **~se** vr
(una persona) to know o.s.; (dos personas) to
(get to) know each other
conocido, a |kono'θiðo, a| adj (well-)
known ♦ nm/f acquaintance
conocimiento |konoθi'mjento| nm
knowledge; (MED) consciousness; **~s** nmpl
(saber) knowledge sg
conozco etc vb ver **conocer**
conque |'konke| conj and so, so then
conquista |kon'kista| nf conquest;
conquistador, a adj conquering ♦ nm
conqueror

conquistar [konkis'tar] vt to conquer

consagrar [konsa'ɣrar] vt (REL) to consecrate; (fig) to devote

consciente [kons'θjente] adj conscious

consecución [konseku'θjon] nf acquisition; (de fin) attainment

consecuencia [konse'kwenθja] nf consequence, outcome; (coherencia) consistency

consecuente [konse'kwente] adj consistent

consecutivo, a [konseku'tiβo, a] adj consecutive

conseguir [konse'ɣir] vt to get, obtain; (objetivo) to attain

consejero, a [konse'xero, a] nm/f adviser, consultant; (POL) councillor

consejo [kon'sexo] nm advice; (POL) council; ~ de administración (COM) board of directors; ~ de guerra court martial; ~ de ministros cabinet meeting

consenso [kon'senso] nm consensus

consentimiento [konsenti'mjento] nm consent

consentir [konsen'tir] vt (permitir, tolerar) to consent to; (mimar) to pamper, spoil; (aguantar) to put up ♦ vi to agree, consent; ~ que uno haga algo to allow sb to do sth

conserje [kon'serxe] nm caretaker; (portero) porter

conservación [konserβa'θjon] nf conservation; (de alimentos, vida) preservation

conservador, a [konserβa'ðor, a] adj (POL) conservative ♦ nm/f conservative

conservante [konser'βante] nm preservative

conservar [konser'βar] vt to conserve, keep; (alimentos, vida) to preserve; ~se vr to survive

conservas [kon'serβas] nfpl canned food(s) (pl)

conservatorio [konserβa'torjo] nm (MUS) conservatoire, conservatory

considerable [konsiðe'raβle] adj considerable

consideración [konsiðera'θjon] nf consideration; (estimación) respect

considerado, a [konsiðe'raðo, a] adj (atento) considerate; (respetado) respected

considerar [konsiðe'rar] vt to consider

consigna [kon'siɣna] nf (orden) order, instruction; (para equipajes) left-luggage office

consigo etc [kon'siɣo] vb ver conseguir ♦ pron (m) with him; (f) with her; (Vd) with you; (reflexivo) with o.s.

consiguiendo etc vb ver conseguir

consiguiente [konsi'ɣjente] adj consequent; **por ~** and so, therefore, consequently

consistente [konsis'tente] adj consistent; (sólido) solid, firm; (válido) sound

consistir [konsis'tir] vi: ~ en (componerse de) to consist of

consola [kon'sola] nf (mueble) console table; (de videojuegos) console

consolación [konsola'θjon] nf consolation

consolar [konso'lar] vt to console

consolidar [konsoli'ðar] vt to consolidate

consomé [konso'me] (pl ~s) nm consommé, clear soup

consonante [konso'nante] adj consonant, harmonious ♦ nf consonant

consorcio [kon'sorθjo] nm consortium

conspiración [konspira'θjon] nf conspiracy

conspirador, a [konspira'ðor, a] nm/f conspirator

conspirar [konspi'rar] vi to conspire

constancia [kon'stanθja] nf constancy; **dejar ~ de** to put on record

constante [kon'stante] adj, nf constant

constar [kons'tar] vi (evidenciarse) to be clear o evident; ~ de to consist of

constatar [konsta'tar] vt to verify

consternación [konsterna'θjon] nf consternation

constipado, a [konsti'paðo, a] adj: **estar ~** to have a cold ♦ nm cold

constitución [konstitu'θjon] nf constitution; **constitucional** adj constitutional

constituir [konstitu'ir] vt (formar, componer) to constitute, make up; (fundar, erigir, ordenar) to constitute, establish

constituyente [konstitu'jente] adj constituent

constreñir [konstre'nir] vt (restringir) to restrict

construcción [konstruk'θjon] nf construction, building

constructor, a [konstruk'tor, a] nm/f builder

construir [konstru'ir] vt to build, construct

construyendo etc vb ver construir

consuelo [kon'swelo] nm consolation, solace

cónsul ['konsul] nm consul; **consulado** nm consulate

consulta [kon'sulta] nf consultation; (MED): **horas de ~** surgery hours

consultar [konsul'tar] vt to consult

consultorio [konsul'torjo] nm (MED) surgery

consumar [konsu'mar] vt to complete, carry out; (crimen) to commit; (sentencia) to carry out

consumición [konsumi'θjon] nf consumption; (bebida) drink; (comida) food; ~ mínima cover charge

consumidor, a [konsumi'ðor, a] nm/f consumer

consumir [konsu'mir] vt to consume; ~se vr

to be consumed; (*persona*) to waste away

consumismo [konsu'mismo] *nm* consumerism

consumo [kon'sumo] *nm* consumption

contabilidad [kontaßili'ðað] *nf* accounting, book-keeping; (*profesión*) accountancy; **contable** *nm/f* accountant

contacto [kon'takto] *nm* contact; (*AUTO*) ignition

contado, a [kon'taðo, a] *adj*: **~s** (*escasos*) numbered, scarce, few ♦ *nm*: **pagar al ~ to** pay (in) cash

contador [konta'ðor] *nm* (*aparato*) meter; (*AM*: *contante*) accountant

contagiar [konta'xjar] *vt* (*enfermedad*) to pass on, transmit; (*persona*) to infect; **~se** *vr* to become infected

contagio [kon'taxjo] *nm* infection; **contagioso, a** *adj* infectious; (*fig*) catching

contaminación [kontamina'θjon] *nf* contamination; (*polución*) pollution

contaminar [kontami'nar] *vt* to contaminate; (*aire, agua*) to pollute

contante [kon'tante] *adj*: **dinero ~ (y sonante)** cash

contar [kon'tar] *vt* (*páginas, dinero*) to count; (*anécdota, chiste etc*) to tell ♦ *vi* to count; **~ con** to rely on, count on

contemplación [kontempla'θjon] *nf* contemplation

contemplar [kontem'plar] *vt* to contemplate; (*mirar*) to look at

contemporáneo, a [kontempo'raneo, a] *adj, nm/f* contemporary

contendiente [konten'djente] *nm/f* contestant

contenedor [kontene'ðor] *nm* container

contener [konte'ner] *vt* (*tener dentro*) to contain, hold; (*retener*) to hold back, contain; **~se** *vr* to control o restrain o.s.

contenido, a [konte'niðo, a] *adj* (*moderado*) restrained; (*risa etc*) suppressed ♦ *nm* contents *pl*, content

contentar [konten'tar] *vt* (*satisfacer*) to satisfy; (*complacer*) to please; **~se** *vr* to be satisfied

contento, a [kon'tento, a] *adj* (*alegre*) pleased; (*feliz*) happy

contestación [kontesta'θjon] *nf* answer, reply

contestador [kontesta'ðor] *nm*: **~ automático** answering machine

contestar [kontes'tar] *vt* to answer, reply; (*JUR*) to corroborate, confirm

contexto [kon'te(k)sto] *nm* context

contienda [kon'tjenda] *nf* contest

contigo [kon'tiɣo] *pron* with you

contiguo, a [kon'tiɣwo, a] *adj* adjacent, adjoining

continente [konti'nente] *adj, nm* continent

contingencia [kontin'xenθja] *nf* contingency; (*riesgo*) risk; **contingente** *adj, nm* contingent

continuación [kontinwa'θjon] *nf* continuation; **a ~** then, next

continuar [konti'nwar] *vt* to continue, go on with ♦ *vi* to continue, go on; **~ hablando** to continue talking o to talk

continuidad [kontinwi'ðað] *nf* continuity

continuo, a [kon'tinwo, a] *adj* (*sin interrupción*) continuous; (*acción perseverante*) continual

contorno [kon'torno] *nm* outline; (*GEO*) contour; **~s** *nmpl* neighbourhood *sg*, surrounding area *sg*

contorsión [kontor'sjon] *nf* contortion

contra ['kontra] *prep, ad* against ♦ *nm inv* **con ♦** *nf*: **la C~** (*de Nicaragua*) the Contras *pl*

contraataque [kontraa'take] *nm* counterattack

contrabajo [kontra'ßaxo] *nm* double bass

contrabandista [kontraßan'dista] *nm/f* smuggler

contrabando [kontra'ßando] *nm* (*acción*) smuggling; (*mercancías*) contraband

contracción [kontrak'θjon] *nf* contraction

contracorriente [kontrako'rrjente]: **(a) ~** *adv* against the current

contradecir [kontraðe'θir] *vt* to contradict

contradicción [kontraðik'θjon] *nf* contradiction

contradictorio, a [kontraðik'torjo, a] *adj* contradictory

contraer [kontra'er] *vt* to contract; (*limitar*) to restrict; **~se** *vr* to contract; (*limitarse*) to limit o.s.

contraluz [kontra'luθ] *nf*: **a ~** against the light

contrapartida [kontrapar'tiða] *nf*: **como ~ (de)** in return (for)

contrapelo [kontra'pelo]: **a ~** *adv* the wrong way

contrapesar [kontrape'sar] *vt* to counterbalance; (*fig*) to offset; **contrapeso** *nm* counterweight

contraportada [kontrapor'taða] *nf* (*de revista*) back cover

contraproducente [kontraproðu'θente] *adj* counterproductive

contrariar [kontra'rjar] *vt* (*oponerse*) to oppose; (*poner obstáculo*) to impede; (*enfadar*) to vex

contrariedad [kontrarje'ðað] *nf* (*obstáculo*) obstacle, setback; (*disgusto*) vexation, annoyance

contrario, a [kon'trarjo, a] *adj* contrary; (*persona*) opposed; (*sentido, lado*) opposite ♦ *nm/f* enemy, adversary; (*DEPORTE*)

opponent; **al/por el ~** on the contrary; **de lo ~**
otherwise

contrarreloj [kontrarre'lo] nf (tb: **prueba ~**)
time trial

contrarrestar [kontrarres'tar] vt to
counteract

contrasentido [kontrasen'tiðo] nm: **es un
~ que él ...** it doesn't make sense for him to ...

contraseña [kontra'seɲa] nf (INFORM)
password

contrastar [kontras'tar] vt, vi to contrast

contraste [kon'traste] nm contrast

contratar [kontra'tar] vt (firmar un acuerdo
para) to contract for; (empleados, obreros) to
hire, engage; **~se** vr to sign on

contratiempo [kontra'tjempo] nm setback

contratista [kontra'tista] nm/f contractor

contrato [kon'trato] nm contract

contravenir [kontraße'nir] vi: **~ a** to
contravene, violate

contraventana [kontraßen'tana] nf shutter

contribución [kontrißu'θjon] nf (municipal
etc) tax; (ayuda) contribution

contribuir [kontrißu'ir] vt, vi to contribute;
(COM) to pay (in taxes)

contribuyente [kontrißu'jente] nm/f (COM)
taxpayer; (que ayuda) contributor

contrincante [kontrin'kante] nm opponent

control [kon'trol] nm control; (inspección)
inspection, check; **~ador, a** nm/f controller;
~ador aéreo air-traffic controller

controlar [kontro'lar] vt to control;
(inspeccionar) to inspect, check

controversia [kontro'ßersja] nf controversy

contundente [kontun'dente] adj
(instrumento) blunt; (argumento, derrota)
overwhelming

contusión [kontu'sjon] nf bruise

convalecencia [kombale'θenθja] nf
convalescence

convalecer [kombale'θer] vi to convalesce,
get better

convaleciente [kombale'θjente] adj, nm/f
convalescent

convalidar [kombali'ðar] vt (título) to
recognize

convencer [komben'θer] vt to convince

convencimiento [kombenθi'mjento] nm
(certidumbre) conviction

convención [komben'θjon] nf convention

conveniencia [kombe'njenθja] nf suitability;
(conformidad) agreement; (utilidad, provecho)
usefulness; **~s** nfpl (convenciones)
conventions; (COM) property sg

conveniente [kombe'njente] adj suitable;
(útil) useful

convenio [kom'benjo] nm agreement, treaty

convenir [kombe'nir] vi (estar de acuerdo) to
agree; (venir bien) to suit, be suitable

convento [kom'bento] nm convent

convenza etc vb ver **convencer**

converger [komber'xer] vi to converge

convergir [komber'xir] vi = **converger**

conversación [kombersa'θjon] nf
conversation

conversar [komber'sar] vi to talk, converse

conversión [komber'sjon] nf conversion

convertir [komber'tir] vt to convert

convicción [kombik'θjon] nf conviction

convicto, a [kom'bikto, a] adj convicted

convidado, a [kombi'ðaðo, a] nm/f guest

convidar [kombi'ðar] vt to invite

convincente [kombin'θente] adj convincing

convite [kom'bite] nm invitation; (banquete)
banquet

convivencia [kombi'ßenθja] nf coexistence,
living together

convivir [kombi'ßir] vi to live together

convocar [kombo'kar] vt to summon, call
(together)

convocatoria [komboka'torja] nf (de
oposiciones, elecciones) notice; (de huelga) call

convulsión [kombul'sjon] nf convulsion

conyugal [konju'xal] adj conjugal; **cónyuge**
['konjuxe] nm/f spouse

coñac [ko'ɲa(k)] (pl **~s**) nm cognac, brandy

coño ['koɲo] (fam!) excl (enfado) shit! (!);
(sorpresa) bloody hell! (!)

cooperación [koopera'θjon] nf cooperation

cooperar [koope'rar] vi to cooperate

cooperativa [koopera'tißa] nf cooperative

coordinadora [koorðina'ðora] nf (comité)
coordinating committee

coordinar [koorði'nar] vt to coordinate

copa ['kopa] nf cup; (vaso) glass; (bebida):
(**tomar una) ~** (to have a) drink; (de árbol)
top; (de sombrero) crown; **~s** nfpl (NAIPES) ≈
hearts

copia ['kopja] nf copy; **~ de respaldo** o
seguridad (INFORM) back-up copy; **copiar** vt
to copy

copioso, a [ko'pjoso, a] adj copious, plentiful

copla ['kopla] nf verse; (canción) (popular)
song

copo ['kopo] nm: **~ de nieve** snowflake; **~s de
maíz** cornflakes

coqueta [ko'keta] adj flirtatious, coquettish;
coquetear vi to flirt

coraje [ko'raxe] nm courage; (ánimo) spirit;
(ira) anger

coral [ko'ral] adj choral ♦ nf (MUS) choir ♦ nm
(ZOOL) coral

coraza [ko'raθa] nf (armadura) armour;
(blindaje) armour-plating

corazón [kora'θon] nm heart

corazonada [koraθo'naða] nf impulse;
(presentimiento) hunch

corbata [kor'ßata] nf tie

corchete [kor'tʃete] nm catch, clasp

corcho ['kortʃo] nm cork; (PESCA) float

cordel [kor'ðel] nm cord, line

cordero [kor'ðero] nm lamb

cordial [kor'ðjal] adj cordial; **~idad** nf warmth, cordiality

cordillera [korði'ʎera] nf range (of mountains)

Córdoba ['korðoβa] n Cordova

cordón [kor'ðon] nm (cuerda) cord, string; (de zapatos) lace; (MIL etc) cordon

cordura [kor'ðura] nf: **con ~** (obrar, hablar) sensibly

corneta [kor'neta] nf bugle

cornisa [kor'nisa] nf (ARQ) cornice

coro ['koro] nm chorus; (conjunto de cantores) choir

corona [ko'rona] nf crown; (de flores) garland; **coronación** nf coronation; **coronar** vt to crown

coronel [koro'nel] nm colonel

coronilla [koro'niʎa] nf (ANAT) crown (of the head)

corporación [korpora'θjon] nf corporation

corporal [korpo'ral] adj corporal, bodily

corpulento, a [korpu'lento] adj (persona) heavily-built

corral [ko'rral] nm farmyard

correa [ko'rrea] nf strap; (cinturón) belt; (de perro) lead, leash

corrección [korrek'θjon] nf correction; (reprensión) rebuke; **correccional** nm reformatory

correcto, a [ko'rrekto] adj correct; (persona) well-mannered

corredizo, a [korre'ðiθo] adj (puerta etc) sliding

corredor, a [korre'ðor] a, nm (pasillo) corridor; (balcón corrido) gallery; (COM) agent, broker ♦ nm/f (DEPORTE) runner

corregir [korre'xir] vt (error) to correct; **~se** vr to reform

correo [ko'rreo] nm post, mail; (persona) courier; **C~s** nmpl Post Office sg; **~ aéreo** airmail; **~ electrónico** electronic mail, e-mail

correr [ko'rrer] vt to run; (cortinas) to draw; (cerrojo) to shoot ♦ vi to run; (líquido) to run, flow; **~se** vr to slide, move; (colores) to run

correspondencia [korrespon'denθja] nf correspondence; (FERRO) connection

corresponder [korrespon'der] vi to correspond; (convenir) to be suitable; (pertenecer) to belong; (concernir) to concern; **~se** vr (por escrito) to correspond; (amarse) to love one another

correspondiente [korrespon'djente] adj corresponding

corresponsal [korrespon'sal] nm/f correspondent

corrida [ko'rriða] nf (de toros) bullfight

corrido, a [ko'rriðo, a] adj (avergonzado) abashed; **3 noches corridas** 3 nights running; **un kilo ~** a good kilo

corriente [ko'rrjente] adj (agua) running; (dinero etc) current; (común) ordinary, normal ♦ nf current ♦ nm current month; **~ eléctrica** electric current

corrija etc vb ver **corregir**

corrillo [ko'rriʎo] nm ring, circle (of people); (fig) clique

corro ['korro] nm ring, circle (of people)

corroborar [korroβo'rar] vt to corroborate

corroer [korro'er] vt to corrode; (GEO) to erode

corromper [korrom'per] vt (madera) to rot; (fig) to corrupt

corrosivo, a [korro'siβo, a] adj corrosive

corrupción [korrup'θjon] nf rot, decay; (fig) corruption

corsé [kor'se] nm corset

cortacésped [korta'θespeð] nm lawn mower

cortado, a [kor'taðo, a] adj (gen) cut; (leche) sour; (tímido) shy; (avergonzado) embarrassed ♦ nm coffee (with a little milk)

cortar [kor'tar] vt to cut; (suministro) to cut off; (un pasaje) to cut out ♦ vi to cut; **~se** vr (avergonzarse) to become embarrassed; (leche) to turn, curdle; **~se el pelo** to have one's hair cut

cortauñas [korta'uɲas] nm inv nail clippers pl

corte ['korte] nm cut, cutting; (de tela) piece, length ♦ nf: **las C~s** the Spanish Parliament; **~ y confección** dressmaking; **~ de luz** power cut

cortejar [korte'xar] vt to court

cortejo [kor'texo] nm entourage; **~ fúnebre** funeral procession

cortés [kor'tes] adj courteous, polite

cortesía [korte'sia] nf courtesy

corteza [kor'teθa] nf (de árbol) bark; (de pan) crust

cortijo [kor'tixo] nm farm, farmhouse

cortina [kor'tina] nf curtain

corto, a ['korto, a] adj (breve) short; (tímido) bashful; **~ de luces** not very bright; **~ de vista** short-sighted; **estar ~ de fondos** to be short of funds; **~circuito** nm short circuit; **~metraje** nm (CINE) short

cosa ['kosa] nf thing; **~ de** about; **eso es ~ mía** that's my business

coscorrón [kosko'rron] nm bump on the head

cosecha [ko'setʃa] nf (AGR) harvest; (de vino) vintage

cosechar [kose'tʃar] vt to harvest, gather (in)

coser [ko'ser] vt to sew

cosmético, a [kos'metiko, a] adj, nm cosmetic

cosquillas [kosˈkiʎas] *nfpl*: **hacer ~** to tickle; **tener ~** to be ticklish

costa [ˈkosta] *nf* (GEO) coast; **C~ Brava** Costa Brava; **C~ Cantábrica** Cantabrian Coast; **C~ del Sol** Costa del Sol; **a toda ~** at all costs

costado [kosˈtaðo] *nm* side

costar [kosˈtar] *vt* (*valer*) to cost; **me cuesta hablarle** I find it hard to talk to him

Costa Rica *nf* Costa Rica; **costarricense** *adj, nm/f* Costa Rican; **costarriqueño, a** *adj, nm/f* Costa Rican

coste [ˈkoste] *nm* = **costo**

costear [kosteˈar] *vt* to pay for

costero, a [kosˈtero, a] *adj* (*pueblecito, camino*) coastal

costilla [kosˈtiʎa] *nf* rib; (CULIN) cutlet

costo [ˈkosto] *nm* cost, price; **~ de la vida** cost of living; **~so, a** *adj* costly, expensive

costra [ˈkostra] *nf* (*corteza*) crust; (MED) scab

costumbre [kosˈtumbre] *nf* custom, habit

costura [kosˈtura] *nf* sewing, needlework; (*zurcido*) seam

costurera [kostuˈrera] *nf* dressmaker

costurero [kostuˈrero] *nm* sewing box o case

cotejar [koteˈxar] *vt* to compare

cotidiano, a [kotiˈðjano, a] *adj* daily, day to day

cotilla [koˈtiʎa] *nm/f* (*fam*) gossip; **cotillear** *vi* to gossip; **cotilleo** *nm* gossip(ing)

cotización [kotiθaˈθjon] *nf* (COM) quotation, price; (*de club*) dues *pl*

cotizar [kotiˈθar] *vt* (COM) to quote, price; **~se** *vr*: **~se a** to sell at, fetch; (BOLSA) to stand at, be quoted at

coto [ˈkoto] *nm* (*terreno cercado*) enclosure; (*de caza*) reserve

cotorra [koˈtorra] *nf* parrot

COU [kou] (ESP) *nm abr* (= *Curso de Orientación Universitaria*) 1 year course leading to final school-leaving certificate and university entrance examinations

coyote [koˈjote] *nm* coyote, prairie wolf

coyuntura [kojunˈtura] *nf* juncture, occasion

coz [koθ] *nf* kick

crack *nm* (*droga*) crack

cráneo [ˈkraneo] *nm* skull, cranium

cráter [ˈkrater] *nm* crater

creación [kreaˈθjon] *nf* creation

creador, a [kreaˈðor, a] *adj* creative ♦ *nm/f* creator

crear [kreˈar] *vt* to create, make

crecer [kreˈθer] *vi* to grow; (*precio*) to rise

creces [ˈkreθes]: **con ~** *adv* amply, fully

crecido, a [kreˈθiðo, a] *adj* (*persona, planta*) full-grown; (*cantidad*) large

creciente [kreˈθjente] *adj* growing; (*cantidad*) increasing; (*luna*) crescent ♦ *nm* crescent

crecimiento [kreθiˈmjento] *nm* growth;

(*aumento*) increase

credenciales [kreðenˈθjales] *nfpl* credentials

crédito [ˈkreðito] *nm* credit

credo [ˈkreðo] *nm* creed

crédulo, a [ˈkreðulo, a] *adj* credulous

creencia [kreˈenθja] *nf* belief

creer [kreˈer] *vt, vi* to think, believe; **~se** *vr* to believe o.s. (to be); **~ en** to believe in; **¡ya lo creo!** I should think so!

creíble [kreˈiβle] *adj* credible, believable

creído, a [kreˈiðo, a] *adj* (*engreído*) conceited

crema [ˈkrema] *nf* cream; **~ pastelera** (confectioner's) custard

cremallera [kremaˈʎera] *nf* zip (fastener)

crematorio [kremaˈtorjo] *nm* (*tb*: *horno ~*) crematorium

crepitar [krepiˈtar] *vi* to crackle

crepúsculo [kreˈpuskulo] *nm* twilight, dusk

cresta [ˈkresta] *nf* (GEO, ZOOL) crest

creyendo *vb ver* **creer**

creyente [kreˈjente] *nm/f* believer

creyó *etc vb ver* **creer**

crezco *etc vb ver* **crecer**

cría *etc* [ˈkria] *vb ver* **criar** ♦ *nf* (*de animales*) rearing, breeding; (*animal*) young; *ver tb* **crío**

criadero [kriaˈðero] *nm* (ZOOL) breeding place

criado, a [kriaˈðo, a] *nm* servant ♦ *nf* servant, maid

criador [kriaˈðor] *nm* breeder

crianza [kriˈanθa] *nf* rearing, breeding; (*fig*) breeding

criar [kriˈar] *vt* (*educar*) to bring up; (*producir*) to grow, produce; (*animales*) to breed

criatura [kriaˈtura] *nf* creature; (*niño*) baby, (small) child

criba [ˈkriβa] *nf* sieve; **cribar** *vt* to sieve

crimen [ˈkrimen] *nm* crime

criminal [krimiˈnal] *adj, nm/f* criminal

crin [krin] *nf* (*tb*: **~es** *nfpl*) mane

crío, a [ˈkrio, a] (*fam*) *nm/f* (*niño*) kid

crisis [ˈkrisis] *nf inv* crisis; **~ nerviosa** nervous breakdown

crispar [krisˈpar] *vt* (*nervios*) to set on edge

cristal [krisˈtal] *nm* crystal; (*de ventana*) glass, pane; (*lente*) lens; **~ino, a** *adj* crystalline; (*fig*) clear ♦ *nm* lens (of the eye); **~izar** *vt, vi* to crystallize

cristiandad [kristjanˈdað] *nf* Christendom

cristianismo [kristjaˈnismo] *nm* Christianity

cristiano, a [krisˈtjano, a] *adj, nm/f* Christian

Cristo [ˈkristo] *nm* Christ; (*crucifijo*) crucifix

criterio [kriˈterjo] *nm* criterion; (*juicio*) judgement

crítica [ˈkritika] *nf* criticism; *ver tb* **crítico**

criticar [kritiˈkar] *vt* to criticize

crítico, a [ˈkritiko, a] *adj* critical ♦ *nm/f* critic

Croacia *nf* Croatia

croar [kroˈar] *vi* to croak

cromo ['kromo] nm chrome

crónica ['kronika] nf chronicle, account

crónico, a ['kroniko, a] adj chronic

cronómetro [kro'nometro] nm stopwatch

croqueta [kro'keta] nf croquette

cruce etc ['kruθe] vb ver **cruzar** ♦ nm crossing; (de carreteras) crossroads

crucificar [kruθifi'kar] vt to crucify

crucifijo [kruθi'fixo] nm crucifix

crucigrama [kruθi'ɣrama] nm crossword (puzzle)

crudo, a ['kruðo, a] adj raw; (no maduro) unripe; (petróleo) crude; (rudo, cruel) cruel ♦ nm crude (oil)

cruel [krwel] adj cruel; **~dad** nf cruelty

crujido [kru'xiðo] nm (de madera etc) creak

crujiente [kru'xjente] adj (galleta etc) crunchy

crujir [kru'xir] vi (madera etc) to creak; (dedos) to crack; (dientes) to grind; (nieve, arena) to crunch

cruz [kruθ] nf cross; (de moneda) tails sg; **~ gamada** swastika

cruzada [kru'θaða] nf crusade

cruzado, a [kru'θaðo, a] adj crossed ♦ nm crusader

cruzar [kru'θar] vt to cross; **~se** vr (líneas etc) to cross; (personas) to pass each other

Cruz Roja nf Red Cross

cuaderno [kwa'ðerno] nm notebook; (de escuela) exercise book; (NAUT) logbook

cuadra ['kwaðra] nf (caballeriza) stable; (AM) block

cuadrado, a [kwa'ðraðo, a] adj square ♦ nm (MAT) square

cuadrar [kwa'ðrar] vt to square ♦ vi: **~ con** to square with, tally with; **~se** vr (soldado) to stand to attention

cuadrilátero [kwaðri'latero] nm (DEPORTE) boxing ring; (GEOM) quadrilateral

cuadrilla [kwa'ðriʎa] nf party, group

cuadro ['kwaðro] nm square; (ARTE) painting; (TEATRO) scene; (diagrama) chart; (DEPORTE, MED) team; **tela a ~s** checked (BRIT) o chequered (US) material

cuádruple ['kwaðruple] adj quadruple

cuajar [kwa'xar] vt (leche) to curdle; (sangre) to congeal; (CULIN) to set; **~se** vr to curdle; to congeal; (llenarse) to fill up

cuajo ['kwaxo] nm: **de ~** (arrancar) by the roots; (cortar) completely

cual [kwal] adv like, as ♦ pron: **el ~** etc which; (persona: sujeto) who; (: objeto) whom ♦ adj such as; **cada ~** each one; **déjalo tal ~** leave it just as it is

cuál [kwal] pron interr which (one)

cualesquier(a) [kwales'kjer(a)] pl de **cualquier(a)**

cualidad [kwali'ðað] nf quality

cualquier [kwal'kjer] adj ver **cualquiera**

cualquiera [kwal'kjera] (pl **cualesquiera**) adj (delante de nm y f: **cualquier**) any ♦ pron anybody; **un coche ~ servirá** any car will do; **no es un hombre ~** he isn't just anybody; **cualquier día/libro** any day/book; **eso ~ lo sabe hacer** anybody can do that; **es un ~** he's a nobody

cuando ['kwando] adv when; (aún si) if, even if ♦ conj (puesto que) since ♦ prep: **yo, ~ niño ...** when I was a child ...; **~ no sea así** even if it is not so; **~ más** at (the) most; **~ menos** at least; **~ no** if not, otherwise; **de ~ en ~** from time to time

cuándo ['kwando] adv when; **¿desde ~?, ¿de ~ acá?** since when?

cuantía [kwan'tia] nf (importe: de pérdidas, deuda, daños) extent

cuantioso, a [kwan'tjoso, a] adj substantial

PALABRA CLAVE

---

cuanto, a ['kwanto, a] adj **1** (todo): **tiene todo ~ desea** he's got everything he wants; **le daremos ~s ejemplares necesite** we'll give him as many copies as o all the copies he needs; **~s hombres la ven** all the men who see her

2 unos **~s**: **había unos ~s periodistas** there were a few journalists

3 (+ más): **~ más vino bebes peor te sentirás** the more wine you drink the worse you'll feel

♦ pron: **tiene ~ desea** he has everything he wants; **tome ~/~s quiera** take as much/many as you want

♦ adv: **en ~: en ~ profesor** as a teacher; **en ~ a mí** as for me; ver tb **antes**

♦ conj **1**: **~ más gana menos gasta** the more he earns the less he spends; **~ más joven más confiado** the younger you are the more trusting you are

2: **en ~: en ~ llegue/llegué** as soon as I arrive/arrived

---

cuánto, a ['kwanto, a] adj (exclamación) what a lot of; (interr: sg) how much?; (: pl) how many? ♦ pron, adv how; (interr: sg) how much?; (: pl) how many?; **¡cuánta gente!** what a lot of people!; **¿~ cuesta?** how much does it cost?; **¿a ~s estamos?** what's the date?; **Señor no sé ~s** Mr. So-and-So

cuarenta [kwa'renta] num forty

cuarentena [kwaren'tena] nf quarantine

cuaresma [kwa'resma] nf Lent

cuarta ['kwarta] nf (MAT) quarter, fourth; (palmo) span

cuartel [kwar'tel] nm (MIL) barracks pl; **~ general** headquarters pl

cuarteto [kwar'teto] nm quartet

cuarto, a ['kwarto, a] adj fourth ♦ nm (MAT) quarter, fourth; (habitación) room; **~ de baño**

bathroom; ~ **de estar** living room; ~ **de hora** quarter (of an) hour; ~ **de kilo** quarter kilo

cuatro ['kwatro] num four

Cuba ['kuβa] nf Cuba; **cubano, a** adj, nm/f Cuban

cuba ['kuβa] nf cask, barrel

cubata [ku'βata] nm (fam) large drink (of rum and coke etc)

cúbico, a ['kuβiko, a] adj cubic

cubierta [ku'βjerta] nf cover, covering; (neumático) tyre; (NAUT) deck

cubierto, a [ku'βjerto, a] pp de **cubrir** ♦ adj covered ♦ nm cover; (lugar en la mesa) place; ~s nmpl cutlery sg; **a ~** under cover

cubil [ku'βil] nm den; **~ete** nm (en juegos) cup

cubito [ku'βito] nm: ~ **de hielo** ice-cube

cubo ['kuβo] nm (MATH) cube; (balde) bucket, tub; (TEC) drum

cubrecama [kuβre'kama] nm bedspread

cubrir [ku'βrir] vt to cover; ~se vr (cielo) to become overcast

cucaracha [kuka'ratʃa] nf cockroach

cuchara [ku'tʃara] nf spoon; (TEC) scoop; ~**da** nf spoonful; ~**dita** nf teaspoonful

cucharilla [kutʃa'riʎa] nf teaspoon

cucharón [kutʃa'ron] nm ladle

cuchichear [kutʃitʃe'ar] vi to whisper

cuchilla [ku'tʃiʎa] nf (large) knife; (de arma blanca) blade; ~ **de afeitar** razor blade

cuchillo [ku'tʃiʎo] nm knife

cuchitril [kutʃi'tril] nm hovel

cuclillas [ku'kliʎas] nfpl: **en ~** squatting

cuco, a ['kuko, a] adj pretty; (astuto) sharp ♦ nm cuckoo

cucurucho [kuku'rutʃo] nm cornet

cuello ['kweʎo] nm (ANAT) neck; (de vestido, camisa) collar

cuenca ['kwenka] nf (ANAT) eye socket; (GEO) bowl, deep valley

cuenco ['kwenko] nm bowl

cuenta etc ['kwenta] vb ver **contar** ♦ nf (cálculo) count, counting; (en café, restaurante) bill (BRIT), check (US); (COM) account; (de collar) bead; **a fin de ~s** in the end; **caer en la ~** to catch on; **darse ~ de** to realize; **tener en ~** to bear in mind; **echar ~s** to take stock; ~ **corriente/de ahorros** current/ savings account; ~ **atrás** countdown; ~**kilómetros** nm inv ≈ milometer; (de velocidad) speedometer

cuento etc ['kwento] vb ver **contar** ♦ nm story

cuerda ['kwerða] nf rope; (fina) string; (de reloj) spring; **dar ~ a un reloj** to wind up a clock; ~ **floja** tightrope

cuerdo, a ['kwerðo, a] adj sane; (prudente) wise, sensible

cuerno ['kwerno] nm horn

cuero ['kwero] nm leather; **en ~s** stark naked; ~ **cabelludo** scalp

cuerpo ['kwerpo] nm body

cuervo ['kwerβo] nm crow

cuesta etc ['kwesta] vb ver **costar** ♦ nf slope; (en camino etc) hill; ~ **arriba/abajo** uphill/ downhill; **a ~s** on one's back

cueste etc vb ver **costar**

cuestión [kwes'tjon] nf matter, question, issue

cueva ['kweβa] nf cave

cuidado [kwi'ðaðo] nm care, carefulness; (preocupación) care, worry ♦ excl careful!, look out!

cuidadoso, a [kwiða'ðoso, a] adj careful; (preocupado) anxious

cuidar [kwi'ðar] vt (MED) to care for; (ocuparse de) to take care of, look after ♦ vi: ~ **de** to take care of, look after; ~**se** vr to look after o.s.; ~**se de hacer algo** to take care to do sth

culata [ku'lata] nf (de fusil) butt

culebra [ku'leβra] nf snake

culebrón [kule'βron] (fam) nm (TV) soap(-opera)

culinario, a [kuli'narjo, a] adj culinary, cooking cpd

culminación [kulmina'θjon] nf culmination

culo ['kulo] nm bottom, backside; (de vaso, botella) bottom

culpa ['kulpa] nf fault; (JUR) guilt; **por ~ de** because of; **tener la ~ (de)** to be to blame (for); ~**bilidad** nf guilt; ~**ble** adj guilty ♦ nm/f culprit

culpar [kul'par] vt to blame; (acusar) to accuse

cultivar [kulti'βar] vt to cultivate

cultivo [kul'tiβo] nm (acto) cultivation; (plantas) crop

culto, a ['kulto, a] adj (que tiene cultura) cultured, educated ♦ nm (homenaje) worship; (religión) cult

cultura [kul'tura] nf culture

culturismo [kultu'rismo] nm body-building

cumbre ['kumbre] nf summit, top

cumpleaños [kumple'aɲos] nm inv birthday

cumplido, a [kum'pliðo, a] adj (abundante) plentiful; (cortés) courteous ♦ nm compliment; **visita de ~** courtesy call

cumplidor, a [kumpli'ðor, a] adj reliable

cumplimentar [kumplimen'tar] vt to congratulate

cumplimiento [kumpli'mjento] nm (de un deber) fulfilment; (acabamiento) completion

cumplir [kum'plir] vt (orden) to carry out, obey; (promesa) to carry out, fulfil; (condena) to serve ♦ vi: ~ **con** (deberes) to carry out, fulfil; ~**se** vr (plazo) to expire; **hoy cumple dieciocho años** he is eighteen today

cúmulo ['kumulo] nm heap

cuna ['kuna] nf cradle, cot
cundir [kun'dir] vi (noticia, rumor, pánico) to spread; (rendir) to go a long way
cuneta [ku'neta] nf ditch
cuña ['kuɲa] nf wedge
cuñado, a [ku'ɲaðo, a] nm/f brother-/sister-in-law
cuota ['kwota] nf (parte proporcional) share; (cotización) fee, dues pl
cupe etc vb ver **caber**
cupiera etc vb ver **caber**
cupo ['kupo] vb ver **caber** ♦ nm quota
cupón [ku'pon] nm coupon
cúpula ['kupula] nf dome
cura ['kura] nf (curación) cure; (método curativo) treatment ♦ nm priest
curación [kura'θjon] nf cure; (acción) curing
curandero, a [kuran'dero, a] nm/f quack
curar [ku'rar] vt (MED: herida) to treat, dress; (: enfermo) to cure; (CULIN) to cure, salt; (cuero) to tan; ~se vr to get well, recover
curiosear [kurjose'ar] vt to glance at, look over ♦ vi to look round, wander round; (explorar) to poke about
curiosidad [kurjosi'ðað] nf curiosity
curioso, a [ku'rjoso, a] adj curious ♦ nm/f bystander, onlooker
currante [ku'rrante] (fam) nm/f worker
currar [ku'rrar] (fam) vi to work
currículo [ku'rrikulo] = **curriculum**
curriculum [ku'rrikulum] nm curriculum vitae
cursi ['kursi] (fam) adj affected
cursillo [kur'siʎo] nm short course
cursiva [kur'siβa] nf italics pl
curso ['kurso] nm course; en ~ (año) current; (proceso) going on, under way
cursor [kur'sor] nm (INFORM) cursor
curtido, a [kur'tiðo, a] adj (cara etc) weather-beaten; (fig: persona) experienced
curtir [kur'tir] vt (cuero etc) to tan
curva ['kurβa] nf curve, bend
cúspide ['kuspiðe] nf (GEO) peak; (fig) top
custodia [kus'toðja] nf safekeeping; custody;
custodiar vt (conservar) to take care of; (vigilar) to guard
cutis ['kutis] nm inv skin, complexion
cutre ['kutre] (fam) adj (lugar) grotty
cuyo, a ['kujo, a] pron (de quien) whose; (de que) whose, of which; en ~ caso in which case
C.V. abr (= caballos de vapor) H.P.

D, d

D. abr (= Don) Esq.
Da. abr = **Doña**
dádiva ['daðiβa] nf (donación) donation;
(regalo) gift; **dadivoso, a** adj generous
dado, a ['daðo, a] pp de **dar** ♦ nm die; ~s nmpl dice; ~ que conj given that
daltónico, a [dal'toniko, a] adj colour-blind
dama ['dama] nf (gen) lady; (AJEDREZ) queen; ~s nfpl (juego) draughts sg
damnificar [damnifi'kar] vt to harm; (persona) to injure
danés, esa [da'nes, esa] adj Danish ♦ nm/f Dane
danzar [dan'θar] vt, vi to dance
dañar [da'ɲar] vt (objeto) to damage; (persona) to hurt; ~se vr (objeto) to get damaged
dañino, a [da'ɲino, a] adj harmful
daño ['daɲo] nm (a un objeto) damage; (a una persona) harm, injury; ~s y perjuicios (JUR) damages; **hacer ~ a** to damage; (persona) to hurt, injure; **hacerse ~** to hurt o.s.

PALABRA CLAVE
---

dar [dar] vt **1** (gen) to give; (obra de teatro) to put on; (film) to show; (fiesta) to hold;
~ **algo a uno** to give sb sth o sth to sb; ~ **de beber a uno** to give sb a drink
2 (producir: intereses) to yield; (fruta) to produce
3 (locuciones + n): **da gusto escucharle** it's a pleasure to listen to him; ver tb **paseo** y otros sustantivos
4 (+ n: = perífrasis de verbo): **me da asco** it sickens me
5 (considerar): ~ **algo por descontado/entendido** to take sth for granted/as read; ~ **algo por concluido** to consider sth finished
6 (hora): **el reloj dio las 6** the clock struck 6 (o'clock)
7: **me da lo mismo** it's all the same to me; ver tb **igual, más**
♦ vi **1**: ~ **con**: **dimos con él dos horas más tarde** we came across him two hours later; **al final di con la solución** I eventually came up with the answer
2: ~ **en** (blanco, suelo) to hit; **el sol me da en la cara** the sun is shining (right) on my face
3: ~ **de sí** (zapatos etc) to stretch, give
♦ ~**se** vr **1**: ~**se por vencido** to give up
2 (ocurrir): **se han dado muchos casos** there have been a lot of cases
3: ~**se a**: **se ha dado a la bebida** he's taken to drinking
4: **se me dan bien/mal las ciencias** I'm good/bad at science
5: **dárselas de**: **se las da de experto** he fancies himself o poses as an expert

---

dardo ['darðo] nm dart
datar [da'tar] vi: ~ **de** to date from

dátil ['datil] *nm* date

dato ['dato] *nm* fact, piece of information; **~s personales** personal details

DC *abbr m* (= *disco compacto*) CD

dcha. *abr* (= *derecha*) r.h.

d. de J.C. *abr* (= *después de Jesucristo*) A.D.

PALABRA CLAVE

---

de [de] *prep* (*de* + *el* = *del*) **1** (*posesión*) of; **la casa ~ Isabel/mis padres** Isabel's/my parents' house; **es ~ ellos** it's theirs

2 (*origen, distancia, con números*) from; **soy ~ Gijón** I'm from Gijón; **~ 8 a 20** from 8 to 20; **salir del cine** to go out *o* leave the cinema; **~ 2 en 2** 2 by 2, 2 at a time

3 (*valor descriptivo*): **una copa ~ vino** a glass of wine; **la mesa ~ la cocina** the kitchen table; **un billete ~ 1000 pesetas** a 1000 peseta note; **un niño ~ tres años** a three-year-old (child); **una máquina ~ coser** a sewing machine; **vestido ~ gris** to be dressed in grey; **la niña del vestido azul** the girl in the blue dress; **trabaja ~ profesora** she works as a teacher; **~ lado** sideways; **~ atrás/delante** rear/front

4 (*hora, tiempo*): **a las 8 ~ la mañana** at 8 o'clock in the morning; **~ día/noche** by day/night; **~ hoy en ocho días** a week from now; **~ niño era gordo** as a child he was fat

5 (*comparaciones*): **más/menos ~ cien personas** more/less than a hundred people; **el más caro ~ la tienda** the most expensive in the shop; **menos/más ~ lo pensado** less/more than expected

6 (*causa*): **del calor** from the heat; **~ puro tonto** out of sheer stupidity

7 (*tema*) about; **clases ~ inglés** English classes; **¿sabes algo ~ él?** do you know anything about him?; **un libro ~ física** a physics book

8 (*adj* + *de* + *infin*): **fácil ~ entender** easy to understand

9 (*oraciones pasivas*): **fue respetado ~ todos** he was loved by all

10 (*condicional* + *infin*) if; **~ ser posible** if possible; **~ no terminarlo hoy** if I *etc* don't finish it today

---

dé *vb ver* **dar**

deambular [deambu'lar] *vi* to wander

debajo [de'βaxo] *adv* underneath; **~ de** below, under; **por ~ de** beneath

debate [de'βate] *nm* debate; **debatir** *vt* to debate

deber [de'βer] *nm* duty ♦ *vt* to owe ♦ *vi*: **debe (de)** it must, it should; **~es** *nmpl* (ESCOL) homework; **debo hacerlo** I must do it; **debe de ir** he should go; **~se** *vr*: **~se a** to be owing *o* due to

debido, a [de'βiðo, a] *adj* proper, just; **~ a**

due to, because of

débil ['deβil] *adj* (*persona, carácter*) weak; (*luz*) dim; **debilidad** *nf* weakness; dimness

debilitar [deβili'tar] *vt* to weaken; **~se** *vr* to grow weak

debutar [deβu'tar] *vi* to make one's debut

década ['dekaða] *nf* decade

decadencia [deka'ðenθja] *nf* (*estado*) decadence; (*proceso*) decline, decay

decaer [deka'er] *vi* (*declinar*) to decline; (*debilitarse*) to weaken

decaído, a [deka'iðo, a] *adj*: **estar ~** (*abatido*) to be down

decaimiento [dekai'mjento] *nm* (*declinación*) decline; (*desaliento*) discouragement; (MED: *estado débil*) weakness

decano, a [de'kano, a] *nm/f* (*de universidad etc*) dean

decapitar [dekapi'tar] *vt* to behead

decena [de'θena] *nf*: **una ~** ten (or so)

decencia [de'θenθja] *nf* decency

decente [de'θente] *adj* decent

decepción [deθep'θjon] *nf* disappointment

decepcionar [deθepθjo'nar] *vt* to disappoint

decidir [deθi'ðir] *vt, vi* to decide; **~se** *vr*: **~se a** to make up one's mind to

décimo, a ['deθimo, a] *adj* tenth ♦ *nm* tenth

decir [de'θir] *vt* to say; (*contar*) to tell; (*hablar*) to speak ♦ *nm* saying; **~se** *vr*: **se dice que** it is said that; **~ para** *o* **entre sí** to say to o.s.; **querer ~** to mean; **¡dígame!** (TEL) hello!; (*en tienda*) can I help you?

decisión [deθi'sjon] *nf* (*resolución*) decision; (*firmeza*) decisiveness

decisivo, a [deθi'siβo, a] *adj* decisive

declaración [deklara'θjon] *nf* (*manifestación*) statement; (*de amor*) declaration; **~ de ingresos** *o* **de la renta** *o* **fiscal** income-tax return

declarar [dekla'rar] *vt* to declare ♦ *vi* to declare; (JUR) to testify; **~se** *vr* to propose

declinar [dekli'nar] *vt* (*gen*) to decline; (JUR) to reject ♦ *vi* (*el día*) to draw to a close

declive [de'kliβe] *nm* (*cuesta*) slope; (*fig*) decline

decodificador [dekoðifika'ðor] *nm* decoder

decolorarse [dekolo'rarse] *vr* to become discoloured

decoración [dekora'θjon] *nf* decoration

decorado [deko'raðo] *nm* (CINE, TEATRO) scenery, set

decorar [deko'rar] *vt* to decorate; **decorativo, a** *adj* ornamental, decorative

decoro [de'koro] *nm* (*respeto*) respect; (*dignidad*) decency; (*recato*) propriety; **~so, a** *adj* (*decente*) decent; (*modesto*) modest; (*digno*) proper

decrecer [dekre'θer] *vi* to decrease, diminish

decrépito, a [de'krepito, a] *adj* decrepit
decretar [dekre'tar] *vt* to decree; **decreto** *nm* decree
dedal [de'ðal] *nm* thimble
dedicación [deðika'θjon] *nf* dedication
dedicar [deði'kar] *vt* (*libro*) to dedicate; (*tiempo, dinero*) to devote; (*palabras: decir, consagrar*) to dedicate, devote; **dedicatoria** *nf* (*de libro*) dedication
dedo ['deðo] *nm* finger; ~ **(del pie)** toe; ~ **pulgar** thumb; ~ **índice** index finger; ~ **corazón** middle finger; ~ **anular** ring finger; ~ **meñique** little finger; **hacer** ~ (*fam*) to hitch (a lift)
deducción [deðuk'θjon] *nf* deduction
deducir [deðu'θir] *vt* (*concluir*) to deduce, infer; (*COM*) to deduct
defecto [de'fekto] *nm* defect, flaw; **defectuoso, a** *adj* defective, faulty
defender [defen'der] *vt* to defend
defensa [de'fensa] *nf* defence ♦ *nm* (*DEPORTE*) defender, back; **defensivo, a** *adj* defensive; **a la defensiva** on the defensive
defensor, a [defen'sor, a] *adj* defending ♦ *nm/f* (*abogado* ~) defending counsel; (*protector*) protector
deficiencia [defi'θjenθja] *nf* deficiency
deficiente [defi'θjente] *adj* (*defectuoso*) defective; ~ **en** lacking *o* deficient in; **ser un** ~ **mental** to be mentally handicapped
déficit ['defiθit] (*pl* ~s) *nm* deficit
definición [defini'θjon] *nf* definition
definir [defi'nir] *vt* (*determinar*) to determine, establish; (*decidir*) to define; (*aclarar*) to clarify; **definitivo, a** *adj* definitive; **en definitiva** definitively; (*en resumen*) in short
deformación [deforma'θjon] *nf* (*alteración*) deformation; (*RADIO etc*) distortion
deformar [defor'mar] *vt* (*gen*) to deform; ~**se** *vr* to become deformed; **deforme** *adj* (*informe*) deformed; (*feo*) ugly; (*malhecho*) misshapen
defraudar [defrau'ðar] *vt* (*decepcionar*) to disappoint; (*estafar*) to defraud
defunción [defun'θjon] *nf* death, demise
degeneración [dexenera'θjon] *nf* (*de las células*) degeneration; (*moral*) degeneracy
degenerar [dexene'rar] *vi* to degenerate
degollar [devo'ʎar] *vt* to behead; (*fig*) to slaughter
degradar [devra'ðar] *vt* to debase, degrade; ~**se** *vr* to demean o.s.
degustación [devusta'θjon] *nf* sampling, tasting
deificar [deifi'kar] *vt* to deify
dejadez [dexa'ðeθ] *nf* (*negligencia*) neglect; (*descuido*) untidiness, carelessness
dejar [de'xar] *vt* to leave; (*permitir*) to allow, let; (*abandonar*) to abandon, forsake;

(*beneficios*) to produce, yield ♦ *vi*: ~ **de** (*parar*) to stop; (*no hacer*) to fail to; **no dejes de comprar un billete** make sure you buy a ticket; ~ **a un lado** to leave *o* set aside
dejo ['dexo] *nm* (*LING*) accent
del [del] (= **de+ el**) *ver* **de**
delantal [delan'tal] *nm* apron
delante [de'lante] *adv* in front, (*enfrente*) opposite; (*adelante*) ahead; ~ **de** in front of, before
delantera [delan'tera] *nf* (*de vestido, casa etc*) front part; (*DEPORTE*) forward line; **llevar la** ~ **(a uno)** to be ahead (of sb)
delantero, a [delan'tero, a] *adj* front ♦ *nm* (*DEPORTE*) forward, striker
delatar [dela'tar] *vt* to inform on *o* against, betray; **delator, a** *nm/f* informer
delegación [deleva'θjon] *nf* (*acción, delegados*) delegation; (*COM: oficina*) office, branch; ~ **de policía** police station
delegado, a [dele'vaðo, a] *nm/f* delegate; (*COM*) agent
delegar [dele'var] *vt* to delegate
deletrear [deletre'ar] *vt* to spell (out)
deleznable [deleθ'naßle] *adj* brittle; (*excusa, idea*) feeble
delfín [del'fin] *nm* dolphin
delgadez [delva'ðeθ] *nf* thinness, slimness
delgado, a [del'vaðo, a] *adj* thin; (*persona*) slim, thin; (*tela etc*) light, delicate
deliberación [delißera'θjon] *nf* deliberation
deliberar [deliße'rar] *vt* to debate, discuss
delicadeza [delika'ðeθa] *nf* (*gen*) delicacy; (*refinamiento, sutileza*) refinement
delicado, a [deli'kaðo, a] *adj* (*gen*) delicate; (*sensible*) sensitive; (*quisquilloso*) touchy
delicia [de'liθja] *nf* delight
delicioso, a [deli'θjoso, a] *adj* (*gracioso*) delightful; (*exquisito*) delicious
delimitar [delimi'tar] *vt* (*funciones, responsabilidades*) to define
delincuencia [delin'kwenθja] *nf* delinquency; **delincuente** *nm/f* delinquent; (*criminal*) criminal
delineante [deline'ante] *nm/f* draughtsman/woman
delinear [deline'ar] *vt* (*dibujo*) to draw; (*fig, contornos*) to outline
delinquir [delin'kir] *vi* to commit an offence
delirante [deli'rante] *adj* delirious
delirar [deli'rar] *vi* to be delirious, rave
delirio [de'lirjo] *nm* (*MED*) delirium; (*palabras insensatas*) ravings *pl*
delito [de'lito] *nm* (*gen*) crime; (*infracción*) offence
delta ['delta] *nm* delta
demacrado, a [dema'kraðo, a] *adj*: **estar** ~ to look pale and drawn, be wasted away
demagogo, a [dema'yoɣo, a] *nm/f*

demagogue

demanda [de'manda] nf (pedido, COM) demand; (petición) request; (JUR) action, lawsuit

demandante [deman'dante] nm/f claimant

demandar [deman'dar] vt (gen) to demand; (JUR) to sue, file a lawsuit against

demarcación |demarka'θjon] nf (de terreno) demarcation

demás |de'mas] adj: los ~ niños the other children, the remaining children ♦ pron: los/ las ~ the others, the rest (of them); lo ~ the rest (of it)

demasía [dema'sia] nf (exceso) excess, surplus; comer en ~ to eat to excess

demasiado, a [dema'sjaðo, a] adj: ~ vino too much wine ♦ adv (antes de adj, adv) too; ~s libros too many books; ¡esto es ~! that's the limit!; hace ~ calor it's too hot; ~ despacio too slowly; ~s too many

demencia [de'menθja] nf (locura) madness; **demente** nm/f lunatic ♦ adj mad, insane

democracia [demo'kraθja] nf democracy

demócrata [de'mokrata] nm/f democrat; **democrático, a** adj democratic

demoler [demo'ler] vt to demolish; **demolición** nf demolition

demonio [de'monjo] nm devil, demon; ¡~s! hell!, damn!; ¿cómo ~s? how the hell?

demora [de'mora] nf delay; **demorar** vt (retardar) to delay, hold back; (detener) to hold up ♦ vi to linger, stay on; ~se vr to be delayed

demos vb ver **dar**

demostración |demostra'θjon] nf (MAT) proof; (de afecto) show, display

demostrar |demos'trar] vt (probar) to prove; (mostrar) to show; (manifestar) to demonstrate

demudado, a [demu'ðaðo, a] adj (rostro) pale

den vb ver **dar**

denegar [dene'xar] vt (rechazar) to refuse; (JUR) to reject

denigrar [deni'xrar] vt (desacreditar, infamar) to denigrate; (injuriar) to insult

denotar [deno'tar] vt to denote

densidad [densi'ðað] nf density; (fig) thickness

denso, a ['denso, a] adj dense; (espeso, pastoso) thick; (fig) heavy

dentadura [denta'ðura] nf (set of) teeth pl; ~ postiza false teeth pl

dentera [den'tera] nf (sensación desagradable) the shivers pl

dentífrico, a |den'tifriko, a] adj dental ♦ nm toothpaste

dentista [den'tista] nm/f dentist

dentro ['dentro] adv inside ♦ prep: ~ de in, inside, within; por ~ (on the) inside; mirar por ~ to look inside; ~ de tres meses within three months

denuncia [de'nunθja] nf (delación) denunciation; (acusación) accusation; (de accidente) report; **denunciar** vt to report; (delatar) to inform on o against

departamento [departa'mento] nm (sección administrativa) department, section; (AM: apartamento) flat (BRIT), apartment

dependencia [depen'denθja] nf dependence; (POL) dependency; (COM) office, section

depender [depen'der] vi: ~ de to depend on

dependienta [depen'djenta] nf saleswoman, shop assistant

dependiente [depen'djente] adj dependent ♦ nm salesman, shop assistant

depilar [depi'lar] vt (con cera) to wax; (cejas) to pluck; **depilatorio** nm hair remover

deplorable |deplo'raßle] adj deplorable

deplorar |deplo'rar] vt to deplore

deponer [depo'ner] vt to lay down ♦ vi (JUR) to give evidence; (declarar) to make a statement

deportar [depor'tar] vt to deport

deporte [de'porte] nm sport; hacer ~ to play sports; **deportista** adj sports cpd ♦ nm/f sportsman/woman; **deportivo, a** adj (club, periódico) sports cpd ♦ nm sports car

depositar [deposi'tar] vt (dinero) to deposit; (mercancías) to put away, store; ~se vr to settle; ~io, a nm/f trustee

depósito [de'posito] nm (gen) deposit; (almacén) warehouse, store; (de agua, gasolina etc) tank; ~ de cadáveres mortuary

depreciar [depre'θjar] vt to depreciate, reduce the value of; ~se vr to depreciate, lose value

depredador, a [depreða'ðor, a] adj predatory ♦ nm predator

depresión [depre'sjon] nf depression

deprimido, a [depri'miðo, a] adj depressed

deprimir [depri'mir] vt to depress; ~se vr (persona) to become depressed

deprisa |de'prisa] adv quickly, hurriedly

depuración [depura'θjon] nf purification; (POL) purge

depurar [depu'rar] vt to purify; (purgar) to purge

derecha [de'retʃa] nf right(-hand) side; (POL) right; a la ~ (estar) on the right; (torcer etc) (to the) right

derecho, a [de'retʃo, a] adj right, right-hand ♦ nm (privilegio) right; (lado) right(-hand) side; (leyes) law ♦ adv straight, directly; ~s nmpl (de aduana) duty sg; (de autor) royalties; tener ~ a to have a right to

deriva [de'rißa] nf: ir o estar a la ~ to drift, be

adrift

derivado [deri'ßaðo] nm (COM) by-product

derivar [deri'ßar] vt to derive; (desviar) to direct ♦ vi to derive, be derived; (NAUT) to drift; **~se** vr to derive, be derived; to drift

derramamiento [derrama'mjento] nm (dispersión) spilling; **~ de sangre** bloodshed

derramar [derra'mar] vt to spill; (verter) to pour out; (esparcir) to scatter; **~se** vr to pour out; **~ lágrimas** to weep

derrame [de'rrame] nm (de líquido) spilling; (de sangre) shedding; (de tubo etc) overflow; (pérdida) leakage; (MED) discharge

derredor [derre'ðor] adv: **al o en ~ de** around, about

derretido, a [derre'tiðo, a] adj melted; (metal) molten

derretir [derre'tir] vt (gen) to melt; (nieve) to thaw; **~se** vr to melt

derribar [derri'ßar] vt to knock down; (construcción) to demolish; (persona, gobierno, político) to bring down

derrocar [derro'kar] vt (gobierno) to bring down, overthrow

derrochar [derro'tʃar] vt to squander; **derroche** nm (despilfarro) waste, squandering

derrota [de'rrota] nf (NAUT) course; (MIL, DEPORTE etc) defeat, rout; **derrotar** vt (gen) to defeat; **derrotero** nm (rumbo) course

derruir [derru'ir] vt (edificio) to demolish

derrumbar [derrum'bar] vt (edificio) to knock down; **~se** vr to collapse

derruyendo etc vb ver **derruir**

des vb ver **dar**

desabotonar [desaßoto'nar] vt to unbutton, undo; **~se** vr to come undone

desabrido, a [desa'ßriðo, a] adj (comida) insipid, tasteless; (persona) rude, surly; (respuesta) sharp; (tiempo) unpleasant

desabrochar [desaßro'tʃar] vt (botones, broches) to undo, unfasten; **~se** vr (ropa etc) to come undone

desacato [desa'kato] nm (falta de respeto) disrespect; (JUR) contempt

desacertado, a [desaθer'taðo, a] adj (equivocado) mistaken; (inoportuno) unwise

desacierto [desa'θjerto] nm mistake, error

desaconsejado, a [desakonse'xaðo, a] adj ill-advised

desaconsejar [desakonse'xar] vt to advise against

desacreditar [desakreði'tar] vt (desprestigiar) to discredit, bring into disrepute; (denigrar) to run down

desacuerdo [desa'kwerðo] nm disagreement, discord

desafiar [desafi'ar] vt (retar) to challenge; (enfrentarse a) to defy

desafilado, a [desafi'laðo, a] adj blunt

desafinado, a [desafi'naðo, a] adj: **estar ~** to be out of tune

desafinar [desafi'nar] vi (al cantar) to be o go out of tune

desafío etc [desa'fio] vb ver **desafiar** ♦ nm (reto) challenge; (combate) duel; (resistencia) defiance

desaforado, a [desafo'raðo, a] adj (grito) ear-splitting; (comportamiento) outrageous

desafortunadamente [desafortunaða'mente] adv unfortunately

desafortunado, a [desafortu'naðo, a] adj (desgraciado) unfortunate, unlucky

desagradable [desaɣra'ðaßle] adj (fastidioso, enojoso) unpleasant; (irritante) disagreeable

desagradar [desaɣra'ðar] vi (disgustar) to displease; (molestar) to bother

desagradecido, a [desaɣraðe'θiðo, a] adj ungrateful

desagrado [desa'ɣraðo] nm (disgusto) displeasure; (contrariedad) dissatisfaction

desagraviar [desaɣra'ßjar] vt to make amends to

desagüe [des'aɣwe] nm (de un líquido) drainage; (cañería) drainpipe; (salida) outlet, drain

desaguisado [desaɣi'saðo] nm outrage

desahogado, a [desao'ɣaðo, a] adj (holgado) comfortable; (espacioso) roomy, large

desahogar [desao'ɣar] vt (aliviar) to ease, relieve; (ira) to vent; **~se** vr (relajarse) to relax; (desfogarse) to let off steam

desahogo [desa'oɣo] nm (alivio) relief; (comodidad) comfort, ease

desahuciar [desau'θjar] vt (enfermo) to give up hope for; (inquilino) to evict; **desahucio** nm eviction

desairar [desai'rar] vt (menospreciar) to slight, snub

desaire [des'aire] nm (menosprecio) slight; (falta de garbo) unattractiveness

desajustar [desaxus'tar] vt (desarreglar) to disarrange; (desconcertar) to throw off balance; **~se** vr to get out of order; (aflojarse) to loosen

desajuste [desa'xuste] nm (de máquina) disorder; (situación) imbalance

desalentador, a [desalenta'ðor, a] adj discouraging

desalentar [desalen'tar] vt (desanimar) to discourage

desaliento etc [desa'ljento] vb ver **desalentar** ♦ nm discouragement

desaliño [desa'liɲo] nm slovenliness

desalmado, a [desal'maðo, a] adj (cruel) cruel, heartless

desalojar [desalo'xar] vt (*expulsar, echar*) to eject; (*abandonar*) to move out of ♦ vi to move out

desamor [desa'mor] nm (*frialdad*) indifference; (*odio*) dislike

desamparado, a [desampa'raðo, a] adj (*persona*) helpless; (*lugar: expuesto*) exposed; (*desierto*) deserted

desamparar [desampa'rar] vt (*abandonar*) to desert, abandon; (*JUR*) to leave defenceless; (*barco*) to abandon

desandar [desan'dar] vt: ~ **lo andado** o **el camino** to retrace one's steps

desangrar [desaŋ'grar] vt to bleed; (*fig: persona*) to bleed dry; ~**se** vr to lose a lot of blood

desanimado, a [desani'maðo, a] adj (*persona*) downhearted; (*espectáculo, fiesta*) dull

desanimar [desani'mar] vt (*desalentar*) to discourage; (*deprimir*) to depress; ~**se** vr to lose heart

desapacible [desapa'θiβle] adj (*gen*) unpleasant

desaparecer [desapare'θer] vi (*gen*) to disappear; (*el sol, la luz*) to vanish; **desaparecido, a** adj missing; **desaparición** nf disappearance

desapasionado, a [desapasjo'naðo, a] adj dispassionate, impartial

desapego [desa'peɣo] nm (*frialdad*) coolness; (*distancia*) detachment

desapercibido, a [desaperθi'βiðo, a] adj (*desprevenido*) unprepared; **pasar ~** to go unnoticed

desaprensivo, a [desapren'siβo, a] adj unscrupulous

desaprobar [desapro'βar] vt (*reprobar*) to disapprove of; (*condenar*) to condemn; (*no consentir*) to reject

desaprovechado, a [desaproβe'tʃaðo, a] adj (*oportunidad, tiempo*) wasted; (*estudiante*) slack

desaprovechar [desaproβe'tʃar] vt to waste

desarmar [desar'mar] vt (*MIL, fig*) to disarm; (*TEC*) to take apart, dismantle; **desarme** nm disarmament

desarraigar [desarrai'xar] vt to uproot; **desarraigo** nm uprooting

desarreglar [desarre'xlar] vt (*desordenar*) to disarrange; (*trastocar*) to upset, disturb

desarreglo [desa'rreɣlo] nm (*de casa, persona*) untidiness; (*desorden*) disorder

desarrollar [desarro'ʎar] vt (*gen*) to develop; ~**se** vr to develop; (*ocurrir*) to take place; (*FOTO*) to develop; **desarrollo** nm development

desarticular [desartiku'lar] vt (*hueso*) to dislocate; (*objeto*) to take apart; (*fig*) to break up

desasir [desa'sir] vt to loosen

desasosegar [desasose'var] vt (*inquietar*) to disturb, make uneasy; ~**se** vr to become uneasy

desasosiego etc [desaso'sjeɣo] vb ver **desasosegar** ♦ nm (*intranquilidad*) uneasiness, restlessness; (*ansiedad*) anxiety

desastrado, a [desas'traðo, a] adj (*desaliñado*) shabby; (*sucio*) dirty

desastre [de'sastre] nm disaster; **desastroso, a** adj disastrous

desatado, a [desa'taðo, a] adj (*desligado*) untied; (*violento*) violent, wild

desatar [desa'tar] vt (*nudo*) to untie; (*paquete*) to undo; (*separar*) to detach; ~**se** vr (*zapatos*) to come untied; (*tormenta*) to break

desatascar [desatas'kar] vt (*cañería*) to unblock, clear

desatender [desaten'der] vt (*no prestar atención a*) to disregard; (*abandonar*) to neglect

desatento, a [desa'tento, a] adj (*distraído*) inattentive; (*descortés*) discourteous

desatinado, a [desati'naðo, a] adj foolish, silly; **desatino** nm (*idiotez*) foolishness, folly; (*error*) blunder

desatornillar [desatorni'ʎar] vt to unscrew

desatrancar [desatran'kar] vt (*puerta*) to unbolt; (*cañería*) to clear, unblock

desautorizado, a [desautori'θaðo, a] adj unauthorized

desautorizar [desautori'θar] vt (*oficial*) to deprive of authority; (*informe*) to deny

desavenencia [desaβe'nenθja] nf (*desacuerdo*) disagreement; (*discrepancia*) quarrel

desayunar [desaju'nar] vi to have breakfast ♦ vt to have for breakfast; **desayuno** nm breakfast

desazón [desa'θon] nf anxiety

desazonarse [desaθo'narse] vr to worry, be anxious

desbandarse [desβan'darse] vr (*MIL*) to disband; (*fig*) to flee in disorder

desbarajuste [desβara'xuste] nm confusion, disorder

desbaratar [desβara'tar] vt (*deshacer, destruir*) to ruin

desbloquear [desβloke'ar] vt (*negociaciones, tráfico*) to get going again; (*COM: cuenta*) to unfreeze

desbocado, a [desβo'kaðo, a] adj (*caballo*) runaway

desbordar [desβor'ðar] vt (*sobrepasar*) to go beyond; (*exceder*) to exceed; ~**se** vr (*río*) to overflow; (*entusiasmo*) to erupt

descabalgar [deskaβal'xar] vi to dismount

descabellado, a |deskaβe'ʎaðo, a| *adj*
(*disparatado*) wild, crazy

descafeinado, a |deskafei'naðo, a| *adj*
decaffeinated ♦ *nm* decaffeinated coffee

descalabro |deska'laβro| *nm* blow;
(*desgracia*) misfortune

descalificar |deskalifi'kar| *vt* to disqualify;
(*desacreditar*) to discredit

descalzar |deskal'θar| *vt* (*zapato*) to take off;
descalzo, a *adj* barefoot(ed)

descambiar |deskam'bjar| *vt* to exchange

descaminado, a |deskami'naðo, a| *adj*
(*equivocado*) on the wrong road; (*fig*)
misguided

descampado |deskam'paðo| *nm* open space

descansado, a |deskan'saðo, a| *adj* (*gen*)
rested; (*que tranquiliza*) restful

descansar |deskan'sar| *vt* (*gen*) to rest ♦ *vi*
to rest, have a rest; (*echarse*) to lie down

descansillo |deskan'siʎo| *nm* (*de escalera*)
landing

descanso |des'kanso| *nm* (*reposo*) rest;
(*alivio*) relief; (*pausa*) break; (*DEPORTE*)
interval, half-time

descapotable |deskapo'taβle| *nm* (*tb: coche*
~) convertible

descarado, a |deska'raðo, a| *adj* shameless;
(*insolente*) cheeky

descarga |des'karɣa| *nf* (*ARQ, ELEC, MIL*)
discharge; (*NAUT*) unloading

descargar |deskar'ɣar| *vt* to unload; (*golpe*)
to let fly; **~se** *vr* to unburden o.s.; **descargo**
nm (*COM*) receipt; (*JUR*) evidence

descaro |des'karo| *nm* nerve

descarriar |deska'rrjar| *vt* (*descaminar*) to
misdirect; (*fig*) to lead astray; **~se** *vr*
(*perderse*) to lose one's way; (*separarse*) to
stray; (*pervertirse*) to err, go astray

descarrilamiento |deskarrila'mjento| *nm*
(*de tren*) derailment

descarrilar |deskarri'lar| *vi* to be derailed

descartar |deskar'tar| *vt* (*rechazar*) to reject;
(*eliminar*) to rule out; **~se** *vr* (*NAIPES*) to
discard; **~se de** to shirk

descascarillado, a |deskaskari'ʎaðo, a| *adj*
(*paredes*) peeling

descendencia |desθen'denθja| *nf* (*origen*)
origin, descent; (*hijos*) offspring

descender |desθen'der| *vt* (*bajar: escalera*)
to go down ♦ *vi* to descend; (*temperatura,
nivel*) to fall, drop; **~ de** to be descended
from

descendiente |desθen'djente| *nm/f*
descendant

descenso |des'θenso| *nm* descent; (*de
temperatura*) drop

descifrar |desθi'frar| *vt* to decipher;
(*mensaje*) to decode

descolgar |deskol'ɣar| *vt* (*bajar*) to take

down; (*teléfono*) to pick up; **~se** *vr* to let o.s.
down

descolorido, a |deskolo'riðo, a| *adj* faded;
(*pálido*) pale

descompasado, a |deskompa'saðo, a| *adj*
(*sin proporción*) out of all proportion;
(*excesivo*) excessive

descomponer |deskompo'ner| *vt*
(*desordenar*) to disarrange, disturb; (*TEC*) to
put out of order; (*dividir*) to break down
(into parts); (*fig*) to provoke; **~se** *vr*
(*corromperse*) to rot, decompose; (*TEC*) to
break down

descomposición |deskomposi'θjon| *nf* (*de
un objeto*) breakdown; (*de fruta etc*)
decomposition; **~ de vientre** stomach upset,
diarrhoea

descompuesto, a |deskom'pwesto, a| *adj*
(*corrompido*) decomposed; (*roto*) broken

descomunal |deskomu'nal| *adj* (*enorme*)
huge

desconcertado, a |deskonθer'taðo, a| *adj*
disconcerted, bewildered

desconcertar |deskonθer'tar| *vt* (*confundir*)
to baffle; (*incomodar*) to upset, put out; **~se**
vr (*turbarse*) to be upset

desconchado, a |deskon't∫aðo, a| *adj*
(*pintura*) peeling

desconcierto *etc* |deskon'θjerto| *vb ver*
desconcertar ♦ *nm* (*gen*) disorder;
(*desorientación*) uncertainty; (*inquietud*)
uneasiness

desconectar |deskonek'tar| *vt* to disconnect

desconfianza |deskon'fjanθa| *nf* distrust

desconfiar |deskon'fjar| *vi* to be distrustful;
~ de to distrust, suspect

descongelar |deskonxe'lar| *vt* to defrost;
(*COM, POL*) to unfreeze

descongestionar |deskonxestjo'nar| *vt*
(*cabeza, tráfico*) to clear

desconocer |deskono'θer| *vt* (*ignorar*) not
to know, be ignorant of

desconocido, a |deskono'θiðo, a| *adj*
unknown ♦ *nm/f* stranger

desconocimiento |deskonoθi'mjento| *nm*
(*falta de conocimientos*) ignorance

desconsiderado, a |deskonsiðe'raðo, a|
adj inconsiderate; (*insensible*) thoughtless

desconsolar |deskonso'lar| *vt* to distress;
~se *vr* to despair

desconsuelo *etc* |deskon'swelo| *vb ver*
desconsolar ♦ *nm* (*tristeza*) distress;
(*desesperación*) despair

descontado, a |deskon'taðo, a| *adj*: **dar por
~ (que)** to take (it) for granted (that)

descontar |deskon'tar| *vt* (*deducir*) to take
away, deduct; (*rebajar*) to discount

descontento, a |deskon'tento, a| *adj*
dissatisfied ♦ *nm* dissatisfaction, discontent

descorazonar [deskoraθo'nar] *vt* to discourage, dishearten

descorchar [deskor'tʃar] *vt* to uncork

descorrer [desko'rrer] *vt* (*cortinas, cerrojo*) to draw back

descortés [deskor'tes] *adj* (*mal educado*) discourteous; (*grosero*) rude

descoser [desko'ser] *vt* to unstitch; **~se** *vr* to come apart (at the seams)

descosido, a [desko'siðo, a] *adj* (*COSTURA*) unstitched

descrédito [des'kreðito] *nm* discredit

descreído, a [deskre'iðo, a] *adj* (*incrédulo*) incredulous; (*falto de fe*) unbelieving

descremado, a [deskre'maðo, a] *adj* skimmed

describir [deskri'βir] *vt* to describe; **descripción** [deskrip'θjon] *nf* description

descrito [des'krito] *pp de* **describir**

descuartizar [deskwarti'θar] *vt* (*animal*) to cut up

descubierto, a [desku'βjerto, a] *pp de* **descubrir** ♦ *adj* uncovered, bare; (*persona*) bareheaded ♦ *nm* (*bancario*) overdraft; **al ~ in** the open

descubrimiento [deskuβri'mjento] *nm* (*hallazgo*) discovery; (*revelación*) revelation

descubrir [desku'βrir] *vt* to discover, find; (*inaugurar*) to unveil; (*vislumbrar*) to detect; (*revelar*) to reveal, show; (*destapar*) to uncover; **~se** *vr* to reveal o.s.; (*quitarse sombrero*) to take off one's hat; (*confesar*) to confess

descuento *etc* [des'kwento] *vb ver* **descontar** ♦ *nm* discount

descuidado, a [deskwi'ðaðo, a] *adj* (*sin cuidado*) careless; (*desordenado*) untidy; (*olvidadizo*) forgetful; (*dejado*) neglected; (*desprevenido*) unprepared

descuidar [deskwi'ðar] *vt* (*dejar*) to neglect; (*olvidar*) to overlook; **~se** *vr* (*distraerse*) to be careless; (*abandonarse*) to let o.s. go; (*desprevenirse*) to drop one's guard; **¡descuida!** don't worry!; **descuido** *nm* (*dejadez*) carelessness; (*olvido*) negligence

desde [ˈdesðe] *prep* **1** (*lugar*) from; **~ Burgos hasta mi casa hay 30 km** it's 30 kms from Burgos to my house

2 (*posición*): **hablaba ~ el balcón** she was speaking from the balcony

3 (*tiempo*: + *ad, n*): **~ ahora** from now on; **~ la boda** since the wedding; **~ niño** since I *etc* was a child; **~ 3 años atrás** since 3 years ago

4 (*tiempo*: + *vb, fecha*) since; for; **nos conocemos ~ 1992/~ hace 20 años** we've known each other since 1992/for 20 years;

no le veo ~ 1997/~ hace 5 años I haven't seen him since 1997/for 5 years

5 (*gama*): **~ los más lujosos hasta los más económicos** from the most luxurious to the most reasonably priced

6: **~ luego (que no)** of course (not)

♦ *conj*: **~ que**: **~ que recuerdo** for as long as I can remember; **~ que llegó no ha salido** he hasn't been out since he arrived

desdecirse [desðe'θirse] *vr* to retract; **~ de** to go back on

desdén [des'ðen] *nm* scorn

desdeñar [desðe'ɲar] *vt* (*despreciar*) to scorn

desdicha [des'ðitʃa] *nf* (*desgracia*) misfortune; (*infelicidad*) unhappiness; **desdichado, a** *adj* (*sin suerte*) unlucky; (*infeliz*) unhappy

desdoblar [desðo'βlar] *vt* (*extender*) to spread out; (*desplegar*) to unfold

desear [dese'ar] *vt* to want, desire, wish for

desecar [dese'kar] *vt* to dry up; **~se** *vr* to dry up

desechar [dese'tʃar] *vt* (*basura*) to throw out o away; (*ideas*) to reject, discard; **desechos** *nmpl* rubbish *sg*, waste *sg*

desembalar [desemba'lar] *vt* to unpack

desembarazar [desembara'θar] *vt* (*desocupar*) to clear; (*desenredar*) to free; **~se** *vr*: **~se de** to free o.s. of, get rid of

desembarcar [desembar'kar] *vt* (*mercancías etc*) to unload ♦ *vi* to disembark; **~se** *vr* to disembark

desembocadura [desemboka'ðura] *nf* (*de río*) mouth; (*de calle*) opening

desembocar [desembo'kar] *vi* (*río*) to flow into; (*fig*) to result in

desembolso [desem'bolso] *nm* payment

desembragar [desembra'var] *vi* to declutch

desembrollar [desembro'ʎar] *vt* (*madeja*) to unravel; (*asunto, malentendido*) to sort out

desemejanza [deseme'xanθa] *nf* dissimilarity

desempaquetar [desempake'tar] *vt* (*regalo*) to unwrap; (*mercancía*) to unpack

desempatar [desempa'tar] *vi* to replay, hold a play-off; **desempate** *nm* (*FÚTBOL*) replay, play-off; (*TENIS*) tie-break(er)

desempeñar [desempe'ɲar] *vt* (*cargo*) to hold; (*papel*) to perform; (*lo empeñado*) to redeem; **~ un papel** (*fig*) to play (a role)

desempeño [desem'peɲo] *nm* redeeming; (*de cargo*) occupation

desempleado, a [desemple'aðo, a] *nm/f* unemployed person; **desempleo** *nm* unemployment

desempolvar [desempol'βar] *vt* (*muebles etc*) to dust; (*lo olvidado*) to revive

desencadenar [desenkaðe'nar] *vt* to

unchain; (*ira*) to unleash; **~se** *vr* to break loose; (*tormenta*) to burst; (*guerra*) to break out

desencajar [desenka'xar] *vt* (*hueso*) to dislocate; (*mecanismo, pieza*) to disconnect, disengage

desencanto [desen'kanto] *nm* disillusionment

desenchufar [desentʃu'far] *vt* to unplug

desenfadado, a [desenfa'ðaðo, a] *adj* (*desenvuelto*) uninhibited; (*descarado*) forward; **desenfado** *nm* (*libertad*) freedom; (*comportamiento*) free and easy manner; (*descaro*) forwardness

desenfocado, a [desenfo'kaðo, a] *adj* (*FOTO*) out of focus

desenfrenado, a [desenfre'naðo, a] *adj* (*descontrolado*) uncontrolled; (*inmoderado*) unbridled; **desenfreno** *nm* wildness; (*de las pasiones*) lack of self-control

desenganchar [desengan'tʃar] *vt* (*gen*) to unhook; (*FERRO*) to uncouple

desengañar [desenga'ɲar] *vt* to disillusion; **~se** *vr* to become disillusioned; **desengaño** *nm* disillusionment; (*decepción*) disappointment

desenlace [desen'laθe] *nm* outcome

desenmarañar [desenmara'ɲar] *vt* (*fig*) to unravel

desenmascarar [desenmaska'rar] *vt* to unmask

desenredar [desenre'ðar] *vt* (*pelo*) to untangle; (*problema*) to sort out

desenroscar [desenros'kar] *vt* to unscrew

desentenderse [desenten'derse] *vr*: **~ de** to pretend not to know about; (*apartarse*) to have nothing to do with

desenterrar [desente'rrar] *vt* to exhume; (*tesoro, fig*) to unearth, dig up

desentonar [desento'nar] *vi* (*MUS*) to sing (*o play*) out of tune; (*color*) to clash

desentrañar [desentra'ɲar] *vt* (*misterio*) to unravel

desentumecer [desentume'θer] *vt* (*pierna etc*) to stretch

desenvoltura [desenβol'tura] *nf* ease

desenvolver [desenβol'βer] *vt* (*paquete*) to unwrap; (*fig*) to develop; **~se** *vr* (*desarrollarse*) to unfold, develop; (*arreglárselas*) to cope

deseo [de'seo] *nm* desire, wish; **~so, a** *adj*: **estar ~so de** to be anxious to

desequilibrado, a [desekili'βraðo, a] *adj* unbalanced

desertar [deser'tar] *vi* to desert

desértico, a [de'sertiko, a] *adj* desert *cpd*

desesperación [desespera'θjon] *nf* (*impaciencia*) desperation, despair; (*irritación*) fury

desesperar [desespe'rar] *vt* to drive to despair; (*exasperar*) to drive to distraction ♦ *vi*: **~ de** to despair of; **~se** *vr* to despair, lose hope

desestabilizar [desestaβili'θar] *vt* to destabilize

desestimar [desesti'mar] *vt* (*menospreciar*) to have a low opinion of; (*rechazar*) to reject

desfachatez [desfatʃa'teθ] *nf* (*insolencia*) impudence; (*descaro*) rudeness

desfalco [des'falko] *nm* embezzlement

desfallecer [desfaʎe'θer] *vi* (*perder las fuerzas*) to become weak; (*desvanecerse*) to faint

desfasado, a [desfa'saðo, a] *adj* (*anticuado*) old-fashioned; **desfase** *nm* (*diferencia*) gap

desfavorable [desfaβo'raβle] *adj* unfavourable

desfigurar [desfixu'rar] *vt* (*cara*) to disfigure; (*cuerpo*) to deform

desfiladero [desfila'ðero] *nm* gorge

desfilar [desfi'lar] *vi* to parade; **desfile** *nm* procession

desfogarse [desfo'xarse] *vr* (*fig*) to let off steam

desgajar [desxa'xar] *vt* (*arrancar*) to tear off; (*romper*) to break off; **~se** *vr* to come off

desgana [des'xana] *nf* (*falta de apetito*) loss of appetite; (*apatía*) unwillingness; **~do, a** *adj*: **estar ~do** (*sin apetito*) to have no appetite; (*sin entusiasmo*) to have lost interest

desgarrador, a [desxarra'ðor, a] *adj* (*fig*) heartrending

desgarrar [desxa'rrar] *vt* to tear (up); (*fig*) to shatter; **desgarro** *nm* (*en tela*) tear; (*aflicción*) grief

desgastar [desxas'tar] *vt* (*deteriorar*) to wear away *o* down; (*estropear*) to spoil; **~se** *vr* to get worn out; **desgaste** *nm* wear (and tear)

desglosar [desxlo'sar] *vt* (*factura*) to break down

desgracia [des'xraθja] *nf* misfortune; (*accidente*) accident; (*vergüenza*) disgrace; (*contratiempo*) setback; **por ~** unfortunately

desgraciado, a [desxra'θjaðo, a] *adj* (*sin suerte*) unlucky, unfortunate; (*miserable*) wretched; (*infeliz*) miserable

desgravación [desxraβa'θjon] *nf* (*COM*): **~ fiscal** tax relief

desgravar [desxra'βar] *vt* (*impuestos*) to reduce the tax *o* duty on

deshabitado, a [desaβi'taðo, a] *adj* uninhabited

deshacer [desa'θer] *vt* (*casa*) to break up; (*TEC*) to take apart; (*enemigo*) to defeat; (*diluir*) to melt; (*contrato*) to break; (*intriga*) to solve; **~se** *vr* (*disolverse*) to melt; (*despedazarse*) to come apart *o* undone; **~se de** to get rid of; **~se en lágrimas** to burst into tears

desharrapado, a [desarra'paðo, a] *adj*
(*persona*) shabby

deshecho, a [des'etʃo, a] *adj* undone; (*roto*)
smashed; (*persona*): **estar ~** to be shattered

desheredar [desere'ðar] *vt* to disinherit

deshidratar [desiðra'tar] *vt* to dehydrate

deshielo [des'jelo] *nm* thaw

deshonesto, a [deso'nesto, a] *adj* indecent

deshonra [des'onra] *nf* (*deshonor*) dishonour; (*vergüenza*) shame

deshora [des'ora]: **a ~** *adv* at the wrong time

deshuesar [deswe'sar] *vt* (*carne*) to bone;
(*fruta*) to stone

desierto, a [de'sjerto, a] *adj* (*casa, calle,
negocio*) deserted ♦ *nm* desert

designar [desiɣ'nar] *vt* (*nombrar*) to
designate; (*indicar*) to fix

designio [de'siɣnjo] *nm* plan

desigual [desi'ɣwal] *adj* (*terreno*) uneven;
(*lucha etc*) unequal

desilusión [desilu'sjon] *nf* disillusionment;
(*decepción*) disappointment; **desilusionar** *vt*
to disillusion; to disappoint; **desilusionarse** *vr*
to become disillusioned

desinfectar [desinfek'tar] *vt* to disinfect

desinflar [desin'flar] *vt* to deflate

desintegración [desinteɣra'θjon] *nf*
disintegration

desinterés [desinte'res] *nm* (*desgana*) lack
of interest; (*altruismo*) unselfishness

desintoxicarse [desintoksi'karse] *vr*
(*drogadicto*) to undergo detoxification

desistir [desis'tir] *vi* (*renunciar*) to stop, desist

desleal [desle'al] *adj* (*infiel*) disloyal; (*COM:
competencia*) unfair; **~tad** *nf* disloyalty

desleír [desle'ir] *vt* (*líquido*) to dilute; (*sólido*)
to dissolve

deslenguado, a [deslen'gwaðo, a] *adj*
(*grosero*) foul-mouthed

desligar [desli'ɣar] *vt* (*desatar*) to untie,
undo; (*separar*) to separate; **~se** *vr* (*de un
compromiso*) to extricate o.s.

desliz [des'liθ] *nm* (*fig*) lapse; **~ar** *vt* to slip,
slide

deslucido, a [deslu'θiðo, a] *adj* dull; (*torpe*)
awkward, graceless; (*deslustrado*) tarnished

deslumbrar [deslum'brar] *vt* to dazzle

desmadrarse [desma'ðrarse] (*fam*) *vr*
(*descontrolarse*) to run wild; (*divertirse*) to let
one's hair down; **desmadre** (*fam*) *nm*
(*desorganización*) chaos; (*jaleo*) commotion

desmán [des'man] *nm* (*exceso*) outrage;
(*abuso de poder*) abuse

desmandarse [desman'darse] *vr* (*portarse
mal*) to behave badly; (*excederse*) to get out
of hand; (*caballo*) to bolt

desmantelar [desmante'lar] *vt* (*deshacer*) to
dismantle; (*casa*) to strip

desmaquillador [desmakiʎa'ðor] *nm*
make-up remover

desmayar [desma'jar] *vi* to lose heart; **~se** *vr*
(*MED*) to faint; **desmayo** *nm* (*MED: acto*)
faint; (: *estado*) unconsciousness

desmedido, a [desme'ðiðo, a] *adj* excessive

desmejorar [desmexo'rar] *vt* (*dañar*) to
impair, spoil; (*MED*) to weaken

desmembrar [desmem'brar] *vt* (*MED*) to
dismember; (*fig*) to separate

desmemoriado, a [desmemo'rjaðo, a] *adj*
forgetful

desmentir [desmen'tir] *vt* (*contradecir*) to
contradict; (*refutar*) to deny

desmenuzar [desmenu'θar] *vt* (*deshacer*) to
crumble; (*carne*) to chop; (*examinar*) to
examine closely

desmerecer [desmere'θer] *vt* to be
unworthy of ♦ *vi* (*deteriorarse*) to deteriorate

desmesurado, a [desmesu'raðo, a] *adj*
disproportionate

desmontable [desmon'taβle] *adj* (*que se
quita: pieza*) detachable; (*que se puede plegar
etc*) collapsible, folding

desmontar [desmon'tar] *vt* (*deshacer*) to
dismantle; (*tierra*) to level ♦ *vi* to dismount

desmoralizar [desmorali'θar] *vt* to
demoralize

desmoronar [desmoro'nar] *vt* to wear
away, erode; **~se** *vr* (*edificio, dique*) to
collapse; (*economía*) to decline

desnatado, a [desna'taðo, a] *adj* skimmed

desnivel [desni'βel] *nm* (*de terreno*)
unevenness

desnudar [desnu'ðar] *vt* (*desvestir*) to
undress; (*despojar*) to strip; **~se** *vr*
(*desvestirse*) to get undressed; **desnudo, a**
adj naked ♦ *nm/f* nude; **desnudo de** devoid o
bereft of

desnutrición [desnutri'θjon] *nf*
malnutrition; **desnutrido, a** *adj*
undernourished

desobedecer [desoβeðe'θer] *vt, vi* to
disobey; **desobediencia** *nf* disobedience

desocupado, a [desoku'paðo, a] *adj* at
leisure; (*desempleado*) unemployed;
(*deshabitado*) empty, vacant

desocupar [desoku'par] *vt* to vacate

desodorante [desoðo'rante] *nm* deodorant

desolación [desola'θjon] *nf* (*de lugar*)
desolation; (*fig*) grief

desolar [deso'lar] *vt* to ruin, lay waste

desorbitado, a [desorβi'taðo, a] *adj*
(*excesivo: ambición*) boundless; (*deseos*)
excessive; (: *precio*) exorbitant

desorden [des'orðen] *nm* confusion;
(*político*) disorder, unrest

desorganizar [desorɣani'θar] *vt*
(*desordenar*) to disorganize;

desorganización nf (de persona) disorganization; (en empresa, oficina) disorder, chaos

desorientar [desorjen'tar] vt (extraviar) to mislead; (confundir, desconcertar) to confuse; **~se** vr (perderse) to lose one's way

despabilado, a [despaβi'laðo, a] adj (despierto) wide-awake; (fig) alert, sharp

despabilar [despaβi'lar] vt (el ingenio) to sharpen ♦ vi to wake up; (fig) to get a move on; **~se** vr to wake up; to get a move on

despachar [despa'tʃar] vt (negocio) to do, complete; (enviar) to send, dispatch; (vender) to sell, deal in; (billete) to issue; (mandar ir) to send away

despacho [des'patʃo] nm (oficina) office; (de paquetes) dispatch; (venta) sale; (comunicación) message

despacio [des'paθjo] adv slowly

desparpajo [despar'paxo] nm self-confidence; (pey) nerve

desparramar [desparra'mar] vt (esparcir) to scatter; (líquido) to spill

despavorido, a [despaβo'riðo, a] adj terrified

despecho [des'petʃo] nm spite; **a ~ de** in spite of

despectivo, a [despek'tiβo, a] adj (despreciativo) derogatory; (LING) pejorative

despedazar [despeða'θar] vt to tear to pieces

despedida [despe'ðiða] nf (adiós) farewell; (de obrero) sacking

despedir [despe'ðir] vt (visita) to see off, show out; (empleado) to dismiss; (inquilino) to evict; (objeto) to hurl; (olor etc) to give out o off; **~se** vr: **~se de** to say goodbye to

despegar [despe'var] vt to unstick ♦ vi (avión) to take off; **~se** vr to come loose, come unstuck; **despego** nm detachment

despegue etc [des'peve] vb ver **despegar** ♦ nm takeoff

despeinado, a [despei'naðo, a] adj dishevelled, unkempt

despejado, a [despe'xaðo, a] adj (lugar) clear, free; (cielo) clear; (persona) wide-awake, bright

despejar [despe'xar] vt (gen) to clear; (misterio) to clear up ♦ vi (el tiempo) to clear; **~se** vr (tiempo, cielo) to clear (up); (misterio) to become clearer; (cabeza) to clear

despellejar [despeʎe'xar] vt (animal) to skin

despensa [des'pensa] nf larder

despeñadero [despeɲa'ðero] nm (GEO) cliff, precipice

despeñarse [despe'ɲarse] vr to hurl o.s. down; (coche) to tumble over

desperdicio [desper'ðiθjo] nm (despilfarro) squandering; **~s** nmpl (basura) rubbish sg

(BRIT), garbage sg (US); (residuos) waste sg

desperdigarse [desperði'varse] vr (rebaño, familia) to scatter, spread out; (granos de arroz, semillas) to scatter

desperezarse [despere'θarse] vr to stretch

desperfecto [desper'fekto] nm (deterioro) slight damage; (defecto) flaw, imperfection

despertador [desperta'ðor] nm alarm clock

despertar [desper'tar] nm awakening ♦ vt (persona) to wake up; (recuerdos) to revive; (sentimiento) to arouse ♦ vi to awaken, wake up; **~se** vr to awaken, wake up

despiadado, a [despja'ðaðo, a] adj (ataque) merciless; (persona) heartless

despido etc [des'piðo] vb ver **despedir** ♦ nm dismissal, sacking

despierto, a etc [des'pjerto, a] vb ver **despertar** ♦ adj awake; (fig) sharp, alert

despilfarro [despil'farro] nm (derroche) squandering; (lujo desmedido) extravagance

despistar [despis'tar] vt to throw off the track o scent; (confundir) to mislead, confuse; **~se** vr to take the wrong road; (confundirse) to become confused

despiste [des'piste] nm absent-mindedness; **un ~** a mistake, slip

desplazamiento [desplaθa'mjento] nm displacement

desplazar [despla'θar] vt to move; (NAUT) to displace; (INFORM) to scroll; (fig) to oust; **~se** vr (persona) to travel

desplegar [desple'var] vt (tela, papel) to unfold, open out; (bandera) to unfurl; **despliegue** etc [des'pleve] vb ver **desplegar** ♦ nm display

desplomarse [desplo'marse] vr (edificio, gobierno, persona) to collapse

desplumar [desplu'mar] vt (ave) to pluck; (fam: estafar) to fleece

despoblado, a [despo'βlaðo, a] adj (sin habitantes) uninhabited

despojar [despo'xar] vt (alguien: de sus bienes) to divest of, deprive of; (casa) to strip, leave bare; (alguien: de su cargo) to strip of

despojo [des'poxo] nm (acto) plundering; (objetos) plunder, loot; **~s** nmpl (de ave, res) offal sg

desposado, a [despo'saðo, a] adj, nm/f newly-wed

desposar [despo'sar] vt to marry; **~se** vr to get married

desposeer [despose'er] vt: **~ a uno de** (puesto, autoridad) to strip sb of

déspota ['despota] nm/f despot

despreciar [despre'θjar] vt (desdeñar) to despise, scorn; (afrentar) to slight; **desprecio** nm scorn, contempt; slight

desprender [despren'der] vt (broche) to

unfasten; (olor) to give off; **~se** vr (botón: caerse) to fall off; (broche) to come unfastened; (olor, perfume) to be given off; **~se de algo que ...** to draw from sth that ...

desprendimiento [desprendi'mjento] nm (gen) loosening; (generosidad) disinterestedness; (de tierra, rocas) landslide

despreocupado, a [despreoku'paðo, a] adj (sin preocupación) unworried, nonchalant; (negligente) careless

despreocuparse [despreoku'parse] vr not to worry; **~ de** to have no interest in

desprestigiar [despresti'xjar] vt (criticar) to run down; (desacreditar) to discredit

desprevenido, a [despreße'niðo, a] adj (no preparado) unprepared, unready

desproporcionado, a [despropor-θjo'naðo, a] adj disproportionate, out of proportion

desprovisto, a [despro'ßisto, a] adj: **~ de** devoid of

después [des'pwes] adv afterwards, later; (próximo paso) next; **~ de comer** after lunch; **un año ~ a** year later; **~ se debatió el tema** next the matter was discussed; **~ de corregido el texto** after the text had been corrected; **~ de todo** after all

desquiciado, a [deski'θjaðo, a] adj deranged

desquite [des'kite] nm (satisfacción) satisfaction; (venganza) revenge

destacar [desta'kar] vt to emphasize, point up; (MIL) to detach, detail ♦ vi (resaltarse) to stand out; (persona) to be outstanding o exceptional; **~se** vr to stand out; to be outstanding o exceptional

destajo [des'taxo] nm: **trabajar a ~** to do piecework

destapar [desta'par] vt (botella) to open; (cacerola) to take the lid off; (descubrir) to uncover; **~se** vr (revelarse) to reveal one's true character

destartalado, a [destarta'laðo, a] adj (desordenado) untidy; (ruinoso) tumbledown

destello [des'teʎo] nm (de estrella) twinkle; (de faro) signal light

destemplado, a [destem'plaðo, a] adj (MUS) out of tune; (voz) harsh; (MED) out of sorts; (tiempo) unpleasant, nasty

desteñir [deste'ɲir] vt to fade ♦ vi to fade; **~se** vr to fade; **esta tela no destiñe** this fabric will not run

desternillarse [desterni'ʎarse] vr: **~ de risa** to split one's sides laughing

desterrar [deste'rrar] vt (exilar) to exile; (fig) to banish, dismiss

destiempo [des'tjempo]: **a ~** adv out of turn

destierro etc [des'tjerro] vb ver **desterrar** ♦ nm exile

destilar [desti'lar] vt to distil; **destilería** nf distillery

destinar [desti'nar] vt (funcionario) to appoint, assign; (fondos): **~ (a)** to set aside (for)

destinatario, a [destina'tarjo, a] nm/f addressee

destino [des'tino] nm (suerte) destiny; (de avión, viajero) destination

destituir [destitu'ir] vt to dismiss

destornillador [destorniʎa'ðor] nm screwdriver

destornillar [destorni'ʎar] vt (tornillo) to unscrew; **~se** vr to unscrew

destreza [des'treθa] nf (habilidad) skill; (maña) dexterity

destrozar [destro'θar] vt (romper) to smash, break (up); (estropear) to ruin; (nervios) to shatter

destrozo [des'troθo] nm (acción) destruction; (desastre) smashing; **~s** nmpl (pedazos) pieces; (daños) havoc sg

destrucción [destruk'θjon] nf destruction

destruir [destru'ir] vt to destroy

desuso [des'uso] nm disuse; **caer en ~** to become obsolete

desvalido, a [desßa'liðo, a] adj (desprotegido) destitute; (sin fuerzas) helpless

desvalijar [desßali'xar] vt (persona) to rob; (casa, tienda) to burgle; (coche) to break into

desván [des'ßan] nm attic

desvanecer [desßane'θer] vt (disipar) to dispel; (borrar) to blur; **~se** vr (humo etc) to vanish, disappear; (color) to fade; (recuerdo, sonido) to fade away; (MED) to pass out; (duda) to be dispelled

desvanecimiento [desßaneθi'mjento] nm (desaparición) disappearance; (de colores) fading; (evaporación) evaporation; (MED) fainting fit

desvariar [desßa'rjar] vi (enfermo) to be delirious; **desvarío** nm delirium

desvelar [desße'lar] vt to keep awake; **~se** vr (no poder dormir) to stay awake; (preocuparse) to be vigilant o watchful

desvelos [des'ßelos] nmpl worrying sg

desvencijado, a [desßenθi'xaðo, a] adj (silla) rickety; (máquina) broken-down

desventaja [desßen'taxa] nf disadvantage

desventura [desßen'tura] nf misfortune

desvergonzado, a [desßerxon'θaðo, a] adj shameless

desvergüenza [desßer'xwenθa] nf (descaro) shamelessness; (insolencia) impudence; (mala conducta) effrontery

desvestir [desßes'tir] vt to undress; **~se** vr to undress

desviación [desßja'θjon] nf deviation; (AUTO) diversion, detour

desviar [des'βjar] vt to turn aside; (*río*) to alter the course of; (*navío*) to divert, re-route; (*conversación*) to sidetrack; **~se** vr (*apartarse del camino*) to turn aside; (: *barco*) to go off course

desvío etc [des'βio] vb ver **desviar** ♦ nm (*desviación*) detour, diversion; (*fig*) indifference

desvirtuar [desβir'twar] vt to distort

desvivirse [desβi'βirse] vr: **~ por** (*anhelar*) to long for, crave for; (*hacer lo posible por*) to do one's utmost for

detallar [deta'ʎar] vt to detail

detalle [de'taʎe] nm detail; (*gesto*) gesture, token; **al ~** in detail; (*COM*) retail

detallista [deta'ʎista] nm/f (*COM*) retailer

detective [detek'tiβe] nm/f detective

detener [dete'ner] vt (*gen*) to stop; (*JUR*) to arrest; (*objeto*) to keep; **~se** vr to stop; (*demorarse*): **~se en** to delay over, linger over

detenidamente [deteniða'mente] adv (*minuciosamente*) carefully; (*extensamente*) at great length

detenido, a [dete'niðo, a] adj (*arrestado*) under arrest ♦ nm/f person under arrest, prisoner

detenimiento [deteni'mjento] nm: **con ~** thoroughly; (*observar, considerar*) carefully

detergente [deter'xente] nm detergent

deteriorar [deterjo'rar] vt to spoil, damage; **~se** vr to deteriorate; **deterioro** nm deterioration

determinación [determina'θjon] nf (*empeño*) determination; (*decisión*) decision; **determinado, a** adj specific

determinar [determi'nar] vt (*plazo*) to fix; (*precio*) to settle; **~se** vr to decide

detestar [detes'tar] vt to detest

detractor, a [detrak'tor, a] nm/f slanderer, libeller

detrás [de'tras] adv behind; (*atrás*) at the back; **~ de** behind

detrimento [detri'mento] nm: **en ~ de** to the detriment of

deuda ['deuða] nf debt

devaluación [deβalwa'θjon] nf devaluation

devastar [deβas'tar] vt (*destruir*) to devastate

devoción [deβo'θjon] nf devotion

devolución [deβolu'θjon] nf (*reenvío*) return, sending back; (*reembolso*) repayment; (*JUR*) devolution

devolver [deβol'βer] vt to return; (*lo extraviado, lo prestado*) to give back; (*carta al correo*) to send back; (*COM*) to repay, refund ♦ vi (*vomitar*) to be sick

devorar [deβo'rar] vt to devour

devoto, a [de'βoto, a] adj devout ♦ nm/f admirer

devuelto pp de **devolver**

devuelva etc vb ver **devolver**

di vb ver **dar**; **decir**

día ['dia] nm day; **¿qué ~ es?** what's the date?; **estar/poner al ~** to be/keep up to date; **el ~ de hoy/de mañana** today/tomorrow; **al ~ siguiente** (on) the following day; **vivir al ~** to live from hand to mouth; **de ~** by day, in daylight; **en pleno ~** in full daylight; **D~ de Reyes** Epiphany; **~ festivo** (*ESP*) o **feriado** (*AM*) holiday; **~ libre** day off

diabetes [dja'βetes] nf diabetes

diablo ['djaβlo] nm devil; **diablura** nf prank

diadema [dja'ðema] nf tiara

diafragma [dja'fraɣma] nm diaphragm

diagnosis [djaɣ'nosis] nf inv diagnosis

diagnóstico [djaɣ'nostiko] nm = **diagnosis**

diagonal [djaɣo'nal] adj diagonal

diagrama [dja'ɣrama] nm diagram; **~ de flujo** flowchart

dial [djal] nm dial

dialecto [dja'lekto] nm dialect

dialogar [djalo'ɣar] vi: **~ con** (*POL*) to hold talks with

diálogo ['djaloɣo] nm dialogue

diamante [dja'mante] nm diamond

diana ['djana] nf (*MIL*) reveille; (*de blanco*) centre, bull's-eye

diapositiva [djaposi'tiβa] nf (*FOTO*) slide, transparency

diario, a ['djarjo, a] adj daily ♦ nm newspaper; **a ~** daily; **de ~** everyday

diarrea [dja'rrea] nf diarrhoea

dibujar [diβu'xar] vt to draw, sketch; **dibujo** nm drawing; **dibujos animados** cartoons

diccionario [dikθjo'narjo] nm dictionary

dice etc vb ver **decir**

dicho, a ['ditʃo, a] pp de **decir** ♦ adj: **en ~s países** in the aforementioned countries ♦ nm saying

dichoso, a [di'tʃoso, a] adj happy

diciembre [di'θjembre] nm December

dictado [dik'taðo] nm dictation

dictador [dikta'ðor] nm dictator; **dictadura** nf dictatorship

dictamen [dik'tamen] nm (*opinión*) opinion; (*juicio*) judgment; (*informe*) report

dictar [dik'tar] vt (*carta*) to dictate; (*JUR: sentencia*) to pronounce; (*decreto*) to issue; (*AM: clase*) to give

didáctico, a [di'ðaktiko, a] adj educational

diecinueve [djeθi'nweβe] num nineteen

dieciocho [djeθi'otʃo] num eighteen

dieciséis [djeθi'seis] num sixteen

diecisiete [djeθi'sjete] num seventeen

diente ['djente] nm (*ANAT, TEC*) tooth; (*ZOOL*) fang; (: *de elefante*) tusk; (*de ajo*) clove; **hablar entre ~s** to mutter, mumble

diera etc vb ver **dar**

diesel ['disel] adj: **motor ~** diesel engine

diestro, a ['djestro, a] adj (*derecho*) right; (*hábil*) skilful

dieta ['djeta] nf diet; **dietética** nf: **tienda de dietética** health food shop; **dietético, a** adj diet (*atr*), dietary

diez [djeθ] num ten

diezmar [djeθ'mar] vt (*población*) to decimate

difamar [difa'mar] vt (*JUR: hablando*) to slander; (*: por escrito*) to libel

diferencia [dife'renθja] nf difference; **diferenciar** vt to differentiate between ♦ vi to differ; **diferenciarse** vr to differ, be different; (*distinguirse*) to distinguish o.s.

diferente [dife'rente] adj different

diferido [dife'riðo] nm: **en ~** (*TV etc*) recorded

difícil [di'fiθil] adj difficult

dificultad [difikul'taθ] nf difficulty; (*problema*) trouble

dificultar [difikul'tar] vt (*complicar*) to complicate, make difficult; (*estorbar*) to obstruct

difteria [dif'terja] nf diphtheria

difundir [difun'dir] vt (*calor, luz*) to diffuse; (*RADIO, TV*) to broadcast; **~ una noticia** to spread a piece of news; **~se** vr to spread (out)

difunto, a [di'funto, a] adj dead, deceased ♦ nm/f deceased (person)

difusión [difu'sjon] nf (*RADIO, TV*) broadcasting

diga etc vb ver **decir**

digerir [dixe'rir] vt to digest; (*fig*) to absorb; **digestión** nf digestion; **digestivo, a** adj digestive

digital [dixi'tal] adj digital

dignarse [div'narse] vr to deign to

dignatario, a [divna'tarjo, a] nm/f dignitary

dignidad [divni'ðaθ] nf dignity

digno, a ['divno, a] adj worthy

digo etc vb ver **decir**

dije etc vb ver **decir**

dilapidar [dilapi'ðar] vt (*dinero, herencia*) to squander, waste

dilatar [dila'tar] vt (*cuerpo*) to dilate; (*prolongar*) to prolong

dilema [di'lema] nm dilemma

diligencia [dili'xenθja] nf diligence; (*ocupación*) errand, job; **~s** nfpl (*JUR*) formalities; **diligente** adj diligent

diluir [dilu'ir] vt to dilute

diluvio [di'lußjo] nm deluge, flood

dimensión [dimen'sjon] nf dimension

diminuto, a [dimi'nuto, a] adj tiny, diminutive

dimitir [dimi'tir] vi to resign

dimos vb ver **dar**

Dinamarca [dina'marka] nf Denmark

dinámico, a [di'namiko, a] adj dynamic

dinamita [dina'mita] nf dynamite

dínamo ['dinamo] nf dynamo

dineral [dine'ral] nm large sum of money, fortune

dinero [di'nero] nm money; **~ contante**, **~ efectivo** (ready) cash; **~ suelto** (loose) change

dio vb ver **dar**

dios [djos] nm god; **¡D~ mío!** (oh,) my God!

diosa ['djosa] nf goddess

diploma [di'ploma] nm diploma

diplomacia [diplo'maθja] nf diplomacy; (*fig*) tact

diplomado, a [diplo'maðo, a] adj qualified

diplomático, a [diplo'matiko, a] adj diplomatic ♦ nm/f diplomat

diputación [diputa'θjon] nf (tb: **~ provincial**) ≈ county council

diputado, a [dipu'taðo, a] nm/f delegate; (*POL*) ≈ member of parliament (*BRIT*), ≈ representative (*US*)

dique ['dike] nm dyke

diré etc vb ver **decir**

dirección [direk'θjon] nf direction; (*señas*) address; (*AUTO*) steering; (*gerencia*) management; (*POL*) leadership; **~ única/ prohibida** one-way street/no entry

directa [di'rekta] nf (*AUT*) top gear

directiva [direk'tißa] nf (*DEP, tb: **junta ~***) board of directors

directo, a [di'rekto, a] adj direct; (*RADIO, TV*) live; **transmitir en ~** to broadcast live

director, a [direk'tor, a] adj leading ♦ nm/f director; (*ESCOL*) head(teacher) (*BRIT*), principal (*US*); (*gerente*) manager(ess); (*PRENSA*) editor; **~ de cine** film director; **~ general** managing director

dirigente [diri'xente] nm/f (*POL*) leader

dirigir [diri'xir] vt to direct; (*carta*) to address; (*obra de teatro, film*) to direct; (*MUS*) to conduct; (*negocio*) to manage; **~se** vr: **~se a** to go towards, make one's way towards; (*hablar con*) to speak to

dirija etc vb ver **dirigir**

discernir [disθer'nir] vt to discern

disciplina [disθi'plina] nf discipline

discípulo, a [dis'θipulo, a] nm/f disciple

disco ['disko] nm disc; (*DEPORTE*) discus; (*TEL*) dial; (*AUTO: semáforo*) light; (*MUS*) record; (*INFORM*): **~ flexible/rígido** floppy/hard disk; **~ compacto/de larga duración** compact disc/ long-playing record; **~ de freno** brake disc

disconforme [diskon'forme] adj differing; **estar ~ (con)** to be in disagreement (with)

discordia [dis'korðja] nf discord

discoteca [disko'teka] nf disco(theque)

discreción [diskre'θjon] nf discretion; (*reserva*) prudence; **comer a ~** to eat as much as one wishes; **discrecional** adj (*facultativo*) discretionary

discrepancia [diskre'panθja] nf (diferencia) discrepancy; (desacuerdo) disagreement

discreto, a [dis'kreto, a] adj discreet

discriminación [diskrimina'θjon] nf discrimination

disculpa [dis'kulpa] nf excuse; (pedir perdón) apology; **pedir ~s a/por** to apologize to/for; **disculpar** vt to excuse, pardon; **disculparse** vr to excuse o.s.; to apologize

discurrir [disku'rrir] vi (pensar, reflexionar) to think, meditate; (el tiempo) to pass, go by

discurso [dis'kurso] nm speech

discusión [disku'sjon] nf (diálogo) discussion; (riña) argument

discutir [disku'tir] vt (debatir) to discuss; (pelear) to argue about; (contradecir) to argue against ♦ vi (debatir) to discuss; (pelearse) to argue

disecar [dise'kar] vt (conservar: animal) to stuff; (: planta) to dry

diseminar [disemi'nar] vt to disseminate, spread

diseñar [dise'ɲar] vt, vi to design

diseño [di'seɲo] nm design

disfraz [dis'fraθ] nm (máscara) disguise; (excusa) pretext; **~ar** vt to disguise; **~arse** vr: **~arse de** to disguise o.s. as

disfrutar [disfru'tar] vt to enjoy ♦ vi to enjoy o.s.; **~ de** to enjoy, possess

disgregarse [disɣre'ɣarse] vr (muchedumbre) to disperse

disgustar [disɣus'tar] vt (no gustar) to displease; (contrariar, enojar) to annoy, upset; **~se** vr (enfadarse) to get upset; (dos personas) to fall out

disgusto [dis'ɣusto] nm (contrariedad) annoyance; (tristeza) grief; (riña) quarrel

disidente [disi'ðente] nm dissident

disimular [disimu'lar] vt (ocultar) to hide, conceal ♦ vi to dissemble

disipar [disi'par] vt to dispel; (fortuna) to squander; **~se** vr (nubes) to vanish; (indisciplinarse) to dissipate

dislocarse [dislo'karse] vr (articulación) to sprain, dislocate

disminución [disminu'θjon] nf decrease, reduction

disminuido, a [disminu'iðo, a] nm/f: **~ mental/físico** mentally/physically handicapped person

disminuir [disminu'ir] vt to decrease, diminish

disociarse [diso'θjarse] vr: **~ (de)** to dissociate o.s. (from)

disolver [disol'ßer] vt (gen) to dissolve; **~se** vr to dissolve; (COM) to go into liquidation

dispar [dis'par] adj different

disparar [dispa'rar] vt, vi to shoot, fire

disparate [dispa'rate] nm (tontería) foolish remark; (error) blunder; **decir ~s** to talk nonsense

disparo [dis'paro] nm shot

dispensar [dispen'sar] vt to dispense; (disculpar) to excuse

dispersar [disper'sar] vt to disperse; **~se** vr to scatter

disponer [dispo'ner] vt (arreglar) to arrange; (ordenar) to put in order; (preparar) to prepare, get ready ♦ vi: **~ de** to have, own; **~se** vr: **~se a o para hacer** to prepare to do

disponible [dispo'nißle] adj available

disposición [disposi'θjon] nf arrangement, disposition; (INFORM) layout; **a la ~ de** at the disposal of; **~ de animo** state of mind

dispositivo [disposi'tißo] nm device, mechanism

dispuesto, a [dis'pwesto, a] pp de **disponer** ♦ adj (arreglado) arranged; (preparado) disposed

disputar [dispu'tar] vt (carrera) to compete in

disquete [dis'kete] nm floppy disk, diskette

distancia [dis'tanθja] nf distance

distanciar [distan'θjar] vt to space out; **~se** vr to become estranged

distante [dis'tante] adj distant

distar [dis'tar] vi: **dista 5km de aquí** it is 5km from here

diste vb ver **dar**

disteis ['disteis] vb ver **dar**

distension [disten'sjon] nf (en las relaciones) relaxation; (POL) détente; (muscular) strain

distinción [distin'θjon] nf distinction; (elegancia) elegance; (honor) honour

distinguido, a [distin'ɡiðo, a] adj distinguished

distinguir [distin'ɡir] vt to distinguish; (escoger) to single out; **~se** vr to be distinguished

distintivo [distin'tißo] nm badge; (fig) characteristic

distinto, a [dis'tinto, a] adj different; (claro) clear

distracción [distrak'θjon] nf distraction; (pasatiempo) hobby, pastime; (olvido) absent-mindedness, distraction

distraer [distra'er] vt (atención) to distract; (divertir) to amuse; (fondos) to embezzle; **~se** vr (entretenerse) to amuse o.s.; (perder la concentración) to allow one's attention to wander

distraído, a [distra'iðo, a] adj (gen) absent-minded; (entretenido) amusing

distribuidor, a [distribui'ðor, a] nm/f distributor; **distribuidora** nf (COM) dealer, agent; (CINE) distributor

distribuir [distribu'ir] vt to distribute

distrito [dis'trito] nm (sector, territorio) region; (barrio) district

disturbio [dis'turßjo] nm disturbance; (desorden) riot

disuadir [diswa'ðir] vt to dissuade

disuelto [di'swelto] pp de **disolver**

disyuntiva [disjun'tißa] nf dilemma

DIU nm abr (= dispositivo intrauterino) IUD

diurno, a [djurno, a] adj day cpd

divagar [dißa'ɣar] vi (desviarse) to digress

diván [di'ßan] nm divan

divergencia [dißer'xenθja] nf divergence

diversidad [dißersi'ðað] nf diversity, variety

diversificar [dißersifi'kar] vt to diversify

diversión [dißer'sjon] nf (gen) entertainment; (actividad) hobby, pastime

diverso, a [di'ßerso, a] adj diverse; ~s libros several books; ~s nmpl sundries

divertido, a [dißer'tiðo, a] adj (chiste) amusing; (fiesta etc) enjoyable

divertir [dißer'tir] vt (entretener, recrear) to amuse; ~se vr (pasarlo bien) to have a good time; (distraerse) to amuse o.s.

dividendos [dißi'ðendos] nmpl (COM) dividends

dividir [dißi'ðir] vt (gen) to divide; (distribuir) to distribute, share out

divierta etc vb ver **divertir**

divino, a [di'ßino, a] adj divine

divirtiendo etc vb ver **divertir**

divisa [di'ßisa] nf (emblema) emblem, badge; ~s nfpl foreign exchange sg

divisar [dißi'sar] vt to make out, distinguish

división [dißi'sjon] nf (gen) division; (de partido) split; (de país) partition

divorciar [dißor'θjar] vt to divorce; ~se vr to get divorced; **divorcio** nm divorce

divulgar [dißul'xar] vt (ideas) to spread; (secreto) to divulge

DNI (ESP) nm abr (= Documento Nacional de Identidad) national identity card

Dña. abr (= doña) Mrs

do [do] nm (MUS) do, C

dobladillo [doßla'ðiʎo] nm (de vestido) hem; (de pantalón: vuelta) turn-up (BRIT), cuff (US)

doblar [do'ßlar] vt to double; (papel) to fold; (caño) to bend; (la esquina) to turn, go round; (film) to dub ♦ vi to turn; (campana) to toll; ~se vr (plegarse) to fold (up), crease; (encorvarse) to bend

doble ['doßle] adj double; (de dos aspectos) dual; (fig) two-faced ♦ nm double ♦ nm/f (TEATRO) stand-in; ~s nmpl (DEPORTE) doubles sg; **con sentido** ~ with a double meaning

doblegar [doßle'xar] vt to fold, crease; ~se vr to yield

doblez [do'ßleθ] nm fold, hem ♦ nf insincerity, duplicity

doce ['doθe] num twelve; ~na nf dozen

docente [do'θente] adj: **centro/personal** ~ teaching establishment/staff

dócil ['doθil] adj (pasivo) docile; (obediente) obedient

docto, a ['dokto, a] adj: ~ **en** instructed in

doctor, a [dok'tor, a] nm/f doctor

doctorado [dokto'raðo] nm doctorate

doctrina [dok'trina] nf doctrine, teaching

documentación [dokumenta'θjon] nf documentation, papers pl

documental [dokumen'tal] adj, nm documentary

documento [doku'mento] nm (certificado) document; ~ **national de identidad** identity card

dólar ['dolar] nm dollar

doler [do'ler] vt, vi to hurt; (fig) to grieve; ~se vr (de su situación) to grieve, feel sorry; (de las desgracias ajenas) to sympathize; **me duele el brazo** my arm hurts

dolor [do'lor] nm pain; (fig) grief, sorrow; ~ **de cabeza** headache; ~ **de estómago** stomachache

domar [do'mar] vt to tame

domesticar [domesti'kar] vt = **domar**

doméstico, a [do'mestiko, a] adj (vida, servicio) home; (tareas) household; (animal) tame, pet

domiciliación [domiθilia'θjon] nf: ~ **de pagos** (COM) standing order

domicilio [domi'θiljo] nm home; ~ **particular** private residence; ~ **social** (COM) head office; **sin** ~ **fijo** of no fixed abode

dominante [domi'nante] adj dominant; (persona) domineering

dominar [domi'nar] vt (gen) to dominate; (idiomas) to be fluent in ♦ vi to dominate, prevail; ~se vr to control o.s.

domingo [do'mingo] nm Sunday

dominio [do'minjo] nm (tierras) domain; (autoridad) power, authority; (de las pasiones) grip, hold; (de idiomas) command

don [don] nm (talento) gift; ~ **Juan Gómez** Mr Juan Gómez, Juan Gómez Esq (BRIT)

donaire [do'naire] nm charm

donar [do'nar] vt to donate

donativo [dona'tißo] nm donation

doncella [don'θeʎa] nf (criada) maid

donde ['donde] adv where ♦ prep: **el coche está allí** ~ **el farol** the car is over there by the lamppost o where the lamppost is; **en** ~ where, in which

dónde ['donde] adv interrogativo where?; ¿a ~ **vas?** where are you going (to)?; ¿de ~ **vienes?** where have you been?; ¿por ~? where?, whereabouts?

dondequiera [donde'kjera] adv anywhere; **por** ~ everywhere, all over the place ♦ conj:

~ **que** wherever

doña ['doɲa] *nf:* ~ **Alicia** Alicia; ~ **Victoria Benito** Mrs Victoria Benito

dorado, a [do'raðo, a] *adj (color)* golden; *(TEC)* gilt

dormir [dor'mir] *vt:* ~ **la siesta** to have an afternoon nap ♦ *vi* to sleep; ~**se** *vr* to fall asleep

dormitar [dormi'tar] *vi* to doze

dormitorio [dormi'torjo] *nm* bedroom; ~ **común** dormitory

dorsal [dor'sal] *nm (DEPORTE)* number

dorso ['dorso] *nm (de mano)* back; *(de hoja)* other side

dos [dos] *num* two

dosis ['dosis] *nf inv* dose, dosage

dotado, a [do'taðo, a] *adj* gifted; ~ **de** endowed with

dotar [do'tar] *vt* to endow; **dote** *nf* dowry; **dotes** *nfpl (talentos)* gifts

doy *vb ver* **dar**

dragar [dra'ɣar] *vt (río)* to dredge; *(minas)* to sweep

drama ['drama] *nm* drama

dramaturgo [drama'turɣo] *nm* dramatist, playwright

drástico, a ['drastiko, a] *adj* drastic

drenaje [dre'naxe] *nm* drainage

droga ['droxa] *nf* drug

drogadicto, a [droɣa'ðikto, a] *nm/f* drug addict

droguería [droɣe'ria] *nf* hardware shop *(BRIT)* o store *(US)*

ducha ['dutʃa] *nf (baño)* shower; *(MED)* douche; **ducharse** *vr* to take a shower

duda ['duða] *nf* doubt; **dudar** *vt, vi* to doubt; **dudoso, a** [du'ðoso, a] *adj (incierto)* hesitant; *(sospechoso)* doubtful

duela *etc vb ver* **doler**

duelo ['dwelo] *vb ver* **doler** ♦ *nm (combate)* duel; *(luto)* mourning

duende ['dwende] *nm* imp, goblin

dueño, a ['dweɲo, a] *nm/f (propietario)* owner; *(de pensión, taberna)* landlord/lady; *(empresario)* employer

duermo *etc vb ver* **dormir**

dulce ['dulθe] *adj* sweet ♦ *adv* gently, softly ♦ *nm* sweet

dulzura [dul'θura] *nf* sweetness; *(ternura)* gentleness

duna ['duna] *nf (GEO)* dune

dúo ['duo] *nm* duet

duplicar [dupli'kar] *vt (hacer el doble de)* to duplicate; ~**se** *vr* to double

duque ['duke] *nm* duke; ~**sa** *nf* duchess

duración [dura'θjon] *nf (de película, disco etc)* length; *(de pila etc)* life; *(curso: de acontecimientos etc)* duration

duradero, a [dura'ðero, a] *adj (tela etc)* hard-wearing; *(fe, paz)* lasting

durante [du'rante] *prep* during

durar [du'rar] *vi* to last; *(recuerdo)* to remain

durazno [du'raθno] *(AM) nm (fruta)* peach; *(árbol)* peach tree

durex ['dureks] *(AM) nm (tira adhesiva)* Sellotape ® *(BRIT)*, Scotch tape ® *(US)*

dureza [du'reθa] *nf (calidad)* hardness

duro, a ['duro, a] *adj* hard; *(carácter)* tough ♦ *adv* hard ♦ *nm (moneda)* five peseta coin o piece

DVD *nm abr (= disco de vídeo digital)* DVD

E, e

E *abr (= este)* E

e |e| *conj* and

ebanista [eßa'nista] *nm/f* cabinetmaker

ébano ['eßano] *nm* ebony

ebrio, a ['eßrjo, a] *adj* drunk

ebullición [eßuʎi'θjon] *nf* boiling

eccema [ek'θema] *nf (MED)* eczema

echar [e'tʃar] *vt* to throw; *(agua, vino)* to pour (out); *(empleado: despedir)* to fire, sack; *(hojas)* to sprout; *(cartas)* to post; *(humo)* to emit, give out ♦ *vi:* ~ **a correr/llorar** to run off/burst into tears; ~**se** *vr* to lie down; ~ **llave a** to lock (up); ~ **abajo** *(gobierno)* to overthrow; *(edificio)* to demolish; ~ **mano a** to lay hands on; ~ **una mano a uno** *(ayudar)* to give sb a hand; ~ **de menos** to miss

eclesiástico, a [ekle'sjastiko, a] *adj* ecclesiastical

eclipse [e'klipse] *nm* eclipse

eco ['eko] *nm* echo; **tener** ~ to catch on

ecología [ekolo'xia] *nf* ecology; **ecológico, a** *adj (producto, método)* environmentally-friendly; *(agricultura)* organic; **ecologista** *adj* ecological, environmental ♦ *nm/f* environmentalist

economato [ekono'mato] *nm* cooperative store

economía [ekono'mia] *nf (sistema)* economy; *(carrera)* economics

económico, a [eko'nomiko, a] *adj (barato)* cheap, economical; *(ahorrativo)* thrifty; *(COM: año etc)* financial; *(: situación)* economic

economista [ekono'mista] *nm/f* economist

ECU [eku] *nm* ECU

ecuador [ekwa'ðor] *nm* equator; **(el) E~** Ecuador

ecuánime [e'kwanime] *adj (carácter)* level-headed; *(estado)* calm

ecuatoriano, a [ekwato'rjano, a] *adj, nm/f* Ecuadorian

ecuestre [e'kwestre] *adj* equestrian

eczema [ek'θema] *nm* = **eccema**

edad [e'ðað] *nf* age; **¿qué ~ tienes?** how old

are you?; **tiene ocho años de ~** he is eight (years old); **de ~ mediana/avanzada** middle-aged/advanced in years; **la E~ Media** the Middle Ages

edición [eði'θjon] *nf* (*acto*) publication; (*ejemplar*) edition

edificar [edifi'kar] *vt, vi* to build

edificio [eði'fiθjo] *nm* building; (*fig*) edifice, structure

Edimburgo [eðim'burɣo] *nm* Edinburgh

editar [eði'tar] *vt* (*publicar*) to publish; (*preparar textos*) to edit

editor, a [eði'tor, a] *nm/f* (*que publica*) publisher; (*redactor*) editor ♦ *adj*: **casa ~a** publishing house, publisher; **~ial** *adj* editorial ♦ *nm* leading article, editorial; **casa ~ial** publishing house, publisher

edredon [eðre'ðon] *nm* duvet

educación [eðuka'θjon] *nf* education; (*crianza*) upbringing; (*modales*) (good) manners *pl*

educado, a [eðu'kaðo, a] *adj*: **bien/mal ~** well/badly behaved

educar [eðu'kar] *vt* to educate; (*criar*) to bring up; (*voz*) to train

EE. UU. *nmpl abr* (= *Estados Unidos*) US(A)

efectista [efek'tista] *adj* sensationalist

efectivamente [efectißa'mente] *adv* (*como respuesta*) exactly, precisely; (*verdaderamente*) really; (*de hecho*) in fact

efectivo, a [efek'tißo, a] *adj* effective; (*real*) actual, real ♦ *nm*: **pagar en ~** to pay (in) cash; **hacer ~ un cheque** to cash a cheque

efecto [e'fekto] *nm* effect, result; **~s** *nmpl* (~*s personales*) effects; (*bienes*) goods, (*COM*) assets; **en ~** in fact; (*respuesta*) exactly, indeed; **~ 2000** millennium bug; **~ invernadero** greenhouse effect

efectuar [efek'twar] *vt* to carry out; (*viaje*) to make

eficacia [efi'kaθja] *nf* (*de persona*) efficiency; (*de medicamento etc*) effectiveness

eficaz [efi'kaθ] *adj* (*persona*) efficient; (*acción*) effective

eficiente [efi'θjente] *adj* efficient

efusivo, a [efu'sißo, a] *adj* effusive; **mis más efusivas gracias** my warmest thanks

EGB (*ESP*) *nf abr* (*ESCOL*) = *Educación General Básica*

egipcio, a [e'xipθjo, a] *adj, nm/f* Egyptian

Egipto [e'xipto] *nm* Egypt

egoísmo [exo'ismo] *nm* egoism

egoísta [exo'ista] *adj* egoistical, selfish ♦ *nm/f* egoist

egregio, a [e'xrexjo, a] *adj* eminent, distinguished

Eire ['eire] *nm* Eire

ej. *abr* (= *ejemplo*) eg

eje ['exe] *nm* (*GEO, MAT*) axis; (*de rueda*) axle;

(*de máquina*) shaft, spindle

ejecución [exeku'θjon] *nf* execution; (*cumplimiento*) fulfilment; (*MUS*) performance; (*JUR*: *embargo de deudor*) attachment

ejecutar [exeku'tar] *vt* to execute, carry out; (*matar*) to execute; (*cumplir*) to fulfil; (*MUS*) to perform; (*JUR*: *embargar*) to attach, distrain (on)

ejecutivo, a [exeku'tißo, a] *adj* executive; **el (poder) ~** the executive (power)

ejemplar [exem'plar] *adj* exemplary ♦ *nm* example; (*ZOOL*) specimen; (*de libro*) copy; (*de periódico*) number, issue

ejemplo [e'xemplo] *nm* example; **por ~** for example

ejercer [exer'θer] *vt* to exercise; (*influencia*) to exert; (*un oficio*) to practise ♦ *vi* (*practicar*): **~ (de)** to practise (as)

ejercicio [exer'θiθjo] *nm* exercise; (*período*) tenure; **~ comercial** financial year

ejército [e'xerθito] *nm* army; **entrar en el ~** to join the army, join up

ejote [e'xote] (*AM*) *nm* green bean

---

el [el] (*f* **la**, *pl* **los, las,** *neutro* **lo**) *art def* **1** the; **el libro/la mesa/los estudiantes** the book/table/students

2 (*con n abstracto: no se traduce*): **el amor/la juventud** love/youth

3 (*posesión: se traduce a menudo por adj posesivo*): **romperse el brazo** to break one's arm; **levantó la mano** he put his hand up; **se puso el sombrero** she put her hat on

4 (*valor descriptivo*): **tener la boca grande/los ojos azules** to have a big mouth/blue eyes

5 (*con días*) on; **me iré el viernes** I'll leave on Friday; **los domingos suelo ir a nadar** on Sundays I generally go swimming

6 (*lo + adj*): **lo difícil/caro** what is difficult/expensive; (= *cuán*): **no se da cuenta de lo pesado que es** he doesn't realise how boring he is

♦ *pron demos* **1**: **mi libro y el de usted** my book and yours; **las de Pepe son mejores** Pepe's are better; **no la(s) blanca(s) sino la(s) gris(es)** not the white one(s) but the grey one(s)

2: **lo de: lo de ayer** what happened yesterday; **lo de las facturas** that business about the invoices

♦ *pron relativo*: **el que** *etc* **1** (*indef*): **el (los) que quiera(n) que se vaya(n)** anyone who wants to can leave; **llévese el que más le guste** take the one you like best

2 (*def*): **el que compré ayer** the one I bought yesterday; **los que se van** those who leave

3: **lo que: lo que pienso yo/más me gusta**

what I think/like most
♦ *conj*: **el que: el que lo diga** the fact that he says so; **el que sea tan vago me molesta** his being so lazy bothers me
♦ *excl*: **¡el susto que me diste!** what a fright you gave me!
♦ *pron personal* **1** (*persona: m*) him; (: *f*) her; (: *pl*) them; **lo/las veo** I can see him/them **2** (*animal, cosa: sg*) it; (: *pl*) them; **lo** (*o* **la**) **veo** I can see it; **los** (*o* **las**) **veo** I can see them
3: **lo** (*como sustituto de frase*): **no lo sabía** I didn't know; **ya lo entiendo** I understand now

él [el] *pron* (*persona*) he; (*cosa*) it; (*después de prep: persona*) him; (: *cosa*) it; **de ~** his
elaborar [elaßo'rar] *vt* (*producto*) to make, manufacture; (*preparar*) to prepare; (*madera, metal etc*) to work; (*proyecto etc*) to work on o out
elasticidad [elastiθi'ðað] *nf* elasticity
elástico, a [e'lastiko, a] *adj* elastic; (*flexible*) flexible ♦ *nm* elastic; (*un ~*) elastic band
elección [elek'θjon] *nf* election; (*selección*) choice, selection
electorado [elekto'raðo] *nm* electorate, voters *pl*
electricidad [elektriθi'ðað] *nf* electricity
electricista [elektri'θista] *nm/f* electrician
eléctrico, a [e'lektriko, a] *adj* electric
electro... [elektro] *prefijo* electro...; **~cardiograma** *nm* electrocardiogram; **~cutar** *vt* to electrocute; **~do** *nm* electrode; **~domésticos** *nmpl* (*electrical*) household appliances; **~magnético, a** *adj* electromagnetic
electrónica [elek'tronika] *nf* electronics *sg*
electrónico, a [elek'troniko, a] *adj* electronic
elefante [ele'fante] *nm* elephant
elegancia [ele'ɣanθja] *nf* elegance, grace; (*estilo*) stylishness
elegante [ele'ɣante] *adj* elegant, graceful; (*estiloso*) stylish, fashionable
elegir [ele'xir] *vt* (*escoger*) to choose, select; (*optar*) to opt for; (*presidente*) to elect
elemental [elemen'tal] *adj* (*claro, obvio*) elementary; (*fundamental*) elemental, fundamental
elemento [ele'mento] *nm* element; (*fig*) ingredient; **~s** *nmpl* elements, rudiments
elepé [ele'pe] (*pl*: **elepés**) *nm* L.P.
elevación [eleßa'θjon] *nf* elevation; (*acto*) raising, lifting; (*de precios*) rise; (*GEO etc*) height, altitude
elevar [ele'ßar] *vt* to raise, lift (up); (*precio*) to put up; **~se** *vr* (*edificio*) to rise; (*precios*) to go up
eligiendo *etc vb ver* **elegir**

elija *etc vb ver* **elegir**
eliminar [elimi'nar] *vt* to eliminate, remove
eliminatoria [elimina'torja] *nf* heat, preliminary (round)
elite [e'lite] *nf* elite
ella ['eʎa] *pron* (*persona*) she; (*cosa*) it; (*después de prep: persona*) her; (: *cosa*) it; **de ~** hers
ellas ['eʎas] *pron* (*personas y cosas*) they; (*después de prep*) them; **de ~** theirs
ello ['eʎo] *pron* it
ellos ['eʎos] *pron* they; (*después de prep*) them; **de ~** theirs
elocuencia [elo'kwenθja] *nf* eloquence
elogiar [elo'xjar] *vt* to praise; **elogio** *nm* praise
elote [e'lote] (*AM*) *nm* corn on the cob
eludir [elu'ðir] *vt* to avoid
emanar [ema'nar] *vi*: **~ de** to emanate from, come from; (*derivar de*) to originate in
emancipar [emanθi'par] *vt* to emancipate; **~se** *vr* to become emancipated, free o.s.
embadurnar [embaður'nar] *vt* to smear
embajada [emba'xaða] *nf* embassy
embajador, a [embaxa'ðor, a] *nm/f* ambassador/ambassadress
embalaje [emba'laxe] *nm* packing
embalar [emba'lar] *vt* to parcel, wrap (up); **~se** *vr* to go fast
embalsamar [embalsa'mar] *vt* to embalm
embalse [em'balse] *nm* (*presa*) dam; (*lago*) reservoir
embarazada [embara'θaða] *adj* pregnant ♦ *nf* pregnant woman
embarazo [emba'raθo] *nm* (*de mujer*) pregnancy; (*impedimento*) obstacle, obstruction; (*timidez*) embarrassment; **embarazoso, a** *adj* awkward, embarrassing
embarcación [embarka'θjon] *nf* (*barco*) boat, craft; (*acto*) embarkation, boarding
embarcadero [embarka'ðero] *nm* pier, landing stage
embarcar [embar'kar] *vt* (*cargamento*) to ship, stow; (*persona*) to embark, put on board; **~se** *vr* to embark, go on board
embargar [embar'ɣar] *vt* (*JUR*) to seize, impound
embargo [em'barɣo] *nm* (*JUR*) seizure; (*COM, POL*) embargo
embargue [em'barɣe] *etc vb ver* **embargar**
embarque *etc* [em'barke] *vb ver* **embarcar** ♦ *nm* shipment, loading
embaucar [embau'kar] *vt* to trick, fool
embeber [embe'ßer] *vt* (*absorber*) to absorb, soak up; (*empapar*) to saturate ♦ *vi* to shrink; **~se** *vr*: **~se en un libro** to be engrossed o absorbed in a book
embellecer [embeʎe'θer] *vt* to embellish, beautify

embestida [embes'tiða] nf attack, onslaught; (carga) charge

embestir [embes'tir] vt to attack, assault; to charge, attack ♦ vi to attack

emblema [em'blema] nm emblem

embobado, a [embo'ßaðo, a] adj (atontado) stunned, bewildered

embolia [em'bolja] nf (MED) clot

émbolo ['embolo] nm (AUTO) piston

embolsar [embol'sar] vt to pocket, put in one's pocket

emborrachar [emborra'tʃar] vt to make drunk, intoxicate; ~se vr to get drunk

emboscada [embos'kaða] nf ambush

embotar [embo'tar] vt to blunt, dull; ~se vr (adormecerse) to go numb

embotellamiento [emboteʎa'mjento] nm (AUTO) traffic jam

embotellar [embote'ʎar] vt to bottle

embrague [em'braxe] nm (tb: pedal de ~) clutch

embriagar [embrja'xar] vt (emborrachar) to make drunk; ~se vr (emborracharse) to get drunk

embrión [em'brjon] nm embryo

embrollar [embro'ʎar] vt (el asunto) to confuse, complicate; (implicar) to involve, embroil; ~se vr (confundirse) to get into a muddle o mess

embrollo [em'broʎo] nm (enredo) muddle, confusion; (aprieto) fix, jam

embrujado, a [embru'xaðo, a] adj bewitched; **casa embrujada** haunted house

embrutecer [embrute'θer] vt (atontar) to stupefy; ~se vr to be stupefied

embudo [em'buðo] nm funnel

embuste [em'buste] nm (mentira) lie; ~**ro, a** adj lying, deceitful ♦ nm/f (mentiroso) liar

embutido [embu'tiðo] nm (CULIN) sausage; (TEC) inlay

emergencia [emer'xenθja] nf emergency; (surgimiento) emergence

emerger [emer'xer] vi to emerge, appear

emigración [emixra'θjon] nf emigration; (de pájaros) migration

emigrar [emi'xrar] vi (personas) to emigrate; (pájaros) to migrate

eminencia [emi'nenθja] nf eminence; **eminente** adj eminent, distinguished; (elevado) high

emisario [emi'sarjo] nm emissary

emisión [emi'sjon] nf (acto) emission; (COM etc) issue; (RADIO, TV: acto) broadcasting; (: programa) broadcast, programme (BRIT), program (US)

emisora [emi'sora] nf radio o broadcasting station

emitir [emi'tir] vt (olor etc) to emit, give off; (moneda etc) to issue; (opinión) to express; (RADIO) to broadcast

emoción [emo'θjon] nf emotion; (excitación) excitement; (sentimiento) feeling

emocionante [emoθjo'nante] adj (excitante) exciting, thrilling

emocionar [emoθjo'nar] vt (excitar) to excite, thrill; (conmover) to move, touch; (impresionar) to impress

emotivo, a [emo'tißo, a] adj emotional

empacar [empa'kar] vt (gen) to pack; (en caja) to bale, crate

empacho [em'patʃo] nm (MED) indigestion; (fig) embarrassment

empadronarse [empaðro'narse] vr (POL: como elector) to register

empalagoso, a [empala'xoso, a] adj cloying; (fig) tiresome

empalmar [empal'mar] vt to join, connect ♦ vi (dos caminos) to meet, join; **empalme** nm joint, connection; junction; (de trenes) connection

empanada [empa'naða] nf pie, pasty

empantanarse [empanta'narse] vr to get swamped; (fig) to get bogged down

empañarse [empa'narse] vr (cristales etc) to steam up

empapar [empa'par] vt (mojar) to soak, saturate; (absorber) to soak up, absorb; ~se vr: ~**se de** to soak up

empapelar [empape'lar] vt (paredes) to paper

empaquetar [empake'tar] vt to pack, parcel up

empastar [empas'tar] vt (embadurnar) to paste; (diente) to fill

empaste [em'paste] nm (de diente) filling

empatar [empa'tar] vi to draw, tie; **empate** nm draw, tie

empecé etc vb ver **empezar**

empedernido, a [empeðer'niðo, a] adj hard, heartless; (fumador) inveterate

empedrado, a [empe'ðraðo, a] adj paved ♦ nm paving

empeine [em'peine] nm (de pie, zapato) instep

empellón [empe'ʎon] nm push, shove

empeñado, a [empe'naðo, a] adj (persona) determined; (objeto) pawned

empeñar [empe'nar] vt (objeto) to pawn, pledge; (persona) to compel; ~se vr (endeudarse) to get into debt; ~**se en** to be set on, be determined to

empeño [em'peno] nm (determinación, insistencia) determination, insistence; **casa de** ~**s** pawnshop

empeorar [empeo'rar] vt to make worse, worsen ♦ vi to get worse, deteriorate

empequeñecer [empekene'θer] vt to dwarf; (minusvalorar) to belittle

emperador [empera'ðor] *nm* emperor;
emperatriz *nf* empress

empezar [empe'θar] *vt*, *vi* to begin, start

empiece *etc vb ver* **empezar**

empiezo *etc vb ver* **empezar**

empinar [empi'nar] *vt* to raise; **~se** *vr*
(*persona*) to stand on tiptoe; (*animal*) to rear
up; (*camino*) to climb steeply

empírico, a [em'piriko, a] *adj* empirical

emplasto [em'plasto] *nm* (*MED*) plaster

emplazamiento [emplaθa'mjento] *nm* site,
location; (*JUR*) summons *sg*

emplazar [empla'θar] *vt* (*ubicar*) to site,
place, locate; (*JUR*) to summons; (*convocar*)
to summon

empleado, a [emple'aðo, a] *nm/f* (*gen*)
employee; (*de banco etc*) clerk

emplear [emple'ar] *vt* (*usar*) to use, employ;
(*dar trabajo a*) to employ; **~se** *vr* (*conseguir
trabajo*) to be employed; (*ocuparse*) to
occupy o.s.

empleo [em'pleo] *nm* (*puesto*) job; (*puestos:
colectivamente*) employment; (*uso*) use,
employment

empobrecer [empoβre'θer] *vt* to
impoverish; **~se** *vr* to become poor *o*
impoverish

empollar [empo'ʎar] (*fam*) *vt*, *vi* to swot
(up); **empollón, ona** (*fam*) *nm/f* swot

emporio [em'porjo] *nm* (*AM: gran almacén*)
department store

empotrado, a [empo'traðo, a] *adj* (*armario
etc*) built-in

emprender [empren'der] *vt* (*empezar*) to
begin, embark on; (*acometer*) to tackle, take
on

empresa [em'presa] *nf* (*de espíritu etc*)
enterprise; (*COM*) company, firm; **~rio, a** *nm/f* (*COM*) businessman/woman

empréstito [em'prestito] *nm* (*public*) loan

empujar [empu'xar] *vt* to push, shove

empujón [empu'xon] *nm* push, shove

empuñar [empu'nar] *vt* (*asir*) to grasp, take
(firm) hold of

emular [emu'lar] *vt* to emulate; (*rivalizar*) to
rival

PALABRA CLAVE
---

en [en] *prep* **1** (*posición*) in; (*: sobre*) on; **está
~ el cajón** it's in the drawer; **~ Argentina/La
Paz** in Argentina/La Paz; **~ la oficina/el
colegio** at the office/school; **está ~ el suelo/
quinto piso** it's on the floor/the fifth floor

2 (*dirección*) into; **entró ~ el aula** she went
into the classroom; **meter algo ~ el bolso** to
put sth into one's bag

3 (*tiempo*) in; on; **~ 1605/3 semanas/invierno**
in 1605/3 weeks/winter; **~ (el mes de) enero**
in (the month of) January; **~ aquella**
ocasión/época on that occasion/at that time

4 (*precio*) for; **lo vendió ~ 20 dólares** he sold
it for 20 dollars

5 (*diferencia*) by; **reducir/aumentar ~ una
tercera parte/un 20 por ciento** to reduce/
increase by a third/20 per cent

6 (*manera*): **~ avión/autobús** by plane/bus;
escrito ~ inglés written in English

7 (*después de vb que indica gastar etc*) on;
han cobrado demasiado ~ dietas they've
charged too much to expenses; **se le va la
mitad del sueldo ~ comida** he spends half his
salary on food

8 (*tema, ocupación*): **experto ~ la materia**
expert on the subject; **trabaja ~ la
construcción** he works in the building
industry

9 (*adj + en + infin*): **lento ~ reaccionar** slow
to react

---

enaguas [e'naɣwas] *nfpl* petticoat *sg*,
underskirt *sg*

enajenación [enaxena'θjon] *nf*: **~ mental**
mental derangement

enajenar [enaxe'nar] *vt* (*volver loco*) to drive
mad

enamorado, a [enamo'raðo, a] *adj* in love
♦ *nm/f* lover

enamorar [enamo'rar] *vt* to win the love of;
~se *vr*: **~se de alguien** to fall in love with sb

enano, a [e'nano, a] *adj* tiny ♦ *nm/f* dwarf

enardecer [enarðe'θer] *vt* (*pasiones*) to fire,
inflame; (*persona*) to fill with enthusiasm; **~se**
vr: **~se por** to get excited about; (*entusiasmarse*) to get enthusiastic about

encabezamiento [enkaβeθa'mjento] *nm*
(*de carta*) heading; (*de periódico*) headline

encabezar [enkaβe'θar] *vt* (*movimiento,
revolución*) to lead, head; (*lista*) to head, be
at the top of; (*carta*) to put a heading to

encadenar [enkaðe'nar] *vt* to chain
(together); (*poner grilletes a*) to shackle

encajar [enka'xar] *vt* (*ajustar*): **~ (en)** to fit
(into); (*fam: golpe*) to take ♦ *vi* to fit (well);
(*fig: corresponder a*) to match; **~se** *vr*: **~se en
un sillón** to squeeze into a chair

encaje [en'kaxe] *nm* (*labor*) lace

encalar [enka'lar] *vt* (*pared*) to whitewash

encallar [enka'ʎar] *vi* (*NAUT*) to run aground

encaminar [enkami'nar] *vt* to direct, send;
~se *vr*: **~se a** to set out for

encantado, a [enkan'taðo, a] *adj*
(*hechizado*) bewitched; (*muy contento*)
delighted; **¡~!** how do you do, pleased to
meet you

encantador, a [enkanta'ðor, a] *adj*
charming, lovely ♦ *nm/f* magician,
enchanter/enchantress

encantar [enkan'tar] *vt* (*agradar*) to charm,

delight; (*hechizar*) to bewitch, cast a spell on; **me encanta eso** I love that; **encanto** *nm* (*hechizo*) spell, charm; (*fig*) charm, delight

encarcelar [enkarθe'lar] *vt* to imprison, jail

encarecer [enkare'θer] *vt* to put up the price of; **~se** *vr* to get dearer

encarecimiento [enkareθi'mjento] *nm* price increase

encargado, a [enkar'βaðo, a] *adj* in charge ♦ *nm/f* agent, representative; (*responsable*) person in charge

encargar [enkar'βar] *vt* to entrust; (*recomendar*) to urge, recommend; **~se** *vr*: **~se de** to look after, take charge of

encargo [en'karβo] *nm* (*tarea*) assignment, job; (*responsabilidad*) responsibility; (*COM*) order

encariñarse [enkari'narse] *vr*: **~ con** to grow fond of, get attached to

encarnación [enkarna'θjon] *nf* incarnation, embodiment

encarnizado, a [enkarni'θaðo, a] *adj* (*lucha*) bloody, fierce

encarrilar [enkarri'lar] *vt* (*tren*) to put back on the rails; (*fig*) to correct, put on the right track

encasillar [enkasi'ʎar] *vt* (*tb fig*) to pigeonhole; (*actor*) to typecast

encauzar [enkau'θar] *vt* to channel

encendedor [enθende'ðor] *nm* lighter

encender [enθen'der] *vt* (*con fuego*) to light; (*luz, radio*) to put on, switch on; (*avivar: pasiones*) to inflame; **~se** *vr* to catch fire; (*excitarse*) to get excited; (*de cólera*) to flare up; (*el rostro*) to blush

encendido [enθen'diðo] *nm* (*AUTO*) ignition

encerado [enθe'raðo] *nm* (*ESCOL*) blackboard

encerar [enθe'rar] *vt* (*suelo*) to wax, polish

encerrar [enθe'rrar] *vt* (*confinar*) to shut in, shut up; (*comprender, incluir*) to include, contain

encharcado, a [entʃar'kaðo, a] *adj* (*terreno*) flooded

encharcarse [entʃar'karse] *vr* to get flooded

enchufado, a [entʃu'faðo, a] (*fam*) *nm/f* well-connected person

enchufar [entʃu'far] *vt* (*ELEC*) to plug in; (*TEC*) to connect, fit together; **enchufe** *nm* (*ELEC: clavija*) plug; (: *toma*) socket; (*de dos tubos*) joint, connection; (*fam: influencia*) contact, connection; (: *puesto*) cushy job

encía [en'θia] *nf* gum

encienda *etc* *vb ver* **encender**

encierro *etc* [en'θjerro] *vb ver* **encerrar** ♦ *nm* shutting in, shutting up; (*calabozo*) prison

encima [en'θima] *adv* (*sobre*) above, over; (*además*) besides; **~ de** (*en*) on, on top of; (*sobre*) above, over; (*además de*) besides, on top of; **por ~ de** over; **¿llevas dinero ~?** have

you (got) any money on you?; **se me vino ~** it took me by surprise

encina [en'θina] *nf* holm oak

encinta [en'θinta] *adj* pregnant

enclenque [en'klenke] *adj* weak, sickly

encoger [enko'xer] *vt* to shrink, contract; **~se** *vr* to shrink, contract; (*fig*) to cringe; **~se de hombros** to shrug one's shoulders

encolar [enko'lar] *vt* (*engomar*) to glue, paste; (*pegar*) to stick down

encolerizar [enkoleri'θar] *vt* to anger, provoke; **~se** *vr* to get angry

encomendar [enkomen'dar] *vt* to entrust, commend; **~se** *vr*: **~se a** to put one's trust in

encomiar [enko'mjar] *vt* to praise, pay tribute to

encomienda *etc* [enko'mjenda] *vb ver* **encomendar** ♦ *nf* (*encargo*) charge, commission; (*elogio*) tribute; **~ postal** (*AM*) parcel post

encontrado, a [enkon'traðo, a] *adj* (*contrario*) contrary, conflicting

encontrar [enkon'trar] *vt* (*hallar*) to find; (*inesperadamente*) to meet, run into; **~se** *vr* to meet (each other); (*situarse*) to be (situated); **~se con** to meet; **~se bien (de salud)** to feel well

encrespar [enkres'par] *vt* (*cabellos*) to curl; (*fig*) to anger, irritate; **~se** *vr* (*el mar*) to get rough; (*fig*) to get cross, get irritated

encrucijada [enkruθi'xaða] *nf* crossroads *sg*

encuadernación [enkwaðerna'θjon] *nf* binding

encuadernador, a [enkwaðerna'ðor, a] *nm/f* bookbinder

encuadrar [enkwa'ðrar] *vt* (*retrato*) to frame; (*ajustar*) to fit, insert; (*contener*) to contain

encubrir [enku'βrir] *vt* (*ocultar*) to hide, conceal; (*criminal*) to harbour, shelter

encuentro *etc* [en'kwentro] *vb ver* **encontrar** ♦ *nm* (*de personas*) meeting; (*AUTO etc*) collision, crash; (*DEPORTE*) match, game; (*MIL*) encounter

encuesta [en'kwesta] *nf* inquiry, investigation; (*sondeo*) (public) opinion poll; **~ judicial** post mortem

encumbrar [enkum'brar] *vt* (*persona*) to exalt

endeble [en'deβle] *adj* (*argumento, excusa, persona*) weak

endémico, a [en'demiko, a] *adj* (*MED*) endemic; (*fig*) rife, chronic

endemoniado, a [endemo'njaðo, a] *adj* possessed (of the devil); (*travieso*) devilish

enderezar [endere'θar] *vt* (*poner derecho*) to straighten (out); (: *verticalmente*) to set upright; (*situación*) to straighten o sort out; (*dirigir*) to direct; **~se** *vr* (*persona sentada*) to straighten up

endeudarse [endeu'ðarse] vr to get into debt

endiablado, a [endja'ßlaðo, a] adj devilish, diabolical; (travieso) mischievous

endilgar [endil'ɣar] (fam) vt: **~le algo a uno** to lumber sb with sth; **~le un sermón a uno** to lecture sb

endiñar [endi'ɲar] (fam) vt (bofetón) to land, belt

endosar [endo'sar] vt (cheque etc) to endorse

endulzar [endul'θar] vt to sweeten; (suavizar) to soften

endurecer [endure'θer] vt to harden; **~se** vr to harden, grow hard

enema [e'nema] nm (MED) enema

enemigo, a [ene'miɣo, a] adj enemy, hostile ♦ nm/f enemy

enemistad [enemis'taθ] nf enmity

enemistar [enemis'tar] vt to make enemies of, cause a rift between; **~se** vr to become enemies; (amigos) to fall out

energía [ener'xia] nf (vigor) energy, drive; (empuje) push; (TEC, ELEC) energy, power; **~ eólica** wind power; **~ solar** solar energy/power

enérgico, a [e'nerxiko, a] adj (gen) energetic; (voz, modales) forceful

energúmeno, a [ener'ɣumeno, a] (fam) nm/f (fig) madman/woman

enero [e'nero] nm January

enfadado, a [enfa'ðaðo, a] adj angry, annoyed

enfadar [enfa'ðar] vt to anger, annoy; **~se** vr to get angry o annoyed

enfado [en'faðo] nm (enojo) anger, annoyance; (disgusto) trouble, bother

énfasis ['enfasis] nm emphasis, stress

enfático, a [en'fatiko, a] adj emphatic

enfermar [enfer'mar] vt to make ill ♦ vi to fall ill, be taken ill

enfermedad [enferme'ðaθ] nf illness; **~ venérea** venereal disease

enfermera [enfer'mera] nf nurse

enfermería [enferme'ria] nf infirmary; (de colegio etc) sick bay

enfermero [enfer'mero] nm (male) nurse

enfermizo, a [enfer'miθo, a] adj (persona) sickly, unhealthy; (fig) unhealthy

enfermo, a [en'fermo, a] adj ill, sick ♦ nm/f invalid, sick person; (en hospital) patient

enflaquecer [enflake'θer] vt (adelgazar) to make thin; (debilitar) to weaken

enfocar [enfo'kar] vt (foto etc) to focus; (problema etc) to approach

enfoque etc [en'foke] vb ver **enfocar** ♦ nm focus.

enfrascarse [enfras'karse] vr: **~ en algo** to bury o.s. in sth

enfrentar [enfren'tar] vt (peligro) to face (up to), confront; (oponer) to bring face to face; **~se** vr (dos personas) to face o confront each other; (DEPORTE: dos equipos) to meet; **~se a** o **con** to face up to, confront

enfrente [en'frente] adv opposite; **la casa de ~** the house opposite, the house across the street; **~ de** opposite, facing

enfriamiento [enfria'mjento] nm chilling, refrigeration; (MED) cold, chill

enfriar [enfri'ar] vt (alimentos) to cool, chill; (algo caliente) to cool down; **~se** vr to cool down; (MED) to catch a chill; (amistad) to cool

enfurecer [enfure'θer] vt to enrage, madden; **~se** vr to become furious, fly into a rage; (mar) to get rough

engalanar [engala'nar] vt (adornar) to adorn; (ciudad) to decorate; **~se** vr to get dressed up

enganchar [engan'tʃar] vt to hook; (dos vagones) to hitch up; (TEC) to couple, connect; (MIL) to recruit; **~se** vr (MIL) to enlist, join up

enganche [en'gantʃe] nm hook; (TEC) coupling, connection; (acto) hooking (up); (MIL) recruitment, enlistment; (AM: depósito) deposit

engañar [enga'ɲar] vt to deceive; (estafar) to cheat, swindle; **~se** vr (equivocarse) to be wrong; (disimular la verdad) to deceive o.s.

engaño [en'gaɲo] nm deceit; (estafa) trick, swindle; (error) mistake, misunderstanding; (ilusión) delusion; **~so, a** adj (tramposo) crooked; (mentiroso) dishonest, deceitful; (aspecto) deceptive; (consejo) misleading

engarzar [engar'θar] vt (joya) to set, mount; (fig) to link, connect

engatusar [engatu'sar] (fam) vt to coax

engendrar [enxen'drar] vt to breed; (procrear) to beget; (causar) to cause, produce; **engendro** nm (BIO) foetus; (fig) monstrosity

englobar [englo'ßar] vt to include, comprise

engordar [engor'ðar] vt to fatten ♦ vi to get fat, put on weight

engorroso, a [engo'rroso, a] adj bothersome, trying

engranaje [engra'naxe] nm (AUTO) gear

engrandecer [engrande'θer] vt to enlarge, magnify; (alabar) to praise, speak highly of; (exagerar) to exaggerate

engrasar [engra'sar] vt (TEC: poner grasa) to grease; (: lubricar) to lubricate, oil; (manchar) to make greasy

engreído, a [engre'iðo, a] adj vain, conceited

engrosar [engro'sar] vt (ensanchar) to enlarge; (aumentar) to increase; (hinchar) to swell

enhebrar [ene'βrar] vt to thread

enhorabuena [enora'βwena] excl: ¡~! congratulations! ♦ nf: **dar la ~ a** to congratulate

enigma [e'niɣma] nm enigma; (problema) puzzle; (misterio) mystery

enjabonar [enxaβo'nar] vt to soap; (fam: adular) to soft-soap

enjambre [en'xambre] nm swarm

enjaular [enxau'lar] vt to (put in a) cage; (fam) to jail, lock up

enjuagar [enxwa'var] vt (ropa) to rinse (out)

enjuague etc [en'xwave] vb ver **enjuagar** ♦ nm (MED) mouthwash; (de ropa) rinse, rinsing

enjugar [enxu'var] vt to wipe (off); (lágrimas) to dry; (déficit) to wipe out

enjuiciar [enxwi'θjar] vt (JUR: procesar) to prosecute, try; (fig) to judge

enjuto, a [en'xuto, a] adj (flaco) lean, skinny

enlace [en'laθe] nm link, connection; (relación) relationship; (tb: ~ matrimonial) marriage; (de carretera, trenes) connection; ~ **sindical** shop steward

enlatado, a [enla'taðo, a] adj (comida, productos) tinned, canned

enlazar [enla'θar] vt (unir con lazos) to bind together; (atar) to tie; (conectar) to link, connect; (AM) to lasso

enlodar [enlo'ðar] vt to cover in mud; (fig: manchar) to stain; (: rebajar) to debase

enloquecer [enloke'θer] vt to drive mad ♦ vi to go mad; ~**se** vr to go mad

enlutado, a [enlu'taðo, a] adj (persona) in mourning

enmarañar [enmara'ɲar] vt (enredar) to tangle (up), entangle; (complicar) to complicate; (confundir) to confuse; ~**se** vr (enredarse) to become entangled; (confundirse) to get confused

enmarcar [enmar'kar] vt (cuadro) to frame

enmascarar [enmaska'rar] vt to mask; ~**se** vr to put on a mask

enmendar [enmen'dar] vt to emend, correct; (constitución etc) to amend; (comportamiento) to reform; ~**se** vr to reform, mend one's ways; **enmienda** nf correction; amendment; reform

enmohecerse [enmoe'θerse] vr (metal) to rust, go rusty; (muro, plantas) to get mouldy

enmudecer [enmuðe'θer] vi (perder el habla) to fall silent; (guardar silencio) to remain silent

ennegrecer [ennexre'θer] vt (poner negro) to blacken; (oscurecer) to darken; ~**se** vr to turn black; (oscurecerse) to get dark, darken

ennoblecer [ennoβle'θer] vt to ennoble

enojar [eno'xar] vt (encolerizar) to anger; (disgustar) to annoy, upset; ~**se** vr to get angry; to get annoyed

enojo [e'noxo] nm (cólera) anger; (irritación) annoyance; ~**so, a** adj annoying

enorgullecerse [enorɣuʎe'θerse] vr to be proud; ~ **de** to pride o.s. on, be proud of

enorme [e'norme] adj enormous, huge; (fig) monstrous; **enormidad** nf hugeness, immensity

enrarecido, a [enrare'θiðo, a] adj (atmósfera, aire) rarefied

enredadera [enreða'ðera] nf (BOT) creeper, climbing plant

enredar [enre'ðar] vt (cables, hilos etc) to tangle (up), entangle; (situación) to complicate, confuse; (meter cizaña) to sow discord among o between; (implicar) to embroil, implicate; ~**se** vr to get entangled, get tangled (up); (situación) to get complicated; (persona) to get embroiled; (AM: fam) to meddle

enredo [en'reðo] nm (maraña) tangle; (confusión) mix-up, confusion; (intriga) intrigue

enrejado [enre'xaðo] nm fence, railings pl

enrevesado, a [enreβe'saðo, a] adj (asunto) complicated, involved

enriquecer [enrike'θer] vt to make rich, enrich; ~**se** vr to get rich

enrojecer [enroxe'θer] vt to redden ♦ vi (persona) to blush; ~**se** vr to blush

enrolar [enro'lar] vt (MIL) to enlist; (reclutar) to recruit; ~**se** vr (MIL) to join up; (afiliarse) to enrol

enrollar [enro'ʎar] vt to roll (up), wind (up)

enroscar [enros'kar] vt (torcer, doblar) to coil (round), wind; (tornillo, rosca) to screw in; ~**se** vr to coil, wind

ensalada [ensa'laða] nf salad; **ensaladilla (rusa)** nf Russian salad

ensalzar [ensal'θar] vt (alabar) to praise, extol; (exaltar) to exalt

ensamblaje [ensam'blaxe] nm assembly; (TEC) joint

ensanchar [ensan'tʃar] vt (hacer más ancho) to widen; (agrandar) to enlarge, expand; (COSTURA) to let out; ~**se** vr to get wider, expand; **ensanche** nm (de calle) widening

ensangrentar [ensangren'tar] vt to stain with blood

ensañar [ensa'ɲar] vt to enrage; ~**se** vr: ~**se con** to treat brutally

ensartar [ensar'tar] vt (cuentas, perlas etc) to string (together)

ensayar [ensa'jar] vt to test, try (out); (TEATRO) to rehearse

ensayo [en'sajo] nm test, trial; (QUÍM) experiment; (TEATRO) rehearsal; (DEPORTE) try; (ESCOL, LITERATURA) essay

enseguida [ense'viða] adv at once, right away

ensenada [ense'naða] nf inlet, cove

enseñanza [ense'nanθa] nf (educación) education; (acción) teaching; (doctrina) teaching, doctrine

enseñar [ense'nar] vt (educar) to teach; (mostrar, señalar) to show

enseres [en'seres] nmpl belongings

ensillar [ensi'ʎar] vt to saddle (up)

ensimismarse [ensimis'marse] vr (abstraerse) to become lost in thought; (AM) to become conceited

ensombrecer [ensombre'θer] vt to darken, cast a shadow over; (fig) to overshadow, put in the shade

ensordecer [ensorðe'θer] vt to deafen ♦ vi to go deaf

ensortijado, a [ensorti'xaðo, a] adj (pelo) curly

ensuciar [ensu'θjar] vt (manchar) to dirty, soil; (fig) to defile; ~se vr to get dirty; (niño) to wet o.s.

ensueño [en'sweɲo] nm (sueño) dream, fantasy; (ilusión) illusion; (soñando despierto) daydream

entablar [enta'βlar] vt (recubrir) to board (up); (AJEDREZ, DAMAS) to set up; (conversación) to strike up; (JUR) to file ♦ vi to draw

entablillar [entaβli'ʎar] vt (MED) to (put in a) splint

entallar [enta'ʎar] vt (traje) to tailor ♦ vi: **el traje entalla bien** the suit fits well

ente ['ente] nm (organización) body, organization; (fam: persona) odd character

entender [enten'der] vt (comprender) to understand; (darse cuenta) to realize ♦ vi to understand; (creer) to think, believe; ~se vr (comprenderse) to be understood; (2 personas) to get on together; (ponerse de acuerdo) to agree, reach an agreement; ~ de to know all about; ~ algo de to know a little about; ~ en to deal with, have to do with; ~se mal (2 personas) to get on badly

entendido, a [enten'diðo, a] adj (comprendido) understood; (hábil) skilled; (inteligente) knowledgeable ♦ nm/f (experto) expert ♦ excl agreed!; **entendimiento** nm (comprensión) understanding; (inteligencia) mind, intellect; (juicio) judgement

enterado, a [ente'raðo, a] adj well-informed; **estar ~ de** to know about, be aware of

enteramente [entera'mente] adv entirely, completely

enterar [ente'rar] vt (informar) to inform, tell; ~se vr to find out, get to know

entereza [ente'reθa] nf (totalidad) entirety; (fig: carácter) strength of mind; (: honradez) integrity

enternecer [enterne'θer] vt (ablandar) to soften; (apiadar) to touch, move; ~se vr to be touched, be moved

entero, a [en'tero, a] adj (total) whole, entire; (fig: honesto) honest; (: firme) firm, resolute ♦ nm (COM: punto) point; (AM: pago) payment

enterrador [enterra'ðor] nm gravedigger

enterrar [ente'rrar] vt to bury

entibiar [enti'βjar] vt (enfriar) to cool; (calentar) to warm; ~se vr (fig) to cool

entidad [enti'ðað] nf (empresa) firm, company; (organismo) body; (sociedad) society; (FILOSOFÍA) entity

entiendo etc vb ver **entender**

entierro [en'tjerro] nm (acción) burial; (funeral) funeral

entonación [entona'θjon] nf (LING) intonation

entonar [ento'nar] vt (canción) to intone; (colores) to tone; (MED) to tone up ♦ vi to be in tune

entonces [en'tonθes] adv then, at that time; **desde ~** since then; **en aquel ~** at that time; **(pues) ~** and so

entornar [entor'nar] vt (puerta, ventana) to half close, leave ajar; (los ojos) to screw up

entorpecer [entorpe'θer] vt (entendimiento) to dull; (impedir) to obstruct, hinder; (: tránsito) to slow down, delay

entrada [en'traða] nf (acción) entry, access; (sitio) entrance, way in; (INFORM) input; (COM) receipts pl, takings pl; (CULIN) starter; (DEPORTE) innings sg; (TEATRO) house, audience; (billete) ticket; (COM): ~s y salidas income and expenditure; (TEC): ~ de aire air intake o inlet; de ~ from the outset

entrado, a [en'traðo, a] adj: ~ **en años** elderly; **una vez ~ el verano** in the summer(time), when summer comes

entramparse [entram'parse] vr to get into debt

entrante [en'trante] adj next, coming; **mes/ año ~** next month/year; ~**s** nmpl starters

entraña [en'traɲa] nf (fig: centro) heart, core; (raíz) root; ~**s** nfpl (ANAT) entrails; (fig) heart sg; **sin ~s** (fig) heartless; **entrañable** adj close, intimate; **entrañar** vt to entail

entrar [en'trar] vt (introducir) to bring in; (INFORM) to input ♦ vi (meterse) to go in, come in, enter; (comenzar): ~ **diciendo** to begin by saying; **hacer ~** to show in; **no me entra** I can't get the hang of it

entre ['entre] prep (dos) between; (más de dos) among(st)

entreabrir [entrea'βrir] vt to half-open, open halfway

entrecejo [entre'θexo] nm: **fruncir el ~** to

frown

entrecortado, a [entrekor'taðo, a] *adj*
(*respiración*) difficult; (*habla*) faltering

entredicho [entre'ðitʃo] *nm* (*JUR*) injunction;
poner en ~ to cast doubt on; **estar en ~** to be
in doubt

entrega [en'treγa] *nf* (*de mercancías*)
delivery; (*de novela etc*) instalment

entregar [entre'γar] *vt* (*dar*) to hand (over),
deliver; **~se** *vr* (*rendirse*) to surrender, give in,
submit; (*dedicarse*) to devote o.s.

entrelazar [entrela'θar] *vt* to entwine

entremeses [entre'meses] *nmpl* hors
d'œuvres

entremeter [entreme'ter] *vt* to insert, put
in; **~se** *vr* to meddle, interfere;
entremetido, a *adj* meddling, interfering

entremezclar [entremeθ'klar] *vt* to
intermingle; **~se** *vr* to intermingle

entrenador, a [entrena'ðor, a] *nm/f* trainer,
coach

entrenarse [entre'narse] *vr* to train

entrepierna [entre'pjerna] *nf* crotch

entresacar [entresa'kar] *vt* to pick out, select

entresuelo [entre'swelo] *nm* mezzanine

entretanto [entre'tanto] *adv* meanwhile,
meantime

entretejer [entrete'xer] *vt* to interweave

entretener [entrete'ner] *vt* (*divertir*) to
entertain, amuse; (*detener*) to hold up, delay;
~se *vr* (*divertirse*) to amuse o.s.; (*retrasarse*)
to delay, linger; **entretenido, a** *adj*
entertaining, amusing; **entretenimiento** *nm*
entertainment, amusement

entrever [entre'ßer] *vt* to glimpse, catch a
glimpse of

entrevista [entre'ßista] *nf* interview;
entrevistar *vt* to interview; **entrevistarse** *vr*
to have an interview

entristecer [entriste'θer] *vt* to sadden,
grieve; **~se** *vr* to grow sad

entrometerse [entrome'terse] *vr*: **~ (en)** to
interfere (in o with)

entroncar [entron'kar] *vi* to be connected o
related

entumecer [entume'θer] *vt* to numb,
benumb; **~se** *vr* (*por el frío*) to become
numb; **entumecido, a** *adj* numb, stiff

enturbiar [entur'ßjar] *vt* (*el agua*) to make
cloudy; (*fig*) to confuse; **~se** *vr* (*oscurecerse*)
to become cloudy; (*fig*) to get confused,
become obscure

entusiasmar [entusjas'mar] *vt* to excite, fill
with enthusiasm; (*gustar mucho*) to delight;
~se *vr*: **~se con** o **por** to get enthusiastic o
excited about

entusiasmo [entu'sjasmo] *nm* enthusiasm;
(*excitación*) excitement

entusiasta [entu'sjasta] *adj* enthusiastic

♦ *nm/f* enthusiast

enumerar [enume'rar] *vt* to enumerate

enunciación [enunθja'θjon] *nf* enunciation

enunciado [enun'θjaðo] *nm* enunciation

envainar [embai'nar] *vt* to sheathe

envalentonar [embalento'nar] *vt* to give
courage to; **~se** *vr* (*pey: jactarse*) to boast,
brag

envanecer [embane'θer] *vt* to make
conceited; **~se** *vr* to grow conceited

envasar [emba'sar] *vt* (*empaquetar*) to pack,
wrap; (*enfrascar*) to bottle; (*enlatar*) to can;
(*embolsar*) to pocket

envase [em'base] *nm* (*en paquete*) packing,
wrapping; (*en botella*) bottling; (*en lata*)
canning; (*recipiente*) container; (*paquete*)
package; (*botella*) bottle; (*lata*) tin (*BRIT*), can

envejecer [embexe'θer] *vt* to make old, age
♦ *vi* (*volverse viejo*) to grow old; (*parecer
viejo*) to age; **~se** *vr* to grow old; to age

envenenar [embene'nar] *vt* to poison; (*fig*)
to embitter

envergadura [emberγa'ðura] *nf* (*fig*) scope,
compass

envés [em'bes] *nm* (*de tela*) back, wrong side

enviar [em'bjar] *vt* to send

enviciarse [embi'θjarse] *vr*: **~ (con)** to get
addicted (to)

envidia [em'biðja] *nf* envy; **tener ~ a** to envy,
be jealous of; **envidiar** *vt* to envy

envío [em'bio] *nm* (*acción*) sending; (*de
mercancías*) consignment; (*de dinero*)
remittance

enviudar [embju'ðar] *vi* to be widowed

envoltura [embol'tura] *nf* (*cobertura*) cover;
(*embalaje*) wrapper, wrapping; **envoltorio**
nm package

envolver [embol'ßer] *vt* to wrap (up);
(*cubrir*) to cover; (*enemigo*) to surround;
(*implicar*) to involve, implicate

envuelto [em'bwelto] *pp de* envolver

enyesar [enje'sar] *vt* (*pared*) to plaster;
(*MED*) to put in plaster

enzarzarse [enθar'θarse] *vr*: **~ en** (*pelea*) to
get mixed up in; (*disputa*) to get involved in

épica ['epika] *nf* epic

épico, a ['epiko, a] *adj* epic

epidemia [epi'ðemja] *nf* epidemic

epilepsia [epi'lepsja] *nf* epilepsy

epílogo [e'piloxo] *nm* epilogue

episodio [epi'soðjo] *nm* episode

epístola [e'pistola] *nf* epistle

época ['epoka] *nf* period, time; (*HISTORIA*)
age, epoch; **hacer ~** to be epoch-making

equilibrar [ekili'ßrar] *vt* to balance;
equilibrio *nm* balance, equilibrium;
equilibrista *nm/f* (*funámbulo*) tightrope
walker; (*acróbata*) acrobat

equipaje [eki'paxe] *nm* luggage; (*avíos*):

~ **de mano** hand luggage

equipar [eki'par] vt (proveer) to equip

equipararse [ekipa'rarse] vr: ~ **con** to be on a level with

equipo [e'kipo] nm (conjunto de cosas) equipment; (DEPORTE) team; (de obreros) shift

equis ['ekis] nf inv (the letter) X

equitación [ekita'θjon] nf horse riding

equitativo, a [ekita'tiβo, a] adj equitable, fair

equivalente [ekiβa'lente] adj, nm equivalent

equivaler [ekiβa'ler] vi to be equivalent o equal

equivocación [ekiβoka'θjon] nf mistake, error

equivocado, a [ekiβo'kaðo, a] adj wrong, mistaken

equivocarse [ekiβo'karse] vr to be wrong, make a mistake; ~ **de camino** to take the wrong road

equívoco, a [e'kiβoko, a] adj (dudoso) suspect; (ambiguo) ambiguous ♦ nm ambiguity; (malentendido) misunderstanding

era ['era] vb ver **ser** ♦ nf era, age

erais vb ver **ser**

éramos vb ver **ser**

eran vb ver **ser**

erario [e'rarjo] nm exchequer (BRIT), treasury

eras vb ver **ser**

erección [erek'θjon] nf erection

eres vb ver **ser**

erguir [er'xir] vt to raise, lift; (poner derecho) to straighten; ~**se** vr to straighten up

erigir [eri'xir] vt to erect, build; ~**se** vr: ~**se en** to set o.s. up as

erizarse [eri'θarse] vr (pelo: de perro) to bristle; (: de persona) to stand on end

erizo [e'riθo] nm (ZOOL) hedgehog; ~ **de mar** sea-urchin

ermita [er'mita] nf hermitage

ermitaño, a [ermi'taɲo, a] nm/f hermit

erosión [ero'sjon] nf erosion

erosionar [erosjo'nar] vt to erode

erótico, a [e'rotiko, a] adj erotic; **erotismo** nm eroticism

erradicar [erraði'kar] vt to eradicate

errante [e'rrante] adj wandering, errant

errar [e'rrar] vi (vagar) to wander, roam; (equivocarse) to be mistaken ♦ vt: ~ **el camino** to take the wrong road; ~ **el tiro** to miss

erróneo, a [e'rroneo, a] adj (equivocado) wrong, mistaken

error [e'rror] nm error, mistake; (INFORM) bug; ~ **de imprenta** misprint

eructar [eruk'tar] vt to belch, burp

erudito, a [eru'ðito, a] adj erudite, learned

erupción [erup'θjon] nf eruption; (MED) rash

es vb ver **ser**

esa ['esa] (pl **esas**) adj demos ver **ese**

ésa ['esa] (pl **ésas**) pron ver **ése**

esbelto, a [es'βelto, a] adj slim, slender

esbozo [es'βoθo] nm sketch, outline

escabeche [eska'βetʃe] nm brine; (de aceitunas etc) pickle; **en** ~ pickled

escabroso, a [eska'βroso, a] adj (accidentado) rough, uneven; (fig) tough, difficult; (: atrevido) risqué

escabullirse [eskaβu'ʎirse] vr to slip away, to clear out

escafandra [eska'fandra] nf (buzo) diving suit; (~ espacial) space suit

escala [es'kala] nf (proporción, MUS) scale; (de mano) ladder; (AVIAT) stopover; **hacer** ~ **en** to stop o call in at

escalafón [eskala'fon] nm (escala de salarios) salary scale, wage scale

escalar [eska'lar] vt to climb, scale

escalera [eska'lera] nf stairs pl, staircase; (escala) ladder; (NAIPES) run; ~ **mecánica** escalator; ~ **de caracol** spiral staircase

escalfar [eskal'far] vt (huevos) to poach

escalinata [eskali'nata] nf staircase

escalofriante [eskalo'frjante] adj chilling

escalofrío [eskalo'frio] nm (MED) chill; ~**s** nmpl (fig) shivers

escalón [eska'lon] nm step, stair; (de escalera) rung

escalope [eska'lope] nm (CULIN) escalope

escama [es'kama] nf (de pez, serpiente) scale; (de jabón) flake; (fig) resentment

escamar [eska'mar] vt (fig) to make wary o suspicious

escamotear [eskamote'ar] vt (robar) to lift, swipe; (hacer desaparecer) to make disappear

escampar [eskam'par] vb impers to stop raining

escandalizar [eskandali'θar] vt to scandalize, shock; ~**se** vr to be shocked; (ofenderse) to be offended

escándalo [es'kandalo] nm scandal; (alboroto, tumulto) row, uproar; **escandaloso, a** adj scandalous, shocking

escandinavo, a [eskandi'naβo, a] adj, nm/f Scandinavian

escaño [es'kaɲo] nm bench; (POL) seat

escapar [eska'par] vi (gen) to escape, run away; (DEPORTE) to break away; ~**se** vr to escape, get away; (agua, gas) to leak (out)

escaparate [eskapa'rate] nm shop window

escape [es'kape] nm (de agua, gas) leak; (de motor) exhaust

escarabajo [eskara'βaxo] nm beetle

escaramuza [eskara'muθa] nf skirmish

escarbar [eskar'βar] vt (tierra) to scratch

escarceos [eskar'θeos] nmpl (fig): **en mis** ~ **con la política ...** in my dealings with politics **...**; ~ **amorosos** love affairs

escarcha [es'kartʃa] nf frost
escarchado, a [eskar'tʃaðo, a] adj (CULIN: fruta) crystallized
escarlata [eskar'lata] adj inv scarlet; **escarlatina** nf scarlet fever
escarmentar [eskarmen'tar] vt to punish severely ♦ vi to learn one's lesson
escarmiento etc [eskar'mjento] vb ver **escarmentar** ♦ nm (ejemplo) lesson; (castigo) punishment
escarnio [es'karnjo] nm mockery; (injuria) insult
escarola [eska'rola] nf endive
escarpado, a [eskar'paðo, a] adj (pendiente) sheer, steep; (rocas) craggy
escasear [eskase'ar] vi to be scarce
escasez [eska'seθ] nf (falta) shortage, scarcity; (pobreza) poverty
escaso, a [es'kaso, a] adj (poco) scarce; (raro) rare; (ralo) thin, sparse; (limitado) limited
escatimar [eskati'mar] vt to skimp (on), be sparing with
escayola [eska'jola] nf plaster
escena [es'θena] nf scene
escenario [esθe'narjo] nm (TEATRO) stage; (CINE) set; (fig) scene; **escenografía** nf set design
escepticismo [esθepti'θismo] nm scepticism; **escéptico, a** adj sceptical ♦ nm/f sceptic
escisión [esθi'sjon] nf (de partido, secta) split
esclarecer [esklare'θer] vt (misterio, problema) to shed light on
esclavitud [esklaβi'tuð] nf slavery
esclavizar [esklaβi'θar] vt to enslave
esclavo, a [es'klaβo, a] nm/f slave
esclusa [es'klusa] nf (de canal) lock; (compuerta) floodgate
escoba [es'koβa] nf broom; **escobilla** nf brush
escocer [esko'θer] vi to burn, sting; ~se vr to chafe, get chafed
escocés, esa [esko'θes, esa] adj Scottish ♦ nm/f Scotsman/woman, Scot
Escocia [es'koθja] nf Scotland
escoger [esko'xer] vt to choose, pick, select; **escogido, a** adj chosen, selected
escolar [esko'lar] adj school cpd ♦ nm/f schoolboy/girl, pupil
escollo [es'koʎo] nm (obstáculo) pitfall
escolta [es'kolta] nf escort; **escoltar** vt to escort
escombros [es'kombros] nmpl (basura) rubbish sg; (restos) debris sg
esconder [eskon'der] vt to hide, conceal; ~se vr to hide; **escondidas** (AM) nfpl: a **escondidas** secretly; **escondite** nm hiding place; (juego) hide-and-seek; **escondrijo** nm

hiding place, hideout
escopeta [esko'peta] nf shotgun
escoria [es'korja] nf (de alto horno) slag; (fig) scum, dregs pl
Escorpio [es'korpjo] nm Scorpio
escorpión [eskor'pjon] nm scorpion
escotado, a [esko'taðo, a] adj low-cut
escote [es'kote] nm (de vestido) low neck; **pagar a ~** to share the expenses
escotilla [esko'tiʎa] nf (NAUT) hatch(way)
escozor [esko'θor] nm (dolor) sting(ing)
escribir [eskri'βir] vt, vi to write; **~ a máquina** to type; **¿cómo se escribe?** how do you spell it?
escrito, a [es'krito, a] pp de **escribir** ♦ nm (documento) document; (manuscrito) text, manuscript; **por ~** in writing
escritor, a [eskri'tor, a] nm/f writer
escritorio [eskri'torjo] nm desk
escritura [eskri'tura] nf (acción) writing; (caligrafía) (hand)writing; (JUR: documento) deed
escrúpulo [es'krupulo] nm scruple; (minuciosidad) scrupulousness; **escrupuloso, a** adj scrupulous
escrutar [eskru'tar] vt to scrutinize, examine; (votos) to count
escrutinio [eskru'tinjo] nm (examen atento) scrutiny; (POL: recuento de votos) count(ing)
escuadra [es'kwaðra] nf (MIL etc) squad; (NAUT) squadron; (de coches etc) fleet; **escuadrilla** nf (de aviones) squadron; (AM: de obreros) gang
escuadrón [eskwa'ðron] nm squadron
escuálido, a [es'kwaliðo, a] adj skinny, scraggy; (sucio) squalid
escuchar [esku'tʃar] vt to listen to ♦ vi to listen
escudilla [esku'ðiʎa] nf bowl, basin
escudo [es'kuðo] nm shield
escudriñar [eskuðri'ɲar] vt (examinar) to investigate, scrutinize; (mirar de lejos) to scan
escuela [es'kwela] nf school; **~ de artes y oficios** (ESP) ≈ technical college; **~ normal** teacher training college
escueto, a [es'kweto, a] adj plain; (estilo) simple
escuincle [es'kwinkle] (AM: fam) nm/f kid
esculpir [eskul'pir] vt to sculpt; (grabar) to engrave; (tallar) to carve; **escultor, a** nm/f sculptor/tress; **escultura** nf sculpture
escupidera [eskupi'ðera] nf spittoon
escupir [esku'pir] vt, vi to spit (out)
escurreplatos [eskurre'platos] nm inv plate rack
escurridizo, a [eskurri'ðiθo, a] adj slippery
escurridor [eskurri'ðor] nm colander
escurrir [esku'rrir] vt (ropa) to wring out; (verduras, platos) to drain ♦ vi (líquidos) to

drip; **~se** vr (secarse) to drain; (resbalarse) to slip, slide; (escaparse) to slip away

ese ['ese] (f **esa**, pl **esos, esas**) adj demos (sg) that; (pl) those

ése ['ese] (f **ésa**, pl **ésos, ésas**) pron (sg) that (one); (pl) those (ones); **~ ... éste ...** the former ... the latter ...; **no me vengas con ésas** don't give me any more of that nonsense

esencia [e'senθja] nf essence; **esencial** adj essential

esfera [es'fera] nf sphere; (de reloj) face; **esférico, a** adj spherical

esforzarse [esfor'θarse] vr to exert o.s., make an effort

esfuerzo etc [es'fwerθo] vb ver esforzar ♦ nm effort

esfumarse [esfu'marse] vr (apoyo, esperanzas) to fade away

esgrima [es'ɣrima] nf fencing

esgrimir [esɣri'mir] vt (arma) to brandish; (argumento) to use

esguince [es'ɣinθe] nm (MED) sprain

eslabón [esla'ɓon] nm link

eslip [ez'lip] nm pants pl (BRIT), briefs pl

eslovaco, a [eslo'ɓako, a] adj, nm/f Slovak, Slovakian ♦ nm (LING) Slovak, Slovakian

Eslovaquia [eslo'ɓakja] nf Slovakia

esmaltar [esmal'tar] vt to enamel; **esmalte** nm enamel; **esmalte de uñas** nail varnish o polish

esmerado, a [esme'raðo, a] adj careful, neat

esmeralda [esme'ralda] nf emerald

esmerarse [esme'rarse] vr (aplicarse) to take great pains, exercise great care; (afanarse) to work hard

esmero [es'mero] nm (great) care

esnob [es'nob] (pl **~s**) adj (persona) snobbish ♦ nm/f snob; **~ismo** nm snobbery

eso ['eso] pron that, that thing o matter; **~ de su coche** that business about his car; **~ de ir al cine** all that about going to the cinema; **a ~ de las cinco** at about five o'clock; **en ~** thereupon, at that point; **~ es** that's it; **¡~ sí que es vida!** now that is really living!; **por ~ te lo dije** that's why I told you; **y ~ que llovía** in spite of the fact it was raining

esos ['esos] adj demos ver ese

ésos ['esos] pron ver ése

espabilar etc [espaβi'lar] = despabilar etc

espacial [espa'θjal] adj (del espacio) space cpd

espaciar [espa'θjar] vt to space (out)

espacio [es'paθjo] nm space; (MUS) interval; (RADIO, TV) programme (BRIT), program (US); **el ~** space; **~so, a** spacious, roomy

espada [es'paða] nf sword; **~s** nfpl (NAIPES) spades

espaguetis [espa'ɣetis] nmpl spaghetti sg

espalda [es'palda] nf (gen) back; **~s** nfpl (hombros) shoulders; **a ~s de uno** behind sb's back; **tenderse de ~s** to lie (down) on one's back; **volver la ~ a alguien** to cold-shoulder sb

espantajo [espan'taxo] nm = espantapájaros

espantapájaros [espanta'paxaros] nm inv scarecrow

espantar [espan'tar] vt (asustar) to frighten, scare; (ahuyentar) to frighten off; (asombrar) to horrify, appal; **~se** vr to get frightened o scared; to be appalled

espanto [es'panto] nm (susto) fright; (terror) terror; (asombro) astonishment; **~so, a** adj frightening; terrifying; astonishing

España [es'paɲa] nf Spain; **español, a** adj Spanish ♦ nm/f Spaniard ♦ nm (LING) Spanish

esparadrapo [espara'ðrapo] nm (sticking) plaster (BRIT), adhesive tape (US)

esparcimiento [esparθi'mjento] nm (dispersión) spreading; (diseminación) scattering; (fig) cheerfulness

esparcir [espar'θir] vt to spread; (diseminar) to scatter; **~se** vr to spread (out); to scatter; (divertirse) to enjoy o.s.

espárrago [es'parraɣo] nm asparagus

esparto [es'parto] nm esparto (grass)

espasmo [es'pasmo] nm spasm

espátula [es'patula] nf spatula

especia [es'peθja] nf spice

especial [espe'θjal] adj special; **~idad** nf speciality (BRIT), specialty (US)

especie [es'peθje] nf (BIO) species; (clase) kind, sort; **en ~** in kind

especificar [espeθifi'kar] vt to specify; **específico, a** adj specific

espécimen [es'peθimen] (pl **especímenes**) nm specimen

espectáculo [espek'takulo] nm (gen) spectacle; (TEATRO etc) show

espectador, a [espekta'ðor, a] nm/f spectator

espectro [es'pektro] nm ghost; (fig) spectre

especular [espeku'lar] vt, vi to speculate

espejismo [espe'xismo] nm mirage

espejo [es'pexo] nm mirror; **~ retrovisor** rear-view mirror

espeluznante [espeluθ'nante] adj horrifying, hair-raising

espera [es'pera] nf (pausa, intervalo) wait; (JUR: plazo) respite; **en ~ de** waiting for; (con expectativa) expecting

esperanza [espe'ranθa] nf (confianza) hope; (expectativa) expectation; **hay pocas ~s de que venga** there is little prospect of his coming

esperar [espe'rar] vt (aguardar) to wait for; (tener expectativa de) to expect; (desear) to hope for ♦ vi to wait; to expect; to hope

esperma [es'perma] nf sperm

espesar [espe'sar] *vt* to thicken; **~se** *vr* to thicken, get thicker

espeso, a [es'peso, a] *adj* thick; **espesor** *nm* thickness

espía [es'pia] *nm/f* spy; **espiar** *vt* (*observar*) to spy on

espiga [es'piɣa] *nf* (BOT: *de trigo etc*) ear

espigón [espi'ɣon] *nm* (BOT) ear; (NAUT) breakwater

espina [es'pina] *nf* thorn; (*de pez*) bone; **~ dorsal** (ANAT) spine

espinaca [espi'naka] *nf* spinach

espinazo [espi'naθo] *nm* spine, backbone

espinilla [espi'niʎa] *nf* (ANAT: *tibia*) shin(bone); (*grano*) blackhead

espinoso, a [espi'noso, a] *adj* (*planta*) thorny, prickly; (*asunto*) difficult

espionaje [espjo'naxe] *nm* spying, espionage

espiral [espi'ral] *adj*, *nf* spiral

espirar [espi'rar] *vt* to breathe out, exhale

espiritista [espiri'tista] *adj*, *nm/f* spiritualist

espíritu [es'piritu] *nm* spirit; **espiritual** *adj* spiritual

espita [es'pita] *nf* tap

espléndido, a [es'plendiðo, a] *adj* (*magnífico*) magnificent, splendid; (*generoso*) generous

esplendor [esplen'dor] *nm* splendour

espolear [espole'ar] *vt* to spur on

espoleta [espo'leta] *nf* (*de bomba*) fuse

espolón [espo'lon] *nm* sea wall

espolvorear [espolβore'ar] *vt* to dust, sprinkle

esponja [es'ponxa] *nf* sponge; (*fig*) sponger; **esponjoso, a** *adj* spongy

espontaneidad [espontanei'ðað] *nf* spontaneity; **espontáneo, a** *adj* spontaneous

esposa [es'posa] *nf* wife; **~s** *nfpl* handcuffs; **esposar** *vt* to handcuff

esposo [es'poso] *nm* husband

espray [es'prai] *nm* spray

espuela [es'pwela] *nf* spur

espuma [es'puma] *nf* foam; (*de cerveza*) froth, head; (*de jabón*) lather; **espumadera** *nf* (*utensilio*) skimmer; **espumoso, a** *adj* frothy, foamy; (*vino*) sparkling

esqueleto [eske'leto] *nm* skeleton

esquema [es'kema] *nm* (*diagrama*) diagram; (*dibujo*) plan; (FILOSOFÍA) schema

esquí [es'ki] (*pl* **~s**) *nm* (*objeto*) ski; (DEPORTE) skiing; **~ acuático** water-skiing; **esquiar** *vi* to ski

esquilar [eski'lar] *vt* to shear

esquimal [eski'mal] *adj*, *nm/f* Eskimo

esquina [es'kina] *nf* corner

esquinazo [eski'naθo] *nm*: **dar ~ a algn** to give sb the slip

esquirol [eski'rol] *nm* blackleg

esquivar [eski'βar] *vt* to avoid

esquivo, a [es'kiβo, a] *adj* evasive; (*tímido*) reserved; (*huraño*) unsociable

esta ['esta] *adj demos ver* **este²**

está *vb ver* **estar**

ésta ['esta] *pron ver* **éste**

estabilidad [estaβili'ðað] *nf* stability; **estable** *adj* stable

establecer [estaβle'θer] *vt* to establish; **~se** *vr* to establish o.s.; (*echar raíces*) to settle (down); **establecimiento** *nm* establishment

establo [es'taβlo] *nm* (AGR) stable

estaca [es'taka] *nf* stake, post; (*de tienda de campaña*) peg

estacada [esta'kaða] *nf* (*cerca*) fence, fencing; (*palenque*) stockade

estación [esta'θjon] *nf* station; (*del año*) season; **~ de autobuses** bus station; **~ balnearia** seaside resort; **~ de servicio** service station

estacionamiento [estaθjona'mjento] *nm* (AUTO) parking; (MIL) stationing

estacionar [estaθjo'nar] *vt* (AUTO) to park; (MIL) to station; **~io, a** *adj* stationary; (COM: *mercado*) slack

estadio [es'taðjo] *nm* (*fase*) stage, phase; (DEPORTE) stadium

estadista [esta'ðista] *nm* (POL) statesman; (ESTADÍSTICA) statistician

estadística [esta'ðistika] *nf* figure, statistic; (*ciencia*) statistics *sg*

estado [es'taðo] *nm* (POL: *condición*) state; **~ de ánimo** state of mind; **~ de cuenta** bank statement; **~ de sitio** state of siege; **~ civil** marital status; **~ mayor** staff; **estar en ~** to be pregnant; **(los) E~s Unidos** *nmpl* the United States (of America) *sg*

estadounidense [estaðouni'ðense] *adj* United States *cpd*, American ♦ *nm/f* American

estafa [es'tafa] *nf* swindle, trick; **estafar** *vt* to swindle, defraud

estafeta [esta'feta] *nf* (*oficina de correos*) post office; **~ diplomática** diplomatic bag

estáis *vb ver* **estar**

estallar [esta'ʎar] *vi* to burst; (*bomba*) to explode, go off; (*epidemia, guerra, rebelión*) to break out; **~ en llanto** to burst into tears; **estallido** *nm* explosion; (*fig*) outbreak

estampa [es'tampa] *nf* print, engraving

estampado, a [estam'paðo, a] *adj* printed ♦ *nm* (*impresión: acción*) printing; (: *efecto*) print; (*marca*) stamping

estampar [estam'par] *vt* (*imprimir*) to print; (*marcar*) to stamp; (*metal*) to engrave; (*poner sello en*) to stamp; (*fig*) to stamp, imprint

estampida [estam'piða] *nf* stampede

estampido [estam'piðo] *nm* bang, report

están *vb ver* **estar**

estancado, a [estaŋ'kaðo, a] *adj* stagnant

estancar [estaŋ'kar] *vt* (*aguas*) to hold up, hold back; (*COM*) to monopolize; (*fig*) to block, hold up; **~se** *vr* to stagnate

estancia [es'tanθja] *nf* (*permanencia*) stay; (*sala*) room; (*AM*) farm, ranch; **estanciero** (*AM*) *nm* farmer, rancher

estanco, a [es'tanko, a] *adj* watertight ♦ *nm* tobacconist's (shop), cigar store (*US*)

estándar [es'tandar] *adj, nm* standard; **estandarizar** *vt* to standardize

estandarte [estan'darte] *nm* banner, standard

estanque [es'tanke] *nm* (*lago*) pool, pond; (*AGR*) reservoir

estanquero, a [estan'kero, a] *nm/f* tobacconist

estante [es'tante] *nm* (*armario*) rack, stand; (*biblioteca*) bookcase; (*anaquel*) shelf; (*AM*) prop; **estantería** *nf* shelving, shelves *pl*

estaño [es'taɲo] *nm* tin

PALABRA CLAVE
---

estar [es'tar] *vi* **1** (*posición*) to be; **está en la plaza** it's in the square; **¿está Juan?** is Juan in?; **estamos a 30 km de Junín** we're 30 kms from Junín

2 (+ *adj: estado*) to be; **~ enfermo** to be ill; **está muy elegante** he's looking very smart; **¿cómo estás?** how are you keeping?

3 (+ *gerundio*) to be; **estoy leyendo** I'm reading

4 (*uso pasivo*): **está condenado a muerte** he's been condemned to death; **está envasado en ...** it's packed in ...

5 (*con fechas*): **¿a cuántos estamos?** what's the date today?; **estamos a 5 de mayo** it's the 5th of May

6 (*locuciones*): **¿estamos?** (*¿de acuerdo?*) okay?; (*¿listo?*) ready?; **¡ya está bien!** that's enough!

7: **~ de**: **~ de vacaciones/viaje** to be on holiday/away o on a trip; **está de camarero** he's working as a waiter

8: **~ para**: **está para salir** he's about to leave; **no estoy para bromas** I'm not in the mood for jokes

9: **~ por** (*propuesta etc*) to be in favour of; (*persona etc*) to support, side with; **está por limpiar** it still has to be cleaned

10: **~ sin**: **~ sin dinero** to have no money; **está sin terminar** it isn't finished yet

♦ **~se** *vr*: **se estuvo en la cama toda la tarde** he stayed in bed all afternoon

---

estas ['estas] *adj demos ver* **este²**
éstas ['estas] *pron ver* **éste**
estatal [esta'tal] *adj* state *cpd*
estático, a [es'tatiko, a] *adj* static

estatua [es'tatwa] *nf* statue

estatura [esta'tura] *nf* stature, height

estatuto [esta'tuto] *nm* (*JUR*) statute; (*de ciudad*) bye-law; (*de comité*) rule

este¹ ['este] *nm* east

este² ['este] (*f* **esta**, *pl* **estos, estas**) *adj demos* (*sg*) this; (*pl*) these

esté *etc vb ver* **estar**

éste ['este] (*f* **ésta**, *pl* **éstos, éstas**) *pron* (*sg*) this (one); (*pl*) these (ones); **ése ... ~ ...** the former ... the latter ....

estelar [este'lar] *adj* (*ASTRO*) stellar; (*actuación, reparto*) star (*atr*)

estepa [es'tepa] *nf* (*GEO*) steppe

estera [es'tera] *nf* mat(ting)

estéreo [es'tereo] *adj inv, nm* stereo; **estereotipo** *nm* stereotype

estéril [es'teril] *adj* sterile, barren; (*fig*) vain, futile; **esterilizar** *vt* to sterilize

esterlina [ester'lina] *adj*: **libra ~** pound sterling

estés *etc vb ver* **estar**

estética [es'tetika] *nf* aesthetics *sg*

estético, a [es'tetiko, a] *adj* aesthetic

estibador [estiβa'ðor] *nm* stevedore, docker

estiércol [es'tjerkol] *nm* dung, manure

estigma [es'tiɣma] *nm* stigma

estilarse [esti'larse] *vr* to be in fashion

estilo [es'tilo] *nm* style; (*TEC*) stylus; (*NATACIÓN*) stroke; **algo por el ~** something along those lines

estima [es'tima] *nf* esteem, respect

estimación [estima'θjon] *nf* (*evaluación*) estimation; (*aprecio, afecto*) esteem, regard

estimar [esti'mar] *vt* (*evaluar*) to estimate; (*valorar*) to value; (*apreciar*) to esteem, respect; (*pensar, considerar*) to think, reckon

estimulante [estimu'lante] *adj* stimulating ♦ *nm* stimulant

estimular [estimu'lar] *vt* to stimulate; (*excitar*) to excite

estímulo [es'timulo] *nm* stimulus; (*ánimo*) encouragement

estipulación [estipula'θjon] *nf* stipulation, condition

estipular [estipu'lar] *vt* to stipulate

estirado, a [esti'raðo, a] *adj* (*tenso*) (stretched o drawn) tight; (*fig: persona*) stiff, pompous

estirar [esti'rar] *vt* to stretch; (*dinero, suma etc*) to stretch out; **~se** *vr* to stretch

estirón [esti'ron] *nm* pull, tug; (*crecimiento*) spurt, sudden growth; **dar un ~** (*niño*) to shoot up

estirpe [es'tirpe] *nf* stock, lineage

estival [esti'βal] *adj* summer *cpd*

esto ['esto] *pron* this, this thing o matter; **~ de la boda** this business about the wedding

Estocolmo [esto'kolmo] *nm* Stockholm

estofado [esto'faðo] *nm* stew

estofar [esto'far] *vt* to stew

estómago [es'tomaxo] *nm* stomach; **tener ~** to be thick-skinned

estorbar [estor'βar] *vt* to hinder, obstruct; (*molestar*) to bother, disturb ♦ *vi* to be in the way, **estorbo** *nm* (*molestia*) bother, nuisance; (*obstáculo*) hindrance, obstacle

estornudar [estornu'ðar] *vi* to sneeze

estos ['estos] *adj demos ver* **este²**

éstos ['estos] *pron ver* **éste**

estoy *vb ver* **estar**

estrado [es'traðo] *nm* platform

estrafalario, a [estrafa'larjo, a] *adj* odd, eccentric

estrago [es'traxo] *nm* ruin, destruction; **hacer ~s en** to wreak havoc among

estragón [estra'xon] *nm* tarragon

estrambótico, a [estram'botiko, a] *adj* (*persona*) eccentric; (*peinado, ropa*) outlandish

estrangulador, a [estrangula'ðor, a] *nm/f* strangler ♦ *nm* (*TEC*) throttle; (*AUTO*) choke

estrangular [estrangu'lar] *vt* (*persona*) to strangle; (*MED*) to strangulate

estratagema [estrata'xema] *nf* (*MIL*) stratagem; (*astucia*) cunning

estrategia [estra'texja] *nf* strategy; **estratégico, a** *adj* strategic

estrato [es'trato] *nm* stratum, layer

estrechamente [es'tretʃamente] *adv* (*íntimamente*) closely, intimately; (*pobremente*: vivir) poorly

estrechar [estre'tʃar] *vt* (*reducir*) to narrow; (*COSTURA*) to take in; (*abrazar*) to hug, embrace; **~se** *vr* (*reducirse*) to narrow, grow narrow; (*abrazarse*) to embrace; **~ la mano** to shake hands

estrechez [estre'tʃeθ] *nf* narrowness; (*de ropa*) tightness; **estrecheces** *nfpl* (*dificultades económicas*) financial difficulties

estrecho, a [es'tretʃo, a] *adj* narrow; (*apretado*) tight; (*íntimo*) close, intimate; (*miserable*) mean ♦ *nm* strait; **~ de miras** narrow-minded

estrella [es'treʎa] *nf* star; **~ de mar** (*ZOOL*) starfish; **~ fugaz** shooting star; **estrellado, a** *adj* (*forma*) star-shaped; (*cielo*) starry

estrellar [estre'ʎar] *vt* (*hacer añicos*) to smash (to pieces); (*huevos*) to fry; **~se** *vr* to smash; (*chocarse*) to crash; (*fracasar*) to fail

estremecer [estreme'θer] *vt* to shake; **~se** *vr* to shake, tremble; **estremecimiento** *nm* (*temblor*) trembling, shaking

estrenar [estre'nar] *vt* (*vestido*) to wear for the first time; (*casa*) to move into; (*película, obra de teatro*) to première; **~se** *vr* (*persona*) to make one's début; **estreno** *nm* (*CINE etc*) première

estreñido, a [estre'ɲiðo, a] *adj* constipated

estreñimiento [estreɲi'mjento] *nm* constipation

estrépito [es'trepito] *nm* noise, racket; (*fig*) fuss; **estrepitoso, a** *adj* noisy; (*fiesta*) rowdy

estría [es'tria] *nf* groove

estribación [estriβa'θjon] *nf* (*GEO*) spur, foothill

estribar [estri'βar] *vi*: **~ en** to lie on

estribillo [estri'βiʎo] *nm* (*LITERATURA*) refrain; (*MUS*) chorus

estribo [es'triβo] *nm* (*de jinete*) stirrup; (*de coche, tren*) step; (*de puente*) support; (*GEO*) spur; **perder los ~s** to fly off the handle

estribor [estri'βor] *nm* (*NAUT*) starboard

estricto, a [es'trikto, a] *adj* (*riguroso*) strict; (*severo*) severe

estridente [estri'ðente] *adj* (*color*) loud; (*voz*) raucous

estropajo [estro'paxo] *nm* scourer

estropear [estrope'ar] *vt* to spoil; (*dañar*) to damage; **~se** *vr* (*objeto*) to get damaged; (*persona*: la piel etc) to be ruined

estructura [estruk'tura] *nf* structure

estruendo [es'trwendo] *nm* (*ruido*) racket, din; (*fig*: alboroto) uproar, turmoil

estrujar [estru'xar] *vt* (*apretar*) to squeeze; (*aplastar*) to crush; (*fig*) to drain, bleed

estuario [es'twarjo] *nm* estuary

estuche [es'tutʃe] *nm* box, case

estudiante [estu'ðjante] *nm/f* student; **estudiantil** *adj* student *cpd*

estudiar [estu'ðjar] *vt* to study

estudio [es'tuðjo] *nm* study; (*CINE, ARTE, RADIO*) studio; **~s** *nmpl* studies; (*erudición*) learning *sg*; **~so, a** *adj* studious

estufa [es'tufa] *nf* heater, fire

estupefaciente [estupefa'θjente] *nm* drug, narcotic

estupefacto, a [estupe'fakto, a] *adj* speechless, thunderstruck

estupendo, a [estu'pendo, a] *adj* wonderful, terrific; (*fam*) great; **¡~!** that's great!, fantastic!

estupidez [estupi'ðeθ] *nf* (*torpeza*) stupidity; (*acto*) stupid thing (to do)

estúpido, a [es'tupiðo, a] *adj* stupid, silly

estupor [estu'por] *nm* stupor; (*fig*) astonishment, amazement

estuve *etc vb ver* **estar**

esvástica [es'βastika] *nf* swastika

ETA ['eta] (*ESP*) *nf abr* (= Euskadi ta Askatasuna) ETA

etapa [e'tapa] *nf* (*de viaje*) stage; (*DEPORTE*) leg; (*parada*) stopping place; (*fase*) stage, phase

etarra [e'tarra] *nm/f* member of ETA

etc. *abr* (= etcétera) etc

etcétera [et'θetera] *adv* etcetera

eternidad [eterni'ðað] *nf* eternity; **eterno, a** *adj* eternal, everlasting

ética ['etika] *nf* ethics *pl*

ético, a ['etiko, a] *adj* ethical

etiqueta [eti'keta] *nf* (*modales*) etiquette; (*rótulo*) label, tag

Eucaristía [eukaris'tia] *nf* Eucharist

eufemismo [eufe'mismo] *nm* euphemism

euforia [eu'forja] *nf* euphoria

euro ['euro] *sm* (*moneda*) euro

eurodiputado, a [eurodipu'taðo, a] *nm/f* Euro MP, MEP

Europa [eu'ropa] *nf* Europe; **europeo, a** *adj, nm/f* European

Euskadi [eus'kaði] *nm* the Basque Country o Provinces *pl*

euskera [eus'kera] *nm* (LING) Basque

evacuación [eßakwa'θjon] *nf* evacuation

evacuar [eßa'kwar] *vt* to evacuate

evadir [eßa'ðir] *vt* to evade, avoid; ~**se** *vr* to escape

evaluar [eßa'lwar] *vt* to evaluate

evangelio [eßan'xeljo] *nm* gospel

evaporar [eßapo'rar] *vt* to evaporate; ~**se** *vr* to vanish

evasión [eßa'sjon] *nf* escape, flight; (*fig*) evasion; ~ **de capitales** flight of capital

evasiva [eßa'sißa] *nf* (*pretexto*) excuse

evasivo, a [eßa'sißo, a] *adj* evasive, non-committal

evento [e'ßento] *nm* event

eventual [eßen'twal] *adj* possible, conditional (upon circumstances); (*trabajador*) casual, temporary

evidencia [eßi'ðenθja] *nf* evidence, proof; **evidenciar** *vt* (*hacer patente*) to make evident; (*probar*) to prove, show; **evidenciarse** *vr* to be evident

evidente [eßi'ðente] *adj* obvious, clear, evident

evitar [eßi'tar] *vt* (*evadir*) to avoid; (*impedir*) to prevent

evocar [eßo'kar] *vt* to evoke, call forth

evolución [eßolu'θjon] *nf* (*desarrollo*) evolution, development; (*cambio*) change; (MIL) manoeuvre; **evolucionar** *vi* to evolve; to manoeuvre

ex [eks] *adj* ex-; **el ~ ministro** the former minister, the ex-minister

exacerbar [eksaθer'ßar] *vt* to irritate, annoy

exactamente [eksakta'mente] *adv* exactly

exactitud [eksakti'tuð] *nf* exactness; (*precisión*) accuracy; (*puntualidad*) punctuality; **exacto, a** *adj* exact; accurate; punctual; **¡exacto!** exactly!

exageración [eksaxera'θjon] *nf* exaggeration

exagerar [eksaxe'rar] *vt, vi* to exaggerate

exaltado, a [eksal'taðo, a] *adj* (*apasionado*) over-excited, worked-up; (POL) extreme

exaltar [eksal'tar] *vt* to exalt, glorify; ~**se** *vr* (*excitarse*) to get excited o worked-up

examen [ek'samen] *nm* examination

examinar [eksami'nar] *vt* to examine; ~**se** *vr* to be examined, take an examination

exasperar [eksaspe'rar] *vt* to exasperate; ~**se** *vr* to get exasperated, lose patience

Exca. *abr* = **Excelencia**

excavadora [ekskaßa'ðora] *nf* excavator

excavar [ekska'ßar] *vt* to excavate

excedencia [eksθe'ðenθja] *nf:* **estar en ~** to be on leave; **pedir** o **solicitar la ~** to ask for leave

excedente [eksθe'ðente] *adj, nm* excess, surplus

exceder [eksθe'ðer] *vt* to exceed, surpass; ~**se** *vr* (*extralimitarse*) to go too far

excelencia [eksθe'lenθja] *nf* excellence; **E~** Excellency; **excelente** *adj* excellent

excentricidad [eksθentriθi'ðað] *nf* eccentricity; **excéntrico, a** *adj, nm/f* eccentric

excepción [eksθep'θjon] *nf* exception; **excepcional** *adj* exceptional

excepto [eks'θepto] *adv* excepting, except (for)

exceptuar [eksθep'twar] *vt* to except, exclude

excesivo, a [eksθe'sißo, a] *adj* excessive

exceso [eks'θeso] *nm* (*gen*) excess; (COM) surplus; ~ **de equipaje/peso** excess luggage/weight

excitación [eksθita'θjon] *nf* (*sensación*) excitement; (*acción*) excitation

excitado, a [eksθi'taðo, a] *adj* excited; (*emociones*) aroused

excitar [eksθi'tar] *vt* to excite; (*incitar*) to urge; ~**se** *vr* to get excited

exclamación [eksklama'θjon] *nf* exclamation

exclamar [ekscla'mar] *vi* to exclaim

excluir [eksklu'ir] *vt* to exclude; (*dejar fuera*) to shut out; (*descartar*) to reject; **exclusión** *nf* exclusion

exclusiva [eksklu'sißa] *nf* (PRENSA) exclusive, scoop; (COM) sole right

exclusivo, a [eksklu'sißo, a] *adj* exclusive; **derecho ~** sole o exclusive right

Excmo. *abr* = **excelentísimo**

excomulgar [ekskomul'var] *vt* (REL) to excommunicate

excomunión [ekskomu'njon] *nf* excommunication

excursión [ekskur'sjon] *nf* excursion, outing; **excursionista** *nm/f* (*turista*) sightseer

excusa [eks'kusa] *nf* excuse; (*disculpa*) apology

excusar [eksku'sar] vt to excuse; **~se** vr (disculparse) to apologize

exhalar [eksa'lar] vt to exhale, breathe out; (olor etc) to give off; (suspiro) to breathe, heave

exhaustivo, a [eksaus'tiβo, a] adj (análisis) thorough; (estudio) exhaustive

exhausto, a [ek'sausto, a] adj exhausted

exhibición [eksiβi'θjon] nf exhibition, display, show

exhibir [eksi'βir] vt to exhibit, display, show

exhortar [eksor'tar] vt: **~ a** to exhort to

exigencia [eksi'xenθja] nf demand, requirement; **exigente** adj demanding

exigir [eksi'xir] vt (gen) to demand, require; **~ el pago** to demand payment

exiliado, a [eksi'ljaðo, a] adj exiled ♦ nm/f exile

exilio [ek'siljo] nm exile

eximir [eksi'mir] vt to exempt

existencia [eksis'tenθja] nf existence; **~s** nfpl stock(s) (pl)

existir [eksis'tir] vi to exist, be

éxito ['eksito] nm (triunfo) success; (MUS etc) hit; **tener ~** to be successful

exonerar [eksone'rar] vt to exonerate; **~ de una obligación** to free from an obligation

exorbitante [eksorβi'tante] adj (precio) exorbitant; (cantidad) excessive

exorcizar [eksorθi'θar] vt to exorcize

exótico, a [ek'sotiko, a] adj exotic

expandir [ekspan'dir] vt to expand

expansión [ekspan'sjon] nf expansion

expansivo, a [ekspan'siβo, a] adj: **onda ~a** shock wave

expatriarse [ekspa'trjarse] vr to emigrate; (POL) to go into exile

expectativa [ekspekta'tiβa] nf (espera) expectation; (perspectiva) prospect

expedición [ekspeði'θjon] nf (excursión) expedition

expediente [ekspe'ðjente] nm expedient; (JUR: procedimento) action, proceedings pl; (: papeles) dossier, file, record

expedir [ekspe'ðir] vt (despachar) to send, forward; (pasaporte) to issue

expendedor, a [ekspende'ðor, a] nm/f (vendedor) dealer

expensas [eks'pensas] nfpl: **a ~ de** at the expense of

experiencia [ekspe'rjenθja] nf experience

experimentado, a [eksperimen'taðo, a] adj experienced

experimentar [eksperimen'tar] vt (en laboratorio) to experiment with; (probar) to test, try out; (notar, observar) to experience; (deterioro, pérdida) to suffer; **experimento** nm experiment

experto, a [eks'perto, a] adj expert, skilled

♦ nm/f expert

expiar [ekspi'ar] vt to atone for

expirar [ekspi'rar] vi to expire

explanada [ekspla'naða] nf (llano) plain

explayarse [ekspla'jarse] vr (en discurso) to speak at length; **~ con uno** to confide in sb

explicación [eksplika'θjon] nf explanation

explicar [ekspli'kar] vt to explain; **~se** vr to explain (o.s.)

explícito, a [eks'pliθito, a] adj explicit

explique etc vb ver **explicar**

explorador, a [eksplora'ðor, a] nm/f (pionero) explorer; (MIL) scout ♦ nm (MED) probe; (TEC) (radar) scanner

explorar [eksplo'rar] vt to explore; (MED) to probe; (radar) to scan

explosión [eksplo'sjon] nf explosion; **explosivo, a** adj explosive

explotación [eksplota'θjon] nf exploitation; (de planta etc) running

explotar [eksplo'tar] vt to exploit; to run, operate ♦ vi to explode

exponer [ekspo'ner] vt to expose; (cuadro) to display; (vida) to risk; (idea) to explain; **~se** vr: **~se a (hacer) algo** to run the risk of (doing) sth

exportación [eksporta'θjon] nf (acción) export; (mercancías) exports pl

exportar [ekspor'tar] vt to export

exposición [eksposi'θjon] nf (gen) exposure; (de arte) show, exhibition; (explicación) explanation; (de declaración) account, statement

expresamente [ekspresa'mente] adv (decir) clearly; (a propósito) expressly

expresar [ekspre'sar] vt to express; **expresión** nf expression

expresivo, a [ekspre'siβo, a] adj (persona, gesto, palabras) expressive; (cariñoso) affectionate

expreso, a [eks'preso, a] pp de **expresar** ♦ adj (explícito) express; (claro) specific, clear; (tren) fast ♦ adv: **mandar ~** to send by express (delivery)

express [eks'pres] (AM) adv: **enviar algo ~** to send sth special delivery

exprimidor [eksprimi'ðor] nm squeezer

exprimir [ekspri'mir] vt (fruta) to squeeze; (zumo) to squeeze out

expropiar [ekspro'pjar] vt to expropriate

expuesto, a [eks'pwesto, a] pp de **exponer** ♦ adj exposed; (cuadro etc) on show, on display

expulsar [ekspul'sar] vt (echar) to eject, throw out; (alumno) to expel; (despedir) to sack, fire; (DEPORTE) to send off; **expulsión** nf expulsion; sending-off

exquisito, a [ekski'sito, a] adj exquisite; (comida) delicious

éxtasis ['ekstasis] *nm* ecstasy

extender [eksten'der] *vt* to extend; (*los brazos*) to stretch out, hold out; (*mapa, tela*) to spread (out), open (out); (*mantequilla*) to spread; (*certificado*) to issue; (*cheque, recibo*) to make out; (*documento*) to draw up; **~se** *vr* (*gen*) to extend; (*persona: en el suelo*) to stretch out; (*epidemia*) to spread; **extendido, a** *adj* (*abierto*) spread out, open; (*brazos*) outstretched; (*costumbre*) widespread

extensión [eksten'sjon] *nf* (*de terreno, mar*) expanse, stretch; (*de tiempo*) length, duration; (*TEL*) extension; **en toda la ~ de la palabra** in every sense of the word

extenso, a [eks'tenso, a] *adj* extensive

extenuar [ekste'nwar] *vt* (*debilitar*) to weaken

exterior [ekste'rjor] *adj* (*de fuera*) external; (*afuera*) outside, exterior; (*apariencia*) outward; (*deuda, relaciones*) foreign ♦ *nm* (*gen*) exterior, outside; (*aspecto*) outward appearance; (*DEPORTE*) wing(er); (*países extranjeros*) abroad; **en el ~** abroad; **al ~** outwardly, on the surface

exterminar [ekstermi'nar] *vt* to exterminate; **exterminio** *nm* extermination

externo, a [eks'terno, a] *adj* (*exterior*) external, outside; (*superficial*) outward ♦ *nm/f* day pupil

extinguir [ekstin'gir] *vt* (*fuego*) to extinguish, put out; (*raza, población*) to wipe out; **~se** *vr* (*fuego*) to go out; (*BIO*) to die out, become extinct

extinto, a [eks'tinto, a] *adj* extinct

extintor [ekstin'tor] *nm* (fire) extinguisher

extirpar [ekstir'par] *vt* (*MED*) to remove (surgically)

extorsión [ekstor'sjon] *nf* extortion

extra ['ekstra] *adj inv* (*tiempo*) extra; (*chocolate, vino*) good-quality ♦ *nm/f* extra ♦ *nm* extra; (*bono*) bonus

extracción [ekstrak'θjon] *nf* extraction; (*en lotería*) draw

extracto [eks'trakto] *nm* extract

extradición [ekstraði'θjon] *nf* extradition

extraer [ekstra'er] *vt* to extract, take out

extraescolar [ekstraesko'lar] *adj*: **actividad ~** extracurricular activity

extralimitarse [ekstralimi'tarse] *vr* to go too far

extranjero, a [ekstran'xero, a] *adj* foreign ♦ *nm/f* foreigner ♦ *nm* foreign countries *pl*; **en el ~** abroad

extrañar [ekstra'ɲar] *vt* (*sorprender*) to find strange o odd; (*echar de menos*) to miss; **~se** *vr* (*sorprenderse*) to be amazed, be surprised

extrañeza [ekstra'ɲeθa] *nf* (*rareza*) strangeness, oddness; (*asombro*) amazement, surprise

extraño, a [eks'traɲo, a] *adj* (*extranjero*) foreign; (*raro, sorprendente*) strange, odd

extraordinario, a [ekstraorði'narjo, a] *adj* extraordinary; (*edición, número*) special ♦ *nm* (*de periódico*) special edition; **horas extraordinarias** overtime *sg*

extrarradio [ekstra'rraðjo] *nm* suburbs

extravagancia [ekstraßa'vanθja] *nf* oddness; outlandishness; **extravagante** *adj* (*excéntrico*) eccentric; (*estrafalario*) outlandish

extraviado, a [ekstra'ßjaðo, a] *adj* lost, missing

extraviar [ekstra'ßjar] *vt* (*persona: desorientar*) to mislead, misdirect; (*perder*) to lose, misplace; **~se** *vr* to lose one's way, get lost; **extravio** *nm* loss; (*fig*) deviation

extremar [ekstre'mar] *vt* to carry to extremes; **~se** *vr* to do one's utmost, make every effort

extremaunción [ekstremaun'θjon] *nf* extreme unction

extremidad [ekstremi'ðað] *nf* (*punta*) extremity; **~es** *nfpl* (*ANAT*) extremities

extremo, a [eks'tremo, a] *adj* extreme; (*último*) last ♦ *nm* end; (*límite, grado sumo*) extreme; **en último ~** as a last resort

extrovertido, a [ekstroßer'tiðo, a] *adj, nm/f* extrovert

exuberancia [eksuße'ranθja] *nf* exuberance; **exuberante** *adj* exuberant; (*fig*) luxuriant, lush

eyacular [ejaku'lar] *vt, vi* to ejaculate

F, f

f.a.b. *abr* (= *franco a bordo*) f.o.b.

fabada [fa'ßaða] *nf* bean and sausage stew

fábrica [fa'ßrika] *nf* factory; **marca de ~** trademark; **precio de ~** factory price

fabricación [faßrika'θjon] *nf* (*manufactura*) manufacture; (*producción*) production; **de ~ casera** home-made; **~ en serie** mass production

fabricante [faßri'kante] *nm/f* manufacturer

fabricar [faßri'kar] *vt* (*manufacturar*) to manufacture, make; (*construir*) to build; (*cuento*) to fabricate, devise

fábula ['faßula] *nf* (*cuento*) fable; (*chisme*) rumour; (*mentira*) fib

fabuloso, a [faßu'loso, a] *adj* (*oportunidad, tiempo*) fabulous, great

facción [fak'θjon] *nf* (*POL*) faction; **facciones** *nfpl* (*del rostro*) features

faceta [fa'θeta] *nf* facet

facha ['fatʃa] *nf* (*fam*) (*aspecto*) look; (*cara*) face

fachada [fa'tʃaða] *nf* (*ARQ*) façade, front

fácil ['faθil] *adj* (*simple*) easy; (*probable*) likely

facilidad [faθili'ðaθ] *nf* (*capacidad*) ease; (*sencillez*) simplicity; (*de palabra*) fluency; **~es** *nfpl* facilities

facilitar [faθili'tar] *vt* (*hacer fácil*) to make easy; (*proporcionar*) to provide

fácilmente [fa'θilmente] *adv* easily

facsímil [fak'simil] *nm* facsimile, fax

factible [fak'tiβle] *adj* feasible

factor [fak'tor] *nm* factor

factura [fak'tura] *nf* (*cuenta*) bill; **facturación** *nf* (*de equipaje*) check-in; **facturar** *vt* (*COM*) to invoice, charge for; (*equipaje*) to check in

facultad [fakul'taθ] *nf* (*aptitud, ESCOL etc*) faculty; (*poder*) power

faena [fa'ena] *nf* (*trabajo*) work; (*quehacer*) task, job

faisán [fai'san] *nm* pheasant

faja ['faxa] *nf* (*para la cintura*) sash; (*de mujer*) corset; (*de tierra*) strip

fajo ['faxo] *nm* (*de papeles*) bundle; (*de billetes*) wad

falacia [fa'laθja] *nf* fallacy

falda ['falda] *nf* (*prenda de vestir*) skirt

falla ['faʎa] *nf* (*defecto*) fault, flaw

fallar [fa'ʎar] *vt* (*JUR*) to pronounce sentence on ♦ *vi* (*memoria*) to fail; (*motor*) to miss

fallecer [faʎe'θer] *vi* to pass away, die; **fallecimiento** *nm* decease, demise

fallido, a [fa'ʎiðo, a] *adj* (*gen*) frustrated, unsuccessful

fallo ['faʎo] *nm* (*JUR*) verdict, ruling; (*fracaso*) failure; **~ cardíaco** heart failure

falsedad [false'ðaθ] *nf* falseness; (*hipocresía*) hypocrisy; (*mentira*) falsehood

falsificar [falsifi'kar] *vt* (*firma etc*) to forge; (*moneda*) to counterfeit

falso, a ['falso, a] *adj* false; (*documento, moneda etc*) fake; **en ~** falsely

falta ['falta] *nf* (*defecto*) fault, flaw; (*privación*) lack, want; (*ausencia*) absence; (*carencia*) shortage; (*equivocación*) mistake; (*DEPORTE*) foul; **echar en ~** to miss; **hacer ~ hacer algo** to be necessary to do sth; **me hace ~ una pluma** I need a pen; **~ de educación** bad manners *pl*

faltar [fal'tar] *vi* (*escasear*) to be lacking, be wanting; (*ausentarse*) to be absent, be missing; **faltan 2 horas para llegar** there are 2 hours to go till arrival; **~ al respeto a uno** to be disrespectful to sb; **¡no faltaba más!** (*no hay de qué*) don't mention it

fama ['fama] *nf* (*renombre*) fame; (*reputación*) reputation

famélico, a [fa'meliko, a] *adj* starving

familia [fa'milja] *nf* family; **~ política** in-laws *pl*

familiar [fami'ljar] *adj* (*relativo a la familia*) family *cpd*; (*conocido, informal*) familiar ♦ *nm* relative, relation; **~idad** *nf* (*gen*) familiarity; (*informalidad*) homeliness; **~izarse** *vr*: **~izarse con** to familiarize o.s. with

famoso, a [fa'moso, a] *adj* (*renombrado*) famous

fanático, a [fa'natiko, a] *adj* fanatical ♦ *nm/f* fanatic; (*CINE, DEPORTE*) fan; **fanatismo** *nm* fanaticism

fanfarrón, ona [fanfa'rron, ona] *adj* boastful

fango ['fango] *nm* mud; **~so, a** *adj* muddy

fantasía [fanta'sia] *nf* fantasy, imagination; **joyas de ~** imitation jewellery *sg*

fantasma [fan'tasma] *nm* (*espectro*) ghost, apparition; (*fanfarrón*) show-off

fantástico, a [fan'tastiko, a] *adj* fantastic

farmacéutico, a [farma'θeutiko, a] *adj* pharmaceutical ♦ *nm/f* chemist (*BRIT*), pharmacist

farmacia [far'maθja] *nf* chemist's (shop) (*BRIT*), pharmacy; **~ de turno** duty chemist; **~ de guardia** all-night chemist

fármaco [far'mako] *nm* drug

faro ['faro] *nm* (*NAUT: torre*) lighthouse; (*AUTO*) headlamp; **~s antiniebla** fog lamps; **~s delanteros/traseros** headlights/rear lights

farol [fa'rol] *nm* lantern, lamp

farola [fa'rola] *nf* street lamp (*BRIT*) o light (*US*)

farsa ['farsa] *nf* (*gen*) farce

farsante [far'sante] *nm/f* fraud, fake

fascículo [fas'θikulo] *nm* (*de revista*) part, instalment

fascinar [fasθi'nar] *vt* (*gen*) to fascinate

fascismo [fas'θismo] *nm* fascism; **fascista** *adj, nm/f* fascist

fase ['fase] *nf* phase

fastidiar [fasti'ðjar] *vt* (*molestar*) to annoy, bother; (*estropear*) to spoil; **~se** *vr*: **¡que se fastidie!** (*fam*) he'll just have to put up with it!

fastidio [fas'tiðjo] *nm* (*molestia*) annoyance; **~so, a** *adj* (*molesto*) annoying

fastuoso, a [fas'twoso, a] *adj* (*banquete, boda*) lavish; (*acto*) pompous

fatal [fa'tal] *adj* (*gen*) fatal; (*desgraciado*) ill-fated; (*fam: malo, pésimo*) awful; **~idad** *nf* (*destino*) fate; (*mala suerte*) misfortune

fatiga [fa'tiɣa] *nf* (*cansancio*) fatigue, weariness

fatigar [fati'ɣar] *vt* to tire, weary; **~se** *vr* to get tired

fatigoso, a [fati'ɣoso, a] *adj* (*cansador*) tiring

fatuo, a ['fatwo, a] *adj* (*vano*) fatuous; (*presuntuoso*) conceited

favor [fa'βor] *nm* favour; **estar a ~ de** to be in favour of; **haga el ~ de...** would you be so good as to..., kindly...; **por ~** please; **~able** *adj* favourable

favorecer [faβore'θer] vt to favour; (vestido etc) to become, flatter; **este peinado le favorece** this hairstyle suits him

favorito, a [faβo'rito, a] adj, nm/f favourite

fax [faks] nm inv fax; **mandar por ~ to** to fax

faz [faθ] nf face; **la ~ de la tierra** the face of the earth

fe [fe] nf (REL) faith; (documento) certificate; **prestar ~ a** to believe, credit; **actuar con buena/mala ~** to act in good/bad faith; **dar ~ de** to bear witness to

fealdad [feal'dað] nf ugliness

febrero [fe'βrero] nm February

febril [fe'βril] adj (fig: actividad) hectic; (mente, mirada) feverish

fecha [ˈfetʃa] nf date; **~ de caducidad** (de producto alimenticio) sell-by date; (de contrato etc) expiry date; **con ~ adelantada** postdated; **en ~ próxima** soon; **hasta la ~** to date, so far; **poner a ~** to date; **fechar** vt to date

fecundar [fekun'dar] vt (generar) to fertilize, make fertile; **fecundo, a** adj (fértil) fertile; (fig) prolific; (productivo) productive

federación [feðera'θjon] nf federation

felicidad [feliθi'ðað] nf happiness; **~es** nfpl (felicitaciones) best wishes, congratulations

felicitación [feliθita'θjon] nf: **¡felicitaciones!** congratulations!

felicitar [feliθi'tar] vt to congratulate

feligrés, esa [feli'ɣres, esa] nm/f parishioner

feliz [fe'liθ] adj happy

felpudo [fel'puðo] nm doormat

femenino, a [feme'nino, a] adj, nm feminine

feminista [femi'nista] adj, nm/f feminist

fenómeno [fe'nomeno] nm phenomenon; (fig) freak, accident ♦ adj great ♦ excl great!, marvellous!; **fenomenal** adj = **fenómeno**

feo, a [ˈfeo, a] adj (gen) ugly; (desagradable) bad, nasty

féretro [ˈferetro] nm (ataúd) coffin; (sarcófago) bier

feria [ˈferja] nf (gen) fair; (descanso) holiday, rest day; (AM: mercado) village market; (: cambio) loose o small change

fermentar [fermen'tar] vi to ferment

ferocidad [feroθi'ðað] nf fierceness, ferocity

feroz [fe'roθ] adj (cruel) cruel; (salvaje) fierce

férreo, a [ˈferreo, a] adj iron

ferretería [ferrete'ria] nf (tienda) ironmonger's (shop) (BRIT), hardware store

ferrocarril [ferroka'rril] nm railway

ferroviario, a [ferro'βjarjo, a] adj rail cpd

fértil [ˈfertil] adj (productivo) fertile; (rico) rich; **fertilidad** nf (gen) fertility; (productividad) fruitfulness

ferviente [fer'βjente] adj fervent

fervor [fer'βor] nm fervour; **~oso, a** adj fervent

festejar [feste'xar] vt (celebrar) to celebrate

festejo [fes'texo] nm celebration; **festejos** nmpl (fiestas) festivals

festín [fes'tin] nm feast, banquet

festival [festi'ßal] nm festival

festividad [festiβi'ðað] nf festivity

festivo, a [fes'tiβo, a] adj (de fiesta) festive; (CINE, LITERATURA) humorous; **día ~** holiday

fétido, a [ˈfetiðo, a] adj foul-smelling

feto [ˈfeto] nm foetus

fiable [ˈfjaβle] adj (persona) trustworthy; (máquina) reliable

fiador, a [fia'ðor, a] nm/f (JUR) surety, guarantor; (COM) backer; **salir ~ por uno** to stand bail for sb

fiambre [ˈfjambre] nm cold meat

fianza [ˈfjanθa] nf surety; (JUR): **libertad bajo ~** release on bail

fiar [fi'ar] vt (salir garante de) to guarantee; (vender a crédito) to sell on credit; (secreto): **~ a** to confide (to) ♦ vi to trust; **~se** vr to trust (in), rely on; **~se de uno** to rely on sb

fibra [ˈfiβra] nf fibre; **~ óptica** optical fibre

ficción [fik'θjon] nf fiction

ficha [ˈfitʃa] nf (TEL) token; (en juegos) counter, marker; (tarjeta) (index) card; **fichar** vt (archivar) to file, index; (DEPORTE) to sign; **estar fichado** to have a record; **fichero** nm box file; (INFORM) file

ficticio, a [fik'tiθjo, a] adj (imaginario) fictitious; (falso) fabricated

fidelidad [fiðeli'ðað] nf (lealtad) fidelity, loyalty; **alta ~** high fidelity, hi-fi

fideos [fi'ðeos] nmpl noodles

fiebre [ˈfjeβre] nf (MED) fever; (fig) fever, excitement; **~ amarilla/del heno** yellow/hay fever; **~ palúdica** malaria; **tener ~** to have a temperature

fiel [fjel] adj (leal) faithful, loyal; (fiable) reliable; (exacto) accurate, faithful ♦ nm: **los ~es** the faithful

fieltro [ˈfjeltro] nm felt

fiera [ˈfjera] nf (animal feroz) wild animal o beast; (fig) dragon; ver tb **fiero**

fiero, a [ˈfjero, a] adj (cruel) cruel; (feroz) fierce; (duro) harsh

fiesta [ˈfjesta] nf party; (de pueblo) festival; (vacaciones, tb: ~s) holiday sg; (REL): **~ de guardar** day of obligation

figura [fi'ɣura] nf (gen) figure; (forma, imagen) shape, form; (NAIPES) face card

figurar [fiɣu'rar] vt (representar) to represent; (fingir) to figure ♦ vi to figure; **~se** vr (imaginarse) to imagine; (suponer) to suppose

fijador [fixa'ðor] nm (FOTO etc) fixative; (de pelo) gel

fijar [fi'xar] vt (gen) to fix; (estampilla) to affix, stick (on); **~se** vr: **~se en** to notice

fijo, a [ˈfixo, a] adj (gen) fixed; (firme) firm;

(*permanente*) permanent ♦ *adv*: **mirar ~ to stare**

fila ['fila] *nf* row; (*MIL*) rank; **ponerse en ~ to line up, get into line**

filántropo, a |fi'lantropo, a| *nm/f* philanthropist

filatelia |fila'telia| *nf* philately, stamp collecting

filete [fi'lete] *nm* (*carne*) fillet steak; (*pescado*) fillet

filiación [filja'θjon] *nf* (*POL*) affiliation

filial [fi'ljal] *adj* filial ♦ *nf* subsidiary

Filipinas [fili'pinas] *nfpl*: **las ~ the Philippines; filipino, a** *adj, nm/f* Philippine

filmar [fil'mar] *vt* to film, shoot

filo ['filo] *nm* (*gen*) edge; **sacar ~ a to sharpen; al ~ del mediodía** at about midday; **de doble ~** double-edged

filón [fi'lon] *nm* (*MINERÍA*) vein, lode; (*fig*) goldmine

filosofía [filoso'fia] *nf* philosophy; **filósofo, a** *nm/f* philosopher

filtrar [fil'trar] *vt, vi* to filter, strain; **~se vr** to filter; **filtro** *nm* (*TEC, utensilio*) filter

fin [fin] *nm* end; (*objetivo*) aim, purpose; **al ~ y al cabo** when all's said and done; **a ~ de** in order to; **por ~** finally; **en ~** in short; **~ de semana** weekend

final [fi'nal] *adj* final ♦ *nm* end, conclusion ♦ *nf* final; **~idad** *nf* (*propósito*) purpose, intention; **~ista** *nm/f* finalist; **~izar** *vt* to end, finish; (*INFORM*) to log out o off ♦ *vi* to end, come to an end

financiar [finan'θjar] *vt* to finance; **financiero, a** *adj* financial ♦ *nm/f* financier

finca ['finka] *nf* (*bien inmueble*) property, land; (*casa de campo*) country house; (*AM*) farm

fingir [fin'xir] *vt* (*simular*) to simulate, feign ♦ *vi* (*aparentar*) to pretend

finlandés, esa [finlan'des, esa] *adj* Finnish ♦ *nm/f* Finn ♦ *nm* (*LING*) Finnish

Finlandia [fin'landja] *nf* Finland

fino, a ['fino, a] *adj* fine; (*delgado*) slender; (*de buenas maneras*) polite, refined; (*jerez*) fino, dry

firma ['firma] *nf* signature; (*COM*) firm, company

firmamento [firma'mento] *nm* firmament

firmar [fir'mar] *vt* to sign

firme ['firme] *adj* firm; (*estable*) stable; (*sólido*) solid; (*constante*) steady; (*decidido*) resolute ♦ *nm* road (surface); **~mente** *adv* firmly; **~za** *nf* firmness; (*constancia*) steadiness; (*solidez*) solidity

fiscal [fis'kal] *adj* fiscal ♦ *nm/f* public prosecutor; **año ~** tax o fiscal year

fisco ['fisko] *nm* (*hacienda*) treasury, exchequer (*BRIT*)

fisgar [fis'var] *vt* to pry into

fisgonear [fisvone'ar] *vt* to poke one's nose into ♦ *vi* to pry, spy

física ['fisika] *nf* physics *sg*; *ver tb* **físico**

físico, a ['fisiko, a] *adj* physical ♦ *nm* physique ♦ *nm/f* physicist

fisura [fi'sural *nf* crack; (*MED*) fracture

flác(c)ido, a ['fla(k)θiðo, a] *adj* flabby

flaco, a ['flako, a] *adj* (*muy delgado*) skinny, thin; (*débil*) weak, feeble

flagrante [fla'vrante] *adj* flagrant

flamante [fla'mante] (*fam*) *adj* brilliant; (*nuevo*) brand-new

flamenco, a [fla'menko, a] *adj* (*de Flandes*) Flemish; (*baile, música*) flamenco ♦ *nm* (*baile, música*) flamenco

flan [flan] *nm* creme caramel

flaqueza [fla'keθa] *nf* (*delgadez*) thinness, leanness; (*fig*) weakness

flash [flaʃ] (*pl* **~s** o **~es**) *nm* (*FOTO*) flash

flauta ['flauta] *nf* (*MUS*) flute

flecha ['fletʃa] *nf* arrow

flechazo [fle'tʃaθo] *nm* love at first sight

fleco ['fleko] *nm* fringe

flema ['flema] *nm* phlegm

flequillo [fle'kiʎo] *nm* (*pelo*) fringe

flexible [flek'siβle] *adj* flexible

flexión [flek'sjon] *nf* press-up

flexo ['flekso] *nm* adjustable table-lamp

flojera [flo'xera] (*AM: fam*) *nf*: **me da ~ I can't be bothered**

flojo, a ['floxo, a] *adj* (*gen*) loose; (*sin fuerzas*) limp; (*débil*) weak

flor [flor] *nf* flower; **a ~ de on the surface of; ~ecer** *vi* (*BOT*) to flower, bloom; (*fig*) to flourish; **~eciente** *adj* (*BOT*) in flower, flowering; (*fig*) thriving; **~ero** *nm* vase; **~istería** *nf* florist's (shop)

flota ['flota] *nf* fleet

flotador [flota'ðor] *nm* (*gen*) float; (*para nadar*) rubber ring

flotar [flo'tar] *vi* (*gen*) to float; **flote** *nm*: **a flote** afloat; **salir a flote** (*fig*) to get back on one's feet

fluctuar [fluk'twar] *vi* (*oscilar*) to fluctuate

fluidez [flui'ðeθ] *nf* fluidity; (*fig*) fluency

flúido, a ['fluiðo, a] *adj, nm* fluid

fluir [flu'ir] *vi* to flow

flujo ['fluxo] *nm* flow; **~ y reflujo** ebb and flow

flúor ['fluor] *nm* fluoride

fluvial [fluβi'al] *adj* (*navegación, cuenca*) fluvial, river *cpd*

foca ['foka] *nf* seal

foco ['foko] *nm* focus; (*ELEC*) floodlight; (*AM*) (light) bulb

fofo, a ['fofo, a] *adj* soft, spongy; (*carnes*) flabby

fogata [fo'vata] *nf* bonfire

fogón [fo'ɣon] nm (de cocina) ring, burner

fogoso, a [fo'ɣoso, a] adj spirited

folio ['foljo] nm folio, page

follaje [fo'ʎaxe] nm foliage

folletín [foʎe'tin] nm newspaper serial

folleto [fo'ʎeto] nm (POL) pamphlet

follón [fo'ʎon] (fam) nm (lío) mess; (conmoción) fuss; **armar un ~** to kick up a row

fomentar [fomen'tar] vt (MED) to foment; **fomento** nm (promoción) promotion

fonda ['fonda] nf inn

fondo ['fondo] nm (de mar) bottom; (de coche, sala) back; (ARTE etc) background; (reserva) fund; **~s** nmpl (COM) funds, resources; **una investigación a ~** a thorough investigation; **en el ~** at bottom, deep down

fonobuzón [fonoβu'θon] nm voice mail

fontanería [fontane'ria] nf plumbing; **fontanero, a** nm/f plumber

footing ['futin] nm jogging; **hacer ~** to jog, go jogging

forastero, a [foras'tero, a] nm/f stranger

forcejear [forθexe'ar] vi (luchar) to struggle

forense [fo'rense] nm/f pathologist

forjar [for'xar] vt to forge

forma ['forma] nf (figura) form, shape; (MED) fitness; (método) way, means; **las ~s** the conventions; **estar en ~** to be fit

formación [forma'θjon] nf (gen) formation; (educación) education; **~ profesional** vocational training

formal [for'mal] adj (gen) formal; (fig: serio) serious; (: de fiar) reliable; **~idad** nf formality; seriousness; **~izar** vt (JUR) to formalize; (situación) to put in order, regularize; **~izarse** vr (situación) to be put in order, be regularized

formar [for'mar] vt (componer) to form, shape; (constituir) to make up, constitute; (ESCOL) to train, educate; **~se** vr (ESCOL) to be trained, educated; (cobrar forma) to form, take form; (desarrollarse) to develop

formatear [formate'ar] vt to format

formativo, a [forma'tiβo, a] adj (lecturas, años) formative

formato [for'mato] nm format

formidable [formi'ðaβle] adj (temible) formidable; (estupendo) tremendous

fórmula ['formula] nf formula

formular [formu'lar] vt (queja) to make, lodge; (petición) to draw up; (pregunta) to pose

formulario [formu'larjo] nm form

fornido, a [for'niðo, a] adj well-built

forrar [fo'rrar] vt (abrigo) to line; (libro) to cover; **forro** nm (de cuaderno) cover; (COSTURA) lining, (de sillón) upholstery

fortalecer [fortale'θer] vt to strengthen

fortaleza [forta'leθa] nf (MIL) fortress; stronghold; (fuerza) strength; (determinación) resolution

fortuito, a [for'twito, a] adj accidental

fortuna [for'tuna] nf (suerte) fortune, (good) luck; (riqueza) fortune, wealth

forzar [for'θar] vt (puerta) to force (open); (compeler) to compel

forzoso, a [for'θoso, a] adj necessary

fosa ['fosa] nf (sepultura) grave; (en tierra) pit; **~s nasales** nostrils

fósforo ['fosforo] nm (QUÍM) phosphorus; (cerilla) match

foso ['foso] nm ditch; (TEATRO) pit; (AUTO): **~ de reconocimiento** inspection pit

foto ['foto] nf photo, snap(shot); **sacar una ~** to take a photo o picture

fotocopia [foto'kopja] nf photocopy; **fotocopiadora** nf photocopier; **fotocopiar** vt to photocopy

fotografía [fotoɣra'fia] nf (ARTE) photography; (una ~) photograph; **fotografiar** vt to photograph

fotógrafo, a [fo'toɣrafo, a] nm/f photographer

fracasar [fraka'sar] vi (gen) to fail

fracaso [fra'kaso] nm failure

fracción [frak'θjon] nf fraction; **fraccionamiento** (AM) nm housing estate

fractura [frak'tura] nf fracture, break

fragancia [fra'ɣanθja] nf (olor) fragrance, perfume

frágil ['fraxil] adj (débil) fragile; (COM) breakable

fragmento [fraɣ'mento] nm (pedazo) fragment

fragua ['fraɣwa] nf forge; **fraguar** vt to forge; (fig) to concoct ♦ vi to harden

fraile ['fraile] nm (REL) friar; (: monje) monk

frambuesa [fram'bwesa] nf raspberry

francamente adv (hablar, decir) frankly; (realmente) really

francés, esa [fran'θes, esa] adj French ♦ nm/f Frenchman/woman ♦ nm (LING) French

Francia ['franθja] nf France

franco, a ['franko, a] adj (cándido) frank, open; (COM: exento) free ♦ nm (moneda) franc

francotirador, a [frankotira'ðor, a] nm/f sniper

franela [fra'nela] nf flannel

franja ['franxa] nf fringe

franquear [franke'ar] vt (camino) to clear; (carta, paquete postal) to frank, stamp; (obstáculo) to overcome

franqueo [fran'keo] nm postage

franqueza [fran'keθa] nf (candor) frankness

frasco ['frasko] nm bottle, flask; **~ al vacío** (vacuum) flask

frase ['frase] *nf* sentence; ~ **hecha** set phrase; (*pey*) stock phrase

fraterno, a [fra'terno, a] *adj* brotherly, fraternal

fraude ['frauðe] *nm* (*cualidad*) dishonesty; (*acto*) fraud; **fraudulento, a** *adj* fraudulent

frazada [fra'saða] (*AM*) *nf* blanket

trecuencia |tre'kwenθja| *nf* frequency; **con ~** frequently, often

frecuentar [frekwen'tar] *vt* to frequent

fregadero |frexa'ðero| *nm* (kitchen) sink

fregar [fre'xar] *vt* (*frotar*) to scrub; (*platos*) to wash (up); (*AM*) to annoy

fregona [fre'xona] *nf* mop

freir |fre'ir| *vt* to fry

frenar [fre'nar] *vt* to brake; (*fig*) to check

frenazo [fre'naθo] *nm*: **dar un ~** to brake sharply

frenesí [frene'si] *nm* frenzy; **frenético, a** *adj* frantic

freno ['freno] *nm* (*TEC, AUTO*) brake; (*de cabalgadura*) bit; (*fig*) check

frente ['frente] *nm* (*ARQ, POL*) front; (*de objeto*) front part ♦ *nf* forehead, brow; ~ **a** in front of; (*en situación opuesta de*) opposite; **al ~ de** (*fig*) at the head of; **chocar de ~** to crash head-on; **hacer ~ a** to face up to

fresa ['fresa] (*ESP*) *nf* strawberry

fresco, a ['fresko, a] *adj* (*nuevo*) fresh; (*frío*) cool; (*descarado*) cheeky ♦ *nm* (*aire*) fresh air; (*ARTE*) fresco; (*AM: jugo*) fruit drink ♦ *nm/f* (*fam*): **ser un ~** to have a nerve; **tomar el ~** to get some fresh air; **frescura** *nf* freshness; (*descaro*) cheek, nerve

frialdad [frial'dað] *nf* (*gen*) coldness; (*indiferencia*) indifference

fricción [frik'θjon] *nf* (*gen*) friction; (*acto*) rub(bing); (*MED*) massage

frigidez [frixi'ðeθ] *nf* frigidity

frigorífico [frixo'rifiko] *nm* refrigerator

frijol [fri'xol] *nm* kidney bean

frío, a *etc* ['frio, a] *vb ver* **freir** ♦ *adj* cold; (*indiferente*) indifferent ♦ *nm* cold; indifference; **hace ~** it's cold; **tener ~** to be cold

frito, a ['frito, a] *adj* fried; **me trae ~ ese hombre** I'm sick and tired of that man; **fritos** *nmpl* fried food

frívolo, a ['frißolo, a] *adj* frivolous

frontal [fron'tal] *adj* frontal; **choque ~** head-on collision

frontera [fron'tera] *nf* frontier; **fronterizo, a** *adj* frontier *cpd*; (*contiguo*) bordering

frontón [fron'ton] *nm* (*DEPORTE: cancha*) pelota court; (: *juego*) pelota

frotar [fro'tar] *vt* to rub; **~se** *vr*: **~se las manos** to rub one's hands

fructífero, a [fruk'tifero, a] *adj* fruitful

fruncir [frun'θir] *vt* to pucker; (*COSTURA*) to

pleat; ~ **el ceño** to knit one's brow

frustrar [frus'trar] *vt* to frustrate

fruta ['fruta] *nf* fruit; **frutería** *nf* fruit shop; **frutero, a** *adj* fruit *cpd* ♦ *nm/f* fruiterer ♦ *nm* fruit bowl

frutilla |fru'tiʎa| (*AM*) *nf* strawberry

fruto ['fruto] *nm* fruit; (*fig: resultado*) result; (: *beneficio*) benefit; **~s secos** nuts; (*pasas etc*) dried fruit *sg*

fue *vb ver* **ser**; **ir**

fuego ['fweɣo] *nm* (*gen*) fire; **a ~ lento** on a low heat; **¿tienes ~?** have you (got) a light?; **~s artificiales** *o* **de artificio** fireworks

fuente ['fwente] *nf* fountain; (*manantial, fig*) spring; (*origen*) source; (*plato*) large dish

fuera *etc* ['fwera] *vb ver* **ser**, **ir** ♦ *adv* out(side); (*en otra parte*) away; (*excepto, salvo*) except, save ♦ *prep*: ~ **de** outside; (*fig*) besides; ~ **de sí** beside o.s.; **por ~** (on the) outside

fuera-borda [fwera'ßorða] *nm* speedboat

fuerte ['fwerte] *adj* strong; (*golpe*) hard; (*ruido*) loud; (*comida*) rich; (*lluvia*) heavy; (*dolor*) intense ♦ *adv* strongly; hard; loud(ly) *sg*

fuerza *etc* ['fwerθa] *nf* (*fortaleza*) strength; (*TEC, ELEC*) power; (*coacción*) force; (*MIL: tb*: **~s**) forces *pl*; **a ~ de** by dint of; **cobrar ~s** to recover one's strength; **tener ~s para** to have the strength to; **a la ~** forcibly, by force; **por ~** of necessity; **~ de voluntad** willpower

fuga ['fuɣa] *nf* (*huida*) flight, escape; (*de gas etc*) leak

fugarse [fu'ɣarse] *vr* to flee, escape

fugaz [fu'ɣaθ] *adj* fleeting

fugitivo, a [fuxi'tißo, a] *adj, nm/f* fugitive

fui *vb ver* **ser**; **ir**

fulano, a [fu'lano, a] *nm/f* so-and-so, what's-his-name/what's-her-name

fulminante [fulmi'nante] *adj* (*fig: mirada*) fierce; (*MED: enfermedad, ataque*) sudden; (*fam: éxito, golpe*) sudden

fumador, a [fuma'ðor, a] *nm/f* smoker

fumar [fu'mar] *vt, vi* to smoke; ~ **en pipa** to smoke a pipe

función [fun'θjon] *nf* function; (*en trabajo*) duties *pl*; (*espectáculo*) show; **entrar en funciones** to take up one's duties

funcionar [funθjo'nar] *vi* (*gen*) to function; (*máquina*) to work; **"no funciona"** "out of order"

funcionario, a [funθjo'narjo, a] *nm/f* civil servant

funda ['funda] *nf* (*gen*) cover; (*de almohada*) pillowcase

fundación [funda'θjon] *nf* foundation

fundamental [fundamen'tal] *adj* fundamental, basic

fundamentar [fundamen'tar] *vt* (*poner*

base) to lay the foundations of; (*establecer*) to found; (*fig*) to base; **fundamento** nm (*base*) foundation

fundar [fun'dar] vt to found; ~se vr: ~se en to be founded on

fundición [fundi'θjon] nf fusing; (*fábrica*) foundry

fundir [fun'dir] vt (*gen*) to fuse; (*metal*) to smelt, melt down; (*nieve etc*) to melt; (*COM*) to merge; (*estatua*) to cast; ~se vr (*colores etc*) to merge, blend; (*unirse*) to fuse together; (*ELEC: fusible, lámpara etc*) to fuse, blow; (*nieve etc*) to melt

fúnebre ['funeßre] adj funeral cpd, funereal

funeral [fune'ral] nm funeral; **funeraria** nf undertaker's

funesto, a [fu'nesto, a] adj (*día*) ill-fated; (*decisión*) fatal

furgón [fur'xon] nm wagon; **furgoneta** nf (*AUTO, COM*) (transit) van (*BRIT*), pick-up (truck) (*US*)

furia ['furja] nf (*ira*) fury; (*violencia*) violence; **furibundo, a** adj furious; **furioso, a** adj (*iracundo*) furious; (*violento*) violent; **furor** nm (*cólera*) rage

furtivo, a [fur'tißo, a] adj furtive ♦ nm poacher

fusible [fu'sißle] nm fuse

fusil [fu'sil] nm rifle; ~**ar** vt to shoot

fusión [fu'sjon] nf (*gen*) melting; (*unión*) fusion; (*COM*) merger

fútbol ['futßol] nm football; **futbolín** nm table football; **futbolista** nm footballer

futuro, a [fu'turo, a] adj, nm future

G, g

gabardina [gaßar'ðina] nf raincoat, gabardine

gabinete [gaßi'nete] nm (*POL*) cabinet; (*estudio*) study; (*de abogados etc*) office

gaceta [ga'θeta] nf gazette

gachas ['gatʃas] nfpl porridge sg

gafas ['gafas] nfpl glasses; ~ **de sol** sunglasses

gafe ['gafe] nm jinx

gaita ['gaita] nf bagpipes pl

gajes ['gaxes] nmpl: **los** ~ **del oficio** occupational hazards

gajo ['gaxo] nm (*de naranja*) segment

gala ['gala] nf (*traje de etiqueta*) full dress; ~**s** nfpl (*ropa*) finery sg; **estar de** ~ to be in one's best clothes; **hacer** ~ **de** to display

galante [ga'lante] adj gallant; **galantería** nf (*caballerosidad*) gallantry; (*cumplido*) politeness; (*comentario*) compliment

galápago [ga'lapaxo] nm (*ZOOL*) turtle

galardón [galar'ðon] nm award, prize

galaxia [ga'laksja] nf galaxy

galera [ga'lera] nf (*nave*) galley; (*carro*) wagon; (*IMPRENTA*) galley

galería [gale'ria] nf (*gen*) gallery; (*balcón*) veranda(h); (*pasillo*) corridor

Gales ['gales] nm (*tb: País de* ~) Wales; **galés, esa** adj Welsh ♦ nm/f Welshman/ woman ♦ nm (*LING*) Welsh

galgo, a ['galxo, a] nm/f greyhound

galimatías [galima'tias] nmpl (*lenguaje*) gibberish sg, nonsense sg

gallardía [gaʎar'ðia] nf (*valor*) bravery

gallego, a [ga'ʎexo, a] adj, nm/f Galician

galleta [ga'ʎeta] nf biscuit (*BRIT*), cookie (*US*)

gallina [ga'ʎina] nf hen ♦ nm/f (*fam: cobarde*) chicken; **gallinero** nm henhouse; (*TEATRO*) top gallery

gallo ['gaʎo] nm cock, rooster

galón [ga'lon] nm (*MIL*) stripe; (*COSTURA*) braid; (*medida*) gallon

galopar [galo'par] vi to gallop

gama ['gama] nf (*fig*) range

gamba ['gamba] nf prawn (*BRIT*), shrimp (*US*)

gamberro, a [gam'berro, a] nm/f hooligan, lout

gamuza [ga'muθa] nf chamois

gana ['gana] nf (*deseo*) desire, wish; (*apetito*) appetite; (*voluntad*) will; (*añoranza*) longing; **de buena** ~ willingly; **de mala** ~ reluctantly; **me da** ~**s de** I feel like, I want to; **no me da la** ~ I don't feel like it; **tener** ~**s de** to feel like

ganadería [ganaðe'ria] nf (*ganado*) livestock; (*ganado vacuno*) cattle pl; (*cría, comercio*) cattle raising

ganado [ga'naðo] nm livestock; ~ **lanar** sheep pl; ~ **mayor** cattle pl; ~ **porcino** pigs pl

ganador, a [gana'ðor, a] adj winning ♦ nm/f winner

ganancia [ga'nanθja] nf (*lo ganado*) gain; (*aumento*) increase; (*beneficio*) profit; ~**s** nfpl (*ingresos*) earnings; (*beneficios*) profit sg, winnings

ganar [ga'nar] vt (*obtener*) to get, obtain; (*sacar ventaja*) to gain; (*salario etc*) to earn; (*DEPORTE, premio*) to win; (*derrotar a*) to beat; (*alcanzar*) to reach ♦ vi (*DEPORTE*) to win; ~**se** vr: ~**se la vida** to earn one's living

ganchillo [gan'tʃiʎo] nm crochet

gancho ['gantʃo] nm (*gen*) hook; (*colgador*) hanger

gandul, a [gan'dul, a] adj, nm/f good-for-nothing, layabout

ganga ['ganga] nf bargain

gangrena [gan'grena] nf gangrene

ganso, a ['ganso, a] nm/f (*ZOOL*) goose; (*fam*) idiot

ganzúa [gan'θua] nf skeleton key

garabatear [garaßate'ar] vi, vt (*al escribir*) to scribble, scrawl

garabato [gara'ßato] nm (*escritura*) scrawl,

scribble
garaje [ga'raxe] *nm* garage
garante [ga'rante] *adj* responsible ♦ *nm/f* guarantor
garantía [garan'tia] *nf* guarantee
garantizar [garanti'θar] *vt* to guarantee
garbanzo [gar'ßanθo] *nm* chickpea (*BRIT*), garbanzo (*US*)
garbo ['garßo] *nm* grace, elegance
garfio ['garfjo] *nm* grappling iron
garganta [gar'vanta] *nf* (*ANAT*) throat; (*de botella*) neck; **gargantilla** *nf* necklace
gárgaras ['garvaras] *nfpl*: **hacer ~** to gargle
garita [ga'rita] *nf* cabin, hut; (*MIL*) sentry box
garra ['garra] *nf* (*de gato, TEC*) claw; (*de ave*) talon; (*fam: mano*) hand, paw
garrafa [ga'rrafa] *nf* carafe, decanter
garrapata [garra'pata] *nf* tick
garrote [ga'rrote] *nm* (*palo*) stick; (*porra*) cudgel; (*suplicio*) garrotte
garza ['garθa] *nf* heron
gas [gas] *nm* gas
gasa ['gasa] *nf* gauze
gaseosa [gase'osa] *nf* lemonade
gaseoso, a [gase'oso, a] *adj* gassy, fizzy
gasoil [ga'soil] *nm* diesel (oil)
gasóleo [ga'soleo] *nm* = **gasoil**
gasolina [gaso'lina] *nf* petrol, gas(oline) (*US*); **gasolinera** *nf* petrol (*BRIT*) o gas (*US*) station
gastado, a [gas'taðo, a] *adj* (*dinero*) spent; (*ropa*) worn out; (*usado: frase etc*) trite
gastar [gas'tar] *vt* (*dinero, tiempo*) to spend; (*fuerzas*) to use up; (*desperdiciar*) to waste; (*llevar*) to wear; **~se** *vr* to wear out; (*estropearse*) to waste; **~ en** to spend on; **~ bromas** to crack jokes; **¿qué número gastas?** what size (shoe) do you take?
gasto ['gasto] *nm* (*desembolso*) expenditure, spending; (*consumo, uso*) use; **~s** *nmpl* (*desembolsos*) expenses; (*cargos*) charges, costs
gastronomía [gastrono'mia] *nf* gastronomy
gatear [gate'ar] *vi* (*andar a gatas*) to go on all fours
gatillo [ga'tiʎo] *nm* (*de arma de fuego*) trigger; (*de dentista*) forceps
gato, a [ga'to, a] *nm/f* cat ♦ *nm* (*TEC*) jack; **andar a gatas** to go on all fours
gaviota [ga'ßjota] *nf* seagull
gay [ge] *adj inv, nm* gay, homosexual
gazpacho [gaθ'patʃo] *nm* gazpacho
gel [xel] *nm* (*tb:* **~ de baño/ducha**) gel
gelatina [xela'tina] *nf* jelly; (*polvos etc*) gelatine
gema ['xema] *nf* gem
gemelo, a [xe'melo, a] *adj, nm/f* twin; **~s** *nmpl* (*de camisa*) cufflinks; (*prismáticos*) field glasses, binoculars

gemido [xe'miðo] *nm* (*quejido*) moan, groan; (*aullido*) howl
Géminis ['xeminis] *nm* Gemini
gemir [xe'mir] *vi* (*quejarse*) to moan, groan; (*aullar*) to howl
generación [xenera'θjon] *nf* generation
general [xene'rral] *adj* general ♦ *nm* general; **por lo** o **en ~** in general; **G~itat** *nf* Catalan parliament; **~izar** *vt* to generalize; **~izarse** *vr* to become generalized, spread; **~mente** *adv* generally
generar [xene'rar] *vt* to generate
género ['xenero] *nm* (*clase*) kind, sort; (*tipo*) type; (*BIO*) genus; (*LING*) gender; (*COM*) material; **~ humano** human race
generosidad [xenerosi'ðað] *nf* generosity; **generoso, a** *adj* generous
genial [xe'njal] *adj* inspired; (*idea*) brilliant; (*afable*) genial
genio ['xenjo] *nm* (*carácter*) nature, disposition; (*humor*) temper; (*facultad creadora*) genius; **de mal ~** bad-tempered
genital [xeni'tal] *adj* genital; **genitales** *nmpl* genitals
gente ['xente] *nf* (*personas*) people *pl*; (*parientes*) relatives *pl*
gentil [xen'til] *adj* (*elegante*) graceful; (*encantador*) charming; **~eza** *nf* grace; charm; (*cortesía*) courtesy
gentío [xen'tio] *nm* crowd, throng
genuino, a [xe'nwino, a] *adj* genuine
geografía [xeovra'fia] *nf* geography
geología [xeolo'xia] *nf* geology
geometría [xeome'tria] *nf* geometry
gerencia [xe'renθja] *nf* management; **gerente** *nm/f* (*supervisor*) manager; (*jefe*) director
geriatría [xeria'tria] *nf* (*MED*) geriatrics *sg*
germen ['xermen] *nm* germ
germinar [xermi'nar] *vi* to germinate
gesticular [xestiku'lar] *vi* to gesticulate; (*hacer muecas*) to grimace; **gesticulación** *nf* gesticulation; (*mueca*) grimace
gestión [xes'tjon] *nf* management; (*diligencia, acción*) negotiation; **gestionar** *vt* (*lograr*) to try to arrange; (*dirigir*) to manage
gesto ['xesto] *nm* (*mueca*) grimace; (*ademán*) gesture
Gibraltar [xißral'tar] *nm* Gibraltar; **gibraltareño, a** *adj, nm/f* Gibraltarian
gigante [xi'vante] *adj, nm/f* giant; **gigantesco, a** *adj* gigantic
gilipollas [xili'poʎas] (*fam*) *adj inv* daft ♦ *nm/f inv* wally
gimnasia [xim'nasja] *nf* gymnastics *pl*; **gimnasio** *nm* gymnasium; **gimnasta** *nm/f* gymnast
gimotear [ximote'ar] *vi* to whine, whimper
ginebra [xi'neßra] *nf* gin

ginecólogo, a [xine'koloɣo, a] nm/f gynaecologist

gira ['xira] nf tour, trip

girar [xi'rar] vt (dar la vuelta) to turn (around); (: rápidamente) to spin; (COM: giro postal) to draw; (: letra de cambio) to issue ♦ vi to turn (round); (rápido) to spin

girasol [xira'sol] nm sunflower

giratorio, a [xira'torjo, a] adj revolving

giro ['xiro] nm (movimiento) turn, revolution; (LING) expression; (COM) draft; ~ **bancario/postal** bank giro/postal order

gis [xis] (AM) nm chalk

gitano, a [xi'tano, a] adj, nm/f gypsy

glacial [gla'θjal] adj icy, freezing

glaciar [gla'θjar] nm glacier

glándula ['glandula] nf gland

global [glo'ßal] adj global

globo ['gloßo] nm (esfera) globe, sphere; (aerostato, juguete) balloon

glóbulo ['gloßulo] nm globule; (ANAT) corpuscle

gloria ['glorja] nf glory

glorieta [glo'rjeta] nf (de jardín) bower, arbour; (plazoleta) roundabout (BRIT), traffic circle (US)

glorificar [glorifi'kar] vt (enaltecer) to glorify, praise

glorioso, a [glo'rjoso, a] adj glorious

glotón, ona [glo'ton, ona] adj gluttonous, greedy ♦ nm/f glutton

glucosa [glu'kosa] nf glucose

gobernador, a [goßerna'ðor, a] adj governing ♦ nm/f governor; **gobernante** adj governing

gobernar [goßer'nar] vt (dirigir) to guide, direct; (POL) to rule, govern ♦ vi to govern; (NAUT) to steer

gobierno etc [go'ßjerno] vb ver **gobernar** ♦ nm (POL) government; (dirección) guidance, direction; (NAUT) steering

goce etc ['goθe] vb ver **gozar** ♦ nm enjoyment

gol [gol] nm goal

golf [golf] nm golf

golfa ['golfa] (fam!) nf (mujer) slut, whore

golfo, a ['golfo, a] nm (GEO) gulf ♦ nm/f (fam: niño) urchin; (gamberro) lout

golondrina [golon'drina] nf swallow

golosina [golo'sina] nf (dulce) sweet; **goloso, a** adj sweet-toothed

golpe ['golpe] nm blow; (de puño) punch; (de mano) smack; (de remo) stroke; (fig: choque) clash; **no dar** ~ to be bone idle; **de un** ~ with one blow; **de** ~ suddenly; ~ **(de estado)** coup (d'état); **golpear** vt, vi to strike, knock; (asestar) to beat; (de puño) to punch; (golpetear) to tap

goma ['goma] nf (caucho) rubber; (elástico) elastic; (una ~) elastic band; ~ **espuma** foam rubber; ~ **de pegar** gum, glue; ~ **de borrar** eraser, rubber (BRIT)

gomina [go'mina] nf hair gel

gordo, a ['gorðo, a] adj (gen) fat; (fam) enormous; **el (premio)** ~ (en lotería) first prize; **gordura** nf fat; (corpulencia) fatness, stoutness

gorila [go'rila] nm gorilla

gorjear [gorxe'ar] vi to twitter, chirp

gorra ['gorra] nf cap; (de niño) bonnet; (militar) bearskin; **entrar de** ~ (fam) to gatecrash; **ir de** ~ to sponge

gorrión [go'rrjon] nm sparrow

gorro ['gorro] nm (gen) cap; (de niño, mujer) bonnet

gorrón, ona [go'rron, ona] nm/f scrounger; **gorronear** (fam) vi to scrounge

gota ['gota] nf (gen) drop; (de sudor) bead; (MED) gout; **gotear** vi to drip; (lloviznar) to drizzle; **gotera** nf leak

gozar [go'θar] vi to enjoy o.s.; ~ **de** (disfrutar) to enjoy; (poseer) to possess

gozne ['goθne] nm hinge

gozo ['goθo] nm (alegría) joy; (placer) pleasure

gr. abr (= gramo, gramos) g

grabación [graßa'θjon] nf recording

grabado [gra'ßaðo] nm print, engraving

grabadora [graßa'ðora] nf tape-recorder

grabar [gra'ßar] vt to engrave; (discos, cintas) to record

gracia ['graθja] nf (encanto) grace, gracefulness; (humor) humour, wit; **¡(muchas) ~s!** thanks (very much)!; **~s a** thanks to; **tener** ~ (chiste etc) to be funny; **no me hace** ~ I am not keen; **gracioso, a** adj (divertido) funny, amusing; (cómico) comical ♦ nm/f (TEATRO) comic character

grada ['graða] nf (de escalera) step; (de anfiteatro) tier, row; **~s** nfpl (DEPORTE: de estadio) terraces

gradería [graðe'ria] nf (gradas) (flight of) steps pl; (de anfiteatro) tiers pl, rows pl; (DEPORTE: de estadio) terraces pl; ~ **cubierta** covered stand

grado ['graðo] nm degree; (de aceite, vino) grade; (grada) step; (MIL) rank; **de buen** ~ willingly

graduación [graðwa'θjon] nf (del alcohol) proof, strength; (ESCOL) graduation; (MIL) rank

gradual [gra'ðwal] adj gradual

graduar [gra'ðwar] vt (gen) to graduate; (MIL) to commission; **~se** vr to graduate; **~se la vista** to have one's eyes tested

gráfica ['grafika] nf graph

gráfico, a ['grafiko, a] adj graphic ♦ nm diagram; **~s** nmpl (INFORM) graphics

grajo ['graxo] nm rook

Gral *abr* (= *General*) Gen.
gramática [gra'matika] *nf* grammar
gramo ['gramo] *nm* gramme (*BRIT*), gram (*US*)
gran [gran] *adj ver* **grande**
grana ['grana] *nf* (*color, tela*) scarlet
granada [gra'naða] *nf* pomegranate; (*MIL*) grenade
granate [gra'nate] *adj* deep red
Gran Bretaña [-bre'taɲa] *nf* Great Britain
grande ['grande] (*antes de nmsg:* **gran**) *adj* (*de tamaño*) big, large; (*alto*) tall; (*distinguido*) great; (*impresionante*) grand ♦ *nm* grandee; **grandeza** *nf* greatness
grandioso, a [gran'djoso, a] *adj* magnificent, grand
granel [gra'nel] : **a ~** *adv* (*COM*) in bulk
granero [gra'nero] *nm* granary, barn
granito [gra'nito] *nm* (*AGR*) small grain; (*roca*) granite
granizado [grani'θaðo] *nm* iced drink
granizar [grani'θar] *vi* to hail; **granizo** *nm* hail
granja ['granxa] *nf* (*gen*) farm; **granjear** *vt* to win, gain; **granjearse** *vr* to win, gain; **granjero, a** *nm/f* farmer
grano ['grano] *nm* grain; (*semilla*) seed; (*de café*) bean; (*MED*) pimple, spot
granuja [gra'nuxa] *nm/f* rogue; (*golfillo*) urchin
grapa ['grapa] *nf* staple; (*TEC*) clamp; **grapadora** *nf* stapler
grasa ['grasa] *nf* (*gen*) grease; (*de cocinar*) fat, lard; (*sebo*) suet; (*mugre*) filth; **grasiento, a** *adj* greasy; (*de aceite*) oily; **graso, a** *adj* (*leche, queso, carne*) fatty; (*pelo, piel*) greasy
gratificación [gratifika'θjon] *nf* (*bono*) bonus; (*recompensa*) reward
gratificar [gratifi'kar] *vt* to reward
gratinar [grati'nar] *vt* to cook au gratin
gratis ['gratis] *adv* free
gratitud [grati'tuð] *nf* gratitude
grato, a ['grato, a] *adj* (*agradable*) pleasant, agreeable
gratuito, a [gra'twito, a] *adj* (*gratis*) free; (*sin razón*) gratuitous
gravamen [gra'ßamen] *nm* (*impuesto*) tax
gravar [gra'ßar] *vt* to tax
grave ['graße] *adj* heavy; (*serio*) grave, serious; **~dad** *nf* gravity
gravilla [gra'ßiʎa] *nf* gravel
gravitar [graßi'tar] *vi* to gravitate; **~ sobre** to rest on
graznar [graθ'nar] *vi* (*cuervo*) to squawk; (*pato*) to quack; (*hablar ronco*) to croak
Grecia ['greθja] *nf* Greece
gremio ['gremjo] *nm* trade, industry
greña ['greɲa] *nf* (*cabellos*) shock of hair
gresca ['greska] *nf* uproar

griego, a ['grjeɣo, a] *adj, nm/f* Greek
grieta ['grjeta] *nf* crack
grifo ['grifo] *nm* tap; (*AM: AUTO*) petrol *o* gas (*US*) station
grilletes [gri'ʎetes] *nmpl* fetters
grillo ['griʎo] *nm* (*ZOOL*) cricket
gripe ['gripe] *nf* flu, influenza
grls [gris] *adj* (*color*) grey
gritar [gri'tar] *vt, vi* to shout, yell; **grito** *nm* shout, yell; (*de horror*) scream
grosella [gro'seʎa] *nf* (*red*)currant; **~ negra** blackcurrant
grosería [grose'ria] *nf* (*actitud*) rudeness; (*comentario*) vulgar comment; **grosero, a** *adj* (*poco cortés*) rude, bad-mannered; (*ordinario*) vulgar, crude
grosor [gro'sor] *nm* thickness
grotesco, a [gro'tesko, a] *adj* grotesque
grúa ['grua] *nf* (*TEC*) crane; (*de petróleo*) derrick
grueso, a ['grweso, a] *adj* thick; (*persona*) stout ♦ *nm* bulk; **el ~ de** the bulk of
grulla ['gruʎa] *nf* crane
grumo ['grumo] *nm* clot, lump
gruñido [gru'ɲiðo] *nm* grunt; (*de persona*) grumble
gruñir [gru'ɲir] *vi* (*animal*) to growl; (*persona*) to grumble
grupa ['grupa] *nf* (*ZOOL*) rump
grupo ['grupo] *nm* group; (*TEC*) unit, set
gruta ['gruta] *nf* grotto
guadaña [gwa'ðaɲa] *nf* scythe
guagua [gwa'ɣwa] (*AM*) *nf* (*niño*) baby; (*bus*) bus
guante ['gwante] *nm* glove; **~ra** *nf* glove compartment
guapo, a ['gwapo, a] *adj* good-looking, attractive; (*elegante*) smart
guarda ['gwarða] *nm/f* (*persona*) guard, keeper ♦ *nf* (*acto*) guarding; (*custodia*) custody; **~bosques** *nm inv* gamekeeper; **~costas** *nm inv* coastguard vessel ♦ *nm/f* guardian, protector; **~espaldas** *nm/f inv* bodyguard; **~meta** *nm/f* goalkeeper; **guardar** *vt* (*gen*) to keep; (*vigilar*) to guard, watch over; (*dinero: ahorrar*) to save; **guardarse** *vr* (*preservarse*) to protect o.s.; (*evitar*) to avoid; **guardar cama** to stay in bed; **~rropa** *nm* (*armario*) wardrobe; (*en establecimiento público*) cloakroom
guardería [gwarðe'ria] *nf* nursery
guardia ['gwarðja] *nf* (*MIL*) guard; (*cuidado*) care, custody ♦ *nm/f* guard; (*policía*) policeman/woman; **estar de ~** to be on guard; **montar ~** to mount guard; **G~ Civil** Civil Guard; **G~ Nacional** National Guard
guardián, ana [gwar'ðjan, ana] *nm/f* (*gen*) guardian, keeper
guarecer [gware'θer] *vt* (*proteger*) to protect;

(*abrigar*) to shelter; **~se** *vr* to take refuge

guarida [gwa'riða] *nf* (*de animal*) den, lair; (*refugio*) refuge

guarnecer [gwarne'θer] *vt* (*equipar*) to provide; (*adornar*) to adorn; (*TEC*) to reinforce; **guarnición** *nf* (*de vestimenta*) trimming; (*de piedra*) mount; (*CULIN*) garnish; (*arneses*) harness; (*MIL*) garrison

guarro, a ['gwarro, a] *nm/f* pig

guasa ['gwasa] *nf* joke; **guasón, ona** *adj* (*bromista*) joking ♦ *nm/f* wit; joker

Guatemala [gwate'mala] *nf* Guatemala

guay [gwai] (*fam*) *adj* super, great

gubernativo, a [gußerna'tißo, a] *adj* governmental

guerra ['gerra] *nf* war; **~ civil** civil war; **~ fría** cold war; **dar ~** to annoy; **guerrear** *vi* to wage war; **guerrero, a** *adj* fighting; (*carácter*) warlike ♦ *nm/f* warrior

guerrilla [ge'rriʎa] *nf* guerrilla warfare; (*tropas*) guerrilla band o group

guía *etc* ['gia] *vb ver* **guiar** ♦ *nm/f* (*persona*) guide ♦ *nf* (*libro*) guidebook; **~ de ferrocarriles** railway timetable; **~ telefónica** telephone directory

guiar [gi'ar] *vt* to guide, direct; (*AUTO*) to steer; **~se** *vr*: **~se por** to be guided by

guijarro [gi'xarro] *nm* pebble

guillotina [giʎo'tina] *nf* guillotine

guinda ['ginda] *nf* morello cherry

guindilla [gin'diʎa] *nf* chilli pepper

guiñapo [gi'ɲapo] *nm* (*harapo*) rag; (*persona*) reprobate, rogue

guiñar [gi'ɲar] *vt* to wink

guión [gi'on] *nm* (*LING*) hyphen, dash; (*CINE*) script; **guionista** *nm/f* scriptwriter

guiri ['giri] (*fam*: *pey*) *nm/f* foreigner

guirnalda [gir'nalda] *nf* garland

guisado [gi'saðo] *nm* stew

guisante [gi'sante] *nm* pea

guisar [gi'sar] *vt, vi* to cook; **guiso** *nm* cooked dish

guitarra [gi'tarra] *nf* guitar

gula ['gula] *nf* gluttony, greed

gusano [gu'sano] *nm* worm; (*lombriz*) earthworm

gustar [gus'tar] *vt* to taste, sample ♦ *vi* to please, be pleasing; **~ de algo** to like o enjoy sth; **me gustan las uvas** I like grapes; **le gusta nadar** she likes o enjoys swimming

gusto ['gusto] *nm* (*sentido, sabor*) taste; (*placer*) pleasure; **tiene ~ a menta** it tastes of mint; **tener buen ~** to have good taste; **sentirse a ~** to feel at ease; **mucho ~ (en conocerle)** pleased to meet you; **el ~ es mío** the pleasure is mine; **con ~** willingly, gladly; **~so, a** *adj* (*sabroso*) tasty; (*agradable*) pleasant

---

ha *vb ver* **haber**

haba ['aßa] *nf* bean

Habana [a'ßana] *nf*: **la ~** Havana

habano [a'ßano] *nm* Havana cigar

habéis *vb ver* **haber**

PALABRA CLAVE

haber [a'ßer] *vb aux* **1** (*tiempos compuestos*) to have; **había comido** I had eaten; **antes/ después de ~lo visto** before seeing/after seeing o having seen it

2: **¡~lo dicho antes!** you should have said so before!

3: **~ de**: **he de hacerlo** I have to do it; **ha de llegar mañana** it should arrive tomorrow

♦ *vb impers* **1** (*existencia*: *sg*) there is; (: *pl*) there are; **hay un hermano/dos hermanos** there is one brother/there are two brothers; **¿cuánto hay de aquí a Sucre?** how far is it from here to Sucre?

2 (*obligación*): **hay que hacer algo** something must be done; **hay que apuntarlo para acordarse** you have to write it down to remember

3: **¡hay que ver!** well I never!

4: **¡no hay de o por** (*AM*) **qué!** don't mention it!, not at all!

5: **¿qué hay?** (*¿qué pasa?*) what's up?, what's the matter?; (*¿qué tal?*) how's it going?

♦ **~se** *vr*: **habérselas con uno** to have it out with sb

♦ *vt*: **he aquí unas sugerencias** here are some suggestions; **no hay cintas blancas pero sí las hay rojas** there aren't any white ribbons but there are some red ones

♦ *nm* (*en cuenta*) credit side; **~es** *nmpl* assets; **¿cuánto tengo en el ~?** how much do I have in my account?; **tiene varias novelas en su ~** he has several novels to his credit

---

habichuela [aßi'tʃwela] *nf* kidney bean

hábil ['aßil] *adj* (*listo*) clever, smart; (*capaz*) fit, capable; (*experto*) expert; **día ~** working day; **habilidad** *nf* skill, ability

habilitar [aßili'tar] *vt* (*capacitar*) to enable; (*dar instrumentos*) to equip; (*financiar*) to finance

hábilmente [aßil'mente] *adv* skilfully, expertly

habitación [aßita'θjon] *nf* (*cuarto*) room; (*BIO*: *morada*) habitat; **~ sencilla** o **individual** single room; **~ doble** o **de matrimonio** double room

habitante [aßi'tante] *nm/f* inhabitant

habitar [aßi'tar] *vt* (*residir en*) to inhabit;

(*ocupar*) to occupy ♦ *vi* to live

hábito [ˈaβito] *nm* habit

habitual [aβiˈtwal] *adj* usual

habituar [aβiˈtwar] *vt* to accustom; **~se** *vr*: **~se a** to get used to

habla [ˈaβla] *nf* (*capacidad de hablar*) speech; (*idioma*) language; (*dialecto*) dialect; **perder el ~ to become speechless; de ~ francesa** French-speaking; **estar al ~** to be in contact; (*TEL*) to be on the line; **¡González al ~!** (*TEL*) González speaking!

hablador, a [aβlaˈðor, a] *adj* talkative ♦ *nm/f* chatterbox

habladuría [aβlaðuˈria] *nf* rumour; **~s** *nfpl* gossip *sg*

hablante [aˈβlante] *adj* speaking ♦ *nm/f* speaker

hablar [aˈβlar] *vt* to speak, talk ♦ *vi* to speak; **~se** *vr* to speak to each other; **~ con** to speak to; **~ de** to speak of o about; **"se habla inglés"** "English spoken here"; **¡ni ~!** it's out of the question!

habré *etc vb ver* **haber**

hacendoso, a [aθenˈdoso, a] *adj* industrious

─────────────
| PALABRA CLAVE |
─────────────

hacer [aˈθer] *vt* **1** (*fabricar, producir*) to make; (*construir*) to build; **~ una película/un ruido** to make a film/noise; **el guisado lo hice yo** I made o cooked the stew

2 (*ejecutar: trabajo etc*) to do; **~ la colada** to do the washing; **~ la comida** to do the cooking; **¿qué haces?** what are you doing?; **~ el malo** o **el papel del malo** (*TEATRO*) to play the villain

3 (*estudios, algunos deportes*) to do; **~ español/económicas** to do o study Spanish/economics; **~ yoga/gimnasia** to do yoga/go to gym

4 (*transformar, incidir en*): **esto lo hará más difícil** this will make it more difficult; **salir te hará sentir mejor** going out will make you feel better

5 (*cálculo*): **2 y 2 hacen 4** 2 and 2 make 4; **éste hace 100** this one makes 100

6 (+ *sub*): **esto hará que ganemos** this will make us win; **harás que no quiera venir** you'll stop him wanting to come

7 (*como sustituto de vb*) to do; **él bebió y yo hice lo mismo** he drank and I did likewise

8: **no hace más que criticar** all he does is criticize

♦ *vb semi-aux*: **hacer** + *infin* **1** (*directo*): **les hice venir** I made o had them come;

~ trabajar a los demás to get others to work

2 (*por intermedio de otros*): **~ reparar algo** to get sth repaired

♦ *vi* **1**: **haz como que no lo sabes** act as if you don't know

2 (*ser apropiado*): **si os hace** if it's alright with you

3: **~ de**: **~ de madre para uno** to be like a mother to sb; (*TEATRO*): **~ de Otelo** to play Othello

♦ *vb impers* **1**: **hace calor/frío** it's hot/cold; *ver tb* **bueno; sol; tiempo**

2 (*tiempo*): **hace 3 años 3 years ago; hace un mes que voy/no voy** I've been going/I haven't been going for a month

3: **¿cómo has hecho para llegar tan rápido?** how did you manage to get here so quickly?

♦ **~se** *vr* **1** (*volverse*) to become; **se hicieron amigos** they became friends

2 (*acostumbrarse*): **~se a** to get used to

3: **se hace con huevos y leche** it's made out of eggs and milk; **eso no se hace** that's not done

4 (*obtener*): **~se de** o **con algo** to get hold of sth

5 (*fingirse*): **~se el sueco** to turn a deaf ear

hacha [ˈatʃa] *nf* axe; (*antorcha*) torch

hachís [aˈtʃis] *nm* hashish

hacia [ˈaθja] *prep* (*en dirección de*) towards; (*cerca de*) near; (*actitud*) towards; **~ arriba/abajo** up(wards)/down(wards); **~ mediodía** about noon

hacienda [aˈθjenda] *nf* (*propiedad*) property; (*finca*) farm; (*AM*) ranch; **~ pública** public finance; **(Ministerio de) H~** Exchequer (*BRIT*), Treasury Department (*US*)

hada [ˈaða] *nf* fairy

hago *etc vb ver* **hacer**

Haití [aiˈti] *nm* Haiti

halagar [alaˈɣar] *vt* to flatter

halago [aˈlaɣo] *nm* flattery; **halagüeño, a** *adj* flattering

halcón [alˈkon] *nm* falcon, hawk

hallar [aˈʎar] *vt* (*gen*) to find; (*descubrir*) to discover; (*toparse con*) to run into; **~se** *vr* to be (situated); **hallazgo** *nm* discovery; (*cosa*) find

halterofilia [alteroˈfilja] *nf* weightlifting

hamaca [aˈmaka] *nf* hammock

hambre [ˈambre] *nf* hunger; (*plaga*) famine; (*deseo*) longing; **tener ~** to be hungry; **hambriento, a** *adj* hungry, starving

hamburguesa [amburˈɣesa] *nf* hamburger; **hamburguesería** *nf* burger bar

han *vb ver* **haber**

harapiento, a [araˈpjento, a] *adj* tattered, in rags

harapos [aˈrapos] *nmpl* rags

haré *etc vb ver* **hacer**

harina [aˈrina] *nf* flour

hartar [arˈtar] *vt* to satiate, glut; (*fig*) to tire, sicken; **~se** *vr* (*de comida*) to fill o.s., gorge o.s.; (*cansarse*) to get fed up (*de* with);

hartazgo nm surfeit, glut; **harto, a** adj (lleno) full; (cansado) fed up ♦ adv (bastante) enough; (muy) very; **estar harto de** to be fed up with

has vb ver **haber**

hasta ['asta] adv even ♦ prep (alcanzando a) as far as; up to; down to; (de tiempo: a tal hora) till, until; (antes de) before ♦ conj: ~ **que** until; ~ **luego/el sábado** see you soon/ on Saturday

hastiar [as'tjar] vt (gen) to weary; (aburrir) to bore; ~**se** vr: ~**se de** to get fed up with; **hastío** nm weariness; boredom

hatillo [a'tiʎo] nm belongings pl, kit; (montón) bundle, heap

hay vb ver **haber**

Haya ['aja] nf: **la ~** The Hague

haya etc ['aja] vb ver **haber** ♦ nf beech tree

haz [aθ] vb ver **hacer** ♦ nm (de luz) beam

hazaña [a'θaɲa] nf feat, exploit

hazmerreír [aθmerre'ir] nm inv laughing stock

he vb ver **haber**

hebilla [e'βiʎa] nf buckle, clasp

hebra ['eβra] nf thread; (BOT: fibra) fibre, grain

hebreo, a [e'βreo, a] adj, nm/f Hebrew ♦ nm (LING) Hebrew

hechizar [etʃi'θar] vt to cast a spell on, bewitch

hechizo [e'tʃiθo] nm witchcraft, magic; (acto de magia) spell, charm

hecho, a ['etʃo, a] pp de **hacer** ♦ adj (carne) done; (COSTURA) ready-to-wear ♦ nm deed, act; (dato) fact; (cuestión) matter; (suceso) event ♦ excl agreed!, done!; **¡bien ~!** well done!; **de ~** in fact, as a matter of fact

hechura [e'tʃura] nf (forma) form, shape; (de persona) build

hectárea [ek'tarea] nf hectare

heder [e'ðer] vi to stink, smell

hediondo, a [e'ðjondo, a] adj stinking

hedor [e'ðor] nm stench

helada [e'laða] nf frost

heladera [ela'ðera] nf (AM) (refrigerador) refrigerator

helado, a [e'laðo, a] adj frozen; (glacial) icy; (fig) chilly, cold ♦ nm ice cream

helar [e'lar] vt to freeze, ice (up); (dejar atónito) to amaze; (desalentar) to discourage ♦ vi to freeze; ~**se** vr to freeze

helecho [e'letʃo] nm fern

hélice ['eliθe] nf (TEC) propeller

helicóptero [eli'koptero] nm helicopter

hembra ['embra] nf (BOT, ZOOL) female; (mujer) woman; (TEC) nut

hemorragia [emo'rraxja] nf haemorrhage

hemorroides [emo'rroiðes] nfpl haemorrhoids, piles

hemos vb ver **haber**

hendidura [endi'ðura] nf crack, split

heno ['eno] nm hay

herbicida [erβi'θiða] nm weedkiller

heredad [ere'ðað] nf landed property; (granja) farm

heredar [ere'ðar] vt to inherit; **heredero, a** nm/f heir(ess)

hereje [e'rexe] nm/f heretic

herencia [e'renθja] nf inheritance

herida [e'riða] nf wound, injury; ver tb **herido**

herido, a [e'riðo, a] adj injured, wounded ♦ nm/f casualty

herir [e'rir] vt to wound, injure; (fig) to offend

hermanastro, a [erma'nastro, a] nm/f stepbrother/sister

hermandad [erman'dað] nf brotherhood

hermano, a [er'mano, a] nm/f brother/sister; ~ **gemelo** twin brother; **hermana gemela** twin sister; ~ **político** brother-in-law; **hermana política** sister-in-law

hermético, a [er'metiko, a] adj hermetic; (fig) watertight

hermoso, a [er'moso, a] adj beautiful, lovely; (estupendo) splendid; (guapo) handsome; **hermosura** nf beauty

hernia ['ernja] nf hernia

héroe ['eroe] nm hero

heroína [ero'ina] nf (mujer) heroine; (droga) heroin

heroísmo [ero'ismo] nm heroism

herradura [erra'ðura] nf horseshoe

herramienta [erra'mjenta] nf tool

herrero [e'rrero] nm blacksmith

herrumbre [e'rrumbre] nf rust

hervidero [erβi'ðero] nm (fig) swarm; (POL etc) hotbed

hervir [er'βir] vi to boil; (burbujear) to bubble; (fig): ~ **de** to teem with; ~ **a fuego lento** to simmer; **hervor** nm boiling; (fig) ardour, fervour

heterosexual [eterosek'swal] adj heterosexual

hice etc vb ver **hacer**

hidratante [iðra'tante] adj: **crema ~** moisturizing cream, moisturizer; **hidratar** vt (piel) to moisturize; **hidrato** nm: **hidratos de carbono** carbohydrates

hidráulica [i'ðraulika] nf hydraulics sg

hidráulico, a [i'ðrauliko, a] adj hydraulic

hidro... [iðro] prefijo hydro..., water-...; ~**eléctrico, a** adj hydroelectric; ~**fobia** nf hydrophobia, rabies; **hidrógeno** nm hydrogen

hiedra ['jeðra] nf ivy

hiel [jel] nf gall, bile; (fig) bitterness

hiela etc vb ver **helar**

hielo ['jelo] nm (gen) ice; (escarcha) frost; (fig) coldness, reserve

hiena ['jena] *nf* hyena

hierba ['jerβa] *nf* (*pasto*) grass; (*CULIN, MED*: *planta*) herb; **mala ~** weed; (*fig*) evil influence; **~buena** *nf* mint

hierro ['jerro] *nm* (*metal*) iron; (*objeto*) iron object

hígado ['iɣaðo] *nm* liver

higiene [i'xjene] *nf* hygiene, **higiénico, a** *adj* hygienic

higo ['iɣo] *nm* fig; **higuera** *nf* fig tree

hijastro, a [i'xastro, a] *nm/f* stepson/daughter

hijo, a ['ixo, a] *nm/f* son/daughter, child; **~s** *nmpl* children, sons and daughters; **~ de papá/mamá** daddy's/mummy's boy; **~ de puta** (*fam!*) bastard (!), son of a bitch (!)

hilar [i'lar] *vt* to spin; **~ fino** to split hairs

hilera [i'lera] *nf* row, file

hilo ['ilo] *nm* thread; (*BOT*) fibre; (*metal*) wire; (*de agua*) trickle, thin stream

hilvanar [ilβa'nar] *vt* (*COSTURA*) to tack (*BRIT*), baste (*US*); (*fig*) to do hurriedly

himno ['imno] *nm* hymn; **~ nacional** national anthem

hincapié [inka'pje] *nm*: **hacer ~ en** to emphasize

hincar [in'kar] *vt* to drive (in), thrust (in); **~se** *vr*: **~se de rodillas** to kneel down

hincha ['intʃa] (*fam*) *nm/f* fan

hinchado, a [in'tʃaðo, a] *adj* (*gen*) swollen; (*persona*) pompous

hinchar [in'tʃar] *vt* (*gen*) to swell; (*inflar*) to blow up, inflate; (*fig*) to exaggerate; **~se** *vr* (*inflarse*) to swell up; (*fam*: *de comer*) to stuff o.s.; **hinchazón** *nf* (*MED*) swelling; (*altivez*) arrogance

hinojo [i'noxo] *nm* fennel

hipermercado [ipermer'kaðo] *nm* hypermarket, superstore

hípico, a ['ipiko, a] *adj* horse *cpd*

hipnotismo [ipno'tismo] *nm* hypnotism; **hipnotizar** *vt* to hypnotize

hipo ['ipo] *nm* hiccups *pl*

hipocresía [ipokre'sia] *nf* hypocrisy; **hipócrita** *adj* hypocritical ♦ *nm/f* hypocrite

hipódromo [i'poðromo] *nm* racetrack

hipopótamo [ipo'potamo] *nm* hippopotamus

hipoteca [ipo'teka] *nf* mortgage

hipótesis [i'potesis] *nf inv* hypothesis

hiriente [i'rjente] *adj* offensive, wounding

hispánico, a [is'paniko, a] *adj* Hispanic

hispano, a [is'pano, a] *adj* Hispanic, Spanish, Hispano- ♦ *nm/f* Spaniard; **H~américa** *nf* Latin America; **~americano, a** *adj, nm/f* Latin American

histeria [is'terja] *nf* hysteria

historia [is'torja] *nf* history; (*cuento*) story, tale; **~s** *nfpl* (*chismes*) gossip *sg*; **dejarse de ~s**

to come to the point; **pasar a la ~** to go down in history; **historial** *nm* (*profesional*) curriculum vitae, C.V.; (*MED*) case history; **histórico, a** *adj* historical; (*memorable*) historic

historieta [isto'rjeta] *nf* tale, anecdote; (*dibujos*) comic strip

hito ['ito] *nm* (*fig*) landmark

hizo *vb ver* **hacer**

Hnos *abr* (= *Hermanos*) Bros.

hocico [o'θiko] *nm* snout

hockey ['xoki] *nm* hockey; **~ sobre hielo** ice hockey

hogar [o'ɣar] *nm* fireplace, hearth; (*casa*) home; (*vida familiar*) home life; **~eño, a** *adj* home *cpd*; (*persona*) home-loving

hoguera [o'ɣera] *nf* (*gen*) bonfire

hoja ['oxa] *nf* (*gen*) leaf; (*de flor*) petal; (*de papel*) sheet; (*página*) page; **~ de afeitar** razor blade

hojalata [oxa'lata] *nf* tin(plate)

hojaldre [o'xaldre] *nm* (*CULIN*) puff pastry

hojear [oxe'ar] *vt* to leaf through, turn the pages of

hola ['ola] *excl* hello!

Holanda [o'landa] *nf* Holland; **holandés, esa** *adj* Dutch ♦ *nm/f* Dutchman/woman ♦ *nm* (*LING*) Dutch

holgado, a [ol'ɣaðo, a] *adj* (*ropa*) loose, baggy; (*rico*) comfortable

holgar [ol'ɣar] *vi* (*descansar*) to rest; (*sobrar*) to be superfluous; **huelga decir que** it goes without saying that

holgazán, ana [olɣa'θan, ana] *adj* idle, lazy ♦ *nm/f* loafer

holgura [ol'ɣura] *nf* looseness, bagginess; (*TEC*) play, free movement; (*vida*) comfortable living

hollín [o'ʎin] *nm* soot

hombre ['ombre] *nm* (*gen*) man; (*raza humana*): **el ~** man(kind) ♦ *excl*: **¡sí ~!** (*claro*) of course!; (*para énfasis*) man, old boy; **~ de negocios** businessman; **~ de pro** honest man; **~-rana** frogman

hombrera [om'brera] *nf* shoulder strap

hombro ['ombro] *nm* shoulder

hombruno, a [om'bruno, a] *adj* mannish

homenaje [ome'naxe] *nm* (*gen*) homage; (*tributo*) tribute

homicida [omi'θiða] *adj* homicidal ♦ *nm/f* murderer; **homicidio** *nm* murder, homicide

homologar [omolo'ðar] *vt* (*COM*: *productos, tamaños*) to standardize; **homólogo, a** *nm/f*: **su** *etc* **homólogo** his *etc* counterpart o opposite number

homosexual [omosek'swal] *adj, nm/f* homosexual

hondo, a ['ondo, a] *adj* deep; **lo ~** the depth(s) (*pl*), the bottom; **~nada** *nf* hollow, depression; (*cañón*) ravine

Honduras [on'duras] *nf* Honduras

hondureño, a [ondu'reɲo, a] *adj, nm/f* Honduran

honestidad [onesti'ðað] *nf* purity, chastity; (*decencia*) decency; **honesto, a** *adj* chaste; decent, honest; (*justo*) just

hongo ['ongo] *nm* (BOT: *gen*) fungus; (: *comestible*) mushroom; (: *venenoso*) toadstool

honor [o'nor] *nm* (*gen*) honour; **en ~ a la verdad** to be fair; **~able** *adj* honourable

honorario, a [ono'rarjo, a] *adj* honorary; **~s** *nmpl* fees

honra ['onra] *nf* (*gen*) honour; (*renombre*) good name; **~dez** *nf* honesty; (*de persona*) integrity; **~do, a** *adj* honest, upright

honrar [on'rar] *vt* to honour; **~se** *vr*: **~se con algo/de hacer algo** to be honoured by sth/to do sth

honroso, a [on'roso, a] *adj* (*honrado*) honourable; (*respetado*) respectable

hora ['ora] *nf* (*una* ~) hour; (*tiempo*) time; **¿qué ~ es?** what time is it?; **¿a qué ~?** at what time?; **media ~** half an hour; **a la ~ de recreo** at playtime; **a primera ~** first thing (in the morning); **a última ~** at the last moment; **a altas ~s** in the small hours; **¡a buena ~!** about time, too!; **dar la ~** to strike the hour; **~s de oficina/de trabajo** office/working hours; **~s de visita** visiting times; **~s extras** o **extraordinarias** overtime *sg*; **~s punta** rush hours

horadar [ora'ðar] *vt* to drill, bore

horario, a [o'rarjo, a] *adj* hourly, hour *cpd* ♦ *nm* timetable; **~ comercial** business hours *pl*

horca ['orka] *nf* gallows *sg*

horcajadas [orka'xaðas]: **a ~** *adv* astride

horchata [or'tʃata] *nf* cold drink made from tiger nuts and water, tiger nut milk

horizontal [oriθon'tal] *adj* horizontal

horizonte [ori'θonte] *nm* horizon

horma ['orma] *nf* mould

hormiga [or'miɣa] *nf* ant; **~s** *nfpl* (MED) pins and needles

hormigón [ormi'ɣon] *nm* concrete; **~ armado/pretensado** reinforced/prestressed concrete

hormigueo [ormi'ɣeo] *nm* (*comezón*) itch

hormona [or'mona] *nf* hormone

hornada [or'naða] *nf* batch (of loaves *etc*)

hornillo [or'niʎo] *nm* (*cocina*) portable stove

horno ['orno] *nm* (CULIN) oven; (TEC) furnace; **alto ~** blast furnace

horóscopo [o'roskopo] *nm* horoscope

horquilla [or'kiʎa] *nf* hairpin; (AGR) pitchfork

horrendo, a [o'rrendo, a] *adj* horrendous, frightful

horrible [o'rriβle] *adj* horrible, dreadful

horripilante [orripi'lante] *adj* hair-raising,

horrifying

horror [o'rror] *nm* horror, dread; (*atrocidad*) atrocity; **¡qué ~!** (*fam*) how awful!; **~izar** *vt* to horrify, frighten; **~izarse** *vr* to be horrified; **~oso, a** *adj* horrifying, ghastly

hortaliza [orta'liθa] *nf* vegetable

hortelano, a [orte'lano, a] *nm/f* (market) gardener

hortera [or'tera] (*fam*) *adj* tacky

hosco, a ['osko, a] *adj* sullen, gloomy

hospedar [ospe'ðar] *vt* to put up; **~se** *vr* to stay, lodge

hospital [ospi'tal] *nm* hospital

hospitalario, a [ospita'larjo, a] *adj* (*acogedor*) hospitable; **hospitalidad** *nf* hospitality

hostal [os'tal] *nm* small hotel

hostelería [ostele'ria] *nf* hotel business o trade

hostia ['ostja] *nf* (REL) host, consecrated wafer; (*fam!*: *golpe*) whack, punch ♦ *excl* (*fam!*): **¡~(s)!** damn!

hostigar [osti'ɣar] *vt* to whip; (*fig*) to harass, pester

hostil [os'til] *adj* hostile; **~idad** *nf* hostility

hotel [o'tel] *nm* hotel; **~ero, a** *adj* hotel *cpd* ♦ *nm/f* hotelier

hoy [oi] *adv* (*este día*) today; (*la actualidad*) now(adays) ♦ *nm* present time; **~ (en) día** now(adays)

hoyo ['ojo] *nm* hole, pit; **hoyuelo** *nm* dimple

hoz [oθ] *nf* sickle

hube *etc vb ver* **haber**

hucha ['utʃa] *nf* money box

hueco, a ['weko, a] *adj* (*vacío*) hollow, empty; (*resonante*) booming ♦ *nm* hollow, cavity

huelga *etc* ['welɣa] *vb ver* **holgar** ♦ *nf* strike; **declararse en ~** to go on strike, come out on strike; **~ de hambre** hunger strike

huelguista [wel'ɣista] *nm/f* striker

huella ['weʎa] *nf* (*pisada*) tread; (*marca del paso*) footprint, footstep; (: *de animal, máquina*) track; **~ digital** fingerprint

huelo *etc vb ver* **oler**

huérfano, a ['werfano, a] *adj* orphan(ed) ♦ *nm/f* orphan

huerta ['werta] *nf* market garden; (*en Murcia y Valencia*) irrigated region

huerto ['werto] *nm* kitchen garden; (*de árboles frutales*) orchard

hueso ['weso] *nm* (ANAT) bone; (*de fruta*) stone

huésped, a ['wespeð, a] *nm/f* guest

huesudo, a [we'suðo, a] *adj* bony, big-boned

hueva ['weβa] *nf* roe

huevera [we'βera] *nf* eggcup

huevo ['weβo] *nm* egg; **~ duro/escalfado/frito**

(*ESP*) o **estrellado** (*AM*)**/pasado por agua** hard-boiled/poached/fried/soft-boiled egg; **~s revueltos** scrambled eggs

huida [u'iða] *nf* escape, flight

huidizo, a [ui'ðiθo, a] *adj* shy

huir [u'ir] *vi* (*escapar*) to flee, escape; (*evitar*) to avoid; **~se** *vr* (*escaparse*) to escape

hule ['ule] *nm* oilskin

humanidad [umani'ðað] *nf* (*género humano*) man(kind); (*cualidad*) humanity

humanitario, a [umani'tarjo, a] *adj* humanitarian

humano, a [u'mano, a] *adj* (*gen*) human; (*humanitario*) humane ♦ *nm* human; **ser ~** human being

humareda [uma'reða] *nf* cloud of smoke

humedad [ume'ðað] *nf* (*del clima*) humidity; (*de pared etc*) dampness; **a prueba de ~** damp-proof; **humedecer** *vt* to moisten, wet; **humedecerse** *vr* to get wet

húmedo, a ['umeðo, a] *adj* (*mojado*) damp, wet; (*tiempo etc*) humid

humildad [umil'dað] *nf* humility, humbleness; **humilde** *adj* humble, modest

humillación [umiʎa'θjon] *nf* humiliation; **humillante** *adj* humiliating

humillar [umi'ʎar] *vt* to humiliate; **~se** *vr* to humble o.s., grovel

humo ['umo] *nm* (*de fuego*) smoke; (*gas nocivo*) fumes *pl*; (*vapor*) steam, vapour; **~s** *nmpl* (*fig*) conceit *sg*

humor [u'mor] *nm* (*disposición*) mood, temper; (*lo que divierte*) humour; **de buen/ mal ~** in a good/bad mood; **~ista** *nm/f* comic; **~ístico, a** *adj* funny, humorous

hundimiento [undi'mjento] *nm* (*gen*) sinking; (*colapso*) collapse

hundir [un'dir] *vt* to sink; (*edificio, plan*) to ruin, destroy; **~se** *vr* to sink, collapse

húngaro, a ['ungaro, a] *adj, nm/f* Hungarian

Hungría [un'gria] *nf* Hungary

huracán [ura'kan] *nm* hurricane

huraño, a [u'raɲo, a] *adj* (*antisocial*) unsociable

hurgar [ur'xar] *vt* to poke, jab; (*remover*) to stir (up); **~se** *vr*: **~se (las narices)** to pick one's nose

hurón, ona [u'ron, ona] *nm* (*ZOOL*) ferret

hurtadillas [urta'ðiʎas]: **a ~** *adv* stealthily, on the sly

hurtar [ur'tar] *vt* to steal; **hurto** *nm* theft, stealing

husmear [usme'ar] *vt* (*oler*) to sniff out, scent; (*fam*) to pry into

huyo *etc vb ver* **huir**

I, i

iba *etc vb ver* **ir**

ibérico, a [i'ßeriko, a] *adj* Iberian

iberoamericano, a [ißeroameri'kano, a] *adj, nm/f* Latin American

Ibiza [i'ßiθa] *nf* Ibiza

iceberg [iθe'ßer] *nm* iceberg

icono [i'kono] *nm* ikon, icon

iconoclasta [ikono'klasta] *adj* iconoclastic ♦ *nm/f* iconoclast

ictericia [ikte'riθja] *nf* jaundice

I + D *abr* (= *Investigación y Desarrollo*) R & D

ida ['iða] *nf* going, departure; **~ y vuelta** round trip, return

idea [i'ðea] *nf* idea; **no tengo la menor ~** I haven't a clue

ideal [iðe'al] *adj, nm* ideal; **~ista** *nm/f* idealist; **~izar** *vt* to idealize

idear [iðe'ar] *vt* to think up; (*aparato*) to invent; (*viaje*) to plan

ídem ['iðem] *pron* ditto

idéntico, a [i'ðentiko, a] *adj* identical

identidad [iðenti'ðað] *nf* identity

identificación [iðentifika'θjon] *nf* identification

identificar [iðentifi'kar] *vt* to identify; **~se** *vr*: **~se con** to identify with

ideología [iðeolo'xia] *nf* ideology

idilio [i'ðiljo] *nm* love-affair

idioma [i'ðjoma] *nm* (*gen*) language

idiota [i'ðjota] *adj* idiotic ♦ *nm/f* idiot; **idiotez** *nf* idiocy

ídolo ['iðolo] *nm* (*tb: fig*) idol

idóneo, a [i'ðoneo, a] *adj* suitable

iglesia [i'ɣlesja] *nf* church

ignorancia [iɣno'ranθja] *nf* ignorance; **ignorante** *adj* ignorant, uninformed ♦ *nm/f* ignoramus

ignorar [iɣno'rar] *vt* not to know, be ignorant of; (*no hacer caso a*) to ignore

igual [i'ɣwal] *adj* (*gen*) equal; (*similar*) like, similar; (*mismo*) (the) same; (*constante*) constant; (*temperatura*) even ♦ *nm/f* equal; **~ que** like, the same as; **me da** o **es ~** I don't care; **son ~es** they're the same; **al ~ que** *prep, conj* like, just like

igualada [iɣwa'laða] *nf* equaliser

igualar [iɣwa'lar] *vt* (*gen*) to equalize, make equal; (*allanar, nivelar*) to level (off), even (out); **~se** *vr* (*platos de balanza*) to balance out

igualdad [iɣwal'dað] *nf* equality; (*similaridad*) sameness; (*uniformidad*) uniformity

igualmente [iɣwal'mente] *adv* equally; (*también*) also, likewise ♦ *excl* the same to you!

ikurriña [iku'rriɲa] nf Basque flag

ilegal [ile'val] adj illegal

ilegítimo, a [ile'xitimo, a] adj illegitimate

ileso, a [i'leso, a] adj unhurt

ilícito, a [i'liθito] adj illicit

ilimitado, a [ilimi'taðo, a] adj unlimited

ilógico, a [i'loxiko, a] adj illogical

iluminación [ilumina'θjon] nf illumination; (alumbrado) lighting

iluminar [ilumi'nar] vt to illuminate, light (up); (fig) to enlighten

ilusión [ilu'sjon] nf illusion; (quimera) delusion; (esperanza) hope; **hacerse ilusiones** to build up one's hopes; **ilusionado, a** adj excited; **ilusionar** vi: **le ilusiona ir de vacaciones** he's looking forward to going on holiday; **ilusionarse** vr: **ilusionarse (con)** to get excited (about)

ilusionista [ilusjo'nista] nm/f conjurer

iluso, a [i'luso, a] adj easily deceived ♦ nm/f dreamer

ilusorio, a [ilu'sorjo, a] adj (de ilusión) illusory, deceptive; (esperanza) vain

ilustración [ilustra'θjon] nf illustration; (saber) learning, erudition; **la I~** the Enlightenment; **ilustrado, a** adj illustrated; learned

ilustrar [ilus'trar] vt to illustrate; (instruir) to instruct; (explicar) to explain, make clear; **~se** vr to acquire knowledge

ilustre [i'lustre] adj famous, illustrious

imagen [i'maxen] nf (gen) image; (dibujo) picture

imaginación [imaxina'θjon] nf imagination

imaginar [imaxi'nar] vt (gen) to imagine; (idear) to think up; (suponer) to suppose; **~se** vr to imagine; **~io, a** adj imaginary; **imaginativo, a** adj imaginative

imán [i'man] nm magnet

imbécil [im'beθil] nm/f imbecile, idiot

imitación [imita'θjon] nf imitation

imitar [imi'tar] vt to imitate; (parodiar, remedar) to mimic, ape

impaciencia [impa'θjenθja] nf impatience; **impaciente** adj impatient; (nervioso) anxious

impacto [im'pakto] nm impact

impar [im'par] adj odd

imparcial [impar'θjal] adj impartial, fair

impartir [impar'tir] vt to impart, give

impasible [impa'siβle] adj impassive

impecable [impe'kaβle] adj impeccable

impedimento [impeði'mento] nm impediment, obstacle

impedir [impe'ðir] vt (obstruir) to impede, obstruct; (estorbar) to prevent

impenetrable [impene'traβle] adj impenetrable; (fig) incomprehensible

imperar [impe'rar] vi (reinar) to rule, reign; (fig) to prevail, reign; (precio) to be current

imperativo, a [impera'tiβo, a] adj (urgente, LING) imperative

imperceptible [imperθep'tiβle] adj imperceptible

imperdible [imper'ðiβle] nm safety pin

imperdonable [imperðo'naβle] adj unforgivable, inexcusable

imperfección [imperfek'θjon] nf imperfection

imperfecto, a [imper'fekto, a] adj imperfect

imperial [impe'rjal] adj imperial; **~ismo** nm imperialism

imperio [im'perjo] nm empire; (autoridad) rule, authority; (fig) pride, haughtiness; **~so, a** adj imperious; (urgente) urgent; (imperativo) imperative

impermeable [imperme'aβle] adj waterproof ♦ nm raincoat, mac (BRIT)

impersonal [imperso'nal] adj impersonal

impertinencia [imperti'nenθja] nf impertinence; **impertinente** adj impertinent

imperturbable [impertur'βaβle] adj imperturbable

ímpetu ['impetu] nm (impulso) impetus, impulse; (impetuosidad) impetuosity; (violencia) violence

impetuoso, a [impe'twoso, a] adj impetuous; (río) rushing; (acto) hasty

impío, a [im'pio, a] adj impious, ungodly

implacable [impla'kaβle] adj implacable

implantar [implan'tar] vt to introduce

implicar [impli'kar] vt to involve; (entrañar) to imply

implícito, a [im'pliθito, a] adj (tácito) implicit; (sobreentendido) implied

implorar [implo'rar] vt to beg, implore

imponente [impo'nente] adj (impresionante) impressive, imposing; (solemne) grand

imponer [impo'ner] vt to impose; (exigir) to exact; **~se** vr to assert o.s.; (prevalecer) to prevail; **imponible** adj (COM) taxable

impopular [impopu'lar] adj unpopular

importación [importa'θjon] nf (acto) importing; (mercancías) imports pl

importancia [impor'tanθja] nf importance; (valor) value, significance; (extensión) size, magnitude; **importante** adj important; valuable, significant

importar [impor'tar] vt (del extranjero) to import; (costar) to amount to ♦ vi to be important, matter; **me importa un rábano** I couldn't care less; **no importa** it doesn't matter; **¿le importa que fume?** do you mind if I smoke?

importe [im'porte] nm (total) amount; (valor) value

importunar [importu'nar] *vt* to bother, pester

imposibilidad [imposiβili'ðað] *nf* impossibility; **imposibilitar** *vt* to make impossible, prevent

imposible [impo'siβle] *adj* (*gen*) impossible; (*insoportable*) unbearable, intolerable

imposición [imposi'θjon] *nf* imposition; (*COM: impuesto*) tax; (: *inversión*) deposit

impostor, a [impos'tor, a] *nm/f* impostor

impotencia [impo'tenθja] *nf* impotence; **impotente** *adj* impotent

impracticable [imprakti'kaβle] *adj* (*irrealizable*) impracticable; (*intransitable*) impassable

impreciso, a [impre'θiso, a] *adj* imprecise, vague

impregnar [impreɣ'nar] *vt* to impregnate; **~se** *vr* to become impregnated

imprenta [im'prenta] *nf* (*acto*) printing; (*aparato*) press; (*casa*) printer's; (*letra*) print

imprescindible [impresθin'diβle] *adj* essential, vital

impresión [impre'sjon] *nf* (*gen*) impression; (*IMPRENTA*) printing; (*edición*) edition; (*FOTO*) print; (*marca*) imprint; **~ digital** fingerprint

impresionable [impresjo'naβle] *adj* (*sensible*) impressionable

impresionante [impresjo'nante] *adj* impressive; (*tremendo*) tremendous; (*maravilloso*) great, marvellous

impresionar [impresjo'nar] *vt* (*conmover*) to move; (*afectar*) to impress, strike; (*película fotográfica*) to expose; **~se** *vr* to be impressed; (*conmoverse*) to be moved

impreso, a [im'preso, a] *pp de* **imprimir** ♦ *adj* printed; **~s** *nmpl* printed matter; **impresora** *nf* printer

imprevisto, a [impre'βisto, a] *adj* (*gen*) unforeseen; (*inesperado*) unexpected

imprimir [impri'mir] *vt* to imprint, impress, stamp; (*textos*) to print; (*INFORM*) to output, print out

improbable [impro'βaβle] *adj* improbable; (*inverosímil*) unlikely

improcedente [improθe'ðente] *adj* inappropriate

improductivo, a [improðuk'tiβo, a] *adj* unproductive

improperio [impro'perjo] *nm* insult

impropio, a [im'propjo, a] *adj* improper

improvisado, a [improβi'saðo, a] *adj* improvised

improvisar [improβi'sar] *vt* to improvise

improviso, a [impro'βiso, a] *adj*: **de ~** unexpectedly, suddenly

imprudencia [impru'ðenθja] *nf* imprudence; (*indiscreción*) indiscretion; (*descuido*) carelessness; **imprudente** *adj*

unwise, imprudent; (*indiscreto*) indiscreet

impúdico, a [im'puðiko, a] *adj* shameless; (*lujurioso*) lecherous

impuesto, a [im'pwesto, a] *adj* imposed ♦ *nm* tax; **~ sobre el valor añadido** value added tax

impugnar [impuɣ'nar] *vt* to oppose, contest; (*refutar*) to refute, impugn

impulsar [impul'sar] *vt* to drive; (*promover*) to promote, stimulate

impulsivo, a [impul'siβo, a] *adj* impulsive; **impulso** *nm* impulse; (*fuerza, empuje*) thrust, drive; (*fig: sentimiento*) urge, impulse

impune [im'pune] *adj* unpunished

impureza [impu'reθa] *nf* impurity; **impuro, a** *adj* impure

imputar [impu'tar] *vt* to attribute

inacabable [inaka'ßaßle] *adj* (*infinito*) endless; (*interminable*) interminable

inaccesible [inakθe'siβle] *adj* inaccessible

inacción [inak'θjon] *nf* inactivity

inaceptable [inaθep'taßle] *adj* unacceptable

inactividad [inaktiβi'ðað] *nf* inactivity; (*COM*) dullness; **inactivo, a** *adj* inactive

inadecuado, a [inaðe'kwaðo, a] *adj* (*insuficiente*) inadequate; (*inapto*) unsuitable

inadmisible [inaðmi'siβle] *adj* inadmissible

inadvertido, a [inaðßer'tiðo, a] *adj* (*no visto*) unnoticed

inagotable [inaɣo'taßle] *adj* inexhaustible

inaguantable [inaɣwan'taßle] *adj* unbearable

inalterable [inalte'raßle] *adj* immutable, unchangeable

inanición [inani'θjon] *nf* starvation

inanimado, a [inani'maðo, a] *adj* inanimate

inapreciable [inapre'ðjaßle] *adj* (*cantidad, diferencia*) imperceptible; (*ayuda, servicio*) invaluable

inaudito, a [inau'ðito, a] *adj* unheard-of

inauguración [inauɣura'θjon] *nf* inauguration; opening

inaugurar [inauɣu'rar] *vt* to inaugurate; (*exposición*) to open

inca ['inka] *nm/f* Inca

incalculable [inkalku'laßle] *adj* incalculable

incandescente [inkandes'θente] *adj* incandescent

incansable [inkan'saßle] *adj* tireless, untiring

incapacidad [inkapaθi'ðað] *nf* incapacity; (*incompetencia*) incompetence; **~ física/mental** physical/mental disability

incapacitar [inkapaθi'tar] *vt* (*inhabilitar*) to incapacitate, render unfit; (*descalificar*) to disqualify

incapaz [inka'paθ] *adj* incapable

incautación [inkauta'θjon] *nf* confiscation

incautarse [inkau'tarse] *vr*: **~ de** to seize, confiscate

incauto, a [in'kauto, a] adj (imprudente) incautious, unwary

incendiar [inθen'djar] vt to set fire to; (fig) to inflame; ~se vr to catch fire; ~io, a adj incendiary

incendio [in'θendjo] nm fire

incentivo [inθen'tiβo] nm incentive

incertidumbre [inθerti'ðumbre] nf (inseguridad) uncertainty; (duda) doubt

incesante [inθe'sante] adj incessant

incesto [in'θesto] nm incest

incidencia [inθi'ðenθja] nf (MAT) incidence

incidente [inθi'ðente] nm incident

incidir [inθi'ðir] vi (influir) to influence; (afectar) to affect; ~ en un error to fall into error

incienso [in'θjenso] nm incense

incierto, a [in'θjerto, a] adj uncertain

incineración [inθinera'θjon] nf incineration; (de cadáveres) cremation

incinerar [inθine'rar] vt to burn; (cadáveres) to cremate

incipiente [inθi'pjente] adj incipient

incisión [inθi'sjon] nf incision

incisivo, a [inθi'siβo, a] adj sharp, cutting; (fig) incisive

incitar [inθi'tar] vt to incite, rouse

inclemencia [inkle'menθja] nf (severidad) harshness, severity; (del tiempo) inclemency

inclinación [inklina'θjon] nf (gen) inclination; (de tierras) slope, incline; (de cabeza) nod, bow; (fig) leaning, bent

inclinar [inkli'nar] vt to incline; (cabeza) to nod, bow ♦ vi to lean, slope; ~se vr to bow; (encorvarse) to stoop; ~se a (parecerse a) to take after, resemble; ~se ante to bow down to; me inclino a pensar que I'm inclined to think that

incluir [inklu'ir] vt to include; (incorporar) to incorporate; (meter) to enclose

inclusive [inklu'siβe] adv inclusive ♦ prep including

incluso [in'kluso] adv even

incógnita [in'koɣnita] nf (MAT) unknown quantity

incógnito [in'koɣnito] nm: de ~ incognito

incoherente [inkoe'rente] adj incoherent

incoloro, a [inko'loro, a] adj colourless

incólume [in'kolume] adj unhurt, unharmed

incomodar [inkomo'ðar] vt to inconvenience; (molestar) to bother, trouble; (fastidiar) to annoy; ~se vr to put o.s. out; (fastidiarse) to get annoyed

incomodidad [inkomoði'ðað] nf inconvenience; (fastidio, enojo) annoyance; (de vivienda) discomfort

incómodo, a [in'komoðo, a] adj (inconfortable) uncomfortable; (molesto) annoying; (inconveniente) inconvenient

incomparable [inkompa'raβle] adj incomparable

incompatible [inkompa'tiβle] adj incompatible

incompetencia [inkompe'tenθja] nf incompetence; **incompetente** adj incompetent

incompleto, a [inkom'pleto, a] adj incomplete, unfinished

incomprensible [inkompren'siβle] adj incomprehensible

incomunicado, a [inkomuni'kaðo, a] adj (aislado) cut off, isolated; (confinado) in solitary confinement

inconcebible [inkonθe'βiβle] adj inconceivable

incondicional [inkondiθjo'nal] adj unconditional; (apoyo) wholehearted; (partidario) staunch

inconexo, a [inko'nekso, a] adj (gen) unconnected; (desunido) disconnected

inconfundible [inkonfun'diβle] adj unmistakable

incongruente [inkon'grwente] adj incongruous

inconsciencia [inkons'θjenθja] nf unconsciousness; (fig) thoughtlessness; **inconsciente** adj unconscious; thoughtless

inconsecuente [inkonse'kwente] adj inconsistent

inconsiderado, a [inkonsiðe'raðo, a] adj inconsiderate

inconsistente [inkonsis'tente] adj weak; (tela) flimsy

inconstancia [inkons'tanθja] nf inconstancy; (inestabilidad) unsteadiness; **inconstante** adj inconstant

incontable [inkon'taβle] adj countless, innumerable

incontestable [inkontes'taβle] adj unanswerable; (innegable) undeniable

incontinencia [inkonti'nenθja] nf incontinence

inconveniencia [inkombe'njenθja] nf unsuitability, inappropriateness; (descortesía) impoliteness; **inconveniente** adj unsuitable; impolite ♦ nm obstacle; (desventaja) disadvantage; el inconveniente es que ... the trouble is that ...

incordiar [inkor'ðjar] (fam) vt to bug, annoy

incorporación [inkorpora'θjon] nf incorporation

incorporar [inkorpo'rar] vt to incorporate; ~se vr to sit up

incorrección [inkorrek'θjon] nf (gen) incorrectness, inaccuracy; (descortesía) bad-mannered behaviour; **incorrecto, a** adj (gen) incorrect, wrong; (comportamiento) bad-mannered

incorregible [inkorre'xiβle] *adj* incorrigible

incredulidad [inkreðuli'ðað] *nf* incredulity; (*escepticismo*) scepticism; **incrédulo, a** *adj* incredulous, unbelieving; sceptical

increíble [inkre'iβle] *adj* incredible

incremento [inkre'mento] *nm* increment; (*aumento*) rise, increase

increpar [inkre'par] *vt* to reprimand

incruento, a [in'krwento, a] *adj* bloodless

incrustar [inkrus'tar] *vt* to incrust; (*piedras: en joya*) to inlay

incubar [inku'βar] *vt* to incubate

inculcar [inkul'kar] *vt* to inculcate

inculpar [inkul'par] *vt* (*acusar*) to accuse; (*achacar, atribuir*) to charge, blame

inculto, a [in'kulto, a] *adj* (*persona*) uneducated; (*grosero*) uncouth ♦ *nm/f* ignoramus

incumplimiento [inkumpli'mjento] *nm* non-fulfilment; **~ de contrato** breach of contract

incurrir [inku'rrir] *vi*: **~ en** to incur; (*crimen*) to commit; **~ en un error** to make a mistake

indagación [indaɣa'θjon] *nf* investigation; (*búsqueda*) search; (*JUR*) inquest

indagar [inda'ɣar] *vt* to investigate; to search; (*averiguar*) to ascertain

indecente [inde'θente] *adj* indecent, improper; (*lascivo*) obscene

indecible [inde'θiβle] *adj* unspeakable; (*indescriptible*) indescribable

indeciso, a [inde'θiso, a] *adj* (*por decidir*) undecided; (*vacilante*) hesitant

indefenso, a [inde'fenso, a] *adj* defenceless

indefinido, a [indefi'niðo, a] *adj* indefinite; (*vago*) vague, undefined

indeleble [inde'leβle] *adj* indelible

indemne [in'demne] *adj* (*objeto*) undamaged; (*persona*) unharmed, unhurt

indemnizar [indemni'θar] *vt* to indemnify; (*compensar*) to compensate

independencia [indepen'denθja] *nf* independence

independiente [indepen'djente] *adj* (*libre*) independent; (*autónomo*) self-sufficient

indeterminado, a [indetermi'naðo, a] *adj* indefinite; (*desconocido*) indeterminate

India ['indja] *nf*: **la ~** India

indicación [indika'θjon] *nf* indication; (*señal*) sign; (*sugerencia*) suggestion, hint

indicado, a [indi'kaðo, a] *adj* (*momento, método*) right; (*tratamiento*) appropriate; (*solución*) likely

indicador [indika'ðor] *nm* indicator; (*TEC*) gauge, meter

indicar [indi'kar] *vt* (*mostrar*) to indicate, show; (*termómetro etc*) to read, register; (*señalar*) to point to

índice ['indiθe] *nm* index; (*catálogo* catalogue; (*ANAT*) index finger, forefinger

indicio [in'diθjo] *nm* indication, sign; (*en pesquisa etc*) clue

indiferencia [indife'renθja] *nf* indifference; (*apatía*) apathy; **indiferente** *adj* indifferent

indígena [in'dixena] *adj* indigenous, native ♦ *nm/f* native

indigencia [indi'xenθja] *nf* poverty, need

indigestión [indixes'tjon] *nf* indigestion

indigesto, a [indi'xesto, a] *adj* (*alimento*) indigestible; (*fig*) turgid

indignación [indiɣna'θjon] *nf* indignation

indignar [indiɣ'nar] *vt* to anger, make indignant; **~se** *vr*: **~se por** to get indignant about

indigno, a [in'diɣno, a] *adj* (*despreciable*) low, contemptible; (*inmerecido*) unworthy

indio, a ['indjo, a] *adj*, *nm/f* Indian

indirecta [indi'rekta] *nf* insinuation, innuendo; (*sugerencia*) hint

indirecto, a [indi'rekto, a] *adj* indirect

indiscreción [indiskre'θjon] *nf* (*imprudencia*) indiscretion; (*irreflexión*) tactlessness; (*acto*) gaffe, faux pas

indiscreto, a [indis'kreto, a] *adj* indiscreet

indiscriminado, a [indiskrimi'naðo, a] *adj* indiscriminate

indiscutible [indisku'tiβle] *adj* indisputable, unquestionable

indispensable [indispen'saβle] *adj* indispensable, essential

indisponer [indispo'ner] *vt* to spoil, upset; (*salud*) to make ill; **~se** *vr* to fall ill; **~se con uno** to fall out with sb

indisposición [indisposi'θjon] *nf* indisposition

indispuesto, a [indis'pwesto, a] *adj* (*enfermo*) unwell, indisposed

indistinto, a [indis'tinto, a] *adj* indistinct; (*vago*) vague

individual [indiβi'ðwal] *adj* individual; (*habitación*) single ♦ *nm* (*DEPORTE*) singles *sg*

individuo, a [indi'βiðwo, a] *adj*, *nm* individual

índole ['indole] *nf* (*naturaleza*) nature; (*clase*) sort, kind

indómito, a [in'domito, a] *adj* indomitable

inducir [indu'θir] *vt* to induce; (*inferir*) to infer; (*persuadir*) to persuade

indudable [indu'ðaβle] *adj* undoubted; (*incuestionable*) unquestionable

indulgencia [indul'xenθja] *nf* indulgence

indultar [indul'tar] *vt* (*perdonar*) to pardon, reprieve; (*librar de pago*) to exempt; **indulto** *nm* pardon; exemption

industria [in'dustrja] *nf* industry; (*habilidad*) skill; **industrial** *adj* industrial ♦ *nm* industrialist

inédito, a [in'eðito, a] *adj* (*texto*)

unpublished; (*nuevo*) new

inefable [ine'faßle] *adj* ineffable, indescribable

ineficaz [inefi'kaθ] *adj* (*inútil*) ineffective; (*ineficiente*) inefficient

ineludible [inelu'ðißle] *adj* inescapable, unavoidable

ineptitud [inepti'tuð] *nf* ineptitude, incompetence; **inepto, a** *adj* inept, incompetent

inequívoco, a [ine'kißoko, a] *adj* unequivocal; (*inconfundible*) unmistakable

inercia [in'erθja] *nf* inertia; (*pasividad*) passivity

inerme [in'erme] *adj* (*sin armas*) unarmed; (*indefenso*) defenceless

inerte [in'erte] *adj* inert; (*inmóvil*) motionless

inesperado, a [inespe'raðo, a] *adj* unexpected, unforeseen

inestable [ines'taßle] *adj* unstable

inevitable [ineßi'taßle] *adj* inevitable

inexactitud [ineksakti'tuð] *nf* inaccuracy; **inexacto, a** *adj* inaccurate; (*falso*) untrue

inexperto, a [inek'sperto, a] *adj* (*novato*) inexperienced

infalible [infa'lißle] *adj* infallible; (*plan*) foolproof

infame [in'fame] *adj* infamous; (*horrible*) dreadful; **infamia** *nf* infamy; (*deshonra*) disgrace

infancia [in'fanθja] *nf* infancy, childhood

infantería [infante'ria] *nf* infantry

infantil [infan'til] *adj* (*pueril, aniñado*) infantile; (*cándido*) childlike; (*literatura, ropa etc*) children's

infarto [in'farto] *nm* (*tb:* ~ *de miocardio*) heart attack

infatigable [infati'vaßle] *adj* tireless, untiring

infección [infek'θjon] *nf* infection; **infeccioso, a** *adj* infectious

infectar [infek'tar] *vt* to infect; **~se** *vr* to become infected

infeliz [infe'liθ] *adj* unhappy, wretched ♦ *nm/f* wretch

inferior [infe'rjor] *adj* inferior; (*situación*) lower ♦ *nm/f* inferior, subordinate

inferir [infe'rir] *vt* (*deducir*) to infer, deduce; (*causar*) to cause

infestar [infes'tar] *vt* to infest

infidelidad [infiðeli'ðað] *nf* (*gen*) infidelity, unfaithfulness

infiel [in'fjel] *adj* unfaithful, disloyal; (*erróneo*) inaccurate ♦ *nm/f* infidel, unbeliever

infierno [in'fjerno] *nm* hell

infiltrarse [infil'trarse] *vr:* ~ **en** to infiltrate in(to); (*persona*) to work one's way in(to)

ínfimo, a ['infimo, ə] *adj* (*más bajo*) lowest; (*despreciable*) vile, mean

infinidad [infini'ðað] *nf* infinity;

(*abundancia*) great quantity

infinito, a [infi'nito, a] *adj, nm* infinite

inflación [infla'θjon] *nf* (*hinchazón*) swelling; (*monetaria*) inflation; (*fig*) conceit; **inflacionario, a** *adj* inflationary

inflamar [infla'mar] *vt* (*MED, fig*) to inflame; **~se** *vr* to catch fire; to become inflamed

inflar [in'flar] *vt* (*hinchar*) to inflate, blow up; (*fig*) to exaggerate; **~se** *vr* to swell (up); (*fig*) to get conceited

inflexible [inflek'sißle] *adj* inflexible; (*fig*) unbending

infligir [infli'xir] *vt* to inflict

influencia [influ'enθja] *nf* influence; **influenciar** *vt* to influence

influir [influ'ir] *vt* to influence

influjo [in'fluxo] *nm* influence

influya *etc vb ver* **influir**

influyente [influ'jente] *adj* influential

información [informa'θjon] *nf* information; (*noticias*) news *sg*; (*JUR*) inquiry; **I~** (*oficina*) Information Office; (*mostrador*) Information Desk; (*TEL*) Directory Enquiries

informal [infor'mal] *adj* (*gen*) informal

informar [infor'mar] *vt* (*gen*) to inform; (*revelar*) to reveal, make known ♦ *vi* (*JUR*) to plead; (*denunciar*) to inform; (*dar cuenta de*) to report on; **~se** *vr* to find out; **~se de** to inquire into

informática [infor'matika] *nf* computer science, information technology

informe [in'forme] *adj* shapeless ♦ *nm* report

infortunio [infor'tunjo] *nm* misfortune

infracción [infrak'θjon] *nf* infraction, infringement

infranqueable [infranke'aßle] *adj* impassable; (*fig*) insurmountable

infravalorar [infrabalo'rar] *vt* to undervalue, underestimate

infringir [infrin'xir] *vt* to infringe, contravene

infructuoso, a [infruk'twoso, a] *adj* fruitless, unsuccessful

infundado, a [infun'daðo, a] *adj* groundless, unfounded

infundir [infun'dir] *vt* to infuse, instil

infusión [infu'sjon] *nf* infusion; ~ **de manzanilla** camomile tea

ingeniar [inxe'njar] *vt* to think up, devise; **~se** *vr:* **~se para** to manage to

ingeniería [inxenje'ria] *nf* engineering; ~ **genética** genetic engineering; **ingeniero, a** *nm/f* engineer; **ingeniero de caminos/de sonido** civil engineer/sound engineer

ingenio [in'xenjo] *nm* (*talento*) talent; (*agudeza*) wit; (*habilidad*) ingenuity, inventiveness; ~ **azucarero** (*AM*) sugar refinery

ingenioso, a [inxe'njoso, a] *adj* ingenious, clever; (*divertido*) witty

ingenuidad [inxenwi'ðað] *nf* ingenuousness;

(*sencillez*) simplicity; **ingenuo, a** *adj*
ingenuous

ingerir [inxe'rir] *vt* to ingest; (*tragar*) to
swallow; (*consumir*) to consume

Inglaterra [ingla'terra] *nf* England

ingle ['ingle] *nf* groin

inglés, esa [in'gles, esa] *adj* English ♦ *nm/f*
Englishman/woman ♦ *nm* (*LING*) English

ingratitud [ingrati'tuð] *nf* ingratitude;
ingrato, a *adj* (*gen*) ungrateful

ingrediente [ingre'ðjente] *nm* ingredient

ingresar [ingre'sar] *vt* (*dinero*) to deposit ♦ *vi*
to come in; ~ **en un club** to join a club; ~ **en
el hospital** to go into hospital

ingreso [in'greso] *nm* (*entrada*) entry; (: *en
hospital etc*) admission; ~**s** *nmpl* (*dinero*)
income *sg*; (: *COM*) takings *pl*

inhabitable [inaßi'taßle] *adj* uninhabitable

inhalar [ina'lar] *vt* to inhale

inherente [ine'rente] *adj* inherent

inhibir [ini'ßir] *vt* to inhibit

inhóspito, a [i'nospito, a] *adj* (*región,
paisaje*) inhospitable

inhumano, a [inu'mano, a] *adj* inhuman

inicial [ini'θjal] *adj, nf* initial

iniciar [ini'θjar] *vt* (*persona*) to initiate;
(*empezar*) to begin, commence;
(*conversación*) to start up

iniciativa [iniθja'tißa] *nf* initiative; **la
~ privada** private enterprise

ininterrumpido, a [ininterrum'piðo, a] *adj*
uninterrupted

injerencia [inxe'renθja] *nf* interference

injertar [inxer'tar] *vt* to graft; **injerto** *nm*
graft

injuria [in'xurja] *nf* (*agravio, ofensa*) offence;
(*insulto*) insult; **injuriar** *vt* to insult;
injurioso, a *adj* offensive; insulting

injusticia [inxus'tiθja] *nf* injustice

injusto, a [in'xusto, a] *adj* unjust, unfair

inmadurez [inmaðu'reθ] *nf* immaturity

inmediaciones [inmeðja'θjones] *nfpl*
neighbourhood *sg*, environs

inmediato, a [inme'ðjato, a] *adj* immediate;
(*contiguo*) adjoining; (*rápido*) prompt;
(*próximo*) neighbouring, next; **de ~**
immediately

inmejorable [inmexo'raßle] *adj*
unsurpassable; (*precio*) unbeatable

inmenso, a [in'menso, a] *adj* immense,
huge

inmerecido, a [inmere'θiðo, a] *adj*
undeserved

inmigración [inmixra'θjon] *nf* immigration

inmiscuirse [inmisku'irse] *vr* to interfere,
meddle

inmobiliaria [inmoßi'ljarja] *nf* estate agency

inmobiliario, a [inmoßi'ljarjo, a] *adj* real-
estate *cpd*, property *cpd*

inmolar [inmo'lar] *vt* to immolate, sacrifice

inmoral [inmo'ral] *adj* immoral

inmortal [inmor'tal] *adj* immortal; ~**izar** *vt*
to immortalize

inmóvil [in'moßil] *adj* immobile

inmueble [in'mweßle] *adj*: **bienes ~s** real
estate, landed property ♦ *nm* property

inmundicia [inmun'diθja] *nf* filth;
inmundo, a *adj* filthy

inmune [in'mune] *adj*: ~ **(a)** (*MED*) immune
(to)

inmunidad [inmuni'ðað] *nf* immunity

inmutarse [inmu'tarse] *vr* to turn pale; **no
se inmutó** he didn't turn a hair

innato, a [in'nato, a] *adj* innate

innecesario, a [inneθe'sarjo, a] *adj*
unnecessary

innoble [in'noßle] *adj* ignoble

innovación [innoßa'θjon] *nf* innovation

innovar [inno'ßar] *vt* to introduce

inocencia [ino'θenθja] *nf* innocence

inocentada [inoθen'taða] *nf* practical joke

inocente [ino'θente] *adj* (*ingenuo*) naive,
innocent; (*inculpable*) innocent; (*sin malicia*)
harmless ♦ *nm/f* simpleton

inodoro [ino'ðoro] *nm* toilet, lavatory (*BRIT*)

inofensivo, a [inofen'sißo, a] *adj*
inoffensive, harmless

inolvidable [inolßi'ðaßle] *adj* unforgettable

inopinado, a [inopi'naðo, a] *adj*
unexpected

inoportuno, a [inopor'tuno, a] *adj*
untimely; (*molesto*) inconvenient

inoxidable [inoksi'ðaßle] *adj*: **acero ~**
stainless steel

inquebrantable [inkeßran'taßle] *adj*
unbreakable

inquietar [inkje'tar] *vt* to worry, trouble; ~**se**
vr to worry, get upset; **inquieto, a** *adj*
anxious, worried; **inquietud** *nf* anxiety,
worry

inquilino, a [inki'lino, a] *nm/f* tenant

inquirir [inki'rir] *vt* to enquire into,
investigate

insaciable [insa'θjaßle] *adj* insatiable

insalubre [insa'lußre] *adj* unhealthy

inscribir [inskri'ßir] *vt* to inscribe; ~ **a uno en**
(*lista*) to put sb on; (*censo*) to register sb on

inscripción [inskrip'θjon] *nf* inscription;
(*ESCOL etc*) enrolment; (*censo*) registration

insecticida [insekti'θiða] *nm* insecticide

insecto [in'sekto] *nm* insect

inseguridad [insexuri'ðað] *nf* insecurity

inseguro, a [inse'xuro, a] *adj* insecure;
(*inconstante*) unsteady; (*incierto*) uncertain

insensato, a [insen'sato, a] *adj* foolish,
stupid

insensibilidad [insensißili'ðað] *nf* (*gen*)
insensitivity; (*dureza de corazón*) callousness

insensible [insen'sißle] adj (gen) insensitive; (movimiento) imperceptible; (sin sentido) numb

insertar [inser'tar] vt to insert

inservible [inser'ßißle] adj useless

insidioso, a [insi'ðjoso, a] adj insidious

insignia [in'siɣnja] nf (señal distintiva) badge; (estandarte) flag

insignificante [insiɣnifi'kante] adj insignificant

insinuar [insi'nwar] vt to insinuate, imply

insípido, a [in'sipiðo, a] adj insipid

insistencia [insis'tenθja] nf insistence

insistir [insis'tir] vi to insist; ~ en algo to insist on sth; (enfatizar) to stress sth

insolación [insola'θjon] nf (MED) sunstroke

insolencia [inso'lenθja] nf insolence; **insolente** adj insolent

insólito, a [in'solito, a] adj unusual

insoluble [inso'lußle] adj insoluble

insolvencia [insol'ßenθja] nf insolvency

insomnio [in'somnjo] nm insomnia

insondable [inson'daßle] adj bottomless; (fig) impenetrable

insonorizado, a [insonori'θaðo, a] adj (cuarto etc) soundproof

insoportable [insopor'taßle] adj unbearable

insospechado, a [insospe'tʃaðo, a] adj (inesperado) unexpected

inspección [inspek'θjon] nf inspection, check; **inspeccionar** vt (examinar) to inspect, examine; (controlar) to check

inspector, a [inspek'tor, a] nm/f inspector

inspiración [inspira'θjon] nf inspiration

inspirar [inspi'rar] vt to inspire; (MED) to inhale; ~se vr: ~se en to be inspired by

instalación [instala'θjon] nf (equipo) fittings pl, equipment; ~ **eléctrica** wiring

instalar [insta'lar] vt (establecer) to instal; (erguir) to set up, erect; ~se vr to establish o.s.; (en una vivienda) to move into

instancia [ins'tanθja] nf (JUR) petition; (ruego) request; **en última** ~ as a last resort

instantánea [instan'tanea] nf snap(shot)

instantáneo, a [instan'taneo, a] adj instantaneous; **café** ~ instant coffee

instante [ins'tante] nm instant, moment

instar [ins'tar] vt to press, urge

instaurar [instau'rar] vt (costumbre) to establish; (normas, sistema) to bring in, introduce; (gobierno) to instal

instigar [insti'ɣar] vt to instigate

instinto [ins'tinto] nm instinct; **por** ~ instinctively

institución [institu'θjon] nf institution, establishment

instituir [institu'ir] vt to establish; (fundar) to found; **instituto** nm (gen) institute; (ESP: ESCOL) ≈ comprehensive (BRIT) o high (US) school

institutriz [institu'triθ] nf governess

instrucción [instruk'θjon] nf instruction

instructivo, a [instruk'tißo, a] adj instructive

instruir [instru'ir] vt (gen) to instruct; (enseñar) to teach, educate

instrumento [instru'mento] nm (gen) instrument; (herramienta) tool, implement

insubordinarse [insußorði'narse] vr to rebel

insuficiencia [insufi'θjenθja] nf (carencia) lack; (inadecuación) inadequacy; **insuficiente** adj (gen) insufficient; (ESCOL: calificación) unsatisfactory

insufrible [insu'frißle] adj insufferable

insular [insu'lar] adj insular

insultar [insul'tar] vt to insult; **insulto** nm insult

insumiso, a [insu'miso, a] nm/f (POL) person who refuses to do military service or its substitute, community service

insuperable [insupe'raßle] adj (excelente) unsurpassable; (problema etc) insurmountable

insurgente [insur'xente] adj, nm/f insurgent

insurrección [insurrek'θjon] nf insurrection, rebellion

intachable [inta'tʃaßle] adj irreproachable

intacto, a [in'takto, a] adj intact

integral [inte'ɣral] adj integral; (completo) complete; **pan** ~ wholemeal (BRIT) o wholewheat (US) bread

integrar [inte'ɣrar] vt to make up, compose; (MAT, fig) to integrate

integridad [inteɣri'ðað] nf wholeness; (carácter) integrity; **íntegro, a** adj whole, entire; (honrado) honest

intelectual [intelek'twal] adj, nm/f intellectual

inteligencia [inteli'xenθja] nf intelligence; (ingenio) ability; **inteligente** adj intelligent

inteligible [inteli'xißle] adj intelligible

intemperie [intem'perje] nf: **a la** ~ out in the open, exposed to the elements

intempestivo, a [intempes'tißo, a] adj untimely

intención [inten'θjon] nf (gen) intention, purpose; **con segundas intenciones** maliciously; **con** ~ deliberately

intencionado, a [intenθjo'naðo, a] adj deliberate; **bien** ~ well-meaning; **mal** ~ ill-disposed, hostile

intensidad [intensi'ðað] nf (gen) intensity; (ELEC, TEC) strength; **llover con** ~ to rain hard

intenso, a [in'tenso, a] adj intense; (sentimiento) profound, deep

intentar [inten'tar] vt (tratar) to try, attempt; **intento** nm attempt

interactivo, a [interak'tißo, a] adj (INFORM)

interactive

intercalar [interka'lar] vt to insert

intercambio [inter'kambjo] nm exchange, swap

interceder [interθe'ðer] vi to intercede

interceptar [interθep'tar] vt to intercept

intercesión [interθe'sjon] nf intercession

interés [inte'roɛ] nm (gen) interest; (parte) share, part; (pey) self-interest; **intereses creados** vested interests

interesado, a [intere'saðo, a] adj interested; (prejuiciado) prejudiced; (pey) mercenary, self-seeking

interesante [intere'sante] adj interesting

interesar [intere'sar] vt, vi to interest, be of interest to; **~se** vr: **~se en** o **por** to take an interest in

interferir [interfe'rir] vt to interfere with; (TEL) to jam ♦ vi to interfere

interfono [inter'fono] nm intercom

interino, a [inte'rino, a] adj temporary ♦ nm/f temporary holder of a post; (MED) locum; (ESCOL) supply teacher

interior [inte'rjor] adj inner, inside; (COM) domestic, internal ♦ nm interior, inside; (fig) soul, mind; **Ministerio del I~** ≈ Home Office (BRIT), ≈ Department of the Interior (US)

interjección [interxek'θjon] nf interjection

interlocutor, a [interloku'tor, a] nm/f speaker

intermediario, a [interme'ðjarjo, a] nm/f intermediary

intermedio, a [inter'meðjo, a] adj intermediate ♦ nm interval

interminable [intermi'naßle] adj endless

intermitente [intermi'tente] adj intermittent ♦ nm (AUTO) indicator

internacional [internaθjo'nal] adj international

internado [inter'naðo] nm boarding school

internar [inter'nar] vt to intern; (en un manicomio) to commit; **~se** vr (penetrar) to penetrate

Internet [inter'net] nm o nf Internet

interno, a [in'terno, a] adj internal, interior; (POL etc) domestic ♦ nm/f (alumno) boarder

interponer [interpo'ner] vt to interpose, put in; **~se** vr to intervene

interpretación [interpreta'θjon] nf interpretation

interpretar [interpre'tar] vt to interpret; (TEATRO, MUS) to perform, play; **intérprete** nm/f (LING) interpreter, translator; (MUS, TEATRO) performer, artist(e)

interrogación [interroxa'θjon] nf interrogation; (LING: tb: **signo de ~**) question mark

interrogar [interro'var] vt to interrogate, question

interrumpir [interrum'pir] vt to interrupt

interrupción [interrup'θjon] nf interruption

interruptor [interrup'tor] nm (ELEC) switch

intersección [intersek'θjon] nf intersection

interurbano, a [interur'ßano, a] adj: **llamada interurbana** long-distance call

intervalo [inter'ßalo] nm interval; (descanso) break; **a ~e** at intervals, every now and then

intervenir [interße'nir] vt (controlar) to control, supervise; (MED) to operate on ♦ vi (participar) to take part, participate; (mediar) to intervene

interventor, a [interßen'tor, a] nm/f inspector; (COM) auditor

intestino [intes'tino] nm intestine

intimar [inti'mar] vi to become friendly

intimidad [intimi'ðað] nf intimacy; (familiaridad) familiarity; (vida privada) private life; (JUR) privacy

íntimo, a ['intimo, a] adj intimate

intolerable [intole'raßle] adj intolerable, unbearable

intoxicación [intoksika'θjon] nf poisoning

intranet [intra'net] nf intranet

intranquilizarse [intrankili'θarse] vr to get worried o anxious; **intranquilo, a** adj worried

intransigente [intransi'xente] adj intransigent

intransitable [intransi'taßle] adj impassable

intrépido, a [in'trepiðo, a] adj intrepid

intriga [in'triva] nf intrigue; (plan) plot; **intrigar** vt, vi to intrigue

intrincado, a [intrin'kaðo, a] adj intricate

intrínseco, a [in'trinseko, a] adj intrinsic

introducción [introðuk'θjon] nf introduction

introducir [introðu'θir] vt (gen) to introduce; (moneda etc) to insert; (INFORM) to input, enter

intromisión [intromi'sjon] nf interference, meddling

introvertido, a [introßer'tiðo, a] adj, nm/f introvert

intruso, a [in'truso, a] adj intrusive ♦ nm/f intruder

intuición [intwi'θjon] nf intuition

inundación [inunda'θjon] nf flood(ing); **inundar** vt to flood; (fig) to swamp, inundate

inusitado, a [inusi'taðo, a] adj unusual, rare

inútil [in'util] adj useless; (esfuerzo) vain, fruitless; **inutilidad** nf uselessness

inutilizar [inutili'θar] vt to make o render useless; **~se** vr to become useless

invadir [imba'ðir] vt to invade

inválido, a [im'baliðo, a] adj invalid ♦ nm/f invalid

invariable [imba'rjaßle] adj invariable

invasión [imba'sjon] nf invasion

invasor, a [imba'sor, a] adj invading ♦ nm/f invader

invención [imben'θjon] nf invention

inventar [imben'tar] vt to invent

inventario [imben'tarjo] nm inventory

inventiva [imben'tißa] nf inventiveness

invento [im'bento] nm invention

inventor, a [imben'tor, a] nm/f inventor

invernadero [imberna'ðero] nm greenhouse

inverosímil [imbero'simil] adj implausible

inversión [imber'sjon] nf (COM) investment

inverso, a [im'berso, a] adj inverse, opposite; **en el orden ~** in reverse order; **a la inversa** inversely, the other way round

inversor, a [imber'sor, a] nm/f (COM) investor

invertir [imber'tir] vt (COM) to invest; (volcar) to turn upside down; (tiempo etc) to spend

investigación [imbestiɣa'θjon] nf investigation; (ESCOL) research; **~ de mercado** market research

investigar [imbesti'var] vt to investigate; (ESCOL) to do research into

invierno [im'bjerno] nm winter

invisible [imbi'sißle] adj invisible

invitado, a [imbi'taðo, a] nm/f guest

invitar [imbi'tar] vt to invite; (incitar) to entice; (pagar) to buy, pay for

invocar [imbo'kar] vt to invoke, call on

involucrar [imbolu'krar] vt: **~ en** to involve in; **~se** vr (persona): **~ en** to get mixed up in

involuntario, a [imbolun'tarjo, a] adj (movimiento, gesto) involuntary; (error) unintentional

inyección [injek'θjon] nf injection

inyectar [injek'tar] vt to inject

PALABRA CLAVE

ir [ir] vi **1** to go; (a pie) to walk; (viajar) to travel; **~ caminando** to walk; **fui en tren** I went o travelled by train; **¡(ahora) voy!** (I'm just) coming!

2: ~ (a) por: ~ (a) por el médico to fetch the doctor

3 (progresar: persona, cosa) to go; **el trabajo va muy bien** work is going very well; **¿cómo te va?** how are things going?; **me va muy bien** I'm getting on very well; **le fue fatal** it went awfully badly for him

4 (funcionar): **el coche no va muy bien** the car isn't running very well

5: te va estupendamente ese color that colour suits you fantastically well

6 (locuciones): **¿vino? – ¡que va!** did he come? – of course not!; **vamos, no llores** come on, don't cry; **¡vaya coche!** what a car!, that's some car!

7: no vaya a ser: tienes que correr, no vaya a ser que pierdas el tren you'll have to run so as not to miss the train

8 (+ pp): **iba vestido muy bien** he was very well dressed

9: no me etc **va ni me viene** I etc don't care

♦ vb aux **1: ~ a: voy/iba a hacerlo hoy** I am/ was going to do it today

2 (+ gerundio): **iba anocheciendo** it was getting dark; **todo se me iba aclarando** everything was gradually becoming clearer to me

3 (+ pp = pasivo): **van vendidos 300 ejemplares** 300 copies have been sold so far

♦ **~se** vr **1: ¿por dónde se va al zoológico?** which is the way to the zoo?

2 (marcharse) to leave; **ya se habrán ido** they must already have left o gone

---

ira ['ira] nf anger, rage

Irak [i'rak] nm = **Iraq**

Irán [i'ran] nm Iran; **iraní** adj, nm/f Iranian

Iraq [i'rak] nm Iraq; **iraquí** adj, nm/f Iraqi

iris ['iris] nm inv (tb: **arco ~**) rainbow; (ANAT) iris

Irlanda [ir'landa] nf Ireland; **irlandés, esa** adj Irish ♦ nm/f Irishman/woman; **los irlandeses** the Irish

ironía [iro'nia] nf irony; **irónico, a** adj ironic(al)

IRPF ['i 'erre 'pe 'efe] n abr (=Impuesto sobre la Renta de las Personas Físicas) (personal) income tax

irreal [irre'al] adj unreal

irrecuperable [irrekupe'raßle] adj irrecoverable, irretrievable

irreflexión [irreflek'sjon] nf thoughtlessness

irregular [irreɣu'lar] adj (gen) irregular; (situación) abnormal

irremediable [irreme'ðjaßle] adj irremediable; (vicio) incurable

irreparable [irrepa'raßle] adj (daños) irreparable; (pérdida) irrecoverable

irresoluto, a [irreso'luto, a] adj irresolute, hesitant

irrespetuoso, a [irrespe'twoso, a] adj disrespectful

irresponsable [irrespon'saßle] adj irresponsible

irreversible [irreßer'sible] adj irreversible

irrigar [irri'var] vt to irrigate

irrisorio, a [irri'sorjo, a] adj derisory, ridiculous

irritar [irri'tar] vt to irritate, annoy

irrupción [irrup'θjon] nf irruption; (invasión) invasion

isla ['isla] nf island

islandés, esa [islan'des, esa] adj Icelandic ♦ nm/f Icelander

Islandia [is'landja] nf Iceland
isleño, a [is'leɲo, a] adj island cpd ♦ nm/f islander
Israel [isra'el] nm Israel; **israelí** adj, nm/f Israeli
istmo ['istmo] nm isthmus
Italia [i'talja] nf Italy; **italiano, a** adj, nm/f Italian
itinerario [itine'rarjo] nm itinerary, route
IVA ['ißa] nm abr (= impuesto sobre el valor añadido) VAT
izar [i'θar] vt to hoist
izdo, a abr (= izquierdo, a) l.
izquierda [iθ'kjerda] nf left; (POL) left (wing); **a la ~** (estar) on the left; (torcer etc) (to the) left
izquierdista [iθkjer'ðista] nm/f left-winger, leftist
izquierdo, a [iθ'kjerðo, a] adj left

J, j

jabalí [xaßa'li] nm wild boar
jabalina [xaßa'lina] nf javelin
jabón [xa'ßon] nm soap; **jabonar** vt to soap
jaca ['xaka] nf pony
jacinto [xa'θinto] nm hyacinth
jactarse [xak'tarse] vr to boast, brag
jadear [xaðe'ar] vi to pant, gasp for breath; **jadeo** nm panting, gasping
jaguar [xa'ɣwar] nm jaguar
jalea [xa'lea] nf jelly
jaleo [xa'leo] nm racket, uproar; **armar un ~** to kick up a racket
jalón [xa'lon] (AM) nm tug
jamás [xa'mas] adv never
jamón [xa'mon] nm ham; **~ dulce, ~ de York** cooked ham; **~ serrano** cured ham
Japón [xa'pon] nm: **el ~** Japan; **japonés, esa** adj, nm/f Japanese ♦ nm (LING) Japanese
jaque ['xake] nm: **~ mate** checkmate
jaqueca [xa'keka] nf (very bad) headache, migraine
jarabe [xa'raße] nm syrup
jarcia ['xarθja] nf (NAUT) ropes pl, rigging
jardín [xar'ðin] nm garden; **~ de infancia** (ESP) o **de niños** (AM) nursery (school); **jardinería** nf gardening; **jardinero, a** nm/f gardener
jarra ['xarra] nf jar; (jarro) jug
jarro ['xarro] nm jug
jarrón [xa'rron] nm vase
jaula ['xaula] nf cage
jauría [xau'ria] nf pack of hounds
jazmín [xaθ'min] nm jasmine
J. C. abr (= Jesucristo) J.C.
jefa ['xefa] nf ver **jefe**
jefatura [xefa'tura] nf: **~ de policía** police headquarters sg

jefe, a ['xefe, a] nm/f (gen) chief, head; (patrón) boss; **~ de cocina** chef; **~ de estación** stationmaster; **~ de estado** head of state
jengibre [xen'xißre] nm ginger
jeque ['xeke] nm sheik
jerarquía [xerar'kia] nf (orden) hierarchy; (rango) rank; **jerárquico, a** adj hierarchic(al)
jerez [xe're θ] nm sherry
jerga ['xerɣa] nf jargon
jeringa [xe'ringa] nf syringe; (AM) annoyance, bother; **~ de engrase** grease gun; **jeringar** vt (fam) to annoy, bother; **jeringuilla** nf syringe
jeroglífico [xero'ɣlifiko] nm hieroglyphic
jersey [xer'sei] (pl **~s**) nm jersey, pullover, jumper
Jerusalén [xerusa'len] n Jerusalem
Jesucristo [xesu'kristo] nm Jesus Christ
jesuita [xe'swita] adj, nm Jesuit
Jesús [xe'sus] nm Jesus; **¡~!** good heavens!; (al estornudar) bless you!
jinete, a [xi'nete, a] nm/f horseman/woman, rider
jipijapa [xipi'xapa] (AM) nm straw hat
jirafa [xi'rafa] nf giraffe
jirón [xi'ron] nm rag, shred
jocoso, a [xo'koso, a] adj humorous, jocular
joder [xo'ðer] (fam!) vt, vi to fuck(!)
jofaina [xo'faina] nf washbasin
jornada [xor'naða] nf (viaje de un día) day's journey; (camino o viaje entero) journey; (día de trabajo) working day
jornal [xor'nal] nm (day's) wage; **~ero** nm (day) labourer
joroba [xo'roßa] nf hump, hunched back; **~do, a** adj hunchbacked ♦ nm/f hunchback
jota ['xota] nf (the letter) J; (danza) Aragonese dance; **no saber ni ~** to have no idea
joven ['xoßen] (pl **jóvenes**) adj young ♦ nm young man, youth ♦ nf young woman, girl
jovial [xo'ßjal] adj cheerful, jolly
joya ['xoja] nf jewel, gem; (fig: persona) gem; **joyería** nf (joyas) jewellery; (tienda) jeweller's (shop); **joyero** nm (persona) jeweller; (caja) jewel case
juanete [xwa'nete] nm (del pie) bunion
jubilación [xußila'θjon] nf (retiro) retirement
jubilado, a [xußi'laðo, a] adj retired ♦ nm/f pensioner (BRIT), senior citizen
jubilar [xußi'lar] vt to pension off, retire; (fam) to discard; **~se** vr to retire
júbilo ['xußilo] nm joy, rejoicing; **jubiloso, a** adj jubilant
judía [xu'ðia] nf (CULIN) bean; **~ verde** French bean; ver tb **judío**
judicial [xuði'θjal] adj judicial
judío, a [xu'ðio, a] adj Jewish ♦ nm/f Jew(ess)
judo ['juðo] nm judo

juego etc ['xweɣo] vb ver **jugar** ♦ nm (gen) play; (pasatiempo, partido) game; (en casino) gambling; (conjunto) set; **fuera de ~** (DEPORTE: persona) offside; (: pelota) out of play; **J~s Olímpicos** Olympic Games

juerga ['xwerɣa] nf binge; (fiesta) party; **ir de ~** to go out on a binge

jueves ['xweβes] nm inv Thursday

juez |xweθ| nm/f judge; **~ de línea** linesman; **~ de salida** starter

jugada [xu'ɣaða] nf play; **buena ~** good move/shot/stroke etc

jugador, a [xuxa'ðor, a] nm/f player; (en casino) gambler

jugar [xu'ɣar] vt, vi to play; (en casino) to gamble; (apostar) to bet; **~ al fútbol** to play football

juglar [xu'ɣlar] nm minstrel

jugo ['xuɣo] nm (BOT) juice; (fig) essence, substance; **~ de fruta** (AM) fruit juice; **~so, a** adj juicy; (fig) substantial, important

juguete [xu'ɣete] nm toy; **~ar** vi to play; **~ría** nf toyshop

juguetón, ona [xuɣe'ton, ona] adj playful

juicio ['xwiθjo] nm judgement; (razón) sanity, reason; (opinión) opinion; **~so, a** adj wise, sensible

julio ['xuljo] nm July

junco ['xunko] nm rush, reed

jungla ['xuŋla] nf jungle

junio ['xunjo] nm June

junta ['xunta] nf (asamblea) meeting, assembly; (comité, consejo) board, council, committee; (TEC) joint

juntar [xun'tar] vt to join, unite; (maquinaria) to assemble, put together; (dinero) to collect; **~se** vr to join, meet; (reunirse: personas) to meet, assemble; (arrimarse) to approach, draw closer; **~se con uno** to join sb

junto, a [a 'xunto, a] adj joined; (unido) united; (anexo) near, close; (contiguo, próximo) next, adjacent ♦ adv: **todo ~** all at once; **~s together**; **~ a** near (to), next to

jurado [xu'raðo] nm (JUR: individuo) juror; (: grupo) jury; (de concurso: grupo) panel (of judges); (: individuo) member of a panel

juramento [xura'mento] nm oath; (maldición) oath, curse; **prestar ~** to take the oath; **tomar ~ a** to swear in, administer the oath to

jurar [xu'rar] vt, vi to swear; **~ en falso** to commit perjury; **jurárselas a uno** to have it in for sb

jurídico, a |xu'riðiko, a| adj legal

jurisdicción [xurisðik'θjon] nf (poder, autoridad) jurisdiction; (territorio) district

jurisprudencia |xurispru'ðenθja| nf jurisprudence

jurista [xu'rista] nm/f jurist

justamente [xusta'mente] adv justly, fairly; (precisamente) just, exactly

justicia [xus'tiθja] nf justice; (equidad) fairness, justice; **justiciero, a** adj just, righteous

justificación [xustifika'θjon] nf justification; **justificar** vt to justify

justo, a ['xusto, a] adj (equitativo) just, fair, right; (preciso) exact, correct; (ajustado) tight ♦ adv (precisamente) exactly, precisely; (AM: apenas a tiempo) just in time

juvenil [xuβe'nil] adj youthful

juventud [xuβen'tuð] nf (adolescencia) youth; (jóvenes) young people pl

juzgado [xuθ'ɣaðo] nm tribunal; (JUR) court

juzgar [xuθ'ɣar] vt to judge; **a ~ por ...** to judge by ..., judging by ...

K, k

kg abr (= kilogramo) kg

kilo ['kilo] nm kilo ♦ pref: **~gramo** nm kilogramme; **~metraje** nm distance in kilometres, ≈ mileage; **kilómetro** nm kilometre; **~vatio** nm kilowatt

kiosco ['kjosko] nm = **quiosco**

km abr (= kilómetro) km

Kosovo [ko'soβo] nm Kosovo

kv abr (= kilovatio) kw

L, l

l abr (= litro) l

la [la] art def the ♦ pron her; (Ud.) you; (cosa) it ♦ nm (MUS) la; **~ del sombrero rojo** the girl in the red hat; tb ver **el**

laberinto [laβe'rinto] nm labyrinth

labia ['laβja] nf fluency; (pey) glib tongue

labio ['laβjo] nm lip

labor [la'βor] nf labour; (AGR) farm work; (tarea) job, task; (COSTURA) needlework; **~able** adj (AGR) workable; **día ~able** working day; **~al** adj (accidente) at work; (jornada) working

laboratorio [laβora'torjo] nm laboratory

laborioso, a [laβo'rjoso, a] adj (persona) hard-working; (trabajo) tough

laborista [laβo'rista] adj: **Partido L~** Labour Party

labrado, a [la'βraðo, a] adj worked; (madera) carved; (metal) wrought

labrador, a [laβra'ðor, a] adj farming cpd ♦ nm/f farmer

labranza [la'βranθa] nf (AGR) cultivation

labrar [la'βrar] vt (gen) to work; (madera etc) to carve; (fig) to cause, bring about

labriego, a [la'βrjeɣo, a] nm/f peasant

laca ['laka] nf lacquer

lacayo [la'kajo] nm lackey

lacio, a ['laθjo, a] adj (pelo) lank, straight

lacón [la'kon] nm shoulder of pork

lacónico, a [la'koniko, a] adj laconic

lacra ['lakra] nf (fig) blot; **lacrar** vt (cerrar) to seal (with sealing wax); **lacre** nm sealing wax

lactancia [lak'tanθja] nf lactation

lactar [lak'tar] vt, vi to suckle

lácteo, a ['lakteo, a] adj: **productos ~s** dairy products

ladear [laðe'ar] vt to tip, tilt ♦ vi to tilt; **~se** vr to lean

ladera [la'ðera] nf slope

lado ['laðo] nm (gen) side; (fig) protection; (MIL) flank; **al ~ de** beside; **poner de ~** to put on its side; **poner a un ~** to put aside; **por todos ~s** on all sides, all round (BRIT)

ladrar [la'ðrar] vi to bark; **ladrido** nm bark, barking

ladrillo [la'ðriʎo] nm (gen) brick; (azulejo) tile

ladrón, ona [la'ðron, ona] nm/f thief

lagartija [laɣar'tixa] nf (ZOOL) (small) lizard

lagarto [la'ɣarto] nm (ZOOL) lizard

lago ['laɣo] nm lake

lágrima ['laɣrima] nf tear

laguna [la'ɣuna] nf (lago) lagoon; (hueco) gap

laico, a ['laiko, a] adj lay

lamentable [lamen'taβle] adj lamentable, regrettable; (miserable) pitiful

lamentar [lamen'tar] vt (sentir) to regret; (deplorar) to lament; **lo lamento mucho** I'm very sorry; **~se** vr to lament; **lamento** nm lament

lamer [la'mer] vt to lick

lámina ['lamina] nf (plancha delgada) sheet; (para estampar, estampa) plate

lámpara ['lampara] nf lamp; **~ de alcohol/gas** spirit/gas lamp; **~ de pie** standard lamp

lamparón [lampa'ron] nm grease spot

lana ['lana] nf wool

lancha ['lantʃa] nf launch; **~ de pesca** fishing boat; **~ salvavidas/torpedera** lifeboat/torpedo boat

langosta [lan'gosta] nf (crustáceo) lobster; (: de río) crayfish; **langostino** nm Dublin Bay prawn

languidecer [langiðe'θer] vi to languish; **languidez** nf languor; **lánguido, a** adj (gen) languid; (sin energía) listless

lanilla [la'niʎa] nf nap

lanza ['lanθa] nf (arma) lance, spear

lanzamiento [lanθa'mjento] nm (gen) throwing; (NAUT, COM) launch, launching; **~ de peso** putting the shot

lanzar [lan'θar] vt (gen) to throw; (DEPORTE: pelota) to bowl; (NAUT, COM) to launch; (JUR) to evict; **~se** vr to throw o.s.

lapa ['lapa] nf limpet

lapicero [lapi'θero] nm pencil; (AM: bolígrafo) Biro ®

lápida ['lapiða] nf stone; **~ mortuoria** headstone; **~ conmemorativa** memorial stone; **lapidario, a** adj nm lapidary

lápiz ['lapiθ] nm pencil; **~ de color** coloured pencil; **~ de labios** lipstick

lapón, ona [la'pon, ona] nm/f Laplander, Lapp

lapso ['lapso] nm (de tiempo) interval; (error) error

lapsus ['lapsus] nm inv error, mistake

largar [lar'ɣar] vt (soltar) to release; (aflojar) to loosen; (lanzar) to launch; (fam) to let fly; (velas) to unfurl; (AM) to-throw; **~se** vr (fam) to beat it; **~se a** (AM) to start to

largo, a ['larɣo, a] adj (longitud) long; (tiempo) lengthy; (fig) generous ♦ nm length; (MUS) largo; **dos años ~s** two long years; **tiene 9 metros de ~** it is 9 metres long; **a lo ~** de along; (tiempo) all through, throughout; **~metraje** nm feature film

laringe [la'rinxe] nf larynx; **laringitis** nf laryngitis

larva ['larβa] nf larva

las [las] art def the ♦ pron them; **~ que cantan** the ones/women/girls who sing; tb ver **el**

lascivo, a [las'θiβo, a] adj lewd

láser ['laser] nm laser

lástima ['lastima] nf (pena) pity; **dar ~** to be pitiful; **es una ~ que** it's a pity that; **¡qué ~!** what a pity!; **ella está hecha una ~** she looks pitiful

lastimar [lasti'mar] vt (herir) to wound; (ofender) to offend; **~se** vr to hurt o.s.; **lastimero, a** adj pitiful, pathetic

lastre ['lastre] nm (TEC, NAUT) ballast; (fig) dead weight

lata ['lata] nf (metal) tin; (caja) tin (BRIT), can; (fam) nuisance; **en ~** tinned (BRIT), canned; **dar (la) ~** to be a nuisance

latente [la'tente] adj latent

lateral [late'ral] adj side cpd, lateral ♦ nm (TEATRO) wings

latido [la'tiðo] nm (del corazón) beat

latifundio [lati'fundjo] nm large estate; **latifundista** nm/f owner of a large estate

latigazo [lati'ɣaθo] nm (golpe) lash; (sonido) crack

látigo ['latiɣo] nm whip

latín [la'tin] nm Latin

latino, a [la'tino, a] adj Latin; **~americano, a** adj, nm/f Latin-American

latir [la'tir] vi (corazón, pulso) to beat

latitud [lati'tuð] nf (GEO) latitude

latón [la'ton] nm brass

latoso, a [la'toso, a] adj (molesto) annoying; (aburrido) boring

laúd [la'uð] nm lute

laurel [lau'rel] nm (BOT) laurel; (CULIN) bay

lava ['laßa] nf lava

lavabo [la'ßaßo] nm (pila) washbasin; (tb: ~s) toilet

lavado [la'ßaðo] nm washing; (de ropa) laundry; (ARTE) wash; **~ de cerebro** brainwashing; **~ en seco** dry-cleaning

lavadora [laßa'ðora] nf washing machine

lavanda [la'ßanda] nf lavender

lavandería [laßande'ria] nf laundry; (automática) launderette

lavaplatos [laßa'platos] nm inv dishwasher

lavar [la'ßar] vt to wash; (borrar) to wipe away; **~se** vr to wash o.s.; **~se las manos** to wash one's hands; **~se los dientes** to brush one's teeth; **~ y marcar** (pelo) to shampoo and set; **~ en seco** to dry-clean; **~ los platos** to wash the dishes

lavavajillas [laßaßa'xiʎas] nm inv dishwasher

laxante [lak'sante] nm laxative

lazada [la'θaða] nf bow

lazarillo [laθa'riʎo] nm: **perro ~** guide dog

lazo ['laθo] nm knot; (lazada) bow; (para animales) lasso; (trampa) snare; (vínculo) tie

le [le] pron (directo) him (o her); (: usted) you; (indirecto) to him (o her o it); (: usted) to you

leal [le'al] adj loyal; **~tad** nf loyalty

lección [lek'θjon] nf lesson

leche ['letʃe] nf milk; **tiene mala ~** (fam!) he's a swine (!); **~ condensada/en polvo** condensed/powdered milk; **~ desnatada** skimmed milk; **~ra** nf (vendedora) milkmaid; (recipiente) (milk) churn; (AM) cow; **~ro, a** adj dairy

lecho ['letʃo] nm (cama, de río) bed; (GEO) layer

lechón [le'tʃon] nm sucking (BRIT) o suckling (US) pig

lechoso, a [le'tʃoso, a] adj milky

lechuga [le'tʃuɣa] nf lettuce

lechuza [le'tʃuθa] nf owl

lector, a [lek'tor, a] nm/f reader ♦ nm: **~ de discos compactos** CD player

lectura [lek'tura] nf reading

leer [le'er] vt to read

legado [le'ɣaðo] nm (don) bequest; (herencia) legacy; (enviado) legate

legajo [le'ɣaxo] nm file

legal [le'ɣal] adj (gen) legal; (persona) trustworthy; **~idad** nf legality

legalizar [leɣali'θar] vt to legalize; (documento) to authenticate

legaña [le'ɣaɲa] nf sleep (in eyes)

legar [le'ɣar] vt to bequeath, leave

legendario, a [lexen'darjo, a] adj legendary

legión [le'xjon] nf legion; **legionario, a** adj legionary ♦ nm legionnaire

legislación [lexisla'θjon] nf legislation

legislar [lexis'lar] vi to legislate

legislatura [lexisla'tura] nf (POL) period of office

legitimar [lexiti'mar] vt to legitimize; **legítimo, a** adj (genuino) authentic; (legal) legitimate

lego, a ['leɣo, a] adj (REL) secular; (ignorante) ignorant ♦ nm layman

legua ['leɣwa] nf league

legumbres [le'ɣumbres] nfpl pulses

leído, a [le'iðo, a] adj well-read

lejanía [lexa'nia] nf distance; **lejano, a** adj far-off; (en el tiempo) distant; (fig) remote

lejía [le'xia] nf bleach

lejos ['lexos] adv far, far away; **a lo ~** in the distance; **de o desde ~** from afar; **~ de** far from

lelo, a ['lelo, a] adj silly ♦ nm/f idiot

lema ['lema] nm motto; (POL) slogan

lencería [lenθe'ria] nf linen, drapery

lengua ['lenɣwa] nf tongue; (LING) language; **morderse la ~** to hold one's tongue

lenguado [len'ɣwaðo] nm sole

lenguaje [len'ɣwaxe] nm language

lengüeta [len'ɣweta] nf (ANAT) epiglottis; (zapatos) tongue, (MUS) reed

lente ['lente] nf lens; (lupa) magnifying glass; **~s** nfpl (gafas) glasses; **~s de contacto** contact lenses

lenteja [len'texa] nf lentil; **lentejuela** nf sequin

lentilla [len'tiʎa] nf contact lens

lentitud [lenti'tuð] nf slowness; **con ~** slowly

lento, a ['lento, a] adj slow

leña ['leɲa] nf firewood; **~dor, a** nm/f woodcutter

leño ['leɲo] nm (trozo de árbol) log; (madera) timber; (fig) blockhead

Leo ['leo] nm Leo

león [le'on] nm lion; **~ marino** sea lion

leopardo [leo'parðo] nm leopard

leotardos [leo'tarðos] nmpl tights

lepra ['lepra] nf leprosy; **leproso, a** nm/f leper

lerdo, a ['lerðo, a] adj (lento) slow; (patoso) clumsy

les [les] pron (directo) them; (: ustedes) you; (indirecto) to them; (: ustedes) to you

lesbiana [les'ßjana] adj, nf lesbian

lesión [le'sjon] nf wound, lesion; (DEPORTE) injury; **lesionado, a** adj injured ♦ nm/f injured person

letal [le'tal] adj lethal

letanía [leta'nia] nf litany

letargo [le'tarɣo] nm lethargy

letra ['letra] nf letter; (escritura) handwriting;

(*MUS*) lyrics *pl*; ~ **de cambio** bill of exchange; ~ **de imprenta** print; **~do, a** *adj* learned ♦ *nm/f* lawyer; **letrero** *nm* (*cartel*) sign; (*etiqueta*) label

letrina [le'trina] *nf* latrine

leucemia [leu'θemja] *nf* leukaemia

levadizo [leβa'ðiθo] *adj*: **puente ~** drawbridge

levadura [leβa'ðura] *nf* (*para el pan*) yeast; (*de la cerveza*) brewer's yeast

levantamiento [leβanta'mjento] *nm* raising, lifting; (*rebelión*) revolt, uprising; **~ de pesos** weight-lifting

levantar [leβan'tar] *vt* (*gen*) to raise; (*del suelo*) to pick up; (*hacia arriba*) to lift (up); (*plan*) to make, draw up; (*mesa*) to clear; (*campamento*) to strike; (*fig*) to cheer up, hearten; **~se** *vr* to get up; (*enderezarse*) to straighten up; (*rebelarse*) to rebel; **~ el ánimo** to cheer up

levante [le'βante] *nm* east coast; **el L~** region of Spain extending from Castellón to Murcia

levar [le'βar] *vt* to weigh

leve [leβe] *adj* light; (*fig*) trivial; **~dad** *nf* lightness

levita [le'βita] *nf* frock coat

léxico ['leksiko] *nm* (*vocabulario*) vocabulary

ley [lei] *nf* (*gen*) law; (*metal*) standard

leyenda [le'jenda] *nf* legend

leyó *etc vb ver* **leer**

liar [li'ar] *vt* to tie (up); (*unir*) to bind; (*envolver*) to wrap (up); (*enredar*) to confuse; (*cigarrillo*) to roll; **~se** *vr* (*fam*) to get involved; **~se a palos** to get involved in a fight

Líbano ['liβano] *nm*: **el ~** (the) Lebanon

libelo [li'βelo] *nm* satire, lampoon

libélula [li'βelula] *nf* dragonfly

liberación [liβera'θjon] *nf* liberation; (*de la cárcel*) release

liboral [liβe'ral] *adj, nm/f* liberal; **~idad** *nf* liberality, generosity

liberar [liβe'rar] *vt* to liberate

libertad [liβer'tað] *nf* liberty, freedom; **~ de culto/de prensa/de comercio** freedom of worship/of the press/of trade; **~ condicional** probation; **~ bajo palabra** parole; **~ bajo fianza** bail

libertar [liβer'tar] *vt* (*preso*) to set free; (*de una obligación*) to release; (*eximir*) to exempt

libertino, a [liβer'tino, a] *adj* permissive ♦ *nm/f* permissive person

libra ['liβra] *nf* pound; (*ASTROLOGÍA*): **L~** Libra; **~ esterlina** pound sterling

librar [li'βrar] *vt* (*de peligro*) to save; (*batalla*) to wage, fight; (*de impuestos*) to exempt; (*cheque*) to make out; (*JUR*) to exempt; **~se** *vr*: **~se de** to escape from, free o.s. from

libre ['liβre] *adj* free; (*lugar*) unoccupied;

(*asiento*) vacant; (*de deudas*) free of debts; **~ de impuestos** free of tax; **tiro ~** free kick; **los 100 metros ~** the 100 metres free-style (race); **al aire ~** in the open air

librería [liβre'ria] *nf* (*tienda*) bookshop; **librero, a** *nm/f* bookseller

libreta [li'βreta] *nf* notebook; **~ de ahorros** savings book

libro ['liβro] *nm* book; **~ de bolsillo** paperback; **~ de caja** cashbook; **~ de cheques** chequebook (*BRIT*), checkbook (*US*); **~ de texto** textbook

Lic. *abr* = **licenciado, a**

licencia [li'θenθja] *nf* (*gen*) licence; (*permiso*) permission; **~ por enfermedad** sick leave; **~ de caza** game licence; **~do, a** *adj* licensed ♦ *nm/f* graduate; **licenciar** *vt* (*empleado*) to dismiss; (*permitir*) to permit, allow; (*soldado*) to discharge; (*estudiante*) to confer a degree upon; **licenciarse** *vr*: **licenciarse en letras** to graduate in arts

licencioso, a [liθen'θjoso, a] *adj* licentious

licitar [liθi'tar] *vt* to bid for; (*AM*) to sell by auction

lícito, a ['liθito, a] *adj* (*legal*) lawful; (*justo*) fair, just; (*permisible*) permissible

licor [li'kor] *nm* spirits *pl* (*BRIT*), liquor (*US*); (*de frutas etc*) liqueur

licuadora [likwa'ðora] *nf* blender

licuar [li'kwar] *vt* to liquidize

líder ['liðer] *nm/f* leader; **liderato** *nm* leadership; **liderazgo** *nm* leadership

lidia ['liðja] *nf* bullfighting; (*una ~*) bullfight; **toros de ~** fighting bulls; **lidiar** *vt, vi* to fight

liebre ['ljeβre] *nf* hare

lienzo ['ljenθo] *nm* linen; (*ARTE*) canvas; (*ARQ*) wall

liga ['liɣa] *nf* (*de medias*) garter, suspender; (*AM: gomita*) rubber band; (*confederación*) league

ligadura [liɣa'ðura] *nf* bond, tie; (*MED, MUS*) ligature

ligamento [liɣa'mento] *nm* ligament

ligar [li'ɣar] *vt* (*atar*) to tie; (*unir*) to join; (*MED*) to bind up; (*MUS*) to slur ♦ *vi* to mix, blend; (*fam*): **(él) liga mucho** he pulls a lot of women; **~se** *vr* to commit o.s.

ligereza [lixe'reθa] *nf* lightness; (*rapidez*) swiftness; (*agilidad*) agility; (*superficialidad*) flippancy

ligero, a [li'xero, a] *adj* (*de peso*) light; (*tela*) thin; (*rápido*) swift, quick; (*ágil*) agile, nimble; (*de importancia*) slight; (*de carácter*) flippant, superficial ♦ *adv*: **a la ligera** superficially

liguero [li'ɣero] *nm* suspender (*BRIT*) o garter (*US*) belt

lija ['lixa] *nf* (*ZOOL*) dogfish; (*tb: papel de ~*) sandpaper

lila ['lila] nf lilac

lima ['lima] nf file; (BOT) lime; ~ **de uñas** nailfile; **limar** vt to file

limitación [limita'θjon] nf limitation, limit; ~ **de velocidad** speed limit

limitar [limi'tar] vt to limit; (reducir) to reduce, cut down ♦ vi: ~ **con** to border on; ~**se** vr: ~**se a** to limit o.s. to

límite ['limite] nm (gen) limit; (fin) end; (frontera) border; ~ **de velocidad** speed limit

limítrofe [li'mitrofe] adj neighbouring

limón [li'mon] nm lemon ♦ adj: **amarillo** ~ lemon-yellow; **limonada** nf lemonade

limosna [li'mosna] nf alms pl; **vivir de** ~ to live on charity

limpiaparabrisas [limpjapara'ßrisas] nm inv windscreen (BRIT) o windshield (US) wiper

limpiar [lim'pjar] vt to clean; (con trapo) to wipe; (quitar) to wipe away; (zapatos) to shine, polish; (fig) to clean up

limpieza [lim'pjeθa] nf (estado) cleanliness; (acto) cleaning; (: de las calles) cleansing; (: de zapatos) polishing; (habilidad) skill; (fig: POLICÍA) clean-up; (pureza) purity; (MIL): **operación de** ~ mopping-up operation; ~ **en seco** dry cleaning

limpio, a ['limpjo, a] adj clean; (moralmente) pure; (COM) clear, net; (fam) honest ♦ adv: **jugar** ~ to play fair; **pasar a** (ESP) o **en** (AM) ~ to make a clean copy

linaje [li'naxe] nm lineage, family

lince ['linθe] nm lynx

linchar [lin'tʃar] vt to lynch

lindar [lin'dar] vi to adjoin; ~ **con** to border on; **linde** nm o f boundary; **lindero, a** adj adjoining ♦ nm boundary

lindo, a ['lindo, a] adj pretty, lovely ♦ adv: **nos divertimos de lo** ~ we had a marvellous time; **canta muy** ~ (AM) he sings beautifully

línea ['linea] nf (gen) line; **en** ~ (INFORM) on line; ~ **aérea** airline; ~ **de meta** goal line; (de carrera) finishing line; ~ **recta** straight line

lingote [lin'gote] nm ingot

lingüista [lin'gwista] nm/f linguist; **lingüística** nf linguistics sg

lino ['lino] nm linen; (BOT) flax

linóleo [li'noleo] nm lino, linoleum

linterna [lin'terna] nf torch (BRIT), flashlight (US)

lío ['lio] nm bundle; (fam) fuss; (desorden) muddle, mess; **armar un** ~ to make a fuss

liquen ['liken] nm lichen

liquidación [likiða'θjon] nf liquidation; **venta de** ~ clearance sale

liquidar [liki'ðar] vt (mercancías) to liquidate; (deudas) to pay off; (empresa) to wind up

líquido, a ['likiðo, a] adj liquid; (ganancia) net ♦ nm liquid; ~ **imponible** net taxable income

lira ['lira] nf (MUS) lyre; (moneda) lira

lírico, a ['liriko, a] adj lyrical

lirio ['lirjo] nm (BOT) iris

lirón [li'ron] nm (ZOOL) dormouse; (fig) sleepyhead

Lisboa [lis'ßoa] n Lisbon

lisiado, a [li'sjaðo, a] adj injured ♦ nm/f cripple

lisiar [li'sjar] vt to maim; ~**se** vr to injure o.s.

liso, a ['liso, a] adj (terreno) flat; (cabello) straight; (superficie) even; (tela) plain

lisonja [li'sonxa] nf flattery

lista ['lista] nf list; (de alumnos) school register; (de libros) catalogue; (de platos) menu; (de precios) price list; **pasar** ~ to call the roll; ~ **de correos** poste restante; ~ **de espera** waiting list; **tela de** ~**s** striped material; **listín** nm: ~ (**telefónico**) telephone directory

listo, a ['listo, a] adj (perspicaz) smart, clever; (preparado) ready

listón [lis'ton] nm (de madera, metal) strip

litera [li'tera] nf (en barco, tren) berth; (en dormitorio) bunk, bunk bed

literal [lite'ral] adj literal

literario, a [lite'rarjo, a] adj literary

literato, a [lite'rato, a] adj literary ♦ nm/f writer

literatura [litera'tura] nf literature

litigar [liti'var] vt to fight ♦ vi (JUR) to go to law; (fig) to dispute, argue

litigio [li'tixjo] nm (JUR) lawsuit; (fig): **en** ~ **con** in dispute with

litografía [litovra'fia] nf lithography; (una ~) lithograph

litoral [lito'ral] adj coastal ♦ nm coast, seaboard

litro ['litro] nm litre

liviano, a [li'ßjano, a] adj (cosa, objeto) trivial

lívido, a ['lißiðo, a] adj livid

llaga ['ʎava] nf wound

llama ['ʎama] nf flame; (ZOOL) llama

llamada [ʎa'maða] nf call; ~ **al orden** call to order; ~ **a pie de página** reference note

llamamiento [ʎama'mjento] nm call

llamar [ʎa'mar] vt to call; (atención) to attract ♦ vi (por teléfono) to telephone; (a la puerta) to knock (o ring); (por señas) to beckon; (MIL) to call up; ~**se** vr to be called, be named; **¿cómo se llama usted?** what's your name?

llamarada [ʎama'raða] nf (llamas) blaze; (rubor) flush

llamativo, a [ʎama'tißo, a] adj showy; (color) loud

llano, a ['ʎano, a] adj (superficie) flat; (persona) straightforward; (estilo) clear ♦ nm plain, flat ground

llanta ['ʎanta] nf (wheel) rim; (AM): ~ (**de**

goma) tyre; (: *cámara*) inner (tube)

llanto [ˈʎanto] *nm* weeping

llanura [ʎaˈnura] *nf* plain

llave [ˈʎaβe] *nf* key; (*del agua*) tap; (*MECÁNICA*) spanner; (*de la luz*) switch; (*MUS*) key; ~ **inglesa** monkey wrench; ~ **maestra** master key; ~ **de contacto** (*AUTO*) ignition key, ~ **de paso** stopcock, **echar la** ~ **a** to lock up; **~ro** *nm* keyring

llegada [ʎeˈɣaða] *nf* arrival

llegar [ʎeˈɣar] *vi* to arrive; (*alcanzar*) to reach; (*bastar*) to be enough; **~se** *vr*: **~se a** to approach; ~ **a** to manage to, succeed in; ~ **a saber** to find out; ~ **a ser** to become; ~ **a las manos de** to come into the hands of

llenar [ʎeˈnar] *vt* to fill; (*espacio*) to cover; (*formulario*) to fill in o up; (*fig*) to heap

lleno, a [ˈʎeno, a] *adj* full, filled; (*repleto*) full up ♦ *nm* (*TEATRO*) full house; **dar de ~ contra un muro** to hit a wall head-on

llevadero, a [ʎeβaˈðero, a] *adj* bearable, tolerable

llevar [ʎeˈβar] *vt* to take; (*ropa*) to wear; (*cargar*) to carry; (*quitar*) to take away; (*en coche*) to drive; (*transportar*) to transport; (*traer: dinero*) to carry; (*conducir*) to lead; (*MAT*) to carry ♦ *vi* (suj: *camino etc*): ~ **a** to lead to; **~se** *vr* to carry off, take away; **llevamos dos días aquí** we have been here for two days; **él me lleva 2 años** he's 2 years older than me; (*COM*): ~ **los libros** to keep the books; **~se bien** to get on well (together)

llorar [ʎoˈrar] *vt, vi* to cry, weep; ~ **de risa** to cry with laughter

lloriquear [ʎorikeˈar] *vi* to snivel, whimper

lloro [ˈʎoro] *nm* crying, weeping; **llorón, ona** *adj* tearful ♦ *nm/f* cry-baby; **~so, a** *adj* (*gen*) weeping, tearful; (*triste*) sad, sorrowful

llover [ʎoˈβer] *vi* to rain

llovizna [ʎoˈβiθna] *nf* drizzle; **lloviznar** *vi* to drizzle

llueve *etc vb ver* **llover**

lluvia [ˈʎuβja] *nf* rain; ~ **radioactiva** (radioactive) fallout; **lluvioso, a** *adj* rainy

lo [lo] *art def:* ~ **bello** the beautiful, what is beautiful, that which is beautiful ♦ *pron* (*persona*) him; (*cosa*) it; *tb ver* **el**

loable [loˈaβle] *adj* praiseworthy; **loar** *vt* to praise

lobo [ˈloβo] *nm* wolf; ~ **de mar** (*fig*) sea dog; ~ **marino** seal

lóbrego, a [ˈloβreɣo, a] *adj* dark; (*fig*) gloomy

lóbulo [ˈloβulo] *nm* lobe

local [loˈkal] *adj* local ♦ *nm* place, site; (*oficinas*) premises *pl*; **~idad** *nf* (*barrio*) locality; (*lugar*) location; (*TEATRO*) seat, ticket; **~izar** *vt* (*ubicar*) to locate, find; (*restringir*) to localize; (*situar*) to place

loción [loˈθjon] *nf* lotion

loco, a [ˈloko, a] *adj* mad ♦ *nm/f* lunatic, mad person

locomotora [lokomoˈtora] *nf* engine, locomotive

locuaz [loˈkwaθ] *adj* loquacious

locución [lokuˈθjon] *nf* expression

locura [loˈkura] *nf* madness; (*acto*) crazy act

locutor, a [lokuˈtor, a] *nm/f* (*RADIO*) announcer; (*comentarista*) commentator; (*TV*) newsreader

locutorio [lokuˈtorjo] *nm* (*en telefónica*) telephone booth

lodo [ˈloðo] *nm* mud

lógica [ˈloxika] *nf* logic

lógico, a [ˈloxiko, a] *adj* logical

logística [loˈxistika] *nf* logistics *sg*

logotipo [loðoˈtipo] *nm* logo

logrado, a [loˈðraðo, a] *adj* (*interpretación, reproducción*) polished, excellent

lograr [loˈɣrar] *vt* to achieve; (*obtener*) to get, obtain; ~ **hacer** to manage to do; ~ **que uno venga** to manage to get sb to come

logro [ˈloɣro] *nm* achievement, success

loma [ˈloma] *nf* hillock (*BRIT*), small hill

lombriz [lomˈbriθ] *nf* worm

lomo [ˈlomo] *nm* (*de animal*) back; (*CULIN: de cerdo*) pork loin; (: *de vaca*) rib steak; (*de libro*) spine

lona [ˈlona] *nf* canvas

loncha [ˈlontʃa] *nf* = **lonja**

lonche [ˈlontʃe] (*AM*) *nm* lunch; **~ría** (*AM*) *nf* snack bar, diner (*US*)

Londres [ˈlondres] *n* London

longaniza [longaˈniθa] *nf* pork sausage

longitud [lonxiˈtuð] *nf* length; (*GEO*) longitude; **tener 3 metros de ~** to be 3 metres long; ~ **de onda** wavelength

lonja [ˈlonxa] *nf* slice; (*de tocino*) rasher; ~ **de pescado** fish market

loro [ˈloro] *nm* parrot

los [los] *art def the* ♦ *pron* them; (*ustedes*) you; **mis libros y ~ tuyos** my books and yours; *tb ver* **el**

losa [ˈlosa] *nf* stone; ~ **sepulcral** gravestone

lote [ˈlote] *nm* portion; (*COM*) lot

lotería [loteˈria] *nf* lottery; (*juego*) lotto

loza [ˈloθa] *nf* crockery

lubina [luˈβina] *nf* sea bass

lubricante [luβriˈkante] *nm* lubricant

lubricar [luβriˈkar] *vt* to lubricate

lucha [ˈlutʃa] *nf* fight, struggle; ~ **de clases** class struggle; ~ **libre** wrestling; **luchar** *vi* to fight

lucidez [luθiˈðeθ] *nf* lucidity

lúcido, a [ˈluθiðo, a] *adj* (*persona*) lucid; (*mente*) logical; (*idea*) crystal-clear

luciérnaga [luˈθjernaɣa] *nf* glow-worm

lucir [luˈθir] *vt* to illuminate, light (up);

(*ostentar*) to show off ♦ vi (*brillar*) to shine;
~se vr (*irónico*) to make a fool of o.s.
lucro ['lukro] nm profit, gain
lúdico, a ['ludiko, a] adj (*aspecto, actividad*)
play cpd
luego ['lwe o] adv (*después*) next; (*más
tarde*) later, afterwards
lugar [lu'ɣar] nm place; (*sitio*) spot; **en ~ de**
instead of; **hacer ~** to make room; **fuera de ~**
out of place; **tener ~** to take place; **~ común**
commonplace
lugareño, a [luɣa'reɲo, a] adj village cpd
♦ nm/f villager
lugarteniente [luɣarte'njente] nm deputy
lúgubre ['luɣuβre] adj mournful
lujo ['luxo] nm luxury; (*fig*) profusion,
abundance; **~so, a** adj luxurious
lujuria [lu'xurja] nf lust
lumbre ['lumbre] nf fire; (*para cigarrillo*) light
lumbrera [lum'brera] nf luminary
luminoso, a [lumi'noso, a] adj luminous,
shining
luna ['luna] nf moon; (*de un espejo*) glass; (*de
gafas*) lens; (*fig*) crescent; **~ llena/nueva** full/
new moon; **estar en la ~** to have one's head
in the clouds; **~ de miel** honeymoon
lunar [lu'nar] adj lunar ♦ nm (*ANAT*) mole;
tela de ~es spotted material
lunes ['lunes] nm inv Monday
lupa ['lupa] nf magnifying glass
lustrar [lus'trar] vt (*mueble*) to polish;
(*zapatos*) to shine; **lustre** nm polish; (*fig*)
lustre; **dar lustre a** to polish; **lustroso, a** adj
shining
luto ['luto] nm mourning; **llevar el o vestirse
de ~** to be in mourning
Luxemburgo [luksem'burɣo] nm Luxembourg
luz [luθ] (*pl* luces) nf light; **dar a ~ un niño** to
give birth to a child; **sacar a la ~** to bring to
light; **dar o encender** (*ESP*) o **prender** (*AM*)/
apagar la ~ to switch the light on/off; **a todas
luces** by any reckoning; **tener pocas luces** to
be dim o stupid; **~ roja/verde** red/green light;
~ de freno brake light; **luces de tráfico** traffic
lights; **traje de luces** bullfighter's costume

M, m

m abr (= *metro*) m; (= *minuto*) m
macarrones [maka'rrones] nmpl macaroni
sg
macedonia [maθe'ðonja] nf: **~ de frutas**
fruit salad
macerar [maθe'rar] vt to macerate
maceta [ma'θeta] nf (*de flores*) pot of
flowers; (*para plantas*) flowerpot
machacar [matʃa'kar] vt to crush, pound

♦ vi (*insistir*) to go on, keep on
machete [ma'tʃete] (*AM*) nm machete,
(large) knife
machismo [ma'tʃismo] nm male
chauvinism; **machista** adj, nm sexist
macho ['matʃo] adj male; (*fig*) virile ♦ nm
male; (*fig*) he-man
macizo, a [ma'θiθo, a] adj (*grande*) massive;
(*fuerte, sólido*) solid ♦ nm mass, chunk
madeja [ma'ðexa] nf (*de lana*) skein, hank;
(*de pelo*) mass, mop
madera [ma'ðera] nf wood; (*fig*) nature,
character; **una ~** a piece of wood
madero [ma'ðero] nm beam
madrastra [ma'ðrastra] nf stepmother
madre ['maðre] adj mother cpd; (*AM*)
tremendous ♦ nf mother; (*de vino etc*) dregs
pl; **~ política/soltera** mother-in-law/unmarried
mother
Madrid [ma'ðrið] n Madrid
madriguera [maðri'ɣera] nf burrow
madrileño, a [maðri'leɲo, a] adj of o from
Madrid ♦ nm/f native of Madrid
madrina [ma'ðrina] nf godmother; (*ARQ*)
prop, shore; (*TEC*) brace; (*de boda*)
bridesmaid
madrugada [maðru'ɣaða] nf early morning;
(*alba*) dawn, daybreak
madrugador, a [maðruxa'ðor, a] adj early-
rising
madrugar [maðru'ɣar] vi to get up early;
(*fig*) to get ahead
madurar [maðu'rar] vt, vi (*fruta*) to ripen;
(*fig*) to mature; **madurez** nf ripeness;
maturity; **maduro, a** adj ripe; mature
maestra [ma'estra] nf ver **maestro**
maestría [maes'tria] nf mastery; (*habilidad*)
skill, expertise
maestro, a [ma'estro, a] adj masterly;
(*principal*) main ♦ nm/f master/mistress;
(*profesor*) teacher ♦ nm (*autoridad*) authority;
(*MUS*) maestro; (*AM*) skilled workman;
~ albañil master mason
magdalena [maɣða'lena] nf fairy cake
magia ['maxja] nf magic; **mágico, a** adj
magic(al) ♦ nm/f magician
magisterio [maxis'terjo] nm (*enseñanza*)
teaching; (*profesión*) teaching profession;
(*maestros*) teachers pl
magistrado [maxis'traðo] nm magistrate
magistral [maxis'tral] adj magisterial; (*fig*)
masterly
magnánimo, a [maɣ'nanimo, a] adj
magnanimous
magnate [maɣ'nate] nm magnate, tycoon
magnético, a [maɣ'netiko, a] adj magnetic;
magnetizar vt to magnetize
magnetofón [maɣneto'fon] nm tape
recorder; **magnetofónico, a** adj: **cinta**

magnetofónica recording tape
magnetófono [maɣne'tofono] *nm* = **magnetófon**
magnífico, a [maɣ'nifiko, a] *adj* splendid, magnificent
magnitud [maɣni'tuð] *nf* magnitude
mago, a ['maɣo, a] *nm/f* magician; **los Reyes M~s** the Magi, the Three Wise Men
magro, a ['maɣro, a] *adj* (*carne*) lean
maguey [ma'ɣei] *nm* agave
magullar [maɣu'ʎar] *vt* (*amoratar*) to bruise; (*dañar*) to damage
mahometano, a [maome'tano, a] *adj* Mohammedan
mahonesa [mao'nesa] *nf* mayonnaise
maíz [ma'iθ] *nm* maize (*BRIT*), corn (*US*); sweet corn
majadero, a [maxa'ðero, a] *adj* silly, stupid
majestad [maxes'taθ] *nf* majesty; **majestuoso, a** *adj* majestic
majo, a ['maxo, a] *adj* nice; (*guapo*) attractive, good-looking; (*elegante*) smart
mal [mal] *adv* badly; (*equivocadamente*) wrongly ♦ *adj* = **malo** ♦ *nm* evil; (*desgracia*) misfortune; (*daño*) harm, damage; (*MED*) illness; **~ que bien** rightly or wrongly; **ir de ~ en peor** to get worse and worse
malabarismo [malaβa'rismo] *nm* juggling; **malabarista** *nm/f* juggler
malaria [ma'larja] *nf* malaria
malcriado, a [mal'krjaðo, a] *adj* spoiled
maldad [mal'daθ] *nf* evil, wickedness
maldecir [malde'θir] *vt* to curse ♦ *vi*: **~ de** to speak ill of
maldición [maldi'θjon] *nf* curse
maldito, a [mal'dito, a] *adj* (*condenado*) damned; (*perverso*) wicked; **¡~ sea!** damn it!
maleante [male'ante] *nm/f* criminal, crook
maledicencia [maleði'θenθja] *nf* slander, scandal
maleducado, a [maleðu'kaðo, a] *adj* bad-mannered, rude
malentendido [malenten'diðo] *nm* misunderstanding
malestar [males'tar] *nm* (*gen*) discomfort; (*fig: inquietud*) uneasiness; (*POL*) unrest
maleta [ma'leta] *nf* case, suitcase; (*AUTO*) boot (*BRIT*), trunk (*US*); **hacer las ~s** to pack; **maletera** (*AM*) *nf*, **maletero** *nm* (*AUTO*) boot (*BRIT*), trunk (*US*); **maletín** *nm* small case, bag
malévolo, a [ma'leβolo, a] *adj* malicious, spiteful
maleza [ma'leθa] *nf* (*hierbas malas*) weeds *pl*; (*arbustos*) thicket
malgastar [malɣas'tar] *vt* (*tiempo, dinero*) to waste; (*salud*) to ruin
malhechor, a [male'tʃor, a] *nm/f* delinquent
malhumorado, a [malumo'raðo, a] *adj* bad-tempered

malicia [ma'liθja] *nf* (*maldad*) wickedness; (*astucia*) slyness, guile; (*mala intención*) malice, spite; (*carácter travieso*) mischievousness; **malicioso, a** *adj* wicked, evil; sly, crafty; malicious, spiteful; mischievous
maligno, a [ma'liɣno, a] *adj* evil; (*malévolo*) malicious; (*MED*) malignant
malla ['maʎa] *nf* mesh; (*de baño*) swimsuit; (*de ballet, gimnasia*) leotard; **~s** *nfpl* tights; **~ de alambre** wire mesh
Mallorca [ma'ʎorka] *nf* Majorca
malo, a ['malo, a] *adj* bad; (*falso*) false ♦ *nm/f* villain; **estar ~** to be ill
malograr [malo'ɣrar] *vt* to spoil; (*plan*) to upset; (*ocasión*) to waste; **~se** *vr* (*plan etc*) to fail, come to grief; (*persona*) to die before one's time
malparado, a [malpa'raðo, a] *adj*: **salir ~** to come off badly
malpensado, a [malpen'saðo, a] *adj* nasty
malsano, a [mal'sano, a] *adj* unhealthy
malteada [malte'aða] (*AM*) *nf* milk shake
maltratar [maltra'tar] *vt* to ill-treat, mistreat
maltrecho, a [mal'tretʃo, a] *adj* battered, damaged
malvado, a [mal'ßaðo, a] *adj* evil, villainous
malversar [malßer'sar] *vt* to embezzle, misappropriate
Malvinas [mal'ßinas]: **Islas ~** *nfpl* Falkland Islands
malvivir [malßi'ßir] *vi* to live poorly
mama ['mama] *nf* (*de animal*) teat; (*de mujer*) breast
mamá [ma'ma] (*pl* **~s**) (*fam*) *nf* mum, mummy
mamar [ma'mar] *vt*, *vi* to suck
mamarracho [mama'rratʃo] *nm* sight, mess
mamífero [ma'mifero] *nm* mammal
mampara [mam'para] *nf* (*entre habitaciones*) partition; (*biombo*) screen
mampostería [mamposte'ria] *nf* masonry
manada [ma'naða] *nf* (*ZOOL*) herd; (*: de leones*) pride; (*: de lobos*) pack
manantial [manan'tjal] *nm* spring
manar [ma'nar] *vi* to run, flow
mancha ['mantʃa] *nf* stain, mark; (*ZOOL*) patch; **manchar** *vt* (*gen*) to stain, mark; (*ensuciar*) to soil, dirty
manchego, a [man'tʃeɣo, a] *adj* of o from La Mancha
manco, a ['manko, a] *adj* (*de un brazo*) one-armed; (*de una mano*) one-handed; (*fig*) defective, faulty
mancomunar [mankomu'nar] *vt* to unite, bring together; (*recursos*) to pool; (*JUR*) to make jointly responsible; **mancomunidad** *nf* union, association; (*comunidad*) community;

(*JUR*) joint responsibility

mandamiento [manda'mjento] *nm* (*orden*) order, command; (*REL*) commandment; **~ judicial** warrant

mandar [man'dar] *vt* (*ordenar*) to order; (*dirigir*) to lead, command; (*enviar*) to send; (*pedir*) to order, ask for ♦ *vi* to be in charge; (*pey*) to be bossy; **¿mande?** pardon?, excuse me?; **~ hacer un traje** to have a suit made

mandarina [manda'rina] *nf* tangerine, mandarin (orange)

mandato [man'dato] *nm* (*orden*) order; (*POL*: *período*) term of office; (: *territorio*) mandate; **~ judicial** (search) warrant

mandíbula [man'dißula] *nf* jaw

mandil [man'dil] *nm* apron

mando ['mando] *nm* (*MIL*) command; (*de país*) rule; (*el primer lugar*) lead; (*POL*) term of office; (*TEC*) control; **~ a la izquierda** left-hand drive

mandón, ona [man'don, ona] *adj* bossy, domineering

manejable [mane'xaßle] *adj* manageable

manejar [mane'xar] *vt* to manage; (*máquina*) to work, operate; (*caballo etc*) to handle; (*casa*) to run, manage; (*AM*: *AUTO*) to drive; **~se** *vr* (*comportarse*) to act, behave; (*arreglárselas*) to manage; **manejo** *nm* management; handling; running; driving; (*facilidad de trato*) ease, confidence; **manejos** *nmpl* (*intrigas*) intrigues

manera [ma'nera] *nf* way, manner, fashion; **~s** *nfpl* (*modales*) manners; **su ~ de ser** the way he is; (*aire*) his manner; **de ninguna ~** no way, by no means; **de otra ~** otherwise; **de todas ~s** at any rate; **no hay ~ de persuadirle** there's no way of convincing him

manga ['manga] *nf* (*de camisa*) sleeve; (*de riego*) hose

mangar [man'gar] (*fam*) *vt* to pinch, nick

mango ['mango] *nm* handle; (*BOT*) mango

mangonear [mangone'ar] *vi* (*meterse*) to meddle, interfere; (*ser mandón*) to boss people about

manguera [man'gera] *nf* hose

manía [ma'nia] *nf* (*MED*) mania; (*fig*: *moda*) rage, craze; (*disgusto*) dislike; (*malicia*) spite; **maníaco, a** *adj* maniac(al) ♦ *nm/f* maniac

maniatar [manja'tar] *vt* to tie the hands of

maniático, a [ma'njatiko, a] *adj* maniac(al) ♦ *nm/f* maniac

manicomio [mani'komjo] *nm* mental hospital (*BRIT*), insane asylum (*US*)

manifestación [manifesta'θjon] *nf* (*declaración*) statement, declaration; (*de emoción*) show, display; (*POL*: *desfile*) demonstration; (: *concentración*) mass meeting

manifestar [manifes'tar] *vt* to show,

manifest; (*declarar*) to state, declare; **manifiesto, a** *adj* clear, manifest ♦ *nm* manifesto

manillar [mani'ʎar] *nm* handlebars *pl*

maniobra [ma'njoßra] *nf* manoeuvre; **~s** *nfpl* (*MIL*) manoeuvres; **maniobrar** *vt* to manoeuvre

manipulación [manipula'θjon] *nf* manipulation

manipular [manipu'lar] *vt* to manipulate; (*manejar*) to handle

maniquí [mani'ki] *nm* dummy ♦ *nm/f* model

manirroto, a [mani'rroto, a] *adj* lavish, extravagant ♦ *nm/f* spendthrift

manivela [mani'ßela] *nf* crank

manjar [man'xar] *nm* (tasty) dish

mano ['mano] *nf* hand; (*ZOOL*) foot, paw; (*de pintura*) coat; (*serie*) lot, series; **a ~** by hand; **a ~ derecha/izquierda** on the right(-hand side)/left(-hand side); **de primera ~** (at) first hand; **de segunda ~** (at) second hand; **robo a ~ armada** armed robbery; **~ de obra** labour, manpower; **estrechar la ~ a uno** to shake sb's hand

manojo [ma'noxo] *nm* handful, bunch; **~ de llaves** bunch of keys

manopla [ma'nopla] *nf* mitten

manoseado, a [manose'aðo, a] *adj* well-worn

manosear [manose'ar] *vt* (*tocar*) to handle, touch; (*desordenar*) to mess up, rumple; (*insistir en*) to overwork; (*AM*) to caress, fondle

manotazo [mano'taθo] *nm* slap, smack

mansalva [man'salβa]: **a ~** *adv* indiscriminately

mansedumbre [manse'ðumbre] *nf* gentleness, meekness

mansión [man'sjon] *nf* mansion

manso, a ['manso, a] *adj* gentle, mild; (*animal*) tame

manta ['manta] *nf* blanket; (*AM*: *poncho*) poncho

manteca [man'teka] *nf* fat; (*AM*) butter; **~ de cacahuete/cacao** peanut/cocoa butter; **~ de cerdo** lard

mantecado [mante'kaðo] (*AM*) *nm* ice cream

mantel [man'tel] *nm* tablecloth

mantendré etc *vb ver* **mantener**

mantener [mante'ner] *vt* to support, maintain; (*alimentar*) to sustain; (*conservar*) to keep; (*TEC*) to maintain, service; **~se** *vr* (*seguir de pie*) to be still standing; (*no ceder*) to hold one's ground; (*subsistir*) to sustain o.s., keep going; **mantenimiento** *nm* maintenance; sustenance; (*sustento*) support

mantequilla [mante'kiʎa] *nf* butter

mantilla [man'tiʎa] *nf* mantilla; **~s** *nfpl* (*de*

bebé) baby clothes

manto ['manto] *nm* (*capa*) cloak; (*de ceremonia*) robe, gown

mantuve *etc vb ver* **mantener**

manual [ma'nwal] *adj* manual ♦ *nm* manual, handbook

manufactura [manufak'tura] *nf* manufacture; (*fábrica*) factory; **manufacturado, a** *adj* (*producto*) manufactured

manuscrito, a [manus'krito, a] *adj* handwritten ♦ *nm* manuscript

manutención [manuten'θjon] *nf* maintenance; (*sustento*) support

manzana [man'θana] *nf* apple; (*ARQ*) block (of houses)

manzanilla [manθa'niʎa] *nf* (*planta*) camomile; (*infusión*) camomile tea

manzano [man'θano] *nm* apple tree

maña ['maɲa] *nf* (*gen*) skill, dexterity; (*pey*) guile; (*destreza*) trick, knack

mañana [ma'ɲana] *adv* tomorrow ♦ *nm* future ♦ *nf* morning; **de** *o* **por la ~** in the morning; **¡hasta ~!** see you tomorrow!; **~ por la ~** tomorrow morning

mañoso, a [ma'ɲoso, a] *adj* (*hábil*) skilful; (*astuto*) smart, clever

mapa ['mapa] *nm* map

maqueta [ma'keta] *nf* (scale) model

maquillaje [maki'ʎaxe] *nm* make-up; (*acto*) making up

maquillar [maki'ʎar] *vt* to make up; **~se** *vr* to put on (some) make-up

máquina ['makina] *nf* machine; (*de tren*) locomotive, engine; (*FOTO*) camera; (*AM: coche*) car; (*fig*) machinery; **escrito a ~** typewritten; **~ de escribir** typewriter; **~ de coser/lavar** sewing/washing machine

maquinación [makina'θjon] *nf* machination, plot

maquinal [maki'nal] *adj* (*fig*) mechanical, automatic

maquinaria [maki'narja] *nf* (*máquinas*) machinery; (*mecanismo*) mechanism, works *pl*

maquinilla [maki'niʎa] *nf*: **~ de afeitar** razor

maquinista [maki'nista] *nm/f* (*de tren*) engine driver; (*TEC*) operator; (*NAUT*) engineer

mar [mar] *nm o f* sea; **~ adentro** *o* **afuera** out at sea; **en alta ~** on the high seas; **la ~ de** (*fam*) lots of; **el M~ Negro/Báltico** the Black/ Baltic Sea

maraña [ma'raɲa] *nf* (*maleza*) thicket; (*confusión*) tangle

maravilla [mara'ßiʎa] *nf* marvel, wonder; (*BOT*) marigold; **maravillar** *vt* to astonish, amaze; **maravillarse** *vr* to be astonished, be amazed; **maravilloso, a** *adj* wonderful, marvellous

marca ['marka] *nf* (*gen*) mark; (*sello*) stamp; (*COM*) make, brand; **de ~** excellent, outstanding; **~ de fábrica** trademark; **~ registrada** registered trademark

marcado, a [mar'kaðo, a] *adj* marked, strong

marcador [marka'ðor] *nm* (*DEPORTE*) scoreboard; (: *persona*) scorer

marcapasos [marka'pasos] *nm inv* pacemaker

marcar [mar'kar] *vt* (*gen*) to mark; (*número de teléfono*) to dial; (*gol*) to score; (*números*) to record, keep a tally of; (*pelo*) to set ♦ *vi* (*DEPORTE*) to score; (*TEL*) to dial

marcha ['martʃa] *nf* march; (*TEC*) running, working; (*AUTO*) gear; (*velocidad*) speed; (*fig*) progress; (*dirección*) course; **poner en ~** to put into gear; (*fig*) to set in motion, get going; **dar ~ atrás** to reverse, put into reverse; **estar en ~** to be under way, be in motion

marchar [mar'tʃar] *vi* (*ir*) to go; (*funcionar*) to work, go; **~se** *vr* to go (away), leave

marchitar [martʃi'tar] *vt* to wither, dry up; **~se** *vr* (*BOT*) to wither; (*fig*) to fade away; **marchito, a** *adj* withered, faded; (*fig*) in decline

marcial [mar'θjal] *adj* martial, military

marciano, a [mar'θjano, a] *adj, nm/f* Martian

marco ['marko] *nm* frame; (*moneda*) mark; (*fig*) framework

marea [ma'rea] *nf* tide

marear [mare'ar] *vt* (*fig*) to annoy, upset; (*MED*): **~ a uno** to make sb feel sick; **~se** *vr* (*tener náuseas*) to feel sick; (*desvanecerse*) to feel faint; (*aturdirse*) to feel dizzy; (*fam: emborracharse*) to get tipsy

maremoto [mare'moto] *nm* tidal wave

mareo [ma'reo] *nm* (*náusea*) sick feeling; (*en viaje*) travel sickness; (*aturdimiento*) dizziness; (*fam: lata*) nuisance

marfil [mar'fil] *nm* ivory

margarina [marɣa'rina] *nf* margarine

margarita [marɣa'rita] *nf* (*BOT*) daisy; (**rueda**) **~** daisywheel

margen ['marxen] *nm* (*borde*) edge, border; (*fig*) margin, space ♦ *nf* (*de río etc*) bank; **dar ~ para** to give an opportunity for; **mantenerse al ~** to keep out (of things)

marginar [marxi'nar] *vt* (*socialmente*) to marginalize, ostracize

marica [ma'rika] (*fam*) *nm* sissy

maricón [mari'kon] (*fam*) *nm* queer

marido [ma'riðo] *nm* husband

marihuana [mari'wana] *nf* marijuana, cannabis

marina [ma'rina] *nf* navy; **~ mercante** merchant navy

marinero, a [mari'nero, a] *adj* sea *cpd* ♦ *nm* sailor, seaman

marino, a [ma'rino, a] *adj* sea *cpd*, marine ♦ *nm* sailor

marioneta [marjo'neta] *nf* puppet

mariposa [mari'posa] *nf* butterfly

mariquita [mari'kita] *nf* ladybird (*BRIT*), ladybug (*US*)

mariscos [ma'riskos] *nmpl* shellfish *inv*, seafood(s)

marítimo, a [ma'ritimo, a] *adj* sea *cpd*, maritime

mármol ['marmol] *nm* marble

marqués, esa [mar'kes, esa] *nm/f* marquis/ marchioness

marrón [ma'rron] *adj* brown

marroquí [marro'ki] *adj, nm/f* Moroccan ♦ *nm* Morocco (leather)

Marruecos [ma'rrwekos] *nm* Morocco

martes ['martes] *nm inv* Tuesday

martillo [mar'tiʎo] *nm* hammer; **~ neumático** pneumatic drill (*BRIT*), jackhammer

mártir ['martir] *nm/f* martyr; **martirio** *nm* martyrdom; (*fig*) torture, torment

marxismo [mark'sismo] *nm* Marxism; **marxista** *adj, nm/f* Marxist

marzo ['marθo] *nm* March

PALABRA CLAVE

---

más [mas] *adj, adv* **1**: **~ (que, de)** (*compar*) more (than), ... + er (than); **~ grande/ inteligente** bigger/more intelligent; **trabaja ~ (que yo)** he works more (than me); *ver tb* **cada**

2 (*superl*): **el ~** the most, ... + est; **el ~ grande/inteligente (de)** the biggest/most intelligent (in)

3 (*negativo*): **no tengo ~ dinero** I haven't got any more money; **no viene ~ por aquí** he doesn't come round here any more

4 (*adicional*): **no le veo ~ solución que ...** I see no other solution than to ...; **¿quién ~?** anybody else?

5 (+ *adj: valor intensivo*): **¡qué perro ~ sucio!** what a filthy dog!; **¡es ~ tonto!** he's so stupid!

6 (*locuciones*): **~ o menos** more or less; **los ~** most people; **es ~** furthermore; **~ bien** rather; **¡qué ~ da!** what does it matter!; *ver tb* **no**

7: **por ~**: **por ~ que te esfuerces** no matter how hard you try; **por ~ que quisiera ...** much as I should like to ...

8: **de ~**: **veo que aquí estoy de ~** I can see I'm not needed here; **tenemos uno de ~** we've got one extra

♦ *prep*: **2 ~ 2 son 4** 2 and 2 are 4, 2 and 2 make 4

♦ *nm inv*: **este trabajo tiene sus ~ y sus menos** this job's got its good points and its bad points

---

mas [mas] *conj* but

masa ['masa] *nf* (*mezcla*) dough; (*volumen*) volume, mass; (*FÍSICA*) mass; **en ~** en masse; **las ~s** (*POL*) the masses

masacre [ma'sakre] *nf* massacre

masaje [ma'saxe] *nm* massage

máscara ['maskara] *nf* mask; **mascarilla** *nf* (*de belleza*, *MED*) mask

masculino, a [masku'lino, a] *adj* masculine; (*BIO*) male

masía [ma'sia] *nf* farmhouse

masificación [masifika'θjon] *nf* overcrowding

masivo, a [ma'siβo, a] *adj* mass *cpd*

masón [ma'son] *nm* (free)mason

masoquista [maso'kista] *nm/f* masochist

masticar [masti'kar] *vt* to chew

mástil ['mastil] *nm* (*de navío*) mast; (*de guitarra*) neck

mastín [mas'tin] *nm* mastiff

masturbación [masturßa'θjon] *nf* masturbation

masturbarse [mastur'ßarse] *vr* to masturbate

mata ['mata] *nf* (*arbusto*) bush, shrub; (*de hierba*) tuft

matadero [mata'ðero] *nm* slaughterhouse, abattoir

matador, a [mata'ðor, a] *adj* killing ♦ *nm/f* killer ♦ *nm* (*TAUR*) matador, bullfighter

matamoscas [mata'moskas] *nm inv* (*palo*) fly swat

matanza [ma'tanθa] *nf* slaughter

matar [ma'tar] *vt, vi* to kill; **~se** *vr* (*suicidarse*) to kill o.s., commit suicide; (*morir*) to be o get killed; **~ el hambre** to stave off hunger

matasellos [mata'seʎos] *nm inv* postmark

mate ['mate] *adj* matt ♦ *nm* (*en ajedrez*) (check)mate; (*AM: hierba*) maté; (: *vasija*) gourd

matemáticas [mate'matikas] *nfpl* mathematics; **matemático, a** *adj* mathematical ♦ *nm/f* mathematician

materia [ma'terja] *nf* (*gen*) matter; (*TEC*) material; (*ESCOL*) subject; **en ~ de** on the subject of; **~ prima** raw material; **material** *adj* material ♦ *nm* material; (*TEC*) equipment; **materialismo** *nm* materialism; **materialista** *adj* materialist(ic); **materialmente** *adv* materially; (*fig*) absolutely

maternal [mater'nal] *adj* motherly, maternal

maternidad [materni'ðað] *nf* motherhood, maternity; **materno, a** *adj* maternal; (*lengua*) mother *cpd*

matinal [mati'nal] *adj* morning *cpd*

matiz [ma'tiθ] *nm* shade; **~ar** *vt* (*variar*) to vary; (*ARTE*) to blend; **~ar de** to tinge with

matón [ma'ton] *nm* bully

matorral [mato'rral] nm thicket

matraca [ma'traka] nf rattle

matrícula [ma'trikula] nf (registro) register; (AUTO) registration number; (: placa) number plate; **matricular** vt to register, enrol

matrimonial [matrimo'njal] adj matrimonial

matrimonio [matri'monjo] nm (pareja) (married) couple; (union) marriage

matriz [ma'triθ] nf (ANAT) womb; (TEC) mould; casa ~ (COM) head office

matrona [ma'trona] nf (persona de edad) matron; (comadrona) midwife

maullar [mau'ʎar] vi to mew, miaow

maxilar [maksi'lar] nm jaw(bone)

máxima ['maksima] nf maxim

máxime ['maksime] adv especially

máximo, a ['maksimo, a] adj maximum; (más alto) highest; (más grande) greatest ♦ nm maximum

mayo ['majo] nm May

mayonesa [majo'nesa] nf mayonnaise

mayor [ma'jor] adj main, chief; (adulto) adult; (de edad avanzada) elderly; (MUS) major; (compar: de tamaño) bigger; (: de edad) older; (superl: de tamaño) biggest; (: de edad) oldest ♦ nm (adulto) adult; **al por ~** wholesale; **~ de edad** adult; **~es** nmpl (antepasados) ancestors

mayoral [majo'ral] nm foreman

mayordomo [major'domo] nm butler

mayoría [majo'ria] nf majority, greater part

mayorista [majo'rista] nm/f wholesaler

mayoritario, a [majori'tarjo, a] adj majority cpd

mayúscula [ma'juskula] nf capital letter

mayúsculo, a [ma'juskulo, a] adj (fig) big, tremendous

mazapán [maθa'pan] nm marzipan

mazo ['maθo] nm (martillo) mallet; (de flores) bunch; (DEPORTE) bat

me [me] pron (directo) me; (indirecto) (to) me; (reflexivo) (to) myself; **¡dámelo!** give it to me!

mear [me'ar] (fam) vi to pee, piss (!)

mecánica [me'kanika] nf (ESCOL) mechanics sg; (mecanismo) mechanism; ver tb **mecánico**

mecánico, a [me'kaniko, a] adj mechanical ♦ nm/f mechanic

mecanismo [meka'nismo] nm mechanism; (marcha) gear

mecanografía [mekanoɣra'fia] nf typewriting; **mecanógrafo, a** nm/f typist

mecate [me'kate] (AM) nm rope

mecedora [meθe'ðora] nf rocking chair

mecer [me'θer] vt (cuna) to rock; **~se** vr to rock; (ramo) to sway

mecha ['metʃa] nf (de vela) wick; (de bomba) fuse

mechero [me'tʃero] nm (cigarette) lighter

mechón [me'tʃon] nm (gen) tuft; (de pelo) lock

medalla [me'ðaʎa] nf medal

media ['meðja] nf (ESP) stocking; (AM) sock; (promedio) average

mediado, a [me'ðjaðo, a] adj half-full; (trabajo) half-completed; **a ~s de** in the middle of, halfway through

mediano, a [me'ðjano, a] adj (regular) medium, average; (mediocre) mediocre

medianoche [meðja'notʃe] nf midnight

mediante [me'ðjante] adv by (means of), through

mediar [me'ðjar] vi (interceder) to mediate, intervene

medicación [meðika'θjon] nf medication, treatment

medicamento [meðika'mento] nm medicine, drug

medicina [meði'θina] nf medicine

medición [meði'θjon] nf measurement

médico, a ['meðiko, a] adj medical ♦ nm/f doctor

medida [me'ðiða] nf measure; (medición) measurement; (prudencia) moderation, prudence; **en cierta/gran ~** up to a point/to a great extent; **un traje a la ~** made-to-measure suit; **~ de cuello** collar size; **a ~ de** in proportion to; (de acuerdo con) in keeping with; **a ~ que** (conforme) as

medio, a ['meðjo, a] adj half (a); (punto) mid, middle; (promedio) average ♦ adv half ♦ nm (centro) middle, centre; (promedio) average; (método) means, way; (ambiente) environment; **~s** nmpl means, resources; **~ litro** half a litre; **las tres y media** half past three; **medio ambiente** environment; **M~ Oriente** Middle East; **a ~ terminar** half finished; **pagar a medias** to share the cost; **~ambiental** adj (política, efectos) environmental

mediocre [me'ðjokre] adj mediocre

mediodía [meðjo'ðia] nm midday, noon

medir [me'ðir] vt, vi (gen) to measure

meditar [meði'tar] vt to ponder, think over, meditate on; (planear) to think out

mediterráneo, a [meðite'rraneo, a] adj Mediterranean ♦ nm: **el M~** the Mediterranean (Sea)

médula ['meðula] nf (ANAT) marrow; **~ espinal** spinal cord

medusa [me'ðusa] (ESP) nf jellyfish

megafonía [meɣafo'nia] nf public address system, PA system; **megáfono** nm megaphone

megalómano, a [meɣa'lomano, a] nm/f megalomaniac

mejicano, a [mexi'kano, a] adj, nm/f Mexican

Méjico ['mexiko] nm Mexico

mejilla [me'xiʎa] nf cheek

mejillón [mexi'ʎon] nm mussel

mejor [me'xor] adj, adv (compar) better; (superl) best; **a lo ~** probably; (quizá) maybe; **~ dicho** rather; **tanto ~** so much the better

mejora [me'xora] nf improvement; **mejorar** vt to improve, make better ♦ vi to improve, get better; **mejorarse** vr to improve, get better

melancólico, a [melan'koliko, a] adj (triste) sad, melancholy; (soñador) dreamy

melena [me'lena] nf (de persona) long hair; (ZOOL) mane

mellizo, a [me'ʎiθo, a] adj, nm/f twin; **~s** nmpl (AM) cufflinks

melocotón [meloko'ton] (ESP) nm peach

melodía [melo'ðia] nf melody, tune

melodrama [melo'ðrama] nm melodrama; **melodramático, a** adj melodramatic

melón [me'lon] nm melon

membrete [mem'brete] nm letterhead

membrillo [mem'briʎo] nm quince; **carne de ~** quince jelly

memorable [memo'raßle] adj memorable

memoria [me'morja] nf (gen) memory; **~s** nfpl (de autor) memoirs; **memorizar** vt to memorize

menaje [me'naxe] nm: **~ de cocina** kitchenware

mencionar [menθjo'nar] vt to mention

mendigar [mendi'yar] vt to beg (for)

mendigo, a [men'diɣo, a] nm/f beggar

mendrugo [men'druɣo] nm crust

menear [mene'ar] vt to move; **~se** vr to shake; (balancearse) to sway; (moverse) to move; (fig) to get a move on

menestra [me'nestra] nf: **~ de verduras** vegetable stew

menguante [men'gwante] adj decreasing, diminishing

menguar [men'gwar] vt to lessen, diminish ♦ vi to diminish, decrease

menopausia [meno'pausja] nf menopause

menor [me'nor] adj (más pequeño: compar) smaller; (: superl) smallest; (más joven: compar) younger; (: superl) youngest; (MUS) minor ♦ nm/f (joven) young person, juvenile; **no tengo la ~ idea** I haven't the faintest idea; **al por ~** retail; **~ de edad** person under age

Menorca [me'norka] nf Minorca

PALABRA CLAVE

menos [menos] adj **1**: **~ (que, de)** (compar: cantidad) less (than); (: número) fewer (than); **con ~ entusiasmo** with less enthusiasm; **~ gente** fewer people; ver tb **cada**

2 (superl): **es el que ~ culpa tiene** he is the least to blame

♦ adv **1** (compar): **~ (que, de)** less (than); **me gusta ~ que el otro** I like it less than the other one

2 (superl): **es el ~ listo (de su clase)** he's the least bright in his class; **de todas ellas es la que ~ me agrada** out of all of them she's the one I like least; **(por) lo ~ at** (the very) least

3 (locuciones): **no quiero verle y ~ visitarle** I don't want to see him let alone visit him; **tenemos 7 de ~** we're seven short

♦ prep except; (cifras) minus; **todos ~ él** everyone except (for) him; **5 ~ 2** 5 minus 2

♦ conj: **a ~ que: a ~ que venga mañana** unless he comes tomorrow

menospreciar [menospre'θjar] vt to underrate, undervalue; (despreciar) to scorn, despise

mensaje [men'saxe] nm message; **~ro, a** nm/f messenger

menstruación [menstrua'θjon] nf menstruation

menstruar [mens'trwar] vi to menstruate

mensual [men'swal] adj monthly; **1000 ptas ~es** 1000 ptas a month; **~idad** nf (salario) monthly salary; (COM) monthly payment, monthly instalment

menta ['menta] nf mint

mental [men'tal] adj mental; **~idad** nf mentality; **~izar** vt (sensibilizar) to make aware; (convencer) to convince; (padres) to prepare (mentally); **~izarse** vr (concienciarse) to become aware; **~izarse (de)** to get used to the idea (of); **~izarse de que ...** (convencerse) to get it into one's head that ...

mentar [men'tar] vt to mention, name

mente ['mente] nf mind

mentir [men'tir] vi to lie

mentira [men'tira] nf (una ~) lie; (acto) lying; (invención) fiction; **parece ~ que ...** it seems incredible that ..., I can't believe that ...

mentiroso, a [menti'roso, a] adj lying ♦ nm/f liar

menú [me'nu] (pl **~s**) nm menu; (AM) set meal; **~ del día** set menu

menudo, a [me'nuðo, a] adj (pequeño) small, tiny; (sin importancia) petty, insignificant; **¡~ negocio!** (fam) some deal!; **a ~** often, frequently

meñique [me'ɲike] nm little finger

meollo [me'oʎo] nm (fig) core

mercado [mer'kaðo] nm market

mercancía [merkan'θia] nf commodity; **~s** nfpl goods, merchandise sg

mercantil [merkan'til] adj mercantile, commercial

mercenario, a [merθe'narjo, a] adj, nm

mercenary

mercería [merθe'ria] nf haberdashery (BRIT), notions (US); (tienda) haberdasher's (BRIT), notions store (US); (AM) drapery

mercurio [mer'kurjo] nm mercury

merecer [mere'θer] vt to deserve, merit ♦ vi to be deserving, be worthy; **merece la pena** it's worthwhile; **merecido, a** adj (well) deserved; **llevar su merecido** to get one's deserts

merendar [meren'dar] vt to have for tea ♦ vi to have tea; (en el campo) to have a picnic; **merendero** nm open-air cafe

merengue [me'renge] nm meringue

meridiano [meri'ðjano] nm (GEO) meridian

merienda [me'rjenda] nf (light) tea, afternoon snack; (de campo) picnic

mérito ['merito] nm merit; (valor) worth, value

merluza [mer'luθa] nf hake

merma ['merma] nf decrease; (pérdida) wastage; **mermar** vt to reduce, lessen ♦ vi to decrease, dwindle

mermelada [merme'laða] nf jam

mero, a ['mero, a] adj mere; (AM: fam) very

merodear [meroðe'ar] vi: ~ **por** to prowl about

mes [mes] nm month

mesa ['mesa] nf table; (de trabajo) desk; (GEO) plateau; ~ **directiva** board; ~ **redonda** (reunión) round table; **poner/quitar la** ~ to lay/clear the table; **mesero, a** (AM) nm/f waiter/waitress

meseta [me'seta] nf (GEO) meseta, tableland

mesilla [me'siʎa] nf: ~ **(de noche)** bedside table

mesón [me'son] nm inn

mestizo, a [mes'tiθo, a] adj half-caste, of mixed race ♦ nm/f half-caste

mesura [me'sura] nf moderation, restraint

meta ['meta] nf goal; (de carrera) finish

metabolismo [metaßo'lismo] nm metabolism

metáfora [me'tafora] nf metaphor

metal [me'tal] nm (materia) metal; (MUS) brass; **metálico, a** adj metallic; (de metal) metal ♦ nm (dinero contante) cash

metalurgia [meta'lurxja] nf metallurgy

meteoro [mete'oro] nm meteor; **~logía** nf meteorology

meter [me'ter] vt (colocar) to put, place; (introducir) to put in, insert; (involucrar) to involve; (causar) to make, cause; **~se** vr: **~se en** to go into, enter; (fig) to interfere in, meddle in; **~se a** to start; **~se a escritor** to become a writer; **~se con uno** to provoke sb, pick a quarrel with sb

meticuloso, a [metiku'loso, a] adj meticulous, thorough

metódico, a [me'toðiko, a] adj methodical

método ['metoðo] nm method

metralleta [metra'ʎeta] nf sub-machine-gun

métrico, a ['metriko, a] adj metric

metro ['metro] nm metre; (tren) underground (BRIT), subway (US)

México ['mexiko] nm Mexico; **Ciudad de ~** Mexico City

mezcla ['meθkla] nf mixture; **mezclar** vt to mix (up); **mezclarse** vr to mix, mingle; **mezclarse en** to get mixed up in, get involved in

mezquino, a [meθ'kino, a] adj mean

mezquita [meθ'kita] nf mosque

mg. abr (= miligramo) mg

mi [mi] adj pos my ♦ nm (MUS) E

mí [mi] pron me; myself

mía ['mia] pron ver **mío**

miaja ['mjaxa] nf crumb

michelín [mitʃe'lin] (fam) nm (de grasa) spare tyre

micro ['mikro] (AM) nm minibus

microbio [mi'kroßjo] nm microbe

micrófono [mi'krofono] nm microphone

microondas [mikro'ondas] nm inv (tb: horno ~) microwave (oven)

microscopio [mikro'skopjo] nm microscope

miedo ['mjeðo] nm fear; (nerviosismo) apprehension, nervousness; **tener** ~ to be afraid; **de** ~ wonderful, marvellous; **hace un frío de** ~ (fam) it's terribly cold; **~so, a** adj fearful, timid

miel [mjel] nf honey

miembro ['mjembro] nm limb; (socio) member; ~ **viril** penis

mientras ['mjentras] conj while; (duración) as long as ♦ adv meanwhile; ~ **tanto** meanwhile; ~ **más tiene, más quiere** the more he has, the more he wants

miércoles ['mjerkoles] nm inv Wednesday

mierda ['mjerða] (fam!) nf shit (!)

miga ['miɣa] nf crumb; (fig: meollo) essence; **hacer buenas ~s** (fam) to get on well

migración [miɣra'θjon] nf migration

mil [mil] num thousand; **dos ~ libras** two thousand pounds

milagro [mi'laɣro] nm miracle; **~so, a** adj miraculous

milésima [mi'lesima] nf (de segundo) thousandth

mili ['mili] (fam) nf: **hacer la ~** to do one's military service

milicia [mi'liθja] nf militia; (servicio militar) military service

milímetro [mi'limetro] nm millimetre

militante [mili'tante] adj militant

militar [mili'tar] adj military ♦ nm/f soldier ♦ vi (MIL) to serve; (en un partido) to be a member

milla ['miʎa] nf mile

millar [mi'ʎar] nm thousand

millón [mi'ʎon] num million; **millonario, a** nm/f millionaire

mimar [mi'mar] vt to spoil, pamper

mimbre ['mimbre] nm wicker

mímica ['mimika] nf (para comunicarse) sign language; (imitación) mimicry

mimo ['mimo] nm (caricia) caress; (de niño) spoiling; (TEATRO) mime; (: actor) mime artist

mina ['mina] nf mine; **minar** vt to mine; (fig) to undermine

mineral [mine'ral] adj mineral ♦ nm (GEO) mineral; (mena) ore

minero, a [mi'nero, a] adj mining cpd ♦ nm/f miner

miniatura [minja'tura] adj inv, nf miniature

MiniDisc® [mini'ðisk] nm MiniDisc®

minifalda [mini'falda] nf miniskirt

mínimo, a ['minimo, a] adj, nm minimum

minino, a [mi'nino, a] (fam) nm/f puss, pussy

ministerio [minis'terjo] nm Ministry; **M~ de Hacienda/de Asuntos Exteriores** Treasury (BRIT), Treasury Department (US)/Foreign Office (BRIT), State Department (US)

ministro, a [mi'nistro, a] nm/f minister

minoría [mino'ria] nf minority

minucioso, a [minu'θjoso, a] adj thorough, meticulous; (prolijo) very detailed

minúscula [mi'nuskula] nf small letter

minúsculo, a [mi'nuskulo, a] adj tiny, minute

minusválido, a [minus'βaliðo, a] adj (physically) handicapped ♦ nm/f (physically) handicapped person

minuta [mi'nuta] nf (de comida) menu

minutero [minu'tero] nm minute hand

minuto [mi'nuto] nm minute

mío, a ['mio, a] pron: **el ~/la mía** mine; **un amigo ~** a friend of mine; **lo ~** what is mine

miope [mi'ope] adj short-sighted

mira ['mira] nf (de arma) sight(s) (pl); (fig) aim, intention

mirada [mi'raða] nf look, glance; (expresión) look, expression; **clavar la ~ en** to stare at; **echar una ~ a** to glance at

mirado, a [mi'raðo, a] adj (sensato) sensible; (considerado) considerate; **bien/mal ~** well/ not well thought of; **bien ~** all things considered

mirador [mira'ðor] nm viewpoint, vantage point

mirar [mi'rar] vt to look at; (observar) to watch; (considerar) to consider, think over; (vigilar, cuidar) to watch, look after ♦ vi to look; (ARQ) to face; **~se** vr (dos personas) to look at each other; **~ bien/mal** to think highly of/have a poor opinion of; **~se al espejo** to

look at o.s. in the mirror

mirilla [mi'riʎa] nf spyhole, peephole

mirlo ['mirlo] nm blackbird

misa ['misa] nf mass

miserable [mise'raβle] adj (avaro) mean, stingy; (nimio) miserable, paltry; (lugar) squalid; (fam) vile, despicable ♦ nm/f (malvado) rogue

miseria [mi'serja] nf (pobreza) poverty; (tacañería) meanness, stinginess; (condiciones) squalor; **una ~** a pittance

misericordia [miseri'korðja] nf (compasión) compassion, pity; (piedad) mercy

misil [mi'sil] nm missile

misión [mi'sjon] nf mission; **misionero, a** nm/f missionary

mismo, a ['mismo, a] adj (semejante) same; (después de pron) -self; (para énfasis) very ♦ adv: **aquí/hoy ~** right here/this very day; **ahora ~** right now ♦ conj: **lo ~ que** just like, just as; **el ~ traje** the same suit; **en ese ~ momento** at that very moment; **vino el ~ Ministro** the minister himself came; **yo ~ lo vi** I saw it myself; **lo ~** the same (thing); **da lo ~** it's all the same; **quedamos en las mismas** we're no further forward; **por lo ~** for the same reason

misterio [mis'terjo] nm mystery; **~so, a** adj mysterious

mitad [mi'tað] nf (medio) half; (centro) middle; **a ~ de precio** (at) half-price; **en o a ~ del camino** halfway along the road; **cortar por la ~** to cut through the middle

mitigar [miti'var] vt to mitigate; (dolor) to ease; (sed) to quench

mitin ['mitin] (pl **mítines**) nm meeting

mito ['mito] nm myth

mixto, a ['miksto, a] adj mixed

ml. abr (= mililitro) ml

mm. abr (= milímetro) mm

mobiliario [moβi'ljarjo] nm furniture

mochila [mo'tʃila] nf rucksack (BRIT), backpack

moción [mo'θjon] nf motion

moco ['moko] nm mucus; **~s** nmpl (fam) snot; **limpiarse los ~s de la nariz** (fam) to wipe one's nose

moda ['moða] nf fashion; (estilo) style; **a la o de ~** in fashion, fashionable; **pasado de ~** out of fashion

modales [mo'ðales] nmpl manners

modalidad [moðali'ðað] nf kind, variety

modelar [moðe'lar] vt to model

modelo [mo'ðelo] adj inv, nm/f model

módem ['moðem] nm (INFORM) modem

moderado, a [moðe'raðo, a] adj moderate

moderar [moðe'rar] vt to moderate; (violencia) to restrain, control; (velocidad) to reduce; **~se** vr to restrain o.s., control o.s.

modernizar [moðerni'θar] vt to modernize

moderno, a [mo'ðerno, a] adj modern; (actual) present-day

modestia [mo'ðestja] nf modesty; **modesto, a** adj modest

módico, a ['moðiko, a] adj moderate, reasonable

modificar [moðifi'kar] vt to modify

modista, a [mo'ðista, a] nm/f (diseñador) couturier, designer; (que confecciona) dressmaker

modo ['moðo] nm way, manner; (MUS) mode; ~s nmpl manners; **de ningún ~** in no way; **de todos ~s** at any rate; **~ de empleo** directions pl (for use)

modorra [mo'ðorra] nf drowsiness

mofa ['mofa] nf: **hacer ~ de** to mock; **mofarse** vr: **mofarse de** to mock, scoff at

mogollón [moɣo'ʎon] (fam) adv a hell of a lot

moho ['moo] nm mould, mildew; (en metal) rust; **~so, a** adj mouldy; rusty

mojar [mo'xar] vt to wet; (humedecer) to damp(en), moisten; (calar) to soak; **~se** vr to get wet

mojón [mo'xon] nm boundary stone

molde ['molde] nm mould; (COSTURA) pattern; (fig) model; **~ado** nm soft perm; **~ar** vt to mould

mole ['mole] nf mass, bulk; (edificio) pile

moler [mo'ler] vt to grind, crush

molestar [moles'tar] vt to bother; (fastidiar) to annoy; (incomodar) to inconvenience, put out ♦ vi to be a nuisance; **~se** vr to bother; (incomodarse) to go to trouble; (ofenderse) to take offence; **¿(no) te molesta si ...?** do you mind if ...?

molestia [mo'lestja] nf bother, trouble; (incomodidad) inconvenience; (MED) discomfort; **es una ~** it's a nuisance; **molesto, a** adj (que fastidia) annoying; (incómodo) inconvenient; (inquieto) uncomfortable, ill at ease; (enfadado) annoyed

molido, a [mo'liðo, a] adj: **estar ~** (fig) to be exhausted o dead beat

molinillo [moli'niʎo] nm: **~ de carne/café** mincer/coffee grinder

molino [mo'lino] nm (edificio) mill; (máquina) grinder

momentáneo, a [momen'taneo, a] adj momentary

momento [mo'mento] nm moment; **de ~** at the moment, for the moment

momia ['momja] nf mummy

monarca [mo'narka] nm/f monarch, ruler; **monarquía** nf monarchy; **monárquico, a** nm/f royalist, monarchist

monasterio [monas'terjo] nm monastery

mondar [mon'dar] vt to peel; **~se** vr: **~se de risa** (fam) to split one's sides laughing

moneda [mo'neða] nf (tipo de dinero) currency, money; (pieza) coin; **una ~ de 5 pesetas** a 5 peseta piece; **monedero** nm purse; **monetario, a** adj monetary, financial

monitor, a [moni'tor, a] nm/f instructor, coach ♦ nm (TV) set; (INFORM) monitor

monja ['monxa] nf nun

monje ['monxe] nm monk

mono, a ['mono, a] adj (bonito) lovely, pretty; (gracioso) nice, charming ♦ nm/f monkey, ape ♦ nm dungarees pl; (overoles) overalls pl

monopatín [monopa'tin] nm skateboard

monopolio [mono'poljo] nm monopoly; **monopolizar** vt to monopolize

monotonía [monoto'nia] nf (sonido) monotone; (fig) monotony

monótono, a [mo'notono, a] adj monotonous

monstruo ['monstrwo] nm monster ♦ adj inv fantastic; **~so, a** adj monstrous

montaje [mon'taxe] nm assembly; (TEATRO) décor; (CINE) montage

montaña [mon'taɲa] nf (monte) mountain; (sierra) mountains pl, mountainous area; (AM: selva) forest; **~ rusa** roller coaster; **montañero, a** nm/f mountaineer; **montañés, esa** nm/f highlander; **montañismo** nm mountaineering

montar [mon'tar] vt (subir a) to mount, get on; (TEC) to assemble, put together; (negocio) to set up; (arma) to cock; (colocar) to lift on to; (CULIN) to beat ♦ vi to mount, get on; (sobresalir) to overlap; **~ en cólera** to get angry; **~ a caballo** to ride, go horseriding

monte ['monte] nm (montaña) mountain; (bosque) woodland; (área sin cultivar) wild area, wild country; **M~ de Piedad** pawnshop

montón [mon'ton] nm heap, pile; (fig): **un ~ de** heaps of, lots of

monumento [monu'mento] nm monument

monzón [mon'θon] nm monsoon

moño ['moɲo] nm bun

moqueta [mo'keta] nf fitted carpet

mora ['mora] nf blackberry; ver tb **moro**

morada [mo'raða] nf (casa) dwelling, abode

morado, a [mo'raðo, a] adj purple, violet ♦ nm bruise

moral [mo'ral] adj moral ♦ nf (ética) ethics pl; (moralidad) morals pl, morality; (ánimo) morale

moraleja [mora'lexa] nf moral

moralidad [morali'ðað] nf morals pl, morality

morboso, a [mor'ßoso, a] adj morbid

morcilla [mor'θiʎa] nf blood sausage, ≈ black pudding (BRIT)

mordaz [mor'ðaθ] adj (crítica) biting, scathing

mordaza [mor'ðaθa] nf (para la boca) gag; (TEC) clamp

morder [mor'ðer] vt to bite; (fig: consumir) to eat away, eat into; **mordisco** nm bite

moreno, a [mo'reno, a] adj (color) (dark) brown; (de tez) dark; (de pelo ~) dark-haired; (negro) black

morfina [mor'fina] nf morphine

moribundo, a [mori'ßundo, a] adj dying

morir [mo'rir] vi to die; (fuego) to die down; (luz) to go out; ~se vr to die; (fig) to be dying; **murió en un accidente** he was killed in an accident; **~se por algo** to be dying for sth

moro, a ['moro, a] adj Moorish ♦ nm/f Moor

moroso, a [mo'roso, a] nm/f bad debtor, defaulter

morral [mo'rral] nm haversack

morro ['morro] nm (ZOOL) snout, nose; (AUTO, AVIAT) nose

morsa ['morsa] nf walrus

mortadela [morta'ðela] nf mortadella

mortaja [mor'taxa] nf shroud

mortal [mor'tal] adj mortal; (golpe) deadly; **~idad** nf mortality

mortero [mor'tero] nm mortar

mortífero, a [mor'tifero, a] adj deadly, lethal

mortificar [mortifi'kar] vt to mortify

mosca ['moska] nf fly

Moscú [mos'ku] n Moscow

mosquearse [moske'arse] (fam) vr (enojarse) to get cross; (ofenderse) to take offence

mosquitero [moski'tero] nm mosquito net

mosquito [mos'kito] nm mosquito

mostaza [mos'taθa] nf mustard

mosto ['mosto] nm (unfermented) grape juice

mostrador [mostra'ðor] nm (de tienda) counter; (de café) bar

mostrar [mos'trar] vt to show; (exhibir) to display, exhibit; (explicar) to explain; ~se vr: ~se amable to be kind; to prove to be kind; no se muestra muy inteligente he doesn't seem (to be) very intelligent

mota ['mota] nf speck, tiny piece; (en diseño) dot

mote ['mote] nm nickname

motín [mo'tin] nm (del pueblo) revolt, rising; (del ejército) mutiny

motivar [moti'ßar] vt (causar) to cause, motivate; (explicar) to explain, justify; **motivo** nm motive, reason

moto ['moto] (fam) nf = **motocicleta**

motocicleta [motoθi'kleta] nf motorbike (BRIT), motorcycle

motor [mo'tor] nm motor, engine; **~ a chorro** o **de reacción/de explosión** jet engine/internal combustion engine

motora [mo'tora] nf motorboat

movedizo, a [moße'ðiθo, a] adj ver **arena**

mover [mo'ßer] vt to move; (palanca) to shake; (accionar) to drive; (fig) to cause, provoke; **~se** vr to move; (fig) to get a move on

móvil ['moßil] adj mobile; (pieza de máquina) moving; (mueble) movable ♦ nm motive; **movilidad** nf mobility; **movilizar** vt to mobilize

movimiento [moßi'mjento] nm movement; (TEC) motion; (actividad) activity

mozo, a ['moθo, a] adj (joven) young ♦ nm/f youth, young man/girl

muchacho, a [mu'tʃatʃo, a] nm/f (niño) boy/girl; (criado) servant; (criada) maid

muchedumbre [mutʃe'ðumbre] nf crowd

PALABRA CLAVE

mucho, a ['mutʃo, a] adj **1** (cantidad) a lot of, much; (número) lots of, a lot of, many; **~ dinero** a lot of money; **hace ~ calor** it's very hot; **muchas amigas** lots o a lot of friends

2 (sg: grande): **ésta es mucha casa para él** this house is much too big for him

♦ pron: **tengo ~ que hacer** I've got a lot to do; **~s dicen que ...** a lot of people say that ...; ver tb **tener**

♦ adv **1**: **me gusta ~** I like it a lot; **lo siento ~** I'm very sorry; **come ~** he eats a lot; **¿te vas a quedar ~?** are you going to be staying long?

2 (respuesta) very; **¿estás cansado? – ¡~!** are you tired? – very!

3 (locuciones): **como ~** at (the) most; **con ~**: **el mejor con ~** by far the best; **ni ~ menos**: **no es rico ni ~ menos** he's far from being rich

4: **por ~ que**: **por ~ que le creas** no matter how o however much you believe her

---

muda ['muða] nf change of clothes

mudanza [mu'ðanθa] nf (de casa) move

mudar [mu'ðar] vt to change; (ZOOL) to shed ♦ vi to change; ~se vr (la ropa) to change; ~se de casa to move house

mudo, a ['muðo, a] adj dumb; (callado, CINE) silent

mueble ['mweßle] nm piece of furniture; **~s** nmpl furniture sg

mueca ['mweka] nf face, grimace; **hacer ~s a** to make faces at

muela ['mwela] nf (back) tooth

muelle ['mweʎe] nm spring; (NAUT) wharf; (malecón) pier

muero etc vb ver **morir**

muerte ['mwerte] nf death; (homicidio) murder; **dar ~ a** to kill

muerto, a ['mwerto, a] pp de **morir** ♦ adj

dead ♦ nm/f dead man/woman; (difunto)
deceased; (cadáver) corpse; estar ~ de
cansancio to be dead tired
muestra ['mwestra] nf (señal) indication,
sign; (demostración) demonstration; (prueba)
proof; (estadística) sample; (modelo) model,
pattern; (testimonio) token
muestreo [mwes'treo] nm sample, sampling
muestro etc vb ver mostrar
muevo etc vb ver mover
mugir [mu'xir] vi (vaca) to moo
mugre ['muxre] nf dirt, filth; mugriento, a
adj dirty, filthy
mujer [mu'xer] nf woman; (esposa) wife;
~iego nm womanizer
mula ['mula] nf mule
muleta [mu'leta] nf (para andar) crutch;
(TAUR) stick with red cape attached
mullido, a [mu'ʎiðo, a] adj (cama) soft;
(hierba) soft, springy
multa ['multa] nf fine; poner una ~ to fine;
multar vt to fine
multicines [multi'θines] nmpl multiscreen
cinema
multinacional [multinaθjo'nal] nf
multinational
múltiple ['multiple] adj multiple; (pl) many,
numerous
multiplicar [multipli'kar] vt (MAT) to
multiply; (fig) to increase; ~se vr (BIO) to
multiply; to be everywhere at once
multitud [multi'tuð] nf (muchedumbre)
crowd; ~ de lots of
mundano, a [mun'dano, a] adj worldly
mundial [mun'djal] adj world-wide,
universal; (guerra, récord) world cpd
mundo ['mundo] nm world; todo el ~
everybody; tener ~ to be experienced, know
one's way around
munición [muni'θjon] nf ammunition
municipal [muniθi'pal] adj municipal, local
municipio [muni'θipjo] nm (ayuntamiento)
town council, corporation; (territorio
administrativo) town, municipality
muñeca [mu'ɲeka] nf (ANAT) wrist; (juguete)
doll
muñeco [mu'ɲeko] nm (figura) figure;
(marioneta) puppet; (fig) puppet, pawn
mural [mu'ral] adj mural, wall cpd ♦ nm
mural
muralla [mu'raʎa] nf (city) wall(s) (pl)
murciélago [mur'θjelaxo] nm bat
murmullo [mur'muʎo] nm murmur(ing);
(cuchicheo) whispering
murmuración [murmura'θjon] nf gossip;
murmurar vi to murmur, whisper; (cotillear)
to gossip
muro ['muro] nm wall
muscular [musku'lar] adj muscular

músculo ['muskulo] nm muscle
museo [mu'seo] nm museum; ~ de arte art
gallery
musgo ['musxo] nm moss
música ['musika] nf music; ver tb músico
músico, a ['musiko, a] adj musical ♦ nm/f
musician
muslo ['muslo] nm thigh
mustio, a ['mustjo, a] adj (persona)
depressed, gloomy; (planta) faded, withered
musulmán, ana [musul'man, ana] nm/f
Moslem
mutación [muta'θjon] nf (BIO) mutation;
(cambio) (sudden) change
mutilar [muti'lar] vt to mutilate; (a una
persona) to maim
mutismo [mu'tismo] nm (de persona)
uncommunicativeness; (de autoridades)
silence
mutuamente [mutwa'mente] adv mutually
mutuo, a ['mutwo, a] adj mutual
muy [mwi] adv very; (demasiado) too;
M~ Señor mío Dear Sir; ~ de noche very late
at night; eso es ~ de él that's just like him

N, n

N abr (= norte) N
nabo ['naβo] nm turnip
nácar ['nakar] nm mother-of-pearl
nacer [na'θer] vi to be born; (de huevo) to
hatch; (vegetal) to sprout; (río) to rise; nací
en Barcelona I was born in Barcelona; nació
una sospecha en su mente a suspicion formed
in her mind; nacido, a adj born; recién
nacido newborn; naciente adj new,
emerging; (sol) rising; nacimiento nm
birth; (de Navidad) Nativity; (de río) source
nación [na'θjon] nf nation; nacional adj
national; nacionalismo nm nationalism;
nacionalista nm/f nationalist; nacionalizar
vt to nationalize; nacionalizarse vr (persona)
to become naturalized
nada ['naða] pron nothing ♦ adv not at all, in
no way; no decir ~ to say nothing, not to say
anything; ~ más nothing else; de ~ don't
mention it
nadador, a [naða'ðor, a] nm/f swimmer
nadar [na'ðar] vi to swim
nadie ['naðje] pron nobody, no-one; ~ habló
nobody spoke; no había ~ there was nobody
there, there wasn't anybody there
nado ['naðo]: a ~ adv: pasar a ~ to swim
across
nafta ['nafta] (AM) nf petrol (BRIT), gas (US)
naipe ['naipe] nm (playing) card; ~s nmpl
cards
nalgas ['nalxas] nfpl buttocks

nana ['nana] nf lullaby

naranja [na'ranxa] adj inv, nf orange; **media ~** (fam) better half; **naranjada** nf orangeade; **naranjo** nm orange tree

narciso [nar'θiso] nm narcissus

narcótico, a [nar'kotiko, a] adj, nm narcotic; **narcotizar** vt to drug; **narcotráfico** nm drug trafficking o running

nardo ['narðo] nm lily

narigudo, a [nari'ɣuðo, a] adj big-nosed

nariz [na'riθ] nf nose

narración [narra'θjon] nf narration; **narrador, a** nm/f narrator

narrar [na'rrar] vt to narrate, recount; **narrativa** nf narrative

nata ['nata] nf cream

natación [nata'θjon] nf swimming

natal [na'tal] adj: **ciudad ~** home town; **~idad** nf birth rate

natillas [na'tiʎas] nfpl custard sg

nativo, a [na'tiβo, a] adj, nm/f native

nato, a ['nato, a] adj born; **un músico ~** a born musician

natural [natu'ral] adj natural; (fruta etc) fresh ♦ nm/f native ♦ nm (disposición) nature

naturaleza [natura'leθa] nf nature; (género) nature, kind; **~ muerta** still life

naturalidad [naturali'ðað] nf naturalness

naturalmente [natural'mente] adv (de modo natural) in a natural way; **¡~!** of course!

naufragar [naufra'ɣar] vi to sink; **naufragio** nm shipwreck; **náufrago, a** nm/f castaway, shipwrecked person

nauseabundo, a [nausea'ßundo, a] adj nauseating, sickening

náuseas ['nauseas] nfpl nausea sg; **me da ~** it makes me feel sick

náutico, a ['nautiko, a] adj nautical

navaja [na'ßaxa] nf knife; (de barbero, peluquero) razor

naval [na'ßal] adj naval

Navarra [na'ßarra] n Navarre

nave ['naße] nf (barco) ship, vessel; (ARQ) nave; **~ espacial** spaceship

navegación [naßeɣa'θjon] nf navigation; (viaje) sea journey; **~ aérea** air traffic; **~ costera** coastal shipping; **navegador** nm (INFORM) browser; **navegante** nm/f navigator; **navegar** vi (barco) to sail; (avión) to fly

navidad [naßi'ðað] nf Christmas; **~es** nfpl Christmas time; **Feliz N~** Merry Christmas; **navideño, a** adj Christmas cpd

navío [na'ßio] nm ship

nazca etc vb ver **nacer**

nazi ['naθi] adj, nm/f Nazi

NE abr (= nor(d)este) NE

neblina [ne'ßlina] nf mist

nebulosa [neßu'losa] nf nebula

necesario, a [neθe'sarjo, a] adj necessary

neceser [neθe'ser] nm toilet bag; (bolsa grande) holdall

necesidad [neθesi'ðað] nf need; (lo inevitable) necessity; (miseria) poverty, need; **en caso de ~** in case of need o emergency; **hacer sus ~es** to relieve o.s.

necesitado, a [neθesi'taðo, a] adj needy, poor; **~ de** in need of

necesitar [neθesi'tar] vt to need, require

necio, a ['neθjo, a] adj foolish

necrópolis [ne'kropolis] nf inv cemetery

nectarina [nekta'rina] nf nectarine

nefasto, a [ne'fasto, a] adj ill-fated, unlucky

negación [neɣa'θjon] nf negation; (rechazo) refusal, denial

negar [ne'ɣar] vt (renegar, rechazar) to refuse; (prohibir) to refuse, deny; (desmentir) to deny; **~se** vr: **~se a** to refuse to

negativa [neɣa'tißa] nf negative; (rechazo) refusal, denial

negativo, a [neɣa'tißo, a] adj, nm negative

negligencia [neɣli'xenθja] nf negligence; **negligente** adj negligent

negociado [neɣo'θjaðo] nm department, section

negociante [neɣo'θjante] nm/f businessman/woman

negociar [neɣo'θjar] vt, vi to negotiate; **~ en** to deal in, trade in

negocio [ne'ɣoθjo] nm (COM) business; (asunto) affair, business; (operación comercial) deal, transaction; (AM) firm; (lugar) place of business; **los ~s** business sg; **hacer ~** to do business

negra ['neɣra] nf (MUS) crotchet; ver tb **negro**

negro, a ['neɣro, a] adj black; (suerte) awful ♦ nm black ♦ nm/f black man/woman

nene, a ['nene, a] nm/f baby, small child

nenúfar [ne'nufar] nm water lily

neologismo [neolo'xismo] nm neologism

neón [ne'on] nm: **luces/lámpara de ~** neon lights/lamp

neoyorquino, a [neojor'kino, a] adj (of) New York

nervio ['nerßjo] nm nerve; **nerviosismo** nm nervousness, nerves pl; **~so, a** adj nervous

neto, a ['neto, a] adj net

neumático, a [neu'matiko, a] adj pneumatic ♦ nm (ESP) tyre (BRIT), tire (US); **~ de recambio** spare tyre

neurasténico, a [neuras'teniko, a] adj (fig) hysterical

neurólogo, a [neu'roloɣo, a] nm/f neurologist

neurona [neu'rona] nf nerve cell

neutral [neu'tral] adj neutral; **~izar** vt to neutralize; (contrarrestar) to counteract

neutro, a ['neutro, a] adj (BIO, LING) neuter

neutrón [neu'tron] *nm* neutron

nevada [ne'βaða] *nf* snowstorm; (*caída de nieve*) snowfall

nevar [ne'ßar] *vi* to snow

nevera [ne'ßera] (*ESP*) *nf* refrigerator (*BRIT*), icebox (*US*)

nevería [neße'ria] (*AM*) *nf* ice-cream parlour

nexo ['nekso] *nm* link, connection

ni [ni] *conj* nor, neither; (*tb: ~ siquiera*) not ... even; **~ aunque que** not even if; **~ blanco ~ negro** neither white nor black

Nicaragua [nika'raɣwa] *nf* Nicaragua; **nicaragüense** *adj*, *nm/f* Nicaraguan

nicho ['nitʃo] *nm* niche

nicotina [niko'tina] *nf* nicotine

nido ['niðo] *nm* nest

niebla ['njeßla] *nf* fog; (*neblina*) mist

niego *etc vb ver* **negar**

nieto, a ['njeto, a] *nm/f* grandson/daughter; **~s** *nmpl* grandchildren

nieve *etc* ['njeße] *vb ver* **nevar** ♦ *nf* snow; (*AM*) icecream

N.I.F. *nm abr* (= *Número de Identificación Fiscal*) *personal identification number used for financial and tax purposes*

nimiedad [nimje'ðað] *nf* triviality

nimio, a [ni'mjo, a] *adj* trivial, insignificant

ninfa ['ninfa] *nf* nymph

ningún [nin'gun] *adj ver* **ninguno**

ninguno, a [nin'guno, a] *adj* (*delante de nm*: **ningún**) *adj* no ♦ *pron* (*nadie*) nobody; (*ni uno*) none, not one; (*ni uno ni otro*) neither; **de ninguna manera** by no means, not at all

niña ['nina] *nf* (*ANAT*) pupil; *ver tb* **niño**

niñera [ni'nera] *nf* nursemaid, nanny; **niñería** *nf* childish act

niñez [ni'neθ] *nf* childhood; (*infancia*) infancy

niño, a ['nino, a] *adj* (*joven*) young; (*inmaduro*) immature ♦ *nm/f* child, boy/girl

nipón, ona [ni'pon, ona] *adj*, *nm/f* Japanese

níquel ['nikel] *nm* nickel; **niquelar** *vt* (*TEC*) to nickel-plate

níspero ['nispero] *nm* medlar

nitidez [niti'ðeθ] *nf* (*claridad*) clarity; (: *de imagen*) sharpness; **nítido, a** *adj* clear; sharp

nitrato [ni'trato] *nm* nitrate

nitrógeno [ni'troxeno] *nm* nitrogen

nivel [ni'ßel] *nm* (*GEO*) level; (*norma*) level, standard; (*altura*) height; **~ de aceite** oil level; **~ de aire** spirit level; **~ de vida** standard of living; **~ar** *vt* to level out; (*fig*) to even up; (*COM*) to balance

NN. UU. *nfpl abr* (= *Naciones Unidas*) UN *sg*

no [no] *adv* no; not; (*con verbo*) not ♦ *excl* no!; **~ tengo nada** I don't have anything, I have nothing; **~ es el mío** it's not mine; **ahora ~** not now; **¿~ lo sabes?** don't you know?; **~ mucho** not much; **~ bien termine, lo entregaré** as soon as I finish I'll hand it

over; **~ más: ayer ~ más** just yesterday; **¡pase ~ más!** come in!; **¡a que ~ lo sabes!** I bet you don't know!; **¡cómo ~!** of course!; **los países ~ alineados** the non-aligned countries; **la ~ intervención** non-intervention

noble ['noßle] *adj*, *nm/f* noble; **~za** *nf* nobility

noche ['notʃe] *nf* night, night time; (*la tarde*) evening; **de ~, por la ~** at night; **es de ~** it's dark

nochebuena [notʃe'ßwena] *nf* Christmas Eve

nochevieja [notʃe'ßjexa] *nf* New Year's Eve

noción [no'θjon] *nf* notion

nocivo, a [no'θißo, a] *adj* harmful

noctámbulo, a [nok'tambulo, a] *nm/f* sleepwalker

nocturno, a [nok'turno, a] *adj* (*de la noche*) nocturnal, night *cpd*; (*de la tarde*) evening *cpd* ♦ *nm* nocturne

nodriza [no'ðriθa] *nf* wet nurse; **buque** o **nave ~** supply ship

nogal [no'ɣal] *nm* walnut tree

nómada ['nomaða] *adj* nomadic ♦ *nm/f* nomad

nombramiento [nombra'mjento] *nm* naming; (*a un empleo*) appointment

nombrar [nom'brar] *vt* (*designar*) to name; (*mencionar*) to mention; (*dar puesto a*) to appoint

nombre ['nombre] *nm* name; (*sustantivo*) noun; **~ y apellidos** name in full; **~ común/ propio** common/proper noun; **~ de pila/de soltera** Christian/maiden name; **poner ~ a** to call, name

nómina ['nomina] *nf* (*lista*) payroll; (*hoja*) payslip

nominal [nomi'nal] *adj* nominal

nominar [nomi'nar] *vt* to nominate

nominativo, a [nomina'tißo, a] *adj* (*COM*): **cheque ~ a X** cheque made out to X

nono, a ['nono, a] *adj* ninth

nordeste [nor'ðeste] *adj* north-east, north-eastern, north-easterly ♦ *nm* north-east

nórdico, a ['norðiko, a] *adj* Nordic

noreste [no'reste] *adj*, *nm* = **nordeste**

noria ['norja] *nf* (*AGR*) waterwheel; (*de carnaval*) big (*BRIT*) o Ferris (*US*) wheel

norma ['norma] *nf* rule (of thumb)

normal [nor'mal] *adj* (*corriente*) normal; (*habitual*) usual, natural; **~idad** *nf* normality; **restablecer la ~idad** to restore order; **~izar** *vt* (*reglamentar*) to normalize; (*TEC*) to standardize; **~izarse** *vr* to return to normal; **~mente** *adv* normally

normando, a [nor'mando, a] *adj*, *nm/f* Norman

normativa [norma'tißa] *nf* (set of) rules *pl*, regulations *pl*

noroeste [noro'este] *adj* north-west, north-

western, north-westerly ♦ *nm* north-west
norte [ˈnorte] *adj* north, northern, northerly
♦ *nm* north; (*fig*) guide
norteamericano, a [norteameriˈkano, a]
adj, nm/f (North) American
Noruega [noˈrweɣa] *nf* Norway
noruego, a [noˈrweɣo, a] *adj, nm/f*
Norwegian
nos [nos] *pron* (*directo*) us; (*indirecto*) us; to
us; for us; from us; (*reflexivo*) (to) ourselves;
(*recíproco*) (to) each other; ~ **levantamos a
las 7** we get up at 7
nosotros, as [noˈsotros, as] *pron* (*sujeto*)
we; (*después de prep*) us
nostalgia [nosˈtalxja] *nf* nostalgia
nota [ˈnota] *nf* note; (*ESCOL*) mark
notable [noˈtaßle] *adj* notable; (*ESCOL*)
outstanding
notar [noˈtar] *vt* to notice, note; ~**se** *vr* to be
obvious; **se nota que** ... one observes that ...
notarial [notaˈrjal] *adj*: **acta ~** affidavit
notario [noˈtarjo] *nm* notary
noticia [noˈtiθja] *nf* (*información*) piece of
news; **las ~s** the news *sg*; **tener ~s de alguien**
to hear from sb
noticiero [notiˈθjero] (*AM*) *nm* news bulletin
notificación [notifikaˈθjon] *nf* notification;
notificar *vt* to notify, inform
notoriedad [notorjeˈðað] *nf* fame, renown;
notorio, a *adj* (*público*) well-known;
(*evidente*) obvious
novato, a [noˈßato, a] *adj* inexperienced
♦ *nm/f* beginner, novice
novecientos, as [noßeˈθjentos, as] *num*
nine hundred
novedad [noßeˈðað] *nf* (*calidad de nuevo*)
newness; (*noticia*) piece of news; (*cambio*)
change, (new) development
novel [noˈßel] *adj* new; (*inexperto*)
inexperienced ♦ *nm/f* beginner
novela [noˈßela] *nf* novel
noveno, a [noˈßeno, a] *adj* ninth
noventa [noˈßenta] *num* ninety
novia [ˈnoßja] *nf ver* **novio**
noviazgo [noˈßjaθɣo] *nm* engagement
novicio, a [noˈßiθjo, a] *nm/f* novice
noviembre [noˈßjembre] *nm* November
novillada [noßiˈʎaða] *nf* (*TAUR*) bullfight with
young bulls; **novillero** *nm* novice bullfighter;
novillo *nm* young bull, bullock; **hacer
novillos** (*fam*) to play truant
novio, a [ˈnoßjo, a] *nm/f* boyfriend/girlfriend;
(*prometido*) fiancé/fiancée; (*recién casado*)
bridegroom/bride; **los ~s** the newly-weds
nubarrón [nußaˈrron] *nm* storm cloud
nube [ˈnuße] *nf* cloud
nublado, a [nuˈßlaðo, a] *adj* cloudy;
nublarse *vr* to grow dark
nubosidad [nußosiˈðað] *nf* cloudiness; **había**

mucha ~ it was very cloudy
nuca [ˈnuka] *nf* nape of the neck
nuclear [nukleˈar] *adj* nuclear
núcleo [ˈnukleo] *nm* (*centro*) core; (*FÍSICA*)
nucleus
nudillo [nuˈðiʎo] *nm* knuckle
nudista [nuˈðista] *adj* nudist
nudo [ˈnuðo] *nm* knot; ~**so, a** *adj* knotty
nuera [ˈnwera] *nf* daughter-in-law
nuestro, a [ˈnwestro, a] *adj pos* our ♦ *pron*
ours; **padre ~** our father; **un amigo ~** a friend
of ours; **es el ~** it's ours
nueva [ˈnweßa] *nf* piece of news
nuevamente [nweßaˈmente] *adv* (*otra vez*)
again; (*de nuevo*) anew
Nueva York [-ˈjɔrk] *n* New York
Nueva Zelanda [-θeˈlanda] *nf* New Zealand
nueve [ˈnweße] *num* nine
nuevo, a [ˈnweßo, a] *adj* (*gen*) new; **de ~**
again
nuez [nweθ] *nf* walnut; ~ **de Adán** Adam's
apple; ~ **moscada** nutmeg
nulidad [nuliˈðað] *nf* (*incapacidad*)
incompetence; (*abolición*) nullity
nulo, a [ˈnulo, a] *adj* (*inepto, torpe*) useless;
(*inválido*) (null and) void; (*DEPORTE*) drawn,
tied
núm. *abr* (= *número*) no
numeración [numeraˈθjon] *nf* (*cifras*)
numbers *pl*; (*arábiga, romana etc*) numerals
pl
numeral [numeˈral] *nm* numeral
numerar [numeˈrar] *vt* to number
número [ˈnumero] *nm* (*gen*) number;
(*tamaño: de zapato*) size; (*ejemplar: de diario*)
number, issue; **sin ~** numberless,
unnumbered; ~ **de matrícula/de teléfono**
registration/telephone number; ~ **atrasado**
back number
numeroso, a [numeˈroso, a] *adj* numerous
nunca [ˈnunka] *adv* (*jamás*) never; ~ **lo pensé**
I never thought it; **no viene** ~ he never
comes; ~ **más** never again; **más que** ~ more
than ever
nupcias [ˈnupθjas] *nfpl* wedding *sg*, nuptials
nutria [ˈnutrja] *nf* otter
nutrición [nutriˈθjon] *nf* nutrition
nutrido, a [nuˈtriðo, a] *adj* (*alimentado*)
nourished; (*fig: grande*) large; (*abundante*)
abundant
nutrir [nuˈtrir] *vt* (*alimentar*) to nourish; (*dar
de comer*) to feed; (*fig*) to strengthen;
nutritivo, a *adj* nourishing, nutritious
nylon [niˈlon] *nm* nylon

Ñ

ñato, a ['ɲato, a] (*AM*) *adj* snub-nosed
ñoñería [ɲoɲe'ria] *nf* insipidness
ñoño, a ['ɲoɲo, a] *adj* (*AM: tonto*) silly, stupid; (*soso*) insipid; (*persona*) spineless

O, o

O *abr* (= *oeste*) W
o [o] *conj* or
o/ *abr* (= *orden*) o.
oasis [o'asis] *nm inv* oasis
obcecarse [oßθe'karse] *vr* to get o become stubborn
obedecer [oßeðe'θer] *vt* to obey; **obediencia** *nf* obedience; **obediente** *adj* obedient
obertura [oßer'tura] *nf* overture
obesidad [oßesi'ðað] *nf* obesity; **obeso, a** *adj* obese
obispo [o'ßispo] *nm* bishop
objeción [oßxe'θjon] *nf* objection; **poner objeciones** to raise objections
objetar [oßxe'tar] *vt, vi* to object
objetivo, a [oßxe'tißo, a] *adj, nm* objective
objeto [oß'xeto] *nm* (*cosa*) object; (*fin*) aim
objetor, a [oßxe'tor, a] *nm/f* objector
oblicuo, a [o'ßlikwo, a] *adj* oblique; (*mirada*) sidelong
obligación [oßliɣa'θjon] *nf* obligation; (*COM*) bond
obligar [oßli'ɣar] *vt* to force; **~se** *vr* to bind o.s.; **obligatorio, a** *adj* compulsory, obligatory
oboe [o'ßoe] *nm* oboe
obra ['oßra] *nf* work; (*ARQ*) construction, building; (*TEATRO*) play; **~ maestra** masterpiece; **~s públicas** public works; **por ~ de** thanks to (the efforts of); **obrar** *vt* to work; (*tener efecto*) to have an effect on ♦ *vi* to act, behave; (*tener efecto*) to have an effect; **la carta obra en su poder** the letter is in his/her possession
obrero, a [o'ßrero, a] *adj* (*clase*) working; (*movimiento*) labour *cpd* ♦ *nm/f* (*gen*) worker; (*sin oficio*) labourer
obscenidad [oßsθeni'ðað] *nf* obscenity; **obsceno, a** *adj* obscene
obscu... = oscu...
obsequiar [oßseki'kjar] *vt* (*ofrecer*) to present with; (*agasajar*) to make a fuss of, lavish attention on; **obsequio** *nm* (*regalo*) gift; (*cortesía*) courtesy, attention
observación [oßserßa'θjon] *nf* observation; (*reflexión*) remark
observador, a [oßserßa'ðor, a] *nm/f* observer
observar [oßser'ßar] *vt* to observe; (*anotar*) to notice; **~se** *vr* to keep to, observe
obsesión [oßse'sjon] *nf* obsession; **obsesivo, a** *adj* obsessive
obsoleto, a [oßso'leto, a] *adj* obsolete
obstáculo [oßs'takulo] *nm* obstacle; (*impedimento*) hindrance, drawback
obstante [oßs'tante]: **no ~** *adv* nevertheless
obstinado, a [oßsti'naðo, a] *adj* obstinate, stubborn
obstinarse [oßsti'narse] *vr* to be obstinate; **~ en** to persist in
obstrucción [oßstruk'θjon] *nf* obstruction; **obstruir** *vt* to obstruct
obtener [oßte'ner] *vt* (*gen*) to obtain; (*premio*) to win
obturador [oßtura'ðor] *nm* (*FOTO*) shutter
obvio, a ['oßßjo, a] *adj* obvious
oca ['oka] *nf* (*animal*) goose; (*juego*) ≈ snakes and ladders
ocasión [oka'sjon] *nf* (*oportunidad*) opportunity, chance; (*momento*) occasion, time; (*causa*) cause; **de ~** secondhand; **ocasionar** *vt* to cause
ocaso [o'kaso] *nm* (*fig*) decline
occidente [okθi'ðente] *nm* west
OCDE *nf abr* (= *Organización de Cooperación y Desarrollo Económico*) OECD
océano [o'θeano] *nm* ocean; **el ~ Índico** the Indian Ocean
ochenta [o'tʃenta] *num* eighty
ocho ['otʃo] *num* eight; **~ días** a week
ocio ['oθjo] *nm* (*tiempo*) leisure; (*pey*) idleness; **~so, a** (*inactivo*) idle; (*inútil*) useless
octavilla [okta'viʎa] *nf* leaflet, pamphlet
octavo, a [ok'taßo, a] *adj* eighth
octubre [ok'tußre] *nm* October
ocular [oku'lar] *adj* ocular, eye *cpd*; **testigo ~** eyewitness
oculista [oku'lista] *nm/f* oculist
ocultar [okul'tar] *vt* (*esconder*) to hide; (*callar*) to conceal; **oculto, a** *adj* hidden; (*fig*) secret
ocupación [okupa'θjon] *nf* occupation
ocupado, a [oku'paðo, a] *adj* (*persona*) busy; (*plaza*) occupied, taken; (*teléfono*) engaged; **ocupar** *vt* (*gen*) to occupy; **ocuparse** *vr*: **ocuparse de o en** (*gen*) to concern o.s. with; (*cuidar*) to look after
ocurrencia [oku'rrenθja] *nf* (*idea*) bright idea
ocurrir [oku'rrir] *vi* to happen; **~se** *vr*: **se me ocurrió que ...** it occurred to me that ...
odiar [o'ðjar] *vt* to hate; **odio** *nm* hate, hatred; **odioso, a** *adj* (*gen*) hateful; (*malo*)

nasty

odontólogo, a [oðon'toloɣo, a] nm/f dentist, dental surgeon

OEA nf abr (= Organización de Estados Americanos) OAS

oeste [o'este] nm west; **una película del ~** a western

ofender [ofen'der] vt (agraviar) to offend; (insultar) to insult; **~se** vr to take offence; **ofensa** nf offence; **ofensiva** nf offensive; **ofensivo, a** adj offensive

oferta [o'ferta] nf offer; (propuesta) proposal; **la ~ y la demanda** supply and demand; **artículos en ~** goods on offer

oficial [ofi'θjal] adj official ♦ nm (MIL) officer

oficina [ofi'θina] nf office; **~ de correos** post office; **~ de turismo** tourist office; **oficinista** nm/f clerk

oficio [o'fiθjo] nm (profesión) profession; (puesto) post; (REL) service; **ser del ~** to be an old hand; **tener mucho ~** to have a lot of experience; **~ de difuntos** funeral service

oficioso, a [ofi'θjoso, a] adj (pey) officious; (no oficial) unofficial, informal

ofimática [ofi'matika] nf office automation

ofrecer [ofre'θer] vt (dar) to offer; (proponer) to propose; **~se** vr (persona) to offer o.s., volunteer; (situación) to present itself; **¿qué se le ofrece?, ¿se le ofrece algo?** what can I do for you?, can I get you anything?

ofrecimiento [ofreθi'mjento] nm offer

oftalmólogo, a [oftal'moloɣo, a] nm/f ophthalmologist

ofuscar [ofus'kar] vt (por pasión) to blind; (por luz) to dazzle

oída [o'iða] nf: **de ~s** by hearsay

oído [o'iðo] nm (ANAT) ear; (sentido) hearing

oigo etc vb ver **oír**

oír [o'ir] vt (gen) to hear; (atender a) to listen to; **¡oiga!** listen!; **~ misa** to attend mass

OIT nf abr (= Organización Internacional del Trabajo) ILO

ojal [o'xal] nm buttonhole

ojalá [oxa'la] excl if only (it were so)!, some hope! ♦ conj if only ...!, would that ...!; **~ (que) venga hoy** I hope he comes today

ojeada [oxe'aða] nf glance

ojera [o'xera] nf: **tener ~s** to have bags under one's eyes

ojeriza [oxe'riθa] nf ill-will

ojeroso, a [oxe'roso, a] adj haggard

ojo ['oxo] nm eye; (de puente) span; (de cerradura) keyhole ♦ excl careful!; **tener ~ para** to have an eye for; **~ de buey** porthole

okupa [o'kupa] (fam) nm/f squatter

ola ['ola] nf wave

olé [o'le] excl bravo!, olé!

oleada [ole'aða] nf big wave, swell; (fig) wave

oleaje [ole'axe] nm swell

óleo ['oleo] nm oil; **oleoducto** nm (oil) pipeline

oler [o'ler] vt (gen) to smell; (inquirir) to pry into; (fig: sospechar) to sniff out ♦ vi to smell; **~ a** to smell of

olfatear [olfate'ar] vt to smell; (inquirir) to pry into; **olfato** nm sense of smell

oligarquía [oliɣar'kia] nf oligarchy

olimpíada [olim'piaða] nf: **las O~s** the Olympics; **olímpico, a** [o'limpiko, a] adj Olympic

oliva [o'liβa] nf (aceituna) olive; **aceite de ~** olive oil; **olivo** nm olive tree

olla ['oʎa] nf pan; (comida) stew; **~ a presión** o **exprés** pressure cooker; **~ podrida** type of Spanish stew

olmo ['olmo] nm elm (tree)

olor [o'lor] nm smell; **~oso, a** adj scented

olvidar [olβi'ðar] vt to forget; (omitir) to omit; **~se** vr (fig) to forget o.s.; **se me olvidó** I forgot

olvido [ol'βiðo] nm oblivion; (despiste) forgetfulness

ombligo [om'bliɣo] nm navel

omisión [omi'sjon] nf (abstención) omission; (descuido) neglect

omiso, a [o'miso, a] adj: **hacer caso ~ de** to ignore, pass over

omitir [omi'tir] vt to omit

omnipotente [omnipo'tente] adj omnipotent

omóplato [o'moplato] nm shoulder blade

OMG nm abr (= Organismo Modificado Genéticamente) GMO

OMS nf abr (= Organización Mundial de la Salud) WHO

once ['onθe] num eleven; **~s** (AM) nfpl tea break

onda ['onda] nf wave; **~ corta/larga/media** short/long/medium wave; **ondear** vt, vi to wave; (tener ondas) to be wavy; (agua) to ripple; **ondearse** vr to swing, sway

ondulación [ondula'θjon] nf undulation; **ondulado, a** adj wavy

ondular [ondu'lar] vt (el pelo) to wave ♦ vi to undulate; **~se** vr to undulate

ONG nf abr (= organización no gubernamental) NGO

ONU ['onu] nf abr (= Organización de las Naciones Unidas) UNO

opaco, a [o'pako, a] adj opaque

opción [op'θjon] nf (gen) option; (derecho) right, option

OPEP ['opep] nf abr (= Organización de Países Exportadores de Petróleo) OPEC

ópera ['opera] nf opera; **~ bufa** o **cómica** comic opera

operación [opera'θjon] nf (gen) operation;

(COM) transaction, deal

operador, a [opera'ðor, a] nm/f operator; (CINE: proyección) projectionist; (: rodaje) cameraman

operar [ope'rar] vt (producir) to produce, bring about; (MED) to operate on ♦ vi (COM) to operate, deal; **~se** vr to occur; (MED) to have an operation

opereta [ope'reta] nf operetta

opinar [opi'nar] vt to think ♦ vi to give one's opinion; **opinión** nf (creencia) belief; (criterio) opinion

opio ['opjo] nm opium

oponente [opo'nente] nm/f opponent

oponer [opo'ner] vt (resistencia) to put up, offer; **~se** vr (objetar) to object; (estar frente a frente) to be opposed; (dos personas) to oppose each other; **~ A a B** to set A against B; **me opongo a pensar que ...** I refuse to believe o think that ...

oportunidad [oportuni'ðað] nf (ocasión) opportunity; (posibilidad) chance

oportuno, a [opor'tuno, a] adj (en su tiempo) opportune, timely; (respuesta) suitable; **en el momento ~** at the right moment

oposición [oposi'θjon] nf opposition; **oposiciones** nfpl (ESCOL) public examinations

opositor, a [oposi'tor, a] nm/f (adversario) opponent; (candidato): **~ (a)** candidate (for)

opresión [opre'sjon] nf oppression; **opresivo, a** adj oppressive; **opresor, a** nm/f oppressor

oprimir [opri'mir] vt to squeeze; (fig) to oppress

optar [op'tar] vi (elegir) to choose; **~ por** to opt for; **optativo, a** adj optional

óptico, a ['optiko, a] adj optic(al) ♦ nm/f optician; **óptica** nf optician's (shop); **desde esta óptica** from this point of view

optimismo [opti'mismo] nm optimism; **optimista** nm/f optimist

óptimo, a ['optimo, a] adj (el mejor) very best

opuesto, a [o'pwesto, a] adj (contrario) opposite; (antagónico) opposing

opulencia [opu'lenθja] nf opulence; **opulento, a** adj opulent

oración [ora'θjon] nf (REL) prayer; (LING) sentence

orador, a [ora'ðor, a] nm/f (conferenciante) speaker, orator

oral [o'ral] adj oral

orangután [orangu'tan] nm orangutan

orar [o'rar] vi to pray

oratoria [ora'torja] nf oratory

órbita ['orßita] nf orbit

orden ['orðen] nm (gen) order ♦ nf (gen) order; (INFORM) command; **~ del día** agenda;

de primer ~ first-rate; **en ~ de prioridad** in order of priority

ordenado, a [orðe'naðo, a] adj (metódico) methodical; (arreglado) orderly

ordenador [orðena'ðor] nm computer; **~ central** mainframe computer

ordenanza [orðe'nanθa] nf ordinance

ordenar [orðe'nar] vt (mandar) to order; (poner orden) to put in order, arrange; **~se** vr (REL) to be ordained

ordeñar [orðe'nar] vt to milk

ordinario, a [orði'narjo, a] adj (común) ordinary, usual; (vulgar) vulgar, common

orégano [o'reɣano] nm oregano

oreja [o'rexa] nf ear; (MECÁNICA) lug, flange

orfanato [orfa'nato] nm orphanage

orfandad [orfan'dað] nf orphanhood

orfebrería [orfeßre'ria] nf gold/silver work

orgánico, a [or'ɣaniko, a] adj organic

organigrama [orɣani'ɣrama] nm flow chart

organismo [orɣa'nismo] nm (BIO) organism; (POL) organization

organización [orɣaniθa'θjon] nf organization; **organizar** vt to organize

órgano ['orɣano] nm organ

orgasmo [or'ɣasmo] nm orgasm

orgía [or'xia] nf orgy

orgullo [or'ɣuʎo] nm pride; **orgulloso, a** adj (gen) proud; (altanero) haughty

orientación [orjenta'θjon] nf (posición) position; (dirección) direction

oriental [orjen'tal] adj eastern; (del Lejano Oriente) oriental

orientar [orjen'tar] vt (situar) to orientate; (señalar) to point; (dirigir) to direct; (guiar) to guide; **~se** vr to get one's bearings

oriente [o'rjente] nm east; **Cercano/Medio/Lejano O~** Near/Middle/Far East

origen [o'rixen] nm origin

original [orixi'nal] adj (nuevo) original; (extraño) odd, strange; **~idad** nf originality

originar [orixi'nar] vt to start, cause; **~se** vr to originate; **~io, a** adj original; **~io de** native of

orilla [o'riʎa] nf (borde) border; (de río) bank; (de bosque, tela) edge; (de mar) shore

orina [o'rina] nf urine; **orinal** nm (chamber) pot; **orinar** vi to urinate; **orinarse** vr to wet o.s.; **orines** nmpl urine

oriundo, a [o'rjundo, a] adj: **~ de** native of

ornitología [ornitolo'xia] nf ornithology, bird-watching

oro ['oro] nm gold; **~s** nmpl (NAIPES) hearts

oropel [oro'pel] nm tinsel

orquesta [or'kesta] nf orchestra; **~ de cámara/sinfónica** chamber/symphony orchestra

orquídea [or'kiðea] nf orchid

ortiga [or'tiɣa] nf nettle

ortodoxo, a [orto'ðokso, a] *adj* orthodox

ortografía [ortoɣra'fia] *nf* spelling

ortopedia [orto'peðja] *nf* orthopaedics *sg*;
ortopédico, a *adj* orthopaedic

oruga [o'ruɣa] *nf* caterpillar

orzuelo [or'θwelo] *nm* stye

os [os] *pron* (*gen*) you; (*a vosotros*) to you

osa ['osa] *nf* (she-)bear; **O~ Mayor/Menor**
Great/Little Bear

osadía [osa'ðia] *nf* daring

osar [o'sar] *vi* to dare

oscilación [osθila'θjon] *nf* (*movimiento*)
oscillation; (*fluctuación*) fluctuation

oscilar [osθi'lar] *vi* to oscillate; to fluctuate

oscurecer [oskure'θer] *vt* to darken ♦ *vi* to
grow dark; **~se** *vr* to grow *o* get dark

oscuridad [oskuri'ðað] *nf* obscurity;
(*tinieblas*) darkness

oscuro, a [os'kuro, a] *adj* dark; (*fig*) obscure;
a oscuras in the dark

óseo, a ['oseo, a] *adj* bone *cpd*

oso ['oso] *nm* bear; **~ de peluche** teddy bear;
~ hormiguero anteater

ostentación [ostenta'θjon] *nf* (*gen*)
ostentation; (*acto*) display

ostentar [osten'tar] *vt* (*gen*) to show;
(*pey*) to flaunt, show off; (*poseer*) to have,
possess

ostra ['ostra] *nf* oyster

OTAN ['otan] *nf abr* (= *Organización del
Tratado del Atlántico Norte*) NATO

otear [ote'ar] *vt* to observe; (*fig*) to look into

otitis [o'titis] *nf* earache

otoñal [oto'ɲal] *adj* autumnal

otoño [o'toɲo] *nm* autumn

otorgar [otor'ɣar] *vt* (*conceder*) to concede;
(*dar*) to grant

otorrino, a [oto'rrino, a], **otorrinolarin-
gólogo, a** [otorrinolarin'ɣoloɣo, a] *nm/f* ear,
nose and throat specialist

PALABRA CLAVE

---

otro, a ['otro, a] *adj* **1** (*distinto: sg*) another;
(*: pl*) other; **con ~s amigos** with other *o*
different friends

2 (*adicional*): **tráigame ~ café (más), por
favor** can I have another coffee please; **~s 10
días más** another ten days

♦ *pron* **1**: **el ~** the other one; (*los*) **~s** (the)
others; **de ~** somebody else's; **que lo haga ~**
let somebody else do it

2 (*recíproco*): **se odian (la) una a (la) otra**
they hate one another *o* each other

3: **~ tanto: comer ~ tanto** to eat the same *o*
as much again; **recibió una decena de
telegramas y otras tantas llamadas** he got
about ten telegrams and as many calls

---

ovación [oβa'θjon] *nf* ovation

oval [o'βal] *adj* oval; **~ado, a** *adj* oval; **óvalo**
nm oval

ovario [o'βarjo] *nm* ovary

oveja [o'βexa] *nf* sheep

overol [oβe'rol] (*AM*) *nm* overalls *pl*

ovillo [o'βiʎo] *nm* (*de lana*) ball of wool;
hacerse un ~ to curl up

OVNI ['oβni] *nm abr* (= *objeto volante no
identificado*) UFO

ovulación [oβula'θjon] *nf* ovulation; **óvulo**
nm ovum

oxidación [oksiða'θjon] *nf* rusting

oxidar [oksi'ðar] *vt* to rust; **~se** *vr* to go rusty

óxido ['oksiðo] *nm* oxide

oxigenado, a [oksixe'naðo, a] *adj* (*QUÍM*)
oxygenated; (*pelo*) bleached

oxígeno [ok'sixeno] *nm* oxygen

oyente [o'jente] *nm/f* listener, hearer

oyes *etc vb ver* **oír**

ozono [o'θono] *nm* ozone

P, p

P *abr* (= *padre*) Fr.

pabellón [paβe'ʎon] *nm* bell tent; (*ARQ*)
pavilion; (*de hospital etc*) block, section;
(*bandera*) flag

pacer [pa'θer] *vi* to graze

paciencia [pa'θjenθja] *nf* patience

paciente [pa'θjente] *adj*, *nm/f* patient

pacificación [paθifika'θjon] *nf* pacification

pacificar [paθifi'kar] *vt* to pacify;
(*tranquilizar*) to calm

pacífico, a [pa'θifiko, a] *adj* (*persona*)
peaceable; (*existencia*) peaceful; **el (océano)
P~** the Pacific (Ocean)

pacifismo [paθi'fismo] *nm* pacifism;
pacifista *nm/f* pacifist

pacotilla [pako'tiʎa] *nf*: **de ~** (*actor, escritor*)
third-rate; (*mueble etc*) cheap

pactar [pak'tar] *vt* to agree to *o* on ♦ *vi* to
come to an agreement

pacto ['pakto] *nm* (*tratado*) pact; (*acuerdo*)
agreement

padecer [paðe'θer] *vt* (*sufrir*) to suffer;
(*soportar*) to endure, put up with;
padecimiento *nm* suffering

padrastro [pa'ðrastro] *nm* stepfather

padre ['paðre] *nm* father ♦ *adj* (*fam*): **un
éxito ~** a tremendous success; **~s** *nmpl*
parents

padrino [pa'ðrino] *nm* (*REL*) godfather; (*tb:
~ de boda*) best man; (*fig*) sponsor, patron;
~s *nmpl* godparents

padrón [pa'ðron] *nm* (*censo*) census, roll

paella [pa'eʎa] *nf* paella, dish of rice with
meat, shellfish etc

paga ['paɣa] *nf* (*pago*) payment; (*sueldo*) pay, wages *pl*

pagano, a [pa'ɣano, a] *adj, nm/f* pagan, heathen

pagar [pa'ɣar] *vt* to pay; (*las compras, crimen*) to pay for; (*fig: favor*) to repay ♦ *vi* to pay; **~ al contado/a plazos** to pay (in) cash/in instalments

pagaré [paɣa're] *nm* I.O.U.

página ['paxina] *nf* page; **~ de inicio** (*INFORM*) home page

pago ['paɣo] *nm* (*dinero*) payment; **~ anticipado/a cuenta/contra reembolso/en especie** advance payment/payment on account/cash on delivery/payment in kind; **en ~ de** in return for

pág(s). *abr* (= *página(s)*) p(p).

pague *etc vb ver* **pagar**

país [pa'is] *nm* (*gen*) country; (*región*) land; **los P~es Bajos** the Low Countries; **el P~ Vasco** the Basque Country

paisaje [pai'saxe] *nm* landscape, scenery

paisano, a [pai'sano, a] *adj* of the same country ♦ *nm/f* (*compatriota*) fellow countryman/woman; **vestir de ~** (*soldado*) to be in civvies; (*guardia*) to be in plain clothes

paja ['paxa] *nf* straw; (*fig*) rubbish (*BRIT*), trash (*US*)

pajarita [paxa'rita] *nf* (*corbata*) bow tie

pájaro ['paxaro] *nm* bird; **~ carpintero** woodpecker

pajita [pa'xita] *nf* (*drinking*) straw

pala ['pala] *nf* spade, shovel; (*raqueta etc*) bat; (*: de tenis*) racquet; (*CULIN*) slice; **~ matamoscas** fly swat

palabra [pa'laßra] *nf* word; (*facultad*) (*power of*) speech; (*derecho de hablar*) right to speak; **tomar la ~** (*en mitin*) to take the floor

palabrota [pala'brota] *nf* swearword

palacio [pa'laθjo] *nm* palace; (*mansión*) mansion, large house; **~ de justicia** courthouse; **~ municipal** town/city hall

paladar [pala'ðar] *nm* palate; **paladear** *vt* to taste

palanca [pa'lanka] *nf* lever; (*fig*) pull, influence

palangana [palan'gana] *nf* washbasin

palco ['palko] *nm* box

Palestina [pales'tina] *nf* Palestine; **palestino, a** *nm/f* Palestinian

paleta [pa'leta] *nf* (*de pintor*) palette; (*de albañil*) trowel; (*de ping-pong*) bat; (*AM*) ice lolly

paleto, a [pa'leto, a] (*fam, pey*) *nm/f* yokel

paliar [pa'ljar] *vt* (*mitigar*) to mitigate, alleviate; **paliativo** *nm* palliative

palidecer [paliðe'θer] *vi* to turn pale; **palidez** *nf* paleness; **pálido, a** *adj* pale

palillo [pa'liʎo] *nm* (*mondadientes*) toothpick; (*para comer*) chopstick

paliza [pa'liθa] *nf* beating, thrashing

palma ['palma] *nf* (*ANAT*) palm; (*árbol*) palm tree; **batir** o **dar ~s** to clap, applaud; **~da** *nf* slap; **~das** *nfpl* clapping *sg*, applause *sg*

palmar [pal'mar] (*fam*) *vi* (*tb: **~la***) to die, kick the bucket

palmear [palme'ar] *vi* to clap

palmera [pal'mera] *nf* (*BOT*) palm tree

palmo ['palmo] *nm* (*medida*) span; (*fig*) small amount; **~ a ~** inch by inch

palo ['palo] *nm* stick; (*poste*) post; (*de tienda de campaña*) pole; (*mango*) handle, shaft; (*golpe*) blow, hit; (*de golf*) club; (*de béisbol*) bat; (*NAUT*) mast; (*NAIPES*) suit

paloma [pa'loma] *nf* dove, pigeon

palomitas [palo'mitas] *nfpl* popcorn *sg*

palpar [pal'par] *vt* to touch, feel

palpitación [palpita'θjon] *nf* palpitation

palpitante [palpi'tante] *adj* palpitating; (*fig*) burning

palpitar [palpi'tar] *vi* to palpitate; (*latir*) to beat

palta ['palta] (*AM*) *nf* avocado (pear)

paludismo [palu'ðismo] *nm* malaria

pamela [pa'mela] *nf* picture hat, sun hat

pampa ['pampa] (*AM*) *nf* pampas, prairie

pan [pan] *nm* bread; (*una barra*) loaf; **~ integral** wholemeal (*BRIT*) o wholewheat (*US*) bread; **~ rallado** breadcrumbs *pl*

pana ['pana] *nf* corduroy

panadería [panaðe'ria] *nf* baker's (shop); **panadero, a** *nm/f* baker

Panamá [pana'ma] *nm* Panama; **panameño, a** *adj* Panamanian

pancarta [pan'karta] *nf* placard, banner

panda ['panda] *nm* (*ZOOL*) panda

pandereta [pande'reta] *nf* tambourine

pandilla [pan'diʎa] *nf* set, group; (*de criminales*) gang; (*pey: camarilla*) clique

panecillo [pane'θiʎo] *nm* (*bread*) roll

panel [pa'nel] *nm* panel; **~ solar** solar panel

panfleto [pan'fleto] *nm* pamphlet

pánico ['paniko] *nm* panic

panorama [pano'rama] *nm* panorama; (*vista*) view

pantalla [pan'taʎa] *nf* (*de cine*) screen; (*de lámpara*) lampshade

pantalón [panta'lon] *nm* trousers; **pantalones** *nmpl* trousers

pantano [pan'tano] *nm* (*ciénaga*) marsh, swamp; (*depósito: de agua*) reservoir; (*fig*) jam, difficulty

panteón [pante'on] *nm*: **~ familiar** family tomb

pantera [pan'tera] *nf* panther

panti(e)s ['pantis] *nmpl* tights

pantomima [panto'mima] *nf* pantomime

pantorrilla [panto'rriʎa] *nf* calf (of the leg)

pantufla [pan'tufla] nf slipper

panty(s) ['panti(s)] nm(pl) tights

panza ['panθa] nf belly, paunch

pañal [pa'ɲal] nm nappy (BRIT), diaper (US); **~es** nmpl (fig) early stages, infancy sg

paño [pa'ɲo] nm (tela) cloth; (pedazo de tela) (piece of) cloth; (trapo) duster, rag; **~ higiénico** sanitary towel; **~s menores** underclothes

pañuelo [pa'ɲwelo] nm handkerchief, hanky (fam); (para la cabeza) (head)scarf

papa ['papa] nm: **el P~** the Pope ♦ nf (AM) potato

papá [pa'pa] (pl **~s**) (fam) nm dad(dy), pa (US)

papada [pa'paða] nf double chin

papagayo [papa'yajo] nm parrot

papanatas [papa'natas] (fam) nm inv simpleton

paparrucha [papa'rrutʃa] nf piece of nonsense

papaya [pa'paja] nf papaya

papear [pape'ar] (fam) vt, vi to scoff

papel [pa'pel] nm paper; (hoja de ~) sheet of paper; (TEATRO, fig) role; **~ de calco/carbón/ de cartas** tracing paper/carbon paper/ stationery; **~ de envolver/pintado** wrapping paper/wallpaper; **~ de aluminio/higiénico** aluminium (BRIT) o aluminum (US) foil/toilet paper; **~ de estaño** o **plata** tinfoil; **~ de lija** sandpaper; **~ moneda** paper money; **~ secante** blotting paper

papeleo [pape'leo] nm red tape

papelera [pape'lera] nf wastepaper basket; (en la calle) litter bin

papelería [papele'ria] nf stationer's (shop)

papeleta [pape'leta] nf (POL) ballot paper; (ESCOL) report

paperas [pa'peras] nfpl mumps sg

papilla [pa'piʎa] nf (para niños) baby food

paquete [pa'kete] nm (de cigarrillos etc) packet; (CORREOS etc) parcel; (AM) package tour; (: fam) nuisance

par [par] adj (igual) like, equal; (MAT) even ♦ nm equal; (de guantes) pair; (de veces) couple; (POL) peer; (GOLF, COM) par; **abrir de ~ en ~** to open wide

para ['para] prep for; **no es ~ comer** it's not for eating; **decir ~ sí** to say to o.s.; **¿~ qué lo quieres?** what do you want it for?; **se casaron ~ separarse otra vez** they married only to separate again; **lo tendré ~ mañana** I'll have it (for) tomorrow; **ir ~ casa** to go home, head for home; **~ profesor es muy estúpido** he's very stupid for a teacher; **¿quién es usted ~ gritar así?** who are you to shout like that?; **tengo bastante ~ vivir** I have enough to live on; ver tb **con**

parabién [para'βjen] nm congratulations pl

parábola [pa'raβola] nf parable; (MAT) parabola; **parabólica** nf (tb: antena ~) satellite dish

parabrisas [para'βrisas] nm inv windscreen (BRIT), windshield (US)

paracaídas [paraka'iðas] nm inv parachute; **paracaidista** nm/f parachutist; (MIL) paratrooper

parachoques [para'tʃokes] nm inv (AUTO) bumper; (MECÁNICA etc) shock absorber

parada [pa'raða] nf stop; (acto) stopping; (de industria) shutdown, stoppage; (lugar) stopping place; **~ de autobús** bus stop

paradero [para'ðero] nm stopping-place; (situación) whereabouts

parado, a [pa'raðo, a] adj (persona) motionless, standing still; (fábrica) closed, at a standstill; (coche) stopped; (AM) standing (up); (sin empleo) unemployed, idle

paradoja [para'ðoxa] nf paradox

parador [para'ðor] nm parador, state-run hotel

paráfrasis [pa'rafrasis] nf inv paraphrase

paraguas [pa'raɣwas] nm inv umbrella

Paraguay [para'ɣwai] nm: **el ~ Paraguay; paraguayo, a** adj, nm/f Paraguayan

paraíso [para'iso] nm paradise, heaven

paraje [pa'raxe] nm place, spot

paralelo, a [para'lelo, a] adj parallel

parálisis [pa'ralisis] nf inv paralysis; **paralítico, a** adj, nm/f paralytic

paralizar [parali'θar] vt to paralyse; **~se** vr to become paralysed; (fig) to come to a standstill

paramilitar [paramili'tar] adj paramilitary

páramo ['paramo] nm bleak plateau

parangón [paran'gon] nm: **sin ~** incomparable

paranoico, a [para'noiko, a] nm/f paranoiac

parapente [para'pente] nm (deporte) paragliding; (aparato) paraglider

parapléjico, a [para'plexiko, a] adj, nm/f paraplegic

parar [pa'rar] vt to stop; (golpe) to ward off ♦ vi to stop; **~se** vr to stop; (AM) to stand up; **ha parado de llover** it has stopped raining; **van a ir a ~ a comisaría** they're going to end up in the police station; **~se en** to pay attention to

pararrayos [para'rrajos] nm inv lightning conductor

parásito, a [pa'rasito, a] nm/f parasite

parcela [par'θela] nf plot, piece of ground

parche ['partʃe] nm (gen) patch

parchís [par'tʃis] nm ludo

parcial [par'θjal] adj (pago) part-; (eclipse) partial; (JUR) prejudiced, biased; (POL) partisan; **~idad** nf prejudice, bias

pardillo, a [par'ðiʎo, a] (pey) adj yokel

parecer [pare'θer] nm (*opinión*) opinion, view; (*aspecto*) looks pl ♦ vi (*tener apariencia*) to seem, look; (*asemejarse*) to look o seem like; (*aparecer, llegar*) to appear; **~se** vr to look alike, resemble each other; **~se a** to look like, resemble; **según parece** evidently, apparently; **me parece que** I think (that), it seems to me that

parecido, a [pare'θiðo, a] adj similar ♦ nm similarity, likeness, resemblance; **bien ~** good-looking, nice-looking

pared [pa'reð] nf wall

pareja [pa'rexa] nf (*par*) pair; (*dos personas*) couple; (*otro: de un par*) other one (of a pair); (*persona*) partner

parentela [paren'tela] nf relations pl

parentesco [paren'tesko] nm relationship

paréntesis [pa'rentesis] nm inv parenthesis; (*en escrito*) bracket

parezco etc vb ver **parecer**

pariente, a [pa'rjente, a] nm/f relative, relation

parir [pa'rir] vt to give birth to ♦ vi (*mujer*) to give birth, have a baby

París [pa'ris] n París

parking ['parkin] nm car park (*BRIT*), parking lot (*US*)

parlamentar [parlamen'tar] vi to parley

parlamentario, a [parlamen'tarjo, a] adj parliamentary ♦ nm/f member of parliament

parlamento [parla'mento] nm parliament

parlanchín, ina [parlan'tʃin, ina] adj indiscreet ♦ nm/f chatterbox

parlar [par'lar] vi to chatter (away)

paro ['paro] nm (*huelga*) stoppage (of work), strike; (*desempleo*) unemployment; **subsidio de ~** unemployment benefit

parodia [pa'roðja] nf parody; **parodiar** vt to parody

parpadear [parpaðe'ar] vi (*ojos*) to blink; (*luz*) to flicker

párpado ['parpaðo] nm eyelid

parque ['parke] nm (*lugar verde*) park; **~ de atracciones/infantil/zoológico** fairground/playground/zoo

parqué [par'ke] nm parquet (flooring)

parquímetro [par'kimetro] nm parking meter

parra ['parra] nf (grape)vine

párrafo ['parrafo] nm paragraph; **echar un ~** (*fam*) to have a chat

parranda [pa'rranda] (*fam*) nf spree, binge

parrilla [pa'rriʎa] nf (*CULIN*) grill; (*de coche*) grille; (**carne a la**) **~** barbecue; **~da** nf barbecue

párroco ['parroko] nm parish priest

parroquia [pa'rrokja] nf parish; (*iglesia*) parish church; (*COM*) clientele, customers pl; **~no, a** nm/f parishioner; client, customer

parsimonia [parsi'monja] nf calmness, level-headedness

parte ['parte] nm message; (*informe*) report ♦ nf part; (*lado, cara*) side; (*de reparto*) share; (*JUR*) party; **en alguna ~ de Europa** somewhere in Europe; **en/por todas ~s** everywhere; **en gran ~** to a large extent; **la mayor ~ de los españoles** most Spaniards; **de un tiempo a esta ~** for some time past; **de ~ de alguien** on sb's behalf; **¿de ~ de quién?** (*TEL*) who is speaking?; **por ~ de** on the part of; **yo por mi ~** I for my part; **por otra ~** on the other hand; **dar ~** to inform; **tomar ~** to take part

partición [parti'θjon] nf division, sharing-out; (*POL*) partition

participación [partiθipa'θjon] nf (*acto*) participation, taking part; (*parte, COM*) share; (*de lotería*) shared prize; (*aviso*) notice, notification

participante [partiθi'pante] nm/f participant

participar [partiθi'par] vt to notify, inform ♦ vi to take part, participate

partícipe [par'tiθipe] nm/f participant

particular [partiku'lar] adj (*especial*) particular, special; (*individual, personal*) private, personal ♦ nm (*punto, asunto*) particular, point; (*individuo*) individual; **tiene coche ~** he has a car of his own

partida [par'tiða] nf (*salida*) departure; (*COM*) entry, item; (*juego*) game; (*grupo de personas*) band, group; **mala ~** dirty trick; **~ de nacimiento / matrimonio / defunción** birth/marriage/death certificate

partidario, a [parti'ðarjo, a] adj partisan ♦ nm/f supporter, follower

partido [par'tiðo] nm (*POL*) party; (*DEPORTE*) game, match; **sacar ~ de** to profit o benefit from; **tomar ~** to take sides

partir [par'tir] vt (*dividir*) to split, divide; (*compartir, distribuir*) to share (out), distribute; (*romper*) to break open, split open; (*rebanada*) to cut (off) ♦ vi (*ponerse en camino*) to set off o out; (*comenzar*) to start (off o out); **~se** vr to crack o split o break (in two etc); **a ~ de** (starting) from

partitura [parti'tura] nf (*MUS*) score

parto ['parto] nm birth; (*fig*) product, creation; **estar de ~** to be in labour

pasa ['pasa] nf raisin; **~ de Corinto/de Esmirna** currant/sultana

pasada [pa'saða] nf passing, passage; **de ~** in passing, incidentally; **una mala ~** a dirty trick

pasadizo [pasa'ðiθo] nm (*pasillo*) passage, corridor; (*callejuela*) alley

pasado, a [pa'saðo, a] adj past; (*malo: comida, fruta*) bad; (*muy cocido*) overdone; (*anticuado*) out of date ♦ nm past; **~ mañana** the day after tomorrow; **el mes ~** last month

pasador [pasa'ðor] nm (cerrojo) bolt; (de pelo) hair slide; (horquilla) grip

pasaje [pa'saxe] nm passage; (pago de viaje) fare; (los pasajeros) passengers pl; (pasillo) passageway

pasajero, a [pasa'xero, a] adj passing; (situación, estado) temporary; (amor, enfermedad) brief ♦ nm/f passenger

pasamontañas [pasamon'taɲas] nm inv balaclava helmet

pasaporte [pasa'porte] nm passport

pasar [pa'sar] vt to pass; (tiempo) to spend; (desgracias) to suffer, endure; (noticia) to give, pass on; (río) to cross; (barrera) to pass through; (falta) to overlook, tolerate; (contrincante) to surpass, do better than; (coche) to overtake; (CINE) to show; (enfermedad) to give, infect with ♦ vi (gen) to pass; (terminarse) to be over; (ocurrir) to happen; ~se vr (flores) to fade; (comida) to go bad o off; (fig) to overdo it, go too far; ~ de to go beyond, exceed; ~ por (AM) to fetch; ~lo bien/mal to have a good/bad time; ¡pase! come in!; hacer ~ to show in; ~se al enemigo to go over to the enemy; se me pasó I forgot; no se le pasa nada he misses nothing; pase lo que pase come what may; ¿qué pasa? what's going on?, what's up?; ¿qué te pasa? what's wrong?

pasarela [pasa'rela] nf footbridge; (en barco) gangway

pasatiempo [pasa'tjempo] nm pastime, hobby

Pascua ['paskwa] nf: ~ (de Resurrección) Easter; ~ de Navidad Christmas; ~s nfpl Christmas (time); ¡felices ~s! Merry Christmas!

pase ['pase] nm pass; (CINE) performance, showing

pasear [pase'ar] vt to take for a walk; (exhibir) to parade, show off ♦ vi to walk, go for a walk; ~se vr to walk, go for a walk; ~ en coche to go for a drive; paseo nm (avenida) avenue; (distancia corta) walk, stroll; dar un o ir de paseo to go for a walk

pasillo [pa'siʎo] nm passage, corridor

pasión [pa'sjon] nf passion

pasivo, a [pa'siβo, a] adj passive; (inactivo) inactive ♦ nm (COM) liabilities pl, debts pl

pasmar [pas'mar] vt (asombrar) to amaze, astonish; **pasmo** nm amazement, astonishment; (resfriado) chill; (fig) wonder, marvel; **pasmoso, a** adj amazing, astonishing

paso, a ['paso, a] adj dried ♦ nm step; (modo de andar) walk; (huella) footprint; (rapidez) speed, pace, rate; (camino accesible) way through, passage; (cruce) crossing; (pasaje) passing, passage; (GEO) pass; (estrecho) strait; ~ a nivel (FERRO) level-crossing; ~ de peatones pedestrian crossing; a ese ~ (fig) at that rate; salir al ~ de o a to waylay; estar de ~ to be passing through; ~ elevado flyover; prohibido el ~ no entry; ceda el ~ give way

pasota [pa'sota] (fam) adj, nm/f ≈ dropout; ser un (tipo) ~ to be a bit of a dropout; (ser indiferente) not to care about anything

pasta ['pasta] nf paste; (CULIN: masa) dough; (: de bizcochos etc) pastry; (fam) dough; ~s nfpl (bizcochos) pastries, small cakes; (fideos, espaguetis etc) pasta; ~ de dientes o dentífrica toothpaste

pastar [pas'tar] vt, vi to graze

pastel [pas'tel] nm (dulce) cake; (ARTE) pastel; ~ de carne meat pie; ~ería nf cake shop

pasteurizado, a [pasteuri'θaðo, a] adj pasteurized

pastilla [pas'tiʎa] nf (de jabón, chocolate) bar; (píldora) tablet, pill

pasto ['pasto] nm (hierba) grass; (lugar) pasture, field

pastor, a [pas'tor, a] nm/f shepherd/ess ♦ nm (REL) clergyman, pastor; ~ alemán Alsatian

pata ['pata] nf (pierna) leg; (pie) foot; (de muebles) leg; ~s arriba upside down; metedura de ~ (fam) gaffe; meter la ~ (fam) to put one's foot in it; (TEC): ~ de cabra crowbar; tener buena/mala ~ to be lucky/unlucky; ~da nf kick; (en el suelo) stamp

patalear [patale'ar] vi (en el suelo) to stamp one's feet

patata [pa'tata] nf potato; ~s fritas chips, French fries; (de bolsa) crisps

paté [pa'te] nm pâté

patear [pate'ar] vt (pisar) to stamp on, trample (on); (pegar con el pie) to kick ♦ vi to stamp (with rage), stamp one's feet

patentar [paten'tar] vt to patent

patente [pa'tente] adj obvious, evident; (COM) patent ♦ nf patent

paternal [pater'nal] adj fatherly, paternal; **paterno, a** adj paternal

patético, a [pa'tetiko, a] adj pathetic, moving

patilla [pa'tiʎa] nf (de gafas) side(piece); ~s nfpl sideburns

patín [pa'tin] nm skate; (de trineo) runner; **patinaje** nm skating; **patinar** vi to skate; (resbalarse) to skid, slip; (fam) to slip up, blunder

patio ['patjo] nm (de casa) patio, courtyard; ~ de recreo playground

pato ['pato] nm duck; **pagar el ~** (fam) to take the blame, carry the can

patológico, a [pato'loxiko, a] adj pathological

patoso, a [pa'toso, a] (fam) adj clumsy

patraña [pa'traɲa] nf story, fib
patria ['patrja] nf native land, mother country
patrimonio [patri'monjo] nm inheritance; (fig) heritage
patriota [pa'trjota] nm/f patriot; **patriotismo** nm patriotism
patrocinar [patroθi'nar] vt to sponsor; **patrocinio** nm sponsorship
patrón, ona [pa'tron, ona] nm/f (jefe) boss, chief, master/mistress; (propietario) landlord/lady; (REL) patron saint ♦ nm (TEC, COSTURA) pattern
patronal [patro'nal] adj: **la clase ~** management
patronato [patro'nato] nm sponsorship; (acto) patronage; (fundación benéfica) trust, foundation
patrulla [pa'truʎa] nf patrol
pausa ['pausa] nf pause, break
pausado, a [pau'saðo, a] adj slow, deliberate
pauta ['pauta] nf line, guide line
pavimento [paβi'mento] nm (con losas) pavement, paving
pavo ['paβo] nm turkey; **~ real** peacock
pavor [pa'βor] nm dread, terror
payaso [pa'jaso, a] nm/f clown
payo, a [pa'jo, a] nm/f non-gipsy
paz [paθ] nf peace; (tranquilidad) peacefulness, tranquillity; **hacer las paces** to make peace; (fig) to make up
pazo ['paθo] nm country house
P.D. abr (= posdata) P.S., p.s.
peaje [pe'axe] nm toll
peatón [pea'ton] nm pedestrian
peca ['peka] nf freckle
pecado [pe'kaðo] nm sin; **pecador, a** adj sinful ♦ nm/f sinner
pecaminoso, a [pekami'noso, a] adj sinful
pecar [pe'kar] vi (REL) to sin; **peca de generoso** he is generous to a fault
pecera [pe'θera] nf fish tank; (redondo) goldfish bowl
pecho ['petʃo] nm (ANAT) chest; (de mujer) breast; **dar el ~ a** to breast-feed; **tomar algo a ~** to take sth to heart
pechuga [pe'tʃuxa] nf breast
peculiar [peku'ljar] adj special, peculiar; (característico) typical, characteristic; **~idad** nf peculiarity; special feature, characteristic
pedal [pe'ðal] nm pedal; **~ear** vi to pedal
pedante [pe'ðante] adj pedantic ♦ nm/f pedant; **~ría** nf pedantry
pedazo [pe'ðaθo] nm piece, bit; **hacerse ~s** to smash, shatter
pedernal [peðer'nal] nm flint
pediatra [pe'ðjatra] nm/f paediatrician
pedido [pe'ðiðo] nm (COM) order; (petición) request
pedir [pe'ðir] vt to ask for, request; (comida, COM: mandar) to order; (necesitar) to need, demand, require ♦ vi to ask; **me pidió que cerrara la puerta** he asked me to shut the door; **¿cuánto piden por el coche?** how much are they asking for the car?
pedo ['peðo] (fam!) nm fart
pega ['peɣa] nf snag; **poner ~s (a)** to complain (about)
pegadizo, a [peɣa'ðiθo, a] adj (MUS) catchy
pegajoso, a [peɣa'xoso, a] adj sticky, adhesive
pegamento [peɣa'mento] nm gum, glue
pegar [pe'ɣar] vt (papel, sellos) to stick (on); (cartel) to stick up; (coser) to sew (on); (unir: partes) to join, fix together; (MED) to give, infect with; (dar: golpe) to give, deal ♦ vi (adherirse) to stick, adhere; (ir juntos: colores) to match, go together; (golpear) to hit; (quemar: el sol) to strike hot, burn (fig); **~se** vr (gen) to stick; (dos personas) to hit each other, fight; (fam): **~ un grito** to let out a yell; **~ un salto** to jump (with fright); **~ en** to touch; **~se un tiro** to shoot o.s.
pegatina [peɣa'tina] nf sticker
pegote [pe'ɣote] (fam) nm eyesore, sight
peinado [pei'naðo] nm hairstyle
peinar [pei'nar] vt to comb; (hacer estilo) to style; **~se** vr to comb one's hair
peine ['peine] nm comb; **~ta** nf ornamental comb
p.ej. abr (= por ejemplo) e.g.
Pekín [pe'kin] n Pekin(g)
pelado, a [pe'laðo, a] adj (fruta, patata etc) peeled; (cabeza) shorn; (campo, fig) bare; (fam: sin dinero) broke
pelaje [pe'laxe] nm (ZOOL) fur, coat; (fig) appearance
pelar [pe'lar] vt (fruta, patatas etc) to peel; (cortar el pelo a) to cut the hair of; (quitar la piel: animal) to skin; **~se** vr (la piel) to peel off; **voy a ~me** I'm going to get my hair cut
peldaño [pel'daɲo] nm step
pelea [pe'lea] nf (lucha) fight; (discusión) quarrel, row
peleado, a [pele'aðo, a] adj: **estar ~ (con uno)** to have fallen out (with sb)
pelear [pele'ar] vi to fight; **~se** vr to fight; (reñirse) to fall out, quarrel
peletería [pelete'ria] nf furrier's, fur shop
pelícano [pe'likano] nm pelican
película [pe'likula] nf film; (cobertura ligera) thin covering; (FOTO: rollo) roll o reel of film
peligro [pe'liɣro] nm danger; (riesgo) risk; **correr ~ de** to run the risk of; **~so, a** adj dangerous; risky
pelirrojo, a [peli'rroxo, a] adj red-haired, red-headed ♦ nm/f redhead
pellejo [pe'ʎexo] nm (de animal) skin, hide
pellizcar [peʎiθ'kar] vt to pinch, nip

pelma ['pelma] (*fam*) *nm/f* pain (in the neck)
pelmazo |pel'maθo| (*fam*) *nm* = **pelma**
pelo ['pelo] *nm* (*cabellos*) hair; (*de barba,
bigote*) whisker; (*de animal: pellejo*) hair, fur,
coat; **al ~** just right; **venir al ~** to be exactly
what one needs; **un hombre de ~ en pecho** a
brave man; **por los ~s** by the skin of one's
teeth; **no tener ~s en la lengua** to be
outspoken, not mince words; **tomar el ~ a
uno** to pull sb's leg
pelota [pe'lota] *nf* ball; **en ~** stark naked;
hacer la ~ (a uno) (*fam*) to creep (to sb);
~ vasca pelota
pelotari [pelo'tari] *nm* pelota player
pelotón [pelo'ton] *nm* (*MIL*) squad,
detachment
peluca [pe'luka] *nf* wig
peluche [pe'lutʃe] *nm*: **oso/muñeco de ~**
teddy bear/soft toy
peludo, a [pe'luðo, a] *adj* hairy, shaggy
peluquería [peluke'ria] *nf* hairdresser's;
peluquero, a *nm/f* hairdresser
pelusa [pe'lusa] *nf* (*BOT*) down; (*en tela*) fluff
pena ['pena] *nf* (*congoja*) grief, sadness;
(*remordimiento*) regret; (*dificultad*) trouble;
(*dolor*) pain; (*JUR*) sentence; **merecer** o **valer
la ~** to be worthwhile; **a duras ~s** with great
difficulty; **~ de muerte** death penalty;
~ pecuniaria fine; **¡qué ~!** what a shame!
penal [pe'nal] *adj* penal ♦ *nm* (*cárcel*) prison
penalidad [penali'ðað] *nf* (*problema,
dificultad*) trouble, hardship; (*JUR*) penalty,
punishment; **~es** *nfpl* trouble, hardship
penalti, penalty [pe'nalti] (*pl* **~s** o **~es**)
nm penalty (kick)
pendiente [pen'djente] *adj* pending,
unsettled ♦ *nm* earring ♦ *nf* hill, slope
pene ['pene] *nm* penis
penetración [penetra'θjon] *nf* (*acto*)
penetration; (*agudeza*) sharpness, insight
penetrante [pene'trante] *adj* (*herida*) deep;
(*persona, arma*) sharp; (*sonido*) penetrating,
piercing; (*mirada*) searching; (*viento, ironía*)
biting
penetrar [pene'trar] *vt* to penetrate, pierce;
(*entender*) to grasp ♦ *vi* to penetrate, go in;
(*entrar*) to enter, go in; (*líquido*) to soak in;
(*fig*) to pierce
penicilina [peniθi'lina] *nf* penicillin
península [pe'ninsula] *nf* peninsula;
peninsular *adj* peninsular
penique [pe'nike] *nm* penny
penitencia [peni'tenθja] *nf* penance
penoso, a [pe'noso, a] *adj* (*lamentable*)
distressing; (*difícil*) arduous, difficult
pensador, a [pensa'ðor, a] *nm/f* thinker
pensamiento [pensa'mjento] *nm* thought;
(*mente*) mind; (*idea*) idea
pensar [pen'sar] *vt* to think; (*considerar*) to

think over, think out; (*proponerse*) to intend,
plan; (*imaginarse*) to think up, invent ♦ *vi* to
think; **~ en** to aim at, aspire to; **pensativo,
a** *adj* thoughtful, pensive
pensión [pen'sjon] *nf* (*casa*) boarding o
guest house; (*dinero*) pension; (*cama y
comida*) board and lodging; **~ completa** full
board; **media ~** half-board; **pensionista**
nm/f (*jubilado*) (old-age) pensioner;
(*huésped*) lodger
penúltimo, a [pe'nultimo, a] *adj*
penultimate, last but one
penumbra [pe'numbra] *nf* half-light
penuria [pe'nurja] *nf* shortage, want
peña ['peɲa] *nf* (*roca*) rock; (*cuesta*) cliff,
crag; (*grupo*) group, circle; (*AM: club*) folk
club
peñasco [pe'ɲasko] *nm* large rock, boulder
peñón [pe'ɲon] *nm* wall of rock; **el P~** the
Rock (of Gibraltar)
peón [pe'on] *nm* labourer; (*AM*) farm
labourer, farmhand; (*AJEDREZ*) pawn
peonza [pe'onθa] *nf* spinning top
peor [pe'or] *adj* (*comparativo*) worse;
(*superlativo*) worst ♦ *adv* worse; worst; **de
mal en ~** from bad to worse
pepinillo [pepi'niʎo] *nm* gherkin
pepino [pe'pino] *nm* cucumber; **(no) me
importa un ~** I don't care one bit
pepita [pe'pita] *nf* (*BOT*) pip; (*MINERÍA*)
nugget
pepito [pe'pito] *nm*: **~ (de ternera)** steak
sandwich
pequeñez [peke'ɲeθ] *nf* smallness, littleness;
(*trivialidad*) trifle, triviality
pequeño, a [pe'keɲo, a] *adj* small, little
pera ['pera] *nf* pear; **peral** *nm* pear tree
percance [per'kanθe] *nm* setback, misfortune
percatarse [perka'tarse] *vr*: **~ de** to notice,
take note of
percebe [per'θeβe] *nm* barnacle
percepción [perθep'θjon] *nf* (*vista*)
perception; (*idea*) notion, idea
percha ['pertʃa] *nf* (*coat*)hanger; (*ganchos*)
coat hooks *pl*; (*de ave*) perch
percibir [perθi'βir] *vt* to perceive, notice;
(*COM*) to earn, get
percusión [perku'sjon] *nf* percussion
perdedor, a [perðe'ðor, a] *adj* losing ♦ *nm/f*
loser
perder [per'ðer] *vt* to lose; (*tiempo, palabras*)
to waste; (*oportunidad*) to lose, miss; (*tren*)
to miss ♦ *vi* to lose; **~se** *vr* (*extraviarse*) to get
lost; (*desaparecer*) to disappear, be lost to
view; (*arruinarse*) to be ruined; **echar a ~**
(*comida*) to spoil, ruin; (*oportunidad*) to
waste
perdición [perði'θjon] *nf* perdition, ruin
pérdida ['perðiða] *nf* loss; (*de tiempo*) waste;

~s *nfpl* (*COM*) losses
perdido, a [per'ðiðo, a] *adj* lost
perdiz [per'ðiθ] *nf* partridge
perdón [per'ðon] *nm* (*disculpa*) pardon, forgiveness; (*clemencia*) mercy; ¡~! sorry!, I beg your pardon!; **perdonar** *vt* to pardon, forgive; (*la vida*) to spare; (*excusar*) to exempt, excuse; **¡perdone (usted)!** sorry!, I beg your pardon!
perdurar [perðu'rar] *vi* (*resistir*) to last, endure; (*seguir existiendo*) to stand, still exist
perecedero, a [pereθe'ðero, a] *adj* perishable
perecer |pere'θer| *vi* to perish, die
peregrinación [pereɣrina'θjon] *nf* (*REL*) pilgrimage
peregrino, a |pere'ɣrino, a] *adj* (*idea*) strange, absurd ♦ *nm/f* pilgrim
perejil [pere'xil] *nm* parsley
perenne [pe'renne] *adj* everlasting, perennial
pereza [pe'reθa] *nf* laziness, idleness; **perezoso, a** *adj* lazy, idle
perfección [perfek'θjon] *nf* perfection; **perfeccionar** *vt* to perfect; (*mejorar*) to improve; (*acabar*) to complete, finish
perfectamente [perfekta'mente] *adv* perfectly
perfecto, a [per'fekto, a] *adj* perfect; (*total*) complete
perfil [per'fil] *nm* profile; (*contorno*) silhouette, outline; (*ARQ*) (cross) section; **~es** *nmpl* features; **~ar** *vt* (*trazar*) to outline; (*fig*) to shape, give character to
perforación [perfora'θjon] *nf* perforation; (*con taladro*) drilling; **perforadora** *nf* punch
perforar [perfo'rar] *vt* to perforate; (*agujero*) to drill, bore; (*papel*) to punch a hole in ♦ *vi* to drill, bore
perfume [per'fume] *nm* perfume, scent
pericia [pe'riθja] *nf* skill, expertise
periferia [peri'ferja] *nf* periphery; (*de ciudad*) outskirts *pl*
periférico |peri'feriko| (*AM*) *nm* ring road (*BRIT*), beltway (*US*)
perímetro [pe'rimetro] *nm* perimeter
periódico, a [pe'rjoðiko, a] *adj* periodic(al) ♦ *nm* newspaper
periodismo [perjo'ðismo] *nm* journalism; **periodista** *nm/f* journalist
periodo [pe'rjoðo] *nm* period
período [pe'rioðo] *nm* = **periodo**
periquito [peri'kito] *nm* budgerigar, budgie
perito, a [pe'rito, a] *adj* (*experto*) expert; (*diestro*) skilled, skilful ♦ *nm/f* expert; skilled worker; (*técnico*) technician
perjudicar [perxuði'kar] *vt* (*gen*) to damage, harm; **perjudicial** *adj* damaging, harmful; (*en detrimento*) detrimental; **perjuicio** *nm* damage, harm

perjurar [perxu'rar] *vi* to commit perjury
perla ['perla] *nf* pearl; **me viene de ~s** it suits me fine
permanecer [permane'θer] *vi* (*quedarse*) to stay, remain; (*seguir*) to continue to be
permanencia [perma'nenθja] *nf* permanence; (*estancia*) stay
permanente [perma'nente] *adj* permanent, constant ♦ *nf* perm
permiso [per'miso] *nm* permission; (*licencia*) permit, licence; **con ~** excuse me; **estar de ~** (*MIL*) to be on leave; **~ de conducir** driving licence (*BRIT*), driver's license (*US*)
permitir [permi'tir] *vt* to permit, allow
pernera [per'nera] *nf* trouser leg
pernicioso, a [perni'θjoso, a] *adj* pernicious
pero ['pero] *conj* but; (*aún*) yet ♦ *nm* (*defecto*) flaw, defect; (*reparo*) objection
perpendicular [perpendiku'lar] *adj* perpendicular
perpetrar [perpe'trar] *vt* to perpetrate
perpetuar [perpe'twar] *vt* to perpetuate; **perpetuo, a** *adj* perpetual
perplejo, a [per'plexo, a] *adj* perplexed, bewildered
perra ['perra] *nf* (*ZOOL*) bitch; **estar sin una ~** to be flat broke
perrera [pe'rrera] *nf* kennel
perrito [pe'rrito] *nm*: **~ caliente** hot dog
perro ['perro] *nm* dog
persa ['persa] *adj, nm/f* Persian
persecución [perseku'θjon] *nf* pursuit, chase; (*REL, POL*) persecution
perseguir [perse'ɣir] *vt* to pursue, hunt; (*cortejar*) to chase after; (*molestar*) to pester, annoy; (*REL, POL*) to persecute
perseverante [perseße'rante] *adj* persevering, persistent
perseverar [perseße'rar] *vi* to persevere, persist
persiana [per'sjana] *nf* (Venetian) blind
persignarse [persiɣ'narse] *vr* to cross o.s.
persistente [persis'tente] *adj* persistent
persistir [persis'tir] *vi* to persist
persona [per'sona] *nf* person; **~ mayor** elderly person
personaje [perso'naxe] *nm* important person, celebrity; (*TEATRO etc*) character
personal [perso'nal] *adj* (*particular*) personal; (*para una persona*) single, for one person ♦ *nm* personnel, staff; **~idad** *nf* personality
personarse [perso'narse] *vr* to appear in person
personificar [personifi'kar] *vt* to personify
perspectiva [perspek'tißa] *nf* perspective; (*vista, panorama*) view, panorama; (*posibilidad futura*) outlook, prospect
perspicacia [perspi'kaθja] *nf* discernment, perspicacity

perspicaz [perspi'kaθ] adj shrewd
persuadir [perswa'ðir] vt (gen) to persuade; (convencer) to convince; **~se** vr to become convinced; **persuasión** nf persuasion; **persuasivo, a** adj persuasive; convincing
pertenecer [pertene'θer] vi to belong; (fig) to concern; **perteneciente** adj: **perteneciente a** belonging to; **pertenencia** nf ownership; **pertenencias** nfpl (bienes) possessions, property sg
pertenezca etc vb ver **pertenecer**
pértiga ['pertixa] nf: **salto de ~** pole vault
pertinente [perti'nente] adj relevant, pertinent; (apropiado) appropriate; **~ a** concerning, relevant to
perturbación [perturßa'θjon] nf (POL) disturbance; (MED) upset, disturbance
perturbado, a [pertur'ßaðo, a] adj mentally unbalanced
perturbar [pertur'ßar] vt (el orden) to disturb; (MED) to upset, disturb; (mentalmente) to perturb
Perú [pe'ru] nm: **el ~** Peru; **peruano, a** adj, nm/f Peruvian
perversión [perßer'sjon] nf perversion; **perverso, a** adj perverse; (depravado) depraved
pervertido, a [perßer'tiðo, a] adj perverted ♦ nm/f pervert
pervertir [perßer'tir] vt to pervert, corrupt
pesa ['pesa] nf weight; (DEPORTE) shot
pesadez [pesa'ðeθ] nf (peso) heaviness; (lentitud) slowness; (aburrimiento) tediousness
pesadilla [pesa'ðiʎa] nf nightmare, bad dream
pesado, a [pe'saðo, a] adj heavy; (lento) slow; (difícil, duro) tough, hard; (aburrido) boring, tedious; (tiempo) sultry
pésame ['pesame] nm expression of condolence, message of sympathy; **dar el ~** to express one's condolences
pesar [pe'sar] vt to weigh ♦ vi to weigh; (ser pesado) to weigh a lot, be heavy; (fig: opinión) to carry weight; **no pesa mucho** it is not very heavy ♦ nm (arrepentimiento) regret; (pena) grief, sorrow; **a ~ de** o **pese a (que)** in spite of, despite
pesca ['peska] nf (acto) fishing; (lo pescado) catch; **ir de ~** to go fishing
pescadería [peskaðe'ria] nf fish shop, fishmonger's (BRIT)
pescadilla [peska'ðiʎa] nf whiting
pescado [pes'kaðo] nm fish
pescador, a [peska'ðor, a] nm/f fisherman/woman
pescar [pes'kar] vt (tomar) to catch; (intentar tomar) to fish for; (conseguir: trabajo) to manage to get ♦ vi to fish, go fishing

pescuezo [pes'kweθo] nm neck
pesebre [pe'seßre] nm manger
peseta [pe'seta] nf peseta
pesimista [pesi'mista] adj pessimistic ♦ nm/f pessimist
pésimo, a ['pesimo, a] adj awful, dreadful
peso ['peso] nm weight; (balanza) scales pl; (moneda) peso; **~ bruto/neto** gross/net weight; **vender al ~** to sell by weight
pesquero, a [pes'kero, a] adj fishing cpd
pesquisa [pes'kisa] nf inquiry, investigation
pestaña [pes'tana] nf (ANAT) eyelash; (borde) rim; **pestañear** vi to blink
peste ['peste] nf plague; (mal olor) stink, stench
pesticida [pesti'θiða] nm pesticide
pestillo [pes'tiʎo] nm (cerrojo) bolt; (picaporte) doorhandle
petaca [pe'taka] nf (de cigarros) cigarette case; (de pipa) tobacco pouch; (AM: maleta) suitcase
pétalo ['petalo] nm petal
petardo [pe'tardo] nm firework, firecracker
petición [peti'θjon] nf (pedido) request, plea; (memorial) petition; (JUR) plea
petrificar [petrifi'kar] vt to petrify
petróleo [pe'troleo] nm oil, petroleum; **petrolero, a** adj petroleum cpd ♦ nm (oil) tanker
peyorativo, a [pejora'tißo, a] adj pejorative
pez [peθ] nm fish
pezón [pe'θon] nm teat, nipple
pezuña [pe'θuna] nf hoof
piadoso, a [pja'ðoso, a] adj (devoto) pious, devout; (misericordioso) kind, merciful
pianista [pja'nista] nm/f pianist
piano ['pjano] nm piano
piar [pjar] vi to cheep
pibe, a ['piße, a] (AM) nm/f boy/girl
picadero [pika'ðero] nm riding school
picadillo [pika'ðiʎo] nm mince, minced meat
picado, a [pi'kaðo, a] adj pricked, punctured; (CULIN) minced, chopped; (mar) choppy; (diente) bad; (tabaco) cut; (enfadado) cross
picador [pika'ðor] nm (TAUR) picador; (minero) faceworker
picadura [pika'ðura] nf (pinchazo) puncture; (de abeja) sting; (de mosquito) bite; (tabaco picado) cut tobacco
picante [pi'kante] adj hot; (comentario) racy, spicy
picaporte [pika'porte] nm (manija) doorhandle; (pestillo) latch
picar [pi'kar] vt (agujerear, perforar) to prick, puncture; (abeja) to sting; (mosquito, serpiente) to bite; (CULIN) to mince, chop; (incitar) to incite, goad; (dañar, irritar) to annoy, bother; (quemar: lengua) to burn,

sting ♦ vi (*pez*) to bite, take the bait; (*sol*) to burn, scorch; (*abeja*, MED) to sting; (*mosquito*) to bite; **~se** vr (*agriarse*) to turn sour, go off; (*ofenderse*) to take offence

picardía [pikar'ðia] nf villainy; (*astucia*) slyness, craftiness; (*una ~*) dirty trick; (*palabra*) rude/bad word o expression

pícaro, a ['pikaro, a] adj (*malicioso*) villainous; (*travieso*) mischievous ♦ nm (*astuto*) crafty sort; (*sinvergüenza*) rascal, scoundrel

pichón [pi'tʃon] nm young pigeon

pico ['piko] nm (*de ave*) beak; (*punta*) sharp point; (TEC) pick, pickaxe; (GEO) peak, summit; **y ~** and a bit

picor [pi'kor] nm itch

picotear [pikote'ar] vt to peck ♦ vi to nibble, pick

picudo, a [pi'kuðo, a] adj pointed, with a point

pidió etc vb ver **pedir**

pido etc vb ver **pedir**

pie [pje] (pl **~s**) nm foot; (*fig: motivo*) motive, basis; (: *fundamento*) foothold; **ir a ~** to go on foot, walk; **estar de ~** to be standing (up); **ponerse de ~** to stand up; **de ~s a cabeza** from top to bottom; **al ~ de la letra** (*citar*) literally, verbatim; (*copiar*) exactly, word for word; **en ~ de guerra** on a war footing; **dar ~ a** to give cause for; **hacer ~** (*en el agua*) to touch (the) bottom

piedad [pje'ðað] nf (*lástima*) pity, compassion; (*clemencia*) mercy; (*devoción*) piety, devotion

piedra ['pjeðra] nf stone; (*roca*) rock; (*de mechero*) flint; (METEOROLOGÍA) hailstone

piel [pjel] nf (ANAT) skin; (ZOOL) skin, hide, fur; (*cuero*) leather; (BOT) skin, peel

pienso etc vb ver **pensar**

pierdo etc vb ver **perder**

pierna ['pjerna] nf leg

pieza ['pjeθa] nf piece; (*habitación*) room; **~ de recambio** o **repuesto** spare (part)

pigmeo, a [piɣ'meo, a] adj, nm/f pigmy

pijama [pi'xama] nm pyjamas pl

pila ['pila] nf (ELEC) battery; (*montón*) heap, pile; (*lavabo*) sink

píldora ['pildora] nf pill; **la ~ (anticonceptiva)** the (contraceptive) pill

pileta [pi'leta] nf basin, bowl; (AM) swimming pool

pillaje [pi'ʎaxe] nm pillage, plunder

pillar [pi'ʎar] vt (*saquear*) to pillage, plunder; (*fam: coger*) to catch; (: *agarrar*) to grasp, seize; (: *entender*) to grasp, catch on to; **~se** vr: **~se un dedo con la puerta** to catch one's finger in the door

pillo, a ['piʎo, a] adj villainous; (*astuto*) sly, crafty ♦ nm/f rascal, rogue, scoundrel

piloto [pi'loto] nm pilot; (*de aparato*) (pilot) light; (AUTO: *luz*) tail o rear light; (: *conductor*) driver

pimentón [pimen'ton] nm paprika

pimienta [pi'mjenta] nf pepper

pimiento [pi'mjento] nm pepper, pimiento

pin [pin] (pl **pins**) nm badge

pinacoteca [pinako'teka] nf art gallery

pinar [pi'nar] nm pine forest (BRIT), pine grove (US)

pincel [pin'θel] nm paintbrush

pinchadiscos [pintʃa'ðiskos] nm/f inv disc-jockey, DJ

pinchar [pin'tʃar] vt (*perforar*) to prick, pierce; (*neumático*) to puncture; (*fig*) to prod

pinchazo [pin'tʃaθo] nm (*perforación*) prick; (*de neumático*) puncture; (*fig*) prod

pincho ['pintʃo] nm savoury (snack); **~ moruno** shish kebab; **~ de tortilla** small slice of omelette

ping-pong ['pin'pon] nm table tennis

pingüino [pin'gwino] nm penguin

pino ['pino] nm pine (tree)

pinta ['pinta] nf spot; (*de líquidos*) spot, drop; (*aspecto*) appearance, look(s) (pl); **~do, a** adj spotted; (*de colores*) colourful; **~das** nfpl graffiti sg

pintar [pin'tar] vt to paint ♦ vi to paint; (*fam*) to count, be important; **~se** vr to put on make-up

pintor, a [pin'tor, a] nm/f painter

pintoresco, a [pinto'resko, a] adj picturesque

pintura [pin'tura] nf painting; **~ a la acuarela** watercolour; **~ al óleo** oil painting

pinza ['pinθa] nf (ZOOL) claw; (*para colgar ropa*) clothes peg; (TEC) pincers pl; **~s** nfpl (*para depilar etc*) tweezers pl

piña ['piɲa] nf (*fruto del pino*) pine cone; (*fruta*) pineapple; (*fig*) group

piñón [pi'ɲon] nm (*fruto*) pine nut; (TEC) pinion

pío, a ['pio, a] adj (*devoto*) pious, devout; (*misericordioso*) merciful

piojo ['pjoxo] nm louse

pionero, a [pjo'nero, a] adj pioneering ♦ nm/f pioneer

pipa ['pipa] nf pipe; **~s** nfpl (BOT) (edible) sunflower seeds

pipí [pi'pi] (fam) nm: **hacer ~** to have a wee(-wee) (BRIT), have to go (wee-wee) (US)

pique ['pike] nm (*resentimiento*) pique, resentment; (*rivalidad*) rivalry, competition; **irse a ~** to sink; (*esperanza, familia*) to be ruined

piqueta [pi'keta] nf pick(axe)

piquete [pi'kete] nm (MIL) squad, party; (*de obreros*) picket

pirado, a [pi'raðo, a] (fam) adj round the

bend ♦ nm/f nutter

piragua [pi'raɣwa] nf canoe; **piragüismo** nm canoeing

pirámide [pi'ramiðe] nf pyramid

pirata [pi'rata] adj, nm pirate ♦ nm/f: ~ **informático/a** hacker

Pirineo(s) [piri'neo(s)] nm(pl) Pyrenees pl

pirómano, a [pi'romano, a] nm/f (MED, JUR) arsonist

piropo [pi'ropo] nm compliment, (piece of) flattery

pirueta [pi'rweta] nf pirouette

pis [pis] (fam) nm pee, piss; **hacer** ~ to have a pee; (para niños) to wee-wee

pisada [pi'saða] nf (paso) footstep; (huella) footprint

pisar [pi'sar] vt (caminar sobre) to walk on, tread on; (apretar con el pie) to press; (fig) to trample on, walk all over ♦ vi to tread, step, walk

piscina [pis'θina] nf swimming pool

Piscis [pis'θis] nm Pisces

piso ['piso] nm (suelo, planta) floor; (apartamento) flat (BRIT), apartment; **primer** ~ (ESP) first floor; (AM) ground floor

pisotear [pisote'ar] vt to trample (on o underfoot)

pista ['pista] nf track, trail; (indicio) clue; ~ **de aterrizaje** runway; ~ **de baile** dance floor; ~ **de hielo** ice rink; ~ **de tenis** tennis court

pistola [pis'tola] nf pistol; (TEC) spray-gun; **pistolero, a** nm/f gunman/woman, gangster

pistón [pis'ton] nm (TEC) piston; (MUS) key

pitar [pi'tar] vt (silbato) to blow; (rechiflar) to whistle at, boo ♦ vi to whistle; (AUTO) to sound o toot one's horn; (AM) to smoke

pitillo [pi'tiʎo] nm cigarette

pito ['pito] nm whistle; (de coche) horn

pitón [pi'ton] nm (ZOOL) python

pitonisa [pito'nisa] nf fortune-teller

pitorreo [pito'rreo] nm joke; **estar de** ~ to be joking

pizarra [pi'θarra] nf (piedra) slate; (encerado) blackboard

pizca ['piθka] nf pinch, spot; (fig) spot, speck; **ni** ~ not a bit

placa ['plaka] nf plate; (distintivo) badge, insignia; ~ **de matrícula** number plate

placentero, a [plaθen'tero, a] adj pleasant, agreeable

placer [pla'θer] nm pleasure ♦ vt to please

plácido, a ['plaθiðo, a] adj placid

plaga ['plaɣa] nf pest; (MED) plague; (abundancia) abundance; **plagar** vt to infest, plague; (llenar) to fill

plagio ['plaxjo] nm plagiarism

plan [plan] nm (esquema, proyecto) plan; (idea, intento) idea, intention; **tener** ~ (fam) to have a date; **tener un** ~ (fam) to have an affair; **en** ~ **económico** (fam) on the cheap; **vamos en** ~ **de turismo** we're going as tourists; **si te pones en ese** ~ ... if that's your attitude ...

plana ['plana] nf sheet (of paper), page; (TEC) trowel; **en primera** ~ on the front page; ~ **mayor** staff

plancha ['plantʃa] nf (para planchar) iron; (rótulo) plate, sheet; (NAUT) gangway; **a la** ~ (CULIN) grilled; ~**do** nm ironing; **planchar** vt to iron ♦ vi to do the ironing

planeador [planea'ðor] nm glider

planear [plane'ar] vt to plan ♦ vi to glide

planeta [pla'neta] nm planet

planicie [pla'niθje] nf plain

planificación [planifika'θjon] nf planning; ~ **familiar** family planning

plano, a ['plano, a] adj flat, level, even ♦ nm (MAT, TEC) plane; (FOTO) shot; (ARQ) plan; (GEO) map; (de ciudad) map, street plan; **primer** ~ close-up; **caer de** ~ to fall flat

planta ['planta] nf (BOT, TEC) plant; (ANAT) sole of the foot, foot; (piso) floor; (AM: personal) staff; ~ **baja** ground floor

plantación [planta'θjon] nf (AGR) plantation; (acto) planting

plantar [plan'tar] vt (BOT) to plant; (levantar) to erect, set up; ~**se** vr to stand firm; ~ **a uno en la calle** to throw sb out; **dejar plantado a uno** (fam) to stand sb up

plantear [plante'ar] vt (problema) to pose; (dificultad) to raise

plantilla [plan'tiʎa] nf (de zapato) insole; (personal) personnel; **ser de** ~ to be on the staff

plantón [plan'ton] nm (MIL) guard, sentry; (fam) long wait; **dar (un)** ~ **a uno** to stand sb up

plasmar [plas'mar] vt (dar forma) to mould, shape; (representar) to represent; ~**se** vr: ~**se en** to take the form of

plasta ['plasta] (fam) adj inv boring ♦ nm/f bore

plástico, a ['plastiko, a] adj plastic ♦ nm plastic

Plastilina ® [plasti'lina] nf Plasticine ®

plata ['plata] nf (metal) silver; (cosas hechas de ~) silverware; (AM) cash, dough; **hablar en** ~ to speak bluntly o frankly

plataforma [plata'forma] nf platform; ~ **de lanzamiento/perforación** launch(ing) pad/ drilling rig

plátano ['platano] nm (fruta) banana; (árbol) plane tree; banana tree

platea [pla'tea] nf (TEATRO) pit

plateado, a [plate'aðo, a] adj silver; (TEC) silver-plated

plática ['platika] nf talk, chat; **platicar** vi to talk, chat

platillo |pla'tiʎo| nm saucer; **~s** nmpl (MUS) cymbals; **~ volador** o **volante** flying saucer

platino |pla'tino| nm platinum; **~s** nmpl (AUTO) contact points

plato |'plato| nm plate, dish; (parte de comida) course; (comida) dish; **~ combinado** set main course (served on one plate); **~ fuerte** main course; **primer ~** first course

playa |'plaja| nf beach; (costa) seaside; **~ de estacionamiento** (AM) car park

playera |pla'jera| nf (AM: camiseta) T-shirt; **~s** nfpl (zapatos) canvas shoes

plaza |'plaθa| nf square; (mercado) market(place); (sitio) room, space; (en vehículo) seat, place; (colocación) post, job; **~ de toros** bullring

plazo |'plaθo| nm (lapso de tiempo) time, period; (fecha de vencimiento) expiry date; (pago parcial) instalment; **a corto/largo ~** short-/long-term; **comprar algo a ~s** to buy sth on hire purchase (BRIT) o on time (US)

plazoleta |plaθo'leta| nf small square

pleamar |plea'mar| nf high tide

plebe |'pleβe| nf: **la ~** the common people pl, the masses pl; (pey) the plebs pl; **~yo, a** adj plebeian; (pey) coarse, common

plebiscito |pleβis'θito| nm plebiscite

plegable |ple'xaβle| adj collapsible; (silla) folding

plegar |ple'xar| vt (doblar) to fold, bend; (COSTURA) to pleat; **~se** vr to yield, submit

pleito |'pleito| nm (JUR) lawsuit, case; (fig) dispute, feud

plenilunio |pleni'lunjo| nm full moon

plenitud |pleni'tuð| nf plenitude, fullness; (abundancia) abundance

pleno, a |'pleno, a| adj full; (completo) complete ♦ nm plenum; **en ~ día** in broad daylight; **en ~ verano** at the height of summer; **en plena cara** full in the face

pliego etc |'pljexo| vb ver **plegar** ♦ nm (hoja) sheet (of paper); (carta) sealed letter/ document; **~ de condiciones** details pl, specifications pl

pliegue etc |'pljexe| vb ver **plegar** ♦ nm fold, crease; (de vestido) pleat

plomero |plo'mero| nm (AM) plumber

plomo |'plomo| nm (metal) lead; (ELEC) fuse; **sin ~** unleaded

pluma |'pluma| nf feather; (para escribir): **~ (estilográfica)** ink pen; **~ fuente** (AM) fountain pen

plumero |plu'mero| nm (para el polvo) feather duster

plumón |plu'mon| nm (de ave) down; (AM: fino) felt-tip pen; (: ancho) marker

plural |plu'ral| adj plural; **~idad** nf plurality

pluriempleo |pluriem'pleo| nm having more than one job

plus |plus| nm bonus; **~valía** nf (COM) appreciation

población |poβla'θjon| nf population; (pueblo, ciudad) town, city

poblado, a |po'βlaðo, a| adj inhabited ♦ nm (aldea) village; (pueblo) (small) town; **densamente ~** densely populated

poblador, a |poβla'ðor, a| nm/f settler, colonist

poblar |po'βlar| vt (colonizar) to colonize; (fundar) to found; (habitar) to inhabit

pobre |'poβre| adj poor ♦ nm/f poor person; **~za** nf poverty

pocilga |po'θilxa| nf pigsty

pócima |'poθima| nf = **poción**

PALABRA CLAVE
---

poco, a |'poko, a| adj **1** (sg) little, not much; **~ tiempo** little o not much time; **de ~ interés** of little interest, not very interesting; **poca cosa** not much

2 (pl) few, not many; **unos ~s** a few, some; **~s niños comen lo que les conviene** few children eat what they should

♦ adv **1** little, not much; **cuesta ~** it doesn't cost much

2 (+ adj: = negativo, antónimo): **~ amable/ inteligente** not very nice/intelligent

3: **por ~ me caigo** I almost fell

4: **a ~: a ~ de haberse casado** shortly after getting married

5: **~ a ~** little by little

♦ nm a little, a bit; **un ~ triste/de dinero** a little sad/money

---
podar |po'ðar| vt to prune

PALABRA CLAVE
---

poder |po'ðer| vi **1** (capacidad) can, be able to; **no puedo hacerlo** I can't do it, I'm unable to do it

2 (permiso) can, may, be allowed to; **¿se puede?** may I (o we)?; **puedes irte ahora** you may go now; **no se puede fumar en este hospital** smoking is not allowed in this hospital

3 (posibilidad) may, might, could; **puede llegar mañana** he may o might arrive tomorrow; **pudiste haberte hecho daño** you might o could have hurt yourself; **¡podías habérmelo dicho antes!** you might have told me before!

4: **puede ser: puede ser** perhaps; **puede ser que lo sepa Tomás** Tomás may o might know

5: **¡no puedo más!** I've had enough!; **no pude menos que dejarlo** I couldn't help but leave it; **es tonto a más no ~** he's as stupid as they come

6: **~ con: no puedo con este crío** this kid's too

much for me
♦ *nm* power; ~ **adquisitivo** purchasing
power; **detentar** *o* **ocupar** *o* **estar en el** ~ to be
in power

poderoso, a |poðe'roso, a| *adj* (*político, país*)
powerful
podio |'poðjo| *nm* (*DEPORTE*) podium
podium |'poðjum| = **podio**
podrido, a |po'ðriðo, a| *adj* rotten, bad;
(*fig*) rotten, corrupt
podrir |po'ðrir| = **pudrir**
poema |po'ema| *nm* poem
poesía |poe'sia| *nf* poetry
poeta |po'eta| *nm/f* poet; **poético, a** *adj*
poetic(al)
poetisa |poe'tisa| *nf* (woman) poet
póker |'poker| *nm* poker
polaco, a |po'lako, a| *adj* Polish ♦ *nm/f*
Pole
polar |po'lar| *adj* polar; **~idad** *nf* polarity;
~izarse *vr* to polarize
polea |po'lea| *nf* pulley
polémica |po'lemika| *nf* polemics *sg*; (*una* ~)
controversy, polemic
polen |'polen| *nm* pollen
policía |poli'θia| *nm/f* policeman/woman
♦ *nf* police; **~co, a** *adj* police *cpd*; **novela
policíaca** detective story; **policial** *adj* police
cpd
polideportivo |poliðepor'tiβo| *nm* sports
centre *o* complex
poligamia |poli'vamja| *nf* polygamy
polígono |po'livono| *nm* (*MAT*) polygon;
~ **industrial** industrial estate
polilla |po'liʎa| *nf* moth
polio |'poljo| *nf* polio
política |po'litika| *nf* politics *sg*; (*económica,
agraria etc*) policy; *ver tb* **político**
político, a |po'litiko, a| *adj* political;
(*discreto*) tactful; (*de familia*) -in-law ♦ *nm/f*
politician; **padre** ~ father-in-law
póliza |'poliθa| *nf* certificate, voucher;
(*impuesto*) tax stamp; ~ **de seguros** insurance
policy
polizón |poli'θon| *nm* stowaway
pollera |po'ʎera| (*AM*) *nf* skirt
pollería |poʎe'ria| *nf* poulterer's (shop)
pollo |'poʎo| *nm* chicken
polo |'polo| *nm* (*GEO, ELEC*) pole; (*helado*) ice
lolly; (*DEPORTE*) polo; (*suéter*) polo-neck;
~ **Norte/Sur** North/South Pole
Polonia |po'lonja| *nf* Poland
poltrona |pol'trona| *nf* easy chair
polución |polu'θjon| *nf* pollution
polvera |pol'βera| *nf* powder compact
polvo |'polβo| *nm* dust; (*QUÍM, CULIN, MED*)
powder; **~s** *nmpl* (*maquillaje*) powder *sg*;
quitar el ~ to dust; ~ **de talco** talcum powder;

estar hecho ~ (*fam*) to be worn out *o*
exhausted
pólvora |'polβora| *nf* gunpowder; (*fuegos
artificiales*) fireworks *pl*
polvoriento, a |polβo'rjento, a| *adj*
(*superficie*) dusty; (*sustancia*) powdery
pomada |po'maða| *nf* cream, ointment
pomelo |po'melo| *nm* grapefruit
pómez |'pomeθ| *nf*: **piedra** ~ pumice stone
pomo |'pomo| *nm* doorknob
pompa |'pompa| *nf* (*burbuja*) bubble;
(*bomba*) pump; (*esplendor*) pomp,
splendour; **pomposo, a** *adj* splendid,
magnificent; (*pey*) pompous
pómulo |'pomulo| *nm* cheekbone
pon |pon| *vb ver* **poner**
ponche |'pontʃe| *nm* punch
poncho |'pontʃo| *nm* poncho
ponderar |ponde'rar| *vt* (*considerar*) to
weigh up, consider; (*elogiar*) to praise highly,
speak in praise of
pondré *etc vb ver* **poner**

| PALABRA CLAVE |
---

poner |po'ner| *vt* **1** (*colocar*) to put;
(*telegrama*) to send; (*obra de teatro*) to put
on; (*película*) to show; **¿qué ponen en el Excelsior?** what's on
at the Excelsior?
2 (*tienda*) to open; (*instalar: gas etc*) to put
in; (*radio, TV*) to switch *o* turn on
3 (*suponer*): **pongamos que ...** let's suppose
that ...
4 (*contribuir*): **el gobierno ha puesto otro
millón** the government has contributed
another million
5 (*TELEC*): **póngame con el Sr. López** can you
put me through to Mr. López?
6: ~ **de**: **le han puesto de director general**
they've appointed him general manager
7 (+ *adj*) to make; **me estás poniendo
nerviosa** you're making me nervous
8 (*dar nombre*): **al hijo le pusieron Diego** they
called their son Diego
♦ *vi* (*gallina*) to lay
♦ **~se** *vr* **1** (*colocarse*): **se puso a mi lado** he
came and stood beside me; **tú ponte en esa
silla** you go and sit on that chair
2 (*vestido, cosméticos*) to put on; **¿por qué no
te pones el vestido nuevo?** why don't you put
on *o* wear your new dress?
3 (+ *adj*) to turn; to get, become; **se puso
muy serio** he got very serious; **después de
lavarla la tela se puso azul** after washing it
the material turned blue
4: **~se a**: **se puso a llorar** he started to cry;
tienes que ~te a estudiar you must get down
to studying
5: **~se a bien con uno** to make it up with sb;

~se a mal con uno to get on the wrong side of sb

pongo etc vb ver **poner**

poniente [po'njente] nm (occidente) west; (viento) west wind

pontífice [pon'tifiθe] nm pope, pontiff

popa ['popa] nf stern

popular [popu'lar] adj popular; (cultura) of the people, folk cpd; **~idad** nf popularity; **~izarse** vr to become popular

---

PALABRA CLAVE

por [por] prep **1** (objetivo) for; **luchar ~ la patria** to fight for one's country

2 (+ infin): **~ no llegar tarde** so as not to arrive late; **~ citar unos ejemplos** to give a few examples

3 (causa) out of, because of; **~ escasez de fondos** through o for lack of funds

4 (tiempo): **~ la mañana/noche** in the morning/at night; **se queda ~ una semana** she's staying (for) a week

5 (lugar): **pasar ~ Madrid** to pass through Madrid; **ir a Guayaquil ~ Quito** to go to Guayaquil via Quito; **caminar ~ la calle** to walk along the street; ver tb **todo**

6 (cambio, precio): **te doy uno nuevo ~ el que tienes** I'll give you a new one (in return) for the one you've got

7 (valor distributivo): **550 pesetas ~ hora/cabeza** 550 pesetas an o per hour/a o per head

8 (modo, medio) by; **~ correo/avión** by post/air; **día ~ día** day by day; **entrar ~ la entrada principal** to go in through the main entrance

9: **10 ~ 10 son 100** 10 times 10 is 100

10 (en lugar de): **vino él ~ su jefe** he came instead of his boss

11: **~ mí que revienten** as far as I'm concerned they can drop dead

12: **¿~ qué?** why?; **¿~ qué no?** why not?

---

porcelana [porθe'lana] nf porcelain; (china) china

porcentaje [porθen'taxe] nm percentage

porción [por'θjon] nf (parte) portion, share; (cantidad) quantity, amount

pordiosero, a [pordjo'sero, a] nm/f beggar

porfiar [por'fjar] vi to persist, insist; (disputar) to argue stubbornly

pormenor [porme'nor] nm detail, particular

pornografía [pornoxra'fia] nf pornography

poro ['poro] nm pore; **~so, a** adj porous

porque ['porke] conj (a causa de) because; (ya que) since; (con el fin de) so that, in order that

porqué [por'ke] nm reason, cause

porquería [porke'ria] nf (suciedad) filth, dirt; (acción) dirty trick; (objeto) small thing, trifle; (fig) rubbish

porra ['porra] nf (arma) stick, club

porrazo [po'rraθo] nm blow, bump

porro ['porro] (fam) nm (droga) joint (fam)

porrón [po'rron] nm glass wine jar with a long spout

portaaviones [porta(a)βjones] nm inv aircraft carrier

portada [por'taða] nf (de revista) cover

portador, a [porta'ðor, a] nm/f carrier, bearer; (COM) bearer, payee

portaequipajes [portaeki'paxes] nm inv (AUTO: maletero) boot; (: baca) luggage rack

portal [por'tal] nm (entrada) vestibule, hall; (portada) porch, doorway; (puerta de entrada) main door

portamaletas [portama'letas] nm inv (AUTO: maletero) boot; (: baca) roof rack

portarse [por'tarse] vr to behave, conduct o.s.

portátil [por'tatil] adj portable

portavoz [porta'βoθ] nm/f spokesman/woman

portazo [por'taθo] nm: **dar un ~** to slam the door

porte ['porte] nm (COM) transport; (precio) transport charges pl

portento [por'tento] nm marvel, wonder; **~so, a** adj marvellous, extraordinary

porteño, a [por'teno, a] adj of o from Buenos Aires

portería [porte'ria] nf (oficina) porter's office; (DEPORTE) goal

portero, a [por'tero, a] nm/f porter; (conserje) caretaker; (ujier) doorman; (DEPORTE) goalkeeper; **~ automático** intercom

pórtico ['portiko] nm (patio) portico, porch; (fig) gateway; (arcada) arcade

portorriqueño, a [portorri'keno, a] adj Puerto Rican

Portugal [portu'val] nm Portugal; **portugués, esa** adj, nm/f Portuguese ♦ nm (LING) Portuguese

porvenir [porβe'nir] nm future

pos [pos] prep: **en ~ de** after, in pursuit of

posada [po'saða] nf (refugio) shelter, lodging; (mesón) guest house; **dar ~ a** to give shelter to, take in

posaderas [posa'ðeras] nfpl backside sg, buttocks

posar [po'sar] vt (en el suelo) to lay down, put down; (la mano) to place, put gently ♦ vi (modelo) to sit, pose; **~se** vr to settle; (pájaro) to perch; (avión) to land, come down

posavasos [posa'basos] nm inv coaster; (para cerveza) beermat

posdata [pos'ðata] nf postscript

pose ['pose] nf pose

poseedor, a [posee'ðor, a] nm/f owner,

possessor; (*de récord, puesto*) holder

poseer [pose'er] *vt* to possess, own; (*ventaja*) to enjoy; (*récord, puesto*) to hold

posesión [pose'sjon] *nf* possession; **posesionarse** *vr:* **posesionarse de** to take possession of, take over

posesivo, a [pose'sißo, a] *adj* possessive

posgrado [pos'graðo] *nm:* **curso de ~** postgraduate course

posibilidad [posißili'ðaθ] *nf* possibility; (*oportunidad*) chance; **posibilitar** *vt* to make possible; (*hacer realizable*) to make feasible

posible [po'sißle] *adj* possible; (*realizable*) feasible; **de ser ~** if possible; **en lo ~** as far as possible

posición [posi'θjon] *nf* position; (*rango social*) status

positivo, a [posi'tißo, a] *adj* positive

poso ['poso] *nm* sediment; (*heces*) dregs *pl*

posponer [pospo'ner] *vt* (*relegar*) to put behind/below; (*aplazar*) to postpone

posta ['posta] *nf:* **a ~** deliberately, on purpose

postal [pos'tal] *adj* postal ♦ *nf* postcard

poste ['poste] *nm* (*de telégrafos etc*) post, pole; (*columna*) pillar

póster ['poster] (*pl* **pósteres, pósters**) *nm* poster

postergar [poster'var] *vt* to postpone, delay

posteridad [posteri'ðaθ] *nf* posterity

posterior [poste'rjor] *adj* back, rear; (*siguiente*) following, subsequent; (*más tarde*) later; **~idad** *nf:* **con ~idad** later, subsequently

postgrado [pos'graðo] *nm* = **posgrado**

postizo, a [pos'tiθo, a] *adj* false, artificial ♦ *nm* hairpiece

postor, a [pos'tor, a] *nm/f* bidder

postre ['postre] *nm* sweet, dessert

postrero, a [pos'trero, a] (*delante de nmsg:* **postrer**) *adj* (*último*) last; (*que viene detrás*) rear

postulado [postu'laðo] *nm* postulate

póstumo, a ['postumo, a] *adj* posthumous

postura [pos'tura] *nf* (*del cuerpo*) posture, position; (*fig*) attitude, position

potable [po'taßle] *adj* drinkable; **agua ~** drinking water

potaje [po'taxe] *nm* thick vegetable soup

pote ['pote] *nm* pot, jar

potencia [po'tenθja] *nf* power; **~l** [poten'θjal] *adj, nm* potential; **~r** *vt* to boost

potente [po'tente] *adj* powerful

potro, a ['potro, a] *nm/f* (*ZOOL*) colt/filly ♦ *nm* (*de gimnasia*) vaulting horse

pozo ['poθo] *nm* well; (*de río*) deep pool; (*de mina*) shaft

P.P. *abr* (= *porte pagado*) CP

práctica ['praktika] *nf* practice; (*método*) method; (*arte, capacidad*) skill; **en la ~** in practice

practicable [prakti'kaßle] *adj* practicable; (*camino*) passable

practicante [prakti'kante] *nm/f* (*MED:* *ayudante de doctor*) medical assistant; (*: enfermero*) nurse; (*quien practica algo*) practitioner ♦ *adj* practising

practicar [prakti'kar] *vt* to practise; (*DEPORTE*) to play; (*realizar*) to carry out, perform

práctico, a ['praktiko, a] *adj* practical; (*instruido: persona*) skilled, expert

practique *etc vb ver* **practicar**

pradera [pra'ðera] *nf* meadow; (*US etc*) prairie

prado ['praðo] *nm* (*campo*) meadow, field; (*pastizal*) pasture

Praga ['praxa] *n* Prague

pragmático, a [prav'matiko, a] *adj* pragmatic

preámbulo [pre'ambulo] *nm* preamble, introduction

precario, a [pre'karjo, a] *adj* precarious

precaución [prekau'θjon] *nf* (*medida preventiva*) preventive measure, precaution; (*prudencia*) caution, wariness

precaver [preka'ßer] *vt* to guard against; (*impedir*) to forestall; **~se** *vr:* **~se de** o **contra algo** to (be on one's) guard against sth; **precavido, a** *adj* cautious, wary

precedente [preθe'ðente] *adj* preceding; (*anterior*) former ♦ *nm* precedent

preceder [preθe'ðer] *vt, vi* to precede, go before, come before

precepto [pre'θepto] *nm* precept

preciado, a [pre'θjaðo, a] *adj* (*estimado*) esteemed, valuable

preciarse [pre'θjarse] *vr* to boast; **~se de** to pride o.s. on, boast of being

precinto [pre'θinto] *nm* (*tb:* **~ de garantía**) seal

precio ['preθjo] *nm* price; (*costo*) cost; (*valor*) value, worth; (*de viaje*) fare; **~ al contado/de coste/de oportunidad** cash/cost/bargain price; **~ al detalle** o **al por menor** retail price; **~ tope** top price

preciosidad [preθjosi'ðaθ] *nf* (*valor*) (high) value, (great) worth; (*encanto*) charm; (*cosa bonita*) beautiful thing; **es una ~** it's lovely, it's really beautiful

precioso, a [pre'θjoso, a] *adj* precious; (*de mucho valor*) valuable; (*fam*) lovely, beautiful

precipicio [preθi'piθjo] *nm* cliff, precipice; (*fig*) abyss

precipitación [preθipita'θjon] *nf* haste; (*lluvia*) rainfall

precipitado, a [preθipi'taðo, a] *adj* (*conducta*) hasty, rash; (*salida*) hasty, sudden

precipitar [preθipi'tar] *vt* (*arrojar*) to hurl down, throw; (*apresurar*) to hasten; (*acelerar*) to speed up, accelerate; **~se** *vr* to throw o.s.; (*apresurarse*) to rush; (*actuar sin pensar*) to act rashly

precisamente [preθisa'mente] *adv* precisely; (*exactamente*) precisely, exactly

precisar [preθi'sar] *vt* (*necesitar*) to need, require; (*fijar*) to determine exactly, fix; (*especificar*) to specify

precisión [preθi'sjon] *nf* (*exactitud*) precision

preciso, a [pre'θiso, a] *adj* (*exacto*) precise; (*necesario*) necessary, essential

preconcebido, a [prekonθe'βiðo, a] *adj* preconceived

precoz [pre'koθ] *adj* (*persona*) precocious; (*calvicie etc*) premature

precursor, a [prekur'sor, a] *nm/f* predecessor, forerunner

predecir [preðe'θir] *vt* to predict, forecast

predestinado, a [preðesti'naðo, a] *adj* predestined

predicar [preði'kar] *vt, vi* to preach

predicción [preðik'θjon] *nf* prediction

predilecto, a [preði'lekto, a] *adj* favourite

predisponer [preðispo'ner] *vt* to predispose; (*pey*) to prejudice; **predisposición** *nf* inclination; prejudice, bias

predominante [preðomi'nante] *adj* predominant

predominar [preðomi'nar] *vt* to dominate ♦ *vi* to predominate; (*prevalecer*) to prevail; **predominio** *nm* predominance; prevalence

preescolar [pre(e)sko'lar] *adj* preschool

prefabricado, a [prefaβri'kaðo, a] *adj* prefabricated

prefacio [pre'faθjo] *nm* preface

preferencia [prefe'renθja] *nf* preference; **de ~** preferably, for preference

preferible [prefe'riβle] *adj* preferable

preferir [prefe'rir] *vt* to prefer

prefiero *etc vb ver* **preferir**

prefijo [pre'fixo] *nm* (*TELEC*) (dialling) code

pregonar [preɣo'nar] *vt* to proclaim, announce

pregunta [pre'ɣunta] *nf* question; **hacer una ~** to ask a question

preguntar [preɣun'tar] *vt* to ask; (*cuestionar*) to question ♦ *vi* to ask; **~se** *vr* to wonder; **~ por alguien** to ask for sb

preguntón, ona [preɣun'ton, ona] *adj* inquisitive

prehistórico, a [preis'toriko, a] *adj* prehistoric

prejuicio [pre'xwiθjo] *nm* (*acto*) prejudgement; (*idea preconcebida*) preconception; (*parcialidad*) prejudice, bias

preliminar [prelimi'nar] *adj* preliminary

preludio [pre'luðjo] *nm* prelude

prematuro, a [prema'turo, a] *adj* premature

premeditación [premeðita'θjon] *nf* premeditation

premeditar [premeði'tar] *vt* to premeditate

premiar [pre'mjar] *vt* to reward; (*en un concurso*) to give a prize to

premio ['premjo] *nm* reward; prize; (*COM*) premium

premonición [premoni'θjon] *nf* premonition

prenatal [prena'tal] *adj* antenatal, prenatal

prenda ['prenda] *nf* (*ropa*) garment, article of clothing; (*garantía*) pledge; **~s** *nfpl* (*talentos*) talents, gifts

prendedor [prende'ðor] *nm* brooch

prender [pren'der] *vt* (*captar*) to catch, capture; (*detener*) to arrest; (*COSTURA*) to pin, attach; (*sujetar*) to fasten ♦ *vi* to catch; (*arraigar*) to take root; **~se** *vr* (*encenderse*) to catch fire

prendido, a [pren'diðo, a] (*AM*) *adj* (*luz etc*) on

prensa ['prensa] *nf* press; **la ~** the press; **prensar** *vt* to press

preñado, a [pre'ɲaðo, a] *adj* pregnant; **~ de** pregnant with, full of

preocupación [preokupa'θjon] *nf* worry, concern; (*ansiedad*) anxiety

preocupado, a [preoku'paðo, a] *adj* worried, concerned; (*ansioso*) anxious

preocupar [preoku'par] *vt* to worry; **~se** *vr* to worry; **~se de algo** (*hacerse cargo*) to take care of sth

preparación [prepara'θjon] *nf* (*acto*) preparation; (*estado*) readiness; (*entrenamiento*) training

preparado, a [prepa'raðo, a] *adj* (*dispuesto*) prepared; (*CULIN*) ready (to serve) ♦ *nm* preparation

preparar [prepa'rar] *vt* (*disponer*) to prepare, get ready; (*TEC: tratar*) to prepare, process; (*entrenar*) to teach, train; **~se** *vr*: **~se a o para** to prepare to o for, get ready to o for; **preparativo, a** *adj* preparatory, preliminary; **preparativos** *nmpl* preparations; **preparatoria** (*AM*) *nf* sixth-form college (*BRIT*), senior high school (*US*)

prerrogativa [prerroɣa'tiβa] *nf* prerogative, privilege

presa ['presa] *nf* (*cosa apresada*) catch; (*víctima*) victim; (*de animal*) prey; (*de agua*) dam

presagiar [presa'xjar] *vt* to presage, forebode; **presagio** *nm* omen

prescindir [presθin'dir] *vi*: **~ de** (*privarse de*) to do without, go without; (*descartar*) to dispense with

prescribir [preskri'βir] *vt* to prescribe; **prescripción** *nf* prescription

presencia [pre'senθja] *nf* presence; **presencial** *adj*: **testigo presencial** eyewitness; **presenciar** *vt* to be present at;

(*asistir a*) to attend; (*ver*) to see, witness

presentación [presenta'θjon] *nf* presentation; (*introducción*) introduction

presentador, a [presenta'ðor, a] *nm/f* presenter, compère

presentar [presen'tar] *vt* to present; (*ofrecer*) to offer; (*mostrar*) to show, display; (*a una persona*) to introduce; **~se** *vr* (*llegar inesperadamente*) to appear, turn up; (*ofrecerse como candidato*) to run, stand; (*aparecer*) to show, appear; (*solicitar empleo*) to apply

presente [pre'sente] *adj* present ♦ *nm* present; **hacer ~** to state, declare; **tener ~** to remember, bear in mind

presentimiento [presenti'mjento] *nm* premonition, presentiment

presentir [presen'tir] *vt* to have a premonition of

preservación [preserßa'θjon] *nf* protection, preservation

preservar [preser'ßar] *vt* to protect, preserve; **preservativo** *nm* sheath, condom

presidencia [presi'ðenθja] *nf* presidency; (*de comité*) chairmanship

presidente [presi'ðente] *nm/f* president; (*de comité*) chairman/woman

presidiario [presi'ðjarjo] *nm* convict

presidio [pre'sidjo] *nm* prison, penitentiary

presidir [presi'ðir] *vt* (*dirigir*) to preside at, preside over; (: *comité*) to take the chair at; (*dominar*) to dominate, rule ♦ *vi* to preside; to take the chair

presión [pre'sjon] *nf* pressure; **presionar** *vt* to press; (*fig*) to press, put pressure on ♦ *vi*: **presionar para** to press for

preso, a [ˈpreso, a] *nm/f* prisoner; **tomar o llevar ~ a uno** to arrest sb, take sb prisoner

prestación [presta'θjon] *nf* service; (*subsidio*) benefit; **prestaciones** *nfpl* (*TEC, AUT*) performance features

prestado, a [pres'taðo, a] *adj* on loan; **pedir ~** to borrow

prestamista [presta'mista] *nm/f* moneylender

préstamo ['prestamo] *nm* loan; **~ hipotecario** mortgage

prestar [pres'tar] *vt* to lend, loan; (*atención*) to pay; (*ayuda*) to give

presteza [pres'teθa] *nf* speed, promptness

prestigio [pres'tixjo] *nm* prestige; **~so, a** *adj* (*honorable*) prestigious; (*famoso, renombrado*) renowned, famous

presumido, a [presu'miðo, a] *adj* (*persona*) vain

presumir [presu'mir] *vt* to presume ♦ *vi* (*tener aires*) to be conceited; **según cabe ~** as may be presumed, presumably; **presunción** *nf* presumption; **presunto, a** *adj* (*supuesto*)

supposed, presumed; (*así llamado*) so-called;

presuntuoso, a *adj* conceited, presumptuous

presuponer [presupo'ner] *vt* to presuppose

presupuesto [presu'pwesto] *pp de* **presuponer** ♦ *nm* (*FINANZAS*) budget; (*estimación: de costo*) estimate

pretencioso, a [preten'θjoso, a] *adj* pretentious

pretender [preten'der] *vt* (*intentar*) to try to, seek to; (*reivindicar*) to claim; (*buscar*) to seek, try for; (*cortejar*) to woo, court; **~ que** to expect that; **pretendiente** *nm/f* (*amante*) suitor; (*al trono*) pretender; **pretensión** *nf* (*aspiración*) aspiration; (*reivindicación*) claim; (*orgullo*) pretension

pretexto [pre'teksto] *nm* pretext; (*excusa*) excuse

prevalecer [preßale'θer] *vi* to prevail

prevención [preßen'θjon] *nf* prevention; (*precaución*) precaution

prevenido, a [preße'niðo, a] *adj* prepared, ready; (*cauteloso*) cautious

prevenir [preße'nir] *vt* (*impedir*) to prevent; (*predisponer*) to prejudice, bias; (*avisar*) to warn; (*preparar*) to prepare, get ready; **~se** *vr* to get ready, prepare; **~se contra** to take precautions against; **preventivo, a** *adj* preventive, precautionary

prever [pre'ßer] *vt* to foresee

previo, a ['preßjo, a] *adj* (*anterior*) previous; (*preliminar*) preliminary ♦ *prep*: **~ acuerdo de los otros** subject to the agreement of the others

previsión [preßi'sjon] *nf* (*perspicacia*) foresight; (*predicción*) forecast; **previsto, a** *adj* anticipated, forecast

prima ['prima] *nf* (*COM*) bonus; **~ de seguro** insurance premium; *ver tb* **primo**

primacía [prima'θia] *nf* primacy

primario, a [pri'marjo, a] *adj* primary

primavera [prima'ßera] *nf* spring(-time)

primera [pri'mera] *nf* (*AUTO*) first gear; (*FERRO: tb*: **~ clase**) first class; **de ~** (*fam*) first-class, first-rate

primero, a [pri'mero, a] (*delante de nmsg*: **primer**) *adj* first; (*principal*) prime ♦ *adv* first; (*más bien*) sooner, rather; **primera plana** front page

primicia [pri'miθja] *nf* (*tb*: **~ informativa**) scoop

primitivo, a [primi'tißo, a] *adj* primitive; (*original*) original

primo, a ['primo, a] *adj* prime ♦ *nm/f* cousin; (*fam*) fool, idiot; **~ hermano** first cousin; **materias primas** raw materials

primogénito, a [primo'xenito, a] *adj* first-born

primordial [primor'ðjal] *adj* basic,

fundamental
primoroso, a [priˈmoroso, a] *adj* exquisite,
delicate
princesa [prinˈθesa] *nf* princess
principal [prinθiˈpal] *adj* principal, main
♦ *nm* (*jefe*) chief, principal
príncipe [ˈprinθipe] *nm* prince
principiante [prinθiˈpjante] *nm/f* beginner
principio [prinˈθipjo] *nm* (*comienzo*)
beginning, start; (*origen*) origin; (*primera
etapa*) rudiment, basic idea; (*moral*)
principle; **a ~s de** at the beginning of
pringoso, a [prinˈɣoso, a] *adj* (*grasiento*)
greasy; (*pegajoso*) sticky
pringue [ˈpringe] *nm* (*grasa*) grease, fat,
dripping
prioridad [prioriˈðað] *nf* priority
prisa [ˈprisa] *nf* (*apresuramiento*) hurry, haste;
(*rapidez*) speed; (*urgencia*) (sense of)
urgency; **a o de ~** quickly; **correr ~** to be
urgent; **darse ~** to hurry up; **estar de o tener
~** to be in a hurry
prisión [priˈsjon] *nf* (*cárcel*) prison; (*período
de cárcel*) imprisonment; **prisionero, a** *nm/f*
prisoner
prismáticos [prisˈmatikos] *nmpl* binoculars
privación [priβaˈθjon] *nf* deprivation; (*falta*)
want, privation
privado, a [priˈβaðo, a] *adj* private
privar [priˈβar] *vt* to deprive; **privativo, a**
adj exclusive
privilegiado, a [priβileˈxjaðo, a] *adj*
privileged; (*memoria*) very good
privilegiar [priβileˈxjar] *vt* to grant a
privilege to; (*favorecer*) to favour
privilegio [priβiˈlexjo] *nm* privilege;
(*concesión*) concession
pro [pro] *nm o f* profit, advantage ♦ *prep*:
asociación ~ ciegos association for the blind
♦ *prefijo*: **~ soviético/americano** pro-Soviet/
American; **en ~ de** on behalf of, for; **los ~s y
los contras** the pros and cons
proa [ˈproa] *nf* bow, prow; **de ~** bow *cpd*, fore
probabilidad [proβaβiliˈðað] *nf* probability,
likelihood; (*oportunidad, posibilidad*) chance,
prospect; **probable** *adj* probable, likely
probador [proβaˈðor] *nm* (*en tienda*) fitting
room
probar [proˈβar] *vt* (*demostrar*) to prove;
(*someter a prueba*) to test, try out; (*ropa*) to
try on; (*comida*) to taste ♦ *vi* to try; **~se un
traje** to try on a suit
probeta [proˈβeta] *nf* test tube
problema [proˈβlema] *nm* problem
procedente [proθeˈðente] *adj* (*razonable*)
reasonable; (*conforme a derecho*) proper,
fitting; **~ de** coming from, originating in
proceder [proθeˈðer] *vi* (*avanzar*) to
proceed; (*actuar*) to act; (*ser correcto*) to be

right (and proper), be fitting ♦ *nm*
(*comportamiento*) behaviour, conduct; **~ de**
to come from, originate in; **procedimiento**
nm procedure; (*proceso*) process; (*método*)
means *pl*, method
procesado, a [proθeˈsaðo, a] *nm/f* accused
procesador [proθesaˈðor] *nm*: **~ de textos**
word processor
procesar [proθeˈsar] *vt* to try, put on trial
procesión [proθeˈsjon] *nf* procession
proceso [proˈθeso] *nm* process; (*JUR*) trial
proclamar [proklaˈmar] *vt* to proclaim
procreación [prokreaˈθjon] *nf* procreation
procrear [prokreˈar] *vt, vi* to procreate
procurador, a [prokuraˈðor, a] *nm/f*
attorney
procurar [prokuˈrar] *vt* (*intentar*) to try,
endeavour; (*conseguir*) to get, obtain;
(*asegurar*) to secure; (*producir*) to produce
prodigio [proˈðixjo] *nm* prodigy; (*milagro*)
wonder, marvel; **~so, a** *adj* prodigious,
marvellous
pródigo, a [ˈproðiɣo, a] *adj*: **hijo ~** prodigal
son
producción [proðukˈθjon] *nf* (*gen*)
production; (*producto*) output; **~ en serie**
mass production
producir [proðuˈθir] *vt* to produce; (*causar*)
to cause, bring about; **~se** *vr* (*cambio*) to
come about; (*accidente*) to take place;
(*problema etc*) to arise; (*hacerse*) to be
produced, be made; (*estallar*) to break out
productividad [proðuktiβiˈðað] *nf*
productivity; **productivo, a** *adj* productive;
(*provechoso*) profitable
producto [proˈðukto] *nm* product
productor, a [proðukˈtor, a] *adj* productive,
producing ♦ *nm/f* producer
proeza [proˈeθa] *nf* exploit, feat
profanar [profaˈnar] *vt* to desecrate, profane;
profano, a *adj* profane ♦ *nm/f* layman/
woman
profecía [profeˈθia] *nf* prophecy
proferir [profeˈrir] *vt* (*palabra, sonido*) to
utter; (*injuria*) to hurl, let fly
profesión [profeˈsjon] *nf* profession;
profesional *adj* professional
profesor, a [profeˈsor, a] *nm/f* teacher;
~ado *nm* teaching profession
profeta [proˈfeta] *nm/f* prophet; **profetizar**
vt, vi to prophesy
prófugo, a [ˈprofuɣo, a] *nm/f* fugitive; (*MIL*:
desertor) deserter
profundidad [profundiˈðað] *nf* depth;
profundizar *vi*: **profundizar en** to go deeply
into; **profundo, a** *adj* deep; (*misterio,
pensador*) profound
progenitor [proxeniˈtor] *nm* ancestor; **~es**
nmpl (*padres*) parents

programa [pro'ɣrama] *nm* programme
(*BRIT*), program (*US*); **~ción** *nf* programming;
~dor, a *nm/f* programmer; **programar** *vt* to
program

progresar [proɣre'sar] *vi* to progress, make
progress; **progresista** *adj, nm/f* progressive;
progresivo, a *adj* progressive; (*gradual*)
gradual; (*continuo*) continuous; **progreso**
nm progress

prohibición [proiβi'θjon] *nf* prohibition, ban

prohibir [proi'βir] *vt* to prohibit, ban, forbid;
se prohibe fumar, prohibido fumar no
smoking; **"prohibido el paso"** "no entry"

prójimo, a ['proximo, a] *nm/f* fellow man;
(*vecino*) neighbour

proletariado [proleta'rjaðo] *nm* proletariat

proletario, a [prole'tarjo, a] *adj, nm/f*
proletarian

proliferación [prolifera'θjon] *nf* proliferation

proliferar [prolife'rar] *vi* to proliferate;
prolífico, a *adj* prolific

prólogo ['proloɣo] *nm* prologue

prolongación [prolonga'θjon] *nf* extension;
prolongado, a *adj* (*largo*) long; (*alargado*)
lengthy

prolongar [prolon'ɣar] *vt* to extend;
(*reunión etc*) to prolong; (*calle, tubo*) to
extend

promedio [pro'meðjo] *nm* average; (*de
distancia*) middle, mid-point

promesa [pro'mesa] *nf* promise

prometer [prome'ter] *vt* to promise ♦ *vi* to
show promise; **~se** *vr* (*novios*) to get
engaged; **prometido, a** *adj* promised;
engaged ♦ *nm/f* fiancé/fiancée

prominente [promi'nente] *adj* prominent

promiscuo, a [pro'miskwo, a] *adj*
promiscuous

promoción [promo'θjon] *nf* promotion

promotor [promo'tor] *nm* promoter;
(*instigador*) instigator

promover [promo'βer] *vt* to promote;
(*causar*) to cause; (*instigar*) to instigate, stir
up

promulgar [promul'ɣar] *vt* to promulgate;
(*anunciar*) to proclaim

pronombre [pro'nombre] *nm* pronoun

pronosticar [pronosti'kar] *vt* to predict,
foretell, forecast; **pronóstico** *nm* prediction,
forecast; **pronóstico del tiempo** weather
forecast

pronto, a ['pronto, a] *adj* (*rápido*) prompt,
quick; (*preparado*) ready ♦ *adv* quickly,
promptly; (*en seguida*) at once, right away;
(*dentro de poco*) soon; (*temprano*) early
♦ *nm*: **tener ~s de enojo** to be quick-
tempered; **de ~** suddenly; **por lo ~**
meanwhile, for the present

pronunciación [pronunθja'θjon] *nf*
pronunciation

pronunciar [pronun'θjar] *vt* to pronounce;
(*discurso*) to make, deliver; **~se** *vr* to revolt,
rebel; (*declararse*) to declare o.s.

propagación [propaɣa'θjon] *nf* propagation

propaganda [propa'ɣanda] *nf* (*política*)
propaganda; (*comercial*) advertising

propagar [propa'ɣar] *vt* to propagate

propensión [propen'sjon] *nf* inclination,
propensity; **propenso, a** *adj* inclined to; **ser
propenso a** to be inclined to, have a tendency
to

propicio, a [pro'piθjo, a] *adj* favourable,
propitious

propiedad [propje'ðað] *nf* property;
(*posesión*) possession, ownership; **~ particular**
private property

propietario, a [propje'tarjo, a] *nm/f* owner,
proprietor

propina [pro'pina] *nf* tip

propio, a ['propjo, a] *adj* own, of one's own;
(*característico*) characteristic, typical; (*debido*)
proper; (*mismo*) selfsame, very; **el ~ ministro**
the minister himself; **¿tienes casa propia?**
have you a house of your own?

proponer [propo'ner] *vt* to propose, put
forward; (*problema*) to pose; **~se** *vr* to
propose, intend

proporción [propor'θjon] *nf* proportion;
(*MAT*) ratio; **proporciones** *nfpl* (*dimensiones*)
dimensions; (*fig*) size say; **proporcionado, a**
adj proportionate; (*regular*) medium,
middling; (*justo*) just right; **proporcionar** *vt*
(*dar*) to give, supply, provide

proposición [proposi'θjon] *nf* proposition;
(*propuesta*) proposal

propósito [pro'posito] *nm* purpose; (*intento*)
aim, intention ♦ *adv*: **a ~** by the way,
incidentally; (*a posta*) on purpose,
deliberately; **a ~ de** about, with regard to

propuesta [pro'pwesta] *vb ver* **proponer** ♦ *nf*
proposal

propulsar [propul'sar] *vt* to drive, propel;
(*fig*) to promote, encourage; **propulsión** *nf*
propulsion; **propulsión a chorro** o **por reacción**
jet propulsion

prórroga ['prorroɣa] *nf* extension; (*JUR*) stay;
(*COM*) deferment; (*DEPORTE*) extra time;
prorrogar *vt* (*período*) to extend; (*decisión*)
to defer, postpone

prorrumpir [prorrum'pir] *vi* to burst forth,
break out

prosa ['prosa] *nf* prose

proscrito, a [pro'skrito, a] *adj* banned

proseguir [prose'ɣir] *vt* to continue, carry on
♦ *vi* to continue, go on

prospección [prospek'θjon] *nf* exploration;
(*del oro*) prospecting

prospecto [pros'pekto] *nm* prospectus

prosperar [prospe'rar] *vi* to prosper, thrive, flourish; **prosperidad** *nf* prosperity; (*éxito*) success; **próspero, a** *adj* prosperous, flourishing; (*que tiene éxito*) successful

prostíbulo [pros'tiβulo] *nm* brothel (*BRIT*), house of prostitution (*US*)

prostitución [prostitu'θjon] *nf* prostitution

prostituir [prosti'twir] *vt* to prostitute; **~se** *vr* to prostitute o.s., become a prostitute

prostituta [prosti'tuta] *nf* prostitute

protagonista [protaγo'nista] *nm/f* protagonist

protagonizar [protaγoni'θar] *vt* to take the chief rôle in

protección [protek'θjon] *nf* protection

protector, a [protek'tor, a] *adj* protective, protecting ♦ *nm/f* protector

proteger [prote'xer] *vt* to protect; **protegido, a** *nm/f* protégé/protégée

proteína [prote'ina] *nf* protein

protesta [pro'testa] *nf* protest; (*declaración*) protestation

protestante [protes'tante] *adj* Protestant

protestar [protes'tar] *vt* to protest, declare ♦ *vi* to protest

protocolo [proto'kolo] *nm* protocol

prototipo [proto'tipo] *nm* prototype

prov. *abr* (= *provincia*) prov

provecho [pro'βetʃo] *nm* advantage, benefit; (*FINANZAS*) profit; **¡buen ~!** bon appétit!; **en ~ de** to the benefit of; **sacar ~ de** to benefit from, profit by

proveer [proβe'er] *vt* to provide, supply ♦ *vi*: **~ a** to provide for

provenir [proβe'nir] *vi*: **~ de** to come from, stem from

proverbio [pro'βerβjo] *nm* proverb

providencia [proβi'ðenθja] *nf* providence

provincia [pro'βinθja] *nf* province; **~no, a** *adj* provincial; (*del campo*) country *cpd*

provisión [proβi'sjon] *nf* provision; (*abastecimiento*) provision, supply; (*medida*) measure, step

provisional [proβisjo'nal] *adj* provisional

provocación [proβoka'θjon] *nf* provocation

provocar [proβo'kar] *vt* to provoke; (*alentar*) to tempt, invite; (*causar*) to bring about, lead to; (*promover*) to promote; (*estimular*) to rouse, stimulate; **¿te provoca un café?** (*AM*) would you like a coffee?; **provocativo, a** *adj* provocative

próximamente [proksima'mente] *adv* shortly, soon

proximidad [proksimi'ðað] *nf* closeness, proximity; **próximo, a** *adj* near, close; (*vecino*) neighbouring; (*siguiente*) next

proyectar [projek'tar] *vt* (*objeto*) to hurl, throw; (*luz*) to cast, shed; (*CINE*) to screen, show; (*planear*) to plan

proyectil [projek'til] *nm* projectile, missile

proyecto [pro'jekto] *nm* plan; (*estimación de costo*) detailed estimate

proyector [projek'tor] *nm* (*CINE*) projector

prudencia [pru'ðenθja] *nf* (*sabiduría*) wisdom; (*cuidado*) care; **prudente** *adj* sensible, wise; (*conductor*) careful

prueba *etc* ['prweβa] *vb ver* **probar** ♦ *nf* proof; (*ensayo*) test, trial; (*degustación*) tasting, sampling; (*de ropa*) fitting; **a ~** on trial; **a ~ de** proof against; **a ~ de agua/fuego** waterproof/fireproof; **someter a ~** to put to the test

prurito [pru'rito] *nm* itch; (*de bebé*) nappy (*BRIT*) o diaper (*US*) rash

psico... [siko] *prefijo* psycho...; **~análisis** *nm inv* psychoanalysis; **~logía** *nf* psychology; **~lógico, a** *adj* psychological; **psicólogo, a** *nm/f* psychologist; **psicópata** *nm/f* psychopath; **~sis** *nf inv* psychosis

psiquiatra [si'kjatra] *nm/f* psychiatrist; **psiquiátrico, a** *adj* psychiatric

psíquico, a [si'kiko, a] *adj* psychic(al)

PSOE [pe'soe] *nm abr* = **Partido Socialista Obrero Español**

pta(s) *abr* = **peseta(s)**

pts *abr* = **pesetas**

púa ['pua] *nf* (*BOT, ZOOL*) prickle, spine; (*para guitarra*) plectrum (*BRIT*), pick (*US*); **alambre de ~** barbed wire

pubertad [puβer'tað] *nf* puberty

publicación [puβlika'θjon] *nf* publication

publicar [puβli'kar] *vt* (*editar*) to publish; (*hacer público*) to publicize; (*divulgar*) to make public, divulge

publicidad [puβliθi'ðað] *nf* publicity; (*COM: propaganda*) advertising; **publicitario, a** *adj* publicity *cpd*; advertising *cpd*

público, a ['puβliko, a] *adj* public ♦ *nm* public; (*TEATRO etc*) audience

puchero [pu'tʃero] *nm* (*CULIN: guiso*) stew; (: *olla*) cooking pot; **hacer ~s** to pout

pude *etc vb ver* **poder**

púdico, a ['puðiko, a] *adj* modest

pudiente [pu'ðjente] *adj* (*rico*) wealthy, well-to-do

pudiera *etc vb ver* **poder**

pudor [pu'ðor] *nm* modesty

pudrir [pu'ðrir] *vt* to rot; **~se** *vr* to rot, decay

pueblo ['pweβlo] *nm* people; (*nación*) nation; (*aldea*) village

puedo *etc vb ver* **poder**

puente ['pwente] *nm* bridge; **hacer ~** (*inf*) to take extra days off work between 2 public holidays; to take a long weekend; **~ aéreo** shuttle service; **~ colgante** suspension bridge

puerco, a ['pwerko, a] *nm/f* pig/sow ♦ *adj* (*sucio*) dirty, filthy; (*obsceno*) disgusting; **~ de mar** porpoise; **~ marino** dolphin

pueril [pwe'ril] adj childish

puerro ['pwerro] nm leek

puerta ['pwerta] nf door; (de jardín) gate; (portal) doorway; (fig) gateway; (portería) goal; **a la ~** at the door; **a ~ cerrada** behind closed doors; **~ giratoria** revolving door

puerto ['pwerto] nm port; (paso) pass; (fig) haven, refuge

Puerto Rico [pwerto'riko] nm Puerto Rico; **puertorriqueño, a** adj, nm/f Puerto Rican

pues [pwes] adv (entonces) then; (bueno) well, well then; (así que) so ♦ conj (ya que) since; ¡~! (sí) yes!, certainly!

puesta ['pwesta] nf (apuesta) bet, stake; **~ en marcha** starting; **~ del sol** sunset

puesto, a ['pwesto, a] pp de poner ♦ adj: **tener algo ~** to have sth on, be wearing sth ♦ nm (lugar, posición) place; (trabajo) post, job; (COM) stall ♦ conj: **~ que** since, as

púgil ['puxil] nm boxer

pugna ['puɣna] nf battle, conflict; **pugnar** vi (luchar) to struggle, fight; (pelear) to fight

pujar [pu'xar] vi (en subasta) to bid; (esforzarse) to struggle, strain

pulcro, a ['pulkro, a] adj neat, tidy

pulga ['pulɣa] nf flea

pulgada [pul'ɣaða] nf inch

pulgar [pul'ɣar] nm thumb

pulir [pu'lir] vt to polish; (alisar) to smooth; (fig) to polish up, touch up

pulla ['puʎa] nf cutting remark

pulmón [pul'mon] nm lung; **pulmonía** nf pneumonia

pulpa ['pulpa] nf pulp; (de fruta) flesh, soft part

pulpería [pulpe'ria] (AM) nf (tienda) small grocery store

púlpito ['pulpito] nm pulpit

pulpo ['pulpo] nm octopus

pulsación [pulsa'θjon] nf beat; **pulsaciones** pulse rate

pulsar [pul'sar] vt (tecla) to touch, tap; (MUS) to play; (botón) to press, push ♦ vi to pulsate; (latir) to beat, throb; (MED): **~ a uno** to take sb's pulse

pulsera [pul'sera] nf bracelet

pulso ['pulso] nm (ANAT) pulse; (fuerza) strength; (firmeza) steadiness, steady hand

pulverizador [pulβeriθa'ðor] nm spray, spray gun

pulverizar [pulβeri'θar] vt to pulverize; (líquido) to spray

puna ['puna] (AM) nf mountain sickness

punitivo, a [puni'tiβo, a] adj punitive

punta ['punta] nf point, tip; (extremidad) end; (fig) touch, trace; **horas ~s** peak hours, rush hours; **sacar ~ a** to sharpen

puntada [pun'taða] nf (COSTURA) stitch

puntal [pun'tal] nm prop, support

puntapié [punta'pje] nm kick

puntear [punte'ar] vt to tick, mark

puntería [punte'ria] nf (de arma) aim, aiming; (destreza) marksmanship

puntero, a [pun'tero, a] adj leading ♦ nm (palo) pointer

puntiagudo, a [puntja'ɣuðo, a] adj sharp, pointed

puntilla [pun'tiʎa] nf (encaje) lace edging o trim; **(andar) de ~s** (to walk) on tiptoe

punto ['punto] nm (gen) point; (señal diminuta) spot, dot; (COSTURA, MED) stitch; (lugar) spot, place; (momento) point, moment; **a ~** ready; **estar a ~ de** to be on the point of o about to; **en ~** on the dot; **~ muerto** dead centre; (AUTO) neutral (gear); **~ final** full stop (BRIT), period (US); **~ y coma** semicolon; **~ de interrogación** question mark; **~ de vista** point of view, viewpoint; **hacer ~** (tejer) to knit

puntuación [puntwa'θjon] nf punctuation; (puntos: en examen) mark(s) (pl); (: DEPORTE) score

puntual [pun'twal] adj (a tiempo) punctual; (exacto) exact, accurate; **~idad** nf punctuality; exactness, accuracy; **~izar** vt to fix, specify

puntuar [pun'twar] vi (DEPORTE) to score, count

punzada [pun'θaða] nf (de dolor) twinge

punzante [pun'θante] adj (dolor) shooting, sharp; (herramienta) sharp; **punzar** vt to prick, pierce ♦ vi to shoot, stab

puñado [pu'ɲaðo] nm handful

puñal [pu'ɲal] nm dagger; **~ada** nf stab

puñetazo [puɲe'taθo] nm punch

puño ['puɲo] nm (ANAT) fist; (cantidad) fistful, handful; (COSTURA) cuff; (de herramienta) handle

pupila [pu'pila] nf pupil

pupitre [pu'pitre] nm desk

puré [pu're] nm puree; (sopa) (thick) soup; **~ de patatas** mashed potatoes

pureza [pu'reθa] nf purity

purga ['purɣa] nf purge; **purgante** adj, nm purgative; **purgar** vt to purge

purgatorio [purɣa'torjo] nm purgatory

purificar [purifi'kar] vt to purify; (refinar) to refine

puritano, a [puri'tano, a] adj (actitud) puritanical; (iglesia, tradición) puritan ♦ nm/f puritan

puro, a ['puro, a] adj pure; (verdad) simple, plain ♦ adv: **de ~ cansado** out of sheer tiredness ♦ nm cigar

púrpura ['purpura] nf purple; **purpúreo, a** adj purple

pus [pus] nm pus

puse etc vb ver **poner**

pusiera etc vb ver **poner**

pústula ['pustula] nf pimple, sore

puta ['puta] (fam!) nf whore, prostitute

putrefacción [putrefak'θjon] nf rotting, putrefaction

PVP abr (ESP: = precio venta al público) RRP

pyme, PYME ['pime] nf abr (= Pequeña y Mediana Empresa) SME

Q, q

que [ke] conj 1 (con oración subordinada: muchas veces no se traduce) that; **dijo ~ vendría** he said (that) he would come; **espero ~ lo encuentres** I hope (that) you find it; ver tb **el**

2 (en oración independiente): **¡~ entre!** send him in; **¡~ se mejore tu padre!** I hope your father gets better

3 (enfático): **¿me quieres? – ¡~ sí!** do you love me? – of course!

4 (consecutivo: muchas veces no se traduce) that; **es tan grande ~ no lo puedo levantar** it's so big (that) I can't lift it

5 (comparaciones) than; **yo ~ tú/él** if I were you/him; ver tb **más; menos; mismo**

6 (valor disyuntivo): **~ le guste o no** whether he likes it or not; **~ venga o ~ no venga** whether he comes or not

7 (porque): **no puedo, ~ tengo ~ quedarme en casa** I can't, I've got to stay in

♦ pron 1 (cosa) that, which; (+ prep) which; **el sombrero ~ te compraste** the hat (that o which) you bought; **la cama en ~ dormí** the bed (that o which) I slept in

2 (persona: suj) that, who; (: objeto) that, whom; **el amigo ~ me acompañó al museo** the friend that o who went to the museum with me: **la chica ~ invité** the girl (that o whom) I invited

qué [ke] adj what?, which? ♦ pron what?; **¡~ divertido!** how funny!; **¿~ edad tienes?** how old are you?; **¿de ~ me hablas?** what are you saying to me?; **¿~ tal?** how are you?, how are things?; **¿~ hay (de nuevo)?** what's new?

quebradizo, a [keβra'ðiθo, a] adj fragile; (persona) frail

quebrado, a [ke'βraðo, a] adj (roto) broken ♦ nm/f bankrupt ♦ nm (MAT) fraction

quebrantar [keβran'tar] vt (infringir) to violate, transgress; **~se** vr (persona) to fail in health

quebranto [ke'βranto] nm damage, harm; (dolor) grief, pain

quebrar [ke'βrar] vt to break, smash ♦ vi to go bankrupt; **~se** vr to break, get broken; (MED) to be ruptured

quedar [ke'ðar] vi to stay, remain; (encontrarse: sitio) to be; (haber aún) to remain, be left; **~se** vr to remain, stay (behind); **~se (con) algo** to keep sth; **~ en** (acordar) to agree on/to; **~ en nada** to come to nothing; **~ por hacer** to be still to be done; **~ ciego/mudo** to be left blind/dumb; **no te queda bien ese vestido** that dress doesn't suit you; **eso queda muy lejos** that's a long way (away); **quedamos a las seis** we agreed to meet at six

quedo, a ['keðo, a] adj still ♦ adv softly, gently

quehacer [kea'θer] nm task, job; **~es (domésticos)** nmpl household chores

queja ['kexa] nf complaint; **quejarse** vr (enfermo) to moan, groan; (protestar) to complain; **quejarse de que** to complain (about the fact) that; **quejido** nm moan

quemado, a [ke'maðo, a] adj burnt

quemadura [kema'ðura] nf burn, scald

quemar [ke'mar] vt to burn; (fig: malgastar) to burn up, squander ♦ vi to be burning hot; **~se** vr (consumirse) to burn (up); (del sol) to get sunburnt

quemarropa [kema'rropa]: **a ~** adv point-blank

quepo etc vb ver **caber**

querella [ke'reʎa] nf (JUR) charge; (disputa) dispute; **~rse** vr (JUR) to file a complaint

querer [ke'rer] vt 1 (desear) to want; **quiero más dinero** I want more money; **quisiera o querría un té** I'd like a tea; **sin ~** unintentionally; **quiero ayudar/que vayas** I want to help/you to go

2 (preguntas: para pedir algo): **¿quiere abrir la ventana?** could you open the window?; **¿quieres echarme una mano?** can you give me a hand?

3 (amar) to love; (tener cariño a) to be fond of; **quiere mucho a sus hijos** he's very fond of his children

4 (requerir): **esta planta quiere más luz** this plant needs more light

5: **le pedí que me dejara ir pero no quiso** I asked him to let me go but he refused

querido, a [ke'riðo, a] adj dear ♦ nm/f darling; (amante) lover

queso ['keso] nm cheese

quicio ['kiθjo] nm hinge; **sacar a uno de ~** to get on sb's nerves

quiebra ['kjeβra] nf break, split; (COM) bankruptcy; (ECON) slump

quiebro ['kjeßro] *nm* (*del cuerpo*) swerve

quien [kjen] *pron* who; **hay ~ piensa que** there are those who think that; **no hay ~ lo haga** no-one will do it

quién [kjen] *pron* who, whom; **¿~ es?** who's there?

quienquiera [kjen'kjera] (*pl* **quienesquiera**) *pron* whoever

quiero *etc vb ver* **querer**

quieto, a ['kjeto, a] *adj* still; (*carácter*) placid; **quietud** *nf* stillness

quilate [ki'late] *nm* carat

quilla ['kiʎa] *nf* keel

quimera [ki'mera] *nf* chimera; **quimérico, a** *adj* fantastic

químico, a ['kimiko, a] *adj* chemical ♦ *nm/f* chemist ♦ *nf* chemistry

quincalla [kin'kaʎa] *nf* hardware, ironmongery (*BRIT*)

quince ['kinθe] *num* fifteen; **~ días** a fortnight; **~añero, a** *nm/f* teenager; **~na** *nf* fortnight; (*pago*) fortnightly pay; **~nal** *adj* fortnightly

quiniela [ki'njela] *nf* football pools *pl*; **~s** *nfpl* (*impreso*) pools coupon *sg*

quinientos, as [ki'njentos, as] *adj, num* five hundred

quinina [ki'nina] *nf* quinine

quinto, a ['kinto, a] *adj* fifth ♦ *nf* country house; (*MIL*) call-up, draft

quiosco ['kjosko] *nm* (*de música*) bandstand; (*de periódicos*) news stand

quirófano [ki'rofano] *nm* operating theatre

quirúrgico, a [ki'rurxiko, a] *adj* surgical

quise *etc vb ver* **querer**

quisiera *etc vb ver* **querer**

quisquilloso, a [kiski'ʎoso, a] *adj* (*susceptible*) touchy; (*meticuloso*) pernickety

quiste ['kiste] *nm* cyst

quitaesmalte [kitaes'malte] *nm* nail-polish remover

quitamanchas [kita'mantʃas] *nm inv* stain remover

quitanieves [kita'njeßes] *nm inv* snowplough (*BRIT*), snowplow (*US*)

quitar [ki'tar] *vt* to remove, take away; (*ropa*) to take off; (*dolor*) to relieve; **¡quita de ahí!** get away!; **~se** *vr* to withdraw; (*ropa*) to take off; **se quitó el sombrero** he took off his hat

quite ['kite] *nm* (*esgrima*) parry; (*evasión*) dodge

Quito ['kito] *n* Quito

quizá(s) [ki'θa(s)] *adv* perhaps, maybe

R, r

rábano ['raßano] *nm* radish; **me importa un ~** I don't give a damn

rabia ['raßja] *nf* (*MED*) rabies *sg*; (*ira*) fury, rage; **rabiar** *vi* to have rabies; to rage, be furious; **rabiar por algo** to long for sth

rabieta [ra'ßjeta] *nf* tantrum, fit of temper

rabino [ra'ßino] *nm* rabbi

rabioso, a [ra'ßjoso, a] *adj* rabid; (*fig*) furious

rabo ['raßo] *nm* tail

racha ['ratʃa] *nf* gust of wind: **buena/mala ~** spell of good/bad luck

racial [ra'θjal] *adj* racial, race *cpd*

racimo [ra'θimo] *nm* bunch

raciocinio [raθjo'θinjo] *nm* reason

ración [ra'θjon] *nf* portion; **raciones** *nfpl* rations

racional [raθjo'nal] *adj* (*razonable*) reasonable; (*lógico*) rational; **~izar** *vt* to rationalize

racionar [raθjo'nar] *vt* to ration (out)

racismo [ra'θismo] *nm* racism; **racista** *adj, nm/f* racist

radar [ra'ðar] *nm* radar

radiactivo, a [raðiak'tißo, a] *adj* = **radioactivo**

radiador [raðja'ðor] *nm* radiator

radiante [ra'ðjante] *adj* radiant

radical [raði'kal] *adj, nm/f* radical

radicar [raði'kar] *vi:* **~ en** (*dificultad, problema*) to lie in; (*solución*) to consist in; **~se** *vr* to establish o.s., put down (one's) roots

radio ['raðjo] *nf* radio; (*aparato*) radio (set) ♦ *nm* (*MAT*) radius; (*QUÍM*) radium; **~actividad** *nf* radioactivity; **~activo, a** *adj* radioactive; **~difusión** *nf* broadcasting; **~emisora** *nf* transmitter, radio station; **~escucha** *nm/f* listener; **~grafía** *nf* X-ray; **~grafiar** *vt* to X-ray; **~terapia** *nf* radiotherapy; **~yente** *nm/f* listener

ráfaga ['rafaxa] *nf* gust; (*de luz*) flash; (*de tiros*) burst

raído, a [ra'iðo, a] *adj* (*ropa*) threadbare

raigambre [rai'xambre] *nf* (*BOT*) roots *pl*; (*fig*) tradition

raíz [ra'iθ] *nf* root; **~ cuadrada** square root; **a ~ de** as a result of

raja ['raxa] *nf* (*de melón etc*) slice; (*grieta*) crack; **rajar** *vt* to split; (*fam*) to slash; **rajarse** *vr* to split, crack; **rajarse de** to back out of

rajatabla [raxa'taßla]: **a ~** *adv* (*estrictamente*) strictly, to the letter

rallador [raʎa'ðor] *nm* grater

rallar [ra'ʎar] *vt* to grate

rama ['rama] *nf* branch; **~je** *nm* branches *pl*, foliage; **ramal** *nm* (*de cuerda*) strand; (*FERRO*) branch line (*BRIT*); (*AUTO*) branch (road) (*BRIT*)

rambla ['rambla] *nf* (*avenida*) avenue

ramificación [ramifika'θjon] *nf* ramification

ramificarse [ramifiˈkarse] vr to branch out

ramillete [ramiˈʎete] nm bouquet

ramo [ˈramo] nm branch; (sección) department, section

rampa [ˈrampa] nf ramp

ramplón, ona [ramˈplon, ona] adj uncouth, coarse

rana [ˈrana] nf frog; **salto de ~** leapfrog

ranchero [ranˈtʃero] nm (AM) rancher; smallholder

rancho [ˈrantʃo] nm (grande) ranch; (pequeño) small farm

rancio, a [ˈranθjo, a] adj (comestibles) rancid; (vino) aged, mellow; (fig) ancient

rango [ˈrango] nm rank, standing

ranura [raˈnura] nf groove; (de teléfono etc) slot

rapar [raˈpar] vt to shave; (los cabellos) to crop

rapaz [raˈpaθ] (nf: **rapaza**) nm/f young boy/girl ♦ adj (ZOOL) predatory

rape [ˈrape] nm (pez) monkfish; **al ~** cropped

rapé [raˈpe] nm snuff

rapidez [rapiˈðeθ] nf speed, rapidity; **rápido, a** adj fast, quick ♦ adv quickly ♦ nm (FERRO) express; **rápidos** nmpl rapids

rapiña [raˈpiɲa] nm robbery; **ave de ~** bird of prey

raptar [rapˈtar] vt to kidnap; **rapto** nm kidnapping; (impulso) sudden impulse; (éxtasis) ecstasy, rapture

raqueta [raˈketa] nf racquet

raquítico, a [raˈkitiko, a] adj stunted; (fig) poor, inadequate; **raquitismo** nm rickets sg

rareza [raˈreθa] nf rarity; (fig) eccentricity

raro, a [ˈraro, a] adj (poco común) rare; (extraño) odd, strange; (excepcional) remarkable

ras [ras] nm: **a ~** de level with; **a ~ de tierra** at ground level

rasar [raˈsar] vt (igualar) to level

rascacielos [raskaˈθjelos] nm inv skyscraper

rascar [rasˈkar] vt (con las uñas etc) to scratch; (raspar) to scrape; **~se** vr to scratch (o.s.)

rasgar [rasˈvar] vt to tear, rip (up)

rasgo [ˈrasvo] nm (con pluma) stroke; **~s** nmpl (facciones) features, characteristics; **a grandes ~s** in outline, broadly

rasguñar [rasvuˈɲar] vt to scratch; **rasguño** nm scratch

raso, a [ˈraso, a] adj (liso) flat, level; (a baja altura) very low ♦ nm satin; **cielo ~** clear sky

raspadura [raspaˈðura] nf (acto) scrape, scraping; (marca) scratch; **~s** nfpl (de papel etc) scrapings

raspar [rasˈpar] vt to scrape; (arañar) to scratch; (limar) to file

rastra [ˈrastra] nf (AGR) rake; **a ~s** by dragging; (fig) unwillingly

rastreador [rastreaˈðor] nm tracker; **~ de minas** minesweeper

rastrear [rastreˈar] vt (seguir) to track

rastrero, a [rasˈtrero, a] adj (BOT, ZOOL) creeping; (fig) despicable, mean

rastrillo [rasˈtriʎo] nm rake

rastro [ˈrastro] nm (AGR) rake, (pista) track, trail; (vestigio) trace; **el R~** the Madrid fleamarket

rastrojo [rasˈtroxo] nm stubble

rasurador [rasuraˈðor] (AM) nm electric shaver

rasuradora [rasuraˈðora] (AM) nf = **rasurador**

rasurarse [rasuˈrarse] vr to shave

rata [ˈrata] nf rat

ratear [rateˈar] vt (robar) to steal

ratero, a [raˈtero, a] adj light-fingered ♦ nm/f (carterista) pickpocket; (AM: de casas) burglar

ratificar [ratifiˈkar] vt to ratify

rato [ˈrato] nm while, short time; **a ~s** from time to time; **hay para ~** there's still a long way to go; **al poco ~** soon afterwards; **pasar el ~** to kill time; **pasar un buen/mal ~** to have a good/rough time; **en mis ~s libres** in my spare time

ratón [raˈton] nm mouse; **ratonera** nf mousetrap

raudal [rauˈðal] nm torrent; **a ~es** in abundance

raya [ˈraja] nf line; (marca) scratch; (en tela) stripe; (de pelo) parting; (límite) boundary; (pez) ray; (puntuación) dash; **a ~s** striped; **pasarse de la ~** to go too far: **tener a ~** to keep in check; **rayar** vt to line; to scratch; (subrayar) to underline ♦ vi: **rayar en** o **con** to border on

rayo [ˈrajo] nm (del sol) ray, beam; (de luz) shaft; (en una tormenta) (flash of) lightning; **~s X** X-rays

raza [ˈraθa] nf race; **~ humana** human race

razón [raˈθon] nf reason; (justicia) right, justice; (razonamiento) reasoning; (motivo) reason, motive; (MAT) ratio; **a ~ de 10 cada día** at the rate of 10 a day; **"~: ..."** "inquiries to ..."; **en ~ de** with regard to; **dar ~ a uno** to agree that sb is right; **tener ~** to be right; **~ directa/inversa** direct/inverse proportion; **~ de ser** raison d'être; **razonable** adj reasonable; (justo, moderado) fair; **razonamiento** nm (juicio) judg(e)ment; (argumento) reasoning; **razonar** vt, vi to reason, argue

reacción [reakˈθjon] nf reaction; **avión a ~** jet plane; **~ en cadena** chain reaction; **reaccionar** vi to react; **reaccionario, a** adj reactionary

reacio, a [reˈaθjo, a] adj stubborn

reactivar [reakti'ßar] *vt* to revitalize

reactor [reak'tor] *nm* reactor

readaptación [reaðapta'θjon] *nf*:
~ **profesional** industrial retraining

reajuste [rea'xuste] *nm* readjustment

real [re'al] *adj* real; (*del rey, fig*) royal

realce [re'alθe] *nm* (*lustre, fig*) splendour;
poner de ~ to emphasize

realidad [reali'ðað] *nf* reality, fact; (*verdad*)
truth

realista [rea'lista] *nm/f* realist

realización [realiθa'θjon] *nf* fulfilment

realizador, a [realiθa'ðor, a] *nm/f* film-
maker

realizar [reali'θar] *vt* (*objetivo*) to achieve;
(*plan*) to carry out; (*viaje*) to make,
undertake; ~**se** *vr* to come about, come
true

realmente [real'mente] *adv* really, actually

realquilar [realki'lar] *vt* to sublet

realzar [real'θar] *vt* to enhance; (*acentuar*) to
highlight

reanimar [reani'mar] *vt* to revive; (*alentar*)
to encourage; ~**se** *vr* to revive

reanudar [reanu'ðar] *vt* (*renovar*) to renew;
(*historia, viaje*) to resume

reaparición [reapari'θjon] *nf* reappearance

rearme [re'arme] *nm* rearmament

rebaja [re'ßaxa] *nf* (COM) reduction; (: *descuento*) discount; ~**s** *nfpl* (COM) sale; **rebajar**
vt (*bajar*) to lower; (*reducir*) to reduce;
(*disminuir*) to lessen; (*humillar*) to humble

rebanada [reßa'naða] *nf* slice

rebañar [reßa'ɲar] *vt* (*comida*) to scrape up;
(*plato*) to scrape clean

rebaño [re'ßaɲo] *nm* herd; (*de ovejas*) flock

rebasar [reßa'sar] *vt* (*tb*: ~ **de**) to exceed

rebatir [reßa'tir] *vt* to refute

rebeca [re'ßeka] *nf* cardigan

rebelarse [reße'larse] *vr* to rebel, revolt

rebelde [re'ßelde] *adj* rebellious; (*niño*)
unruly ♦ *nm/f* rebel; **rebeldía** *nf*
rebelliousness; (*desobediencia*) disobedience

rebelión [reße'ljon] *nf* rebellion

reblandecer [reßlande'θer] *vt* to soften

rebobinar [reßoßi'nar] *vt* (*cinta, película de
video*) to rewind

rebosante [reßo'sante] *adj* overflowing

rebosar [reßo'sar] *vi* (*líquido, recipiente*) to
overflow; (*abundar*) to abound, be plentiful

rebotar [reßo'tar] *vt* to bounce; (*rechazar*) to
repel ♦ *vi* (*pelota*) to bounce; (*bala*) to
ricochet; **rebote** *nm* rebound; **de rebote** on
the rebound

rebozado, a [reßo'θaðo, a] *adj* fried in
batter *o* breadcrumbs

rebozar [reßo'θar] *vt* to wrap up; (CULIN) to
fry in batter *o* breadcrumbs

rebuscado, a [reßus'kaðo, a] *adj*

(*amanerado*) affected; (*palabra*) recherché;
(*idea*) far-fetched

rebuscar [reßus'kar] *vi*: ~ **(en/por)** to search
carefully (in/for)

rebuznar [reßuθ'nar] *vi* to bray

recado [re'kaðo] *nm* (*mensaje*) message;
(*encargo*) errand; **tomar un ~** (TEL) to take a
message

recaer [reka'er] *vi* to relapse; ~ **en** to fall to *o*
on; (*criminal etc*) to fall back into, relapse
into; **recaída** *nf* relapse

recalcar [rekal'kar] *vt* (*fig*) to stress,
emphasize

recalcitrante [rekalθi'trante] *adj* recalcitrant

recalentar [rekalen'tar] *vt* (*volver a calentar*)
to reheat; (*calentar demasiado*) to overheat

recámara [re'kamara] (AM) *nf* bedroom

recambio [re'kambjo] *nm* spare; (*de pluma*)
refill

recapacitar [rekapaθi'tar] *vi* to reflect

recargado, a [rekar'ɣaðo, a] *adj* overloaded

recargar [rekar'ɣar] *vt* to overload; (*batería*)
to recharge; **recargo** *nm* surcharge;
(*aumento*) increase

recatado, a [reka'taðo, a] *adj* (*modesto*)
modest, demure; (*prudente*) cautious

recato [re'kato] *nm* (*modestia*) modesty,
demureness; (*cautela*) caution

recaudación [rekauða'θjon] *nf* (*acción*)
collection; (*cantidad*) takings *pl*; (*en deporte*)
gate; **recaudador, a** *nm/f* tax collector

recelar [reθe'lar] *vt*: ~ **que** (*sospechar*) to
suspect that; (*temer*) to fear that ♦ *vi*: ~ **de** to
distrust; **recelo** *nm* distrust, suspicion;
receloso, a *adj* distrustful, suspicious

recepción [reθep'θjon] *nf* reception;
recepcionista *nm/f* receptionist

receptáculo [reθep'takulo] *nm* receptacle

receptivo, a [reθep'tißo, a] *adj* receptive

receptor, a [reθep'tor, a] *nm/f* recipient
♦ *nm* (TEL) receiver

recesión [reθe'sjon] *nf* (COM) recession

receta [re'θeta] *nf* (CULIN) recipe; (MED)
prescription

rechazar [retʃa'θar] *vt* to reject; (*oferta*) to
turn down; (*ataque*) to repel

rechazo [re'tʃaθo] *nm* rejection

rechifla [re'tʃifla] *nf* hissing, booing; (*fig*)
derision

rechinar [retʃi'nar] *vi* to creak; (*dientes*) to
grind

rechistar [retʃis'tar] *vi*: **sin ~** without a
murmur

rechoncho, a [re'tʃontʃo, a] (*fam*) *adj*
thickset (BRIT), heavy-set (US)

rechupete [retʃu'pete]: **de ~** (*comida*)
delicious, scrumptious

recibidor, a [reθißi'ðor, a] *nm* entrance hall

recibimiento [reθißi'mjento] *nm* reception,

welcome

recibir [reθi'ßir] vt to receive; (dar la bienvenida) to welcome ♦ vi to entertain; **~se** vr: **~se de** to qualify as; **recibo** nm receipt

reciclar [reθi'klar] vt to recycle

recién [re'θjen] adv recently, newly; **los ~ casados** the newly-weds; **el ~ llegado** the newcomer; **el ~ nacido** the newborn child

reciente [re'θjente] adj recent; (fresco) fresh; **~mente** adv recently

recinto [re'θinto] nm enclosure; (área) area, place

recio, a ['reθjo, a] adj strong, tough; (voz) loud ♦ adv hard; loud(ly)

recipiente [reθi'pjente] nm receptacle

reciprocidad [reθiproθi'ðað] nf reciprocity; **recíproco, a** adj reciprocal

recital [reθi'tal] nm (MUS) recital; (LITERATURA) reading

recitar [reθi'tar] vt to recite

reclamación [reklama'θjon] nf claim, demand; (queja) complaint

reclamar [rekla'mar] vt to claim, demand ♦ vi: **~ contra** to complain about; **~ a uno en justicia** to take sb to court; **reclamo** nm (anuncio) advertisement; (tentación) attraction

reclinar [rekli'nar] vt to recline, lean; **~se** vr to lean back

recluir [reklu'ir] vt to intern, confine

reclusión [reklu'sjon] nf (prisión) prison; (refugio) seclusion; **~ perpetua** life imprisonment

recluta [re'kluta] nm/f recruit ♦ nf recruitment; **reclutar** vt (datos) to collect; (dinero) to collect up; **~miento** [rekluta'mjento] nm recruitment

recobrar [reko'ßrar] vt (salud) to recover; (rescatar) to get back; **~se** vr to recover

recodo [re'koðo] nm (de río, camino) bend

recogedor [rekoxe'ðor] nm dustpan

recoger [reko'xer] vt to collect; (AGR) to harvest; (levantar) to pick up; (juntar) to gather; (pasar a buscar) to come for, get; (dar asilo) to give shelter to; (faldas) to gather up; (pelo) to put up; **~se** vr (retirarse) to retire; **recogido, a** adj (lugar) quiet, secluded; (pequeño) small ♦ nf (CORREOS) collection; (AGR) harvest

recolección [rekolek'θjon] nf (AGR) harvesting; (colecta) collection

recomendación [rekomenda'θjon] nf (sugerencia) suggestion, recommendation; (referencia) reference

recomendar [rekomen'dar] vt to suggest, recommend; (confiar) to entrust

recompensa [rekom'pensa] nf reward, recompense; **recompensar** vt to reward, recompense

recomponer [rekompo'ner] vt to mend

reconciliación [rekonθilja'θjon] nf reconciliation

reconciliar [rekonθi'ljar] vt to reconcile; **~se** vr to become reconciled

recóndito, a [re'kondito, a] adj (lugar) hidden, secret

reconfortar [rekonfor'tar] vt to comfort

reconocer [rekono'θer] vt to recognize; (registrar) to search; (MED) to examine; **reconocido, a** adj recognized; (agradecido) grateful; **reconocimiento** nm recognition; search; examination; gratitude; (confesión) admission

reconquista [rekon'kista] nf reconquest; **la R~** the Reconquest (of Spain)

reconstituyente [rekonstitu'jente] nm tonic

reconstruir [rekonstru'ir] vt to reconstruct

reconversión [rekonßer'sjon] nf: **~ industrial** industrial rationalization

recopilación [rekopila'θjon] nf (resumen) summary; (compilación) compilation; **recopilar** vt to compile

récord ['rekorð] (pl ~s) adj inv, nm record

recordar [rekor'ðar] vt (acordarse de) to remember; (acordar a otro) to remind ♦ vi to remember

recorrer [reko'rrer] vt (país) to cross, travel through; (distancia) to cover; (registrar) to search; (repasar) to look over; **recorrido** nm run, journey; **tren de largo recorrido** main-line train

recortado, a [rekor'taðo, a] adj uneven, irregular

recortar [rekor'tar] vt to cut out; **recorte** nm (acción, de prensa) cutting; (de telas, chapas) trimming; **recorte presupuestario** budget cut

recostado, a [rekos'taðo, a] adj leaning; **estar ~** to be lying down

recostar [rekos'tar] vt to lean; **~se** vr to lie down

recoveco [reko'ßeko] nm (de camino, río etc) bend; (en casa) cubby hole

recreación [rekrea'θjon] nf recreation

recrear [rekre'ar] vt (entretener) to entertain; (volver a crear) to recreate; **recreativo, a** adj recreational; **recreo** nm recreation; (ESCOL) break, playtime

recriminar [rekrimi'nar] vt to reproach ♦ vi to recriminate; **~se** vr to reproach each other

recrudecer [rekruðe'θer] vt, vi to worsen; **~se** vr to worsen

recrudecimiento [rekruðeθi'mjento] nm upsurge

recta ['rekta] nf straight line

rectángulo, a [rek'tangulo, a] adj rectangular ♦ nm rectangle

rectificar [rektifi'kar] vt to rectify; (volverse

recto) to straighten ♦ *vi* to correct o.s.

rectitud [rekti'tuð] *nf* straightness; (*fig*) rectitude

recto, a ['rekto, a] *adj* straight; (*persona*) honest, upright ♦ *nm* rectum

rector, a [rek'tor, a] *adj* governing

recuadro [re'kwaðro] *nm* box; (*TIPOGRAFÍA*) inset

recubrir [reku'ßrir] *vt*: ~ **(con)** (*pintura, crema*) to cover (with)

recuento [re'kwento] *nm* inventory; **hacer el ~ de** to count o reckon up

recuerdo [re'kwerðo] *nm* souvenir; **~s** *nmpl* (*memorias*) memories; **¡~s a tu madre!** give my regards to your mother!

recular [reku'lar] *vi* to back down

recuperable [rekupe'raßle] *adj* recoverable

recuperación [rekupera'θjon] *nf* recovery

recuperar [rekupe'rar] *vt* to recover; (*tiempo*) to make up; **~se** *vr* to recuperate

recurrir [reku'rrir] *vi* (*JUR*) to appeal; **~ a** to resort to; (*persona*) to turn to; **recurso** *nm* resort; (*medios*) means *pl*, resources *pl*; (*JUR*) appeal

recusar [reku'sar] *vt* to reject, refuse

red [reð] *nf* net, mesh; (*FERRO etc*) network; (*trampa*) trap; **la R~** (*Internet*) the Net

redacción [reðak'θjon] *nf* (*acción*) editing; (*personal*) editorial staff; (*ESCOL*) essay, composition

redactar [reðak'tar] *vt* to draw up, draft; (*periódico*) to edit

redactor, a [reðak'tor, a] *nm/f* editor

redada [re'ðaða] *nf*: **~ policial** police raid, round-up

rededor [reðe'ðor] *nm*: **al** o **en ~** around, round about

redención [reðen'θjon] *nf* redemption

redicho, a [re'ðiʧo, a] *adj* affected

redil [re'ðil] *nm* sheepfold

redimir [reði'mir] *vt* to redeem

rédito ['reðito] *nm* interest, yield

redoblar [reðo'ßlar] *vt* to redouble ♦ *vi* (*tambor*) to roll

redomado, a [reðo'maðo, a] *adj* (*astuto*) sly, crafty; (*perfecto*) utter

redonda [re'ðonda] *nf*: **a la ~** around, round about

redondear [reðonde'ar] *vt* to round, round off

redondel [reðon'del] *nm* (*círculo*) circle; (*TAUR*) bullring, arena

redondo, a [re'ðondo, a] *adj* (*circular*) round; (*completo*) complete

reducción [reðuk'θjon] *nf* reduction

reducido, a [reðu'θiðo, a] *adj* reduced; (*limitado*) limited; (*pequeño*) small

reducir [reðu'θir] *vt* to reduce; to limit; **~se** *vr* to diminish

redundancia [reðun'danθja] *nf* redundancy

reembolsar [re(e)mbol'sar] *vt* (*persona*) to reimburse; (*dinero*) to repay, pay back; (*depósito*) to refund; **reembolso** *nm* reimbursement; refund

reemplazar [re(e)mpla'θar] *vt* to replace; **reemplazo** *nm* replacement; **de reemplazo** (*MIL*) reserve

reencuentro [re(e)n'kwentro] *nm* reunion

referencia [refe'renθja] *nf* reference; **con ~ a** with reference to

referéndum [refe'rendum] (*pl* **~s**) *nm* referendum

referente [refe'rente] *adj*: **~ a** concerning, relating to

referir [refe'rir] *vt* (*contar*) to tell, recount; (*relacionar*) to refer, relate; **~se** *vr*: **~se a** to refer to

refilón [refi'lon]: **de ~** *adv* obliquely

refinado, a [refi'naðo, a] *adj* refined

refinamiento [refina'mjento] *nm* refinement

refinar [refi'nar] *vt* to refine; **refinería** *nf* refinery

reflejar [refle'xar] *vt* to reflect; **reflejo, a** *adj* reflected; (*movimiento*) reflex ♦ *nm* reflection; (*ANAT*) reflex

reflexión [reflek'sjon] *nf* reflection; **reflexionar** *vt* to reflect on ♦ *vi* to reflect; (*detenerse*) to pause (to think)

reflexivo, a [reflek'sißo, a] *adj* thoughtful; (*LING*) reflexive

reflujo [re'fluxo] *nm* ebb

reforma [re'forma] *nf* reform; (*ARQ etc*) repair; **~ agraria** agrarian reform

reformar [refor'mar] *vt* to reform; (*modificar*) to change, alter; (*ARQ*) to repair; **~se** *vr* to mend one's ways

reformatorio [reforma'torjo] *nm* reformatory

reforzar [refor'θar] *vt* to strengthen; (*ARQ*) to reinforce; (*fig*) to encourage

refractario, a [refrak'tarjo, a] *adj* (*TEC*) heat-resistant

refrán [re'fran] *nm* proverb, saying

refregar [refre'xar] *vt* to scrub

refrenar [refre'nar] *vt* to check, restrain

refrendar [refren'dar] *vt* (*firma*) to endorse, countersign; (*ley*) to approve

refrescante [refres'kante] *adj* refreshing, cooling

refrescar [refres'kar] *vt* to refresh ♦ *vi* to cool down; **~se** *vr* to get cooler; (*tomar aire fresco*) to go out for a breath of fresh air; (*beber*) to have a drink

refresco [re'fresko] *nm* soft drink, cool drink; **"~s"** "refreshments"

refriega [re'frjexa] *nf* scuffle, brawl

refrigeración [refrixera'θjon] *nf*

refrigeration; (*de sala*) air-conditioning

refrigerador [refrixera'ðor] *nm* refrigerator (*BRIT*), icebox (*US*)

refrigerar [refrixe'rar] *vt* to refrigerate; (*sala*) to air-condition

refuerzo [re'fwerθo] *nm* reinforcement; (*TEC*) support

refugiado, a [refu'xjaðo, a] *nm/f* refugee

refugiarse [refu'xjarse] *vr* to take refuge, shelter

refugio [re'fuxjo] *nm* refuge; (*protección*) shelter

refunfuñar [refunfu'ɲar] *vi* to grunt, growl; (*quejarse*) to grumble

refutar [refu'tar] *vt* to refute

regadera [reɣa'ðera] *nf* watering can

regadío [reɣa'ðio] *nm* irrigated land

regalado, a [reɣa'laðo, a] *adj* comfortable, luxurious; (*gratis*) free, for nothing

regalar [reɣa'lar] *vt* (*dar*) to give (as a present); (*entregar*) to give away; (*mimar*) to pamper, make a fuss of

regaliz [reɣa'liθ] *nm* liquorice

regalo [re'ɣalo] *nm* (*obsequio*) gift, present; (*gusto*) pleasure

regañadientes [reɣaɲa'ðjentes]: **a ~** *adv* reluctantly

regañar [reɣa'ɲar] *vt* to scold ♦ *vi* to grumble; **regañón, ona** *adj* nagging

regar [re'ɣar] *vt* to water, irrigate; (*fig*) to scatter, sprinkle

regatear [reɣate'ar] *vt* (*COM*) to bargain over; (*escatimar*) to be mean with ♦ *vi* to bargain, haggle; (*DEPORTE*) to dribble; **regateo** *nm* bargaining; dribbling; (*del cuerpo*) swerve, dodge

regazo [re'ɣaθo] *nm* lap

regeneración [rexenera'θjon] *nf* regeneration

regenerar [rexene'rar] *vt* to regenerate

regentar [rexen'tar] *vt* to direct, manage; **regente** *nm* (*COM*) manager; (*POL*) regent

régimen ['reximen] (*pl* **regímenes**) *nm* regime; (*MED*) diet

regimiento [rexi'mjento] *nm* regiment

regio, a ['rexjo, a] *adj* royal, regal; (*fig: suntuoso*) splendid; (*AM: fam*) great, terrific

región [re'xjon] *nf* region

regir [re'xir] *vt* to govern, rule; (*dirigir*) to manage, run ♦ *vi* to apply, be in force

registrar [rexis'trar] *vt* (*buscar*) to search; (: *en cajón*) to look through; (*inspeccionar*) to inspect; (*anotar*) to register, record; (*INFORM*) to log; **~se** *vr* to register; (*ocurrir*) to happen

registro [re'xistro] *nm* (*acto*) registration; (*MUS, libro*) register; (*inspección*) inspection, search; **~ civil** registry office

regla ['reɣla] *nf* (*ley*) rule, regulation; (*de medir*) ruler, rule; (*MED: período*) period

reglamentación [reɣlamenta'θjon] *nf* (*acto*) regulation; (*lista*) rules *pl*

reglamentar [reɣlamen'tar] *vt* to regulate; **reglamentario, a** *adj* statutory; **reglamento** *nm* rules *pl*, regulations *pl*

regocijarse [reɣoθi'xarse] *vr*: **~ de** to rejoice at, be happy about; **regocijo** *nm* joy, happiness

regodearse [reɣoðe'arse] *vr* to be glad, be delighted; **regodeo** *nm* delight

regresar [reɣre'sar] *vi* to come back, go back, return; **regresivo, a** *adj* backward; (*fig*) regressive; **regreso** *nm* return

reguero [re'ɣero] *nm* (*de sangre etc*) trickle; (*de humo*) trail

regulador [reɣula'ðor] *nm* regulator; (*de radio etc*) knob, control

regular [reɣu'lar] *adj* regular; (*normal*) normal, usual; (*común*) ordinary; (*organizado*) regular, orderly; (*mediano*) average; (*fam*) not bad, so-so ♦ *adv* so-so, alright ♦ *vt* (*controlar*) to control, regulate; (*TEC*) to adjust; **por lo ~** as a rule; **~idad** *nf* regularity; **~izar** *vt* to regularize

regusto [re'ɣusto] *nm* aftertaste

rehabilitación [reaβilita'θjon] *nf* rehabilitation; (*ARQ*) restoration

rehabilitar [reaβili'tar] *vt* to rehabilitate; (*ARQ*) to restore; (*reintegrar*) to reinstate

rehacer [rea'θer] *vt* (*reparar*) to mend, repair; (*volver a hacer*) to redo, repeat; **~se** *vr* (*MED*) to recover

rehén [re'en] *nm* hostage

rehuir [reu'ir] *vt* to avoid, shun

rehusar [reu'sar] *vt, vi* to refuse

reina ['reina] *nf* queen; **~do** *nm* reign

reinante [rei'nante] *adj* (*fig*) prevailing

reinar [rei'nar] *vi* to reign

reincidir [reinθi'ðir] *vi* to relapse

reincorporarse [reinkorpo'rarse] *vr*: **~ a** to rejoin

reino ['reino] *nm* kingdom; **el R~ Unido** the United Kingdom

reintegrar [reinte'ɣrar] *vt* (*reconstituir*) to reconstruct; (*persona*) to reinstate; (*dinero*) to refund, pay back; **~se** *vr*: **~se a** to return to

reír [re'ir] *vi* to laugh; **~se** *vr* to laugh; **~se de** to laugh at

reiterar [reite'rar] *vt* to reiterate

reivindicación [reiβindika'θjon] *nf* (*demanda*) claim, demand; (*justificación*) vindication

reivindicar [reiβindi'kar] *vt* to claim

reja ['rexa] *nf* (*de ventana*) grille, bars *pl*; (*en la calle*) grating

rejilla [re'xiʎa] *nf* grating, grille; (*muebles*) wickerwork; (*de ventilación*) vent; (*de coche etc*) luggage rack

rejoneador [rexonea'ðor] *nm* mounted

bullfighter

rejuvenecer |rexuβene'θer| vt, vi to rejuvenate

relación |rela'θjon| nf relation, relationship; (MAT) ratio; (narración) report; **relaciones públicas** public relations; **con ~ a, en ~ con** in relation to; **relacionar** vt to relate, connect; **relacionarse** vr to be connected, be linked

relajación |relaxa'θjon| nf relaxation

relajado, a |rela'xaðo, a| adj (disoluto) loose; (cómodo) relaxed; (MED) ruptured

relajar |rela'xar| vt to relax; **~se** vr to relax

relamerse |rela'merse| vr to lick one's lips

relamido, a |rela'miðo, a| adj (pulcro) overdressed; (afectado) affected

relámpago |re'lampaɣo| nm flash of lightning; **visita/huelga ~** lightning visit/strike; **relampaguear** vi to flash

relatar |rela'tar| vt to tell, relate

relativo, a |rela'tiβo, a| adj relative; **en lo ~ a** concerning

relato |re'lato| nm (narración) story, tale

relegar |rele'xar| vt to relegate

relevante |rele'βante| adj eminent, outstanding

relevar |rele'βar| vt (sustituir) to relieve; **~se** vr to relay; **~ a uno de un cargo** to relieve sb of his post

relevo |re'leβo| nm relief; **carrera de ~s** relay race

relieve |re'ljeβe| nm (ARTE, TEC) relief; (fig) prominence, importance; **bajo ~** bas-relief

religión |reli'xjon| nf religion; **religioso, a** adj religious ♦ nm/f monk/nun

relinchar |relin'tʃar| vi to neigh; **relincho** nm neigh; (acto) neighing

reliquia |re'likja| nf relic; **~ de familia** heirloom

rellano |re'ʎano| nm (ARQ) landing

rellenar |reʎe'nar| vt (llenar) to fill up; (CULIN) to stuff; (COSTURA) to pad; **relleno, a** adj full up; stuffed ♦ nm stuffing; (de tapicería) padding

reloj |re'lo(x)| nm clock; **~ (de pulsera)** wristwatch; **~ despertador** alarm (clock); **poner el ~** to set one's watch (o the clock); **~ero, a** nm/f clockmaker; watchmaker

reluciente |relu'θjente| adj brilliant, shining

relucir |relu'θir| vi to shine; (fig) to excel

relumbrar |relum'brar| vi to dazzle, shine brilliantly

remachar |rema'tʃar| vt to rivet; (fig) to hammer home, drive home; **remache** nm rivet

remanente |rema'nente| nm remainder; (COM) balance; (de producto) surplus

remangar |reman'gar| vt to roll up

remanso |re'manso| nm pool

remar |re'mar| vi to row

rematado, a |rema'taðo, a| adj complete, utter

rematar |rema'tar| vt to finish off; (COM) to sell off cheap ♦ vi to end, finish off; (DEPORTE) to shoot

remate |re'mate| nm end, finish; (punta) tip; (DEPORTE) shot; (ARQ) top; **de o para ~** to crown it all (BRIT), to top it off

remedar |reme'ðar| vt to imitate

remediar |reme'ðjar| vt to remedy; (subsanar) to make good, repair; (evitar) to avoid

remedio |re'meðjo| nm remedy; (alivio) relief, help; (JUR) recourse, remedy; **poner ~ a** to correct, stop; **no tener más ~** to have no alternative; **¡qué ~!** there's no choice!; **sin ~** hopeless

remedo |re'meðo| nm imitation; (pey) parody

remendar |remen'dar| vt to repair; (con parche) to patch

remesa |re'mesa| nf remittance; (COM) shipment

remiendo |re'mjendo| nm mend; (con parche) patch; (cosido) darn

remilgado, a |remil'ɣaðo, a| adj prim; (afectado) affected

remilgo |re'milɣo| nm primness; (afectación) affectation

reminiscencia |reminis'θenθja| nf reminiscence

remiso, a |re'miso, a| adj slack, slow

remite |re'mite| nm (en sobre) name and address of sender

remitir |remi'tir| vt to remit, send ♦ vi to slacken; (en carta): **remite: X** sender: X; **remitente** nm/f sender

remo |'remo| nm (de barco) oar; (DEPORTE) rowing

remojar |remo'xar| vt to steep, soak; (galleta etc) to dip, dunk

remojo |re'moxo| nm: **dejar la ropa en ~** to leave clothes to soak

remolacha |remo'latʃa| nf beet, beetroot

remolcador |remolka'ðor| nm (NAUT) tug; (AUTO) breakdown lorry

remolcar |remol'kar| vt to tow

remolino |remo'lino| nm eddy; (de agua) whirlpool; (de viento) whirlwind; (de gente) crowd

remolque |re'molke| nm tow, towing; (cuerda) towrope; **llevar a ~** to tow

remontar |remon'tar| vt to mend; **~se** vr to soar; **~se a** (COM) to amount to; **~ el vuelo** to soar

remorder |remor'ðer| vt to distress, disturb; **~le la conciencia a uno** to have a guilty conscience; **remordimiento** nm remorse

remoto, a |re'moto, a| adj remote

remover [remoˈβer] *vt* to stir; (*tierra*) to turn over; (*objetos*) to move round

remozar [remoˈθar] *vt* (*ARQ*) to refurbish

remuneración [remuneraˈθjon] *nf* remuneration

remunerar [remuneˈrar] *vt* to remunerate; (*premiar*) to reward

renacer [renaˈθer] *vi* to be reborn; (*fig*) to revive; **renacimiento** *nm* rebirth; **el Renacimiento** the Renaissance

renacuajo [renaˈkwaxo] *nm* (*ZOOL*) tadpole

renal [reˈnal] *adj* renal, kidney *cpd*

rencilla [renˈθiʎa] *nf* quarrel

rencor [renˈkor] *nm* rancour, bitterness; **~oso, a** *adj* spiteful

rendición [rendiˈθjon] *nf* surrender

rendido, a [renˈdiðo, a] *adj* (*sumiso*) submissive; (*cansado*) worn-out, exhausted

rendija [renˈdixa] *nf* (*hendedura*) crack, cleft

rendimiento [rendiˈmjento] *nm* (*producción*) output; (*TEC, COM*) efficiency

rendir [renˈdir] *vt* (*vencer*) to defeat; (*producir*) to produce; (*dar beneficio*) to yield; (*agotar*) to exhaust ♦ *vi* to pay; **~se** *vr* (*someterse*) to surrender; (*cansarse*) to wear o.s. out; **~ homenaje** o **culto a** to pay homage to

renegar [reneˈvar] *vi* (*renunciar*) to renounce; (*blasfemar*) to blaspheme; (*quejarse*) to complain

RENFE ['renfe] *nf abr* (= *Red Nacional de los Ferrocarriles Españoles*) ≈ BR (*BRIT*)

renglón [renˈglon] *nm* (*línea*) line; (*COM*) item, article; **a ~ seguido** immediately after

renombrado, a [renomˈbraðo, a] *adj* renowned

renombre [reˈnombre] *nm* renown

renovación [renoβaˈθjon] *nf* (*de contrato*) renewal; (*ARQ*) renovation

renovar [renoˈβar] *vt* to renew; (*ARQ*) to renovate

renta ['renta] *nf* (*ingresos*) income; (*beneficio*) profit; (*alquiler*) rent; **~ vitalicia** annuity; **rentable** *adj* profitable; **rentar** *vt* to produce, yield

renuncia [reˈnunθja] *nf* resignation

renunciar [renunˈθjar] *vt* to renounce; (*tabaco, alcohol etc*): **~ a** to give up; (*oferta, oportunidad*) to turn down; (*puesto*) to resign ♦ *vi* to resign

reñido, a [reˈɲiðo, a] *adj* (*batalla*) bitter, hard-fought; **estar ~ con uno** to be on bad terms with sb

reñir [reˈɲir] *vt* (*regañar*) to scold ♦ *vi* (*estar peleado*) to quarrel, fall out; (*combatir*) to fight

reo ['reo] *nm/f* culprit, offender; **~ de muerte** prisoner condemned to death

reojo [reˈoxo]: **de ~** *adv* out of the corner of one's eye

reparación [reparaˈθjon] *nf* (*acto*) mending, repairing; (*TEC*) repair; (*fig*) amends, reparation

reparar [repaˈrar] *vt* to repair; (*fig*) to make amends for; (*observar*) to observe ♦ *vi*: **~ en** (*darse cuenta de*) to notice; (*prestar atención a*) to pay attention to

reparo [reˈparo] *nm* (*advertencia*) observation; (*duda*) doubt; (*dificultad*) difficulty; **poner ~s (a)** to raise objections (to)

repartición [repartiˈθjon] *nf* distribution; (*división*) division; **repartidor, a** *nm/f* distributor

repartir [reparˈtir] *vt* to distribute, share out; (*CORREOS*) to deliver; **reparto** *nm* distribution; delivery; (*TEATRO, CINE*) cast; (*AM: urbanización*) housing estate (*BRIT*), real estate development (*US*)

repasar [repaˈsar] *vt* (*ESCOL*) to revise; (*MECÁNICA*) to check, overhaul; (*COSTURA*) to mend; **repaso** *nm* revision; overhaul, checkup; mending

repatriar [repaˈtrjar] *vt* to repatriate

repecho [reˈpetʃo] *nm* steep incline

repelente [repeˈlente] *adj* repellent, repulsive

repeler [repeˈler] *vt* to repel

repensar [repenˈsar] *vt* to reconsider

repente [reˈpente] *nm*: **de ~** suddenly; **~ de ira** fit of anger

repentino, a [repenˈtino, a] *adj* sudden

repercusión [reperkuˈsjon] *nf* repercussion

repercutir [reperkuˈtir] *vi* (*objeto*) to rebound; (*sonido*) to echo; **~ en** (*fig*) to have repercussions on

repertorio [reperˈtorjo] *nm* list; (*TEATRO*) repertoire

repetición [repetiˈθjon] *nf* repetition

repetir [repeˈtir] *vt* to repeat; (*plato*) to have a second helping of ♦ *vi* to repeat; (*sabor*) to come back; **~se** *vr* (*volver sobre un tema*) to repeat o.s.

repetitivo, a [repetiˈtiβo, a] *adj* repetitive, repetitious

repicar [repiˈkar] *vt* (*campanas*) to ring

repique [reˈpike] *nm* pealing, ringing; **~teo** *nm* pealing; (*de tambor*) drumming

repisa [reˈpisa] *nf* ledge, shelf; (*de ventana*) windowsill; **~ de chimenea** mantelpiece

repito *etc vb ver* **repetir**

replantearse [replanteˈarse] *vr*: **~ un problema** to reconsider a problem

replegarse [repleˈvarse] *vr* to fall back, retreat

repleto, a [reˈpleto, a] *adj* replete, full up

réplica ['replika] *nf* answer; (*ARTE*) replica

replicar [repliˈkar] *vi* to answer; (*objetar*) to argue, answer back

repliegue [reˈpljeʝe] *nm* (*MIL*) withdrawal

repoblación [repoβla'θjon] *nf* repopulation; (*de río*) restocking; ~ **forestal** reafforestation

repoblar [repo'βlar] *vt* to repopulate; (*con árboles*) to reafforest

repollo [re'poλo] *nm* cabbage

reponer [repo'ner] *vt* to replace, put back; (*TEATRO*) to revive; ~**se** *vr* to recover; ~ **que** to reply that

reportaje [repor'taxe] *nm* report, article

reportero, a [repor'tero, a] *nm/f* reporter

reposacabezas [reposaka'βeθas] *nm inv* headrest

reposado, a [repo'saðo, a] *adj* (*descansado*) restful; (*tranquilo*) calm

reposar [repo'sar] *vi* to rest, repose

reposición [reposi'θjon] *nf* replacement; (*CINE*) remake

reposo [re'poso] *nm* rest

repostar [repos'tar] *vt* to replenish; (*AUTO*) to fill up (with petrol (*BRIT*) o gasoline (*US*))

repostería [reposte'ria] *nf* confectioner's (shop); **repostero, a** *nm/f* confectioner

reprender [repren'der] *vt* to reprimand

represa [re'presa] *nf* dam; (*lago artificial*) lake, pool

represalia [repre'salja] *nf* reprisal

representación [representa'θjon] *nf* representation; (*TEATRO*) performance; **representante** *nm/f* representative; performer

representar [represen'tar] *vt* to represent; (*TEATRO*) to perform; (*edad*) to look; ~**se** *vr* to imagine; **representativo, a** *adj* representative

represión [repre'sjon] *nf* repression

reprimenda [repri'menda] *nf* reprimand, rebuke

reprimir [repri'mir] *vt* to repress

reprobar [repro'βar] *vt* to censure, reprove

reprochar [repro'tʃar] *vt* to reproach; **reproche** *nm* reproach

reproducción [reproðuk'θjon] *nf* reproduction

reproducir [reproðu'θir] *vt* to reproduce; ~**se** *vr* to breed; (*situación*) to recur

reproductor, a [reproðuk'tor, a] *adj* reproductive

reptil [rep'til] *nm* reptile

república [re'puβlika] *nf* republic; **R~ Dominicana** Dominican Republic; **republicano, a** *adj, nm/f* republican

repudiar [repu'ðjar] *vt* to repudiate; (*fe*) to renounce

repuesto [re'pwesto] *nm* (*pieza de recambio*) spare (part); (*abastecimiento*) supply; **rueda de** ~ spare wheel

repugnancia [repuˈnanθja] *nf* repugnance; **repugnante** *adj* repugnant, repulsive

repugnar [repuˈnar] *vt* to disgust

repulsa [re'pulsa] *nf* rebuff

repulsión [repul'sjon] *nf* repulsion, aversion; **repulsivo, a** *adj* repulsive

reputación [reputa'θjon] *nf* reputation

requemado, a [reke'maðo, a] *adj* (*quemado*) scorched; (*bronceado*) tanned

requerimiento [rekeri'mjento] *nm* request; (*JUR*) summons

requerir [reke'rir] *vt* (*pedir*) to ask, request; (*exigir*) to require; (*llamar*) to send for, summon

requesón [reke'son] *nm* cottage cheese

requete... [re'kete] *prefijo* extremely

réquiem ['rekjem] (*pl* ~**s**) *nm* requiem

requisito [reki'sito] *nm* requirement, requisite

res [res] *nf* beast, animal

resaca [re'saka] *nf* (*en el mar*) undertow, undercurrent; (*fam*) hangover

resaltar [resal'tar] *vi* to project, stick out; (*fig*) to stand out

resarcir [resar'θir] *vt* to compensate; ~**se** *vr* to make up for

resbaladizo, a [resβala'ðiθo, a] *adj* slippery

resbalar [resβa'lar] *vi* to slip, slide; (*fig*) to slip (up); ~**se** *vr* to slip, slide; to slip (up); **resbalón** *nm* (*acción*) slip

rescatar [reska'tar] *vt* (*salvar*) to save, rescue; (*objeto*) to get back, recover; (*cautivos*) to ransom

rescate [res'kate] *nm* rescue; (*de objeto*) recovery; **pagar un** ~ to pay a ransom

rescindir [resθin'dir] *vt* to rescind

rescisión [resθi'sjon] *nf* cancellation

rescoldo [res'koldo] *nm* embers *pl*

resecar [rese'kar] *vt* to dry thoroughly; (*MED*) to cut out, remove; ~**se** *vr* to dry up

reseco, a [re'seko, a] *adj* very dry; (*fig*) skinny

resentido, a [resen'tiðo, a] *adj* resentful

resentimiento [resenti'mjento] *nm* resentment, bitterness

resentirse [resen'tirse] *vr* (*debilitarse: persona*) to suffer; ~ **de** (*consecuencias*) to feel the effects of; ~ **de** (*o por*) **algo** to resent sth, be bitter about sth

reseña [re'sena] *nf* (*cuenta*) account; (*informe*) report; (*LITERATURA*) review

reseñar [rese'nar] *vt* to describe; (*LITERATURA*) to review

reserva [re'serβa] *nf* reserve; (*reservación*) reservation; **a** ~ **de que ... unless ...; con toda** ~ in strictest confidence

reservado, a [reser'βaðo, a] *adj* reserved; (*retraído*) cold, distant ♦ *nm* private room

reservar [reser'βar] *vt* (*guardar*) to keep; (*habitación, entrada*) to reserve; ~**se** *vr* to save o.s.; (*callar*) to keep to o.s.

resfriado [resfri'aðo] *nm* cold; **resfriarse** *vr*

to cool; (MED) to catch (a) cold

resguardar [resɣwar'ðar] vt to protect, shield; **~se** vr: **~se de** to guard against; **resguardo** nm defence; (vale) voucher; (recibo) receipt, slip

residencia [resi'ðenθja] nf residence; **~l** nf (urbanización) housing estate

residente [resi'ðente] adj, nm/f resident

residir [resi'ðir] vi to reside, live; **~ en** to reside in, lie in

residuo [re'siðwo] nm residue

resignación [resiɣna'θjon] nf resignation; **resignarse** vr: **resignarse a** o **con** to resign o.s. to, be resigned to

resina [re'sina] nf resin

resistencia [resis'tenθja] nf (dureza) endurance, strength; (oposición, ELEC) resistance; **resistente** adj strong, hardy; resistant

resistir [resis'tir] vt (soportar) to bear; (oponerse a) to resist, oppose; (aguantar) to put up with ♦ vi to resist; (aguantar) to last, endure; **~se** vr: **~se a** to refuse to, resist

resolución [resolu'θjon] nf resolution; (decisión) decision; **resoluto, a** adj resolute

resolver [resol'ßer] vt to resolve; (solucionar) to solve, resolve; (decidir) to decide, settle; **~se** vr to make up one's mind

resonancia [reso'nanθja] nf (del sonido) resonance; (repercusión) repercussion

resonar [reso'nar] vi to ring, echo

resoplar [reso'plar] vi to snort; **resoplido** nm heavy breathing

resorte [re'sorte] nm spring; (fig) lever

respaldar [respal'dar] vt to back (up), support; **~se** vr to lean back; **~se con** o **en** (fig) to take one's stand on; **respaldo** nm (de sillón) back; (fig) support, backing

respectivo, a [respek'tißo, a] adj respective; **en lo ~ a** with regard to

respecto [res'pekto] nm: **al ~** on this matter; **con ~ a**, **~ de** with regard to, in relation to

respetable [respe'taßle] adj respectable

respetar [respe'tar] vt to respect; **respeto** nm respect; (acatamiento) deference; **respetos** nmpl respects; **respetuoso, a** adj respectful

respingo [res'pingo] nm start, jump

respiración [respira'θjon] nf breathing; (MED) respiration; (ventilación) ventilation

respirar [respi'rar] vi to breathe; **respiratorio, a** adj respiratory; **respiro** nm breathing; (fig: descanso) respite

resplandecer [resplande'θer] vi to shine; **resplandeciente** adj resplendent, shining; **resplandor** nm brilliance, brightness; (de luz, fuego) blaze

responder [respon'der] vt to answer ♦ vi to answer; (fig) to respond; (pey) to answer

back; **~ de** o **por** to answer for; **respondón, ona** adj cheeky

responsabilidad [responsaßili'ðað] nf responsibility

responsabilizarse [responsaßili'θarse] vr to make o.s. responsible, take charge

responsable [respon'saßle] adj responsible

respuesta [res'pwesta] nf answer, reply

resquebrajar [reskeßra'xar] vt to crack, split; **~se** vr to crack, split

resquemor [reske'mor] nm resentment

resquicio [res'kiθjo] nm chink; (hendedura) crack

resta ['resta] nf (MAT) remainder

restablecer [restaßle'θer] vt to re-establish, restore; **~se** vr to recover

restallar [resta'ʎar] vi to crack

restante [res'tante] adj remaining; **lo ~** the remainder

restar [res'tar] vt (MAT) to subtract; (fig) to take away ♦ vi to remain, be left

restauración [restaura'θjon] nf restoration

restaurante [restau'rante] nm restaurant

restaurar [restau'rar] vt to restore

restitución [restitu'θjon] nf return, restitution

restituir [restitu'ir] vt (devolver) to return, give back; (rehabilitar) to restore

resto ['resto] nm (residuo) rest, remainder; (apuesta) stake; **~s** nmpl remains

restregar [restre'xar] vt to scrub, rub

restricción [restrik'θjon] nf restriction

restrictivo, a [restrik'tißo, a] adj restrictive

restringir [restrin'xir] vt to restrict, limit

resucitar [resuθi'tar] vt, vi to resuscitate, revive

resuello [re'sweʎo] nm (aliento) breath; **estar sin ~** to be breathless

resuelto, a [re'swelto, a] pp de **resolver** ♦ adj resolute, determined

resultado [resul'taðo] nm result; (conclusión) outcome; **resultante** adj resulting, resultant

resultar [resul'tar] vi (ser) to be; (llegar a ser) to turn out to be; (salir bien) to turn out well; (COM) to amount to; **~ de** to stem from; **me resulta difícil hacerlo** it's difficult for me to do it

resumen [re'sumen] (pl **resúmenes**) nm summary, résumé; **en ~** in short

resumir [resu'mir] vt to sum up; (cortar) to abridge, cut down; (condensar) to summarize

resurgir [resur'xir] vi (reaparecer) to reappear

resurrección [resurre(k)'θjon] nf resurrection

retablo [re'taßlo] nm altarpiece

retaguardia [reta'ɣwarðja] nf rearguard

retahíla [reta'ila] nf series, string

retal [re'tal] nm remnant

retar [re'tar] vt to challenge; (desafiar) to

defy, dare

retardar [retar'ðar] vt (*demorar*) to delay; (*hacer más lento*) to slow down; (*retener*) to hold back

retazo [re'taθo] nm snippet (*BRIT*), fragment

retener [rete'ner] vt (*intereses*) to withhold

reticente [reti'θente] adj (*tono*) insinuating; (*postura*) reluctant; **ser ~ a hacer algo** to be reluctant o unwilling to do sth

retina [re'tina] nf retina

retintín [retin'tin] nm jangle, jingle

retirada [reti'raða] nf (*MIL, refugio*) retreat; (*de dinero*) withdrawal; (*de embajador*) recall; **retirado, a** adj (*lugar*) remote; (*vida*) quiet; (*jubilado*) retired

retirar [reti'rar] vt to withdraw; (*quitar*) to remove; (*jubilar*) to retire, pension off; **~se** vr to retreat, withdraw; to retire; (*acostarse*) to retire, go to bed; **retiro** nm retreat; retirement; (*pago*) pension

reto ['reto] nm dare, challenge

retocar [reto'kar] vt (*fotografía*) to touch up, retouch

retoño [re'toɲo] nm sprout, shoot; (*fig*) offspring, child

retoque [re'toke] nm retouching

retorcer [retor'θer] vt to twist; (*manos, lavado*) to wring; **~se** vr to become twisted; (*mover el cuerpo*) to writhe

retorcido, a [retor'θiðo, a] adj (*persona*) devious

retórica [re'torika] nf rhetoric; (*pey*) affectedness; **retórico, a** adj rhetorical

retornar [retor'nar] vt to return, give back ♦ vi to return, go/come back; **retorno** nm return

retortijón [retorti'xon] nm twist, twisting

retozar [reto'θar] vi (*juguetear*) to frolic, romp; (*saltar*) to gambol; **retozón, ona** adj playful

retracción [retrak'θjon] nf retraction

retractarse [retrak'tarse] vr to retract; **me retracto** I take that back

retraerse [retra'erse] vr to retreat, withdraw; **retraído, a** adj shy, retiring; **retraimiento** nm retirement; (*timidez*) shyness

retransmisión [retransmi'sjon] nf repeat (broadcast)

retransmitir [retransmi'tir] vt (*mensaje*) to relay; (*TV etc*) to repeat, retransmit; (: *en vivo*) to broadcast live

retrasado, a [retra'saðo, a] adj late; (*MED*) mentally retarded; (*país etc*) backward, underdeveloped

retrasar [retra'sar] vt (*demorar*) to postpone, put off; (*retardar*) to slow down ♦ vi (*atrasarse*) to be late; (*reloj*) to be slow; (*producción*) to fall (off); (*quedarse atrás*) to lag behind; **~se** vr to be late; to be slow; to

fall (off); to lag behind

retraso [re'traso] nm (*demora*) delay; (*lentitud*) slowness; (*tardanza*) lateness; (*atraso*) backwardness; **~s** (*FINANZAS*) nmpl arrears; **llegar con ~** to arrive late; **~ mental** mental deficiency

retratar [retra'tar] vt (*ARTE*) to paint the portrait of; (*fotografiar*) to photograph; (*fig*) to depict, describe; **~se** vr to have one's portrait painted; to have one's photograph taken; **retrato** nm portrait; (*fig*) likeness; **retrato-robot** nm Identikit ® picture

retreta [re'treta] nf retreat

retrete [re'trete] nm toilet

retribución [retriβu'θjon] nf (*recompensa*) reward; (*pago*) pay, payment

retribuir [retri'βwir] vt (*recompensar*) to reward; (*pagar*) to pay

retro... ['retro] prefijo retro...

retroactivo, a [retroak'tiβo, a] adj retroactive, retrospective

retroceder [retroθe'ðer] vi (*echarse atrás*) to move back(wards); (*fig*) to back down

retroceso [retro'θeso] nm backward movement; (*MED*) relapse; (*fig*) backing down

retrógrado, a [re'troxraðo, a] adj retrograde, retrogressive; (*POL*) reactionary

retrospectivo, a [retrospek'tiβo, a] adj retrospective

retrovisor [retroβi'sor] nm (*tb: espejo ~*) rear-view mirror

retumbar [retum'bar] vi to echo, resound

reúma [re'uma], **reuma** ['reuma] nm rheumatism

reumatismo [reuma'tismo] nm = **reúma**

reunificar [reunifi'kar] vt to reunify

reunión [reu'njon] nf (*asamblea*) meeting; (*fiesta*) party

reunir [reu'nir] vt (*juntar*) to reunite, join (together); (*recoger*) to gather (together); (*personas*) to get together; (*cualidades*) to combine; **~se** vr (*personas: en asamblea*) to meet, gather

revalidar [reβali'ðar] vt (*ratificar*) to confirm, ratify

revalorizar [reβalori'θar] vt to revalue, reassess

revancha [re'βantʃa] nf revenge

revelación [reβela'θjon] nf revelation

revelado [reβe'laðo] nm developing

revelar [reβe'lar] vt to reveal; (*FOTO*) to develop

reventa [re'βenta] nf (*de entradas: para concierto*) touting

reventar [reβen'tar] vt to burst, explode

reventón [reβen'ton] nm (*AUTO*) blow-out (*BRIT*), flat (*US*)

reverencia [reβe'renθja] nf reverence;

reverenciar vt to revere
reverendo, a [reße'rendo, a] adj reverend
reverente [reße'rente] adj reverent
reversible [reßer'sißle] adj (prenda) reversible
reverso [re'ßerso] nm back, other side; (de moneda) reverse
revertir [reßer'tir] vi to revert
revés [re'ßes] nm back, wrong side; (fig) reverse, setback; (DEPORTE) backhand; **al ~** the wrong way round; (de arriba abajo) upside down; (ropa) inside out; **volver algo del ~** to turn sth round; (ropa) to turn sth inside out
revestir [reßes'tir] vt (cubrir) to cover, coat
revisar [reßi'sar] vt (examinar) to check; (texto etc) to revise; **revisión** nf revision
revisor, a [reßi'sor, a] nm/f inspector; (FERRO) ticket collector
revista [re'ßista] nf magazine, review; (TEATRO) revue; (inspección) inspection; **pasar ~ a** to review, inspect
revivir [reßi'ßir] vi to revive
revocación [reßoka'θjon] nf repeal
revocar [reßo'kar] vt to revoke
revolcarse [reßol'karse] vr to roll about
revolotear [reßolote'ar] vi to flutter
revoltijo [reßol'tixo] nm mess, jumble
revoltoso, a [reßol'toso, a] adj (travieso) naughty, unruly
revolución [reßolu'θjon] nf revolution; **revolucionar** vt to revolutionize; **revolucionario, a** adj, nm/f revolutionary
revolver [reßol'ßer] vt (desordenar) to disturb, mess up; (mover) to move about ♦ vi: **~ en** to go through, rummage (about) in; **~se** vr (volver contra) to turn on o against
revólver [re'ßolßer] nm revolver
revuelo [re'ßwelo] nm fluttering; (fig) commotion
revuelta [re'ßwelta] nf (motín) revolt; (agitación) commotion
revuelto, a [re'ßwelto, a] pp de **revolver** ♦ adj (mezclado) mixed-up, in disorder
rey [rei] nm king; **Día de R~es** Twelfth Night
reyerta [re'jerta] nf quarrel, brawl
rezagado, a [reθa'xaðo, a] nm/f straggler
rezagar [reθa'xar] vt (dejar atrás) to leave behind; (retrasar) to delay, postpone
rezar [re'θar] vi to pray; **~ con** (fam) to concern, have to do with; **rezo** nm prayer
rezongar [reθon'gar] vi to grumble
rezumar [reθu'mar] vt to ooze
ría ['ria] nf estuary
riada [ri'aða] nf flood
ribera [ri'ßera] nf (de río) bank; (: área) riverside
ribete [ri'ßete] nm (de vestido) border; (fig) addition; **~ar** vt to edge, border
ricino [ri'θino] nm: **aceite de ~** castor oil

rico, a ['riko, a] adj rich; (adinerado) wealthy, rich; (lujoso) luxurious; (comida) delicious; (niño) lovely, cute ♦ nm/f rich person
rictus ['riktus] nm (mueca) sneer, grin
ridiculez [riðiku'leθ] nf absurdity
ridiculizar [riðikuli'θar] vt to ridicule
ridículo, a [ri'ðikulo, a] adj ridiculous; **hacer el ~** to make a fool of o.s.; **poner a uno en ~** to make a fool of sb
riego ['rjexo] nm (aspersión) watering; (irrigación) irrigation
riel [rjel] nm rail
rienda ['rjenda] nf rein; **dar ~ suelta a** to give free rein to
riesgo ['rjesxo] nm risk; **correr el ~ de** to run the risk of
rifa ['rifa] nf (lotería) raffle; **rifar** vt to raffle
rifle ['rifle] nm rifle
rigidez [rixi'ðeθ] nf rigidity, stiffness; (fig) strictness; **rígido, a** adj rigid, stiff; strict, inflexible
rigor [ri'xor] nm strictness, rigour; (inclemencia) harshness; **de ~** de rigueur, essential; **riguroso, a** adj rigorous; harsh; (severo) severe
rimar [ri'mar] vi to rhyme
rimbombante [rimbom'bante] adj pompous
rímel ['rimel] nm mascara
rímmel ['rimel] nm = **rímel**
rincón [rin'kon] nm corner (inside)
rinoceronte [rinoθe'ronte] nm rhinoceros
riña ['riɲa] nf (disputa) argument; (pelea) brawl
riñón [ri'ɲon] nm kidney
río etc ['rio] vb ver **reir** ♦ nm river; (fig) torrent, stream; **~ abajo/arriba** downstream/ upstream; **~ de la Plata** River Plate
rioja [ri'oxa] nm (vino) rioja (wine)
rioplatense [riopla'tense] adj of o from the River Plate region
riqueza [ri'keθa] nf wealth, riches pl; (cualidad) richness
risa ['risa] nf laughter; (una ~) laugh; **¡qué ~!** what a laugh!
risco ['risko] nm crag, cliff
risible [ri'sißle] adj ludicrous, laughable
risotada [riso'taða] nf guffaw, loud laugh
ristra ['ristra] nf string
risueño, a [ri'sweɲo, a] adj (sonriente) smiling; (contento) cheerful
ritmo ['ritmo] nm rhythm; **a ~ lento** slowly; **trabajar a ~ lento** to go slow
rito ['rito] nm rite
ritual [ri'twal] adj, nm ritual
rival [ri'ßal] adj, nm/f rival; **~idad** nf rivalry; **~izar** vi: **~izar con** to rival, vie with
rizado, a [ri'θaðo, a] adj curly ♦ nm curls pl
rizar [ri'θar] vt to curl; **~se** vr (pelo) to curl;

(*agua*) to ripple; **rizo** *nm* curl; ripple

RNE *nf abr* = **Radio Nacional de España**

robar [ro'βar] *vt* to rob; (*objeto*) to steal; (*casa etc*) to break into; (*NAIPES*) to draw

roble ['roβle] *nm* oak; **~dal** *nm* oakwood

robo ['roβo] *nm* robbery, theft

robot [ro'βot] *nm* robot; **~ (de cocina)** food processor

robustecer [roβuste'θer] *vt* to strengthen

robusto, a [ro'βusto, a] *adj* robust, strong

roca ['roka] *nf* rock

roce ['roθe] *nm* (*caricia*) brush; (*TEC*) friction; (*en la piel*) graze; **tener ~ con** to be in close contact with

rociar [ro'θjar] *vt* to spray

rocín [ro'θin] *nm* nag, hack

rocío [ro'θio] *nm* dew

rocoso, a [ro'koso, a] *adj* rocky

rodaballo [roða'βaʎo] *nm* turbot

rodado, a [ro'ðaðo, a] *adj* (*con ruedas*) wheeled

rodaja [ro'ðaxa] *nf* slice

rodaje [ro'ðaxe] *nm* (*CINE*) shooting, filming; (*AUTO*): **en ~** running in

rodar [ro'ðar] *vt* (*vehículo*) to wheel (along); (*escalera*) to roll down; (*viajar por*) to travel (over) ♦ *vi* to roll; (*coche*) to go, run; (*CINE*) to shoot, film

rodear [roðe'ar] *vt* to surround ♦ *vi* to go round; **~se** *vr*: **~se de amigos** to surround o.s. with friends

rodeo [ro'ðeo] *nm* (*ruta indirecta*) detour; (*evasión*) evasion; (*AM*) rodeo; **hablar sin ~s** to come to the point, speak plainly

rodilla [ro'ðiʎa] *nf* knee; **de ~s** kneeling; **ponerse de ~s** to kneel (down)

rodillo [ro'ðiʎo] *nm* roller; (*CULIN*) rolling-pin

roedor, a [roe'ðor, a] *adj* gnawing ♦ *nm* rodent

roer [ro'er] *vt* (*masticar*) to gnaw; (*corroer, fig*) to corrode

rogar [ro'xar] *vt, vi* (*pedir*) to ask for; (*suplicar*) to beg, plead; **se ruega no fumar** please do not smoke

rojizo, a [ro'xiθo, a] *adj* reddish

rojo, a ['roxo, a] *adj, nm* red; **al ~ vivo** red-hot

rol [rol] *nm* list, roll; (*papel*) role

rollito [ro'ʎito] *nm*: **~ de primavera** spring roll

rollizo, a [ro'ʎiθo, a] *adj* (*objeto*) cylindrical; (*persona*) plump

rollo ['roʎo] *nm* roll; (*de cuerda*) coil; (*madera*) log; (*fam*) bore; **¡qué ~!** what a carry-on!

Roma ['roma] *n* Rome

romance [ro'manθe] *nm* (*amoroso*) romance; (*LITERATURA*) ballad

romano, a [ro'mano, a] *adj, nm/f* Roman; **a la romana** in batter

romanticismo [romanti'θismo] *nm* romanticism

romántico, a [ro'mantiko, a] *adj* romantic

rombo ['rombo] *nm* (*GEOM*) rhombus

romería [rome'ria] *nf* (*REL*) pilgrimage; (*excursión*) trip, outing

romero, a [ro'mero, a] *nm/f* pilgrim ♦ *nm* rosemary

romo, a ['romo, a] *adj* blunt; (*fig*) dull

rompecabezas [rompeka'βeθas] *nm inv* riddle, puzzle; (*juego*) jigsaw (puzzle)

rompeolas [rompe'olas] *nm inv* breakwater

romper [rom'per] *vt* to break; (*hacer pedazos*) to smash; (*papel, tela etc*) to tear, rip ♦ *vi* (*olas*) to break; (*sol, diente*) to break through; **~ un contrato** to break a contract; **~ a** (*empezar a*) to start (suddenly) to; **~ a llorar** to burst into tears; **~ con uno** to fall out with sb

ron [ron] *nm* rum

roncar [ron'kar] *vi* to snore

ronco, a ['ronko, a] *adj* (*afónico*) hoarse; (*áspero*) raucous

ronda ['ronda] *nf* (*gen*) round; (*patrulla*) patrol; **rondar** *vt* to patrol ♦ *vi* to patrol; (*fig*) to prowl round

ronquido [ron'kiðo] *nm* snore, snoring

ronronear [ronrone'ar] *vi* to purr; **ronroneo** *nm* purr

roña ['roɲa] *nf* (*VETERINARIA*) mange; (*mugre*) dirt, grime; (*óxido*) rust

roñoso, a [ro'ɲoso, a] *adj* (*mugriento*) filthy; (*tacaño*) mean

ropa ['ropa] *nf* clothes *pl*, clothing; **~ blanca** linen; **~ de cama** bed linen; **~ interior** underwear; **~ para lavar** washing; **~je** *nm* gown, robes *pl*

ropero [ro'pero] *nm* linen cupboard; (*guardarropa*) wardrobe

rosa ['rosa] *adj* pink ♦ *nf* rose; **~ de los vientos** the compass

rosado, a [ro'saðo, a] *adj* pink ♦ *nm* rosé

rosal [ro'sal] *nm* rosebush

rosario [ro'sarjo] *nm* (*REL*) rosary; **rezar el ~** to say the rosary

rosca ['roska] *nf* (*de tornillo*) thread; (*de humo*) coil, spiral; (*pan, postre*) ring-shaped roll/pastry

rosetón [rose'ton] *nm* rosette; (*ARQ*) rose window

rosquilla [ros'kiʎa] *nf* doughnut-shaped fritter

rostro ['rostro] *nm* (*cara*) face

rotación [rota'θjon] *nf* rotation; **~ de cultivos** crop rotation

rotativo, a [rota'tiβo, a] *adj* rotary

roto, a ['roto, a] *pp de* **romper** ♦ *adj* broken

rotonda [ro'tonda] *nf* roundabout

rótula ['rotula] *nf* kneecap; (*TEC*) ball-and-socket joint

rotulador [rotula'ðor] *nm* felt-tip pen

rotular [rotu'lar] *vt* (*carta, documento*) to head, entitle; (*objeto*) to label; **rótulo** *nm* heading, title; label; (*letrero*) sign

rotundamente [rotunda'mente] *adv* (*negar*) flatly; (*responder, afirmar*) emphatically; **rotundo, a** *adj* round; (*enfático*) emphatic

rotura [ro'tura] *nf* (*acto*) breaking; (*MED*) fracture

roturar [rotu'rar] *vt* to plough

rozadura [roθa'ðura] *nf* abrasion, graze

rozar [ro'θar] *vt* (*frotar*) to rub; (*arañar*) to scratch; (*tocar ligeramente*) to shave, touch lightly; **~se** *vr* to rub (together); **~se con** (*fam*) to rub shoulders with

rte. *abr* (= *remite, remitente*) sender

RTVE *nf abr* = **Radiotelevisión Española**

rubí [ru'ßi] *nm* ruby; (*de reloj*) jewel

rubio, a ['rußjo, a] *adj* fair-haired, blond(e) ♦ *nm/f* blond/blonde; **tabaco ~** Virginia tobacco

rubor [ru'ßor] *nm* (*sonrojo*) blush; (*timidez*) bashfulness; **~izarse** *vr* to blush

rúbrica ['rußrika] *nf* (*de la firma*) flourish; **rubricar** *vt* (*firmar*) to sign with a flourish; (*concluir*) to sign and seal

rudimentario, a [ruðimen'tarjo, a] *adj* rudimentary; **rudimento** *nm* rudiment

rudo, a ['ruðo, a] *adj* (*sin pulir*) unpolished; (*grosero*) coarse; (*violento*) violent; (*sencillo*) simple

rueda ['rweða] *nf* wheel; (*círculo*) ring, circle; (*rodaja*) slice, round; **~ delantera/trasera/de repuesto** front/back/spare wheel; **~ de prensa** press conference

ruedo ['rweðo] *nm* (*círculo*) circle; (*TAUR*) arena, bullring

ruego *etc* ['rweɣo] *vb ver* **rogar** ♦ *nm* request

rufián [ru'fjan] *nm* scoundrel

rugby ['ruɣßi] *nm* rugby

rugido [ru'xiðo] *nm* roar

rugir [ru'xir] *vi* to roar

rugoso, a [ru'ɣoso, a] *adj* (*arrugado*) wrinkled; (*áspero*) rough; (*desigual*) ridged

ruido ['rwiðo] *nm* noise; (*sonido*) sound; (*alboroto*) racket, row; (*escándalo*) commotion, rumpus; **~so, a** *adj* noisy, loud; (*fig*) sensational

ruin [rwin] *adj* contemptible, mean

ruina ['rwina] *nf* ruin; (*colapso*) collapse; (*de persona*) ruin, downfall

ruindad [rwin'dað] *nf* lowness, meanness; (*acto*) low o mean act

ruinoso, a [rwi'noso, a] *adj* ruinous; (*destartalado*) dilapidated, tumbledown; (*COM*) disastrous

ruiseñor [rwise'ɲor] *nm* nightingale

ruleta [ru'leta] *nf* roulette

rulo ['rulo] *nm* (*para el pelo*) curler

Rumanía [ruma'nia] *nf* Rumania

rumba ['rumba] *nf* rumba

rumbo ['rumbo] *nm* (*ruta*) route, direction; (*ángulo de dirección*) course, bearing; (*fig*) course of events; **ir con ~ a** to be heading for

rumboso, a [rum'boso, a] *adj* generous

rumiante [ru'mjante] *nm* ruminant

rumiar [ru'mjar] *vt* to chew; (*fig*) to chew over ♦ *vi* to chew the cud

rumor [ru'mor] *nm* (*ruido sordo*) low sound; (*murmuración*) murmur, buzz

rumorearse *vr*: **se rumorea que** it is rumoured that

runrún [run'run] *nm* (*voces*) murmur, sound of voices; (*fig*) rumour

rupestre [ru'pestre] *adj* rock *cpd*

ruptura [rup'tura] *nf* rupture

rural [ru'ral] *adj* rural

Rusia ['rusja] *nf* Russia; **ruso, a** *adj, nm/f* Russian

rústica ['rustika] *nf*: **libro en ~** paperback (book); *ver tb* **rústico**

rústico, a ['rustiko, a] *adj* rustic; (*ordinario*) coarse, uncouth ♦ *nm/f* yokel

ruta ['ruta] *nf* route

rutina [ru'tina] *nf* routine; **~rio, a** *adj* routine

S, s

S *abr* (= *santo, a*) St; (= *sur*) S

s. *abr* (= *siglo*) C.; (= *siguiente*) foll

S.A. *abr* (= *Sociedad Anónima*) Ltd. (*BRIT*), Inc. (*US*)

sábado ['saßaðo] *nm* Saturday

sábana ['saßana] *nf* sheet

sabandija [saßan'dixa] *nf* bug, insect

sabañón [saßa'ɲon] *nm* chilblain

saber [sa'ßer] *vt* to know; (*llegar a conocer*) to find out, learn; (*tener capacidad de*) to know how to ♦ *vi*: **~ a** to taste of, taste like ♦ *nm* knowledge, learning; **a ~** namely; **¿sabes conducir/nadar?** can you drive/swim?; **¿sabes francés?** do you speak French?; **~ de memoria** to know by heart; **hacer ~ algo a uno** to inform sb of sth, let sb know sth

sabiduría [saßiðu'ria] *nf* (*conocimientos*) wisdom; (*instrucción*) learning

sabiendas [sa'ßjendas]: **a ~** *adv* knowingly

sabio, a ['saßjo,a] *adj* (*docto*) learned; (*prudente*) wise, sensible

sabor [sa'ßor] *nm* taste, flavour; **~ear** *vt* to taste, savour; (*fig*) to relish

sabotaje [saßo'taxe] *nm* sabotage

saboteador, a [saßotea'ðor, a] *nm/f* saboteur

sabotear [saßote'ar] *vt* to sabotage

sabré etc vb ver **saber**

sabroso, a [sa'ßroso, a] adj tasty; (fig: fam) racy, salty

sacacorchos [saka'kortʃos] nm inv corkscrew

sacapuntas [saka'puntas] nm inv pencil sharpener

sacar [sa'kar] vt to take out; (fig: extraer) to get (out); (quitar) to remove, get out; (hacer salir) to bring out; (conclusión) to draw; (novela etc) to publish, bring out; (ropa) to take off; (obra) to make; (premio) to receive; (entradas) to get; (TENIS) to serve; **~ adelante** (niño) to bring up; (negocio) to carry on, go on with; **~ a uno a bailar** to get sb up to dance; **~ una foto** to take a photo; **~ la lengua** to stick out one's tongue; **~ buenas/malas notas** to get good/bad marks

sacarina [saka'rina] nf saccharin(e)

sacerdote [saθer'ðote] nm priest

saciar [sa'θjar] vt (hambre, sed) to satisfy; **~se** vr (de comida) to get full up; **comer hasta ~se** to eat one's fill

saco [sako] nm bag; (grande) sack; (su contenido) bagful; (AM) jacket; **~ de dormir** sleeping bag

sacramento [sakra'mento] nm sacrament

sacrificar [sakrifi'kar] vt to sacrifice; **sacrificio** nm sacrifice

sacrilegio [sakri'lexjo] nm sacrilege; **sacrílego, a** adj sacrilegious

sacristía [sakris'tia] nf sacristy

sacro, a [sakro, a] adj sacred

sacudida [saku'ðiða] nf (agitación) shake, shaking; (sacudimiento) jolt, bump; **~ eléctrica** electric shock

sacudir [saku'ðir] vt to shake; (golpear) to hit

sádico, a ['saðiko, a] adj sadistic ♦ nm/f sadist; **sadismo** nm sadism

saeta [sa'eta] nf (flecha) arrow

sagacidad [saɣaθi'ðað] nf shrewdness, cleverness; **sagaz** adj shrewd, clever

sagitario [saxi'tarjo] nm Sagittarius

sagrado, a [sa'ɣraðo, a] adj sacred, holy

Sáhara ['saara] nm: **el ~** the Sahara (desert)

sal [sal] vb ver **salir** ♦ nf salt

sala ['sala] nf room; (~ de estar) living room; (TEATRO) house, auditorium; (de hospital) ward; **~ de apelación** court; **~ de espera** waiting room; **~ de estar** living room; **~ de fiestas** dance hall

salado, a [sa'laðo, a] adj salty; (fig) witty, amusing; **agua salada** salt water

salar [sa'lar] vt to salt, add salt to

salarial [sala'rjal] adj (aumento, revisión) wage cpd, salary cpd

salario [sa'larjo] nm wage, pay

salchicha [sal'tʃitʃa] nf (pork) sausage; **salchichón** nm (salami-type) sausage

saldar [sal'dar] vt to pay; (vender) to sell off; (fig) to settle, resolve; **saldo** nm (pago) settlement; (de una cuenta) balance; (lo restante) remnant(s) (pl), remainder; **saldos** nmpl (en tienda) sale

saldré etc vb ver **salir**

salero [sa'lero] nm salt cellar

salgo etc vb ver **salir**

salida [sa'liða] nf (puerta etc) exit, way out; (acto) leaving, going out; (de tren, AVIAT) departure; (TEC) output, production; (fig) way out; (COM) opening; (GEO, válvula) outlet; (de gas) leak; **calle sin ~** cul-de-sac; **~ de incendios** fire escape

saliente [sa'ljente] adj (ARQ) projecting; (sol) rising; (fig) outstanding

---

PALABRA CLAVE

salir [sa'lir] vi 1 (partir: tb: **~ de**) to leave; **Juan ha salido** Juan is out; **salió de la cocina** he came out of the kitchen

2 (aparecer) to appear; (disco, libro) to come out; **anoche salió en la tele** she appeared o was on TV last night; **salió en todos los periódicos** it was in all the papers

3 (resultar): **la muchacha nos salió muy trabajadora** the girl turned out to be a very hard worker; **la comida te ha salido exquisita** the food was delicious; **sale muy caro** it's very expensive

4: **~le a uno algo: la entrevista que hice me salió bien/mal** the interview I did went o turned out well/badly

5: **~ adelante: no sé como haré para ~ adelante** I don't know how I'll get by

♦ **~se** vr (líquido) to spill; (animal) to escape

---

salmo ['salmo] nm psalm

salmón [sal'mon] nm salmon

salmonete [salmo'nete] nm red mullet

salmuera [sal'mwera] nf pickle, brine

salón [sa'lon] nm (de casa) living room, lounge; (muebles) lounge suite; **~ de belleza** beauty parlour; **~ de baile** dance hall

salpicadero [salpika'ðero] nm (AUTO) dashboard

salpicar [salpi'kar] vt (rociar) to sprinkle, spatter; (esparcir) to scatter

salpicón [salpi'kon] nm: **~ de mariscos** seafood salad

salsa ['salsa] nf sauce; (con carne asada) gravy; (fig) spice

saltamontes [salta'montes] nm inv grasshopper

saltar [sal'tar] vt to jump (over), leap (over); (dejar de lado) to skip, miss out ♦ vi to jump, leap; (pelota) to bounce; (al aire) to fly up; (quebrarse) to break; (al agua) to dive; (fig) to explode, blow up

salto ['salto] nm jump, leap; (al agua) dive; ~ **de agua** waterfall; ~ **de altura** high jump

saltón, ona [sal'ton, ona] adj (ojos) bulging, popping; (dientes) protruding

salud [sa'luð] nf health; ¡(a su) ~! cheers!, good health!; **~able** adj (de buena ~) healthy; (provechoso) good, beneficial

saludar [salu'ðar] vt to greet; (MIL) to salute; **saludo** nm greeting; "**saludos**" (en carta) "best wishes", "regards"

salva ['salßa] nf: ~ **de aplausos** ovation

salvación [salßa'θjon] nf salvation; (rescate) rescue

salvado [sal'ßaðo] nm bran

salvaguardar [salßaɣwar'ðar] vt to safeguard

salvajada [salßa'xaða] nf atrocity

salvaje [sal'ßaxe] adj wild; (tribu) savage; **salvajismo** nm savagery

salvamento [salßa'mento] nm rescue

salvar [sal'ßar] vt (rescatar) to save, rescue; (resolver) to overcome, resolve; (cubrir distancias) to cover, travel; (hacer excepción) to except, exclude; (barco) to salvage

salvavidas [salßa'ßiðas] adj inv: **bote/ chaleco/cinturón ~** lifeboat/life jacket/life belt

salvo, a ['salßo, a] adj safe ♦ adv except (for), save; **a ~** out of danger; ~ **que** unless; **~conducto** nm safe-conduct

san [san] adj saint; **S~ Juan** St John

sanar [sa'nar] vt (herida) to heal; (persona) to cure ♦ vi (persona) to get well, recover; (herida) to heal

sanatorio [sana'torjo] nm sanatorium

sanción [san'θjon] nf sanction; **sancionar** vt to sanction

sandalia [san'dalja] nf sandal

sandez [san'deθ] nf foolishness

sandía [san'dia] nf watermelon

sandwich ['sandwitʃ] (pl **~s**, **~es**) nm sandwich

saneamiento [sanea'mjento] nm sanitation

sanear [sane'ar] vt to clean up; (terreno) to drain

sangrar [san'grar] vt, vi to bleed; **sangre** nf blood

sangría [san'gria] nf sangría, sweetened drink of red wine with fruit

sangriento, a [san'grjento, a] adj bloody

sanguijuela [sangi'xwela] nf (ZOOL, fig) leech

sanguinario, a [sangi'narjo, a] adj bloodthirsty

sanguíneo, a [san'gineo, a] adj blood cpd

sanidad [sani'ðað] nf: ~ **(pública)** public health

sanitario, a [sani'tarjo, a] adj health cpd; **~s** nmpl toilets (BRIT), washroom (US)

sano, a ['sano, a] adj healthy; (sin daños)

sound; (comida) wholesome; (entero) whole, intact; ~ **y salvo** safe and sound

Santiago [san'tjaɣo] nm: ~ **(de Chile)** Santiago

santiamén [santja'men] nm: **en un ~** in no time at all

santidad [santi'ðað] nf holiness, sanctity

santiguarse [santi'xwarse] vr to make the sign of the cross

santo, a ['santo, a] adj holy; (fig) wonderful, miraculous ♦ nm/f saint ♦ nm saint's day; ~ **y seña** password

santuario [san'twarjo] nm sanctuary, shrine

saña ['sana] nf rage, fury

sapo ['sapo] nm toad

saque ['sake] nm (TENIS) service, serve; (FÚTBOL) throw-in; ~ **de esquina** corner (kick)

saquear [sake'ar] vt (MIL) to sack; (robar) to loot, plunder; (fig) to ransack; **saqueo** nm sacking; looting, plundering; ransacking

sarampión [saram'pjon] nm measles sg

sarcasmo [sar'kasmo] nm sarcasm; **sarcástico, a** adj sarcastic

sardina [sar'ðina] nf sardine

sargento [sar'xento] nm sergeant

sarmiento [sar'mjento] nm (BOT) vine shoot

sarna ['sarna] nf itch; (MED) scabies

sarpullido [sarpu'ʎiðo] nm (MED) rash

sarro ['sarro] nm (en dientes) tartar, plaque

sartén [sar'ten] nf frying pan

sastre ['sastre] nm tailor; **~ría** nf (arte) tailoring; (tienda) tailor's (shop)

Satanás [sata'nas] nm Satan

satélite [sa'telite] nm satellite

sátira ['satira] nf satire

satisfacción [satisfak'θjon] nf satisfaction

satisfacer [satisfa'θer] vt to satisfy; (gastos) to meet; (pérdida) to make good; **~se** vr to satisfy o.s., be satisfied; (vengarse) to take revenge; **satisfecho, a** adj satisfied; (contento) content(ed), happy; (tb: satisfecho de sí mismo) self-satisfied, smug

saturar [satu'rar] vt to saturate; **~se** vr (mercado, aeropuerto) to reach saturation point

sauce ['sauθe] nm willow; ~ **llorón** weeping willow

sauna ['sauna] nf sauna

savia ['saßja] nf sap

saxofón [sakso'fon] nm saxophone

sazonar [saθo'nar] vt to ripen; (CULIN) to flavour, season

SE abr (= sudeste) SE

PALABRA CLAVE
---

se [se] pron **1** (reflexivo: sg: m) himself; (: f) herself; (: pl) themselves; (: cosa) itself; (: de Vd) yourself; (: de Vds) yourselves; ~ **está preparando** she's preparing herself; **para usos**

léxicos del pron ver el vb en cuestión, p.ej.
arrepentirse
2 (*con complemento indirecto*) to him; to her;
to them; to it; to you; **a usted ~ lo dije ayer** I
told you yesterday; **~ compró un sombrero** he
bought himself a hat; **~ rompió la pierna** he
broke his leg
3 (*uso recíproco*) each other, one another;
~ miraron (el uno al otro) they looked at each
other o one another
4 (*en oraciones pasivas*): **se han vendido
muchos libros** a lot of books have been sold
5 (*impers*): **~ dice que** people say that, it is
said that; **allí ~ come muy bien** the food there
is very good, you can eat very well there

sé *vb ver* **saber; ser**
sea *etc vb ver* **ser**
sebo ['seßo] *nm* fat, grease
secador [seka'ðor] *nm*: **~ de pelo** hair-dryer
secadora [seka'ðora] *nf* tumble dryer
secar [se'kar] *vt* to dry; **~se** *vr* to dry (off);
(*río, planta*) to dry up
sección [sek'θjon] *nf* section
seco, a ['seko, a] *adj* dry; (*carácter*) cold;
(*respuesta*) sharp, curt; **habrá pan a secas**
there will be just bread; **decir algo a secas** to
say sth curtly; **parar en ~** to stop dead
secretaría [sekreta'ria] *nf* secretariat
secretario, a [sekre'tarjo, a] *nm/f* secretary
secreto, a [se'kreto, a] *adj* secret; (*persona*)
secretive ♦ *nm* secret; (*calidad*) secrecy
secta ['sekta] *nf* sect; **~rio, a** *adj* sectarian
sector [sek'tor] *nm* sector
secuela [se'kwela] *nf* consequence
secuencia [se'kwenθja] *nf* sequence
secuestrar [sekwes'trar] *vt* to kidnap;
(*bienes*) to seize, confiscate; **secuestro** *nm*
kidnapping; seizure, confiscation
secular [seku'lar] *adj* secular
secundar [sekun'dar] *vt* to second, support
secundario, a [sekun'darjo, a] *adj*
secondary
sed [seð] *nf* thirst; **tener ~** to be thirsty
seda ['seða] *nf* silk
sedal [se'ðal] *nm* fishing line
sedante [se'ðante] *nm* sedative
sede ['seðe] *nf* (*de gobierno*) seat; (*de
compañía*) headquarters *pl*; **Santa S~** Holy
See
sedentario, a [seðen'tarjo, a] *adj* sedentary
sediento, a [se'ðjento, a] *adj* thirsty
sedimento [seði'mento] *nm* sediment
sedoso, a [se'ðoso, a] *adj* silky, silken
seducción [seðuk'θjon] *nf* seduction
seducir [seðu'θir] *vt* to seduce; (*cautivar*) to
charm, fascinate; (*atraer*) to attract;
seductor, a *adj* seductive; charming,
fascinating; attractive ♦ *nm/f* seducer

segar [se'ɣar] *vt* (*mies*) to reap, cut; (*hierba*)
to mow, cut
seglar [se'ɣlar] *adj* secular, lay
segregación [seɣreɣa'θjon] *nf* segregation.
~ racial racial segregation
segregar [seɣre'ɣar] *vt* to segregate, separate
seguida [se'ɣiða] *nf*: **en ~** at once, right away
seguido, a [se'ɣiðo, a] *adj* (*continuo*)
continuous, unbroken; (*recto*) straight ♦ *adv*
(*directo*) straight (on); (*después*) after; (AM: *a
menudo*) often; **~s** consecutive, successive; **5
días ~s** 5 days running, 5 days in a row
seguimiento [seɣi'mjento] *nm* chase,
pursuit; (*continuación*) continuation
seguir [se'ɣir] *vt* to follow; (*venir después*) to
follow on, come after; (*proseguir*) to
continue; (*perseguir*) to chase, pursue ♦ *vi*
(*gen*) to follow; (*continuar*) to continue, carry
o go on; **~se** *vr* to follow; **sigo sin
comprender** I still don't understand; **sigue
lloviendo** it's still raining
según [se'ɣun] *prep* according to ♦ *adv*:
¿**irás?** — **~ ¿are you going?** — it all depends
♦ *conj* as; **~ caminamos** while we walk
segundo, a [se'ɣundo, a] *adj* second ♦ *nm*
second ♦ *nf* second meaning; **de segunda
mano** second-hand; **segunda (clase)** second
class; **segunda enseñanza** secondary
education; **segunda (marcha)** (AUT) second
(gear)
seguramente [seɣura'mente] *adv* surely;
(*con certeza*) for sure, with certainty
seguridad [seɣuri'ðað] *nf* safety; (*del estado,
de casa etc*) security; (*certidumbre*) certainty;
(*confianza*) confidence; (*estabilidad*) stability;
~ social social security
seguro, a [se'ɣuro, a] *adj* (*cierto*) sure,
certain; (*fiel*) trustworthy; (*libre de peligro*)
safe; (*bien defendido, firme*) secure ♦ *adv* for
sure, certainly ♦ *nm* (COM) insurance;
~ contra terceros/a todo riesgo third party/
comprehensive insurance; **~s sociales** social
security *sg*
seis [seis] *num* six
seísmo [se'ismo] *nm* tremor, earthquake
selección [selek'θjon] *nf* selection;
seleccionar *vt* to pick, choose, select
selectividad [selektiβi'ðað] (ESP) *nf*
university entrance examination
selecto, a [se'lekto, a] *adj* select, choice;
(*escogido*) selected
sellar [se'ʎar] *vt* (*documento oficial*) to seal;
(*pasaporte, visado*) to stamp
sello ['seʎo] *nm* stamp; (*precinto*) seal
selva ['selβa] *nf* (*bosque*) forest, woods *pl*;
(*jungla*) jungle
semáforo [se'maforo] *nm* (AUTO) traffic lights
pl; (FERRO) signal
semana [se'mana] *nf* week; **entre ~** during

the week; **S~ Santa** Holy Week; **semanal** *adj*
weekly; **~rio** *nm* weekly magazine
semblante [sem'blante] *nm* face; (*fig*) look
sembrar [sem'brar] *vt* to sow; (*objetos*) to
sprinkle, scatter about; (*noticias etc*) to spread
semejante [seme'xante] *adj* (*parecido*)
similar ♦ *nm* fellow man, fellow creature; **~s**
alike, similar; **nunca hizo cosa ~** he never did
any such thing; **semejanza** *nf* similarity,
resemblance
semejar [seme'xar] *vi* to seem like, resemble;
~se *vr* to look alike, be similar
semen ['semen] *nm* semen
semestral [semes'tral] *adj* half-yearly, bi-
annual
semicírculo [semi'θirkulo] *nm* semicircle
semidesnatado, a [semiðesna'taðo, a] *adj*
semi-skimmed
semifinal [semifi'nal] *nf* semifinal
semilla [se'miʎa] *nf* seed
seminario [semi'narjo] *nm* (*REL*) seminary;
(*ESCOL*) seminar
sémola ['semola] *nf* semolina
Sena ['sena] *nm*: **el ~** the (river) Seine
senado [se'naðo] *nm* senate; **senador, a**
nm/f senator
sencillez [senθi'ʎeθ] *nf* simplicity; (*de
persona*) naturalness; **sencillo, a** *adj* simple;
natural, unaffected
senda ['senda] *nf* path, track
senderismo [sende'rismo] *nm* hiking
sendero [sen'dero] *nm* path, track
sendos, as ['sendos, as] *adj pl*: **les dio
~ golpes** he hit both of them
senil [se'nil] *adj* senile
seno ['seno] *nm* (*ANAT*) bosom, bust; (*fig*)
bosom; **~s** breasts
sensación [sensa'θjon] *nf* sensation;
(*sentido*) sense; (*sentimiento*) feeling;
sensacional *adj* sensational
sensato, a [sen'sato, a] *adj* sensible
sensible [sen'sible] *adj* sensitive; (*apreciable*)
perceptible, appreciable; (*pérdida*)
considerable; **~ro, a** *adj* sentimental
sensitivo, a [sensi'tißo, a] *adj* sense *cpd*
sensorial [senso'rjal] *adj* sensory
sensual [sen'swal] *adj* sensual
sentada [sen'taða] *nf* sitting; (*protesta*) sit-in
sentado, a [sen'taðo, a] *adj*: **estar ~** to sit,
be sitting (down); **dar por ~** to take for
granted, assume
sentar [sen'tar] *vt* to sit, seat; (*fig*) to
establish ♦ *vi* (*vestido*) to suit; (*alimento*):
~ bien/mal a to agree/disagree with; **~se** *vr*
(*persona*) to sit, sit down; (*los depósitos*) to
settle
sentencia [sen'tenθja] *nf* (*máxima*) maxim,
saying; (*JUR*) sentence; **sentenciar** *vt* to
sentence

sentido, a [sen'tiðo, a] *adj* (*pérdida*)
regrettable; (*carácter*) sensitive ♦ *nm* sense;
(*sentimiento*) feeling; (*significado*) sense,
meaning; (*dirección*) direction; **mi más
~ pésame** my deepest sympathy; **~ del humor**
sense of humour; **~ único** one-way (street);
tener ~ to make sense
sentimental [sentimen'tal] *adj* sentimental;
vida ~ love life
sentimiento [senti'mjento] *nm* feeling
sentir [sen'tir] *vt* to feel; (*percibir*) to
perceive, sense; (*lamentar*) to regret, be sorry
for ♦ *vi* (*tener la sensación*) to feel;
(*lamentarse*) to feel sorry ♦ *nm* opinion,
judgement; **~se bien/mal** to feel well/ill; **lo
siento** I'm sorry
seña ['seɲa] *nf* sign; (*MIL*) password; **~s** *nfpl*
(*dirección*) address *sg*; **~s personales** personal
description *sg*
señal [se'ɲal] *nf* sign; (*síntoma*) symptom;
(*FERRO, TELEC*) signal; (*marca*) mark; (*COM*)
deposit; **en ~ de** as a token of, as a sign of;
~ar *vt* to mark; (*indicar*) to point out,
indicate
señor [se'ɲor] *nm* (*hombre*) man; (*caballero*)
gentleman; (*dueño*) owner, master; (*trato:
antes de nombre propio*) Mr; (: *hablando
directamente*) sir; **muy ~ mío** Dear Sir; **el
~ alcalde/presidente** the mayor/president
señora [se'ɲora] *nf* (*dama*) lady; (*trato: antes
de nombre propio*) Mrs; (: *hablando
directamente*) madam; (*esposa*) wife; **Nuestra
S~** Our Lady
señorita [seɲo'rita] *nf* (*con nombre y/o
apellido*) Miss; (*mujer joven*) young lady
señorito [seɲo'rito] *nm* young gentleman;
(*pey*) rich kid
señuelo [se'ɲwelo] *nm* decoy
sepa *etc vb ver* **saber**
separación [separa'θjon] *nf* separation;
(*división*) division; (*hueco*) gap
separar [sepa'rar] *vt* to separate; (*dividir*) to
divide; **~se** *vr* (*parte*) to come away; (*partes*)
to come apart; (*persona*) to leave, go away;
(*matrimonio*) to separate; **separatismo** *nm*
separatism
sepia ['sepja] *nf* cuttlefish
septentrional [septentrjo'nal] *adj* northern
septiembre [sep'tjembre] *nm* September
séptimo, a ['septimo, a] *adj, nm* seventh
sepulcral [sepul'kral] *adj* (*fig: silencio,
atmósfera*) deadly; **sepulcro** *nm* tomb, grave
sepultar [sepul'tar] *vt* to bury; **sepultura** *nf*
(*acto*) burial; (*tumba*) grave, tomb
sequedad [seke'ðað] *nf* dryness; (*fig*)
brusqueness, curtness
sequía [se'kia] *nf* drought
séquito ['sekito] *nm* (*de rey etc*) retinue;
(*seguidores*) followers *pl*

PALABRA CLAVE

ser [ser] *vi* **1** (*descripción*) to be; **es médica/
muy alta** she's a doctor/very tall; **la familia es
de Cuzco** this (o her *etc*) family is from Cuzco;
soy Ana (*TELEC*) Ana speaking o here
2 (*propiedad*): **es de Joaquín** it's Joaquín's, it
belongs to Joaquín
3 (*horas, fechas, números*): **es la una** it's one
o'clock; **son las seis y media** it's half-past six;
es el 1 de junio it's the first of June; **somos/
son seis** there are six of us/them
4 (*en oraciones pasivas*): **ha sido descubierto
ya** it's already been discovered
5: **es de esperar que ...** it is to be hoped o I
etc hope that ...
6 (*locuciones con sub*): **o sea** that is to say;
sea él sea su hermana either him or his sister
7: **a no ~ por él** ... but for him ...
8: **a no ~ que**: **a no ~ que tenga uno ya** unless
he's got one already
♦ *nm* being; **~ humano** human being

serenarse [sere'narse] *vr* to calm down
sereno, a [se'reno, a] *adj* (*persona*) calm,
unruffled; (*el tiempo*) fine, settled; (*ambiente*)
calm, peaceful ♦ *nm* night watchman
serial [ser'jal] *nm* serial
serie ['serje] *nf* series; (*cadena*) sequence,
succession; **fuera de ~** out of order; (*fig*)
special, out of the ordinary; **fabricación en ~**
mass production
seriedad [serje'ðað] *nf* seriousness;
(*formalidad*) reliability; **serio, a** *adj* serious;
reliable, dependable; grave, serious; **en serio**
adv seriously
serigrafía [serixra'fia] *nf* silk-screen printing
sermón [ser'mon] *nm* (*REL*) sermon
seropositivo, a [seroposi'tiβo] *adj* HIV
positive
serpentear [serpente'ar] *vi* to wriggle;
(*camino, río*) to wind, snake↘
serpentina [serpen'tina] *nf* streamer
serpiente [ser'pjente] *nf* snake; **~ de
cascabel** rattlesnake
serranía [serra'nia] *nf* mountainous area
serrar [se'rrar] *vt* = aserrar
serrín [se'rrin] *nm* = aserrín
serrucho [se'rrutʃo] *nm* saw
servicio [ser'ßiθjo] *nm* service; **~s** *nmpl*
toilet(s); **~ incluido** service charge included;
~ militar military service
servidumbre [serßi'ðumbre] *nf* (*sujeción*)
servitude; (*criados*) servants *pl*, staff
servil [ser'ßil] *adj* servile
servilleta [serßi'ʎeta] *nf* serviette, napkin
servir [ser'ßir] *vt* to serve ♦ *vi* to serve; (*tener
utilidad*) to be of use, be useful; **~se** *vr* to
serve o help o.s.; **~se de algo** to make use of

sth, use sth; **sírvase pasar** please come in
sesenta [se'senta] *num* sixty
sesgo ['sesɣo] *nm* slant; (*fig*) slant, twist
sesión [se'sjon] *nf* (*POL*) session, sitting;
(*CINE*) showing
seso ['seso] *nm* brain; **sesudo, a** *adj* sensible,
wise
seta ['seta] *nf* mushroom; **~ venenosa**
toadstool
setecientos, as [sete'θjentos, as] *adj, num*
seven hundred
setenta [se'tenta] *num* seventy
seto ['seto] *nm* hedge
seudónimo [seu'ðonimo] *nm* pseudonym
severidad [seßeri'ðað] *nf* severity; **severo, a**
adj severe
Sevilla [se'ßiʎa] *n* Seville; **sevillano, a** *adj* of
o from Seville ♦ *nm/f* native o inhabitant of
Seville
sexo ['sekso] *nm* sex
sexto, a ['seksto, a] *adj, nm* sixth
sexual [sek'swal] *adj* sexual; **vida ~** sex life
si [si] *conj* if; **me pregunto ~ ...** I wonder if o
whether ...
sí [si] *adv* yes ♦ *nm* consent ♦ *pron* (*uso
impersonal*) oneself; (*sg: m*) himself; (: *f*)
herself; (: *de cosa*) itself; (*de usted*) yourself;
(*pl*) themselves; (*de ustedes*) yourselves;
(*recíproco*) each other; **él no quiere pero yo ~**
he doesn't want to but I do; **ella ~ vendrá** she
will certainly come, she is sure to come; **claro
que ~** of course; **creo que ~** I think so
siamés, esa [sja'mes, esa] *adj, nm/f* Siamese
SIDA ['siða] *nm abr* (= *Síndrome de
Inmunodeficiencia Adquirida*) AIDS
siderúrgico, a [siðe'rurxico, a] *adj* iron and
steel *cpd*
sidra ['siðra] *nf* cider
siembra ['sjembra] *nf* sowing
siempre ['sjempre] *adv* always; (*todo el
tiempo*) all the time; **~ que** (*cada vez*)
whenever; (*dado que*) provided that; **como ~**
as usual; **para ~** for ever
sien [sjen] *nf* temple
siento *etc vb ver* sentar; sentir
sierra ['sjerra] *nf* (*TEC*) saw; (*cadena de
montañas*) mountain range
siervo, a ['sjerßo, a] *nm/f* slave
siesta ['sjesta] *nf* siesta, nap; **echar la ~** to
have an afternoon nap o a siesta
siete ['sjete] *num* seven
sífilis ['sifilis] *nf* syphilis
sifón [si'fon] *nm* syphon; **whisky con ~** whisky
and soda
sigla ['siɣla] *nf* abbreviation; acronym
siglo ['siɣlo] *nm* century; (*fig*) age
significación [siɣnifika'θjon] *nf* significance
significado [siɣnifi'kaðo] *nm* (*de palabra
etc*) meaning

significar [siɣnifiˈkar] vt to mean, signify; (notificar) to make known, express; **significativo, a** adj significant

signo [ˈsiɣno] nm sign; ~ **de admiración** o **exclamación** exclamation mark; ~ **de interrogación** question mark

sigo etc vb ver **seguir**

siguiente [siˈɣjente] adj next, following

siguió etc vb ver **seguir**

sílaba [ˈsilaβa] nf syllable

silbar [silˈβar] vt, vi to whistle; **silbato** nm whistle; **silbido** nm whistle, whistling

silenciador [silenθjaˈðor] nm silencer

silenciar [silenˈθjar] vt (persona) to silence; (escándalo) to hush up; **silencio** nm silence, quiet; **silencioso, a** adj silent, quiet

silla [ˈsiʎa] nf (asiento) chair; (tb: ~ **de montar**) saddle; ~ **de ruedas** wheelchair

sillón [siˈʎon] nm armchair, easy chair

silueta [siˈlweta] nf silhouette; (de edificio) outline; (figura) figure

silvestre [silˈβestre] adj wild

simbólico, a [simˈboliko, a] adj symbolic(al)

simbolizar [simboliˈθar] vt to symbolize

símbolo [ˈsimbolo] nm symbol

simetría [simeˈtria] nf symmetry

simiente [siˈmjente] nf seed

similar [simiˈlar] adj similar

simio [ˈsimjo] nm ape

simpatía [simpaˈtia] nf liking; (afecto) affection; (amabilidad) kindness; **simpático, a** adj nice, pleasant; kind

simpatizante [simpatiˈθante] nm/f sympathizer

simpatizar [simpatiˈθar] vi: ~ **con** to get on well with

simple [ˈsimple] adj simple; (elemental) simple, easy; (mero) mere; (puro) pure, sheer ♦ nm/f simpleton; ~**za** nf simpleness; (necedad) silly thing; **simplificar** vt to simplify

simposio [simˈposjo] nm symposium

simular [simuˈlar] vt to simulate

simultáneo, a [simulˈtaneo, a] adj simultaneous

sin [sin] prep without; **la ropa está ~ lavar** the clothes are unwashed; ~ **que** without; ~ **embargo** however, still

sinagoga [sinaˈɣoɣa] nf synagogue

sinceridad [sinθeriˈðað] nf sincerity; **sincero, a** adj sincere

sincronizar [sinkroniˈθar] vt to synchronize

sindical [sindiˈkal] adj union cpd, trade-union cpd; ~**ista** adj, nm/f trade unionist

sindicato [sindiˈkato] nm (de trabajadores) trade(s) union; (de negociantes) syndicate

síndrome [ˈsindrome] nm (MED) syndrome; ~ **de abstinencia** (MED) withdrawal symptoms

sinfín [sinˈfin] nm: **un ~ de** a great many, no end of

sinfonía [sinfoˈnia] nf symphony

singular [singuˈlar] adj singular; (fig) outstanding, exceptional; (raro) peculiar, odd; ~**idad** nf singularity, peculiarity; ~**izarse** vr to distinguish o.s., stand out

siniestro, a [siˈnjestro, a] adj sinister ♦ nm (accidente) accident

sinnúmero [sinˈnumero] nm = **sinfín**

sino [ˈsino] nm fate, destiny ♦ conj (pero) but; (salvo) except, save

sinónimo, a [siˈnonimo, a] adj synonymous ♦ nm synonym

síntesis [ˈsintesis] nf synthesis; **sintético, a** adj synthetic

sintetizar [sintetiˈθar] vt to synthesize

sintió vb ver **sentir**

síntoma [ˈsintoma] nm symptom

sintonía [sintoˈnia] nf (RADIO, MUS: de programa) tuning; **sintonizar** vt (RADIO: emisora) to tune (in)

sinvergüenza [simberˈɣwenθa] nm/f rogue, scoundrel; **¡es un ~!** he's got a nerve!

siquiera [siˈkjera] conj even if, even though ♦ adv at least; **ni ~** not even

sirena [siˈrena] nf siren

Siria [ˈsirja] nf Syria

sirviente, a [sirˈβjente, a] nm/f servant

sirvo etc vb ver **servir**

sisear [siseˈar] vt, vi to hiss

sistema [sisˈtema] nm system; (método) method; **sistemático, a** adj systematic

sitiar [siˈtjar] vt to besiege, lay siege to

sitio [ˈsitjo] nm (lugar) place; (espacio) room, space; (MIL) siege; ~ **Web** (INFORM) website

situación [sitwaˈθjon] nf situation, position; (estatus) position, standing

situado, a [situˈaðo, a] adj situated, placed

situar [siˈtwar] vt to place, put; (edificio) to locate, situate

slip [slip] nm pants pl, briefs pl

smoking [ˈsmokin, esˈmokin] (pl ~**s**) nm dinner jacket (BRIT), tuxedo (US)

snob [esˈnob] = **esnob**

SO abr (= suroeste) SW

sobaco [soˈβako] nm armpit

sobar [soˈβar] vt (ropa) to rumple; (comida) to play around with

soberanía [soβeraˈnia] nf sovereignty; **soberano, a** adj sovereign; (fig) supreme ♦ nm/f sovereign

soberbia [soˈβerβja] nf pride; haughtiness, arrogance; magnificence

soberbio, a [soˈβerβjo, a] adj (orgulloso) proud; (altivo) haughty, arrogant; (estupendo) magnificent, superb

sobornar [soβorˈnar] vt to bribe; **soborno** nm bribe

sobra [ˈsoβra] nf excess, surplus; ~**s** nfpl leftovers, scraps; **de ~** surplus, extra; **tengo de ~** I've more than enough; **~do, a** adj (más que suficiente) more than enough; (superfluo) excessive; **sobrante** adj remaining, extra ♦ nm surplus, remainder

sobrar [so'βrar] vt to exceed, surpass ♦ vi (tener de más) to be more than enough; (quedar) to remain, be left (over)

sobrasada [soβra'saða] nf pork sausage spread

sobre ['soβre] prep (gen) on; (encima) on (top of); (por encima de, arriba de) over, above; (más que) more than; (además) in addition to, besides; (alrededor de) about ♦ nm envelope; **~ todo** above all

sobrecama [soβre'kama] nf bedspread

sobrecargar [soβrekar'γar] vt (camión) to overload; (COM) to surcharge

sobredosis [soβre'ðosis] nf inv overdose

sobreentender [soβre(e)nten'der] vt to deduce, infer; **~se** vr: **se sobreentiende que ...** it is implied that ...

sobrehumano, a [soβreu'mano, a] adj superhuman

sobrellevar [soβreʎe'βar] vt to bear, endure

sobremesa [soβre'mesa] nf: **durante la ~** after dinner; **ordenador de ~** desktop computer

sobrenatural [soβrenatu'ral] adj supernatural

sobrenombre [soβre'nombre] nm nickname

sobrepasar [soβrepa'sar] vt to exceed, surpass

sobreponerse [soβrepo'nerse] vr: **~ a** to overcome

sobresaliente [soβresa'ljente] adj outstanding, excellent

sobresalir [soβresa'lir] vi to project, jut out; (fig) to stand out, excel

sobresaltar [soβresal'tar] vt (asustar) to scare, frighten; (sobrecoger) to startle; **sobresalto** nm (movimiento) start; (susto) scare; (turbación) sudden shock

sobretodo [soβre'toðo] nm overcoat

sobrevenir [soβreβe'nir] vi (ocurrir) to happen (unexpectedly); (resultar) to follow, ensue

sobreviviente [soβreβi'βjente] adj surviving ♦ nm/f survivor

sobrevivir [soβreβi'βir] vi to survive

sobrevolar [soβreβo'lar] vt to fly over

sobriedad [soβrje'ðað] nf sobriety, soberness; (moderación) moderation, restraint

sobrino, a [so'βrino, a] nm/f nephew/niece

sobrio, a ['soβrjo, a] adj sober; (moderado) moderate, restrained

socarrón, ona [soka'rron, ona] adj (sarcástico) sarcastic, ironic(al)

socavar [soka'βar] vt (tb fig) to undermine

socavón [soka'βon] nm (hoyo) hole

sociable [so'θjaβle] adj (persona) sociable, friendly; (animal) social

social [so'θjal] adj social; (COM) company cpd

socialdemócrata [soθjalde'mokrata] nm/f social democrat

socialista [soθja'lista] adj, nm/f socialist

socializar [soθjali'θar] vt to socialize

sociedad [soθje'ðað] nf society; (COM) company; **~ anónima** limited company; **~ de consumo** consumer society

socio, a ['soθjo, a] nm/f (miembro) member; (COM) partner

sociología [soθjolo'xia] nf sociology; **sociólogo, a** nm/f sociologist

socorrer [soko'rrer] vt to help; **socorrista** nm/f first aider; (en piscina, playa) lifeguard; **socorro** nm (ayuda) help, aid; (MIL) relief; **¡socorro!** help!

soda ['soða] nf (sosa) soda; (bebida) soda (water)

sofá [so'fa] (pl **~s**) nm sofa, settee; **~-cama** nm studio couch; sofa bed

sofisticación [sofistika'θjon] nf sophistication

sofocar [sofo'kar] vt to suffocate; (apagar) to smother, put out; **~se** vr to suffocate; (fig) to blush, feel embarrassed; **sofoco** nm suffocation; embarrassment

sofreír [sofre'ir] vt (CULIN) to fry lightly

soga ['soγa] nf rope

sois vb ver **ser**

soja ['soxa] nf soya

sol [sol] nm sun; (luz) sunshine, sunlight; **hace ~** it is sunny

solamente [sola'mente] adv only, just

solapa [so'lapa] nf (de chaqueta) lapel; (de libro) jacket

solapado, a [sola'paðo, a] adj (intenciones) underhand; (gestos, movimiento) sly

solar [so'lar] adj solar, sun cpd

solaz [so'laθ] nm recreation, relaxation; **~ar** vt (divertir) to amuse

soldado [sol'daðo] nm soldier; **~ raso** private

soldador [solda'ðor] nm soldering iron; (persona) welder

soldar [sol'dar] vt to solder, weld

soleado, a [sole'aðo, a] adj sunny

soledad [sole'ðað] nf solitude; (estado infeliz) loneliness

solemne [so'lemne] adj solemn; **solemnidad** nf solemnity

soler [so'ler] vi to be in the habit of, be accustomed to; **suele salir a las ocho** she usually goes out at 8 o'clock

solfeo [sol'feo] nm solfa

solicitar [soliθi'tar] vt (permiso) to ask for, seek; (puesto) to apply for; (votos) to canvass for; (atención) to attract

solícito, a [so'liθito, a] *adj* (*diligente*) diligent; (*cuidadoso*) careful; **solicitud** *nf* (*calidad*) great care; (*petición*) request; (*a un puesto*) application

solidaridad [soliðari'ðað] *nf* solidarity; **solidario, a** *adj* (*participación*) joint, common; (*compromiso*) mutually binding

solidez [soli'ðeθ] *nf* solidity; **sólido, a** *adj* solid

soliloquio [soli'lokjo] *nm* soliloquy

solista [so'lista] *nm/f* soloist

solitario, a [soli'tarjo, a] *adj* (*persona*) lonely, solitary; (*lugar*) lonely, desolate ♦ *nm/f* (*reclusa*) recluse; (*en la sociedad*) loner ♦ *nm* solitaire

sollozar [soλo'θar] *vi* to sob; **sollozo** *nm* sob

solo, a ['solo, a] *adj* (*único*) single, sole; (*sin compañía*) alone; (*solitario*) lonely; **hay una sola dificultad** there is just one difficulty; **a solas** alone, by oneself

sólo ['solo] *adv* only, just

solomillo [solo'miλo] *nm* sirloin

soltar [sol'tar] *vt* (*dejar ir*) to let go of; (*desprender*) to unfasten, loosen; (*librar*) to release, set free; (*risa etc*) to let out

soltero, a [sol'tero, a] *adj* single, unmarried ♦ *nm/f* bachelor/single woman; **solterón, ona** *nm/f* old bachelor/spinster

soltura [sol'tura] *nf* looseness, slackness; (*de los miembros*) agility, ease of movement; (*en el hablar*) fluency, ease

soluble [so'luβle] *adj* (QUÍM) soluble; (*problema*) solvable; **~ en agua** soluble in water

solución [solu'θjon] *nf* solution; **solucionar** *vt* (*problema*) to solve; (*asunto*) to settle, resolve

solventar [solβen'tar] *vt* (*pagar*) to settle, pay; (*resolver*) to resolve; **solvente** *adj* (ECON: *empresa, persona*) solvent

sombra ['sombra] *nf* shadow; (*como protección*) shade; **~s** *nfpl* (*oscuridad*) darkness *sg*, shadows; **tener buena/mala ~** to be lucky/unlucky

sombrero [som'brero] *nm* hat

sombrilla [som'briλa] *nf* parasol, sunshade

sombrío, a [som'brio, a] *adj* (*oscuro*) dark; (*triste*) sombre, sad; (*persona*) gloomy

somero, a [so'mero, a] *adj* superficial

someter [some'ter] *vt* (*país*) to conquer; (*persona*) to subject to one's will; (*informe*) to present, submit; **~se** *vr* to give in, yield, submit; **~ a** to subject to

somier [so'mjer] (*pl* **somiers**) *n* spring mattress

somnífero [som'nifero] *nm* sleeping pill

somnolencia [somno'lenθja] *nf* sleepiness, drowsiness

somos *vb ver* **ser**

son [son] *vb ver* **ser** ♦ *nm* sound; **en ~ de broma** as a joke

sonajero [sona'xero] *nm* (baby's) rattle

sonambulismo [sonambu'lismo] *nm* sleepwalking; **sonámbulo, a** *nm/f* sleepwalker

sonar [so'nar] *vt* to ring ♦ *vi* to sound; (*hacer ruido*) to make a noise; (*pronunciarse*) to be sounded, be pronounced; (*ser conocido*) to sound familiar; (*campana*) to ring; (*reloj*) to strike, chime; **~se** *vr*: **~se (las narices)** to blow one's nose; **me suena ese nombre** that name rings a bell

sonda ['sonda] *nf* (NAUT) sounding; (TEC) bore, drill; (MED) probe

sondear [sonde'ar] *vt* to sound; to bore (into), drill; to probe, sound; (*fig*) to sound out; **sondeo** *nm* sounding; boring, drilling; (*fig*) poll, enquiry

sonido [so'niðo] *nm* sound

sonoro, a [so'noro, a] *adj* sonorous; (*resonante*) resonant, loud

sonreír [sonre'ir] *vi* to smile; **~se** *vr* to smile; **sonriente** *adj* smiling; **sonrisa** *nf* smile

sonrojarse [sonro'xarse] *vr* to blush, go red; **sonrojo** *nm* blush

soñador, a [sona'ðor, a] *nm/f* dreamer

soñar [so'nar] *vt, vi* to dream; **~ con** to dream about o of

soñoliento, a [sono'ljento, a] *adj* sleepy, drowsy

sopa ['sopa] *nf* soup

sopesar [sope'sar] *vt* to consider, weigh up

soplar [so'plar] *vt* (*polvo*) to blow away, blow off; (*inflar*) to blow up; (*vela*) to blow out ♦ *vi* to blow; **soplo** *nm* blow, puff; (*de viento*) puff, gust

soplón, ona [so'plon, ona] (*fam*), *nm/f* (*niño*) telltale; (*de policía*) grass (*fam*)

sopor [so'por] *nm* drowsiness

soporífero [sopo'rifero] *nm* sleeping pill

soportable [sopor'taβle] *adj* bearable

soportar [sopor'tar] *vt* to bear, carry; (*fig*) to bear, put up with; **soporte** *nm* support; (*fig*) pillar, support

soprano [so'prano] *nf* soprano

sorber [sor'βer] *vt* (*chupar*) to sip; (*absorber*) to soak up, absorb

sorbete [sor'βete] *nm* iced fruit drink

sorbo [sor'βo] *nm* (*trago: grande*) gulp, swallow; (: *pequeño*) sip

sordera [sor'ðera] *nf* deafness

sórdido, a ['sorðiðo, a] *adj* dirty, squalid

sordo, a ['sorðo, a] *adj* (*persona*) deaf ♦ *nm/f* deaf person; **~mudo, a** *adj* deaf and dumb

sorna ['sorna] *nf* sarcastic tone

soroche [so'rotʃe] (AM) *nm* mountain sickness

sorprendente [sorpren'dente] *adj* surprising

sorprender [sorpren'der] *vt* to surprise;

sorpresa *nf* surprise
sortear [sorte'ar] *vt* to draw lots for; (*rifar*) to raffle; (*dificultad*) to avoid; **sorteo** *nm* (*en lotería*) draw; (*rifa*) raffle
sortija [sor'tixa] *nf* ring; (*rizo*) ringlet, curl
sosegado, a [sose'vaðo, a] *adj* quiet, calm
sosegar [sose'var] *vt* to quieten, calm; (*el ánimo*) to reassure ♦ *vi* to rest; **sosiego** *nm* quiet(ness), calm(ness)
soslayo [sos'lajo]: **de ~** *adv* obliquely, sideways
soso, a ['soso, a] *adj* (*CULIN*) tasteless; (*aburrido*) dull, uninteresting
sospecha [sos'petʃa] *nf* suspicion; **sospechar** *vt* to suspect; **sospechoso, a** *adj* suspicious; (*testimonio, opinión*) suspect ♦ *nm/f* suspect
sostén [sos'ten] *nm* (*apoyo*) support; (*sujetador*) bra; (*alimentación*) sustenance, food
sostener [soste'ner] *vt* to support; (*mantener*) to keep up, maintain; (*alimentar*) to sustain, keep going; **~se** *vr* to support o.s.; (*seguir*) to continue, remain; **sostenido, a** *adj* continuous, sustained; (*prolongado*) prolonged
sotana [so'tana] *nf* (*REL*) cassock
sótano ['sotano] *nm* basement
soviético, a [so'ßjetiko, a] *adj* Soviet; **los ~s** the Soviets
soy *vb ver* **ser**
Sr. *abr* (= *Señor*) Mr
Sra. *abr* (= *Señora*) Mrs
S.R.C. *abr* (= *se ruega contestación*) R.S.V.P.
Sres. *abr* (= *Señores*) Messrs
Srta. *abr* (= *Señorita*) Miss
Sta. *abr* (= *Santo*) St
status ['status, e'status] *nm inv* status
Sto. *abr* (= *Santo*) St
su [su] *pron* (*de él*) his; (*de ella*) her; (*de una cosa*) its; (*de ellos, ellas*) their; (*de usted, ustedes*) your
suave ['swaße] *adj* gentle; (*superficie*) smooth; (*trabajo*) easy; (*música, voz*) soft, sweet; **suavidad** *nf* gentleness; smoothness, softness, sweetness; **suavizante** *nm* (*de ropa*) softener; (*del pelo*) conditioner; **suavizar** *vt* to soften; (*quitar la aspereza*) to smooth (out)
subalimentado, a [sußalimen'taðo, a] *adj* undernourished
subasta [su'ßasta] *nf* auction; **subastar** *vt* to auction (off)
subcampeón, ona [sußkampe'on, ona] *nm/f* runner-up
subconsciente [sußkon'sθjente] *adj, nm* subconscious
subdesarrollado, a [sußðesarro'ʎaðo, a] *adj* underdeveloped

subdesarrollo [sußðesa'rroʎo] *nm* underdevelopment
subdirector, a [sußðirek'tor, a] *nm/f* assistant director
súbdito, a ['sußðito, a] *nm/f* subject
subestimar [sußesti'mar] *vt* to underestimate, underrate
subida [su'ßiða] *nf* (*de montaña etc*) ascent, climb; (*de precio*) rise, increase; (*pendiente*) slope, hill
subir [su'ßir] *vt* (*objeto*) to raise, lift up; (*cuesta, calle*) to go up; (*colina, montaña*) to climb; (*precio*) to raise, put up ♦ *vi* to go up, come up; (*a un coche*) to get in; (*a un autobús, tren o avión*) to get on, board; (*precio*) to rise, go up; (*río, marea*) to rise; **~se** *vr* to get up, climb
súbito, a ['sußito, a] *adj* (*repentino*) sudden; (*imprevisto*) unexpected
subjetivo, a [sußxe'tißo, a] *adj* subjective
sublevación [sußleßa'θjon] *nf* revolt, rising
sublevar [sußle'ßar] *vt* to rouse to revolt; **~se** *vr* to revolt, rise
sublime [su'ßlime] *adj* sublime
submarinismo [sußmari'nismo] *nm* scuba diving
submarino, a [sußma'rino, a] *adj* underwater ♦ *nm* submarine
subnormal [sußnor'mal] *adj* subnormal ♦ *nm/f* subnormal person
subordinado, a [sußorði'naðo, a] *adj, nm/f* subordinate
subrayar [sußra'jar] *vt* to underline
subsanar [sußsa'nar] *vt* to rectify
subscribir [sußskri'ßir] *vt* = **suscribir**
subsidio [suß'siðjo] *nm* (*ayuda*) aid, financial help; (*subvención*) subsidy, grant; (*de enfermedad, paro etc*) benefit, allowance
subsistencia [sußsis'tenθja] *nf* subsistence
subsistir [sußsis'tir] *vi* to subsist; (*sobrevivir*) to survive, endure
subterráneo, a [sußte'rraneo, a] *adj* underground, subterranean ♦ *nm* underpass, underground passage
subtítulo [suß'titulo] *nm* (*CINE*) subtitle
suburbano, a [sußur'ßano, a] *adj* suburban
suburbio [su'ßurßjo] *nm* (*barrio*) slum quarter
subvención [sußßen'θjon] *nf* (*ECON*) subsidy, grant; **subvencionar** *vt* to subsidize
subversión [sußßer'sjon] *nf* subversion; **subversivo, a** *adj* subversive
subyugar [sußju'var] *vt* (*país*) to subjugate, subdue; (*enemigo*) to overpower; (*voluntad*) to dominate
sucedáneo, a [suße'ðaneo, a] *adj* substitute ♦ *nm* substitute (food)
suceder [suße'ðer] *vt, vi* to happen; (*seguir*) to succeed, follow; **lo que sucede es que ...**

the fact is that ...; **sucesión** nf succession;
(serie) sequence, series

sucesivamente [suθesißa'mente] adv: **y así
~** and so on

sucesivo, a [suθe'sißo, a] adj successive,
following; **en lo ~** in future, from now on

suceso [su'θeso] nm (hecho) event,
happening; (incidente) incident

suciedad [suθje'ðað] nf (estado) dirtiness;
(mugre) dirt, filth

sucinto, a [su'θinto, a] adj (conciso)
succinct, concise

sucio, a ['suθjo, a] adj dirty

suculento, a [suku'lento, a] adj succulent

sucumbir [sukum'bir] vi to succumb

sucursal [sukur'sal] nf branch (office)

sudadera [suða'ðera] nf sweatshirt

Sudáfrica [suð'afrika] nf South Africa

Sudamérica [suða'merika] nf South
America; **sudamericano, a** adj, nm/f South
American

sudar [su'ðar] vt, vi to sweat

sudeste [su'ðeste] nm south-east

sudoeste [suðo'este] nm south-west

sudor [su'ðor] nm sweat; **~oso, a** adj sweaty,
sweating

Suecia ['sweθja] nf Sweden; **sueco, a** adj
Swedish ♦ nm/f Swede

suegro, a ['sweɣro, a] nm/f father-/mother-
in-law

suela ['swela] nf sole

sueldo ['sweldo] nm pay, wage(s) (pl)

suele etc vb ver **soler**

suelo ['swelo] nm (tierra) ground; (de casa)
floor

suelto, a ['swelto, a] adj loose; (libre) free;
(separado) detached; (ágil) quick, agile ♦ nm
(loose) change, small change

sueño etc ['sweɲo] vb ver **soñar** ♦ nm sleep;
(somnolencia) sleepiness, drowsiness; (lo
soñado, fig) dream; **tener ~** to be sleepy

suero ['swero] nm (MED) serum; (de leche)
whey

suerte ['swerte] nf (fortuna) luck; (azar)
chance; (destino) fate, destiny; (especie) sort,
kind; **tener ~** to be lucky; **de otra ~** otherwise,
if not; **de ~ que** so that, in such a way that

suéter ['sweter] nm sweater

suficiente [sufi'θjente] adj enough, sufficient
♦ nm (ESCOL) pass

sufragio [su'fraxjo] nm (voto) vote; (derecho
de voto) suffrage

sufrido, a [su'friðo, a] adj (persona) tough;
(paciente) long-suffering, patient

sufrimiento [sufri'mjento] nm (dolor)
suffering

sufrir [su'frir] vt (padecer) to suffer; (soportar)
to bear, put up with; (apoyar) to hold up,
support ♦ vi to suffer

sugerencia [suxe'renθja] nf suggestion

sugerir [suxe'rir] vt to suggest; (sutilmente)
to hint

sugestión [suxes'tjon] nf suggestion; (sutil)
hint; **sugestionar** vt to influence

sugestivo, a [suxes'tißo, a] adj stimulating;
(fascinante) fascinating

suicida [sui'θiða] adj suicidal ♦ nm/f suicidal
person; (muerto) suicide, person who has
committed suicide; **suicidarse** vr to commit
suicide, kill o.s.; **suicidio** nm suicide

Suiza ['swiθa] nf Switzerland; **suizo, a** adj,
nm/f Swiss

sujeción [suxe'θjon] nf subjection

sujetador [suxeta'ðor] nm (sostén) bra

sujetar [suxe'tar] vt (fijar) to fasten; (detener)
to hold down; **~se** vr to subject o.s.; **sujeto,
a** adj fastened, secure ♦ nm subject;
(individuo) individual; **sujeto a** subject to

suma ['suma] nf (cantidad) total, sum; (de
dinero) sum; (acto) adding (up), addition; **en
~** in short

sumamente [suma'mente] adv extremely,
exceedingly

sumar [su'mar] vt to add (up) ♦ vi to add up

sumario, a [su'marjo, a] adj brief, concise
♦ nm summary

sumergir [sumer'xir] vt to submerge;
(hundir) to sink

suministrar [sumini'strar] vt to supply,
provide; **suministro** nm supply; (acto)
supplying, providing

sumir [su'mir] vt to sink, submerge; (fig) to
plunge

sumisión [sumi'sjon] nf (acto) submission;
(calidad) submissiveness, docility; **sumiso, a**
adj submissive, docile

sumo, a ['sumo, a] adj great, extreme;
(autoridad) highest, supreme

suntuoso, a [sun'twoso, a] adj sumptuous,
magnificent

supe etc vb ver **saber**

supeditar [supeði'tar] vt: **~ algo a algo** to
subordinate sth to sth

super... [super] prefijo super..., over...;
~bueno adj great, fantastic

súper ['super] nf (gasolina) three-star (petrol)

superar [supe'rar] vt (sobreponerse a) to
overcome; (rebasar) to surpass, do better
than; (pasar) to go beyond; **~se** vr to excel
o.s.

superávit [supe'raßit] nm inv surplus

superficial [superfi'θjal] adj superficial;
(medida) surface cpd, of the surface

superficie [superfi'θje] nf surface; (área)
area

superfluo, a [su'perflwo, a] adj superfluous

superior [supe'rjor] adj (piso, clase) upper;
(temperatura, número, nivel) higher; (mejor:

calidad, producto) superior, better ♦ *nm/f* superior; **~idad** *nf* superiority

supermercado [supermer'kaðo] *nm* supermarket

superponer [superpo'ner] *vt* to superimpose

supersónico, a [super'soniko, a] *adj* supersonic

superstición [supersti'θjon] *nf* superstition; **supersticioso, a** *adj* superstitious

supervisar [superßi'sar] *vt* to supervise

supervivencia [superßi'ßenθja] *nf* survival

superviviente [superßi'ßjente] *adj* surviving

supiera *etc vb ver* **saber**

suplantar [suplan'tar] *vt* to supplant

suplemento [suple'mento] *nm* supplement

suplente [su'plente] *adj, nm/f* substitute

supletorio, a [suple'torjo, a] *adj* supplementary ♦ *nm* supplement; **teléfono ~** extension

súplica ['suplika] *nf* request; (*JUR*) petition

suplicar [supli'kar] *vt* (*cosa*) to beg (for), plead for; (*persona*) to beg, plead with

suplicio [su'pliθjo] *nm* torture

suplir [su'plir] *vt* (*compensar*) to make good, make up for; (*reemplazar*) to replace, substitute ♦ *vi*: **~ a** to take the place of, substitute for

supo *etc vb ver* **saber**

suponer [supo'ner] *vt* to suppose; **suposición** *nf* supposition

supremacía [suprema'θia] *nf* supremacy

supremo, a [su'premo, a] *adj* supreme

supresión [supre'sjon] *nf* suppression; (*de derecho*) abolition; (*de palabra etc*) deletion; (*de restricción*) cancellation, lifting

suprimir [supri'mir] *vt* to suppress; (*derecho, costumbre*) to abolish; (*palabra etc*) to delete; (*restricción*) to cancel, lift

supuesto, a [su'pwesto, a] *pp de* **suponer** ♦ *adj* (*hipotético*) supposed ♦ *nm* assumption, hypothesis; **~ que** since; **por ~ de** course

sur [sur] *nm* south

surcar [sur'kar] *vt* to plough; **surco** *nm* (*en metal, disco*) groove; (*AGR*) furrow

surgir [sur'xir] *vi* to arise, emerge; (*dificultad*) to come up, crop up

suroeste [suro'este] *nm* south-west

surtido, a [sur'tiðo, a] *adj* mixed, assorted ♦ *nm* (*selección*) selection, assortment; (*abastecimiento*) supply, stock; **~r** *nm* (*also:* **~r de gasolina**) petrol pump (*BRIT*), gas pump (*US*)

surtir [sur'tir] *vt* to supply, provide ♦ *vi* to spout, spurt

susceptible [susθep'tißle] *adj* susceptible; (*sensible*) sensitive; **~ de** capable of

suscitar [susθi'tar] *vt* to cause, provoke; (*interés, sospechas*) to arouse

suscribir [suskri'ßir] *vt* (*firmar*) to sign; (*respaldar*) to subscribe to, endorse; **~se** *vr* to subscribe; **suscripción** *nf* subscription

susodicho, a [suso'ðitʃo, a] *adj* above-mentioned

suspender [suspen'der] *vt* (*objeto*) to hang (up), suspend; (*trabajo*) to stop, suspend; (*ESCOL*) to fail; (*interrumpir*) to adjourn; (*atrasar*) to postpone; **suspensión** *nf* suspension; (*fig*) stoppage, suspension

suspenso, a [sus'penso, a] *adj* hanging, suspended; (*ESCOL*) failed ♦ *nm* (*ESCOL*) fail; **quedar o estar en ~** to be pending

suspicacia [suspi'kaθja] *nf* suspicion, mistrust; **suspicaz** *adj* suspicious, distrustful

suspirar [suspi'rar] *vi* to sigh; **suspiro** *nm* sigh

sustancia [sus'tanθja] *nf* substance

sustentar [susten'tar] *vt* (*alimentar*) to sustain, nourish; (*objeto*) to hold up, support; (*idea, teoría*) to maintain, uphold; (*fig*) to sustain, keep going; **sustento** *nm* support; (*alimento*) sustenance, food

sustituir [sustitu'ir] *vt* to substitute, replace; **sustituto, a** *nm/f* substitute, replacement

susto ['susto] *nm* fright, scare

sustraer [sustra'er] *vt* to remove, take away; (*MAT*) to subtract

susurrar [susu'rrar] *vi* to whisper; **susurro** *nm* whisper

sutil [su'til] *adj* (*aroma, diferencia*) subtle; (*tenue*) thin; (*inteligencia, persona*) sharp; **~eza** *nf* subtlety; thinness

suyo, a ['sujo, a] (*con artículo o después del verbo* **ser**) *adj* (*de él*) his; (*de ella*) hers; (*de ellos, ellas*) theirs; (*de Ud, Uds*) yours; **un amigo ~** a friend of his (*o* hers *o* theirs *o* yours)

T, t

tabacalera [taßaka'lera] *nf*: **T~** Spanish state tobacco monopoly

tabaco [ta'ßako] *nm* tobacco; (*fam*) cigarettes *pl*

taberna [ta'ßerna] *nf* bar, pub (*BRIT*)

tabique [ta'ßike] *nm* partition (wall)

tabla ['taßla] *nf* (*de madera*) plank; (*estante*) shelf; (*de vestido*) pleat; (*ARTE*) panel; **~s** *nfpl*: **estar o quedar en ~s** to draw; **~do** *nm* (*plataforma*) platform; (*TEATRO*) stage

tablao [ta'ßlao] *nm* (*tb*: **~ flamenco**) flamenco show

tablero [ta'ßlero] *nm* (*de madera*) plank, board; (*de ajedrez, damas*) board; **~ de anuncios** notice (*BRIT*) *o* bulletin (*US*) board

tableta [ta'ßleta] *nf* (*MED*) tablet; (*de chocolate*) bar

tablón [ta'ßlon] nm (de suelo) plank; (de techo) beam; ~ **de anuncios** notice board (BRIT), bulletin board (US)

tabú [ta'ßu] nm taboo

tabular [taßu'lar] vt to tabulate

taburete [taßu'rete] nm stool

tacaño, a [ta'kaɲo, a] adj mean

tacha ['tatʃa] nf flaw; (TEC) stud; **tachar** vt (borrar) to cross out; **tachar de** to accuse of

tácito, a ['taθito, a] adj tacit

taciturno, a [taθi'turno, a] adj silent

taco ['tako] nm (BILLAR) cue; (libro de billetes) book; (AM: de zapato) heel; (tarugo) peg; (palabrota) swear word

tacón [ta'kon] nm heel; **de ~ alto** high-heeled; **taconeo** nm (heel) stamping

táctica ['taktika] nf tactics pl

táctico, a ['taktiko, a] adj tactical

tacto ['takto] nm touch; (fig) tact

taimado, a [tai'maðo, a] adj (astuto) sly

tajada [ta'xaða] nf slice

tajante [ta'xante] adj sharp

tajo ['taxo] nm (corte) cut; (GEO) cleft

tal [tal] adj such; ~ **vez** perhaps ♦ pron (persona) someone, such a one; (cosa) something, such a thing; ~ **como** such as; ~ **para cual** (dos iguales) two of a kind ♦ adv: ~ **como** (igual) just as; ~ **cual** (como es) just as it is; **¿qué ~?** how are things?; **¿qué te gusta?** how do you like it? ♦ conj: **con ~ de que** provided that

taladrar [tala'ðrar] vt to drill; **taladro** nm drill

talante [ta'lante] nm (humor) mood; (voluntad) will, willingness

talar [ta'lar] vt to fell, cut down; (devastar) to devastate

talco ['talko] nm (polvos) talcum powder

talego [ta'leɣo] nm sack

talento [ta'lento] nm talent; (capacidad) ability

TALGO ['talɣo] (ESP) nm abr (= tren articulado ligero Goicoechea-Oriol) ≈ HST (BRIT)

talismán [talis'man] nm talisman

talla ['taʎa] nf (estatura, fig, MED) height, stature; (palo) measuring rod; (ARTE) carving; (medida) size

tallado, a [ta'ʎaðo, a] adj carved ♦ nm carving

tallar [ta'ʎar] vt (madera) to carve; (metal etc) to engrave; (medir) to measure

tallarines [taʎa'rines] nmpl noodles

talle ['taʎe] nm (ANAT) waist; (fig) appearance

taller [ta'ʎer] nm (TEC) workshop; (de artista) studio

tallo ['taʎo] nm (de planta) stem; (de hierba) blade; (brote) shoot

talón [ta'lon] nm (ANAT) heel; (COM) counterfoil; (cheque) cheque (BRIT), check (US)

talonario [talo'narjo] nm (de cheques) chequebook (BRIT), checkbook (US); (de recibos) receipt book

tamaño, a [ta'maɲo, a] adj (tan grande) such a big; (tan pequeño) such a small ♦ nm size; **de ~ natural** full-size

tamarindo [tama'rindo] nm tamarind

tambalearse [tambale'arse] vr (persona) to stagger; (vehículo) to sway

también [tam'bjen] adv (igualmente) also, too, as well; (además) besides

tambor [tam'bor] nm drum; (ANAT) eardrum; ~ **del freno** brake drum

tamiz [ta'miθ] nm sieve; ~**ar** vt to sieve

tampoco [tam'poko] adv nor, neither; **yo ~ lo compré** I didn't buy it either

tampón [tam'pon] nm tampon

tan [tan] adv so; ~ **es así que ...** so much so that ....

tanda ['tanda] nf (gen) series; (turno) shift

tangente [tan'xente] nf tangent

Tánger ['tanxer] n Tangier(s)

tangible [tan'xiße] adj tangible

tanque ['tanke] nm (cisterna, MIL) tank; (AUTO) tanker

tantear [tante'ar] vt (calcular) to reckon (up); (medir) to take the measure of; (probar) to test, try out; (tomar la medida: persona) to take the measurements of; (situación) to weigh up; (persona: opinión) to sound out ♦ vi (DEPORTE) to score; **tanteo** nm (cálculo) (rough) calculation; (prueba) test, trial; (DEPORTE) scoring

tanto, a ['tanto, a] adj (cantidad) so much, as much; ~**s** so many, as many; **20 y ~s** 20-odd ♦ adv (cantidad) so much, as much; (tiempo) so long, as long ♦ conj: **en ~ que** while; **hasta ~ (que)** until such time as ♦ nm (suma) certain amount; (proporción) so much; (punto) point; (gol) goal; **un ~ perezoso** somewhat lazy ♦ pron: **cado uno paga ~** each one pays so much; ~ **tú como yo** both you and I; ~ **como eso** as much as that; ~ **más ... cuanto que** all the more ... because; ~ **mejor/peor** so much the better/the worse; ~ **si viene como si va** whether he comes or whether he goes; ~ **es así que** so much so that; **por o por lo ~** therefore; **me he vuelto ronco de o con ~ hablar** I have become hoarse with so much talking; **a ~s de agosto** on such and such a day in August

tapa ['tapa] nf (de caja, olla) lid; (de botella) top; (de libro) cover; (comida) snack

tapadera [tapa'ðera] nf lid, cover

tapar [ta'par] vt (cubrir) to cover; (envolver) to wrap o cover up; (la vista) to obstruct; (persona, falta) to conceal; (AM) to fill; ~**se** vr to wrap o.s. up

taparrabo [tapa'rraβo] nm loincloth

tapete [ta'pete] nm table cover

tapia ['tapja] nf (garden) wall; **tapiar** vt to wall in

tapicería [tapiθe'ria] nf tapestry; (para muebles) upholstery; (tienda) upholsterer's (shop)

tapiz [ta'piθ] nm (alfombra) carpet; (tela tejida) tapestry; **~ar** vt (muebles) to upholster

tapón [ta'pon] nm (de botella) top; (de lavabo) plug; **~ de rosca** screw-top

taquigrafía [takiɣra'fia] nf shorthand; **taquígrafo, a** nm/f shorthand writer, stenographer

taquilla [ta'kiʎa] nf (donde se compra) booking office; (suma recogida) takings pl; **taquillero, a** adj: **función taquillera** box office success ♦ nm/f ticket clerk

tara ['tara] nf (defecto) defect; (COM) tare

tarántula [ta'rantula] nf tarantula

tararear [tarare'ar] vi to hum

tardar [tar'ðar] vi (tomar tiempo) to take a long time; (llegar tarde) to be late; (demorar) to delay; **¿tarda mucho el tren?** does the train take (very) long?; **a más ~** at the latest; **no tardes en venir** come soon

tarde ['tarðe] adv late ♦ nf (de día) afternoon; (al anochecer) evening; **de ~ en ~** from time to time; **¡buenas ~s!** good afternoon!; **a o por la ~** in the afternoon; in the evening

tardío, a [tar'ðio, a] adj (retrasado) late; (lento) slow (to arrive)

tarea [ta'rea] nf task; (faena) chore; (ESCOL) homework

tarifa [ta'rifa] nf (lista de precios) price list; (precio) tariff

tarima [ta'rima] nf (plataforma) platform

tarjeta [tar'xeta] nf card; **~ postal/de crédito/de Navidad** postcard/credit card/Christmas card; **~ cliente** loyalty card

tarro ['tarro] nm jar, pot

tarta ['tarta] nf (pastel) cake; (de base dura) tart

tartamudear [tartamuðe'ar] vi to stammer; **tartamudo, a** adj stammering ♦ nm/f stammerer

tártaro, a ['tartaro, a] adj: **salsa tártara** tartar(e) sauce

tasa ['tasa] nf (precio) (fixed) price, rate; (valoración) valuation; (medida, norma) measure, standard; **~ de cambio/interés** exchange/interest rate; **~s universitarias** university fees; **~s de aeropuerto** airport tax; **~ción** nf valuation; **~dor, a** nm/f valuer

tasar [ta'sar] vt (arreglar el precio) to fix a price for; (valorar) to value, assess

tasca ['taska] (fam) nf pub

tatarabuelo, a [tatara'ßwelo, a] nm/f great-

great-grandfather/mother

tatuaje [ta'twaxe] nm (dibujo) tattoo; (acto) tattooing

tatuar [ta'twar] vt to tattoo

taurino, a [tau'rino, a] adj bullfighting cpd

Tauro ['tauro] nm Taurus

tauromaquia [tauro'makja] nf tauromachy, (art of) bullfighting

taxi ['taksi] nm taxi

taxista [tak'sista] nm/f taxi driver

taza ['taθa] nf cup; (de retrete) bowl; **~ para café** coffee cup; **tazón** nm (taza grande) mug, large cup; (de fuente) basin

te [te] pron (complemento de objeto) you; (complemento indirecto) (to) you; (reflexivo) (to) yourself; **¿~ duele mucho el brazo?** does your arm hurt a lot?; **~ equivocas** you're wrong; **¡cálma~!** calm down!

té [te] nm tea

tea ['tea] nf torch

teatral [tea'tral] adj theatre cpd; (fig) theatrical

teatro [te'atro] nm theatre; (LITERATURA) plays pl, drama

tebeo [te'ßeo] nm comic

techo ['tetʃo] nm (externo) roof; (interno) ceiling; **~ corredizo** sunroof

tecla ['tekla] nf key; **~do** nm keyboard; **teclear** vi (MUS) to strum; (con los dedos) to tap ♦ vt (INFORM) to key in

técnica ['teknika] nf technique; (tecnología) technology; ver tb **técnico**

técnico, a ['tekniko, a] adj technical ♦ nm/f technician; (experto) expert

tecnología [teknolo'xia] nf technology; **tecnológico, a** adj technological

tedio ['teðjo] nm boredom, tedium; **~so, a** adj boring, tedious

teja ['texa] nf tile; (BOT) lime (tree); **~do** nm (tiled) roof

tejemaneje [texema'nexe] nm (lío) fuss; (intriga) intrigue

tejer [te'xer] vt to weave; (hacer punto) to knit; (fig) to fabricate; **tejido** nm (tela) material, fabric; (telaraña) web; (ANAT) tissue

tel [tel] abr (= teléfono) tel

tela ['tela] nf (tejido) material; (telaraña) web; (en líquido) skin; (de máquina) loom

telaraña [tela'rana] nf cobweb

tele ['tele] (fam) nf telly (BRIT), tube (US)

tele... ['tele] pref tele...; **~comunicación** nf telecommunication; **~control** nm remote control; **~diario** nm television news; **~difusión** nf (television) broadcast; **~dirigido, a** adj remote-controlled

teléf abr (= teléfono) tel

teleférico [tele'feriko] nm (de esquí) ski-lift

telefonear [telefone'ar] vi to telephone

telefónico, a [tele'foniko, a] adj telephone

cpd

telefonillo [telefo'niʎo] *nm* (*de puerta*) intercom

telefonista [telefo'nista] *nm/f* telephonist

teléfono [te'lefono] *nm* (tele)phone; **estar hablando al ~** to be on the phone; **llamar a uno por ~** to ring sb (up) o phone sb (up); **~ móvil** car phone; **~ portátil** mobile phone

telegrafía [teleɣra'fia] *nf* telegraphy

telégrafo [te'leɣrafo] *nm* telegraph

telegrama [tele'ɣrama] *nm* telegram

tele: ~impresor *nm* teleprinter (*BRIT*), teletype (*US*); **~novela** *nf* soap (opera); **~objetivo** *nm* telephoto lens; **~patía** *nf* telepathy; **~pático, a** *adj* telepathic; **~scópico, a** *adj* telescopic; **~scopio** *nm* telescope; **~silla** *nm* chairlift; **~spectador, a** *nm/f* viewer; **~squí** *nm* ski-lift; **~tarjeta** *nf* phonecard; **~tipo** *nm* teletype; **~ventas** *nfpl* telesales

televidente [teleßi'ðente] *nm/f* viewer

televisar [teleßi'sar] *vt* to televise

televisión [teleßi'sjon] *nf* television; **~ en colores** colour television; **~ digital** digital television

televisor [teleßi'sor] *nm* television set

télex ['teleks] *nm inv* telex

telón [te'lon] *nm* curtain; **~ de acero** (*POL*) iron curtain; **~ de fondo** backcloth, background

tema ['tema] *nm* (*asunto*) subject, topic; (*MUS*) theme; **temática** *nf* (*social, histórica, artística*) range of topics; **temático, a** *adj* thematic

temblar [tem'blar] *vi* to shake, tremble; (*de frío*) to shiver; **temblón, ona** *adj* shaking; **temblor** *nm* trembling; (*de tierra*) earthquake; **tembloroso, a** *adj* trembling

temer [te'mer] *vt* to fear ♦ *vi* to be afraid; **temo que llegue tarde** I am afraid he may be late

temerario, a [teme'rarjo, a] *adj* (*descuidado*) reckless; (*irreflexivo*) hasty; **temeridad** *nf* (*imprudencia*) rashness; (*audacia*) boldness

temeroso, a [teme'roso, a] *adj* (*miedoso*) fearful; (*que inspira temor*) frightful

temible [te'mißle] *adj* fearsome

temor [te'mor] *nm* (*miedo*) fear; (*duda*) suspicion

témpano ['tempano] *nm*: **~ de hielo** ice-floe

temperamento [tempera'mento] *nm* temperament

temperatura [tempera'tura] *nf* temperature

tempestad [tempes'taθ] *nf* storm; **tempestuoso, a** *adj* stormy

templado, a [tem'plaðo, a] *adj* (*moderado*) moderate; (*frugal*) frugal; (*agua*) lukewarm; (*clima*) mild; (*MUS*) well-tuned; **templanza** *nf* moderation; mildness

templar [tem'plar] *vt* (*moderar*) to moderate; (*furia*) to restrain; (*calor*) to reduce; (*afinar*) to tune (up); (*acero*) to temper; (*tuerca*) to tighten up; **temple** *nm* (*ajuste*) tempering; (*afinación*) tuning; (*pintura*) tempera

templo ['templo] *nm* (*iglesia*) church; (*pagano etc*) temple

temporada [tempo'raða] *nf* time, period; (*estación*) season

temporal [tempo'ral] *adj* (*no permanente*) temporary; (*REL*) temporal ♦ *nm* storm

tempranero, a [tempra'nero, a] *adj* (*BOT*) early; (*persona*) early-rising

temprano, a [tem'prano, a] *adj* early; (*demasiado pronto*) too soon, too early

ten *vb ver* **tener**

tenaces [te'naθes] *adj pl ver* **tenaz**

tenacidad [tenaθi'ðaθ] *nf* tenacity; (*dureza*) toughness; (*terquedad*) stubbornness

tenacillas [tena'θiʎas] *nfpl* tongs; (*para el pelo*) curling tongs (*BRIT*) o iron *sg* (*US*); (*MED*) forceps

tenaz [te'naθ] *adj* (*material*) tough; (*persona*) tenacious; (*creencia, resistencia*) stubborn

tenaza(s) [te'naθa(s)] *nf(pl)* (*MED*) forceps; (*TEC*) pliers; (*ZOOL*) pincers

tendedero [tende'ðero] *nm* (*para ropa*) drying place; (*cuerda*) clothes line

tendencia [ten'denθja] *nf* tendency; **tener ~ a** to tend to, have a tendency to; **tendencioso, a** *adj* tendentious

tender [ten'der] *vt* (*extender*) to spread out; (*colgar*) to hang out; (*vía férrea, cable*) to lay; (*estirar*) to stretch ♦ *vi*: **~ a** to tend to, have a tendency towards; **~se** *vr* to lie down; **~ la cama/la mesa** (*AM*) to make the bed/lay (*BRIT*) o set (*US*) the table

tenderete [tende'rete] *nm* (*puesto*) stall; (*exposición*) display of goods

tendero, a [ten'dero, a] *nm/f* shopkeeper

tendido, a [ten'diðo, a] *adj* (*acostado*) lying down, flat; (*colgado*) hanging ♦ *nm* (*TAUR*) front rows of seats; **a galope ~** flat out

tendón [ten'don] *nm* tendon

tendré *etc vb ver* **tener**

tenebroso, a [tene'ßroso, a] *adj* (*oscuro*) dark; (*fig*) gloomy

tenedor [tene'ðor] *nm* (*CULIN*) fork; **~ de libros** book-keeper

tenencia [te'nenθja] *nf* (*de casa*) tenancy; (*de oficio*) tenure; (*de propiedad*) possession

---

PALABRA CLAVE

---

tener [te'ner] *vt* **1** (*poseer, gen*) to have; (*en la mano*) to hold; **¿tienes un boli?** have you got a pen?; **va a ~ un niño** she's going to have a baby; **¡ten** (o **tenga**)!, **¡aquí tienes** (o **tiene**)! here you are!

2 (*edad, medidas*) to be; **tiene 7 años** she's 7

(years old); **tiene 15 cm de largo** it's 15 cm
long; *ver* **calor; hambre** *etc*
3 (*considerar*): **lo tengo por brillante** I
consider him to be brilliant; **~ en mucho a
uno** to think very highly of sb
4 (+ *pp*: = *pretérito*): **tengo terminada ya la
mitad del trabajo** I've done half the work
already
5: **~ que hacer algo** to have to do sth; **tengo
que acabar este trabajo hoy** I have to finish
this job today
6: **¿qué tienes, estás enfermo?** what's the
matter with you, are you ill?
♦ **~se** *vr* **1**: **~se en pie** to stand up
2: **~se por** to think o.s.; **se tiene por muy listo**
he thinks himself very clever

tengo *etc vb ver* **tener**
tenia ['tenja] *nf* tapeworm
teniente [te'njente] *nm* (*rango*) lieutenant;
(*ayudante*) deputy
tenis ['tenis] *nm* tennis; **~ de mesa** table
tennis; **~ta** *nm/f* tennis player
tenor [te'nor] *nm* (*sentido*) meaning; (*MUS*)
tenor; **a ~ de** on the lines of
tensar [ten'sar] *vt* to tighten; (*arco*) to draw
tensión [ten'sjon] *nf* tension; (*TEC*) stress;
(*MED*): **~ arterial** blood pressure; **tener la
~ alta** to have high blood pressure
tenso, a ['tenso, a] *adj* tense
tentación [tenta'θjon] *nf* temptation
tentáculo [ten'takulo] *nm* tentacle
tentador, a [tenta'ðor, a] *adj* tempting
tentar [ten'tar] *vt* (*seducir*) to tempt; (*atraer*)
to attract; **tentativa** *nf* attempt; **tentativa de
asesinato** attempted murder
tentempié [tentem'pje] *nm* snack
tenue ['tenwe] *adj* (*delgado*) thin, slender;
(*neblina*) light; (*lazo, vínculo*) slight
teñir [te'ɲir] *vt* to dye; (*fig*) to tinge; **~se** *vr*
to dye; **~se el pelo** to dye one's hair
teología [teolo'xia] *nf* theology
teoría [teo'ria] *nf* theory; **en ~** in theory;
teóricamente *adv* theoretically; **teórico,
a** *adj* theoretic(al) ♦ *nm/f* theoretician,
theorist; **teorizar** *vi* to theorize
terapéutico, a [tera'peutiko, a] *adj*
therapeutic
terapia [te'rapja] *nf* therapy
tercer [ter'θer] *adj ver* **tercero**
tercermundista [terθermun'dista] *adj* Third
World *cpd*
tercero, a [ter'θero, a] *adj* (*delante de nmsg*:
tercer) third ♦ *nm* (*JUR*) third party
terceto [ter'θeto] *nm* trio
terciar [ter'θjar] *vi* (*participar*) to take part;
(*hacer de árbitro*) to mediate; **~se** *vr* to come
up; **~io, a** *adj* tertiary
tercio ['terθjo] *nm* third

terciopelo [terθjo'pelo] *nm* velvet
terco, a ['terko, a] *adj* obstinate
tergal ® [ter'val] *nm* type of polyester
tergiversar [terxiβer'sar] *vt* to distort
termal [ter'mal] *adj* thermal
termas ['termas] *nfpl* hot springs
térmico, a ['termiko, a] *adj* thermal
terminación [termina'θjon] *nf* (*final*) end;
(*conclusión*) conclusion, ending
terminal [termi'nal] *adj, nm, nf* terminal
terminante [termi'nante] *adj* (*final*) final,
definitive; (*tajante*) categorical; **~mente** *adv*:
~mente prohibido strictly forbidden
terminar [termi'nar] *vt* (*completar*) to
complete, finish; (*concluir*) to end ♦ *vi* (*llegar
a su fin*) to end; (*parar*) to stop; (*acabar*) to
finish; **~se** *vr* to come to an end; **~ por hacer
algo** to end up (by) doing sth
término ['termino] *nm* end, conclusion;
(*parada*) terminus; (*límite*) boundary;
~ medio average; (*fig*) middle way; **en último
~** (*a fin de cuentas*) in the last analysis; (*como
último recurso*) as a last resort
terminología [terminolo'xia] *nf*
terminology
termodinámico, a [termoði'namiko, a] *adj*
thermodynamic
termómetro [ter'mometro] *nm* thermometer
termonuclear [termonukle'ar] *adj*
thermonuclear
termo(s) ® ['termo(s)] *nm* Thermos ®
(flask)
termostato [termo'stato] *nm* thermostat
ternero, a [ter'nero, a] *nm/f* (*animal*) calf
♦ *nf* (*carne*) veal
ternura [ter'nura] *nf* (*trato*) tenderness;
(*palabra*) endearment; (*cariño*) fondness
terquedad [terke'ðað] *nf* obstinacy
terrado [te'rraðo] *nm* terrace
terraplén [terra'plen] *nm* embankment
terrateniente [terrate'njente] *nm/f*
landowner
terraza [te'rraθa] *nf* (*balcón*) balcony;
(*tejado*) (flat) roof; (*AGR*) terrace
terremoto [terre'moto] *nm* earthquake
terrenal [terre'nal] *adj* earthly
terreno [te'rreno] *nm* (*tierra*) land; (*parcela*)
plot; (*suelo*) soil; (*fig*) field; **un ~** a piece of
land
terrestre [te'rrestre] *adj* terrestrial; (*ruta*)
land *cpd*
terrible [te'rriβle] *adj* terrible, awful
territorio [terri'torjo] *nm* territory
terrón [te'rron] *nm* (*de azúcar*) lump; (*de
tierra*) clod, lump
terror [te'rror] *nm* terror; **~ífico, a** *adj*
terrifying; **~ista** *adj, nm/f* terrorist
terso, a ['terso, a] *adj* (*liso*) smooth; (*pulido*)

polished; **tersura** nf smoothness

tertulia [ter'tulja] nf (reunión informal) social gathering; (grupo) group, circle

tesis ['tesis] nf inv thesis

tesón [te'son] nm (firmeza) firmness; (tenacidad) tenacity

tesorero, a [teso'rero, a] nm/f treasurer

tesoro [te'soro] nm treasure; (COM, POL) treasury

testaferro [testa'ferro] nm figurehead

testamentario, a [testamen'tarjo, a] adj testamentary ♦ nm/f executor/executrix

testamento [testa'mento] nm will

testar [tes'tar] vi to make a will

testarudo, a [testa'ruðo, a] adj stubborn

testículo [tes'tikulo] nm testicle

testificar [testifi'kar] vt to testify; (fig) to attest ♦ vi to give evidence

testigo [tes'tiɣo] nm/f witness; ~ **de cargo/ descargo** witness for the prosecution/defence; ~ **ocular** eye witness

testimoniar [testimo'njar] vt to testify to; (fig) to show; **testimonio** nm testimony

teta ['teta] nf (de biberón) teat; (ANAT: fam) breast

tétanos ['tetanos] nm tetanus

tetera [te'tera] nf teapot

tétrico, a ['tetriko, a] adj gloomy, dismal

textil [teks'til] adj textile

texto ['teksto] nm text; **textual** adj textual

textura [teks'tura] nf (de tejido) texture

tez [teθ] nf (cutis) complexion

ti [ti] pron you; (reflexivo) yourself

tía ['tia] nf (pariente) aunt; (fam) chick, bird

tibieza [ti'ßjeθa] nf (temperatura) tepidness; (actitud) coolness; **tibio, a** adj lukewarm

tiburón [tißu'ron] nm shark

tic [tik] nm (ruido) click; (de reloj) tick; (MED): ~ **nervioso** nervous tic

tictac [tik'tak] nm (de reloj) tick tock

tiempo ['tjempo] nm time; (época, período) age, period; (METEOROLOGÍA) weather; (LING) tense; (DEPORTE) half; **a** ~ in time; **a un** o **al mismo** ~ at the same time; **al poco** ~ very soon (after); **se quedó poco** ~ he didn't stay very long; **hace poco** ~ not long ago; **mucho** ~ a long time; **de** ~ **en** ~ from time to time; **hace buen/mal** ~ the weather is fine/bad; **estar a** ~ to be in time; **hace** ~ some time ago; **hacer** ~ to while away the time; **motor de 2** ~**s** two-stroke engine; **primer** ~ first half

tienda ['tjenda] nf shop, store; ~ (**de campaña**) tent; ~ **de alimentación** o **comestibles** grocer's (BRIT), grocery store (US)

tienes etc vb ver **tener**

tienta etc ['tjenta] vb ver **tentar** ♦ nf: **andar a** ~**s** to grope one's way along

tiento ['tjento] vb ver **tentar** ♦ nm (tacto) touch; (precaución) wariness

tierno, a ['tjerno, a] adj (blando) tender; (fresco) fresh; (amable) sweet

tierra ['tjerra] nf earth; (suelo) soil; (mundo) earth, world; (país) country, land; ~ **adentro** inland

tieso, a ['tjeso, a] adj (rígido) rigid; (duro) stiff; (fam: orgulloso) conceited

tiesto ['tjesto] nm flowerpot

tifoidea [tifoi'ðea] nf typhoid

tifón [ti'fon] nm typhoon

tifus ['tifus] nm typhus

tigre ['tiɣre] nm tiger

tijera [ti'xera] nf scissors pl; (ZOOL) claw; ~**s** nfpl scissors; (para plantas) shears

tijeretear [tixerete'ar] vt to snip

tila ['tila] nf lime blossom tea

tildar [til'dar] vt: ~ **de** to brand as

tilde ['tilde] nf (TIP) tilde

tilín [ti'lin] nm tinkle

tilo ['tilo] nm lime tree

timar [ti'mar] vt (estafar) to swindle

timbal [tim'bal] nm small drum

timbrar [tim'brar] vt to stamp

timbre ['timbre] nm (sello) stamp; (campanilla) bell; (tono) timbre; (COM) stamp duty

timidez [timi'ðeθ] nf shyness; **tímido, a** adj shy

timo ['timo] nm swindle

timón [ti'mon] nm helm, rudder; **timonel** nm helmsman

tímpano ['timpano] nm (ANAT) eardrum; (MUS) small drum

tina ['tina] nf tub; (baño) bath(tub); **tinaja** nf large jar

tinglado [tin'glaðo] nm (cobertizo) shed; (fig: truco) trick; (intriga) intrigue

tinieblas [ti'njeßlas] nfpl darkness sg; (sombras) shadows

tino ['tino] nm (habilidad) skill; (juicio) insight

tinta ['tinta] nf ink; (TEC) dye; (ARTE) colour

tinte ['tinte] nm dye

tintero [tin'tero] nm inkwell

tintinear [tintine'ar] vt to tinkle

tinto ['tinto] nm red wine

tintorería [tintore'ria] nf dry cleaner's

tintura [tin'tura] nf (QUÍM) dye; (farmacéutico) tincture

tío ['tio] nm (pariente) uncle; (fam: individuo) bloke (BRIT), guy

tiovivo [tio'ßißo] nm merry-go-round

típico, a ['tipiko, a] adj typical

tipo ['tipo] nm (clase) type, kind; (hombre) fellow; (ANAT: de hombre) build; (: de mujer) figure; (IMPRENTA) type; ~ **bancario/de descuento/de interés/de cambio** bank/ discount/interest/exchange rate

tipografía [tipoɣra'fia] nf printing cpd; **tipográfico, a** adj printing cpd

tíquet ['tiket] (pl ~s) nm ticket; (en tienda) cash slip

tiquismiquis |tikis'mikis| nm inv fussy person ♦ nmpl (querellas) squabbling sg; (escrúpulos) silly scruples

tira ['tira] nf strip; (fig) abundance; **~ y afloja** give and take

tirabuzón [tiraβu'θon] nm (rizo) curl

tirachinas [tira'tʃinas] nm inv catapult

tirada [ti'raða] nf (acto) cast, throw; (serie) series; (TIP) printing, edition; **de una ~** at one go

tirado, a [ti'raðo, a] adj (barato) dirt-cheap; (fam: fácil) very easy

tirador [tira'ðor] nm (mango) handle

tiranía [tira'nia] nf tyranny; **tirano, a** adj tyrannical ♦ nm/f tyrant

tirante [ti'rante] adj (cuerda etc) tight, taut; (relaciones) strained ♦ nm (ARQ) brace; (TEC) stay; **~s** nmpl (de pantalón) braces (BRIT), suspenders (US); **tirantez** nf tightness; (fig) tension

tirar [ti'rar] vt to throw; (dejar caer) to drop; (volcar) to upset; (derribar) to knock down o over; (desechar) to throw out o away; (dinero) to squander; (imprimir) to print ♦ vi (disparar) to shoot; (de la puerta etc) to pull; (fam: andar) to go; (tender a, buscar realizar) to tend to; (DEPORTE) to shoot; **~se** vr to throw o.s.; **~ abajo** to bring down, destroy; **tira más a su padre** he takes more after his father; **ir tirando** to manage; **a todo ~** at the most

tirita [ti'rita] nf (sticking) plaster (BRIT), bandaid (US)

tiritar [tiri'tar] vi to shiver

tiro ['tiro] nm (lanzamiento) throw; (disparo) shot; (DEPORTE) shot; (GOLF, TENIS) drive; (alcance) range; **~ al blanco** target practice; **caballo de ~** cart-horse; **andar de ~s largos** to be all dressed up; **al ~** (AM) at once

tirón [ti'ron] nm (sacudida) pull, tug; **de un ~** in one go, all at once

tiroteo [tiro'teo] nm exchange of shots, shooting

tísico, a [ˈtisiko, a] adj consumptive

tisis ['tisis] nf inv consumption, tuberculosis

títere ['titere] nm puppet

titiritero, a [titiri'tero, a] nm/f puppeteer

titubeante [tituße'ante] adj (al andar) shaky, tottering; (al hablar) stammering; (dudoso) hesitant

titubear [tituße'ar] vi to stagger; to stammer; (fig) to hesitate; **titubeo** nm staggering; stammering; hesitation

titulado, a [titu'laðo, a] adj (libro) entitled; (persona) titled

titular [titu'lar] adj titular ♦ nm/f holder ♦ nm headline ♦ vt to title; **~se** vr to be entitled;

título nm title; (de diario) headline; (certificado) professional qualification; (universitario) (university) degree; **a título de** in the capacity of

tiza ['tiθa] nf chalk

tiznar [tiθ'nar] vt to blacken

tizón [ti'θon] nm brand

toalla [to'aʎa] nf towel

tobillo [to'ßiʎo] nm ankle

tobogán [toßo'ɣan] nm (montaña rusa) roller-coaster; (de niños) chute, slide

tocadiscos [toka'ðiskos] nm inv record player

tocado, a [to'kaðo, a] adj (fam) touched ♦ nm headdress

tocador [toka'ðor] nm (mueble) dressing table; (cuarto) boudoir; (fam) ladies' toilet (BRIT) o room (US)

tocante |to'kante|: **~ a** prep with regard to

tocar [to'kar] vt to touch; (MUS) to play; (referirse a) to allude to; (timbre) to ring ♦ vi (a la puerta) to knock (on o at the door); (ser de turno) to fall to, be the turn of; (ser hora) to be due; **~se** vr (cubrirse la cabeza) to cover one's head; (tener contacto) to touch (each other); **por lo que a mí me toca** as far as I am concerned; **te toca a ti** it's your turn

tocayo, a [to'kajo, a] nm/f namesake

tocino [to'θino] nm bacon

todavía [toða'ßia] adv (aun) even; (aún) still, yet; **~ más** yet more; **~ no** not yet

---

PALABRA CLAVE

todo, a ['toðo, a] adj **1** (con artículo sg) all; **toda la carne** all the meat; **toda la noche** all night, the whole night; **~ el libro** the whole book; **toda una botella** a whole bottle; **~ lo contrario** quite the opposite; **está toda sucia** she's all dirty; **por ~ el país** throughout the whole country

2 (con artículo pl) all; every; **~s los libros** all the books; **todas las noches** every night; **~s los que quieran salir** all those who want to leave

♦ pron **1** everything, all; **~s** everyone, everybody; **lo sabemos ~** we know everything; **~s querían más tiempo** everybody o everyone wanted more time; **nos marchamos ~s** all of us left

2: **con ~**: **con ~ él me sigue gustando** even so I still like him

♦ adv all; **vaya ~ seguido** keep straight on o ahead

♦ nm: **como un ~** as a whole; **del ~**: **no me agrada del ~** I don't entirely like it

---

todopoderoso, a [toðopoðe'roso, a] adj all powerful; (REL) almighty

toga ['toɣa] nf toga; (ESCOL) gown

Tokio ['tokjo] n Tokyo

toldo ['toldo] nm (para el sol) sunshade (BRIT), parasol; (tienda) marquee

tolerancia [tole'ranθja] nf tolerance; **tolerante** adj (sociedad) liberal; (persona) open-minded

tolerar [tole'rar] vt to tolerate; (resistir) to endure

toma ['toma] nf (acto) taking; (MED) dose; ~ **(de corriente)** socket

tomar [to'mar] vt to take; (aspecto) to take on; (beber) to drink ♦ vi to take; (AM) to drink; ~**se** vr to take; ~**se por** to consider o.s. to be; ~ **a bien/a mal** to take well/badly; ~ **en serio** to take seriously; ~ **el pelo a alguien** to pull sb's leg; ~**la con uno** to pick a quarrel with sb; **¡tome!** here you are!; ~ **el sol** to sunbathe

tomate [to'mate] nm tomato

tomillo [to'miʎo] nm thyme

tomo ['tomo] nm (libro) volume

ton [ton] abr = **tonelada** ♦ nm: **sin ~ ni son** without rhyme or reason

tonada [to'naða] nf tune

tonalidad [tonali'ðað] nf tone

tonel [to'nel] nm barrel

tonelada [tone'laða] nf ton; **tonelaje** nm tonnage

tónica ['tonika] nf (MUS) tonic; (fig) keynote

tónico, a ['toniko, a] adj tonic ♦ nm (MED) tonic

tonificar [tonifi'kar] vt to tone up

tono ['tono] nm tone; **fuera de ~** inappropriate; **darse ~** to put on airs

tontería [tonte'ria] nf (estupidez) foolishness; (cosa) stupid thing; (acto) foolish act; ~**s** nfpl (disparates) rubbish sg, nonsense sg

tonto, a ['tonto, a] adj stupid, silly ♦ nm/f fool

topar [to'par] vi: ~ **contra** o **en** to run into; ~ **con** to run up against

tope ['tope] adj maximum ♦ nm (fin) end; (límite) limit; (FERRO) buffer; (AUTO) bumper; **al ~** end to end

tópico, a ['topiko, a] adj topical ♦ nm platitude

topo ['topo] nm (ZOOL) mole; (fig) blunderer

topografía [topoɣra'fia] nf topography; **topógrafo, a** nm/f topographer

toque etc ['toke] vb ver **tocar** ♦ nm touch; (MUS) beat; (de campana) peal; **dar un ~ a** to warn; ~ **de queda** curfew

toqué vb ver **tocar**

toquetear [tokete'ar] vt to finger

toquilla [to'kiʎa] nf (pañuelo) headscarf; (chal) shawl

tórax ['toraks] nm thorax

torbellino [torbe'ʎino] nm whirlwind; (fig) whirl

torcedura [torθe'ðura] nf twist; (MED) sprain

torcer [tor'θer] vt to twist; (la esquina) to turn; (MED) to sprain ♦ vi (desviar) to turn off; ~**se** vr (ladearse) to bend; (desviarse) to go astray; (fracasar) to go wrong; **torcido, a** adj twisted; (fig) crooked ♦ nm curl

tordo, a ['torðo, a] adj dappled ♦ nm thrush

torear [tore'ar] vt (fig: evadir) to avoid; (jugar con) to tease ♦ vi to fight bulls; **toreo** nm bullfighting; **torero, a** nm/f bullfighter

tormenta [tor'menta] nf storm; (fig: confusión) turmoil

tormento [tor'mento] nm torture; (fig) anguish

tornar [tor'nar] vt (devolver) to return, give back; (transformar) to transform ♦ vi to go back; ~**se** vr (ponerse) to become

tornasolado, a [tornaso'laðo, a] adj (brillante) iridescent; (reluciente) shimmering

torneo [tor'neo] nm tournament

tornillo [tor'niʎo] nm screw

torniquete [torni'kete] nm (MED) tourniquet

torno ['torno] nm (TEC) winch; (tambor) drum; **en ~ (a)** round, about

toro ['toro] nm bull; (fam) he-man; **los ~s** bullfighting

toronja [to'ronxa] nf grapefruit

torpe ['torpe] adj (poco hábil) clumsy, awkward; (necio) dim; (lento) slow

torpedo [tor'peðo] nm torpedo

torpeza [tor'peθa] nf (falta de agilidad) clumsiness; (lentitud) slowness; (error) mistake

torre ['torre] nf tower; (de petróleo) derrick

torrefacto, a [torre'facto, a] adj roasted

torrente [to'rrente] nm torrent

tórrido, a ['torriðo, a] adj torrid

torrija [to'rrixa] nf French toast

torsión [tor'sjon] nf twisting

torso ['torso] nm torso

torta ['torta] nf cake; (fam) slap

tortícolis [tor'tikolis] nm inv stiff neck

tortilla [tor'tiʎa] nf omelette; (AM) maize pancake; ~ **francesa/española** plain/potato omelette

tórtola ['tortola] nf turtledove

tortuga [tor'tuxa] nf tortoise

tortuoso, a [tor'twoso, a] adj winding

tortura [tor'tura] nf torture; **torturar** vt to torture

tos [tos] nf cough; ~ **ferina** whooping cough

tosco, a ['tosko, a] adj coarse

toser [to'ser] vi to cough

tostada [tos'taða] nf piece of toast; **tostado, a** adj toasted; (por el sol) dark brown; (piel) tanned

tostador [tosta'ðor] nm toaster

tostar [tos'tar] vt to toast; (café) to roast; (persona) to tan; ~**se** vr to get brown

total [to'tal] *adj* total ♦ *adv* in short; (*al fin y al cabo*) when all is said and done ♦ *nm* total; ~ **que** to cut (*BRIT*) o make (*US*) a long story short

totalidad [totali'ðað] *nf* whole

totalitario, a [totali'tarjo, a] *adj* totalitarian

tóxico, a [t'toksiko, a] *adj* toxic ♦ *nm* poison; **toxicómano, a** *nm/f* drug addict

toxina [to'ksina] *nf* toxin

tozudo, a [to'θuðo, a] *adj* obstinate

traba ['traßa] *nf* bond, tie; (*cadena*) shackle

trabajador, a [traßaxa'ðor, a] *adj* hard-working ♦ *nm/f* worker

trabajar [traßa'xar] *vt* to work; (*AGR*) to till; (*empeñarse en*) to work at; (*convencer*) to persuade ♦ *vi* to work; (*esforzarse*) to strive; **trabajo** *nm* work; (*tarea*) task; (*POL*) labour; (*fig*) effort; **tomarse el trabajo de** to take the trouble to; **trabajo por turno/a destajo** shift work/piecework; **trabajoso, a** *adj* hard

trabalenguas [traßa'lengwas] *nm inv* tongue twister

trabar [tra'ßar] *vt* (*juntar*) to join, unite; (*atar*) to tie down, fetter; (*agarrar*) to seize; (*amistad*) to strike up; **~se** *vr* to become entangled; **trabársele a uno la lengua** to be tongue-tied

tracción [trak'θjon] *nf* traction; ~ **delantera/ trasera** front-wheel/rear-wheel drive

tractor [trak'tor] *nm* tractor

tradición [traði'θjon] *nf* tradition; **tradicional** *adj* traditional

traducción [traðuk'θjon] *nf* translation

traducir [traðu'θir] *vt* to translate; **traductor, a** *nm/f* translator

traer [tra'er] *vt* to bring; (*llevar*) to carry; (*llevar puesto*) to wear; (*incluir*) to carry; (*causar*) to cause; **~se** *vr*: **~se algo** to be up to sth

traficar [trafi'kar] *vi* to trade

tráfico ['trafiko] *nm* (*COM*) trade; (*AUTO*) traffic

tragaluz [traxa'luθ] *nm* skylight

tragaperras [traxa'perras] *nm o f inv* slot machine

tragar [tra'xar] *vt* to swallow; (*devorar*) to devour, bolt down; **~se** *vr* to swallow

tragedia [tra'xeðja] *nf* tragedy; **trágico, a** *adj* tragic

trago ['traxo] *nm* (*líquido*) drink; (*bocado*) gulp; (*fam: de bebida*) swig; (*desgracia*) blow

traición [trai'θjon] *nf* treachery; (*JUR*) treason; (*una ~*) act of treachery; **traicionar** *vt* to betray

traicionero, a [traiθjo'nero, a] *adj* treacherous

traidor, a [trai'ðor, a] *adj* treacherous ♦ *nm/f* traitor

traigo *etc vb ver* **traer**

traje ['traxe] *vb ver* **traer** ♦ *nm* (*de hombre*) suit; (*de mujer*) dress; (*vestido típico*) costume; ~ **de baño** swimsuit; ~ **de luces** bullfighter's costume

trajera *etc vb ver* **traer**

trajín [tra'xin] *nm* (*fam: movimiento*) bustle; **trajinar** *vi* (*moverse*) to bustle about

trama ['trama] *nf* (*intriga*) plot; (*de tejido*) weft (*BRIT*), woof (*US*); **tramar** *vt* to plot; (*TEC*) to weave

tramitar [trami'tar] *vt* (*asunto*) to transact; (*negociar*) to negotiate

trámite ['tramite] *nm* (*paso*) step; (*JUR*) transaction; **~s** *nmpl* (*burocracia*) procedure *sg*; (*JUR*) proceedings

tramo ['tramo] *nm* (*de tierra*) plot; (*de escalera*) flight; (*de vía*) section

tramoya [tra'moja] *nf* (*TEATRO*) piece of stage machinery; **tramoyista** *nm/f* scene shifter; (*fig*) trickster

trampa ['trampa] *nf* trap; (*en el suelo*) trapdoor; (*truco*) trick; (*engaño*) fiddle; **trampear** *vt, vi* to cheat

trampolín [trampo'lin] *nm* (*de piscina etc*) diving board

tramposo, a [tram'poso, a] *adj* crooked, cheating ♦ *nm/f* crook, cheat

tranca ['tranka] *nf* (*palo*) stick; (*de puerta, ventana*) bar; **trancar** *vt* to bar

trance ['tranθe] *nm* (*momento difícil*) difficult moment o juncture; (*estado hipnotizado*) trance

tranquilidad [trankili'ðað] *nf* (*calma*) calmness, stillness; (*paz*) peacefulness

tranquilizar [trankili'θar] *vt* (*calmar*) to calm (down); (*asegurar*) to reassure; **~se** *vr* to calm down; **tranquilo, a** *adj* (*calmado*) calm; (*apacible*) peaceful; (*mar*) calm; (*mente*) untroubled

transacción [transak'θjon] *nf* transaction

transbordador [transßorða'ðor] *nm* ferry

transbordar [transßor'ðar] *vt* to transfer; **transbordo** *nm* transfer; **hacer transbordo** to change (trains etc)

transcurrir [transku'rrir] *vi* (*tiempo*) to pass; (*hecho*) to take place

transcurso [trans'kurso] *nm*: ~ **del tiempo** lapse (of time)

transeúnte [transe'unte] *nm/f* passer-by

transferencia [transfe'renθja] *nf* transference; (*COM*) transfer

transferir [transfe'rir] *vt* to transfer

transformador [transforma'ðor] *nm* (*ELEC*) transformer

transformar [transfor'mar] *vt* to transform; (*convertir*) to convert

tránsfuga ['transfuxa] *nm/f* (*MIL*) deserter; (*POL*) turncoat

transfusión [transfu'sjon] *nf* transfusion

transgénico, a [trans'xeniko, a] *adj*
genetically modified, GM
transición [transi'θjon] *nf* transition
transigir [transi'xir] *vi* to compromise, make
concessions
transistor [transis'tor] *nm* transistor
transitar [transi'tar] *vi* to go (from place to
place); **tránsito** *nm* transit; (*AUTO*) traffic;
transitorio, a *adj* transitory
transmisión [transmi'sjon] *nf* (*TEC*)
transmission; (*transferencia*) transfer; ~ **en
directo/exterior** live/outside broadcast
transmitir [transmi'tir] *vt* to transmit;
(*RADIO, TV*) to broadcast
transparencia [transpa'renθja] *nf*
transparency; (*claridad*) clearness, clarity;
(*foto*) slide
transparentar [transparen'tar] *vt* to reveal
♦ *vi* to be transparent; **transparente** *adj*
transparent; (*claro*) clear
transpirar [transpi'rar] *vi* to perspire
transportar [transpor'tar] *vt* to transport;
(*llevar*) to carry; **transporte** *nm* transport;
(*COM*) haulage
transversal [transßer'sal] *adj* transverse,
cross
tranvía [tram'bia] *nm* tram
trapecio [tra'peθjo] *nm* trapeze; **trapecista**
nm/f trapeze artist
trapero, a [tra'pero, a] *nm/f* ragman
trapicheo [trapi'tʃeo] (*fam*) *nm* scheme,
fiddle
trapo ['trapo] *nm* (*tela*) rag; (*de cocina*) cloth
tráquea ['trakea] *nf* windpipe
traqueteo [trake'teo] *nm* rattling
tras [tras] *prep* (*detrás*) behind; (*después*) after
trasatlántico [trasat'lantiko] *nm* (*barco*)
(cabin) cruiser
trascendencia [trasθen'denθja] *nf*
(*importancia*) importance; (*FILOSOFÍA*)
transcendence
trascendental [trasθenden'tal] *adj*
important; (*FILOSOFÍA*) transcendental
trascender [trasθen'der] *vi* (*noticias*) to
come out; (*suceso*) to have a wide effect
trasero, a [tra'sero, a] *adj* back, rear ♦ *nm*
(*ANAT*) bottom
trasfondo [tras'fondo] *nm* background
trasgredir [trasɣre'ðir] *vt* to contravene
trashumante [trasu'mante] *adj* (*animales*)
migrating
trasladar [trasla'ðar] *vt* to move; (*persona*)
to transfer; (*postergar*) to postpone; (*copiar*)
to copy; **~se** *vr* (*mudarse*) to move; **traslado** *nm* move; (*mudanza*) move, removal
traslucir [traslu'θir] *vt* to show; **~se** *vr* to be
translucent; (*fig*) to be revealed
trasluz [tras'luθ] *nm* reflected light; **al ~**
against o up to the light

trasnochador, a [trasnotʃa'ðor, a] *nm/f*
night owl
trasnochar [trasno'tʃar] *vi* (*acostarse tarde*)
to stay up late
traspapelar [traspape'lar] *vt* (*document,
carta*) to mislay, misplace
traspasar [traspa'sar] *vt* (*suj: bala etc*) to
pierce, go through; (*propiedad*) to sell,
transfer; (*calle*) to cross over; (*límites*) to go
beyond; (*ley*) to break; **traspaso** *nm* (*venta*)
transfer, sale
traspié [tras'pje] *nm* (*tropezón*) trip; (*error*)
blunder
trasplantar [trasplan'tar] *vt* to transplant
traste ['traste] *nm* (*MUS*) fret; **dar al ~ con
algo** to ruin sth
trastero [tras'tero] *nm* storage room
trastienda [tras'tjenda] *nf* back of shop
trasto ['trasto] (*pey*) *nm* (*cosa*) piece of junk;
(*persona*) dead loss
trastornado, a [trastor'naðo, a] *adj* (*loco*)
mad, crazy
trastornar [trastor'nar] *vt* (*fig: planes*) to
disrupt; (: *nervios*) to shatter; (: *persona*) to
drive crazy; **~se** *vr* (*volverse loco*) to go mad o
crazy; **trastorno** *nm* (*acto*) overturning;
(*confusión*) confusion
tratable [tra'taßle] *adj* friendly
tratado [tra'taðo] *nm* (*POL*) treaty; (*COM*)
agreement
tratamiento [trata'mjento] *nm* treatment;
~ de textos (*INFORM*) word processing *cpd*
tratar [tra'tar] *vt* (*ocuparse de*) to treat;
(*manejar, TEC*) to handle; (*MED*) to treat;
(*dirigirse a: persona*) to address ♦ *vi*: ~ **de**
(*hablar sobre*) to deal with, be about;
(*intentar*) to try to; **~se** *vr* to treat each other;
~ con (*COM*) to trade in; (*negociar*) to
negotiate with; (*tener contactos*) to have
dealings with; **¿de qué se trata?** what's it
about?; **trato** *nm* dealings *pl*; (*relaciones*)
relationship; (*comportamiento*) manner;
(*COM*) agreement
trauma ['trauma] *nm* trauma
través [tra'ßes] *nm* (*fig*) reverse; **al ~** across,
crossways; **a ~ de** across; (*sobre*) over; (*por*)
through
travesaño [traße'saɲo] *nm* (*ARQ*) crossbeam;
(*DEPORTE*) crossbar
travesía [traße'sia] *nf* (*calle*) cross-street;
(*NAUT*) crossing
travesura [traße'sura] *nf* (*broma*) prank;
(*ingenio*) wit
traviesa [tra'ßjesa] *nf* (*ARQ*) crossbeam
travieso, a [tra'ßjeso, a] *adj* (*niño*) naughty
trayecto [tra'jekto] *nm* (*ruta*) road, way;
(*viaje*) journey; (*tramo*) stretch; **~ria** *nf*
trajectory; (*fig*) path
traza ['traθa] *nf* (*aspecto*) looks *pl*; (*señal*)

sign; ~**do, a** adj: **bien** ~**do** shapely, well-formed ♦ nm (ARQ) plan, design; (fig) outline

trazar [tra'θar] vt (ARQ) to plan; (ARTE) to sketch; (fig) to trace; (plan) to draw up; **trazo** nm (línea) line; (bosquejo) sketch

trébol ['treβol] nm (BOT) clover

trece ['treθe] num thirteen

trecho ['tretʃo] nm (distancia) distance; (de tiempo) while; **de ~ en ~** at intervals

tregua ['treɣwa] nf (MIL) truce; (fig) respite

treinta ['treinta] num thirty

tremendo, a [tre'mendo, a] adj (terrible) terrible; (imponente: cosa) imposing; (fam: fabuloso) tremendous

trémulo, a ['tremulo, a] adj quivering

tren [tren] nm train; **~ de aterrizaje** undercarriage

trenca ['trenka] nf duffel coat

trenza ['trenθa] nf (de pelo) plait (BRIT), braid (US); **trenzar** vt (pelo) to plait, braid; **trenzarse** vr (AM) to become involved

trepadora [trepa'ðora] nf (BOT) climber

trepar [tre'par] vt, vi to climb

trepidante [trepi'ðante] adj (acción) fast; (ritmo) hectic

tres [tres] num three

tresillo [tre'siʎo] nm three-piece suite; (MUS) triplet

treta ['treta] nf trick

triángulo ['trjangulo] nm triangle

tribu ['triβu] nf tribe

tribuna [tri'βuna] nf (plataforma) platform; (DEPORTE) (grand)stand

tribunal [triβu'nal] nm (JUR) court; (comisión, fig) tribunal

tributar [triβu'tar] vt (gen) to pay; **tributo** nm (COM) tax

tricotar [triko'tar] vi to knit

trigal [tri'ɣal] nm wheat field

trigo ['triɣo] nm wheat

trigueño, a [tri'ɣeɲo, a] adj (pelo) corn-coloured

trillado, a [tri'ʎaðo, a] adj threshed; (asunto) trite, hackneyed; **trilladora** nf threshing machine

trillar [tri'ʎar] vt (AGR) to thresh

trimestral [trimes'tral] adj quarterly; (ESCOL) termly

trimestre [tri'mestre] nm (ESCOL) term

trinar [tri'nar] vi (pájaros) to sing; (rabiar) to fume, be angry

trinchar [trin'tʃar] vt to carve

trinchera [trin'tʃera] nf (fosa) trench

trineo [tri'neo] nm sledge

trinidad [trini'ðað] nf trio; (REL): **la T~** the Trinity

trino ['trino] nm trill

tripa ['tripa] nf (ANAT) intestine; (fam: tb: ~s) insides pl

triple ['triple] adj triple

triplicado, a [tripli'kaðo, a] adj: **por ~** in triplicate

triplicación [tripula'θjon] nf crew

tripulante [tripu'lante] nm/f crewman/woman

tripular [tripu'lar] vt (barco) to man; (AUTO) to drive

triquiñuela [triki'ɲwela] nf trick

tris [tris] nm inv crack; **en un ~** in an instant

triste ['triste] adj sad; (lamentable) sorry, miserable; **~za** nf (aflicción) sadness; (melancolía) melancholy

triturar [tritu'rar] vt (moler) to grind; (mascar) to chew

triunfar [trjun'far] vi (tener éxito) to triumph; (ganar) to win; **triunfo** nm triumph

trivial [tri'βjal] adj trivial; **~izar** vt to minimize, play down

triza ['triθa] nf: **hacer ~s** to smash to bits; (papel) to tear to shreds

trocar [tro'kar] vt to exchange

trocear [troθe'ar] vt (carne, manzana) to cut up, cut into pieces

trocha ['trotʃa] nf short cut

troche ['trotʃe]: **a ~ y moche** adv helter-skelter, pell-mell

trofeo [tro'feo] nm (premio) trophy; (éxito) success

tromba ['tromba] nf downpour

trombón [trom'bon] nm trombone

trombosis [trom'bosis] nf inv thrombosis

trompa ['trompa] nf horn; (trompo) humming top; (hocico) snout; (fam): **cogerse una ~** to get tight

trompazo [trom'paθo] nm bump, bang

trompeta [trom'peta] nf trumpet; (clarín) bugle

trompicón [trompi'kon]: **a ~es** adv in fits and starts

trompo ['trompo] nm spinning top

trompón [trom'pon] nm bump

tronar [tro'nar] vt (AM) to shoot ♦ vi to thunder; (fig) to rage

tronchar [tron'tʃar] vt (árbol) to chop down; (fig: vida) to cut short; (: esperanza) to shatter; (persona) to tire out; **~se** vr to fall down

tronco ['tronko] nm (de árbol, ANAT) trunk

trono ['trono] nm throne

tropa ['tropa] nf (MIL) troop; (soldados) soldiers pl

tropel [tro'pel] nm (muchedumbre) crowd

tropezar [trope'θar] vi to trip, stumble; (errar) to slip up; **~ con** to run into; (topar con) to bump into; **tropezón** nm trip; (fig) blunder

tropical [tropi'kal] adj tropical

trópico ['tropiko] nm tropic

tropiezo [tro'pjeθo] *vb ver* **tropezar ♦** *nm*
(*error*) slip, blunder; (*desgracia*) misfortune;
(*obstáculo*) snag

trotamundos [trota'mundos] *nm inv*
globetrotter

trotar [tro'tar] *vi* to trot; **trote** *nm* trot; (*fam*)
travelling; **de mucho trote** hard-wearing

trozo ['troθo] *nm* bit, piece

trucha ['trutʃa] *nf* trout

truco ['truko] *nm* (*habilidad*) knack; (*engaño*)
trick

trueno ['trweno] *nm* thunder; (*estampido*)
bang

trueque *etc* ['trweke] *vb ver* **trocar ♦** *nm*
exchange; (*COM*) barter

trufa ['trufa] *nf* (*BOT*) truffle

truhán, ana [tru'an, ana] *nm/f* rogue

truncar [trun'kar] *vt* (*cortar*) to truncate; (*fig:
la vida etc*) to cut short; (: *el desarrollo*) to
stunt

tu [tu] *adj* your

tú [tu] *pron* you

tubérculo [tu'ßerkulo] *nm* (*BOT*) tuber

tuberculosis [tußerku'losis] *nf inv*
tuberculosis

tubería [tuße'ria] *nf* pipes *pl*; (*conducto*)
pipeline

tubo ['tußo] *nm* tube, pipe; **~ de ensayo** test
tube; **~ de escape** exhaust (pipe)

tuerca ['twerka] *nf* nut

tuerto, a ['twerto, a] *adj* blind in one eye
♦ *nm/f* one-eyed person

tuerza *etc vb ver* **torcer**

tuétano ['twetano] *nm* marrow; (*BOT*) pith

tufo ['tufo] *nm* (*hedor*) stench

tul [tul] *nm* tulle

tulipán [tuli'pan] *nm* tulip

tullido, a [tu'ʎiðo, a] *adj* crippled

tumba ['tumba] *nf* (*sepultura*) tomb

tumbar [tum'bar] *vt* to knock down; **~se** *vr*
(*echarse*) to lie down; (*extenderse*) to stretch
out

tumbo ['tumbo] *nm*: **dar ~s** to stagger

tumbona [tum'bona] *nf* (*butaca*) easy chair;
(*de playa*) deckchair (*BRIT*), beach chair (*US*)

tumor [tu'mor] *nm* tumour

tumulto [tu'multo] *nm* turmoil

tuna ['tuna] *nf* (*MUS*) student music group; *ver
tb* **tuno**

tunante [tu'nante] *nm/f* rascal

tunda ['tunda] *nf* (*golpeo*) beating

túnel ['tunel] *nm* tunnel

Túnez ['tuneθ] *nm* Tunisia; (*ciudad*) Tunis

tuno, a ['tuno, a] *nm/f* (*fam*) rogue **♦** *nm*
member of student music group

tupido, a [tu'piðo, a] *adj* (*denso*) dense;
(*tela*) close-woven

turba ['turßa] *nf* crowd

turbante [tur'ßante] *nm* turban

turbar [tur'ßar] *vt* (*molestar*) to disturb;
(*incomodar*) to upset; **~se** *vr* to be disturbed

turbina [tur'ßina] *nf* turbine

turbio, a ['turßjo, a] *adj* cloudy; (*tema etc*)
confused

turbulencia [turßu'lenθja] *nf* turbulence;
(*fig*) restlessness; **turbulento, a** *adj*
turbulent; (*fig: intranquilo*) restless; (: *ruidoso*) noisy

turco, a ['turko, a] *adj* Turkish **♦** *nm/f* Turk

turismo [tu'rismo] *nm* tourism; (*coche*) car;
turista *nm/f* tourist; **turístico, a** *adj* tourist
cpd

turnar [tur'nar] *vi* to take (it in) turns; **~se** *vr*
to take (it in) turns; **turno** *nm* (*de trabajo*)
shift; (*juegos etc*) turn

turquesa [tur'kesa] *nf* turquoise

Turquía [tur'kia] *nf* Turkey

turrón [tu'rron] *nm* (*dulce*) nougat

tutear [tute'ar] *vt* to address as familiar "tú";
~se *vr* to be on familiar terms

tutela [tu'tela] *nf* (*legal*) guardianship;
tutelar *adj* tutelary **♦** *vt* to protect

tutor, a [tu'tor, a] *nm/f* (*legal*) guardian;
(*ESCOL*) tutor

tuve *etc vb ver* **tener**

tuviera *etc vb ver* **tener**

tuyo, a ['tujo, a] *adj* yours, of yours **♦** *pron*
yours; **un amigo ~** a friend of yours; **los ~s**
(*fam*) your relations, your family

TV ['te'ße] *nf abr* (= *televisión*) TV

TVE *nf abr* = **Televisión Española**

U, u

u [u] *conj* or

ubicar [ußi'kar] *vt* to place, situate; (*AM:
encontrar*) to find; **~se** *vr* to lie, be located

ubre ['ußre] *nf* udder

UCI *nf abr* (= *Unidad de Cuidados Intensivos*)
ICU

Ud(s) *abr* = **usted(es)**

UE *nf abr* (= *Unión Europea*) EU

ufanarse [ufa'narse] *vr* to boast; **~ de** to
pride o.s. on; **ufano, a** *adj* (*arrogante*)
arrogant; (*presumido*) conceited

UGT *nf abr* = **Unión General de Trabajadores**

ujier [u'xjer] *nm* usher; (*portero*) doorkeeper

úlcera ['ulθera] *nf* ulcer

ulcerar [ulθe'rar] *vt* to make sore; **~se** *vr* to
ulcerate

ulterior [ulte'rjor] *adj* (*más allá*) farther,
further; (*subsecuente, siguiente*) subsequent

últimamente ['ultimamente] *adv*
(*recientemente*) lately, recently

ultimar [ulti'mar] *vt* to finish; (*finalizar*) to
finalize; (*AM: rematar*) to finish off

ultimátum [ulti'matum] (*pl* **~s**) ultimatum

último, a ['ultimo, a] *adj* last; (*más reciente*) latest, most recent; (*más bajo*) bottom; (*más alto*) top; **en las últimas** on one's last legs; **por ~** finally

ultra ['ultra] *adj* ultra ♦ *nm/f* extreme right-winger

ultrajar [ultra'xar] *vt* (*ofender*) to outrage; (*insultar*) to insult, abuse; **ultraje** *nm* outrage; insult

ultramar [ultra'mar] *nm*: **de o en ~** abroad, overseas

ultramarinos [ultrama'rinos] *nmpl* groceries; **tienda de ~** grocer's (shop)

ultranza [ul'tranθa]: **a ~** *adv* (*a todo trance*) at all costs; (*completo*) outright

ultratumba [ultra'tumba] *nf*: **la vida de ~** the next life

umbral [um'bral] *nm* (*gen*) threshold

umbrío, a [um'brio, a] *adj* shady

un, una [un, 'una] *art indef* a; (*antes de vocal*) an; **una mujer/naranja** a woman/an orange
♦ *adj*: **unos** (*o* **unas**): **hay unos regalos para ti** there are some presents for you; **hay unas cervezas en la nevera** there are some beers in the fridge

unánime [u'nanime] *adj* unanimous; **unanimidad** *nf* unanimity

undécimo, a [un'deθimo, a] *adj* eleventh

ungir [un'xir] *vt* to anoint

ungüento [un'gwento] *nm* ointment

únicamente ['unikamente] *adv* solely, only

único, a ['uniko, a] *adj* only, sole; (*sin par*) unique

unidad [uni'ðað] *nf* unity; (*COM, TEC etc*) unit

unido, a [u'niðo, a] *adj* joined, linked; (*fig*) united

unificar [unifi'kar] *vt* to unite, unify

uniformar [unifor'mar] *vt* to make uniform, level up; (*persona*) to put into uniform

uniforme [uni'forme] *adj* uniform, equal; (*superficie*) even ♦ *nm* uniform; **uniformidad** *nf* uniformity; (*de terreno*) levelness, evenness

unilateral [unilate'ral] *adj* unilateral

unión [u'njon] *nf* union; (*acto*) uniting, joining; (*unidad*) unity; (*TEC*) joint; **la U~ Europea** the European Union; **la U~ Soviética** the Soviet Union

unir [u'nir] *vt* (*juntar*) to join, unite; (*atar*) to tie, fasten; (*combinar*) to combine; **~se** *vr* to join together, unite; (*empresas*) to merge

unísono [u'nisono] *nm*: **al ~** in unison

universal [uniβer'sal] *adj* universal; (*mundial*) world *cpd*

universidad [uniβersi'ðað] *nf* university

universitario, a [uniβersi'tarjo, a] *adj* university *cpd* ♦ *nm/f* (*profesor*) lecturer; (*estudiante*) (university) student; (*graduado*) graduate

universo [uni'βerso] *nm* universe

uno, a ['uno, a] *adj* one; **es todo ~** it's all one and the same; **~s pocos** a few; **~s cien** about a hundred
♦ *pron* **1** one; **quiero sólo ~** I only want one; **~ de ellos** one of them
2 (*alguien*) somebody, someone; **conozco a ~ que se te parece** I know somebody *o* someone who looks like you; **~ mismo** oneself; **~s querían quedarse** some (people) wanted to stay
3: **(los) ~s ... (los) otros ...** some ... others; **una y otra son muy agradables** they're both very nice
♦ *nf* one; **es la una** it's one o'clock
♦ *nm* (number) one

untar [un'tar] *vt* (*mantequilla*) to spread; (*engrasar*) to grease, oil

uña ['uɲa] *nf* (*ANAT*) nail; (*garra*) claw; (*casco*) hoof; (*arrancaclavos*) claw

uranio [u'ranjo] *nm* uranium

urbanidad [urβani'ðað] *nf* courtesy, politeness

urbanismo [urβa'nismo] *nm* town planning

urbanización [urβaniθa'θjon] *nf* (*barrio, colonia*) housing estate

urbanizar [urβani'θar] *vt* (*zona*) to develop, urbanize

urbano, a [ur'βano, a] *adj* (*de ciudad*) urban; (*cortés*) courteous, polite

urbe ['urβe] *nf* large city

urdimbre [ur'ðimbre] *nf* (*de tejido*) warp; (*intriga*) intrigue

urdir [ur'ðir] *vt* to warp; (*complot*) to plot, contrive

urgencia [ur'xenθja] *nf* urgency; (*prisa*) haste, rush; (*emergencia*) emergency; **servicios de ~** emergency services; **"Urgencias"** "Casualty"; **urgente** *adj* urgent

urgir [ur'xir] *vi* to be urgent; **me urge** I'm in a hurry for it

urinario, a [uri'narjo, a] *adj* urinary ♦ *nm* urinal

urna ['urna] *nf* urn; (*POL*) ballot box

urraca [u'rraka] *nf* magpie

URSS *nf*: **la ~** the USSR

Uruguay [uru'ɣwai] *nm*: **el ~** Uruguay; **uruguayo, a** *adj, nm/f* Uruguayan

usado, a [u'saðo, a] *adj* used; (*de segunda mano*) secondhand

usar [u'sar] *vt* to use; (*ropa*) to wear; (*tener costumbre*) to be in the habit of; **~se** *vr* to be

used; **uso** *nm* use; wear; (*costumbre*) usage,
custom; (*moda*) fashion; **al uso** in keeping
with custom; **al uso de** in the style of
usted [us'teð] *pron* (*sg*) you *sg*; (*pl*): **~es** you
pl
usual [u'swal] *adj* usual
usuario, a [usu'arjo, a] *nm/f* user
usura [u'sura] *nf* usury; **usurero, a** *nm/f*
usurer
usurpar [usur'par] *vt* to usurp
utensilio [uten'siljo] *nm* tool; (*CULIN*) utensil
útero ['utero] *nm* uterus, womb
útil ['util] *adj* useful ♦ *nm* tool; **utilidad** *nf*
usefulness; (*COM*) profit; **utilizar** *vt* to use,
utilize
utopía [uto'pia] *nf* Utopia; **utópico, a** *adj*
Utopian
uva ['ußa] *nf* grape

V, v

v *abr* (= *voltio*) v
va *vb ver* **ir**
vaca ['baka] *nf* (*animal*) cow; **carne de ~** beef
vacaciones [baka'θjones] *nfpl* holidays
vacante [ba'kante] *adj* vacant, empty ♦ *nf*
vacancy
vaciar [ba'θjar] *vt* to empty out; (*ahuecar*) to
hollow out; (*moldear*) to cast; **~se** *vr* to
empty
vacilante [baθi'lante] *adj* unsteady; (*habla*)
faltering; (*dudoso*) hesitant
vacilar [baθi'lar] *vi* to be unsteady; (*al
hablar*) to falter; (*dudar*) to hesitate, waver;
(*memoria*) to fail
vacío, a [ba'θio, a] *adj* empty; (*puesto*)
vacant; (*desocupado*) idle; (*vano*) vain ♦ *nm*
emptiness; (*FÍSICA*) vacuum; (*un ~*) (empty)
space
vacuna [ba'kuna] *nf* vaccine; **vacunar** *vt* to
vaccinate
vacuno, a [ba'kuno, a] *adj* cow *cpd*; **ganado
~** cattle
vacuo, a ['bakwo, a] *adj* empty
vadear [baðe'ar] *vt* (*río*) to ford; **vado** *nm*
ford
vagabundo, a [baɣa'ßundo, a] *adj*
wandering ♦ *nm* tramp
vagamente [baɣa'mente] *adv* vaguely
vagancia [ba'ɣanθja] *nf* (*pereza*) idleness,
laziness
vagar [ba'ɣar] *vi* to wander; (*no hacer nada*)
to idle
vagina [ba'xina] *nf* vagina
vago, a ['baɣo, a] *adj* vague; (*perezoso*) lazy
♦ *nm/f* (*vagabundo*) tramp; (*flojo*) lazybones
sg, idler
vagón [ba'ɣon] *nm* (*FERRO: de pasajeros*)

carriage; (: *de mercancías*) wagon
vaguedad [baɣe'ðað] *nf* vagueness
vaho ['bao] *nm* (*vapor*) vapour, steam;
(*respiración*) breath
vaina ['baina] *nf* sheath
vainilla [bai'niʎa] *nf* vanilla
vainita [bai'nita] (*AM*) *nf* green o French bean
vals *vb ver* **ir**
vaivén [bai'ßen] *nm* to-and-fro movement;
(*de tránsito*) coming and going; **vaivenes**
nmpl (*fig*) ups and downs
vajilla [ba'xiʎa] *nf* crockery, dishes *pl*; **lavar la
~** to do the washing-up (*BRIT*), wash the
dishes (*US*)
valdré *etc vb ver* **valer**
vale ['bale] *nm* voucher; (*recibo*) receipt;
(*pagaré*) IOU
valedero, a [bale'ðero, a] *adj* valid
valenciano, a [balen'θjano, a] *adj* Valencian
valentía [balen'tia] *nf* courage, bravery
valer [ba'ler] *vt* to equal; (*MAT*) to equal;
(*costar*) to cost ♦ *vi* (*ser útil*) to be useful;
(*ser válido*) to be valid; **~se** *vr* to take care of
oneself; **~se de** to make use of, take
advantage of; **~ la pena** to be worthwhile;
¿vale? (*ESP*) OK?
valeroso, a [bale'roso, a] *adj* brave, valiant
valgo *etc vb ver* **valer**
valía [ba'lia] *nf* worth, value
validar [bali'ðar] *vt* to validate; **validez** *nf*
validity; **válido, a** *adj* valid
valiente [ba'ljente] *adj* brave, valiant ♦ *nm*
hero
valioso, a [ba'ljoso, a] *adj* valuable
valla ['baʎa] *nf* fence; (*DEPORTE*) hurdle;
~ publicitaria hoarding; **vallar** *vt* to fence in
valle ['baʎe] *nm* valley
valor [ba'lor] *nm* value, worth; (*precio*) price;
(*valentía*) valour, courage; (*importancia*)
importance; **~es** *nmpl* (*COM*) securities; **~ar** *vt*
to value
vals [bals] *nm inv* waltz
válvula ['balßula] *nf* valve
vamos *vb ver* **ir**
vampiro, resa [bam'piro, 'resa] *nm/f*
vampire
van *vb ver* **ir**
vanagloriarse [banaɣlo'rjarse] *vr* to boast
vandalismo [banda'lismo] *nm* vandalism;
vándalo, a *nm/f* vandal
vanguardia [ban'gwardja] *nf* vanguard;
(*ARTE etc*) avant-garde
vanidad [bani'ðað] *nf* vanity; **vanidoso, a**
adj vain, conceited
vano, a ['bano, a] *adj* vain
vapor [ba'por] *nm* vapour; (*vaho*) steam; **al ~**
(*CULIN*) steamed; **~izador** *nm* atomizer;
~izar *vt* to vaporize; **~oso, a** *adj* vaporous
vapulear [bapule'ar] *vt* to beat, thrash

vaquero, a [ba'kero, a] adj cattle cpd ♦ nm cowboy; **~s** nmpl (pantalones) jeans

vaquilla [ba'kiʎa] nf (ZOOL) heifer

vara ['bara] nf stick; (TEC) rod; **~ mágica** magic wand

variable [ba'rjaβle] adj, nf variable

variación [barja'θjon] nf variation

variar [bar'jar] vt to vary; (modificar) to modify; (cambiar de posición) to switch around ♦ vi to vary

varicela [bari'θela] nf chickenpox

varices [ba'riθes] nfpl varicose veins

variedad [barje'ðað] nf variety

varilla [ba'riʎa] nf stick; (BOT) twig; (TEC) rod; (de rueda) spoke

vario, a ['barjo, a] adj varied; **~s** various, several

varita [ba'rita] nf: **~ mágica** magic wand

varón [ba'ron] nm male, man; **varonil** adj manly, virile

Varsovia [bar'soβja] n Warsaw

vas vb ver **ir**

vasco, a ['basko, a] adj, nm/f Basque

vascongado, a [baskon'gaðo, a] adj Basque; **las Vascongadas** the Basque Country

vascuence [bas'kwenθe] adj = **vascongado**

vaselina [base'lina] nf Vaseline ®

vasija [ba'sixa] nf container, vessel

vaso ['baso] nm glass, tumbler; (ANAT) vessel

vástago ['bastaxo] nm (BOT) shoot; (TEC) rod; (fig) offspring

vasto, a ['basto, a] adj vast, huge

Vaticano [bati'kano] nm: **el ~** the Vatican

vatio ['batjo] nm (ELEC) watt

vaya etc vb ver **ir**

Vd(s) abr = **usted(es)**

ve vb ver **ir; ver**

vecindad [beθin'dað] nf neighbourhood; (habitantes) residents pl

vecindario [beθin'darjo] nm neighbourhood; residents pl

vecino, a [be'θino, a] adj neighbouring ♦ nm/f neighbour; (residente) resident

veda ['beða] nf prohibition

vedar [be'ðar] vt (prohibir) to ban, prohibit; (impedir) to stop, prevent

vegetación [bexeta'θjon] nf vegetation

vegetal [bexe'tal] adj, nm vegetable

vegetariano, a [bexeta'rjano, a] adj, nm/f vegetarian

vehemencia [be(e)'menθja] nf vehemence; **vehemente** adj vehement

vehículo [be'ikulo] nm vehicle; (MED) carrier

veía etc vb ver **ver**

veinte ['beinte] num twenty

vejación [bexa'θjon] nf vexation; (humillación) humiliation

vejar [be'xar] vt (irritar) to annoy, vex; (humillar) to humiliate

vejez [be'xeθ] nf old age

vejiga [be'xiɣa] nf (ANAT) bladder

vela ['bela] nf (de cera) candle; (NAUT) sail; (insomnio) sleeplessness; (vigilia) vigil; (MIL) sentry duty; **estar a dos ~s** (fam: sin dinero) to be skint

velado, a [be'laðo, a] adj veiled; (sonido) muffled; (FOTO) blurred ♦ nf soirée

velar [be'lar] vt (vigilar) to keep watch over ♦ vi to stay awake; **~ por** to watch over, look after

velatorio [bela'torjo] nm (funeral) wake

veleidad [belei'ðað] nf (ligereza) fickleness; (capricho) whim

velero [be'lero] nm (NAUT) sailing ship; (AVIAT) glider

veleta [be'leta] nf weather vane

veliz [be'lis] (AM) nm suitcase

vello ['beʎo] nm down, fuzz

velo ['belo] nm veil

velocidad [beloθi'ðað] nf speed; (TEC, AUTO) gear

velocímetro [belo'θimetro] nm speedometer

veloz [be'loθ] adj fast

ven vb ver **venir**

vena ['bena] nf vein

venado [be'naðo] nm deer

vencedor, a [benθe'ðor, a] adj victorious ♦ nm/f victor, winner

vencer [ben'θer] vt (dominar) to defeat, beat; (derrotar) to vanquish; (superar, controlar) to overcome, master ♦ vi (triunfar) to win (through), triumph; (plazo) to expire; **vencido, a** adj (derrotado) defeated, beaten; (COM) due ♦ adv: **pagar vencido** to pay in arrears; **vencimiento** nm (COM) maturity

venda ['benda] nf bandage; **vendaje** nm bandage, dressing; **vendar** vt to bandage; **vendar los ojos** to blindfold

vendaval [benda'βal] nm (viento) gale

vendedor, a [bende'ðor, a] nm/f seller

vender [ben'der] vt to sell; **~ al contado/al por mayor/al por menor** to sell for cash/ wholesale/retail

vendimia [ben'dimja] nf grape harvest

vendré etc vb ver **venir**

veneno [be'neno] nm poison; (de serpiente) venom; **~so, a** adj poisonous; venomous

venerable [bene'raβle] adj venerable; **venerar** vt (respetar) to revere; (adorar) to worship

venéreo, a [be'nereo, a] adj: **enfermedad venérea** venereal disease

venezolano, a [beneθo'lano, a] adj Venezuelan

Venezuela [bene'θwela] nf Venezuela

venganza [ben'ganθa] nf vengeance, revenge; **vengar** vt to avenge; **vengarse** vr to take revenge; **vengativo, a** adj (persona) vindictive

vengo etc vb ver **venir**

venia ['benja] nf (perdón) pardon; (permiso) consent

venial [be'njal] adj venial

venida [be'niða] nf (llegada) arrival; (regreso) return

venidero, a [beni'ðero, a] adj coming, future

venir [be'nir] vi to come; (llegar) to arrive; (ocurrir) to happen; (fig): **~ de** to stem from; **~ bien/mal** to be suitable/unsuitable; **el año que viene** next year; **~se abajo** to collapse

venta ['benta] nf (COM) sale; **~ a plazos** hire purchase; **~ al contado/al por mayor/al por menor** o **al detalle** cash sale/wholesale/retail; **~ con derecho a retorno** sale or return; "**en ~**" "for sale"

ventaja [ben'taxa] nf advantage; **ventajoso, a** adj advantageous

ventana [ben'tana] nf window; **ventanilla** nf (de taquilla) window (of booking office etc)

ventilación [bentila'θjon] nf ventilation; (corriente) draught

ventilador [bentila'ðor] nm fan

ventilar [benti'lar] vt to ventilate; (para secar) to put out to dry; (asunto) to air, discuss

ventisca [ben'tiska] nf blizzard

ventrílocuo, a [ben'trilokwo, a] nm/f ventriloquist

ventura [ben'tura] nf (felicidad) happiness; (buena suerte) luck; (destino) fortune; **a la (buena) ~** at random; **venturoso, a** adj happy; (afortunado) lucky, fortunate

veo etc vb ver **ver**

ver [ber] vt to see; (mirar) to look at, watch; (entender) to understand; (investigar) to look into; ♦ vi to see; to understand; **~se** vr (encontrarse) to meet; (dejarse **~**) to be seen; (hallarse: en un apuro) to find o.s., be; **a ~** let's see; **no tener nada que ~ con** to have nothing to do with; **a mi modo de ~** as I see it

vera ['bera] nf edge, verge; (de río) bank

veracidad [beraθi'ðað] nf truthfulness

veranear [berane'ar] vi to spend the summer; **veraneo** nm summer holiday; **veraniego, a** adj summer cpd

verano [be'rano] nm summer

veras ['beras] nfpl truth sg; **de ~** really, truly

veraz [be'raθ] adj truthful

verbal [ber'ßal] adj verbal

verbena [ber'ßena] nf (baile) open-air dance

verbo ['berßo] nm verb; **~so, a** adj verbose

verdad [ber'ðað] nf truth; (fiabilidad) reliability, truth, proper; **a decir ~** to tell the truth; **~ero, a** adj (veraz) true, truthful; (fiable) reliable; (fig) real

verde ['berðe] adj green; (chiste) blue, dirty

♦ nm green; **viejo ~** dirty old man; **~ar** vi to turn green; **verdor** nm greenness

verdugo [ber'ðuxo] nm executioner

verdulero, a [berðu'lero, a] nm/f greengrocer

verduras [ber'ðuras] nfpl (CULIN) greens

vereda [be'reða] nf path; (AM) pavement (BRIT), sidewalk (US)

veredicto [bere'ðikto] nm verdict

vergonzoso, a [bervon'θoso, a] adj shameful; (tímido) timid, bashful

vergüenza [ber'xwenθa] nf shame, sense of shame; (timidez) bashfulness; (pudor) modesty; **me da ~** I'm ashamed

verídico, a [be'riðiko, a] adj true, truthful

verificar [berifi'kar] vt to check; (corroborar) to verify; (llevar a cabo) to carry out; **~se** vr (predicción) to prove to be true

verja ['berxa] nf (cancela) iron gate; (valla) iron railings pl; (de ventana) grille

vermut [ber'mut] (pl **~s**) nm vermouth

verosímil [bero'simil] adj likely, probable; (relato) credible

verruga [be'rruxa] nf wart

versado, a [ber'saðo, a] adj: **~ en** versed in

versátil [ber'satil] adj versatile

versión [ber'sjon] nf version

verso ['berso] nm verse; **un ~** a line of poetry

vértebra ['berteßra] nf vertebra

verter [ber'ter] vt (líquido: adrede) to empty, pour (out); (: sin querer) to spill; (basura) to dump ♦ vi to flow

vertical [berti'kal] adj vertical

vértice ['bertiθe] nm vertex, apex

vertidos [ber'tiðos] nmpl waste sg

vertiente [ber'tjente] nf slope; (fig) aspect

vertiginoso, a [bertixi'noso, a] adj giddy, dizzy

vértigo ['bertixo] nm vertigo; (mareo) dizziness

vesícula [be'sikula] nf blister

vespino ® [bes'pino] nm o nf moped

vestíbulo [bes'tißulo] nm hall; (de teatro) foyer

vestido [bes'tiðo] pp de **vestir**; **~ de azul/ marinero** dressed in blue/as a sailor ♦ nm (ropa) clothes pl, clothing; (de mujer) dress, frock

vestigio [bes'tixjo] nm (huella) trace; **~s** nmpl (restos) remains

vestimenta [besti'menta] nf clothing

vestir [bes'tir] vt (poner: ropa) to put on; (llevar: ropa) to wear; (proveer de ropa a) to clothe; (suj: sastre) to make clothes for ♦ vi to dress; (verse bien) to look good; **~se** vr to get dressed, dress o.s.

vestuario [bes'twarjo] nm clothes pl, wardrobe; (TEATRO: cuarto) dressing room; (DEPORTE) changing room

veta ['beta] *nf* (*vena*) vein, seam; (*en carne*) streak; (*de madera*) grain

vetar [be'tar] *vt* to veto

veterano, a [bete'rano, a] *adj, nm* veteran

veterinaria [beteri'narja] *nf* veterinary science; *ver tb* **veterinario**

veterinario, a [beteri'narjo, a] *nm/f* vet(erinary surgeon)

veto ['beto] *nm* veto

vez [beθ] *nf* time; (*turno*) turn; **a la ~ que** at the same time as; **a su ~** in its turn; **otra ~** again; **una ~** once; **de una ~** in one go; **de una ~ para siempre** once and for all; **en ~ de** instead of; **a o algunas veces** sometimes; **una y otra ~** repeatedly; **de ~ en cuando** from time to time; **7 veces 9** 7 times 9; **hacer las veces de** to stand in for; **tal ~** perhaps

vía ['bia] *nf* track, route; (*FERRO*) line; (*fig*) way; (*ANAT*) passage, tube ♦ *prep* via, by way of; **por ~ judicial** by legal means; **por ~ oficial** through official channels; **en ~s de** in the process of; **~ aérea** airway; **V~ Láctea** Milky Way; **~ pública** public road o thoroughfare

viable ['bjaβle] *adj* (*solución, plan, alternativa*) feasible

viaducto [bja'ðukto] *nm* viaduct

viajante [bja'xante] *nm* commercial traveller

viajar [bja'xar] *vi* to travel; **viaje** *nm* journey; (*gira*) tour; (*NAUT*) voyage; **estar de viaje** to be on a trip; **viaje de ida y vuelta** round trip; **viaje de novios** honeymoon; **viajero, a** *adj* travelling; (*ZOOL*) migratory ♦ *nm/f* (*quien viaja*) traveller; (*pasajero*) passenger

vial [bjal] *adj* road *cpd*, traffic *cpd*

víbora ['biβora] *nf* viper; (*AM*) poisonous snake

vibración [biβra'θjon] *nf* vibration

vibrar [bi'βrar] *vt, vi* to vibrate

vicario [bi'karjo] *nm* curate

vicepresidente [biθepresi'ðente] *nm/f* vice-president

viceversa [biθe'βersa] *adv* vice versa

viciado, a [bi'θjaðo, a] *adj* (*corrompido*) corrupt; (*contaminado*) foul, contaminated; **viciar** *vt* (*pervertir*) to pervert; (*JUR*) to nullify; (*estropear*) to spoil; **viciarse** *vr* to become corrupted

vicio ['biθjo] *nm* vice; (*mala costumbre*) bad habit; **~so, a** *adj* (*muy malo*) vicious; (*corrompido*) depraved ♦ *nm/f* depraved person

vicisitud [biθisi'tuð] *nf* vicissitude

víctima ['biktima] *nf* victim

victoria [bik'torja] *nf* victory; **victorioso, a** *adj* victorious

vid [bið] *nf* vine

vida ['biða] *nf* (*gen*) life; (*duración*) lifetime; **de por ~** for life; **en la/mi ~** never; **estar con ~** to be still alive; **ganarse la ~** to earn one's living

vídeo ['biðeo] *nm* video ♦ *adj inv*: **película ~** video film; **~cámara** *nf* camcorder; **~casete** *nm* video cassette, videotape; **~club** *nm* video club; **~juego** *nm* video game

vidriero, a [bi'ðrjero, a] *nm/f* glazier ♦ *nf* (*ventana*) stained-glass window; (*AM*: *de tienda*) shop window; (*puerta*) glass door

vidrio ['biðrjo] *nm* glass

vieira ['bjeira] *nf* scallop

viejo, a ['bjexo, a] *adj* old ♦ *nm/f* old man/woman; **hacerse ~** to get old

Viena ['bjena] *n* Vienna

vienes *etc vb ver* **venir**

vienés, esa [bje'nes, esa] *adj* Viennese

viento ['bjento] *nm* wind; **hacer ~** to be windy

vientre ['bjentre] *nm* belly; (*matriz*) womb

viernes ['bjernes] *nm inv* Friday; **V~ Santo** Good Friday

Vietnam [bjet'nam] *nm*: **el ~** Vietnam; **vietnamita** *adj* Vietnamese

viga ['biɣa] *nf* beam, rafter; (*de metal*) girder

vigencia [bi'xenθja] *nf* validity; **estar en ~** to be in force; **vigente** *adj* valid, in force; (*imperante*) prevailing

vigésimo, a [bi'xesimo, a] *adj* twentieth

vigía [bi'xia] *nm* look-out

vigilancia [bixi'lanθja] *nf*: **tener a uno bajo ~** to keep watch on sb

vigilar [bixi'lar] *vt* to watch over ♦ *vi* (*gen*) to be vigilant; (*hacer guardia*) to keep watch; **~ por** to take care of

vigilia [vi'xilja] *nf* wakefulness, being awake; (*REL*) fast

vigor [bi'vor] *nm* vigour, vitality; **en ~** in force; **entrar/poner en ~** to come/put into effect; **~oso, a** *adj* vigorous

VIH *nm abr* (= *virus de la inmunodeficiencia humana*) HIV; **~ positivo/negativo** HIV-positive/-negative

vil [bil] *adj* vile, low; **~eza** *nf* vileness; (*acto*) base deed

vilipendiar [bilipen'djar] *vt* to vilify, revile

villa ['biʎa] *nf* (*casa*) villa; (*pueblo*) small town; (*municipalidad*) municipality; **~ miseria** (*AM*) shantytown

villancico [biʎan'θiko] *nm* (Christmas) carol

villorrio [bi'ʎorrjo] *nm* shantytown

vilo ['bilo]: **en ~** *adv* in the air, suspended; (*fig*) on tenterhooks, in suspense

vinagre [bi'naɣre] *nm* vinegar

vinagreta [bina'ɣreta] *nf* vinaigrette, French dressing

vinculación [binkula'θjon] *nf* (*lazo*) link, bond; (*acción*) linking

vincular [binku'lar] *vt* to link, bind; **vínculo** *nm* link, bond

vine *etc vb ver* **venir**

vinicultura [binikul'tura] nf wine growing

viniera etc vb ver **venir**

vino ['bino] vb ver **venir** ♦ nm wine; ~ **blanco/tinto** white/red wine

viña ['biɲa] nf vineyard; **viñedo** nm vineyard

viola ['bjola] nf viola

violación [bjola'θjon] nf violation; ~ **(sexual)** rape

violar [bjo'lar] vt to violate; (sexualmente) to rape

violencia [bjo'lenθja] nf violence, force; (incomodidad) embarrassment; (acto injusto) unjust act; **violentar** vt to force; (casa) to break into; (agredir) to assault; (violar) to violate; **violento, a** adj violent; (furioso) furious; (situación) embarrassing; (acto) forced, unnatural

violeta [bjo'leta] nf violet

violín [bjo'lin] nm violin

violón [bjo'lon] nm double bass

viraje [bi'raxe] nm turn; (de vehículo) swerve; (fig) change of direction; **virar** vi to change direction

virgen ['birxen] adj, nf virgin

Virgo ['birxo] nm Virgo

viril [bi'ril] adj virile; **~idad** nf virility

virtud [bir'tuð] nf virtue; **en ~ de** by virtue of; **virtuoso, a** adj virtuous ♦ nm/f virtuoso

viruela [bi'rwela] nf smallpox

virulento, a [biru'lento, a] adj virulent

virus ['birus] nm inv virus

visa ['bisa] (AM) nf = **visado**

visado [bi'saðo] nm visa

víscera ['bisθera] nf (ANAT, ZOOL) gut, bowel; **~s** nfpl entrails

visceral [bisθe'ral] adj (odio) intense; **reacción ~** gut reaction

viscoso, a [bis'koso, a] adj viscous

visera [bi'sera] nf visor

visibilidad [bisiβili'ðað] nf visibility; **visible** adj visible; (fig) obvious

visillos [bi'siʎos] nmpl lace curtains

visión [bi'sjon] nf (ANAT) vision, (eye)sight; (fantasía) vision, fantasy

visita [bi'sita] nf call, visit; (persona) visitor; **hacer una ~** to pay a visit

visitar [bisi'tar] vt to visit, call on

vislumbrar [bislum'brar] vt to glimpse, catch a glimpse of

viso ['biso] nm (del metal) glint, gleam; (de tela) sheen; (aspecto) appearance

visón [bi'son] nm mink

visor [bi'sor] nm (FOTO) viewfinder

víspera ['bispera] nf: **la ~ de** ... the day before ...

vista ['bista] nf sight, vision; (capacidad de ver) (eye)sight; (mirada) look(s) (pl); **a primera ~** at first glance; **hacer la ~ gorda** to turn a blind eye; **volver la ~** to look back;

está a la ~ que it's obvious that; **en ~ de** in view of; **en ~ de que** in view of the fact that; **¡hasta la ~!** so long!, see you!; **con ~s a** with a view to; **~zo** nm glance; **dar** o **echar un ~zo a** to glance at

visto, a ['bisto, a] pp de **ver** ♦ vb ver tb **vestir** ♦ adj seen; (considerado) considered ♦ nm: **~ bueno** approval; **"~ bueno"** "approved"; **por lo ~** apparently; **está ~ que** it's clear that; **está bien/mal** it's acceptable/unacceptable; **~ que** since, considering that

vistoso, a [bis'toso, a] adj colourful

visual [bi'swal] adj visual

vital [bi'tal] adj life cpd, living cpd; (fig) vital; (persona) lively, vivacious; **~icio, a** adj for life; **~idad** nf (de persona, negocio) energy; (de ciudad) liveliness

vitamina [bita'mina] nf vitamin

viticultor, a [bitikul'tor, a] nm/f wine grower; **viticultura** nf wine growing

vitorear [bitore'ar] vt to cheer, acclaim

vitrina [bi'trina] nf show case; (AM) shop window

viudez nf widowhood

viudo, a ['bjuðo, a] nm/f widower/widow

viva ['biβa] excl hurrah!: **¡~ el rey!** long live the king!

vivacidad [biβaθi'ðað] nf (vigor) vigour; (vida) liveliness

vivaracho, a [biβa'ratʃo, a] adj jaunty, lively; (ojos) bright, twinkling

vivaz [bi'βaθ] adj lively

víveres ['biβeres] nmpl provisions

vivero [bi'βero] nm (para plantas) nursery; (para peces) fish farm; (fig) hotbed

viveza [bi'βeθa] nf liveliness; (agudeza: mental) sharpness

vivienda [bi'βjenda] nf housing; (una ~) house; (piso) flat (BRIT), apartment (US)

viviente [bi'βjente] adj living

vivir [bi'βir] vt, vi to live ♦ nm life, living

vivo, a ['biβo, a] adj living, alive; (fig: descripción) vivid; (persona: astuto) smart, clever; **en ~** (transmisión etc) live

vocablo [bo'kaβlo] nm (palabra) word; (término) term

vocabulario [bokaβu'larjo] nm vocabulary

vocación [boka'θjon] nf vocation; **vocacional** (AM) nf ≈ technical college

vocal [bo'kal] adj vocal ♦ nf vowel; **~izar** vt to vocalize

vocear [boθe'ar] vt (para vender) to cry; (aclamar) to acclaim; (fig) to proclaim ♦ vi to yell; **vocerío** nm shouting

vocero [bo'θero] nm/f spokesman/woman

voces ['boθes] pl de **voz**

vociferar [boθife'rar] vt to shout ♦ vi to yell

vodka ['boðka] nm o f vodka

vol abr = **volumen**

volador, a [bola'ðor, a] *adj* flying
volandas [bo'landas]: **en ~** *adv* in the air
volante [bo'lante] *adj* flying ♦ *nm* (*de coche*) steering wheel; (*de reloj*) balance
volar [bo'lar] *vt* (*edificio*) to blow up ♦ *vi* to fly
volátil ['bo'latil] *adj* volatile
volcán [bol'kan] *nm* volcano; **~ico, a** *adj* volcanic
volcar [bol'kar] *vt* to upset, overturn; (*tumbar, derribar*) to knock over; (*vaciar*) to empty out ♦ *vi* to overturn; **~se** *vr* to tip over
voleibol [bolei'ßol] *nm* volleyball
volqué *etc vb ver* **volcar**
voltaje [bol'taxe] *nm* voltage
voltear [bolte'ar] *vt* to turn over; (*volcar*) to turn upside down
voltereta [bolte'reta] *nf* somersault
voltio ['boltjo] *nm* volt
voluble [bo'lußle] *adj* fickle
volumen [bo'lumen] (*pl* **volúmenes**) *nm* volume; **voluminoso, a** *adj* voluminous; (*enorme*) massive
voluntad [bolun'tað] *nf* will; (*resolución*) willpower; (*deseo*) desire, wish
voluntario, a [bolun'tarjo, a] *adj* voluntary ♦ *nm/f* volunteer
voluntarioso, a [bolunta'rjoso, a] *adj* headstrong
voluptuoso, a [bolup'twoso, a] *adj* voluptuous
volver [bol'ßer] *vt* (*gen*) to turn; (*dar vuelta a*) to turn (over); (*voltear*) to turn round, turn upside down; (*poner al revés*) to turn inside out; (*devolver*) to return ♦ *vi* to return, go back, come back; **~se** *vr* to turn round; **~ la espalda** to turn one's back; **~ triste** *etc* **a uno** to make sb sad *etc*; **~ a hacer** to do again; **~ en sí** to come to; **~se insoportable/ muy caro** to get o become unbearable/very expensive; **~se loco** to go mad
vomitar [bomi'tar] *vt, vi* to vomit; **vómito** *nm* vomit
voraz [bo'raθ] *adj* voracious
vos [bos] (*AM*) *pron* you
vosotros, as [bo'sotros, as] *pron* you; (*reflexivo*): **entre/para ~** among/for yourselves
votación [bota'θjon] *nf* (*acto*) voting; (*voto*) vote
votar [bo'tar] *vi* to vote; **voto** *nm* vote; (*promesa*) vow; **votos** (good) wishes
voy *vb ver* **ir**
voz [boθ] *nf* voice; (*grito*) shout; (*rumor*) rumour; (*LING*) word; **dar voces** to shout, yell; **a media ~** in a low voice; **a ~ en cuello** *o* **en grito** at the top of one's voice; **de viva ~** verbally; **en ~ alta** aloud; **~ de mando** command
vuelco ['bwelko] *vb ver* **volcar** ♦ *nm* spill, overturning
vuelo ['bwelo] *vb ver* **volar** ♦ *nm* flight; (*encaje*) lace, frill; **coger al ~** to catch in flight; **~ charter/regular** charter/scheduled flight; **~ libre** (*DEPORTE*) hang-gliding
vuelque *etc vb ver* **volcar**
vuelta ['bwelta] *nf* (*gen*) turn; (*curva*) bend, curve; (*regreso*) return; (*revolución*) revolution; (*de circuito*) lap; (*de papel, tela*) reverse; (*cambio*) change; **a la ~** on one's return; **a ~ de correo** by return of post; **dar ~s** (*suj: cabeza*) to spin; **dar ~s a una idea** to turn over an idea (in one's head); **estar de ~** to be back; **dar una ~** to go for a walk; (*en coche*) to go for a drive; **~ ciclista** (*DEPORTE*) (cycle) tour
vuelto *pp de* **volver**
vuelvo *etc vb ver* **volver**
vuestro, a ['bwestro, a] *adj* your; **un amigo ~** a friend of yours ♦ *pron*: **el ~/la vuestra, los ~s/las vuestras** yours
vulgar [bul'xar] *adj* (*ordinario*) vulgar; (*común*) common; **~idad** *nf* commonness; (*acto*) vulgarity; (*expresión*) coarse expression; **~izar** *vt* to popularize
vulgo ['bulxo] *nm* common people
vulnerable [bulne'raßle] *adj* vulnerable
vulnerar [bulne'rar] *vt* (*ley, acuerdo*) to violate, breach; (*derechos, intimidad*) to violate; (*reputación*) to damage

W, w

Walkman ® [wak'man] *nm* Walkman ®
wáter ['bater] *nm* toilet
whisky ['wiski] *nm* whisky, whiskey
WWW *nm o nf abr* (*INFORM*: = *World Wide Web*) WWW

X, x

xenofobia [kseno'foßja] *nf* xenophobia
xilófono [ksi'lofono] *nm* xylophone

Y, y

y [i] *conj* and
ya [ja] *adv* (*gen*) already; (*ahora*) now; (*en seguida*) at once; (*pronto*) soon ♦ *excl* all right! ♦ *conj* (*ahora que*) now that; **~ lo sé** I know; **~ que** since
yacer [ja'θer] *vi* to lie
yacimiento [jaθi'mjento] *nm* (*de mineral*) deposit; (*arqueológico*) site
yanqui ['janki] *adj, nm/f* Yankee
yate ['jate] *nm* yacht

yazco *etc vb ver* **yacer**

yedra ['jeðra] *nf* ivy

yegua ['jeɣwa] *nf* mare

yema ['jema] *nf* (*del huevo*) yolk; (*BOT*) leaf bud; (*fig*) best part; **~ del dedo** fingertip

yergo *etc vb ver* **erguir**

yermo, a ['jermo, a] *adj* (*estéril, fig*) barren ♦ *nm* wasteland

yerno ['jerno] *nm* son-in-law

yerro *etc vb ver* **errar**

yeso ['jeso] *nm* plaster

yo [jo] *pron* I; **soy ~** it's me, it is I

yodo ['joðo] *nm* iodine

yoga ['joɣa] *nm* yoga

yogur(t) [jo'ɣur(t)] *nm* yoghurt

yugo ['juɣo] *nm* yoke

Yugoslavia [juɣos'laßja] *nf* Yugoslavia

yugular [juɣu'lar] *adj* jugular

yunque ['junke] *nm* anvil

yunta ['junta] *nf* yoke

yuxtaponer [jukstapo'ner] *vt* to juxtapose; **yuxtaposición** *nf* juxtaposition

Z, z

zafar [θa'far] *vt* (*soltar*) to untie; (*superficie*) to clear; **~se** *vr* (*escaparse*) to escape; (*TEC*) to slip off

zafio, a ['θafjo, a] *adj* coarse

zafiro [θa'firo] *nm* sapphire

zaga ['θaɣa] *nf*: **a la ~** behind, in the rear

zaguán [θa'ɣwan] *nm* hallway

zaherir [θae'rir] *vt* (*criticar*) to criticize

zaino, a ['θaino, a] *adj* (*caballo*) chestnut

zalamería [θalame'ria] *nf* flattery; **zalamero, a** *adj* flattering; (*cobista*) suave

zamarra [θa'marra] *nf* (*chaqueta*) sheepskin jacket

zambullirse [θambu'ʎirse] *vr* to dive

zampar [θam'par] *vt* to gobble down

zanahoria [θana'orja] *nf* carrot

zancada [θan'kaða] *nf* stride

zancadilla [θanka'ðiʎa] *nf* trip

zanco ['θanko] *nm* stilt

zancudo, a [θan'kuðo, a] *adj* long-legged ♦ *nm* (*AM*) mosquito

zángano ['θangano] *nm* drone

zanja ['θanxa] *nf* ditch; **zanjar** *vt* (*resolver*) to resolve

zapata [θa'pata] *nf* (*MECÁNICA*) shoe

zapatear [θapate'ar] *vi* to tap with one's feet

zapatería [θapate'ria] *nf* (*oficio*) shoemaking; (*tienda*) shoe shop; (*fábrica*) shoe factory; **zapatero, a** *nm/f* shoemaker

zapatilla [θapa'tiʎa] *nf* slipper; **~ de deporte** training shoe

zapato [θa'pato] *nm* shoe

zapping ['θapin] *nm* channel-hopping; **hacer ~** to flick through the channels

zar [θar] *nm* tsar, czar

zarandear [θarande'ar] (*fam*) *vt* to shake vigorously

zarpa ['θarpa] *nf* (*garra*) claw

zarpar [θar'par] *vi* to weigh anchor

zarza ['θarθa] *nf* (*BOT*) bramble; **zarzal** *nm* (*matorral*) bramble patch

zarzamora [θarθa'mora] *nf* blackberry

zarzuela [θar'θwela] *nf* Spanish light opera

zigzag [θix'θax] *nm* zigzag; **zigzaguear** *vi* to zigzag

zinc [θink] *nm* zinc

zócalo ['θokalo] *nm* (*ARQ*) plinth, base

zodíaco [θo'ðiako] *nm* (*ASTRO*) zodiac

zona ['θona] *nf* zone; **~ fronteriza** border area

zoo ['θoo] *nm* zoo

zoología [θoolo'xia] *nf* zoology; **zoológico, a** *adj* zoological ♦ *nm* (*tb: parque ~*) zoo; **zoólogo, a** *nm/f* zoologist

zoom [θum] *nm* zoom lens

zopilote [θopi'lote] (*AM*) *nm* buzzard

zoquete [θo'kete] *nm* (*fam*) blockhead

zorro, a ['θorro, a] *adj* crafty ♦ *nm/f* fox/vixen

zozobra [θo'θoßra] *nf* (*fig*) anxiety; **zozobrar** *vi* (*hundirse*) to capsize; (*fig*) to fail

zueco ['θweko] *nm* clog

zumbar [θum'bar] *vt* (*golpear*) to hit ♦ *vi* to buzz; **zumbido** *nm* buzzing

zumo ['θumo] *nm* juice

zurcir [θur'θir] *vt* (*coser*) to darn

zurdo, a ['θurðo, a] *adj* (*persona*) left-handed

zurrar [θu'rrar] (*fam*) *vt* to wallop

ENGLISH – SPANISH
INGLÉS – ESPAÑOL

A, a

A [eɪ] *n* (*MUS*) la *m*

a [ə] *indef art* (*before vowel or silent h:* an)
 1 un(a); **~ book** un libro; **an apple** una
 manzana; **she's ~ doctor** (ella) es médica
 2 (*instead of the number "one"*) un(a); **~ year
 ago** hace un año; **~ hundred/thousand** *etc*
 pounds cien/mil *etc* libras
 3 (*in expressing ratios, prices etc*): **3 ~ day/
 week** 3 al día/a la semana; **10 km an hour** 10
 km por hora; **£5 ~ person** £5 por persona;
 30p ~ kilo 30p el kilo

A.A. *n abbr* (= *Automobile Association: BRIT*) ≈
 RACE *m* (*SP*); (= *Alcoholics Anonymous*)
 Alcohólicos Anónimos

A.A.A. (*US*) *n abbr* (= *American Automobile
 Association*) ≈ RACE *m* (*SP*)

aback [ə'bæk] *adv*: **to be taken ~** quedar
 desconcertado

abandon [ə'bændən] *vt* abandonar; (*give up*)
 renunciar a

abate [ə'beɪt] *vi* (*storm*) amainar; (*anger*)
 aplacarse; (*terror*) disminuir

abattoir ['æbətwɑː*] (*BRIT*) *n* matadero

abbey ['æbɪ] *n* abadía

abbot ['æbət] *n* abad *m*

abbreviation [ə'briːvɪ'eɪʃən] *n* (*short form*)
 abreviatura

abdicate ['æbdɪkeɪt] *vt* renunciar a ♦ *vi*
 abdicar

abdomen ['æbdəmən] *n* abdomen *m*

abduct [æb'dʌkt] *vt* raptar, secuestrar

abeyance [ə'beɪəns] *n*: **in ~** (*law*) en desuso;
 (*matter*) en suspenso

abide [ə'baɪd] *vt*: **I can't ~ it/him** no lo/le
 puedo ver; **~ by** *vt fus* atenerse a

ability [ə'bɪlɪtɪ] *n* habilidad *f*, capacidad *f*;
 (*talent*) talento

abject ['æbdʒɛkt] *adj* (*poverty*) miserable;
 (*apology*) rastrero

ablaze [ə'bleɪz] *adj* en llamas, ardiendo

able ['eɪbl] *adj* capaz; (*skilled*) hábil; **to be
 ~ to do sth** poder hacer algo; **~-bodied** *adj*
 sano; **ably** *adv* hábilmente

abnormal [æb'nɔːməl] *adj* anormal

aboard [ə'bɔːd] *adv* a bordo ♦ *prep* a bordo
 de

abode [ə'bəud] *n*: **of no fixed ~** sin domicilio

abolish [ə'bɔlɪʃ] *vt* suprimir, abolir

aborigine [æbə'rɪdʒɪnɪ] *n* aborigen *m/f*

abort [ə'bɔːt] *vt*, *vi* abortar; **~ion** [ə'bɔːʃən] *n*
 aborto; **to have an ~ion** abortar, hacerse
 abortar; **~ive** *adj* malogrado

about [ə'baut] *adv* **1** (*approximately*) más o
 menos, aproximadamente; **~ a hundred/
 thousand** *etc* unos(unas) cien/mil *etc*; **it takes
 ~ 10 hours** se tarda unas *or* más o menos 10
 horas; **at ~ 2 o'clock** sobre las dos; **I've just
 ~ finished** casi he terminado
 2 (*referring to place*) por todas partes; **to
 leave things lying ~** dejar las cosas (tiradas)
 por ahí; **to run ~** correr por todas partes; **to
 walk ~** pasearse, ir y venir
 3: **to be ~ to do sth** estar a punto de hacer
 algo
 ♦ *prep* **1** (*relating to*) de, sobre, acerca de; **a
 book ~ London** un libro sobre *or* acerca de
 Londres; **what is it ~?** ¿de qué se trata?, ¿qué
 pasa?; **we talked ~ it** hablamos de eso *or* ello;
 what or how ~ doing this? ¿qué tal si
 hacemos esto?
 2 (*referring to place*) por; **to walk ~ the town**
 caminar por la ciudad

above [ə'bʌv] *adv* encima, por encima, arriba
 ♦ *prep* encima de; (*: greater than: in number*)
 más de; (*: in rank*) superior a; **mentioned ~**
 susodicho; **~ all** sobre todo; **~ board** *adj*
 legítimo

abrasive [ə'breɪzɪv] *adj* abrasivo; (*manner*)
 brusco

abreast [ə'brɛst] *adv* de frente; **to keep ~ of**
 (*fig*) mantenerse al corriente de

abroad [ə'brɔːd] *adv* (*to be*) en el extranjero;
 (*to go*) al extranjero

abrupt [ə'brʌpt] *adj* (*sudden*) brusco; (*curt*)
 áspero

abruptly [ə'brʌptlɪ] *adv* (*leave*)
 repentinamente; (*speak*) bruscamente

abscess ['æbsɪs] *n* absceso

abscond [əb'skɔnd] *vi* (*thief*): **to ~ with**
 fugarse con; (*prisoner*): **to ~ (from)** escaparse
 (de)

absence ['æbsəns] *n* ausencia

absent ['æbsənt] *adj* ausente; **~ee** [-'tiː] *n*

ausente *m/f*; **~-minded** *adj* distraído

absolute [ˈæbsəluːt] *adj* absoluto; **~ly**
[-ˈluːtlɪ] *adv* (*totally*) totalmente; (*certainly!*)
¡por supuesto (que sí)!

absolve [əbˈzɔlv] *vt*: **to ~ sb (from)** absolver
a alguien (de)

absorb [əbˈzɔːb] *vt* absorber; **to be ~ed in a
book** estar absorto en un libro; **~ent cotton**
(*US*) *n* algodón *m* hidrófilo; **~ing** *adj*
absorbente

absorption [əbˈzɔːpʃən] *n* absorción *f*

abstain [əbˈsteɪn] *vi*: **to ~ (from)** abstenerse
(de)

abstinence [ˈæbstɪnəns] *n* abstinencia

abstract [ˈæbstrækt] *adj* abstracto

absurd [əbˈsəːd] *adj* absurdo

abundance [əˈbʌndəns] *n* abundancia

abuse [*n* əˈbjuːs, *vb* əˈbjuːz] *n* (*insults*) insultos
mpl, injurias *fpl*; (*ill-treatment*) malos tratos
mpl; (*misuse*) abuso ♦ *vt* insultar; maltratar;
abusar de; **abusive** *adj* ofensivo

abysmal [əˈbɪzməl] *adj* pésimo; (*failure*)
garrafal; (*ignorance*) supino

abyss [əˈbɪs] *n* abismo

AC *abbr* (= *alternating current*) corriente *f*
alterna

academic [ækəˈdemɪk] *adj* académico,
universitario; (*pej: issue*) puramente teórico
♦ *n* estudioso/a; profesor(a) *m/f*
universitario/a

academy [əˈkædəmɪ] *n* (*learned body*)
academia; (*school*) instituto, colegio; **~ of
music** conservatorio

accelerate [ækˈseləreɪt] *vt, vi* acelerar;
accelerator (*BRIT*) *n* acelerador *m*

accent [ˈæksent] *n* acento; (*fig*) énfasis *m*

accept [əkˈsept] *vt* aceptar; (*responsibility,
blame*) admitir; **~able** *adj* aceptable; **~ance**
n aceptación *f*

access [ˈækses] *n* acceso; **to have ~** tener
libre acceso a; **~ible** [-ˈsesəbl] *adj* (*place,
person*) accesible; (*knowledge etc*) asequible

accessory [ækˈsesərɪ] *n* accesorio, (*LAW*):
~ to cómplice de

accident [ˈæksɪdənt] *n* accidente *m*; (*chance
event*) casualidad *f*; **by ~** (*unintentionally*) sin
querer; (*by chance*) por casualidad; **~al**
[-ˈdentl] *adj* accidental, fortuito; **~ally**
[-ˈdentəlɪ] *adv* sin querer; por casualidad;
~ insurance *n* seguro contra accidentes;
~-prone *adj* propenso a los accidentes

acclaim [əˈkleɪm] *vt* aclamar, aplaudir ♦ *n*
aclamación *f*, aplausos *mpl*

acclimatize [əˈklaɪmətaɪz] (*US*: **acclimate**) *vt*:
to become ~d aclimatarse

accommodate [əˈkɔmədeɪt] *vt* (*subj:
person*) alojar, hospedar; (: *car, hotel etc*)
tener cabida para; (*oblige, help*) complacer;
accommodating *adj* servicial, complaciente

accommodation [əkɔməˈdeɪʃən] *n* (*US*
accommodations *npl*) alojamiento

accompany [əˈkʌmpənɪ] *vt* acompañar

accomplice [əˈkʌmplɪs] *n* cómplice *m/f*

accomplish [əˈkʌmplɪʃ] *vt* (*finish*) concluir;
(*achieve*) lograr; **~ed** *adj* experto, hábil;
~ment *n* (*skill: gen pl*) talento; (*completion*)
realización *f*

accord [əˈkɔːd] *n* acuerdo ♦ *vt* conceder; **of
his own ~** espontáneamente; **~ance** *n*: **in
~ance with** de acuerdo con; **~ing**: **~ing to**
prep según; (*in accordance with*) conforme a;
~ingly *adv* (*appropriately*) de acuerdo con
esto; (*as a result*) en consecuencia

accordion [əˈkɔːdɪən] *n* acordeón *m*

accost [əˈkɔst] *vt* abordar, dirigirse a

account [əˈkaunt] *n* (*COMM*) cuenta; (*report*)
informe *m*; **~s** *npl* (*COMM*) cuentas *fpl*; **on ~
de ninguna importancia; **on ~** a cuenta; **on
no ~** bajo ningún concepto; **on ~ of** a causa
de, por motivo de; **to take into ~, take ~ of**
tener en cuenta; **~ for** *vt fus* (*explain*)
explicar; (*represent*) representar; **~able** *adj*:
~able (to) responsable (ante); **~ancy**
n contabilidad *f*; **~ant** *n* contable *m/f*,
contador(a) *m/f*; **~ number** *n* (*at bank etc*)
número de cuenta

accrued interest [əˈkruːd-] *n* interés *m*
acumulado

accumulate [əˈkjuːmjuleɪt] *vt* acumular ♦ *vi*
acumularse

accuracy [ˈækjurəsɪ] *n* (*of total*) exactitud *f*;
(*of description etc*) precisión *f*

accurate [ˈækjurɪt] *adj* (*total*) exacto;
(*description*) preciso; (*person*) cuidadoso;
(*device*) de precisión; **~ly** *adv* con precisión

accusation [ækjuˈzeɪʃən] *n* acusación *f*

accuse [əˈkjuːz] *vt*: **to ~ sb (of sth)** acusar a
uno (de algo); **~d** *n* (*LAW*) acusado/a

accustom [əˈkʌstəm] *vt* acostumbrar; **~ed**
adj: **~ed to** acostumbrado a

ace [eɪs] *n* as *m*

ache [eɪk] *n* dolor *m* ♦ *vi* doler; **my head ~s**
me duele la cabeza

achieve [əˈtʃiːv] *vt* (*aim, result*) alcanzar;
(*success*) lograr, conseguir; **~ment** *n*
(*completion*) realización *f*; (*success*) éxito

acid [ˈæsɪd] *adj* ácido; (*taste*) agrio ♦ *n* (*CHEM,
inf: LSD*) ácido; **~ rain** *n* lluvia ácida

acknowledge [əkˈnɔlɪdʒ] *vt* (*letter: also:
~ receipt of*) acusar recibo de; (*fact, situation,
person*) reconocer; **~ment** *n* acuse *m* de
recibo

acne [ˈækni] *n* acné *m*

acorn [ˈeɪkɔːn] *n* bellota

acoustic [əˈkuːstɪk] *adj* acústico; **~s** *n, npl*
acústica *sg*

acquaint [əˈkweɪnt] *vt*: **to ~ sb with sth**
(*inform*) poner a uno al corriente de algo; **to**

be ~ed with conocer; ~ance n (person) conocido/a; (with person, subject) conocimiento

acquire [ə'kwaɪə*] vt adquirir; **acquisition** [ækwɪ'zɪʃən] n adquisición f

acquit [ə'kwɪt] vt absolver, exculpar; **to ~ o.s. well** salir con éxito

acre ['eɪkə*] n acre m

acrid ['ækrɪd] adj acre

acrobat ['ækrəbæt] n acróbata m/f

across [ə'krɒs] prep (on the other side of) al otro lado de, del otro lado de; (crosswise) a través de ♦ adv de un lado a otro, de una parte a otra; a través, al través; (measurement): **the road is 10m ~** la carretera tiene 10m de ancho; **to run/swim ~** atravesar corriendo/nadando; **~ from** enfrente de

acrylic [ə'krɪlɪk] adj acrílico ♦ n acrílica f

act [ækt] n acto, acción f; (of play) acto; (in music hall etc) número; (LAW) decreto, ley f ♦ vi (behave) comportarse; (have effect: drug, chemical) hacer efecto; (THEATRE) actuar; (pretend) fingir; (take action) obrar ♦ vt (part) hacer el papel de, en **the ~ of** en el momento sb **in the ~ of** pillar a uno en el momento en que ...; **to ~ as** actuar or hacer de; **~ing** adj suplente ♦ n (activity) actuación f; (profession) profesión f de actor

action ['ækʃən] n acción f, acto; (MIL) acción f, batalla; (LAW) proceso, demanda; **out of ~** (person) fuera de combate; (thing) estropeado; **to take ~** tomar medidas; **~ replay** n (TV) repetición f

activate ['æktɪveɪt] vt activar

active ['æktɪv] adj activo, enérgico; (volcano) en actividad; **~ly** adv (participate) activamente; (discourage, dislike) enérgicamente; **activity** [-'tɪvɪtɪ] n actividad f; **activity holiday** n vacaciones fpl con actividades organizadas

actor ['æktə*] n actor m

actress ['æktrɪs] n actriz f

actual ['æktjuəl] adj verdadero, real; (emphatic use) propiamente dicho; **~ly** adv realmente, en realidad; (even) incluso

acumen ['ækjumən] n perspicacia

acute [ə'kjuːt] adj agudo

ad [æd] n abbr = **advertisement**

A.D. adv abbr (= anno Domini) A.C.

adamant ['ædəmənt] adj firme, inflexible

adapt [ə'dæpt] vt adaptar ♦ vi: **to ~ (to)** adaptarse (a), ajustarse (a); **~able** adj adaptable; **~er, ~or** n (ELEC) adaptador m

add [æd] vt añadir, agregar; (figures: also: ~ up) sumar ♦ vi: **to ~ to** (increase) aumentar, acrecentar; **it doesn't ~ up** (fig) no tiene sentido

adder ['ædə*] n víbora

addict ['ædɪkt] n adicto/a; (enthusiast)

entusiasta m/f; **~ed** ['ə'dɪktɪd] adj: **to be ~ed to** ser adicto a; (football etc) ser fanático de; **~ion** [ə'dɪkʃən] n (to drugs etc) adicción f; **~ive** [ə'dɪktɪv] adj que causa adicción

addition [ə'dɪʃən] n (adding up) adición f; (thing added) añadidura, añadido; **in ~** además, por añadidura; **in ~ to** además de; **~al** adj adicional

additive ['ædɪtɪv] n aditivo

address [ə'drɛs] n dirección f, señas fpl; (speech) discurso ♦ vt (letter) dirigir; (speak to) dirigirse a, dirigir la palabra a; (problem) tratar

adept ['ædept] adj: **~ at** experto or hábil en

adequate ['ædɪkwɪt] adj (satisfactory) adecuado; (enough) suficiente

adhere [əd'hɪə*] vi: **to ~ to** (stick to) pegarse a; (fig: abide by) observar; (: belief etc) ser partidario de

adhesive [əd'hiːzɪv] n adhesivo; **~ tape** n (BRIT) cinta adhesiva; (US: MED) esparadrapo

ad hoc [æd'hɔk] adj ad hoc

adjacent [ə'dʒeɪsənt] adj: **~ to** contiguo a, inmediato a

adjective ['ædʒektɪv] n adjetivo

adjoining [ə'dʒɔɪnɪŋ] adj contiguo, vecino

adjourn [ə'dʒəːn] vt aplazar ♦ vi suspenderse

adjudicate [ə'dʒuːdɪkeɪt] vi sentenciar

adjust [ə'dʒʌst] vt (change) modificar; (clothing) arreglar; (machine) ajustar ♦ vi: **to ~ (to)** adaptarse (a); **~able** adj ajustable; **~ment** n adaptación f; (to machine, prices) ajuste m

ad-lib [æd'lɪb] vt, vi improvisar; **ad lib** adv de forma improvisada

administer [əd'mɪnɪstə*] vt administrar; **administration** [-'treɪʃən] n (management) administración f; (government) gobierno; **administrative** [-trətɪv] adj administrativo

admiral ['ædmərəl] n almirante m; **A~ty** (BRIT) n Ministerio de Marina, Almirantazgo

admiration [ædmə'reɪʃən] n admiración f

admire [əd'maɪə*] vt admirar; **~r** n (fan) admirador(a) m/f

admission [əd'mɪʃən] n (to university, club) ingreso; (entry fee) entrada; (confession) confesión f

admit [əd'mɪt] vt (confess) confesar; (permit to enter) dejar entrar, dar entrada a; (to club, organization) admitir; (accept: defeat) reconocer; **to be ~ted to hospital** ingresar en el hospital; **~ to** vt fus confesarse culpable de; **~tance** n entrada; **~tedly** adv es cierto or verdad que

admonish [əd'mɔnɪʃ] vt amonestar

ad nauseam [æd'nɔːsɪæm] adv hasta el cansancio

ado [ə'duː] n: **without (any) more ~** sin más (ni más)

adolescent [ædəu'lɛsnt] *adj, n* adolescente *m/f*

adopt [ə'dɔpt] *vt* adoptar; **~ed** *adj* adoptivo; **~ion** [ə'dɔpʃən] *n* adopción *f*

adore [ə'dɔ:*] *vt* adorar

Adriatic [eɪdrɪ'ætɪk] *n*: **the ~ (Sea)** el (Mar) Adriático

adrift [ə'drɪft] *adv* a la deriva

adult ['ædʌlt] *n* adulto/a ♦ *adj* (*grown-up*) adulto; (*for adults*) para adultos

adultery [ə'dʌltərɪ] *n* adulterio

advance [əd'vɑ:ns] *n* (*progress*) adelanto, progreso; (*money*) anticipo, préstamo; (*MIL*) avance *m* ♦ *adj*: **~ booking** venta anticipada; **~ notice, ~ warning** previo aviso ♦ *vt* (*money*) anticipar; (*theory, idea*) proponer (para la discusión) ♦ *vi* avanzar, adelantarse; **to make ~s (to sb)** hacer proposiciones (a alguien); **in ~** por adelantado; **~d** *adj* avanzado; (*SCOL: studies*) adelantado

advantage [əd'vɑ:ntɪdʒ] *n* (*also TENNIS*) ventaja; **to take ~ of** (*person*) aprovecharse de; (*opportunity*) aprovechar

Advent ['ædvənt] *n* (*REL*) Adviento

adventure [əd'vɛntʃə*] *n* aventura; **adventurous** [-tʃərəs] *adj* atrevido; aventurero

adverb ['ædvə:b] *n* adverbio

adverse ['ædvə:s] *adj* adverso, contrario

adversity [əd'və:sɪtɪ] *n* infortunio

advert ['ædvə:t] (*BRIT*) *n abbr* = **advertisement**

advertise ['ædvətaɪz] *vi* (*in newspaper etc*) anunciar, hacer publicidad; **to ~ for** (*staff, accommodation etc*) buscar por medio de anuncios ♦ *vt* anunciar; **~ment** [əd'və:tɪsmənt] *n* (*COMM*) anuncio; **~r** *n* anunciante *m/f*; **advertising** *n* publicidad *f*, anuncios *mpl*; (*industry*) industria publicitaria

advice [əd'vaɪs] *n* consejo, consejos *mpl*; (*notification*) aviso; **a piece of ~** un consejo; **to take legal ~** consultar con un abogado

advisable [əd'vaɪzəbl] *adj* aconsejable, conveniente

advise [əd'vaɪz] *vt* aconsejar; (*inform*): **to ~ sb of sth** informar a uno de algo; **to ~ against sth/doing sth** desaconsejar algo a uno/aconsejar a uno que no haga algo; **~dly** [əd'vaɪzɪdlɪ] *adv* (*deliberately*) deliberadamente; **~r** *n* = **advisor**; **advisor** *n* consejero/a; (*consultant*) asesor(a) *m/f*; **advisory** *adj* consultivo

advocate ['ædvəkeɪt] *vt* abogar por ♦ *n* [-kɪt] (*lawyer*) abogado/a; (*supporter*): **~ of** defensor(a) *m/f* de

Aegean [iː'dʒiːən] *n*: **the ~ (Sea)** el (Mar) Egeo

aerial ['ɛərɪəl] *n* antena ♦ *adj* aéreo

aerobics [ɛə'rəubɪks] *n* aerobic *m*

aeroplane ['ɛərəpleɪn] (*BRIT*) *n* avión *m*

aerosol ['ɛərəsɔl] *n* aerosol *m*

aesthetic [iːs'θɛtɪk] *adj* estético

afar [ə'fɑ:*] *adv*: **from ~** desde lejos

affair [ə'fɛə*] *n* asunto; (*also*: **love ~**) aventura (amorosa)

affect [ə'fɛkt] *vt* (*influence*) afectar, influir en; (*afflict, concern*) afectar; (*move*) conmover; **~ed** *adj* afectado

affection [ə'fɛkʃən] *n* afecto, cariño; **~ate** *adj* afectuoso, cariñoso

affinity [ə'fɪnɪtɪ] *n* (*bond, rapport*): **to feel an ~ with** sentirse identificado con; (*resemblance*) afinidad *f*

afflict [ə'flɪkt] *vt* afligir

affluence ['æfluəns] *n* opulencia, riqueza

affluent ['æfluənt] *adj* (*wealthy*) acomodado; **the ~ society** la sociedad opulenta

afford [ə'fɔ:d] *vt* (*provide*) proporcionar; **can we ~ (to buy) it?** ¿tenemos bastante dinero para comprarlo?

Afghanistan [æf'gænɪstæn] *n* Afganistán *m*

afield [ə'fiːld] *adv*: **far ~** muy lejos

afloat [ə'fləut] *adv* (*floating*) a flote

afoot [ə'fut] *adv*: **there is something ~** algo está tramando

afraid [ə'freɪd] *adj*: **to be ~ of** (*person*) tener miedo a; (*thing*) tener miedo de; **to be ~ to** tener miedo de, temer; **I am ~ that** me temo que; **I am ~ not/so** lo siento, pero no/es así

afresh [ə'frɛʃ] *adv* de nuevo, otra vez

Africa ['æfrɪkə] *n* África; **~n** *adj, n* africano/a *m/f*

after ['ɑ:ftə*] *prep* (*time*) después de; (*place, order*) detrás de, tras ♦ *adv* después ♦ *conj* después (de) que; **what/who are you ~?** ¿qué/a quién busca usted?; **~ having done/he left** después de haber hecho/después de que se marchó; **to name sb ~ sb** llamar a uno por uno; **it's twenty ~ eight** (*US*) son las ocho y veinte; **to ask ~ sb** preguntar por alguien; **~ all** después de todo, al fin y al cabo; **~ you!** ¡pase usted!; **~-effects** *npl* consecuencias *fpl*, efectos *mpl*; **~math** *n* consecuencias *fpl*, resultados *mpl*; **~noon** *n* tarde *f*; **~s** (*inf*) *n* (*dessert*) postre *m*; **~-sales service** (*BRIT*) *n* servicio de asistencia pos-venta; **~-shave (lotion)** *n* aftershave *m*; **~sun (lotion/cream)** *n* loción *f*/crema para después del sol, aftersun *m*; **~thought** *n* ocurrencia (tardía); **~wards** (*US* **~ward**) *adv* después, más tarde

again [ə'gɛn] *adv* otra vez, de nuevo; **to do sth ~** volver a hacer algo; **~ and ~** una y otra vez

against [ə'gɛnst] *prep* (*in opposition to*) en contra de; (*leaning on, touching*) contra, junto a

age [eɪdʒ] *n* edad *f*; (*period*) época ♦ *vi*

envejecer(se) ♦ vt envejecer; **she is 20 years of ~** tiene 20 años; **to come of ~** llegar a la mayoría de edad; **it's been ~s since I saw you** hace siglos que no te veo; **~d 10** de 10 años de edad; **the ~d** ['eɪdʒɪd] npl los ancianos; **~ group** n: **to be in the same ~ group** tener la misma edad; **~ limit** n edad f mínima (or máxima)

agency ['eɪdʒənsɪ] n agencia

agenda [ə'dʒɛndə] n orden m del día

agent ['eɪdʒənt] n agente m/f; (COMM: holding concession) representante m/f, delegado/a; (CHEM, fig) agente m

aggravate ['ægrəveɪt] vt (situation) agravar; (person) irritar

aggregate ['ægrɪgeɪt] n conjunto

aggressive [ə'gresɪv] adj (belligerent) agresivo; (assertive) enérgico

aggrieved [ə'griːvd] adj ofendido, agraviado

aghast [ə'gɑːst] adj horrorizado

agile ['ædʒaɪl] adj ágil

agitate ['ædʒɪteɪt] vt (trouble) inquietar ♦ vi: **to ~ for/against** hacer campaña pro or en favor de/en contra de

AGM n abbr (= annual general meeting) asamblea anual

ago [ə'gəu] adv: **2 days ~** hace 2 días; **not long ~** hace poco; **how long ~?** ¿hace cuánto tiempo?

agog [ə'gɔg] adj (eager) ansioso; (excited) emocionado

agonizing ['ægənaɪzɪŋ] adj (pain) atroz; (decision, wait) angustioso

agony ['ægənɪ] n (pain) dolor m agudo; (distress) angustia; **to be in ~** retorcerse de dolor

agree [ə'griː] vt (price, date) acordar, quedar en ♦ vi (have same opinion): **to ~ (with/that)** estar de acuerdo (con/que); (correspond) coincidir, concordar; (consent) acceder; **to ~ with** (subj: person) estar de acuerdo con, ponerse de acuerdo con; (: food) sentar bien a; (LING) concordar con; **to ~ to sth/to do sth** consentir en algo/aceptar hacer algo; **to ~ that** (admit) estar de acuerdo en que; **~able** adj (sensation) agradable; (person) simpático; (willing) de acuerdo, conforme; **~d** adj (time, place) convenido; **~ment** n acuerdo; (contract) contrato; **in ~ment** de acuerdo, conforme

agricultural [ægrɪ'kʌltʃərəl] adj agrícola

agriculture ['ægrɪkʌltʃə*] n agricultura

aground [ə'graund] adv: **to run ~** (NAUT) encallar, embarrancar

ahead [ə'hed] adv (in front) delante; (into the future): **she had no time to think ~** no tenía tiempo de hacer planes para el futuro; **~ of** delante de; (in advance of) antes de; **~ of time** antes de la hora; **go right** or **straight ~**

(direction) siga adelante; (permission) hazlo (or hágalo)

aid [eɪd] n ayuda, auxilio; (device) aparato ♦ vt ayudar, auxiliar; **in ~ of** a beneficio de

aide [eɪd] n (person, also: MIL) ayudante m/f

AIDS [eɪdz] n abbr (= acquired immune deficiency syndrome) SIDA m

ailment ['eɪlmənt] n enfermedad f, achaque m

aim [eɪm] vt (gun, camera) apuntar; (missile, remark) dirigir; (blow) asestar ♦ vi (also: take ~) apuntar ♦ n (in shooting: skill) puntería; (objective) propósito, meta; **to ~ at** (with weapon) apuntar a; (objective) aspirar a, pretender; **to ~ to do** tener la intención de hacer; **~less** adj sin propósito, sin objeto

ain't [eɪnt] (inf) = **am not; aren't; isn't**

air [ɛə*] n aire m; (appearance) aspecto ♦ vt (room) ventilar; (clothes, ideas) airear ♦ cpd aéreo; **to throw sth into the ~** (ball etc) lanzar algo al aire; **by ~** (travel) en avión; **to be on the ~** (RADIO, TV) estar en antena; **~bed** (BRIT) n colchón m neumático; **~-conditioned** adj climatizado; **~ conditioning** n aire acondicionado; **~craft** n inv avión m; **~craft carrier** n porta(a)viones m inv; **~field** n campo de aviación; **A~ Force** n fuerzas fpl aéreas, aviación f; **~ freshener** n ambientador m; **~gun** n escopeta de aire comprimido; **~ hostess** (BRIT) n azafata; **~ letter** (BRIT) n carta aérea; **~lift** n puente m aéreo; **~line** n línea aérea; **~liner** n avión m de pasajeros; **~mail** n: **by ~mail** por avión; **~plane** (US) n avión m; **~port** n aeropuerto; **~ raid** n ataque m aéreo; **~sick** adj: **to be ~sick** marearse (en avión); **~space** n espacio aéreo; **~tight** adj hermético; **~-traffic controller** n controlador(a) m/f aéreo/a; **~y** adj (room) bien ventilado; (fig: manner) desenfadado

aisle [aɪl] n (of church) nave f; (of theatre, supermarket) pasillo; **~ seat** n (on plane) asiento de pasillo

ajar [ə'dʒɑː*] adj entreabierto

alarm [ə'lɑːm] n (in shop, bank) alarma; (anxiety) inquietud f ♦ vt asustar, inquietar; **~ call** n (in hotel etc) alarma; **~ clock** n despertador m

alas [ə'læs] adv desgraciadamente

albeit [ɔːl'biːɪt] conj aunque

album ['ælbəm] n álbum m; (L.P.) elepé m

alcohol ['ælkəhɔl] n alcohol m; **~ic** [-'hɔlɪk] adj, n alcohólico/a m/f

ale [eɪl] n cerveza

alert [ə'ləːt] adj (attentive) atento; (to danger, opportunity) alerta ♦ n alerta m, alarma ♦ vt poner sobre aviso; **to be on the ~** (also MIL) estar alerta or sobre aviso

algebra ['ældʒɪbrə] n álgebra

Algeria [æl'dʒɪərɪə] n Argelia
alias ['eɪlɪəs] adv alias, conocido por ♦ n (of criminal) apodo; (of writer) seudónimo
alibi ['ælɪbaɪ] n coartada
alien ['eɪlɪən] n (foreigner) extranjero/a; (extraterrestrial) extraterrestre m/f ♦ adj: ~ to ajeno a; **~ate** vt enajenar, alejar
alight [ə'laɪt] adj ardiendo; (eyes) brillante ♦ vi (person) apearse, bajar; (bird) posarse
align [ə'laɪn] vt alinear
alike [ə'laɪk] adj semejantes, iguales ♦ adv igualmente, del mismo modo; **to look ~** parecerse
alimony ['ælɪmənɪ] n manutención f
alive [ə'laɪv] adj vivo; (lively) alegre

KEYWORD

all [ɔːl] adj (sg) todo/a; (pl) todos/as; **~ day** todo el día; **~ night** toda la noche; **~ men** todos los hombres; **~ five came** vinieron los cinco; **~ the books** todos los libros; **~ his life** toda su vida
♦ pron 1 todo; **I ate it ~, I ate ~ of it** me lo comí todo; **~ of us went** fuimos todos; **~ the boys went** fueron todos los chicos; **is that ~?** ¿eso es todo?, ¿algo más?; (in shop) ¿algo más?, ¿alguna cosa más?
2 (in phrases): **above ~** sobre todo; por encima de todo; **after ~** después de todo; **at ~: not at ~** (in answer to question) en absoluto; (in answer to thanks) ¡de nada!, ¡no hay de qué!; **I'm not at ~ tired** no estoy nada cansado/a; **anything at ~ will do** cualquier cosa viene bien; **~ in ~** a fin de cuentas
♦ adv: **~ alone** completamente solo/a; **it's not as hard as ~ that** no es tan difícil como lo pintas; **~ the more/the better** tanto más/ mejor; **~ but** casi; **the score is 2 ~** están empatados a 2

all clear n (after attack etc) fin m de la alerta; (fig) luz f verde
allege [ə'ledʒ] vt pretender; **~dly** [ə'ledʒɪdlɪ] adv supuestamente, según se afirma
allegiance [ə'liːdʒəns] n lealtad f
allergy ['æ1ədʒɪ] n alergia
alleviate [ə'liːvɪeɪt] vt aliviar
alley ['ælɪ] n callejuela
alliance [ə'laɪəns] n alianza
allied ['ælaɪd] adj aliado
alligator ['ælɪɡeɪtə*] n (ZOOL) caimán m
all-in (BRIT) adj, adv (charge) todo incluido
all-night adj (café, shop) abierto toda la noche; (party) que dura toda la noche
allocate ['æləkeɪt] vt (money etc) asignar
allot [ə'lɔt] vt asignar; **~ment** n ración f; (garden) parcela
all-out adj (effort etc) supremo; **all out** adv con todas las fuerzas

allow [ə'lau] vt permitir, dejar; (a claim) admitir; (sum, time etc) dar, conceder; (concede): **to ~ that** reconocer que; **to ~ sb to do** permitir a alguien hacer; **he is ~ed to ...** se le permite ...; **~ for** vt fus tener en cuenta; **~ance** n subvención f; (welfare payment) subsidio, pensión f; (pocket money) dinero de bolsillo; (tax ~ance) desgravación f; **to make ~ances for** (person) disculpar a; (thing) tener en cuenta
alloy ['ælɔɪ] n mezcla
all: ~ right adv bien; (as answer) ¡conforme!, ¡está bien!; **~-rounder** n: **he's a good ~-rounder** se le da bien todo; **~-time** adj (record) de todos los tiempos
alluring [ə'ljuərɪŋ] adj atractivo, tentador(a)
ally ['ælaɪ] n aliado/a ♦ vt: **to ~ o.s. with** aliarse con
almighty [ɔːl'maɪtɪ] adj todopoderoso; (row etc) imponente
almond ['ɑːmənd] n almendra
almost ['ɔːlməust] adv casi
alone [ə'ləun] adj, adv solo; **to leave sb ~** dejar a uno en paz; **to leave sth ~** no tocar algo, dejar algo sin tocar; **let ~ ...** y mucho menos ...
along [ə'lɔŋ] prep a lo largo de, por ♦ adv: **is he coming ~ with us?** ¿viene con nosotros?; **he was limping ~** iba cojeando; **~ with** junto con; **all ~** (all the time) desde el principio; **~side** prep al lado de ♦ adv al lado
aloof [ə'luːf] adj reservado ♦ adv: **to stand ~** mantenerse apartado
aloud [ə'laud] adv en voz alta
alphabet ['ælfəbet] n alfabeto
Alps [ælps] npl: **the ~** los Alpes
already [ɔːl'redɪ] adv ya
alright [ɔːl'raɪt] (BRIT) adv = **all right**
Alsatian [æl'seɪʃən] n (dog) pastor m alemán
also ['ɔːlsəu] adv también, además
altar ['ɔltə*] n altar m
alter ['ɔltə*] vt cambiar, modificar ♦ vi cambiar; **~ation** [ɔltə'reɪʃən] n cambio; (to clothes) arreglo; (to building) arreglos mpl
alternate [adj ɔl'tɜːnɪt, vb 'ɔltə:neɪt] adj (actions etc) alternativo; (events) alterno; (US) = **alternative** ♦ vi: **to ~ (with)** alternar (con); **on ~ days** un día sí y otro no; **alternating current** [-neɪtɪŋ] n corriente f alterna
alternative [ɔl'tɜːnətɪv] adj alternativo ♦ n alternativa; **~ medicine** medicina alternativa; **~ly** adv: **~ly one could ...** por otra parte se podría ...
although [ɔːl'ðəu] conj aunque
altitude ['æltɪtjuːd] n altura
alto ['æltəu] n (female) contralto f; (male) alto
altogether [ɔːltə'ɡeðə*] adv completamente, del todo; (on the whole) en total, en conjunto
aluminium [ælju'mɪnɪəm] (BRIT), **alumi-**

num [ə'lu:mɪnəm] (US) n aluminio
always ['ɔ:lweɪz] adv siempre
Alzheimer's (disease) ['æltshaɪməz-] n enfermedad f de Alzheimer
AM n abbr (= Assembly Member) parlamentario/a m/f
am [æm] vb see be
a.m. adv abbr (= ante meridiem) de la mañana
amalgamate [ə'mælɡəmeɪt] vi amalgamarse ♦ vt amalgamar, unir
amateur ['æmətə*] n aficionado/a, amateur m/f; **~ish** adj inexperto, superficial
amaze [ə'meɪz] vt asombrar, pasmar; **to be ~d (at)** quedar pasmado (de); **~ment** n asombro, sorpresa; **amazing** adj extraordinario; (fantastic) increíble
Amazon ['æməzən] n (GEO) Amazonas m
ambassador [æm'bæsədə*] n embajador(a) m/f
amber ['æmbə*] n ámbar m; **at ~** (BRIT: AUT) en el amarillo
ambiguous [æm'bɪɡjuəs] adj ambiguo
ambition [æm'bɪʃən] n ambición f; **ambitious** [-ʃəs] adj ambicioso
ambulance ['æmbjuləns] n ambulancia
ambush ['æmbuʃ] n emboscada ♦ vt tender una emboscada a
amenable [ə'mi:nəbl] adj: **to be ~ to** dejarse influir por
amend [ə'mend] vt enmendar; **to make ~s** dar cumplida satisfacción
amenities [ə'mi:nɪtɪz] npl comodidades fpl
America [ə'merɪkə] n (USA) Estados mpl Unidos; **~n** adj, n norteamericano/a m/f; estadounidense m/f
amiable ['eɪmɪəbl] adj amable, simpático
amicable ['æmɪkəbl] adj amistoso, amigable
amid(st) [ə'mɪd(st)] prep entre, en medio de
amiss [ə'mɪs] adv: **to take sth ~** tomar algo a mal; **there's something ~** pasa algo
ammonia [ə'məʊnɪə] n amoníaco
ammunition [æmju'nɪʃən] n municiones fpl
amnesty ['æmnɪstɪ] n amnistía
amok [ə'mɔk] adv: **to run ~** enloquecerse, desbocarse
among(st) [ə'mʌŋ(st)] prep entre, en medio de
amorous ['æmərəs] adj amoroso
amount [ə'maʊnt] n (gen) cantidad f; (of bill etc) suma, importe m ♦ vi: **to ~ to** sumar; (be same as) equivaler a, significar
amp(ère) ['æmp(ɛə*)] n amperio
ample ['æmpl] adj (large) grande; (abundant) abundante; (enough) bastante, suficiente
amplifier ['æmplɪfaɪə*] n amplificador m
amuse [ə'mju:z] vt divertir; (distract) distraer, entretener; **~ment** n diversión f; (pastime) pasatiempo; (laughter) risa; **~ment arcade** n salón m de juegos; **~ment park** n parque m de

atracciones
an [æn] indef art see a
anaemic [ə'ni:mɪk] (US anemic) adj anémico; (fig) soso, insípido
anaesthetic [ænɪs'θetɪk] n (US anesthetic) anestesia
analog(ue) ['ænəlɔɡ] adj (computer, watch) analógico
analyse ['ænəlaɪz] (US analyze) vt analizar; **analysis** [ə'næləsɪs] (pl **analyses**) n análisis m inv; **analyst** [-lɪst] n (political analyst, psychoanalyst) analista m/f
analyze ['ænəlaɪz] (US) vt = **analyse**
anarchist ['ænəkɪst] n anarquista m/f
anatomy [ə'nætəmɪ] n anatomía
ancestor ['ænsɪstə*] n antepasado
anchor ['æŋkə*] n ancla, áncora ♦ vi (also: to drop ~) anclar ♦ vt anclar; **to weigh ~** levar anclas
anchovy ['æntʃəvɪ] n anchoa
ancient ['eɪnʃənt] adj antiguo
ancillary [æn'sɪlərɪ] adj auxiliar
and [ænd] conj y; (before i-, hi- + consonant) e; **men ~ women** hombres y mujeres; **father ~ son** padre e hijo; **trees ~ grass** árboles y hierba; **~ so on** etcétera, y así sucesivamente; **try ~ come** procura venir; **he talked ~ talked** habló sin parar; **better ~ better** cada vez mejor
Andes ['ændi:z] npl: **the ~** los Andes
anemic etc [ə'ni:mɪk] (US) = **anaemic** etc
anesthetic etc [ænɪs'θetɪk] (US) = **anaesthetic** etc
anew [ə'nju:] adv de nuevo, otra vez
angel ['eɪndʒəl] n ángel m
anger ['æŋɡə*] n cólera
angina [æn'dʒaɪnə] n angina (del pecho)
angle ['æŋɡl] n ángulo; **from their ~** desde su punto de vista
angler ['æŋɡlə*] n pescador(a) m/f (de caña)
Anglican ['æŋɡlɪkən] adj, n anglicano/a m/f
angling ['æŋɡlɪŋ] n pesca con caña
Anglo... ['æŋɡləʊ] prefix anglo...
angrily ['æŋɡrɪlɪ] adv coléricamente, airadamente
angry ['æŋɡrɪ] adj enfadado, airado; (wound) inflamado; **to be ~ with sb/at sth** estar enfadado con alguien/por algo; **to get ~** enfadarse, enojarse
anguish ['æŋɡwɪʃ] n (physical) tormentos mpl; (mental) angustia
animal ['ænɪməl] n animal m; (pej: person) bestia ♦ adj animal
animate ['ænɪmɪt] adj vivo; **~d** [-meɪtɪd] adj animado
aniseed ['ænɪsi:d] n anís m
ankle ['æŋkl] n tobillo m; **~ sock** n calcetín m corto
annex [n 'æneks, vb æ'neks] n (also: BRIT: annexe) (building) edificio anexo ♦ vt

(*territory*) anexionar
annihilate [ə'naɪəleɪt] *vt* aniquilar
anniversary [ænɪ'vɜːsərɪ] *n* aniversario
announce [ə'naʊns] *vt* anunciar; **~ment** *n* anuncio; (*official*) declaración *f*; **~r** *n* (*RADIO*) locutor(a) *m/f*; (*TV*) presentador(a) *m/f*
annoy [ə'nɔɪ] *vt* molestar, fastidiar; **don't get ~ed!** ¡no se enfade!; **~ance** *n* enojo; **~ing** *adj* molesto, fastidioso; (*person*) pesado
annual ['ænjuəl] *adj* anual ♦ *n* (*BOT*) anual *m*; (*book*) anuario; **~ly** *adv* anualmente, cada año
annul [ə'nʌl] *vt* anular
annum ['ænəm] *n see* per
anonymous [ə'nɒnɪməs] *adj* anónimo
anorak ['ænəræk] *n* anorak *m*
anorexia [ænə'rɛksɪə] *n* (*MED: also:* **~ nervosa**) anorexia
another [ə'nʌðə*] *adj* (*one more, a different one*) otro ♦ *pron* otro; *see* one
answer ['ɑːnsə*] *n* contestación *f*, respuesta; (*to problem*) solución *f* ♦ *vi* contestar, responder ♦ *vt* (*reply to*) contestar a, responder a; (*problem*) resolver; (*prayer*) escuchar; **in ~ to your letter** contestando or en contestación a su carta; **to ~ the phone** contestar or coger el teléfono; **to ~ the bell** or **the door** acudir a la puerta; **~ back** *vi* replicar, ser respondón/ona; **~ for** *vt fus* responder de or por; **~ to** *vt fus* (*description*) corresponder a; **~able** *adj*: **~able to sb for sth** responsable ante uno de algo; **~ing machine** *n* contestador *m* automático
ant [ænt] *n* hormiga
antagonism [æn'tægənɪzm] *n* antagonismo, hostilidad *f*
antagonize [æn'tægənaɪz] *vt* provocar la enemistad de
Antarctic [ænt'ɑːktɪk] *n*: **the ~** el Antártico
antelope ['æntɪləʊp] *n* antílope *m*
antenatal ['æntɪ'neɪtl] *adj* antenatal, prenatal; **~ clinic** *n* clínica prenatal
anthem ['ænθəm] *n*: **national ~** himno nacional
anthropology [ænθrə'pɒlədʒɪ] *n* antropología
anti... [ænti] *prefix* anti...; **~-aircraft** [-'eəkrɑːft] *adj* antiaéreo; **~biotic** [-baɪ'ɒtɪk] *n* antibiótico; **~body** ['æntɪbɒdɪ] *n* anticuerpo
anticipate [æn'tɪsɪpeɪt] *vt* prever; (*expect*) esperar, contar con; (*look forward to*) esperar con ilusión a; (*do first*) anticiparse a, adelantarse a; **anticipation** [-'peɪʃən] *n* (*expectation*) previsión *f*; (*eagerness*) ilusión *f*, expectación *f*
anticlimax [æntɪ'klaɪmæks] *n* decepción *f*
anticlockwise [æntɪ'klɒkwaɪz] (*BRIT*) *adv* en dirección contraria a la de las agujas del reloj
antics ['æntɪks] *npl* gracias *fpl*

anticyclone [æntɪ'saɪkləʊn] *n* anticiclón *m*
antidepressant ['æntɪdɪ'prɛsnt] *n* antidepresivo
antidote ['æntɪdəʊt] *n* antídoto
antifreeze ['æntɪfriːz] *n* anticongelante *m*
antihistamine [æntɪ'hɪstəmiːn] *n* antihistamínico
antiquated ['æntɪkweɪtɪd] *adj* anticuado
antique [æn'tiːk] *n* antigüedad *f* ♦ *adj* antiguo; **~ dealer** *n* anticuario/a; **~ shop** *n* tienda de antigüedades
antiquity [æn'tɪkwɪtɪ] *n* antigüedad *f*
antiseptic [æntɪ'sɛptɪk] *adj*, *n* antiséptico
antlers ['æntləz] *npl* cuernas *fpl*, cornamenta *sg*
anus ['eɪnəs] *n* ano
anvil ['ænvɪl] *n* yunque *m*
anxiety [æŋ'zaɪətɪ] *n* inquietud *f*; (*MED*) ansiedad *f*; **~ to do** deseo de hacer
anxious ['æŋkʃəs] *adj* inquieto, preocupado; (*worrying*) preocupante; (*keen*): **to be ~ to do** tener muchas ganas de hacer

---

KEYWORD

---

any ['ɛnɪ] *adj* **1** (*in questions etc*) algún/ alguna; **have you ~ butter/children?** ¿tienes mantequilla/hijos?; **if there are ~ tickets left** si quedan billetes, si queda algún billete
2 (*with negative*): **I haven't ~ money/books** no tengo dinero/libros
3 (*no matter which*) cualquier; **~ excuse will do** valdrá or servirá cualquier excusa; **choose ~ book you like** escoge el libro que quieras; **~ teacher you ask will tell you** cualquier profesor al que preguntes te lo dirá
4 (*in phrases*): **in ~ case** de todas formas, en cualquier caso; **~ day now** cualquier día (de estos); **at ~ moment** en cualquier momento, de un momento a otro; **at ~ rate** en todo caso; **~ time: come (at) ~ time** ven cuando quieras; **he might come (at) ~ time** podría llegar de un momento a otro
♦ *pron* **1** (*in questions etc*): **have you got ~?** ¿tienes alguno(s)/a(s)?; **can ~ of you sing?** ¿sabe cantar alguno de vosotros/ustedes?
2 (*with negative*): **I haven't ~ (of them)** no tengo ninguno
3 (*no matter which one(s)*): **take ~ of those books (you like)** toma el libro que quieras de ésos
♦ *adv* **1** (*in questions etc*): **do you want ~ more soup/sandwiches?** ¿quieres más sopa/bocadillos?; **are you feeling ~ better?** ¿te sientes algo mejor?
2 (*with negative*): **I can't hear him ~ more** ya no le oigo; **don't wait ~ longer** no esperes más

---

anybody ['ɛnɪbɒdɪ] *pron* cualquiera; (*in*

interrogative sentences) alguien; (*in negative sentences*): **I don't see ~** no veo a nadie; **if ~ should phone ...** si llama alguien ...

anyhow ['ɛnɪhau] *adv* (*at any rate*) de todos modos, de todas formas; (*haphazard*): **do it ~ you like** hazlo como quieras; **she leaves things just ~** deja las cosas como quiera *or* de cualquier modo; **I shall go ~** de todos modos iré

anyone ['ɛnɪwʌn] *pron* = **anybody**

anything ['ɛnɪθɪŋ] *pron* (*in questions etc*) algo, alguna cosa; (*with negative*) nada; **can you see ~?** ¿le ves por algún lado?; **if ~ happens to me ...** si algo me ocurre ...; (*no matter what*): **you can say ~ you like** puedes decir lo que quieras; **~ will do** vale todo *or* cualquier cosa; **he'll eat ~** come de todo *or* lo que sea

anyway ['ɛnɪweɪ] *adv* (*at any rate*) de todos modos, de todas formas; **I shall go ~** iré de todos modos; (*besides*): **~, I couldn't come even if I wanted to** además, no podría venir aunque quisiera; **why are you phoning, ~?** ¿entonces, por qué llamas?, ¿por qué llamas, pues?

anywhere ['ɛnɪwɛə*] *adv* (*in questions etc*): **can you see him ~?** ¿le ves por algún lado?; **are you going ~?** ¿vas a algún sitio?; (*with negative*): **I can't see him ~** no le veo por ninguna parte; **~ in the world** (*no matter where*) en cualquier parte (del mundo); **put the books down ~** deja los libros donde quieras

apart [ə'pɑːt] *adv* (*aside*) aparte; (*situation*): **~ (from)** separado (de); (*movement*): **to pull ~** separar; **10 miles ~** separados por 10 millas; **to take ~** desmontar; **~ from** *prep* aparte de

apartheid [ə'pɑːteɪt] *n* apartheid *m*

apartment [ə'pɑːtmənt] *n* (*US*) piso (*SP*), departamento (*AM*), apartamento; (*room*) cuarto; **~ building** (*US*) *n* edificio de apartamentos

apathetic [æpə'θɛtɪk] *adj* apático, indiferente

ape [eɪp] *n* mono ♦ *vt* imitar, remedar

aperitif [ə'pɛrɪtiːf] *n* aperitivo

aperture ['æpətʃjuə*] *n* rendija, resquicio; (*PHOT*) abertura

APEX ['eɪpɛks] *n abbr* (= *Advanced Purchase Excursion Fare*) tarifa APEX *f*

apex *n* ápice *m*; (*fig*) cumbre *f*

apiece [ə'piːs] *adv* cada uno

aplomb [ə'plɔm] *n* aplomo

apologetic [əpɔlə'dʒɛtɪk] *adj* de disculpa, (*person*) arrepentido

apologize [ə'pɔlədʒaɪz] *vi*: **to ~ (for sth to sb)** disculparse (con alguien de algo)

apology [ə'pɔlədʒɪ] *n* disculpa, excusa

apostrophe [ə'pɔstrəfɪ] *n* apóstrofo *m*

appal [ə'pɔːl] *vt* horrorizar, espantar; **~ling** *adj* espantoso; (*awful*) pésimo

apparatus [æpə'reɪtəs] *n* (*equipment*) equipo; (*organization*) aparato; (*in gymnasium*) aparatos *mpl*

apparel [ə'pærəl] (*US*) *n* ropa

apparent [ə'pærənt] *adj* aparente; (*obvious*) evidente; **~ly** *adv* por lo visto, al parecer

appeal [ə'piːl] *vi* (*LAW*) apelar ♦ *n* (*LAW*) apelación *f*; (*request*) llamamiento; (*plea*) petición *f*; (*charm*) atractivo; **to ~ for** reclamar; **to ~ to** (*be attractive to*) atraer; **it doesn't ~ to me** no me atrae, no me llama la atención; **~ing** *adj* (*attractive*) atractivo

appear [ə'pɪə*] *vi* aparecer, presentarse; (*LAW*) comparecer; (*publication*) salir (a luz), publicarse; (*seem*) parecer; **to ~ on TV/in "Hamlet"** salir por la tele/hacer un papel en "Hamlet"; **it would ~ that** parecería que; **~ance** *n* aparición *f*; (*look*) apariencia, aspecto

appease [ə'piːz] *vt* (*pacify*) apaciguar; (*satisfy*) satisfacer

appendices [ə'pɛndɪsiːz] *npl of* **appendix**

appendicitis [əpɛndɪ'saɪtɪs] *n* apendicitis *f*

appendix [ə'pɛndɪks] (*pl* **appendices**) *n* apéndice *m*

appetite ['æpɪtaɪt] *n* apetito; (*fig*) deseo, anhelo

appetizer ['æpɪtaɪzə*] *n* (*drink*) aperitivo; (*food*) tapas *fpl* (*SP*)

applaud [ə'plɔːd] *vt, vi* aplaudir

applause [ə'plɔːz] *n* aplausos *mpl*

apple ['æpl] *n* manzana; **~ tree** *n* manzano

appliance [ə'plaɪəns] *n* aparato

applicable [ə'plɪkəbl] *adj* (*relevant*): **to be ~ (to)** referirse a

applicant ['æplɪkənt] *n* candidato/a; solicitante *m/f*

application [æplɪ'keɪʃən] *n* aplicación *f*; (*for a job etc*) solicitud *f*, petición *f*; **~ form** *n* solicitud *f*

applied [ə'plaɪd] *adj* aplicado

apply [ə'plaɪ] *vt* (*paint etc*) poner; (*law etc*: *put into practice*) poner en vigor ♦ *vi*: **to ~ to** (*ask*) dirigirse a; (*be applicable*) ser aplicable a; **to ~ for** (*permit, grant, job*) solicitar; **to ~ o.s. to** aplicarse a, dedicarse a

appoint [ə'pɔɪnt] *vt* (*to post*) nombrar; **~ed** *adj*: **at the ~ed time** a la hora señalada; **~ment** *n* (*with client*) cita; (*act*) nombramiento; (*post*) puesto; (*at hairdresser etc*): **to have an ~ment** tener hora; **to make an ~ment (with sb)** citarse (con uno)

appraisal [ə'preɪzl] *n* valoración *f*

appreciate [ə'priːʃɪeɪt] *vt* apreciar, tener en mucho; (*be grateful for*) agradecer; (*be aware of*) comprender ♦ *vi* (*COMM*) aumentar(se) en valor; **appreciation** [-'eɪʃən] *n* apreciación *f*; (*gratitude*) reconocimiento, agradecimiento; (*COMM*) aumento en valor

appreciative [ə'pri:ʃɪətɪv] adj apreciativo; (comment) agradecido

apprehensive [æprɪ'hensɪv] adj aprensivo

apprentice [ə'prɛntɪs] n aprendiz/a m/f; ~ship n aprendizaje m

approach [ə'prəutʃ] vi acercarse ♦ vt acercarse a; (ask, apply to) dirigirse a; (situation, problem) abordar ♦ n acercamiento; (access) acceso; (to problem, situation): ~ (to) actitud f (ante); ~able adj (person) abordable; (place) accesible

appropriate [adj ə'prəuprɪɪt, vb ə'prəuprɪeɪt] adj apropiado, conveniente ♦ vt (take) apropiarse de

approval [ə'pru:vəl] n aprobación f, visto bueno; (permission) consentimiento; on ~ (COMM) a prueba

approve [ə'pru:v] vt aprobar; ~ of vt fus (thing) aprobar; (person): they don't ~ of her (ella) no les parece bien

approximate [ə'prɔksɪmɪt] adj aproximado; ~ly adv aproximadamente, más o menos

apricot ['eɪprɪkɔt] n albaricoque m (SP), damasco (AM)

April ['eɪprəl] n abril m; ~ Fools' Day n el primero de abril; ≈ día m de los Inocentes (28 December)

apron ['eɪprən] n delantal m

apt [æpt] adj acertado, apropiado; (likely): ~ to do propenso a hacer

aquarium [ə'kwɛərɪəm] n acuario

Aquarius [ə'kwɛərɪəs] n Acuario

Arab ['ærəb] adj, n árabe m/f

Arabian [ə'reɪbɪən] adj árabe

Arabic ['ærəbɪk] adj árabe; (numerals) arábigo ♦ n árabe m

arable ['ærəbl] adj cultivable

Aragon ['ærəgən] n Aragón m

arbitrary ['ɑ:bɪtrərɪ] adj arbitrario

arbitration [ɑ:bɪ'treɪʃən] n arbitraje m

arcade [ɑ:'keɪd] n (round a square) soportales mpl; (shopping mall) galería comercial

arch [ɑ:tʃ] n arco; (of foot) arco del pie ♦ vt arquear

archaeologist [ɑ:kɪ'ɔlədʒɪst] (US archeologist) n arqueólogo/a

archaeology [ɑ:kɪ'ɔlədʒɪ] (US archeology) n arqueología

archbishop [ɑ:tʃ'bɪʃəp] n arzobispo

archeology etc [ɑ:kɪ'ɔlədʒɪ] (US) = **archaeology** etc

archery ['ɑ:tʃərɪ] n tiro al arco

architect ['ɑ:kɪtɛkt] n arquitecto/a; ~ure n arquitectura

archives ['ɑ:kaɪvz] npl archivo

Arctic ['ɑ:ktɪk] adj ártico ♦ n: the ~ el Ártico

ardent ['ɑ:dənt] adj ardiente, apasionado

arduous ['ɑ:djuəs] adj (task) arduo; (journey) agotador(a)

are [ɑ:*] vb see **be**

area ['ɛərɪə] n área, región f; (part of place) zona; (MATH etc) área, superficie f; (in room: e.g. dining ~) parte f; (of knowledge, experience) campo

arena [ə'ri:nə] n estadio; (of circus) pista

aren't [ɑ:nt] = **are not**

Argentina [ɑ:dʒən'ti:nə] n Argentina; **Argentinian** [-'tɪnɪən] adj, n argentino/a m/f

arguably ['ɑ:gjuəblɪ] adv posiblemente

argue ['ɑ:gju:] vi (quarrel) discutir, pelearse; (reason) razonar, argumentar; to ~ that sostener que

argument ['ɑ:gjumənt] n discusión f, pelea; (reasons) argumento; ~ative [-'mɛntətɪv] adj discutidor(a)

Aries ['ɛərɪz] n Aries m

arise [ə'raɪz] (pt arose, pp arisen) vi surgir, presentarse

arisen [ə'rɪzn] pp of **arise**

aristocrat ['ærɪstəkræt] n aristócrata m/f

arithmetic [ə'rɪθmətɪk] n aritmética

ark [ɑ:k] n: Noah's A~ el Arca f de Noé

arm [ɑ:m] n brazo ♦ vt armar; ~s npl armas fpl; ~ in ~ cogidos del brazo

armaments ['ɑ:məmənts] npl armamento

armchair ['ɑ:mtʃɛə*] n sillón m, butaca

armed [ɑ:md] adj armado; ~ robbery n robo a mano armada

armour ['ɑ:mə*] (US armor) n armadura; (MIL: tanks) blindaje m; ~ed car n coche m (SP) o carro (AM) blindado

armpit ['ɑ:mpɪt] n sobaco, axila

armrest ['ɑ:mrɛst] n apoyabrazos m inv

army ['ɑ:mɪ] n ejército; (fig) multitud f

aroma [ə'rəumə] n aroma m, fragancia; ~therapy n aromaterapia

arose [ə'rəuz] pt of **arise**

around [ə'raund] adv alrededor; (in the area): there is no one else ~ no hay nadie más por aquí ♦ prep alrededor de

arouse [ə'rauz] vt despertar; (anger) provocar

arrange [ə'reɪndʒ] vt arreglar, ordenar; (organize) organizar; to ~ to do sth quedar en hacer algo; ~ment n arreglo; (agreement) acuerdo; ~ments npl (preparations) preparativos mpl

array [ə'reɪ] n: ~ of (things) serie f de; (people) conjunto de

arrears [ə'rɪəz] npl atrasos mpl; to be in ~ with one's rent estar retrasado en el pago del alquiler

arrest [ə'rɛst] vt detener; (sb's attention) llamar ♦ n detención f; under ~ detenido

arrival [ə'raɪvəl] n llegada; new ~ recién llegado/a; (baby) recién nacido

arrive [ə'raɪv] vi llegar; (baby) nacer

arrogant ['ærəgənt] adj arrogante

arrow ['ærəu] n flecha

arse [ɑːs] (*BRIT: inf!*) *n* culo, trasero

arson ['ɑːsn] *n* incendio premeditado

art [ɑːt] *n* arte *m*; (*skill*) destreza; **A~s** *npl* (*SCOL*) Letras *fpl*

artery ['ɑːtəri] *n* arteria

art gallery *n* pinacoteca; (*saleroom*) galería de arte

arthritis [ɑː'θraɪtɪs] *n* artritis *f*

artichoke ['ɑːtɪtʃəuk] *n* alcachofa; **Jerusalem ~** aguaturma

article ['ɑːtɪkl] *n* artículo; (*BRIT: LAW: training*): **~s** *npl* contrato de aprendizaje; **~ of clothing** prenda de vestir

articulate [*adj* ɑː'tɪkjulɪt, *vb* ɑː'tɪkjuleɪt] *adj* claro, bien expresado ♦ *vt* expresar; **~d lorry** (*BRIT*) *n* trailer *m*

artificial [ɑːtɪ'fɪʃəl] *adj* artificial; (*affected*) afectado

artillery [ɑː'tɪlərɪ] *n* artillería

artisan ['ɑːtɪzæn] *n* artesano

artist ['ɑːtɪst] *n* artista *m/f*; (*MUS*) intérprete *m/f*; **~ic** [ɑː'tɪstɪk] *adj* artístico; **~ry** *n* arte *m*, habilidad *f* (artística)

art school *n* escuela de bellas artes

KEYWORD

as [æz] *conj* **1** (*referring to time*) cuando, mientras; a medida que; **~ the years went by** con el paso de los años; **he came in ~ I was leaving** entró cuando me marchaba; **~ from tomorrow** desde *or* a partir de mañana

2 (*in comparisons*): **~ big ~** tan grande como; **twice ~ big ~** el doble de grande que; **~ much money/many books ~** tanto dinero/ tantos libros como; **~ soon ~** en cuanto

3 (*since, because*) como, ya que; **he left early ~ he had to be home by 10** se fue temprano ya que tenía que estar en casa a las 10

4 (*referring to manner, way*): **do ~ you wish** haz lo que quieras; **~ she said** como dijo; **he gave it to me ~ a present** me lo dio de regalo

5 (*in the capacity of*): **he works ~ a barman** trabaja de barman; **~ chairman of the company, he ...** como presidente de la compañía, ...

6 (*concerning*): **~ for** *or* **to that** por *or* en lo que respecta a eso

7: **~ if** *or* **though** como si; **he looked ~ if he was ill** parecía como si estuviera enfermo, tenía aspecto de enfermo; *see also* **long**; **such**; **well**

---

a.s.a.p. *abbr* (= *as soon as possible*) cuanto antes

asbestos [æz'bɛstəs] *n* asbesto, amianto

ascend [ə'sɛnd] *vt* subir; (*throne*) ascender *or* subir a

ascent [ə'sɛnt] *n* subida; (*slope*) cuesta, pendiente *f*

ascertain [æsə'teɪn] *vt* averiguar

ash [æʃ] *n* ceniza; (*tree*) fresno

ashamed [ə'feɪmd] *adj* avergonzado, apenado (*AM*); **to be ~ of** avergonzarse de

ashore [ə'ʃɔː*] *adv* en tierra; (*swim etc*) a tierra

ashtray ['æʃtreɪ] *n* cenicero

Ash Wednesday *n* miércoles *m* de Ceniza

Asia ['eɪʃə] *n* Asia; **~n** *adj, n* asiático/a *m/f*

aside [ə'saɪd] *adv* a un lado ♦ *n* aparte *m*

ask [ɑːsk] *vt* (*question*) preguntar; (*invite*) invitar; **to ~ sb sth/to do sth** preguntar algo a alguien/pedir a alguien que haga algo; **to ~ sb about sth** preguntar algo a alguien; **to ~ (sb) a question** hacer una pregunta (a alguien); **to ~ sb out to dinner** invitar a cenar a uno; **~ after** *vt fus* preguntar por; **~ for** *vt fus* pedir; (*trouble*) buscar

asking price *n* precio inicial

asleep [ə'sliːp] *adj* dormido; **to fall ~** dormirse, quedarse dormido

asparagus [əs'pærəgəs] *n* (*plant*) espárrago; (*food*) espárragos *mpl*

aspect ['æspekt] *n* aspecto, apariencia; (*direction in which a building etc faces*) orientación *f*

aspersions [əs'pəːʃənz] *npl*: **to cast ~ on** difamar a, calumniar a

asphyxiation [æsfɪksɪ'eɪʃən] *n* asfixia

aspire [əs'paɪə*] *vi*: **to ~ to** aspirar a, ambicionar

aspirin ['æsprɪn] *n* aspirina

ass [æs] *n* asno, burro; (*inf: idiot*) imbécil *m/f*; (*US: inf!*) culo, trasero

assailant [ə'seɪlənt] *n* asaltador(a) *m/f*, agresor(a) *m/f*

assassinate [ə'sæsɪneɪt] *vt* asesinar; **assassination** [əsæsɪ'neɪʃən] *n* asesinato

assault [ə'sɔːlt] *n* asalto; (*LAW*) agresión *f* ♦ *vt* asaltar, atacar; (*sexually*) violar

assemble [ə'sɛmbl] *vt* reunir, juntar; (*TECH*) montar ♦ *vi* reunirse, juntarse

assembly [ə'sɛmblɪ] *n* reunión *f*, asamblea; (*parliament*) parlamento; (*construction*) montaje *m*; **~ line** *n* cadena de montaje

assent [ə'sɛnt] *n* asentimiento, aprobación *f*

assert [ə'səːt] *vt* afirmar; (*authority*) hacer valer; **~ion** [-ʃən] *n* afirmación *f*

assess [ə'sɛs] *vt* valorar, calcular; (*tax, damages*) fijar; (*for tax*) gravar; **~ment** *n* valoración *f*; (*for tax*) gravamen *m*; **~or** *n* asesor(a) *m/f*

asset ['æsɛt] *n* ventaja; **~s** *npl* (*COMM*) activo; (*property, funds*) fondos *mpl*

assign [ə'saɪn] *vt*: **to ~ (to)** (*date*) fijar (para); (*task*) asignar (a); (*resources*) destinar (a); **~ment** *n* tarea

assist [ə'sɪst] *vt* ayudar; **~ance** *n* ayuda, auxilio; **~ant** *n* ayudante *m/f*; (*BRIT: also:*

shop ~ant) dependiente/a *m/f*
associate [*adj, n* ə'səʊʃɪɪt, *vb* ə'səʊʃɪeɪt] *adj*
asociado ♦ *n* (*at work*) colega *m/f* ♦ *vt*
asociar; (*ideas*) relacionar ♦ *vi*: **to ~ with sb**
tratar con alguien
association [əsəʊsɪ'eɪʃən] *n* asociación *f*
assorted [ə'sɔːtɪd] *adj* surtido, variado
assortment [ə'sɔːtmənt] *n* (*of shapes,
colours*) surtido; (*of books*) colección *f*; (*of
people*) mezcla
assume [ə'sjuːm] *vt* suponer; (*responsibilities*)
asumir; (*attitude*) adoptar, tomar
assumption [ə'sʌmpʃən] *n* suposición *f*,
presunción *f*; (*of power etc*) toma
assurance [ə'ʃʊərəns] *n* garantía, promesa;
(*confidence*) confianza, aplomo; (*insurance*)
seguro
assure [ə'ʃʊə*] *vt* asegurar
asthma ['æsmə] *n* asma
astonish [ə'stɒnɪʃ] *vt* asombrar, pasmar;
~ment *n* asombro, sorpresa
astound [ə'staʊnd] *vt* asombrar, pasmar
astray [ə'streɪ] *adv*: **to go ~** extraviarse; **to
lead ~** (*morally*) llevar por mal camino
astride [ə'straɪd] *prep* a caballo or horcajadas
sobre
astrology [æs'trɒlədʒɪ] *n* astrología
astronaut ['æstrənɔːt] *n* astronauta *m/f*
astronomy [æs'trɒnəmɪ] *n* astronomía
asylum [ə'saɪləm] *n* (*refuge*) asilo; (*mental
hospital*) manicomio

KEYWORD
---

at [æt] *prep* **1** (*referring to position*) en;
(*direction*) a; **~ the top** en lo alto; **~ home/
school** en casa/la escuela; **to look ~ sth/sb**
mirar algo/a uno
2 (*referring to time*): **~ 4 o'clock** a las 4;
~ night por la noche; **~ Christmas** en
Navidad; **~ times** a veces
3 (*referring to rates, speed etc*): **~ £1 a kilo** a
una libra el kilo; **two ~ a time** de dos en dos;
~ 50 km/h a 50 km/h
4 (*referring to manner*): **~ a stroke** de un
golpe; **~ peace** en paz
5 (*referring to activity*): **to be ~ work** estar
trabajando; (*in the office etc*) estar en el
trabajo; **to play ~ cowboys** jugar a los
vaqueros; **to be good ~ sth** ser bueno en algo
6 (*referring to cause*): **shocked/surprised/
annoyed ~ sth** asombrado/sorprendido/
fastidiado por algo; **I went ~ his suggestion**
fui a instancias suyas

ate [eɪt] *pt of* **eat**
atheist ['eɪθɪɪst] *n* ateo/a
Athens ['æθɪnz] *n* Atenas
athlete ['æθliːt] *n* atleta *m/f*
athletic [æθ'lɛtɪk] *adj* atlético; **~s** *n* atletismo

Atlantic [ət'læntɪk] *adj* atlántico ♦ *n*: **the
~ (Ocean)** el (Océano) Atlántico
atlas ['ætləs] *n* atlas *m*
A.T.M. *n abbr* (= *automated telling machine*)
cajero automático
atmosphere ['ætməsfɪə*] *n* atmósfera; (*of
place*) ambiente *m*
atom ['ætəm] *n* átomo; **~ic** [ə'tɒmɪk] *adj*
atómico; **~(ic) bomb** *n* bomba atómica;
~izer ['ætəmaɪzə*] *n* atomizador *m*
atone [ə'təʊn] *vi*: **to ~ for** expiar
atrocious [ə'trəʊʃəs] *adj* atroz
attach [ə'tætʃ] *vt* (*fasten*) atar; (*join*) unir,
sujetar; (*document, letter*) adjuntar;
(*importance etc*) dar, conceder; **to be ~ed to
sb/sth** (*like*) tener cariño a alguien/algo
attaché case [ə'tæʃeɪ-] *n* maletín *m*
attachment [ə'tætʃmənt] *n* (*tool*) accesorio;
(*love*): **~ (to)** apego (a)
attack [ə'tæk] *vt* (*MIL*) atacar; (*subj: criminal*)
agredir, asaltar; (*criticize*) criticar; (*task*)
emprender ♦ *n* ataque *m*, asalto; (*on sb's life*)
atentado; (*fig: criticism*) crítica; (*of illness*)
ataque *m*; **heart ~** infarto (de miocardio); **~er**
n agresor(a) *m/f*, asaltante *m/f*
attain [ə'teɪn] *vt* (*also*: **~ to**) alcanzar;
(*achieve*) lograr, conseguir
attempt [ə'tɛmpt] *n* tentativa, intento;
(*attack*) atentado ♦ *vt* intentar; **~ed** *adj*: **~ed
burglary/murder/suicide** tentativa *or* intento
de robo/asesinato/suicidio
attend [ə'tɛnd] *vt* asistir a; (*patient*) atender;
~ to *vt fus* ocuparse de; (*customer, patient*)
atender a; **~ance** *n* asistencia, presencia;
(*people present*) concurrencia; **~ant** *n*
ayudante *m/f*; (*in garage etc*) encargado/a
♦ *adj* (*dangers*) concomitante
attention [ə'tɛnʃən] *n* atención *f*; (*care*)
atenciones *fpl* ♦ *excl* (*MIL*) ¡firme(s)!; **for the
~ of ...** (*ADMIN*) atención ...
attentive [ə'tɛntɪv] *adj* atento
attic ['ætɪk] *n* desván *m*
attitude ['ætɪtjuːd] *n* actitud *f*; (*disposition*)
disposición *f*
attorney [ə'tɜːnɪ] *n* (*lawyer*) abogado/a;
A~ General *n* (*BRIT*) ≈ Presidente *m* del
Consejo del Poder Judicial (*SP*); (*US*) ≈
ministro de justicia
attract [ə'trækt] *vt* atraer; (*sb's attention*)
llamar; **~ion** [ə'trækʃən] *n* encanto; (*gen pl:
amusements*) diversiones *fpl*; (*PHYSICS*)
atracción *f*; (*fig: towards sb, sth*) atractivo;
~ive *adj* guapo; (*interesting*) atrayente
attribute [*n* 'ætrɪbjuːt, *vb* ə'trɪbjuːt] *n*
atributo ♦ *vt*: **to ~ sth to** atribuir algo a
attrition [ə'trɪʃən] *n*: **war of ~** guerra de
agotamiento
aubergine ['əʊbəʒiːn] (*BRIT*) *n* berenjena;
(*colour*) morado

auburn ['ɔːbən] adj color castaño rojizo

auction ['ɔːkʃən] n (also: sale by ~) subasta ♦ vt subastar; **~eer** [-'nɪə*] n subastador(a) m/f

audible ['ɔːdɪbl] adj audible, que se puede oír

audience ['ɔːdɪəns] n público; (RADIO) radioescuchas mpl; (TV) telespectadores mpl; (interview) audiencia

audio-visual [ɔːdɪəu'vɪzjuəl] adj audiovisual; **~ aid** n ayuda audiovisual

audit ['ɔːdɪt] vt revisar, intervenir

audition [ɔː'dɪʃən] n audición f

auditor ['ɔːdɪtə*] n interventor(a) m/f, censor(a) m/f de cuentas

augment [ɔːg'mɛnt] vt aumentar

augur ['ɔːgə*] vi: **it ~s well** es un buen augurio

August ['ɔːgəst] n agosto

aunt [ɑːnt] n tía; **~ie**, **~y** n diminutive of aunt

au pair ['əu'pɛə*] n (also: ~ girl) (chica) au pair f

auspicious [ɔːs'pɪʃəs] adj propicio, de buen augurio

Australia [ɔs'treɪlɪə] n Australia; **~n** adj, n australiano/a m/f

Austria ['ɔstrɪə] n Austria; **~n** adj, n austríaco/a m/f

authentic [ɔː'θɛntɪk] adj auténtico

author ['ɔːθə*] n autor(a) m/f

authoritarian [ɔːθɔrɪ'tɛərɪən] adj autoritario

authoritative [ɔː'θɔrɪtətɪv] adj autorizado; (manner) autoritario

authority [ɔː'θɔrɪtɪ] n autoridad f; (official permission) autorización f; **the authorities** npl las autoridades

authorize ['ɔːθəraɪz] vt autorizar

auto ['ɔːtəu] (US) n coche m (SP), carro (AM), automóvil m

auto-: **~biography** [ɔːtəbaɪ'ɔgrəfɪ] n autobiografía; **~graph** ['ɔːtəgrɑːf] n autógrafo ♦ vt (photo etc) dedicar; (programme) firmar; **~mated** ['ɔːtəmeɪtɪd] adj automatizado; **~matic** [ɔːtə'mætɪk] adj automático ♦ n (gun) pistola automática; (car) coche m automático, **~matically** adv automáticamente; **~mation** [ɔː'tɔmeɪʃən] n reconversión f; **~mobile** ['ɔːtəmɔbiːl] (US) n coche m (SP), carro (AM), automóvil m; **~nomy** [ɔː'tɔnəmɪ] n autonomía

autumn ['ɔːtəm] n otoño

auxiliary [ɔːg'zɪlɪərɪ] adj, n auxiliar m/f

avail [ə'veɪl] vt: **to ~ o.s. of** aprovechar(se) de ♦ n: **to no ~** en vano, sin resultado

available [ə'veɪləbl] adj disponible; (unoccupied) libre; (person: unattached) soltero y sin compromiso

avalanche ['ævəlɑːnʃ] n alud m, avalancha

avant-garde ['ævãŋ'gɑːd] adj de vanguardia

Ave. abbr = avenue

avenge [ə'vɛndʒ] vt vengar

avenue ['ævənjuː] n avenida; (fig) camino

average ['ævərɪdʒ] n promedio, término medio ♦ adj medio, de término medio; (ordinary) regular, corriente ♦ vt sacar un promedio de; **on ~** por regla general; **~ out** vi: **to ~ out at** salir en un promedio de

averse [ə'vɜːs] adj: **to be ~ to sth/doing** sentir aversión or antipatía por algo/por hacer

avert [ə'vɜːt] vt prevenir; (blow) desviar; (one's eyes) apartar

aviary ['eɪvɪərɪ] n pajarera, avería

avocado [ævə'kɑːdəu] n (also: BRIT: ~ pear) aguacate m (SP), palta (AM)

avoid [ə'vɔɪd] vt evitar, eludir

await [ə'weɪt] vt esperar, aguardar

awake [ə'weɪk] (pt awoke, pp awoken or awaked) adj despierto ♦ vt despertar ♦ vi despertarse; **to be ~** estar despierto; **~ning** n el despertar

award [ə'wɔːd] n premio; (LAW: damages) indemnización f ♦ vt otorgar, conceder; (LAW: damages) adjudicar

aware [ə'wɛə*] adj: **~ (of)** consciente (de); **to become ~ of/that** (realize) darse cuenta de/de que; (learn) enterarse de/de que; **~ness** n conciencia; (knowledge) conocimiento

away [ə'weɪ] adv fuera; (movement): **she went ~** se marchó; (far ~) lejos; **two kilometres ~** a dos kilómetros de distancia; **two hours ~ by car** a dos horas en coche; **the holiday was two weeks ~** faltaban dos semanas para las vacaciones; **he's ~ for a week** estará ausente una semana; **to take ~ (from)** quitar (a); (subtract) substraer (de); **to work/pedal ~** seguir trabajando/ pedaleando; **to fade ~** (colour) desvanecerse; (sound) apagarse; **~ game** n (SPORT) partido de fuera

awe [ɔː] n admiración f respetuosa; **~-inspiring** adj imponente

awful ['ɔːfəl] adj horroroso; (quantity): **an ~ lot (of)** cantidad (de); **~ly** adv (very) terriblemente

awkward ['ɔːkwəd] adj desmañado, torpe; (shape) incómodo; (embarrassing) delicado, difícil

awning ['ɔːnɪŋ] n (of tent, caravan, shop) toldo

awoke [ə'wəuk] pt of awake

awoken [ə'wəukən] pp of awake

awry [ə'raɪ] adv: **to be ~** estar descolocado or mal puesto

axe [æks] (US ax) n hacha ♦ vt (project) cortar; (jobs) reducir

axes ['æksiːz] npl of axis

axis ['æksɪs] (pl axes) n eje m

axle ['æksl] n eje m, árbol m

ay(e) [aɪ] *excl* sí

B, b

B [bi:] *n* (MUS) si *m*

B.A. *abbr* = **Bachelor of Arts**

baby ['beɪbɪ] *n* bebé *m/f*; (US: *inf: darling*) mi amor; **~ carriage** (US) *n* cochecito; **~-sit** *vi* hacer de canguro; **~-sitter** *n* canguro/a; **~ wipe** *n* toallita húmeda (*para bebés*)

bachelor ['bætʃələ*] *n* soltero; **B~ of Arts/ Science** licenciado/a en Filosofía y Letras/ Ciencias

back [bæk] *n* (*of person*) espalda; (*of animal*) lomo; (*of hand*) dorso; (*as opposed to front*) parte *f* de atrás; (*of chair*) respaldo; (*of page*) reverso; (*of book*) final *m*; (FOOTBALL) defensa *m*; (*of crowd*): **the ones at the ~** los del fondo ♦ *vt* (*candidate: also:* ~ **up**) respaldar, apoyar; (*horse: at races*) apostar a; (*car*) dar marcha atrás a or con ♦ *vi* (*car etc*) ir (*or salir or entrar*) marcha atrás ♦ *adj* (*payment, rent*) atrasado; (*seats, wheels*) de atrás ♦ *adv* (*not forward*) (*hacia*) atrás; (*returned*): **he's ~** está de vuelta, ha vuelto; **he ran ~** volvió corriendo; (*restitution*): **throw the ball ~** devuelve la pelota; **can I have it ~?** ¿me lo devuelve?; (*again*): **he called ~** llamó de nuevo; **~ down** *vi* echarse atrás; **~ out** *vi* (*of promise*) volverse atrás; **~ up** *vt* (*person*) apoyar, respaldar; (*theory*) defender; (COMPUT) hacer una copia preventiva or de reserva; **~bencher** (BRIT) *n* miembro del parlamento sin cargo relevante; **~bone** *n* columna vertebral; **~date** *vt* (*pay rise*) dar efecto retroactivo a; (*letter*) poner fecha atrasada a; **~drop** *n* telón *m* de fondo; **~fire** *vi* (AUT) petardear; (*plans*) fallar, salir mal; **~ground** *n* fondo; (*of events*) antecedentes *mpl*; (*basic knowledge*) bases *fpl*; (*experience*) conocimientos *mpl*, educación *f*; **family ~ground** origen *m*, antecedentes *mpl*; **~hand** *n* (TENNIS: *also:* ~hand stroke) revés *m*; **~hander** (BRIT) *n* (*bribe*) soborno; **~ing** *n* (*fig*) apoyo, respaldo; **~lash** *n* reacción *f*; **~log** *n*: **~log of work** trabajo atrasado; **~ number** *n* (*of magazine etc*) número atrasado; **~pack** *n* mochila; **~packer** *n* mochilero(a); **~ pay** *n* pago atrasado; **~side** (*inf*) *n* trasero, culo; **~stage** *adv* entre bastidores; **~stroke** *n* espalda; **~up** *adj* suplementario; (COMPUT) de reserva ♦ *n* (*support*) apoyo; (*also:* ~-up file) copia preventiva or de reserva; **~ward** *adj* (*person, country*) atrasado; **~wards** *adv* hacia atrás; (*read a list*) al revés; (*fall*) de espaldas; **~yard** *n* traspatio

bacon ['beɪkən] *n* tocino, beicon *m*

bad [bæd] *adj* malo; (*mistake, accident*) grave; (*food*) podrido, pasado; **his ~ leg** su pierna lisiada; **to go ~** (*food*) pasarse

badge [bædʒ] *n* insignia; (*policeman's*) chapa, placa

badger ['bædʒə*] *n* tejón *m*

badly ['bædlɪ] *adv* mal; **to reflect ~ on sb** influir negativamente en la reputación de uno; **~ wounded** gravemente herido; **he needs it ~** le hace gran falta; **to be ~ off (for money)** andar mal de dinero

badminton ['bædmɪntən] *n* bádminton *m*

bad-tempered *adj* de mal genio or carácter; (*temporarily*) de mal humor

bag [bæg] *n* bolsa; (*handbag*) bolso; (*satchel*) mochila; (*case*) maleta; **~s of** (*inf*) un montón de; **~gage** *n* equipaje *m*; **~gage allowance** *n* límite *m* de equipaje; **~gage reclaim** *n* recogida de equipajes; **~gy** *adj* amplio; **~pipes** *npl* gaita

Bahamas [bə'hɑ:məz] *npl*: **the ~** las Islas Bahamas

bail [beɪl] *n* fianza ♦ *vt* (*prisoner: gen: grant* ~ *to*) poner en libertad bajo fianza; (*boat: also:* ~ **out**) achicar; **on ~** (*prisoner*) bajo fianza; **to ~ sb out** obtener la libertad de uno bajo fianza; *see also* **bale**

bailiff ['beɪlɪf] *n* alguacil *m*

bait [beɪt] *n* cebo ♦ *vt* poner cebo en; (*tease*) tomar el pelo a

bake [beɪk] *vt* cocer (al horno) ♦ *vi* cocerse; **~d beans** *npl* judías *fpl* en salsa de tomate; **~d potato** *n* patata al horno; **~r** *n* panadero; **~ry** *n* panadería; (*for cakes*) pastelería; **baking** *n* (*act*) amasar *m*; (*batch*) hornada; **baking powder** *n* levadura (en polvo)

balance ['bæləns] *n* equilibrio; (COMM: *sum*) balance *m*; (*remainder*) resto; (*scales*) balanza ♦ *vt* equilibrar; (*budget*) nivelar; (*account*) saldar; (*make equal*) equilibrar; **~ of trade/ payments** balanza de comercio/pagos; **~d** *adj* (*personality, diet*) equilibrado; (*report*) objetivo; **~ sheet** *n* balance *m*

balcony ['bælkənɪ] *n* (*open*) balcón *m*; (*closed*) galería; (*in theatre*) anfiteatro

bald [bɔ:ld] *adj* calvo; (*tyre*) liso

bale [beɪl] *n* (AGR) paca, fardo; (*of papers etc*) fajo; **~ out** *vi* lanzarse en paracaídas

Balearics [bælɪ'ærɪks] *npl*: **the ~** las Baleares

ball [bɔ:l] *n* pelota; (*football*) balón *m*; (*of wool, string*) ovillo; (*dance*) baile *m*; **to play ~** (*fig*) cooperar

ballast ['bæləst] *n* lastre *m*

ball bearings *npl* cojinetes *mpl* de bolas

ballerina [bælə'ri:nə] *n* bailarina

ballet ['bæleɪ] *n* ballet *m*; **~ dancer** *n* bailarín/ina *m/f*

balloon [bə'lu:n] *n* globo

ballot ['bælət] n votación f; ~ **paper** n papeleta (para votar)

ballpoint (pen) ['bɔːlpɔɪnt-] n bolígrafo

ballroom ['bɔːlrum] n salón m de baile

Baltic ['bɔːltɪk] n: **the ~ (Sea)** el (Mar) Báltico

ban [bæn] n prohibición f, proscripción f ♦ vt prohibir, proscribir

banal [bə'nɑːl] adj banal, vulgar

banana [bə'nɑːnə] n plátano (SP), banana (AM)

band [bænd] n grupo; (strip) faja, tira; (stripe) lista; (MUS: jazz) orquesta; (: rock) grupo; (: MIL) banda; ~ **together** vi juntarse, asociarse

bandage ['bændɪdʒ] n venda, vendaje m ♦ vt vendar

Bandaid ® ['bændeɪd] (US) n tirita

bandit ['bændɪt] n bandido

bandy-legged ['bændɪ'legd] adj estevado

bang [bæŋ] n (of gun, exhaust) estallido, detonación f; (of door) portazo; (blow) golpe m ♦ vt (door) cerrar de golpe; (one's head) golpear ♦ vi estallar; (door) cerrar de golpe

Bangladesh [bɑːŋglə'deʃ] n Bangladesh m

bangs [bæŋz] (US) npl flequillo

banish ['bænɪʃ] vt desterrar

banister(s) ['bænɪstə(z)] n(pl) barandilla, pasamanos m inv

bank [bæŋk] n (COMM) banco; (of river, lake) ribera, orilla; (of earth) terraplén m ♦ vi (AVIAT) ladearse; ~ **on** vt fus contar con; ~ **account** n cuenta de banco; ~ **card** n tarjeta bancaria; ~**er** n banquero; ~**er's card** (BRIT) n = ~ **card**; **B~ holiday** (BRIT) n día m festivo; ~**ing** n banca; ~**note** n billete m de banco; ~ **rate** n tipo de interés bancario

bankrupt ['bæŋkrʌpt] adj quebrado, insolvente; **to go ~** hacer bancarrota; **to be ~** estar en quiebra; ~**cy** n quiebra

bank statement n balance m or detalle m de cuenta

banner ['bænə*] n pancarta

bannister(s) ['bænɪstə(z)] n(pl) = **banister(s)**

baptism ['bæptɪzəm] n bautismo; (act) bautizo

bar [bɑː*] n (pub) bar m; (counter) mostrador m; (rod) barra; (of window, cage) reja; (of soap) pastilla; (of chocolate) tableta; (fig: hindrance) obstáculo; (prohibition) proscripción f; (MUS) barra ♦ vt (road) obstruir; (person) excluir; (activity) prohibir; **the B~** (LAW) la abogacía; **behind ~s** entre rejas; ~ **none** sin excepción

barbaric [bɑː'bærɪk] adj bárbaro

barbecue ['bɑːbɪkjuː] n barbacoa

barbed wire ['bɑːbd-] n alambre m de púas

barber ['bɑːbə*] n peluquero, barbero

bar code n código de barras

bare [beə*] adj desnudo; (trees) sin hojas; (necessities etc) básico ♦ vt desnudar; (teeth) enseñar; ~**back** adv a pelo, sin silla; ~**faced** adj descarado; ~**foot** adj, adv descalzo; ~**ly** adv apenas

bargain ['bɑːgɪn] n pacto, negocio; (good buy) ganga ♦ vi negociar; (haggle) regatear; **into the ~** además, por añadidura; ~ **for** vi fus: **he got more than he ~ed for** le resultó peor de lo que esperaba

barge [bɑːdʒ] n barcaza; ~ **in** vi irrumpir; (interrupt: conversation) interrumpir

bark [bɑːk] n (of tree) corteza; (of dog) ladrido ♦ vi ladrar

barley ['bɑːlɪ] n cebada

barmaid ['bɑːmeɪd] n camarera

barman ['bɑːmən] n camarero, barman m

barn [bɑːn] n granero

barometer [bə'rɔmɪtə*] n barómetro

baron ['bærən] n barón m; (press ~ etc) magnate m; ~**ess** n baronesa

barracks ['bærəks] npl cuartel m

barrage ['bærɑːʒ] n (MIL) descarga, bombardeo; (dam) presa; (of criticism) lluvia, aluvión m

barrel ['bærəl] n barril m; (of gun) cañón m

barren ['bærən] adj estéril

barricade [bærɪ'keɪd] n barricada

barrier ['bærɪə*] n barrera

barring ['bɑːrɪŋ] prep excepto, salvo

barrister ['bærɪstə*] (BRIT) n abogado/a

barrow ['bærəu] n (cart) carretilla (de mano)

bartender ['bɑːtɛndə*] (US) n camarero, barman m

barter ['bɑːtə*] vt: **to ~ sth for sth** trocar algo por algo

base [beɪs] n base f ♦ vt: **to ~ sth on** basar or fundar algo en ♦ adj bajo, infame

baseball ['beɪsbɔːl] n béisbol m

basement ['beɪsmənt] n sótano

bases[1] ['beɪsiːz] npl of **basis**

bases[2] ['beɪsɪz] npl of **base**

bash [bæʃ] (inf) vt golpear

bashful ['bæʃful] adj tímido, vergonzoso

basic ['beɪsɪk] adj básico; ~**ally** adv fundamentalmente, en el fondo; (simply) sencillamente; ~**s** npl: **the ~s** los fundamentos

basil ['bæzl] n albahaca

basin ['beɪsn] n cuenco, tazón m; (GEO) cuenca; (also: wash~) lavabo

basis ['beɪsɪs] (pl **bases**) n base f; **on a part-time/trial ~** a tiempo parcial/a prueba

bask [bɑːsk] vi: **to ~ in the sun** tomar el sol

basket ['bɑːskɪt] n cesta, cesto; canasta; ~**ball** n baloncesto

Basque [bæsk] adj, n vasco/a m/f; ~ **Country** n Euskadi m, País m Vasco

bass [beɪs] n (MUS: instrument) bajo; (double ~) contrabajo; (singer) bajo

bassoon [bəˈsuːn] n fagot m

bastard [ˈbɑːstəd] n bastardo; (inf!) hijo de puta (!)

bat [bæt] n (ZOOL) murciélago; (for ball games) palo; (BRIT: for table tennis) pala ♦ vt: **he didn't ~ an eyelid** ni pestañeó

batch [bætʃ] n (of bread) hornada; (of letters etc) lote m

bated [ˈbeɪtɪd] adj: **with ~ breath** sin respirar

bath [bɑːθ, pl bɑːðz] n (action) baño; (~tub) baño (SP), bañera (SP), tina (AM) ♦ vt bañar; **to have a ~** bañarse, tomar un baño; see also **baths**

bathe [beɪð] vi bañarse ♦ vt (wound) lavar; **~r** n bañista m/f

bathing [ˈbeɪðɪŋ] n el bañarse; **~ costume** (US = **suit**) n traje m de baño

bath: **~robe** n (man's) batín m; (woman's) bata; **~room** n (cuarto de) baño; **~s** [bɑːðz] npl (also: swimming ~s) piscina; **~ towel** n toalla de baño

baton [ˈbætən] n (MUS) batuta; (ATHLETICS) testigo; (weapon) porra

batter [ˈbætə*] vt maltratar; (subj: rain etc) azotar ♦ n masa (para rebozar); **~ed** adj (hat, pan) estropeado

battery [ˈbætərɪ] n (AUT) batería; (of torch) pila

battle [ˈbætl] n batalla; (fig) lucha ♦ vi luchar; **~ship** n acorazado

bawl [bɔːl] vi chillar, gritar; (child) berrear

bay [beɪ] n (GEO) bahía; **B~ of Biscay** ≈ mar Cantábrico; **to hold sb at ~** mantener a alguien a raya; **~ leaf** n hoja de laurel

bay window n ventana sa lediza

bazaar [bəˈzɑː*] n bazar m; (fete) venta con fines benéficos

B. & B. n abbr (= bed and breakfast) cama y desayuno

BBC n abbr (= British Broadcasting Corporation) cadena de radio y televisión estatal británica

B.C. adv abbr (= before Christ) a. de C.

KEYWORD

be [biː] (pt **was, were**, pp **been**) aux vb 1 (with present participle: forming continuous tenses): **what are you doing?** ¿qué estás haciendo?, ¿qué haces?; **they're coming tomorrow** vienen mañana; **I've been waiting for you for hours** llevo horas esperándote

2 (with pp: forming passives) ser (but often replaced by active or reflective constructions); **to ~ murdered** ser asesinado; **the box had been opened** habían abierto la caja; **the thief was nowhere to ~ seen** no se veía al ladrón por ninguna parte

3 (in tag questions): **it was fun, wasn't it?** fue divertido, ¿no? or ¿verdad?; **he's good-**

looking, isn't he? es guapo, ¿no te parece?; **she's back again, is she?** entonces, ¿ha vuelto?

4 (+ to + infin): **the house is to ~ sold** (necessity) hay que vender la casa; (future) van a vender la casa; **he's not to open it** no tiene que abrirlo

♦ vb + complement 1 (with n or num complement, but see also 3, 4, 5 and impers vb below) ser; **he's a doctor** es médico; **2 and 2 are 4** 2 y 2 son 4

2 (with adj complement: expressing permanent or inherent quality) ser; (: expressing state seen as temporary or reversible) estar; **I'm English** soy inglés/esa; **she's tall/pretty** es alta/bonita; **he's young** es joven; **~ careful/good/quiet** ten cuidado/pórtate bien/cállate; **I'm tired** estoy cansado/a; **it's dirty** está sucio/a

3 (of health) estar; **how are you?** ¿cómo estás?; **he's very ill** está muy enfermo; **I'm better now** ya estoy mejor

4 (of age) tener; **how old are you?** ¿cuántos años tienes?; **I'm sixteen (years old)** tengo dieciséis años

5 (cost) costar; ser; **how much was the meal?** ¿cuánto fue or costó la comida?; **that'll ~ £5.75, please** son £5.75, por favor; **this shirt is £17** esta camisa cuesta £17

♦ vi 1 (exist, occur etc) existir, haber; **the best singer that ever was** el mejor cantante que existió jamás; **is there a God?** ¿hay un Dios?, ¿existe Dios?; **~ that as it may** sea como sea; **so ~ it** así sea

2 (referring to place) estar; **I won't ~ here tomorrow** no estaré aquí mañana

3 (referring to movement): **where have you been?** ¿dónde has estado?

♦ impers vb 1 (referring to time): **it's 5 o'clock** son las 5; **it's the 28th of April** estamos a 28 de abril

2 (referring to distance): **it's 10 km to the village** el pueblo está a 10 km

3 (referring to the weather): **it's too hot/cold** hace demasiado calor/frío; **it's windy today** hace viento hoy

4 (emphatic): **it's me** soy yo; **it was Maria who paid the bill** fue María la que pagó la cuenta

---

beach [biːtʃ] n playa ♦ vt varar

beacon [ˈbiːkən] n (lighthouse) faro; (marker) guía

bead [biːd] n cuenta; (of sweat etc) gota

beak [biːk] n pico

beaker [ˈbiːkə*] n vaso de plástico

beam [biːm] n (ARCH) viga, travesaño; (of light) rayo, haz m de luz ♦ vi brillar; (smile) sonreír

bean [biːn] n judía; **runner/broad ~**

habichuela/haba; **coffee ~** grano de café;
~sprouts *npl* brotes *mpl* de soja
bear [bɛə*] (*pt* **bore**, *pp* **borne**) *n* oso ♦ *vt*
(*weight etc*) llevar; (*cost*) pagar;
(*responsibility*) tener; (*endure*) soportar,
aguantar; (*children*) parir, tener; (*fruit*) dar
♦ *vi*: **to ~ right/left** torcer a la derecha/
izquierda; **~ out** *vt* (*suspicions*) corroborar,
confirmar; (*person*) dar la razón a; **~ up** *vi*
(*remain cheerful*) mantenerse animado
beard [bɪəd] *n* barba; **~ed** *adj* con barba,
barbudo
bearer ['bɛərə*] *n* portador(a) *m/f*
bearing ['bɛərɪŋ] *n* porte *m*,
comportamiento; (*connection*) relación *f*; **~s**
npl (*also:* **ball ~s**) cojinetes *mpl* a bolas; **to
take a ~** tomar marcaciones; **to find one's ~s**
orientarse
beast [biːst] *n* bestia; (*inf*) bruto, salvaje *m*;
~ly (*inf*) *adj* horrible
beat [biːt] (*pt* **beat**, *pp* **beaten**) *n* (*of heart*)
latido; (*MUS*) ritmo, compás *m*; (*of
policeman*) ronda ♦ *vt* pegar, golpear; (*eggs*)
batir; (*defeat: opponent*) vencer, derrotar;
(*: record*) sobrepasar ♦ *vi* (*heart*) latir; (*drum*)
redoblar; (*rain, wind*) azotar; **off the ~en
track** aislado; **to ~ it** (*inf*) largarse; **~ off** *vt*
rechazar; **~ up** *vt* (*attack*) dar una paliza a;
~ing *n* paliza
beautiful ['bjuːtɪful] *adj* precioso, hermoso,
bello; **~ly** *adv* maravillosamente
beauty ['bjuːtɪ] *n* belleza; **~ salon** *n* salón *m*
de belleza; **~ spot** *n* (*TOURISM*) lugar *m*
pintoresco
beaver ['biːvə*] *n* castor *m*
became [bɪ'keɪm] *pt of* **become**
because [bɪ'kɔz] *conj* porque; **~ of** debido a,
a causa de
beckon ['bɛkən] *vt* (*also:* **~ to**) llamar con
señas
become [bɪ'kʌm] (*irreg: like* **come**) *vt* (*suit*)
favorecer, sentar bien a ♦ *vi* (+ *n*) hacerse,
llegar a ser; (+ *adj*) ponerse, volverse; **to ~
fat** engordar
becoming [bɪ'kʌmɪŋ] *adj* (*behaviour*)
decoroso; (*clothes*) favorecedor/a
bed [bɛd] *n* cama; (*of flowers*) macizo; (*of
coal, clay*) capa; (*of river*) lecho; (*of sea*)
fondo; **to go to ~** acostarse; **~ and
breakfast** *n* (*place*) pensión *f*; (*terms*) cama
y desayuno; **~clothes** *npl* ropa de cama;
~ding *n* ropa de cama
bedraggled [bɪ'drægld] *adj* (*untidy: person*)
desastrado; (*clothes, hair*) desordenado
bed: **~ridden** *adj* postrado (en cama);
~room *n* dormitorio; **~side** *n*: **at the ~side
of** a la cabecera de; **~sit(ter)** (*BRIT*) *n* estudio
(*SP*), suite *m* (*AM*); **~spread** *n* cubrecama *m*,
colcha; **~time** *n* hora de acostarse

bee [biː] *n* abeja
beech [biːtʃ] *n* haya
beef [biːf] *n* carne *f* de vaca; **roast ~** rosbif *m*;
~burger *n* hamburguesa; **B~eater** *n*
alabardero de la Torre de Londres
beehive ['biːhaɪv] *n* colmena
beeline ['biːlaɪn] *n*: **to make a ~ for** ir
derecho a
been [biːn] *pp of* **be**
beer [bɪə*] *n* cerveza
beet [biːt] (*US*) *n* (*also:* **red ~**) remolacha
beetle ['biːtl] *n* escarabajo
beetroot ['biːtruːt] (*BRIT*) *n* remolacha
before [bɪ'fɔː*] *prep* (*of time*) antes de; (*of
space*) delante de ♦ *conj* antes (de) que
♦ *adv* antes, anteriormente; delante,
adelante; **~ going** antes de marcharse; **~ she
goes** antes de que se vaya; **the week ~** la
semana anterior; **I've never seen it ~** no lo he
visto nunca; **~hand** *adv* de antemano, con
anticipación
beg [bɛg] *vi* pedir limosna ♦ *vt* pedir, rogar;
(*entreat*) suplicar; **to ~ sb to do sth** rogar a
uno que haga algo; *see also* **pardon**
began [bɪ'gæn] *pt of* **begin**
beggar ['bɛgə*] *n* mendigo/a
begin [bɪ'gɪn] (*pt* **began**, *pp* **begun**) *vt*, *vi*
empezar, comenzar; **to ~ doing** *or* **to do sth**
empezar a hacer algo; **~ner** *n* principiante
m/f; **~ning** *n* principio, comienzo
begun [bɪ'gʌn] *pp of* **begin**
behalf [bɪ'hɑːf] *n*: **on ~ of** en nombre de, por;
(*for benefit of*) en beneficio de; **on my/his ~**
por mí/él
behave [bɪ'heɪv] *vi* (*person*) portarse,
comportarse; (*well: also:* **~ o.s.**) portarse
bien; **behaviour** (*US* **behavior**) *n*
comportamiento, conducta
behind [bɪ'haɪnd] *prep* detrás de;
(*supporting*): **to be ~ sb** apoyar a alguien
♦ *adv* detrás, por detrás, atrás ♦ *n* trasero; **to
be ~ (schedule)** ir retrasado; **~ the scenes**
(*fig*) entre bastidores
behold [bɪ'həuld] (*irreg: like* **hold**) *vt*
contemplar
beige [beɪʒ] *adj* color beige
Beijing ['beɪ'dʒɪŋ] *n* Pekín *m*
being ['biːɪŋ] *n* ser *m*; (*existence*): **in ~**
existente; **to come into ~** aparecer
Beirut [beɪ'ruːt] *n* Beirut *m*
Belarus [bɛlə'rus] *n* Bielorrusia
belated [bɪ'leɪtɪd] *adj* atrasado, tardío
belch [bɛltʃ] *vi* eructar ♦ *vt* (*gen:* **~ out:** *smoke
etc*) arrojar
Belgian ['bɛldʒən] *adj*, *n* belga *m/f*
Belgium ['bɛldʒəm] *n* Bélgica
belief [bɪ'liːf] *n* opinión *f*; (*faith*) fe *f*
believe [bɪ'liːv] *vt*, *vi* creer; **to ~ in** creer en;
~r *n* partidario/a; (*REL*) creyente *m/f*, fiel *m/f*

belittle |bɪ'lɪtl| vt quitar importancia a
bell |bel| n campana; (small) campanilla; (on door) timbre m
belligerent |bɪ'lɪdʒərənt| adj agresivo
bellow |'beləu| vi bramar; (person) rugir
belly |'belɪ| n barriga, panza
belong |bɪ'lɔŋ| vi: **to ~ to** pertenecer a; (club etc) ser socio de; **this book ~s here** este libro va aquí; **~ings** npl pertenencias fpl
beloved |bɪ'lʌvɪd| adj querido/a
below |bɪ'ləu| prep bajo, debajo de; (less than) inferior a ♦ adv abajo, (por) debajo; **see ~** véase más abajo
belt |belt| n cinturón m; (TECH) correa, cinta ♦ vt (thrash) pegar con correa; **~way** (US) n (AUT) carretera de circunvalación
bench |bentʃ| n banco; (BRIT: POL): **the Government/Opposition ~es** (los asientos de) los miembros del Gobierno/de la Oposición; **the B~** (LAW: judges) magistratura
bend |bend| (pt, pp **bent**) vt doblar ♦ vi inclinarse ♦ n (BRIT: in road, river) curva; (in pipe) codo; **~ down** vi inclinarse, doblarse; **~ over** vi inclinarse
beneath |bɪ'ni:θ| prep bajo, debajo de; (unworthy of) indigno de ♦ adv abajo, (por) debajo
benefactor |'benɪfæktə*| n bienhechor m
beneficial |benɪ'fɪʃəl| adj beneficioso
benefit |'benɪfɪt| n beneficio; (allowance of money) subsidio ♦ vt beneficiar ♦ vi: **he'll ~ from it** le sacará provecho
benevolent |bɪ'nevələnt| adj (person) benévolo
benign |bɪ'naɪn| adj benigno; (smile) afable
bent |bent| pt, pp of **bend** ♦ n inclinación f ♦ adj: **to be ~ on** estar empeñado en
bequest |bɪ'kwest| n legado
bereaved |bɪ'ri:vd| npl: **the ~** los íntimos de una persona afligidos por su muerte
beret |'bereɪ| n boina
Berlin |bə:'lɪn| n Berlín
berm |bə:m| (US) n (AUT) arcén m
Bermuda |bə:'mju:də| n las Bermudas
berry |'berɪ| n baya
berserk |bə'sə:k| adj: **to go ~** perder los estribos
berth |bə:θ| n (bed) litera; (cabin) camarote m; (for ship) amarradero ♦ vi atracar, amarrar
beseech |bɪ'si:tʃ| (pt, pp **besought**) vt suplicar
beset |bɪ'set| (pt, pp **beset**) vt (person) acosar
beside |bɪ'saɪd| prep junto a, al lado de; **to be ~ o.s. with anger** estar fuera de sí; **that's ~ the point** eso no tiene nada que ver; **~s** adv además ♦ prep además de
besiege |bɪ'si:dʒ| vt sitiar; (fig) asediar
best |best| adj (el/la) mejor ♦ adv (lo) mejor; **the ~ part of** (quantity) la mayor parte de; **at ~** en el mejor de los casos; **to make the ~ of sth** sacar el mejor partido de algo; **to do one's ~** hacer todo lo posible; **to the ~ of my knowledge** que yo sepa; **to the ~ of my ability** como mejor pueda; **~-before date** n fecha de consumo preferente; **~ man** n padrino de boda
bestow |bɪ'stəu| vt (title) otorgar
bestseller |'best'selə*| n éxito de librería, bestseller m
bet |bet| (pt, pp **bet** or **betted**) n apuesta ♦ vt: **to ~ money on** apostar dinero por; **to ~ sb sth** apostar algo a uno ♦ vi apostar
betray |bɪ'treɪ| vt traicionar; (trust) faltar a; **~al** n traición f
better |'betə*| adj, adv mejor ♦ vt superar ♦ n: **to get the ~ of sb** quedar por encima de alguien; **you had ~ do it** más vale que lo hagas; **he thought ~ of it** cambió de parecer; **to get ~** (MED) mejorar(se); **~ off** adj mejor; (wealthier) más acomodado
betting |'betɪŋ| n juego, el apostar; **~ shop** (BRIT) n agencia de apuestas
between |bɪ'twi:n| prep entre ♦ adv (time) mientras tanto; (place) en medio
beverage |'bevərɪdʒ| n bebida
beware |bɪ'weə*| vi: **to ~ (of)** tener cuidado (con); **"~ of the dog"** "perro peligroso"
bewildered |bɪ'wɪldəd| adj aturdido, perplejo
beyond |bɪ'jɔnd| prep más allá de; (past: understanding) fuera de; (after: date) después de, más allá de; (above) superior a ♦ adv (in space) más allá; (in time) posteriormente; **~ doubt** fuera de toda duda; **~ repair** irreparable
bias |'baɪəs| n (prejudice) prejuicio, pasión f; (preference) predisposición f; **~(s)ed** adj parcial
bib |bɪb| n babero
Bible |'baɪbl| n Biblia
bicarbonate of soda |baɪ'kɑ:bənɪt-| n bicarbonato sódico
bicker |'bɪkə*| vi pelearse
bicycle |'baɪsɪkl| n bicicleta
bid |bɪd| (pt **bade** or **bid**, pp **bidden** or **bid**) n oferta, postura; (in tender) licitación f; (attempt) tentativa, conato ♦ vi hacer una oferta ♦ vt (offer) ofrecer; **to ~ sb good day** dar a uno los buenos días; **~der** n: **the highest ~der** el mejor postor; **~ding** n (at auction) ofertas fpl
bide |baɪd| vt: **to ~ one's time** esperar el momento adecuado
bifocals |baɪ'fəuklz| npl gafas fpl (SP) or anteojos mpl (AM) bifocales
big |bɪg| adj grande; (brother, sister) mayor
bigheaded |'bɪg'hedɪd| adj engreído
bigot |'bɪgət| n fanático/a, intolerante m/f;

~ed adj fanático, intolerante; **~ry** n fanatismo, intolerancia

big top n (at circus) carpa

bike |baɪk| n bici f

bikini |bɪˈkiːnɪ| n bikini m

bilingual |baɪˈlɪŋgwəl| adj bilingüe

bill |bɪl| n cuenta; (invoice) factura; (POL) proyecto de ley, (US: banknote) billete m, (of bird) pico; (of show) programa m; "**post no ~s**" "prohibido fijar carteles"; **to fit** or **fill the ~** (fig) cumplir con los requisitos; **~board** (US) n cartelera

billet |ˈbɪlɪt| n alojamiento

billfold |ˈbɪlfəʊld| (US) n cartera

billiards |ˈbɪljədz| n billar m

billion |ˈbɪljən| n (BRIT) billón m (millón de millones); (US) mil millones mpl

bimbo |ˈbɪmbəʊ| (inf) n tía buena sin seso

bin |bɪn| n (for rubbish) cubo (SP) or bote m (AM) de la basura; (container) recipiente m

bind |baɪnd| (pt, pp **bound**) vt atar; (book) encuadernar; (oblige) obligar ♦ n (inf: nuisance) lata; **~ing** adj (contract) obligatorio

binge |bɪndʒ| (inf) n: **to go on a ~** ir de juerga

bingo |ˈbɪngəʊ| n bingo m

binoculars |bɪˈnɒkjʊləz| npl prismáticos mpl

bio... |baɪə| prefix **~chemistry** n bioquímica; **~degradable** |baɪəʊdɪˈgreɪdəbl| adj biodegradable; **~graphy** |baɪˈɒgrəfɪ| n biografía; **~logical** |baɪəˈlɒdʒɪkl| adj biológico; **~logy** |baɪˈɒlədʒɪ| n biología

birch |bɜːtʃ| n (tree) abedul m

bird |bɜːd| n ave f, pájaro; (BRIT: inf: girl) chica; **~'s eye view** n (aerial view) vista de pájaro; (overview) visión f de conjunto; **~ watcher** n ornitólogo/a

Biro ® |ˈbaɪrəʊ| n bolígrafo

birth |bɜːθ| n nacimiento; **to give ~ to** parir, dar a luz; **~ certificate** n partida de nacimiento; **~ control** n (policy) control m de natalidad; (methods) métodos mpl anticonceptivos; **~day** n cumpleaños m inv ♦ cpd (cake, card etc) de cumpleaños; **~place** n lugar m de nacimiento; **~ rate** n (tasa de) natalidad f

biscuit |ˈbɪskɪt| (BRIT) n galleta, bizcocho (AM)

bisect |baɪˈsekt| vt bisecar

bishop |ˈbɪʃəp| n obispo; (CHESS) alfil m

bit |bɪt| pt of **bite** ♦ n trozo, pedazo, pedacito; (COMPUT) bit m, bitio; (for horse) freno, bocado; **a ~ of** un poco de; **a ~ mad** un poco loco; **~ by ~** poco a poco

bitch |bɪtʃ| n perra; (inf!: woman) zorra (!)

bite |baɪt| (pt **bit**, pp **bitten**) vt, vi morder; (insect etc) picar ♦ n (insect ~) picadura; (mouthful) bocado; **to ~ one's nails** comerse las uñas; **let's have a ~ (to eat)** (inf) vamos a comer algo

bitter |ˈbɪtə*| adj amargo; (wind) cortante, penetrante; (battle) encarnizado ♦ n (BRIT: beer) cerveza típica británica a base de lúpulos; **~ness** n lo amargo, amargura; (anger) rencor m

bizarre |bɪˈzɑː*| adj raro, extraño

black |blæk| adj negro; (tea, coffee) solo ♦ n color m negro, (person). **B~** negro/a ♦ vi (BRIT: INDUSTRY) boicotear; **to give sb a ~ eye** ponerle a uno el ojo morado; **~ and blue** (bruised) amoratado; **to be in the ~** (bank account) estar en números negros; **~berry** n zarzamora; **~bird** n mirlo; **~board** n pizarra; **~ coffee** n café m solo; **~currant** n grosella negra; **~en** vt (fig) desacreditar; **~ ice** n hielo invisible en la carretera; **~leg** (BRIT) n esquirol m, rompehuelgas m inv; **~list** n lista negra; **~mail** n chantaje m ♦ vt chantajear; **~ market** n mercado negro; **~out** n (MIL) oscurecimiento; (power cut) apagón m; (TV, RADIO) interrupción f de programas; (faint) desvanecimiento; **B~ Sea** n: **the B~ Sea** el Mar Negro; **~ sheep** n (fig) oveja negra; **~smith** n herrero; **~ spot** n (AUT) lugar m peligroso; (for unemployment etc) punto negro

bladder |ˈblædə*| n vejiga

blade |bleɪd| n hoja; (of propeller) paleta; **a ~ of grass** una brizna de hierba

blame |bleɪm| n culpa ♦ vt: **to ~ sb for sth** echar a uno la culpa de algo; **to be to ~** tener la culpa de

bland |blænd| adj (music, taste) soso

blank |blæŋk| adj en blanco; (look) sin expresión ♦ n (of memory): **my mind is a ~** no puedo recordar nada; (on form) blanco, espacio en blanco; (cartridge) cartucho sin bala or de fogueo; **~ cheque** n cheque m en blanco

blanket |ˈblæŋkɪt| n manta (SP), cobija (AM); (of snow) capa; (of fog) manto

blare |bleə*| vi sonar estrepitosamente

blasé |ˈblɑːzeɪ| adj hastiado

blast |blɑːst| n (of wind) ráfaga, soplo; (of explosive) explosión f ♦ vt (blow up) volar; **~-off** n (SPACE) lanzamiento

blatant |ˈbleɪtənt| adj descarado

blaze |bleɪz| n (fire) fuego; (: of glory) despliegue m; (: of colour) esplendor m ♦ vi arder en llamas; (fig) brillar ♦ vt: **to ~ a trail** (fig) abrir (un) camino; **in a ~ of publicity** con gran publicidad

blazer |ˈbleɪzə*| n chaqueta de uniforme de colegial o de socio de club

bleach |bliːtʃ| n (also: household ~) lejía ♦ vt blanquear; **~ed** adj (hair) teñido (de rubio); **~ers** (US) npl (SPORT) gradas fpl al sol

bleak |bliːk| adj (countryside) desierto; (prospect) poco prometedor(a); (weather) crudo; (*smile*) triste

bleat [bli:t] *vi* balar

bleed [bli:d] (*pt, pp* **bled**) *vt, vi* sangrar; **my nose is ~ing** me está sangrando la nariz

bleeper ['bli:pə*] *n* busca *m*

blemish ['blemɪʃ] *n* marca, mancha; (*on reputation*) tacha

blend [blend] *n* mezcla ♦ *vt* mezclar; (*colours etc*) combinar, mezclar ♦ *vi* (*colours etc: also:* ~ *in*) combinarse, mezclarse

bless [bles] (*pt, pp* **blessed** *or* **blest**) *vt* bendecir; ~ **you!** (*after sneeze*) ¡Jesús!; **~ing** *n* (*approval*) aprobación *f*; (*godsend*) don *m* del cielo, bendición *f*; (*advantage*) beneficio, ventaja

blew [blu:] *pt of* **blow**

blind [blaɪnd] *adj* ciego; (*fig*): ~ (**to**) ciego (a) ♦ *n* (*for window*) persiana ♦ *vt* cegar; (*dazzle*) deslumbrar; (*deceive*): **to ~ sb to ...** cegar a uno a ...; **the ~** *npl* los ciegos; ~ **alley** *n* callejón *m* sin salida; ~ **corner** (*BRIT*) *n* esquina escondida; **~fold** *n* venda ♦ *adv* con los ojos vendados ♦ *vt* vendar los ojos a; **~ly** *adv* a ciegas, ciegamente; **~ness** *n* ceguera; ~ **spot** (*AUT*) ángulo ciego

blink [blɪŋk] *vi* parpadear, pestañear; (*light*) oscilar; **~ers** *npl* anteojeras *fpl*

bliss [blɪs] *n* felicidad *f*

blister ['blɪstə*] *n* ampolla ♦ *vi* (*paint*) ampollarse

blizzard ['blɪzəd] *n* ventisca

bloated ['bləʊtɪd] *adj* hinchado; (*person: full*) ahíto

blob [blɒb] *n* (*drop*) gota; (*indistinct object*) bulto

bloc [blɒk] *n* (*POL*) bloque *m*

block [blɒk] *n* bloque *m*; (*in pipes*) obstáculo; (*of buildings*) manzana (*SP*), cuadra (*AM*) ♦ *vt* obstruir, cerrar; (*progress*) estorbar; ~ **of flats** (*BRIT*) bloque *m* de pisos; **mental** ~ bloqueo mental; **~ade** [-'keɪd] *n* bloqueo ♦ *vt* bloquear; **~age** *n* estorbo, obstrucción *f*; **~buster** *n* (*book*) bestseller *m*; (*film*) éxito de público; ~ **letters** *npl* letras *fpl* de molde

bloke [bləʊk] (*BRIT: inf*) *n* tipo, tío

blond(e) [blɒnd] *adj, n* rubio/a *m/f*

blood [blʌd] *n* sangre *f*; ~ **donor** *n* donante *m/f* de sangre; ~ **group** *n* grupo sanguíneo; **~hound** *n* sabueso; ~ **poisoning** *n* envenenamiento de la sangre; ~ **pressure** *n* presión *f* sanguínea; **~shed** *n* derramamiento de sangre; **~shot** *adj* inyectado en sangre; **~stream** *n* corriente *f* sanguínea; ~ **test** *n* análisis *m inv* de sangre; **~thirsty** *adj* sanguinario; ~ **vessel** *n* vaso sanguíneo; **~y** *adj* sangriento; (*nose etc*) lleno de sangre; (*BRIT: inf!*): **this ~y...** este condenado *o* puñetero ... (*!*) ♦ *adv*: **~y strong/good** (*BRIT: inf!*) terriblemente fuerte/bueno; **~y-minded**

(*BRIT: inf*) *adj* puñetero (*!*)

bloom [blu:m] *n* flor *f* ♦ *vi* florecer

blossom ['blɒsəm] *n* flor *f* ♦ *vi* (*also fig*) florecer

blot [blɒt] *n* borrón *m*; (*fig*) mancha ♦ *vt* (*stain*) manchar; ~ **out** *vt* (*view*) tapar

blotchy ['blɒtʃi] *adj* (*complexion*) lleno de manchas

blotting paper ['blɒtɪŋ-] *n* papel *m* secante

blouse [blauz] *n* blusa

blow [bləʊ] (*pt* **blew**, *pp* **blown**) *n* golpe *m*; (*with sword*) espadazo ♦ *vi* soplar; (*dust, sand etc*) volar; (*fuse*) fundirse ♦ *vt* (*subj: wind*) llevarse; (*fuse*) quemar; (*instrument*) tocar; **to ~ one's nose** sonarse; ~ **away** *vt* llevarse, arrancar; ~ **down** *vt* derribar; ~ **off** *vt* arrebatar; ~ **out** *vi* apagarse; ~ **over** *vi* amainar; ~ **up** *vi* estallar ♦ *vt* volar; (*tyre*) inflar; (*PHOT*) ampliar; **~-dry** *n* moldeado (con secador); **~lamp** (*BRIT*) *n* soplete *m*, lámpara de soldar; **~-out** *n* (*of tyre*) pinchazo; **~torch** *n* = **~lamp**

blue [blu:] *adj* azul; (*depressed*) deprimido; ~ **film/joke** película/chiste *m* verde; **out of the** ~ (*fig*) de repente; **~bell** *n* campanilla, campánula azul; **~bottle** *n* moscarda, mosca azul; **~print** *n* (*fig*) anteproyecto

bluff [blʌf] *vi* tirarse un farol, farolear ♦ *n* farol *m*; **to call sb's ~** coger a uno la palabra

blunder ['blʌndə*] *n* patinazo, metedura de pata ♦ *vi* cometer un error, meter la pata

blunt [blʌnt] *adj* (*pencil*) despuntado; (*knife*) desafilado, romo; (*person*) franco, directo

blur [blə:*] *n* (*shape*): **to become a ~** hacerse borroso ♦ *vt* (*vision*) enturbiar; (*distinction*) borrar

blush [blʌʃ] *vi* ruborizarse, ponerse colorado ♦ *n* rubor *m*

blustery ['blʌstərɪ] *adj* (*weather*) tempestuoso, tormentoso

boar [bɔ:*] *n* verraco, cerdo

board [bɔ:d] *n* (*card~*) cartón *m*; (*wooden*) tabla, tablero; (*on wall*) tablón *m*; (*for chess etc*) tablero; (*committee*) junta, consejo; (*in firm*) mesa *or* junta directiva; (*NAUT, AVIAT*): **on ~** a bordo ♦ *vt* (*ship*) embarcarse en; (*train*) subir a; **full ~** (*BRIT*) pensión completa; **half ~** (*BRIT*) media pensión; **to go by the ~** (*fig*) ser abandonado *or* olvidado; ~ **up** *vt* (*door*) tapiar; **~er** *n* (*SCOL*) interno/a; **~ing card** (*BRIT*) *n* tarjeta de embarque; **~ing house** *n* casa de huéspedes; **~ing pass** (*US*) *n* = **~ing card**; **~ing school** *n* internado; ~ **room** *n* sala de juntas

boast [bəʊst] *vi*: **to ~** (**about** *or* **of**) alardear (de)

boat [bəʊt] *n* barco, buque *m*; (*small*) barca, bote *m*

bob [bɔb] vi (also: ~ up and down) menearse, balancearse; ~ up vi (re)aparecer de repente
bobby ['bɔbɪ] (BRIT: inf) n poli m
bobsleigh ['bɔbsleɪ] n bob m
bode [bəud] vi: to ~ well/ill (for) ser prometedor/poco prometedor (para)
bodily ['bɔdɪlɪ] adj corporal ♦ adv (move: person) en peso
body ['bɔdɪ] n cuerpo; (corpse) cadáver m; (of car) caja, carrocería; (fig: group) grupo; (: organization) organismo; ~-**building** n culturismo; ~**guard** n guardaespaldas m inv; ~**work** n carrocería
bog [bɔg] n pantano, ciénaga ♦ vt: to get ~ged down (fig) empantanarse, atascarse
bogus ['bəugəs] adj falso, fraudulento
boil [bɔɪl] vt (water) hervir; (eggs) pasar por agua, cocer ♦ vi hervir; (fig: with anger) estar furioso; (: with heat) asfixiarse ♦ n (MED) furúnculo, divieso; **to come to the ~, to come to a ~** (US) comenzar a hervir; **to ~ down to** (fig) reducirse a; ~ **over** vi salirse, rebosar; (anger etc) llegar al colmo; ~**ed egg** n huevo cocido (SP) or pasado (AM); ~**ed potatoes** npl patatas fpl (SP) or papas fpl (AM) hervidas; ~**er** n caldera; ~**er suit** (BRIT) n mono; ~**ing point** n punto de ebullición
boisterous ['bɔɪstərəs] adj (noisy) bullicioso; (excitable) exuberante; (crowd) tumultuoso
bold [bəuld] adj valiente, audaz; (pej) descarado; (colour) llamativo
Bolivia [bə'lɪvɪə] n Bolivia; ~**n** adj, n boliviano/a m/f
bollard ['bɔləd] (BRIT) n (AUT) poste m
bolt [bəult] n (lock) cerrojo; (with nut) perno, tornillo ♦ adv: ~ **upright** rígido, erguido ♦ vt (door) echar el cerrojo a; (also: ~ together) sujetar con tornillos; (food) engullir ♦ vi fugarse; (horse) desbocarse
bomb [bɔm] n bomba ♦ vt bombardear; ~ **disposal** n desmontaje m de explosivos; ~**er** n (AVIAT) bombardero; ~**shell** n (fig) bomba
bond [bɔnd] n (promise) fianza; (FINANCE) bono; (link) vínculo, lazo; (COMM): **in ~** en depósito bajo fianza
bondage ['bɔndɪdʒ] n esclavitud f
bone [bəun] n hueso; (of fish) espina ♦ vt deshuesar; quitar las espinas a; ~ **idle** adj gandul; ~ **marrow** n médula
bonfire ['bɔnfaɪə*] n hoguera, fogata
bonnet ['bɔnɪt] n gorra; (BRIT: of car) capó m
bonus ['bəunəs] n (payment) paga extraordinaria, plus m; (fig) bendición f
bony ['bəunɪ] adj (arm, face) huesudo; (MED: tissue) óseo; (meat) lleno de huesos; (fish) lleno de espinas
boo [buː] excl ¡uh! ♦ vt abuchear, rechiflar
booby trap ['buːbɪ-] n trampa explosiva

book [buk] n libro; (of tickets) taco; (of stamps etc) librito ♦ vt (ticket) sacar; (seat, room) reservar; ~**s** npl (COMM) cuentas fpl, contabilidad f; ~**case** n librería, estante m para libros; ~**ing office** n (BRIT: RAIL) despacho de billetes (SP) or boletos (AM); (THEATRE) taquilla (SP), boletería (AM); ~-**keeping** n contabilidad f; ~**let** n folleto; ~**maker** n corredor m de apuestas; ~**seller** n librero; ~**shop**, ~ **store** n librería
boom [buːm] n (noise) trueno, estampido; (in prices etc) alza rápida; (ECON: in population) boom m ♦ vi (cannon) hacer gran estruendo, retumbar; (ECON) estar en alza
boon [buːn] n favor m, beneficio
boost [buːst] n estímulo, empuje m ♦ vt estimular, empujar; ~**er** n (MED) reinyección f
boot [buːt] n bota; (BRIT: of car) maleta, maletero ♦ vt (COMPUT) arrancar; **to ~** (in addition) además, por añadidura
booth [buːð] n (telephone ~, voting ~) cabina
booze [buːz] (inf) n bebida
border ['bɔːdə*] n borde m, margen m; (of a country) frontera; (for flowers) arriate m ♦ vt (road) bordear; (another country: also: ~ on) lindar con; B~**s** n: **the B~s** región fronteriza entre Escocia e Inglaterra; ~ **on** vt fus (insanity etc) rayar en; ~**line** n: **on the ~line** en el límite; ~**line case** n caso dudoso
bore [bɔː*] pt of bear ♦ vt (hole) hacer un agujero en; (well) perforar; (person) aburrir ♦ n (person) pelmazo, pesado; (of gun) calibre m; **to be ~d** estar aburrido; ~**dom** n aburrimiento
boring ['bɔːrɪŋ] adj aburrido
born [bɔːn] adj: **to be ~** nacer; **I was ~ in 1960** nací en 1960
borne [bɔːn] pp of bear
borough ['bʌrə] n municipio
borrow ['bɔrəu] vt: **to ~ sth (from sb)** tomar algo prestado (a alguien)
Bosnia(-Herzegovina) ['bɔːsnɪə(hɜːzə'gəuvɪːnə)] n Bosnia (-Herzegovina)
bosom ['buzəm] n pecho
boss [bɔs] n jefe m ♦ vt (also: ~ about or around) mangonear; ~**y** adj mandón/ona
bosun ['bəusn] n contramaestre m
botany ['bɔtənɪ] n botánica
botch [bɔtʃ] vt (also: ~ up) arruinar, estropear
both [bəuθ] adj, pron ambos/as, los/las dos; ~ **of us went, we ~ went** fuimos los dos, ambos fuimos ♦ adv: ~ **A and B** tanto A como B
bother ['bɔðə*] vt (worry) preocupar; (disturb) molestar, fastidiar ♦ vi (also: ~ o.s.) molestarse ♦ n (trouble) dificultad f; (nuisance) molestia, lata; **to ~ doing** tomarse la molestia de hacer

bottle ['bɔtl] n botella; (small) frasco; (baby's) biberón m ♦ vt embotellar; ~ **up** vt suprimir; ~ **bank** n contenedor m de vidrio; ~**neck** n (AUT) embotellamiento; (in supply) obstáculo; ~-**opener** n abrebotellas m inv

bottom ['bɔtəm] n (of box, sea) fondo; (buttocks) trasero, culo; (of page) pie m; (of list) final m; (of class) último/a ♦ adj (lowest) más bajo; (last) último

bough [bau] n rama

bought [bɔːt] pt, pp of **buy**

boulder ['bəuldə*] n canto rodado

bounce [bauns] vi (ball) (re)botar; (cheque) ser rechazado ♦ vt hacer (re)botar ♦ n (rebound) (re)bote m; ~**r** (inf) n gorila m (que echa a los alborotadores de un bar, club etc)

bound [baund] pt, pp of **bind** ♦ n (leap) salto; (gen pl: limit) límite m ♦ vi (leap) saltar ♦ vt (border) rodear ♦ adj: ~ **by** rodeado de; **to be ~ to do sth** (obliged) tener el deber de hacer algo; **he's ~ to come** es seguro que vendrá; **out of ~s** prohibido el paso; ~ **for** con destino a

boundary ['baundrɪ] n límite m

bouquet ['bukeɪ] n (of flowers) ramo

bourgeois ['buəʒwɑː] adj burgués/esa m/f

bout [baut] n (of malaria etc) ataque m; (of activity) período; (BOXING etc) combate m, encuentro

bow¹ [bəu] n (knot) lazo; (weapon, MUS) arco

bow² [bau] n (of the head) reverencia; (NAUT: also: ~**s**) proa ♦ vi inclinarse, hacer una reverencia; (yield): **to ~ to** or **before** ceder ante, someterse a

bowels [bauəlz] npl intestinos mpl, vientre m; (fig) entrañas fpl

bowl [bəul] n tazón m, cuenco; (ball) bola ♦ vi (CRICKET) arrojar la pelota; see also **bowls**

bow-legged ['bəu'lɛgɪd] adj estevado

bowler ['bəulə*] n (CRICKET) lanzador m (de la pelota); (BRIT: also: ~ **hat**) hongo, bombín m

bowling ['bəulɪŋ] n (game) bochas fpl, bolos mpl; ~ **alley** n bolera; ~ **green** n pista para bochas

bowls [bəulz] n juego de las bochas, bolos mpl

bow tie ['bəu-] n corbata de lazo, pajarita

box [bɔks] n (also: cardboard ~) caja, cajón m; (THEATRE) palco ♦ vt encajonar ♦ vi (SPORT) boxear; ~**er** ['bɔksə*] n (person) boxeador m; ~**ing** ['bɔksɪŋ] n (SPORT) boxeo; **B~ing Day** (BRIT) n día en que se dan los aguinaldos, 26 de diciembre; ~**ing gloves** npl guantes mpl de boxeo; ~**ing ring** n ring m, cuadrilátero; ~ **office** n taquilla (SP), boletería (AM); ~**room** n trastero

boy [bɔɪ] n (young) niño; (older) muchacho, chico; (son) hijo

boycott ['bɔɪkɔt] n boicot m ♦ vt boicotear

boyfriend ['bɔɪfrɛnd] n novio

boyish ['bɔɪʃ] adj juvenil; (girl) con aspecto de muchacho

B.R. n abbr (formerly = British Rail) ≈ RENFE f (SP)

bra [brɑː] n sostén m, sujetador m

brace [breɪs] n (BRIT: also: ~**s**: on teeth) corrector m, aparato; (tool) berbiquí m ♦ vt (knees, shoulders) tensionar; ~**s** npl (BRIT) tirantes mpl; **to ~ o.s.** (fig) prepararse

bracelet ['breɪslɪt] n pulsera, brazalete m

bracing ['breɪsɪŋ] adj vigorizante, tónico

bracket ['brækɪt] n (TECH) soporte m, puntal m; (group) clase f, categoría; (also: **brace ~**) soporte m, abrazadera; (also: **round ~**) paréntesis m inv; (also: **square ~**) corchete m ♦ vt (word etc) poner entre paréntesis

brag [bræg] vi jactarse

braid [breɪd] n (trimming) galón m; (of hair) trenza

brain [breɪn] n cerebro; ~**s** npl sesos mpl; **she's got ~s** es muy lista; ~**wash** vt lavar el cerebro; ~**wave** n idea luminosa; ~**y** adj muy inteligente

braise [breɪz] vt cocer a fuego lento

brake [breɪk] n (on vehicle) freno ♦ vi frenar; ~ **light** n luz f de frenado

bran [bræn] n salvado

branch [brɑːntʃ] n rama; (COMM) sucursal f; ~ **out** vi (fig) extenderse

brand [brænd] n marca; (fig: type) tipo ♦ vt (cattle) marcar con hierro candente; ~-**new** adj flamante, completamente nuevo

brandy ['brændɪ] n coñac m

brash [bræʃ] adj (forward) descarado

brass [brɑːs] n latón m; **the ~** (MUS) los cobres; ~ **band** n banda de metal

brat [bræt] (pej) n mocoso/a

brave [breɪv] adj valiente, valeroso ♦ vt (face up to) desafiar; ~**ry** n valor m, valentía

brawl [brɔːl] n pelea, reyerta

brazen ['breɪzn] adj descarado, cínico ♦ vt: **to ~ it out** echarle cara

Brazil [brə'zɪl] n (el) Brasil; ~**ian** adj, n brasileño/a m/f

breach [briːtʃ] vt abrir brecha en ♦ n (gap) brecha; (breaking): ~ **of contract** infracción f de contrato; ~ **of the peace** perturbación f del órden público

bread [brɛd] n pan m; ~ **and butter** n pan con mantequilla; (fig) pan (de cada día); ~**bin** n panera; ~**crumbs** npl migajas fpl; (CULIN) pan rallado; ~**line** n: **on the ~line** en la miseria

breadth [brɛtθ] n anchura; (fig) amplitud f

breadwinner ['brɛdwɪnə*] n sustento m de la familia

break [breɪk] (pt **broke**, pp **broken**) vt romper;

(*promise*) faltar a; (*law*) violar, infringir; (*record*) batir ♦ vi romperse, quebrarse; (*storm*) estallar; (*weather*) cambiar; (*dawn*) despuntar; (*news etc*) darse a conocer ♦ n (*gap*) abertura; (*fracture*) fractura; (*time*) intervalo; (: *at school*) (período de) recreo; (*chance*) oportunidad f; **to ~ the news to sb** comunicar la noticia a uno; **~ down** vt (*figures, data*) analizar, descomponer ♦ vi (*machine*) averiarse; (*AUT*) averiarse; (*person*) romper a llorar; (*talks*) fracasar; **~ even** vi cubrir los gastos; **~ free** or **loose** vi escaparse; **~ in** vt (*horse etc*) domar ♦ vi (*burglar*) forzar una entrada; (*interrupt*) interrumpir; **~ into** vt fus (*house*) forzar; **~ off** vi (*speaker*) pararse, detenerse; (*branch*) partir; **~ open** vt (*door etc*) abrir por la fuerza, forzar; **~ out** vi estallar; (*prisoner*) escaparse; **to ~ out in spots** salirle a uno granos; **~ up** vi (*ship*) hacerse pedazos; (*crowd, meeting*) disolverse; (*marriage*) deshacerse; (*SCOL*) terminar (el curso) ♦ vt (*rocks etc*) partir; (*journey*) partir; (*fight etc*) acabar con; **~age** n rotura; **~down** n (*AUT*) avería; (*in communications*) interrupción f; (*MED: also: nervous ~down*) colapso, crisis f nerviosa; (*of marriage, talks*) fracaso; (*of statistics*) análisis m inv; **~down van** (*BRIT*) n (camión m) grúa; **~er** n (ola) rompiente f

breakfast ['brɛkfəst] n desayuno

break: **~-in** n robo con allanamiento de morada; **~ing and entering** n (*LAW*) violación f de domicilio, allanamiento de morada; **~through** n (*also fig*) avance m; **~water** n rompeolas m inv

breast [brɛst] n (*of woman*) pecho, seno; (*chest*) pecho; (*of bird*) pechuga; **~-feed** (*irreg: like* feed) vt, vi amamantar, criar a los pechos; **~-stroke** n braza (de pecho)

breath [brɛθ] n aliento, respiración f; **to take a deep ~** respirar hondo; **out of ~** sin aliento, sofocado

Breathalyser ® ['brɛθəlaɪzə*] (*BRIT*) n alcoholímetro m

breathe [briːð] vt, vi respirar; **~ in** vt, vi aspirar; **~ out** vt, vi espirar; **~r** n respiro; **breathing** n respiración f

breath: **~less** adj sin aliento, jadeante; **~taking** adj imponente, pasmoso

breed [briːd] (*pt, pp* bred) vt criar ♦ vi reproducirse, procrear ♦ n (*ZOOL*) raza, casta; (*type*) tipo; **~ing** n (*of person*) educación f

breeze [briːz] n brisa

breezy ['briːzɪ] adj de mucho viento, ventoso; (*person*) despreocupado

brevity ['brɛvɪtɪ] n brevedad f

brew [bruː] vt (*tea*) hacer; (*beer*) elaborar ♦ vi (*fig: trouble*) prepararse; (*storm*) amenazar; **~ery** n fábrica de cerveza, cervecería

bribe [braɪb] n soborno ♦ vt sobornar, cohechar; **~ry** n soborno, cohecho

bric-a-brac ['brɪkəbræk] n inv baratijas fpl

brick [brɪk] n ladrillo; **~layer** n albañil m

bridal ['braɪdl] adj nupcial

bride [braɪd] n novia; **~groom** n novio; **~smaid** n dama de honor

bridge [brɪdʒ] n puente m; (*NAUT*) puente m de mando; (*of nose*) caballete m; (*CARDS*) bridge m ♦ vt (*fig*): **to ~ a gap** llenar un vacío

bridle ['braɪdl] n brida, freno; **~ path** n camino de herradura

brief [briːf] adj breve, corto ♦ n (*LAW*) escrito; (*task*) cometido, encargo ♦ vt informar; **~s** npl (*for men*) calzoncillos mpl; (*for women*) bragas fpl; **~case** n cartera (*SP*), portafolio (*AM*); **~ing** n (*PRESS*) informe m; **~ly** adv (*glance*) fugazmente; (*say*) en pocas palabras

brigadier [brɪɡə'dɪə*] n general m de brigada

bright [braɪt] adj brillante; (*room*) luminoso; (*day*) de sol; (*person: clever*) listo, inteligente; (: *lively*) alegre; (*colour*) vivo; (*future*) prometedor(a); **~en** (*also: ~en up*) vt (*room*) hacer más alegre; (*event*) alegrar ♦ vi (*weather*) despejarse; (*person*) animarse, alegrarse; (*prospects*) mejorar

brilliance ['brɪljəns] n brillo, brillantez f; (*of talent etc*) brillantez

brilliant ['brɪljənt] adj brillante; (*inf*) fenomenal

brim [brɪm] n borde m; (*of hat*) ala

brine [braɪn] n (*CULIN*) salmuera

bring [brɪŋ] (*pt, pp* brought) vt (*thing, person: with you*) traer; (: *to sb*) llevar, conducir; (*trouble, satisfaction*) causar; **~ about** vt ocasionar, producir; **~ back** vt volver a traer; (*return*) devolver; **~ down** vt (*government, plane*) derribar; (*price*) rebajar; **~ forward** vt adelantar; **~ off** vt (*task, plan*) lograr, conseguir; **~ out** vt sacar; (*book etc*) publicar; (*meaning*) subrayar; **~ round** vt (*unconscious person*) hacer volver en sí; **~ up** vt subir; (*person*) educar, criar; (*question*) sacar a colación; (*food: vomit*) devolver, vomitar

brink [brɪŋk] n borde m

brisk [brɪsk] adj (*abrupt: tone*) brusco; (*person*) enérgico, vigoroso; (*pace*) rápido; (*trade*) activo

bristle ['brɪsl] n cerda ♦ vi: **to ~ in anger** temblar de rabia

Britain ['brɪtən] n (*also: Great ~*) Gran Bretaña

British ['brɪtɪʃ] adj británico ♦ npl: **the ~** los británicos; **~ Isles** npl: **the ~ Isles** las Islas Británicas; **~ Rail** n ≈ RENFE f (*SP*)

Briton ['brɪtən] n británico/a

brittle ['brɪtl] adj quebradizo, frágil

broach [brəʊtʃ] vt (subject) abordar

broad [brɔːd] adj ancho; (range) amplio; (smile) abierto; (general: outlines etc) general; (accent) cerrado; **in ~ daylight** en pleno día; **~cast** (irreg: like **cast**) n emisión f ♦ vt (RADIO) emitir; (TV) transmitir ♦ vi emitir; transmitir; **~en** vt ampliar ♦ vi ensancharse; **to ~en one's mind** hacer más tolerante a uno; **~ly** adv en general; **~-minded** adj tolerante, liberal

broccoli ['brɔkəlɪ] n brécol m

brochure ['brəʊʃjʊə*] n folleto

broil [brɔɪl] vt (CULIN) asar a la parrilla

broke [brəʊk] pt of **break** ♦ adj (inf) pelado, sin blanca

broken ['brəʊkən] pp of **break** ♦ adj roto; (machine: also: ~ **down**) averiado; **~ leg** pierna rota; **in ~ English** en un inglés imperfecto; **~-hearted** adj con el corazón partido

broker ['brəʊkə*] n agente m/f, bolsista m/f; (insurance ~) agente de seguros

brolly ['brɔlɪ] (BRIT: inf) n paraguas m inv

bronchitis [brɔŋ'kaɪtɪs] n bronquitis f

bronze [brɔnz] n bronce m

brooch [brəʊtʃ] n prendedor m, broche m

brood [bruːd] n camada, cría ♦ vi (person) dejarse obsesionar

broom [brum] n escoba; (BOT) retama

Bros. abbr (= **Brothers**) Hnos

broth [brɔθ] n caldo

brothel ['brɔθl] n burdel m

brother ['brʌðə*] n hermano; **~-in-law** n cuñado

brought [brɔːt] pt, pp of **bring**

brow [brau] n (forehead) frente m; (eye~) ceja; (of hill) cumbre f

brown [braun] adj (colour) marrón m; (hair) castaño; (tanned) bronceado, moreno ♦ n (colour) color m marrón or pardo ♦ vt (CULIN) dorar; **~ bread** n pan integral

Brownie ['braunɪ] n niña exploradora; **b~** (US: cake) pastel de chocolate con nueces

brown paper n papel m de estraza

brown sugar n azúcar m terciado

browse [brauz] vi (through book) hojear; (in shop) mirar; **~r** n (COMPUT) navegador m

bruise [bruːz] n cardenal m (SP), moretón m (AM) ♦ vt magullar

brunch [brʌntʃ] n desayuno-almuerzo

brunette [bruː'net] n morena

brunt [brʌnt] n: **to bear the ~ of** llevar el peso de

brush [brʌʃ] n cepillo; (for painting, shaving etc) brocha; (artist's) pincel m; (with police etc) roce m ♦ vt (sweep) barrer; (groom) cepillar; (also: ~ **against**) rozar al pasar; **~ aside** vt rechazar, no hacer caso a; **~ up** vt (knowledge) repasar, refrescar; **~wood** n (sticks) leña

Brussels ['brʌslz] n Bruselas; **~ sprout** n col f de Bruselas

brute [bruːt] n bruto; (person) bestia ♦ adj: **by ~ force** a fuerza bruta

B.Sc. abbr (= **Bachelor of Science**) licenciado en Ciencias

BSE n abbr (= **bovine spongiform encephalopathy**) encefalopatía espongiforme bovina

bubble ['bʌbl] n burbuja ♦ vi burbujear, borbotar; **~ bath** n espuma para el baño; **~ gum** n chicle m de globo

buck [bʌk] n (rabbit) conejo macho; (deer) gamo; (US: inf) dólar m ♦ vi corcovear; **to pass the ~ (to sb)** echar (a uno) el muerto; **~ up** vi (cheer up) animarse, cobrar ánimo

bucket ['bʌkɪt] n cubo, balde m

buckle ['bʌkl] n hebilla ♦ vt abrochar con hebilla ♦ vi combarse

bud [bʌd] n (of plant) brote m, yema; (of flower) capullo ♦ vi brotar, echar brotes

Buddhism ['budɪzm] n Budismo

budding ['bʌdɪŋ] adj en ciernes, en embrión

buddy ['bʌdɪ] (US) n compañero, compinche m

budge [bʌdʒ] vt mover; (fig) hacer ceder ♦ vi moverse, ceder

budgerigar ['bʌdʒərɪgɑː*] n periquito

budget ['bʌdʒɪt] n presupuesto ♦ vi: **to ~ for sth** presupuestar algo

budgie ['bʌdʒɪ] n = **budgerigar**

buff [bʌf] adj (colour) color de ante ♦ n (inf: enthusiast) entusiasta m/f

buffalo ['bʌfələu] (pl ~ or ~**es**) n (BRIT) búfalo; (US: bison) bisonte m

buffer ['bʌfə*] n (COMPUT) memoria intermedia; (RAIL) tope m

buffet[1] ['bufeɪ] n (BRIT: in station) bar m, cafetería; (food) buffet m; **~ car** (BRIT) n (RAIL) coche-comedor m

buffet[2] ['bʌfɪt] vt golpear

bug [bʌg] n (esp US: insect) bicho, sabandija; (COMPUT) error m; (germ) microbio, bacilo; (spy device) micrófono oculto ♦ vt (inf: annoy) fastidiar; (room) poner micrófono oculto en

buggy ['bʌgɪ] n cochecito de niño

bugle ['bjuːgl] n corneta, clarín m

build [bɪld] (pt, pp **built**) n (of person) tipo ♦ vt construir, edificar; **~ up** vt (morale, forces, production) acrecentar; (stocks) acumular; **~er** n (contractor) contratista m/f; **~ing** n construcción f; (structure) edificio; **~ing society** (BRIT) n sociedad f inmobiliaria

built [bɪlt] pt, pp of **build** ♦ adj: **~-in** (wardrobe etc) empotrado; **~-up area** n zona urbanizada

bulb [bʌlb] n (BOT) bulbo; (ELEC) bombilla (SP), foco (AM)

Bulgaria [bʌl'gɛərɪə] n Bulgaria; **~n** adj, n búlgaro/a m/f

bulge [bʌldʒ] n bulto, protuberancia ♦ vi bombearse, pandearse; (pocket etc): **to ~ (with)** rebosar (de)

bulk [bʌlk] n masa, mole f; **in ~** (COMM) a granel; **the ~ of** la mayor parte de; **~y** adj voluminoso, abultado

bull [bul] n toro; (male elephant, whale) macho; **~dog** n dogo

bulldozer ['buldəuzə*] n bulldozer m

bullet ['bulɪt] n bala

bulletin ['bulɪtɪn] n anuncio, parte m; (journal) boletín m; **~ board** n (US) tablón m de anuncios; (COMPUT) tablero de noticias

bulletproof ['bulɪtpruːf] adj a prueba de balas

bullfight ['bulfaɪt] n corrida de toros; **~er** n torero; **~ing** n los toros, el toreo

bullion ['buljən] n oro (or plata) en barras

bullock ['buljək] n novillo

bullring ['bulrɪŋ] n plaza de toros

bull's-eye n centro del blanco

bully ['bulɪ] n valentón m, matón m ♦ vt intimidar, tiranizar

bum [bʌm] n (inf: backside) culo; (esp US: tramp) vagabundo

bumblebee ['bʌmblbiː] n abejorro

bump [bʌmp] n (blow) tope m, choque m; (jolt) sacudida; (on road etc) bache m; (on head etc) chichón m ♦ vt (strike) chocar contra; **~ into** vt fus chocar contra, tropezar con; (person) topar con; **~er** n (AUT) parachoques m inv ♦ adj: **~er crop/harvest** cosecha abundante; **~er cars** npl coches mpl de choque; **~y** adj (road) lleno de baches

bun [bʌn] n (BRIT: cake) pastel m; (US: bread) bollo; (of hair) moño

bunch [bʌntʃ] n (of flowers) ramo; (of keys) manojo; (of bananas) piña; (of people) grupo; (pej) pandilla; **~es** npl (in hair) coletas fpl

bundle ['bʌndl] n bulto, fardo; (of sticks) haz m; (of papers) legajo ♦ vt (also: ~ up) atar, envolver; **to ~ sth/sb into** meter algo/a alguien precipitadamente en

bungalow ['bʌŋgələu] n bungalow m, chalé m

bungle ['bʌŋgl] vt hacer mal

bunion ['bʌnjən] n juanete m

bunk [bʌŋk] n litera; **~ beds** npl literas fpl

bunker ['bʌŋkə*] n (coal store) carbonera; (MIL) refugio; (GOLF) bunker m

bunny ['bʌnɪ] n (also: ~ rabbit) conejito

buoy [bɔɪ] n boya; **~ant** adj (ship) capaz de flotar; (economy) boyante; (person) optimista

burden ['bəːdn] n carga ♦ vt cargar

bureau [bjuə'rəu] (pl bureaux) n (BRIT: writing desk) escritorio, buró m; (US: chest of drawers) cómoda; (office) oficina, agencia

bureaucracy [bjuə'rɔkrəsɪ] n burocracia

burglar ['bəːglə*] n ladrón/ona m/f; **~ alarm** n alarma f antirrobo; **~y** n robo con allanamiento, robo de una casa

burial ['bɛrɪəl] n entierro

burly ['bəːlɪ] adj fornido, membrudo

Burma ['bəːmə] n Birmania

burn [bəːn] (pt, pp burned or burnt) vt quemar; (house) incendiar ♦ vi quemarse, arder; incendiarse; (sting) escocer ♦ n quemadura; **~ down** vt incendiar; **~er** n (on cooker etc) quemador m; **~ing** adj (building etc) en llamas; (hot: sand etc) abrasador(a); (ambition) ardiente

burrow ['bʌrəu] n madriguera ♦ vi hacer una madriguera; (rummage) hurgar

bursary ['bəːsərɪ] n (BRIT) beca

burst [bəːst] (pt, pp burst) vt reventar; (subj: river: banks etc) romper ♦ vi reventarse; (tyre) pincharse ♦ n (of gunfire) ráfaga; (also: ~ pipe) reventón m; **a ~ of energy/speed/ enthusiasm** una explosión de energía/un ímpetu de velocidad/un arranque de entusiasmo; **to ~ into flames** estallar en llamas; **to ~ into tears** deshacerse en lágrimas; **to ~ out laughing** soltar la carcajada; **to ~ open** abrirse de golpe; **to be ~ing with** (subj: container) estar lleno a rebosar de; (person) reventar por or de; **~ into** vt fus (room etc) irrumpir en

bury ['bɛrɪ] vt enterrar; (body) enterrar, sepultar

bus [bʌs] (pl ~es) n autobús m

bush [buʃ] n arbusto; (scrub land) monte m; **to beat about the ~** andar(se) con rodeos

bushy ['buʃɪ] adj (thick) espeso, poblado

busily ['bɪzɪlɪ] adv afanosamente

business ['bɪznɪs] n (matter) asunto; (trading) comercio, negocios mpl; (firm) empresa, casa; (occupation) oficio; **to be away on ~** estar en viaje de negocios; **it's my ~ to ...** me toca or corresponde ...; **it's none of my ~** yo no tengo nada que ver; **he means ~** habla en serio; **~like** adj eficiente; **~man** n hombre m de negocios; **~ trip** n viaje m de negocios; **~woman** n mujer f de negocios

busker ['bʌskə*] n (BRIT) músico/a ambulante

bus: **~ shelter** n parada cubierta; **~ station** n estación f de autobuses; **~-stop** n parada de autobús

bust [bʌst] n (ANAT) pecho; (sculpture) busto ♦ adj (inf: broken) roto, estropeado; **to go ~** quebrar

bustle ['bʌsl] n bullicio, movimiento ♦ vi menearse, apresurarse; **bustling** adj (town) animado, bullicioso

busy ['bɪzɪ] *adj* ocupado, atareado; (*shop, street*) concurrido, animado; (*TEL: line*) comunicando ♦ *vt*: **to ~ o.s. with** ocuparse en; **~body** *n* entrometido/a; **~ signal** (*US*) *n* (*TEL*) señal *f* de comunicando

but [bʌt] *conj* **1** pero; **he's not very bright, ~ he's hard-working** no es muy inteligente, pero es trabajador
2 (*in direct contradiction*) sino; **he's not English ~ French** no es inglés sino francés; **he didn't sing ~ he shouted** no cantó sino que gritó **3** (*showing disagreement, surprise etc*): **~ that's far too expensive!** ¡pero eso es carísimo!; **~ it does work!** ¡(pero) sí que funciona!
♦ *prep* (*apart from, except*) menos, salvo; **we've had nothing ~ trouble** no hemos tenido más que problemas; **no-one ~ him can do it** nadie más que él puede hacerlo; **who ~ a lunatic would do such a thing?** ¡sólo un loco haría una cosa así!; **~ for you/your help** si no fuera por ti/tu ayuda; **anything ~ that** cualquier cosa menos eso
♦ *adv* (*just, only*): **she's ~ a child** no es más que una niña; **had I ~ known** si lo hubiera sabido; **I can ~ try** al menos lo puedo intentar; **it's all ~ finished** está casi acabado

butcher ['butʃə*] *n* carnicero ♦ *vt* hacer una carnicería con; (*cattle etc*) matar; **~'s (shop)** *n* carnicería
butler ['bʌtlə*] *n* mayordomo
butt [bʌt] *n* (*barrel*) tonel *m*; (*of cigarette*) colilla; (*BRIT: fig: target*) blanco ♦ *vt* dar cabezadas contra, top(et)ar; **~ in** *vi* (*interrupt*) interrumpir
butter ['bʌtə*] *n* mantequilla ♦ *vt* untar con mantequilla; **~cup** *n* botón *m* de oro
butterfly ['bʌtəflaɪ] *n* mariposa; (*SWIMMING: also*: **~ stroke**) braza de mariposa
buttocks ['bʌtəks] *npl* nalgas *fpl*
button ['bʌtn] *n* botón *m*; (*US*) placa, chapa ♦ *vt* (*also*: **~ up**) abotonar, abrochar ♦ *vi* abrocharse
buttress ['bʌtrɪs] *n* contrafuerte *m*
buy [baɪ] (*pt, pp* **bought**) *vt* comprar ♦ *n* compra; **to ~ sb sth/sth from sb** comprarle algo a alguien; **to ~ sb a drink** invitar a alguien a tomar algo; **~er** *n* comprador(a) *m/f*
buzz [bʌz] *n* zumbido *m*; (*inf: phone call*) llamada (por teléfono) ♦ *vi* zumbar; **~er** *n* timbre *m*; **~ word** *n* palabra que está de moda

by [baɪ] *prep* **1** (*referring to cause, agent*) por; de; **killed ~ lightning** muerto por un relámpago; **a painting ~ Picasso** un cuadro de Picasso
2 (*referring to method, manner, means*): **~ bus/car/train** en autobús/coche/tren; **to pay ~ cheque** pagar con un cheque; **~ moonlight/candlelight** a la luz de la luna/una vela; **~ saving hard, he ...** ahorrando, ...
3 (*via, through*) por; **we came ~ Dover** vinimos por Dover
4 (*close to, past*): **the house ~ the river** la casa junto al río; **she rushed ~ me** pasó a mi lado como una exhalación; **I go ~ the post office every day** paso por delante de Correos todos los días
5 (*time: not later than*) para; (: *during*): **~ daylight** de día; **~ 4 o'clock** para las cuatro; **~ this time tomorrow** mañana a estas horas; **~ the time I got here it was too late** cuando llegué ya era demasiado tarde
6 (*amount*): **~ the metre/kilo** por metro/kilo; **paid ~ the hour** pagado por hora
7 (*MATH, measure*): **to divide/multiply ~ 3** dividir/multiplicar por 3; **a room 3 metres ~ 4** una habitación de 3 metros por 4; **it's broader ~ a metre** es un metro más ancho
8 (*according to*) según, de acuerdo con; **it's 3 o'clock ~ my watch** según mi reloj, son las tres; **it's all right ~ me** por mí, está bien
9: (**all**) **~ oneself** *etc* todo solo; **he did it (all) ~ himself** lo hizo él solo; **he was standing (all) ~ himself in a corner** estaba de pie solo en un rincón
10: **~ the way** a propósito, por cierto; **this wasn't my idea, ~ the way** pues, no fue idea mía
♦ *adv* **1** *see* go; pass *etc*
2: **~ and ~** finalmente; **they'll come back ~ and ~** acabarán volviendo; **~ and large** en líneas generales, en general

bye(-bye) ['baɪ('baɪ)] *excl* adiós, hasta luego
by(e)-law *n* ordenanza municipal
by: **~-election** (*BRIT*) *n* elección *f* parcial; **~gone** ['baɪgɒn] *adj* pasado, del pasado ♦ *n*: **let ~gones be ~gones** lo pasado, pasado está; **~pass** ['baɪpɑːs] *n* carretera de circunvalación; (*MED*) (operación *f* de) by-pass *m* ♦ *vt* evitar; **~-product** *n* subproducto, derivado; (*of situation*) consecuencia; **~stander** ['baɪstændə*] *n* espectador(a) *m/f*
byte [baɪt] *n* (*COMPUT*) byte *m*, octeto
byword ['baɪwɜːd] *n*: **to be a ~ for** ser conocidísimo por

C, c

C |si:| n (MUS) do m

C. abbr (= centigrade) C.

C.A. abbr = **chartered accountant**

cab [kæb] n taxi m; (of truck) cabina

cabbage ['kæbɪdʒ] n col f, berza

cabin ['kæbɪn] n cabaña; (on ship) camarote m; (on plane) cabina; **~ crew** n tripulación f de cabina; **~ cruiser** n yate m de motor

cabinet ['kæbɪnɪt] n (POL) consejo de ministros; (furniture) armario; (also: display ~) vitrina

cable ['keɪbl] n cable m ♦ vt cablegrafiar; **~-car** n teleférico; **~ television** n televisión f por cable

cache [kæʃ] n (of arms, drugs etc) alijo

cackle ['kækl] vi lanzar risotadas; (hen) cacarear

cactus ['kæktəs] (pl cacti) n cacto

cadge [kædʒ] (inf) vt gorronear

Caesarean [si:'zeərɪən] adj: **~ (section)** cesárea

café ['kæfeɪ] n café m

cafeteria [kæfɪ'tɪərɪə] n cafetería

cage [keɪdʒ] n jaula

cagey ['keɪdʒɪ] (inf) adj cauteloso, reservado

cagoule [kə'gu:l] n chubasquero

cajole [kə'dʒəul] vt engatusar

cake [keɪk] n (CULIN: large) tarta; (: small) pastel m; (of soap) pastilla; **~d** adj: **~d with** cubierto de

calculate ['kælkjuleɪt] vt calcular; **calculation** [-'leɪʃən] n cálculo, cómputo; **calculator** n calculadora

calendar ['kæləndə*] n calendario; **~ month/year** n mes m/año civil

calf [kɑ:f] (pl calves) n (of cow) ternero, becerro; (of other animals) cría; (also: ~skin) piel f de becerro; (ANAT) pantorrilla

calibre ['kælɪbə*] (US caliber) n calibre m

call [kɔ:l] vt llamar; (meeting) convocar ♦ vi (shout) llamar; (TEL) llamar (por teléfono), telefonear (esp AM); (visit: also: **~ in**, **~ round**) hacer una visita ♦ n llamada; (of bird) canto; **to be ~ed** llamarse; **on ~** (on duty) de guardia; **~ back** vi (return) volver; (TEL) volver a llamar; **~ for** vt fus (demand) pedir, exigir; (fetch) venir por (SP), pasar por (AM); **~ off** vt (cancel: meeting, race) cancelar; (: deal) anular; (: strike) desconvocar; **~ on** vt fus (visit) visitar; (turn to) acudir a; **~ out** vi gritar; **~ up** vt (MIL) llamar al servicio militar; (TEL) llamar; **~box** (BRIT) n cabina telefónica; **~ centre** (BRIT) n centro de llamadas; **~er** n visita; (TEL) usuario/a; **~ girl** n prostituta; **~-in** (US) n

(programa m) coloquio (por teléfono); **~ing** n vocación f; (occupation) profesión f; **~ing card** (US) n tarjeta de visita

callous ['kæləs] adj insensible, cruel

calm [kɑ:m] adj tranquilo; (sea) liso, en calma ♦ n calma, tranquilidad f ♦ vt calmar, tranquilizar; **~ down** vi calmarse, tranquilizarse ♦ vt calmar, tranquilizar

Calor gas ® ['kælə*-] n butano

calorie ['kælərɪ] n caloría

calves [kɑ:vz] npl of **calf**

Cambodia [kæm'bəudjə] n Camboya

camcorder ['kæmkɔ:də*] n videocámara

came [keɪm] pt of **come**

camel ['kæməl] n camello

camera ['kæmərə] n máquina fotográfica; (CINEMA, TV) cámara; **in ~** (LAW) a puerta cerrada; **~man** n cámara m

camouflage ['kæməflɑ:ʒ] n camuflaje m ♦ vt camuflar

camp [kæmp] n campamento, camping m; (MIL) campamento; (for prisoners) campo; (fig: faction) bando ♦ vi acampar ♦ adj afectado, afeminado

campaign [kæm'peɪn] n (MIL, POL etc) campaña ♦ vi hacer campaña

camp: ~bed (BRIT) n cama de campaña; **~er** n campista m/f; (vehicle) caravana; **~ing** n camping m; **to go ~ing** hacer camping; **~site** n camping m

campus ['kæmpəs] n ciudad f universitaria

can¹ [kæn] n (of oil, water) bidón m; (tin) lata, bote m ♦ vt enlatar

---

KEYWORD

---

can² [kæn] (negative **cannot, can't**; conditional and pt **could**) aux vb **1** (be able to) poder; **you ~ do it if you try** puedes hacerlo si lo intentas; **I ~'t see you** no te veo

2 (know how to) saber; **I ~ swim/play tennis/drive** sé nadar/jugar al tenis/conducir; **~ you speak French?** ¿hablas or sabes hablar francés?

3 (may) poder; **~ I use your phone?** ¿me dejas or puedo usar tu teléfono?

4 (expressing disbelief, puzzlement etc): **it ~'t be true!** ¡no puede ser (verdad)!; **what** CAN **he want?** ¿qué querrá?

5 (expressing possibility, suggestion etc): **he could be in the library** podría estar en la biblioteca; **she could have been delayed** pudo haberse retrasado

Canada ['kænədə] n (el) Canadá; **Canadian** [kə'neɪdɪən] adj, n canadiense m/f

canal [kə'næl] n canal m

canary [kə'neərɪ] n canario; **the C~ Islands** npl las (Islas) Canarias

cancel ['kænsəl] vt cancelar; (train) suprimir;

(*cross out*) tachar, borrar; **~lation** [-'leɪʃən] *n* cancelación *f*; supresión *f*

cancer ['kænsə*] *n* cáncer *m*; **C~** (*ASTROLOGY*) Cáncer *m*

candid ['kændɪd] *adj* franco, abierto

candidate ['kændɪdeɪt] *n* candidato/a

candle ['kændl] *n* vela; (*in church*) cirio; **~light** *n*: **by ~light** a la luz de una vela; **~stick** *n* (*single*) candelero; (*low*) palmatoria; (*bigger, ornate*) candelabro

candour ['kændə*] (*US* **candor**) *n* franqueza

candy ['kændɪ] *n* azúcar *m* cande; (*US*) caramelo; **~floss** (*BRIT*) *n* algodón *m* (azucarado)

cane [keɪn] *n* (*BOT*) caña; (*stick*) vara, palmeta; (*for furniture*) mimbre *f* ♦ (*BRIT*) *vt* (*SCOL*) castigar (con vara)

canister ['kænɪstə*] *n* bote *m*, lata; (*of gas*) bombona

cannabis ['kænəbɪs] *n* marijuana

canned [kænd] *adj* en lata, de lata

cannon ['kænən] (*pl* ~ *or* ~**s**) *n* cañón *m*

cannot ['kænɔt] = **can not**

canoe [kə'nu:] *n* canoa; (*SPORT*) piragua; **~ing** *n* piragüismo

canon ['kænən] *n* (*clergyman*) canónigo; (*standard*) canon *m*

can-opener *n* abrelatas *m inv*

canopy ['kænəpɪ] *n* dosel *m*; toldo

can't [kænt] = **can not**

canteen [kæn'ti:n] *n* (*eating place*) cantina; (*BRIT: of cutlery*) juego

canter ['kæntə*] *vi* ir a medio galope

canvas ['kænvəs] *n* (*material*) lona; (*painting*) lienzo; (*NAUT*) velas *fpl*

canvass ['kænvəs] *vi* (*POL*): **to ~ for** solicitar votos por ♦ *vt* (*COMM*) sondear

canyon ['kænjən] *n* cañón *m*

cap [kæp] *n* (*hat*) gorra; (*of pen*) capuchón *m*; (*of bottle*) tapa, tapón *m*; (*contraceptive*) diafragma *m*; (*for toy gun*) cápsula ♦ *vt* (*outdo*) superar; (*limit*) recortar

capability [keɪpə'bɪlɪtɪ] *n* capacidad *f*

capable ['keɪpəbl] *adj* capaz

capacity [kə'pæsɪtɪ] *n* capacidad *f*; (*position*) calidad *f*

cape [keɪp] *n* capa; (*GEO*) cabo

caper ['keɪpə*] *n* (*CULIN: gen*: ~**s**) alcaparra; (*prank*) broma

capital ['kæpɪtl] *n* (*also*: ~ *city*) capital *f*; (*money*) capital *m*; (*also*: ~ *letter*) mayúscula; **~ gains tax** *n* impuesto sobre las ganancias de capital; **~ism** *n* capitalismo; **~ist** *adj*, *n* capitalista *m/f*; **~ize on** *vt fus* aprovechar; **~ punishment** *n* pena de muerte

Capricorn ['kæprɪkɔ:n] *n* (*ASTROLOGY*) Capricornio

capsize [kæp'saɪz] *vt* volcar, hacer zozobrar ♦ *vi* volcarse, zozobrar

capsule ['kæpsju:l] *n* cápsula

captain ['kæptɪn] *n* capitán *m*

caption ['kæpʃən] *n* (*heading*) título; (*to picture*) leyenda

captive ['kæptɪv] *adj*, *n* cautivo/a *m/f*

capture ['kæptʃə*] *vt* prender, apresar; (*animal, COMPUT*) capturar; (*place*) tomar; (*attention*) captar, llamar ♦ *n* apresamiento; captura; toma; (*data* ~) formulación *f* de datos

car [kɑ:*] *n* coche *m*, carro (*AM*), automóvil *m*; (*US: RAIL*) vagón *m*

carafe [kə'ræf] *n* jarra

carat ['kærət] *n* quilate *m*

caravan ['kærəvæn] *n* (*BRIT*) caravana, ruló *f*; (*in desert*) caravana; **~ning** *n*: **to go ~ning** ir de vacaciones en caravana, viajar en caravana; **~ site** (*BRIT*) *n* camping *m* para caravanas

carbohydrate [kɑ:bəu'haɪdreɪt] *n* hidrato de carbono; (*food*) fécula

carbon ['kɑ:bən] *n* carbono; **~ paper** *n* papel *m* carbón

car boot sale *n* mercadillo organizado en un aparcamiento, en el que se exponen las mercancías en el maletero del coche

carburettor [kɑ:bju'retə*] (*US* **carburetor**) *n* carburador *m*

card [kɑ:d] *n* (*material*) cartulina; (*index* ~ *etc*) ficha; (*playing* ~) carta, naipe *m*; (*visiting* ~, *greetings* ~ *etc*) tarjeta; **~board** *n* cartón *m*

cardiac ['kɑ:dɪæk] *adj* cardíaco

cardigan ['kɑ:dɪgən] *n* rebeca

cardinal ['kɑ:dɪnl] *adj* cardinal; (*importance, principal*) esencial ♦ *n* cardenal *m*

card index *n* fichero

care [keə*] *n* cuidado; (*worry*) inquietud *f*; (*charge*) cargo, custodia ♦ *vi*: **to ~ about** (*person, animal*) tener cariño a; (*thing, idea*) preocuparse por; ♦ **of** en casa de, al cuidado de; **in sb's ~** a cargo de uno; **to take ~ to** cuidarse de, tener cuidado de; **to take ~ of** cuidar; (*problem etc*) ocuparse de; **I don't ~** no me importa; **I couldn't ~ less** eso me trae sin cuidado; **~ for** *vt fus* cuidar a; (*like*) querer

career [kə'rɪə*] *n* profesión *f*; (*in work, school*) carrera ♦ *vi* (*also*: ~ *along*) correr a toda velocidad; **~ woman** *n*: mujer *f* dedicada a su profesión

care: **~free** *adj* despreocupado; **~ful** *adj* cuidadoso; (*cautious*) cauteloso; (**be**) **~ful!** ¡tenga cuidado!; **~fully** *adv* con cuidado, cuidadosamente; con cautela; **~less** *adj* descuidado; (*heedless*) poco atento; **~lessness** *n* descuido; falta de atención; **~r** ['keərə*] *n* enfermero/a *m/f* (*official*); (*unpaid*) *persona que cuida a un pariente o* vecino

caress [kə'rɛs] n caricia ♦ vt acariciar

caretaker ['kɛəteɪkə*] n portero/a, conserje m/f

car-ferry n transbordador m para coches

cargo ['kɑ:gəu] (pl **-es**) n cargamento, carga

car hire n alquiler m de automóviles

Caribbean [kærɪ'bi:ən] n: **the ~ (Sea)** el (Mar) Caribe

caring ['kɛərɪŋ] adj humanitario; (behaviour) afectuoso

carnation [kɑ:'neɪʃən] n clavel m

carnival ['kɑ:nɪvəl] n carnaval m; (US: funfair) parque m de atracciones

carol ['kærəl] n: (Christmas) ~ villancico

carp [kɑ:p] n (fish) carpa

car park (BRIT) n aparcamiento, parking m

carpenter ['kɑ:pɪntə*] n carpintero/a

carpet ['kɑ:pɪt] n alfombra; (fitted) moqueta ♦ vt alfombrar

car phone n teléfono movil

car rental (US) n alquiler m de coches

carriage ['kærɪdʒ] n (BRIT: RAIL) vagón m; (horse-drawn) coche m; (of goods) transporte m; (: cost) porte m, flete m; **~way** (BRIT) n (part of road) calzada

carrier ['kærɪə*] n (transport company) transportista, empresa de transportes; (MED) portador m; **~ bag** (BRIT) n bolsa de papel or plástico

carrot ['kærət] n zanahoria

carry ['kærɪ] vt (subj: person) llevar; (transport) transportar; (involve: responsibilities etc) entrañar, implicar; (MED) ser portador de ♦ vi (sound) oírse; **to get carried away** (fig) entusiasmarse; **~ on** vi (continue) seguir (adelante), continuar ♦ vt (continue) seguir, continuar; **~ out** vt (orders) cumplir; (investigation) llevar a cabo, realizar; **~ cot** (BRIT) n cuna portátil; **~-on** (inf) n (fuss) lío

cart [kɑ:t] n carro, carreta ♦ vt (inf: transport) acarrear

carton ['kɑ:tən] n (box) caja (de cartón); (of milk etc) bote m; (of yogurt) tarrina

cartoon [kɑ:'tu:n] n (PRESS) caricatura; (comic strip) tira cómica; (film) dibujos mpl animados

cartridge ['kɑ:trɪdʒ] n cartucho; (of pen) recambio; (of record player) cápsula

carve [kɑ:v] vt (meat) trinchar; (wood, stone) cincelar, esculpir; (initials etc) grabar; **~ up** vt dividir, repartir; **carving** n (object) escultura; (design) talla; (art) tallado; **carving knife** n trinchante m

car wash n lavado de coches

case [keɪs] n (container) caja; (MED) caso; (for jewels etc) estuche m; (LAW) causa, proceso; (BRIT: also: suit~) maleta; **in ~ of** en caso de;

in any ~ en todo caso; **just in ~** por si acaso

cash [kæʃ] n dinero en efectivo, dinero contante ♦ vt cobrar, hacer efectivo; **to pay (in) ~** pagar al contado; **~ on delivery** cóbrese al entregar; **~book** n libro de caja; **~ card** n tarjeta f dinero; **~ desk** (BRIT) n caja; **~ dispenser** n cajero automático

cashew [kæ'ju:] n (also: ~ nut) anacardo

cash flow n flujo de fondos, cash-flow m

cashier [kæ'ʃɪə*] n cajero/a

cashmere ['kæʃmɪə*] n cachemira

cash register n caja

casing ['keɪsɪŋ] n revestimiento

casino [kə'si:nəu] n casino

casket ['kɑ:skɪt] n cofre m, estuche m; (US: coffin) ataúd m

casserole ['kæsərəul] n (food, pot) cazuela

cassette [kæ'sɛt] n cassette f; **~ player/ recorder** n tocacassettes m inv, cassette m

cast [kɑ:st] (pt, pp **cast**) vt (throw) echar, arrojar, lanzar; (glance, eyes) dirigir; (THEATRE): **to ~ sb as Othello** dar a uno el papel de Otelo ♦ vi (FISHING) lanzar ♦ n (THEATRE) reparto; (also: plaster ~) vaciado; **to ~ one's vote** votar; **to ~ doubt on** suscitar dudas acerca de; **~ off** vi (NAUT) desamarrar; (KNITTING) cerrar (los puntos); **~ on** vi (KNITTING) poner los puntos

castanets [kæstə'nɛts] npl castañuelas fpl

castaway ['kɑ:stəwəɪ] n náufrago/a

caster sugar ['kɑ:stə*-] (BRIT) n azúcar m extrafino

Castile [kæs'ti:l] n Castilla; **Castilian** adj, n castellano/a m/f

casting vote ['kɑ:stɪŋ-] (BRIT) n voto decisivo

cast iron n hierro fundido

castle ['kɑ:sl] n castillo; (CHESS) torre f

castor oil ['kɑ:stə*-] n aceite m de ricino

casual ['kæʒjul] adj fortuito; (irregular: work etc) eventual, temporero; (unconcerned) despreocupado; (clothes) de sport; **~ly** adv de manera despreocupada; (dress) de sport

casualty ['kæʒjultɪ] n víctima, herido; (dead) muerto; (MED: department) urgencias fpl

cat [kæt] n gato; (big ~) felino

Catalan ['kætələn] adj, n catalán/ana m/f

catalogue ['kætəlɔg] (US **catalog**) n catálogo ♦ vt catalogar

Catalonia [kætə'ləunɪə] n Cataluña

catalyst ['kætəlɪst] n catalizador m

catalytic convertor [kætə'lɪtɪk kən'vɜ:tə*] n catalizador m

catapult ['kætəpʌlt] n tirachinas m inv

catarrh [kə'tɑ:*] n catarro

catastrophe [kə'tæstrəfɪ] n catástrofe f

catch [kætʃ] (pt, pp **caught**) vt coger (SP), agarrar (AM); (arrest) detener; (grasp) asir; (breath) contener; (surprise: person) sorprender; (*attract: attention*) captar; (*hear*) oír; (*MED*) contagiarse de, coger; (*also*: ~ up) alcanzar ♦ *vi* (*fire*) encenderse; (*in branches etc*) enredarse ♦ *n* (*fish etc*) pesca; (*act of catching*) cogida; (*hidden problem*) dificultad f; (*game*) pilla-pilla; (*of lock*) pestillo, cerradura; **to ~ fire** encenderse; **to ~ sight of** divisar; **~ on** *vi* (*understand*) caer en la cuenta; (*grow popular*) hacerse popular; **~ up** *vi* (*fig*) ponerse al día; **~ing** ['kætʃɪŋ] *adj* (*MED*) contagioso; **~ment area** ['kætʃmənt-] (*BRIT*) *n* zona de captación; **~phrase** ['kætʃfreɪz] *n* lema m, eslogan m; **~y** ['kætʃɪ] *adj* (*tune*) pegadizo

category ['kætɪgərɪ] *n* categoría, clase f

cater ['keɪtə*] *vi*: **to ~ for** (*BRIT*) abastecer a; (*needs*) atender a; (*COMM: parties etc*) proveer comida a; **~er** *n* abastecedor(a) m/f, proveedor(a) m/f; **~ing** *n* (*trade*) hostelería

caterpillar ['kætəpɪlə*] *n* oruga, gusano

cathedral [kə'θiːdrəl] *n* catedral f

catholic ['kæθəlɪk] *adj* (*tastes etc*) amplio; **C~** *adj, n* (*REL*) católico/a m/f

CAT scan [kæt-] *n* TAC f, tomografía

Cat'seye ® ['kæts'aɪ] (*BRIT*) *n* (*AUT*) catafoto

cattle ['kætl] *npl* ganado

catty ['kætɪ] *adj* malicioso, rencoroso

caucus ['kɔːkəs] *n* (*POL*) camarilla política; (*: US: to elect candidates*) comité m electoral

caught [kɔːt] *pt, pp of* **catch**

cauliflower ['kɔlɪflauə*] *n* coliflor f

cause [kɔːz] *n* causa, motivo, razón f; (*principle: also: POL*) causa ♦ *vt* causar

caution ['kɔːʃən] *n* cautela, prudencia; (*warning*) advertencia, amonestación f ♦ *vt* amonestar; **cautious** *adj* cauteloso, prudente, precavido

cavalry ['kævəlrɪ] *n* caballería

cave [keɪv] *n* cueva, caverna; **~ in** *vi* (*roof etc*) derrumbarse, hundirse

caviar(e) ['kævɪɑ:*] *n* caviar m

CB *n abbr* (= *Citizens' Band (Radio*)) banda ciudadana

CBI *n abbr* (= *Confederation of British Industry*) ≈ C.E.O.E. f (*SP*)

cc *abbr* = **cubic centimetres**; = **carbon copy**

CD *n abbr* (= *compact disc*) DC m; (*player*) (reproductor m de) disco compacto; **~ player** *n* lector m de discos compactos; **~-ROM** [si:di:'rɔm] *n abbr* CD-ROM m

cease [si:s] *vt, vi* cesar; **~fire** *n* alto m el fuego; **~less** *adj* incesante

cedar ['si:də*] *n* cedro

ceiling ['si:lɪŋ] *n* techo; (*fig*) límite m

celebrate ['sɛlɪbreɪt] *vt* celebrar ♦ *vi* divertirse; **~d** *adj* célebre; **celebration** [-'breɪʃən] *n* fiesta, celebración f

celery ['sɛlərɪ] *n* apio

cell [sɛl] *n* celda; (*BIOL*) célula; (*ELEC*) elemento

cellar ['sɛlə*] *n* sótano; (*for wine*) bodega

cello ['tʃɛləu] *n* violoncelo

Cellophane ® ['sɛləfeɪn] *n* celofán m

cellphone ['sɛlfəun] *n* teléfono celular

Celt [kɛlt, sɛlt] *adj, n* celta m/f; **~ic** *adj* celta

cement [sə'mɛnt] *n* cemento; **~ mixer** *n* hormigonera

cemetery ['sɛmɪtrɪ] *n* cementerio

censor ['sɛnsə*] *n* censor m ♦ *vt* (*cut*) censurar; **~ship** *n* censura

censure ['sɛnʃə*] *vt* censurar

census ['sɛnsəs] *n* censo

cent [sɛnt] *n* (*unit of dollar*) centavo, céntimo; (*unit of euro*) céntimo; *see also* **per**

centenary [sɛn'ti:nərɪ] *n* centenario

center ['sɛntə*] (*US*) = **centre**

centi... [sɛntɪ] *prefix*: **~grade** *adj* centígrado; **~litre** (*US* **~liter**) *n* centilitro; **~metre** (*US* **~meter**) *n* centímetro

centipede ['sɛntɪpi:d] *n* ciempiés m inv

central ['sɛntrəl] *adj* central; (*of house etc*) céntrico; **C~ America** *n* Centroamérica; **~ heating** *n* calefacción f central; **~ize** *vt* centralizar

centre ['sɛntə*] (*US* **center**) *n* centro; (*fig*) núcleo ♦ *vt* centrar; **~-forward** *n* (*SPORT*) delantero centro; **~-half** *n* (*SPORT*) medio centro

century ['sɛntjurɪ] *n* siglo; **20th ~** siglo veinte

ceramic [sɪ'ræmɪk] *adj* cerámico; **~s** *n* cerámica

cereal ['si:rɪəl] *n* cereal m

ceremony ['sɛrɪmənɪ] *n* ceremonia; **to stand on ~** hacer ceremonias, estar de cumplido

certain ['sə:tən] *adj* seguro; (*person*): **a ~ Mr Smith** un tal Sr Smith; (*particular, some*) cierto; **for ~** a ciencia cierta; **~ly** *adv* (*undoubtedly*) ciertamente; (*of course*) desde luego, por supuesto; **~ty** *n* certeza, certidumbre f, seguridad f; (*inevitability*) certeza

certificate [sə'tɪfɪkɪt] *n* certificado

certified ['sə:tɪfaɪd]: **~ mail** (*US*) *n* correo certificado; **~ public accountant** (*US*) *n* contable m/f diplomado/a

certify ['sə:tɪfaɪ] *vt* certificar; (*award diploma to*) conceder un diploma a; (*declare insane*) declarar loco

cervical ['sə:vɪkl] *adj* cervical

cervix ['sə:vɪks] *n* cuello del útero

cf. *abbr* (= *compare*) cfr

CFC *n abbr* (= *chlorofluorocarbon*) CFC m

ch. *abbr* (= *chapter*) cap

chain [tʃeɪn] *n* cadena; (*of mountains*) cordillera; (*of events*) sucesión f ♦ *vt* (*also*: ~ up) encadenar; **~ reaction** *n* reacción f en cadena; **~-smoke** *vi* fumar un cigarrillo tras otro; **~ store** *n* tienda de una cadena, ≈

gran almacén

chair [tʃeə*] n silla; (*armchair*) sillón m, butaca; (*of university*) cátedra; (*of meeting etc*) presidencia ♦ vt (*meeting*) presidir; **~lift** n telesilla; **~man** n presidente m

chalk [tʃɔːk] n (*GEO*) creta; (*for writing*) tiza (*SP*), qis m (*AM*)

challenge ['tʃælɪndʒ] n desafío, reto ♦ vt desafiar, retar; (*statement, right*) poner en duda; **to ~ sb to do sth** retar a uno a que haga algo; **challenging** adj exigente; (*tone*) de desafío

chamber ['tʃeɪmbə*] n cámara, sala; (*POL*) cámara; (*BRIT: LAW: gen pl*) despacho; **~ of commerce** cámara de comercio; **~maid** n camarera; **~ music** n música de cámara

chamois ['ʃæmwɑː] n gamuza

champagne [ʃæm'peɪn] n champaña m, champán m

champion ['tʃæmpɪən] n campeón/ona m/f; (*of cause*) defensor(a) m/f; **~ship** n campeonato

chance [tʃɑːns] n (*opportunity*) ocasión f, oportunidad f; (*likelihood*) posibilidad f; (*risk*) riesgo ♦ vt arriesgar, probar ♦ adj fortuito, casual; **to ~ it** arriesgarse, intentarlo; **to take a ~** arriesgarse; **by ~** por casualidad

chancellor ['tʃɑːnsələ*] n canciller m; **C~ of the Exchequer** (*BRIT*) n Ministro de Hacienda

chandelier [ʃændə'lɪə*] n araña (de luces)

change [tʃeɪndʒ] vt cambiar; (*replace*) cambiar, reemplazar; (*gear, clothes, job*) cambiar de; (*transform*) transformar ♦ vi cambiar(se); (*trains*) hacer transbordo; (*traffic lights*) cambiar de color; (*be transformed*) **to ~ into** transformarse en ♦ n cambio; (*alteration*) modificación f, transformación f; (*of clothes*) muda; (*coins*) suelto, sencillo; (*money returned*) vuelta; **to ~ gear** (*AUT*) cambiar de marcha; **to ~ one's mind** cambiar de opinión *or* idea; **for a ~** para variar; **~able** adj (*weather*) cambiable; **~ machine** n máquina de cambio; **~over** n (*to new system*) cambio; **changing** adj cambiante; **changing room** (*BRIT*) n vestuario

channel ['tʃænl] n (*TV*) canal m; (*of river*) cauce m; (*groove*) conducto; (*fig: medium*) medio ♦ vt (*river etc*) encauzar; **the (English) C~** el Canal (de la Mancha); **the C~ Islands** las Islas Normandas; **the C~ Tunnel** el túnel del Canal de la Mancha, el Eurotúnel; **~-hopping** n (*TV*) zapping m

chant [tʃɑːnt] n (*of crowd*) gritos mpl; (*REL*) canto ♦ vt (*slogan, word*) repetir a gritos

chaos ['keɪɒs] n caos m

chap [tʃæp] (*BRIT: inf*) n (*man*) tío, tipo

chapel ['tʃæpəl] n capilla

chaperone ['ʃæpərəun] n carabina

chaplain ['tʃæplɪn] n capellán m

chapped [tʃæpt] adj agrietado

chapter ['tʃæptə*] n capítulo

char [tʃɑː*] vt (*burn*) carbonizar, chamuscar

character ['kærɪktə*] n carácter m, naturaleza, índole f; (*moral strength, personality*) carácter m; (*in novel, film*) personaje m; **~istic** [-'rɪstɪk] adj característico ♦ n característica

charcoal ['tʃɑːkəul] n carbón m vegetal; (*ART*) carboncillo

charge [tʃɑːdʒ] n (*LAW*) cargo, acusación f; (*cost*) precio, coste m; (*responsibility*) cargo ♦ vt (*LAW*): **to ~ (with)** acusar (de); (*battery*) cargar; (*price*) pedir; (*customer*) cobrar ♦ vi precipitarse; (*MIL*) cargar, atacar; **~s** npl: **to reverse the ~s** (*BRIT: TEL*) revertir el cobro; **to take ~ of** hacerse cargo de, encargarse de; **to be in ~ of** estar encargado de; (*business*) mandar; **how much do you ~?** ¿cuánto cobra usted?; **to ~ an expense (up) to sb's account** cargar algo a cuenta de alguien; **~ card** n tarjeta de cuenta

charity ['tʃærɪtɪ] n caridad f; (*organization*) sociedad f benéfica; (*money, gifts*) limosnas fpl

charm [tʃɑːm] n encanto, atractivo; (*talisman*) hechizo; (*on bracelet*) dije m ♦ vt encantar; **~ing** adj encantador(a)

chart [tʃɑːt] n (*diagram*) cuadro; (*graph*) gráfica; (*map*) carta de navegación ♦ vt (*course*) trazar; (*progress*) seguir; **~s** npl (*Top 40*): **the ~s** ≈ los 40 principales (*SP*)

charter ['tʃɑːtə*] vt (*plane*) alquilar; (*ship*) fletar ♦ n (*document*) carta; (*of university, company*) estatutos mpl; **~ed accountant** (*BRIT*) n contable m/f diplomado/a; **~ flight** n vuelo chárter

chase [tʃeɪs] vt (*pursue*) perseguir; (*also: ~ away*) ahuyentar ♦ n persecución f

chasm ['kæzəm] n sima

chassis ['ʃæsɪ] n chasis m

chat [tʃæt] vi (*also: have a ~*) charlar ♦ n charla; **~ show** (*BRIT*) n programa m de entrevistas

chatter ['tʃætə*] vi (*person*) charlar; (*teeth*) castañetear ♦ n (*of birds*) parloteo; (*of people*) charla, cháchara; **~box** (*inf*) n parlanchín/ina m/f

chatty ['tʃætɪ] adj (*style*) informal; (*person*) hablador(a)

chauffeur ['ʃəufə*] n chófer m

chauvinist ['ʃəuvɪnɪst] n (*male ~*) machista m; (*nationalist*) chovinista m/f

cheap [tʃiːp] adj barato; (*joke*) de mal gusto; (*poor quality*) de mala calidad ♦ adv barato; **~ day return** n billete m de ida y vuelta el mismo día; **~er** adj más barato; **~ly** adv barato, a bajo precio

cheat [tʃiːt] vi hacer trampa ♦ vt: **to ~ sb (out of sth)** estafar (algo) a uno ♦ n (person) tramposo/a

check [tʃɛk] vt (examine) controlar; (facts) comprobar; (halt) parar, detener; (restrain) refrenar, restringir ♦ n (inspection) control m, inspección f; (curb) freno; (US: bill) nota, cuenta; (US) = **cheque**; (pattern: gen pl) cuadro ♦ adj (also: ~ed: pattern, cloth) a cuadros ♦ **~ in** vi (at hotel) firmar el registro; (at airport) facturar el equipaje ♦ vt (luggage) facturar; **~ out** vi (of hotel) marcharse; **~ up** vi: **to ~ up on sth** comprobar algo; **to ~ up on sb** investigar a alguien; **~ered** (US) adj = **check**; **chequered**; **~ers** (US) n juego de damas; **~-in (desk)** n mostrador m de facturación; **~ing account** (US) n cuenta corriente; **~mate** n jaque m mate; **~out** n caja; **~point** n (punto de) control m; **~room** (US) n consigna; **~up** n (MED) reconocimiento general

cheek [tʃiːk] n mejilla; (impudence) descaro; **what a ~!** ¡qué cara!; **~bone** n pómulo; **~y** adj fresco, descarado

cheep [tʃiːp] vi piar

cheer [tʃɪə*] vt vitorear, aplaudir; (gladden) alegrar, animar ♦ vi dar vivas ♦ n viva m; **~s** npl aplausos mpl; **~s!** ¡salud!; **~ up** vi animarse ♦ vt alegrar, animar; **~ful** adj alegre

cheerio [tʃɪərɪˈəu] (BRIT) excl ¡hasta luego!

cheese [tʃiːz] n queso; **~board** n tabla de quesos

cheetah [tʃiːtə] n leopardo cazador

chef [ʃɛf] n jefe/a m/f de cocina

chemical [ˈkɛmɪkəl] adj químico ♦ n producto químico

chemist [ˈkɛmɪst] n (BRIT: pharmacist) farmacéutico/a; (scientist) químico/a; **~ry** n química; **~'s (shop)** (BRIT) n farmacia

cheque [tʃɛk] (US check) n cheque m; **~book** n talonario de cheques (SP), chequera (AM); **~ card** n tarjeta de cheque

chequered [ˈtʃɛkəd] (US checkered) adj (fig) accidentado

cherish [ˈtʃɛrɪʃ] vt (love) querer, apreciar; (protect) cuidar; (hope etc) abrigar

cherry [ˈtʃɛrɪ] n cereza; (also: ~ tree) cerezo

chess [tʃɛs] n ajedrez m; **~board** n tablero (de ajedrez)

chest [tʃɛst] n (ANAT) pecho; (box) cofre m, cajón m; **~ of drawers** n cómoda

chestnut [ˈtʃɛsnʌt] n castaña; **~ (tree)** n castaño

chew [tʃuː] vt mascar, masticar; **~ing gum** n chicle m

chic [ʃiːk] adj elegante

chick [tʃɪk] n pollito, polluelo; (inf: girl) chica

chicken [ˈtʃɪkɪn] n gallina, pollo; (food) pollo;

(inf: coward) gallina m/f; **~ out** (inf) vi rajarse; **~pox** n varicela

chicory [ˈtʃɪkərɪ] n (for coffee) achicoria; (salad) escarola

chief [tʃiːf] n jefe/a m/f ♦ adj principal; **~ executive** n director(a) m/f general; **~ly** adv principalmente

chilblain [ˈtʃɪlbleɪn] n sabañón m

child [tʃaɪld] (pl **children**) n niño/a; (offspring) hijo/a; **~birth** n parto; **~hood** n niñez f, infancia; **~ish** adj pueril, aniñado; **~like** adj de niño; **~ minder** (BRIT) n madre f de día; **~ren** [ˈtʃɪldrən] npl of **child**

Chile [ˈtʃɪlɪ] n Chile m; **~an** adj, n chileno/a m/f

chill [tʃɪl] n frío; (MED) resfriado ♦ vt enfriar; (CULIN) congelar

chil(l)i [ˈtʃɪlɪ] (BRIT) n chile m (SP), ají m (AM)

chilly [ˈtʃɪlɪ] adj frío

chime [tʃaɪm] n repique m; (of clock) campanada ♦ vi repicar; sonar

chimney [ˈtʃɪmnɪ] n chimenea; **~ sweep** n deshollinador m

chimpanzee [tʃɪmpænˈziː] n chimpancé m

chin [tʃɪn] n mentón m, barbilla

china [ˈtʃaɪnə] n porcelana; (crockery) loza

China [ˈtʃaɪnə] n China; **Chinese** [tʃaɪˈniːz] adj chino ♦ n inv chino/a; (LING) chino

chink [tʃɪŋk] n (opening) grieta, hendedura; (noise) tintineo

chip [tʃɪp] n (gen pl: CULIN: BRIT) patata (SP) or papa (AM) frita; (: US: also: potato ~) patata or papa frita; (of wood) astilla; (of glass, stone) lasca; (at poker) ficha; (COMPUT) chip m ♦ vt (cup, plate) desconchar

chiropodist [kɪˈrɔpədɪst] (BRIT) n pedicuro/a, callista m/f

chirp [tʃəːp] vi (bird) gorjear, piar

chisel [ˈtʃɪzl] n (for wood) escoplo; (for stone) cincel m

chit [tʃɪt] n nota

chitchat [ˈtʃɪttʃæt] n chismes mpl, habladurías fpl

chivalry [ˈʃɪvəlrɪ] n caballerosidad f

chives [tʃaɪvz] npl cebollinos mpl

chlorine [ˈklɔːriːn] n cloro

chock-a-block [ˈtʃɔkəˈblɔk] adj atestado

chock-full [ˈtʃɔkˈful] adj atestado

chocolate [ˈtʃɔklɪt] n chocolate m; (sweet) bombón m

choice [tʃɔɪs] n elección f, selección f; (option) opción f; (preference) preferencia ♦ adj escogido

choir [ˈkwaɪə*] n coro; **~boy** n niño de coro

choke [tʃəuk] vi ahogarse; (on food) atragantarse ♦ vt estrangular, ahogar; (block): **to be ~d with** estar atascado de ♦ n (AUT) estárter m

cholesterol [kəˈlɛstərɔl] n colesterol m

choose [tʃuːz] (pt **chose**, pp **chosen**) vt escoger, elegir; (team) seleccionar; **to ~ to do sth** optar por hacer algo

choosy ['tʃuːzɪ] adj delicado

chop [tʃɔp] vt (wood) cortar, tajar; (CULIN: also: ~ up) picar ♦ n (CULIN) chuleta; **~s** npl (jaws) boca, labios mpl

chopper ['tʃɔpə*] n (helicopter) helicóptero

choppy ['tʃɔpɪ] adj (sea) picado, agitado

chopsticks ['tʃɔpstɪks] npl palillos mpl

chord [kɔːd] n (MUS) acorde m

chore [tʃɔː*] n faena, tarea; (routine task) trabajo rutinario

chorus ['kɔːrəs] n coro; (repeated part of song) estribillo

chose [tʃəuz] pt of **choose**

chosen ['tʃəuzn] pp of **choose**

chowder ['tʃaudə*] n (esp US) sopa de pescado

Christ [kraɪst] n Cristo

christen ['krɪsn] vt bautizar

Christian ['krɪstɪən] adj, n cristiano/a m/f; **~ity** [-'ænɪtɪ] n cristianismo; **~ name** n nombre m de pila

Christmas ['krɪsməs] n Navidad f; **Merry ~!** ¡Felices Pascuas!; **~ card** n crismas m inv, tarjeta de Navidad; **~ Day** n día m de Navidad; **~ Eve** n Nochebuena; **~ tree** n árbol m de Navidad

chrome [krəum] n cromo

chronic ['krɔnɪk] adj crónico

chronological [krɔnə'lɔdʒɪkəl] adj cronológico

chubby ['tʃʌbɪ] adj regordete

chuck [tʃʌk] (inf) vt lanzar, arrojar; (BRIT: also: ~ up) abandonar; **~ out** vt (person) echar (fuera); (rubbish etc) tirar

chuckle ['tʃʌkl] vi reírse entre dientes

chug [tʃʌg] vi resoplar; (car, boat: also: ~ along) avanzar traqueteando

chum [tʃʌm] n compañero/a

chunk [tʃʌŋk] n pedazo, trozo

church [tʃəːtʃ] n iglesia; **~yard** n cementerio

churn [tʃəːn] n (for milk) mantequera; (for milk) lechera; **~ out** vt producir en serie

chute [ʃuːt] n (also: rubbish ~) vertedero; (for coal etc) rampa de caída

chutney ['tʃʌtnɪ] n condimento a base de frutas de la India

CIA (US) n abbr (= Central Intelligence Agency) CIA f

CID (BRIT) n abbr (= Criminal Investigation Department) ≈ B.I.C. f (SP)

cider ['saɪdə*] n sidra

cigar [sɪ'gɑː*] n puro

cigarette [sɪgə'rɛt] n cigarrillo (SP), cigarro (AM); pitillo; **~ case** n pitillera; **~ end** n colilla

Cinderella [sɪndə'rɛlə] n Cenicienta

cinders ['sɪndəz] npl cenizas fpl

cine camera ['sɪnɪ-] (BRIT) n cámara cinematográfica

cinema ['sɪnəmə] n cine m

cinnamon ['sɪnəmən] n canela

circle ['səːkl] n círculo; (in theatre) anfiteatro ♦ vi dar vueltas ♦ vt (surround) rodear, cercar; (move round) dar la vuelta a

circuit ['səːkɪt] n circuito; (tour) gira; (track) pista; (lap) vuelta; **~ous** [səː'kjuɪtəs] adj indirecto

circular ['səːkjulə*] adj circular ♦ n circular f

circulate ['səːkjuleɪt] vi circular; (person: at party etc) hablar con los invitados ♦ vt poner en circulación; **circulation** [-'leɪʃən] n circulación f; (of newspaper) tirada

circumstances ['səːkəmstənsɪz] npl circunstancias fpl; (financial condition) situación f económica

circus ['səːkəs] n circo

CIS n abbr (= Commonwealth of Independent States) CEI f

cistern ['sɪstən] n tanque m, depósito; (in toilet) cisterna

citizen ['sɪtɪzn] n (POL) ciudadano/a; (of city) vecino/a, habitante m/f; **~ship** n ciudadanía

citrus fruits ['sɪtrəs-] npl agrios mpl

city ['sɪtɪ] n ciudad f; **the C~** centro financiero de Londres

civic ['sɪvɪk] adj cívico; (authorities) municipal; **~ centre** (BRIT) n centro público

civil ['sɪvɪl] adj civil; (polite) atento, cortés; **~ engineer** n ingeniero de caminos(, canales y puertos); **~ian** [sɪ'vɪlɪən] adj civil (no military) ♦ n civil m/f, paisano/a

civilization [sɪvɪlaɪ'zeɪʃən] n civilización f

civilized ['sɪvɪlaɪzd] adj civilizado

civil: ~ law n derecho civil; **~ servant** n funcionario/a del Estado; **C~ Service** n administración f pública; **~ war** n guerra civil

claim [kleɪm] vt exigir, reclamar; (rights etc) reivindicar; (assert) pretender ♦ vi (for insurance) reclamar ♦ n reclamación f; pretensión f; **~ant** n demandante m/f

clairvoyant [klɛə'vɔɪənt] n clarividente m/f

clam [klæm] n almeja

clamber ['klæmbə*] vi trepar

clammy ['klæmɪ] adj frío y húmedo

clamour ['klæmə*] (US **clamor**) vi: **to ~ for** clamar por, pedir a voces

clamp [klæmp] n abrazadera, grapa ♦ vt (2 things together) cerrar fuertemente; (one thing on another) afianzar (con abrazadera); (AUT: wheel) poner el cepo a; **~ down on** vt fus (subj: government, police) reforzar la lucha contra

clang [klæŋ] vi sonar, hacer estruendo

clap [klæp] vi aplaudir; **~ping** n aplausos mpl

claret ['klærət] n burdeos m inv

clarify ['klærɪfaɪ] vt aclarar

clarinet [klærɪ'net] n clarinete m

clash [klæʃ] n enfrentamiento; choque m; desacuerdo; estruendo ♦ vi (fight) enfrentarse; (beliefs) chocar; (disagree) estar en desacuerdo; (colours) desentonar; (two events) coincidir

clasp [klɑːsp] n (hold) apretón m; (of necklace, bag) cierre m ♦ vt apretar; abrazar

class [klɑːs] n clase f ♦ vt clasificar

classic ['klæsɪk] adj, n clásico; **~al** adj clásico

classified ['klæsɪfaɪd] adj (information) reservado; **~ advertisement** n anuncio por palabras

classmate ['klɑːsmeɪt] n compañero/a de clase

classroom ['klɑːsrum] n aula

clatter ['klætə*] n estrépito ♦ vi hacer ruido or estrépito

clause [klɔːz] n cláusula; (LING) oración f

claw [klɔː] n (of cat) uña; (of bird of prey) garra; (of lobster) pinza

clay [kleɪ] n arcilla

clean [kliːn] adj limpio; (record, reputation) bueno, intachable; (joke) decente ♦ vt limpiar; (hands etc) lavar; **~ out** vt limpiar; **~ up** vt limpiar, asear; **~cut** adj (person) bien parecido; **~er** n (person) asistenta; (substance) producto para la limpieza; **~er's** n tintorería; **~ing** n limpieza; **~liness** ['klenlɪnɪs] n limpieza

cleanse [klenz] vt limpiar; **~r** n (for face) crema limpiadora

clean-shaven adj sin barba, afeitado

cleansing department (BRIT) n departamento de limpieza

clear [klɪə*] adj claro; (road, way) libre; (conscience) limpio, tranquilo; (skin) terso; (sky) despejado ♦ vt (space) despejar, limpiar; (LAW: suspect) absolver; (obstacle) salvar, saltar por encima de; (cheque) aceptar ♦ vi (fog etc) despejarse ♦ adv: **~ of** a distancia de; **to ~ the table** recoger or levantar la mesa; **~ up** vt limpiar; (mystery) aclarar, resolver; **~ance** n (removal) despeje m; (permission) acreditación f; **~-cut** adj bien definido, nítido; **~ing** n (in wood) claro; **~ing bank** (BRIT) n cámara de compensación; **~ly** adv claramente; (evidently) sin duda; **~way** (BRIT) n carretera donde no se puede parar

clef [klef] n (MUS) clave f

cleft [kleft] n (in rock) grieta, hendedura

clench [klentʃ] vt apretar, cerrar

clergy ['klɜːdʒɪ] n clero; **~man** n clérigo

clerical ['klerɪkəl] adj de oficina; (REL) clerical

clerk [klɑːk, (US) klɜːrk] n (BRIT) oficinista m/f; (US) dependiente/a m/f

clever ['klevə*] adj (intelligent) inteligente,

listo; (skilful) hábil; (device, arrangement) ingenioso

click [klɪk] vt (tongue) chasquear; (heels) taconear ♦ vi (COMPUT) hacer clic

client ['klaɪənt] n cliente m/f

cliff [klɪf] n acantilado

climate ['klaɪmɪt] n clima m

climax ['klaɪmæks] n (of battle, career) apogeo; (of film, book) punto culminante; (sexual) orgasmo

climb [klaɪm] vi subir; (plant) trepar; (move with effort): **to ~ over a wall/into a car** trepar a una tapia/subir a un coche ♦ vt (stairs) subir; (tree) trepar a; (mountain) escalar ♦ n subida; **~-down** n vuelta atrás; **~er** n alpinista m/f (SP), andinista m/f (AM); **~ing** n alpinismo (SP), andinismo (AM)

clinch [klɪntʃ] vt (deal) cerrar; (argument) remachar

cling [klɪŋ] (pt, pp clung) vi: **to ~** agarrarse a; (clothes) pegarse a

clinic ['klɪnɪk] n clínica; **~al** adj clínico; (fig) frío

clink [klɪŋk] vi tintinar

clip [klɪp] n (for hair) horquilla; (also: paper ~) sujetapapeles m inv, clip m; (TV, CINEMA) fragmento ♦ vt (cut) cortar; (also: ~ together) unir; **~pers** npl (for gardening) tijeras fpl; **~ping** n (newspaper) recorte m

clique [kliːk] n camarilla

cloak [kləuk] n capa, manto ♦ vt (fig) encubrir, disimular; **~room** n guardarropa; (BRIT: WC) lavabo (SP), aseos mpl (SP), baño (AM)

clock [klɔk] n reloj m; **~ in** or **on** vi fichar, picar; **~ off** or **out** vi fichar or picar la salida; **~wise** adv en el sentido de las agujas del reloj; **~work** n aparato de relojería ♦ adj (toy) de cuerda

clog [klɔg] n zueco, chanclo ♦ vt atascar ♦ vi (also: ~ up) atascarse

cloister ['klɔɪstə*] n claustro

close¹ [kləus] adj (near): **~ (to)** cerca (de); (friend) íntimo; (connection) estrecho; (examination) detallado, minucioso; (weather) bochornoso; **to have a ~ shave** (fig) escaparse por un pelo ♦ adv cerca; **~ by, ~ at hand** muy cerca; **~ to** prep cerca de

close² [kləuz] vt (shut) cerrar; (end) concluir, terminar ♦ vi (shop etc) cerrarse; (end) concluirse, terminarse ♦ n (end) fin m, final m, conclusión f; **~ down** vi cerrarse definitivamente; **~d** adj (shop etc) cerrado; **~d shop** n taller m gremial

close-knit [kləus'nɪt] adj (fig) muy unido

closely ['kləuslɪ] adv (study) con detalle; (watch) de cerca; (resemble) estrechamente

closet ['klɔzɪt] n armario

close-up ['kləusʌp] n primer plano

closure ['kləʊʒə*] n cierre m
clot [klɔt] n (gen: blood ~) coágulo; (inf: idiot) imbécil m/f ♦ vi (blood) coagularse
cloth [klɔθ] n (material) tela, paño; (rag) trapo
clothe [kləʊð] vt vestir; **~s** npl ropa; **~s brush** n cepillo (para la ropa); **~s line** n cuerda (para tender la ropa); **~s peg** (US **~s pin**) n pinza
clothing ['kləʊðɪŋ] n = **clothes**
cloud [klaʊd] n nube f; **~burst** n aguacero; **~y** adj nublado, nubloso; (liquid) turbio
clout [klaʊt] vt dar un tortazo a
clove [kləʊv] n clavo; ~ **of garlic** diente m de ajo
clover ['kləʊvə*] n trébol m
clown [klaʊn] n payaso ♦ vi (also: ~ **about**, ~ **around**) hacer el payaso
cloying ['klɔɪɪŋ] adj empalagoso
club [klʌb] n (society) club m; (weapon) porra, cachiporra; (also: golf ~) palo ♦ vt aporrear ♦ vi: **to ~ together** (for gift) comprar entre todos; **~s** npl (CARDS) tréboles mpl; ~ **class** n (AVIAT) clase f preferente; **~house** n local social, sobre todo en clubs deportivos
cluck [klʌk] vi cloquear
clue [kluː] n pista; (in crosswords) indicación f; **I haven't a ~** no tengo ni idea
clump [klʌmp] n (of trees) grupo
clumsy ['klʌmzɪ] adj (person) torpe, desmañado; (tool) difícil de manejar; (movement) desgarbado
clung [klʌŋ] pt, pp of **cling**
cluster ['klʌstə*] n grupo ♦ vi agruparse, apiñarse
clutch [klʌtʃ] n (AUT) embrague m; (grasp): **~es** garras fpl ♦ vt asir; agarrar
clutter ['klʌtə*] vt atestar
cm abbr (= centimetre) cm
CND n abbr (= Campaign for Nuclear Disarmament) plataforma pro desarme nuclear
Co. abbr = **county; company**
c/o abbr (= care of) c/a, a/c
coach [kəʊtʃ] n autocar m (SP), coche m de línea; (horse-drawn) coche m; (of train) vagón m, coche m; (SPORT) entrenador(a) m/f, instructor(a) m/f; (tutor) profesor(a) m/f particular ♦ vt (SPORT) entrenar; (student) preparar, enseñar; ~ **trip** n excursión f en autocar
coal [kəʊl] n carbón m; ~ **face** n frente m de carbón; **~field** n yacimiento de carbón
coalition [kəʊə'lɪʃən] n coalición f
coalman ['kəʊlmən] (irreg) n carbonero
coalmine ['kəʊlmaɪn] n mina de carbón
coarse [kɔːs] adj basto, burdo; (vulgar) grosero, ordinario
coast [kəʊst] n costa, litoral m ♦ vi (AUT) ir en punto muerto; **~al** adj costero, costanero;

~guard n guardacostas m inv; **~line** n litoral m
coat [kəʊt] n abrigo; (of animal) pelaje m, lana; (of paint) mano f, capa ♦ vt cubrir, revestir; ~ **of arms** n escudo de armas; ~ **hanger** n percha (SP), gancho (AM); **~ing** n capa, baño
coax [kəʊks] vt engatusar
cobbler ['kɔblə*] n zapatero (remendón)
cobbles ['kɔblz] npl, **cobblestones** ['kɔblstəʊnz] npl adoquines mpl
cobweb ['kɔbwɛb] n telaraña
cocaine [kə'keɪn] n cocaína
cock [kɔk] n (rooster) gallo; (male bird) macho ♦ vt (gun) amartillar; **~erel** n gallito
cockle ['kɔkl] n berberecho
cockney ['kɔknɪ] n habitante de ciertos barrios de Londres
cockpit ['kɔkpɪt] n cabina
cockroach ['kɔkrəʊtʃ] n cucaracha
cocktail ['kɔkteɪl] n coctel m, cóctel m; ~ **cabinet** n mueble-bar m; ~ **party** n coctel m, cóctel m
cocoa ['kəʊkəʊ] n cacao; (drink) chocolate m
coconut ['kəʊkənʌt] n coco
cod [kɔd] n bacalao
C.O.D. abbr (= cash on delivery) C.A.E.
code [kəʊd] n código; (cipher) clave f; (dialling ~) prefijo; (post ~) código postal
cod-liver oil ['kɔdlɪvər-] n aceite m de hígado de bacalao
coercion [kəʊ'əːʃən] n coacción f
coffee ['kɔfɪ] n café m; ~ **bar** n (BRIT) cafetería; ~ **bean** n grano de café; ~ **break** n descanso (para tomar café); **~pot** n cafetera; ~ **table** n mesita (para servir el café)
coffin ['kɔfɪn] n ataúd m
cog [kɔg] n (wheel) rueda dentada; (tooth) diente m
cogent ['kəʊdʒənt] adj convincente
cognac ['kɔnjæk] n coñac m
coil [kɔɪl] n rollo; (ELEC) bobina, carrete m; (contraceptive) espiral f ♦ vt enrollar
coin [kɔɪn] n moneda ♦ vt (word) inventar, idear; **~age** n moneda; **~-box** (BRIT) n cabina telefónica
coincide [kəʊɪn'saɪd] vi coincidir; (agree) estar de acuerdo; **coincidence** [kəʊ'ɪnsɪdəns] n casualidad f
Coke ® [kəʊk] n Coca-Cola ®
coke [kəʊk] n (coal) coque m
colander ['kɔləndə*] n colador m, escurridor m
cold [kəʊld] adj frío ♦ n frío; (MED) resfriado; **it's ~** hace frío; **to be ~** (person) tener frío; **to catch ~** enfriarse; **to catch a ~** resfriarse, acatarrarse; **in ~ blood** a sangre fría; **~-shoulder** vt dar or volver la espalda a;

~ **sore** n herpes mpl or fpl

coleslaw ['kəulslɔ:] n especie de ensalada de col

colic ['kɒlɪk] n cólico

collapse [kə'læps] vi hundirse, derrumbarse; (MED) sufrir un colapso ♦ n hundimiento, derrumbamiento; (MED) colapso; **collapsible** adj plegable

collar ['kɒlə*] n (of coat, shirt) cuello; (of dog etc) collar; **~bone** n clavícula

collateral [kɒ'lætərəl] n garantía colateral

colleague ['kɒli:g] n colega m/f; (at work) compañero, a

collect [kə'lɛkt] vt (litter, mail etc) recoger; (as a hobby) coleccionar; (BRIT: call and pick up) recoger; (debts, subscriptions etc) recaudar ♦ vi reunirse; (dust) acumularse; **to call ~** (US: TEL) llamar a cobro revertido; **~ion** [kə'lɛkʃən] n colección f; (of mail, for charity) recogida; **~or** n coleccionista m/f

college ['kɒlɪdʒ] n colegio mayor; (of agriculture, technology) escuela universitaria

collide [kə'laɪd] vi chocar

colliery ['kɒlɪərɪ] (BRIT) n mina de carbón

collision [kə'lɪʒən] n choque m

colloquial [kə'ləukwɪəl] adj familiar, coloquial

Colombia [kə'lɒmbɪə] n Colombia; **~n** adj, n colombiano/a

colon ['kəulən] n (sign) dos puntos; (MED) colon m

colonel ['kə:nl] n coronel m

colonial [kə'ləunɪəl] adj colonial

colony ['kɒlənɪ] n colonia

colour ['kʌlə*] (US **color**) n color m ♦ vt color(e)ar; (dye) teñir; (fig: account) adornar; (: judgement) distorsionar ♦ vi (blush) sonrojarse; **~s** npl (of party, club) colores mpl; **in ~** en color; **~ in** vt colorear; **~ bar** n segregación f racial; **~-blind** adj daltónico; **~ed** adj de color; (photo) en color; **~ film** n película en color; **~ful** adj lleno de color; (story) fantástico; (person) excéntrico; **~ing** n (complexion) tez f; (in food) colorante m; **~ scheme** n combinación f de colores; **~ television** n televisión f en color

colt [kəult] n potro

column ['kɒləm] n columna; **~ist** ['kɒləmnɪst] n columnista m/f

coma ['kəumə] n coma m

comb [kəum] n peine m; (ornamental) peineta ♦ vt (hair) peinar; (area) registrar a fondo

combat ['kɒmbæt] n combate m ♦ vt combatir

combination [kɒmbɪ'neɪʃən] n combinación f

combine [vb kəm'baɪn, n 'kɒmbaɪn] vt combinar; (qualities) reunir ♦ vi combinarse

♦ n (ECON) cartel m; ~ (**harvester**) n cosechadora

come [kʌm] (pt **came**, pp **come**) vi **1** (movement towards) venir; **to ~ running** venir corriendo

2 (arrive) llegar; **he's ~ here to work** ha venido aquí para trabajar; **to ~ home** volver a casa

3 (reach): **to ~ to** llegar a; **the bill came to £40** la cuenta ascendía a cuarenta libras

4 (occur): **an idea came to me** se me ocurrió una idea

5 (be, become): **to ~ loose/undone** etc aflojarse/desabrocharse, desatarse etc; **I've ~ to like him** por fin ha llegado a gustarme

come about vi suceder, ocurrir

come across vt fus (person) topar con; (thing) dar con

come away vi (leave) marcharse; (become detached) desprenderse

come back vi (return) volver

come by vt fus (acquire) conseguir

come down vi (price) bajar; (tree, building) ser derribado

come forward vi presentarse

come from vt fus (place, source) ser de

come in vi (visitor) entrar; (train, report) llegar; (fashion) ponerse de moda; (on deal etc) entrar

come in for vt fus (criticism etc) recibir

come into vt fus (money) heredar; (be involved) tener que ver con; **to ~ into fashion** ponerse de moda

come off vi (button) soltarse, desprenderse; (attempt) salir bien

come on vi (pupil) progresar; (work, project) desarrollarse; (lights) encenderse; (electricity) volver; ~ **on!** ¡vamos!

come out vi (fact) salir a la luz; (book, sun) salir; (stain) quitarse

come round vi (after faint, operation) volver en sí

come to vi (wake) volver en sí

come up vi (sun) salir; (problem) surgir; (event) aproximarse; (in conversation) mencionarse

come up against vt fus (resistance etc) tropezar con

come up with vt fus (idea) sugerir; (money) conseguir

come upon vt fus (find) dar con

comeback ['kʌmbæk] n: **to make a ~** (THEATRE) volver a las tablas

comedian [kə'mi:dɪən] n cómico; **comedienne** [-'ɛn] n cómica

comedy ['kɒmɪdɪ] n comedia; (humour)

comicidad f

comet ['kɔmɪt] n cometa m

comeuppance [kʌm'ʌpəns] n: **to get one's ~** llevar su merecido

comfort ['kʌmfət] n bienestar m; (relief) alivio ♦ vt consolar; **~s** npl (of home etc) comodidades fpl; **~able** adj cómodo; (financially) acomodado; (easy) fácil; **~ably** adv (sit) cómodamente; (live) holgadamente; **~ station** (US) n servicios mpl

comic ['kɔmɪk] adj (also: ~al) cómico ♦ n (comedian) cómico; (BRIT: for children) tebeo; (BRIT: for adults) comic m; **~ strip** n tira cómica

coming ['kʌmɪŋ] n venida, llegada ♦ adj que viene; **~(s) and going(s)** n(pl) ir y venir m, ajetreo

comma ['kɔmə] n coma

command [kə'mɑːnd] n orden f, mandato; (MIL: authority) mando; (mastery) dominio ♦ vt (troops) mandar; (give orders to): **to ~ sb to do** mandar or ordenar a uno hacer; **~eer** [kɔmən'dɪə*] comandante m/f, jefe/a m/f

commemorate [kə'meməreɪt] vt conmemorar

commence [kə'mens] vt, vi comenzar, empezar

commend [kə'mend] vt elogiar, alabar; (recommend) recomendar

commensurate [kə'menʃərɪt] adj: **~ with** en proporción a, que corresponde a

comment ['kɔment] n comentario ♦ vi: **to ~ on** hacer comentarios sobre; **"no ~"** (written) "sin comentarios"; (spoken) "no tengo nada que decir"; **~ary** ['kɔməntəri] n comentario; **~ator** ['kɔməntertə*] n comentarista m/f

commerce ['kɔməːs] n comercio

commercial [kə'məːʃəl] adj comercial ♦ n (TV, RADIO) anuncio

commiserate [kə'mɪzəreɪt] vi: **to ~ with** compadecerse de, condolerse de

commission [kə'mɪʃən] n (committee, fee) comisión f ♦ vt (work of art) encargar; **out of ~** fuera de servicio; **~aire** [kəmɪʃə'neə*] (BRIT) n portero; **~er** n (POLICE) comisario de policía

commit [kə'mɪt] vt (act) cometer; (resources) dedicar; (to sb's care) entregar; **to ~ o.s. (to do)** comprometerse (a hacer); **to ~ suicide** suicidarse; **~ment** n compromiso; (to ideology etc) entrega

committee [kə'mɪtɪ] n comité m

commodity [kə'mɔdɪtɪ] n mercancía

common ['kɔmən] adj común; (pej) ordinario ♦ n campo común; **the C~s** npl (BRIT) (la Cámara de) los Comunes mpl; **in ~** en común; **~er** n plebeyo; **~ law** n ley f consuetudinaria; **~ly** adv comúnmente;

C~ Market n Mercado Común; **~place** adj de lo más común; **~room** n sala común; **~ sense** n sentido común; **the C~wealth** n la Commonwealth

commotion [kə'məuʃən] n tumulto, confusión f

commune [n 'kɔmjuːn, vb kə'mjuːn] n (group) comuna ♦ vi: **to ~ with** comulgar or conversar con

communicate [kə'mjuːnɪkeɪt] vt comunicar ♦ vi: **to ~ (with)** comunicarse (con); (in writing) estar en contacto (con)

communication [kəmjuːnɪ'keɪʃən] n comunicación f; **~ cord** (BRIT) n timbre m de alarma

communion [kə'mjuːnɪən] n (also: Holy C~) comunión f

communiqué [kə'mjuːnɪkeɪ] n comunicado, parte f

communism ['kɔmjunɪzəm] n comunismo; **communist** adj, n comunista m/f

community [kə'mjuːnɪtɪ] n comunidad f; (large group) colectividad f; **~ centre** n centro social; **~ chest** (US) n arca comunitaria, fondo común

commutation ticket [kɔmju'teɪʃən-] (US) n billete m de abono

commute [kə'mjuːt] vi viajar a diario de la casa al trabajo ♦ vt conmutar; **~r** n persona (que viaja ... see vi)

compact [adj kəm'pækt, n 'kɔmpækt] adj compacto ♦ n (also: powder ~) polvera; **~ disc** n compact disc m; **~ disc player** n reproductor m de disco compacto, compact disc m

companion [kəm'pænɪən] n compañero/a; **~ship** n compañerismo

company ['kʌmpənɪ] n compañía; (COMM) sociedad f, compañía; **to keep sb ~** acompañar a uno; **~ secretary** (BRIT) n secretario/a de compañía

comparative [kəm'pærətɪv] adj relativo; (study) comparativo; **~ly** adv (relatively) relativamente

compare [kəm'peə*] vt: **to ~ sth/sb with/to** comparar algo/a uno con ♦ vi: **to ~ (with)** compararse (con); **comparison** [-'pærɪsn] n comparación f

compartment [kəm'pɑːtmənt] n (also: RAIL) compartim(i)ento

compass ['kʌmpəs] n brújula; **~es** npl (MATH) compás m

compassion [kəm'pæʃən] n compasión f; **~ate** adj compasivo

compatible [kəm'pætɪbl] adj compatible

compel [kəm'pel] vt obligar

compensate ['kɔmpenseɪt] vt compensar ♦ vi: **to ~ for** compensar; **compensation** [-'seɪʃən] n (for loss) indemnización f

compère ['kɔmpeə*] n presentador m
compete [kəm'pi:t] vi (take part) tomar parte, concurrir; (vie with): **to ~ with** competir con, hacer competencia a
competent ['kɔmpɪtənt] adj competente, capaz
competition [kɔmpɪ'tɪʃən] n (contest) concurso; (rivalry) competencia
competitive [kəm'petɪtɪv] adj (ECON, SPORT) competitivo
competitor [kəm'petɪtə*] n (rival) competidor(a) m/f; (participant) concursante m/f
complacency [kəm'pleɪsnsɪ] n autosatisfacción f
complacent [kəm'pleɪsənt] adj autocomplaciente
complain [kəm'pleɪn] vi quejarse; (COMM) reclamar; **~t** n queja; reclamación f; (MED) enfermedad f
complement [n 'kɔmplɪmənt, vb 'kɔmplɪment] n complemento; (esp of ship's crew) dotación f ♦ vt (enhance) complementar; **~ary** [kɔmplɪ'mentərɪ] adj complementario
complete [kəm'pli:t] adj (full) completo; (finished) acabado ♦ vt (fulfil) completar; (finish) acabar; (a form) llenar; **~ly** adv completamente; **completion** [-'pli:ʃən] n terminación f; (of contract) realización f
complex ['kɔmpleks] adj, n complejo
complexion [kəm'plekʃən] n (of face) tez f, cutis m
compliance [kəm'plaɪəns] n (submission) sumisión f; (agreement) conformidad f; **in ~ with** de acuerdo con
complicate ['kɔmplɪkeɪt] vt complicar; **~d** adj complicado; **complication** [-'keɪʃən] n complicación f
compliment ['kɔmplɪmənt] n (formal) cumplido ♦ vt felicitar; **~s** npl (regards) saludos mpl; **to pay sb a ~** hacer cumplidos a uno; **~ary** [-'mentərɪ] adj lisonjero; (free) de favor
comply [kəm'plaɪ] vi: **to ~ with** cumplir con
component [kəm'pəunənt] adj componente ♦ n (TECH) pieza
compose [kəm'pəuz] vt: **to be ~d of** componerse de; (music etc) componer; **to ~ o.s.** tranquilizarse; **~d** adj sosegado; **~r** n (MUS) compositor(a) m/f; **composition** [kɔmpə'zɪʃən] n composición f
compost ['kɔmpɔst] n abono (vegetal)
composure [kəm'pəuʒə*] n serenidad f, calma
compound ['kɔmpaund] n (CHEM) compuesto; (LING) palabra compuesta; (enclosure) recinto ♦ adj compuesto; (fracture) complicado

comprehend [kɔmprɪ'hend] vt comprender; **comprehension** [-'henʃən] n comprensión f
comprehensive [kɔmprɪ'hensɪv] adj exhaustivo; (INSURANCE) contra todo riesgo; **~ (school)** n centro estatal de enseñanza secundaria; ≈ Instituto Nacional de Bachillerato (SP)
compress [vb kəm'pres, n 'kɔmpres] vt comprimir; (information) condensar ♦ n (MED) compresa
comprise [kəm'praɪz] vt (also: **be ~d of**) comprender, constar de; (constitute) constituir
compromise ['kɔmprəmaɪz] n (agreement) arreglo ♦ vt comprometer ♦ vi transigir
compulsion [kəm'pʌlʃən] n compulsión f; (force) obligación f
compulsive [kəm'pʌlsɪv] adj compulsivo; (viewing, reading) obligado
compulsory [kəm'pʌlsərɪ] adj obligatorio
computer [kəm'pju:tə*] n ordenador m, computador m, computadora; **~ game** n juego para ordenador; **~-generated** adj realizado por ordenador, creado por ordenador; **~ize** vt (data) computerizar; (system) informatizar; **~ programmer** n programador(a) m/f; **~ programming** n programación f; **~ science** n informática; **computing** [kəm'pju:tɪŋ] n (activity, science) informática
comrade ['kɔmrɪd] n (POL, MIL) camarada; (friend) compañero/a; **~ship** n camaradería, compañerismo
con [kɔn] vt (deceive) engañar; (cheat) estafar ♦ n estafa
conceal [kən'si:l] vt ocultar
conceit [kən'si:t] n presunción f; **~ed** adj presumido
conceive [kən'si:v] vt, vi concebir
concentrate ['kɔnsəntreɪt] vi concentrarse ♦ vt concentrar
concentration [kɔnsən'treɪʃən] n concentración f
concept ['kɔnsept] n concepto
concern [kən'sə:n] n (matter) asunto; (COMM) empresa; (anxiety) preocupación f ♦ vt (worry) preocupar; (involve) afectar; (relate to) tener que ver con; **to be ~ed (about)** interesarse (por), preocuparse (por); **~ing** prep sobre, acerca de
concert ['kɔnsət] n concierto; **~ed** [kən'sə:tɪd] adj (efforts etc) concertado; **~ hall** n sala de conciertos
concerto [kən'tʃə:təu] n concierto
concession [kən'seʃən] n concesión f; **tax ~** privilegio fiscal
conclude [kən'klu:d] vt concluir; (treaty etc) firmar; (agreement) llegar a; (decide) llegar a la conclusión de; **conclusion** [-'klu:ʒən] n

conclusión f; firma; **conclusive** [-'kluːsɪv] adj decisivo, concluyente

concoct [kən'kɔkt] vt confeccionar; (plot) tramar; **~ion** [-'kɔkʃən] n mezcla

concourse ['kɔŋkɔːs] n vestíbulo

concrete ['kɔnkriːt] n hormigón m ♦ adj de hormigón, (fig) concreto

concur [kən'kəː*] vi estar de acuerdo, asentir

concurrently [kən'kʌrntlɪ] adv al mismo tiempo

concussion [kən'kʌʃən] n conmoción f cerebral

condemn [kən'dem] vt condenar; (building) declarar en ruina

condense [kən'dens] vi condensarse ♦ vt condensar, abreviar; **~d milk** n leche f condensada

condition [kən'dɪʃən] n condición f, estado; (requirement) condición f ♦ vt condicionar; **on ~ that** a condición (de) que; **~er** n suavizante

condolences [kən'dəulənsɪz] npl pésame m

condom ['kɔndəm] n condón m

condone [kən'dəun] vt condonar

conducive [kən'djuːsɪv] adj: **~ to** conducente a

conduct [n 'kɔndʌkt, vb kən'dʌkt] n conducta, comportamiento ♦ vt (lead) conducir; (manage) llevar a cabo, dirigir; (MUS) dirigir; **to ~ o.s.** comportarse; **~ed tour** (BRIT) n visita acompañada; **~or** n (of orchestra) director m; (US: on train) revisor(a) m/f; (on bus) cobrador m; (ELEC) conductor m; **~ress** n (on bus) cobradora

cone [kəun] n cono; (pine ~) piña; (on road) pivote m; (for ice-cream) cucurucho

confectioner [kən'fekʃənə*] n repostero/a; **~'s (shop)** n confitería; **~y** n dulces mpl

confer [kən'fəː*] vt: **to ~ sth on** otorgar algo a ♦ vi conferenciar

conference ['kɔnfərns] n (meeting) reunión f; (convention) congreso

confess [kən'fes] vt confesar ♦ vi admitir; **~ion** [-'feʃən] n confesión f

confetti [kən'fetɪ] n confeti m

confide [kən'faɪd] vi: **to ~ in** confiar en

confidence ['kɔnfɪdns] n (also: self-~) confianza; (secret) confidencia; **in ~** (speak, write) en confianza; **~ trick** n timo; **confident** adj seguro de sí mismo; (certain) seguro; **confidential** [kɔnfɪ'denʃəl] adj confidencial

confine [kən'faɪn] vt (limit) limitar; (shut up) encerrar; **~d** adj (space) reducido; **~ment** n (prison) prisión f; **~s** ['kɔnfaɪnz] npl confines mpl

confirm [kən'fəːm] vt confirmar; **~ation** [kɔnfə'meɪʃən] n confirmación f; **~ed** adj empedernido

confiscate ['kɔnfɪskeɪt] vt confiscar

conflict [n 'kɔnflɪkt, vb kən'flɪkt] n conflicto ♦ vi (opinions) chocar; **~ing** adj contradictorio

conform [kən'fɔːm] vi conformarse; **to ~ to** ajustarse a

confound [kən'faund] vt confundir

confront [kən'frʌnt] vt (problems) hacer frente a; (enemy, danger) enfrentarse con; **~ation** [kɔnfrən'teɪʃən] n enfrentamiento

confuse [kən'fjuːz] vt (perplex) aturdir, desconcertar; (mix up) confundir; (complicate) complicar; **~d** adj confuso; (person) perplejo; **confusing** adj confuso; **confusion** [-'fjuːʒən] n confusión f

congeal [kən'dʒiːl] vi (blood) coagularse; (sauce etc) cuajarse

congested [kən'dʒestɪd] adj congestionado; **congestion** n congestión f

congratulate [kən'grætjuleɪt] vt: **to ~ sb (on)** felicitar a uno (por); **congratulations** [-'leɪʃənz] npl felicitaciones fpl; **congratulations!** ¡enhorabuena!

congregate ['kɔŋgrɪgeɪt] vi congregarse; **congregation** [-'geɪʃən] n (of a church) feligreses mpl

congress ['kɔŋgres] n congreso; (US): **C~** Congreso; **C~man** (irreg) (US) n miembro del Congreso

conifer ['kɔnɪfə*] n conífera

conjunctivitis [kəndʒʌŋktɪ'vaɪtɪs] n conjuntivitis f

conjure ['kʌndʒə*] vi hacer juegos de manos; **~ up** vt (ghost, spirit) hacer aparecer; (memories) evocar; **~r** n ilusionista m/f

con man ['kɔn-] n estafador m

connect [kə'nekt] vt juntar, unir; (ELEC) conectar; (TEL: subscriber) poner; (: caller) poner al habla; (fig) relacionar, asociar ♦ vi: **to ~ with** (train) enlazar con; **to be ~ed with** (associated) estar relacionado con; **~ion** [-ʃən] n juntura, unión f; (ELEC) conexión f; (RAIL) enlace m; (TEL) comunicación f; (fig) relación f

connive [kə'naɪv] vi: **to ~ at** hacer la vista gorda a

connoisseur [kɔnɪ'sə*] n experto/a, entendido/a

conquer ['kɔŋkə*] vt (territory) conquistar; (enemy, feelings) vencer; **~or** n conquistador m

conquest ['kɔŋkwest] n conquista

cons [kɔnz] npl see **convenience**; **pro**

conscience ['kɔnʃəns] n conciencia

conscientious [kɔnʃɪ'enʃəs] adj concienzudo; (objection) de conciencia

conscious ['kɔnʃəs] adj (deliberate) deliberado; (awake, aware) consciente; **~ness** n conciencia; (MED) conocimiento

conscript ['kɒnskrɪpt] n recluta m; **~ion** [kən'skrɪpʃən] n servicio militar (obligatorio)

consensus [kən'sɛnsəs] n consenso

consent [kən'sɛnt] n consentimiento ♦ vi: **to ~ (to)** consentir (en)

consequence ['kɒnsɪkwəns] n consecuencia; (significance) importancia

consequently ['kɒnsɪkwəntlɪ] adv por consiguiente

conservation [kɒnsə'veɪʃən] n conservación f

conservative [kən'sɜ:vətɪv] adj conservador(a); (estimate etc) cauteloso; **C~** (BRIT) adj, n (POL) conservador(a) m/f

conservatory [kən'sɜ:vətrɪ] n invernadero; (MUS) conservatorio

conserve [kən'sɜ:v] vt conservar ♦ n conserva

consider [kən'sɪdə*] vt considerar; (take into account) tener en cuenta; (study) estudiar, examinar; **to ~ doing sth** pensar en (la posibilidad de) hacer algo; **~able** adj considerable; **~ably** adv notablemente; **~ate** adj considerado; **consideration** [-'reɪʃən] n consideración f; (factor) factor m; **to give sth further consideration** estudiar algo más a fondo; **~ing** prep teniendo en cuenta

consign [kən'saɪn] vt: **to ~ to** (sth unwanted) relegar a; (person) destinar a; **~ment** n envío

consist [kən'sɪst] vi: **to ~ of** consistir en

consistency [kən'sɪstənsɪ] n (of argument etc) coherencia; consecuencia; (thickness) consistencia

consistent [kən'sɪstənt] adj (person) consecuente; (argument etc) coherente

consolation [kɒnsə'leɪʃən] n consuelo

console¹ [kən'səul] vt consolar

console² ['kɒnsəul] n consola

consonant ['kɒnsənənt] n consonante f

consortium [kən'sɔ:tɪəm] n consorcio

conspicuous [kən'spɪkjuəs] adj (visible) visible

conspiracy [kən'spɪrəsɪ] n conjura, complot m

constable ['kʌnstəbl] (BRIT) n policía m/f; **chief ~** jefe m de policía

constabulary [kən'stæbjulərɪ] n ≈ policía

constant ['kɒnstənt] adj constante; **~ly** adv constantemente

constipated ['kɒnstɪpeɪtəd] adj estreñido; **constipation** [kɒnstɪ'peɪʃən] n estreñimiento

constituency [kən'stɪtjuənsɪ] n (POL: area) distrito electoral; (: electors) electorado; **constituent** [-ənt] n (POL) elector(a) m/f; (part) componente m

constitution [kɒnstɪ'tju:ʃən] n constitución f; **~al** adj constitucional

constraint [kən'streɪnt] n obligación f; (limit) restricción f

construct [kən'strʌkt] vt construir; **~ion** [-ʃən] n construcción f; **~ive** adj constructivo

consul ['kɒnsl] n cónsul m/f; **~ate** ['kɒnsjulɪt] n consulado

consult [kən'sʌlt] vt consultar; **~ant** n (BRIT: MED) especialista m/f; (other specialist) asesor(a) m/f; **~ation** [kɒnsəl'teɪʃən] n consulta; **~ing room** (BRIT) n consultorio

consume [kən'sju:m] vt (eat) comerse; (drink) beberse; (fire etc, COMM) consumir; **~r** n consumidor(a) m/f; **~r goods** npl bienes mpl de consumo

consummate ['kɒnsʌmeɪt] vt consumar

consumption [kən'sʌmpʃən] n consumo

cont. abbr (= continued) sigue

contact ['kɒntækt] n contacto; (person) contacto; (: pej) enchufe m ♦ vt ponerse en contacto con; **~ lenses** npl lentes fpl de contacto

contagious [kən'teɪdʒəs] adj contagioso

contain [kən'teɪn] vt contener; **to ~ o.s.** contenerse; **~er** n recipiente m; (for shipping etc) contenedor m

contaminate [kən'tæmɪneɪt] vt contaminar

cont'd abbr (= continued) sigue

contemplate ['kɒntəmpleɪt] vt contemplar; (reflect upon) considerar

contemporary [kən'tɛmpərərɪ] adj, n contemporáneo/a m/f

contempt [kən'tɛmpt] n desprecio; **~ of court** (LAW) desacato (a los tribunales); **~ible** adj despreciable; **~uous** adj desdeñoso

contend [kən'tɛnd] vt (argue) afirmar ♦ vi: **to ~ with/for** luchar contra/por; **~er** n (SPORT) contendiente m/f

content [adj, vb kən'tɛnt, n 'kɒntɛnt] adj (happy) contento; (satisfied) satisfecho ♦ vt contentar; satisfacer ♦ n contenido; **~s** npl contenido; (table of) **~s** índice m de materias; **~ed** adj contento; satisfecho

contention [kən'tɛnʃən] n (assertion) aseveración f; (disagreement) discusión f

contest [n 'kɒntest, vb kən'test] n lucha; (competition) concurso ♦ vt (dispute) impugnar; (POL) presentarse como candidato/a en; **~ant** [kən'testənt] n concursante m/f; (in fight) contendiente m/f

context ['kɒntekst] n contexto

continent ['kɒntɪnənt] n continente m; **the C~** (BRIT) el continente europeo; **~al** [-'nentl] adj continental; **~al breakfast** n desayuno estilo europeo; **~al quilt** (BRIT) n edredón m

contingency [kən'tɪndʒənsɪ] n contingencia

continual [kən'tɪnjuəl] adj continuo; **~ly** adv constantemente

continuation [kəntɪnju'eɪʃən] n prolongación f; (after interruption) reanudación f

continue [kən'tɪnju:] vi, vt seguir, continuar

continuous [kən'tɪnjuəs] *adj* continuo
contort [kən'tɔːt] *vt* retorcer
contour ['kɒntuə*] *n* contorno; (*also:* ~ *line*) curva de nivel
contraband ['kɒntrəbænd] *n* contrabando
contraceptive [kɒntrə'septɪv] *adj, n* anticonceptivo
contract [*n* 'kɒntrækt, *vb* kən'trækt] *n* contrato ♦ *vi* (COMM): **to ~ to do sth** comprometerse por contrato a hacer algo; (*become smaller*) contraerse, encogerse ♦ *vt* contraer; **~ion** [kən'trækʃən] *n* contracción *f*; **~or** *n* contratista *m/f*
contradict [kɒntrə'dɪkt] *vt* contradecir; **~ion** [-ʃən] *n* contradicción *f*
contraption [kən'træpʃən] (*pej*) *n* artilugio *m*
contrary¹ ['kɒntrərɪ] *adj* contrario ♦ *n* lo contrario; **on the ~** al contrario; **unless you hear to the ~** a no ser que le digan lo contrario
contrary² [kən'trεərɪ] *adj* (*perverse*) terco
contrast [*n* 'kɒntrɑːst, *vt* kən'trɑːst] *n* contraste *m* ♦ *vt* comparar; **in ~ to** en contraste con
contravene [kɒntrə'viːn] *vt* infringir
contribute [kən'trɪbjuːt] *vi* contribuir ♦ *vt*: **to ~ £10/an article to** contribuir con 10 libras/un artículo a; **to ~ to** (*charity*) donar a; (*newspaper*) escribir para; (*discussion*) intervenir en; **contribution** [kɒntrɪ'bjuːʃən] *n* (*donation*) donativo; (BRIT: *for social security*) cotización *f*; (*to debate*) intervención *f*, (*to journal*) colaboración *f*; **contributor** *n* contribuyente *m/f*; (*to newspaper*) colaborador(a) *m/f*
contrive [kən'traɪv] *vt* (*invent*) idear ♦ *vi*: **to ~ to do** lograr hacer
control [kən'trəul] *vt* controlar; (*process etc*) dirigir; (*machinery*) manejar; (*temper*) dominar; (*disease*) contener ♦ *n* control *m*; **~s** *npl* (*of vehicle*) instrumentos *mpl* de mando; (*of radio*) controles *mpl*; (*governmental*) medidas *fpl* de control; **under ~** bajo control; **to be in ~ of** tener el mando de; **the car went out of ~** se perdió el control del coche; **~led substance** *n* sustancia controlada; **~ panel** *n* tablero de instrumentos; **~ room** *n* sala de mando; **~ tower** *n* (AVIAT) torre *f* de control
controversial [kɒntrə'vɜːʃl] *adj* polémico
controversy ['kɒntrəvɜːsɪ] *n* polémica
convalesce [kɒnvə'les] *vi* convalecer
convector [kən'vektə*] *n* calentador *m* de aire
convene [kən'viːn] *vt* convocar ♦ *vi* reunirse
convenience [kən'viːnɪəns] *n* (*easiness*) comodidad *f*; (*suitability*) idoneidad *f*; (*advantage*) ventaja; **at your ~** cuando le sea

conveniente; **all modern ~s, all mod cons** (BRIT) todo confort
convenient [kən'viːnɪənt] *adj* (*useful*) útil; (*place, time*) conveniente
convent ['kɒnvənt] *n* convento
convention [kən'venʃən] *n* convención *f*; (*meeting*) asamblea; (*agreement*) convenio; **~al** *adj* convencional
converge [kən'vɜːdʒ] *vi* convergir; (*people*): **to ~ on** dirigirse todos a
conversant [kən'vɜːsnt] *adj*: **to be ~ with** estar al tanto de
conversation [kɒnvə'seɪʃən] *n* conversación *f*; **~al** *adj* familiar; **~al skill** facilidad *f* de palabra
converse [*n* 'kɒnvɜːs, *vb* kən'vɜːs] *n* inversa ♦ *vi* conversar; **~ly** [-'vɜːslɪ] *adv* a la inversa
conversion [kən'vɜːʃən] *n* conversión *f*
convert [*vb* kən'vɜːt, *n* 'kɒnvɜːt] *vt* (REL, COMM) convertir; (*alter*): **to ~ sth into/to** transformar algo en/convertir algo a ♦ *n* converso/a; **~ible** *adj* convertible ♦ *n* descapotable *m*
convey [kən'veɪ] *vt* llevar; (*thanks*) comunicar; (*idea*) expresar; **~or belt** *n* cinta transportadora
convict [*vb* kən'vɪkt, *n* 'kɒnvɪkt] *vt* (*find guilty*) declarar culpable a ♦ *n* presidiario/a; **~ion** [-ʃən] *n* condena; (*belief, certainty*) convicción *f*
convince [kən'vɪns] *vt* convencer; **~d** *adj*: **~d of/that** convencido de/de que; **convincing** *adj* convincente
convoluted ['kɒnvəluːtɪd] *adj* (*argument etc*) enrevesado
convoy ['kɒnvɔɪ] *n* convoy *m*
convulse [kən'vʌls] *vt*: **to be ~d with laughter** desternillarse de risa; **convulsion** [-'vʌlʃən] *n* convulsión *f*
cook [kuk] *vt* (*stew etc*) guisar; (*meal*) preparar ♦ *vi* cocer; (*person*) cocinar ♦ *n* cocinero/a; **~ book** *n* libro de cocina; **~er** *n* cocina; **~ery** *n* cocina; **~ery book** (BRIT) *n* = **~ book**; **~ie** (US) *n* galleta; **~ing** *n* cocina
cool [kuːl] *adj* fresco; (*not afraid*) tranquilo; (*unfriendly*) frío ♦ *vt* enfriar ♦ *vi* enfriarse; **~ness** *n* frescura; tranquilidad *f*; (*indifference*) falta de entusiasmo
coop [kuːp] *n* gallinero ♦ *vt*: **to ~ up** (*fig*) encerrar
cooperate [kəu'ɔpəreɪt] *vi* cooperar, colaborar; **cooperation** [-'reɪʃən] *n* cooperación *f*, colaboración *f*; **cooperative** [-'ɔpərətɪv] *adj* (*business*) cooperativo; (*person*) servicial ♦ *n* cooperativa
coordinate [*vb* kəu'ɔːdɪneɪt, *n* kəu'ɔːdɪnət] *vt* coordinar ♦ *n* (MATH) coordenada; **~s** *npl* (*clothes*) coordinados *mpl*; **coordination** [-'neɪʃən] *n* coordinación *f*

co-ownership [kəu'əunəʃip] *n* co-propiedad *f*

cop [kɔp] (*inf*) *n* poli *m* (*SP*), tira *m* (*AM*)

cope [kəup] *vi*: **to ~ with** (*problem*) hacer frente a

copper ['kɔpə*] *n* (*metal*) cobre *m*; (*BRIT: inf*) poli *m*; **~s** *npl* (*money*) calderilla (*SP*), centavos *mpl* (*AM*)

copulate ['kɔpjuleit] *vi* copularse

copy ['kɔpi] *n* copia; (*of book etc*) ejemplar *m* ♦ *vt* copiar; **~right** *n* derechos *mpl* de autor

coral ['kɔrəl] *n* coral *m*

cord [kɔ:d] *n* cuerda; (*ELEC*) cable *m*; (*fabric*) pana

cordial ['kɔ:dɪəl] *adj* cordial ♦ *n* cordial *m*

cordon ['kɔ:dn] *n* cordón *m*; **~ off** *vt* acordonar

corduroy ['kɔ:dərɔɪ] *n* pana

core [kɔ:*] *n* centro, núcleo; (*of fruit*) corazón *m*; (*of problem*) meollo ♦ *vt* quitar el corazón de

coriander [kɔrɪ'ændə*] *n* culantro

cork [kɔ:k] *n* corcho; (*tree*) alcornoque *m*; **~screw** *n* sacacorchos *m inv*

corn [kɔ:n] *n* (*BRIT: cereal crop*) trigo; (*US: maize*) maíz *m*; (*on foot*) callo; **~ on the cob** (*CULIN*) maíz en la mazorca (*SP*), choclo (*AM*)

corned beef ['kɔ:nd-] *n* carne *f* acecinada (en lata)

corner ['kɔ:nə*] *n* (*outside*) esquina; (*inside*) rincón *m*; (*in road*) curva; (*FOOTBALL*) córner *m*; (*BOXING*) esquina ♦ *vt* (*trap*) arrinconar; (*COMM*) acaparar ♦ *vi* (*in car*) tomar las curvas; **~stone** *n* (*also fig*) piedra angular

cornet ['kɔ:nit] *n* (*MUS*) corneta; (*BRIT: of ice-cream*) cucurucho

cornflakes ['kɔ:nfleiks] *npl* copos *mpl* de maíz, cornflakes *mpl*

cornflour ['kɔ:nflauə*] (*BRIT*), **cornstarch** ['kɔ:nstɑ:tʃ] (*US*) *n* harina de maíz

Cornwall ['kɔ:nwəl] *n* Cornualles *m*

corny ['kɔ:ni] (*inf*) *adj* gastado

coronary ['kɔrənəri] *n* (*also*: **~ thrombosis**) infarto

coronation [kɔrə'neiʃən] *n* coronación *f*

coroner ['kɔrənə*] *n* juez *m* (de instrucción)

corporal ['kɔ:pərl] *n* cabo ♦ *adj*: **~ punishment** castigo corporal

corporate ['kɔ:pərit] *adj* (*action, ownership*) colectivo; (*finance, image*) corporativo

corporation [kɔ:pə'reiʃən] *n* (*of town*) ayuntamiento; (*COMM*) corporación *f*

corps [kɔ:*, *pl* kɔ:z] *n inv* cuerpo; **diplomatic ~** cuerpo diplomático; **press ~** gabinete *m* de prensa

corpse [kɔ:ps] *n* cadáver *m*

correct [kə'rekt] *adj* justo, exacto; (*proper*) correcto ♦ *vt* corregir; (*exam*) corregir, calificar; **~ion** [-ʃən] *n* (*act*) corrección *f*; (*instance*) rectificación *f*

correspond [kɔris'pɔnd] *vi* (*write*): **to ~ (with)** escribirse (con); (*be equivalent to*): **to ~ (to)** corresponder (a); (*be in accordance*): **to ~ (with)** corresponder (con); **~ence** *n* correspondencia; **~ence course** *n* curso por correspondencia; **~ent** *n* corresponsal *m/f*

corridor ['kɔridɔ:*] *n* pasillo

corrode [kə'rəud] *vt* corroer ♦ *vi* corroerse

corrugated ['kɔrəgeitid] *adj* ondulado; **~ iron** *n* chapa ondulada

corrupt [kə'rʌpt] *adj* (*person*) corrupto; (*COMPUT*) corrompido ♦ *vt* corromper; (*COMPUT*) degradar

Corsica ['kɔ:sikə] *n* Córcega

cosmetic [kɔz'metik] *adj, n* cosmético

cosmopolitan [kɔzmə'pɔlitn] *adj* cosmopolita

cost [kɔst] (*pt, pp* cost) *n* (*price*) precio; **~s** *npl* (*COMM*) costes *mpl*; (*LAW*) costas *fpl* ♦ *vi* costar, valer ♦ *vt* preparar el presupuesto de; **how much does it ~?** ¿cuánto cuesta?; **to ~ sb time/effort** costarle a uno tiempo/esfuerzo; **it ~ him his life** le costó la vida; **at all ~s** cueste lo que cueste

co-star ['kəustɑ:*] *n* coprotagonista *m/f*

Costa Rica ['kɔstə'ri:kə] *n* Costa Rica; **~n** *adj, n* costarriqueño/a *m/f*

cost-effective [kɔsti'fektiv] *adj* rentable

costly ['kɔstli] *adj* costoso

cost-of-living [kɔstəv'liviŋ] *adj*: **~ allowance** plus *m* de carestía de vida; **~ index** índice *m* del costo de vida

cost price (*BRIT*) *n* precio de coste

costume ['kɔstju:m] *n* traje *m*; (*BRIT: also: swimming ~*) traje de baño; **~ jewellery** *n* bisutería

cosy ['kəuzi] (*US* cozy) *adj* (*person*) cómodo; (*room*) acogedor(a)

cot [kɔt] *n* (*BRIT: child's*) cuna; (*US: campbed*) cama de campaña

cottage ['kɔtidʒ] *n* casita de campo; (*rustic*) barraca; **~ cheese** *n* requesón *m*

cotton ['kɔtn] *n* algodón *m*; (*thread*) hilo; **~ on to** (*inf*) *vt fus* caer en la cuenta de; **~ candy** (*US*) *n* algodón *m* (azucarado); **~ wool** (*BRIT*) *n* algodón *m* (hidrófilo)

couch [kautʃ] *n* sofá *m*; (*doctor's etc*) diván *m*

couchette [ku:'ʃet] *n* litera

cough [kɔf] *vi* toser ♦ *n* tos *f*; **~ drop** *n* pastilla para la tos

could [kud] *pt of* **can²**; **~n't = could not**

council ['kaunsl] *n* consejo; **city or town ~** consejo municipal; **~ estate** (*BRIT*) *n* urbanización *f* de viviendas municipales de alquiler; **~ house** (*BRIT*) *n* vivienda municipal de alquiler; **~lor** *n* concejal(a) *m/f*

counsel ['kaunsl] *n* (*advice*) consejo; (*lawyer*)

abogado/a ♦ vt aconsejar; **~lor** n consejero/a; **~or** (US) n abogado/a

count [kaunt] vt contar; (*include*) incluir ♦ vi contar ♦ n cuenta; (*of votes*) escrutinio; (*level*) nivel m; (*nobleman*) conde m; **~ on** vt fus contar con; **~down** n cuenta atrás

countenance ['kauntɪnəns] n semblante m, rostro ♦ vt (*tolerate*) aprobar, tolerar

counter ['kauntə*] n (*in shop*) mostrador m; (*in games*) ficha ♦ vt contrarrestar ♦ adv: **to run ~ to** ser contrario a, ir en contra de; **~act** vt contrarrestar

counterfeit ['kauntəfɪt] n falsificación f, simulación f ♦ vt falsificar ♦ adj falso, falsificado

counterfoil ['kauntəfɔɪl] n talón m

counterpart ['kauntəpɑ:t] n homólogo/a

counter-productive [kauntəprə'dʌktɪv] adj contraproducente

countersign ['kauntəsaɪn] vt refrendar

countess ['kauntɪs] n condesa

countless ['kauntlɪs] adj innumerable

country ['kʌntrɪ] n país m; (*native land*) patria; (*as opposed to town*) campo; (*region*) región f, tierra; **~ dancing** (*BRIT*) n baile m regional; **~ house** n casa de campo; **~man** n (*irreg*) (*compatriot*) compatriota m; (*rural*) campesino, paisano; **~side** n campo

county ['kauntɪ] n condado

coup [ku:] (pl **~s**) n (*also*: ~ d'état) golpe m (de estado); (*achievement*) éxito

couple ['kʌpl] n (*of things*) par m; (*of people*) pareja; (*married ~*) matrimonio; **a ~ of** un par de

coupon ['ku:pɔn] n cupón m; (*voucher*) valé m

courage ['kʌrɪdʒ] n valor m, valentía; **~ous** [kə'reɪdʒəs] adj valiente

courgette [kuə'ʒet] (*BRIT*) n calabacín m (*SP*), calabacita (*AM*)

courier ['kurɪə*] n mensajero/a; (*for tourists*) guía m/f (de turismo)

course [kɔ:s] n (*direction*) dirección f; (*of river, SCOL*) curso; (*process*) transcurso; (*MED*): **~ of treatment** tratamiento; (*of ship*) rumbo; (*part of meal*) plato; (*GOLF*) campo; **of ~** desde luego, naturalmente; **of ~!** ¡claro!

court [kɔ:t] n (*royal*) corte f; (*LAW*) tribunal m, juzgado; (*TENNIS etc*) pista, cancha ♦ vt (*woman*) cortejar a; **to take to ~** demandar

courteous ['kɜ:tɪəs] adj cortés

courtesy ['kɜ:təsɪ] n cortesía; (**by**) **~** por cortesía de; **~ bus, ~ coach** n autobús m gratuito

court-house ['kɔ:thaus] (US) n palacio de justicia

courtier ['kɔ:tɪə*] n cortesano

court-martial (pl **courts-martial**) n consejo de guerra

courtroom ['kɔ:trum] n sala de justicia

courtyard ['kɔ:tjɑ:d] n patio

cousin ['kʌzn] n primo/a; **first ~** primo/a carnal, primo/a hermano/a

cove [kəuv] n cala, ensenada

covenant ['kʌvənənt] n pacto

cover ['kʌvə*] n cubrir; (*feelings, mistake*) ocultar; (*with lid*) tapar; (*book etc*) forrar; (*distance*) recorrer; (*include*) abarcar; (*protect: also: INSURANCE*) cubrir; (*PRESS*) investigar; (*discuss*) tratar ♦ n cubierta; (*lid*) tapa; (*for chair etc*) funda; (*envelope*) sobre m; (*for book*) forro; (*of magazine*) portada; (*shelter*) abrigo; (*INSURANCE*) cobertura; (*of spy*) cobertura; **~s** npl (*on bed*) sábanas; mantas; **to take ~** (*shelter*) protegerse, resguardarse; **under ~** (*indoors*) bajo techo; **under ~ of darkness** al amparo de la oscuridad; **under separate ~** (*COMM*) por separado; **~ up** vi: **to ~ up for sb** encubrir a uno; **~age** n (*TV, PRESS*) cobertura; **~alls** (*US*) npl mono; **~ charge** n precio del cubierto; **~ing** n capa; **~ing letter** (*US* = **letter**) n carta de explicación; **~ note** n (*INSURANCE*) póliza provisional

covert ['kʌuvət] adj secreto, encubierto

cover-up n encubrimiento

cow [kau] n vaca; (*inf!: woman*) bruja ♦ vt intimidar

coward ['kauəd] n cobarde m/f; **~ice** [-ɪs] n cobardía; **~ly** adj cobarde

cowboy ['kaubɔɪ] n vaquero

cower ['kauə*] vi encogerse (de miedo)

coy [kɔɪ] adj tímido

cozy ['kəuzɪ] (*US*) adj = **cosy**

CPA (*US*) n abbr = **certified public accountant**

crab [kræb] n cangrejo; **~ apple** n manzana silvestre

crack [kræk] n grieta; (*noise*) crujido; (*drug*) crack m ♦ vt agrietar, romper; (*nut*) cascar; (*solve: problem*) resolver; (: *code*) descifrar; (*whip etc*) chasquear; (*knuckles*) crujir; (*joke*) contar ♦ adj (*expert*) de primera; **~ down on** vt fus adoptar fuertes medidas contra; **~ up** vi (*MED*) sufrir una crisis nerviosa; **~er** n (*biscuit*) crácker m; (*Christmas ~er*) petardo sorpresa

crackle ['krækl] vi crepitar

cradle ['kreɪdl] n cuna

craft [krɑ:ft] n (*skill*) arte m; (*trade*) oficio; (*cunning*) astucia; (*boat: pl inv*) barco; (*plane: pl inv*) avión m

craftsman ['krɑ:ftsmən] n artesano; **~ship** n (*quality*) destreza

crafty ['krɑ:ftɪ] adj astuto

crag [kræg] n peñasco

cram [kræm] vt (*fill*): **to ~ sth with** llenar algo (a reventar) de; (*put*): **to ~ sth into** meter algo a la fuerza en ♦ vi (*for exams*) empollar

cramp [kræmp] *n* (*MED*) calambre *m*; **~ed**
adj apretado, estrecho

cranberry ['krænbərɪ] *n* arándano agrio

crane [kreɪn] *n* (*TECH*) grúa; (*bird*) grulla

crank [kræŋk] *n* manivela; (*person*) chiflado

cranny ['krænɪ] *n see* **nook**

crash [kræʃ] *n* (*noise*) estrépito; (*of cars etc*)
choque *m*; (*of plane*) accidente *m* de
aviación; (*COMM*) quiebra ♦ *vt* (*car, plane*)
estrellar ♦ *vi* (*car, plane*) estrellarse; (*two
cars*) chocar; (*COMM*) quebrar; **~ course** *n*
curso acelerado; **~ helmet** *n* casco
(protector); **~ landing** *n* aterrizaje *m* forzado

crass [kræs] *adj* grosero, maleducado

crate [kreɪt] *n* cajón *m* de embalaje; (*for
bottles*) caja

cravat(e) [krə'væt] *n* pañuelo

crave [kreɪv] *vt, vi*: **to ~ (for)** ansiar, anhelar

crawl [krɔːl] *vi* (*drag o.s.*) arrastrarse; (*child*)
andar a gatas, gatear; (*vehicle*) avanzar
(lentamente) ♦ *n* (*SWIMMING*) crol *m*

crayfish ['kreɪfɪʃ] *n inv* (*freshwater*) cangrejo
de río; (*saltwater*) cigala

crayon ['kreɪən] *n* lápiz *m* de color

craze [kreɪz] *n* (*fashion*) moda

crazy ['kreɪzɪ] *adj* (*person*) loco; (*idea*)
disparatado; (*inf: keen*): **~ about sb/sth** loco
por uno/algo

creak [kriːk] *vi* (*floorboard*) crujir; (*hinge etc*)
chirriar, rechinar

cream [kriːm] *n* (*of milk*) nata, crema; (*lotion*)
crema; (*fig*) flor *f* y nata ♦ *adj* (*colour*) color
crema; **~ cake** *n* pastel *m* de nata;
~ cheese *n* queso blanco; **~y** *adj* cremoso;
(*colour*) color crema

crease [kriːs] *n* (*fold*) pliegue *m*; (*in trousers*)
raya; (*wrinkle*) arruga ♦ *vt* (*wrinkle*) arrugar
♦ *vi* (*wrinkle up*) arrugarse

create [kriː'eɪt] *vt* crear; **creation** [-ʃən] *n*
creación *f*; **creative** *adj* creativo; **creator** *n*
creador(a) *m/f*

creature ['kriːtʃə*] *n* (*animal*) animal *m*,
bicho; (*person*) criatura

crèche [krɛʃ] *n* guardería (infantil)

credence ['kriːdəns] *n*: **to lend** *or* **give ~ to**
creer en, dar crédito a

credentials [krɪ'dɛnʃlz] *npl* (*references*)
referencias *fpl*; (*identity papers*) documentos
mpl de identidad

credible ['krɛdɪbl] *adj* creíble; (*trustworthy*)
digno de confianza

credit ['krɛdɪt] *n* crédito; (*merit*) honor *m*,
mérito ♦ *vt* (*COMM*) abonar; (*believe: also*:
give ~ to) creer, prestar fe a ♦ *adj* crediticio;
~s *npl* (*CINEMA*) fichas *fpl* técnicas; **to be in ~**
(*person*) tener saldo a favor; **to ~ sb with** (*fig*)
reconocer a uno el mérito de; **~ card** *n*
tarjeta de crédito; **~or** *n* acreedor(a) *m/f*

creed [kriːd] *n* credo

creek [kriːk] *n* cala, ensenada; (*US*) riachuelo

creep [kriːp] (*pt, pp* **crept**) *vi* arrastrarse; **~er**
n enredadera; **~y** *adj* (*frightening*)
horripilante

cremate [krɪ'meɪt] *vt* incinerar

crematorium [krɛmə'tɔːrɪəm] (*pl
crematoria*) *n* crematorio

crêpe [kreɪp] *n* (*fabric*) crespón *m*; (*also*:
~ rubber) crepé *m*; **~ bandage** (*BRIT*) *n*
venda de crepé

crept [krɛpt] *pt, pp of* **creep**

crescent ['krɛsnt] *n* media luna; (*street*) calle
f (*en forma de semicírculo*)

cress [krɛs] *n* berro

crest [krɛst] *n* (*of bird*) cresta; (*of hill*) cima,
cumbre *f*; (*of coat of arms*) blasón *m*; **~fallen**
adj alicaído

crevice ['krɛvɪs] *n* grieta, hendedura

crew [kruː] *n* (*of ship etc*) tripulación *f*; (*TV,
CINEMA*) equipo; **~-cut** *n* corte *m* al rape; **~-
neck** *n* cuello a la caja

crib [krɪb] *n* cuna ♦ *vt* (*inf*) plagiar

crick [krɪk] *n* (*in neck*) tortícolis *f*

cricket ['krɪkɪt] *n* (*insect*) grillo; (*game*)
críquet *m*

crime [kraɪm] *n* (*no pl: illegal activities*)
crimen *m*; (*illegal action*) delito; **criminal**
['krɪmɪnl] *n* criminal *m/f*, delincuente *m/f*
♦ *adj* criminal; (*illegal*) delictivo; (*law*) penal

crimson ['krɪmzn] *adj* carmesí

cringe [krɪndʒ] *vi* agacharse, encogerse

crinkle ['krɪŋkl] *vt* arrugar

cripple ['krɪpl] *n* lisiado/a, cojo/a ♦ *vt* lisiar,
mutilar

crisis ['kraɪsɪs] (*pl crises*) *n* crisis *f inv*

crisp [krɪsp] *adj* fresco; (*vegetables etc*)
crujiente; (*manner*) seco; **~s** (*BRIT*) *npl*
patatas *fpl* (*SP*) *or* papas (*AM*) fritas

crisscross ['krɪskrɔs] *adj* entrelazado

criterion [kraɪ'tɪərɪən] (*pl criteria*) *n* criterio

critic ['krɪtɪk] *n* crítico/a; **~al** *adj* crítico;
(*illness*) grave; **~ally** *adv* (*speak etc*) en tono
crítico; (*ill*) gravemente; **~ism** ['krɪtɪsɪzm] *n*
crítica; **~ize** ['krɪtɪsaɪz] *vt* criticar

croak [krəuk] *vi* (*frog*) croar; (*raven*) graznar;
(*person*) gruñir

Croatia [krəu'eɪʃə] *n* Croacia

crochet ['krəuʃeɪ] *n* ganchillo

crockery ['krɔkərɪ] *n* loza, vajilla

crocodile ['krɔkədaɪl] *n* cocodrilo

crocus ['krəukəs] *n* croco, crocus *m*

croft [krɔft] *n* granja pequeña

crony ['krəunɪ] (*inf: pej*) *n* compinche *m/f*

crook [kruk] *n* ladrón/ona *m/f*; (*of shepherd*)
cayado; **~ed** ['krukɪd] *adj* torcido; (*dishonest*)
nada honrado

crop [krɔp] *n* (*produce*) cultivo; (*amount
produced*) cosecha; (*riding ~*) látigo de
montar ♦ *vt* cortar, recortar; **~ up** *vi* surgir,

presentarse

cross [krɔs] n cruz f; (hybrid) cruce m ♦ vt (street etc) cruzar, atravesar ♦ adj de mal humor, enojado; **~ out** vt tachar; **~ over** vi cruzar; **~bar** n travesaño; **~country (race)** n carrera a campo traviesa, cross m; **~examine** vt interrogar; **~-eyed** adj bizco; **~fire** n fuego cruzado; **~ing** n (sea passage) travesía; (also: pedestrian ~ing) paso para peatones; **~ing guard** (US) n persona encargada de ayudar a los niños a cruzar la calle; **~ purposes** npl: **to be at ~ purposes** no comprenderse uno a otro; **~-reference** n referencia, llamada; **~roads** n cruce m, encrucijada; **~ section** n corte m transversal; (of population) muestra (representativa); **~walk** (US) n paso de peatones; **~wind** n viento de costado; **~word** n crucigrama m

crotch [krɔtʃ] n (ANAT, of garment) entrepierna

crotchet ['krɔtʃɪt] n (MUS) negra

crouch [krautʃ] vi agacharse, acurrucarse

crow [krəu] n (bird) cuervo; (of cock) canto, cacareo ♦ vi (cock) cantar

crowbar ['krəubɑː*] n palanca

crowd [kraud] n muchedumbre f, multitud f ♦ vt (fill) llenar ♦ vi (gather): **to ~ round** reunirse en torno a; (cram): **to ~ in** entrar en tropel; **~ed** adj (full) atestado; (densely populated) superpoblado

crown [kraun] n corona; (of head) coronilla; (for tooth) funda; (of hill) cumbre f ♦ vt coronar; (fig) completar, rematar; **~ jewels** npl joyas fpl reales; **~ prince** n príncipe m heredero

crow's feet npl patas fpl de gallo

crucial ['kruːʃl] adj decisivo

crucifix ['kruːsɪfɪks] n crucifijo; **~ion** [-'fɪkʃən] n crucifixión f

crude [kruːd] adj (materials) bruto; (fig: basic) tosco; (: vulgar) ordinario; **~ (oil)** n (petróleo) crudo

cruel ['kruəl] adj cruel; **~ty** n crueldad f

cruise [kruːz] n crucero ♦ vi (ship) hacer un crucero; (car) ir a velocidad de crucero; **~r** n (motorboat) yate m de motor; (warship) crucero

crumb [krʌm] n miga, migaja

crumble ['krʌmbl] vt desmenuzar ♦ vi (building, also fig) desmoronarse; **crumbly** adj que se desmigaja fácilmente

crumpet ['krʌmpɪt] n ≈ bollo para tostar

crumple ['krʌmpl] vt (paper) estrujar; (material) arrugar

crunch [krʌntʃ] vt (with teeth) mascar; (underfoot) hacer crujir ♦ n (fig) hora or momento de la verdad; **~y** adj crujiente

crusade [kruːˈseɪd] n cruzada

crush [krʌʃ] n (crowd) aglomeración f;

(infatuation): **to have a ~ on sb** estar loco por uno; (drink): **lemon ~** limonada ♦ vt aplastar; (paper) estrujar; (cloth) arrugar; (fruit) exprimir; (opposition) aplastar; (hopes) destruir

crust [krʌst] n corteza; (of snow, ice) costra

crutch [krʌtʃ] n muleta

crux [krʌks] n: **the ~ of** lo esencial de, el quid de

cry [kraɪ] vi llorar; (shout: also: ~ out) gritar ♦ n (shriek) chillido; (shout) grito; **~ off** vi echarse atrás

cryptic ['krɪptɪk] adj enigmático, secreto

crystal ['krɪstl] n cristal m; **~-clear** adj claro como el agua

cub [kʌb] n cachorro; (also: ~ scout) niño explorador

Cuba ['kjuːbə] n Cuba; **~n** adj, n cubano/a m/f

cube [kjuːb] n cubo ♦ vt (MATH) cubicar; **cubic** adj cúbico

cubicle ['kjuːbɪkl] n (at pool) caseta; (for bed) cubículo

cuckoo ['kukuː] n cuco; **~ clock** n reloj m de cucú

cucumber ['kjuːkʌmbə*] n pepino

cuddle ['kʌdl] vt abrazar ♦ vi abrazarse

cue [kjuː] n (snooker ~) taco; (THEATRE etc) señal f

cuff [kʌf] n (of sleeve) puño; (US: of trousers) vuelta; (blow) bofetada; **off the ~** adv de improviso; **~links** npl gemelos mpl

cuisine [kwɪˈziːn] n cocina

cul-de-sac ['kʌldəsæk] n callejón m sin salida

cull [kʌl] vt (idea) sacar ♦ n (of animals) matanza selectiva

culminate ['kʌlmɪneɪt] vi: **to ~ in** terminar en; **culmination** [-'neɪʃən] n culminación f, colmo

culottes [kuːˈlɔts] npl falda pantalón f

culprit ['kʌlprɪt] n culpable m/f

cult [kʌlt] n culto

cultivate ['kʌltɪveɪt] vt (also fig) cultivar; **~d** adj culto; **cultivation** [-'veɪʃən] n cultivo

cultural ['kʌltʃərəl] adj cultural

culture ['kʌltʃə*] n (also fig) cultura; (BIO) cultivo; **~d** adj culto

cumbersome ['kʌmbəsəm] adj de mucho bulto, voluminoso; (process) enrevesado

cunning ['kʌnɪŋ] n astucia ♦ adj astuto

cup [kʌp] n taza; (as prize) copa

cupboard ['kʌbəd] n armario; (kitchen) alacena

cup tie (BRIT) n partido de copa

curate ['kjuərɪt] n cura m

curator [kjuəˈreɪtə*] n director(a) m/f

curb [kɜːb] vt refrenar; (person) reprimir ♦ n freno; (US) bordillo

curdle ['kɜːdl] vi cuajarse

cure [kjuə*] vt curar ♦ n cura, curación f; (fig: solution) remedio

curfew ['kə:fju:] n toque m de queda

curiosity [kjuərɪ'ɒsɪtɪ] n curiosidad f

curious ['kjuərɪəs] adj curioso; (person: interested): **to be ~** sentir curiosidad

curl [kə:l] n rizo ♦ vt (hair) rizar ♦ vi rizarse; **~ up** vi (person) hacerse un ovillo; **~er** n rulo; **~y** adj rizado

currant ['kʌrnt] n pasa (de Corinto); (black~, red~) grosella

currency ['kʌrnsɪ] n moneda; **to gain ~** (fig) difundirse

current ['kʌrnt] n corriente f ♦ adj (accepted) corriente; (present) actual; **~ account** (BRIT) n cuenta corriente; **~ affairs** npl noticias fpl de actualidad; **~ly** adv actualmente

curriculum [kə'rɪkjuləm] (pl **~s** or **curricula**) n plan m de estudios; **~ vitae** n currículum m

curry ['kʌrɪ] n curry m ♦ vt: **to ~ favour with** buscar favores con; **~ powder** n curry m en polvo

curse [kə:s] vi soltar tacos ♦ vt maldecir ♦ n maldición f; (swearword) palabrota, taco

cursor ['kə:sə*] n (COMPUT) cursor m

cursory ['kə:sərɪ] adj rápido, superficial

curt [kə:t] adj corto, seco

curtail [kə:'teɪl] vt (visit etc) acortar; (freedom) restringir; (expenses etc) reducir

curtain ['kə:tn] n cortina; (THEATRE) telón m

curts(e)y ['kə:tsɪ] vi hacer una reverencia

curve [kə:v] n curva ♦ vi (road) hacer una curva; (line etc) curvarse

cushion ['kuʃən] n cojín m; (of air) colchón m ♦ vt (shock) amortiguar

custard ['kʌstəd] n natillas fpl

custody ['kʌstədɪ] n custodia; **to take into ~** detener

custom ['kʌstəm] n costumbre f; (COMM) clientela; **~ary** adj acostumbrado

customer ['kʌstəmə*] n cliente m/f

customized ['kʌstəmaɪzd] adj (car etc) hecho a encargo

custom-made adj hecho a la medida

customs ['kʌstəmz] npl aduana; **~ officer** n aduanero/a

cut [kʌt] (pt, pp **cut**) vt cortar; (price) rebajar; (text, programme) acortar; (reduce) reducir ♦ vi cortar ♦ n (of garment) corte m; (in skin) cortadura; (in salary etc) rebaja; (in spending) reducción f, recorte m; (slice of meat) tajada; **to ~ a tooth** echar un diente; **~ down** vt (tree) derribar; (reduce) reducir; **~ off** vt cortar; (person, place) aislar; (TEL) desconectar; **~ out** vt (shape) recortar; (stop: activity etc) dejar; (remove) quitar; **~ up** vt cortar (en pedazos); **~back** n reducción f

cute [kju:t] adj mono

cuticle ['kju:tɪkl] n cutícula

cutlery ['kʌtlərɪ] n cubiertos mpl

cutlet ['kʌtlɪt] n chuleta; (nut etc ~) plato vegetariano hecho con nueces y verdura en forma de chuleta

cut: **~out** n (switch) dispositivo de seguridad, disyuntor m; (cardboard ~out) recortable m; **~-price** (US **~rate**) adj a precio reducido; **~throat** n asesino/a ♦ adj feroz

cutting ['kʌtɪŋ] adj (remark) mordaz ♦ n (BRIT: from newspaper) recorte m; (from plant) esqueje m

CV n abbr = **curriculum vitae**

cwt abbr = **hundredweight(s)**

cyanide ['saɪənaɪd] n cianuro

cybercafé ['saɪbəkæfeɪ] n cibercafé m

cycle ['saɪkl] n ciclo; (bicycle) bicicleta ♦ vi ir en bicicleta; **~ lane** n carril-bici m; **~ path** n carril-bici m; **cycling** n ciclismo; **cyclist** n ciclista m/f

cyclone ['saɪkləun] n ciclón m

cygnet ['sɪgnɪt] n pollo de cisne

cylinder ['sɪlɪndə*] n cilindro; (of gas) bombona; **~-head gasket** n junta de culata

cymbals ['sɪmblz] npl platillos mpl

cynic ['sɪnɪk] n cínico/a; **~al** adj cínico; **~ism** ['sɪnɪsɪzəm] n cinismo

Cyprus ['saɪprəs] n Chipre f

cyst [sɪst] n quiste m; **~itis** [-'taɪtɪs] n cistitis f

czar [zɑ:*] n zar m

Czech [tʃek] adj, n checo/a m/f; **~ Republic** n la República Checa

D, d

D [di:] n (MUS) re m

dab [dæb] vt (eyes, wound) tocar (ligeramente); (paint, cream) poner un poco de

dabble ['dæbl] vi: **to ~ in** ser algo aficionado a

dad [dæd] n = **daddy**

daddy ['dædɪ] n papá m

daffodil ['dæfədɪl] n narciso

daft [dɑ:ft] adj tonto

dagger ['dægə*] n puñal m, daga

daily ['deɪlɪ] adj diario, cotidiano ♦ adv todos los días, cada día

dainty ['deɪntɪ] adj delicado

dairy ['dɛərɪ] n (shop) lechería; (on farm) vaquería; **~ farm** n granja; **~ products** npl productos mpl lácteos; **~ store** n (US) n lechería

daisy ['deɪzɪ] n margarita

dale [deɪl] n valle m

dam [dæm] n presa ♦ vt construir una presa sobre, represar

damage ['dæmɪdʒ] n lesión f; daño; (dents etc) desperfectos mpl; (fig) perjuicio ♦ vt dañar, perjudicar; (*spoil, break*) estropear; **~s** *npl* (*LAW*) daños *mpl* y perjuicios

damn [dæm] *vt* condenar; (*curse*) maldecir ♦ *n* (*inf*): **I don't give a ~** me importa un pito ♦ *adj* (*inf: also: ~ed*) maldito; **~ (it)!** ¡maldito sea!; **~ing** *adj* (*evidence*) irrecusable

damp [dæmp] *adj* húmedo, mojado ♦ *n* humedad *f* ♦ *vt* (*also: ~en: cloth, rag*) mojar; (*: enthusiasm*) enfriar

damson ['dæmzən] *n* ciruela damascena

dance [dɑ:ns] *n* baile *m* ♦ *vi* bailar; **~ hall** *n* salón *m* de baile; **~r** *n* bailador(a) *m/f*; (*professional*) bailarín/ina *m/f*; **dancing** *n* baile *m*

dandelion ['dændɪlaɪən] *n* diente *m* de león

dandruff ['dændrəf] *n* caspa

Dane [deɪn] *n* danés/esa *m/f*

danger ['deɪndʒə*] *n* peligro; (*risk*) riesgo; **~!** (*on sign*) ¡peligro de muerte!; **to be in ~ of** correr riesgo de; **~ous** *adj* peligroso; **~ously** *adv* peligrosamente

dangle ['dæŋgl] *vt* colgar ♦ *vi* pender, colgar

Danish ['deɪnɪʃ] *adj* danés/esa ♦ *n* (*LING*) danés *m*

dare [dɛə*] *vt*: **to ~ sb to do** desafiar a uno a hacer ♦ *vi*: **to ~ (to) do sth** atreverse a hacer algo; **I ~ say** (*I suppose*) puede ser (que); **daring** *adj* atrevido, osado ♦ *n* atrevimiento, osadía

dark [dɑ:k] *adj* oscuro; (*hair, complexion*) moreno ♦ *n*: **in the ~** a oscuras; **to be in the ~ about** (*fig*) no saber nada de; **after ~** después del anochecer; **~en** *vt* (*colour*) hacer más oscuro ♦ *vi* oscurecerse; **~ glasses** *npl* gafas *fpl* negras (*SP*), anteojos *mpl* negros (*AM*); **~ness** *n* oscuridad *f*; **~room** *n* cuarto oscuro

darling ['dɑ:lɪŋ] *adj, n* querido/a *m/f*

darn [dɑ:n] *vt* zurcir

dart [dɑ:t] *n* dardo; (*in sewing*) sisa ♦ *vi* precipitarse; **~ away/along** *vi* salir/marchar disparado; **~board** *n* diana; **~s** *n* dardos *mpl*

dash [dæʃ] *n* (*small quantity: of liquid*) gota, chorrito; (*: of solid*) pizca; (*sign*) raya ♦ *vt* (*throw*) tirar; (*hopes*) defraudar ♦ *vi* precipitarse, ir de prisa; **~ away** *or* **off** *vi* marcharse apresuradamente

dashboard ['dæʃbɔ:d] *n* (*AUT*) salpicadero

dashing ['dæʃɪŋ] *adj* gallardo

data ['deɪtə] *npl* datos *mpl*; **~base** *f* de datos; **~ processing** *n* proceso de datos

date [deɪt] *n* (*day*) fecha; (*with friend*) cita; (*fruit*) dátil *m* ♦ *vt* fechar; (*person*) salir con; **~ of birth** fecha de nacimiento; **to ~** *adv* hasta la fecha; **~d** *adj* anticuado; **~ rape** *n* violación ocurrida durante una cita con un conocido

daub [dɔ:b] *vt* embadurnar

daughter ['dɔ:tə*] *n* hija; **~-in-law** *n* nuera,

hija política

daunting ['dɔ:ntɪŋ] *adj* desalentador(a)

dawdle ['dɔ:dl] *vi* (*go slowly*) andar muy despacio

dawn [dɔ:n] *n* alba, amanecer *m*; (*fig*) nacimiento ♦ *vi* (*day*) amanecer; (*fig*): **it ~ed on him that ...** cayó en la cuenta de que ...

day [deɪ] *n* día *m*; (*working ~*) jornada; (*hey~*) tiempos *mpl*, días *mpl*; **the ~ before** el día anterior/siguiente; **the ~ after tomorrow** pasado mañana; **the ~ before yesterday** anteayer; **the following ~** el día siguiente; **by ~ de** día; **~break** *n* amanecer *m*; **~dream** *vi* soñar despierto; **~light** *n* luz *f* (del día); **~ return** (*BRIT*) *n* billete *m* de ida y vuelta (en un día); **~time** *n* día *m*; **~-to-~** *adj* cotidiano

daze [deɪz] *vt* (*stun*) aturdir ♦ *n*: **in a ~** aturdido

dazzle ['dæzl] *vt* deslumbrar

DC *abbr* (= *direct current*) corriente *f* continua

dead [dɛd] *adj* muerto; (*limb*) dormido; (*telephone*) cortado; (*battery*) agotado ♦ *adv* (*completely*) totalmente; (*exactly*) exactamente; **to shoot sb ~** matar a uno a tiros; **~ tired** muerto (de cansancio); **to stop ~** parar en seco; **the ~** *npl* los muertos; **to be a ~ loss** (*inf: person*) ser un inútil; **~en** *vt* (*blow, sound*) amortiguar; (*pain etc*) aliviar; **~ end** *n* callejón *m* sin salida; **~ heat** *n* (*SPORT*) empate *m*; **~line** *n* fecha (or hora) tope; **~lock** *n*: **to reach ~lock** llegar a un punto muerto; **~ly** *adj* mortal, fatal; **~pan** *adj* sin expresión; **the D~ Sea** *n* el Mar Muerto

deaf [dɛf] *adj* sordo; **~en** *vt* ensordecer; **~ness** *n* sordera

deal [di:l] (*pt, pp* **dealt**) *n* (*agreement*) pacto, convenio; (*business ~*) trato ♦ *vt* dar; (*card*) repartir; **a great ~ (of)** bastante, mucho; **~ in** *vt fus* tratar en, comerciar en; **~ with** *vt fus* (*people*) tratar con; (*problem*) ocuparse de; (*subject*) tratar de; **~ings** *npl* (*COMM*) transacciones *fpl*; (*relations*) relaciones *fpl*

dealt [dɛlt] *pt, pp* de **deal**

dean [di:n] *n* (*REL*) deán *m*; (*SCOL: BRIT*) decano; (*: US*) decano; rector *m*

dear [dɪə*] *adj* querido; (*expensive*) caro ♦ *n*: **my ~** mi querido/a ♦ *excl*: **~ me!** ¡Dios mío!; **D~ Sir/Madam** (*in letter*) Muy Señor Mío, Estimado Señor/Estimada Señora; **D~ Mr/Mrs X** Estimado/a Señor(a) X; **~ly** *adv* (*love*) mucho; (*pay*) caro

death [dɛθ] *n* muerte *f*; **~ certificate** *n* partida de defunción; **~ly** *adj* (*white*) como un muerto; (*silence*) sepulcral; **~ penalty** *n* pena de muerte; **~ rate** *n* mortalidad *f*; **~ toll** *n* número de víctimas

debacle [deɪ'bɑ:kl] *n* desastre *m*

debase [dɪ'beɪs] vt degradar
debatable [dɪ'beɪtəbl] adj discutible
debate [dɪ'beɪt] n debate m ♦ vt discutir
debit ['debɪt] n debe m ♦ vt: **to ~ a sum to sb**
or **to sb's account** cargar una suma en cuenta
a alguien
debris ['debriː] n escombros mpl
debt |det| n deuda; **to be in ~** tener deudas;
~or n deudor(a) m/f
début ['deɪbjuː] n presentación f
decade ['dekeɪd] n decenio, década
decadence ['dekədəns] n decadencia
decaff ['diːkæf] (inf) n descafeinado
decaffeinated [dɪ'kæfɪneɪtɪd] adj
descafeinado
decanter [dɪ'kæntə*] n garrafa
decay [dɪ'keɪ] n (of building)
desmoronamiento; (of tooth) caries f inv ♦ vi
(rot) pudrirse
deceased [dɪ'siːst] n: **the ~** el/la difunto/a
deceit [dɪ'siːt] n engaño; **~ful** adj engañoso;
deceive [dɪ'siːv] vt engañar
December [dɪ'sembə*] n diciembre m
decent ['diːsənt] adj (proper) decente;
(person: kind) amable, bueno
deception [dɪ'sepʃən] n engaño
deceptive [dɪ'septɪv] adj engañoso
decibel ['desɪbel] n decibel(io) m
decide [dɪ'saɪd] vt (person) decidir; (question,
argument) resolver ♦ vi decidir; **to ~ to do/
that** decidir hacer/que; **to ~ on sth** decidirse
por algo; **~d** adj (resolute) decidido; (clear,
definite) indudable; **~dly** |-dɪdlɪ| adv
decididamente; (emphatically) con resolución
deciduous [dɪ'sɪdjuəs] adj de hoja caduca
decimal ['desɪməl] adj decimal ♦ n decimal
m; **~ point** n coma decimal
decipher [dɪ'saɪfə*] vt descifrar
decision [dɪ'sɪʒən] n decisión f
decisive [dɪ'saɪsɪv] adj decisivo; (person)
decidido
deck [dek] n (NAUT) cubierta; (of bus) piso;
(record ~) platina; (of cards) baraja; **~chair** n
tumbona
declaration [deklə'reɪʃən] n declaración f
declare [dɪ'klɛə*] vt declarar
decline [dɪ'klaɪn] n disminución f, descenso
♦ vt rehusar ♦ vi (person, business) decaer;
(strength) disminuir
decoder [diː'kəudə*] n (TV) decodificador m
décor ['deɪkɔː*] n decoración f; (THEATRE)
decorado
decorate ['dekəreɪt] vt (adorn): **to ~ (with)**
adornar (de), decorar (de); (paint) pintar;
(paper) empapelar; **decoration** [-'reɪʃən] n
adorno; (act) decoración f; (medal)
condecoración f; **decorator** n (workman)
pintor m (decorador)
decorum [dɪ'kɔːrəm] n decoro

decoy ['diːkɔɪ] n señuelo
decrease [n 'diːkriːs, vb dɪ'kriːs] n: **~ (in)**
disminución f (de) ♦ vt disminuir, reducir ♦ vi
reducirse
decree [dɪ'kriː] n decreto; **~ nisi** n sentencia
provisional de divorcio
dedicate ['dedɪkeɪt] vt dedicar; **dedication**
[-'keɪʃən] n (devotion) dedicación f; (in book)
dedicatoria
deduce [dɪ'djuːs] vt deducir
deduct [dɪ'dʌkt] vt restar; descontar; **~ion**
[dɪ'dʌkʃən] n (amount deducted) descuento;
(conclusion) deducción f, conclusión f
deed [diːd] n hecho, acto; (feat) hazaña;
(LAW) escritura
deep [diːp] adj profundo; (expressing
measurements) de profundidad; (voice) bajo;
(breath) profundo; (colour) intenso ♦ adv:
the spectators stood 20 ~ los espectadores se
formaron de 20 en fondo; **to be 4 metres ~**
tener 4 metros de profundidad; **~en** vt
ahondar, profundizar ♦ vi aumentar, crecer;
~-freeze n congelador m; **~-fry** vt freír en
aceite abundante; **~ly** adv (breathe) a pleno
pulmón; (interested, moved, grateful)
profundamente, hondamente; **~-sea diving**
n buceo de altura; **~-seated** adj (beliefs)
(profundamente) arraigado
deer [dɪə*] n inv ciervo
deface [dɪ'feɪs] vt (wall, surface) estropear,
pintarrajear
default [dɪ'fɔːlt] n: **by ~** (win) por
incomparecencia ♦ adj (COMPUT) por defecto
defeat [dɪ'fiːt] n derrota ♦ vt derrotar, vencer;
~ist adj, n derrotista m/f
defect [n 'diːfekt, vb dɪ'fekt] n defecto ♦ vi: **to
~ to the enemy** pasarse al enemigo; **~ive**
[dɪ'fektɪv] adj defectuoso
defence [dɪ'fens] (US defense) n defensa;
~less adj indefenso
defend [dɪ'fend] vt defender; **~ant** n
acusado/a; (in civil case) demandado/a; **~er**
n defensor(a) m/f; (SPORT) defensa m/f
defense [dɪ'fens] (US) n = **defence**
defensive [dɪ'fensɪv] adj defensivo ♦ n: **on
the ~** a la defensiva
defer [dɪ'fɜː*] vt aplazar
defiance [dɪ'faɪəns] n desafío; **in ~ of** en
contra de; **defiant** [dɪ'faɪənt] adj
(challenging) desafiante, retador(a)
deficiency [dɪ'fɪʃənsɪ] n (lack) falta; (defect)
defecto; **deficient** [dɪ'fɪʃənt] adj deficiente
deficit ['defɪsɪt] n déficit m
define [dɪ'faɪn] vt (word etc) definir; (limits
etc) determinar
definite ['defɪnɪt] adj (fixed) determinado;
(obvious) claro; (certain) indudable; **he was
~ about it** no dejó lugar a dudas (sobre ello);
~ly adv desde luego, por supuesto

definition [dɛfɪ'nɪʃən] *n* definición *f*;
(*clearness*) nitidez *f*
deflate [diː'fleɪt] *vt* desinflar
deflect [dɪ'flɛkt] *vt* desviar
defraud [dɪ'frɔːd] *vt*: **to ~ sb of sth** estafar
algo a uno
defrost [diː'frɒst] *vt* descongelar; **~er** (*US*) *n*
(*demister*) eliminador *m* de vaho
deft [dɛft] *adj* diestro, hábil
defunct [dɪ'fʌŋkt] *adj* difunto; (*organization
etc*) ya que no existe
defuse [diː'fjuːz] *vt* desactivar; (*situation*)
calmar
defy [dɪ'faɪ] *vt* (*resist*) oponerse a; (*challenge*)
desafiar; (*fig*): **it defies description** resulta
imposible describirlo
degenerate [*vb* dɪ'dʒɛnəreɪt, *adj* dɪ'dʒɛnərɪt]
vi degenerar ♦ *adj* degenerado
degree [dɪ'griː] *n* grado; (*SCOL*) título; **to
have a ~ in maths** tener una licenciatura en
matemáticas; **by ~s** (*gradually*) poco a poco,
por etapas; **to some ~** hasta cierto punto
dehydrated [diːhaɪ'dreɪtɪd] *adj*
deshidratado; (*milk*) en polvo
de-ice [diː'aɪs] *vt* deshelar
deign [deɪn] *vi*: **to ~ to do** dignarse hacer
dejected [dɪ'dʒɛktɪd] *adj* abatido,
desanimado
delay [dɪ'leɪ] *vt* demorar, aplazar; (*person*)
entretener; (*train*) retrasar ♦ *vi* tardar ♦ *n*
demora, retraso; **to be ~ed** retrasarse; **without
~** en seguida, sin tardar
delectable [dɪ'lɛktəbl] *adj* (*person*)
encantador(a); (*food*) delicioso
delegate [*n* 'dɛlɪgɪt, *vb* 'dɛlɪgeɪt] *n* delegado/
a ♦ *vt* (*person*) delegar en; (*task*) delegar
delete [dɪ'liːt] *vt* suprimir, tachar
deliberate [*adj* dɪ'lɪbərɪt, *vb* dɪ'lɪbəreɪt] *adj*
(*intentional*) intencionado; (*slow*) pausado,
lento ♦ *vi* deliberar; **~ly** *adv* (*on purpose*) a
propósito
delicacy ['dɛlɪkəsɪ] *n* delicadeza; (*choice
food*) manjar *m*
delicate ['dɛlɪkɪt] *adj* delicado; (*fragile*) frágil
delicatessen [dɛlɪkə'tɛsn] *n* ultramarinos
mpl finos
delicious [dɪ'lɪʃəs] *adj* delicioso
delight [dɪ'laɪt] *n* (*feeling*) placer *m*, deleite
m; (*person, experience etc*) encanto, delicia
♦ *vt* encantar, deleitar; **to take ~ in** deleitarse
en; **~ed** *adj*: **~ed** (**at** *or* **with/to do**)
encantado (con/de hacer); **~ful** *adj*
encantador(a), delicioso
delinquent [dɪ'lɪŋkwənt] *adj, n* delincuente
m/f
delirious [dɪ'lɪrɪəs] *adj*: **to be ~** delirar,
desvariar; **to be ~ with** estar loco de
deliver [dɪ'lɪvə*] *vt* (*distribute*) repartir; (*hand
over*) entregar; (*message*) comunicar;

(*speech*) pronunciar; (*MED*) asistir al parto de;
~y *n* reparto; entrega; (*of speaker*) modo de
expresarse; (*MED*) parto, alumbramiento; **to
take ~y of** recibir
delude [dɪ'luːd] *vt* engañar
deluge ['dɛljuːdʒ] *n* diluvio
delusion [dɪ'luːʒən] *n* ilusión *f*, engaño
de luxe [də'lʌks] *adj* de lujo
demand [dɪ'mɑːnd] *vt* (*gen*) exigir; (*rights*)
reclamar ♦ *n* exigencia; (*claim*) reclamación
f; (*ECON*) demanda; **to be in ~** ser muy
solicitado; **on ~** a solicitud; **~ing** *adj* (*boss*)
exigente; (*work*) absorbente
demean [dɪ'miːn] *vt*: **to ~ o.s.** rebajarse
demeanour [dɪ'miːnə*] (*US* **demeanor**) *n*
porte *m*, conducta
demented [dɪ'mɛntɪd] *adj* demente
demise [dɪ'maɪz] *n* (*death*) fallecimiento
demister [diː'mɪstə*] *n* (*AUT*) eliminador *m*
de vaho
demo ['dɛməu] (*inf*) *n abbr* (= *demonstration*) manifestación *f*
democracy [dɪ'mɒkrəsɪ] *n* democracia;
democrat ['dɛməkræt] *n* demócrata *m/f*;
democratic [dɛmə'krætɪk] *adj* democrático;
(*US*) demócrata
demolish [dɪ'mɒlɪʃ] *vt* derribar, demoler;
(*fig: argument*) destruir
demon ['diːmən] *n* (*evil spirit*) demonio
demonstrate ['dɛmənstreɪt] *vt* demostrar;
(*skill, appliance*) mostrar ♦ *vi* manifestarse;
demonstration [-'streɪʃən] *n* (*POL*)
manifestación *f*; (*proof, exhibition*)
demostración *f*; **demonstrator** *n* (*POL*)
manifestante *m/f*; (*COMM*) demostrador(a)
m/f; vendedor(a) *m/f*
demote [dɪ'məut] *vt* degradar
demure [dɪ'mjuə*] *adj* recatado
den [dɛn] *n* (*of animal*) guarida; (*room*)
habitación *f*
denial [dɪ'naɪəl] *n* (*refusal*) negativa; (*of
report etc*) negación *f*
denim ['dɛnɪm] *n* tela vaquera; **~s** *npl*
vaqueros *mpl*
Denmark ['dɛnmɑːk] *n* Dinamarca
denomination [dɪnɒmɪ'neɪʃən] *n* valor *m*;
(*REL*) confesión *f*
denounce [dɪ'nauns] *vt* denunciar
dense [dɛns] *adj* (*crowd*) denso; (*thick*)
espeso; (: *foliage etc*) tupido; (*inf: stupid*)
torpe; **~ly** *adv*: **~ly populated** con una alta
densidad de población
density ['dɛnsɪtɪ] *n* densidad *f*; **single/
double-~ disk** *n* (*COMPUT*) disco de
densidad sencilla/doble densidad
dent [dɛnt] *n* abolladura ♦ *vt* (*also: make a
~ in*) abollar
dental ['dɛntl] *adj* dental; **~ surgeon** *n*
odontólogo/a

dentist ['dɛntɪst] n dentista m/f

dentures ['dɛntʃəz] npl dentadura (postiza)

deny [dɪ'naɪ] vt negar; (charge) rechazar

deodorant [di:'əudərənt] n desodorante m

depart [dɪ'pa:t] vi irse, marcharse; (train) salir; **to ~ from** (fig: differ from) apartarse de

department [dɪ'pa:tmənt] n (COMM) sección f; (SCOL) departamento; (POL) ministerio; **~ store** n gran almacén m

departure [dɪ'pa:tʃə*] n partida, ida; (of train) salida; (of employee) marcha; **a new ~** un nuevo rumbo; **~ lounge** n (at airport) sala de embarque

depend [dɪ'pɛnd] vi: **to ~ on** depender de; (rely on) contar con; **it ~s** depende, según; **~ing on the result** según el resultado; **~able** adj (person) formal, serio; (watch) exacto; (car) seguro; **~ant** n dependiente m/f; **~ent** adj: **to be ~ent on** depender de ♦ n = dependant

depict [dɪ'pɪkt] vt (in picture) pintar; (describe) representar

depleted [dɪ'pli:tɪd] adj reducido

deploy [dɪ'plɔɪ] vt desplegar

deport [dɪ'pɔ:t] vt deportar

deposit [dɪ'pɔzɪt] n depósito; (CHEM) sedimento; (of ore, oil) yacimiento ♦ vt (gen) depositar; **~ account** n cuenta de ahorros

depot ['dɛpəu] n (storehouse) depósito; (for vehicles) parque m; (US) estación f

depreciate [dɪ'pri:ʃɪeɪt] vi depreciarse, perder valor

depress [dɪ'prɛs] vt deprimir; (wages etc) hacer bajar; (press down) apretar; **~ed** adj deprimido; **~ing** adj deprimente; **~ion** [dɪ'prɛʃən] n depresión f

deprivation [dɛprɪ'veɪʃən] n privación f

deprive [dɪ'praɪv] vt: **to ~ sb of** privar a uno de; **~d** adj necesitado

depth [dɛpθ] n profundidad f; (of cupboard) fondo; **to be in the ~s of despair** sentir la mayor desesperación; **to be out of one's ~** (in water) no hacer pie; (fig) sentirse totalmente perdido

deputize ['dɛpjutaɪz] vi: **to ~ for sb** suplir a uno

deputy ['dɛpjutɪ] adj: **~ head** subdirector(a) m/f ♦ n sustituto/a, suplente m/f; (US: POL) diputado/a; (US: also: **~ sheriff**) agente m (del sheriff)

derail [dɪ'reɪl] vt: **to be ~ed** descarrilarse

deranged [dɪ'reɪndʒd] adj trastornado

derby ['dɑ:bɪ] (US) n (hat) hongo

derelict ['dɛrɪlɪkt] adj abandonado

derisory [dɪ'raɪzərɪ] adj (sum) irrisorio

derive [dɪ'raɪv] vt (benefit etc) obtener ♦ vi: **to ~ from** derivarse de

derogatory [dɪ'rɔgətərɪ] adj despectivo

descend [dɪ'sɛnd] vt, vi descender, bajar; **to ~ from** descender de; **to ~ to** rebajarse a; **~ant** n descendiente m/f

descent [dɪ'sɛnt] n descenso; (origin) descendencia

describe [dɪs'kraɪb] vt describir; **description** [-'krɪpʃən] n descripción f; (sort) clase f, género

desecrate ['dɛsɪkreɪt] vt profanar

desert [n 'dɛzət, vb dɪ'zə:t] n desierto ♦ vt abandonar ♦ vi (MIL) desertar; **~er** [dɪ'zə:tə*] n desertor(a) m/f; **~ion** [dɪ'zə:ʃən] n deserción f; (LAW) abandono; **~ island** n isla desierta; **~s** [dɪ'zə:ts] npl: **to get one's just ~s** llevar su merecido

deserve [dɪ'zə:v] vt merecer, ser digno de; **deserving** adj (person) digno; (action, cause) meritorio

design [dɪ'zaɪn] n (sketch) bosquejo; (layout, shape) diseño; (pattern) dibujo; (intention) intención f ♦ vt diseñar

designate [vb 'dɛzɪgneɪt, adj 'dɛzɪgnɪt] vt (appoint) nombrar; (destine) designar ♦ adj designado

designer [dɪ'zaɪnə*] n diseñador(a) m/f; (fashion ~) modisto/a, diseñador(a) m/f de moda

desirable [dɪ'zaɪərəbl] adj (proper) deseable; (attractive) atractivo

desire [dɪ'zaɪə*] n deseo ♦ vt desear

desk [dɛsk] n (in office) escritorio; (for pupil) pupitre m; (in hotel, at airport) recepción f; (BRIT: in shop, restaurant) caja

desk-top publishing ['dɛsktɔp-] n autoedición f

desolate ['dɛsəlɪt] adj (place) desierto; (person) afligido

despair [dɪs'pɛə*] n desesperación f ♦ vi: **to ~ of** perder la esperanza de

despatch [dɪs'pætʃ] n, vt = **dispatch**

desperate ['dɛspərɪt] adj desesperado; (fugitive) peligroso; **to be ~ for sth/to do** necesitar urgentemente algo/hacer; **~ly** adv desesperadamente; (very) terriblemente, gravemente

desperation [dɛspə'reɪʃən] n desesperación f; **in** (sheer) **~** (absolutamente) desesperado

despicable [dɪs'pɪkəbl] adj vil, despreciable

despise [dɪs'paɪz] vt despreciar

despite [dɪs'paɪt] prep a pesar de, pese a

despondent [dɪs'pɔndənt] adj deprimido, abatido

dessert [dɪ'zə:t] n postre m; **~spoon** n cuchara (de postre)

destination [dɛstɪ'neɪʃən] n destino

destiny ['dɛstɪnɪ] n destino

destitute ['dɛstɪtju:t] adj desamparado, indigente

destroy [dɪs'trɔɪ] vt destruir; (animal)

sacrificar; **~er** n (NAUT) destructor m

destruction [dɪs'trʌkʃən] n destrucción f

detach [dɪ'tætʃ] vt separar; (unstick)
despegar; **~ed** adj (attitude) objetivo,
imparcial; **~ed house** n ≈ chalé m, ≈ chalet
m; **~ment** n (aloofness) frialdad f; (MIL)
destacamento

detail ['diːteɪl] n detalle m; (no pl: in picture
etc) detalles mpl; (trifle) pequeñez f ♦ vt
detallar; (MIL) destacar; **in ~** detalladamente;
~ed adj detallado

detain [dɪ'teɪn] vt retener; (in captivity)
detener

detect [dɪ'tekt] vt descubrir; (MED, POLICE)
identificar; (MIL, RADAR, TECH) detectar; **~ion**
[dɪ'tekʃən] n descubrimiento; identificación f;
~ive n detective m/f; **~ive story** n novela
policíaca; **~or** n detector m

detention [dɪ'tenʃən] n detención f, arresto;
(SCOL) castigo

deter [dɪ'təː] vt (dissuade) disuadir

detergent [dɪ'təːdʒənt] n detergente m

deteriorate [dɪ'tɪərɪəreɪt] vi deteriorarse;
deterioration [-'reɪʃən] n deterioro

determination [dɪtəːmɪ'neɪʃən] n resolución
f

determine [dɪ'təːmɪn] vt determinar; **~d** adj
(person) resuelto, decidido; **~d to do** resuelto
a hacer

deterrent [dɪ'terənt] n (MIL) fuerza de
disuasión

detest [dɪ'test] vt aborrecer

detonate ['detəneɪt] vi estallar ♦ vt hacer
detonar

detour ['diːtuə] n (gen, US: AUT) desviación f

detract [dɪ'trækt] vt: **to ~ from** quitar mérito
a, desvirtuar

detriment ['detrɪmənt] n: **to the ~ of** en
perjuicio de; **~al** [detrɪ'mentl] adj: **~al (to)**
perjudicial (a)

devaluation [dɪvælju'eɪʃən] n devaluación f

devalue [diː'væljuː] vt (currency) devaluar;
(fig) quitar mérito a

devastate ['devəsteɪt] vt devastar; (fig): **to
be ~d by** quedar destrozado por;
devastating adj devastador(a); (fig)
arrollador(a)

develop [dɪ'veləp] vt desarrollar; (PHOT)
revelar; (disease) coger; (habit) adquirir;
(fault) empezar a tener ♦ vi desarrollarse;
(advance) progresar; (facts, symptoms)
aparecer; **~er** n promotor m; **~ing country**
n país m en (vías de) desarrollo; **~ment** n
desarrollo; (advance) progreso; (of affair,
case) desenvolvimiento; (of land)
urbanización f

deviation [diːvɪ'eɪʃən] n desviación f

device [dɪ'vaɪs] n (apparatus) aparato,
mecanismo

devil ['devl] n diablo, demonio

devious ['diːvɪəs] adj taimado

devise [dɪ'vaɪz] vt idear, inventar

devoid [dɪ'vɔɪd] adj: **~ of** desprovisto de

devolution [diːvə'luːʃən] n (POL)
descentralización f

devote [dɪ'vəut] vt: **to ~ sth to** dedicar algo
a; **~d** adj (loyal) leal, fiel; **to be ~d to sb**
querer con devoción a alguien; **the book is ~d
to politics** el libro trata de la política; **~e**
[devəu'tiː] n entusiasta m/f; (REL) devoto/a;
devotion n dedicación f; (REL) devoción f

devour [dɪ'vauə] vt devorar

devout [dɪ'vaut] adj devoto

dew [djuː] n rocío

diabetes [daɪə'biːtiːz] n diabetes f; **diabetic**
[-'betɪk] adj, n diabético/a m/f

diabolical [daɪə'bɔlɪkəl] (inf) adj (weather,
behaviour) pésimo

diagnosis [daɪəg'nəusɪs] (pl -ses) n
diagnóstico

diagonal [daɪ'ægənl] adj, n diagonal f

diagram ['daɪəgræm] n diagrama m,
esquema m

dial ['daɪəl] n esfera, cuadrante m, cara (AM);
(on radio etc) selector m; (of phone) disco
♦ vt (number) marcar

dialling ['daɪəlɪŋ]: **~ code** n prefijo; **~ tone**
(US **dial tone**) n (BRIT) señal f o tono de
marcar

dialogue ['daɪəlɔg] (US **dialog**) n diálogo

diameter [daɪ'æmɪtə] n diámetro

diamond ['daɪəmənd] n diamante m; (shape)
rombo; **~s** npl (CARDS) diamantes mpl

diaper ['daɪəpə] (US) n pañal m

diaphragm ['daɪəfræm] n diafragma m

diarrhoea [daɪə'riːə] (US **diarrhea**) n diarrea

diary ['daɪərɪ] n (daily account) diario; (book)
agenda

dice [daɪs] n inv dados mpl ♦ vt (CULIN) cortar
en cuadritos

Dictaphone ® ['dɪktəfəun] n dictáfono ®

dictate [dɪk'teɪt] vt dictar; (conditions)
imponer; **dictation** [-'teɪʃən] n dictado;
(giving of orders) órdenes fpl

dictator [dɪk'teɪtə] n dictador m; **~ship** n
dictadura

dictionary ['dɪkʃənrɪ] n diccionario

did [dɪd] pt of **do**

didn't ['dɪdənt] = **did not**

die [daɪ] vi morir; (fig: fade) desvanecerse,
desaparecer; **to be dying for sth/to do sth**
morirse por algo/de ganas de hacer algo;
~ away vi (sound, light) perderse; **~ down**
vi apagarse; (wind) amainar; **~ out** vi
desaparecer

diesel ['diːzəl] n vehículo con motor Diesel;
~ engine n motor m Diesel; **~ (oil)** n gasoil
m

diet ['daɪət] n dieta; (restricted food) régimen m ♦ vi (also: be on a ~) estar a dieta, hacer régimen

differ ['dɪfə*] vi: to ~ (from) (be different) ser distinto (a), diferenciarse (de); (disagree) discrepar (de); ~ence n diferencia; (disagreement) desacuerdo; ~ent adj diferente, distinto; ~entiate [-'renʃɪeɪt] vi: to ~entiate (between) distinguir (entre); ~ently adv de otro modo, en forma distinta

difficult ['dɪfɪkəlt] adj difícil; ~y n dificultad f

diffident ['dɪfɪdənt] adj tímido

dig [dɪg] (pt, pp dug) vt (hole, ground) cavar ♦ n (prod) empujón m; (archaeological) excavación f; (remark) indirecta; to ~ one's nails into clavar las uñas en; ~ into vt fus (savings) consumir; ~ up vt (information) desenterrar; (plant) desarraigar

digest [vb daɪ'dʒɛst, n 'daɪdʒɛst] vt (food) digerir; (facts) asimilar ♦ n resumen m; ~ion [dɪ'dʒɛstʃən] n digestión f

digit ['dɪdʒɪt] n (number) dígito; (finger) dedo; ~al adj digital; ~al TV n televisión f digital

dignified ['dɪgnɪfaɪd] adj grave, solemne

dignity ['dɪgnɪtɪ] n dignidad f

digress [daɪ'grɛs] vi: to ~ from apartarse de

digs [dɪgz] (BRIT: inf) npl pensión f, alojamiento

dilapidated [dɪ'læpɪdeɪtɪd] adj desmoronado, ruinoso

dilemma [daɪ'lɛmə] n dilema m

diligent ['dɪlɪdʒənt] adj diligente

dilute [daɪ'luːt] vt diluir

dim [dɪm] adj (light) débil; (outline) indistinto; (room) oscuro; (inf: stupid) lerdo ♦ vt (light) bajar

dime [daɪm] (US) n moneda de diez centavos

dimension [dɪ'mɛnʃən] n dimensión f

diminish [dɪ'mɪnɪʃ] vt, vi disminuir

diminutive [dɪ'mɪnjutɪv] adj diminuto ♦ n (LING) diminutivo

dimmers ['dɪməz] (US) npl (AUT: dipped headlights) luces fpl cortas; (: parking lights) luces fpl de posición

dimple ['dɪmpl] n hoyuelo

din [dɪn] n estruendo, estrépito

dine [daɪn] vi cenar; ~r n (person) comensal m/f; (US) restaurante m económico

dinghy ['dɪŋgɪ] n bote m; (also: rubber ~) lancha (neumática)

dingy ['dɪndʒɪ] adj (room) sombrío; (colour) sucio

dining car ['daɪnɪŋ-] (BRIT) n (RAIL) coche-comedor m

dining room n comedor m

dinner ['dɪnə*] n (evening meal) cena; (lunch) comida; (public) cena, banquete m; ~ jacket n smoking m; ~ party n cena; ~ time n

(evening) hora de cenar; (midday) hora de comer

dinosaur ['daɪnəsɔː*] n dinosaurio

diocese ['daɪəsɪs] n diócesis f inv

dip [dɪp] n (slope) pendiente m; (in sea) baño; (CULIN) salsa ♦ vt (in water) mojar; (ladle etc) meter; (BRIT: AUT): to ~ one's lights poner luces de cruce ♦ vi (road etc) descender, bajar

diploma [dɪ'pləumə] n diploma m

diplomacy [dɪ'pləuməsɪ] n diplomacia

diplomat ['dɪpləmæt] n diplomático/a; ~ic [dɪplə'mætɪk] adj diplomático

diprod ['dɪprəd] (US) n = dipstick

dipstick ['dɪpstɪk] (BRIT) n (AUT) varilla de nivel (del aceite)

dipswitch ['dɪpswɪtʃ] (BRIT) n (AUT) interruptor m

dire [daɪə*] adj calamitoso

direct [daɪ'rɛkt] adj directo; (challenge) claro; (person) franco ♦ vt dirigir; (order): to ~ sb to do sth mandar a uno hacer algo ♦ adv derecho; can you ~ me to...? ¿puede indicarme dónde está...?; ~ debit (BRIT) n domiciliación f bancaria de recibos

direction [dɪ'rɛkʃən] n dirección f; sense of ~ sentido de la dirección; ~s npl (instructions) instrucciones fpl; ~s for use modo de empleo

directly [dɪ'rɛktlɪ] adv (in straight line) directamente; (at once) en seguida

director [dɪ'rɛktə*] n director(a) m/f

directory [dɪ'rɛktərɪ] n (TEL) guía (telefónica); (COMPUT) directorio; ~ enquiries, ~ assistance (US) n (servicio de) información f

dirt [dɜːt] n suciedad f; (earth) tierra; ~-cheap adj baratísimo; ~y adj sucio; (joke) verde (SP), colorado (AM) ♦ vt ensuciar; (stain) manchar; ~y trick n juego sucio

disability [dɪsə'bɪlɪtɪ] n incapacidad f

disabled [dɪs'eɪbld] adj: to be physically ~ ser minusválido/a; to be mentally ~ ser deficiente mental

disadvantage [dɪsəd'vɑːntɪdʒ] n desventaja, inconveniente m

disagree [dɪsə'griː] vi (differ) discrepar; to ~ (with) no estar de acuerdo (con); ~able adj desagradable; (person) antipático; ~ment n desacuerdo

disallow [dɪsə'lau] vt (goal) anular; (claim) rechazar

disappear [dɪsə'pɪə*] vi desaparecer; ~ance n desaparición f

disappoint [dɪsə'pɔɪnt] vt decepcionar, defraudar; ~ed adj decepcionado; ~ing adj decepcionante; ~ment n decepción f

disapproval [dɪsə'pruːvəl] n desaprobación f

disapprove [dɪsə'pruːv] vi: to ~ of ver mal

disarmament [dɪs'ɑːməmənt] n desarme m

disarray [dɪsə'reɪ] n: in ~ (army, organization)

desorganizado; (*hair, clothes*) desarreglado

disaster |dɪˈzɑːstə*| n desastre m

disband |dɪsˈbænd| vt disolver ♦ vi desbandarse

disbelief |dɪsbəˈliːf| n incredulidad f

disc |dɪsk| n disco; (COMPUT) = **disk**

discard |dɪsˈkɑːd| vt (*old things*) tirar; (*fig*) descartar

discern |dɪˈsɜːn| vt percibir, discernir; (*understand*) comprender; **~ing** adj perspicaz

discharge |vb dɪsˈtʃɑːdʒ, n ˈdɪstʃɑːdʒ| vt (*task, duty*) cumplir; (*waste*) verter; (*patient*) dar de alta; (*employee*) despedir; (*soldier*) licenciar; (*defendant*) poner en libertad ♦ n (ELEC) descarga; (MED) supuración f; (*dismissal*) despedida; (*of duty*) desempeño; (*of debt*) pago, descargo

discipline |ˈdɪsɪplɪn| n disciplina ♦ vt disciplinar; (*punish*) castigar

disc jockey n pinchadiscos m/f inv

disclaim |dɪsˈkleɪm| vt negar

disclose |dɪsˈkləuz| vt revelar; **disclosure** [-ˈkləuʒə*] n revelación f

disco |ˈdɪskəu| n abbr = **discothèque**

discomfort |dɪsˈkʌmfət| n incomodidad f; (*unease*) inquietud f; (*physical*) malestar m

disconcert |dɪskənˈsɜːt| vt desconcertar

disconnect |dɪskəˈnekt| vt separar; (ELEC etc) desconectar

discontent |dɪskənˈtent| n descontento; **~ed** adj descontento

discontinue |dɪskənˈtɪnjuː| vt interrumpir; (*payments*) suspender; "**~d**" (COMM) "ya no se fabrica"

discord |ˈdɪskɔːd| n discordia; (MUS) disonancia

discothèque |ˈdɪskəutek| n discoteca

discount |n ˈdɪskaunt, vb dɪsˈkaunt| n descuento ♦ vt descontar

discourage |dɪsˈkʌrɪdʒ| vt desalentar; (*advise against*): **to ~ sb from doing** disuadir a uno de hacer

discover |dɪsˈkʌvə*| vt descubrir; (*error*) darse cuenta de; **~y** n descubrimiento

discredit |dɪsˈkredɪt| vt desacreditar

discreet |dɪˈskriːt| adj (*tactful*) discreto; (*careful*) circunspecto, prudente

discrepancy |dɪˈskrepənsɪ| n diferencia

discretion |dɪˈskreʃən| n (*tact*) discreción f; **at the ~ of** a criterio de

discriminate |dɪˈskrɪmɪneɪt| vi: **to ~ between** distinguir entre; **to ~ against** discriminar contra; **discriminating** adj entendido; **discrimination** [-ˈneɪʃən] n (*discernment*) perspicacia; (*bias*) discriminación f

discuss |dɪˈskʌs| vt discutir; (*a theme*) tratar; **~ion** |dɪˈskʌʃən| n discusión f

disdain |dɪsˈdeɪn| n desdén m

disease |dɪˈziːz| n enfermedad f

disembark |dɪsɪmˈbɑːk| vt, vi desembarcar

disentangle |dɪsɪnˈtæŋgl| vt soltar; (*wire, thread*) desenredar

disfigure |dɪsˈfɪgə*| vt (*person*) desfigurar; (*object*) afear

disgrace |dɪsˈgreɪs| n ignominia; (*shame*) vergüenza, escándalo ♦ vt deshonrar; **~ful** adj vergonzoso

disgruntled |dɪsˈgrʌntld| adj disgustado, descontento

disguise |dɪsˈgaɪz| n disfraz m ♦ vt disfrazar; **in ~** disfrazado

disgust |dɪsˈgʌst| n repugnancia ♦ vt repugnar, dar asco a; **~ing** adj repugnante, asqueroso; (*behaviour etc*) vergonzoso

dish |dɪʃ| n (*gen*) plato; **to do** o **wash the ~es** fregar los platos; **~ out** vt repartir; **~ up** vt servir; **~cloth** n estropajo

dishearten |dɪsˈhɑːtn| vt desalentar

dishevelled |dɪˈʃevəld| (US **disheveled**) adj (*hair*) despeinado; (*appearance*) desarreglado

dishonest |dɪsˈɒnɪst| adj (*person*) poco honrado, tramposo; (*means*) fraudulento; **~y** n falta de honradez

dishonour |dɪsˈɒnə*| (US **dishonor**) n deshonra; **~able** adj deshonroso

dishtowel |ˈdɪʃtauəl| (US) n estropajo

dishwasher |ˈdɪʃwɒʃə*| n lavaplatos m inv

disillusion |dɪsɪˈluːʒən| vt desilusionar

disinfect |dɪsɪnˈfekt| vt desinfectar; **~ant** n desinfectante m

disintegrate |dɪsˈɪntɪgreɪt| vi disgregarse, desintegrarse

disinterested |dɪsˈɪntrəstɪd| adj desinteresado

disjointed |dɪsˈdʒɔɪntɪd| adj inconexo

disk |dɪsk| n (*esp US*) = **disc**; (COMPUT) disco, disquete m; **single-/double-sided ~** disco de una cara/dos caras; **~ drive** n disc drive m; **~ette** n = **disk**

dislike |dɪsˈlaɪk| n antipatía, aversión f ♦ vt tener antipatía a

dislocate |ˈdɪsləkeɪt| vt dislocar

dislodge |dɪsˈlɒdʒ| vt sacar

disloyal |dɪsˈlɔɪəl| adj desleal

dismal |ˈdɪzml| adj (*gloomy*) deprimente, triste; (*very bad*) malísimo, fatal

dismantle |dɪsˈmæntl| vt desmontar, desarmar

dismay |dɪsˈmeɪ| n consternación f ♦ vt consternar

dismiss |dɪsˈmɪs| vt (*worker*) despedir; (*pupils*) dejar marchar; (*soldiers*) dar permiso para irse; (*idea, LAW*) rechazar; (*possibility*) descartar; **~al** n despido

dismount |dɪsˈmaunt| vi apearse

disobedient |dɪsəˈbiːdɪənt| adj desobediente

disobey |dɪsəˈbeɪ| vt desobedecer

disorder |dɪsˈɔːdə*| n desorden m; (rioting) disturbios mpl; (MED) trastorno; **~ly** adj desordenado; (meeting) alborotado; (conduct) escandaloso

disorientated |dɪsˈɔːrɪənteɪtəd| adj desorientado

disown |dɪsˈəʊn| vt (action) renegar de; (person) negar cualquier tipo de relación con

disparaging |dɪsˈpærɪdʒɪŋ| adj despreciativo

dispassionate |dɪsˈpæʃənɪt| adj (unbiased) imparcial

dispatch |dɪsˈpætʃ| vt enviar ♦ n (sending) envío; (PRESS) información m; (MIL) parte m

dispel |dɪsˈpel| vt disipar

dispense |dɪsˈpens| vt (medicines) preparar; **~ with** vt fus prescindir de; **~r** n (container) distribuidor m automático; **dispensing chemist** (BRIT) n farmacia

disperse |dɪsˈpɜːs| vt dispersar ♦ vi dispersarse

dispirited |dɪˈspɪrɪtɪd| adj desanimado, desalentado

displace |dɪsˈpleɪs| vt desplazar, reemplazar; **~d person** n (POL) desplazado/a

display |dɪsˈpleɪ| n (in shop window) escaparate m; (exhibition) exposición f; (COMPUT) visualización f; (of feeling) manifestación f ♦ vt exponer; manifestar; (ostentatiously) lucir

displease |dɪsˈpliːz| vt (offend) ofender; (annoy) fastidiar; **~d** adj: **~d with** disgustado con; **displeasure** |-ˈpleʒə*| n disgusto

disposable |dɪsˈpəʊzəbl| adj desechable; (income) disponible; **~ nappy** n pañal m desechable

disposal |dɪsˈpəʊzl| n (of rubbish) destrucción f; **at one's ~** a su disposición

dispose |dɪsˈpəʊz| vi: **to ~ of** (unwanted goods) deshacerse de; (problem etc) resolver; **~d** adj: **~d to do** dispuesto a hacer; **to be well-~d towards sb** estar bien dispuesto hacia uno; **disposition** |dɪspəˈzɪʃən| n (nature) temperamento; (inclination) propensión f

disprove |dɪsˈpruːv| vt refutar

dispute |dɪsˈpjuːt| n disputa; (also: industrial ~) conflicto (laboral) ♦ vt (argue) disputar, discutir; (question) cuestionar

disqualify |dɪsˈkwɒlɪfaɪ| vt (SPORT) desclasificar; **to ~ sb for sth/from doing sth** incapacitar a alguien para algo/hacer algo

disquiet |dɪsˈkwaɪət| n preocupación f, inquietud f

disregard |dɪsrɪˈɡɑːd| vt (ignore) no hacer caso de

disrepair |dɪsrɪˈpeə*| n: **to fall into ~** (building) desmoronarse

disreputable |dɪsˈrepjʊtəbl| adj (person) de mala fama; (behaviour) vergonzoso

disrespectful |dɪsrɪˈspektful| adj irrespetuoso

disrupt |dɪsˈrʌpt| vt (plans) desbaratar, trastornar; (conversation) interrumpir

dissatisfaction |dɪssætɪsˈfækʃən| n disgusto, descontento

dissect |dɪˈsekt| vt disecar

dissent |dɪˈsent| n disensión f

dissertation |dɪsəˈteɪʃən| n tesina

disservice |dɪsˈsɜːvɪs| n: **to do sb a ~** perjudicar a alguien

dissimilar |dɪˈsɪmɪlə*| adj distinto

dissipate |ˈdɪsɪpeɪt| vt disipar; (waste) desperdiciar

dissolve |dɪˈzɒlv| vt disolver ♦ vi disolverse; **to ~ in(to) tears** deshacerse en lágrimas

dissuade |dɪˈsweɪd| vt: **to ~ sb (from)** disuadir a uno (de)

distance |ˈdɪstəns| n distancia; **in the ~** a lo lejos

distant |ˈdɪstənt| adj lejano; (manner) reservado, frío

distaste |dɪsˈteɪst| n repugnancia; **~ful** adj repugnante, desagradable

distended |dɪˈstendɪd| adj (stomach) hinchado

distil |dɪsˈtɪl| (US **distill**) vt destilar; **~lery** n destilería

distinct |dɪsˈtɪŋkt| adj (different) distinto; (clear) claro; (unmistakeable) inequívoco; **as ~ from** a diferencia de; **~ion** |dɪsˈtɪŋkʃən| n distinción f; (honour) honor m; (in exam) sobresaliente m; **~ive** adj distintivo

distinguish |dɪsˈtɪŋɡwɪʃ| vt distinguir; **to ~ o.s.** destacarse; **~ed** adj (eminent) distinguido; **~ing** adj (feature) distintivo

distort |dɪsˈtɔːt| vt distorsionar; (shape, image) deformar; **~ion** |dɪsˈtɔːʃən| n distorsión f; deformación f

distract |dɪsˈtrækt| vt distraer; **~ed** adj distraído; **~ion** |dɪsˈtrækʃən| n distracción f; (confusion) aturdimiento

distraught |dɪsˈtrɔːt| adj loco de inquietud

distress |dɪsˈtres| n (anguish) angustia, aflicción f ♦ vt afligir; **~ing** adj angustioso; doloroso; **~ signal** n señal f de socorro

distribute |dɪsˈtrɪbjuːt| vt distribuir; (share out) repartir; **distribution** |-ˈbjuːʃən| n distribución f, reparto; **distributor** n (AUT) distribuidor m; (COMM) distribuidora

district |ˈdɪstrɪkt| n (of country) zona, región f; (of town) barrio; (ADMIN) distrito; **~ attorney** (US) n fiscal m/f; **~ nurse** (BRIT) n enfermera que atiende a pacientes a domicilio

distrust |dɪsˈtrʌst| n desconfianza ♦ vt desconfiar de

disturb |dɪsˈtɜːb| vt (person: bother, interrupt) molestar; (: upset) perturbar, inquietar; (disorganize) alterar; **~ance** n (upheaval) perturbación f; (political etc: gen pl) disturbio; (of mind) trastorno; **~ed** adj (worried, upset) preocupado, angustiado; **emotionally ~ed** trastornado; (childhood) inseguro; **~ing** adj inquietante, perturbador(a)

disuse [dɪsˈjuːs] n: **to fall into ~** caer en desuso

disused [dɪsˈjuːzd] adj abandonado

ditch [dɪtʃ] n zanja; (irrigation ~) acequia ♦ vt (inf: partner) deshacerse de; (: plan, car etc) abandonar

dither [ˈdɪðə*] (pej) vi vacilar

ditto [ˈdɪtəu] adv ídem, lo mismo

divan [dɪˈvæn] n (also: ~ bed) cama turca

dive [daɪv] n (from board) salto; (underwater) buceo; (of submarine) sumersión f ♦ vi (swimmer: into water) saltar; (: under water) zambullirse, bucear; (fish, submarine) sumergirse; (bird) lanzarse en picado; **to ~ into** (bag etc) meter la mano en; (place) meterse de prisa en; **~r** n (underwater) buzo

diverse [daɪˈvəːs] adj diversos/as, varios/as

diversion [daɪˈvəːʃən] n (BRIT: AUT) desviación f; (distraction, MIL) diversión f; (of funds) distracción f

divert [daɪˈvəːt] vt (turn aside) desviar

divide [dɪˈvaɪd] vt dividir; (separate) separar ♦ vi dividirse; (road) bifurcarse; **~d highway** (US) n carretera de doble calzada

dividend [ˈdɪvɪdend] n dividendo; (fig): **to pay ~s** proporcionar beneficios

divine [dɪˈvaɪn] adj (also fig) divino

diving [ˈdaɪvɪŋ] n (SPORT) salto; (underwater) buceo; **~ board** n trampolín m

divinity [dɪˈvɪnɪtɪ] n divinidad f; (SCOL) teología

division [dɪˈvɪʒən] n división f; (sharing out) reparto; (disagreement) diferencias fpl; (COMM) sección f

divorce [dɪˈvɔːs] n divorcio ♦ vt divorciarse de; **~d** adj divorciado; **~e** [-ˈsiː] n divorciado/a

divulge [daɪˈvʌldʒ] vt divulgar, revelar

D.I.Y. [BRIT] adj, n abbr = **do-it-yourself**

dizzy [ˈdɪzɪ] adj (spell) de mareo; **to feel ~** marearse

DJ n abbr = **disc jockey**

KEYWORD
---

do [duː] (pt **did**, pp **done**) n (inf: party etc): **we're having a little ~ on Saturday** damos una fiestecita el sábado; **it was rather a grand ~** fue un acontecimiento a lo grande
♦ aux vb **1** (in negative constructions: not translated) **I don't understand** no entiendo
2 (to form questions: not translated) **didn't you know?** ¿no lo sabías?; **what ~ you think?** ¿qué opinas?
3 (for emphasis, in polite expressions): **people**

~ **make mistakes sometimes** sí que se cometen errores a veces; **she does seem rather late** a mí también me parece que se ha retrasado; **~ sit down/help yourself** siéntate/sírvete por favor; **~ take care!** ¡ten cuidado (, te pido)!
4 (used to avoid repeating vb): **she sings better than I ~** canta mejor que yo; **~ you agree? — yes, I ~/no, I don't** ¿estás de acuerdo? — sí (lo estoy)/no (lo estoy); **she lives in Glasgow — so ~ I** vive en Glasgow — yo también; **he didn't like it and neither did we** no le gustó y a nosotros tampoco; **who made this mess? — I did** ¿quién hizo esta chapuza? — yo; **he asked me to help him and I did** me pidió que le ayudara y lo hice
5 (in question tags): **you like him, don't you?** te gusta, ¿verdad? or ¿no?; **I don't know him, ~ I?** creo que no le conozco
♦ vt **1** (gen, carry out, perform etc): **what are you ~ing tonight?** ¿qué haces esta noche?; **what can I ~ for you?** ¿en qué puedo servirle?; **to ~ the washing-up/cooking** fregar los platos/cocinar; **to ~ one's teeth/hair/nails** lavarse los dientes/arreglarse el pelo/arreglarse las uñas
2 (AUT etc): **the car was ~ing 100** el coche iba a 100; **we've done 200 km already** ya hemos hecho 200 km; **he can ~ 100 in that car** puede ir a 100 en ese coche
♦ vi **1** (act, behave) hacer; **~ as I ~** haz como yo
2 (get on, fare): **he's ~ing well/badly at school** va bien/mal en la escuela; **the firm is ~ing well** la empresa anda or va bien; **how ~ you ~?** mucho gusto; (less formal) ¿qué tal?
3 (suit): **will it ~?** ¿sirve?, ¿está or va bien?
4 (be sufficient) bastar; **will £10 ~?** ¿será bastante con £10?; **that'll ~** así está bien; **that'll ~!** (in annoyance) ¡ya está bien!, ¡basta ya!; **to make ~ (with)** arreglárselas (con)

do away with vt fus (kill, disease) eliminar; (abolish: law etc) abolir; (withdraw) retirar

do up vt (laces) atar; (zip, dress, shirt) abrochar; (renovate: room, house) renovar

do with vt fus (need): **I could ~ with a drink/some help** no me vendría mal un trago/un poco de ayuda; (be connected) tener que ver con; **what has it got to ~ with you?** ¿qué tiene que ver contigo?

do without vi pasar sin; **if you're late for tea then you'll ~ without** si llegas tarde tendrás que quedarte sin cenar ♦ vt fus pasar sin; **I can ~ without a car** puedo pasar sin coche

---

dock [dɔk] n (NAUT) muelle m; (LAW) banquillo (de los acusados); **~s** npl (NAUT) muelles mpl, puerto sg ♦ vi (enter) atracar (la) muelle; (SPACE) acoplarse; **~er** n trabajador *m* portuario, estibador *m*; **~yard** *n* astillero

doctor ['dɔktə*] *n* médico/a; (*Ph.D. etc*) doctor(a) *m/f* ♦ *vt* (*drink etc*) adulterar; **D~ of Philosophy** *n* Doctor en Filosofía y Letras

document ['dɔkjumənt] *n* documento; **~ary** [-'mentərɪ] *adj* documental ♦ *n* documental *m*

dodge [dɔdʒ] *n* (*fig*) truco ♦ *vt* evadir; (*blow*) esquivar

dodgems ['dɔdʒəmz] (*BRIT*) *npl* coches *mpl* de choque

doe [dəu] *n* (*deer*) cierva, gama; (*rabbit*) coneja

does [dʌz] *vb see* **do**; **~n't** = **does not**

dog [dɔg] *n* perro ♦ *vt* seguir los pasos de; (*subj: bad luck*) perseguir; **~ collar** *n* collar *m* de perro; (*of clergyman*) alzacuellos *m inv*; **~-eared** *adj* sobado

dogged ['dɔgɪd] *adj* tenaz, obstinado

dogsbody ['dɔgzbɔdɪ] (*BRIT: inf*) *n* burro de carga

doings ['duɪŋz] *npl* (*activities*) actividades *fpl*

do-it-yourself *n* bricolaje *m*

doldrums ['dɔldrəmz] *npl*: **to be in the ~** (*person*) estar abatido; (*business*) estar estancado

dole [dəul] (*BRIT*) *n* (*payment*) subsidio de paro; **on the ~** parado; **~ out** *vt* repartir

doll [dɔl] *n* muñeca; (*US: inf: woman*) muñeca, gachí *f*

dollar ['dɔlə*] *n* dólar *m*

dolled up (*inf*) *adj* arreglado

dolphin ['dɔlfɪn] *n* delfín *m*

domain [də'meɪn] *n* (*fig*) campo, competencia; (*land*) dominios *mpl*

dome [dəum] *n* (*ARCH*) cúpula

domestic [də'mestɪk] *adj* (*animal, duty*) doméstico; (*flight, policy*) nacional; **~ated** *adj* domesticado; (*home-loving*) casero, hogareño

dominate ['dɔmɪneɪt] *vt* dominar

domineering [dɔmɪ'nɪərɪŋ] *adj* dominante

dominion [də'mɪnɪən] *n* dominio

domino ['dɔmɪnəu] (*pl* **~es**) *n* ficha de dominó; **~es** *n* (*game*) dominó

don [dɔn] (*BRIT*) *n* profesor(a) *m/f* universitario/a

donate [də'neɪt] *vt* donar; **donation** [də'neɪʃən] *n* donativo

done [dʌn] *pp of* **do**

donkey ['dɔŋkɪ] *n* burro

donor ['dəunə*] *n* donante *m/f*; **~ card** *n* carnet *m* de donante de órganos

don't [dəunt] = **do not**

donut ['dəunʌt] (*US*) *n* = **doughnut**

doodle ['du:dl] *vi* hacer dibujitos *or* garabatos

doom [du:m] *n* (*fate*) suerte *f* ♦ *vt*: **to be ~ed to failure** estar condenado al fracaso

door [dɔ:*] *n* puerta; **~bell** *n* timbre *m*;

~ handle *n* tirador *m*; (*of car*) manija; **~man** (*irreg*) *n* (*in hotel*) portero; **~mat** *n* felpudo, estera; **~step** *n* peldaño; **~-to-~** *adj* de puerta en puerta; **~way** *n* entrada, puerta

dope [dəup] *n* (*inf: illegal drug*) droga; (*: person*) imbécil *m/f* ♦ *vt* (*horse etc*) drogar

dormant ['dɔ:mənt] *adj* inactivo

dormitory ['dɔ:mɪtrɪ] *n* (*BRIT*) dormitorio; (*US*) colegio mayor

dormouse ['dɔ:maus] (*pl* **-mice**) *n* lirón *m*

DOS *n abbr* (= *disk operating system*) DOS *m*

dosage ['dəusɪdʒ] *n* dosis *f inv*

dose [dəus] *n* dósis *f inv*

doss house ['dɔs-] (*BRIT*) *n* pensión *f* de mala muerte

dossier ['dɔsɪeɪ] *n* expediente *m*, dosier *m*

dot [dɔt] *n* punto ♦ *vi*: **~ted with** salpicado de; **on the ~** en punto

double ['dʌbl] *adj* doble ♦ *adv* (*twice*): **to cost ~** costar el doble ♦ *n* doble *m* ♦ *vt* doblar ♦ *vi* doblarse; **on the ~**, **at the ~** (*BRIT*) corriendo; **~ bass** *n* contrabajo; **~ bed** *n* cama de matrimonio; **~ bend** (*BRIT*) *n* doble curva; **~-breasted** *adj* cruzado; **~-click** *vi* (*COMPUT*) hacer doble clic; **~cross** *vt* (*trick*) engañar; (*betray*) traicionar; **~decker** *n* autobús *m* de dos pisos; **~ glazing** (*BRIT*) *n* doble acristalamiento; **~ room** *n* habitación *f* doble; **~s** *n* (*TENNIS*) juego de dobles; **doubly** *adv* doblemente

doubt [daut] *n* duda ♦ *vt* dudar; (*suspect*) dudar de; **to ~ that** dudar que; **~ful** *adj* dudoso; (*person*): **to be ~ful about sth** tener dudas sobre algo; **~less** *adv* sin duda

dough [dəu] *n* masa, pasta; **~nut** (*US* **donut**) *n* ≈ rosquilla

dove [dʌv] *n* paloma

dovetail ['dʌvteɪl] *vi* (*fig*) encajar

dowdy ['daudɪ] *adj* (*person*) mal vestido; (*clothes*) pasado de moda

down [daun] *n* (*feathers*) plumón *m*, flojel *m* ♦ *adv* (*~wards*) abajo, hacia abajo; (*on the ground*) por *or* en tierra ♦ *prep* abajo ♦ *vt* (*inf: drink*) beberse; **~ with X!** ¡abajo X!; **~-and-out** *n* vagabundo/a; **~-at-heel** *adj* venido a menos; (*appearance*) desaliñado; **~cast** *adj* abatido; **~fall** *n* caída, ruina; **~hearted** *adj* desanimado; **~hill** *adv*: **to go ~hill** (*also fig*) ir cuesta abajo; **~ payment** *n* entrada, pago al contado; **~pour** *n* aguacero; **~right** *adj* (*nonsense, lie*) manifiesto; (*refusal*) terminante; **~size** *vi* (*ECON: company*) reducir la plantilla de

Down's syndrome ['daunz-] *n* síndrome *m* de Down

down: **~stairs** *adv* (*below*) (en la casa de) abajo; (*~wards*) escaleras abajo; **~stream** *adv* aguas *or* río abajo; **~-to-earth** *adj* práctico; **~town** *adv* en el centro de la ciudad; **~ under** adv en Australia (or Nueva Zelanda); **~ward** [-wəd] adj, adv hacia abajo; **~wards** [-wədz] adv hacia abajo

dowry ['dauri] n dote f

doz. abbr = **dozen**

doze [dəuz] vi dormitar; **~ off** vi quedarse medio dormido

dozen ['dʌzn] n docena; **a ~ books** una docena de libros; **~s of** cantidad de

Dr. abbr = **doctor; drive**

drab [dræb] adj gris, monótono

draft [drɑ:ft] n (first copy) borrador m; (POL: of bill) anteproyecto; (US: call-up) quinta ♦ vt (plan) preparar; (write roughly) hacer un borrador de; see also **draught**

draftsman ['drɑ:ftsmən] (US) = **draughtsman**

drag [dræg] vt arrastrar; (river) dragar, rastrear ♦ vi (time) pasar despacio; (play, film etc) hacerse pesado ♦ n (inf) lata; (women's clothing): **in ~** vestido de travesti; **~ on** vi ser interminable; **~ and drop** vt (COMPUT) arrastrar y soltar

dragon ['drægən] n dragón m

dragonfly ['drægənflaɪ] n libélula

drain [dreɪn] n desaguadero, (in street) sumidero; (source of loss): **to be a ~ on** consumir, agotar ♦ vt (land, marshes) desaguar; (reservoir) desecar; (vegetables) escurrir ♦ vi escurrirse; **~age** n (act) desagüe m; (MED, AGR) drenaje m; (sewage) alcantarillado; **~ing board** (US **~board**) n escurridera, escurridor m; **~pipe** n tubo de desagüe

drama ['drɑ:mə] n (art) teatro; (play) drama m; (excitement) emoción f; **~tic** [drə'mætɪk] adj dramático; (sudden, marked) espectacular; **~tist** ['dræmətɪst] n dramaturgo/a; **~tize** ['dræmətaɪz] vt (events) dramatizar

drank [dræŋk] pt of **drink**

drape [dreɪp] vt (cloth) colocar; (flag) colgar; **~s** (US) npl cortinas fpl

drastic ['dræstɪk] adj (measure) severo; (change) radical, drástico

draught [drɑ:ft] (US **draft**) n (of air) corriente f de aire; (NAUT) calado; **on ~** (of beer) de barril; **~ beer** n cerveza de barril; **~board** (BRIT) n tablero de damas; **~s** (BRIT) n (game) juego de damas

draughtsman ['drɑ:ftsmən] (US **draftsman**) (irreg) n delineante m

draw [drɔ:] (pt **drew**, pp **drawn**) vt (picture) dibujar; (cart) tirar de; (curtain) correr; (take out) sacar; (attract) atraer; (money) retirar; (wages) cobrar ♦ vi (SPORT) empatar ♦ n (SPORT) empate m; (lottery) sorteo; **~ near** vi acercarse; **~ out** vi (lengthen) alargarse ♦ vt sacar; **~ up** vi (stop) pararse ♦ vt (chair)

acercar; (document) redactar; **~back** n inconveniente m, desventaja; **~bridge** n puente m levadizo

drawer [drɔ:*] n cajón m

drawing ['drɔ:ɪŋ] n dibujo; **~ board** n tablero (de dibujante); **~ pin** (BRIT) n chincheta; **~ room** n salón m

drawl [drɔ:l] n habla lenta y cansina

drawn [drɔ:n] pp of **draw**

dread [dred] n pavor m, terror m ♦ vt temer, tener miedo or pavor a; **~ful** adj horroroso

dream [dri:m] (pt, pp **dreamed** or **dreamt**) n sueño ♦ vt, vi soñar; **~y** adj (distracted) soñador(a), distraído; (music) suave

dreary ['drɪərɪ] adj monótono

dredge [dredʒ] vt dragar

dregs [dregz] npl posos mpl; (of humanity) hez f

drench [drentʃ] vt empapar

dress [dres] n vestido; (clothing) ropa ♦ vt vestir; (wound) vendar ♦ vi vestirse; **to get ~ed** vestirse; **~ up** vi vestirse de etiqueta; (in fancy dress) disfrazarse; **~ circle** (BRIT) n principal m; **~er** n (furniture) aparador m; (: US) cómoda (con espejo); **~ing** n (MED) vendaje m; (CULIN) aliño; **~ing gown** (BRIT) n bata; **~ing room** n (THEATRE) camarín m; (SPORT) vestuario; **~ing table** n tocador m; **~maker** n modista, costurera; **~ rehearsal** n ensayo general

drew [dru:] pt of **draw**

dribble ['drɪbl] vi (baby) babear ♦ vt (ball) regatear

dried [draɪd] adj (fruit) seco; (milk) en polvo

drier ['draɪə*] n = **dryer**

drift [drɪft] n (of current etc) flujo; (of snow) ventisquero; (meaning) significado ♦ vi (boat) ir a la deriva; (sand, snow) amontonarse; **~wood** n madera de deriva

drill [drɪl] n (~ bit) broca; (tool for DIY etc) taladro; (of dentist) fresa; (for mining etc) perforadora, barrena; (MIL) instrucción f ♦ vt perforar, taladrar; (troops) enseñar la instrucción a ♦ vi (for oil) perforar

drink [drɪŋk] (pt **drank**, pp **drunk**) n bebida; (sip) trago ♦ vt, vi beber; **to have a ~** tomar algo; tomar una copa or un trago; **a ~ of water** un trago de agua; **~er** n bebedor(a) m/f; **~ing water** n agua potable

drip [drɪp] n (act) goteo; (one by one) gota; (MED) gota a gota ♦ vi gotear; **~-dry** adj (shirt) inarrugable; **~ping** n (animal fat) pringue m

drive [draɪv] (pt **drove**, pp **driven**) n (journey) viaje m (en coche); (also: **~way**) entrada; (energy) energía, vigor m; (COMPUT: also: **disk ~**) drive m ♦ vt (car) conducir (SP), manejar (AM); (nail) clavar; (push) empujar; (TECH: motor) impulsar ♦ vi (AUT: at controls) conducir; (: travel) pasearse en coche; **left-/**

right-hand ~ conducción f a la izquierda/derecha; **to ~ sb mad** volverle loco a uno

drivel ['drɪvl] (inf) n tonterías fpl

driven ['drɪvn] pp of **drive**

driver ['draɪvə*] n conductor(a) m/f (SP), chofer m (AM); (of taxi, bus) chofer; **~'s license** (US) n carnet m de conducir

driveway ['draɪvweɪ] n entrada

driving ['draɪvɪŋ] n el conducir (SP), el manejar (AM); **~ instructor** n instructor(a) m/f de conducción or manejo; **~ lesson** n clase f de conducción or manejo; **~ licence** (BRIT) n permiso de conducir; **~ school** n autoescuela; **~ test** n examen m de conducción or manejo

drizzle ['drɪzl] n llovizna

drool [dru:l] vi babear

droop [dru:p] vi (flower) marchitarse; (shoulders) encorvarse; (head) inclinarse

drop [drɒp] n (of water) gota; (lessening) baja; (fall) caída ♦ vt dejar caer; (voice, eyes, price) bajar; (passenger) dejar; (omit) omitir ♦ vi (object) caer; (wind) amainar; **~s** npl (MED) gotas fpl; **~ off** vi (sleep) dormirse ♦ vt (passenger) dejar; **~ out** vi (withdraw) retirarse; **~out** n marginado/a; (SCOL) estudiante que abandona los estudios; **~per** n cuentagotas m inv; **~pings** npl excremento

drought [draut] n sequía

drove [drəuv] pt of **drive**

drown [draun] vt ahogar ♦ vi ahogarse

drowsy ['drauzɪ] adj soñoliento; **to be ~** tener sueño

drug [drʌg] n medicamento; (narcotic) droga ♦ vt drogar; **to be on ~s** drogarse; **~ addict** n drogadicto/a; **~gist** (US) n farmacéutico; **~store** (US) n farmacia

drum [drʌm] n tambor m; (for oil, petrol) bidón m; **~s** npl batería; **~mer** n tambor m

drunk [drʌŋk] pp of **drink** ♦ adj borracho ♦ n (also: ~ard) borracho/a; **~en** adj borracho; (laughter, party) de borrachos

dry [draɪ] adj seco; (day) sin lluvia; (climate) árido, seco ♦ vt secar; (tears) enjugarse ♦ vi secarse; **~ up** vi (river) secarse; **~-cleaner's** n tintorería; **~-cleaning** n lavado en seco; **~er** n (for hair) secador m; (US: for clothes) secadora; **~ rot** n putrefacción f fungoide

DSS n abbr = Department of Social Security

DTP n abbr (= desk-top publishing) autoedición f

dual ['djuəl] adj doble; **~ carriageway** (BRIT) n carretera de doble calzada; **~-purpose** adj de doble uso

dubbed [dʌbd] adj (CINEMA) doblado

dubious ['dju:bɪəs] adj indeciso; (reputation, company) sospechoso/a

duchess ['dʌtʃɪs] n duquesa

duck [dʌk] n pato ♦ vi agacharse; **~ling** n

patito

duct [dʌkt] n conducto, canal m

dud [dʌd] n (object, tool) engaño, engañifa ♦ adj: **~ cheque** (BRIT) cheque m sin fondos

due [dju:] adj (owed): **he is ~ £10** se le deben 10 libras; (expected: event): **the meeting is ~ on Wednesday** la reunión tendrá lugar el miércoles; (: arrival): **the train is ~ at 8am** el tren tiene su llegada para las 8; (proper) debido ♦ n: **to give sb his** (or her) **~** ser justo con alguien ♦ adv: **~ north** derecho al norte; **~s** npl (for club, union) cuota; (in harbour) derechos mpl; **in ~ course** a su debido tiempo; **to ~** debido a; **to be ~ to** deberse a

duet [dju:'et] n dúo

duffel bag ['dʌfəl] n bolsa de lona

duffel coat n trenca, abrigo de tres cuartos

dug [dʌg] pt, pp of **dig**

duke [dju:k] n duque m

dull [dʌl] adj (light) débil; (stupid) torpe; (boring) pesado; (sound, pain) sordo; (weather, day) gris ♦ vt (pain, grief) aliviar; (mind, senses) entorpecer

duly ['dju:lɪ] adv debidamente; (on time) a su debido tiempo

dumb [dʌm] adj mudo; (pej: stupid) estúpido; **~founded** [dʌm'faundɪd] adj pasmado

dummy ['dʌmɪ] n (tailor's ~) maniquí m; (mock-up) maqueta; (BRIT: for baby) chupete m ♦ adj falso, postizo

dump [dʌmp] n (also: rubbish ~) basurero, vertedero; (inf: place) cuchitril m ♦ vt (put down) dejar; (get rid of) deshacerse de; (COMPUT: data) transferir

dumpling ['dʌmplɪŋ] n bola de masa hervida

dumpy ['dʌmpɪ] adj regordete/a

dunce [dʌns] n zopenco

dung [dʌŋ] n estiércol m

dungarees [dʌŋgə'ri:z] npl mono

dungeon ['dʌndʒən] n calabozo

duplex ['dju:pleks] n dúplex m

duplicate [n 'dju:plɪkət, vb 'dju:plɪkeɪt] n duplicado ♦ vt duplicar; (photocopy) fotocopiar; (repeat) repetir; **in ~** por duplicado

durable ['djuərəbl] adj duradero

duration [djuə'reɪʃən] n duración f

during ['djuərɪŋ] prep durante

dusk [dʌsk] n crepúsculo, anochecer m

dust [dʌst] n polvo ♦ vt quitar el polvo a, desempolvar; (cake etc): **to ~ with** espolvorear de; **~bin** (BRIT) n cubo de la basura (SP), balde m (AM); **~er** n paño, trapo; **~man** (BRIT irreg) n basurero; **~y** adj polvoriento

Dutch [dʌtʃ] adj holandés/esa ♦ n (LING) holandés m; **the ~** npl los holandeses; **to go ~** (inf) pagar cada uno lo suyo; **~man/**

woman (*irreg*) *n* holandés/esa *m/f*
duty ['dju:tɪ] *n* deber *m*; (*tax*) derechos *mpl* de aduana; **on** ~ de servicio; (*at night etc*) de guardia; **off** ~ libre (de servicio); **~-free** *adj* libre de impuestos
duvet ['du:veɪ] (*BRIT*) *n* edredón *m*
DVD *n abbr* (= *digital versatile or video disc*) DVD *m*
dwarf [dwɔ:f] (*pl* **dwarves**) *n* enano/a ♦ *vt* empequeñecer
dwell [dwɛl] (*pt, pp* **dwelt**) *vi* morar; ~ **on** *vt fus* explayarse en
dwindle ['dwɪndl] *vi* menguar, disminuir
dye [daɪ] *n* tinte *m* ♦ *vt* teñir
dying ['daɪɪŋ] *adj* moribundo, agonizante
dyke [daɪk] (*BRIT*) *n* dique *m*
dynamic [daɪ'næmɪk] *adj* dinámico
dynamite ['daɪnəmaɪt] *n* dinamita
dynamo ['daɪnəməu] *n* dínamo *f*
dynasty ['dɪnəstɪ] *n* dinastía

E, e

E [iː] *n* (*MUS*) mi *m*
each [iːtʃ] *adj* cada *inv* ♦ *pron* cada uno; ~ **other** el uno al otro; **they hate ~ other** se odian (entre ellos *or* mutuamente); **they have 2 books ~** tienen 2 libros por persona
eager ['iːgə*] *adj* (*keen*) entusiasmado; **to be ~ to do sth** tener muchas ganas de hacer algo, impacientarse por hacer algo; **to be ~ for** tener muchas ganas de
eagle ['iːgl] *n* águila
ear [ɪə*] *n* oreja; oído; (*of corn*) espiga; **~ache** *n* dolor *m* de oídos; **~drum** *n* tímpano
earl [əːl] *n* conde *m*
earlier ['əːlɪə*] *adj* anterior ♦ *adv* antes
early ['əːlɪ] *adv* temprano; (*before time*) con tiempo, con anticipación ♦ *adj* temprano; (*settlers etc*) primitivo; (*death, departure*) prematuro; (*reply*) pronto; **to have an ~ night** acostarse temprano; **in the ~** *or* **~ in the spring/19th century** a principios de primavera/del siglo diecinueve; **~ retirement** *n* jubilación *f* anticipada
earmark ['ɪəmɑːk] *vt*: **to ~ (for)** reservar (para), destinar (a)
earn [əːn] *vt* (*salary*) percibir; (*interest*) devengar; (*praise*) merecerse
earnest ['əːnɪst] *adj* (*wish*) fervoroso; (*person*) serio, formal; **in ~** en serio
earnings ['əːnɪŋz] *npl* (*personal*) sueldo, ingresos *mpl*; (*company*) ganancias *fpl*
ear: ~phones *npl* auriculares *mpl*; **~ring** *n* pendiente *m*, arete *m*; **~shot** *n*: **within ~shot** al alcance del oído
earth [əːθ] *n* tierra; (*BRIT: ELEC*) cable *m* de toma de tierra ♦ *vt* (*BRIT: ELEC*) conectar a

tierra; **~enware** *n* loza (de barro); **~quake** *n* terremoto; **~y** *adj* (*fig: vulgar*) grosero
ease [iːz] *n* facilidad *f*; (*comfort*) comodidad *f* ♦ *vt* (*lessen: problem*) mitigar; (: *pain*) aliviar; (: *tension*) reducir; **to ~ sth in/out** meter/sacar algo con cuidado; **at ~!** (*MIL*) ¡descansen!; **~ off** *or* **up** *vi* (*wind, rain*) amainar; (*slow down*) aflojar la marcha
easel ['iːzl] *n* caballete *m*
easily ['iːzɪlɪ] *adv* fácilmente
east [iːst] *n* este *m* ♦ *adj* del este, oriental; (*wind*) este ♦ *adv* al este, hacia el este; **the E~** el Oriente; (*POL*) los países del Este
Easter ['iːstə*] *n* Pascua (de Resurrección); **~ egg** *n* huevo de Pascua
east: ~erly ['iːstəlɪ] *adj* (*to the east*) al este; (*from the east*) del este; **~ern** ['iːstən] *adj* del este, oriental; (*oriental*) oriental; (*communist*) del este; **~ward(s)** ['iːstwəd(z)] *adv* hacia el este
easy ['iːzɪ] *adj* fácil; (*simple*) sencillo, (*comfortable*) holgado, cómodo; (*relaxed*) tranquilo ♦ *adv*: **to take it** *or* **things ~** (*not worry*) tomarlo con calma; (*rest*) descansar; **~ chair** *n* sillón *m*; **~-going** *adj* acomodadizo
eat [iːt] (*pt* **ate**, *pp* **eaten**) *vt* comer; ~ **away at** *vt fus* corroer; mermar; ~ **into** *vt fus* corroer; (*savings*) mermar
eaves [iːvz] *npl* alero
eavesdrop ['iːvzdrɔp] *vi*: **to ~ (on)** escuchar a escondidas
ebb [ɛb] *n* reflujo ♦ *vi* bajar; (*fig: also*: ~ *away*) decaer
ebony ['ɛbənɪ] *n* ébano
EC *n abbr* (= *European Community*) CE *f*
ECB *n abbr* (= *European Central Bank*) BCE *m*
eccentric [ɪk'sɛntrɪk] *adj, n* excéntrico/a *m/f*
echo ['ɛkəu] (*pl* **~es**) *n* eco *m* ♦ *vt* (*sound*) repetir ♦ *vi* resonar, hacer eco
éclair [ɪ'klɛə*] *n* pastelillo relleno de crema y con chocolate por encima
eclipse [ɪ'klɪps] *n* eclipse *m*
ecology [ɪ'kɔlədʒɪ] *n* ecología
e-commerce *n abbr* (= *electronic commerce*) comercio electrónico
economic [iːkə'nɔmɪk] *adj* económico; (*business etc*) rentable; **~al** *adj* económico; **~s** *n* (*SCOL*) economía ♦ *npl* (*of project etc*) rentabilidad *f*
economize [ɪ'kɔnəmaɪz] *vi* economizar, ahorrar
economy [ɪ'kɔnəmɪ] *n* economía; ~ **class** *n* (*AVIAT*) clase *f* económica; ~ **size** *n* tamaño económico
ecstasy ['ɛkstəsɪ] *n* éxtasis *m inv*; (*drug*) éxtasis *m inv*; **ecstatic** [ɛks'tætɪk] *adj* extático
ECU ['eɪkjuː] *n* (= *European Currency Unit*) ECU *m*
Ecuador ['ɛkwədɔːr] *n* Ecuador *m*; **~ian** *adj, n* ecuatoriano/a *m/f*

eczema [ˈɛksɪmə] n eczema m

edge [ɛdʒ] n (of knife) filo; (of object) borde m; (of lake) orilla ♦ vt (SEWING) ribetear; **on ~** (fig) = **edgy**; **to ~ away from** alejarse poco a poco de; **~ways** adv: **he couldn't get a word in ~ways** no pudo meter ni baza

edgy [ˈɛdʒɪ] adj nervioso, inquieto

edible [ˈɛdɪbl] adj comestible

Edinburgh [ˈɛdɪnbərə] n Edimburgo

edit [ˈɛdɪt] vt (be editor of) dirigir; (text, report) corregir, preparar; **~ion** [ɪˈdɪʃən] n edición f; **~or** n (of newspaper) director(a) m/f; (of column): **foreign/political ~or** encargado de la sección de extranjero/política; (of book) redactor(a) m/f; **~orial** [-ˈtɔːrɪəl] adj editorial ♦ n editorial m

educate [ˈɛdjukeɪt] vt (gen) educar; (instruct) instruir

education [ɛdjuˈkeɪʃən] n educación f; (schooling) enseñanza; (SCOL) pedagogía; **~al** adj (policy etc) educacional; (experience) docente; (toy) educativo

EEC n abbr (= European Economic Community) CEE f

eel [iːl] n anguila

eerie [ˈɪərɪ] adj misterioso

effect [ɪˈfɛkt] n efecto ♦ vt efectuar, llevar a cabo; **to take ~** (law) entrar en vigor or vigencia; (drug) surtir efecto; **in ~** en realidad; **~ive** adj eficaz; (actual) verdadero; **~ively** adv eficazmente; (in reality) efectivamente; **~iveness** n eficacia

effeminate [ɪˈfɛmɪnɪt] adj afeminado

efficiency [ɪˈfɪʃənsɪ] n eficiencia; rendimiento

efficient [ɪˈfɪʃənt] adj eficiente; (machine) de buen rendimiento

effort [ˈɛfət] n esfuerzo; **~less** adj sin ningún esfuerzo; (style) natural

effusive [ɪˈfjuːsɪv] adj efusivo

e.g. adv abbr (= exempli gratia) p. ej.

egg [ɛg] n huevo; **hard-boiled/soft-boiled ~** huevo duro/pasado por agua; **~ on** vt incitar; **~cup** n huevera; **~ plant** (esp US) n berenjena; **~shell** n cáscara de huevo

ego [ˈiːgəu] n ego; **~tism** n egoísmo; **~ tist** n egoísta m/f

Egypt [ˈiːdʒɪpt] n Egipto; **~ian** [ɪˈdʒɪpʃən] adj, n egipcio/a m/f

eiderdown [ˈaɪdədaun] n edredón m

eight [eɪt] num ocho; **~een** num diez y ocho, dieciocho; **eighth** [eɪtθ] num octavo; **~y** num ochenta

Eire [ˈɛərə] n Eire m

either [ˈaɪðə*] adj cualquiera de los dos; (both, each) cada ♦ pron: **~ (of them)** cualquiera (de los dos) ♦ adv tampoco; **on ~ side** en ambos lados; **I don't like ~** no me gusta ninguno/a de los/las dos; **no, I don't ~** no, yo tampoco ♦ conj: **~ yes or no** o sí o no

eject [ɪˈdʒɛkt] vt echar, expulsar; (tenant) desahuciar; **~or seat** n asiento proyectable

elaborate [adj ɪˈlæbərɪt, vb ɪˈlæbəreɪt] adj (complex) complejo ♦ vt (expand) ampliar; (refine) refinar ♦ vi explicar con más detalles

elastic [ɪˈlæstɪk] n elástico ♦ adj elástico; (fig) flexible; **~ band** (BRIT) n gomita

elated [ɪˈleɪtɪd] adj: **to be ~** regocijarse

elbow [ˈɛlbəu] n codo

elder [ˈɛldə*] adj mayor ♦ n (tree) saúco; (person) mayor; **~ly** adj de edad, mayor ♦ npl: **the ~ly** los mayores

eldest [ˈɛldɪst] adj, n el/la mayor

elect [ɪˈlɛkt] vt elegir ♦ adj: **the president ~** el presidente electo; **to ~** **to do** optar por hacer; **~ion** [ɪˈlɛkʃən] n elección f; **~ioneering** [ɪlɛkʃə-ˈnɪərɪŋ] n campaña electoral; **~or** n elector(a) m/f; **~oral** adj electoral; **~orate** n electorado

electric [ɪˈlɛktrɪk] adj eléctrico; **~al** adj eléctrico; **~ blanket** n manta eléctrica; **~ fire** n estufa eléctrica; **~ian** [ɪlɛkˈtrɪʃən] n electricista m/f; **~ity** [ɪlɛkˈtrɪsɪtɪ] n electricidad f; **electrify** [ɪˈlɛktrɪfaɪ] vt (RAIL) electrificar; (fig: audience) electrizar

electronic [ɪlɛkˈtrɒnɪk] adj electrónico; **~ mail** n correo electrónico; **~s** n electrónica

elegant [ˈɛlɪgənt] adj elegante

element [ˈɛlɪmənt] n elemento; (of kettle etc) resistencia; **~ary** [-ˈmɛntərɪ] adj elemental; (primitive) rudimentario; (school) primario

elephant [ˈɛlɪfənt] n elefante m

elevation [ɛlɪˈveɪʃən] n elevación f; (height) altura

elevator [ˈɛlɪveɪtə*] n (US) ascensor m; (in warehouse etc) montacargas m inv

eleven [ɪˈlɛvn] num once; **~ses** (BRIT) npl café m de las once; **~th** num undécimo

elicit [ɪˈlɪsɪt] vt: **to ~ (from)** sacar (de)

eligible [ˈɛlɪdʒəbl] adj: **an ~ young man/woman** un buen partido; **to be ~ for sth** llenar los requisitos para algo

elm [ɛlm] n olmo

elongated [ˈiːlɔŋgeɪtɪd] adj alargado

elope [ɪˈləup] vi fugarse (para casarse)

eloquent [ˈɛləkwənt] adj elocuente

else [ɛls] adv: **something ~** otra cosa; **somewhere ~** en otra parte; **everywhere ~** en todas partes menos aquí; **where ~?** ¿dónde más?, ¿en qué otra parte?; **there was little ~ to do** apenas quedaba otra cosa que hacer; **nobody ~ spoke** no habló nadie más; **~where** adv (be) en otra parte; (go) a otra parte

elude [ɪˈluːd] vt (subj: idea etc) escaparse a; (capture) esquivar

elusive [ɪˈluːsɪv] adj esquivo; (quality) difícil de encontrar

emaciated [ɪˈmeɪsɪeɪtɪd] adj demacrado

E-mail, e-mail [ˈiːmeɪl] n abbr (= electronic mail) correo electrónico, e-mail m

emancipate [ɪ'mænsɪpeɪt] vt emancipar
embankment [ɪm'bæŋkmənt] nterraplén m
embark [ɪm'bɑːk] vi embarcarse ♦ vt
embarcar; **to ~ on** (journey) emprender;
(course of action) lanzarse a; **~ation**
[embɑː'keɪʃən] n (people) embarco; (goods)
embarque m
embarrass [ɪm'bærəs] vt avergonzar;
(government etc) dejar en mal lugar; **~ed** adj
(laugh, silence) embarazoso; **~ing** adj
(situation) violento; (question) embarazoso;
~ment n (shame) vergüenza; (problem): **to
be an ~ment for sb** poner en un aprieto a uno
embassy ['embəsɪ] n embajada
embedded [ɪm'bedɪd] adj (object)
empotrado; (thorn etc) clavado
embellish [ɪm'belɪʃ] vt embellecer; (story)
adornar
embers ['embəz] npl rescoldo, ascua
embezzle [ɪm'bezl] vt desfalcar, malversar
embitter [ɪm'bɪtə*] vt (fig: sour) amargar
embody [ɪm'bɒdɪ] vt (spirit) encarnar;
(include) incorporar
embossed [ɪm'bɒst] adj realzado
embrace [ɪm'breɪs] vt abrazar, dar un abrazo
a; (include) abarcar ♦ vi abrazarse ♦ n abrazo
embroider [ɪm'brɔɪdə*] vt bordar; **~y** n
bordado
embryo ['embrɪəʊ] n embrión m
emerald ['emərəld] n esmeralda
emerge [ɪ'mɜːdʒ] vi salir; (arise) surgir
emergency [ɪ'mɜːdʒənsɪ] n crisis f inv; **in an
~** en caso de urgencia; **state of ~** estado de
emergencia; **~ cord** (US) n timbre m de
alarma; **~ exit** n salida de emergencia;
~ landing n aterrizaje m forzoso; **~ services**
npl (fire, police, ambulance) servicios mpl de
urgencia or emergencia
emery board ['emərɪ-] n lima de uñas
emigrate ['emɪgreɪt] vi emigrar
emissions [ɪ'mɪʃənz] npl emisión f
emit [ɪ'mɪt] vt emitir; (smoke) arrojar; (smell)
despedir; (sound) producir
emotion [ɪ'məʊʃən] n emoción f; **~al** adj
(needs) emocional; (person) sentimental;
(scene) conmovedor(a), emocionante;
(speech) emocionado
emperor ['empərə*] n emperador m
emphasis ['emfəsɪs] (pl **-ses**) n énfasis m inv
emphasize ['emfəsaɪz] vt (word, point)
subrayar, recalcar; (feature) hacer resaltar
emphatic [em'fætɪk] adj (reply) categórico;
(person) insistente
empire ['empaɪə*] n (also fig) imperio
employ [ɪm'plɔɪ] vt emplear; **~ee** [-'iː] n
empleado/a; **~er** n patrón/ona m/f;
empresario; **~ment** n (work) trabajo;
~ment agency n agencia de colocaciones
empower [ɪm'paʊə*] vt: **to ~ sb to do sth**

autorizar a uno para hacer algo
empress ['emprɪs] n emperatriz f
emptiness ['emptɪnɪs] n vacío; (of life etc)
vaciedad f
empty ['emptɪ] adj vacío; (place) desierto;
(house) desocupado; (threat) vano ♦ vt
vaciar; (place) dejar vacío ♦ vi vaciarse;
(house etc) quedar desocupado; **~-handed**
adj con las manos vacías
EMU n abbr (= European Monetary Union)
UME f
emulate ['emjʊleɪt] vt emular
emulsion [ɪ'mʌlʃən] n emulsión f; (also:
~ paint) pintura emulsión
enable [ɪ'neɪbl] vt: **to ~ sb to do sth** permitir
a uno hacer algo
enamel [ɪ'næməl] n esmalte m; (also:
~ paint) pintura esmaltada
enchant [ɪn'tʃɑːnt] vt encantar; **~ing** adj
encantador(a)
encl. abbr (= enclosed) adj
enclose [ɪn'kləʊz] vt (land) cercar; (letter etc)
adjuntar; **please find ~d** le mandamos adjunto
enclosure [ɪn'kləʊʒə*] n cercado, recinto
encompass [ɪn'kʌmpəs] vt abarcar
encore [ɔŋ'kɔː*] excl ¡otra!, ¡bis! ♦ n bis m
encounter [ɪn'kaʊntə*] n encuentro ♦ vt
encontrar, encontrarse con; (difficulty)
tropezar con
encourage [ɪn'kʌrɪdʒ] vt alentar, animar;
(activity) fomentar; (growth) estimular;
~ment n estímulo; (of industry) fomento
encroach [ɪn'krəʊtʃ] vi: **to ~ (up)on** invadir;
(rights) usurpar; (time) adueñarse de
encyclop(a)edia [ensaɪkləʊ'piːdɪə] n
enciclopedia
end [end] n (gen, also aim) fin m; (of table)
extremo; (of street) final m; (SPORT) lado ♦ vt
terminar, acabar; (also: **bring to an ~**, **put an
~ to**) acabar con ♦ vi terminar, acabar; **in the
~** al fin; **on ~** (object) de punta, de cabeza; **to
stand on ~** (hair) erizarse; **for hours on ~** hora
tras hora; **~ up** vi: **to ~ up in** terminar en;
(place) ir a parar en
endanger [ɪn'deɪndʒə*] vt poner en peligro;
an ~ed species una especie en peligro de
extinción
endearing [ɪn'dɪərɪŋ] adj simpático, atractivo
endeavour [ɪn'devə*] (US **endeavor**) n
esfuerzo; (attempt) tentativa ♦ vi: **to ~ to do**
esforzarse por hacer; (try) procurar hacer
ending ['endɪŋ] n (of book) desenlace m;
(LING) terminación f
endive ['endaɪv] n (chicory) endibia; (curly)
escarola
endless ['endlɪs] adj interminable, inacabable
endorse [ɪn'dɔːs] vt (cheque) endosar;
(approve) aprobar; **~ment** n (on driving
licence) nota de inhabilitación

endure [ɪn'djuə*] vt (bear) aguantar, soportar ♦ vi (last) durar

enemy ['enəmɪ] adj, n enemigo/a m/f

energetic [enə'dʒetɪk] adj enérgico

energy ['enədʒɪ] n energía

enforce [ɪn'fɔːs] vt (LAW) hacer cumplir

engage [ɪn'geɪdʒ] vt (attention) llamar; (interest) ocupar; (in conversation) abordar; (worker) contratar; (AUT): **to ~ the clutch** embragar ♦ vi (TECH) engranar; **to ~ in** dedicarse a, ocuparse en; **~d** adj (BRIT: busy, in use) ocupado; (betrothed) prometido; **to get ~d** prometerse; **~d tone** (BRIT) n (TEL) señal f de comunicando; **~ment** n (appointment) compromiso, cita; (booking) contratación f; (to marry) compromiso; (period) noviazgo; **~ment ring** n anillo de prometida

engaging [ɪn'geɪdʒɪŋ] adj atractivo

engine ['endʒɪn] n (AUT) motor m; (RAIL) locomotora; **~ driver** n maquinista m/f

engineer [endʒɪ'nɪə*] n (BRIT: for repairs) mecánico; (on ship, US: RAIL) maquinista m; **~ing** n ingeniería

England ['ɪŋglənd] n Inglaterra

English ['ɪŋglɪʃ] adj inglés/esa ♦ n (LING) inglés m; **the ~** npl los ingleses mpl; **the ~ Channel** n (el Canal de) la Mancha; **~man/woman** (irreg) n inglés/esa m/f

engraving [ɪn'greɪvɪŋ] n grabado

engrossed [ɪn'grəust] adj: **~ in** absorto en

engulf [ɪn'gʌlf] vt (subj: water) sumergir, hundir; (: fire) prender; (: fear) apoderarse de

enhance [ɪn'hɑːns] vt (gen) aumentar; (beauty) realzar

enjoy [ɪn'dʒɔɪ] vt (health, fortune) disfrutar de, gozar de; (like) gustarle a uno; **to ~ o.s.** divertirse; **~able** adj agradable; (amusing) divertido; **~ment** n (joy) placer m; (activity) diversión f

enlarge [ɪn'lɑːdʒ] vt aumentar; (broaden) extender; (PHOT) ampliar ♦ vi: **to ~ on** (subject) tratar con más detalles; **~ment** n (PHOT) ampliación f

enlighten [ɪn'laɪtn] vt (inform) informar; **~ed** adj comprensivo; **the E~ment** n (HISTORY) ≈ la Ilustración, ≈ el Siglo de las Luces

enlist [ɪn'lɪst] vt alistar; (support) conseguir ♦ vi alistarse

enmity ['enmɪtɪ] n enemistad f

enormous [ɪ'nɔːməs] adj enorme

enough [ɪ'nʌf] adj: **~ time/books** bastante tiempo/bastantes libros ♦ pron bastante(s) ♦ adv: **big ~** bastante grande; **he has not worked ~** no ha trabajado bastante; **have you got ~?** ¿tiene usted bastante(s)?; **~ to eat** (lo) suficiente or (lo) bastante para comer; **~!** ¡basta ya!; **that's ~, thanks** con eso basta, gracias; **I've had ~ of him** estoy harto de él; ... **which, funnily** or **oddly ~** ... ... lo que, por extraño que parezca ...

enquire [ɪn'kwaɪə*] vt, vi = **inquire**

enrage [ɪn'reɪdʒ] vt enfurecer

enrol [ɪn'rəul] (US **enroll**) vt (members) inscribir; (SCOL) matricular ♦ vi inscribirse; matricularse; **~ment** (US **enrollment**) n inscripción f; matriculación f

en route [ɔn'ruːt] adv durante el viaje

en suite [ɔn'swiːt] adj: **with ~ bathroom** con baño

ensure [ɪn'ʃuə*] vt asegurar

entail [ɪn'teɪl] vt suponer

entangled [ɪn'tæŋgld] adj: **to become ~** (in) quedarse enredado (en) or enmarañado (en)

enter ['entə*] vt (room) entrar en; (club) hacerse socio de; (army) alistarse en; (sb for a competition) inscribir; (write down) anotar, apuntar; (COMPUT) meter ♦ vi entrar; **~ for** vt fus presentarse para; **~ into** vt fus (discussion etc) entablar; (agreement) llegar a, firmar

enterprise ['entəpraɪz] n empresa; (spirit) iniciativa; **free ~** la libre empresa; **private ~** la iniciativa privada; **enterprising** adj emprendedor(a)

entertain [entə'teɪn] vt (amuse) divertir; (invite: guest) invitar (a casa); (idea) abrigar; **~er** n artista m/f; **~ing** adj divertido, entretenido; **~ment** n (amusement) diversión f; (show) espectáculo

enthralled [ɪn'θrɔːld] adj encantado

enthusiasm [ɪn'θuːzɪæzəm] n entusiasmo

enthusiast [ɪn'θuːzɪæst] n entusiasta m/f; **~ic** [-'æstɪk] adj entusiasta; **to be ~ic about** entusiasmarse por

entire [ɪn'taɪə*] adj entero; **~ly** adv totalmente, por completo; **~ty** [ɪn'taɪərətɪ] n: **in its ~ty** en su totalidad

entitle [ɪn'taɪtl] vt: **to ~ sb to sth** dar a uno derecho a algo; **~d** adj (book) titulado; **to be ~d to do** tener derecho a hacer

entrance [n 'entrəns, vb ɪn'trɑːns] n entrada ♦ vt encantar, hechizar; **to gain ~ to** (university etc) ingresar en; **~ examination** n examen m de ingreso; **~ fee** n cuota; **~ ramp** (US) n (AUT) rampa de acceso

entrant ['entrənt] n (in race, competition) participante m/f; (in examination) candidato/a

entrenched [en'trentʃd] adj inamovible

entrepreneur [ɔntrəprə'nɜː] n empresario

entrust [ɪn'trʌst] vt: **to ~ sth to sb** confiar algo a uno

entry ['entrɪ] n entrada; (in competition) participación f; (in register) apunte m; (in account) partida; (in reference book) artículo; **"no ~"** "prohibido el paso"; (AUT) "dirección prohibida"; **~ form** n hoja de inscripción; **~ phone** n portero automático

envelop [ɪn'vɛləp] vt envolver

envelope ['ɛnvələup] n sobre m

envious ['ɛnvɪəs] adj envidioso; (look) de envidia

environment [ɪn'vaɪərnmənt] n (surroundings) entorno; (natural world): **the ~** el medio ambiente; **~al** [-'mɛntl] adj ambiental, medioambiental; **~ friendly** adj no perjudicial para el medio ambiente

envisage [ɪn'vɪzɪdʒ] vt prever

envoy ['ɛnvɔɪ] n enviado

envy ['ɛnvɪ] n envidia ♦ vt tener envidia a; **to ~ sb sth** envidiar algo a uno

epic ['ɛpɪk] n épica ♦ adj épico

epidemic [ɛpɪ'dɛmɪk] n epidemia

epilepsy ['ɛpɪlɛpsɪ] n epilepsia

episode ['ɛpɪsəud] n episodio

epitomize [ɪ'pɪtəmaɪz] vt epitomar, resumir

equal ['i:kwl] adj igual; (treatment) equitativo ♦ n igual m/f ♦ vt ser igual a; (fig) igualar; **to be ~ to** (task) estar a la altura de; **~ity** [iː'kwɔlɪtɪ] n igualdad f; **~ize** vi (SPORT) empatar; **~ly** adv igualmente; (share etc) a partes iguales

equate [ɪ'kweɪt] vt: **to ~ sth with** equiparar algo con; **equation** [ɪ'kweɪʒən] n (MATH) ecuación f

equator [ɪ'kweɪtə*] n ecuador m

equilibrium [i:kwɪ'lɪbrɪəm] n equilibrio

equip [ɪ'kwɪp] vt equipar; (person) proveer; **to be well ~ped** estar bien equipado; **~ment** n equipo; (tools) avíos mpl

equities ['ɛkwɪtɪz] (BRIT) npl (COMM) derechos mpl sobre or en el activo

equivalent [ɪ'kwɪvələnt] adj: **~ (to)** equivalente (a) ♦ n equivalente m

era ['ɪərə] n era, época

eradicate [ɪ'rædɪkeɪt] vt erradicar

erase [ɪ'reɪz] vt borrar; **~r** n goma de borrar

erect [ɪ'rɛkt] adj erguido ♦ vt erigir, levantar; (assemble) montar; **~ion** [-ʃən] n construcción f; (assembly) montaje m; (PHYSIOL) erección f

ERM n abbr (= Exchange Rate Mechanism) tipo de cambio europeo

erode [ɪ'rəud] vt (GEO) erosionar; (metal) corroer, desgastar; (fig) desgastar

erotic [ɪ'rɔtɪk] adj erótico

errand ['ɛrnd] n recado (SP), mandado (AM)

erratic [ɪ'rætɪk] adj desigual, poco uniforme

error ['ɛrə*] n error m, equivocación f

erupt [ɪ'rʌpt] vi entrar en erupción; (fig) estallar; **~ion** [ɪ'rʌpʃən] n erupción f; (of war) estallido

escalate ['ɛskəleɪt] vi extenderse, intensificarse

escalator ['ɛskəleɪtə*] n escalera móvil

escapade [ɛskə'peɪd] n travesura

escape [ɪ'skeɪp] n fuga ♦ vi escaparse; (flee) huir, evadirse; (leak) fugarse ♦ vt (respon-

sibility etc) evitar, eludir; (consequences) escapar a; (elude): **his name ~s me** no me sale su nombre; **to ~ from** (place) escaparse de; (person) escaparse a

escort [n 'ɛskɔːt, vb ɪ'skɔːt] n acompañante m/f; (MIL) escolta ♦ vt acompañar

Eskimo ['ɛskɪməu] n esquimal m/f

especially [ɪ'spɛʃlɪ] adv (above all) sobre todo; (particularly) en particular, especialmente

espionage ['ɛspɪənɑːʒ] n espionaje m

esplanade [ɛsplə'neɪd] n (by sea) paseo marítimo

Esquire [ɪ'skwaɪə] (abbr **Esq.**) n: **J. Brown, ~ Sr.** D. J. Brown

essay ['ɛseɪ] n (LITERATURE) ensayo; (SCOL: short) redacción f; (: long) trabajo

essence ['ɛsns] n esencia

essential [ɪ'sɛnʃl] adj (necessary) imprescindible; (basic) esencial; **~s** npl lo imprescindible, lo esencial; **~ly** adv esencialmente

establish [ɪ'stæblɪʃ] vt establecer; (prove) demostrar; (relations) entablar; (reputation) ganarse; **~ed** adj (business) conocido; (practice) arraigado; **~ment** n establecimiento; **the E~ment** n clase dirigente

estate [ɪ'steɪt] n (land) finca, hacienda; (inheritance) herencia; (BRIT: also: housing ~) urbanización f; **~ agent** (BRIT) n agente m/f inmobiliario/a; **~ car** (BRIT) n furgoneta

esteem [ɪ'stiːm] n: **to hold sb in high ~** estimar en mucho a uno

esthetic [ɪs'θɛtɪk] (US) adj = **aesthetic**

estimate [n 'ɛstɪmət, vb 'ɛstɪmeɪt] n estimación f, apreciación f; (assessment) tasa, cálculo; (COMM) presupuesto ♦ vt estimar, tasar; calcular; **estimation** [-'meɪʃən] n opinión f, juicio; cálculo

estranged [ɪ'streɪndʒd] adj separado

estuary ['ɛstjuərɪ] n estuario, ría

etc abbr (= et cetera) etc

eternal [ɪ'təːnl] adj eterno

eternity [ɪ'təːnɪtɪ] n eternidad f

ethical ['ɛθɪkl] adj ético; **ethics** ['ɛθɪks] n ética ♦ npl moralidad f

Ethiopia [i:θɪ'əupɪə] n Etiopia

ethnic ['ɛθnɪk] adj étnico; **~ minority** n minoría étnica

ethos ['i:θɔs] n genio, carácter m

etiquette ['ɛtɪkɛt] n etiqueta

EU n abbr (= European Union) UE f

euro n euro

Eurocheque ['juərəutʃɛk] n Eurocheque m

Euroland ['juərəulænd] n Eurolandia

Europe ['juərəp] n Europa; **~an** [-'pi:ən] adj, n europeo/a m/f; **~an Community** n Comunidad f Europea; **~an Union** n Unión f Europea

evacuate |ɪ'vækjueɪt| vt (people) evacuar; (place) desocupar

evade |ɪ'veɪd| vt evadir, eludir

evaporate |ɪ'væpəreɪt| vi evaporarse; (fig) desvanecerse; **~d milk** n leche f evaporada

evasion |ɪ'veɪʒən| n evasión f

eve |iːv| n: **on the ~ of** en vísperas de

even |'iːvn| adj (level) llano; (smooth) liso; (speed, temperature) uniforme; (number) par ♦ adv hasta, incluso; (introducing a comparison) aún, todavía; **~ if**, **~ though** aunque + sub; **~ more** aun más; **~ so** aun así; **not ~** ni siquiera; **~ he was there** hasta él estuvo allí; **~ on Sundays** incluso los domingos; **to get ~ with sb** ajustar cuentas con uno

evening |'iːvnɪŋ| n tarde f; (late) noche f; **in the ~** por la tarde; **~ class** n clase f nocturna; **~ dress** n (no pl: formal clothes) traje m de etiqueta; (woman's) traje m de noche

event |ɪ'vent| n suceso, acontecimiento; (SPORT) prueba; **in the ~ of** en caso de; **~ful** adj (life) activo; (day) ajetreado

eventual |ɪ'ventʃuəl| adj final; **~ity** |-'ælɪtɪ| n eventualidad f; **~ly** adv (finally) finalmente; (in time) con el tiempo

ever |'evə*| adv (at any time) nunca, jamás; (at all times) siempre; (in question): **why ~ not?** ¿y por qué no?; **the best ~** lo nunca visto; **have you ~ seen it?** ¿lo ha visto usted alguna vez?; **better than ~** mejor que nunca; **~ since** adv desde entonces ♦ conj después de que; **~green** n árbol m de hoja perenne; **~lasting** adj eterno, perpetuo

---

KEYWORD

every |'evrɪ| adj **1** (each) cada; **~ one of them** (persons) todos ellos/as; (objects) cada uno de ellos/as; **~ shop in the town was closed** todas las tiendas de la ciudad estaban cerradas

2 (all possible) todo/a; **I gave you ~ assistance** te di toda la ayuda posible; **I have ~ confidence in him** tiene toda mi confianza; **we wish you ~ success** te deseamos toda suerte de éxitos

3 (showing recurrence) todo/a; **~ day/week** todos los días/todas las semanas; **~ other car had been broken into** habían forzado uno de cada dos coches; **she visits me ~ other/third day** me visita cada dos/tres días; **~ now and then** de vez en cuando

---

every: **~body** pron = **everyone**; **~day** adj (daily) cotidiano, de todos los días; (usual) acostumbrado; **~one** pron todos/as, todo el mundo; **~thing** pron todo; **this shop sells ~thing** esta tienda vende de todo; **~where** adv: **I've been looking for you ~where** te he

estado buscando por todas partes; **~where you go you meet ... en todas partes encuentras ...

evict |ɪ'vɪkt| vt desahuciar; **~ion** |ɪ'vɪkʃən| n desahucio

evidence |'evɪdəns| n (proof) prueba; (of witness) testimonio; (sign) indicios mpl; **to give ~** prestar declaración, dar testimonio

evident |'evɪdənt| adj evidente, manifiesto; **~ly** adv por lo visto

evil |'iːvl| adj malo; (influence) funesto ♦ n mal m

evoke |ɪ'vəuk| vt evocar

evolution |iːvə'luːʃən| n evolución f

evolve |ɪ'vɔlv| vt desarrollar ♦ vi evolucionar, desarrollarse

ewe |juː| n oveja

ex- |eks| prefix ex

exact |ɪg'zækt| adj exacto; (person) meticuloso ♦ vt: **to ~ sth (from)** exigir algo (de); **~ing** adj exigente; (conditions) arduo; **~ly** adv exactamente; (indicating agreement) exacto

exaggerate |ɪg'zædʒəreɪt| vt, vi exagerar; **exaggeration** |-'reɪʃən| n exageración f

exalted |ɪg'zɔːltɪd| adj eminente

exam |ɪg'zæm| n abbr (SCOL) = **examination**

examination |ɪgzæmɪ'neɪʃən| n examen m; (MED) reconocimiento

examine |ɪg'zæmɪn| vt examinar; (inspect) inspeccionar, escudriñar; (MED) reconocer; **~r** n examinador(a) m/f

example |ɪg'zɑːmpl| n ejemplo; **for ~** por ejemplo

exasperate |ɪg'zɑːspəreɪt| vt exasperar, irritar; **exasperation** |-ʃən| n exasperación f, irritación f

excavate |'ekskəveɪt| vt excavar

exceed |ɪk'siːd| vt (amount) exceder; (number) pasar de; (speed limit) sobrepasar; (powers) excederse en; (hopes) superar; **~ingly** adv sumamente, sobremanera

excellent |'eksələnt| adj excelente

except |ɪk'sept| prep (also: ~ for, ~ing) excepto, salvo ♦ vt exceptuar, excluir; **~ if/ when** excepto si/cuando; **~ that** salvo que; **~ion** |ɪk'sepʃən| n excepción f; **to take ~ion to** ofenderse por; **~ional** |ɪk'sepʃənl| adj excepcional

excerpt |'eksəːpt| n extracto

excess |ɪk'ses| n exceso; **~es** npl (of cruelty etc) atrocidades fpl; **~ baggage** n exceso de equipaje; **~ fare** n suplemento; **~ive** adj excesivo

exchange |ɪks'tʃeɪndʒ| n intercambio; (conversation) diálogo; (also: telephone ~) central f (telefónica) ♦ vt: **to ~ (for)** cambiar (por); **~ rate** n tipo de cambio

exchequer |ɪks'tʃekə*| (BRIT) n: **the E~** la

Hacienda del Fisco

excise ['ɛksaɪz] n impuestos mpl sobre el alcohol y el tabaco

excite [ɪk'saɪt] vt (stimulate) estimular; (arouse) excitar; ~d adj: **to get ~d** emocionarse; ~**ment** n (agitation) excitación f; (exhilaration) emoción f; **exciting** adj emocionante

exclaim [ɪk'skleɪm] vi exclamar; **exclamation** [ɛksklə'meɪʃən] n exclamación f; **exclamation mark** n punto de admiración

exclude [ɪk'sklu:d] vt excluir; exceptuar

exclusive [ɪk'sklu:sɪv] adj exclusivo; (club, district) selecto; ~ **of tax** excluyendo impuestos; ~**ly** adv únicamente

excruciating [ɪk'skru:ʃieɪtɪŋ] adj (pain) agudísimo, atroz; (noise, embarrassment) horrible

excursion [ɪk'skə:ʃən] n (tourist ~) excursión f

excuse [n ɪk'skju:s, vb ɪk'skju:z] n disculpa, excusa; (pretext) pretexto ♦ vt (justify) justificar; (forgive) disculpar, perdonar; **to ~ sb from doing sth** dispensar a uno de hacer algo; ~ **me!** (attracting attention) ¡por favor!; (apologizing) ¡perdón!; **if you will ~ me** con su permiso

ex-directory ['ɛksdɪ'rɛktərɪ] (BRIT) adj que no consta en la guía

execute ['ɛksɪkju:t] vt (plan) realizar; (order) cumplir; (person) ajusticiar, ejecutar; **execution** [-'kju:ʃən] n realización f; cumplimiento; ejecución f

executive [ɪg'zɛkjutɪv] n (person, committee) ejecutivo; (POL: committee) poder m ejecutivo ♦ adj ejecutivo

exemplify [ɪg'zɛmplɪfaɪ] vt ejemplificar; (illustrate) ilustrar

exempt [ɪg'zɛmpt] adj: ~ **from** exento de ♦ vt: **to ~ sb from** eximir a uno de; ~**ion** [-ʃən] n exención f

exercise ['ɛksəsaɪz] n ejercicio ♦ vt (patience) usar de; (right) valerse de; (dog) llevar de paseo; (mind) preocupar ♦ vi (also: **to take ~**) hacer ejercicio(s); ~ **bike** n ciclostático ®ᵐ, bicicleta estática; ~ **book** n cuaderno

exert [ɪg'zə:t] vt ejercer; **to ~ o.s.** esforzarse; ~**ion** [-ʃən] n esfuerzo

exhale [ɛks'heɪl] vt despedir ♦ vi exhalar

exhaust [ɪg'zɔ:st] n (AUT: also: ~ **pipe**) escape m; (: fumes) gases mpl de escape ♦ vt agotar; ~**ed** adj agotado; ~**ion** [ɪg'zɔ:stʃən] n agotamiento; **nervous ~ion** postración f nerviosa; ~**ive** adj exhaustivo

exhibit [ɪg'zɪbɪt] n (ART) obra expuesta; (LAW) objeto expuesto ♦ vt (show: emotions) manifestar; (: courage, skill) demostrar; (paintings) exponer; ~**ion** [ɛksɪ'bɪʃən] n

exposición f; (of talent etc) demostración f

exhilarating [ɪg'zɪləreɪtɪŋ] adj estimulante, tónico

exile ['ɛksaɪl] n exilio; (person) exiliado/a ♦ vt desterrar, exiliar

exist [ɪg'zɪst] vi existir; (live) vivir; ~**ence** n existencia; ~**ing** adj existente, actual

exit ['ɛksɪt] n salida ♦ vi (THEATRE) hacer mutis; (COMPUT) salir (al sistema); ~ **poll** n encuesta a la salida de los colegios electorales; ~ **ramp** (US) n (AUT) vía de acceso

exodus ['ɛksədəs] n éxodo

exonerate [ɪg'zɔnəreɪt] vt: **to ~ from** exculpar de

exotic [ɪg'zɔtɪk] adj exótico

expand [ɪk'spænd] vt ampliar; (number) aumentar ♦ vi (population) aumentar; (trade etc) expandirse; (gas, metal) dilatarse

expanse [ɪk'spæns] n extensión f

expansion [ɪk'spænʃən] n (of population) aumento; (of trade) expansión f

expect [ɪk'spɛkt] vt esperar; (require) contar con; (suppose) suponer ♦ vi: **to be ~ing** (pregnant woman) estar embarazada; ~**ancy** n (anticipation) esperanza; **life ~ancy** esperanza de vida; ~**ant mother** n futura madre f; ~**ation** [ɛkspɛk'teɪʃən] n (hope) esperanza; (belief) expectativa

expedient [ɪk'spi:dɪənt] adj conveniente, oportuno ♦ n recurso, expediente m

expedition [ɛkspə'dɪʃən] n expedición f

expel [ɪk'spɛl] vt arrojar; (from place) expulsar

expend [ɪk'spɛnd] vt (money) gastar; (time, energy) consumir; ~**iture** n gastos mpl, desembolso; consumo

expense [ɪk'spɛns] n gasto, gastos mpl; (high cost) costa; ~**s** npl (COMM) gastos mpl; **at the ~ of** a costa de; ~ **account** n cuenta de gastos

expensive [ɪk'spɛnsɪv] adj caro, costoso

experience [ɪk'spɪərɪəns] n experiencia ♦ vt experimentar; (suffer) sufrir; ~**d** adj experimentado

experiment [ɪk'spɛrɪmənt] n experimento ♦ vi hacer experimentos

expert ['ɛkspə:t] adj experto, perito ♦ n experto/a, perito/a; (specialist) especialista m/f; ~**ise** [-'ti:z] n pericia

expire [ɪk'spaɪə*] vi caducar, vencer; **expiry** n vencimiento

explain [ɪk'spleɪn] vt explicar; **explanation** [ɛksplə'neɪʃən] n explicación f; **explanatory** [ɪk'splænətrɪ] adj explicativo; aclaratorio

explicit [ɪk'splɪsɪt] adj explícito

explode [ɪk'spləud] vi estallar, explotar; (population) crecer rápidamente; (with anger) reventar

exploit [n 'ɛksplɔɪt, vb ɪk'splɔɪt] n hazaña ♦ vt explotar; ~**ation** [-'teɪʃən] n explotación f

exploratory [ɪkˈsplɔrətrɪ] *adj* de exploración; *(fig: talks)* exploratorio, preliminar

explore [ɪkˈsplɔː*] *vt* explorar; *(fig)* examinar; investigar; **~r** *n* explorador(a) *m/f*

explosion [ɪkˈspləuʒən] *n (also fig)* explosión *f*; **explosive** [ɪksˈpləusɪv] *adj*, *n* explosivo

exponent [ɪkˈspəunənt] *n (of theory etc)* partidario/a; *(of skill etc)* exponente *m/f*

export [*vb* ekˈspɔːt, *n* ˈekspɔːt] *vt* exportar ♦ *n (process)* exportación *f*; *(product)* producto de exportación ♦ *cpd* de exportación; **~er** *n* exportador *m*

expose [ɪkˈspəuz] *vt* exponer; *(unmask)* desenmascarar; **~d** *adj* expuesto

exposure [ɪkˈspəuʒə*] *n* exposición *f*; *(publicity)* publicidad *f*; *(PHOT: speed)* velocidad *f* de obturación; *(: shot)* fotografía; **to die from ~** *(MED)* morir de frío; **~ meter** *n* fotómetro

express [ɪkˈspres] *adj (definite)* expreso, explícito; *(BRIT: letter etc)* urgente ♦ *n (train)* rápido ♦ *vt* expresar; **~ion** [ɪkˈspreʃən] *n* expresión *f*; *(of actor etc)* sentimiento; **~ly** *adv* expresamente; **~way** *(US)* *n (urban motorway)* autopista

exquisite [ekˈskwɪzɪt] *adj* exquisito

extend [ɪkˈstend] *vt (visit, street)* prolongar; *(building)* ampliar; *(invitation)* ofrecer ♦ *vi (land)* extenderse; *(period of time)* prolongarse

extension [ɪkˈstenʃən] *n* extensión *f*; *(building)* ampliación *f*; *(of time)* prolongación *f*; *(TEL: in private house)* línea derivada; *(: in office)* extensión *f*

extensive [ɪkˈstensɪv] *adj* extenso; *(damage)* importante; *(knowledge)* amplio; **~ly** *adv*: **he's travelled ~ly** ha viajado por muchos países

extent [ɪkˈstent] *n (breadth)* extensión *f*; *(scope)* alcance *m*; **to some ~** hasta cierto punto; **to the ~ of...** hasta el punto de...; **to such an ~ that...** hasta tal punto que...; **to what ~?** ¿hasta qué punto?

extenuating [ɪkˈstenjueitɪŋ] *adj*: **~ circumstances** circunstancias *fpl* atenuantes

exterior [ekˈstiəriə*] *adj* exterior, externo ♦ *n* exterior *m*

external [ekˈstəːnl] *adj* externo

extinct [ɪkˈstɪŋkt] *adj (volcano)* extinguido; *(race)* extinto

extinguish [ɪkˈstɪŋgwɪʃ] *vt* extinguir, apagar; **~er** *n* extintor *m*

extort [ɪkˈstɔːt] *vt* obtener por fuerza; **~ionate** *adj* excesivo, exorbitante

extra [ˈekstrə] *adj* adicional ♦ *adv (in addition)* de más ♦ *n (luxury, addition)* extra *m*; *(CINEMA, THEATRE)* extra *m/f*, comparsa *m/f*

extra... [ˈekstrə] *prefix* extra...

extract [*vb* ɪkˈstrækt, *n* ˈekstrækt] *vt* sacar; *(tooth)* extraer; *(money, promise)* obtener ♦ *n* extracto

extracurricular [ekstrəkəˈrɪkjulə*] *adj* extraescolar, extra-académico

extradite [ˈekstrədaɪt] *vt* extraditar

extra-: ~marital *adj* extramatrimonial; **~mural** [ekstrəˈmjuərl] *adj* extraescolar; **~ordinary** [ɪkˈstrɔːdnrɪ] *adj* extraordinario; *(odd)* raro

extravagance [ɪkˈstrævəgəns] *n* derroche *m*, despilfarro; *(thing bought)* extravagancia

extravagant [ɪkˈstrævəgənt] *adj (lavish: person)* pródigo; *(: gift)* (demasiado) caro; *(wasteful)* despilfarrador(a)

extreme [ɪkˈstriːm] *adj* extremo, extremado ♦ *n* extremo; **~ly** *adv* sumamente, extremadamente

extricate [ˈekstrɪkeɪt] *vt*: **to ~ sth/sb from** librar algo/a uno de

extrovert [ˈekstrəvəːt] *n* extrovertido/a

eye [aɪ] *n* ojo ♦ *vt* mirar de soslayo, ojear; **to keep an ~ on** vigilar; **~bath** *n* ojera; **~brow** *n* ceja; **~drops** *npl* gotas *fpl* para los ojos, colirio; **~lash** *n* pestaña; **~lid** *n* párpado; **~liner** *n* lápiz *m* de ojos; **~-opener** *n* revelación *f*, gran sorpresa; **~shadow** *n* sombreador *m* de ojos; **~sight** *n* vista; **~sore** *n* monstruosidad *f*; **~ witness** *n* testigo *m/f* presencial

F, f

F [ef] *n (MUS)* fa *m*

F. *abbr* = Fahrenheit

fable [ˈfeɪbl] *n* fábula

fabric [ˈfæbrɪk] *n* tejido, tela

fabulous [ˈfæbjuləs] *adj* fabuloso

façade [fəˈsɑːd] *n* fachada

face [feɪs] *n (ANAT)* cara, rostro; *(of clock)* esfera *(SP)*, cara *(AM)*; *(of mountain)* cara, ladera; *(of building)* fachada ♦ *vt (direction)* estar de cara a; *(situation)* hacer frente a; *(facts)* aceptar; **~ down** *(person, card)* boca abajo; **to lose ~** desprestigiarse; **to make** *or* **pull a ~** hacer muecas; **in the ~ of** *(difficulties etc)* ante; **on the ~ of it** a primera vista; **~ to ~ cara a cara; **~ up to** *vt fus* hacer frente a, arrostrar; **~ cloth** *(BRIT)* *n* manopla; **~ cream** *n* crema (de belleza); **~ lift** *n* estirado facial; *(of building)* renovación *f*; **~ powder** *n* polvos *mpl*; **~-saving** *adj* para salvar las apariencias; **~ value** *n (of stamp)* valor *m* nominal; **to take sth at ~ value** *(fig)* tomar algo en sentido literal

facilities [fəˈsɪlɪtɪz] *npl (buildings)* instalaciones *fpl*; *(equipment)* servicios *mpl*; **credit ~** facilidades *fpl* de crédito

facing [ˈfeɪsɪŋ] *prep* frente a

facsimile [fæk'sımılı] n (replica) facsímil(e) m; (machine) telefax m; (fax) fax m

fact [fækt] n hecho; **in ~** en realidad

factor ['fæktə*] n factor m

factory ['fæktərı] n fábrica

factual ['fæktjuəl] adj basado en los hechos

faculty ['fækəltı] n facultad f; (US: teaching staff) personal m docente

fad [fæd] n novedad f, moda

fade [feɪd] vi desteñirse; (sound, smile) desvanecerse; (light) apagarse; (flower) marchitarse; (hope, memory) perderse

fag [fæg] (BRIT: inf) n (cigarette) pitillo (SP), cigarro

fail [feɪl] vt (candidate) suspender; (exam) no aprobar (SP), reprobar (AM); (subj: memory etc) fallar a ♦ vi suspender; (be unsuccessful) fracasar; (brakes) fallar; (light) acabarse; **to ~ to do sth** (neglect) dejar de hacer algo; (be unable) no poder hacer algo; **without ~** sin falta; **~ing** n falta, defecto ♦ prep a falta de; **~ure** ['feɪljə*] n fracaso; (person) fracasado/a; (mechanical etc) fallo

faint [feɪnt] adj débil; (recollection) vago; (mark) apenas visible ♦ n desmayo ♦ vi desmayarse; **to feel ~** estar mareado, marearse

fair [feə*] adj justo; (hair, person) rubio; (weather) bueno; (good enough) regular; (considerable) considerable ♦ adv (play) limpio ♦ n feria; (BRIT: funfair) parque de atracciones; **~ly** adv (justly) con justicia; (quite) bastante; **~ness** n justicia, imparcialidad f; **~ play** n juego limpio

fairy ['feərı] n hada; **~ tale** n cuento de hadas

faith [feɪθ] n fe f; (trust) confianza; (sect) religión f; **~ful** adj (loyal: troops etc) leal; (spouse) fiel; (account) exacto; **~fully** adv fielmente; **yours ~fully** (BRIT: in letters) le saluda atentamente

fake [feɪk] n (painting etc) falsificación f; (person) impostor(a) m/f ♦ adj falso ♦ vt fingir; (painting etc) falsificar

falcon ['fɔ:lkən] n halcón m

fall [fɔ:l] (pt fell, pp fallen) n caída; (in price etc) descenso; (US) otoño ♦ vi caer(se); (price) bajar, descender; **~s** npl (water~) cascada, salto de agua; **to ~ flat** (on one's face) caerse (boca abajo); (plan) fracasar; (joke, story) no hacer gracia; **~ back** vi retroceder; **~ back on** vt fus (remedy etc) recurrir a; **~ behind** vi quedarse atrás; **~ down** vi (person) caerse; (building, hopes) derrumbarse; **~ for** vt fus (trick) dejarse engañar por; (person) enamorarse de; **~ in** vi (roof) hundirse; (MIL) alinearse; **~ off** vi caerse; (diminish) disminuir; **~ out** vi (friends etc) reñir; (hair, teeth) caerse; **~ through** vi (plan, project) fracasar

fallacy ['fæləsı] n error m

fallen ['fɔ:lən] pp of fall

fallout ['fɔ:laut] n lluvia radioactiva

fallow ['fæləu] adj en barbecho

false [fɔ:ls] adj falso; **under ~ pretences** con engaños; **~ alarm** n falsa alarma; **~ teeth** (BRIT) npl dentadura postiza

falter ['fɔ:ltə*] vi vacilar; (engine) fallar

fame [feɪm] n fama

familiar [fə'mılıə*] adj conocido, familiar; (tone) de confianza; **to be ~ with** (subject) conocer (bien)

family ['fæmılı] n familia; **~ business** n negocio familiar; **~ doctor** n médico/a de cabecera

famine ['fæmın] n hambre f, hambruna

famished ['fæmıʃt] adj hambriento

famous ['feɪməs] adj famoso, célebre; **~ly** adv (get on) estupendamente

fan [fæn] n abanico; (ELEC) ventilador m; (of pop star) fan m/f; (SPORT) hincha m/f ♦ vt abanicar; (fire, quarrel) atizar

fanatic [fə'nætık] n fanático/a

fan belt n correa del ventilador

fanciful ['fænsıful] adj (design, name) fantástico

fancy ['fænsı] n (whim) capricho, antojo; (imagination) imaginación f ♦ adj (luxury) lujoso, de lujo ♦ vt (feel like, want) tener ganas de; (imagine) imaginarse; (think) creer; **to take a ~ to sb** tomar cariño a uno; **he fancies her** (inf) le gusta (ella) mucho; **~ dress** n disfraz m; **~-dress ball** n baile m de disfraces

fanfare ['fænfeə*] n fanfarria (de trompeta)

fang [fæŋ] n colmillo

fantastic [fæn'tæstık] adj (enormous) enorme; (strange, wonderful) fantástico

fantasy ['fæntəzı] n (dream) sueño; (unreality) fantasía

far [fɑ:*] adj (distant) lejano ♦ adv lejos; (much, greatly) mucho; **~ away, ~ off** (a lo) lejos; **~ better** mucho mejor; **~ from** lejos de; **by ~** con mucho; **go as ~ as the farm** vaya hasta la granja; **as ~ as I know** que yo sepa; **how ~?** ¿hasta dónde?; (fig) ¿hasta qué punto?; **~away** adj remoto; (look) distraído

farce [fɑ:s] n farsa

fare [feə*] n (on trains, buses) precio (del billete); (in taxi: cost) tarifa; (food) comida; **half ~** medio pasaje m; **full ~** pasaje completo

Far East n: **the ~** el Extremo Oriente

farewell [feə'wel] excl, n adiós m

farm [fɑ:m] n granja (SP), finca (AM), estancia (AM) ♦ vt cultivar; **~er** n granjero (SP), estanciero (AM); **~hand** n peón m; **~house** n granja, casa de hacienda (AM); **~ing** n agricultura; (of crops) cultivo; (of animals) cría; **~land** n tierra de cultivo; **~ worker** n

= ~**hand**; ~**yard** n corral m
far-reaching [fɑːˈriːtʃɪŋ] adj (reform, effect) de gran alcance
fart [fɑːt] (inf!) vi tirarse un pedo (!)
farther [ˈfɑːðə*] adv más lejos, más allá ♦ adj más lejano
farthest [ˈfɑːðɪst] superlative of **far**
fascinate [ˈfæsɪneɪt] vt fascinar; **fascination** [-ˈneɪʃən] n fascinación f
fascism [ˈfæʃɪzəm] n fascismo
fashion [ˈfæʃən] n moda; (~ industry) industria de la moda; (manner) manera ♦ vt formar; **in ~** a la moda; **out of ~** pasado de moda; ~**able** adj de moda; ~ **show** n desfile m de modelos
fast [fɑːst] adj rápido; (dye, colour) resistente; (clock): **to be ~** estar adelantado ♦ adv rápidamente, de prisa; (stuck, held) firmemente ♦ n ayuno ♦ vi ayunar; ~ **asleep** profundamente dormido
fasten [ˈfɑːsn] vt atar, sujetar; (coat, belt) abrochar ♦ vi atarse; abrocharse; ~**er**, ~**ing** n cierre m; (of door etc) cerrojo
fast food n comida rápida, platos mpl preparados
fastidious [fæsˈtɪdɪəs] adj (fussy) quisquilloso
fat [fæt] adj gordo; (book) grueso; (profit) grande, pingüe ♦ n grasa; (on person) carnes fpl; (lard) manteca
fatal [ˈfeɪtl] adj (mistake) fatal; (injury) mortal; ~**ity** [fəˈtælɪtɪ] n (road death etc) víctima f; ~**ly** adv fatalmente; mortalmente
fate [feɪt] n destino; (of person) suerte f; ~**ful** adj fatídico
father [ˈfɑːðə*] n padre m; ~**-in-law** n suegro; ~**ly** adj paternal
fathom [ˈfæðəm] n braza ♦ vt (mystery) desentrañar; (understand) lograr comprender
fatigue [fəˈtiːg] n fatiga, cansancio
fatten [ˈfætn] vt, vi engordar
fatty [ˈfætɪ] adj (food) graso ♦ n (inf) gordito/a, gordinflón/ona m/f
fatuous [ˈfætjuəs] adj fatuo, necio
faucet [ˈfɔːsɪt] (US) n grifo (SP), llave f (AM)
fault [fɔːlt] n (blame) culpa; (defect: in person, machine) defecto; (GEO) falla ♦ vt criticar; **it's my ~** es culpa mía; **to find ~ with** criticar, poner peros a; **at ~** culpable; ~**y** adj defectuoso
fauna [ˈfɔːnə] n fauna
favour [ˈfeɪvə*] (US **favor**) n favor m; (approval) aprobación f ♦ vt (proposition) estar a favor de, aprobar; (assist) ser propicio a; **to do sb a ~** hacer un favor a uno; **to find ~ with sb** caer en gracia a uno; **in ~ of** a favor de; ~**able** adj favorable; ~**ite** [ˈfeɪvrɪt] adj, n favorito, preferido
fawn [fɔːn] n cervato ♦ adj (also: ~-coloured) color de cervato, leonado ♦ vi: **to ~ (up)on**

adular
fax [fæks] n (document) fax m; (machine) telefax m ♦ vt mandar por telefax
FBI (US) n abbr (= Federal Bureau of Investigation) ≈ BIC f (SP)
fear [fɪə*] n miedo, temor m ♦ vt tener miedo de, temer; **for ~ of** por si; ~**ful** adj temeroso, miedoso; (awful) terrible; ~**less** adj audaz
feasible [ˈfiːzəbl] adj factible
feast [fiːst] n banquete m; (REL: also: ~ **day**) fiesta ♦ vi festejar
feat [fiːt] n hazaña
feather [ˈfeðə*] n pluma
feature [ˈfiːtʃə*] n característica; (article) artículo de fondo ♦ vt (subj: film) presentar ♦ vi: **to ~ in** tener un papel destacado en; ~**s** npl (of face) facciones fpl; ~ **film** n largometraje m
February [ˈfebruərɪ] n febrero
fed [fed] pt, pp of **feed**
federal [ˈfedərəl] adj federal
fed up [fedˈʌp] adj: **to be ~ (with)** estar harto (de)
fee [fiː] n pago; (professional) derechos mpl, honorarios mpl; (of club) cuota; **school ~s** matrícula
feeble [ˈfiːbl] adj débil; (joke) flojo
feed [fiːd] (pt, pp **fed**) n comida; (of animal) pienso; (on printer) dispositivo de alimentación ♦ vt alimentar; (BRIT: baby: breast~) dar el pecho a; (animal) dar de comer a; (data, information): **to ~ into** meter en; ~ **on** vt fus alimentarse de; ~**back** n reacción f, feedback m
feel [fiːl] (pt, pp **felt**) n (sensation) sensación f; (sense of touch) tacto; (impression): **to have the ~ of** parecerse a ♦ vt tocar; (pain etc) sentir; (think, believe) creer; **to ~ hungry/cold** tener hambre/frío; **to ~ lonely/better** sentirse solo/mejor; **I don't ~ well** no me siento bien; **it ~s soft** es suave al tacto; **to ~ like** (want) tener ganas de; ~ **about** or **around** vi tantear; ~**er** n (of insect) antena; ~**ing** n (physical) sensación f; (foreboding) presentimiento; (emotion) sentimiento
feet [fiːt] npl of **foot**
feign [feɪn] vt fingir
fell [fel] pt of **fall** ♦ vt (tree) talar
fellow [ˈfeləu] n tipo, tío (SP); (comrade) compañero; (of learned society) socio/a ♦ cpd: ~ **citizen** n conciudadano/a; ~ **countryman** (irreg) n compatriota m; ~ **men** npl semejantes mpl; ~**ship** n compañerismo; (grant) beca
felony [ˈfelənɪ] n crimen m
felt [felt] pt, pp of **feel** ♦ n fieltro; ~**-tip pen** n rotulador m
female [ˈfiːmeɪl] n (pej: woman) mujer f, tía; (ZOOL) hembra ♦ adj femenino; hembra

feminine ['femɪnɪn] *adj* femenino

feminist ['femɪnɪst] *n* feminista

fence [fens] *n* valla, cerca ♦ *vt* (*also:* ~ *in*) cercar ♦ *vi* (*SPORT*) hacer esgrima; **fencing** *n* esgrima

fend [fend] *vi:* **to ~ for o.s.** valerse por sí mismo; ~ **off** *vt* (*attack*) rechazar; (*questions*) evadir

fender ['fendə*] *n* guardafuego; (*US:* AUT) parachoques *m inv*

ferment [*vb* fə'ment, *n* 'fɜːment] *vi* fermentar ♦ *n* (*fig*) agitación *f*

fern [fɜːn] *n* helecho

ferocious [fə'rəʊʃəs] *adj* feroz

ferret ['ferɪt] *n* hurón *m*

ferry ['ferɪ] *n* (*small*) barca (de pasaje), balsa; (*large: also:* ~*boat*) transbordador *m* (*SP*), embarcadero (AM) ♦ *vt* transportar

fertile ['fɜːtaɪl] *adj* fértil; (BIOL) fecundo; **fertilize** ['fɜːtɪlaɪz] *vt* (BIOL) fecundar; (AGR) abonar; **fertilizer** *n* abono

fester ['festə*] *vi* ulcerarse

festival ['festɪvəl] *n* (REL) fiesta; (ART, MUS) festival *m*

festive ['festɪv] *adj* festivo; **the ~ season** (BRIT: Christmas) las Navidades

festivities [fes'tɪvɪtɪz] *npl* fiestas *fpl*

festoon [fes'tuːn] *vt:* **to ~ with** engalanar de

fetch [fetʃ] *vt* ir a buscar; (*sell for*) venderse por

fête [feɪt] *n* fiesta

fetus ['fiːtəs] (*US*) *n* = **foetus**

feud [fjuːd] *n* (*hostility*) enemistad *f*; (*quarrel*) disputa

fever ['fiːvə*] *n* fiebre *f*; ~**ish** *adj* febril

few [fjuː] *adj* (*not many*) pocos ♦ *pron* pocos; algunos; **a ~** *adj* unos pocos, algunos; ~**er** *adj* menos; ~**est** *adj* los/las menos

fiancé [fɪ'ɑːnseɪ] *n* novio, prometido; ~**e** *n* novia, prometida

fib [fɪb] *n* mentirilla

fibre ['faɪbə*] (*US* **fiber**) *n* fibra; ~**glass** (Fiberglass ® *US*) *n* fibra de vidrio

fickle ['fɪkl] *adj* inconstante

fiction ['fɪkʃən] *n* ficción *f*; ~**al** *adj* novelesco; **fictitious** [fɪk'tɪʃəs] *adj* ficticio

fiddle ['fɪdl] *n* (MUS) violín *m*; (*cheating*) trampa ♦ *vt* (BRIT: *accounts*) falsificar; ~ **with** *vt fus* juguetear con

fidget ['fɪdʒɪt] *vi* enredar; **stop** ~**ing** ¡estáte quieto!

field [fiːld] *n* campo; (*fig*) campo, esfera; (SPORT) campo, cancha (AM); ~ **marshal** *n* mariscal *m*; ~**work** *n* trabajo de campo

fiend [fiːnd] *n* demonio

fierce [fɪəs] *adj* feroz; (*wind, heat*) fuerte; (*fighting, enemy*) encarnizado

fiery ['faɪərɪ] *adj* (*burning*) ardiente; (*temperament*) apasionado

fifteen [fɪf'tiːn] *num* quince

fifth [fɪfθ] *num* quinto

fifty ['fɪftɪ] *num* cincuenta; ~-~ *adj* (*deal, split*) a medias ♦ *adv* a medias, mitad por mitad

fig [fɪg] *n* higo

fight [faɪt] (*pt, pp* **fought**) *n* (*gen*) pelea; (MIL) combate *m*; (*struggle*) lucha ♦ *vt* luchar contra; (*cancer, alcoholism*) combatir; (*election*) intentar ganar; (*emotion*) resistir ♦ *vi* pelear, luchar; ~**er** *n* combatiente *m/f*; (*plane*) caza *m*; ~**ing** *n* combate *m*, pelea

figment ['fɪgmənt] *n:* **a ~ of the imagination** una quimera

figurative ['fɪgjʊrətɪv] *adj* (*meaning*) figurado; (*style*) figurativo

figure ['fɪgə*] *n* (DRAWING, GEOM) figura, dibujo; (*number, cipher*) cifra; (*body, outline*) tipo; (*personality*) figura ♦ *vt* (*esp US*) imaginar ♦ *vi* (*appear*) figurar; ~ **out** *vt* (*work out*) resolver; ~**head** *n* (NAUT) mascarón *m* de proa; (*pej: leader*) figura decorativa; ~ **of speech** *n* figura retórica

file [faɪl] *n* (*tool*) lima; (*dossier*) expediente *m*; (*folder*) carpeta; (COMPUT) fichero; (*row*) fila ♦ *vt* limar; (LAW: *claim*) presentar; (*store*) archivar; ~ **in/out** *vi* entrar/salir en fila; **filing cabinet** *n* fichero, archivador *m*

fill [fɪl] *vt* (*space*): **to ~ (with)** llenar (de); (*vacancy, need*) cubrir ♦ *n:* **to eat one's ~** llenarse; ~ **in** *vt* rellenar; ~ **up** *vt* llenar (hasta el borde) ♦ *vi* (AUT) poner gasolina

fillet ['fɪlɪt] *n* filete *m*; ~ **steak** *n* filete *m* de ternera

filling ['fɪlɪŋ] *n* (CULIN) relleno; (*for tooth*) empaste *m*; ~ **station** *n* estación *f* de servicio

film [fɪlm] *n* película ♦ *vt* (*scene*) filmar ♦ *vi* rodar (una película); ~ **star** *n* astro, estrella de cine

filter ['fɪltə*] *n* filtro ♦ *vt* filtrar; ~ **lane** (BRIT) *n* carril *m* de selección; ~**-tipped** *adj* con filtro

filth [fɪlθ] *n* suciedad *f*; ~**y** *adj* sucio; (*language*) obsceno

fin [fɪn] *n* (*gen*) aleta

final ['faɪnl] *adj* (*last*) final, último; (*definitive*) definitivo, terminante ♦ *n* (BRIT: SPORT) final *f*; ~**s** *npl* (SCOL) examen *m* final; (*US:* SPORT) final *f*

finale [fɪ'nɑːlɪ] *n* final *m*

final: ~**ist** *n* (SPORT) finalista *m/f*; ~**ize** *vt* concluir, completar; ~**ly** *adv* (*lastly*) por último, finalmente; (*eventually*) por fin

finance [faɪ'næns] *n* (*money*) fondos *mpl*; ~**s** *npl* finanzas *fpl*; (*personal* ~*s*) situación *f* económica ♦ *vt* financiar; **financial** [-'nænʃəl] *adj* financiero

find [faɪnd] (*pt, pp* **found**) *vt* encontrar, hallar; (*come upon*) descubrir ♦ *n* hallazgo;

descubrimiento; **to ~ sb guilty** (*LAW*) declarar culpable a uno; **~ out** *vt* averiguar; (*truth, secret*) descubrir; **to ~ out about** (*subject*) informarse sobre; (*by chance*) enterarse de; **~ings** *npl* (*LAW*) veredicto, fallo; (*of report*) recomendaciones *fpl*

fine [faɪn] *adj* excelente; (*thin*) fino ♦ *adv* (*well*) bien ♦ *n* (*LAW*) multa ♦ *vt* (*LAW*) multar; **to be ~** (*person*) estar bien; (*weather*) hacer buen tiempo; **~ arts** *npl* bellas artes *fpl*

finery ['faɪnərɪ] *n* adornos *mpl*

finger ['fɪŋgə*] *n* dedo ♦ *vt* (*touch*) manosear; **little/index ~** (dedo) meñique *m*/ índice *m*; **~nail** *n* uña; **~print** *n* huella dactilar; **~tip** *n* yema del dedo

finish ['fɪnɪʃ] *n* (*end*) fin *m*; (*SPORT*) meta; (*polish etc*) acabado ♦ *vt*, *vi* terminar; **to ~ doing sth** acabar de hacer algo; **to ~ third** llegar el tercero; **~ off** *vt* acabar, terminar; (*kill*) acabar con; **~ up** *vt* acabar, terminar ♦ *vi* ir a parar, terminar; **~ing line** *n* línea de llegada or meta

finite ['faɪnaɪt] *adj* finito; (*verb*) conjugado

Finland ['fɪnlənd] *n* Finlandia

Finn [fɪn] *n* finlandés/esa *m/f*; **~ish** *adj* finlandés/esa ♦ *n* (*LING*) finlandés *m*

fir [fɜ:*] *n* abeto

fire ['faɪə*] *n* fuego; (*in hearth*) lumbre *f*; (*accidental*) incendio; (*heater*) estufa ♦ *vt* (*gun*) disparar; (*interest*) despertar; (*inf: dismiss*) despedir ♦ *vi* (*shoot*) disparar; **on ~** ardiendo, en llamas; **~ alarm** *n* alarma de incendios; **~arm** *n* arma de fuego; **~ brigade** (*US* **~ department**) *n* (cuerpo de) bomberos *mpl*; **~ engine** *n* coche *m* de bomberos; **~ escape** *n* escalera de incendios; **~ extinguisher** *n* extintor *m* (de incendios); **~guard** *n* rejilla de protección; **~man** (*irreg*) *n* bombero; **~place** *n* chimenea; **~side** *n*: **by the ~side** al lado de la chimenea; **~ station** *n* parque *m* de bomberos; **~wood** *n* leña; **~works** *npl* fuegos *mpl* artificiales

firing squad ['faɪrɪŋ-] *n* pelotón *m* de ejecución

firm [fɜ:m] *adj* firme; (*look, voice*) resuelto ♦ *n* firma, empresa; **~ly** *adv* firmemente; resueltamente

first [fɜ:st] *adj* primero ♦ *adv* (*before others*) primero; (*when listing reasons etc*) en primer lugar, primeramente ♦ *n* (*person: in race*) primero/a; (*AUT*) primera; (*BRIT: SCOL*) título de licenciado con calificación de sobresaliente; **at ~** al principio; **~ of all** ante todo; **~ aid** *n* primera ayuda, primeros auxilios *mpl*; **~-aid kit** *n* botiquín *m*; **~-class** *adj* (*excellent*) de primera (categoría); (*ticket etc*) de primera clase; **~-hand** *adj* de primera mano; **F~ Lady** (*esp US*) *n* primera dama; **~ly** *adv*

en primer lugar; **~ name** *n* nombre *m* (de pila); **~-rate** *adj* estupendo

fish [fɪʃ] *n inv* pez *m*; (*food*) pescado ♦ *vt*, *vi* pescar; **to go ~ing** ir de pesca; **~erman** (*irreg*) *n* pescador *m*; **~ farm** *n* criadero de peces; **~ fingers** (*BRIT*) *npl* croquetas *fpl* de pescado; **~ing boat** *n* barca de pesca; **~ing line** *n* sedal *m*; **~ing rod** *n* caña (de pescar); **~monger's (shop)** (*BRIT*) *n* pescadería; **~ sticks** (*US*) *npl* = **~ fingers**; **~y** (*inf*) *adj* sospechoso

fist [fɪst] *n* puño

fit [fɪt] *adj* (*healthy*) en (buena) forma; (*proper*) adecuado, apropiado ♦ *vt* (*subj: clothes*) estar or sentar bien a; (*instal*) poner; (*equip*) proveer, dotar; (*facts*) cuadrar or corresponder con ♦ *vi* (*clothes*) sentar bien; (*in space, gap*) caber; (*facts*) coincidir ♦ *n* (*MED*) ataque *m*; **~ to** (*ready*) a punto de; **~ for** apropiado para; **a ~ of anger/pride** un arranque de cólera/orgullo; **this dress is a good ~** este vestido me sienta bien; **by ~s and starts** a rachas; **~ in** *vi* (*fig: person*) llevarse bien (con todos); **~ful** *adj* espasmódico, intermitente; **~ment** *n* módulo adosable; **~ness** *n* (*MED*) salud *f*; **~ted carpet** *n* moqueta; **~ted kitchen** *n* cocina amueblada; **~ter** *n* ajustador *m*; **~ting** *adj* apropiado ♦ *n* (*of dress*) prueba; (*of piece of equipment*) instalación *f*; **~ting room** *n* probador *m*; **~tings** *npl* instalaciones *fpl*

five [faɪv] *num* cinco; **~r** (*inf*) *n* (*BRIT*) billete *m* de cinco libras; (*US*) billete *m* de cinco dólares

fix [fɪks] *vt* (*secure*) fijar, asegurar; (*mend*) arreglar; (*prepare*) preparar ♦ *n*: **to be in a ~** estar en un aprieto; **~ up** *vt* (*meeting*) arreglar; **to ~ sb up with sth** proveer a uno de algo; **~ation** [fɪk'seɪʃən] *n* obsesión *f*; **~ed** *adj* (*prices etc*) fijo; **~ture** *n* (*SPORT*) encuentro; **~tures** *npl* (*cupboards etc*) instalaciones *fpl* fijas

fizzy ['fɪzɪ] *adj* (*drink*) gaseoso

fjord [fjɔːd] *n* fiordo

flabbergasted ['flæbəgɑːstɪd] *adj* pasmado, alucinado

flabby ['flæbɪ] *adj* gordo

flag [flæg] *n* bandera; (*stone*) losa ♦ *vi* decaer; **to ~ sb down** hacer señas a uno para que se pare; **~pole** *n* asta de bandera; **~ship** *n* buque *m* insignia; (*fig*) bandera

flair [fleə*] *n* aptitud *f* especial

flak [flæk] *n* (*MIL*) fuego antiaéreo; (*inf: criticism*) lluvia de críticas

flake [fleɪk] *n* (*of rust, paint*) escama; (*of snow, soap powder*) copo ♦ *vi* (*also: ~ off*) desconcharse

flamboyant [flæm'bɔɪənt] *adj* (*dress*) vistoso; (*person*) extravagante

flame [fleɪm] n llama
flamingo [fləˈmɪŋgəʊ] n flamenco
flammable [ˈflæməbl] adj inflamable
flan [flæn] (BRIT) n tarta
flank [flæŋk] n (of animal) ijar m; (of army) flanco ♦ vt flanquear
flannel [ˈflænl] n (BRIT: also: face ~) manopla; (fabric) franela
flap [flæp] n (of pocket, envelope) solapa ♦ vt (wings, arms) agitar ♦ vi (sail, flag) ondear
flare [flɛə*] n llamarada; (MIL) bengala; (in skirt etc) vuelo; **~ up** vi encenderse; (fig: person) encolerizarse; (: revolt) estallar
flash [flæʃ] n relámpago; (also: news ~) noticias fpl de última hora; (PHOT) flash m ♦ vt (light, headlights) lanzar un destello con; (news, message) transmitir; (smile) lanzar ♦ vi brillar; (hazard light etc) lanzar destellos; **in a ~** en un instante; **he ~ed by** or **past** pasó como un rayo; **~back** n (CINEMA) flashback m; **~bulb** n bombilla fusible; **~ cube** n cubo de flash; **~light** n linterna
flashy [ˈflæʃɪ] (pej) adj ostentoso
flask [flɑːsk] n frasco; (also: vacuum ~) termo
flat [flæt] adj llano; (smooth) liso; (tyre) desinflado; (battery) descargado; (beer) muerto; (refusal etc) rotundo; (MUS) desafinado; (rate) fijo ♦ n (BRIT: apartment) piso (SP), departamento (AM), apartamento (AUT) pinchazo; (MUS) bemol m; **to work ~ out** trabajar a toda mecha; **~ly** adv terminantemente, de plano; **~ten** vt (also: ~ten out) allanar; (smooth out) alisar; (building, plants) arrasar
flatter [ˈflætə*] vt adular, halagar; **~ing** adj halagüeño; (dress) que favorece; **~y** n adulación f
flaunt [flɔːnt] vt ostentar, lucir
flavour [ˈfleɪvə*] (US flavor) n sabor m, gusto ♦ vt sazonar, condimentar; **strawberry-~ed** con sabor a fresa; **~ing** n (in product) aromatizante m
flaw [flɔː] n defecto; **~less** adj impecable
flax [flæks] n lino
flea [fliː] n pulga
fleck [flɛk] n (mark) mota
flee [fliː] (pt, pp **fled**) vt huir de ♦ vi huir, fugarse
fleece [fliːs] n vellón m; (wool) lana ♦ vt (inf) desplumar
fleet [fliːt] n flota; (of lorries etc) escuadra
fleeting [ˈfliːtɪŋ] adj fugaz
Flemish [ˈflɛmɪʃ] adj flamenco
flesh [flɛʃ] n carne f; (skin) piel f; (of fruit) pulpa; **~ wound** n herida superficial
flew [fluː] pt of **fly**
flex [flɛks] n cordón m ♦ vt (muscles) tensar; **~ible** adj flexible
flick [flɪk] n capirotazo; chasquido ♦ vt (with

hand) dar un capirotazo a; (whip etc) chasquear; (switch) accionar; **~ through** vt fus hojear
flicker [ˈflɪkə*] vi (light) parpadear; (flame) vacilar
flier [ˈflaɪə*] n aviador(a) m/f
flight [flaɪt] n vuelo; (escape) huida, fuga; (also: ~ of steps) tramo (de escaleras); **~ attendant** (US) n camarero/azafata; **~ deck** n (AVIAT) cabina de mandos; (NAUT) cubierta de aterrizaje
flimsy [ˈflɪmzɪ] adj (thin) muy ligero; (building) endeble; (excuse) flojo
flinch [flɪntʃ] vi encogerse; **to ~ from** retroceder ante
fling [flɪŋ] (pt, pp **flung**) vt arrojar
flint [flɪnt] n pedernal m; (in lighter) piedra
flip [flɪp] vt dar la vuelta a; (switch: turn on) encender; (: turn off) apagar; (coin) echar a cara o cruz
flippant [ˈflɪpənt] adj poco serio
flipper [ˈflɪpə*] n aleta
flirt [flɜːt] vi coquetear, flirtear ♦ n coqueta
float [fləʊt] n flotador m; (in procession) carroza; (money) reserva ♦ vi flotar; (swimmer) hacer la plancha
flock [flɒk] n (of sheep) rebaño; (of birds) bandada ♦ vi: **to ~ to** acudir en tropel a
flog [flɒg] vt azotar
flood [flʌd] n inundación f; (of letters, imports etc) avalancha ♦ vt inundar ♦ vi (place) inundarse; (people): **to ~ into** inundar; **~ing** n inundaciones fpl; **~light** n foco
floor [flɔː*] n suelo; (storey) piso; (of sea) fondo ♦ vt (subj: question) dejar sin respuesta; (: blow) derribar; **ground ~**, **first ~** (US) planta baja; **first ~**, **second ~** (US) primer piso; **~board** n tabla; **~ show** n cabaret m
flop [flɒp] n fracaso ♦ vi (fail) fracasar; (fall) derrumbarse; **~py** adj flojo ♦ n (COMPUT: also: ~py disk) floppy m
flora [ˈflɔːrə] n flora
floral [ˈflɔːrl] adj (pattern) floreado
florid [ˈflɒrɪd] adj florido; (complexion) rubicundo
florist [ˈflɒrɪst] n florista m/f; **~'s (shop)** n florería
flounder [ˈflaʊndə*] vi (swimmer) patalear; (fig: economy) estar en dificultades ♦ n (ZOOL) platija
flour [ˈflaʊə*] n harina
flourish [ˈflʌrɪʃ] vi florecer ♦ n ademán m, movimiento (ostentoso)
flout [flaʊt] vt burlarse de
flow [fləʊ] n (movement) flujo; (of traffic) circulación f; (tide) corriente f ♦ vi (river, blood) fluir; (traffic) circular; **~ chart** n organigrama m
flower [ˈflaʊə*] n flor f ♦ vi florecer; **~ bed** n

macizo; **~pot** n tiesto; **~y** adj (fragrance)
floral; (pattern) floreado; (speech) florido
flown [fləun] pp of **fly**
flu [flu:] n: **to have ~** tener la gripe
fluctuate ['flʌktjueɪt] vi fluctuar
fluent ['flu:ənt] adj (linguist) que habla
perfectamente; (speech) elocuente; **he speaks
~ French, he's ~ in French** domina el francés;
~ly adv con fluidez
fluff [flʌf] n pelusa; **~y** adj de pelo suave
fluid ['flu:ɪd] adj (movement) fluido, líquido;
(situation) inestable ♦ n fluido, líquido
fluke [flu:k] (inf) n chiripa
flung [flʌŋ] pt, pp of **fling**
fluoride ['fluəraɪd] n fluoruro
flurry ['flʌrɪ] n (of snow) temporal m; **~ of
activity** frenesí m de actividad
flush [flʌʃ] n rubor m; (fig: of youth etc)
resplandor m; (speech) elocuente ♦ vt limpiar con agua ♦ vi
ruborizarse ♦ adj: **~ with** a ras de; **to ~ the
toilet** hacer funcionar la cisterna; **~ed** adj
ruborizado
flustered ['flʌstəd] adj aturdido
flute [flu:t] n flauta
flutter ['flʌtə*] n (of wings) revoloteo, aleteo;
a ~ of panic/excitement una oleada de
pánico/excitación ♦ vi revolotear
flux [flʌks] n: **to be in a state of ~** estar
continuamente cambiando
fly [flaɪ] (pt **flew**, pp **flown**) n mosca; (on
trousers: also: **flies**) bragueta ♦ vt (plane)
pilot(e)ar; (cargo) transportar (en avión);
(distances) recorrer (en avión) ♦ vi volar;
(passengers) ir en avión; (escape) evadirse;
(flag) ondear; **~ away** or **off** vi emprender
el vuelo; **~-drive** n: **~-drive holiday**
vacaciones que incluyen vuelo y alquiler de
coche; **~ing** n (activity) (el) volar; (action)
vuelo ♦ adj: **~ing visit** visita relámpago; **with
~ing colours** con lucimiento; **~ing saucer** n
platillo volante; **~ing start** n: **to get off to a
~ing start** empezar con buen pie; **~over**
(BRIT) n paso a desnivel or superior; **~sheet** n
(for tent) doble techo
foal [fəul] n potro
foam [fəum] n espuma ♦ vi hacer espuma;
~ rubber n goma espuma
fob [fɔb] vt: **to ~ sb off with sth** despachar a
uno con algo
focal point ['fəukl-] n (fig) centro de
atención
focus ['fəukəs] (pl **~es**) n foco; (centre) centro
♦ vt (field glasses etc) enfocar ♦ vi: **to ~ (on)**
enfocar (a); (issue etc) centrarse en; **in/out of
~** enfocado/desenfocado
fodder ['fɔdə*] n pienso
foetus ['fi:təs] (US **fetus**) n feto
fog [fɔg] n niebla; **~gy** adj: **it's ~gy** hay niebla,
está brumoso; **~ lamp** (US **~ light**) n (AUT)

faro de niebla
foil [fɔɪl] vt frustrar ♦ n hoja; (kitchen ~) papel
m (de) aluminio; (complement)
complemento; (FENCING) florete m
fold [fəuld] n (bend, crease) pliegue m; (AGR) redil
m ♦ vt doblar; (arms) cruzar; **~ up** vi plegarse,
doblarse; (business) quebrar ♦ vt (map etc)
plegar; **~er** n (for papers) carpeta; (COMPUT)
directorio; **~ing** adj (chair, bed) plegable
foliage ['fəulɪdʒ] n follaje m
folk [fəuk] npl gente f ♦ adj popular,
folklórico; **~s** npl (family) familia sg, parientes
mpl; **~lore** ['fəuklɔ:*] n folklore m; **~ song** n
canción f popular or folklórica
follow ['fɔləu] vt seguir ♦ vi seguir; (result)
resultar; **to ~ suit** hacer lo mismo; **~ up** vt
(letter, offer) responder a; (case) investigar;
~er n (of person, belief) partidario/a; **~ing**
adj siguiente ♦ n afición f, partidarios mpl
folly ['fɔlɪ] n locura
fond [fɔnd] adj (memory, smile etc) cariñoso;
(hopes) ilusorio; **to be ~ of** tener cariño a;
(pastime, food) ser aficionado a
fondle ['fɔndl] vt acariciar
font [fɔnt] n pila bautismal; (TYP) fundición f
food [fu:d] n comida; **~ mixer** n batidora;
~ poisoning n intoxicación f alimenticia;
~ processor n robot m de cocina; **~stuffs**
npl comestibles mpl
fool [fu:l] n tonto/a; (CULIN) puré m de frutas
con nata ♦ vt engañar ♦ vi (gen: **~ around**)
bromear; **~hardy** adj temerario; **~ish** adj
tonto; (careless) imprudente; **~proof** adj
(plan etc) infalible
foot [fut] (pl **feet**) n pie m; (measure) pie m
(= 304 mm); (of animal) pata ♦ vt (bill)
pagar; **on ~** a pie; **~age** n (CINEMA) imágenes
fpl; **~ball** n balón m; (game: BRIT) fútbol m;
(: US) fútbol m americano; **~ball player** n
(BRIT: also: **~baller**) futbolista m; (US) jugador
m de fútbol americano; **~brake** n freno de
pie; **~bridge** n puente m para peatones;
~hills npl estribaciones fpl; **~hold** n pie m
firme; **~ing** n (fig) posición f; **to lose one's
~ing** perder el pie; **~lights** npl candilejas fpl;
~note n nota (al pie de la página); **~path** n
sendero; **~print** n huella, pisada; **~step** n
paso; **~wear** n calzado

─────── KEYWORD ───────

for [fɔ:] prep 1 (indicating destination,
intention) para; **the train ~ London** el tren con
destino a or de Londres; **he left ~ Rome**
marchó para Roma; **he went ~ the paper** fue
por el periódico; **is this ~ me?** ¿es esto para
mí?; **it's time ~ lunch** es la hora de comer
2 (indicating purpose) para; **what('s it) ~?**
¿para qué (es)?; **to pray ~ peace** rezar por la
paz

3 (*on behalf of, representing*): **the MP ~ Hove** el diputado por Hove; **he works ~ the government/a local firm** trabaja para el gobierno/en una empresa local; **I'll ask him ~ you** se lo pediré por ti; **G ~ George** G de Gerona

4 (*because of*) por esta razón; **~ fear of being criticized** por temor a ser criticado

5 (*with regard to*) para; **it's cold ~ July** hace frío para julio; **he has a gift ~ languages** tiene don de lenguas

6 (*in exchange for*) por; **I sold it ~ £5** lo vendí por £5; **to pay 50 pence ~ a ticket** pagar 50 peniques por un billete

7 (*in favour of*): **are you ~ or against us?** ¿estás con nosotros o contra nosotros?; **I'm all ~ it** estoy totalmente a favor; **vote ~ X** vote (a) X

8 (*referring to distance*): **there are roadworks ~ 5 km** hay obras en 5 km; **we walked ~ miles** caminamos kilómetros y kilómetros

9 (*referring to time*): **he was away ~ 2 years** estuvo fuera (durante) dos años; **it hasn't rained ~ 3 weeks** no ha llovido durante *or* en 3 semanas; **I have known her ~ years** la conozco desde hace años; **can you do it ~ tomorrow?** ¿lo podrás hacer para mañana?

10 (*with infinitive clauses*): **it is not ~ me to decide** la decisión no es cosa mía; **it would be best ~ you to leave** sería mejor que te fueras; **there is still time ~ you to do it** todavía te queda tiempo para hacerlo; **~ this to be possible ...** para que esto sea posible ...

11 (*in spite of*) a pesar de; **~ all his complaints** a pesar de sus quejas
♦ *conj* (*since, as: rather formal*) puesto que

forage ['fɔrɪdʒ] *vi* (*animal*) forrajear; (*person*): **to ~ for** hurgar en busca de

foray ['fɔreɪ] *n* incursión *f*

forbid [fəˈbɪd] (*pt* **forbad(e)**, *pp* **forbidden**) *vt* prohibir; **to ~ sb to do sth** prohibir a uno hacer algo; **~ding** *adj* amenazador(a)

force [fɔːs] *n* fuerza ♦ *vt* forzar; (*push*) meter a la fuerza; **to ~ o.s.** to do hacer un esfuerzo por hacer; **the F~s** *npl* (*BRIT*) las Fuerzas Armadas; **in ~** en vigor; **~d** [fɔːst] *adj* forzado; **~-feed** *vt* alimentar a la fuerza; **~ful** *adj* enérgico

forcibly ['fɔːsəblɪ] *adv* a la fuerza; (*speak*) enérgicamente

ford [fɔːd] *n* vado

fore [fɔːˀ] *n*: **to come to the ~** empezar a destacar

fore: ~arm *n* antebrazo; **~boding** *n* presentimiento; **~cast** *n* pronóstico ♦ *vt* (*irreg: like cast*) pronosticar; **~court** *n* patio; **~finger** *n* (dedo) índice *m*; **~front** *n*: **in the ~front of** en la vanguardia de

forego *vt* = forgo

foregone ['fɔːgɔn] *pp* of forego ♦ *adj*: **it's a ~ conclusion** es una conclusión evidente

foreground ['fɔːgraund] *n* primer plano

forehead ['fɔrɪd] *n* frente *f*

foreign ['fɔrɪn] *adj* extranjero; (*trade*) exterior; (*object*) extraño; **~er** *n* extranjero/a; **~ exchange** *n* divisas *fpl*; **F~ Office** (*BRIT*) *n* Ministerio de Asuntos Exteriores; **F~ Secretary** (*BRIT*) *n* Ministro de Asuntos Exteriores

fore: ~leg *n* pata delantera; **~man** (*irreg*) *n* capataz *m*; (*in construction*) maestro de obras; **~most** *adj* principal ♦ *adv*: **first and ~most** ante todo

forensic [fəˈrensɪk] *adj* forense

fore: ~runner *n* precursor(a) *m/f*; **~see** (*pt* **foresaw**, *pp* **foreseen**) *vt* prever; **~seeable** *adj* previsible; **~shadow** *vt* prefigurar, anunciar; **~sight** *n* previsión *f*

forest ['fɔrɪst] *n* bosque *m*

forestry ['fɔrɪstrɪ] *n* silvicultura

foretaste ['fɔːteɪst] *n* muestra

foretell [fɔːˈtel] (*pt, pp* **foretold**) *vt* predecir, pronosticar

forever [fəˈrevəˀ] *adv* para siempre; (*endlessly*) constantemente

foreword ['fɔːwəːd] *n* prefacio

forfeit ['fɔːfɪt] *vt* perder

forgave [fəˈgeɪv] *pt* of forgive

forge [fɔːdʒ] *n* herrería ♦ *vt* (*signature, money*) falsificar; (*metal*) forjar; **~ ahead** *vi* avanzar mucho; **~ry** *n* falsificación *f*

forget [fəˈget] (*pt* **forgot**, *pp* **forgotten**) *vt* olvidar ♦ *vi* olvidarse; **~ful** *adj* despistado; **~-me-not** *n* nomeolvides *f inv*

forgive [fəˈgɪv] (*pt* **forgave**, *pp* **forgiven**) *vt* perdonar; **to ~ sb for sth** perdonar algo a uno; **~ness** *n* perdón *m*

forgo [fɔːˈgəu] (*pt* **forwent**, *pp* **forgone**) *vt* (*give up*) renunciar a; (*go without*) privarse de

forgot [fəˈgɔt] *pt* of forget

forgotten [fəˈgɔtn] *pp* of forget

fork [fɔːk] *n* (*for eating*) tenedor *m*; (*for gardening*) horca; (*of roads*) bifurcación *f* ♦ *vi* (*road*) bifurcarse; **~ out** (*inf*) *vt* (*pay*) desembolsar; **~-lift truck** *n* máquina elevadora

forlorn [fəˈlɔːn] *adj* (*person*) triste, melancólico; (*place*) abandonado; (*attempt, hope*) desesperado

form [fɔːm] *n* forma; (*BRIT: SCOL*) clase *f*; (*document*) formulario ♦ *vt* formar; (*idea*) concebir; (*habit*) adquirir; **in top ~** en plena forma; **to ~ a queue** hacer cola

formal ['fɔːməl] *adj* (*offer, receipt*) por escrito; (*person etc*) correcto; (*occasion, dinner*) de etiqueta; (*dress*) correcto; (*garden*) (de estilo) clásico; **~ity** [-ˈmælɪtɪ] *n* (*procedure*) trámite *m*; corrección *f*; etiqueta; **~ly** *adv* oficialmente

format ['fɔːmæt] *n* formato ♦ *vt* (COMPUT) formatear

formative ['fɔːmətɪv] *adj* (*years*) de formación; (*influence*) formativo

former ['fɔːmə*] *adj* anterior; (*earlier*) antiguo; (*ex*) ex; **the ~ ... the latter ...** aquél ... éste ...; **~ly** *adv* antes

formula ['fɔːmjulə] *n* fórmula

forsake [fə'seɪk] (*pt* **forsook**, *pp* **forsaken**) *vt* (*gen*) abandonar; (*plan*) renunciar a

fort [fɔːt] *n* fuerte *m*

forte ['fɔːtɪ] *n* fuerte *m*

forth [fɔːθ] *adv*: **back and ~** de acá para allá; **and so ~** y así sucesivamente; **~coming** *adj* próximo, venidero; (*help, information*) disponible; (*character*) comunicativo; **~right** *adj* franco; **~with** *adv* en el acto

fortify ['fɔːtɪfaɪ] *vt* (*city*) fortificar; (*person*) fortalecer

fortitude ['fɔːtɪtjuːd] *n* fortaleza

fortnight ['fɔːtnaɪt] (BRIT) *n* quince días *mpl*; quincena; **~ly** *adj* de cada quince días, quincenal ♦ *adv* cada quince días, quincenalmente

fortress ['fɔːtrɪs] *n* fortaleza

fortunate ['fɔːtʃənɪt] *adj* afortunado; **it is ~ that ...** (es una) suerte que ...; **~ly** *adv* afortunadamente

fortune ['fɔːtʃən] *n* suerte *f*; (*wealth*) fortuna; **~-teller** *n* adivino/a

forty ['fɔːtɪ] *num* cuarenta

forum ['fɔːrəm] *n* foro

forward ['fɔːwəd] *adj* (*movement, position*) avanzado; (*front*) delantero; (*in time*) adelantado; (*not shy*) atrevido ♦ *n* (SPORT) delantero ♦ *vt* (*letter*) remitir; (*career*) promocionar; **to move ~** avanzar; **~(s)** *adv* (hacia) adelante

fossil ['fɔsl] *n* fósil *m*

foster ['fɔstə*] *vt* (*child*) acoger en una familia; fomentar; **~ child** *n* hijo/a adoptivo/a

fought [fɔːt] *pt, pp of* **fight**

foul [faul] *adj* sucio, puerco; (*weather, smell etc*) asqueroso; (*language*) grosero; (*temper*) malísimo ♦ *n* (SPORT) falta ♦ *vt* (*dirty*) ensuciar; **~ play** *n* (LAW) muerte *f* violenta

found [faund] *pt, pp of* **find** ♦ *vt* fundar; **~ation** [-'deɪʃən] *n* (*act*) fundación *f*; (*basis*) base *f*; (*also:* **~ation cream**) crema base; **~ations** *npl* (*of building*) cimientos *mpl*

founder ['faundə*] *n* fundador(a) *m/f* ♦ *vi* hundirse

foundry ['faundrɪ] *n* fundición *f*

fountain ['fauntɪn] *n* fuente *f*; **~ pen** *n* pluma (estilográfica) (SP), pluma-fuente *f* (AM)

four [fɔː*] *num* cuatro; **on all ~s** a gatas; **~-poster (bed)** *n* cama de dosel; **~teen** *num* catorce; **~th** *num* cuarto

fowl [faul] *n* ave *f* (de corral)

fox [fɔks] *n* zorro ♦ *vt* confundir

foyer ['fɔɪeɪ] *n* vestíbulo

fraction ['frækʃən] *n* fracción *f*

fracture ['fræktʃə*] *n* fractura

fragile ['frædʒaɪl] *adj* frágil

fragment ['frægmənt] *n* fragmento

fragrant ['freɪgrənt] *adj* fragante, oloroso

frail [freɪl] *adj* frágil; (*person*) débil

frame [freɪm] *n* (TECH) armazón *m*; (*of person*) cuerpo; (*of picture, door etc*) marco; (*of spectacles: also:* **~s**) montura ♦ *vt* enmarcar; **~ of mind** *n* estado de ánimo; **~work** *n* marco

France [frɑːns] *n* Francia

franchise ['fræntʃaɪz] *n* (POL) derecho de votar, sufragio; (COMM) licencia, concesión *f*

frank [fræŋk] *adj* franco ♦ *vt* (*letter*) franquear; **~ly** *adv* francamente

frantic ['fræntɪk] *adj* (*distraught*) desesperado; (*hectic*) frenético

fraternity [frə'tɜːnɪtɪ] *n* (*feeling*) fraternidad *f*; (*group of people*) círculos *mpl*

fraud [frɔːd] *n* fraude *m*; (*person*) impostor(a) *m/f*

fraught [frɔːt] *adj*: **~ with** lleno de

fray [freɪ] *vi* deshilacharse

freak [friːk] *n* (*person*) fenómeno; (*event*) suceso anormal

freckle ['frekl] *n* peca

free [friː] *adj* libre; (*gratis*) gratuito ♦ *vt* (*prisoner etc*) poner en libertad; (*jammed object*) soltar; **~ (of charge), for ~** gratis; **~dom** ['friːdəm] *n* libertad *f*; **F~fone** ® ['friːfəun] *n* número gratuito; **~-for-all** *n* riña general; **~ gift** *n* prima; **~hold** *n* propiedad *f* vitalicia; **~ kick** *n* tiro libre; **~lance** *adj* independiente ♦ *adv* por cuenta propia; **~ly** *adv* libremente; (*liberally*) generosamente; **F~mason** *n* francmasón *m*; **F~post** ® *n* porte *m* pagado; **~-range** *adj* (*hen, eggs*) de granja; **~ trade** *n* libre comercio; **~way** (US) *n* autopista; **~ will** *n* libre albedrío; **of one's own ~ will** por su propia voluntad

freeze [friːz] (*pt* **froze**, *pp* **frozen**) *vi* (*weather*) helar; (*liquid, pipe, person*) helarse, congelarse ♦ *vt* helar; (*food, prices, salaries*) congelar ♦ *n* helada; (*on arms, wages*) congelación *f*; **~-dried** *adj* liofilizado; **~r** *n* congelador *m* (SP), congeladora (AM)

freezing ['friːzɪŋ] *adj* helado; **3 degrees below ~** tres grados bajo cero; **~ point** *n* punto de congelación

freight [freɪt] *n* (*goods*) carga; (*money charged*) flete *m*; **~ train** (US) *n* tren *m* de mercancías

French [frɛntʃ] *adj* francés/esa ◆ *n* (*LING*)
francés *m*; **the ~** *npl* los franceses; **~ bean** *n*
judía verde; **~ fried potatoes** *npl* patatas *fpl*
(*SP*) *or* papas *fpl* (*AM*) fritas; **~ fries** (*US*) *npl*
= **~ fried potatoes**; **~man/woman** (*irreg*) *n*
francés/esa *m/f*; **~ window** *n* puerta de
cristal

frenzy [ˈfrɛnzɪ] *n* frenesí *m*

frequent [*adj* ˈfriːkwənt, *vb* frɪˈkwɛnt] *adj*
frecuente ◆ *vt* frecuentar; **~ly** [-əntlɪ] *adv*
frecuentemente, a menudo

fresh [frɛʃ] *adj* fresco; (*bread*) tierno; (*new*)
nuevo; **~en** *vi* (*wind, air*) soplar más recio;
~en up *vi* (*person*) arreglarse, lavarse; **~er**
(*BRIT*: *inf*) *n* (*UNIV*) estudiante *m/f* de primer
año; **~ly** *adv* (*made, painted etc*) recién;
~man (*US irreg*) *n* = **~er**; **~ness** *n* frescura;
~water *adj* (*fish*) de agua dulce

fret [frɛt] *vi* inquietarse

friar [ˈfraɪə*] *n* fraile *m*; (*before name*) fray *m*

friction [ˈfrɪkʃən] *n* fricción *f*

Friday [ˈfraɪdɪ] *n* viernes *m inv*

fridge [frɪdʒ] (*BRIT*) *n* nevera (*SP*),
refrigeradora (*AM*)

fried [fraɪd] *adj* frito

friend [frɛnd] *n* amigo/a; **~ly** *adj* simpático;
(*government*) amigo; (*place*) acogedor(a);
(*match*) amistoso; **~ly fire** fuego amigo,
disparos *mpl* del propio bando; **~ship** *n*
amistad *f*

frieze [friːz] *n* friso

fright [fraɪt] *n* (*terror*) terror *m*; (*scare*) susto;
to take ~ asustarse; **~en** *vt* asustar; **~ened**
adj asustado; **~ening** *adj* espantoso; **~ful** *adj*
espantoso, horrible

frill [frɪl] *n* volante *m*

fringe [frɪndʒ] *n* (*BRIT*: *of hair*) flequillo; (*on*
lampshade etc) flecos *mpl*; (*of forest etc*)
borde *m*, margen *m*; **~ benefits** *npl*
beneficios *mpl* marginales

frisk [frɪsk] *vt* cachear, registrar

frisky [ˈfrɪskɪ] *adj* juguetón/ona

fritter [ˈfrɪtə*] *n* buñuelo; **~ away** *vt*
desperdiciar

frivolous [ˈfrɪvələs] *adj* frívolo

frizzy [ˈfrɪzɪ] *adj* rizado

fro [frəu] *see* **to**

frock [frɔk] *n* vestido

frog [frɔg] *n* rana; **~man** *n* hombre-rana *m*

frolic [ˈfrɔlɪk] *vi* juguetear

KEYWORD
---

from [frɔm] *prep* **1** (*indicating starting place*)
de, desde; **where do you come ~?** ¿de dónde
eres?; **~ London to Glasgow** de Londres a
Glasgow; **to escape ~ sth/sb** escaparse de
algo/alguien
2 (*indicating origin etc*) de; **a letter/telephone**
call ~ my sister una carta/llamada de mi

hermana; **tell him ~ me that ...** dígale de mi
parte que ...
3 (*indicating time*): **~ one o'clock to** *or* **until** *or*
till two de(sde) la una a *or* hasta las dos;
~ January (on) a partir de enero
4 (*indicating distance*) de; **the hotel is 1 km**
~ the beach el hotel está a 1 km de la playa
5 (*indicating price, number etc*) de; **prices**
range ~ £10 to £50 los precios van desde £10
a *or* hasta £50; **the interest rate was**
increased ~ 9% to 10% el tipo de interés fue
incrementado de un 9% a un 10%
6 (*indicating difference*) de; **he can't tell red**
~ green no sabe distinguir el rojo del verde;
to be different ~ sb/sth ser diferente a algo/
alguien
7 (*because of, on the basis of*): **~ what he**
says por lo que dice; **weak ~ hunger**
debilitado por el hambre

---

front [frʌnt] *n* (*foremost part*) parte *f*
delantera; (*of house*) fachada; (*of dress*)
delantero; (*promenade: also: sea ~*) paseo
marítimo; (*MIL, POL, METEOROLOGY*) frente *m*;
(*fig: appearances*) apariencias *fpl* ◆ *adj*
(*wheel, leg*) delantero; (*row, line*) primero; **in**
~ (of) delante (de); **~ door** *n* puerta
principal; **~ier** [ˈfrʌntɪə*] *n* frontera; **~ page**
n primera plana; **~ room** (*BRIT*) *n* salón *m*,
sala; **~-wheel drive** *n* tracción *f* delantera

frost [frɔst] *n* helada; (*also: hoar~*) escarcha;
~bite *n* congelación *f*; **~ed** *adj* (*glass*)
deslustrado; **~y** *adj* (*weather*) de helada;
(*welcome etc*) glacial

froth [frɔθ] *n* espuma

frown [fraun] *vi* fruncir el ceño

froze [frəuz] *pt of* **freeze**

frozen [ˈfrəuzn] *pp of* **freeze**

fruit [fruːt] *n inv* fruta; fruto; (*fig*) fruto;
resultados *mpl*; **~erer** *n* frutero/a; **~erer's**
(**shop**) *n* frutería; **~ful** *adj* provechoso; **~ion**
[fruːˈɪʃən] *n*: **to come to ~ion** realizarse;
~ juice *n* zumo (*SP*) *or* jugo (*AM*) de fruta;
~ machine (*BRIT*) *n* máquina *f* tragaperras;
~ salad *n* macedonia (*SP*) *or* ensalada (*AM*)
de frutas

frustrate [frʌsˈtreɪt] *vt* frustrar

fry [fraɪ] (*pt, pp* **fried**) *vt* freír; **small ~** gente *f*
menuda; **~ing pan** *n* sartén *f*

ft. *abbr* = **foot; feet**

fudge [fʌdʒ] *n* (*CULIN*) caramelo blando

fuel [fjuəl] *n* (*for heating*) combustible *m*;
(*coal*) carbón *m*; (*wood*) leña; (*for engine*)
carburante *m*; **~ oil** *n* fuel oil *m*; **~ tank** *n*
depósito (de combustible)

fugitive [ˈfjuːdʒɪtɪv] *n* fugitivo/a

fulfil [fulˈfɪl] *vt* (*function*) cumplir con;
(*condition*) satisfacer; (*wish, desire*) realizar;
~ment (*US* **fulfillment**) *n* satisfacción *f*; (*of*

promise, desire) realización f

full [ful] *adj* lleno; (*fig*) pleno; (*complete*) completo; (*maximum*) máximo; (*information*) detallado; (*price*) íntegro; (*skirt*) amplio ♦ *adv*: **to know ~ well that** saber perfectamente que; **I'm ~ (up)** no puedo más; **~ employment** pleno empleo; **a ~ two hours** dos horas completas; **at ~ speed** a máxima velocidad; **in ~** (*reproduce, quote*) íntegramente; **~-length** *adj* (*novel etc*) entero; (*coat*) largo; (*portrait*) de cuerpo entero; **~ moon** *n* luna llena; **~-scale** *adj* (*attack, war*) en gran escala; (*model*) de tamaño natural; **~ stop** *n* punto; **~-time** *adj* (*work*) de tiempo completo ♦ *adv*: **to work ~-time** trabajar a tiempo completo; **~y** *adv* completamente; (*at least*) por lo menos; **~y-fledged** *adj* (*teacher, barrister*) diplomado

fumble ['fʌmbl] *vi*: **to ~ with** manejar torpemente

fume [fju:m] *vi* (*rage*) estar furioso; **~s** *npl* humo, gases *mpl*

fun [fʌn] *n* (*amusement*) diversión f; **to have ~** divertirse; **for ~** en broma; **to make ~ of** burlarse de

function ['fʌŋkʃən] *n* función f ♦ *vi* funcionar; **~al** *adj* (*operational*) en buen estado; (*practical*) funcional

fund [fʌnd] *n* fondo; (*reserve*) reserva; **~s** *npl* (*money*) fondos *mpl*

fundamental [fʌndə'mɛntl] *adj* fundamental

funeral ['fju:nərəl] *n* (*burial*) entierro; (*ceremony*) funerales *mpl*; **~ parlour** (*BRIT*) *n* funeraria; **~ service** *n* misa de difuntos, funeral *m*

funfair ['fʌnfeə*] (*BRIT*) *n* parque *m* de atracciones

fungus ['fʌŋgəs] (*pl* **fungi**) *n* hongo; (*mould*) moho

funnel ['fʌnl] *n* embudo; (*of ship*) chimenea

funny ['fʌni] *adj* gracioso, divertido; (*strange*) curioso, raro

fur [fə:*] *n* piel f; (*BRIT: in kettle etc*) sarro; **~ coat** *n* abrigo de pieles

furious ['fjuəriəs] *adj* furioso; (*effort*) violento

furlong ['fə:lɔŋ] *n* octava parte de una milla, = 201.17 m

furnace ['fə:nɪs] *n* horno

furnish ['fə:nɪʃ] *vt* amueblar; (*supply*) suministrar; (*information*) facilitar; **~ings** *npl* muebles *mpl*

furniture ['fə:nɪtʃə*] *n* muebles *mpl*; **piece of ~** mueble *m*

furrow ['fʌrəu] *n* surco

furry ['fə:rɪ] *adj* peludo

further ['fə:ðə*] *adj* (*new*) nuevo, adicional ♦ *adv* más lejos; (*more*) más; (*moreover*) además ♦ *vt* promover, adelantar; **~ education** *n* educación f superior; **~more** [fə:ðə'mɔ:*] *adv* además

furthest ['fə:ðɪst] *superlative of* **far**

fury ['fjuərɪ] *n* furia

fuse [fju:z] (*US* **fuze**) *n* fusible *m*; (*for bomb etc*) mecha ♦ *vt* (*metal*) fundir; (*fig*) fusionar ♦ *vi* fundirse; fusionarse; (*BRIT: ELEC*): **to ~ the lights** fundir los plomos; **~ box** *n* caja de fusibles

fuss [fʌs] *n* (*excitement*) conmoción f; (*trouble*) alboroto; **to make a ~** armar un lío or jaleo; **to make a ~ of sb** mimar a uno; **~y** *adj* (*person*) exigente; (*too ornate*) recargado

futile ['fju:taɪl] *adj* vano

future ['fju:tʃə*] *adj* futuro; (*coming*) venidero ♦ *n* futuro; (*prospects*) porvenir; **in ~** de ahora en adelante

fuze [fju:z] (*US*) = **fuse**

fuzzy ['fʌzɪ] *adj* (*PHOT*) borroso; (*hair*) muy rizado

G, g

G [dʒi:] *n* (*MUS*) sol *m*

g. *abbr* (= **gram(s)**) gr.

G8 *abbr* (= **Group of Eight**) el grupo de los 8

gabble ['gæbl] *vi* hablar atropelladamente

gable ['geɪbl] *n* aguilón *m*

gadget ['gædʒɪt] *n* aparato

Gaelic ['geɪlɪk] *adj, n* (*LING*) gaélico

gag [gæg] *n* (*on mouth*) mordaza; (*joke*) chiste *m* ♦ *vt* amordazar

gaiety ['geɪtɪ] *n* alegría

gaily ['geɪlɪ] *adv* alegremente

gain [geɪn] *n*: **~ (in)** aumento (de); (*profit*) ganancia ♦ *vt* ganar ♦ *vi* (*watch*) adelantarse; **to ~ from/by sth** sacar provecho de algo; **to ~ on sb** ganar terreno a uno; **to ~ 3 lbs (in weight)** engordar 3 libras

gal. *abbr* = **gallon**

gala ['gɑ:lə] *n* fiesta

gale [geɪl] *n* (*wind*) vendaval *m*

gallant ['gælənt] *adj* valiente; (*towards ladies*) atento

gall bladder ['gɔ:l-] *n* vesícula biliar

gallery ['gælərɪ] *n* (*also: art ~: public*) pinacoteca; (: *private*) galería de arte; (*for spectators*) tribuna

gallon ['gælən] *n* galón *m* (*BRIT* = 4,546 litros, *US* = 3,785 litros)

gallop ['gæləp] *n* galope *m* ♦ *vi* galopar

gallows ['gæləuz] *n* horca

gallstone ['gɔ:lstəun] *n* cálculo biliar

galore [gə'lɔ:*] *adv* en cantidad, en abundancia

gambit ['gæmbɪt] *n* (*fig*): **(opening) ~** estrategia (inicial)

gamble ['gæmbl] *n* (*risk*) riesgo ♦ *vt* jugar,

apostar ♦ vi (*take a risk*) jugárselas; (*bet*) apostar; **to ~ on** apostar a; (*success etc*) contar con; **~r** n jugador(a) m/f; **gambling** n juego

game [geɪm] n juego; (*match*) partido; (*of cards*) partida; (*HUNTING*) caza ♦ adj (*willing*): **to be ~ for anything** atreverse a todo; **big ~** caza mayor; **~keeper** n guardabosques m inv

gammon ['gæmən] n (*bacon*) tocino ahumado; (*ham*) jamón m ahumado

gamut ['gæmət] n gama

gang [gæŋ] n (*of criminals*) pandilla; (*of friends etc*) grupo; (*of workmen*) brigada; **~ up** vi: **to ~ up on sb** aliarse contra uno

gangster ['gæŋstə*] n gángster m

gangway ['gæŋweɪ] n (*on ship*) pasarela; (*BRIT: in theatre, bus etc*) pasillo

gaol [dʒeɪl] (*BRIT*) n, vt = **jail**

gap [gæp] n vacío, hueco (*AM*); (*in trees, traffic*) claro; (*in time*) intervalo; (*difference*): **~ (between)** diferencia (entre)

gape [geɪp] vi mirar boquiabierto; (*shirt etc*) abrirse (completamente); **gaping** adj (completamente) abierto

garage ['gærɑːʒ] n garaje m; (*for repairs*) taller m

garbage ['gɑːbɪdʒ] (*US*) n basura; (*inf: nonsense*) tonterías fpl; **~ can** n cubo (*SP*) or bote m (*AM*) de la basura

garbled ['gɑːbld] adj (*distorted*) falsificado, amañado

garden ['gɑːdn] n jardín m; **~s** npl (*park*) parque m; **~er** n jardinero/a; **~ing** n jardinería

gargle ['gɑːgl] vi hacer gárgaras, gargarear (*AM*)

garish ['gɛərɪʃ] adj chillón/ona

garland ['gɑːlənd] n guirnalda

garlic ['gɑːlɪk] n ajo

garment ['gɑːmənt] n prenda (de vestir)

garnish ['gɑːnɪʃ] vt (*CULIN*) aderezar

garrison ['gærɪsn] n guarnición f

garter ['gɑːtə*] n (*for sock*) liga; (*US*) liguero

gas [gæs] n gas m; (*fuel*) combustible m; (*US: gasoline*) gasolina ♦ vt asfixiar con gas; **~ cooker** (*BRIT*) n cocina de gas; **~ cylinder** n bombona de gas; **~ fire** n estufa de gas

gash [gæʃ] n raja; (*wound*) cuchillada ♦ vt rajar; acuchillar

gasket ['gæskɪt] n (*AUT*) junta de culata

gas mask n careta antigás

gas meter n contador m de gas

gasoline ['gæsəliːn] (*US*) n gasolina

gasp [gɑːsp] n boqueada; (*of shock etc*) grito sofocado ♦ vi (*pant*) jadear

gas station (*US*) n gasolinera

gastric ['gæstrɪk] adj gástrico

gate [geɪt] n puerta; (*iron ~*) verja; **~crash** (*BRIT*) vt colarse en; **~way** n (*also fig*) puerta

gather ['gæðə*] vt (*flowers, fruit*) coger (*SP*), recoger; (*assemble*) reunir; (*pick up*) recoger; (*SEWING*) fruncir; (*understand*) entender ♦ vi (*assemble*) reunirse; **to ~ speed** ganar velocidad; **~ing** n reunión f, asamblea

gaudy ['gɔːdɪ] adj chillón/ona

gauge [geɪdʒ] n (*instrument*) indicador m ♦ vt medir; (*fig*) juzgar

gaunt [gɔːnt] adj (*haggard*) demacrado; (*stark*) desolado

gauntlet ['gɔːntlɪt] n (*fig*): **to run the ~ of** exponerse a; **to throw down the ~** arrojar el guante

gauze [gɔːz] n gasa

gave [geɪv] pt of **give**

gay [geɪ] adj (*homosexual*) gay; (*joyful*) alegre; (*colour*) vivo

gaze [geɪz] n mirada fija ♦ vi: **to ~ at sth** mirar algo fijamente

gazelle [gə'zɛl] n gacela

gazumping [gə'zʌmpɪŋ] (*BRIT*) n la subida del precio de una casa una vez que ya ha sido apalabrado

GB abbr = **Great Britain**

GCE n abbr (*BRIT*) = **General Certificate of Education**

GCSE (*BRIT*) n abbr (= **General Certificate of Secondary Education**) examen de reválida que se hace a los 16 años

gear [gɪə*] n equipo, herramientas fpl; (*TECH*) engranaje m; (*AUT*) velocidad f, marcha ♦ vt (*fig: adapt*): **to ~ sth to** adaptar or ajustar algo a; **top** or **high** (*US*)/**low** ~ cuarta/primera velocidad; **in ~** en marcha; **~ box** n caja de cambios; **~ lever** n palanca de cambio; **~ shift** (*US*) n = **~ lever**

geese [giːs] npl of **goose**

gel [dʒɛl] n gel m

gem [dʒɛm] n piedra preciosa

Gemini ['dʒɛmɪnaɪ] n Géminis m, Gemelos mpl

gender ['dʒɛndə*] n género

gene [dʒiːn] n gen(e) m

general ['dʒɛnərl] n general m ♦ adj general; **in ~** en general; **~ delivery** (*US*) n lista de correos; **~ election** n elecciones fpl generales; **~ly** adv generalmente, en general; **~ practitioner** n médico general

generate ['dʒɛnəreɪt] vt (*ELEC*) generar; (*jobs, profits*) producir

generation [dʒɛnə'reɪʃən] n generación f

generator ['dʒɛnəreɪtə*] n generador m

generosity [dʒɛnə'rɔsɪtɪ] n generosidad f

generous ['dʒɛnərəs] adj generoso

genetic [dʒɪ'nɛtɪk] adj: **~ engineering** ingeniería genética; **~ fingerprinting** identificación f genética

Geneva [dʒɪ'niːvə] n Ginebra

genial ['dʒiːnɪəl] adj afable, simpático

genitals ['dʒenɪtlz] npl (órganos mpl)
genitales mpl

genius ['dʒiːnɪəs] n genio

genteel [dʒen'tiːl] adj fino, elegante

gentle ['dʒentl] adj apacible, dulce; (animal)
manso; (breeze, curve etc) suave

gentleman ['dʒentlmən] (irreg) n señor m;
(well-bred man) caballero

gently ['dʒentlɪ] adv dulcemente; suavemente

gentry ['dʒentrɪ] n alta burguesía

gents [dʒents] n aseos mpl (de caballeros)

genuine ['dʒenjuɪn] adj auténtico; (person)
sincero

geography [dʒɪ'ɔɡrəfɪ] n geografía

geology [dʒɪ'ɔlədʒɪ] n geología

geometric(al) [dʒɪə'metrɪk(l)] adj
geométrico

geranium [dʒɪ'reɪnjəm] n geranio

geriatric [dʒerɪ'ætrɪk] adj, n geriátrico/a m/f

germ [dʒɜːm] n (microbe) microbio, bacteria;
(seed, fig) germen m

German ['dʒɜːmən] adj alemán/ana ♦ n
alemán/ana m/f; (LING) alemán m;
~ **measles** n rubéola

Germany ['dʒɜːmənɪ] n Alemania

gesture ['dʒestjə*] n gesto; (symbol) muestra

┌─ KEYWORD ─────────────────────────────┐

get [ɡet] (pt, pp got, pp gotten (US)) vi
1 (become, be) ponerse, volverse; to ~ old/
tired envejecer/cansarse; to ~ drunk
emborracharse; to ~ dirty ensuciarse; to ~
married casarse; when do I ~ paid? ¿cuándo
me pagan o se me paga?; it's ~ting late se
está haciendo tarde
2 (go): to ~ to/from llegar a/de; to ~ home
llegar a casa
3 (begin) empezar a; to ~ to know sb (llegar
a) conocer a uno; I'm ~ting to like him me
está empezando a gustar; let's ~ going o
started ¡vamos (a empezar)!
4 (modal aux vb): you've got to do it tienes
que hacerlo
♦ vt **1**: to ~ sth done (finish) terminar algo;
(have done) mandar hacer algo; to ~ one's
hair cut cortarse el pelo; to ~ the car going o
to go arrancar el coche; to ~ sb to do sth
conseguir o hacer que alguien haga algo; to
~ sth/sb ready preparar algo/a alguien
2 (obtain: money, permission, results)
conseguir; (find: job, flat) encontrar; (fetch:
person, doctor) buscar; (object) ir a buscar,
traer; to ~ sth for sb conseguir algo para
alguien; ~ me Mr Jones, please (TEL)
póngame o comuníqueme con el Sr.
Jones, por favor; can I ~ you a drink? ¿quieres
algo de beber?
3 (receive: present, letter) recibir; (acquire:
reputation) alcanzar; (: prize) ganar; what did

you ~ for your birthday? ¿qué te regalaron
por tu cumpleaños?; how much did you ~ for
the painting? ¿cuánto sacaste por el cuadro?
4 (catch) coger (SP), agarrar (AM); (hit: target
etc) dar en; to ~ sb by the arm/throat coger
or agarrar a uno por el brazo/cuello; ~ him!
¡cógelo! (SP), ¡atrápalo! (AM); the bullet got
him in the leg la bala le dio en la pierna
5 (take, move) llevar; to ~ sth to sb hacer
llegar algo a alguien; do you think we'll ~ it
through the door? ¿crees que lo podremos
meter por la puerta?
6 (catch, take: plane, bus etc) coger (SP),
tomar (AM); where do I ~ the train for
Birmingham? ¿dónde se coge or se toma el
tren para Birmingham?
7 (understand) entender; (hear) oír; I've got
it! ¡ya lo tengo!, ¡eureka!; I don't ~ your
meaning no te entiendo; I'm sorry, I didn't
~ your name lo siento, no cogí tu nombre
8 (have, possess): to have got tener
get about vi salir mucho; (news) divulgarse
get along vi (agree) llevarse bien; (depart)
marcharse; (manage) = get by
get at vt fus (attack) atacar; (reach) alcanzar
get away vi marcharse; (escape) escaparse
get away with vt fus hacer impunemente
get back vi (return) volver ♦ vt recobrar
get by vi (pass) (lograr) pasar; (manage)
arreglárselas
get down vi bajarse ♦ vt fus bajar ♦ vt
bajar; (depress) deprimir
get down to vt fus (work) ponerse a
get in vi entrar; (train) llegar; (arrive home)
volver a casa, regresar
get into vt fus entrar en; (vehicle) subir a; to
~ into a rage enfadarse
get off vi (from train etc) bajar; (depart:
person, car) marcharse ♦ vt (remove) quitar
♦ vt fus (train, bus) bajar de
get on vi (at exam etc): how are you ~ting
on? ¿cómo te va?; (agree): to ~ on (with)
llevarse bien (con) ♦ vt fus subir a
get out vi salir; (of vehicle) bajar ♦ vt sacar
get out of vt fus salir de; (duty etc)
escaparse de
get over vt fus (illness) recobrarse de
get round vt fus rodear; (fig: person)
engatusar a
get through vi (TEL) (lograr) comunicarse
get through to vt fus (TEL) comunicar con
get together vi reunirse ♦ vt reunir, juntar
get up vi (rise) levantarse ♦ vt fus subir
get up to vt fus (reach) llegar a; (prank)
hacer

└──┘

geyser ['ɡiːzə*] n (water heater) calentador m
de agua; (GEO) géiser m

ghastly ['ɡɑːstlɪ] adj horrible

gherkin ['gə:kɪn] n pepinillo
ghetto blaster ['getəʊblɑːstə*] n cassette m portátil de gran tamaño
ghost [gəʊst] n fantasma m
giant ['dʒaɪənt] n gigante m/f ♦ adj gigantesco, gigante
gibberish ['dʒɪbərɪʃ] n galimatías m
giblets ['dʒɪblɪts] npl menudillos mpl
Gibraltar [dʒɪ'brɔːltə*] n Gibraltar m
giddy ['gɪdɪ] adj mareado
gift [gɪft] n regalo; (ability) talento; ~**ed** adj dotado; ~ **token** or **voucher** n vale m canjeable por un regalo
gigantic [dʒaɪ'gæntɪk] adj gigantesco
giggle ['gɪgl] vi reírse tontamente
gill [dʒɪl] n (measure) = 0.25 pints (BRIT = 0.148l, US = 0.118l)
gills [gɪlz] npl (of fish) branquias fpl, agallas fpl
gilt [gɪlt] adj, n dorado; ~**-edged** adj (COMM) de máxima garantía
gimmick ['gɪmɪk] n truco
gin [dʒɪn] n ginebra
ginger ['dʒɪndʒə*] n jengibre m; ~ **ale** = ~ **beer**; ~ **beer** (BRIT) n gaseosa de jengibre; ~**bread** n pan m (or galleta) de jengibre
gingerly ['dʒɪndʒəlɪ] adv con cautela
gipsy ['dʒɪpsɪ] n = **gypsy**
giraffe [dʒɪ'rɑːf] n jirafa
girder ['gə:də*] n viga
girl [gə:l] n (small) niña; (young woman) chica, joven f, muchacha; (daughter) hija; **an English ~** una (chica) inglesa; ~**friend** n (of girl) amiga; (of boy) novia; ~**ish** adj de niña
giro ['dʒaɪrəʊ] n (BRIT: bank ~) giro bancario; (post office ~) giro postal; (state benefit) cheque quincenal del subsidio de desempleo
gist [dʒɪst] n lo esencial
give [gɪv] (pt **gave**, pp **given**) vt dar; (deliver) entregar; (as gift) regalar ♦ vi (break) romperse; (stretch: fabric) dar de sí; **to ~ sb sth, ~ sth to sb** dar algo a uno; ~ **away** vt (give free) regalar; (betray) traicionar; (disclose) revelar; ~ **back** vt devolver; ~ **in** vi ceder ♦ vt entregar; ~ **off** vt despedir; ~ **out** vt distribuir; ~ **up** vi rendirse, darse por vencido ♦ vt renunciar a; **to ~ up smoking** dejar de fumar; **to ~ o.s. up** entregarse; ~ **way** vi ceder; (BRIT: AUT) ceder el paso
glacier ['glæsɪə*] n glaciar m
glad [glæd] adj contento
gladly ['glædlɪ] adv con mucho gusto
glamorous ['glæmərəs] adj encantador(a), atractivo; **glamour** ['glæmə*] n encanto, atractivo
glance [glɑːns] n ojeada, mirada ♦ vi: **to ~ at** echar una ojeada a; **glancing** adj (blow) oblicuo
gland [glænd] n glándula
glare [gleə*] n (of anger) mirada feroz; (of light) deslumbramiento, brillo; **to be in the ~ of publicity** ser el foco de la atención pública ♦ vi deslumbrar; **to ~ at** mirar con odio a; **glaring** adj (mistake) manifiesto
glass [glɑːs] n vidrio, cristal m; (for drinking) vaso; (: with stem) copa; ~**es** npl (spectacles) gafas fpl; ~**house** n invernadero; ~**ware** n cristalería
glaze [gleɪz] vt (window) poner cristales a; (pottery) vidriar ♦ n vidriado; **glazier** ['gleɪzɪə*] n vidriero/a
gleam [gliːm] vi brillar
glean [gliːn] vt (information) recoger
glee [gliː] n alegría, regocijo
glen [glen] n cañada
glib [glɪb] adj de mucha labia; (promise, response) poco sincero
glide [glaɪd] vi deslizarse; (AVIAT, birds) planear; ~**r** n (AVIAT) planeador m; **gliding** n (AVIAT) vuelo sin motor
glimmer ['glɪmə*] n luz f tenue; (of interest) muestra; (of hope) rayo
glimpse [glɪmps] n vislumbre m ♦ vt vislumbrar, entrever
glint [glɪnt] vi centellear
glisten ['glɪsn] vi relucir, brillar
glitter ['glɪtə*] vi relucir, brillar
gloat [gləʊt] vi: **to ~ over** recrearse en
global ['gləʊbl] adj mundial; ~ **warming** (re)calentamiento global or de la tierra
globe [gləʊb] n globo; (model) globo terráqueo
gloom [gluːm] n tinieblas fpl, oscuridad f; (sadness) tristeza, melancolía; ~**y** adj (dark) oscuro; (sad) triste; (pessimistic) pesimista
glorious ['glɔːrɪəs] adj glorioso; (weather etc) magnífico
glory ['glɔːrɪ] n gloria
gloss [glɔs] n (shine) brillo; (paint) pintura de aceite; ~ **over** vt fus disimular
glossary ['glɔsərɪ] n glosario
glossy ['glɔsɪ] adj lustroso; (magazine) de lujo
glove [glʌv] n guante m; ~ **compartment** n (AUT) guantera
glow [gləʊ] vi brillar
glower ['glaʊə*] vi: **to ~ at** mirar con ceño
glue [gluː] n goma (de pegar), cemento ♦ vt pegar
glum [glʌm] adj (person, tone) melancólico
glut [glʌt] n superabundancia
glutton ['glʌtn] n glotón/ona m/f; **a ~ for work** un(a) trabajador(a) incansable
GM adj abbr (= genetically modified) transgénico
gnat [næt] n mosquito
gnaw [nɔː] vt roer
gnome [nəʊm] n gnomo
go [gəʊ] (pt **went**, pp **gone**, pl ~**es**) vi ir; (travel) viajar; (depart) irse, marcharse; (work) funcionar, marchar; (be sold) venderse; (time) pasar; (fit, suit): **to ~ with**

hacer juego con; (*become*) ponerse; (*break etc*) romperse ♦ *n*: **to have a ~ (at)** probar suerte (con); **to be on the ~** parar; **whose ~ is it?** ¿a quién le toca?; **he's going to do it** va a hacerlo; **to ~ for a walk** ir de paseo; **to ~ dancing** ir a bailar; **how did it ~?** ¿qué tal salió or resultó?, ¿cómo ha ido?; **to ~ round the back** pasar por detrás; **~ about** *vi* (*rumour*) propagarse ♦ *vt fus*: **how do I ~ about this?** ¿cómo me las arreglo para hacer esto?; **~ ahead** *vi* seguir adelante; **~ along** *vi* ir ♦ *vt fus* bordear; **to ~ along with** (*agree*) estar de acuerdo con; **~ away** *vi* irse, marcharse; **~ back** *vi* volver; **~ back on** *vt fus* (*promise*) faltar a; **~ by** *vi* (*time*) pasar ♦ *vt fus* guiarse por; **~ down** *vi* bajar; (*ship*) hundirse; (*sun*) ponerse ♦ *vt fus* bajar; **~ for** *vt fus* (*fetch*) ir por; (*like*) gustar; (*attack*) atacar; **~ in** *vi* entrar; **~ in for** *vt fus* (*competition*) presentarse a; **~ into** *vt fus* entrar en; (*investigate*) investigar; (*embark on*) dedicarse a; **~ off** *vi* irse, marcharse; (*food*) pasarse; (*explode*) estallar; (*event*) realizarse ♦ *vt fus* dejar de gustar; **I'm going off him/the idea** ya no me gusta tanto él/la idea; **~ on** *vi* (*continue*) seguir, continuar; (*happen*) pasar, ocurrir; **to ~ on doing sth** seguir haciendo algo; **~ out** *vi* salir; (*fire, light*) apagarse; **~ over** *vi* (*ship*) zozobrar ♦ *vt fus* (*check*) revisar; **~ through** *vt fus* (*town etc*) atravesar; **~ up** *vi, vt fus* subir; **~ without** *vt fus* pasarse sin

goad [gəud] *vt* aguijonear

go-ahead *adj* (*person*) dinámico; (*firm*) innovador(a) ♦ *n* luz *f* verde

goal [gəul] *n* meta; (*score*) gol *m*; **~keeper** *n* portero; **~-post** *n* poste *m* (de la portería)

goat [gəut] *n* cabra

gobble ['gɔbl] *vt* (*also*: **~ down, ~ up**) tragarse, engullir

go-between *n* intermediario/a

god [gɔd] *n* dios *m*; **G~** *n* Dios *m*; **~child** *n* ahijado/a; **~daughter** *n* ahijada; **~dess** *n* diosa; **~father** *n* padrino; **~-forsaken** *adj* dejado de la mano de Dios; **~mother** *n* madrina; **~send** *n* don *m* del cielo; **~son** *n* ahijado

goggles ['gɔglz] *npl* gafas *fpl*

going ['gəuɪŋ] *n* (*conditions*) estado del terreno ♦ *adj*: **the ~ rate** la tarifa corriente or en vigor

gold [gəuld] *n* oro ♦ *adj* de oro; **~en** *adj* (*made of ~*) de oro; (*~ in colour*) dorado; **~fish** *n* pez *m* de colores; **~mine** *n* (*also fig*) mina de oro; **~-plated** *adj* chapado en oro; **~smith** *n* orfebre *m/f*

golf [gɔlf] *n* golf *m*; **~ ball** *n* (*for game*) pelota de golf; (*on typewriter*) esfera; **~ club** *n* club *m* de golf; (*stick*) palo (de golf);

~ course *n* campo de golf; **~er** *n* golfista *m/f*

gone [gɔn] *pp* of **go**

good [gud] *adj* bueno; (*pleasant*) agradable; (*kind*) bueno, amable; (*well-behaved*) educado ♦ *n* bien *m*, provecho; **~s** *npl* (COMM) mercancías *fpl*; **~!** ¡qué bien!; **to be ~ at** tener aptitud para; **to be ~ for** servir para; **it's ~ for you** te hace bien; **would you be ~ enough to ...?** ¿podría hacerme el favor de ...?, ¿sería tan amable de ...?; **a ~ deal (of)** mucho; **a ~ many muchos**; **to make ~** reparar; **it's no ~ complaining** no vale la pena (de) quejarse; **for ~** para siempre, definitivamente; **~ morning/afternoon** ¡buenos días/buenas tardes!; **~ evening!** ¡buenas noches!; **~ night!** ¡buenas noches!; **~bye!** ¡adiós!; **to say ~bye** despedirse; **G~ Friday** *n* Viernes *m* Santo; **~-looking** *adj* guapo; **~-natured** *adj* amable, simpático; **~ness** *n* (*of person*) bondad *f*; **for ~ness sake!** ¡por Dios!; **~ness gracious!** ¡Dios mío!; **~s train** (BRIT) *n* tren *m* de mercancías; **~will** *n* buena voluntad *f*

goose [guːs] (*pl* **geese**) *n* ganso, oca

gooseberry ['guzbəri] *n* grosella espinosa; **to play ~** hacer de carabina

gooseflesh ['guːsfleʃ] *n* = **goose pimples**

goose pimples *npl* carne *f* de gallina

gore [gɔː*] *vt* cornear ♦ *n* sangre *f*

gorge [gɔːdʒ] *n* barranco ♦ *vr*: **to ~ o.s. (on)** atracarse (de)

gorgeous ['gɔːdʒəs] *adj* (*thing*) precioso; (*weather*) espléndido; (*person*) guapísimo

gorilla [gə'rɪlə] *n* gorila *m*

gorse [gɔːs] *n* tojo

gory ['gɔːrɪ] *adj* sangriento

go-slow (BRIT) *n* huelga de manos caídas

gospel ['gɔspl] *n* evangelio

gossip ['gɔsɪp] *n* (*scandal*) cotilleo, chismes *mpl*; (*chat*) charla; (*scandalmonger*) cotilla *m/f*, chismoso/a ♦ *vi* cotillear

got [gɔt] *pt, pp* of **get**; **~ten** (US) *pp* of **get**

gout [gaut] *n* gota

govern ['gʌvən] *vt* gobernar; (*influence*) dominar; **~ess** *n* institutriz *f*; **~ment** *n* gobierno; **~or** *n* gobernador(a) *m/f*; (*of school etc*) miembro del consejo; (*of jail*) director(a) *m/f*

gown [gaun] *n* traje *m*; (*of teacher*, BRIT: *of judge*) toga

G.P. *n abbr* = **general practitioner**

grab [græb] *vt* coger (SP) or agarrar (AM), arrebatar ♦ *vi*: **to ~ at** intentar agarrar

grace [greɪs] *n* gracia ♦ *vt* honrar; (*adorn*) adornar; **5 days' ~** un plazo de 5 días; **~ful** *adj* grácil, ágil; (*style, shape*) elegante, gracioso; **gracious** ['greɪʃəs] *adj* amable

grade [greɪd] *n* (*quality*) clase *f*, calidad *f*; (*in* *hierarchy*) grado; (*SCOL: mark*) nota; (*US: school class*) curso ♦ vt clasificar; **~ crossing** (*US*) *n* paso a nivel; **~ school** (*US*) *n* escuela primaria

gradient ['greidiənt] *n* pendiente *f*

gradual ['grædjuəl] *adj* paulatino; **~ly** *adv* paulatinamente

graduate [*n* 'grædjuit, *vb* 'grædjueit] *n* (*US: of high school*) graduado/a; (*of university*) licenciado/a ♦ *vi* graduarse; licenciarse; **graduation** [-'eiʃən] *n* (*ceremony*) entrega del título

graffiti [grə'fi:ti] *n* pintadas *fpl*

graft [grɑ:ft] *n* (*AGR, MED*) injerto; (*BRIT: inf*) trabajo duro; (*bribery*) corrupción *f* ♦ *vt* injertar

grain [grein] *n* (*single particle*) grano; (*corn*) granos *mpl*, cereales *mpl*; (*of wood*) fibra

gram [græm] *n* gramo

grammar ['græmə*] *n* gramática; **~ school** (*BRIT*) *n* ≈ instituto de segunda enseñanza, liceo (*SP*)

grammatical [grə'mætikl] *adj* gramatical

gramme [græm] *n* = **gram**

gramophone ['græməfəun] (*BRIT*) *n* tocadiscos *m inv*

grand [grænd] *adj* magnífico, imponente; (*wonderful*) estupendo; **G~ Britain** *n* Gran Bretaña; **~children** *npl* nietos *mpl*; **~dad** (*inf*) *n* yayo, abuelito; **~daughter** *n* nieta; **~eur** ['grændjə*] *n* magnificencia, lo grandioso; **~father** *n* abuelo; **~ma** (*inf*) *n* yaya, abuelita; **~mother** *n* abuela; **~pa** (*inf*) *n* = **~dad**; **~parents** *npl* abuelos *mpl*; **~ piano** *n* piano de cola; **~son** *n* nieto; **~stand** *n* (*SPORT*) tribuna

granite ['grænit] *n* granito

granny ['græni] (*inf*) *n* abuelita, yaya

grant [grɑ:nt] *vt* (*concede*) conceder; (*admit*) reconocer ♦ *n* (*SCOL*) beca; (*ADMIN*) subvención *f*; **to take sth/sb for ~ed** dar algo por sentado/no hacer ningún caso a uno

granulated sugar ['grænju:leitid-] (*BRIT*) *n* azúcar *m* blanquilla

grape [greip] *n* uva

grapefruit ['greipfru:t] *n* pomelo (*SP*), toronja (*AM*)

graph [grɑ:f] *n* gráfica; **~ic** ['græfik] *adj* gráfico; **~ics** *n* artes *fpl* gráficas ♦ *npl* (*drawings*) dibujos *mpl*

grapple ['græpl] *vi*: **to ~ with sth/sb** agarrar a algo/uno

grasp [grɑ:sp] *vt* agarrar, asir; (*understand*) comprender ♦ *n* (*grip*) asimiento; (*understanding*) comprensión *f*; **~ing** *adj* (*mean*) avaro

grass [grɑ:s] *n* hierba; (*lawn*) césped *m*; **~hopper** *n* saltamontes *m inv*; **~-roots** *adj* (*fig*) popular

grate [greit] *n* parrilla de chimenea ♦ *vi*: **to ~ (on)** chirriar (sobre) ♦ *vt* (*CULIN*) rallar

grateful ['greitful] *adj* agradecido

grater ['greitə*] *n* rallador *m*

gratifying ['grætifaiiŋ] *adj* grato

grating ['greitiŋ] *n* (*iron bars*) reja ♦ *adj* (*noise*) áspero

gratitude ['grætitju:d] *n* agradecimiento

gratuity [grə'tju:iti] *n* gratificación *f*

grave [greiv] *n* tumba ♦ *adj* serio, grave

gravel ['grævl] *n* grava

gravestone ['greivstəun] *n* lápida

graveyard ['greivjɑ:d] *n* cementerio

gravity ['græviti] *n* gravedad *f*

gravy ['greivi] *n* salsa de carne

gray [grei] *adj* = **grey**

graze [greiz] *vi* pacer ♦ *vt* (*touch lightly*) rozar; (*scrape*) raspar ♦ *n* (*MED*) abrasión *f*

grease [gri:s] *n* (*fat*) grasa; (*lubricant*) lubricante *m* ♦ *vt* engrasar; lubrificar; **~proof paper** (*BRIT*) *n* papel *m* apergaminado; **greasy** *adj* grasiento

great [greit] *adj* grande; (*inf*) magnífico, estupendo; **G~ Britain** *n* Gran Bretaña; **~-grandfather** *n* bisabuelo; **~-grandmother** *n* bisabuela; **~ly** *adv* muy; (*with verb*) mucho; **~ness** *n* grandeza

Greece [gri:s] *n* Grecia

greed [gri:d] *n* (*also: ~iness*) codicia, avaricia; (*for food*) gula; (*for power etc*) avidez *f*; **~y** *adj* avaro; (*for food*) glotón/ona

Greek [gri:k] *adj* griego ♦ *n* griego/a; (*LING*) griego

green [gri:n] *adj* (*also POL*) verde; (*inexperienced*) novato ♦ *n* verde *m*; (*stretch of grass*) césped *m*; (*GOLF*) green *m*; **~s** *npl* (*vegetables*) verduras *fpl*; **~ belt** *n* zona verde; **~ card** *n* (*AUT*) carta verde; (*US: work permit*) permiso de trabajo para los extranjeros en EE. UU.; **~ery** *n* verdura; **~grocer** (*BRIT*) *n* verdulero/a; **~house** *n* invernadero; **~house effect** *n* efecto invernadero; **~house gas** *n* gases *mpl* de invernadero; **~ish** *adj* verdoso

Greenland ['gri:nlənd] *n* Groenlandia

greet [gri:t] *vt* (*welcome*) dar la bienvenida a; (*receive: news*) recibir; **~ing** *n* (*welcome*) bienvenida; **~ing(s) card** *n* tarjeta de felicitación

grenade [grə'neid] *n* granada

grew [gru:] *pt of* **grow**

grey [grei] *adj* gris; (*weather*) sombrío; **~-haired** *adj* canoso; **~hound** *n* galgo

grid [grid] *n* reja; (*ELEC*) red *f*; **~lock** *n* (*traffic jam*) retención *f*

grief [gri:f] *n* dolor *m*, pena

grievance ['gri:vəns] *n* motivo de queja, agravio

grieve [gri:v] *vi* afligirse, acongojarse ♦ *vt* dar pena a; **to ~ for** llorar por

grievous ['gri:vəs] adj: ~ **bodily harm** (LAW) daños mpl corporales graves

grill [grɪl] n (on cooker) parrilla; (also: mixed ~) parrillada ♦ vt (BRIT) asar a la parrilla; (inf: question) interrogar

grille [grɪl] n reja; (AUT) rejilla

grim [grɪm] adj (place) sombrío; (situation) triste; (person) ceñudo

grimace [grɪ'meɪs] n mueca ♦ vi hacer muecas

grime [graɪm] n mugre f, suciedad f

grin [grɪn] n sonrisa abierta ♦ vi sonreír abiertamente

grind [graɪnd] (pt, pp ground) vt (coffee, pepper etc) moler; (US: meat) picar; (make sharp) afilar ♦ n (work) rutina

grip [grɪp] n (hold) asimiento; (control) control m, dominio; (of tyre etc): **to have a good/bad ~** agarrarse bien/mal; (handle) asidero; (holdall) maletín m ♦ vt agarrar; (viewer, reader) fascinar; **to get to ~s with** enfrentarse con; **~ping** adj absorbente

grisly ['grɪzlɪ] adj horripilante, horrible

gristle ['grɪsl] n ternilla

grit [grɪt] n gravilla; (courage) valor m ♦ vt (road) poner gravilla en; **to ~ one's teeth** apretar los dientes

groan [grəun] n gemido; quejido ♦ vi gemir; quejarse

grocer ['grəusə*] n tendero (de ultramarinos (SP)); **~ies** npl comestibles mpl; **~'s (shop)** n tienda de ultramarinos or de abarrotes (AM)

groin [grɔɪn] n ingle f

groom [gru:m] n mozo/a de cuadra; (also: bride~) novio ♦ vt (horse) almohazar; (fig): **to ~ sb for** preparar a uno para; **well-~ed** de buena presencia

groove [gru:v] n ranura, surco

grope [grəup]: **to ~ for** vt fus buscar a tientas

gross [grəus] adj (neglect, injustice) grave; (vulgar: behaviour) grosero; (: appearance) de mal gusto; (COMM) bruto; **~ly** adv (greatly) enormemente

grotto ['grɔtəu] n gruta

grotty ['grɔtɪ] (inf) adj horrible

ground [graund] pt, pp of grind ♦ n suelo, tierra; (SPORT) campo, terreno; (reason: gen pl) causa, razón f; (US: also: ~ wire) tierra ♦ vt (plane) mantener en tierra; (US: ELEC) conectar con tierra; **~s** npl (of coffee etc) poso; (gardens etc) jardines mpl, parque m; **on the ~** en el suelo; **to the ~** al suelo; **to gain/lose ~** ganar/perder terreno; **~ cloth** (US) n = **~sheet**; **~ing** n (in education) conocimientos mpl básicos; **~less** adj infundado; **~sheet** (BRIT) n tela impermeable; suelo; **~ staff** n personal m de tierra; **~work** n preparación f

group [gru:p] n grupo; (musical) conjunto ♦ vt (also: ~ together) agrupar ♦ vi (also: ~ together) agruparse

grouse [graus] n inv (bird) urogallo ♦ vi (complain) quejarse

grove [grəuv] n arboleda

grovel ['grɔvl] vi (fig): **to ~ before** humillarse ante

grow [grəu] (pt grew, pp grown) vi crecer; (increase) aumentar; (expand) desarrollarse; (become) volverse; **to ~ rich/weak** enriquecerse/debilitarse ♦ vt cultivar; (hair, beard) dejar crecer; **~ up** vi crecer, hacerse hombre/mujer; **~er** n cultivador(a) m/f, productor(a) m/f; **~ing** adj creciente

growl [graul] vi gruñir

grown [grəun] pp of grow; **~-up** n adulto, mayor m/f

growth [grəuθ] n crecimiento, desarrollo; (what has grown) brote m; (MED) tumor m

grub [grʌb] n larva, gusano; (inf: food) comida

grubby ['grʌbɪ] adj sucio, mugriento

grudge [grʌdʒ] n (motivo de) rencor m ♦ vt: **to ~ sb sth** dar algo a uno de mala gana; **to bear sb a ~** guardar rencor a uno

gruelling ['gruəlɪŋ] (US **grueling**) adj penoso, duro

gruesome ['gru:səm] adj horrible

gruff [grʌf] adj (voice) ronco; (manner) brusco

grumble ['grʌmbl] vi refunfuñar, quejarse

grumpy ['grʌmpɪ] adj gruñón/ona

grunt [grʌnt] vi gruñir

G-string ['dʒi:strɪŋ] n taparrabo

guarantee [gærən'ti:] n garantía ♦ vt garantizar

guard [gɑːd] n (squad) guardia; (one man) guardia m; (BRIT: RAIL) jefe m de tren; (on machine) dispositivo de seguridad; (also: fire~) rejilla de protección ♦ vt guardar; (prisoner) vigilar; **to be on one's ~** estar alerta; **~ against** vt fus (prevent) protegerse de; **~ed** adj (fig) cauteloso; **~ian** n guardián/ana m/f; (of minor) tutor(a) m/f; **~'s van** n (BRIT: RAIL) furgón m

Guatemala [gwætɪ'mɑːlə] n Guatemala; **~n** adj, n guatemalteco/a m/f

guerrilla [gə'rɪlə] n guerrillero/a

guess [gɛs] vi adivinar; (US) suponer ♦ vt adivinar; suponer ♦ n suposición f, conjetura; **to take** or **have a ~** tratar de adivinar; **~work** n conjeturas fpl

guest [gɛst] n invitado/a; (in hotel) huésped(a) m/f; **~ house** n casa de huéspedes, pensión f; **~ room** n cuarto de huéspedes

guffaw [gʌ'fɔ:] vi reírse a carcajadas

guidance ['gaɪdəns] n (advice) consejos mpl

guide [gaɪd] n (person) guía m/f; (book, fig) guía ♦ vt (round museum etc) guiar; (lead) conducir; (*direct*) orientar; (**girl**) ~ *n* exploradora; **~book** *n* guía; ~ **dog** *n* perro *m* guía; **~lines** *npl* (*advice*) directrices *fpl*

guild [gɪld] *n* gremio

guilt [gɪlt] *n* culpabilidad *f*; **~y** *adj* culpable

guinea pig ['gɪnɪ-] *n* cobaya; (*fig*) conejillo de Indias

guise [gaɪz] *n*: in or under the ~ of bajo apariencia de

guitar [gɪ'tɑː*] *n* guitarra

gulf [gʌlf] *n* golfo; (*abyss*) abismo

gull [gʌl] *n* gaviota

gullible ['gʌlɪbl] *adj* crédulo

gully ['gʌlɪ] *n* barranco

gulp [gʌlp] *vi* tragar saliva ♦ *vt* (*also*: ~ **down**) tragarse

gum [gʌm] *n* (*ANAT*) encía; (*glue*) goma, cemento; (*sweet*) caramelo de goma; (*also*: *chewing-~*) chicle *m* ♦ *vt* pegar con goma; **~boots** (*BRIT*) *npl* botas *fpl* de goma

gun [gʌn] *n* (*small*) pistola, revólver *m*; (*shotgun*) escopeta; (*rifle*) fusil *m*; (*cannon*) cañón *m*; **~boat** *n* cañonero; **~fire** *n* disparos *mpl*; **~man** *n* pistolero; **~point** *n*: at **~point** a mano armada; **~powder** *n* pólvora; **~shot** *n* escopetazo

gurgle ['gəːgl] *vi* (*baby*) gorgotear; (*water*) borbotear

gush [gʌʃ] *vi* salir a raudales; (*person*) deshacerse en efusiones

gust [gʌst] *n* (*of wind*) ráfaga

gusto ['gʌstəu] *n* entusiasmo

gut [gʌt] *n* intestino; **~s** *npl* (*ANAT*) tripas *fpl*; (*courage*) valor *m*

gutter ['gʌtə*] *n* (*of roof*) canalón *m*; (*in street*) cuneta

guy [gaɪ] *n* (*also*: *~rope*) cuerda; (*inf*: *man*) tío (*SP*), tipo; (*figure*) monigote *m*

guzzle ['gʌzl] *vi* tragar ♦ *vt* engullir

gym [dʒɪm] *n* (*also*: *gymnasium*) gimnasio; (*also*: *gymnastics*) gimnasia; **~nast** *n* gimnasta *m/f*; **~ shoes** *npl* zapatillas *fpl* (de deporte); **~ slip** (*BRIT*) *n* túnica de colegiala

gynaecologist [gaɪnɪ'kɔlədʒɪst] (*US* **gynecologist**) *n* ginecólogo/a

gypsy ['dʒɪpsɪ] *n* gitano/a

H, h

haberdashery [hæbə'dæʃərɪ] (*BRIT*) *n* mercería

habit ['hæbɪt] *n* hábito, costumbre *f*; (*drug* ~) adicción *f*; (*costume*) hábito

habitual [hə'bɪtjuəl] *adj* acostumbrado, habitual; (*drinker, liar*) empedernido

hack [hæk] *vt* (*cut*) cortar; (*slice*) tajar ♦ *n* (*pej*: *writer*) escritor(a) *m/f* a sueldo; **~er** *n* (*COMPUT*) pirata *m/f* informático/a

hackneyed ['hæknɪd] *adj* trillado

had [hæd] *pt, pp* of **have**

haddock ['hædək] (*pl* ~ *or* ~s) *n especie de merluza*

hadn't ['hædnt] = **had not**

haemorrhage ['hemərɪdʒ] (*US* **hemorrhage**) *n* hemorragia

haemorrhoids ['hemərɔɪdz] (*US* **hemorrhoids**) *npl* hemorroides *fpl*

haggle ['hægl] *vi* regatear

Hague [heɪg] *n*: The ~ La Haya

hail [heɪl] *n* granizo; (*fig*) lluvia ♦ *vt* saludar; (*taxi*) llamar a; (*acclaim*) aclamar ♦ *vi* granizar; **~stone** *n* (piedra de) granizo

hair [hɛə*] *n* pelo, cabellos *mpl*; (*one* ~) pelo, cabello; (*on legs etc*) vello; **to do one's ~** arreglarse el pelo; **to have grey ~** tener canas *fpl*; **~brush** *n* cepillo (para el pelo); **~cut** *n* corte *m* (de pelo); **~do** *n* peinado; **~dresser** *n* peluquero/a; **~dresser's** *n* peluquería; **~ dryer** *n* secador *m* de pelo; **~grip** *n* horquilla; **~net** *n* redecilla; **~piece** *n* postizo; **~pin** *n* horquilla; **~pin bend** (*US* **~pin curve**) *n* curva de herquilla; **~raising** *adj* espeluznante; **~ removing cream** *n* crema depilatoria; **~ spray** *n* laca; **~style** *n* peinado; **~y** *adj* peludo; velludo; (*inf*: *frightening*) espeluznante

hake [heɪk] (*pl inv or* ~s) *n* merluza

half [hɑːf] (*pl halves*) *n* mitad *f*; (*of beer*) = caña (*SP*), media pinta; (*RAIL, BUS*) billete *m* de niño ♦ *adj* medio ♦ *adv* medio, a medias; **two and a ~** dos y media; **~ a dozen** media docena; **~ a pound** media libra; **to cut sth in ~** cortar algo por la mitad; **~-caste** ['hɑːfkɑːst] *n* mestizo/a; **~-hearted** *adj* indiferente, poco entusiasta; **~-hour** *n* media hora; **~-mast** *n*: at **~-mast** (*flag*) a media asta; **~-price** *adj, adv* a mitad de precio; **~ term** (*BRIT*) *n* (*SCOL*) vacaciones *fpl* de mediados del trimestre; **~-time** *n* descanso; **~way** *adv* a medio camino; (*in period of time*) a mitad de

hall [hɔːl] *n* (*for concerts*) sala; (*entrance way*) hall *m*; vestíbulo; **~ of residence** (*BRIT*) *n* residencia

hallmark ['hɔːlmɑːk] *n* sello

hallo [hə'ləu] *excl* = **hello**

Hallowe'en [hæləu'iːn] *n* víspera de Todos los Santos

hallucination [həluːsɪ'neɪʃən] *n* alucinación *f*

hallway ['hɔːlweɪ] *n* vestíbulo

halo ['heɪləu] *n* (*of saint*) halo, aureola

halt [hɔːlt] *n* (*stop*) alto, parada ♦ *vt* parar; interrumpir ♦ *vi* pararse

halve [hɑːv] *vt* partir por la mitad

halves [hɑːvz] *npl of* **half**

ham [hæm] *n* jamón *m* (cocido)

hamburger ['hæmbə:gə*] n hamburguesa

hamlet ['hæmlɪt] n aldea

hammer ['hæmə*] n martillo ♦ vt (nail)
clavar; (force): **to ~ an idea into sb/a message
across** meter una idea en la cabeza a uno/
machacar una idea ♦ vi dar golpes

hammock ['hæmək] n hamaca

hamper ['hæmpə*] vt estorbar ♦ n cesto

hand [hænd] n mano f; (of clock) aguja;
(writing) letra; (worker) obrero ♦ vt dar,
pasar; **to give** or **lend sb a ~** echar una mano
a uno, ayudar a uno; **at ~** a mano; **in ~** (time)
libre; (job etc) entre manos; **on ~** (person,
services) a mano, al alcance; **to ~** (information
etc) a mano; **on the one ~ ...**, **on the other
~ ...** por una parte ... por otra (parte) ...; **~ in**
vt entregar; **~ out** vt distribuir; **~ over** vt
(deliver) entregar; **~bag** n bolso (SP), cartera
(AM); **~book** n manual m; **~brake** n freno
de mano; **~cuffs** npl esposas fpl; **~ful** n
puñado

handicap ['hændɪkæp] n minusvalía;
(disadvantage) desventaja; (SPORT) handicap
m ♦ vt estorbar; **mentally/physically ~ped**
deficiente m/f (mental)/minusválido/a
(físico/a)

handicraft ['hændɪkrɑ:ft] n artesanía;
(object) objeto de artesanía

handiwork ['hændɪwə:k] n obra

handkerchief ['hæŋkətʃɪf] n pañuelo

handle ['hændl] n (of door etc) tirador m; (of
cup etc) asa; (of knife etc) mango; (for
winding) manivela ♦ vt (touch) tocar; (deal
with) encargarse de; (treat: people) manejar;
"**~ with care**" "(manéjese) con cuidado"; **to
fly off the ~** perder los estribos; **~bar(s)** n(pl)
manillar m

hand: ~ luggage n equipaje m de mano;
~made adj hecho a mano; **~out** n (money
etc) limosna; (leaflet) folleto; **~rail** n
pasamanos m inv; **~shake** n apretón m de
manos

handsome ['hænsəm] adj guapo; (building)
bello; (fig: profit) considerable

handwriting ['hændraɪtɪŋ] n letra

handy ['hændɪ] adj (close at hand) a la
mano; (tool etc) práctico; (skilful) hábil,
diestro

hang [hæŋ] (pt, pp hung) vt colgar; (criminal:
pt, pp hanged) ahorcar ♦ vi (painting, coat
etc) colgar; (hair, drapery) caer; **to get the
~ of sth** (inf) lograr dominar algo; **~ about**
or **around** vi haraganear; **~ on** vi (wait)
esperar; **~ up** vi (TEL) colgar ♦ vt colgar

hanger ['hæŋə*] n percha; **~on** n parásito

hang: ~-gliding ['-glaɪdɪŋ] n vuelo libre;
~over n (after drinking) resaca; **~-up** n
complejo

hanker ['hæŋkə*] vi: **to ~ after** añorar

hankie ['hæŋkɪ], **hanky** ['hæŋkɪ] n abbr =
handkerchief

haphazard [hæp'hæzəd] adj fortuito

happen ['hæpən] vi suceder, ocurrir;
(chance): **he ~ed to hear/see** dió la casualidad
de que oyó/vió; **as it ~s** da la casualidad de
que; **~ing** n suceso, acontecimiento

happily ['hæpɪlɪ] adv (luckily) afortunadamente; (cheerfully) alegremente

happiness ['hæpɪnɪs] n felicidad f;
(cheerfulness) alegría

happy ['hæpɪ] adj feliz; (cheerful) alegre; **to
be ~ (with)** estar contento (con); **to be ~ to
do** estar encantado de hacer; **~ birthday!** ¡feliz
cumpleaños!; **~-go-lucky** adj despreocupado; **~ hour** n horas en las que la bebida es
más barata, happy hour f

harass ['hærəs] vt acosar, hostigar; **~ment** n
persecución f

harbour ['hɑːbə*] (US **harbor**) n puerto ♦ vt
(fugitive) dar abrigo a; (hope etc) abrigar

hard [hɑːd] adj duro; (difficult) difícil; (work)
arduo; (person) severo; (fact) innegable
♦ adv (work) mucho, duro; (think)
profundamente; **to look ~ at** clavar los ojos
en; **to try ~** esforzarse; **no ~ feelings!** ¡sin
rencor(es)!; **to be ~ of hearing** ser duro de
oído; **to be ~ done by** ser tratado
injustamente; **~back** n libro en cartoné;
~ cash n dinero contante; **~ disk** n
(COMPUT) disco duro o rígido; **~en** vt
endurecer; (fig) curtir ♦ vi endurecerse;
curtirse; **~-headed** adj realista; **~ labour** n
trabajos mpl forzados

hardly ['hɑːdlɪ] adv apenas; **~ ever** casi nunca

hard: ~ship n privación f; **~ shoulder** (BRIT)
n (AUT) arcén m; **~-up** (inf) adj sin un duro
(SP), sin plata (AM); **~ware** n ferretería;
(COMPUT) hardware m; (MIL) armamento;
~ware shop n ferretería; **~-wearing** adj
resistente, duradero; **~-working** adj
trabajador(a)

hardy ['hɑːdɪ] adj fuerte; (plant) resistente

hare [hɛə*] n liebre f; **~-brained** adj
descabellado

harm [hɑːm] n daño, mal m ♦ vt (person)
hacer daño a; (health, interests) perjudicar;
(thing) dañar; **out of ~'s way** a salvo; **~ful** adj
dañino; **~less** adj (person) inofensivo; (joke
etc) inocente

harmony ['hɑːmənɪ] n armonía

harness ['hɑːnɪs] n arreos mpl; (for child)
arnés m; (safety ~) arneses mpl ♦ vt (horse)
enjaezar; (resources) aprovechar

harp [hɑːp] n arpa ♦ vi: **to ~ on (about)**
machacar (con)

harrowing ['hærəʊɪŋ] adj angustioso

harsh [hɑːʃ] adj (cruel) duro, cruel; (severe)
severo; (sound) áspero; (light)

deslumbrador(a)

harvest ['hɑːvɪst] n (~ time) siega; (of cereals etc) cosecha; (of grapes) vendimia ♦ vt cosechar

has [hæz] vb see **have**

hash [hæʃ] n (CULIN) picadillo; (fig: mess) lío

hashish ['hæʃiʃ] n hachís m

hasn't ['hæznt] = has not

hassle ['hæsl] (inf) n lata

haste [heɪst] n prisa; **~n** ['heɪsn] vt acelerar ♦ vi darse prisa; **hastily** adv de prisa; precipitadamente; **hasty** adj apresurado; (rash) precipitado

hat [hæt] n sombrero

hatch [hætʃ] n (NAUT: also: ~way) escotilla; (also: service ~) ventanilla ♦ vi (bird) salir del cascarón ♦ vt incubar; (plot) tramar; **5 eggs have ~ed** han salido 5 pollos

hatchback ['hætʃbæk] n (AUT) tres or cinco puertas m

hatchet ['hætʃɪt] n hacha

hate [heɪt] vt odiar, aborrecer ♦ n odio; **~ful** adj odioso; **hatred** ['heɪtrɪd] n odio

haughty ['hɔːtɪ] adj altanero

haul [hɔːl] vt tirar ♦ n (of fish) redada; (of stolen goods etc) botín m; **~age** (BRIT) n transporte m; (costs) gastos mpl de transporte; **~ier** (US **~er**) n transportista m/f

haunch [hɔːntʃ] n anca; (of meat) pierna

haunt [hɔːnt] vt (subj: ghost) aparecerse en; (obsess) obsesionar ♦ n guarida

KEYWORD

have [hæv] (pt, pp had) aux vb 1 (gen) haber; **to ~ arrived/eaten** haber llegado/comido; **having finished** or **when he had finished, he left** cuando hubo acabado, se fue
2 (in tag questions): **you've done it, ~n't you?** lo has hecho, ¿verdad? or ¿no?
3 (in short answers and questions): **I ~n't** no; **so I ~** pues, es verdad; **we ~n't paid — yes we ~!** no hemos pagado — ¡sí que hemos pagado!; **I've been there before, ~ you?** he estado allí antes, ¿y tú?
♦ modal aux vb (be obliged): **to ~ (got) to do sth** tener que hacer algo; **you ~n't to tell her** no hay que or no debes decírselo
♦ vt 1 (possess): **he has (got) blue eyes/dark hair** tiene los ojos azules/el pelo negro
2 (referring to meals etc): **to ~ breakfast/lunch/dinner** desayunar/comer/cenar; **to ~ a drink/a cigarette** tomar algo/fumar un cigarrillo
3 (receive) recibir; (obtain) obtener; **may I ~ your address?** ¿puedes darme tu dirección?; **you can ~ it for £5** te lo puedes quedar por £5; **I must ~ it by tomorrow** lo necesito para mañana; **to ~ a baby** tener un niño or bebé
4 (maintain, allow): **I won't ~ it/this**

nonsense! ¡no lo permitiré!/¡no permitiré estas tonterías!; **we can't ~ that** no podemos permitir eso
5: **to ~ sth done** hacer or mandar hacer algo; **to ~ one's hair cut** cortarse el pelo; **to ~ sb do sth** hacer que alguien haga algo
6 (experience, suffer): **to ~ a cold/flu** tener un resfriado/la gripe; **she had her bag stolen/her arm broken** le robaron el bolso/se rompió un brazo; **to ~ an operation** operarse
7 (+ noun): **to ~ a swim/walk/bath/rest** nadar/dar un paseo/darse un baño/descansar; **let's ~ a look** vamos a ver; **to ~ a meeting/party** celebrar una reunión/una fiesta; **let me ~ a try** déjame intentarlo

have out vt: **to ~ it out with sb** (settle a problem etc) dejar las cosas en claro con alguien

haven ['heɪvn] n puerto; (fig) refugio

haven't ['hævnt] = have not

havoc ['hævək] n estragos mpl

hawk [hɔːk] n halcón m

hay [heɪ] n heno; **~ fever** n fiebre f del heno; **~stack** n almiar m

haywire ['heɪwaɪə*] (inf) adj: **to go ~** (plan) embrollarse

hazard ['hæzəd] n peligro ♦ vt aventurar; **~ous** adj peligroso; **~ warning lights** npl (AUT) señales fpl de emergencia

haze [heɪz] n neblina

hazelnut ['heɪzlnʌt] n avellana

hazy ['heɪzɪ] adj brumoso; (idea) vago

he [hiː] pron él; **~ who ...** él que ..., quien ...

head [hed] n cabeza; (leader) jefe/a m/f; (of school) director(a) m/f ♦ vt (list) encabezar; (group) capitanear; (company) dirigir; **~s (or tails)** cara (o cruz); **~ first** de cabeza; **~ over heels** (in love) perdidamente; **to ~ the ball** cabecear (la pelota); **~ for** vt fus dirigirse a; (disaster) ir camino de; **~ache** n dolor m de cabeza; **~dress** n tocado; **~ing** n título; **~lamp** (BRIT) n = **~light**; **~land** n promontorio; **~light** n faro; **~line** n titular m; **~long** adv (fall) de cabeza; (rush) precipitadamente; **~master/mistress** n director(a) m/f (de escuela); **~ office** n oficina central, central f; **~-on** adj (collision) de frente; **~phones** npl auriculares mpl; **~quarters** npl sede f central; (MIL) cuartel m general; **~rest** n reposa-cabezas m inv; **~room** n (in car) altura interior; (under bridge) (límite m de) altura; **~scarf** n pañuelo; **~strong** adj testarudo; **~ waiter** n maître m; **~way** n: **to make ~way** (fig) hacer progresos; **~wind** n viento contrario; **~y** adj (experience, period) apasionante; (wine) cabezón; (atmosphere) embriagador(a)

heal [hiːl] vt curar ♦ vi cicatrizarse

health [hɛlθ] n salud f; ~ **food** n alimentos mpl orgánicos; **the H~ Service** (BRIT) n el servicio de salud pública; ≈ el Insalud (SP); ~**y** adj sano, saludable

heap [hi:p] n montón m ♦ vt: **to ~ (up)** amontonar; **to ~ sth with** llenar algo hasta arriba de; ~**s of** un montón de

hear [hɪə*] (pt, pp **heard**) vt (also LAW) oír; (news) saber ♦ vi oír; **to ~ about** oír hablar de; **to ~ from sb** tener noticias de uno; ~**ing** n (sense) oído m; (LAW) vista; ~**ing aid** n audífono; ~**say** n rumores mpl, hablillas fpl

hearse [hə:s] n coche m fúnebre

heart [hɑ:t] n corazón m; (fig) valor m; (of lettuce) cogollo; ~**s** npl (CARDS) corazones mpl; **to lose/take** ~ descorazonarse/cobrar ánimo; **at** ~ en el fondo; **by** ~ (learn, know) de memoria; ~ **attack** n infarto de miocardio); ~**beat** n latido (del corazón); ~**breaking** adj desgarrador(a); ~**broken** adj: **she was** ~**broken about it** esto le se partió el corazón; ~**burn** n acedía; ~ **failure** n fallo cardíaco; ~**felt** adj (deeply felt) más sentido

hearth [hɑ:θ] n (fireplace) chimenea

hearty ['hɑ:tɪ] adj (person) campechano; (laugh) sano; (dislike, support) absoluto

heat [hi:t] n calor m; (SPORT: also: qualifying ~) prueba eliminatoria ♦ vt calentar; ~ **up** vi calentarse ♦ vt calentar; ~**ed** adj caliente; (fig) acalorado; ~**er** n estufa; (in car) calefacción f

heath [hi:θ] (BRIT) n brezal m

heather ['hɛðə*] n brezo

heating ['hi:tɪŋ] n calefacción f

heatstroke ['hi:tstrəuk] n insolación f

heatwave ['hi:tweɪv] n ola de calor

heave [hi:v] vt (pull) tirar; (push) empujar con esfuerzo; (lift) levantar (con esfuerzo) ♦ vi (chest) palpitar; (retch) tener náuseas ♦ n tirón m; empujón m; **to ~ a sigh** suspirar

heaven ['hɛvn] n cielo m; (fig) una maravilla; ~**ly** adj celestial; (fig) maravilloso

heavily ['hɛvɪlɪ] adv pesadamente; (drink, smoke) con exceso; (sleep, sigh) profundamente; (depend) mucho

heavy ['hɛvɪ] adj pesado; (work, blow) duro; (sea, rain, meal) fuerte; (drinker, smoker) grande; (responsibility) grave; (schedule) ocupado; (weather) bochornoso; ~ **goods vehicle** n vehículo pesado; ~**weight** n (SPORT) peso pesado

Hebrew ['hi:bru:] adj, n (LING) hebreo

heckle ['hɛkl] vt interrumpir

hectic ['hɛktɪk] adj agitado

he'd [hi:d] = **he would; he had**

hedge [hɛdʒ] n seto ♦ vi contestar con evasivas; **to ~ one's bets** (fig) cubrirse

hedgehog ['hɛdʒhɔg] n erizo

heed [hi:d] vt (also: **take ~ of**) (pay attention to) hacer caso de; ~**less** adj: **to be ~less (of)** no hacer caso de (de)

heel [hi:l] n talón m; (of shoe) tacón m ♦ vt (shoe) poner tacón a

hefty ['hɛftɪ] adj (person) fornido; (parcel, profit) gordo

heifer ['hɛfə*] n novilla, ternera

height [haɪt] n (of person) estatura; (of building) altura; (high ground) cerro; (altitude) altitud f; (fig: of season): **at the ~ of summer** en los días más calurosos del verano; (: of power etc) cúspide f; (: of stupidity etc) colmo; ~**en** vt elevar; (fig) aumentar

heir [ɛə*] n heredero; ~**ess** n heredera; ~**loom** n reliquia de familia

held [hɛld] pt, pp of **hold**

helicopter ['hɛlɪkɔptə*] n helicóptero

hell [hɛl] n infierno; ~**!** (inf) ¡demonios!

he'll [hi:l] = **he will; he shall**

hello [hə'ləu] excl ¡hola!; (to attract attention) ¡oiga!; (surprise) ¡caramba!

helm [hɛlm] n (NAUT) timón m

helmet ['hɛlmɪt] n casco

help [hɛlp] n ayuda; (cleaner etc) criada, asistenta ♦ vt ayudar; ~**!** ¡socorro!; ~ **yourself** sírvete; **he can't ~ it** no es culpa suya; ~**er** n ayudante m/f; ~**ful** adj útil; (person) servicial; (advice) útil; ~**ing** n ración f; ~**less** adj (incapable) incapaz; (defenceless) indefenso

hem [hɛm] n dobladillo ♦ vt poner or coser el dobladillo; ~ **in** vt cercar

hemorrhage ['hɛmərɪdʒ] (US) n = **haemorrhage**

hemorrhoids ['hɛmərɔɪdz] (US) npl = **haemorrhoids**

hen [hɛn] n gallina; (female bird) hembra

hence [hɛns] adv (therefore) por lo tanto; **2 years** ~ de aquí a 2 años; ~**forth** adv de hoy en adelante

hepatitis [hɛpə'taɪtɪs] n hepatitis f

her [hə:*] pron (direct) la; (indirect) le; (stressed, after prep) ella ♦ adj su; see also **me; my**

herald ['hɛrəld] n heraldo ♦ vt anunciar; ~**ry** n heráldica

herb [hə:b] n hierba

herd [hə:d] n rebaño

here [hɪə*] adv aquí; (at this point) en este punto; ~**!** (present) ¡presente!; ~ **is/are** aquí está/están; ~ **she is** aquí está; ~**after** adv en el futuro; ~**by** adv (in letter) por la presente

heritage ['hɛrɪtɪdʒ] n patrimonio

hermit ['hə:mɪt] n ermitaño/a

hernia ['hə:nɪə] n hernia

hero ['hɪərəu] (pl ~**es**) n héroe m; (in book, film) protagonista m

heroin ['hɛrəuɪn] n heroína

heroine ['hɛrəuɪn] n heroína; (in book, film) protagonista

heron ['herən] *n* garza

herring ['herɪŋ] *n* arenque *m*

hers [həːz] *pron* (el) suyo/(la) suya *etc*; *see also* mine¹

herself [həː'self] *pron* (*reflexive*) se; (*emphatic*) ella misma; (*after prep*) sí (misma); *see also* oneself

he's [hiːz] = he is; he has

hesitant ['hezɪtənt] *adj* vacilante

hesitate ['hezɪteɪt] *vi* vacilar; (*in speech*) titubear; (*be unwilling*) resistirse a;

hesitation ['-teɪʃən] *n* indecisión *f*; titubeo; dudas *fpl*

heterosexual [hetərəu'seksjuəl] *adj* heterosexual

heyday ['heɪdeɪ] *n*: **the ~ of** el apogeo de

HGV *n abbr* = **heavy goods vehicle**

hi [haɪ] *excl* ¡hola!; (*to attract attention*) ¡oiga!

hiatus [haɪ'eɪtəs] *n* vacío

hibernate ['haɪbəneɪt] *vi* invernar

hiccough ['hɪkʌp] = **hiccup**

hiccup ['hɪkʌp] *vi* hipar; ~**s** *npl* hipo

hide [haɪd] (*pt* hid, *pp* hidden) *n* (*skin*) piel *f* ♦ *vt* esconder, ocultar ♦ *vi*: **to ~ (from sb)** esconderse *u* ocultarse (de uno); ~**-and-seek** *n* escondite *m*

hideous ['hɪdɪəs] *adj* horrible

hiding ['haɪdɪŋ] *n* (*beating*) paliza; **to be in ~** (*concealed*) estar escondido

hierarchy ['haɪərɑːkɪ] *n* jerarquía

hi-fi ['haɪfaɪ] *n* estéreo, hifi *m* ♦ *adj* de alta fidelidad

high [haɪ] *adj* alto; (*speed, number*) grande; (*price*) elevado; (*wind*) fuerte; (*voice*) agudo ♦ *adv* alto, a gran altura; **it is 20 m ~** tiene 20 m de altura; **~ in the air** en las alturas; **~brow** *adj* intelectual; **~chair** *n* silla alta; **~er education** *n* educación *f* o enseñanza superior; **~-handed** *adj* despótico; **~-heeled** *adj* de tacón alto; **~ jump** *n* (*SPORT*) salto de altura; **the H~lands** *npl* las tierras altas de Escocia; **~light** *n* (*fig: of event*) punto culminante; (*in hair*) reflejo ♦ *vt* subrayar; **~ly** *adv* (*critical, confidential*) sumamente; (*a lot*): **to speak/think ~ly of** hablar muy bien de/tener en mucho a; **~ly strung** *adj* hipertenso; **~ness** *n* altura; **Her** or **His H~ness** Su Alteza; **~-pitched** *adj* agudo; **~-rise block** *n* torre *f* de pisos; **~ school** *n* ≈ Instituto Nacional de Bachillerato (*SP*); **~ season** (*BRIT*) *n* temporada alta; **~ street** (*BRIT*) *n* calle *f* mayor; **~way** *n* carretera; (*US*) carretera nacional; autopista; **H~way Code** (*BRIT*) *n* código de la circulación

hijack ['haɪdʒæk] *vt* secuestrar; **~er** *n* secuestrador(a) *m/f*

hike [haɪk] *vi* (*go walking*) ir de excursión (a pie) ♦ *n* caminata; **~r** *n* excursionista *m/f*;

hiking *n* senderismo

hilarious [hɪ'leərɪəs] *adj* divertidísimo

hill [hɪl] *n* colina; (*high*) montaña; (*slope*) cuesta; **~side** *n* ladera; **~ walking** *n* senderismo (de montaña); **~y** *adj* montañoso

hilt [hɪlt] *n* (*of sword*) empuñadura; **to the ~** (*fig: support*) incondicionalmente

him [hɪm] *pron* (*direct*) le, lo; (*indirect*) le; (*stressed, after prep*) él; *see also* me; **~self** *pron* (*reflexive*) se; (*emphatic*) él mismo; (*after prep*) sí (mismo); *see also* oneself

hinder ['hɪndə*] *vt* estorbar, impedir; **hindrance** ['hɪndrəns] *n* estorbo

hindsight ['haɪndsaɪt] *n*: **with ~** en retrospectiva

Hindu ['hɪnduː] *n* hindú *m/f*

hinge [hɪndʒ] *n* bisagra, gozne *m* ♦ *vi* (*fig*): **to ~ on** depender de

hint [hɪnt] *n* indirecta; (*advice*) consejo; (*sign*) dejo ♦ *vt*: **to ~ that** insinuar que ♦ *vi*: **to ~ at** hacer alusión a

hip [hɪp] *n* cadera

hippopotamus [hɪpə'pɔtəməs] (*pl* **~es** or **hippopotami**) *n* hipopótamo

hire ['haɪə*] *vt* (*BRIT: car, equipment*) alquilar; (*worker*) contratar ♦ *n* alquiler *m*; **for ~** se alquila; (*taxi*) libre; **~(d) car** (*BRIT*) *n* coche *m* de alquiler; **~ purchase** (*BRIT*) *n* compra a plazos

his [hɪz] *pron* (el) suyo/(la) suya *etc* ♦ *adj* su; *see also* mine¹; **my**

Hispanic [hɪs'pænɪk] *adj* hispánico

hiss [hɪs] *vi* silbar

historian [hɪ'stɔːrɪən] *n* historiador(a) *m/f*

historic(al) [hɪ'stɔrɪk(l)] *adj* histórico

history ['hɪstərɪ] *n* historia

hit [hɪt] (*pt, pp* hit) *vt* (*strike*) golpear, pegar; (*reach: target*) alcanzar; (*collide with: car*) chocar contra; (*fig: affect*) afectar ♦ *n* golpe *m*; (*success*) éxito; **to ~ it off with sb** llevarse bien con uno; **~-and-run driver** *n* conductor(a) que atropella y huye

hitch [hɪtʃ] *vt* (*fasten*) atar, amarrar; (*also: ~ up*) remangar ♦ *n* (*difficulty*) dificultad *f*; **to ~ a lift** hacer autostop

hitch-hike *vi* hacer autostop, **~hiking** *n* autostop *m*

hi-tech ['haɪtek] *adj* de alta tecnología

hitherto ['hɪðə'tuː] *adv* hasta ahora

HIV *n abbr* (= *human immunodeficiency virus*) VIH *m*; **~-negative/positive** *adj* VIH negativo/positivo

hive [haɪv] *n* colmena

HMS *abbr* = **His (Her) Majesty's Ship**

hoard [hɔːd] *n* (*treasure*) tesoro; (*stockpile*) provisión *f* ♦ *vt* acumular; (*goods in short supply*) acaparar; **~ing** *n* (*for posters*) cartelera

hoarse [hɔːs] *adj* ronco

hoax [həʊks] n trampa

hob [hɒb] n quemador m

hobble ['hɒbl] vi cojear

hobby ['hɒbɪ] n pasatiempo, afición f

hobo ['həʊbəʊ] (US) n vagabundo

hockey ['hɒkɪ] n hockey m

hog [hɒg] n cerdo, puerco ♦ vt (fig) acaparar; **to go the whole ~** poner toda la carne en el asador

hoist [hɔɪst] n (crane) grúa ♦ vt levantar, alzar; (flag, sail) izar

hold [həʊld] (pt, pp held) vt sostener; (contain) contener; (have: power, qualification) tener; (keep back) retener; (believe) sostener; (consider) considerar; (keep in position): **to ~ one's head up** mantener la cabeza alta; (meeting) celebrar ♦ vi (withstand pressure) resistir; (be valid) valer ♦ n (grasp) asimiento; (fig) dominio; **~ the line!** (TEL) ¡no cuelgue!; **to ~ one's own** (fig) defenderse; **to catch** or **get (a) ~ of** agarrarse or asirse de; **~ back** vt retener; (secret) ocultar; **~ down** vt (person) sujetar; (job) mantener; **~ off** vt (enemy) rechazar; **~ on** vi agarrarse bien; (wait) esperar; **~ on!** (TEL) ¡(espere) un momento!; **~ on to** vt fus agarrarse a; (keep) guardar; **~ out** vt ofrecer ♦ vi (resist) resistir; **~ up** vt (raise) levantar; (support) apoyar; (delay) retrasar; (rob) asaltar; **~all** (BRIT) n bolsa; **~er** n (container) receptáculo; (of ticket, record) poseedor(a) m/f; (of office, title etc) titular m/f; **~ing** n (share) interés m; (farmland) parcela; **~up** n (robbery) atraco; (delay) retraso; (BRIT: in traffic) embotellamiento

hole [həʊl] n agujero

holiday ['hɒlədɪ] n vacaciones fpl; (public ~) (día m de) fiesta, día m feriado; **on ~** de vacaciones; **~ camp** n (BRIT: also: **~ centre**) centro de vacaciones; **~-maker** (BRIT) n turista m/f; **~ resort** n centro turístico

holiness ['həʊlɪnɪs] n santidad f

Holland ['hɒlənd] n Holanda

hollow ['hɒləʊ] adj hueco; (claim) vacío; (eyes) hundido; (sound) sordo ♦ n hueco; (in ground) hoyo ♦ vt: **to ~ out** excavar

holly ['hɒlɪ] n acebo

holocaust ['hɒləkɔːst] n holocausto

holy ['həʊlɪ] adj santo, sagrado; (water) bendito

homage ['hɒmɪdʒ] n homenaje m

home [həʊm] n casa; (country) patria; (institution) asilo ♦ cpd (domestic) casero, de casa; (ECON, POL) nacional ♦ adv (direction) a casa; (right in: nail etc) a fondo; **at ~** en casa; (in country) en el país; (fig) como pez en el agua; **to go/come ~** ir/volver a casa; **make yourself at ~** ¡estás en tu casa!; **~ address** n domicilio; **~land** n tierra natal; **~less** adj sin

hogar, sin casa; **~ly** adj (simple) sencillo; **~-made** adj casero; **H~ Office** (BRIT) n Ministerio del Interior; **~ page** n página de inicio; **~ rule** n autonomía; **H~ Secretary** (BRIT) n Ministro del Interior; **~sick** adj: **to be ~sick** tener morriña, sentir nostalgia; **~ town** n ciudad f natal; **~ward** ['həʊmwəd] adj (journey) hacia casa; **~work** n deberes mpl

homoeopathic [həʊmɪə'pæθɪk] (US **homeopathic**) adj homeopático

homosexual [hɒməʊ'seksjʊəl] adj, n homosexual m/f

Honduran [hɒn'djʊərən] adj, a hondureño/a m/f

Honduras [hɒn'djʊərəs] n Honduras f

honest ['ɒnɪst] adj honrado; (sincere) franco, sincero; **~ly** adv honradamente; francamente; **~y** n honradez f

honey ['hʌnɪ] n miel f; **~comb** n panal m; **~moon** n luna de miel; **~suckle** n madreselva

honk [hɒŋk] vi (AUT) tocar el pito, pitar

honorary ['ɒnərərɪ] adj (member, president) de honor; (title) honorífico; **~ degree** doctorado honoris causa

honour ['ɒnə*] (US **honor**) vt honrar; (commitment, promise) cumplir con ♦ n honor m, honra; **~able** adj honorable; **~s degree** n (SCOL) título de licenciado con calificación alta

hood [hʊd] n capucha; (BRIT: AUT) capota; (US: AUT) capó m; (of cooker) campana de humos

hoof [huːf] (pl **hooves**) n pezuña

hook [hʊk] n gancho; (on dress) corchete m, broche m; (for fishing) anzuelo ♦ vt enganchar; (fish) pescar

hooligan ['huːlɪgən] n gamberro

hoop [huːp] n aro

hooray [huː'reɪ] excl = **hurray**

hoot [huːt] (BRIT) vi (AUT) tocar el pito, pitar; (siren) sonar la sirena; (owl) ulular; **~er** (BRIT) n (AUT) pito, claxon m; (NAUT) sirena

Hoover ® ['huːvə*] (BRIT) n aspiradora ♦ vt: **h~** pasar la aspiradora por

hooves [huːvz] npl of **hoof**

hop [hɒp] vi saltar, brincar; (on one foot) saltar con un pie

hope [həʊp] vt, vi esperar ♦ n esperanza; **I ~ so/not** espero que sí/no; **~ful** adj (person) optimista; (situation) prometedor(a); **~fully** adv con esperanza; (one hopes): **~fully he will recover** esperamos que se recupere; **~less** adj desesperado; (person): **to be ~less** ser un desastre

hops [hɒps] npl lúpulo

horizon [hə'raɪzn] n horizonte m; **~tal** [hɒrɪ'zɒntl] adj horizontal

hormone ['hɔːməʊn] n hormona

horn [hɔːn] n cuerno; (MUS: also: French ~) trompa; (AUT) pito, claxon m
hornet ['hɔːnɪt] n avispón m
horoscope ['hɔrəskəup] n horóscopo
horrible ['hɔrɪbl] adj horrible
horrid ['hɔrɪd] adj horrible, horroroso
horrify ['hɔrɪfaɪ] vt horrorizar
horror ['hɔrə*] n horror m; ~ **film** n película de horror
hors d'œuvre [ɔː'dəːvrə] n entremeses mpl
horse [hɔːs] n caballo; ~**back** n: **on ~back** a caballo; ~ **chestnut** n (tree) castaño de Indias; (nut) castaña de Indias; ~**man/woman** (irreg) n jinete/a m/f; ~**power** n caballo (de fuerza); ~-**racing** n carreras fpl de caballos; ~**radish** n rábano picante; ~**shoe** n herradura
hose [həuz] n (also: ~-pipe) manguera
hospitable [hɔs'pɪtəbl] adj hospitalario
hospital ['hɔspɪtl] n hospital m
hospitality [hɔspɪ'tælɪtɪ] n hospitalidad f
host [həust] n anfitrión m; (TV, RADIO) presentador m; (REL) hostia; (large number): **a ~ of** multitud de
hostage ['hɔstɪdʒ] n rehén m
hostel ['hɔstl] n hostal m; (youth) ~ albergue m juvenil
hostess ['həustɪs] n anfitriona; (BRIT: air ~) azafata; (TV, RADIO) presentadora
hostile ['hɔstaɪl] adj hostil
hot [hɔt] adj caliente; (weather) caluroso, de calor; (as opposed to warm) muy caliente; (spicy) picante; **to be ~** (person) tener calor; (object) estar caliente; (weather) hacer calor; ~**bed** n (fig) semillero; ~ **dog** n perro caliente
hotel [həu'tel] n hotel m
hot: ~**house** n invernadero; ~ **line** n (POL) teléfono rojo; ~**ly** adv con pasión, apasionadamente; ~-**water bottle** n bolsa de agua caliente
hound [haund] vt acosar ♦ n perro (de caza)
hour ['auə*] n hora; ~**ly** adj (de) cada hora
house [n haus, pl 'hauzɪz, vb hauz] n (gen, firm) casa; (POL) cámara; (THEATRE) sala ♦ vt (person) alojar; (collection) albergar; **on the ~** (fig) la casa invita; ~ **arrest** n arresto domiciliario; ~**boat** n casa flotante; ~**bound** adj confinado en casa; ~**breaking** n allanamiento de morada; ~**hold** n familia; (home) casa; ~**keeper** n ama de llaves; ~**keeping** n (work) trabajos mpl domésticos; ~**keeping (money)** n dinero para gastos domésticos; ~-**warming party** n fiesta de estreno de una casa; ~**wife** (irreg) n ama de casa; ~**work** n faenas fpl (de la casa)
housing ['hauzɪŋ] n (act) alojamiento; (houses) viviendas fpl; ~ **development** n urbanización f; ~ **estate** (BRIT) n =

~ **development**
hovel ['hɔvl] n casucha
hover ['hɔvə*] vi flotar (en el aire); ~**craft** n aerodeslizador m
how [hau] adv (in what way) cómo; ~ **are you?** ¿cómo estás?; ~ **much milk/many people?** ¿cuánta leche/gente?; ~ **much does it cost?** ¿cuánto cuesta?; ~ **long have you been here?** ¿cuánto hace que estás aquí?; ~ **old are you?** ¿cuántos años tienes?; ~ **tall is he?** ¿cómo es de alto?; ~ **is school?** ¿cómo (te) va (en) la escuela?; ~ **was the film?** ¿qué tal la película?; ~ **lovely/awful!** ¡qué bonito/horror!
however [hau'evə*] adv: ~ **I do it** lo haga como lo haga; ~ **cold it is** por mucho frío que haga; ~ **fast he runs** por muy rápido que corra; ~ **did you do it?** ¿cómo lo hiciste? ♦ conj sin embargo, no obstante
howl [haul] n aullido ♦ vi aullar; (person) dar alaridos; (wind) ulular
H.P. n abbr = **hire purchase**
h.p. abbr = **horse power**
HQ n abbr = **headquarters**
hub [hʌb] n (of wheel) cubo; (fig) centro
hubcap ['hʌbkæp] n tapacubos m inv
huddle ['hʌdl] vi: **to ~ together** acurrucarse
hue [hjuː] n color m, matiz m
huff [hʌf] n: **in a ~** enojado
hug [hʌg] vt abrazar; (thing) apretar con los brazos
huge [hjuːdʒ] adj enorme
hull [hʌl] n (of ship) casco
hullo [hə'ləu] excl = **hello**
hum [hʌm] vt tararear, canturrear ♦ vi tararear, canturrear; (insect) zumbar
human ['hjuːmən] adj, n humano; ~**e** [hjuː'meɪn] adj humano, humanitario; ~**itarian** [hjuːmænɪ'tɛərɪən] adj humanitario; ~**ity** [hjuː'mænɪtɪ] n humanidad f
humble ['hʌmbl] adj humilde
humdrum ['hʌmdrʌm] adj (boring) monótono, aburrido
humid ['hjuːmɪd] adj húmedo
humiliate [hjuː'mɪlɪeɪt] vt humillar
humorous ['hjuːmərəs] adj gracioso, divertido
humour ['hjuːmə*] (US **humor**) n humorismo, sentido del humor; (mood) humor m ♦ vt (person) complacer
hump [hʌmp] n (in ground) montículo; (camel's) giba
hunch [hʌntʃ] n (premonition) presentimiento; ~**back** n joroba m/f; ~**ed** adj jorobado
hundred ['hʌndrəd] num ciento; (before n) cien; ~**s of** centenares de; ~**weight** n (BRIT) = 50.8 kg; 112 lb; (US) = 45.3 kg; 100 lb
hung [hʌŋ] pt, pp of **hang**

Hungarian [hʌŋ'gɛərɪən] *adj, n* húngaro/a
m/f
Hungary ['hʌŋgərɪ] *n* Hungría
hunger ['hʌŋgə*] *n* hambre *f* ♦ *vi*: **to ~ for**
(*fig*) tener hambre de, anhelar; **~ strike** *n*
huelga de hambre
hungry ['hʌŋgrɪ] *adj*: **~ (for)** hambriento
(de); **to be ~** tener hambre
hunk [hʌŋk] *n* (*of bread etc*) trozo, pedazo
hunt [hʌnt] *vt* (*seek*) buscar; (*SPORT*) cazar
♦ *vi* (*search*): **to ~ (for)** buscar; (*SPORT*) cazar
♦ *n* búsqueda; caza, cacería; **~er** *n*
cazador(a) *m/f*; **~ing** *n* caza
hurdle ['hɜːdl] *n* (*SPORT*) valla; (*fig*) obstáculo
m
hurl [hɜːl] *vt* lanzar, arrojar
hurrah [hu'rɑː] *excl* = **hurray**
hurray [hu'reɪ] *excl* ¡viva!
hurricane ['hʌrɪkən] *n* huracán *m*
hurried ['hʌrɪd] *adj* (*rushed*) hecho de prisa;
~ly *adv* con prisa, apresuradamente
hurry ['hʌrɪ] *n* prisa ♦ *vi* (*also*: **~ up**)
apresurarse, darse prisa ♦ *vt* (*also*: **~ up**:
person) dar prisa a; (: *work*) apresurar, hacer
de prisa; **to be in a ~** tener prisa
hurt [hɜːt] (*pt, pp* **hurt**) *vt* hacer daño a ♦ *vi*
doler ♦ *adj* lastimado; **~ful** *adj* (*remark etc*)
hiriente
hurtle ['hɜːtl] *vi*: **to ~ past** pasar como un
rayo; **to ~ down** ir a toda velocidad
husband ['hʌzbənd] *n* marido
hush [hʌʃ] *n* silencio ♦ *vt* hacer callar; **~!**
¡chitón!, ¡cállate!; **~ up** *vt* encubrir
husk [hʌsk] *n* (*of wheat*) cáscara
husky ['hʌskɪ] *adj* ronco ♦ *n* perro esquimal
hustle ['hʌsl] *vt* (*hurry*) dar prisa a ♦ *n*: **~ and
bustle** ajetreo
hut [hʌt] *n* cabaña; (*shed*) cobertizo
hutch [hʌtʃ] *n* conejera
hyacinth ['haɪəsɪnθ] *n* jacinto
hydrant ['haɪdrənt] *n* (*also*: *fire* **~**) boca de
incendios
hydraulic [haɪ'drɔːlɪk] *adj* hidráulico
hydroelectric [haɪdrəʊ'lektrɪk] *adj*
hidroeléctrico
hydrofoil ['haɪdrəfɔɪl] *n* aerodeslizador *m*
hydrogen ['haɪdrədʒən] *n* hidrógeno
hygiene ['haɪdʒiːn] *n* higiene *f*; **hygienic**
[-'dʒiːnɪk] *adj* higiénico
hymn [hɪm] *n* himno
hype [haɪp] (*inf*) *n* bombardeo publicitario
hypermarket ['haɪpəmɑːkɪt] *n*
hipermercado
hyphen ['haɪfn] *n* guión *m*
hypnotize ['hɪpnətaɪz] *vt* hipnotizar
hypocrisy [hɪ'pɒkrɪsɪ] *n* hipocresía;
hypocrite ['hɪpəkrɪt] *n* hipócrita *m/f*;
hypocritical [hɪpə'krɪtɪkl] *adj* hipócrita
hypothesis [haɪ'pɒθɪsɪs] (*pl* **hypotheses**) *n*
hipótesis *f inv*

hysteria [hɪ'stɪərɪə] *n* histeria; **hysterical**
[-'sterɪkl] *adj* histérico; (*funny*) para morirse
de risa; **hysterics** [-'sterɪks] *npl* histeria; **to
be in hysterics** (*fig*) morirse de risa

I, i

I [aɪ] *pron* yo
ice [aɪs] *n* hielo; (~ *cream*) helado ♦ *vt* (*cake*)
alcorzar ♦ *vi* (*also*: **~ over**, **~ up**) helarse;
~berg *n* iceberg *m*; **~box** *n* (*BRIT*)
congelador *m*; (*US*) nevera (*SP*), refrigeradora
(*AM*); **~ cream** *n* helado; **~ cube** *n* cubito
de hielo; **~d** *adj* (*cake*) escarchado; (*drink*)
helado; **~ hockey** *n* hockey *m* sobre hielo
Iceland ['aɪslənd] *n* Islandia
ice: ~ lolly (*BRIT*) *n* polo; **~ rink** *n* pista de
hielo; **~ skating** *n* patinaje *m* sobre hielo
icicle ['aɪsɪkl] *n* carámbano
icing ['aɪsɪŋ] *n* (*CULIN*) alcorza; **~ sugar** (*BRIT*)
n azúcar *m* glas(eado)
icy ['aɪsɪ] *adj* helado
I'd [aɪd] = **I would**; **I had**
idea [aɪ'dɪə] *n* idea
ideal [aɪ'dɪəl] *n* ideal *m* ♦ *adj* ideal
identical [aɪ'dentɪkl] *adj* idéntico
identification [aɪdentɪfɪ'keɪʃən] *n*
identificación *f*; (*means of*) **~** documentos
mpl personales
identify [aɪ'dentɪfaɪ] *vt* identificar
Identikit ® [aɪ'dentɪkɪt] *n*: **~ (picture)**
retrato-robot *m*
identity [aɪ'dentɪtɪ] *n* identidad *f*; **~ card** *n*
carnet *m* de identidad
ideology [aɪdɪ'ɒlədʒɪ] *n* ideología
idiom ['ɪdɪəm] *n* modismo; (*style of speaking*)
lenguaje *m*
idiosyncrasy [ɪdɪəʊ'sɪŋkrəsɪ] *n* idiosincrasia
idiot ['ɪdɪət] *n* idiota *m/f*; **~ic** [-'ɔtɪk] *adj* tonto
idle ['aɪdl] *adj* (*inactive*) ocioso; (*lazy*)
holgazán/ana; (*unemployed*) parado,
desocupado; (*machinery etc*) parado; (*talk
etc*) frívolo ♦ *vi* (*machine*) marchar en vacío
idol ['aɪdl] *n* ídolo; **~ize** *vt* idolatrar
i.e. *abbr* (= *that is*) esto es
if [ɪf] *conj* si; **~ necessary** si fuera necesario, si
hiciese falta; **~ I were you** yo en tu lugar;
~ so/not de ser así/si no; **~ only I could!** ¡ojalá
pudiera!; *see also* **as**; **even**
igloo ['ɪgluː] *n* iglú *m*
ignite [ɪg'naɪt] *vt* (*set fire to*) encender ♦ *vi*
encenderse
ignition [ɪg'nɪʃən] *n* (*AUT*: *process*) ignición *f*;
(: *mechanism*) encendido; **to switch on/off
the ~** arrancar/apagar el motor; **~ key** *n*
(*AUT*) llave *f* de contacto
ignorant ['ɪgnərənt] *adj* ignorante; **to be ~ of**
ignorar

ignore [ɪɡ'nɔː*] vt (person, advice) no hacer caso de; (fact) pasar por alto

I'll [aɪl] = **I will; I shall**

ill [ɪl] adj enfermo, malo ♦ n mal m ♦ adv mal; **to be taken ~** ponerse enfermo; **~-advised** adj (decision) imprudente; **~-at-ease** adj incómodo

illegal [ɪ'liːɡl] adj ilegal

illegible [ɪ'ledʒɪbl] adj ilegible

illegitimate [ɪlɪ'dʒɪtɪmət] adj ilegítimo

ill-fated adj malogrado

ill feeling n rencor m

illicit [ɪ'lɪsɪt] adj ilícito

illiterate [ɪ'lɪtərət] adj analfabeto

ill: ~-mannered adj mal educado; **~ness** n enfermedad f; **~-treat** vt maltratar

illuminate [ɪ'luːmɪneɪt] vt (room, street) iluminar, alumbrar; **illumination** [-'neɪʃən] n alumbrado; **illuminations** npl (decorative lights) iluminaciones fpl, luces fpl

illusion [ɪ'luːʒən] n ilusión f; (trick) truco

illustrate ['ɪləstreɪt] vt ilustrar

illustration [ɪlə'streɪʃən] n (act of illustrating) ilustración f; (example) ejemplo, ilustración f; (in book) lámina

illustrious [ɪ'lʌstrɪəs] adj ilustre

I'm [aɪm] = **I am**

image ['ɪmɪdʒ] n imagen f; **~ry** [-ərɪ] n imágenes fpl

imaginary [ɪ'mædʒɪnərɪ] adj imaginario

imagination [ɪmædʒɪ'neɪʃən] n imaginación f; (inventiveness) inventiva

imaginative [ɪ'mædʒɪnətɪv] adj imaginativo

imagine [ɪ'mædʒɪn] vt imaginarse

imbalance [ɪm'bæləns] n desequilibrio

imitate ['ɪmɪteɪt] vt imitar; **imitation** [ɪmɪ'teɪʃən] n imitación f; (copy) copia

immaculate [ɪ'mækjulət] adj inmaculado

immaterial [ɪmə'tɪərɪəl] adj (unimportant) sin importancia

immature [ɪmə'tjuə*] adj (person) inmaduro

immediate [ɪ'miːdɪət] adj inmediato; (pressing) urgente, apremiante; (nearest: family) próximo; (: neighbourhood) inmediato; **~ly** adv (at once) en seguida; (directly) inmediatamente; **~ly next to** muy junto a

immense [ɪ'mɛns] adj inmenso, enorme; (importance) enorme

immerse [ɪ'mɜːs] vt (submerge) sumergir; **to be ~d in** (fig) estar absorto en

immersion heater [ɪ'mɜːʃən-] (BRIT) n calentador m de inmersión

immigrant ['ɪmɪɡrənt] n inmigrante m/f; **immigration** [ɪmɪ'ɡreɪʃən] n inmigración f

imminent ['ɪmɪnənt] adj inminente

immobile [ɪ'məubaɪl] adj inmóvil

immoral [ɪ'mɔrl] adj inmoral

immortal [ɪ'mɔːtl] adj inmortal

immune [ɪ'mjuːn] adj: **~ (to)** inmune (a); **immunity** n (MED, of diplomat) inmunidad f

immunize ['ɪmjunaɪz] vt inmunizar

impact ['ɪmpækt] n impacto

impair [ɪm'pɛə*] vt perjudicar

impart [ɪm'paːt] vt comunicar; (flavour) proporcionar

impartial [ɪm'paːʃl] adj imparcial

impassable [ɪm'paːsəbl] adj (barrier) infranqueable; (river, road) intransitable

impassive [ɪm'pæsɪv] adj impasible

impatience [ɪm'peɪʃəns] n impaciencia

impatient [ɪm'peɪʃənt] adj impaciente; **to get or grow ~** impacientarse

impeccable [ɪm'pekəbl] adj impecable

impede [ɪm'piːd] vt estorbar

impediment [ɪm'pedɪmənt] n obstáculo, estorbo; (also: speech ~) defecto (del habla)

impending [ɪm'pendɪŋ] adj inminente

imperative [ɪm'perətɪv] adj (tone) imperioso; (need) imprescindible

imperfect [ɪm'pɜːfɪkt] adj (goods etc) defectuoso ♦ n (LING: also: ~ tense) imperfecto

imperial [ɪm'pɪərɪəl] adj imperial

impersonal [ɪm'pɜːsənl] adj impersonal

impersonate [ɪm'pɜːsəneɪt] vt hacerse pasar por; (THEATRE) imitar

impertinent [ɪm'pɜːtɪnənt] adj impertinente, insolente

impervious [ɪm'pɜːvɪəs] adj impermeable; (fig): **~ to** insensible a

impetuous [ɪm'petjuəs] adj impetuoso

impetus ['ɪmpətəs] n ímpetu m; (fig) impulso

impinge [ɪm'pɪndʒ]: **to ~ on** vt fus (affect) afectar a

implement [n 'ɪmplɪmənt, vb 'ɪmplɪment] n herramienta; (for cooking) utensilio ♦ vt (regulation) hacer efectivo; (plan) realizar

implicit [ɪm'plɪsɪt] adj implícito; (belief, trust) absoluto

imply [ɪm'plaɪ] vt (involve) suponer; (hint) dar a entender que

impolite [ɪmpə'laɪt] adj mal educado

import [vb ɪm'pɔːt, n 'ɪmpɔːt] vt importar ♦ n (COMM) importación f; (: article) producto importado; (meaning) significado, sentido

importance [ɪm'pɔːtəns] n importancia

important [ɪm'pɔːtənt] adj importante; **it's not ~** no importa, no tiene importancia

importer [ɪm'pɔːtə*] n importador(a) m/f

impose [ɪm'pəuz] vt imponer ♦ vi: **to ~ on sb** abusar de uno; **imposing** adj imponente, impresionante

imposition [ɪmpə'zɪʃn] n (of tax etc) imposición f; **to be an ~ on** (person) molestar a

impossible [ɪm'pɔsɪbl] adj imposible; (person) insoportable

impotent ['ɪmpətənt] *adj* impotente

impound [ɪm'paund] *vt* embargar

impoverished [ɪm'pɔvərɪʃt] *adj* necesitado

impractical [ɪm'præktɪkl] *adj* (*person, plan*) poco práctico

imprecise [ɪmprɪ'saɪs] *adj* impreciso

impregnable [ɪm'pregnəbl] *adj* (*castle*) inexpugnable

impress [ɪm'pres] *vt* impresionar; (*mark*) estampar; **to ~ sth on sb** hacer entender algo a uno

impression [ɪm'preʃən] *n* impresión *f*; (*imitation*) imitación *f*; **to be under the ~ that** tener la impresión de que; **~ist** *n* impresionista *m/f*

impressive [ɪm'presɪv] *adj* impresionante

imprint ['ɪmprɪnt] *n* (*outline*) huella; (*PUBLISHING*) pie *m* de imprenta

imprison [ɪm'prɪzn] *vt* encarcelar; **~ment** *n* encarcelamiento; (*term of ~ment*) cárcel *f*

improbable [ɪm'prɔbəbl] *adj* improbable, inverosímil

improper [ɪm'prɔpə*] *adj* (*unsuitable: conduct etc*) incorrecto; (: *activities*) deshonesto

improve [ɪm'pru:v] *vt* mejorar; (*foreign language*) perfeccionar ♦ *vi* mejorarse; **~ment** *n* mejoramiento; perfección *f*; progreso

improvise ['ɪmprəvaɪz] *vt, vi* improvisar

impulse ['ɪmpʌls] *n* impulso; **to act on ~** obrar sin reflexión; **impulsive** [-'pʌlsɪv] *adj* irreflexivo

impure [ɪm'pjuə*] *adj* (*adulterated*) adulterado; (*morally*) impuro; **impurity** *n* impureza

---

KEYWORD

in [ɪn] *prep* **1** (*indicating place, position, with place names*) en; **~ the house/garden** en (la) casa/el jardín; **~ here/there** aquí/ahí or allí dentro; **~ London/England** en Londres/Inglaterra

2 (*indicating time*) en; **~ spring** en (la) primavera; **~ the afternoon** por la tarde; **at 4 o'clock ~ the afternoon** a las 4 de la tarde; **I did it ~ 3 hours/days** lo hice en 3 horas/días; **I'll see you ~ 2 weeks** *or* **~ 2 weeks' time** te veré dentro de 2 semanas

3 (*indicating manner etc*) en; **~ a loud/soft voice** en voz alta/baja; **~ pencil/ink** a lápiz/bolígrafo; **the boy ~ the blue shirt** el chico de la camisa azul

4 (*indicating circumstances*): **~ the sun/shade/rain** al sol/a la sombra/bajo la lluvia; **a change ~ policy** un cambio de política

5 (*indicating mood, state*): **~ tears** en lágrimas, llorando; **~ anger/despair** enfadado/desesperado; **to live ~ luxury** vivir lujosamente

6 (*with ratios, numbers*): **1 ~ 10 households, 1 household ~ 10** una de cada 10 familias; **20 pence ~ the pound** 20 peniques por libra; **they lined up ~ twos** se alinearon de dos en dos

7 (*referring to people, works*) en; entre; **the disease is common ~ children** la enfermedad es común entre los niños; **~ (the works of) Dickens** en (las obras de) Dickens

8 (*indicating profession etc*): **to be ~ teaching** estar en la enseñanza

9 (*after superlative*) de; **the best pupil ~ the class** el/la mejor alumno/a de la clase

10 (*with present participle*): **~ saying this** al decir esto

♦ *adv*: **to be ~** (*person: at home*) estar en casa; (*work*) estar; (*train, ship, plane*) haber llegado; (*in fashion*) estar de moda; **she'll be ~ later today** llegará más tarde hoy; **to ask sb ~** hacer pasar a uno; **to run/limp etc ~** entrar corriendo/cojeando *etc*

♦ *n*: **the ~s and outs** (*of proposal, situation etc*) los detalles

---

in. *abbr* = **inch**

inability [ɪnə'bɪlɪtɪ] *n*: **~ (to do)** incapacidad *f* (de hacer)

inaccurate [ɪn'ækjurət] *adj* inexacto, incorrecto

inadequate [ɪn'ædɪkwət] *adj* (*income, reply etc*) insuficiente; (*person*) incapaz

inadvertently [ɪnəd'vɜːtntlɪ] *adv* por descuido

inadvisable [ɪnəd'vaɪzəbl] *adj* poco aconsejable

inane [ɪ'neɪn] *adj* necio, fatuo

inanimate [ɪn'ænɪmət] *adj* inanimado

inappropriate [ɪnə'prəuprɪət] *adj* inadecuado; (*improper*) poco oportuno

inarticulate [ɪnɑː'tɪkjulət] *adj* (*person*) incapaz de expresarse; (*speech*) mal pronunciado

inasmuch as [ɪnəz'mʌtʃ-] *conj* puesto que, ya que

inauguration [ɪnɔːgju'reɪʃən] *n* ceremonia de apertura

inborn [ɪn'bɔːn] *adj* (*quality*) innato

inbred [ɪn'bred] *adj* innato; (*family*) engendrado por endogamia

Inc. *abbr* (*US*: = **incorporated**) S.A.

incapable [ɪn'keɪpəbl] *adj* incapaz

incapacitate [ɪnkə'pæsɪteɪt] *vt*: **to ~ sb** incapacitar a uno

incense [*n* 'ɪnsens, *vb* ɪn'sens] *n* incienso ♦ *vt* (*anger*) indignar, encolerizar

incentive [ɪn'sentɪv] *n* incentivo, estímulo

incessant [ɪn'sesnt] *adj* incesante, continuo; **~ly** *adv* constantemente

incest ['ɪnsest] n incesto

inch [ɪntʃ] n pulgada; **to be within an ~ of** estar a dos dedos de; **he didn't give an ~** no dio concesión alguna

incident ['ɪnsɪdnt] n incidente m

incidental [ɪnsɪ'dentl] adj accesorio; **~ to** relacionado con; **~ly** [-'dentəlɪ] adv (by the way) a propósito

incite [ɪn'saɪt] vt provocar

inclination [ɪnklɪ'neɪʃən] n (tendency) tendencia, inclinación f; (desire) deseo; (disposition) propensión f

incline [n 'ɪnklaɪn, vb ɪn'klaɪn] n pendiente m, cuesta ♦ vt (head) poner de lado ♦ vi inclinarse; **to be ~d to** (tend) ser propenso a

include [ɪn'kluːd] vt (incorporate) incluir; (in letter) adjuntar; **including** prep incluso, inclusive

inclusion [ɪn'kluːʒən] n inclusión f

inclusive [ɪn'kluːsɪv] adj inclusivo; **~ of tax** incluidos los impuestos

income ['ɪŋkʌm] n (earned) ingresos mpl; (from property etc) renta; (from investment etc) rédito; **~ tax** n impuesto sobre la renta

incoming ['ɪnkʌmɪŋ] adj (flight, government etc) entrante

incomparable [ɪn'kɔmpərəbl] adj incomparable, sin par

incompatible [ɪnkəm'pætɪbl] adj incompatible

incompetent [ɪn'kɔmpɪtənt] adj incompetente

incomplete [ɪnkəm'pliːt] adj (partial: achievement etc) incompleto; (unfinished: painting etc) inacabado

incongruous [ɪn'kɔŋgruəs] adj (strange) discordante; (inappropriate) incongruente

inconsiderate [ɪnkən'sɪdərət] adj desconsiderado

inconsistent [ɪnkən'sɪstənt] adj inconsecuente; (contradictory) incongruente; **~ with** (que) no concuerda con

inconspicuous [ɪnkən'spɪkjuəs] adj (colour, building etc) discreto; (person) que llama poco la atención

inconvenience [ɪnkən'viːnjəns] n inconvenientes mpl; (trouble) molestia, incomodidad f ♦ vt incomodar

inconvenient [ɪnkən'viːnjənt] adj incómodo, poco práctico; (time, place, visitor) inoportuno

incorporate [ɪn'kɔːpəreɪt] vt incorporar; (contain) comprender; (add) agregar; **~d** adj: **~d company** (US) ≈ sociedad f anónima

incorrect [ɪnkə'rekt] adj incorrecto

increase [n 'ɪnkriːs, vb ɪn'kriːs] n aumento ♦ vi aumentar; (grow) crecer; (price) subir ♦ vt aumentar; (price) subir; **increasing** adj creciente; **increasingly** adv cada vez más,

más y más

incredible [ɪn'kredɪbl] adj increíble

incubator ['ɪnkjubeɪtə*] n incubadora

incumbent [ɪn'kʌmbənt] adj: **it is ~ on him to ...** le incumbe ...

incur [ɪn'kɜː*] vt (expenditure) incurrir; (loss) sufrir; (anger, disapproval) provocar

indebted [ɪn'detɪd] adj: **to be ~ to sb** estar agradecido a uno

indecent [ɪn'diːsnt] adj indecente; **~ assault** (BRIT) n atentado contra el pudor; **~ exposure** n exhibicionismo

indecisive [ɪndɪ'saɪsɪv] adj indeciso

indeed [ɪn'diːd] adv efectivamente, en realidad; (in fact) en efecto; (furthermore) es más; **yes ~!** ¡claro que sí!

indefinitely [ɪn'defɪnɪtlɪ] adv (wait) indefinidamente

indemnity [ɪn'demnɪtɪ] n (insurance) indemnidad f; (compensation) indemnización f

independence [ɪndɪ'pendns] n independencia

independent [ɪndɪ'pendənt] adj independiente

index ['ɪndeks] (pl **~es**) n (in book) índice m; (: in library etc) catálogo; (pl **indices**: ratio, sign) exponente m; **~ card** n ficha; **~ed** (US) adj = **~-linked**; **~ finger** n índice m; **~-linked** (BRIT) adj vinculado al índice del coste de la vida

India ['ɪndɪə] n la India; **~n** adj, n indio/a m/f; **Red ~n** piel roja m/f; **~n Ocean** n: **the ~n Ocean** el Océano Índico

indicate ['ɪndɪkeɪt] vt indicar; **indication** [-'keɪʃən] n indicio, señal f; **indicative** [ɪn'dɪkətɪv] adj: **to be indicative of** indicar; **indicator** n indicador m; (AUT) intermitente m

indices ['ɪndɪsiːz] npl of **index**

indictment [ɪn'daɪtmənt] n acusación f

indifferent [ɪn'dɪfrənt] adj indiferente; (mediocre) regular

indigenous [ɪn'dɪdʒɪnəs] adj indígena

indigestion [ɪndɪ'dʒestʃən] n indigestión f

indignant [ɪn'dɪgnənt] adj: **to be ~ at sth/ with sb** indignarse por algo/con uno

indigo ['ɪndɪgəu] adj de color añil ♦ n añil m

indirect [ɪndɪ'rekt] adj indirecto

indiscreet [ɪndɪ'skriːt] adj indiscreto, imprudente

indiscriminate [ɪndɪ'skrɪmɪnət] adj indiscriminado

indisputable [ɪndɪ'spjuːtəbl] adj incontestable

indistinct [ɪndɪ'stɪŋkt] adj (noise, memory etc) confuso

individual [ɪndɪ'vɪdjuəl] n individuo ♦ adj individual; (personal) personal; (particular)

particular; **~ly** adv (*singly*) individualmente
indoctrinate [ɪn'dɒktrɪneɪt] vt adoctrinar
indoor ['ɪndɔ:*] adj (*swimming pool*) cubierto;
(*plant*) de interior; (*sport*) bajo cubierta; **~s**
[ɪn'dɔ:z] adv dentro
induce [ɪn'dju:s] vt inducir, persuadir; (*bring
about*) producir; (*birth*) provocar; **~ment** n
(*incentive*) incentivo; (*pej: bribe*) soborno
indulge [ɪn'dʌldʒ] vt (*whim*) satisfacer;
(*person*) complacer; (*child*) mimar ♦ vi: **to
~ in** darse el gusto de; **~nce** n vicio;
(*leniency*) indulgencia; **~nt** adj indulgente
industrial [ɪn'dʌstrɪəl] adj industrial;
~ action n huelga; **~ estate** (*BRIT*) n
polígono (*SP*) or zona (*AM*) industrial; **~ist** n
industrial m/f; **~ize** vt industrializar; **~ park**
(*US*) n = **~ estate**
industrious [ɪn'dʌstrɪəs] adj trabajador(a);
(*student*) aplicado
industry ['ɪndəstrɪ] n industria; (*diligence*)
aplicación f
inebriated [ɪ'ni:brɪeɪtɪd] adj borracho
inedible [ɪn'ɛdɪbl] adj incomible; (*poisonous*)
no comestible
ineffective [ɪnɪ'fɛktɪv] adj ineficaz, inútil
ineffectual [ɪnɪ'fɛktjuəl] adj = **ineffective**
inefficient [ɪnɪ'fɪʃənt] adj ineficaz, ineficiente
inept [ɪ'nɛpt] adj incompetente
inequality [ɪnɪ'kwɔlɪtɪ] n desigualdad f
inert [ɪ'nɜ:t] adj inerte, inactivo; (*immobile*)
inmóvil
inescapable [ɪnɪ'skeɪpəbl] adj ineludible
inevitable [ɪn'ɛvɪtəbl] adj inevitable;
inevitably adv inevitablemente
inexcusable [ɪnɪks'kju:zəbl] adj
imperdonable
inexpensive [ɪnɪk'spɛnsɪv] adj económico
inexperienced [ɪnɪk'spɪərɪənst] adj
inexperto
infallible [ɪn'fælɪbl] adj infalible
infamous ['ɪnfəməs] adj infame
infancy ['ɪnfənsɪ] n infancia
infant ['ɪnfənt] n niño/a; (*baby*) niño
pequeño, bebé m; (*pej*) aniñado
infantry ['ɪnfəntrɪ] n infantería
infant school (*BRIT*) n parvulario
infatuated [ɪn'fætjueɪtɪd] adj: **~ with** (*in
love*) loco por
infatuation [ɪnfætu'eɪʃən] n enamoramiento,
pasión f
infect [ɪn'fɛkt] vt (*wound*) infectar; (*food*)
contaminar; (*person, animal*) contagiar;
~ion [ɪn'fɛkʃən] n infección f; (*fig*) contagio;
~ious [ɪn'fɛkʃəs] adj (*also fig*) contagioso
infer [ɪn'fɜ:*] vt deducir, inferir
inferior [ɪn'fɪərɪə*] adj, n inferior m/f; **~ity**
[-rɪ'ɔrɪtɪ] n inferioridad f
infertile [ɪn'fɜ:taɪl] adj estéril; (*person*)
infecundo

infested [ɪn'fɛstɪd] adj: **~ with** plagado de
in-fighting n (*fig*) lucha(s) f(pl) interna(s)
infinite ['ɪnfɪnɪt] adj infinito
infinitive [ɪn'fɪnɪtɪv] n infinitivo
infinity [ɪn'fɪnɪtɪ] n infinito; (*an ~*) infinidad f
infirmary [ɪn'fɜ:mərɪ] n hospital m
inflamed [ɪn'fleɪmd] adj: **to become ~**
inflamarse
inflammable [ɪn'flæməbl] adj inflamable
inflammation [ɪnflə'meɪʃən] n inflamación f
inflatable [ɪn'fleɪtəbl] adj (*ball, boat*) inflable
inflate [ɪn'fleɪt] vt (*tyre, price etc*) inflar; (*fig*)
hinchar; **inflation** [ɪn'fleɪʃən] n (*ECON*)
inflación f
inflexible [ɪn'flɛksəbl] adj (*rule*) rígido;
(*person*) inflexible
inflict [ɪn'flɪkt] vt: **to ~ sth on sb** infligir algo
en uno
influence ['ɪnfluəns] n influencia ♦ vt influir
en, influenciar; **under the ~ of alcohol** en
estado de embriaguez; **influential** [-'ɛnʃl]
adj influyente
influenza [ɪnflu'ɛnzə] n gripe f
influx ['ɪnflʌks] n afluencia
inform [ɪn'fɔ:m] vt: **to ~ sb of sth** informar a
uno sobre or de algo ♦ vi: **to ~ on sb** delatar
a uno
informal [ɪn'fɔ:məl] adj (*manner, tone*)
familiar; (*dress, interview, occasion*) informal;
(*visit, meeting*) extraoficial; **~ity** [-'mælɪtɪ] n
informalidad f; sencillez f
informant [ɪn'fɔ:mənt] n informante m/f
information [ɪnfə'meɪʃən] n información f;
(*knowledge*) conocimientos mpl; **a piece of ~**
un dato; **~ desk** n (mostrador m de)
información f; **~ office** n información f
informative [ɪn'fɔ:mətɪv] adj informativo
informer [ɪn'fɔ:mə*] n (*also: police ~*)
soplón/ona m/f
infra-red [ɪnfrə'rɛd] adj infrarrojo
infrastructure ['ɪnfrəstrʌktʃə*] n (*of system
etc*) infraestructura
infringe [ɪn'frɪndʒ] vt infringir, violar ♦ vi: **to
~ on** abusar de; **~ment** n infracción f; (*of
rights*) usurpación f
infuriating [ɪn'fjuərɪeɪtɪŋ] adj (*habit, noise*)
enloquecedor(a)
ingenious [ɪn'dʒi:njəs] adj ingenioso;
ingenuity [-dʒɪ'nju:ɪtɪ] n ingeniosidad f
ingenuous [ɪn'dʒɛnjuəs] adj ingenuo
ingot ['ɪŋgət] n lingote m, barra
ingrained [ɪn'greɪnd] adj arraigado
ingratiate [ɪn'greɪʃɪeɪt] vt: **to ~ o.s. with**
congraciarse con
ingredient [ɪn'gri:dɪənt] n ingrediente m
inhabit [ɪn'hæbɪt] vt vivir en; **~ant** n
habitante m/f
inhale [ɪn'heɪl] vt inhalar ♦ vi (*breathe in*)
aspirar; (*in smoking*) tragar

inherent [ɪn'hɪərənt] *adj*: ~ **in** *or* **to** inherente a

inherit [ɪn'herɪt] *vt* heredar; **~ance** *n* herencia; (*fig*) patrimonio

inhibit [ɪn'hɪbɪt] *vt* inhibir, impedir; **~ed** *adj* (*PSYCH*) cohibido; **~ion** [-'bɪʃən] *n* cohibición *f*

inhospitable [ɪnhɔs'pɪtəbl] *adj* (*person*) inhospitalario; (*place*) inhóspito

inhuman [ɪn'hju:mən] *adj* inhumano

initial [ɪ'nɪʃl] *adj* primero ♦ *n* inicial *f* ♦ *vt* firmar con las iniciales; **~s** *npl* (*as signature*) iniciales *fpl*; (*abbreviation*) siglas *fpl*; **~ly** *adv* al principio

initiate [ɪ'nɪʃɪeɪt] *vt* iniciar; **to ~ proceedings against sb** (*LAW*) entablar proceso contra uno

initiative [ɪ'nɪʃɪətɪv] *n* iniciativa

inject [ɪn'dʒekt] *vt* inyectar; **to ~ sb with sth** inyectar algo a uno; **~ion** [ɪn'dʒekʃən] *n* inyección *f*

injunction [ɪn'dʒʌŋkʃən] *n* interdicto

injure ['ɪndʒə*] *vt* (*hurt*) herir, lastimar; (*fig: reputation etc*) perjudicar; **~d** *adj* (*person, arm*) herido, lastimado; **injury** *n* herida, lesión *f*; (*wrong*) perjuicio, daño; **injury time** *n* (*SPORT*) (tiempo de) descuento

injustice [ɪn'dʒʌstɪs] *n* injusticia

ink [ɪŋk] *n* tinta

inkling ['ɪŋklɪŋ] *n* sospecha; (*idea*) idea

inlaid ['ɪnleɪd] *adj* (*with wood, gems etc*) incrustado

inland [*adj* 'ɪnlənd, *adv* ɪn'lænd] *adj* (*waterway, port etc*) interior ♦ *adv* tierra adentro; **I~ Revenue** (*BRIT*) *n* departamento de impuestos; ≈ Hacienda (*SP*)

in-laws *npl* suegros *mpl*

inlet ['ɪnlet] *n* (*GEO*) ensenada, cala; (*TECH*) admisión *f*, entrada

inmate ['ɪnmeɪt] *n* (*in prison*) preso/a; presidiario/a; (*in asylum*) internado/a

inn [ɪn] *n* posada, mesón *m*

innate [ɪ'neɪt] *adj* innato

inner ['ɪnə*] *adj* (*courtyard, calm*) interior; (*feelings*) íntimo; **~ city** *n* barrios deprimidos del centro de una ciudad; **~ tube** *n* (*of tyre*) cámara (*SP*), llanta (*AM*)

innings ['ɪnɪŋz] *n* (*CRICKET*) entrada, turno

innocent ['ɪnəsnt] *adj* inocente

innocuous [ɪ'nɔkjuəs] *adj* inocuo

innovation [ɪnəu'veɪʃən] *n* novedad *f*

innuendo [ɪnju'endəu] (*pl* **~es**) *n* indirecta

inoculation [ɪnɔkju'leɪʃən] *n* inoculación *f*

in-patient *n* paciente *m/f* interno/a

input ['ɪnput] *n* entrada; (*of resources*) inversión *f*; (*COMPUT*) entrada de datos

inquest ['ɪnkwest] *n* (*coroner's*) encuesta judicial

inquire [ɪn'kwaɪə*] *vi* preguntar ♦ *vt*: **to ~ whether** preguntar si; **to ~ about** (*person*) preguntar por; (*fact*) informarse de; **~ into** *vt fus* investigar, indagar; **inquiry** *n* pregunta; (*investigation*) investigación *f*, pesquisa; **"inquiries"** "Información"; **inquiry office** (*BRIT*) *n* oficina de información

inquisitive [ɪn'kwɪzɪtɪv] *adj* (*curious*) curioso

ins. *abbr* = **inches**

insane [ɪn'seɪn] *adj* loco; (*MED*) demente

insanity [ɪn'sænɪtɪ] *n* demencia, locura

inscription [ɪn'skrɪpʃən] *n* inscripción *f*; (*in book*) dedicatoria

inscrutable [ɪn'skru:təbl] *adj* inescrutable, insondable

insect ['ɪnsekt] *n* insecto; **~icide** [ɪn'sektɪsaɪd] *n* insecticida *m*; **~ repellent** *n* loción *f* contra insectos

insecure [ɪnsɪ'kjuə*] *adj* inseguro

insemination [ɪnsemɪ'neɪʃn] *n*: **artificial ~** inseminación *f* artificial

insensitive [ɪn'sensɪtɪv] *adj* insensible

insert [*vb* ɪn'sə:t, *n* 'ɪnsə:t] *vt* (*into sth*) introducir ♦ *n* encarte *m*; **~ion** [ɪn'sə:ʃən] *n* inserción *f*

in-service ['ɪnsə:vɪs] *adj* (*training, course*) a cargo de la empresa

inshore [ɪn'ʃɔ:*] *adj* de bajura ♦ *adv* (*be*) cerca de la orilla; (*move*) hacia la orilla

inside ['ɪn'saɪd] *n* interior *m* ♦ *adj* interior, interno ♦ *adv* (*be*) (por) dentro; (*go*) hacia dentro ♦ *prep* dentro de; (*of time*): **~ 10 minutes** en menos de 10 minutos; **~s** *npl* (*inf: stomach*) tripas *fpl*; **~ information** *n* información *f* confidencial; **~ lane** *n* (*AUT: in Britain*) carril *m* izquierdo; (: *in US, Europe etc*) carril *m* derecho; **~ out** *adv* (*turn*) al revés; (*know*) a fondo

insider dealing, insider trading *n* (*STOCK EXCHANGE*) abuso de información privilegiada

insight ['ɪnsaɪt] *n* perspicacia

insignificant [ɪnsɪg'nɪfɪknt] *adj* insignificante

insincere [ɪnsɪn'sɪə*] *adj* poco sincero

insinuate [ɪn'sɪnjueɪt] *vt* insinuar

insipid [ɪn'sɪpɪd] *adj* soso, insulso

insist [ɪn'sɪst] *vi* insistir; **to ~ on** insistir en; **to ~ that** insistir en que; (*claim*) exigir que; **~ent** *adj* insistente; (*noise, action*) persistente

insole ['ɪnsəul] *n* plantilla

insolent ['ɪnsələnt] *adj* insolente, descarado

insomnia [ɪn'sɔmnɪə] *n* insomnio

inspect [ɪn'spekt] *vt* inspeccionar, examinar; (*troops*) pasar revista a; **~ion** [ɪn'spekʃən] *n* inspección *f*, examen *m*; (*of troops*) revista; **~or** *n* inspector(a) *m/f*; (*BRIT: on buses, trains*) revisor(a) *m/f*

inspiration [ɪnspə'reɪʃən] *n* inspiración *f*; **inspire** [ɪn'spaɪə*] *vt* inspirar

instability [ɪnstə'bɪlɪtɪ] *n* inestabilidad *f*

install [ɪn'stɔ:l] *vt* instalar; (*official*) nombrar;

~ation [ɪnstə'leɪʃən] n instalación f
instalment [ɪn'stɔːlmənt] (US **installment**) n plazo; (of story) entrega; (of TV serial etc) capítulo; **in ~s** (pay, receive) a plazos
instance ['ɪnstəns] n ejemplo, caso; **for ~** por ejemplo; **in the first ~** en primer lugar
instant ['ɪnstənt] n instante m, momento ♦ adj inmediato; (coffee etc) instantáneo; **~ly** adv en seguida
instead [ɪn'sted] adv en cambio; **~ of** en lugar de, en vez de
instep ['ɪnstep] n empeine m
instil [ɪn'stɪl] vt: **to ~ sth into** inculcar algo a
instinct ['ɪnstɪŋkt] n instinto
institute ['ɪnstɪtjuːt] n instituto; (professional body) colegio ♦ vt (begin) iniciar, empezar; (proceedings) entablar; (system, rule) establecer
institution [ɪnstɪ'tjuːʃən] n institución f; (MED: home) asilo; (: asylum) manicomio; (of system etc) establecimiento; (of custom) iniciación f
instruct [ɪn'strʌkt] vt: **to ~ sb in sth** instruir a uno en or sobre algo; **to ~ sb to do sth** dar instrucciones a uno de hacer algo; **~ion** [ɪn'strʌkʃən] n (teaching) instrucción f; **~ions** npl (orders) órdenes fpl; **~ions (for use)** modo de empleo; **~or** n instructor(a) m/f
instrument ['ɪnstrəmənt] n instrumento; **~al** [-'mentl] adj (MUS) instrumental; **to be ~al in ser** (el) artífice de; **~ panel** n tablero (de instrumentos)
insufficient [ɪnsə'fɪʃənt] adj insuficiente
insular ['ɪnsjulə*] adj insular; (person) estrecho de miras
insulate ['ɪnsjuleɪt] vt aislar; **insulation** [-'leɪʃən] n aislamiento
insulin ['ɪnsjulɪn] n insulina
insult [n 'ɪnsʌlt, vb ɪn'sʌlt] n insulto ♦ vt insultar; **~ing** adj insultante
insurance [ɪn'ʃuərəns] n seguro; **fire/life ~** seguro contra incendios/sobre la vida; **~ agent** n agente m/f de seguros; **~ policy** n póliza (de seguros)
insure [ɪn'ʃuə*] vt asegurar
intact [ɪn'tækt] adj íntegro; (unharmed) intacto
intake ['ɪnteɪk] n (of food) ingestión f; (of air) consumo; (BRIT: SCOL): **an ~ of 200 a year** 200 matriculados al año
integral ['ɪntɪɡrəl] adj (whole) íntegro; (part) integrante
integrate ['ɪntɪɡreɪt] vt integrar ♦ vi integrarse
integrity [ɪn'teɡrɪtɪ] n honradez f, rectitud f
intellect ['ɪntəlekt] n intelecto; **~ual** [-'lektjuəl] adj, n intelectual m/f
intelligence [ɪn'telɪdʒəns] n inteligencia
intelligent [ɪn'telɪdʒənt] adj inteligente

intelligible [ɪn'telɪdʒɪbl] adj inteligible, comprensible
intend [ɪn'tend] vt (gift etc): **to ~ sth for** destinar algo a; **to ~ to do sth** tener intención de or pensar hacer algo
intense [ɪn'tens] adj intenso; **~ly** adv (extremely) sumamente
intensify [ɪn'tensɪfaɪ] vt intensificar; (increase) aumentar
intensive [ɪn'tensɪv] adj intensivo; **~ care unit** n unidad f de vigilancia intensiva
intent [ɪn'tent] n propósito; (LAW) premeditación f ♦ adj (absorbed) absorto; (attentive) atento; **to all ~s and purposes** prácticamente; **to be ~ on doing sth** estar resuelto a hacer algo
intention [ɪn'tenʃən] n intención f, propósito; **~al** adj deliberado; **~ally** adv a propósito
intently [ɪn'tentlɪ] adv atentamente, fijamente
interact [ɪntər'ækt] vi influirse mutuamente; **~ive** adj (COMPUT) interactivo
interchange ['ɪntətʃeɪndʒ] n intercambio; (on motorway) intersección f; **~able** adj intercambiable
intercom ['ɪntəkɔm] n interfono
intercourse ['ɪntəkɔːs] n (sexual) relaciones fpl sexuales
interest ['ɪntrɪst] n (also COMM) interés m ♦ vt interesar; **to be ~ed in** interesarse por; **~ing** adj interesante; **~ rate** n tipo or tasa de interés
interface ['ɪntəfeɪs] n (COMPUT) junción f
interfere [ɪntə'fɪə*] vi: **to ~ in** (quarrel, other people's business) entrometerse en; **to ~ with** (hinder) estorbar; (damage) estropear
interference [ɪntə'fɪərəns] n intromisión f; (RADIO, TV) interferencia
interim ['ɪntərɪm] n: **in the ~** en el ínterin ♦ adj provisional
interior [ɪn'tɪərɪə*] n interior m ♦ adj interior; **~ designer** n interiorista m/f
interjection [ɪntə'dʒekʃən] n interposición f; (LING) interjección f
interlock [ɪntə'lɔk] vi entrelazarse
interlude ['ɪntəluːd] n intervalo; (THEATRE) intermedio
intermediate [ɪntə'miːdɪət] adj intermedio
intermission [ɪntə'mɪʃən] n intermisión f; (THEATRE) descanso
intern [vb ɪn'təːn, n 'ɪntəːn] vt internar ♦ n (US) interno/a
internal [ɪn'təːnl] adj (layout, pipes, security) interior; (injury, structure, memo) internal; **~ly** adv: **"not to be taken ~ly"** "uso externo"; **I~ Revenue Service** (US) n departamento de impuestos; ≈ Hacienda (SP)
international [ɪntə'næʃənl] adj internacional

♦ n (BRIT: match) partido internacional
Internet ['ɪntənɛt] n: the ~ Internet m or f;
~ **café** n cibercafé m; ~ **Service Provider** n
proveedor m de (acceso a) Internet
interplay ['ɪntəpleɪ] n interacción f
interpret [ɪn'tɜːprɪt] vt interpretar; (translate)
traducir; (understand) entender ♦ vi hacer de
intérprete; ~**er** n intérprete m/f
interrogate [ɪn'tɛrəugeɪt] vt interrogar;
interrogation [-'geɪʃən] n interrogatorio
interrupt [ɪntə'rʌpt] vt, vi interrumpir; ~**ion**
[-'rʌpʃən] n interrupción f
intersect [ɪntə'sɛkt] vi (roads) cruzarse; ~**ion**
[-'sɛkʃən] n (of roads) cruce m
intersperse [ɪntə'spəːs] vt: to ~ with salpicar
de
intertwine [ɪntə'twaɪn] vt entrelazarse
interval ['ɪntəvl] n intervalo; (BRIT: THEATRE,
SPORT) descanso; (: SCOL) recreo; **at ~s** a
ratos, de vez en cuando
intervene [ɪntə'viːn] vi intervenir; (event)
interponerse; (time) transcurrir;
intervention n intervención f
interview ['ɪntəvjuː] n entrevista ♦ vt
entrevistar con; ~**er** n entrevistador(a) m/f
intestine [ɪn'tɛstɪn] n intestino
intimacy ['ɪntɪməsɪ] n intimidad f
intimate [adj 'ɪntɪmət, vb 'ɪntɪmeɪt] adj
íntimo; (friendship) estrecho; (knowledge)
profundo ♦ vt dar a entender
into ['ɪntuː] prep en; (towards) a; (inside)
hacia el interior de; ~ **3 pieces/French** en 3
pedazos/al francés
intolerable [ɪn'tɔlərəbl] adj intolerable,
insoportable
intolerant [ɪn'tɔlərənt] adj: ~ (of) intolerante
(con o para)
intoxicated [ɪn'tɔksɪkeɪtɪd] adj embriagado
intractable [ɪn'træktəbl] adj (person)
intratable; (problem) espinoso
intranet ['ɪntrənɛt] n intranet f
intransitive [ɪn'trænsɪtɪv] adj intransitivo
intravenous [ɪntrə'viːnəs] adj intravenoso
in-tray n bandeja de entrada
intricate ['ɪntrɪkət] adj (design, pattern)
intrincado
intrigue [ɪn'triːg] n intriga ♦ vt fascinar;
intriguing adj fascinante
intrinsic [ɪn'trɪnsɪk] adj intrínseco
introduce [ɪntrə'djuːs] vt introducir, meter;
(speaker, TV show etc) presentar; **to ~ sb (to
sb)** presentar uno (a otro); **to ~ sb to**
(pastime, technique) introducir a uno a;
introduction [-'dʌkʃən] n introducción f; (of
person) presentación f; **introductory**
[-'dʌktərɪ] adj introductorio; (lesson, offer) de
introducción
introvert ['ɪntrəvəːt] n introvertido/a ♦ adj
(also: ~ed) introvertido

intrude [ɪn'truːd] vi (person) entrometerse;
to ~ on estorbar; ~**r** n intruso/a; **intrusion**
[-ʒən] n invasión f
intuition [ɪntjuː'ɪʃən] n intuición f
inundate ['ɪnʌndeɪt] vt: **to ~ with** inundar de
invade [ɪn'veɪd] vt invadir
invalid [n 'ɪnvəlɪd, adj ɪn'vælɪd] n (MED)
minusválido/a ♦ adj (not valid) inválido, nulo
invaluable [ɪn'væljuəbl] adj inestimable
invariable [ɪn'vɛərɪəbl] adj invariable
invent [ɪn'vɛnt] vt inventar; ~**ion** [ɪn'vɛnʃən]
n invento; (lie) ficción f, mentira; ~**ive** adj
inventivo; ~**or** n inventor(a) m/f
inventory ['ɪnvəntrɪ] n inventario
invert [ɪn'vəːt] vt invertir
inverted commas (BRIT) npl comillas fpl
invest [ɪn'vɛst] vt invertir ♦ vi: **to ~ in**
(company etc) invertir dinero en; (fig: sth
useful) comprar
investigate [ɪn'vɛstɪgeɪt] vt investigar;
investigation [-'geɪʃən] n investigación f,
pesquisa
investment [ɪn'vɛstmənt] n inversión f
investor [ɪn'vɛstə*] n inversionista m/f
invigilator [ɪn'vɪdʒɪleɪtə*] n persona que
vigila en un examen
invigorating [ɪn'vɪgəreɪtɪŋ] adj vigorizante
invisible [ɪn'vɪzɪbl] adj invisible
invitation [ɪnvɪ'teɪʃən] n invitación f
invite [ɪn'vaɪt] vt invitar; (opinions etc) solicitar,
pedir; **inviting** adj atractivo; (food) apetitoso
invoice ['ɪnvɔɪs] n factura ♦ vt facturar
involuntary [ɪn'vɔləntrɪ] adj involuntario
involve [ɪn'vɔlv] vt suponer, implicar; tener
que ver con; (concern, affect) corresponder;
to ~ sb (in sth) comprometer a uno (con
algo); ~**d** adj complicado; **to be ~d in** (take
part) tomar parte en; (be engrossed) estar
muy metido en; ~**ment** n participación f;
dedicación f
inward ['ɪnwəd] adj (movement) interior,
interno; (thought, feeling) íntimo; ~**(s)** adv
hacia dentro
I/O abbr (COMPUT = input/output) entrada/
salida
iodine ['aɪəudiːn] n yodo
ion ['aɪən] n ion m; **ioniser** ['aɪənaɪzə*] n
ionizador m
iota [aɪ'əutə] n jota, ápice m
IOU n abbr (= I owe you) pagaré m
IQ n abbr (= intelligence quotient) cociente m
intelectual
IRA n abbr (= Irish Republican Army) IRA m
Iran [ɪ'rɑːn] n Irán m; ~**ian** [ɪ'reɪnɪən] adj, n
iraní m/f
Iraq [ɪ'rɑːk] n Iraq; ~**i** adj, n iraquí m/f
irate [aɪ'reɪt] adj enojado, airado
Ireland ['aɪələnd] n Irlanda
iris ['aɪrɪs] (pl ~**es**) n (ANAT) iris m; (BOT) lirio

Irish [ˈaɪrɪʃ] *adj* irlandés/esa ♦ *npl*: **the ~** los irlandeses; **~man/woman** *(irreg)* n irlandés/esa *m/f*; **~ Sea** n: **the ~ Sea** el mar de Irlanda

iron [ˈaɪən] *n* hierro; *(for clothes)* plancha ♦ *cpd* de hierro ♦ *vt (clothes)* planchar; **~ out** *vt (fig)* allanar

ironic(al) [aɪˈrɒnɪk(l)] *adj* irónico

ironing [ˈaɪənɪŋ] *n (activity)* planchado; *(clothes: ironed)* ropa planchada; *(: to be ironed)* ropa por planchar; **~ board** n tabla de planchar

ironmonger's (shop) [ˈaɪənmʌŋgəz] *(BRIT)* n ferretería, quincallería

irony [ˈaɪrənɪ] n ironía

irrational [ɪˈræʃənl] *adj* irracional

irreconcilable [ɪrekənˈsaɪləbl] *adj (ideas)* incompatible; *(enemies)* irreconciliable

irregular [ɪˈregjulə*] *adj* irregular; *(surface)* desigual; *(action, event)* anómalo; *(behaviour)* poco ortodoxo

irrelevant [ɪˈreləvənt] *adj* fuera de lugar, inoportuno

irresolute [ɪˈrezəluːt] *adj* indeciso

irrespective [ɪrɪˈspektɪv]: **~ of** *prep* sin tener en cuenta, no importa

irresponsible [ɪrɪˈspɒnsɪbl] *adj (act)* irresponsable; *(person)* poco serio

irrigate [ˈɪrɪgeɪt] *vt* regar; **irrigation** [-ˈgeɪʃən] *n* riego

irritable [ˈɪrɪtəbl] *adj (person)* de mal humor

irritate [ˈɪrɪteɪt] *vt* fastidiar; *(MED)* picar; **irritating** *adj* fastidioso; **irritation** [-ˈteɪʃən] *n* fastidio; irritación; picazón *f*, picor *m*

IRS *(US)* n abbr = **Internal Revenue Service**

is [ɪz] *vb see* **be**

Islam [ˈɪzlɑːm] *n* Islam *m*; **~ic** [ɪzˈlæmɪk] *adj* islámico

island [ˈaɪlənd] *n* isla; **~er** *n* isleño/a

isle [aɪl] *n* isla

isn't [ˈɪznt] = **is not**

isolate [ˈaɪsəleɪt] *vt* aislar; **~d** *adj* aislado; **isolation** [-ˈleɪʃən] *n* aislamiento

ISP *n abbr* = **Internet Service Provider**

Israel [ˈɪzreɪl] *n* Israel *m*; **~i** [ɪzˈreɪlɪ] *adj, n* israelí *m/f*

issue [ˈɪsjuː] *n (problem, subject, most important part)* cuestión *f*; *(outcome)* resultado; *(of banknotes etc)* emisión *f*; *(of newspaper etc)* edición *f* ♦ *vt (rations, equipment)* distribuir, repartir; *(orders)* dar; *(certificate, passport)* expedir; *(decree)* promulgar; *(magazine)* publicar; *(cheques)* extender; *(banknotes, stamps)* emitir; **at ~** en cuestión; **to take ~ with sb (over)** estar en desacuerdo con uno (sobre); **to make an ~ of sth** hacer una cuestión de algo

Istanbul [ɪstænˈbuːl] *n* Estambul *m*

---

it [ɪt] *pron* **1** *(specific: subject: not generally translated)* él/ella; *(: direct object)* lo, la; *(: indirect object)* le; *(after prep)* él/ella; *(abstract concept)* ello; **~'s on the table** está en la mesa; **I can't find ~** no lo *(or* la*)* encuentro; **give ~ to me** dámelo *(or* dámela*)*; **I spoke to him about ~** le hablé del asunto; **what did you learn from ~?** ¿qué aprendiste de él *(or* ella*)*?; **did you go to ~?** *(party, concert etc)* ¿fuiste?

2 *(impersonal)* **~'s raining** llueve, está lloviendo; **~'s 6 o'clock/the 10th of August** son las 6/es el 10 de agosto; **how far is ~?** — **~'s 10 miles/2 hours on the train** ¿a qué distancia está? — a 10 millas/2 horas en tren; **who is ~?** — **~'s me** ¿quién es? — soy yo

Italian [ɪˈtæljən] *adj* italiano ♦ *n* italiano/a; *(LING)* italiano

italics [ɪˈtælɪks] *npl* cursiva

Italy [ˈɪtəlɪ] *n* Italia

itch [ɪtʃ] *n* picazón *f* ♦ *vi (part of body)* picar; **to ~ to do sth** rabiar por hacer algo; **~y** *adj*: **my hand is ~y** me pica la mano

it'd [ˈɪtd] = **it would**; **it had**

item [ˈaɪtəm] *n* artículo; *(on agenda)* asunto *(a tratar)*; *(also: news ~)* noticia; **~ize** *vt* detallar

itinerary [aɪˈtɪnərərɪ] *n* itinerario

it'll [ˈɪtl] = **it will**; **it shall**

its [ɪts] *adj* su; sus *pl*

it's [ɪts] = **it is**; **it has**

itself [ɪtˈself] *pron (reflexive)* sí mismo/a; *(emphatic)* él mismo/ella misma

ITV *n abbr (BRIT: = Independent Television)* cadena de televisión comercial independiente del Estado

I.U.D. *n abbr (= intra-uterine device)* DIU *m*

I've [aɪv] = **I have**

ivory [ˈaɪvərɪ] *n* marfil *m*

ivy [ˈaɪvɪ] *n (BOT)* hiedra

J, j

jab [dʒæb] *vt*: **to ~ sth into sth** clavar algo en algo ♦ *n (inf) (MED)* pinchazo

jack [dʒæk] *n (AUT)* gato; *(CARDS)* sota; **~ up** *vt (AUT)* levantar con gato

jackal [ˈdʒækɔːl] *n (ZOOL)* chacal *m*

jacket [ˈdʒækɪt] *n* chaqueta, americana, saco *(AM)*; *(of book)* sobrecubierta

jack: ~-knife *vi* colear; **~ plug** *n (ELEC)* enchufe *m* de clavija; **~pot** *n* premio gordo

jaded [ˈdʒeɪdɪd] *adj (tired)* cansado; *(fed-up)* hastiado

jagged [ˈdʒægɪd] *adj* dentado

jail |dʒeɪl| *n* cárcel *f* ♦ *vt* encarcelar

jam |dʒæm| *n* mermelada; (*also: traffic ~*) embotellamiento; (*inf: difficulty*) apuro ♦ *vt* (*passage etc*) obstruir; (*mechanism, drawer etc*) atascar; (*RADIO*) interferir ♦ *vi* atascarse, trabarse; **to ~ sth into sth** meter algo a la fuerza en algo

Jamaica |dʒə'meɪkə| *n* Jamaica

jangle ['dʒæŋgl] *vi* entrechocar (ruidosamente)

janitor ['dʒænɪtə*] *n* (*caretaker*) portero, conserje *m*

January ['dʒænjuərɪ] *n* enero

Japan |dʒə'pæn| *n* (el) Japón; **~ese** |dʒæpə'niːz| *adj* japonés/esa ♦ *n inv* japonés/esa *m/f*; (*LING*) japonés *m*

jar |dʒɑː*| *n* tarro, bote *m* ♦ *vi* (*sound*) chirriar; (*colours*) desentonar

jargon ['dʒɑːgən] *n* jerga

jasmine ['dʒæzmɪn] *n* jazmín *m*

jaundice ['dʒɔːndɪs] *n* ictericia

jaunt |dʒɔːnt| *n* excursión *f*

javelin ['dʒævlɪn] *n* jabalina

jaw |dʒɔː| *n* mandíbula

jay |dʒeɪ| *n* (*ZOOL*) arrendajo

jaywalker ['dʒeɪwɔːkə*] *n* peatón/ona *m/f* imprudente

jazz |dʒæz| *n* jazz *m*; **~ up** *vt* (*liven up*) animar, avivar

jealous ['dʒeləs] *adj* celoso; (*envious*) envidioso; **~y** *n* celos *mpl*; envidia

jeans |dʒiːnz| *npl* vaqueros *mpl*, tejanos *mpl*

Jeep ® |dʒiːp| *n* jeep *m*

jeer |dʒɪə*| *vi*: **to ~ (at)** (*mock*) mofarse (de)

jelly ['dʒelɪ] *n* (*jam*) jalea; (*dessert etc*) gelatina; **~fish** *n inv* medusa (*SP*), aguaviva (*AM*)

jeopardy ['dʒepədɪ] *n*: **to be in ~** estar en peligro

jerk |dʒɜːk| *n* (*jolt*) sacudida; (*wrench*) tirón *m*; (*inf*) imbécil *m/f* ♦ *vt* tirar bruscamente de ♦ *vi* (*vehicle*) traquetear

jersey ['dʒɜːzɪ] *n* jersey *m*; (*fabric*) (tejido de) punto

Jesus ['dʒiːzəs] *n* Jesús *m*

jet |dʒet| *n* (*of gas, liquid*) chorro; (*AVIAT*) avión *m* a reacción; **~-black** *adj* negro como el azabache; **~ engine** *n* motor *m* a reacción; **~ lag** *n* desorientación *f* después de un largo vuelo

jettison ['dʒetɪsn] *vt* desechar

jetty ['dʒetɪ] *n* muelle *m*, embarcadero

Jew |dʒuː| *n* judío

jewel ['dʒuːəl] *n* joya; (*in watch*) rubí *m*; **~ler** (*US* **~er**) *n* joyero/a; **~ler's (shop)** (*US* **~ry store**) *n* joyería; **~lery** (*US* **~ry**) *n* joyas *fpl*, alhajas *fpl*

Jewess ['dʒuːɪs] *n* judía

Jewish ['dʒuːɪʃ] *adj* judío

jibe |dʒaɪb| *n* mofa

jiffy ['dʒɪfɪ] (*inf*) *n*: **in a ~** en un santiamén

jigsaw ['dʒɪgsɔː] *n* (*also: ~ puzzle*) rompecabezas *m inv*, puzle *m*

jilt |dʒɪlt| *vt* dejar plantado a

jingle ['dʒɪŋgl] *n* musiquilla ♦ *vi* tintinear

jinx |dʒɪŋks| *n*: **there's a ~ on it** está gafado

jitters ['dʒɪtəz] (*inf*) *npl*: **to get the ~** ponerse nervioso

job |dʒɔb| *n* (*task*) tarea; (*post*) empleo; **it's not my ~** no me incumbe a mí; **it's a good ~ that ...** menos mal que ...; **just the ~!** ¡estupendo!; **~ centre** (*BRIT*) *n* oficina estatal de colocaciones; **~less** *adj* sin trabajo

jockey ['dʒɔkɪ] *n* jockey *m/f* ♦ *vi*: **to ~ for position** maniobrar para conseguir una posición

jog |dʒɔg| *vt* empujar (ligeramente) ♦ *vi* (*run*) hacer footing; **to ~ sb's memory** refrescar la memoria a uno; **~ along** *vi* (*fig*) ir tirando; **~ging** *n* footing *m*

join |dʒɔɪn| *vt* (*things*) juntar, unir; (*club*) hacerse socio de; (*POL: party*) afiliarse a; (*queue*) ponerse en; (*meet: people*) reunirse con ♦ *vi* (*roads*) juntarse; (*rivers*) confluir ♦ *n* juntura; **~ in** *vi* tomar parte, participar ♦ *vt fus* tomar parte or participar en; **~ up** *vi* reunirse; (*MIL*) alistarse

joiner ['dʒɔɪnə*] (*BRIT*) *n* carpintero/a; **~y** *n* carpintería

joint |dʒɔɪnt| *n* (*TECH*) junta, unión *f*; (*ANAT*) articulación *f*; (*BRIT: CULIN*) pieza de carne (para asar); (*inf: place*) tugurio; (: *of cannabis*) porro ♦ *adj* (*common*) común; (*combined*) combinado; **~ account** (*with bank etc*) cuenta común

joke |dʒəuk| *n* chiste *m*; (*also: practical ~*) broma ♦ *vi* bromear; **to play a ~ on** gastar una broma a; **~r** *n* (*CARDS*) comodín *m*

jolly ['dʒɔlɪ] *adj* (*merry*) alegre; (*enjoyable*) divertido ♦ *adv* (*BRIT: inf*) muy, terriblemente

jolt |dʒəult| *n* (*jerk*) sacudida; (*shock*) susto ♦ *vt* (*physically*) sacudir; (*emotionally*) asustar

jostle ['dʒɔsl] *vt* dar empellones a, codear

jot |dʒɔt| *n*: **not one ~** ni jota, ni pizca; **~ down** *vt* apuntar; **~ter** (*BRIT*) *n* bloc *m*

journal ['dʒɜːnl] *n* (*magazine*) revista; (*diary*) periódico, diario; **~ism** *n* periodismo; **~ist** *n* periodista *m/f*, reportero/a

journey ['dʒɜːnɪ] *n* viaje *m*; (*distance covered*) trayecto

jovial ['dʒəuvɪəl] *adj* risueño, jovial

joy |dʒɔɪ| *n* alegría; **~ful** *adj* alegre; **~ous** *adj* alegre; **~ ride** *n* (*illegal*) paseo en coche robado; **~rider** *n* gamberro que roba un coche para dar una vuelta y luego abandonarlo; **~ stick** *n* (*AVIAT*) palanca de mando; (*COMPUT*) palanca de control

JP *n abbr* = **Justice of the Peace**

Jr *abbr* = junior
jubilant ['dʒu:bɪlnt] *adj* jubiloso
judge [dʒʌdʒ] *n* juez *m/f*; (*fig: expert*) perito
♦ *vt* juzgar; (*consider*) considerar;
judg(e)ment *n* juicio
judiciary [dʒu:'dɪʃɪərɪ] *n* poder *m* judicial
judicious [dʒu:'dɪʃəs] *adj* juicioso
judo ['dʒu:dəu] *n* judo
jug [dʒʌg] *n* jarra
juggernaut ['dʒʌgənɔ:t] (*BRIT*) *n* (*huge truck*)
trailer *m*
juggle ['dʒʌgl] *vi* hacer juegos malabares; **~r**
n malabarista *m/f*
juice [dʒu:s] *n* zumo, jugo (*esp AM*); **juicy** *adj*
jugoso
jukebox ['dʒu:kbɔks] *n* máquina de discos
July [dʒu:'laɪ] *n* julio
jumble ['dʒʌmbl] *n* revoltijo ♦ *vt* (*also:* ~ up)
revolver; **~ sale** (*BRIT*) *n* venta de objetos
usados con fines benéficos
jumbo (jet) ['dʒʌmbəu-] *n* jumbo
jump [dʒʌmp] *vi* saltar, dar saltos; (*with fear
etc*) pegar un bote; (*increase*) aumentar ♦ *vt*
saltar ♦ *n* salto; aumento; **to ~ the queue**
(*BRIT*) colarse
jumper ['dʒʌmpə*] *n* (*BRIT: pullover*) suéter *m*,
jersey *m*; (*US: dress*) mandil *m*; **~ cables**
(*US*) *npl* = **jump leads**
jump leads (*BRIT*) *npl* cables *mpl* puente de
batería
jumpy ['dʒʌmpɪ] (*inf*) *adj* nervioso
Jun. *abbr* = junior
junction ['dʒʌŋkʃən] *n* (*BRIT: of roads*) cruce
m; (*RAIL*) empalme *m*
juncture ['dʒʌŋktʃə*] *n*: **at this ~** en este
momento, en esta coyuntura
June [dʒu:n] *n* junio
jungle ['dʒʌŋgl] *n* selva, jungla
junior ['dʒu:nɪə*] *adj* (*in age*) menor, más
joven; (*brother/sister etc*): **7 years her ~** siete
años menor que ella; (*position*) subalterno
♦ *n* menor *m/f*, joven *m/f*; **~ school** (*BRIT*) *n*
escuela primaria
junk [dʒʌŋk] *n* (*cheap goods*) baratijas *fpl*;
(*rubbish*) basura; **~ food** *n* alimentos
preparados y envasados de escaso valor
nutritivo
junkie ['dʒʌŋkɪ] (*inf*) *n* drogadicto/a, yonqui
m/f
junk mail *n* propaganda de buzón
junk shop *n* tienda de objetos usados
Junr *abbr* = junior
juror ['dʒuərə*] *n* jurado
jury ['dʒuərɪ] *n* jurado
just [dʒʌst] *adj* justo ♦ *adv* (*exactly*)
exactamente; (*only*) sólo, solamente; **he's
~ done it/left** acaba de hacerlo/irse; **~ right**
perfecto; **~ two o'clock** las dos en punto;
she's ~ as clever as you (ella) es tan lista

como tú; **~ as well that ...** menos mal que ...;
~ as he was leaving en el momento en que se
marchaba; **~ before/enough** justo antes/lo
suficiente; **~ here** aquí mismo; **he ~ missed**
ha fallado por poco; **~ listen to this** escucha
esto un momento
justice ['dʒʌstɪs] *n* justicia; (*US: judge*) juez *m*;
to do ~ to (*fig*) hacer justicia a; **J~ of the
Peace** *n* juez *m* de paz
justify ['dʒʌstɪfaɪ] *vt* justificar; (*text*) alinear
jut [dʒʌt] *vi* (*also:* ~ out) sobresalir
juvenile ['dʒu:vənaɪl] *adj* (*court*) de menores;
(*humour, mentality*) infantil ♦ *n* menor *m* de
edad

K, k

K *abbr* (= *one thousand*) mil; (= *kilobyte*)
kilobyte *m*, kilocteto
kangaroo [kæŋgə'ru:] *n* canguro
karate [kə'rɑ:tɪ] *n* karate *m*
kebab [kə'bæb] *n* pincho moruno
keel [ki:l] *n* quilla; **on an even ~** (*fig*) en
equilibrio
keen [ki:n] *adj* (*interest, desire*) grande, vivo;
(*eye, intelligence*) agudo; (*competition*)
reñido; (*edge*) afilado; (*eager*) entusiasta; **to
be ~ to do** *or* **on doing sth** tener muchas
ganas de hacer algo; **to be ~ on sth/sb**
interesarse por algo/uno
keep [ki:p] (*pt, pp* kept) *vt* (*preserve, store*)
guardar; (*hold back*) quedarse con;
(*maintain*) mantener; (*detain*) detener;
(*shop*) ser propietario de; (*feed: family etc*)
mantener; (*promise*) cumplir; (*chickens, bees
etc*) criar; (*accounts*) llevar; (*diary*) escribir;
(*prevent*): **to ~ sb from doing sth** impedir a
uno hacer algo ♦ *vi* (*food*) conservar;
(*remain*) seguir, continuar ♦ *n* (*of castle*)
torreón *m*; (*food etc*) comida, subsistencia;
(*inf*): **for ~s** para siempre; **to ~ doing sth**
seguir haciendo algo; **to ~ sb happy** tener a
uno contento; **to ~ a place tidy** mantener un
lugar limpio; **to ~ sth to o.s.** guardar algo
para sí mismo; **to ~ sth (back) from sb** ocultar
algo a uno; **to ~ time** (*clock*) mantener la
hora exacta; **~ on** *vi*: **to ~ on doing** seguir *or*
continuar haciendo; **to ~ on (about sth)** no
parar de hablar (de algo); **~ out** *vi* (*stay out*)
permanecer fuera; **"~ out"** "prohibida la
entrada"; **~ up** *vt* mantener, conservar ♦ *vi*
no retrasarse; **to ~ up with** (*pace*) ir al paso
de; (*level*) mantenerse a la altura de; **~er** *n*
guardián/ana *m/f*; **~-fit** *n* gimnasia (para
mantenerse en forma); **~ing** *n* (*care*)
cuidado; **in ~ing with** de acuerdo con; **~sake**
n recuerdo
kennel ['kɛnl] *n* perrera; **~s** *npl* residencia

canina

Kenya ['kɛnjə] n Kenia

kept [kɛpt] pt, pp of keep

kerb [kɜːb] (BRIT) n bordillo

kernel ['kɜːnl] n (nut) almendra; (fig) meollo

ketchup ['kɛtʃəp] n salsa de tomate, catsup m

kettle ['kɛtl] n hervidor m de agua; ~ **drum** n (MUS) timbal m

key [kiː] n llave f; (MUS) tono; (of piano, typewriter) tecla ♦ adj (issue etc) clave inv ♦ vt (also: ~ **in**) teclear; **~board** n teclado; **~ed up** adj (person) nervioso; **~hole** n ojo (de la cerradura); **~hole surgery** n cirugía cerrada, cirugía no invasiva; **~note** n (MUS) tónica; (of speech) punto principal or clave; **~ring** n llavero

khaki ['kɑːkɪ] n caqui

kick [kɪk] vt dar una patada or un puntapié a; (inf: habit) quitarse de ♦ vi (horse) dar coces ♦ n patada; puntapié m; (of animal) coz f; (thrill): **he does it for ~s** lo hace por pura diversión; **~ off** vi (SPORT) hacer el saque inicial

kid [kɪd] n (inf: child) chiquillo/a; (animal) cabrito; (leather) cabritilla ♦ vi (inf) bromear

kidnap ['kɪdnæp] vt secuestrar; **~per** n secuestrador(a) m/f; **~ping** n secuestro

kidney ['kɪdnɪ] n riñón m

kill [kɪl] vt matar; (murder) asesinar ♦ n matanza; **to ~ time** matar el tiempo; **~er** n asesino/a; **~ing** n (one) asesinato; (several) matanza; **to make a ~ing** (fig) hacer su agosto; **~joy** (BRIT) n aguafiestas m/f inv

kiln [kɪln] n horno

kilo ['kiːləu] n kilo; **~byte** n (COMPUT) kilobyte m, kilocteto; **~gram(me)** ['kɪləugræm] n kilo, kilogramo; **~metre** ['kɪləmiːtə*] (US **~meter**) n kilómetro; **~watt** ['kɪləuwɔt] n kilovatio

kilt [kɪlt] n falda escocesa

kin [kɪn] n see next

kind [kaɪnd] adj amable, atento ♦ n clase f, especie f; (species) género; **in ~** (COMM) en especie; **a ~ of** una especie de; **to be two of a ~** ser tal para cual

kindergarten ['kɪndəgɑːtn] n jardín m de la infancia

kind-hearted adj bondadoso, de buen corazón

kindle ['kɪndl] vt encender; (arouse) despertar

kindly ['kaɪndlɪ] adj bondadoso; cariñoso ♦ adv bondadosamente, amablemente; **will you ~ ...** sea usted tan amable de ...

kindness ['kaɪndnɪs] n (quality) bondad f, amabilidad f; (act) favor m

king [kɪŋ] n rey m; **~dom** n reino; **~fisher** n martín m pescador; **~-size** adj de tamaño extra

kiosk ['kiːɔsk] n quiosco; (BRIT: TEL) cabina

kipper ['kɪpə*] n arenque m ahumado

kiss [kɪs] n beso ♦ vt besar; **to ~** (**each other**) besarse; **~ of life** n respiración f boca a boca

kit [kɪt] n (equipment) equipo; (tools etc) (caja de) herramientas fpl; (assembly ~) juego de armar

kitchen ['kɪtʃɪn] n cocina; **~ sink** n fregadero

kite [kaɪt] n (toy) cometa

kitten ['kɪtn] n gatito/a

kitty ['kɪtɪ] n (pool of money) fondo común

km abbr (= kilometre) km

knack [næk] n: **to have the ~ of doing sth** tener el don de hacer algo

knapsack ['næpsæk] n mochila

knead [niːd] vt amasar

knee [niː] n rodilla; **~cap** n rótula

kneel [niːl] (pt, pp knelt) vi (also: ~ **down**) arrodillarse

knew [njuː] pt of know

knickers ['nɪkəz] (BRIT) npl bragas fpl

knife [naɪf] (pl **knives**) n cuchillo ♦ vt acuchillar

knight [naɪt] n caballero; (CHESS) caballo; **~hood** (BRIT) n (title): **to receive a ~hood** recibir el título de Sir

knit [nɪt] vt tejer, tricotar ♦ vi hacer punto, tricotar; (bones) soldarse; **to ~ one's brows** fruncir el ceño; **~ting** n labor f de punto; **~ting machine** n máquina de tricotar; **~ting needle** n aguja de hacer punto; **~wear** n prendas fpl de punto

knives [naɪvz] npl of knife

knob [nɔb] n (of door) tirador m; (of stick) puño; (on radio, TV) botón m

knock [nɔk] vt (strike) golpear; (bump into) chocar contra; (inf) criticar ♦ vi (at door etc): **to ~ at/on** llamar a ♦ n golpe m; (on door) llamada; **~ down** vt atropellar; **~ off** vi (finish) salir del trabajo ♦ vt (from price) descontar; (inf: steal) birlar; **~ out** vt dejar sin sentido; (BOXING) poner fuera de combate, dejar K.O.; (in competition) eliminar; **~ over** vt (object) tirar; (person) atropellar; **~er** n (on door) aldabón m; **~out** n (BOXING) K.O. m, knockout m ♦ cpd (competition etc) eliminatorio

knot [nɔt] n nudo ♦ vt anudar

know [nəu] (pt knew, pp known) vt (facts) saber; (be acquainted with) conocer; (recognize) reconocer, conocer; **to ~ how to swim** saber nadar; **to ~ about** or **of sb/sth** saber de uno/algo; **~-all** n sabelotodo m/f; **~-how** n conocimientos mpl; **~ing** adj (look) de complicidad; **~ingly** adv (purposely) adrede; (smile, look) con complicidad

knowledge ['nɔlɪdʒ] n conocimiento; (learning) saber m, conocimientos mpl; **~able** adj entendido

knuckle ['nʌkl] n nudillo
Koran [kɔ'rɑːn] n Corán m
Korea [kə'rɪə] n Corea
kosher ['kəʊʃə*] adj autorizado por la ley judía
Kosovo ['kɒsəvəʊ] n Kosovo m

L, l

L (BRIT) abbr = **learner driver**
l. abbr (= litre) l
lab [læb] n abbr = **laboratory**
label ['leɪbl] n etiqueta ♦ vt poner etiqueta a
labor etc ['leɪbə*] (US) = **labour**
laboratory [lə'bɒrətəri] n laboratorio
laborious [lə'bɔːrɪəs] adj penoso
labour ['leɪbə*] (US **labor**) n (hard work) trabajo; (~ force) mano f de obra; (MED): **to be in ~** estar de parto ♦ vi: **to ~ (at sth)** trabajar (en algo) ♦ vt: **to ~ a point** insistir en un punto; **L~, the L~ party** (BRIT) el partido laborista, los laboristas mpl; **~ed** adj (breathing) fatigoso; **~er** n peón m; **farm ~er** peón m; (day ~er) jornalero
lace [leɪs] n encaje m; (of shoe etc) cordón m ♦ vt (shoes: also: ~ up) atarse (los zapatos)
lack [læk] n (absence) falta ♦ vt faltarle a uno, carecer de; **through** or **for ~ of** por falta de; **to be ~ing** faltar, no haber; **to be ~ing in sth** faltarle a uno algo
lacquer ['lækə*] n laca
lad [læd] n muchacho, chico
ladder ['lædə*] n escalera (de mano); (BRIT: in tights) carrera
laden ['leɪdn] adj: ~ **(with)** cargado (de)
ladle ['leɪdl] n cucharón m
lady ['leɪdɪ] n señora; (dignified, graceful) dama; "**ladies and gentlemen** ..." "señoras y caballeros ..."; **young ~** señorita; **the ladies' (room)** los servicios de señoras; **~bird** (US **~bug**) n mariquita; **~like** adj fino; **L~ship** n: **your L~ship** su Señoría
lag [læg] n retraso ♦ vi (also: ~ **behind**) retrasarse, quedarse atrás ♦ vt (pipes) revestir
lager ['lɑːgə*] n cerveza (rubia)
lagoon [lə'guːn] n laguna
laid [leɪd] pt, pp of **lay**; ~ **back** (inf) adj relajado; ~ **up** adj: **to be ~ up (with)** tener que guardar cama (a causa de)
lain [leɪn] pp of **lie**
lake [leɪk] n lago
lamb [læm] n cordero; (meat) carne f de cordero; ~ **chop** n chuleta de cordero; **lambswool** n lana de cordero
lame [leɪm] adj cojo; (excuse) poco convincente
lament [lə'ment] n quejo ♦ vt lamentarse de
laminated ['læmɪneɪtɪd] adj (metal)

laminado; (wood) contrachapado; (surface) plastificado
lamp [læmp] n lámpara; **~post** (BRIT) n (poste m de) farol m; **~shade** n pantalla
lance [lɑːns] vt (MED) abrir con lanceta
land [lænd] n tierra; (country) país m; (piece of ~) terreno; (estate) tierras fpl, finca ♦ vi (from ship) desembarcar; (AVIAT) aterrizar; (fig: fall) caer, terminar ♦ vt (passengers, goods) desembarcar; **to ~ sb with sth** (inf) hacer cargar a uno con algo; ~ **up** vi: **to ~ up in/at** ir a parar a/en; **~fill site** ['lændfɪl-] n vertedero; **~ing** n aterrizaje m; (of staircase) rellano; **~ing gear** n (AVIAT) tren m de aterrizaje; **~lady** n (of rented house, pub etc) dueña; **~lord** n propietario; (of pub etc) patrón m; **~mark** n lugar m conocido; **to be a ~mark** (fig) marcar un hito histórico; **~owner** n terrateniente m/f; **~scape** n paisaje m; **~scape gardener** n arquitecto de jardines; **~slide** n (GEO) corrimiento de tierras; (fig: POL) victoria arrolladora
lane [leɪn] n (in country) camino; (AUT) carril m; (in race) calle f
language ['læŋgwɪdʒ] n lenguaje m; (national tongue) idioma m, lengua; **bad ~** palabrotas fpl; ~ **laboratory** n laboratorio de idiomas
lank [læŋk] adj (hair) lacio
lanky ['læŋkɪ] adj larguirucho
lantern ['læntn] n linterna, farol m
lap [læp] n (of track) vuelta; (of body) regazo; **to sit on sb's ~** sentarse en las rodillas de uno ♦ vt (also: ~ **up**) beber a lengüetadas ♦ vi (waves) chapotear; ~ **up** vt (fig) tragarse
lapel [lə'pel] n solapa
Lapland ['læplænd] n Laponia
lapse [læps] n fallo; (moral) desliz m; (of time) intervalo ♦ vi (expire) caducar; (time) pasar, transcurrir; **to ~ into bad habits** caer en malos hábitos
laptop (computer) ['læptɒp-] n (ordenador m) portátil m
larch [lɑːtʃ] n alerce m
lard [lɑːd] n manteca (de cerdo)
larder ['lɑːdə*] n despensa
large [lɑːdʒ] adj grande; **at ~** (free) en libertad; (generally) en general; **~ly** adv (mostly) en su mayor parte; (introducing reason) en gran parte; **~-scale** adj (map) en gran escala; (fig) importante
lark [lɑːk] n (bird) alondra; (joke) broma
laryngitis [lærɪn'dʒaɪtɪs] n laringitis f
laser ['leɪzə*] n láser m; ~ **printer** n impresora (por) láser
lash [læʃ] n latigazo; (also: eye~) pestaña ♦ vt azotar; (tie): **to ~ to/together** atar a/atar; ~ **out** vi: **to ~ out (at sb)** (hit) arremeter (contra uno); **to ~ out against sb** lanzar invectivas contra uno

lass [læs] (BRIT) n chica
lasso [læˈsuː] n lazo
last [lɑːst] adj último; (end: of series etc) final ♦ adv (most recently) la última vez; (finally) por último ♦ vi durar; (continue) continuar, seguir; ~ **night** anoche; ~ **week** la semana pasada; **at ~** por fin; ~ **but one** penúltimo; ~**-ditch** adj (attempt) último, desesperado; ~**ing** adj duradero; ~**ly** adv por último, finalmente; ~**-minute** adj de última hora
latch [lætʃ] n pestillo
late [leɪt] adj (far on: in time, process etc) al final de; (not on time) tarde, atrasado; (dead) fallecido ♦ adv tarde; (behind time, schedule) con retraso; **of ~** últimamente; ~ **at night** a última hora de la noche; **in ~ May** hacia fines de mayo; **the ~ Mr X** el difunto Sr X; ~**comer** n recién llegado/a; ~**ly** adv últimamente; ~**r** adj (date etc) posterior; (version etc) más reciente ♦ adv más tarde, después; ~**st** [ˈleɪtɪst] adj último; **at the ~st** a más tardar
lathe [leɪð] n torno
lather [ˈlɑːðə*] n espuma (de jabón) ♦ vt enjabonar
Latin [ˈlætɪn] n latín m ♦ adj latino; ~ **America** n América latina; ~**-American** adj, n latinoamericano/a
latitude [ˈlætɪtjuːd] n latitud f; (fig) libertad f
latter [ˈlætə*] adj último; (of two) segundo ♦ n: **the ~** el último, éste; ~**ly** adv últimamente
laudable [ˈlɔːdəbl] adj loable
laugh [lɑːf] n risa ♦ vi reír(se); **(to do sth) for a ~** (hacer algo) en broma; ~ **at** vt fus reírse de; ~ **off** vt tomar algo a risa; ~**able** adj ridículo; ~**ing stock** n: **the ~ing stock of** el hazmerreír de; ~**ter** n risa
launch [lɔːntʃ] n lanzamiento; (boat) lancha ♦ vt (ship) botar; (rocket etc) lanzar; (fig) comenzar; ~ **into** vt fus lanzarse a; ~**(ing) pad** n plataforma de lanzamiento
launder [ˈlɔːndə*] vt lavar
Launderette ® [lɔːnˈdrɛt] (BRIT) n lavandería (automática)
Laundromat ® [ˈlɔːndrəmæt] (US) n = **Launderette**
laundry [ˈlɔːndrɪ] n (dirty) ropa sucia; (clean) colada; (room) lavadero
lavatory [ˈlævətərɪ] n wáter m
lavender [ˈlævəndə*] n lavanda
lavish [ˈlævɪʃ] adj (amount) abundante; (person): ~ **with** pródigo en ♦ vt: **to ~ sth on sb** colmar a uno de algo
law [lɔː] n ley f; (SCOL) derecho; (a rule) regla; (professions connected with ~) jurisprudencia; ~**-abiding** adj respetuoso de la ley; ~ **and order** n orden m público; ~ **court** n tribunal m (de justicia); ~**ful** adj legítimo, lícito;

~**less** adj (action) criminal
lawn [lɔːn] n césped m; ~**mower** n cortacésped m; ~ **tennis** n tenis m sobre hierba
law school (US) n (SCOL) facultad f de derecho
lawsuit [ˈlɔːsuːt] n pleito
lawyer [ˈlɔːjə*] n abogado/a; (for sales, wills etc) notario/a
lax [læks] adj laxo
laxative [ˈlæksətɪv] n laxante m
lay [leɪ] (pt, pp **laid**) pt of **lie** ♦ adj laico; (not expert) lego ♦ vt (place) colocar; (eggs, table) poner; (cable) tender; (carpet) extender; ~ **aside** or **by** vt dejar a un lado; ~ **down** vt (pen etc) dejar; (rules etc) establecer; **to ~ down the law** (pej) imponer las normas; ~ **off** vt (workers) despedir; ~ **on** vt (meal, facilities) proveer; ~ **out** vt (spread out) disponer, exponer; ~**about** (inf) n vago/a; ~**-by** n (BRIT: AUT) área de aparcamiento
layer [ˈleɪə*] n capa
layman [ˈleɪmən] (irreg) n lego
layout [ˈleɪaʊt] n (design) plan m, trazado; (PRESS) composición f
laze [leɪz] vi (also: ~ **about**) holgazanear
lazy [ˈleɪzɪ] adj perezoso, vago; (movement) lento
lb. abbr = **pound** (weight)
lead¹ [liːd] (pt, pp **led**) n (front position) delantera; (clue) pista; (ELEC) cable m; (for dog) correa; (THEATRE) papel m principal ♦ vt (walk etc in front of) ir a la cabeza de; (guide): **to ~ sb somewhere** conducir a uno a algún sitio; (be leader of) dirigir; (start, guide: activity) protagonizar ♦ vi (road, pipe etc) conducir a; (SPORT) ir primero; **to be in the ~** (SPORT) llevar la delantera; (fig) ir a la cabeza; **to ~ the way** (also fig) llevar la delantera; ~ **away** vt llevar; ~ **back** vt (person, route) llevar de vuelta; ~ **on** vt (tease) engañar; ~ **to** vt fus producir, provocar; ~ **up to** vt fus (events) conducir a; (in conversation) preparar el terreno para
lead² [lɛd] n (metal) plomo; (in pencil) mina; ~**ed petrol** n gasolina con plomo
leader [ˈliːdə*] n jefe/a m/f, líder m; (SPORT) líder m; ~**ship** n dirección f; (position) mando; (quality) iniciativa
leading [ˈliːdɪŋ] adj (main) principal; (first) primero; (front) delantero; ~ **lady** n (THEATRE) primera actriz f; ~ **light** n (person) figura principal; ~ **man** (irreg) n (THEATRE) primer galán m
lead singer [liːd-] n cantante m/f
leaf [liːf] (pl **leaves**) n hoja ♦ vi: **to ~ through** hojear; **to turn over a new ~** reformarse
leaflet [ˈliːflɪt] n folleto
league [liːg] n sociedad f; (FOOTBALL) liga; **to**

be in ~ with haberse confabulado con

leak [liːk] n (of liquid, gas) escape m, fuga; (in pipe) agujero; (in roof) gotera; (in security) filtración f ♦ vi (shoes, ship) hacer agua; (pipe) tener (un) escape; (roof) gotear; (liquid, gas) escaparse, fugarse; (fig) divulgarse ♦ vt (fig) filtrar

lean [liːn] (pt, pp leaned or leant) adj (thin) flaco; (meat) magro ♦ vt: to ~ sth on sth apoyar algo en algo ♦ vi (slope) inclinarse; to ~ against apoyarse contra; to ~ on apoyarse en; ~ back/forward vi inclinarse hacia atrás/adelante; ~ out vi asomarse; ~ over vi inclinarse; ~ing n: ~ing (towards) inclinación f (hacia); **leant** [lent] pt, pp of lean

leap [liːp] (pt, pp leaped or leapt) n salto ♦ vi saltar; ~frog n pídola; ~ year n año bisiesto

learn [ləːn] (pt, pp learned or learnt) vt aprender ♦ vi aprender; to ~ about sth enterarse de algo; to ~ to do sth aprender a hacer algo; ~ed ['ləːnɪd] adj erudito; ~er n (BRIT: also: ~er driver) principiante m/f; ~ing n el saber m, conocimientos mpl

lease [liːs] n arriendo ♦ vt arrendar

leash [liːʃ] n correa

least [liːst] adj: the ~ (slightest) el menor, el más pequeño; (smallest amount of) mínimo ♦ adv (+ vb) menos; (+ adj): the ~ expensive el/la menos costoso/a; the ~ possible effort el menor esfuerzo posible; at ~ por lo menos, al menos; you could at ~ have written por lo menos podías haber escrito; not in the ~ en absoluto

leather ['lɛðə*] n cuero

leave [liːv] (pt, pp left) vt dejar; (go away from) abandonar; (place etc: permanently) salir de ♦ vi irse; (train etc) salir ♦ n permiso; to ~ sth to sb (money etc) legar algo a uno; (responsibility etc) encargar a uno de algo; to be left quedar, sobrar; there's some milk left over sobra or queda algo de leche; on ~ de permiso; ~ behind vt (on purpose) dejar; (accidentally) dejarse; ~ out vt omitir; ~ of absence n permiso de ausentarse

leaves [liːvz] npl of leaf

Lebanon ['lɛbənən] n: the ~ el Líbano

lecherous ['lɛtʃərəs] (pej) adj lascivo

lecture ['lɛktʃə*] n conferencia; (SCOL) clase f ♦ vi dar una clase ♦ vt (scold): to ~ sb on or about sth echar una reprimenda a uno por algo; to give a ~ on dar una conferencia sobre; ~r n conferenciante m/f; (BRIT: at university) profesor(a) m/f

led [lɛd] pt, pp of lead

ledge [lɛdʒ] n repisa; (of window) alféizar m; (of mountain) saliente m

ledger ['lɛdʒə*] n libro mayor

leech [liːtʃ] n sanguijuela

leek [liːk] n puerro

leer [lɪə*] vi: to ~ at sb mirar de manera lasciva a uno

leeway ['liːweɪ] n (fig): to have some ~ tener cierta libertad de acción

left [lɛft] pt, pp of leave ♦ adj izquierdo; (remaining): there are 2 ~ quedan dos ♦ n izquierda ♦ adv a la izquierda; on or to the ~ a la izquierda; the L~ (POL) la izquierda; ~-handed adj zurdo; the ~-hand side n la izquierda; ~-luggage (office) (BRIT) n consigna; ~-overs npl sobras fpl; ~-wing adj (POL) de izquierdas, izquierdista

leg [lɛg] n (pierna; (of animal, chair) pata; (trouser ~) pernera; (CULIN: of lamb) pierna; (of chicken) pata; (of journey) etapa

legacy ['lɛgəsɪ] n herencia

legal ['liːgl] adj (permitted by law) lícito; (of law) legal; ~ holiday (US) n fiesta oficial; ~ize vt legalizar; ~ly adv legalmente; ~ tender n moneda de curso legal

legend ['lɛdʒənd] n (also fig: person) leyenda

legislation [lɛdʒɪs'leɪʃən] n legislación f

legislature ['lɛdʒɪslətʃə*] n cuerpo legislativo

legitimate [lɪ'dʒɪtɪmət] adj legítimo

leg-room n espacio para las piernas

leisure ['lɛʒə*] n ocio, tiempo libre; at ~ con tranquilidad; ~ centre n centro de recreo; ~ly adj sin prisa; lento

lemon ['lɛmən] n limón m; ~ade n (fizzy) gaseosa; ~ tea n té m con limón

lend [lɛnd] (pt, pp lent) vt: to ~ sth to sb prestar algo a alguien; ~ing library n biblioteca de préstamo

length [lɛŋθ] n (size) largo, longitud f; (distance): the ~ of todo lo largo de; (of swimming pool, cloth) largo; (of wood, string) trozo; (amount of time) duración f; at ~ (at last) por fin, finalmente; (lengthily) largamente; ~en vt alargar ♦ vi alargarse; ~ways adv a lo largo; ~y adj largo, extenso

lenient ['liːnɪənt] adj indulgente

lens [lɛnz] n (of spectacles) lente f; (of camera) objetivo

Lent [lɛnt] n Cuaresma

lent [lɛnt] pt, pp of lend

lentil ['lɛntl] n lenteja

Leo ['liːəu] n Leo

leotard ['liːətɑːd] n mallas fpl

leprosy ['lɛprəsɪ] n lepra

lesbian ['lɛzbɪən] n lesbiana

less [lɛs] adj (in size, degree etc) menor; (in quality) menos ♦ pron, adv menos ♦ prep: ~ tax/10% discount menos impuestos/el 10 por ciento de descuento; ~ than half menos de la mitad; ~ than ever menos que nunca; ~ and ~ cada vez menos; the ~ he works ... cuanto menos trabaja ...; ~en vi disminuir, reducirse ♦ vt disminuir, reducir; ~er ['lɛsə*] adj menor; to a ~er extent en menor grado

lesson ['lɛsn] n clase f; (warning) lección f
let [lɛt] (pt, pp **let**) vt (allow) dejar, permitir;
(BRIT: lease) alquilar; **to ~ sb do sth** dejar que
uno haga algo; **to ~ sb know sth** comunicar
algo a uno; **~'s go** ¡vamos!; **~ him come** que
venga; **"to ~"** "se alquila"; **~ down** vt (tyre)
desinflar; (disappoint) defraudar; **~ go** vi, vt
soltar; **~ in** vt dejar entrar; (visitor etc) hacer
pasar; **~ off** vt (culprit) dejar escapar; (gun)
disparar; (bomb) accionar; (firework) hacer
estallar; **~ on** (inf) vi divulgar; **~ out** vt dejar
salir; (sound) soltar; **~ up** vi amainar,
disminuir
lethal ['li:θl] adj (weapon) mortífero; (poison,
wound) mortal
letter ['lɛtə*] n (of alphabet) letra;
(correspondence) carta; **~ bomb** n carta-
bomba; **~box** (BRIT) n buzón m; **~ing** n
letras fpl
lettuce ['lɛtɪs] n lechuga
let-up n disminución f
leukaemia [lu:'ki:mɪə] (US **leukemia**) n
leucemia
level ['lɛvl] adj (flat) llano ♦ adv: **to draw
~ with** llegar a la altura de ♦ n nivel m;
(height) altura ♦ vt nivelar; allanar; (destroy:
building) derribar; (: forest) arrasar; **to be
~ with** estar a nivel de; **"A" ~s** (BRIT) npl ≈
exámenes mpl de bachillerato superior,
B.U.P.; **"O" ~s** (BRIT) npl ≈ exámenes mpl de
octavo de básica; **on the ~** (fig: honest) serio;
~ off or **out** vi (prices etc) estabilizarse;
~ crossing (BRIT) n paso a nivel; **~-headed**
adj sensato
lever ['li:və*] n (also fig) palanca ♦ vt: **to ~ up**
levantar con palanca; **~age** n (using bar etc)
apalancamiento; (fig: influence) influencia
levy ['lɛvɪ] n impuesto ♦ vt exigir, recaudar
lewd [lu:d] adj lascivo; (joke) obsceno,
colorado (AM)
liability [laɪə'bɪlətɪ] n (pej: person, thing)
estorbo, lastre m; (JUR: responsibility)
responsabilidad f; **liabilities** npl (COMM) pasivo
liable ['laɪəbl] adj (subject): **~ to** sujeto a;
(responsible): **~ for** responsable de; (likely):
~ to do propenso a hacer
liaise [lɪ'eɪz] vi: **to ~ with** enlazar con; **liaison**
[lɪ:'eɪzɔn] n (coordination) enlace m; (affair)
relaciones fpl amorosas
liar ['laɪə*] n mentiroso/a
libel ['laɪbl] n calumnia ♦ vt calumniar
liberal ['lɪbərəl] adj liberal; (offer, amount etc)
generoso
liberate ['lɪbəreɪt] vt (people: from poverty
etc) librar; (prisoner) libertar; (country) liberar
liberty ['lɪbətɪ] n libertad f; (criminal): **to be
at ~** estar en libertad; **to be at ~ to do** estar
libre para hacer; **to take the ~ of doing sth**
tomarse la libertad de hacer algo

Libra ['li:brə] n Libra
librarian [laɪ'brɛərɪən] n bibliotecario/a
library ['laɪbrərɪ] n biblioteca
libretto [lɪ'brɛtəu] n libreto
Libya ['lɪbɪə] n Libia; **~n** adj, n libio/a m/f
lice [laɪs] npl of **louse**
licence ['laɪsəns] (US **license**) n licencia;
(permit) permiso; (also: driving ~, (US) driver's
~) carnet m de conducir (SP), permiso (AM)
license ['laɪsəns] n (US) = **licence** ♦ vt
autorizar, dar permiso a; **~d** adj (for alcohol)
autorizado para vender bebidas alcohólicas;
(car) matriculado; **~ plate** (US) n placa (de
matrícula)
lick [lɪk] vt lamer; (inf: defeat) dar una paliza
a; **to ~ one's lips** relamerse
licorice ['lɪkərɪs] (US) n = **liquorice**
lid [lɪd] n (of box, case) tapa; (of pan)
tapadera
lido ['laɪdəu] n (BRIT) piscina
lie [laɪ] (pt **lay**, pp **lain**) vi (rest) estar echado,
estar acostado; (of object: be situated) estar,
encontrarse; (tell lies: pt, pp **lied**) mentir ♦ n
mentira; **to ~ low** (fig) mantenerse a
escondidas; **~ about** or **around** vi (things)
estar tirado; (people) estar tumbado; **~
down** (BRIT) n: **to have a ~down** echarse
(una siesta); **~-in** (BRIT) n: **to have a ~-in**
quedarse en la cama
lieu [lu:]: **in ~ of** prep en lugar de
lieutenant [lɛf'tɛnənt, (US) lu:'tɛnənt] n
(MIL) teniente m
life [laɪf] (pl **lives**) n vida; **to come to ~**
animarse; **~ assurance** (BRIT) n seguro de
vida; **~belt** (BRIT) n salvavidas m inv; **~boat**
n lancha de socorro; **~guard** n vigilante m/f,
socorrista m/f; **~ insurance** n = **~ assurance**; **~ jacket** n chaleco salvavidas;
~less adj sin vida; (dull) soso; **~like** adj
(model etc) que parece vivo; (realistic)
realista; **~long** adj de toda la vida;
~ preserver (US) n cinturón m/chaleco
salvavidas; **~ sentence** n cadena perpetua;
~-size adj de tamaño natural; **~ span** n
vida; **~style** n estilo de vida; **~ support
system** n (MED) sistema m de respiración
asistida; **~time** n (of person) vida; (of thing)
período de vida
lift [lɪft] vt levantar; (end: ban, rule) levantar,
suprimir ♦ vi (fog) disiparse ♦ n (BRIT:
machine) ascensor m; **to give sb a ~** (BRIT)
llevar a uno en el coche; **~-off** n despegue m
light [laɪt] (pt, pp **lighted** or **lit**) n luz f; (lamp)
luz f, lámpara; (AUT) faro; (for cigarette etc):
have you got a ~? ¿tienes fuego? ♦ vt (candle,
cigarette, fire) encender (SP), prender (AM);
(room) alumbrar ♦ adj (colour) claro; (not
heavy, also fig) ligero; (room) con mucha luz;
(gentle, graceful) ágil; **~s** npl (traffic ~s)

semáforos *mpl*; **to come to ~** salir a luz; **in the ~ of** (*new evidence etc*) a la luz de; **~ up** *vi* (*smoke*) encender un cigarrillo; (*face*) iluminarse ♦ *vt* (*illuminate*) iluminar, alumbrar; (*set fire to*) encender; **~ bulb** *n* bombilla (*SP*), foco (*AM*); **~en** *vt* (*make less heavy*) aligerar; **~er** *n* (*also: cigarette ~er*) encendedor *m*, mechero; **~-headed** *adj* (*dizzy*) mareado; (*excited*) exaltado; **~-hearted** *adj* (*person*) alegre; (*remark etc*) divertido; **~house** *n* faro; **~ing** *n* (*system*) alumbrado; **~ly** *adv* ligeramente; (*not seriously*) con poca seriedad; **to get off ~ly** ser castigado con poca severidad; **~ness** *n* (*in weight*) ligereza

lightning ['laɪtnɪŋ] *n* relámpago, rayo; **~ conductor** (*US* → **rod**) *n* pararrayos *m inv*

light: ~ pen *n* lápiz *m* óptico; **~weight** *adj* (*suit*) ligero ♦ *n* (*BOXING*) peso ligero; **~ year** *n* año luz

like [laɪk] *vt* gustarle a uno ♦ *prep* como ♦ *adj* parecido, semejante ♦ *n*: **and the ~** y otros por el estilo; **his ~s and dislikes** sus gustos y aversiones; **I would ~, I'd ~** me gustaría; (*for purchase*) quisiera; **would you ~ a coffee?** ¿te apetece un café?; **I ~ swimming** me gusta nadar; **she ~s apples** le gustan las manzanas; **to be** *or* **look ~ sb/sth** parecerse a alguien/ algo; **what does it look/taste/sound ~?** ¿cómo es/a qué sabe/cómo suena?; **that's just ~ him** es muy de él, es característico de él; **do it ~ this** hazlo así; **it is nothing ~ ...** no tiene parecido alguno con ...; **~able** *adj* simpático, agradable

likelihood ['laɪklɪhʊd] *n* probabilidad *f*

likely ['laɪklɪ] *adj* probable; **he's ~ to leave** es probable que se vaya; **not ~!** ¡ni hablar!

likeness ['laɪknɪs] *n* semejanza, parecido; **that's a good ~** se parece mucho

likewise ['laɪkwaɪz] *adv* igualmente; **to do ~** hacer lo mismo

liking ['laɪkɪŋ] *n*: **~ (for)** (*person*) cariño (a); (*thing*) afición (a); **to be to sb's ~** ser del gusto de uno

lilac ['laɪlək] *n* (*tree*) lilo; (*flower*) lila

lily ['lɪlɪ] *n* lirio, azucena; **~ of the valley** *n* lirio de los valles

limb [lɪm] *n* miembro

limber ['lɪmbə*] : **to ~ up** *vi* (*SPORT*) hacer ejercicios de calentamiento

limbo ['lɪmbəʊ] *n*: **to be in ~** (*fig*) quedar a la expectativa

lime [laɪm] *n* (*tree*) limero; (*fruit*) lima; (*GEO*) cal *f*

limelight ['laɪmlaɪt] *n*: **to be in the ~** (*fig*) ser el centro de atención

limerick ['lɪmərɪk] *n* especie de poema humorístico

limestone ['laɪmstəʊn] *n* piedra caliza

limit ['lɪmɪt] *n* límite *m* ♦ *vt* limitar; **~ed** *adj* limitado; **to be ~ed to** limitarse a; **~ed (liability) company** (*BRIT*) *n* sociedad *f* anónima

limousine ['lɪməzi:n] *n* limusina

limp [lɪmp] *n*: **to have a ~** tener cojera ♦ *vi* cojear ♦ *adj* flojo; (*material*) fláccido

limpet ['lɪmpɪt] *n* lapa

line [laɪn] *n* línea; (*rope*) cuerda; (*for fishing*) sedal *m*; (*wire*) hilo; (*row, series*) fila, hilera; (*of writing*) renglón *m*, línea; (*of song*) verso; (*on face*) arruga; (*RAIL*) vía ♦ *vt* (*road etc*) llenar; (*SEWING*) forrar; **to ~ the streets** llenar las aceras; **in ~ with** alineado con; (*according to*) de acuerdo con; **~ up** *vi* hacer cola ♦ *vt* alinear; (*prepare*) preparar; organizar

lined [laɪnd] *adj* (*face*) arrugado; (*paper*) rayado

linen ['lɪnɪn] *n* ropa blanca; (*cloth*) lino

liner ['laɪnə*] *n* vapor *m* de línea, transatlántico; (*for bin*) bolsa (de basura)

linesman ['laɪnzmən] *n* (*SPORT*) juez *m* de línea

line-up *n* (*US: queue*) cola; (*SPORT*) alineación *f*

linger ['lɪŋgə*] *vi* retrasarse, tardar en marcharse; (*smell, tradition*) persistir

lingerie ['lænʒəri:] *n* lencería

linguist ['lɪŋgwɪst] *n* lingüista *m/f*; **~ics** *n* lingüística

lining ['laɪnɪŋ] *n* forro; (*ANAT*) (*membrana*) mucosa

link [lɪŋk] *n* (*of a chain*) eslabón *m*; (*relationship*) relación *f*, vínculo ♦ *vt* vincular, unir; (*associate*): **to ~ with** *or* **to** relacionar con; **~s** *npl* (*GOLF*) campo de golf; **~ up** *vt* acoplar ♦ *vi* unirse

lino ['laɪnəʊ] *n* = **linoleum**

linoleum [lɪ'nəʊlɪəm] *n* linóleo

lion ['laɪən] *n* león *m*; **~ess** *n* leona

lip [lɪp] *n* labio

liposuction ['lɪpəʊsʌkʃən] *n* liposucción *f*

lip: ~read *vi* leer los labios; **~ salve** *n* crema protectora para labios; **~ service** *n*: **to pay ~ service to sth** (*pej*) prometer algo de boquilla; **~stick** *n* lápiz *m* de labios, carmín *m*

liqueur [lɪ'kjʊə*] *n* licor *m*

liquid ['lɪkwɪd] *adj, n* líquido; **~ize** [-aɪz] *vt* (*CULIN*) licuar; **~izer** [-aɪzə*] *n* licuadora

liquor ['lɪkə*] *n* licor *m*, bebidas *fpl* alcohólicas

liquorice ['lɪkərɪs] (*BRIT*) *n* regaliz *m*

liquor store (*US*) *n* bodega, tienda de vinos y bebidas alcohólicas

Lisbon ['lɪzbən] *n* Lisboa

lisp [lɪsp] *n* ceceo ♦ *vi* cecear

list [lɪst] *n* lista ♦ *vt* (*mention*) enumerar; (*put on a list*) poner en una lista; **~ed building** (*BRIT*) *n* monumento declarado de interés *histórico-artístico*

listen |'lɪsn| *vi* escuchar, oír; **to ~ to sb/sth** escuchar a uno/algo; **~er** *n* oyente *m/f*; (*RADIO*) radioyente *m/f*

listless ['lɪstlɪs] *adj* apático, indiferente

lit |lɪt| *pt, pp* of **light**

liter ['liːtə*] (*US*) *n* = **litre**

literacy ['lɪtərəsɪ] *n* capacidad *f* de leer y escribir

literal ['lɪtərl] *adj* literal

literary ['lɪtərərɪ] *adj* literario

literate ['lɪtərɪt] *adj* que sabe leer y escribir; (*educated*) culto

literature ['lɪtrɪtʃə*] *n* literatura; (*brochures etc*) folletos *mpl*

lithe |laɪð| *adj* ágil

litigation [lɪtɪ'geɪʃən] *n* litigio

litre ['liːtə*] (*US* **liter**) *n* litro

litter ['lɪtə*] *n* (*rubbish*) basura; (*young animals*) camada, cría; **~ bin** (*BRIT*) *n* papelera; **~ed** *adj*: **~ed with** (*scattered*) lleno de

little ['lɪtl] *adj* (*small*) pequeño; (*not much*) poco ♦ *adv* poco; **a ~** un poco (de); **~ house/bird** casita/pajarito; **a ~ bit** un poquito; **~ by ~** poco a poco; **~ finger** *n* dedo meñique

live¹ |laɪv| *adj* (*animal*) vivo; (*wire*) conectado; (*broadcast*) en directo; (*shell*) cargado

live² |lɪv| *vi* vivir; **~ down** *vt* hacer olvidar; **~ on** *vt fus* (*food, salary*) vivir de; **~ together** *vi* vivir juntos; **~ up to** *vt fus* (*fulfil*) cumplir con

livelihood ['laɪvlɪhud] *n* sustento

lively ['laɪvlɪ] *adj* vivo; (*interesting: place, book etc*) animado

liven up ['laɪvn-] *vt* animar ♦ *vi* animarse

liver ['lɪvə*] *n* hígado

lives |laɪvz| *npl* of **life**

livestock ['laɪvstɔk] *n* ganado

livid ['lɪvɪd] *adj* lívido; (*furious*) furioso

living ['lɪvɪŋ] *adj* (*alive*) vivo ♦ *n*: **to earn** or **make a ~** ganarse la vida; **~ conditions** *npl* condiciones *fpl* de vida; **~ room** *n* sala (de estar); **~ standards** *npl* nivel *m* de vida; **~ wage** *n* jornal *m* suficiente para vivir

lizard ['lɪzəd] *n* lagarto; (*small*) lagartija

load |ləud| *n* carga; (*weight*) peso ♦ *vt* (*COMPUT*) cargar; (*also: ~ up*): **to ~ (with)** cargar (con or de); **a ~ of rubbish** (*inf*) tonterías *fpl*; **a ~ of, ~s of** (*fig*) (gran) cantidad *f*, montones de; **~ed** *adj* (*vehicle*): **to be ~ed with** estar cargado de; (*question*) intencionado; (*inf: rich*) forrado (de dinero)

loaf |ləuf| (*pl* **loaves**) *n* (barra de) pan *m*

loan |ləun| *n* préstamo ♦ *vt* prestar; **on ~** prestado

loath |ləuθ| *adj*: **to be ~ to do sth** estar poco

dispuesto a hacer algo

loathe [ləuð] *vt* aborrecer; (*person*) odiar; **loathing** *n* aversión *f*; odio

loaves [ləuvz] *npl* of **loaf**

lobby ['lɔbɪ] *n* vestíbulo, sala de espera; (*POL: pressure group*) grupo de presión ♦ *vt* presionar

lobster ['lɔbstə*] *n* langosta

local ['ləukl] *adj* local ♦ *n* (*pub*) bar *m*; **the ~s** los vecinos, los del lugar; **~ anaesthetic** *n* (*MED*) anestesia local; **~ authority** *n* municipio, ayuntamiento (*SP*); **~ call** *n* (*TEL*) llamada local; **~ government** *n* gobierno municipal; **~ity** [-'kælɪtɪ] *n* localidad *f*; **~ly** [-kəlɪ] *adv* en la vecindad; por aquí

locate |ləu'keɪt| *vt* (*find*) localizar; (*situate*): **to be ~d in** estar situado en

location |ləu'keɪʃən| *n* situación *f*; **on ~** (*CINEMA*) en exteriores

loch |lɔx| *n* lago

lock |lɔk| *n* (*of door, box*) cerradura; (*of canal*) esclusa; (*of hair*) mechón *m* ♦ *vt* (*with key*) cerrar (con llave) ♦ *vi* (*door etc*) cerrarse (con llave); (*wheels*) trabarse; **~ in** *vt* encerrar; **~ out** *vt* (*person*) cerrar la puerta a; **~ up** *vt* (*criminal*) meter en la cárcel; (*mental patient*) encerrar; (*house*) cerrar (con llave) ♦ *vi* echar la llave

locker ['lɔkə*] *n* casillero

locket ['lɔkɪt] *n* medallón *m*

locksmith ['lɔksmɪθ] *n* cerrajero/a

lockup ['lɔkʌp] *n* (*jail, cell*) cárcel *f*

locum ['ləukəm] *n* (*MED*) (médico/a) interino/a

locust ['ləukəst] *n* langosta

lodge [lɔdʒ] *n* casita (del guarda) ♦ *vi* (*person*): **to ~ (with)** alojarse (en casa de); (*bullet, bone*) incrustarse ♦ *vt* (*complaint*) presentar; **~r** *n* huésped(a) *m/f*

lodgings ['lɔdʒɪŋz] *npl* alojamiento

loft |lɔft| *n* desván *m*

lofty ['lɔftɪ] *adj* (*noble*) sublime; (*haughty*) altanero

log |lɔg| *n* (*of wood*) leño, tronco; (*written account*) diario ♦ *vt* anotar

logbook ['lɔgbuk] *n* (*NAUT*) diario de a bordo; (*AVIAT*) libro de vuelo; (*of car*) documentación *f* (del coche (*SP*) or carro (*AM*))

loggerheads ['lɔgəhedz] *npl*: **to be at ~ (with)** estar en desacuerdo (con)

logic ['lɔdʒɪk] *n* lógica; **~al** *adj* lógico

logo ['ləugəu] *n* logotipo

loin |lɔɪn| *n* (*CULIN*) lomo, solomillo

loiter ['lɔɪtə*] *vi* (*linger*) entretenerse

loll |lɔl| *vi* (*also: ~ about*): repantigarse

lollipop ['lɔlɪpɔp] *n* chupa-chups ® *m inv*, piruli *m*; **~ man/lady** (*BRIT irreg*) *n* persona encargada de ayudar a los niños a cruzar la *calle*

London ['lʌndən] *n* Londres; **~er** *n*
londinense *m/f*

lone [ləun] *adj* solitario

loneliness ['ləunlınıs] *n* soledad *f*;
aislamiento

lonely ['ləunlı] *adj* (*situation*) solitario;
(*person*) solo; (*place*) aislado

long [lɒŋ] *adj* largo ♦ *adv* mucho tiempo,
largamente ♦ *vi*: **to ~ for sth** anhelar algo; **so
or as ~ as** mientras, con tal que; **don't be ~!**
¡no tardes!, ¡vuelve pronto!; **how ~ is the
street?** ¿cuánto tiene la calle de largo?; **how
~ is the lesson?** ¿cuánto dura la clase?; **6
metres ~** que mide 6 metros, de 6 metros de
largo; **6 months ~** que dura 6 meses, de 6
meses de duración; **all night ~** toda la noche;
he no ~er comes ya no viene; **~ before** mucho
antes; **before ~** (+ *future*) dentro de poco;
(+ *past*) poco tiempo después; **at ~ last** al
fin, por fin; **~-distance** *adj* (*race*) de larga
distancia; (*call*) interurbano; **~-haired** *adj* de
pelo largo; **~hand** *n* escritura sin
abreviaturas; **~ing** *n* anhelo, ansia;
(*nostalgia*) nostalgia ♦ *adj* anhelante

longitude ['lɒŋgıtju:d] *n* longitud *f*

long: **~ jump** *n* salto de longitud; **~-life** *adj*
(*batteries*) de larga duración; (*milk*)
uperizado; **~-lost** *adj* desaparecido hace
mucho tiempo; **~-range** *adj* (*plan*) de gran
alcance; (*missile*) de largo alcance; **~-
sighted** (*BRIT*) *adj* présbita; **~-standing** *adj*
de mucho tiempo; **~-suffering** *adj* sufrido;
~-term *adj* a largo plazo; **~ wave** *n* onda
larga; **~-winded** *adj* prolijo

loo [lu:] (*BRIT: inf*) *n* wáter *m*

look [luk] *vi* mirar; (*seem*) parecer; (*building
etc*) **to ~ south/on to the sea** dar al sur/al
mar ♦ *n* (*gen*): **to have a ~** mirar; (*glance*)
mirada; (*appearance*) aire *m*, aspecto; **~s** *npl*
(*good ~s*) belleza; **~ (here)!** (*expressing
annoyance etc*) ¡oye!; **~!** (*expressing surprise*)
¡mira!; **~ after** *vt fus* (*care for*) cuidar a; (*deal
with*) encargarse de; **~ at** *vt fus* mirar; (*read
quickly*) echar un vistazo a; **~ back** *vi* mirar
hacia atrás; **~ down on** *vt fus* (*fig*)
despreciar, mirar con desprecio; **~ for** *vt fus*
buscar; **~ forward to** *vt fus* esperar con
ilusión; (*in letters*): **we ~ forward to hearing
from you** quedamos a la espera de sus gratas
noticias; **~ into** *vt* investigar; **~ on** *vi* mirar
(como espectador); **~ out** *vi* (*beware*): **to
~ out (for)** tener cuidado (de); **~ out for** *vt
fus* (*seek*) buscar; (*await*) esperar; **~ round** *vi*
volver la cabeza; **~ through** *vt fus* (*examine*)
examinar; **~ to** *vt fus* (*rely on*) contar con;
~ up *vi* mirar hacia arriba; (*improve*) mejorar
♦ *vt* (*word*) buscar; **~ up to** *vt fus* admirar;
~-out *n* (*tower etc*) puesto de observación;

(*person*) vigía *m/f*; **to be on the ~-out for sth**
estar al acecho de algo

loom [lu:m] *vi*: **~ (up)** (*threaten*) surgir,
amenazar; (*event: approach*) aproximarse

loony ['lu:nı] (*inf*) *n, adj* loco/a *m/f*

loop [lu:p] *n* lazo ♦ *vt*: **to ~ sth round sth**
pasar algo alrededor de algo; **~hole** *n*
escapatoria

loose [lu:s] *adj* suelto; (*clothes*) ancho;
(*morals, discipline*) relajado; **to be on the ~**
estar en libertad; **to be at a ~ end** or **at
~ ends** (*US*) no saber qué hacer; **~ change** *n*
cambio; **~ chippings** *npl* (*on road*) gravilla
suelta; **~ly** *adv* libremente,
aproximadamente; **~n** *vt* aflojar

loot [lu:t] *n* botín *m* ♦ *vt* saquear

lop off [lɒp-] *vt* (*branches*) podar

lop-sided *adj* torcido

lord [lɔ:d] *n* señor *m*; **L~ Smith** Lord Smith;
the L~ el Señor; **my ~** (*to bishop*) Ilustrísima;
(*to noble etc*) Señor; **good L~!** ¡Dios mío!; **the
(House of) L~s** (*BRIT*) la Cámara de los Lores;
~ship *n*: **your L~ship** su Señoría

lore [lɔ:*] *n* tradiciones *fpl*

lorry ['lɒrı] (*BRIT*) *n* camión *m*; **~ driver** *n*
camionero/a

lose [lu:z] (*pt, pp* **lost**) *vt* perder ♦ *vi* perder,
ser vencido; **to ~ (time)** (*clock*) atrasarse; **~r** *n*
perdedor(a) *m/f*

loss [lɒs] *n* pérdida; **heavy ~es** (*MIL*) grandes
pérdidas; **to be at a ~** no saber qué hacer; **to
make a ~** sufrir pérdidas

lost [lɒst] *pt, pp of* **lose** ♦ *adj* perdido;
~ property (*US* **~ and found**) *n* objetos *mpl*
perdidos

lot [lɒt] *n* (*group: of things*) grupo; (*at
auctions*) lote *m*; **the ~** el todo, todos; **a ~**
(*large number: of books etc*) muchos; (*a great
deal*) mucho, bastante; **a ~ of** mucho(s) (*pl*); **I read a ~** leo bastante; **to
draw ~s (for sth)** echar suertes (para decidir
algo)

lotion ['ləuʃən] *n* loción *f*

lottery ['lɒtərı] *n* lotería

loud [laud] *adj* (*voice, sound*) fuerte; (*laugh,
shout*) estrepitoso; (*condemnation etc*)
enérgico; (*gaudy*) chillón/ona ♦ *adv* (*speak
etc*) fuerte; **out ~** en voz alta; **~hailer** (*BRIT*) *n*
megáfono; **~ly** *adv* (*noisily*) fuerte; (*aloud*)
en voz alta; **~speaker** *n* altavoz *m*

lounge [laundʒ] *n* salón *m*, sala (de estar);
(*at airport etc*) sala; (*BRIT: also:* **~-bar**) salón-
bar *m* ♦ *vi* (*also:* **~ about** or **around**) reposar,
holgazanear

louse [laus] (*pl* **lice**) *n* piojo

lousy ['lauzı] (*inf*) *adj* (*bad quality*) malísimo,
asqueroso; (*ill*) fatal

lout [laut] *n* gamberro/a

lovable ['lʌvəbl] *adj* amable, simpático

love [lʌv] n (romantic, sexual) amor m; (kind, caring) cariño ♦ vt amar, querer; (thing, activity) encantarle a uno; "~ from Anne" (on letter) "un abrazo (de) Anne"; **to ~ to do** encantarle a uno hacer; **to be/fall in ~ with** estar enamorado/enamorarse de; **to make ~** hacer el amor; **for the ~ of** por amor de; "15 ♦" (TENNIS) "15 a cero"; **I ~ paella me** encanta la paella; **~ affair** n aventura sentimental; **~ letter** n carta de amor; **~ life** n vida sentimental

lovely ['lʌvlɪ] adj (delightful) encantador(a); (beautiful) precioso

lover ['lʌvə*] n amante m/f; (person in love) enamorado; (amateur): **a ~ of** un(a) aficionado/a or un(a) amante de

loving ['lʌvɪŋ] adj amoroso, cariñoso; (action) tierno

low [ləu] adj, ad bajo ♦ n (METEOROLOGY) área de baja presión; **to be ~ on** (supplies etc) andar mal de; **to feel ~** sentirse deprimido; **to turn (down) ~** bajar; **~-alcohol** adj de bajo contenido en alcohol; **~-calorie** adj bajo en calorías; **~-cut** adj (dress) escotado

lower ['ləuə*] adj más bajo; (less important) menos importante ♦ vt bajar; (reduce) reducir ♦ vr: **to ~ o.s. to** (fig) rebajarse a

low: **~-fat** adj (milk, yoghurt) desnatado; (diet) bajo en calorías; **~lands** npl (GEO) tierras fpl bajas; **~ly** adj humilde, inferior; **~ season** n la temporada baja

loyal ['lɔɪəl] adj leal; **~ty** lealtad f; **~ty card** n tarjeta cliente

lozenge ['lɔzɪndʒ] n (MED) pastilla

L.P. n abbr (= long-playing record) elepé m

L-plates ['ɛl-] (BRIT) npl placas fpl de aprendiz de conductor

Ltd abbr (= limited company) S.A.

lubricate ['lu:brɪkeɪt] vt lubricar, engrasar

luck [lʌk] n suerte f; **bad ~** mala suerte; **good ~!** ¡que tengas suerte!, ¡suerte!; **bad or hard or tough ~!** ¡qué pena!; **~ily** adv afortunadamente; **~y** adj afortunado; (at cards etc) con suerte; (object) que trae suerte

ludicrous ['lu:dɪkrəs] adj absurdo

lug [lʌg] vt (drag) arrastrar

luggage ['lʌgɪdʒ] n equipaje m; **~ rack** n (on car) baca, portaequipajes m inv

lukewarm ['lu:kwɔ:m] adj tibio

lull [lʌl] n tregua ♦ vt: **to ~ sb to sleep** arrullar a uno; **to ~ sb into a false sense of security** dar a alguien una falsa sensación de seguridad

lullaby ['lʌləbaɪ] n nana

lumbago [lʌm'beɪgəu] n lumbago

lumber ['lʌmbə*] n (junk) trastos mpl viejos; (wood) maderos mpl; **~ with** vt: **to be ~ed with** tener que cargar con algo; **~jack** n maderero

luminous ['lu:mɪnəs] adj luminoso

lump [lʌmp] n terrón m; (fragment) trozo; (swelling) bulto ♦ vt (also: ~ together) juntar; **~ sum** n suma global; **~y** adj (sauce) lleno de grumos; (mattress) lleno de bultos

lunatic ['lu:nətɪk] adj loco

lunch [lʌntʃ] n almuerzo, comida ♦ vi almorzar

luncheon ['lʌntʃən] n almuerzo; **~ voucher** (BRIT) n vale m de comida

lunch time n hora de comer

lung [lʌŋ] n pulmón m

lunge [lʌndʒ] vi (also: ~ forward) abalanzarse; **to ~ at** arremeter contra

lurch [lə:tʃ] vi dar sacudidas ♦ n sacudida; **to leave sb in the ~** dejar a uno plantado

lure [luə*] n (attraction) atracción f ♦ vt tentar

lurid ['luərɪd] adj (colour) chillón/ona; (account) espeluznante

lurk [lə:k] vi (person, animal) estar al acecho; (fig) acechar

luscious ['lʌʃəs] adj (attractive: person, thing) precioso; (food) delicioso

lush [lʌʃ] adj exuberante

lust [lʌst] n lujuria; (greed) codicia

lustre ['lʌstə*] (US luster) n lustre m, brillo

lusty ['lʌstɪ] adj robusto, fuerte

Luxembourg ['lʌksəmbə:g] n Luxemburgo

luxuriant [lʌg'zjuərɪənt] adj exuberante

luxurious [lʌg'zjuərɪəs] adj lujoso

luxury ['lʌkʃərɪ] n lujo ♦ cpd de lujo

lying ['laɪɪŋ] n mentiras fpl ♦ adj mentiroso

lyrical ['lɪrɪkl] adj lírico

lyrics ['lɪrɪks] npl (of song) letra

M, m

m. abbr = metre; mile; million

M.A. abbr = Master of Arts

mac [mæk] (BRIT) n impermeable m

macaroni [mækə'rəunɪ] n macarrones mpl

machine [mə'ʃi:n] n máquina ♦ vt (dress etc) coser a máquina; (TECH) hacer a máquina; **~ gun** n ametralladora; **~ language** n (COMPUT) lenguaje m máquina; **~ry** n maquinaria; (fig) mecanismo

macho ['mætʃəu] adj machista

mackerel ['mækrl] n inv caballa

mackintosh ['mækɪntʃ] (BRIT) n impermeable m

mad [mæd] adj loco; (idea) disparatado; (angry) furioso; (keen): **to be ~ about sth** volverle loco a uno algo

madam ['mædəm] n señora

madden ['mædn] vt volver loco

made [meɪd] pt, pp of **make**

Madeira [mə'dɪərə] n (GEO) Madera; (wine) vino de Madera

made-to-measure (BRIT) adj hecho a la

medida

madly ['mædlɪ] *adv* locamente

madman ['mædmən] (*irreg*) *n* loco

madness ['mædnɪs] *n* locura

Madrid [mə'drɪd] *n* Madrid

magazine [mægə'ziːn] *n* revista; (*RADIO, TV*) programa *m* magazina

maggot ['mægət] *n* gusano

magic ['mædʒɪk] *n* magia ♦ *adj* mágico; **~ian** [mə'dʒɪʃən] *n* mago/a; (*conjurer*) prestidigitador(a) *m/f*

magistrate ['mædʒɪstreɪt] *n* juez *m/f* (*municipal*)

magnet ['mægnɪt] *n* imán *m*; **~ic** [-'netɪk] *adj* magnético; (*personality*) atrayente

magnificent [mæg'nɪfɪsənt] *adj* magnífico

magnify ['mægnɪfaɪ] *vt* (*object*) ampliar; (*sound*) aumentar; **~ing glass** *n* lupa

magpie ['mægpaɪ] *n* urraca

mahogany [mə'hɔgənɪ] *n* caoba

maid [meɪd] *n* criada; **old ~** (*pej*) solterona

maiden ['meɪdn] *n* doncella ♦ *adj* (*aunt etc*) solterona; (*speech, voyage*) inaugural; **~ name** *n* nombre *m* de soltera

mail [meɪl] *n* correo; (*letters*) cartas *fpl* ♦ *vt* echar al correo; **~box** (*US*) *n* buzón *m*; **~ing list** *n* lista de direcciones; **~-order** *n* pedido postal

maim [meɪm] *vt* mutilar, lisiar

main [meɪn] *adj* principal, mayor ♦ *n* (*pipe*) cañería maestra; (*US*) red *f* eléctrica; **the ~s** *npl* (*BRIT: ELEC*) la red eléctrica; **in the ~** en general; **~frame** *n* (*COMPUT*) ordenador *m* central; **~land** *n* tierra firme; **~ly** *adv* principalmente; **~ road** *n* carretera; **~stay** *n* (*fig*) pilar *m*; **~stream** *n* corriente *f* principal

maintain [meɪn'teɪn] *vt* mantener; **maintenance** ['meɪntənəns] *n* mantenimiento; (*LAW*) manutención *f*

maize [meɪz] *n* (*BRIT*) maíz *m* (*SP*), choclo (*AM*)

majestic [mə'dʒestɪk] *adj* majestuoso

majesty ['mædʒɪstɪ] *n* majestad *f*; (*title*): **Your M~** Su Majestad

major ['meɪdʒə*] *n* (*MIL*) comandante *m* ♦ *adj* principal; (*MUS*) mayor

Majorca [mə'jɔːkə] *n* Mallorca

majority [mə'dʒɔrɪtɪ] *n* mayoría

make [meɪk] (*pt, pp* **made**) *vt* hacer; (*manufacture*) fabricar; (*mistake*) cometer; (*speech*) pronunciar; (*cause to be*): **to ~ sb sad** poner triste a alguien; (*force*): **to ~ sb do sth** obligar a alguien a hacer algo; (*earn*) ganar; (*equal*): **2 and 2 ~ 4** 2 y 2 son 4 ♦ *n* marca; **to ~ the bed** hacer la cama; **to ~ a fool of sb** poner a alguien en ridículo; **to ~ a profit/loss** obtener ganancias/sufrir pérdidas; **to ~ it** (*arrive*) llegar; (*achieve sth*) tener éxito; **what time do you ~ it?** ¿qué hora

tienes?; **to ~ do with** contentarse con; **~ for** *vt fus* (*place*) dirigirse a; **~ out** *vt* (*decipher*) descifrar; (*understand*) entender; (*see*) distinguir; (*cheque*) extender; **~ up** *vt* (*invent*) inventar; (*prepare*) hacer; (*constitute*) constituir ♦ *vi* reconciliarse; (*with cosmetics*) maquillarse; **~ up for** *vt fus* compensar; **~believe** *n* ficción *f*, invención *f*; **~r** *n* fabricante *m/f*; (*of film, programme*) autor(a) *m/f*; **~shift** *adj* improvisado; **~-up** *n* maquillaje *m*; **~-up remover** *n* desmaquillador *m*

making ['meɪkɪŋ] *n* (*fig*): **in the ~** en vías de formación; **to have the ~s of** (*person*) tener madera de

Malaysia [mə'leɪzɪə] *n* Malasia, Malaysia

male [meɪl] *n* (*BIOL*) macho ♦ *adj* (*sex, attitude*) masculino; (*child etc*) varón

malfunction [mæl'fʌŋkʃən] *n* mal funcionamiento

malice ['mælɪs] *n* malicia; **malicious** [mə'lɪʃəs] *adj* malicioso; rencoroso

malignant [mə'lɪgnənt] *adj* (*MED*) maligno

mall [mɔːl] (*US*) *n* (*also*: *shopping ~*) centro comercial

mallet ['mælɪt] *n* mazo

malnutrition [mælnjuː'trɪʃən] *n* desnutrición *f*

malpractice [mæl'præktɪs] *n* negligencia profesional

malt [mɔːlt] *n* malta; (*whisky*) whisky *m* de malta

Malta ['mɔːltə] *n* Malta; **Maltese** [-'tiːz] *adj*, *n inv* maltés/esa *m/f*

mammal ['mæml] *n* mamífero

mammoth ['mæməθ] *n* mamut *m* ♦ *adj* gigantesco

man [mæn] (*pl* **men**) *n* hombre *m*; (*~kind*) el hombre ♦ *vt* (*NAUT*) tripular; (*MIL*) guarnecer; (*operate: machine*) manejar; **an old ~** un viejo; **~ and wife** marido y mujer

manage ['mænɪdʒ] *vi* arreglárselas, ir tirando ♦ *vt* (*be in charge of*) dirigir; (*control: person*) manejar; (: *ship*) gobernar; **~able** *adj* manejable; **~ment** *n* dirección *f*; **~r** *n* director(a) *m/f*; (*of pop star*) mánayer *m/f*; (*SPORT*) entrenador(a) *m/f*; **~ress** *n* directora; entrenadora; **~rial** [-ə'dʒɪərɪəl] *adj* directivo; **managing director** *n* director(a) *m/f* general

mandarin ['mændərɪn] *n* (*also*: **~ orange**) mandarina; (*person*) mandarín *m*

mandatory ['mændətərɪ] *adj* obligatorio

mane [meɪn] *n* (*of horse*) crin *f*; (*of lion*) melena

maneuver [mə'nuːvə*] (*US*) = **manoeuvre**

manfully ['mænfəlɪ] *adv* valientemente

mangle ['mæŋgl] *vt* mutilar, destrozar

man: **~handle** *vt* maltratar; **~hole** *n* agujero

de acceso; **~hood** n edad f viril; (state) virilidad f; **~hour** n hora-hombre f; **~hunt** n (POLICE) búsqueda y captura

mania ['meɪnɪə] n manía; **~c** ['meɪnɪæk] n maníaco/a; (fig) maniático

manic ['mænɪk] adj frenético; **~-depressive** n maníaco/a depresivo/a

manicure ['mænɪkjʊə*] n manicura

manifest ['mænɪfest] vt manifestar, mostrar ♦ adj manifiesto

manifesto [mænɪ'festəʊ] n manifiesto

manipulate [mə'nɪpjʊleɪt] vt manipular

man: **~kind** [mæn'kaɪnd] n humanidad f, género humano; **~ly** adj varonil; **~-made** adj artificial

manner ['mænə*] n manera, modo; (behaviour) conducta, manera de ser; (type): **all ~ of things** toda clase de cosas; **~s** npl (behaviour) modales mpl; **bad ~s** mala educación; **~ism** n peculiaridad f de lenguaje (or de comportamiento)

manoeuvre [mə'nu:və*] (US **maneuver**) vt, vi maniobrar ♦ n maniobra

manor ['mænə*] n (also: **~ house**) casa solariega

manpower ['mænpaʊə*] n mano f de obra

mansion ['mænʃən] n palacio, casa grande

manslaughter ['mænslɔ:tə*] n homicidio no premeditado

mantelpiece ['mæntlpi:s] n repisa, chimenea

manual ['mænjʊəl] adj manual ♦ n manual m

manufacture [mænju'fæktʃə*] vt fabricar ♦ n fabricación f; **~r** n fabricante m/f

manure [mə'njʊə*] n estiércol m

manuscript ['mænjʊskrɪpt] n manuscrito

many ['menɪ] adj, pron muchos/as; **a great ~** muchísimos, un buen número de; **~ a time** muchas veces

map [mæp] n mapa m; **to ~ out** vt proyectar

maple ['meɪpl] n arce m (SP), maple m (AM)

mar [mɑ:*] vt estropear

marathon ['mærəθən] n maratón m

marble ['mɑ:bl] n mármol m; (toy) canica

March [mɑ:tʃ] n marzo

march [mɑ:tʃ] vi (MIL) marchar; (demonstrators) manifestarse ♦ n marcha; (demonstration) manifestación f

mare [meə*] n yegua

margarine [mɑ:dʒə'ri:n] n margarina

margin ['mɑ:dʒɪn] n margen m; (COMM: profit ~) margen m de beneficios; **~al** adj marginal; **~al seat** n (POL) escaño electoral difícil de asegurar

marigold ['mærɪgəʊld] n caléndula

marijuana [mærɪ'wɑ:nə] n marijuana

marina [mə'ri:nə] n puerto deportivo

marinate ['mærɪneɪt] vt marinar

marine [mə'ri:n] adj marino ♦ n soldado de marina

marital ['mærɪtl] adj matrimonial; **~ status** estado civil

marjoram ['mɑ:dʒərəm] n mejorana

mark [mɑ:k] n marca, señal f; (in snow, mud etc) huella; (stain) mancha; (BRIT: SCOL) nota; (currency) marco ♦ vt marcar; manchar; (damage: furniture) rayar; (indicate: place etc) señalar; (BRIT: SCOL) calificar, corregir; **to ~ time** marcar el paso; (fig) marcar(se) un ritmo; **~ed** adj (obvious) marcado, acusado; **~er** n (sign) marcador m; (bookmark) señal f (de libro)

market ['mɑ:kɪt] n mercado ♦ vt (COMM) comercializar; **~ garden** (BRIT) n huerto; **~ing** n márketing m; **~place** n mercado; **~ research** n análisis m inv de mercados

marksman ['mɑ:ksmən] n tirador m

marmalade ['mɑ:məleɪd] n mermelada de naranja

maroon [mə'ru:n] vt: **to be ~ed** quedar aislado; (fig) quedar abandonado

marquee [mɑ:'ki:] n entoldado

marriage ['mærɪdʒ] n (relationship, institution) matrimonio; (wedding) boda; (act) casamiento; **~ certificate** n partida de casamiento

married ['mærɪd] adj casado; (life, love) conyugal

marrow ['mærəʊ] n médula; (vegetable) calabacín m

marry ['mærɪ] vt casarse con; (subj: father, priest etc) casar ♦ vi (also: **get married**) casarse

Mars [mɑ:z] n Marte m

marsh [mɑ:ʃ] n pantano; (salt ~) marisma

marshal ['mɑ:ʃl] n (MIL) mariscal m; (at sports meeting etc) oficial m; (US: of police, fire department) jefe/a m/f ♦ vt (thoughts etc) ordenar; (soldiers) formar

marshy ['mɑ:ʃɪ] adj pantanoso

martial law ['mɑ:ʃl-] n ley f marcial

martyr ['mɑ:tə*] n mártir m/f; **~dom** n martirio

marvel ['mɑ:vl] n maravilla, prodigio ♦ vi: **to ~ (at)** maravillarse (de); **~lous** (US **~ous**) adj maravilloso

Marxist ['mɑ:ksɪst] adj, n marxista m/f

marzipan ['mɑ:zɪpæn] n mazapán m

mascara [mæs'kɑ:rə] n rímel m

masculine ['mæskjʊlɪn] adj masculino

mash [mæʃ] vt machacar; **~ed potatoes** npl puré m de patatas (SP) or papas (AM)

mask [mɑ:sk] n máscara ♦ vt (cover): **to ~ one's face** ocultarse la cara; (hide: feelings) esconder

mason ['meɪsn] n (also: **stone~**) albañil m; (also: **free~**) masón m; **~ry** n (in building) mampostería

masquerade |mæskə'reɪd| vi: **to ~ as** disfrazarse de, hacerse pasar por

mass |mæs| n (*people*) muchedumbre f; (*of air, liquid etc*) masa; (*of detail, hair etc*) gran cantidad f; (*REL*) misa ♦ cpd masivo ♦ vi reunirse; concentrarse; **the ~es** npl las masas; **~es of** (*inf*) montones de

massacre |'mæsəkə*| n masacre f

massage |'mæsɑːʒ| n masaje m ♦ vt dar masaje en

masseur |mæ'sɜː*| n masajista m

masseuse |mæ'sɜːz| n masajista f

massive |'mæsɪv| adj enorme; (*support, changes*) masivo

mass media npl medios mpl de comunicación

mass production n fabricación f en serie

mast |mɑːst| n (*NAUT*) mástil m; (*RADIO etc*) torre f

master |'mɑːstə*| n (*of servant*) amo; (*of situation*) dueño, maestro; (*in primary school*) maestro; (*in secondary school*) profesor m; (*title for boys*): **M~ X** Señorito X ♦ vt dominar; **M~ of Arts/Science** n licenciatura superior en Letras/Ciencias; **~ly** adj magistral; **~mind** n inteligencia superior ♦ vt dirigir, planear; **~piece** n obra maestra; **~y** n maestría

mat |mæt| n estera; (*also: door~*) felpudo; (*also: table ~*) salvamanteles m inv, posavasos m inv ♦ adj = **matt**

match |mætʃ| n cerilla, fósforo; (*game*) partido; (*equal*) igual m/f ♦ vt (*go well with*) hacer juego con; (*equal*) igualar; (*correspond to*) corresponderse con; (*pair: also: ~ up*) casar con ♦ vi hacer juego; **to be a good ~** hacer juego; **~box** n caja de cerillas; **~ing** adj que hace juego

mate |meɪt| n (*work~*) colega m/f; (*inf: friend*) amigo/a; (*animal*) macho m/hembra f; (*in merchant navy*) segundo de a bordo ♦ vi acoplarse, aparearse ♦ vt aparear

material |mə'tɪərɪəl| n (*substance*) materia; (*information*) material m; (*cloth*) tela, tejido ♦ adj material; (*important*) esencial; **~s** npl materiales mpl

maternal |mə'tɜːnl| adj maternal

maternity |mə'tɜːnɪtɪ| n maternidad f; **~ dress** n vestido premamá

math |mæθ| (*US*) n = **mathematics**

mathematical |mæθə'mætɪkl| adj matemático

mathematician |mæθəmə'tɪʃən| n matemático/a

mathematics |mæθə'mætɪks| n matemáticas fpl

maths |mæθs| (*BRIT*) n = **mathematics**

matinée |'mætɪneɪ| n sesión f de tarde

matrices |'meɪtrɪsiːz| npl of **matrix**

matriculation |mətrɪkju'leɪʃən| n (formalización f de) matrícula

matrimony |'mætrɪmənɪ| n matrimonio

matrix |'meɪtrɪks| (*pl* **matrices**) n matriz f

matron |'meɪtrən| n enfermera f jefe; (*in school*) ama de llaves

mat(t) |mæt| adj mate

matted |'mætɪd| adj enmarañado

matter |'mætə*| n cuestión f, asunto; (*PHYSICS*) sustancia, materia; (*reading ~*) material m; (*MED: pus*) pus m ♦ vi importar; **~s** npl (*affairs*) asuntos mpl, temas mpl; **it doesn't ~** no importa; **what's the ~?** ¿qué pasa?; **no ~ what** pase lo que pase; **as a ~ of course** por rutina; **as a ~ of fact** de hecho; **~-of-fact** adj prosaico, práctico

mattress |'mætrɪs| n colchón m

mature |mə'tjuə*| adj maduro ♦ vi madurar; **maturity** n madurez f

maul |mɔːl| vt magullar

mauve |məuv| adj de color malva (*SP*) or guinda (*AM*)

maximum |'mæksɪməm| (*pl* **maxima**) adj máximo ♦ n máximo

May |meɪ| n mayo

may |meɪ| (*conditional: might*) vi (*indicating possibility*): **he ~ come** puede que venga; (*be allowed to*): **~ I smoke?** ¿puedo fumar?; (*wishes*): **~ God bless you!** ¡que Dios le bendiga!; **you ~ as well go** bien puedes irte

maybe |'meɪbiː| adv quizá(s)

May Day n el primero de Mayo

mayhem |'meɪhem| n caos m total

mayonnaise |meɪə'neɪz| n mayonesa

mayor |meə*| n alcalde m; **~ess** n alcaldesa

maze |meɪz| n laberinto

M.D. abbr = **Doctor of Medicine**

me |miː| pron (*direct*) me; (*stressed, after prep*) mí; **can you hear ~?** ¿me oyes?; **he heard ME!** me oyó a mí; **it's ~** soy yo; **give them to ~** dámelos/las; **with/without ~** conmigo/sin mí

meadow |'medəu| n prado, pradera

meagre |'miːgə*| (*US* **meager**) adj escaso, pobre

meal |miːl| n comida; (*flour*) harina; **~time** n hora de comer

mean |miːn| (*pt, pp* **meant**) adj (*with money*) tacaño; (*unkind*) mezquino, malo; (*shabby*) humilde; (*average*) medio ♦ vt (*signify*) querer decir, significar; (*refer to*) referirse a; (*intend*): **to ~ to do sth** pensar or pretender hacer algo ♦ n medio, término medio; **~s** npl (*way*) medio, manera; (*money*) recursos mpl, medios mpl; **by ~s of** mediante, por medio de; **by all ~s!** ¡naturalmente!, ¡claro que sí!; **do you ~ it?** ¿lo dices en serio?; **what do you ~?** ¿qué quiere decir?; **to be meant for sb/sth** ser para uno/algo

meander |mɪ'ændə*| vi (*river*) serpentear

meaning ['mi:nɪŋ] n significado, sentido; (*purpose*) sentido, propósito; **~ful** adj significativo; **~less** adj sin sentido

meanness ['mi:nnɪs] n (*with money*) tacañería; (*unkindness*) maldad f, mezquindad f; (*shabbiness*) humildad f

meant [mɛnt] pt, pp of **mean**

meantime ['mi:ntaɪm] adv (*also:* in the **~**) mientras tanto

meanwhile ['mi:nwaɪl] adv = **meantime**

measles ['mi:zlz] n sarampión m

measure ['mɛʒə*] vt, vi medir ♦ n medida; (*ruler*) regla; **~ments** npl medidas fpl

meat [mi:t] n carne f; **cold ~** fiambre m; **~ball** n albóndiga; **~ pie** n pastel m de carne

Mecca ['mɛkə] n La Meca

mechanic [mɪ'kænɪk] n mecánico/a; **~s** n mecánica ♦ npl mecanismo; **~al** adj mecánico

mechanism ['mɛkənɪzəm] n mecanismo

medal ['mɛdl] n medalla; **~lion** [mɪ'dælɪən] n medallón m; **~list** (US **~ist**) n (SPORT) medallista m/f

meddle ['mɛdl] vi: **to ~ in** entrometerse en; **to ~ with sth** manosear algo

media ['mi:dɪə] npl medios mpl de comunicación ♦ npl of **medium**

mediaeval [mɛdɪ'i:vl] adj = **medieval**

mediate ['mi:dɪeɪt] vi mediar; **mediator** n intermediario/a, mediador(a) m/f

Medicaid ® ['mɛdɪkeɪd] n (US) n programa de ayuda médica para los pobres

medical ['mɛdɪkl] adj médico ♦ n reconocimiento médico

Medicare ® ['mɛdɪkeə*] n (US) n programa de ayuda médica para los ancianos

medication [mɛdɪ'keɪʃən] n medicación f

medicine ['mɛdsɪn] n medicina; (*drug*) medicamento

medieval [mɛdɪ'i:vl] adj medieval

mediocre [mi:dɪ'əukə*] adj mediocre

meditate ['mɛdɪteɪt] vi meditar

Mediterranean [mɛdɪtə'reɪnɪən] adj mediterráneo; **the ~** (*Sea*) el (Mar) Mediterráneo

medium ['mi:dɪəm] (pl **media**) adj mediano, regular ♦ n (*means*) medio; (pl **mediums**: *person*) médium m/f; **~ wave** n onda media

meek [mi:k] adj manso, sumiso

meet [mi:t] (pt, pp **met**) vt encontrar; (*accidentally*) encontrarse con, tropezar con; (*by arrangement*) reunirse con; (*for the first time*) conocer; (*go and fetch*) ir a buscar; (*opponent*) enfrentarse con; (*obligations*) cumplir; (*encounter: problem*) hacer frente a; (*need*) satisfacer ♦ vi encontrarse; (*in session*) reunirse; (*join: objects*) unirse; (*for the first time*) conocerse; **~ with** vt fus (*difficulty*) tropezar con; **to ~ with success** tener éxito; **~ing** n

encuentro; (*arranged*) cita, compromiso; (*business ~ing*) reunión f; (POL) mítin m

megabyte ['mɛgəbaɪt] n (COMPUT) megabyte m, megaocteto

megaphone ['mɛgəfəun] n megáfono

melancholy ['mɛlənkəlɪ] n melancolía ♦ adj melancólico

mellow ['mɛləu] adj (*wine*) añejo; (*sound, colour*) suave ♦ vi (*person*) ablandar

melody ['mɛlədɪ] n melodía

melon ['mɛlən] n melón m

melt [mɛlt] vi (*metal*) fundirse; (*snow*) derretirse ♦ vt fundir; **~down** n (*in nuclear reactor*) fusión f de un reactor (nuclear); **~ing pot** n (fig) crisol m

member ['mɛmbə*] n (gen, ANAT) miembro; (*of club*) socio/a; **M~ of Parliament** (BRIT) diputado/a; **M~ of the European Parliament** (BRIT) eurodiputado/a; **M~ of the Scottish Parliament** (BRIT) diputado/a del Parlamento escocés; **~ship** n (*members*) número de miembros; (*state*) filiación f; **~ship card** n carnet m de socio

memento [mə'mɛntəu] n recuerdo

memo ['mɛməu] n apunte m, nota

memoirs ['mɛmwa:z] npl memorias fpl

memorandum [mɛmə'rændəm] (pl **memoranda**) n apunte m, nota; (*official note*) acta

memorial [mɪ'mɔ:rɪəl] n monumento conmemorativo ♦ adj conmemorativo

memorize ['mɛməraɪz] vt aprender de memoria

memory ['mɛmərɪ] n (*also:* COMPUT) memoria; (*instance*) recuerdo; (*of dead person*): **in ~ of** a la memoria de

men [mɛn] npl of **man**

menace ['mɛnəs] n amenaza ♦ vt amenazar; **menacing** adj amenazador(a)

mend [mɛnd] vt reparar, arreglar; (*darn*) zurcir ♦ vi reponerse n arreglo, reparación f; zurcido ♦ n: **to be on the ~** ir mejorando; **to ~ one's ways** enmendarse; **~ing** n reparación f; (*clothes*) ropa por remendar

meningitis [mɛnɪn'dʒaɪtɪs] n meningitis f

menopause ['mɛnəupɔ:z] n menopausia

menstruation [mɛnstru'eɪʃən] n menstruación f

mental ['mɛntl] adj mental; **~ity** [-'tælɪtɪ] n mentalidad f

mention ['mɛnʃən] n mención f ♦ vt mencionar; (*speak of*) hablar de; **don't ~ it!** ¡de nada!

menu ['mɛnju:] n (*set ~*) menú m; (*printed*) carta; (COMPUT) menú m

MEP n abbr = **Member of the European Parliament**

merchandise ['mə:tʃəndaɪz] n mercancías fpl

merchant ['mə:tʃənt] n comerciante m/f;

~ bank (*BRIT*) *n* banco comercial; **~ navy** (*US* **~ marine**) *n* marina mercante

merciful ['mɜːsɪful] *adj* compasivo; (*fortunate*) afortunado

merciless ['mɜːsɪlɪs] *adj* despiadado

mercury ['mɜːkjurɪ] *n* mercurio

mercy ['mɜːsɪ] *n* compasión *f*; (*REL*) misericordia; **at the ~ of** a la merced de

merely ['mɪəlɪ] *adv* simplemente, sólo

merge [mɜːdʒ] *vt* (*join*) unir ♦ *vi* unirse; (*COMM*) fusionarse; (*colours etc*) fundirse; **~r** *n* (*COMM*) fusión *f*

meringue [məˈræŋ] *n* merengue *m*

merit ['merɪt] *n* mérito ♦ *vt* merecer

mermaid ['mɜːmeɪd] *n* sirena

merry ['merɪ] *adj* alegre; **M~ Christmas!** ¡Felices Pascuas!; **~-go-round** *n* tiovivo

mesh [meʃ] *n* malla

mesmerize ['mezməraɪz] *vt* hipnotizar

mess [mes] *n* (*muddle: of situation*) confusión *f*; (: *of room*) revoltijo; (*dirt*) porquería; (*MIL*) comedor *m*; **~ about** or **around** (*inf*) *vi* perder el tiempo; (*pass the time*) entretenerse; **~ about** or **around with** (*inf*) *vt fus* divertirse con; **~ up** *vt* (*spoil*) estropear; (*dirty*) ensuciar

message ['mesɪdʒ] *n* recado, mensaje *m*

messenger ['mesɪndʒə*] *n* mensajero/a

Messrs *abbr* (*on letters*: = *Messieurs*) Sres

messy ['mesɪ] *adj* (*dirty*) sucio; (*untidy*) desordenado

met [met] *pt, pp of* **meet**

metal ['metl] *n* metal *m*; **~lic** [-'tælɪk] *adj* metálico

metaphor ['metəfə*] *n* metáfora

meteor ['miːtɪə*] *n* meteoro; **~ite** [-aɪt] *n* meteorito

meteorology [miːtɪəˈrɒlədʒɪ] *n* meteorología

meter ['miːtə*] *n* (*instrument*) contador *m*; (*US: unit*) = **metre** ♦ *vt* (*US: POST*) franquear

method ['meθəd] *n* método

meths [meθs] (*BRIT*) *n*, **methylated spirit** ['meθɪleɪtɪd-] (*BRIT*) *n* alcohol *m* metilado or desnaturalizado

metre ['miːtə*] (*US* **meter**) *n* metro

metric ['metrɪk] *adj* métrico

metropolitan [metrəˈpɒlɪtən] *adj* metropolitano; **the M~ Police** (*BRIT*) la policía londinense

mettle ['metl] *n*: **to be on one's ~** estar dispuesto a mostrar todo lo que uno vale

mew [mjuː] *vi* (*cat*) maullar

mews [mjuːz] *n*: **~ flat** (*BRIT*) piso acondicionado en antiguos establos o cocheras

Mexican ['meksɪkən] *adj, n* mejicano/a *m/f*, mexicano/a *m/f*

Mexico ['meksɪkəu] *n* Méjico (*SP*), México (*AM*); **~ City** *n* Ciudad *f* de Méjico or México

miaow [miːˈau] *vi* maullar

mice [maɪs] *npl of* **mouse**

micro... [maɪkrəu] *prefix* micro...; **~chip** *n* microplaqueta; **~(computer)** *n* microordenador *m*; **~phone** *n* micrófono; **~processor** *n* microprocesador *m*; **~scope** *n* microscopio; **~wave** *n* (*also*: **~wave oven**) horno microondas

mid [mɪd] *adj*: **in ~ May** a mediados de mayo; **in ~ afternoon** a media tarde; **in ~ air** en el aire; **~day** *n* mediodía *m*

middle ['mɪdl] *n* centro; (*half-way point*) medio; (*waist*) cintura ♦ *adj* de en medio; (*course, way*) intermedio; **in the ~ of the night** en plena noche; **~-aged** *adj* de mediana edad; **the M~ Ages** *npl* la Edad Media; **~ class** *adj* de clase media; **the ~ class(es)** *n*(*pl*) la clase media; **M~ East** *n* Oriente *m* Medio; **~man** *n* intermediario; **~ name** *n* segundo nombre; **~-of-the-road** *adj* moderado; **~weight** *n* (*BOXING*) peso medio

middling ['mɪdlɪŋ] *adj* mediano

midge [mɪdʒ] *n* mosquito

midget ['mɪdʒɪt] *n* enano/a

Midlands ['mɪdləndz] *npl*: **the ~** la región central de Inglaterra

midnight ['mɪdnaɪt] *n* medianoche *f*

midst [mɪdst] *n*: **in the ~ of** (*crowd*) en medio de; (*situation, action*) en mitad de

midsummer [mɪd'sʌmə*] *n*: **in ~** en pleno verano

midway [mɪd'weɪ] *adj, adv*: **~ (between)** a medio camino (entre); **~ through** a la mitad (de)

midweek [mɪd'wiːk] *adv* entre semana

midwife ['mɪdwaɪf] (*pl* **midwives**) *n* comadrona, partera

might [maɪt] *vb see* **may** ♦ *n* fuerza, poder *m*; **~y** *adj* fuerte, poderoso

migraine ['miːgreɪn] *n* jaqueca

migrant ['maɪgrənt] *n adj* (*bird*) migratorio; (*worker*) emigrante

migrate [maɪ'greɪt] *vi* emigrar

mike [maɪk] *n abbr* (= *microphone*) micro

mild [maɪld] *adj* (*person*) apacible; (*climate*) templado; (*slight*) ligero; (*taste*) suave; (*illness*) leve; **~ly** *adv* ligeramente; suavemente; **to put it ~ly** para no decir más

mile [maɪl] *n* milla; **~age** *n* número de millas, ≈ kilometraje *m*; **~ometer** [maɪ'lɒmɪtə*] *n* ≈ cuentakilómetros *m inv*; **~stone** *n* mojón *m*

militant ['mɪlɪtnt] *adj, n* militante *m/f*

military ['mɪlɪtərɪ] *adj* militar

militia [mɪ'lɪʃə] *n* milicia

milk [mɪlk] *n* leche *f* ♦ *vt* (*cow*) ordeñar; (*fig*) chupar; **~ chocolate** *n* chocolate *m* con leche; **~man** (*irreg*) *n* lechero; **~ shake** *n* batido, malteada (*AM*); **~y** *adj* lechoso; **M~y Way** *n* Vía Láctea

mill [mɪl] n (windmill etc) molino; (coffee ~) molinillo; (factory) fábrica ♦ vt moler ♦ vi (also: ~ about) arremolinarse

millennium [mɪˈlɛnɪəm] (pl ~s or **millennia**) n milenio, milenario; **the ~ bug** el (problema del) efecto 2000

miller [ˈmɪlə*] n molinero

milli... [ˈmɪlɪ] prefix: **~gram(me)** n miligramo; **~metre** (US **~meter**) n milímetro

million [ˈmɪljən] n millón m; **a ~ times** un millón de veces; **~aire** [-jəˈnɛə*] n millonario/a

milometer [maɪˈlɒmɪtə*] (BRIT) n = **mileometer**

mime [maɪm] n mímica; (actor) mimo/a ♦ vt remedar ♦ vi actuar de mimo

mimic [ˈmɪmɪk] n imitador(a) m/f ♦ adj mímico ♦ vt remedar, imitar

min. abbr = **minimum**; **minute(s)**

mince [mɪns] vt picar ♦ n (BRIT: CULIN) carne f picada; **~meat** n conserva de fruta picada; (US: meat) carne f picada; **~ pie** n empanadilla rellena de fruta picada; **~r** n picadora de carne

mind [maɪnd] n mente f; (intellect) intelecto; (contrasted with matter) espíritu m ♦ vt (attend to, look after) ocuparse de, cuidar; (be careful of) tener cuidado con; (object to): **I don't ~ the noise** no me molesta el ruido; **it is on my ~** me preocupa; **to bear sth in ~** tomar o tener algo en cuenta; **to make up one's ~** decidirse; **I don't ~** me es igual; **~ you, ...** te advierto que ...; **never ~!** ¡es igual!, ¡no importa!; (don't worry) ¡no te preocupes!; **"~ the step"** "cuidado con el escalón"; **~er** n guardaespaldas m inv; (child ~er) ≈ niñera; **~ful** adj: **~ful of** consciente de; **~less** adj (crime) sin motivo; (work) de autómata

mine¹ [maɪn] pron el mío/la mía etc; **a friend of ~** un(a) amigo/a mío/mía ♦ adj: **this book is ~** este libro es mío

mine² [maɪn] n mina ♦ vt (coal) extraer; (bomb: beach etc) minar; **~field** n campo de minas; **miner** n minero/a

mineral [ˈmɪnərəl] adj mineral ♦ n mineral m; **~s** npl (BRIT: soft drinks) refrescos mpl; **~ water** n agua mineral

mingle [ˈmɪŋgl] vi: **to ~ with** mezclarse con

miniature [ˈmɪnətʃə*] adj (en) miniatura ♦ n miniatura

minibus [ˈmɪnɪbʌs] n microbús m

minimal [ˈmɪnɪml] adj mínimo

minimize [ˈmɪnɪmaɪz] vt minimizar; (play down) empequeñecer

minimum [ˈmɪnɪməm] (pl **minima**) n, adj mínimo

mining [ˈmaɪnɪŋ] n explotación f minera

miniskirt [ˈmɪnɪskəːt] n minifalda

minister [ˈmɪnɪstə*] n (BRIT: POL) ministro/a

(SP), secretario/a (AM); (REL) pastor m ♦ vi: **to ~ to** atender a

ministry [ˈmɪnɪstrɪ] n (BRIT: POL) ministerio (SP), secretaría (AM); (REL) sacerdocio

mink [mɪŋk] n visón m

minnow [ˈmɪnəu] n pececillo (de agua dulce)

minor [ˈmaɪnə*] adj (repairs, injuries) leve; (poet, planet) menor; (MUS) menor ♦ n (LAW) menor m de edad

Minorca [mɪˈnɔːkə] n Menorca

minority [maɪˈnɒrɪtɪ] n minoría

mint [mɪnt] n (plant) menta, hierbabuena; (sweet) caramelo de menta ♦ vt (coins) acuñar; **the (Royal) M~, the (US) M~** la Casa de la Moneda; **in ~ condition** en perfecto estado

minus [ˈmaɪnəs] n (also: ~ **sign**) signo de menos ♦ prep menos; **12 ~ 6 equals 6** 12 menos 6 son 6; **~ 24°C** menos 24 grados

minute¹ [ˈmɪnɪt] n minuto; (fig) momento; **~s** npl (of meeting) actas fpl; **at the last ~** a última hora

minute² [maɪˈnjuːt] adj diminuto; (search) minucioso

miracle [ˈmɪrəkl] n milagro

mirage [ˈmɪrɑːʒ] n espejismo

mirror [ˈmɪrə*] n espejo; (in car) retrovisor m

mirth [mɜːθ] n alegría

misadventure [mɪsədˈventʃə*] n desgracia

misapprehension [mɪsæprɪˈhenʃən] n equivocación f

misappropriate [mɪsəˈprəuprɪeɪt] vt malversar

misbehave [mɪsbɪˈheɪv] vi portarse mal

miscalculate [mɪsˈkælkjuleɪt] vt calcular mal

miscarriage [ˈmɪskærɪdʒ] n (MED) aborto; **~ of justice** error m judicial

miscellaneous [mɪsɪˈleɪnɪəs] adj varios/as, diversos/as

mischief [ˈmɪstʃɪf] n travesuras fpl, diabluras fpl; (maliciousness) malicia; **mischievous** [-ʃɪvəs] adj travieso

misconception [mɪskənˈsepʃən] n idea equivocada, equivocación f

misconduct [mɪsˈkɒndʌkt] n mala conducta; **professional ~** falta profesional

misdemeanour [mɪsdɪˈmiːnə*] (US **misdemeanor**) n delito, ofensa

miser [ˈmaɪzə*] n avaro/a

miserable [ˈmɪzərəbl] adj (unhappy) triste, desgraciado; (unpleasant, contemptible) miserable

miserly [ˈmaɪzəlɪ] adj avariento, tacaño

misery [ˈmɪzərɪ] n tristeza; (wretchedness) miseria, desdicha

misfire [mɪsˈfaɪə*] vi fallar

misfit [ˈmɪsfɪt] n inadaptado/a

misfortune [mɪsˈfɔːtʃən] n desgracia

misgiving [mɪsˈgɪvɪŋ] n (apprehension) presentimiento; **to have ~s about sth** tener

dudas acerca de algo
misguided [mɪsˈgaɪdɪd] *adj* equivocado
mishandle [mɪsˈhændl] *vt* (*mismanage*)
manejar mal
mishap [ˈmɪshæp] *n* desgracia, contratiempo
misinform [mɪsɪnˈfɔːm] *vt* informar mal
misinterpret [mɪsɪnˈtɜːprɪt] *vt* interpretar
mal
misjudge [mɪsˈdʒʌdʒ] *vt* juzgar mal
mislay [mɪsˈleɪ] (*irreg*) *vt* extraviar, perder
mislead [mɪsˈliːd] (*irreg*) *vt* llevar a
conclusiones erróneas; **~ing** *adj* engañoso
mismanage [mɪsˈmænɪdʒ] *vt* administrar
mal
misplace [mɪsˈpleɪs] *vt* extraviar
misprint [ˈmɪsprɪnt] *n* errata, error *m* de
imprenta
Miss [mɪs] *n* Señorita
miss [mɪs] *vt* (*train etc*) perder; (*fail to hit*:
target) errar; (*regret the absence of*): **I ~ him**
(yo) le echo de menos or a faltar; (*fail to*
see): **you can't ~ it** no tiene pérdida ♦ *vi* fallar
♦ *n* (*shot*) tiro fallido *or* perdido; **~ out** (*BRIT*)
vt omitir
misshapen [mɪsˈʃeɪpən] *adj* deforme
missile [ˈmɪsaɪl] *n* (*AVIAT*) mísil *m*; (*object*
thrown) proyectil *m*
missing [ˈmɪsɪŋ] *adj* (*pupil*) ausente; (*thing*)
perdido; (*MIL*): **~ in action** desaparecido en
combate
mission [ˈmɪʃən] *n* misión *f*; (*official*
representation) delegación *f*; **~ary** *n*
misionero/a
mist [mɪst] *n* (*light*) neblina; (*heavy*) niebla;
(*at sea*) bruma ♦ *vi* (*eyes: also*: ~ **over**, ~ **up**)
llenarse de lágrimas; (*BRIT*: *windows: also*:
~ **over**, ~ **up**) empañarse
mistake [mɪsˈteɪk] (*vt*: *irreg*) *n* error *m* ♦ *vt*
entender mal; **by ~** por equivocación; **to**
make a ~ equivocarse; **to ~ A for B** confundir
A con B; **mistaken** *pp* of **mistake** ♦ *adj*
equivocado; **to be mistaken** equivocarse,
engañarse
mister [ˈmɪstə*] (*inf*) *n* señor *m*; *see* **Mr**
mistletoe [ˈmɪsltəu] *n* muérdago
mistook [mɪsˈtuk] *pt* of **mistake**
mistress [ˈmɪstrɪs] *n* (*lover*) amante *f*; (*of*
house) señora (de la casa); (*BRIT*: *in primary*
school) maestra; (*in secondary school*)
profesora; (*of situation*) dueña
mistrust [mɪsˈtrʌst] *vt* desconfiar de
misty [ˈmɪstɪ] *adj* (*day*) de niebla; (*glasses*
etc) empañado
misunderstand [mɪsʌndəˈstænd] (*irreg*) *vt*,
vi entender mal; **~ing** *n* malentendido
misuse [*n* mɪsˈjuːs, *vb* mɪsˈjuːz] *n* mal uso; (*of*
power) abuso; (*of funds*) malversación *f* ♦ *vt*
abusar de; malversar
mitt(en) [ˈmɪt(n)] *n* manopla

mix [mɪks] *vt* mezclar; (*combine*) unir ♦ *vi*
mezclarse; (*people*) llevarse bien ♦ *n* mezcla;
~ up *vt* mezclar; (*confuse*) confundir; **~ed**
adj mixto; (*feelings etc*) encontrado; **~ed-up**
adj (*confused*) confuso, revuelto; **~er** *n* (*for*
food) licuadora; (*for drinks*) coctelera;
(*person*): **he's a good ~er** tiene don de
gentes; **~ture** *n* mezcla; (*also*: **cough ~ture**)
jarabe *m*; **~-up** *n* confusión *f*
mm *abbr* (= *millimetre*) mm
moan [məun] *n* gemido ♦ *vi* gemir; (*inf*:
complain): **to ~ (about)** quejarse (de)
moat [məut] *n* foso
mob [mɔb] *n* multitud *f* ♦ *vt* acosar
mobile [ˈməubaɪl] *adj* móvil ♦ *n* móvil *m*;
~ home *n* caravana; **~ phone** *n* teléfono
portátil
mock [mɔk] *vt* (*ridicule*) ridiculizar; (*laugh at*)
burlarse de ♦ *adj* fingido; **~ exam** *examen*
preparatorio antes de los exámenes oficiales;
~ery *n* burla; **~-up** *n* maqueta
mod [mɔd] *adj see* **convenience**
mode [məud] *n* modo
model [ˈmɔdl] *n* modelo; (*fashion ~*, *artist's*
~) modelo *m/f* ♦ *adj* modelo ♦ *vt* (*with clay*
etc) modelar (*copy*): **to ~ o.s. on** tomar como
modelo a ♦ *vi* ser modelo; **to ~ clothes** pasar
modelos, ser modelo; **~ railway** *n* ferrocarril
m de juguete
modem [ˈməudəm] *n* modem *m*
moderate [*adj* ˈmɔdərət, *vb* ˈmɔdəreɪt] *adj*
moderado/a ♦ *vi* moderarse, calmarse ♦ *vt*
moderar
modern [ˈmɔdən] *adj* moderno; **~ize** *vt*
modernizar
modest [ˈmɔdɪst] *adj* modesto; (*small*)
módico; **~y** *n* modestia
modify [ˈmɔdɪfaɪ] *vt* modificar
mogul [ˈməugəl] *n* (*fig*) magnate *m*
mohair [ˈməuhɛə*] *n* mohair *m*
moist [mɔɪst] *adj* húmedo; **~en** [ˈmɔɪsn] *vt*
humedecer; **~ure** [ˈmɔɪstʃə*] *n* humedad *f*;
~urizer [ˈmɔɪstʃəraɪzə*] *n* crema hidratante
molar [ˈməulə*] *n* muela
mold [məuld] (*US*) *n*, *vt* = **mould**
mole [məul] *n* (*animal*, *spy*) topo; (*spot*) lunar
m
molest [məuˈlest] *vt* importunar; (*assault*
sexually) abusar sexualmente de
mollycoddle [ˈmɔlɪkɔdl] *vt* mimar
molt [məult] (*US*) *vi* = **moult**
molten [ˈməultən] *adj* fundido; (*lava*) líquido
mom [mɔm] (*US*) *n* = **mum**
moment [ˈməumənt] *n* momento; **at the ~**
de momento, por ahora; **~ary** *adj*
momentáneo; **~ous** [-ˈmentəs] *adj*
trascendental, importante
momentum [məuˈmentəm] *n* momento;
(*fig*) ímpetu *m*; **to gather ~** cobrar velocidad;

(fig) ganar fuerza

mommy ['mɔmɪ] *(US) n* = **mummy**

Monaco ['mɔnəkəʊ] *n* Mónaco

monarch ['mɔnək] *n* monarca *m/f;* **~y** *n* monarquía

monastery ['mɔnəstərɪ] *n* monasterio

Monday ['mʌndɪ] *n* lunes *m inv*

monetary ['mʌnɪtərɪ] *adj* monetario

money ['mʌnɪ] *n* dinero; *(currency)* moneda; **to make ~** ganar dinero; **~ order** *n* giro; **~-spinner** *(inf) n:* **to be a ~-spinner** dar mucho dinero

mongrel ['mʌŋgrəl] *n (dog)* perro mestizo

monitor ['mɔnɪtə*] *n (SCOL)* monitor *m;* *(also: television ~)* receptor *m* de control; *(of computer)* monitor *m* ♦ *vt* controlar

monk [mʌŋk] *n* monje *m*

monkey ['mʌŋkɪ] *n* mono; **~ nut** *(BRIT) n* cacahuete *(SP)*, maní *m (AM);* **~ wrench** *n* llave *f* inglesa

monopoly [mə'nɔpəlɪ] *n* monopolio

monotone ['mɔnətəʊn] *n* voz *f (or* tono) monocorde

monotonous [mə'nɔtənəs] *adj* monótono

monsoon [mɔn'suːn] *n* monzón *m*

monster ['mɔnstə*] *n* monstruo

monstrous ['mɔnstrəs] *adj (huge)* enorme; *(atrocious, ugly)* monstruoso

month [mʌnθ] *n* mes *m;* **~ly** *adj* mensual ♦ *adv* mensualmente

monument ['mɔnjumənt] *n* monumento

moo [muː] *vi* mugir

mood [muːd] *n* humor *m;* *(of crowd, group)* clima *m;* **to be in a good/bad ~** estar de buen/mal humor; **~y** *adj (changeable)* de humor variable; *(sullen)* malhumorado

moon [muːn] *n* luna; **~light** *n* luz *f* de la luna; **~lighting** *n* pluriempleo; **~lit** *adj:* **a ~lit night** una noche de luna

Moor [muə*] *n* moro/a

moor [muə*] *n* páramo ♦ *vt (ship)* amarrar ♦ *vi* echar las amarras

Moorish ['muərɪʃ] *adj* moro; *(architecture)* árabe, morisco

moorland ['muələnd] *n* páramo, brezal *m*

moose [muːs] *n inv* alce *m*

mop [mɔp] *n* fregona; *(of hair)* greña, melena ♦ *vt* fregar; **~ up** *vt* limpiar

mope [məʊp] *vi* estar *or* andar deprimido

moped ['məʊped] *n* ciclomotor *m*

moral ['mɔrl] *adj* moral ♦ *n* moraleja; **~s** *npl* moralidad *f,* moral *f*

morale [mɔ'rɑːl] *n* moral *f*

morality [mə'rælɪtɪ] *n* moralidad *f*

morass [mə'ræs] *n* pantano

more [mɔː*] *adj* **1** *(greater in number etc)* más; **~ people/work than before** más gente/

trabajo que antes

2 *(additional)* más; **do you want (some) ~ tea?** ¿quieres más té?; **is there any ~ wine?** ¿queda vino?; **it'll take a few ~ weeks** tardará unas semanas más; **it's 2 kms ~ to the house** faltan 2 kms para la casa; **~ time/letters than we expected** más tiempo del que/más cartas de las que esperábamos

♦ *pron (greater amount, additional amount)* más; **~ than 10** más de 10; **it cost ~ than the other one/than we expected** costó más que el otro/más de lo que esperábamos; **is there any ~?** ¿hay más?; **many/much ~** muchos(as)/mucho(a) más

♦ *adv* más; **~ dangerous/easily (than)** más peligroso/fácilmente (que); **~ and ~ expensive** cada vez más caro; **~ or less** más o menos; **~ than ever** más que nunca

━━━━━━━━━━━━━━━━━━━━━━━━━━━

moreover [mɔː'rəʊvə*] *adv* además, por otra parte

morning ['mɔːnɪŋ] *n* mañana; *(early ~)* madrugada ♦ *cpd* matutino, de la mañana; **in the ~** por la mañana; **7 o'clock in the ~** las 7 de la mañana; **~ sickness** *n* náuseas *fpl* matutinas

Morocco [mə'rɔkəʊ] *n* Marruecos *m*

moron ['mɔːrɔn] *(inf) n* imbécil *m/f*

morphine ['mɔːfiːn] *n* morfina

Morse [mɔːs] *n (also:* **~ code)** (código) Morse

morsel ['mɔːsl] *n (of food)* bocado

mortar ['mɔːtə*] *n* argamasa

mortgage ['mɔːgɪdʒ] *n* hipoteca ♦ *vt* hipotecar; **~ company** *(US) n* ≈ banco hipotecario

mortuary ['mɔːtjuərɪ] *n* depósito de cadáveres

Moscow ['mɔskəʊ] *n* Moscú

Moslem ['mɔzləm] *adj, n* = **Muslim**

mosque [mɔsk] *n* mezquita

mosquito [mɔs'kiːtəʊ] *(pl ~es) n* mosquito *(SP)*, zancudo *(AM)*

moss [mɔs] *n* musgo

most [məʊst] *adj* la mayor parte de, la mayoría de ♦ *pron* la mayor parte, la mayoría ♦ *adv* el más; *(very)* muy; **the ~** *(also: + adj)* el más; **~ of them** la mayor parte de ellos; **I saw the ~** yo vi el que más; **at the (very) ~** a lo sumo, todo lo más; **to make the ~ of** aprovechar (al máximo); **a ~ interesting book** un libro interesantísimo; **~ly** *adv* en su mayor parte, principalmente

MOT *(BRIT) n abbr (= Ministry of Transport):* **the ~ (test)** *inspección (anual) obligatoria de coches y camiones*

motel [məʊ'tel] *n* motel *m*

moth [mɔθ] *n* mariposa nocturna; *(clothes ~)* polilla

mother ['mʌðə*] *n* madre *f* ♦ *adj* materno

♦ vt (care for) cuidar (como una madre);
~hood n maternidad f; **~-in-law** n suegra; **~-ly** adj maternal; **~-of-pearl** n nácar m; **~-to-be** n futura madre f; **~ tongue** n lengua materna

motion ['məʊʃən] n movimiento; (gesture) ademán m, señal f; (at meeting) moción f ♦ vt, vi: **to ~ (to) sb to do sth** hacer señas a uno para que haga algo; **~less** adj inmóvil; **~ picture** n película

motivated ['məʊtɪveɪtɪd] adj motivado

motive ['məʊtɪv] n motivo

motley ['mɒtlɪ] adj variado

motor ['məʊtə*] n motor m; (BRIT: inf: vehicle) coche m (SP), carro (AM), automóvil m ♦ adj motor (f: motora or motriz); **~bike** n moto f; **~boat** n lancha motora; **~car** (BRIT) n coche m, carro, automóvil m; **~cycle** n motocicleta; **~cycle racing** n motociclismo; **~cyclist** n motociclista m/f; **~ing** (BRIT) n automovilismo; **~ist** n conductor(a) m/f, automovilista m/f; **~ racing** (BRIT) n carreras fpl de coches, automovilismo; **~ vehicle** n automóvil m; **~way** (BRIT) n autopista

mottled ['mɒtld] adj abigarrado, multicolor

motto ['mɒtəʊ] n (pl **~es**) n lema m; (watchword) consigna

mould [məʊld] (US **mold**) n molde m; (mildew) moho ♦ vt moldear; (fig) formar; **~y** adj enmohecido

moult [məʊlt] (US **molt**) vi mudar la piel (or las plumas)

mound [maʊnd] n montón m, montículo

mount [maʊnt] n monte m ♦ vt montar, subir a; (jewel) engarzar; (picture) enmarcar; (exhibition etc) organizar ♦ vi (increase) aumentar; **~ up** vi aumentar

mountain ['maʊntɪn] n montaña ♦ cpd de montaña; **~ bike** n bicicleta de montaña; **~eer** [-'nɪə*] n montañero/a (SP), andinista m/f (AM); **~eering** [-'nɪərɪŋ] n montañismo, andinismo; **~ous** [-əs] adj montañoso; **~ rescue team** n equipo de rescate de montaña; **~side** n ladera de la montaña

mourn [mɔːn] vt llorar, lamentar ♦ vi: **to ~ for** llorar la muerte de; **~er** n doliente m/f; dolorido/a; **~ing** n luto; **in ~ing** de luto

mouse [maʊs] (pl **mice**) n (ZOOL, COMPUT) ratón m; **~ mat** n (COMPUT) alfombrilla; **~trap** n ratonera

mousse [muːs] n (CULIN) crema batida; (for hair) espuma (moldeadora)

moustache [məs'tɑːʃ] (US **mustache**) n bigote m

mousy ['maʊsɪ] adj (hair) pardusco

mouth [maʊθ] (pl **mouths** [maʊðz]) n boca; (of river) desembocadura; **~ful** n bocado; **~ organ** n armónica; **~piece** n (of musical instrument) boquilla; (spokesman) portavoz m/f; **~wash** n enjuague m; **~-watering** adj apetitoso

movable ['muːvəbl] adj movible

move [muːv] n (movement) movimiento; (in game) jugada; (: turn to play) turno; (change: of house) mudanza; (: of job) cambio de trabajo ♦ vt mover; (emotionally) conmover; (POL: resolution etc) proponer ♦ vi moverse; (traffic) circular; (also: ~ house) trasladarse, mudarse; **to ~ sb to do sth** mover a uno a hacer algo; **to get a ~ on** darse prisa; **~ about** or **around** vi moverse; (travel) viajar; **~ along** vi avanzar, adelantarse; **~ away** vi alejarse; **~ back** vi retroceder; **~ forward** vi avanzar; **~ in** vi (to a house) instalarse; (police, soldiers) intervenir; **~ on** vi ponerse en camino; **~ out** vi (of house) mudarse; **~ over** vi apartarse, hacer sitio; **~ up** vi (employee) ser ascendido

moveable ['muːvəbl] adj = **movable**

movement ['muːvmənt] n movimiento

movie ['muːvɪ] n película; **to go to the ~s** ir al cine

moving ['muːvɪŋ] adj (emotional) conmovedor(a); (that moves) móvil

mow [məʊ] (pt **mowed**, pp **mowed** or **mown**) vt (grass, corn) cortar, segar; **~ down** vt (shoot) acribillar; **~er** n (also: lawn-er) cortacésped m inv, segadora

MP n abbr = **Member of Parliament**

m.p.h. abbr = **miles per hour** (60 m.p.h. = 96 k.p.h.)

Mr ['mɪstə*] (US **Mr.**) n: **~ Smith** (el) Sr. Smith

Mrs ['mɪsɪz] (US **Mrs.**) n: **~ Smith** (la) Sra. Smith

Ms [mɪz] (US **Ms.**) n (= **Miss** or **Mrs**): **~ Smith** (la) Sr(t)a. Smith

M.Sc. abbr = **Master of Science**

MSP n abbr = **Member of the Scottish Parliament**

much [mʌtʃ] adj mucho ♦ adv mucho; (before pp) muy ♦ n or pron mucho; **how ~ is it?** ¿cuánto es?, ¿cuánto cuesta?; **too ~** demasiado; **it's not ~** no es mucho; **as ~ as** tanto como; **however ~ he tries** por mucho que se esfuerce

muck [mʌk] n suciedad f; **~ about** or **around** (inf) vi perder el tiempo; (enjoy o.s.) entretenerse; **~ up** (inf) vt arruinar, estropear

mud [mʌd] n barro, lodo

muddle ['mʌdl] n desorden m, confusión f; (mix-up) embrollo, lío ♦ vt (also: ~ up) embrollar, confundir; **~ through** vi salir del paso

muddy ['mʌdɪ] adj fangoso, cubierto de lodo

mudguard ['mʌdgɑːd] n guardabarros m inv

muffin ['mʌfɪn] n panecillo dulce

muffle ['mʌfl] vt (sound) amortiguar; (against cold) embozar; **~d** adj (noise etc) amortiguado, apagado; **~r** (US) n (AUT) silenciador m

mug [mʌg] n taza grande (sin platillo); (for beer) jarra; (inf: face) jeta; (: fool) bobo ♦ vt

(*assault*) asaltar; **~ging** *n* asalto
muggy ['mʌgi] *adj* bochornoso
mule [mju:l] *n* mula
multi... [mʌlti] *prefix* multi...
multi-level [mʌlti'levl] (*US*) *adj* = **multi-storey**
multiple ['mʌltɪpl] *adj* múltiple ♦ *n* múltiplo; **~ sclerosis** *n* esclerosis *f* múltiple
multiplex cinema ['mʌltɪpleks-] *n* multicines *mpl*
multiplication [mʌltɪplɪ'keɪʃən] *n* multiplicación *f*
multiply ['mʌltɪplaɪ] *vt* multiplicar ♦ *vi* multiplicarse
multistorey [mʌltɪ'stɔːrɪ] (*BRIT*) *adj* de muchos pisos
multitude ['mʌltɪtjuːd] *n* multitud *f*
mum [mʌm] (*BRIT: inf*) *n* mamá ♦ *adj*: **to keep ~** mantener la boca cerrada
mumble ['mʌmbl] *vt, vi* hablar entre dientes, refunfuñar
mummy ['mʌmɪ] *n* (*BRIT: mother*) mamá; (*embalmed*) momia
mumps [mʌmps] *n* paperas *fpl*
munch [mʌntʃ] *vt, vi* mascar
mundane [mʌn'deɪn] *adj* trivial
municipal [mjuː'nɪsɪpl] *adj* municipal
murder ['mɜːdə*] *n* asesinato; (*in law*) homicidio ♦ *vt* asesinar, matar; **~er/ess** *n* asesino/a; **~ous** *adj* homicida
murky ['mɜːkɪ] *adj* (*water*) turbio; (*street, night*) lóbrego
murmur ['mɜːmə*] *n* murmullo ♦ *vt, vi* murmurar
muscle ['mʌsl] *n* músculo; (*fig: strength*) garra, fuerza; **~ in** *vi* entrometerse; **muscular** ['mʌskjulə*] *adj* muscular; (*person*) musculoso
muse [mjuːz] *vi* meditar ♦ *n* musa
museum [mjuː'zɪəm] *n* museo
mushroom ['mʌʃrum] *n* seta, hongo; (*CULIN*) champiñón *m* ♦ *vi* crecer de la noche a la mañana
music ['mjuːzɪk] *n* música; **~al** *adj* musical; (*sound*) melodioso; (*person*) con talento musical ♦ *n* (*show*) comedia musical; **~al instrument** *n* instrumento musical; **~ hall** *n* teatro de variedades; **~ian** [-'zɪʃən] *n* músico/a
Muslim ['mʌzlɪm] *adj, n* musulmán/ana *m/f*
muslin ['mʌzlɪn] *n* muselina
mussel ['mʌsl] *n* mejillón *m*
must [mʌst] *aux vb* (*obligation*): **I ~ do it** debo hacerlo, tengo que hacerlo; (*probability*): **he ~ be there by now** ya debe (de) estar allí ♦ *n*: **it's a ~** es imprescindible
mustache ['mʌstæʃ] (*US*) *n* = **moustache**
mustard ['mʌstəd] *n* mostaza
muster ['mʌstə*] *vt* juntar, reunir

mustn't ['mʌsnt] = **must not**
mute [mjuːt] *adj, n* mudo/a *m/f*
muted ['mjuːtɪd] *adj* callado; (*colour*) apagado
mutiny ['mjuːtɪnɪ] *n* motín *m* ♦ *vi* amotinarse
mutter ['mʌtə*] *vt, vi* murmurar
mutton ['mʌtn] *n* carne *f* de cordero
mutual ['mjuːtʃuəl] *adj* mutuo; (*interest*) común; **~ly** *adv* mutuamente
muzzle ['mʌzl] *n* hocico; (*for dog*) bozal *m*; (*of gun*) boca ♦ *vt* (*dog*) poner un bozal a
my [maɪ] *adj* mi(s); **~ house/brother/sisters** mi casa/mi hermano/mis hermanas; **I've washed ~ hair/cut ~ finger** me he lavado el pelo/cortado un dedo; **is this ~ pen or yours?** ¿es este bolígrafo mío o tuyo?
myself [maɪ'self] *pron* (*reflexive*) me; (*emphatic*) yo mismo; (*after prep*) mí (mismo); *see also* **oneself**
mysterious [mɪs'tɪərɪəs] *adj* misterioso
mystery ['mɪstərɪ] *n* misterio
mystify ['mɪstɪfaɪ] *vt* (*perplex*) dejar perplejo
myth [mɪθ] *n* mito

N, n

n/a *abbr* (= *not applicable*) no interesa
nag [næg] *vt* (*scold*) regañar; **~ging** *adj* (*doubt*) persistente; (*pain*) continuo
nail [neɪl] *n* (*human*) uña; (*metal*) clavo ♦ *vt* clavar; **to ~ sth to sth** clavar algo en algo; **to ~ sb down to doing sth** comprometer a uno a que haga algo; **~brush** *n* cepillo para las uñas; **~file** *n* lima para las uñas; **~ polish** *n* esmalte *m or* laca para las uñas; **~ polish remover** *n* quitaesmalte *m*; **~ scissors** *npl* tijeras *fpl* para las uñas; **~ varnish** (*BRIT*) *n* = **~ polish**
naïve [naɪ'iːv] *adj* ingenuo
naked ['neɪkɪd] *adj* (*nude*) desnudo; (*flame*) expuesto al aire
name [neɪm] *n* nombre *m*; (*surname*) apellido; (*reputation*) fama, renombre *m* ♦ *vt* (*child*) poner nombre a; (*criminal*) identificar; (*price, date etc*) fijar; **what's your ~?** ¿cómo se llama?; **by ~ de** nombre; **in the ~ of** en nombre de; **to give one's ~ and address** dar sus señas; **~ly** *adv* a saber; **~sake** *n* tocayo/a
nanny ['nænɪ] *n* niñera
nap [næp] *n* (*sleep*) sueñecito, siesta
nape [neɪp] *n*: **~ of the neck** nuca, cogote *m*
napkin ['næpkɪn] *n* (*also*: **table ~**) servilleta
nappy ['næpɪ] (*BRIT*) *n* pañal *m*; **~ rash** *n* prurito
narcotic [naː'kɔtɪk] *adj, n* narcótico
narrow ['nærəu] *adj* estrecho, angosto; (*fig: majority etc*) corto; (: *ideas etc*) estrecho ♦ *vi* (*road*) estrecharse; (*diminish*) reducirse; **to**

have a ~ **escape** escaparse por los pelos; **to ~ sth down** reducir algo; **~ly** adv (miss) por poco; **~-minded** adj de miras estrechas

nasty ['nɑːstɪ] adj (remark) feo; (person) antipático; (revolting: taste, smell) asqueroso; (wound, disease etc) peligroso, grave

nation ['neɪʃən] n nación f

national ['næʃənl] adj, n nacional m/f; **~ dress** n vestido nacional; **N~ Health Service** (BRIT) n servicio nacional de salud pública; ≈ Insalud m (SP); **N~ Insurance** (BRIT) n seguro social nacional; **~ism** n nacionalismo; **~ist** adj, n nacionalista m/f; **~ity** [-'nælɪtɪ] n nacionalidad f; **~ize** vt nacionalizar; **~ly** adv (nationwide) en escala nacional; (as a nation) nacionalmente, como nación; **~ park** (BRIT) n parque m nacional

nationwide ['neɪʃənwaɪd] adj en escala or a nivel nacional

native ['neɪtɪv] n (local inhabitant) natural m/f, nacional m/f ♦ adj (indigenous) indígena; (country) natal; (innate) natural, innato; a **~ of Russia** un(a) natural m/f de Rusia; a **~ speaker of French** un hablante nativo de francés; **N~ American** adj, n americano/a indígena, amerindio/a; **~ language** n lengua materna

Nativity [nə'tɪvɪtɪ] n: the **~** Navidad f

NATO ['neɪtəu] n abbr (= North Atlantic Treaty Organization) OTAN f

natural ['nætʃrəl] adj natural; **~ly** adv (speak etc) naturalmente; (of course) desde luego, por supuesto

nature ['neɪtʃə*] n (also: N~) naturaleza; (group, sort) género, clase f; (character) carácter m, genio; **by ~** por or de naturaleza

naught [nɔːt] = nought

naughty ['nɔːtɪ] adj (child) travieso

nausea ['nɔːsɪə] n náuseas fpl

nautical ['nɔːtɪkl] adj náutico, marítimo; (mile) marino

naval ['neɪvl] adj naval, de marina; **~ officer** n oficial m/f de marina

nave [neɪv] n nave f

navel ['neɪvl] n ombligo

navigate ['nævɪgeɪt] vt gobernar ♦ vi navegar; (AUT) ir de copiloto; **navigation** [-'geɪʃən] n (action) navegación f; (science) náutica; **navigator** n navegador(a) m/f, navegante m/f; (AUT) copiloto m/f

navvy ['nævɪ] (BRIT) n peón m caminero

navy ['neɪvɪ] n marina de guerra; (ships) armada, flota; **~(-blue)** adj azul marino

Nazi ['nɑːtsɪ] n nazi m/f

NB abbr (= nota bene) nótese

near [nɪə*] adj (place, relation) cercano; (time) próximo ♦ adv cerca ♦ prep (also: ~ to: space) cerca de, junto a; (: time) cerca de ♦ vt acercarse a, aproximarse a; **~by** [nɪə'baɪ]

adj cercano, próximo ♦ adv cerca; **~ly** adv casi, por poco; **I ~ly fell** por poco me caigo; **~ miss** n tiro cercano; **~side** n (AUT: in Britain) lado izquierdo; (: in US, Europe etc) lado derecho; **~-sighted** adj miope, corto de vista

neat [niːt] adj (place) ordenado, bien cuidado; (person) pulcro; (plan) ingenioso; (spirits) solo; **~ly** adv (tidily) con esmero; (skilfully) ingeniosamente

necessarily ['nesɪsrɪlɪ] adv necesariamente

necessary ['nesɪsrɪ] adj necesario, preciso

necessitate [nɪ'sesɪteɪt] vt hacer necesario

necessity [nɪ'sesɪtɪ] n necesidad f; **necessities** npl artículos mpl de primera necesidad

neck [nek] n (ANAT) cuello; (of person, garment, bottle) cuello; (of animal) pescuezo ♦ vi (inf) besuquearse; **~ and ~** parejos; **~lace** ['neklɪs] n collar m; **~line** n escote m; **~tie** ['nektaɪ] n corbata

née [neɪ] adj: **~ Scott** de soltera Scott

need [niːd] n (lack) escasez f, falta; (necessity) necesidad f ♦ vt (require) necesitar; **I ~ to do it** tengo que or debo hacerlo; **you don't ~ to go** no hace falta que (tú) vayas

needle ['niːdl] n aguja ♦ vt (fig: inf) picar, fastidiar

needless ['niːdlɪs] adj innecesario; **~ to say** huelga decir que

needlework ['niːdlwɜːk] n (activity) costura, labor f de aguja

needn't ['niːdnt] = need not

needy ['niːdɪ] adj necesitado

negative ['negətɪv] n (PHOT) negativo; (LING) negación f ♦ adj negativo; **~ equity** n situación que se da cuando el valor de la vivienda es menor que el de la hipoteca que pesa sobre ella

neglect [nɪ'glekt] vt (one's duty) faltar a, no cumplir con; (child) descuidar, desatender ♦ n (of house, garden etc) abandono; (of child) desatención f; (of duty) incumplimiento

negligee ['neglɪʒeɪ] n (nightgown) salto de cama

negotiate [nɪ'gəuʃɪeɪt] vt (treaty, loan) negociar; (obstacle) franquear; (bend in road) tomar ♦ vi: **to ~ (with)** negociar (con); **negotiation** [-'eɪʃən] n negociación f, gestión f

neigh [neɪ] vi relinchar

neighbour ['neɪbə*] (US neighbor) n vecino/a; **~hood** n (place) vecindad f, barrio; (people) vecindario; **~ing** adj vecino; **~ly** adj (person) amable; (attitude) de buen vecino

neither ['naɪðə*] adj ♦ conj: **I didn't move and ~ did John** no me he movido, ni Juan tampoco ♦ pron ninguno ♦ adv: **~ good nor bad** ni bueno ni malo; **~ is true** ninguno/a de los/las dos es cierto/a

neon ['niːɔn] n neón m; **~ light** n lámpara de neón

nephew ['nevjuː] n sobrino

nerve [nəːv] n (ANAT) nervio; (courage) valor m; (impudence) descaro, frescura; **a fit of ~s** un ataque de nervios; **~-racking** adj desquiciante

nervous ['nəːvəs] adj (anxious, ANAT) nervioso; (timid) tímido, miedoso; **~ breakdown** n crisis f nerviosa

nest [nest] n (of bird) nido; (wasps' ~) avispero ♦ vi anidar; **~ egg** n (fig) ahorros mpl

nestle ['nesl] vi: **to ~ down** acurrucarse

net [net] n (gen) red f; (fabric) tul m ♦ adj (COMM) neto, líquido ♦ vt coger (SP) or agarrar (AM) con red; (SPORT) marcar; **the N~** (Internet) la Red; **~ball** n básquet m

Netherlands ['neðələndz] npl: **the ~** los Países Bajos

nett [net] adj = **net**

netting ['netɪŋ] n red f, redes fpl

nettle ['netl] n ortiga

network ['netwəːk] n red f

neurotic [njuə'rɔtɪk] adj, n neurótico/a m/f

neuter ['njuːtə*] adj (LING) neutro ♦ vt castrar, capar

neutral ['njuːtrəl] adj (person) neutral; (colour etc, ELEC) neutro ♦ n (AUT) punto muerto; **~ize** vt neutralizar

never ['nevə*] adv nunca, jamás; **I ~ went** no fui nunca; **~ in my life** jamás en la vida; see also **mind**; **~-ending** adj interminable, sin fin; **~theless** [nevəðə'les] adv sin embargo, no obstante

new [njuː] adj nuevo; (brand new) a estrenar; (recent) reciente; **N~ Age** n Nueva Era; **~born** adj recién nacido; **~comer** ['njuːkʌmə*] n recién venido/a or llegado/a; **~-fangled** (pej) adj modernísimo; **~-found** adj (friend) nuevo; (enthusiasm) recién adquirido; **~ly** adv nuevamente, recién; **~lyweds** npl recién casados mpl

news [njuːz] n noticias fpl; **a piece of ~** una noticia; **the ~** (RADIO, TV) las noticias fpl; **~ agency** n agencia de noticias; **~agent** (BRIT) n vendedor(a) m/f de periódicos; **~caster** n presentador(a) m/f, locutor(a) m/f; **~ flash** n noticia de última hora; **~letter** n hoja informativa, boletín m; **~paper** n periódico, diario; **~print** n papel m de periódico; **~reader** n = **~caster**; **~reel** n noticiario; **~ stand** n quiosco or puesto de periódicos

newt [njuːt] n tritón m

New Year n Año Nuevo; **~'s Day** n Día m de Año Nuevo; **~'s Eve** n Nochevieja

New York ['njuː'jɔːk] n Nueva York

New Zealand [njuː'ziːlənd] n Nueva Zelanda; **~er** n neozelandés/esa m/f

next [nekst] adj (house, room) vecino; (bus stop, meeting) próximo; (following: page etc) siguiente ♦ adv después; **the ~ day** el día siguiente; **~ time** la próxima vez; **~ year** el año próximo or que viene; **~ to** junto a, al lado de; **~ to nothing** casi nada; **~ please!** ¡el siguiente! **~ door** adv en la casa de al lado ♦ adj vecino, de al lado; **~-of-kin** n pariente m más cercano

NHS n abbr = **National Health Service**

nib [nɪb] n plumilla

nibble ['nɪbl] vt mordisquear, mordiscar

Nicaragua [nɪkə'ræɡjuə] n Nicaragua; **~n** adj, n nicaragüense m/f

nice [naɪs] adj (likeable) simpático; (kind) amable; (pleasant) agradable; (attractive) bonito, mono, lindo (AM); **~ly** adv amablemente; bien

nick [nɪk] n (wound) rasguño; (cut, indentation) mella, muesca ♦ vt (inf) birlar, robar; **in the ~ of time** justo a tiempo

nickel ['nɪkl] n níquel m; (US) moneda de 5 centavos

nickname ['nɪkneɪm] n apodo, mote m ♦ vt apodar

nicotine ['nɪkətiːn] n nicotina

niece [niːs] n sobrina

Nigeria [naɪ'dʒɪərɪə] n Nigeria; **~n** adj, n nigeriano/a m/f

niggling ['nɪɡlɪŋ] adj (trifling) nimio, insignificante; (annoying) molesto

night [naɪt] n noche f; (evening) tarde f; **the ~ before last** anteanoche; **at ~, by ~** de noche, por la noche; **~cap** n (drink) bebida que se toma antes de acostarse; **~ club** n cabaret m; **~dress** (BRIT) n camisón m; **~fall** n anochecer m; **~gown** n = **~dress**; **~ie** ['naɪtɪ] n = **~dress**

nightingale ['naɪtɪŋɡeɪl] n ruiseñor m

night: **~life** n vida nocturna; **~ly** adj de todas las noches ♦ adv todas las noches, cada noche; **~mare** n pesadilla; **~ porter** n portero de noche; **~ school** n clase(s) f(pl) nocturna(s); **~ shift** n turno nocturno or de noche; **~time** n noche f; **~ watchman** n vigilante m nocturno

nil [nɪl] (BRIT) n (SPORT) cero, nada

Nile [naɪl] n: **the ~** el Nilo

nimble ['nɪmbl] adj (agile) ágil, ligero; (skilful) diestro

nine [naɪn] num nueve; **~teen** num diecinueve, diez y nueve; **~ty** num noventa

ninth [naɪnθ] adj noveno

nip [nɪp] vt (pinch) pellizcar; (bite) morder

nipple ['nɪpl] n (ANAT) pezón m

nitrogen ['naɪtrədʒən] n nitrógeno

no [nəu] (*pl* **~es**) *adv* (*opposite of "yes"*) no;
are you coming? — **~** (I'm not) ¿vienes? —
no; would you like some more? — **~** thank
you ¿quieres más? — no gracias
♦ *adj* (*not any*): **I have ~ money/time/books**
no tengo dinero/tiempo/libros; **~ other man**
would have done it ningún otro lo hubiera
hecho; "**~ entry**" "prohibido el paso";
"**~ smoking**" "prohibido fumar"
♦ *n* no *m*

nobility [nəu'bılıtı] *n* nobleza
noble ['nəubl] *adj* noble
nobody ['nəubədı] *pron* nadie
nod [nɔd] *vi* saludar con la cabeza; (*in*
agreement) decir que sí con la cabeza; (*doze*)
dar cabezadas ♦ *vt*: **to ~ one's head** inclinar la
cabeza ♦ *n* inclinación f de cabeza; **~ off** *vi*
dar cabezadas

noise [nɔız] *n* ruido; (*din*) escándalo,
estrépito; **noisy** *adj* ruidoso; (*child*)
escandaloso
nominate ['nɔmıneıt] *vt* (*propose*) proponer;
(*appoint*) nombrar; **nominee** [-'niː] *n*
candidato/a
non... [nɔn] *prefix* no, des..., in...; **~-**
alcoholic *adj* no alcohólico; **~chalant** *adj*
indiferente; **~-committal** *adj* evasivo;
~descript *adj* soso
none [nʌn] *pron* ninguno/a ♦ *adv* de ninguna
manera; **~ of you** ninguno de vosotros; **I've**
~ left no me queda ninguno/a; **he's ~ the**
worse for it no le ha hecho ningún mal
nonentity [nɔ'nentıtı] *n* cero a la izquierda,
nulidad f
nonetheless [nʌnðə'les] *adv* sin embargo,
no obstante
non-existent *adj* inexistente
non-fiction *n* literatura no novelesca
nonplussed [nɔn'plʌst] *adj* perplejo
nonsense ['nɔnsəns] *n* tonterías *fpl*,
disparates *fpl*; **~!** ¡qué tonterías!
non: ~-smoker *n* no fumador(a) *m/f*; **~-**
smoking *adj* (de) no fumador; **~-stick** *adj*
(*pan, surface*) antiadherente; **~-stop** *adj*
continuo; (*RAIL*) directo ♦ *adv* sin parar
noodles ['nuːdlz] *npl* tallarines *mpl*
nook [nuk] *n*: **~s and crannies** escondrijos *mpl*
noon [nuːn] *n* mediodía *m*
no-one *pron* = **nobody**
noose [nuːs] *n* (*hangman's*) dogal *m*
nor [nɔː*] *conj* = **neither** ♦ *adv see* **neither**
norm [nɔːm] *n* norma
normal ['nɔːml] *adj* normal; **~ly** *adv*
normalmente
north [nɔːθ] *n* norte *m* ♦ *adj* del norte,
norteño ♦ *adv* al *or* hacia el norte; **N~**

Africa *n* África del Norte; **N~ America** *n*
América del Norte; **~-east** *n* nor(d)este *m*;
~erly ['nɔːðəlı] *adj* (*point, direction*) norteño;
~ern ['nɔːðən] *adj* norteño, del norte;
N~ern Ireland *n* Irlanda del Norte; **N~ Pole**
n Polo Norte; **N~ Sea** *n* Mar *m* del Norte;
~ward(s) ['nɔːθwəd(z)] *adv* hacia el norte;
~-west *n* nor(d)oeste *m*
Norway ['nɔːweı] *n* Noruega; **Norwegian**
[-'wiːdʒən] *adj* noruego/a ♦ *n* noruego/a;
(*LING*) noruego
nose [nəuz] *n* (*ANAT*) nariz f; (*ZOOL*) hocico;
(*sense of smell*) olfato ♦ *vi*: **to ~ about**
curiosear; **~bleed** *n* hemorragia nasal; **~-**
dive *n* (*of plane: deliberate*) picado vertical;
(*: involuntary*) caída en picado; **~y** (*inf*) *adj*
curioso, fisgón/ona
nostalgia [nɔs'tældʒıə] *n* nostalgia
nostril ['nɔstrıl] *n* ventana de la nariz
nosy ['nəuzı] (*inf*) *adj* = **nosey**
not [nɔt] *adv* no; **~ that** ... no es que ...; **it's**
too late, isn't it? es demasiado tarde, ¿verdad
or no?; **~ yet/now** todavía/ahora no; **why ~?**
¿por qué no?; *see also* **all; only**
notably ['nəutəblı] *adv* especialmente
notary ['nəutərı] *n* notario/a
notch [nɔtʃ] *n* muesca, corte *m*
note [nəut] *n* (*MUS, record, letter*) nota;
(*banknote*) billete *m*; (*tone*) tono ♦ *vt*
(*observe*) notar, observar; (*write down*)
apuntar, anotar; **~book** *n* libreta, cuaderno;
~d ['nəutıd] *adj* célebre, conocido; **~pad** *n*
bloc *m*; **~paper** *n* papel *m* para cartas
nothing ['nʌθıŋ] *n* nada; (*zero*) cero; **he**
does ~ no hace nada; **~ new** nada nuevo;
~ much no mucho; **for ~** (*free*) gratis, sin
pago; (*in vain*) en balde
notice ['nəutıs] *n* (*announcement*) anuncio;
(*warning*) aviso; (*dismissal*) despido;
(*resignation*) dimisión f; (*period of time*) plazo
♦ *vt* (*observe*) notar, observar; **to bring sth to**
sb's ~ (*attention*) llamar la atención de uno
sobre algo; **to take ~ of** tomar nota de,
prestar atención a; **at short ~** con poca
anticipación; **until further ~** hasta nuevo
aviso; **to hand in one's ~** dimitir; **~able** *adj*
evidente, obvio; **~ board** (*BRIT*) *n* tablón *m*
de anuncios
notify ['nəutıfaı] *vt*: **to ~ sb (of sth)**
comunicar (algo) a uno
notion ['nəuʃən] *n* idea; (*opinion*) opinión f
notorious [nəu'tɔːrıəs] *adj* notorio
nougat ['nuːgɑː] *n* turrón *m*
nought [nɔːt] *n* cero
noun [naun] *n* nombre *m*, sustantivo
nourish ['nʌrıʃ] *vt* nutrir; (*fig*) alimentar;
~ing *adj* nutritivo; **~ment** *n* alimento,
sustento
novel ['nɔvl] *n* novela ♦ *adj* (*new*) nuevo,

original; (*unexpected*) insólito; ~**ist** *n*
novelista *m/f*; ~**ty** *n* novedad *f*
November [nəu'vɛmbə*] *n* noviembre
m
novice ['nɔvɪs] *n* (*REL*) novicio/a
now [nau] *adv* (*at the present time*) ahora;
(*these days*) actualmente, hoy día ♦ *conj*:
~ (**that**) ya que, ahora que; **right** ~ ahora
mismo; **by** ~ ya; **just** ~ ahora mismo; ~
and then, ~ **and again** de vez en cuando;
from ~ **on** de ahora en adelante;
~**adays** ['nauədeɪz] *adv* hoy (en) día,
actualmente
nowhere ['nəuwɛə*] *adv* (*direction*) a
ninguna parte; (*location*) en ninguna parte
nozzle ['nɔzl] *n* boquilla
nuance ['njuːɑːns] *n* matiz *m*
nuclear ['njuːklɪə*] *adj* nuclear
nucleus ['njuːklɪəs] (*pl* **nuclei**) *n* núcleo
nude [njuːd] *adj*, *n* desnudo/a *m/f*; **in the** ~
desnudo
nudge [nʌdʒ] *vt* dar un codazo a
nudist ['njuːdɪst] *n* nudista *m/f*
nuisance ['njuːsns] *n* molestia, fastidio;
(*person*) pesado, latoso; **what a** ~! ¡qué lata!
null [nʌl] *adj*: ~ **and void** nulo y sin efecto
numb [nʌm] *adj*: ~ **with cold/fear**
entumecido por el frío/paralizado de miedo
number ['nʌmbə*] *n* número; (*quantity*)
cantidad *f* ♦ *vt* (*pages etc*) numerar, poner
número a; (*amount to*) sumar, ascender a;
to be ~**ed among** figurar entre; **a** ~ **of** varios,
algunos; **they were ten in** ~ eran diez;
~ **plate** (*BRIT*) *n* matrícula, placa
numeral ['njuːmərəl] *n* número, cifra
numerate ['njuːmərɪt] *adj* competente en la
aritmética
numerous ['njuːmərəs] *adj* numeroso
nun [nʌn] *n* monja, religiosa
nurse [nəːs] *n* enfermero/a; (*also*: ~**maid**)
niñera ♦ *vt* (*patient*) cuidar, atender
nursery ['nəːsərɪ] *n* (*institution*) guardería
infantil; (*room*) cuarto de los niños; (*for
plants*) criadero, semillero; ~ **rhyme** *n*
canción *f* infantil; ~ **school** *n* parvulario,
escuela de párvulos; ~ **slope** (*BRIT*) *n* (*SKI*)
cuesta para principiantes
nursing ['nəːsɪŋ] *n* (*profession*) profesión *f* de
enfermera; (*care*) asistencia, cuidado;
~ **home** *n* clínica de reposo
nut [nʌt] *n* (*TECH*) tuerca; (*BOT*) nuez *f*;
~**crackers** *npl* cascanueces *m inv*
nutmeg ['nʌtmɛg] *n* nuez *f* moscada
nutritious [njuː'trɪʃəs] *adj* nutritivo,
alimenticio
nuts [nʌts] (*inf*) *adj* loco
nutshell ['nʌtʃɛl] *n*: **in a** ~ en resumidas
cuentas
nylon ['naɪlɔn] *n* nilón *m* ♦ *adj* de nilón

O, o

oak [əuk] *n* roble *m* ♦ *adj* de roble
O.A.P. (*BRIT*) *n abbr* = **old-age pensioner**
oar [ɔː*] *n* remo
oasis [əu'eɪsɪs] (*pl* **oases**) *n* oasis *m inv*
oath [əuθ] *n* juramento; (*swear word*)
palabrota; **on** (*BRIT*) or **under** ~ bajo
juramento
oatmeal ['əutmiːl] *n* harina de avena
oats [əuts] *n* avena
obedience [ə'biːdɪəns] *n* obediencia
obedient [ə'biːdɪənt] *adj* obediente
obey [ə'beɪ] *vt* obedecer; (*instructions,
regulations*) cumplir
obituary [ə'bɪtjuərɪ] *n* necrología
object [*n* 'ɔbdʒɪkt, *vb* əb'dʒɛkt] *n* objeto;
(*purpose*) objeto, propósito; (*LING*)
complemento ♦ *vi*: **to** ~ **to** estar en contra
de; (*proposal*) oponerse a; **to** ~ **that** objetar
que; **expense is no** ~ no importa cuánto
cuesta; **I** ~! ¡yo protesto!; ~**ion** [əb'dʒɛkʃən] *n*
protesta; **I have no** ~**ion to** ... no tengo
inconveniente en que ...; ~**ionable**
[əb'dʒɛkʃənəbl] *adj* desagradable; (*conduct*)
censurable; ~**ive** *adj*, *n* objetivo
obligation [ɔblɪ'geɪʃən] *n* obligación *f*; (*debt*)
deber *m*; **without** ~ sin compromiso
oblige [ə'blaɪdʒ] *vt* (*do a favour for*)
complacer, hacer un favor a; **to** ~ **sb to do
sth** forzar *or* obligar a uno a hacer algo; **to be
** ~**d to sb for sth** estarle agradecido a uno por
algo; **obliging** *adj* servicial, atento
oblique [ə'bliːk] *adj* oblicuo; (*allusion*)
indirecto
obliterate [ə'blɪtəreɪt] *vt* borrar
oblivion [ə'blɪvɪən] *n* olvido; **oblivious** [-ɪəs]
adj: **oblivious of** inconsciente de
oblong ['ɔblɔŋ] *adj* rectangular ♦ *n*
rectángulo
obnoxious [əb'nɔkʃəs] *adj* odioso,
detestable; (*smell*) nauseabundo
oboe ['əubəu] *n* oboe *m*
obscene [əb'siːn] *adj* obsceno
obscure [əb'skjuə*] *adj* oscuro ♦ *vt*
oscurecer; (*hide: sun*) esconder
observant [əb'zəːvnt] *adj* observador(a)
observation [ɔbzə'veɪʃən] *n* observación *f*;
(*MED*) examen *m*
observe [əb'zəːv] *vt* observar; (*rule*) cumplir;
~**r** *n* observador(a) *m/f*
obsess [əb'sɛs] *vt* obsesionar; ~**ive** *adj*
obsesivo, obsesionante
obsolete ['ɔbsəliːt] *adj*: **to be** ~ estar en
desuso
obstacle ['ɔbstəkl] *n* obstáculo; (*nuisance*)
estorbo; ~ **race** *n* carrera de obstáculos

obstinate ['ɔbstɪnɪt] adj terco, porfiado; (determined) obstinado

obstruct [əb'strʌkt] vt obstruir; (hinder) estorbar, obstaculizar; **~ion** [əb'strʌkʃən] n (action) obstrucción f; (object) estorbo, obstáculo

obtain [əb'teɪn] vt obtener; (achieve) conseguir

obvious ['ɔbvɪəs] adj obvio, evidente; **~ly** adv evidentemente, naturalmente; **~ly not** por supuesto que no

occasion [ə'keɪʒən] n oportunidad f, ocasión f; (event) acontecimiento; **~al** adj poco frecuente, ocasional; **~ally** adv de vez en cuando

occupant ['ɔkjupənt] n (of house) inquilino/a; (of car) ocupante m/f

occupation [ɔkju'peɪʃən] n ocupación f; (job) trabajo; (pastime) ocupaciones fpl; **~al hazard** n riesgo profesional

occupier ['ɔkjupaɪə*] n inquilino/a

occupy ['ɔkjupaɪ] vt (seat, post, time) ocupar; (house) habitar; **to ~ o.s. in doing** pasar el tiempo haciendo

occur [ə'kə:*] vi pasar, suceder; **to ~ to sb** ocurrírsele a uno; **~rence** [ə'kʌrəns] n acontecimiento; (existence) existencia

ocean ['əuʃən] n océano

o'clock [ə'klɔk] adv: **it is 5 ~** son las 5

OCR n abbr = **optical character recognition/reader**

October [ɔk'təubə*] n octubre m

octopus ['ɔktəpəs] n pulpo

odd [ɔd] adj extraño, raro; (number) impar; (sock, shoe etc) suelto; **60-~** 60 y pico; **at ~ times** de vez en cuando; **to be the ~ one out** estar de más; **~ity** n rareza; (person) excéntrico; **~-job man** n chico para todo; **~ jobs** npl bricolaje m; **~ly** adv curiosamente, extrañamente; see also **enough**; **~ments** npl (COMM) retales mpl; **~s** npl (in betting) puntos mpl de ventaja; **it makes no ~s** da lo mismo; **at ~s** reñidos/as; **~s and ends** minucias fpl

odometer [ɔ'dɔmɪtə*] (US) n cuenta-kilómetros m inv

odour ['əudə*] (US **odor**) n olor m; (unpleasant) hedor m

KEYWORD

of [ɔv, əv] prep **1** (gen) de; **a friend ~ ours** un amigo nuestro; **a boy ~ 10** un chico de 10 años; **that was kind ~ you** eso fue muy amable por or de tu parte

2 (expressing quantity, amount, dates etc) de; **a kilo ~ flour** un kilo de harina; **there were 3 ~ them** había tres; **3 ~ us went** tres de nosotros fuimos; **the 5th ~ July** el 5 de julio

3 (from, out of) de; **made ~ wood** (hecho) de madera

---

off [ɔf] adj, adv (engine) desconectado; (light) apagado; (tap) cerrado; (BRIT: food: bad) pasado, malo; (: milk) cortado; (cancelled) cancelado ♦ prep de; **to be ~** (to leave) irse, marcharse; **to be ~ sick** estar enfermo or de baja; **a day ~** un día libre or sin trabajar; **to have an ~ day** tener un día malo; **he had his coat ~** se había quitado el abrigo; **10% ~** (COMM) (con el) 10% de descuento; **5 km ~ (the road)** a 5 km (de la carretera); **~ the coast** frente a la costa; **I'm ~ meat** (no longer eat/like it) paso de la carne; **on the ~ chance** por si acaso; **~ and on** de vez en cuando

offal ['ɔfl] (BRIT) n (CULIN) menudencias fpl

off-colour [ɔf'kʌlə*] (BRIT) adj (ill) indispuesto

offence [ə'fens] (US **offense**) n (crime) delito; **to take ~ at** ofenderse por

offend [ə'fend] vt (person) ofender; **~er** n delincuente m/f

offensive [ə'fensɪv] adj ofensivo; (smell etc) repugnante ♦ n (MIL) ofensiva

offer ['ɔfə*] n oferta, ofrecimiento; (proposal) propuesta ♦ vt ofrecer; (opportunity) facilitar; **"on ~"** (COMM) "en oferta"; **~ing** n ofrenda

offhand [ɔf'hænd] adj informal ♦ adv de improviso

office ['ɔfɪs] n (place) oficina; (room) despacho; (position) carga, oficio; **doctor's ~** (US) consultorio; **to take ~** entrar en funciones; **~ block** (US **~ building**) n bloque m de oficinas; **~ hours** npl horas fpl de oficina; (US: MED) horas fpl de consulta

officer ['ɔfɪsə*] n (MIL etc) oficial m/f; (also: **police ~**) agente m/f de policía; (of organization) director(a) m/f

office worker n oficinista m/f

official [ə'fɪʃl] adj oficial, autorizado ♦ n funcionario, oficial m

offing ['ɔfɪŋ] n: **in the ~** (fig) en perspectiva

off: **~-licence** (BRIT) n (shop) bodega, tienda de vinos y bebidas alcohólicas; **~-line** adj, adv (COMPUT) fuera de línea; **~-peak** adj (electricity) de banda económica; (ticket) billete de precio reducido por viajar fuera de las horas punta; **~-putting** (BRIT) adj (person) asqueroso; (remark) desalentador(a); **~-season** adj, adv fuera de temporada

offset ['ɔfset] (irreg) vt contrarrestar, compensar

offshoot ['ɔfʃuːt] n (fig) ramificación f

offshore [ɔf'ʃɔː*] adj (breeze, island) costera; (fishing) de bajura

offside ['ɔf'saɪd] adj (SPORT) fuera de juego; (AUT: in UK) del lado derecho; (: in US, Europe etc) del lado izquierdo

offspring ['ɔfsprɪŋ] n inv descendencia

off: **~stage** adv entre bastidores; **~-the-peg** (US **~-the-rack**) adv confeccionado; **~-white** adj color crudo

often ['ɔfn] adv a menudo, con frecuencia; **how ~ do you go?** ¿cada cuánto vas?

oh [əu] excl ¡ah!

oil [ɔɪl] n aceite m; (petroleum) petróleo; (for heating) aceite m combustible ♦ vt engrasar; **~can** n lata de aceite; **~field** n campo petrolífero; **~ filter** n (AUT) filtro de aceite; **~ painting** n pintura al óleo; **~ rig** n torre f de perforación; **~ tanker** n petrolero; (truck) camión m cisterna; **~ well** n pozo (de petróleo); **~y** adj aceitoso; (food) grasiento

ointment ['ɔɪntmənt] n ungüento

O.K., okay ['əu'keɪ] excl O.K., ¡está bien!, ¡vale! (SP) ♦ adj bien ♦ vt dar el visto bueno a

old [əuld] adj viejo; (former) antiguo; **how ~ are you?** ¿cuántos años tienes?, ¿qué edad tienes?; **he's 10 years ~** tiene 10 años; **~er brother** hermano mayor; **~ age** n vejez f; **~-age pensioner** (BRIT) n jubilado/a; **~-fashioned** adj anticuado, pasado de moda

olive ['ɔlɪv] n (fruit) aceituna; (tree) olivo ♦ adj (also: **~-green**) verde oliva; **~ oil** n aceite m de oliva

Olympic [əu'lɪmpɪk] adj olímpico; **the ~ Games, the ~s** las Olimpíadas

omelet(te) ['ɔmlɪt] n tortilla (SP), tortilla de huevo (AM)

omen ['əumən] n presagio

ominous ['ɔmɪnəs] adj de mal agüero, amenazador(a)

omit [əu'mɪt] vt omitir

KEYWORD

on [ɔn] prep **1** (indicating position) en; sobre; **~ the wall** en la pared; **it's ~ the table** está sobre or en la mesa; **~ the left** a la izquierda **2** (indicating means, method, condition etc): **~ foot** a pie; **~ the train/plane** (go) en tren/ avión; (be) en el tren/el avión; **~ the radio/ television/telephone** por or en la radio/ televisión/al teléfono; **to be ~ drugs** drogarse; (MED) estar a tratamiento; **to be ~ holiday/ business** estar de vacaciones/en viaje de negocios **3** (referring to time): **~ Friday** el viernes; **~ Fridays** los viernes; **~ June 20th** el 20 de junio; **a week ~ Friday** del viernes en una semana; **~ arrival** al llegar; **~ seeing this** al ver esto **4** (about, concerning) sobre, acerca de; **a book ~ physics** un libro de or sobre física ♦ adv **1** (referring to dress): **to have one's coat ~** tener or llevar el abrigo puesto; **she put her gloves ~** se puso los guantes **2** (referring to covering): **"screw the lid ~ tightly"** "cerrar bien la tapa" **3** (further, continuously): **to walk** etc **~** seguir caminando etc ♦ adj **1** (functioning, in operation: machine, radio, TV, light) encendido/a (SP), prendido/a (AM); (: tap) abierto/a; (: brakes) echado/a, puesto/a; **is the meeting still ~?** (in progress) ¿todavía continúa la reunión?; (not cancelled) ¿va a haber reunión al fin?; **there's a good film ~ at the cinema** ponen una buena película en el cine **2: that's not ~!** (inf: not possible) ¡eso ni hablar!; (: not acceptable) ¡eso no se hace!

once [wʌns] adv una vez; (formerly) antiguamente ♦ conj una vez que; **~ he had left/it was done** una vez que se había marchado/se hizo; **at ~** en seguida, inmediatamente; (simultaneously) a la vez; **~ a week** una vez por semana; **~ more** otra vez; **~ and for all** de una vez por todas; **~ upon a time** érase una vez

oncoming ['ɔnkʌmɪŋ] adj (traffic) que viene de frente

KEYWORD

one [wʌn] num un(o)/una; **~ hundred and fifty** ciento cincuenta; **~ by ~** uno a uno ♦ adj **1** (sole) único; **the ~ book which** el único libro que; **the ~ man who** el único que **2** (same) mismo/a; **they came in the ~ car** vinieron en un solo coche ♦ pron **1: this ~** éste/ésta; **that ~** ése/ésa; (more remote) aquél/aquella; **I've already got (a red) ~** ya tengo uno/a (rojo/a); **~ by ~** uno/a por uno/a **2: ~ another** os (SP), se (+ el uno al otro, unos a otros etc); **do you two ever see ~ another?** ¿vosotros dos os veis alguna vez? (SP), ¿se ven ustedes dos alguna vez?; **the boys didn't dare look at ~ another** los chicos no se atrevieron a mirarse (el uno al otro); **they all kissed ~ another** se besaron unos a otros **3** (impers): **~ never knows** nunca se sabe; **to cut ~'s finger** cortarse el dedo; **~ needs to eat** hay que comer

one: **~-day excursion** (US) n billete m de ida y vuelta en un día; **~-man** adj (business) individual; **~-man band** n hombre-orquesta m; **~-off** (BRIT: inf) n (event) acontecimiento único

oneself [wʌn'self] pron (reflexive) se; (after prep) sí; (emphatic) uno/a mismo/a; **to hurt ~** hacerse daño; **to keep sth for ~** guardarse algo; **to talk to ~** hablar solo

one: **~-sided** adj (argument) parcial; **~-to-~**

adj (*relationship*) de dos; **~-way** *adj* (*street*) de sentido único

ongoing ['ɒngəʊɪŋ] *adj* continuo

onion ['ʌnjən] *n* cebolla

on-line *adj, adv* (COMPUT) en línea

onlooker ['ɒnlʊkə*] *n* espectador(a) *m/f*

only ['əʊnlɪ] *adv* solamente, sólo ♦ *adj* único, solo ♦ *conj* solamente que, pero; **an ~ child** un hijo único; **not ~ ... but also ...** no sólo ... sino también ...

onset ['ɒnsɛt] *n* comienzo

onshore ['ɒnʃɔ:*] *adj* (*wind*) que sopla del mar hacia la tierra

onslaught ['ɒnslɔ:t] *n* ataque *m*, embestida

onto ['ɒntu] *prep* = **on to**

onward(s) ['ɒnwəd(z)] *adv* (*move*) (hacia) adelante; **from that time ~** desde entonces en adelante

onyx ['ɒnɪks] *n* ónice *m*

ooze [u:z] *vi* rezumar

opaque [əʊ'peɪk] *adj* opaco

OPEC ['əʊpɛk] *n abbr* (= *Organization of Petroleum-Exporting Countries*) OPEP *f*

open ['əʊpən] *adj* abierto; (*car*) descubierto; (*road, view*) despejado; (*meeting*) público; (*admiration*) manifiesto ♦ *vt* abrir ♦ *vi* abrirse; (*book etc: commence*) comenzar; **in the ~** (**air**) al aire libre; **~ on to** *vt fus* (*subj: room, door*) dar a; **~ up** *vt* abrir; (*blocked road*) despejar ♦ *vi* abrirse, empezar; **~ing** *n* abertura; (*start*) comienzo; (*opportunity*) oportunidad *f*; **~ing hours** *npl* horario de apertura; **~ learning** *n* enseñanza flexible a tiempo parcial; **~ly** *adv* abiertamente; **~-minded** *adj* imparcial; **~-necked** *adj* (*shirt*) desabrochado; sin corbata; **~-plan** *adj:* **~-plan office** gran oficina sin particiones

opera ['ɒpərə] *n* ópera; **~ house** *n* teatro de la ópera

operate ['ɒpəreɪt] *vt* (*machine*) hacer funcionar; (*company*) dirigir ♦ *vi* funcionar; **to ~ on sb** (MED) operar a uno

operatic [ɒpə'rætɪk] *adj* de ópera

operating table ['ɒpəreɪtɪŋ-] *n* mesa de operaciones

operating theatre *n* sala de operaciones

operation [ɒpə'reɪʃən] *n* operación *f*; (*of machine*) funcionamiento; **to be in ~** estar funcionando o en funcionamiento; **to have an ~** (MED) ser operado; **~al** *adj* operacional, en buen estado

operative ['ɒpərətɪv] *adj* en vigor

operator ['ɒpəreɪtə*] *n* (*of machine*) maquinista *m/f*, operario/a; (TEL) operador(a) *m/f*, telefonista *m/f*

opinion [ə'pɪnɪən] *n* opinión *f*; **in my ~** en mi opinión, a mi juicio; **~ated** *adj* testarudo; **~ poll** *n* encuesta, sondeo

opponent [ə'pəʊnənt] *n* adversario/a,

contrincante *m/f*

opportunity [ɒpə'tju:nɪtɪ] *n* oportunidad *f*; **to take the ~ of doing** aprovechar la ocasión para hacer

oppose [ə'pəʊz] *vt* oponerse a; **to be ~d to sth** oponerse a algo; **as ~d to** a diferencia de; **opposing** *adj* opuesto, contrario

opposite ['ɒpəzɪt] *adj* opuesto, contrario a; (*house etc*) de enfrente ♦ *adv* en frente ♦ *prep* en frente de, frente a ♦ *n* lo contrario

opposition [ɒpə'zɪʃən] *n* oposición *f*

oppressive [ə'prɛsɪv] *adj* opresivo; (*weather*) agobiante

opt [ɒpt] *vi:* **~ for** optar por; **to ~ to do** optar por hacer; **~ out** *vi:* **to ~ out of** optar por no hacer

optical ['ɒptɪkl] *adj* óptico

optician [ɒp'tɪʃən] *n* óptico *m/f*

optimist ['ɒptɪmɪst] *n* optimista *m/f*; **~ic** [-'mɪstɪk] *adj* optimista

option ['ɒpʃən] *n* opción *f*; **~al** *adj* facultativo, discrecional

or [ɔ:*] *conj* o; (*before o, ho*) u; (*with negative*): **he hasn't seen ~ heard anything** no ha visto ni oído nada; **~ else** si no

oral ['ɔ:rəl] *adj* oral ♦ *n* examen *m* oral

orange ['ɒrɪndʒ] *n* (*fruit*) naranja ♦ *adj* color naranja

orbit ['ɔ:bɪt] *n* órbita ♦ *vt, vi* orbitar

orchard ['ɔ:tʃəd] *n* huerto

orchestra ['ɔ:kɪstrə] *n* orquesta; (US: *seating*) platea

orchid ['ɔ:kɪd] *n* orquídea

ordain [ɔ:'deɪn] *vt* (REL) ordenar, decretar

ordeal [ɔ:'di:l] *n* experiencia horrorosa

order ['ɔ:də*] *n* orden *m*; (*command*) orden *f*; (*good ~*) buen estado; (COMM) pedido ♦ *vt* (*also: put in ~*) arreglar, poner en orden; (COMM) pedir; (*command*) mandar, ordenar; **in ~** en orden; (*of document*) en regla; **in (working) ~** en funcionamiento; **in ~ to do/ that** para hacer/que; **on ~** (COMM) pedido; **to be out of ~** estar desordenado; (*not working*) no funcionar; **to ~ sb to do sth** mandar a uno hacer algo; **~ form** *n* hoja de pedido; **~ly** *n* (MIL) ordenanza *m*; (MED) enfermero/a (auxiliar) ♦ *adj* ordenado

ordinary ['ɔ:dnrɪ] *adj* corriente, normal; (*pej*) común y corriente; **out of the ~** fuera de lo común

Ordnance Survey ['ɔ:dnəns-] (BRIT) *n* servicio oficial de topografía

ore [ɔ:*] *n* mineral *m*

organ ['ɔ:gən] *n* órgano; **~ic** [ɔ:'gænɪk] *adj* orgánico; **~ism** *n* organismo

organization [ɔ:gənaɪ'zeɪʃən] *n* organización *f*

organize ['ɔ:gənaɪz] *vt* organizar; **~r** *n* organizador(a) *m/f*

orgasm ['ɔːgæzəm] n orgasmo

orgy ['ɔːdʒɪ] n orgía

Orient ['ɔːrɪənt] n Oriente m; **oriental** [-'ɛntl] adj oriental

orientate ['ɔːrɪənteɪt] vt: **to ~ o.s.** orientarse

origin ['ɒrɪdʒɪn] n origen m

original [ə'rɪdʒɪnl] adj original; (first) primero; (earlier) primitivo ♦ n original m; **~ly** adv al principio

originate [ə'rɪdʒɪneɪt] vi: **to ~ from, to ~ in** surgir de, tener su origen en

Orkneys ['ɔːknɪz] npl: **the ~** (also: **the Orkney Islands**) las Orcadas

ornament ['ɔːnəmənt] n adorno; (trinket) chuchería; **~al** [-'mɛntl] adj decorativo, de adorno

ornate [ɔː'neɪt] adj muy ornado, vistoso

orphan ['ɔːfn] n huérfano/a

orthopaedic [ɔːθə'piːdɪk] (US **orthopedic**) adj ortopédico

ostensibly [ɒs'tɛnsɪblɪ] adv aparentemente

ostentatious [ɒstɛn'teɪʃəs] adj ostentoso

osteopath ['ɒstɪəpæθ] n osteópata m/f

ostracize ['ɒstrəsaɪz] vt hacer el vacío a

ostrich ['ɒstrɪtʃ] n avestruz m

other ['ʌðə*] adj otro ♦ pron: **the ~ (one)** el/la otro/a ♦ adv: **~ than** aparte de; **~s** (~ people) otros; **the ~ day** el otro día; **~wise** adv de otra manera ♦ conj (if not) si no

otter ['ɒtə*] n nutria

ouch [autʃ] excl ¡ay!

ought [ɔːt] (pt **ought**) aux vb: **I ~ to do it** debería hacerlo; **this ~ to have been corrected** esto debiera haberse corregido; **he ~ to win** (probability) debe or debiera ganar

ounce [auns] n onza (28.35g)

our ['auə*] adj nuestro; see also **my**; **~s** pron (el) nuestro/(la) nuestra etc; see also **mine**¹; **~selves** pron pl (reflexive, after prep) nosotros; (emphatic) nosotros mismos; see also **oneself**

oust [aust] vt desalojar

out [aut] adv fuera, afuera; (not at home) fuera (de casa); (light, fire) apagado; **~ there** allí (fuera); **he's ~** (absent) no está, ha salido; **to be ~ in one's calculations** equivocarse en sus cálculos); **to run ~** salir corriendo; **~ loud** en alta voz; **~ of** (outside) fuera de; (because of: anger etc) por; **~ of petrol** sin gasolina; **"~ of order"** "no funciona"; **~-and-~** adj (liar, thief etc) redomado, empedernido; **~back** n interior m; **~board** adj: **~board motor** (motor m) fuera borda m; **~break** n (of war) comienzo; (of disease) epidemia; (of violence etc) ola; **~burst** n explosión f, arranque m; **~cast** n paria m/f; **~come** n resultado; **~crop** n (of rock) afloramiento; **~cry** n protestas fpl; **~dated** adj anticuado, fuera de moda; **~do** (irreg) vt superar;

~door adj exterior, de aire libre; (clothes) de calle; **~doors** adv al aire libre

outer ['autə*] adj exterior, externo; **~ space** n espacio exterior

outfit ['autfɪt] n (clothes) conjunto

out: **~going** adj (character) extrovertido; (retiring: president etc) saliente; **~goings** (BRIT) npl gastos mpl; **~grow** (irreg) vt: **he has ~grown his clothes** su ropa le queda pequeña ya; **~house** n dependencia; **~ing** ['autɪŋ] n excursión f, paseo

out: **~law** n proscrito ♦ vt proscribir; **~lay** n inversión f; **~let** n salida; (of pipe) desagüe m; (US: ELEC) toma de corriente; (also: retail **~let**) punto de venta; **~line** n (shape) contorno, perfil m; (sketch, plan) esbozo ♦ vt (plan etc) esbozar; **in ~line** (fig) a grandes rasgos; **~live** vt sobrevivir a; **~look** n (fig: prospects) perspectivas fpl; (: for weather) pronóstico; **~lying** adj remoto, aislado; **~moded** adj anticuado, pasado de moda; **~number** vt superar en número; **~-of-date** adj (passport) caducado; (clothes) pasado de moda; **~-of-the-way** adj apartado; **~patient** n paciente m/f externo/a; **~post** n puesto avanzado; **~put** n (volumen m de) producción f, rendimiento; (COMPUT) salida

outrage ['autreɪdʒ] n escándalo; (atrocity) atrocidad f ♦ vt ultrajar; **~ous** [-'reɪdʒəs] adj monstruoso

outright [adv aut'raɪt, adj 'autraɪt] adv (ask, deny) francamente; (refuse) rotundamente; (win) de manera absoluta; (be killed) en el acto ♦ adj franco; rotundo

outset ['autsɛt] n principio

outside [aut'saɪd] n exterior m ♦ adj exterior, externo ♦ adv fuera ♦ prep fuera de; (beyond) más allá de; **at the ~** (fig) a lo sumo; **~ lane** n (AUT: in Britain) carril m de la derecha; (: in US, Europe etc) carril m de la izquierda; **~ line** n (TEL) línea (exterior); **~r** n (stranger) extraño, forastero

out: **~size** adj (clothes) de talla grande; **~skirts** npl alrededores mpl, afueras fpl; **~spoken** adj muy franco; **~standing** adj excepcional, destacado; (remaining) pendiente; **~stay** vt: **to ~stay one's welcome** quedarse más de la cuenta; **~stretched** adj (hand) extendido; **~strip** vt (competitors, demand) dejar atrás, aventajar; **~-tray** n bandeja de salida

outward ['autwəd] adj externo; (journey) de ida

outweigh [aut'weɪ] vt pesar más que

outwit [aut'wɪt] vt ser más listo que

oval ['əuvl] adj ovalado ♦ n óvalo

ovary ['əuvərɪ] n ovario

oven ['ʌvn] n horno; **~proof** adj resistente al horno

over ['əuvə*] adv encima, por encima ♦ adj (or adv) (finished) terminado; (surplus) de sobra ♦ prep (por) encima de; (above) sobre; (on the other side of) al otro lado de; (more than) más de; (during) durante; ~ **here** (por) aquí; ~ **there** (por) allí or allá; **all** ~ (everywhere) por todas partes; ~ **and** ~ (again) una y otra vez; ~ **and above** además de; **to ask sb** ~ invitar a uno a casa; **to bend** ~ inclinarse

overall [adj, n 'əuvərɔːl, adv əuvər'ɔːl] adj (length etc) total; (study) de conjunto ♦ adv en conjunto ♦ n (BRIT) guardapolvo; ~**s** npl mono (SP), overol m (AM)

over: ~**awe** vt: **to be** ~**awed (by)** quedar impresionado (con); ~**balance** vi perder el equilibrio; ~**board** adv (NAUT) por la borda; ~**book** [əuvə'buk] vt sobrereservar

overcast ['əuvəkɑːst] adj encapotado

overcharge [əuvə'tʃɑːdʒ] vt: **to** ~ **sb** cobrar un precio excesivo a uno

overcoat ['əuvəkəut] n abrigo, sobretodo

overcome [əuvə'kʌm] (irreg) vt vencer; (difficulty) superar

over: ~**crowded** adj atestado de gente; (city, country) superpoblado; ~**do** (irreg) vt exagerar; (overcook) cocer demasiado; **to** ~**do it** (work etc) pasarse; ~**dose** n sobredosis f inv; ~**draft** n saldo deudor; ~**drawn** adj (account) en descubierto; ~**due** adj retrasado; ~**estimate** [əuvər'estɪmeɪt] vt sobreestimar

overflow [vb əuvə'fləu, n 'əuvəfləu] vi desbordarse ♦ n (also: ~ **pipe**) (cañería de) desagüe m

overgrown [əuvə'grəun] adj (garden) invadido por la vegetación

overhaul [vb əuvə'hɔːl, n 'əuvəhɔːl] vt revisar, repasar ♦ n revisión f

overhead [adv əuvə'hed, adj, n 'əuvəhed] adv por arriba or encima ♦ adj (cable) aéreo ♦ n (US) = ~**s**; ~**s** npl (expenses) gastos mpl generales

over: ~**hear** (irreg) vt oír por casualidad; ~**heat** vi (engine) recalentarse; ~**joyed** adj encantado, lleno de alegría

overland ['əuvəlænd] adj, adv por tierra

overlap [əuvə'læp] vi traslaparse

over: ~**leaf** adv al dorso; ~**load** vt sobrecargar; ~**look** vt (have view of) dar a, tener vistas a; (miss: by mistake) pasar por alto; (excuse) perdonar

overnight [əuvə'naɪt] adv durante la noche; (fig) de la noche a la mañana ♦ adj de noche; **to stay** ~ pasar la noche

overpass ['əuvəpɑːs] (US) n paso superior

overpower [əuvə'pauə*] vt dominar; (fig) embargar; ~**ing** adj (heat) agobiante; (smell) penetrante

over: ~**rate** vt sobreestimar; ~**ride** (irreg) vt no hacer caso de; ~**riding** adj predominante; ~**rule** vt (decision) anular; (claim) denegar; ~**run** (irreg) vt (country) invadir; (time limit) rebasar, exceder

overseas [əuvə'siːz] adv (abroad: live) en el extranjero; (: travel) al extranjero ♦ adj (trade) exterior; (visitor) extranjero

overshadow [əuvə'ʃædəu] vt: **to be** ~**ed by** estar a la sombra de

overshoot [əuvə'ʃuːt] (irreg) vt excederse

oversight ['əuvəsaɪt] n descuido

oversleep [əuvə'sliːp] (irreg) vi quedarse dormido

overstep [əuvə'step] vt: **to** ~ **the mark** pasarse de la raya

overt [əu'vɜːt] adj abierto

overtake [əuvə'teɪk] (irreg) vt sobrepasar; (BRIT: AUT) adelantar

over: ~**throw** (irreg) vt (government) derrocar; ~**time** n horas fpl extraordinarias; ~**tone** n (fig) tono

overture ['əuvətʃuə*] n (MUS) obertura; (fig) preludio

over: ~**turn** vt volcar; (fig: plan) desbaratar; (: government) derrocar ♦ vi volcar; ~**weight** adj demasiado gordo or pesado; ~**whelm** vt aplastar; (subj: emotion) sobrecoger; ~**whelming** adj (victory, defeat) arrollador(a); (feeling) irresistible; ~**work** vi trabajar demasiado; ~**wrought** [əuvə'rɔːt] adj sobreexcitado

owe [əu] vt: **to** ~ **sb sth**, **to** ~ **sth to sb** deber algo a uno; **owing to** prep debido a, por causa de

owl [aul] n búho, lechuza

own [əun] vt tener, poseer ♦ adj propio; **a room of my** ~ una habitación propia; **to get one's** ~ **back** tomar revancha; **on one's** ~ solo, a solas; ~ **up** vi confesar; ~**er** n dueño/a; ~**ership** n posesión f

ox [ɔks] (pl ~**en**) n buey m; ~**tail** n: ~**tail soup** sopa de rabo de buey

oxygen ['ɔksɪdʒən] n oxígeno

oyster ['ɔɪstə*] n ostra

oz. abbr = **ounce(s)**

ozone ['əuzəun]: ~ **friendly** adj que no daña la capa de ozono; ~ **hole** n agujero m de/en la capa de ozono; ~ **layer** n capa f de ozono

P, p

p [piː] abbr = **penny**; **pence**

P.A. n abbr = **personal assistant**; **public address system**

p.a. abbr = **per annum**

pa [pɑː] (inf) n papá m

pace [peɪs] n paso ♦ vi: **to** ~ **up and down**

pasearse de un lado a otro; **to keep ~ with** llevar el mismo paso que; **~maker** n (MED) regulador m cardíaco, marcapasos m inv; (SPORT: also: **~setter**) liebre f

Pacific [pə'sɪfɪk] n: **the ~ (Ocean)** el (Océano) Pacífico

pack [pæk] n (packet) paquete m; (of hounds) jauría; (of people) manada, bando; (of cards) baraja; (bundle) fardo; (US: of cigarettes) paquete m; (back ~) mochila ♦ vt (fill) llenar; (in suitcase etc) meter, poner; (cram) llenar, atestar; **to ~ sb off** despachar a uno; **~ it in!** (inf) ¡déjalo!

package ['pækɪdʒ] n paquete m; (bulky) bulto; (also: ~ **deal**) acuerdo global; **~ holiday** n vacaciones fpl organizadas; **~ tour** n viaje m organizado

packed lunch n almuerzo frío

packet ['pækɪt] n paquete m

packing ['pækɪŋ] n embalaje m; **~ case** n cajón m de embalaje

pact [pækt] n pacto

pad [pæd] n (of paper) bloc m; (cushion) cojinete m; (inf: home) casa ♦ vt rellenar; **~ding** n (material) relleno

paddle ['pædl] n (oar) canalete m; (US: for table tennis) paleta ♦ vt impulsar con canalete ♦ vi (with feet) chapotear; **paddling pool** (BRIT) n estanque m de juegos

paddock ['pædək] n corral m

padlock ['pædlɔk] n candado

paediatrics [pi:dɪ'ætrɪks] (US **pediatrics**) n pediatría

pagan ['peɪgən] adj, n pagano/a m/f

page [peɪdʒ] n (of book) página; (of newspaper) plana; (also: ~ **boy**) paje m ♦ vt (in hotel etc) llamar por altavoz a

pageant ['pædʒənt] n (procession) desfile m; (show) espectáculo; **~ry** n pompa

pager ['peɪdʒə*] n (TEL) busca m

paging device ['peɪdʒɪŋ-] n = **pager**

paid [peɪd] pt, pp of **pay** ♦ adj (work) remunerado; (holiday) pagado; (official etc) a sueldo; **to put ~ to** (BRIT) acabar con

pail [peɪl] n cubo, balde m

pain [peɪn] n dolor m; **to be in ~** sufrir; **to take ~s to do sth** tomarse grandes molestias en hacer algo; **~ed** adj (expression) afligido; **~ful** adj doloroso; (difficult) penoso; (disagreeable) desagradable; **~fully** adv (fig: very) terriblemente; **~killer** n analgésico; **~less** adj que no causa dolor; **~staking** ['peɪnzteɪkɪŋ] adj (person) concienzudo, esmerado

paint [peɪnt] n pintura ♦ vt pintar; **to ~ the door blue** pintar la puerta de azul; **~brush** n (artist's) pincel m; (decorator's) brocha; **~er** n pintor(a) m/f; **~ing** n pintura; **~work** n

pintura

pair [peə*] n (of shoes, gloves etc) par m; (of people) pareja; **a ~ of scissors** unas tijeras; **a ~ of trousers** unos pantalones, un pantalón

pajamas [pə'dʒɑ:məz] (US) npl pijama m

Pakistan [pɑ:kɪ'stɑ:n] n Paquistán m; **~i** adj, n paquistaní m/f

pal [pæl] (inf) n compinche m/f, compañero/a

palace ['pæləs] n palacio

palatable ['pælɪtəbl] adj sabroso

palate ['pælɪt] n paladar m

pale [peɪl] adj (gen) pálido; (colour) claro ♦ n: **to be beyond the ~** pasarse de la raya

Palestine ['pælɪstaɪn] n Palestina; **Palestinian** [-'tɪnɪən] adj, n palestino/a m/f

palette ['pælɪt] n paleta

pall [pɔːl] vi perder el sabor

pallet ['pælɪt] n (for goods) pallet m

pallid ['pælɪd] adj pálido

palm [pɑːm] n (ANAT) palma; (also: ~ **tree**) palmera, palma ♦ vt: **to ~ sth off on sb** (inf) encajar algo a uno; **P~ Sunday** n Domingo de Ramos

paltry ['pɔːltrɪ] adj irrisorio

pamper ['pæmpə*] vt mimar

pamphlet ['pæmflət] n folleto

pan [pæn] n (also: sauce~) cacerola, cazuela, olla; (also: frying ~) sartén f

Panama ['pænəmɑː] n Panamá m; **the ~ Canal** el Canal de Panamá

pancake ['pænkeɪk] n crepe f

panda ['pændə] n panda m; **~ car** (BRIT) n coche m Z (SP)

pandemonium [pændɪ'məʊnɪəm] n jaleo

pander ['pændə*] vi: **to ~ to** complacer a

pane [peɪn] n cristal m

panel ['pænl] n (of wood etc) panel m; (RADIO, TV) panel m de invitados; **~ling** (US **~ing**) n paneles mpl

pang [pæŋ] n: **a ~ of regret** (una punzada de) remordimiento; **hunger ~s** dolores mpl del hambre

panic ['pænɪk] n (terror m) pánico ♦ vi dejarse llevar por el pánico; **~ky** adj (person) asustadizo; **~-stricken** adj preso de pánico

pansy ['pænzɪ] n (BOT) pensamiento; (inf: pej) maricón m

pant [pænt] vi jadear

panther ['pænθə*] n pantera

panties ['pæntɪz] npl bragas fpl, pantis mpl

pantihose ['pæntɪhəʊz] (US) n pantimedias fpl

pantomime ['pæntəmaɪm] (BRIT) n revista musical representada en Navidad, basada en cuentos de hadas

pantry ['pæntrɪ] n despensa

pants [pænts] n (BRIT: underwear: woman's) bragas fpl; (: man's) calzoncillos mpl; (US: trousers) pantalones mpl

paper [ˈpeɪpə*] n papel m; (also: news~) periódico, diario; (academic essay) ensayo; (exam) examen m ♦ adj de papel ♦ vt empapelar (SP), tapizar (AM); ~s npl (also: identity ~s) papeles mpl, documentos mpl; ~**back** n libro en rústica; ~ **bag** n bolsa de papel; ~ **clip** n clip m; ~ **hankie** n pañuelo de papel; ~**weight** n pisapapeles m inv; ~**work** n trabajo administrativo

paprika [ˈpæprɪkə] n pimentón m

par [pɑː*] n par f; (GOLF) par m; **to be on a ~ with** estar a la par con

parachute [ˈpærəʃuːt] n paracaídas m inv

parade [pəˈreɪd] n desfile m ♦ vt (show off) hacer alarde de ♦ vi desfilar; (MIL) pasar revista

paradise [ˈpærədaɪs] n paraíso

paradox [ˈpærədɔks] n paradoja; ~**ically** [-ˈdɔksɪklɪ] adv paradójicamente

paraffin [ˈpærəfɪn] (BRIT) n (also: ~ oil) parafina

paragon [ˈpærəgən] n modelo

paragraph [ˈpærəgrɑːf] n párrafo

parallel [ˈpærəlɛl] adj en paralelo; (fig) semejante ♦ n (line) paralela; (fig, GEO) paralelo

paralyse [ˈpærəlaɪz] vt paralizar

paralysis [pəˈrælɪsɪs] n parálisis f inv

paralyze [ˈpærəlaɪz] (US) vt = **paralyse**

paramount [ˈpærəmaunt] adj: **of ~ importance** de suma importancia

paranoid [ˈpærənɔɪd] adj (person, feeling) paranoico

paraphernalia [pærəfəˈneɪlɪə] n (gear) avíos mpl

parasite [ˈpærəsaɪt] n parásito/a

parasol [ˈpærəsɔl] n sombrilla, quitasol m

paratrooper [ˈpærətruːpə*] n paracaidista m/f

parcel [ˈpɑːsl] n paquete m ♦ vt (also: ~ up) empaquetar, embalar

parched [pɑːtʃt] adj (person) muerto de sed

parchment [ˈpɑːtʃmənt] n pergamino

pardon [ˈpɑːdn] n (LAW) indulto ♦ vt perdonar; ~ **me!, I beg your ~!** (I'm sorry!) ¡perdone usted!; (I beg your) ~?, ~ **me?** (US) (what did you say?) ¿cómo?

parent [ˈpɛərənt] n (mother) madre f; (father) padre m; ~**s** npl padres mpl; ~**al** [pəˈrɛntl] adj paternal/maternal

parenthesis [pəˈrɛnθɪsɪs] (pl **parentheses**) n paréntesis m inv

Paris [ˈpærɪs] n París

parish [ˈpærɪʃ] n parroquia

Parisian [pəˈrɪzɪən] adj, n parisiense m/f

park [pɑːk] n parque m ♦ vt aparcar, estacionar ♦ vi aparcar, estacionarse

parking [ˈpɑːkɪŋ] n aparcamiento, estacionamiento; "**no ~**" "prohibido estacionarse"; ~ **lot** (US) n parking m; ~ **meter** n parquímetro; ~ **ticket** n multa de aparcamiento

parliament [ˈpɑːləmənt] n parlamento; (Spanish) Cortes fpl; ~**ary** [-ˈmɛntərɪ] adj parlamentario

parlour [ˈpɑːlə*] (US **parlor**) n sala de recibo, salón m, living m (AM)

parochial [pəˈrəukɪəl] (pej) adj de miras estrechas

parole [pəˈrəul] n: **on ~** libre bajo palabra

parquet [ˈpɑːkeɪ] n: ~ **floor(ing)** parquet m

parrot [ˈpærət] n loro, papagayo

parry [ˈpærɪ] vt parar

parsley [ˈpɑːslɪ] n perejil m

parsnip [ˈpɑːsnɪp] n chirivía

parson [ˈpɑːsn] n cura m

part [pɑːt] n (gen, MUS) parte f; (bit) trozo; (of machine) pieza; (THEATRE etc) papel m; (of serial) entrega; (US: in hair) raya ♦ adv = **partly** ♦ vt separar ♦ vi (people) separarse; (crowd) apartarse; **to take ~ in** tomar parte or participar en; **to take sth in good ~** tomar algo en buena parte; **to take sb's ~** defender a uno; **for my ~** por mi parte; **for the most ~** en su mayor parte; **to ~ one's hair** hacerse la raya; ~ **with** vt fus ceder, entregar; (money) pagar; ~ **exchange** (BRIT) n: **in ~ exchange** como parte del pago

partial [ˈpɑːʃl] adj parcial; **to be ~ to** ser aficionado a

participant [pɑːˈtɪsɪpənt] n (in competition) concursante m/f; (in campaign etc) participante m/f

participate [pɑːˈtɪsɪpeɪt] vi: **to ~ in** participar en; **participation** [-ˈpeɪʃən] n participación f

participle [ˈpɑːtɪsɪpl] n participio

particle [ˈpɑːtɪkl] n partícula; (of dust) grano

particular [pəˈtɪkjulə*] adj (special) particular; (concrete) concreto; (given) determinado; (fussy) quisquilloso; (demanding) exigente; ~**s** npl (information) datos mpl; (details) pormenores mpl; **in ~** en particular; ~**ly** adv (in particular) sobre todo; (difficult, good etc) especialmente

parting [ˈpɑːtɪŋ] n (act of) separación f; (farewell) despedida; (BRIT: in hair) raya ♦ adj de despedida

partisan [pɑːtɪˈzæn] adj partidista ♦ n partidario/a

partition [pɑːˈtɪʃən] n (POL) división f; (wall) tabique m

partly [ˈpɑːtlɪ] adv en parte

partner [ˈpɑːtnə*] n (COMM) socio/a; (SPORT, at dance) pareja; (spouse) cónyuge m/f; (lover) compañero/a; ~**ship** n asociación f; (COMM) sociedad f

partridge [ˈpɑːtrɪdʒ] n perdiz f

part-time adj, adv a tiempo parcial

party ['pɑːtɪ] n (POL) partido; (celebration) fiesta; (group) grupo; (LAW) parte f interesada ♦ cpd (POL) de partido; **~ dress** n vestido de fiesta

pass [pɑːs] vt (time, object) pasar; (place) pasar por; (overtake) rebasar; (exam) aprobar; (approve) aprobar ♦ vi pasar; (SCOL) aprobar, ser aprobado ♦ n (permit) permiso; (membership card) carnet m; (in mountains) puerto, desfiladero; (SPORT) pase m; (SCOL: also: ~ mark): **to get a ~ in** aprobar en; **to ~ sth through sth** pasar algo por algo; **to make a ~ at sb** (inf) hacer proposiciones a uno; **~ away** vi fallecer; **~ by** vi pasar ♦ vt (ignore) pasar por alto; **~ for** vt fus pasar por; **~ on** vt transmitir; **~ out** vi desmayarse; **~ up** vt (opportunity) renunciar a; **~able** adj (road) transitable; (tolerable) pasable

passage ['pæsɪdʒ] n (also: ~way) pasillo; (act of passing) tránsito; (fare, in book) pasaje m; (by boat) travesía; (ANAT) tubo

passbook ['pɑːsbʊk] n libreta de banco

passenger ['pæsɪndʒə*] n pasajero/a, viajero/a

passer-by [pɑːsə'baɪ] n transeúnte m/f

passing ['pɑːsɪŋ] adj pasajero; **in ~** de paso; **~ place** n (AUT) apartadero

passion ['pæʃən] n pasión f; **~ate** adj apasionado

passive ['pæsɪv] adj (gen, also LING) pasivo; **~ smoking** n efectos del tabaco en fumadores pasivos

Passover ['pɑːsəʊvə*] n Pascua (de los judíos)

passport ['pɑːspɔːt] n pasaporte m; **~ control** n control m de pasaporte; **~ office** n oficina de pasaportes

password ['pɑːswɜːd] n contraseña

past [pɑːst] prep (in front of) por delante de; (further than) más allá de; (later than) después de ♦ adj pasado; (president etc) antiguo ♦ n (time) pasado; (of person) antecedentes mpl; **he's ~ forty** tiene más de cuarenta años; **ten/quarter ~ eight** las ocho y diez/cuarto; **for the ~ few/3 days** durante los últimos días/últimos 3 días; **to run ~ sb** pasar a uno corriendo

pasta ['pæstə] n pasta

paste [peɪst] n pasta; (glue) engrudo ♦ vt pegar

pasteurized ['pæstəraɪzd] adj pasteurizado

pastille ['pæstl] n pastilla

pastime ['pɑːstaɪm] n pasatiempo

pastry ['peɪstrɪ] n (dough) pasta; (cake) pastel m

pasture ['pɑːstʃə*] n pasto

pasty¹ ['pæstɪ] n empanada

pasty² ['peɪstɪ] adj (complexion) pálido

pat [pæt] vt dar una palmadita a; (dog etc)

acariciar

patch [pætʃ] n (of material, eye ~) parche m; (mended part) remiendo; (of land) terreno ♦ vt remendar; **(to go through) a bad ~** (pasar por) una mala racha; **~ up** vt reparar; (quarrel) hacer las paces en; **~work** n labor m de retazos; **~y** adj desigual

pâté ['pæteɪ] n paté m

patent ['peɪtnt] n patente f ♦ vt patentar ♦ adj patente, evidente; **~ leather** n charol m

paternal [pə'tɜːnl] adj paternal; (relation) paterno

path [pɑːθ] n camino, sendero; (trail, track) pista; (of missile) trayectoria

pathetic [pə'θetɪk] adj patético, lastimoso; (very bad) malísimo

pathological [pæθə'lɔdʒɪkəl] adj patológico

pathway ['pɑːθweɪ] n sendero, vereda

patience ['peɪʃns] n paciencia; (BRIT: CARDS) solitario

patient ['peɪʃnt] n paciente m/f ♦ adj paciente, sufrido

patio ['pætɪəʊ] n patio

patriot ['peɪtrɪət] n patriota m/f; **~ic** [pætrɪ'ɔtɪk] adj patriótico

patrol [pə'trəʊl] n patrulla ♦ vt patrullar por; **~ car** n coche m patrulla; **~man** (US irreg) n policía m

patron ['peɪtrən] n (in shop) cliente m/f; (of charity) patrocinador(a) m/f; **~ of the arts** mecenas m; **~ize** ['pætrənaɪz] vt (shop) ser cliente de; (artist etc) proteger; (look down on) condescender con; **~ saint** n santo/a patrón/ona m/f

patter ['pætə*] n golpeteo; (sales talk) labia ♦ vi (rain) tamborilear

pattern ['pætən] n (SEWING) patrón m; (design) dibujo

pauper ['pɔːpə*] n pobre m/f

pause [pɔːz] n pausa ♦ vi hacer una pausa

pave [peɪv] vt pavimentar; **to ~ the way for** preparar el terreno para

pavement ['peɪvmənt] n (BRIT) acera (SP), vereda (AM)

pavilion [pə'vɪlɪən] n (SPORT) caseta

paving ['peɪvɪŋ] n pavimento, enlosado; **~ stone** n losa

paw [pɔː] n pata

pawn [pɔːn] n (CHESS) peón m; (fig) instrumento ♦ vt empeñar; **~ broker** n prestamista m/f; **~shop** n monte m de piedad

pay [peɪ] (pt, pp paid) n (wage etc) sueldo, salario ♦ vt pagar ♦ vi (be profitable) rendir; **to ~ attention (to)** prestar atención (a); **to ~ sb a visit** hacer una visita a uno; **to ~ one's respects to sb** presentar sus respetos a uno; **~ back** vt (money) reembolsar; (person) pagar; **~ for** vt fus pagar; **~ in** vt ingresar; **~ off** vt saldar ♦ vi (scheme, decision) dar resultado; **~ up** vt pagar (de mala gana); **~able** adj: **~able to** pagadero a; **~ day** n día m de paga; **~ee** n portador(a) m/f; **~ envelope** (US) n = **~ packet**; **~ment** n pago; **monthly ~ment** mensualidad f; **~ packet** (BRIT) n sobre m (de paga); **~ phone** n teléfono público; **~roll** n nómina; **~ slip** n recibo de sueldo; **~ television** n televisión f de pago

PC n abbr = **personal computer**; (BRIT) = **police constable** ♦ adv abbr = **politically correct**

p.c. abbr = **per cent**

pea [pi:] n guisante m (SP), chícharo (AM), arveja (AM)

peace [pi:s] n paz f; (calm) paz f, tranquilidad f; **~ful** adj (gentle) pacífico; (calm) tranquilo, sosegado

peach [pi:tʃ] n melocotón m (SP), durazno (AM)

peacock ['pi:kɔk] n pavo real

peak [pi:k] n (of mountain) cumbre f, cima; (of cap) visera; (fig) cumbre f; **~ hours** npl, **~ period** n horas fpl punta

peal [pi:l] n (of bells) repique m; **~ of laughter** carcajada

peanut ['pi:nʌt] n cacahuete m (SP), maní n (AM); **~ butter** manteca de cacahuete or maní

pear [peə*] n pera

pearl [pə:l] n perla

peasant ['peznt] n campesino/a

peat [pi:t] n turba

pebble ['pebl] n guijarro

peck [pek] vt (also: **~ at**) picotear ♦ n picotazo; (kiss) besito; **~ing order** n orden m de jerarquía; **~ish** (BRIT: inf) adj: **I feel ~ish** tengo ganas de picar algo

peculiar [pɪ'kju:lɪə*] adj (odd) extraño, raro; (typical) propio, característico; **~ to** propio de

pedal ['pedl] n pedal m ♦ vi pedalear

pedantic [pɪ'dæntɪk] adj pedante

peddler ['pedlə*] n: **drug ~** traficante m/f; camello

pedestrian [pɪ'destrɪən] n peatón/ona m/f ♦ adj pedestre; **~ crossing** (BRIT) n paso de peatones; **~ precinct** (BRIT), **~ zone** (US) n zona peatonal

pediatrics [pi:dɪ'ætrɪks] (US) n = **paediatrics**

pedigree ['pedɪgri:] n genealogía; (of animal) raza, pedigrí m ♦ cpd (animal) de raza, de casta

pee [pi:] (inf) vi mear

peek [pi:k] vi mirar a hurtadillas

peel [pi:l] n piel f; (of orange, lemon) cáscara; (: removed) peladuras fpl ♦ vt pelar ♦ vi (paint etc) desconcharse; (wallpaper)

despegarse, desprenderse; (skin) pelar

peep [pi:p] n (BRIT: look) mirada furtiva; (sound) pío ♦ vi (BRIT: look) mirar furtivamente; **~ out** vi salir (un poco); **~hole** n mirilla

peer [pɪə*] vi: **to ~ at** esudriñar ♦ n (noble) par m; (equal) igual m; (contemporary) contemporáneo/a; **~age** n nobleza

peeved [pi:vd] adj enojado

peg [peg] n (for coat etc) gancho, colgadero; (BRIT: also: **clothes ~**) pinza

Pekingese [pi:kɪ'ni:z] n (dog) pequinés/esa m/f

pelican ['pelɪkən] n pelícano; **~ crossing** (BRIT) n (AUT) paso de peatones señalizado

pellet ['pelɪt] n bolita; (bullet) perdigón m

pelt [pelt] vt: **to ~ sb with sth** arrojarle algo a uno ♦ vi (rain) llover a cántaros; (inf: run) correr ♦ n pellejo

pen [pen] n (fountain ~) pluma; (ballpoint ~) bolígrafo; (for sheep) redil m

penal ['pi:nl] adj penal; **~ize** vt castigar

penalty ['penltɪ] n (gen) pena; (fine) multa; **~ (kick)** n (FOOTBALL) penalty m; (RUGBY) golpe m de castigo

penance ['penəns] n penitencia

pence [pens] npl of **penny**

pencil ['pensl] n lápiz m, lapicero (AM); **~ case** n estuche m; **~ sharpener** n sacapuntas m inv

pendant ['pendnt] n pendiente m

pending ['pendɪŋ] prep antes de ♦ adj pendiente

pendulum ['pendjuləm] n péndulo

penetrate ['penɪtreɪt] vt penetrar

penfriend ['penfrend] (BRIT) n amigo/a por carta

penguin ['peŋgwɪn] n pingüino

penicillin [penɪ'sɪlɪn] n penicilina

peninsula [pə'nɪnsjulə] n península

penis ['pi:nɪs] n pene m

penitentiary [penɪ'tenʃərɪ] (US) n cárcel f, presidio

penknife ['pennaɪf] n navaja

pen name n seudónimo

penniless ['penɪlɪs] adj sin dinero

penny ['penɪ] (pl **pennies** or (BRIT) **pence**) n penique m; (US) centavo

penpal ['penpæl] n amigo/a por carta

pension ['penʃən] n (state benefit) jubilación f; **~er** (BRIT) n jubilado/a; **~ fund** n caja or fondo de pensiones

pentagon ['pentəgən] n: **the P~** (US: POL) el Pentágono

Pentecost ['pentɪkɔst] n Pentecostés m

penthouse ['penthaus] n ático de lujo

pent-up ['pentʌp] adj reprimido

people ['pi:pl] npl gente f; (citizens) pueblo, ciudadanos mpl; (POL): **the ~** el pueblo ♦ n (*nation, race*) pueblo, nación f; **several ~ came** vinieron varias personas; **~ say that ...** dice la gente que ...

pep |pep| (*inf*): **~ up** vt animar

pepper ['pepə*] n (*spice*) pimienta; (*vegetable*) pimiento ♦ vt: **to ~ with** (*fig*) salpicar de; **~mint** n (*sweet*) pastilla de menta

peptalk ['peptɔːk] n: **to give sb a ~** darle a uno una inyección de ánimo

per [pə:*] prep por; **~ day/person** por día/persona; **~ annum** al año; **~ capita** adj, adv per cápita

perceive [pə'siːv] vt percibir; (*realize*) darse cuenta de

per cent n por ciento

percentage [pə'sentɪdʒ] n porcentaje m

perception [pə'sepʃən] n percepción f; (*insight*) perspicacia; (*opinion etc*) opinión f; **perceptive** [-'septɪv] adj perspicaz

perch [pə:tʃ] n (*fish*) perca; (*for bird*) percha ♦ vi: **to ~ (on)** (*bird*) posarse (en); (*person*) encaramarse (en)

percolator ['pə:kəleɪtə*] n (*also: coffee ~*) cafetera de filtro

perennial [pə'renɪəl] adj perenne

perfect [*adj, n* 'pə:fɪkt, *vb* pə'fekt] adj perfecto ♦ n (*also: ~ tense*) perfecto ♦ vt perfeccionar; **~ly** ['pə:fɪktlɪ] adv perfectamente

perforate ['pə:fəreɪt] vt perforar

perform [pə'fɔːm] vt (*carry out*) realizar, llevar a cabo; (*THEATRE*) representar; (*piece of music*) interpretar ♦ vi (*well, badly*) funcionar; **~ance** n (*of a play*) representación f; (*of actor, athlete etc*) actuación f; (*of car, engine, company*) rendimiento m; (*of economy*) resultados mpl; **~er** n (*actor*) actor m, actriz f

perfume ['pə:fjuːm] n perfume m

perhaps [pə'hæps] adv quizá(s), tal vez

peril ['perɪl] n peligro, riesgo

perimeter [pə'rɪmɪtə*] n perímetro

period ['pɪərɪəd] n período; (*SCOL*) clase f; (*full stop*) punto; (*MED*) regla ♦ adj (*costume, furniture*) de época; **~ic(al)** [-'ɔdɪk(l)] adj periódico; **~ical** [-'ɔdɪkl] n periódico; **~ically** [-'ɔdɪklɪ] adv de vez en cuando, cada cierto tiempo

peripheral [pə'rɪfərəl] adj periférico ♦ n (*COMPUT*) periférico, unidad f periférica

perish ['perɪʃ] vi perecer; (*decay*) echarse a perder; **~able** adj perecedero

perjury ['pə:dʒərɪ] n (*LAW*) perjurio

perk [pə:k] n extra m; **~ up** vi (*cheer up*) animarse

perm [pə:m] n permanente f

permanent ['pə:mənənt] adj permanente

permeate ['pə:mɪeɪt] vi penetrar, trascender ♦ vt penetrar, trascender a

permissible [pə'mɪsɪbl] adj permisible, lícito

permission [pə'mɪʃən] n permiso

permissive [pə'mɪsɪv] adj permisivo

permit [*n* 'pə:mɪt, *vt* pə'mɪt] n permiso, licencia ♦ vt permitir

perplex [pə'pleks] vt dejar perplejo

persecute ['pə:sɪkjuːt] vt perseguir

persevere [pə:sɪ'vɪə*] vi persistir

Persian ['pə:ʃən] adj, n persa m/f; **the ~ Gulf** el Golfo Pérsico

persist [pə'sɪst] vi: **to ~ (in doing sth)** persistir (en hacer algo); **~ence** n empeño; **~ent** adj persistente; (*determined*) porfiado

person ['pə:sn] n persona; **in ~** en persona; **~al** adj personal; individual; (*visit*) en persona; **~al assistant** n ayudante m/f personal; **~al column** n anuncios mpl personales; **~al computer** n ordenador m personal; **~ality** [-'nælɪtɪ] n personalidad f; **~ally** adv personalmente; (*in person*) en persona; **to take sth ~ally** tomarse algo a mal; **~al organizer** n agenda; **~al stereo** n Walkman ® m; **~ify** [-'sɔnɪfaɪ] vt encarnar

personnel [pə:sə'nel] n personal m

perspective [pə'spektɪv] n perspectiva

Perspex ® ['pə:speks] n plexiglás ® m

perspiration [pə:spɪ'reɪʃən] n transpiración f

persuade [pə'sweɪd] vt: **to ~ sb to do sth** persuadir a uno para que haga algo

Peru [pə'ruː] n el Perú; **Peruvian** adj, n peruano/a m/f

perverse [pə'və:s] adj perverso; (*wayward*) travieso

pervert [*n* 'pə:və:t, *vb* pə'və:t] n pervertido/a ♦ vt pervertir; (*truth, sb's words*) tergiversar

pessimist ['pesɪmɪst] n pesimista m/f; **~ic** [-'mɪstɪk] adj pesimista

pest [pest] n (*insect*) insecto nocivo; (*fig*) lata, molestia

pester ['pestə*] vt molestar, acosar

pesticide ['pestɪsaɪd] n pesticida m

pet [pet] n animal m doméstico ♦ cpd favorito ♦ vt acariciar; **teacher's ~** favorito/a (del profesor); **~ hate** manía

petal ['petl] n pétalo

peter ['piːtə*]: **to ~ out** vi agotarse, acabarse

petite [pə'tiːt] adj chiquita

petition [pə'tɪʃən] n petición f

petrified ['petrɪfaɪd] adj horrorizado

petrol ['petrəl] (*BRIT*) n gasolina; **two/four-star ~** gasolina normal/súper; **~ can** n bidón m de gasolina

petroleum [pə'trəulɪəm] n petróleo

petrol: ~ pump (*BRIT*) n (*in garage*) surtidor m de gasolina; **~ station** (*BRIT*) n gasolinera; **~ tank** (*BRIT*) n depósito (de gasolina)

petticoat ['petɪkəut] n enaguas fpl

petty ['petɪ] adj (*mean*) mezquino; (*unimportant*) insignificante; **~ cash** n dinero para gastos menores; **~ officer** *n* contramaestre *m*

petulant ['petjulənt] *adj* malhumorado

pew [pju:] *n* banco

pewter ['pju:tə*] *n* peltre *m*

phantom ['fæntəm] *n* fantasma *m*

pharmacist ['fɑ:məsıst] *n* farmacéutico/a

pharmacy ['fɑ:məsı] *n* farmacia

phase [feız] *n* fase *f* ♦ *vt*: **to ~ sth in/out** introducir/retirar algo por etapas

Ph.D. *abbr* = **Doctor of Philosophy**

pheasant ['feznt] *n* faisán *m*

phenomenon [fə'nɔmınən] (*pl* **phenomena**) *n* fenómeno

philanthropist |fı'lænθrəpıst] *n* filántropo/a

Philippines ['fılıpi:nz] *npl*: **the ~** las Filipinas

philosopher [fı'lɔsəfə*] *n* filósofo/a

philosophy [fı'lɔsəfı] *n* filosofía

phobia ['fəubjə] *n* fobia

phone |fəun] *n* teléfono ♦ *vt* telefonear, llamar por teléfono; **to be on the ~** tener teléfono; (*be calling*) estar hablando por teléfono; **~ back** *vt, vi* volver a llamar; **~ up** *vt, vi* llamar por teléfono; **~ book** *n* guía telefónica; **~ booth** *n* cabina telefónica; **~ box** (*BRIT*) *n* = **~ booth**; **~ call** *n* llamada (telefónica); **~card** *n* teletarjeta; **~-in** (*BRIT*) *n* (*RADIO, TV*) programa *m* de participación (telefónica)

phonetics [fə'netıks] *n* fonética

phoney ['fəunı] *adj* falso

photo ['fəutəu] *n* foto *f*; **~copier** *n* fotocopiadora; **~copy** *n* fotocopia ♦ *vt* fotocopiar

photograph ['fəutəgrɑ:f] *n* fotografía ♦ *vt* fotografiar; **~er** [fə'tɔgrəfə*] *n* fotógrafo; **~y** [fə'tɔgrəfı] *n* fotografía

phrase [freız] *n* frase *f* ♦ *vt* expresar; **~ book** *n* libro de frases

physical ['fızıkl] *adj* físico; **~ education** *n* educación *f* física; **~ly** *adv* físicamente

physician [fı'zıʃən] *n* médico/a

physicist ['fızısıst] *n* físico/a

physics ['fızıks] *n* física

physiotherapy [fızıəu'θerəpı] *n* fisioterapia

physique [fı'zi:k] *n* físico

pianist ['pi:ənıst] *n* pianista *m/f*

piano |pı'ænəu] *n* piano

pick [pık] *n* (*tool: also*: **~-axe**) pico, piqueta ♦ *vt* (*select*) elegir, escoger; (*gather*) coger (*SP*), recoger; (*remove, take out*) sacar, quitar; (*lock*) abrir con ganzúa; **take your ~** escoja lo que quiera; **the ~ of** lo mejor de; **to ~ one's nose/teeth** hurgarse las narices/limpiarse los dientes; **to ~ a quarrel with sb** meterse con alguien; **~ at** *vt fus*: **to ~ at one's food** comer con poco apetito; **~ on** *vt fus* (*person*) meterse con; **~ out** *vt* escoger; (*distinguish*) identificar; **~ up** *vi* (*improve: sales*) ir mejor;

(: *patient*) reponerse; (: *FINANCE*) recobrarse ♦ *vt* recoger; (*learn*) aprender; (*POLICE: arrest*) detener; (*person: for sex*) ligar; (*RADIO*) captar; **to ~ up speed** acelerarse; **to ~ o.s. up** levantarse

picket ['pıkıt] *n* piquete *m* ♦ *vt* piquetear

pickle ['pıkl] *n* (*also*: **~s**: *as condiment*) escabeche *m*; (*fig: mess*) apuro ♦ *vt* encurtir

pickpocket ['pıkpɔkıt] *n* carterista *m/f*

pickup ['pıkʌp] *n* (*small truck*) furgoneta

picnic ['pıknık] *n* merienda ♦ *vi* ir de merienda; **~ area** *n* zona de picnic; (*AUT*) área de descanso

picture ['pıktʃə*] *n* cuadro; (*painting*) pintura; (*photograph*) fotografía; (*TV*) imagen *f*; (*film*) película; (*fig: description*) descripción *f*; (: *situation*) situación *f* ♦ *vt* (*imagine*) imaginar; **~s** *npl*: **the ~s** (*BRIT*) el cine; **~ book** *n* libro de dibujos

picturesque [pıktʃə'resk] *adj* pintoresco

pie [paı] *n* pastel *m*; (*open*) tarta; (*small: of meat*) empanada

piece |pi:s] *n* pedazo, trozo; (*of cake*) trozo; (*item*): **a ~ of clothing/furniture/advice** una prenda (de vestir)/un mueble/un consejo ♦ *vt*: **to ~ together** juntar; (*TECH*) armar; **to take to ~s** desmontar; **~meal** *adv* poco a poco; **~work** *n* trabajo a destajo

pie chart *n* gráfico de sectores or tarta

pier [pıə*] *n* muelle *m*, embarcadero

pierce [pıəs] *vt* perforar

piercing ['pıəsıŋ] *adj* penetrante

pig [pıg] *n* cerdo (*SP*), puerco (*SP*), chancho (*AM*); (*pej: unkind person*) asqueroso; (: *greedy person*) glotón/ona *m/f*

pigeon ['pıdʒən] *n* paloma; (*as food*) pichón *m*; **~hole** *n* casilla

piggy bank ['pıgı-] *n* hucha (*en forma de cerdito*)

pig: ~headed ['pıg'hedıd] *adj* terco, testarudo; **~let** ['pıglıt] *n* cochinillo; **~skin** *n* piel *f* de cerdo; **~sty** ['pıgstaı] *n* pocilga; **~tail** (*girl's*) trenza; (*Chinese, TAUR*) coleta

pike [paık] *n* (*fish*) lucio

pilchard ['pıltʃəd] *n* sardina

pile [paıl] *n* montón *m*; (*of carpet, cloth*) pelo ♦ *vt* (*also*: **~ up**) amontonar; (*fig*) acumular ♦ *vi* (*also*: **~ up**) amontonarse; acumularse; **~ into** *vt fus* (*car*) meterse en; **~s** [paılz] *npl* (*MED*) almorranas *fpl*, hemorroides *mpl*; **~-up** *n* (*AUT*) accidente *m* múltiple

pilfering ['pılfərıŋ] *n* ratería

pilgrim ['pılgrım] *n* peregrino/a; **~age** *n* peregrinación *f*, romería

pill [pıl] *n* píldora; **the ~** la píldora

pillage ['pılıdʒ] *vt* pillar, saquear

pillar ['pılə*] *n* pilar *m*; **~ box** (*BRIT*) *n* buzón *m*

pillion ['pıljən] *n* (*of motorcycle*) asiento

trasero
pillow ['pɪləu] n almohada; **~case** n funda
pilot ['paɪlət] n piloto ♦ cpd (scheme etc)
piloto ♦ vt pilotar; **~ light** n piloto
pimp [pɪmp] n chulo (SP), cafiche m (AM)
pimple ['pɪmpl] n grano
PIN n abbr (= personal identification number)
número personal
pin [pɪn] n alfiler m ♦ vt prender (con alfiler);
~s and needles hormigueo; **to ~ sb down** (fig)
hacer que uno concrete; **to ~ sth on sb** (fig)
colgarle a uno el sambenito de algo
pinafore ['pɪnəfɔ:*] n delantal m; **~ dress**
(BRIT) n mandil m
pinball ['pɪnbɔ:l] n mesa americana
pincers ['pɪnsəz] npl pinzas fpl, tenazas fpl
pinch [pɪntʃ] n (of salt etc) pizca ♦ vt
pellizcar; (inf: steal) birlar; **at a ~** en caso de
apuro
pincushion ['pɪnkuʃən] n acerico
pine [paɪn] n (also: ~ tree, wood) pino ♦ vi: **to
~ for** suspirar por; **~ away** vi morirse de
pena
pineapple ['paɪnæpl] n piña, ananás m
ping [pɪŋ] n (noise) sonido agudo; **~-pong** ®
n pingpong ® m
pink [pɪŋk] adj rosado, (color de) rosa ♦ n
(colour) rosa; (BOT) clavel m, clavellina
pinpoint ['pɪnpɔɪnt] vt precisar
pint [paɪnt] n pinta (BRIT = 568cc; US =
473cc); (BRIT: inf: of beer) pinta de cerveza,
≈ jarra (SP)
pin-up n fotografía erótica
pioneer [paɪə'nɪə*] n pionero/a
pious ['paɪəs] adj piadoso, devoto
pip [pɪp] n (seed) pepita; **the ~s** (BRIT) la señal
pipe [paɪp] n tubo, caño; (for smoking) pipa
♦ vt conducir en cañerías; **~s** npl (gen)
cañería; (also: bag~s) gaita; **~ cleaner** n
limpiapipas m inv; **~ dream** n sueño
imposible; **~line** n (for oil) oleoducto; (for
gas) gasoducto; **~r** n gaitero/a
piping ['paɪpɪŋ] adv: **to be ~ hot** estar que
quema
piquant ['pi:kənt] adj picante; (fig) agudo
pique [pi:k] n pique m, resentimiento
pirate ['paɪərət] n pirata m/f ♦ vt (cassette,
book) piratear; **~ radio** (BRIT) n emisora
pirata
Pisces ['paɪsi:z] n Piscis m
piss [pɪs] (inf!) vi mear; **~ed** (inf!) adj (drunk)
borracho
pistol ['pɪstl] n pistola
piston ['pɪstən] n pistón m, émbolo
pit [pɪt] n hoyo; (also: coal ~) mina; (in
garage) foso de inspección; (also: orchestra
~) platea ♦ vt: **to ~ one's wits against sb**
medir fuerzas con uno; **~s** npl (AUT) box m
pitch [pɪtʃ] n (MUS) tono; (BRIT: SPORT) campo,

terreno; (fig) punto; (tar) brea ♦ vt (throw)
arrojar, lanzar ♦ vi (fall) caer(se); **to ~ a tent**
montar una tienda (de campaña); **~-black**
adj negro como boca de lobo; **~ed battle** n
batalla campal
pitfall ['pɪtfɔ:l] n riesgo
pith [pɪθ] n (of orange) médula
pithy ['pɪθɪ] adj (fig) jugoso
pitiful ['pɪtɪful] adj (touching) lastimoso,
conmovedor(a)
pitiless ['pɪtɪlɪs] adj despiadado
pittance ['pɪtns] n miseria
pity ['pɪtɪ] n compasión f, piedad f ♦ vt
compadecer(se de); **what a ~!** ¡qué pena!
pizza ['pi:tsə] n pizza
placard ['plækɑ:d] n letrero; (in march etc)
pancarta
placate [plə'keɪt] vt apaciguar
place [pleɪs] n lugar m, sitio; (seat) plaza,
asiento; (post) puesto; (home): **at/to his ~**
en/a su casa; (role: in society etc) papel m
♦ vt (object) poner, colocar; (identify)
reconocer; **to take ~** tener lugar; **to be ~d** (in
race, exam) colocarse; **out of ~** (not suitable)
fuera de lugar; **in the first ~** en primer lugar;
to change ~s with sb cambiarse de sitio con
uno; **~ of birth** lugar m de nacimiento
placid ['plæsɪd] adj apacible
plague [pleɪg] n plaga; (MED) peste f ♦ vt
(fig) acosar, atormentar
plaice [pleɪs] n inv platija
plaid [plæd] n (material) tartán m
plain [pleɪn] adj (unpatterned) liso; (clear)
claro, evidente; (simple) sencillo; (not
handsome) poco atractivo ♦ adv claramente
♦ n llano, llanura; **~ chocolate** n chocolate
m amargo; **~-clothes** adj (police) vestido de
paisano; **~ly** adv claramente
plaintiff ['pleɪntɪf] n demandante m/f
plait [plæt] n trenza
plan [plæn] n (drawing) plano; (scheme) plan
m, proyecto ♦ vt proyectar, planificar ♦ vi
hacer proyectos; **to ~ to do** pensar hacer
plane [pleɪn] n (AVIAT) avión m; (MATH, fig)
plano; (also: ~ tree) plátano; (tool) cepillo
planet ['plænɪt] n planeta m
plank [plæŋk] n tabla
planner ['plænə*] n planificador(a) m/f
planning ['plænɪŋ] n planificación f; **family ~**
planificación familiar; **~ permission** n
permiso para realizar obras
plant [plɑ:nt] n (BOT) planta; (machinery)
maquinaria; (factory) fábrica ♦ vt plantar;
(field) sembrar; (bomb) colocar
plaster ['plɑ:stə*] n (for walls) yeso; (also:
~ of Paris) yeso mate; (BRIT: also: sticking ~)
tirita (SP), esparadrapo, curita (AM) ♦ vt
enyesar; (cover): **to ~ with** llenar or cubrir de;
~ed (inf) adj borracho; **~er** n yesero

plastic ['plæstɪk] n plástico ♦ adj de plástico;
~ **bag** n bolsa de plástico
Plasticine ® ['plæstɪsiːn] (BRIT) n plastilina
®
plastic surgery n cirujía plástica
plate [pleɪt] n (dish) plato; (metal, in book)
lámina; (dental ~) placa de dentadura postiza
plateau [pla'təu] (pl ~s or ~x) n meseta,
altiplanicie f
plateaux ['plætəuz] npl of **plateau**
plate glass n vidrio cilindrado
platform ['plætfɔːm] n (RAIL) andén m;
(stage, BRIT: on bus) plataforma; (at meeting)
tribuna; (POL) programa m (electoral)
platinum ['plætɪnəm] adj, n platino
platoon [pla'tuːn] n pelotón m
platter ['plætə*] n fuente f
plausible ['plɔːzɪbl] adj verosímil; (person)
convincente
play [pleɪ] n (THEATRE) obra, comedia ♦ vt
(game) jugar; (compete against) jugar contra;
(instrument) tocar; (part: in play etc) hacer el
papel de; (tape, record) poner ♦ vi jugar;
(band) tocar; (tape, record) sonar; **to ~ safe**
ir a lo seguro; ~ **down** vt quitar importancia
a; ~ **up** vi (cause trouble to) dar guerra;
~**boy** n playboy m; ~**er** n jugador(a) m/f;
(THEATRE) actor/actriz m/f; (MUS) músico/a;
~**ful** adj juguetón/ona; ~**ground** n (in
school) patio de recreo; (in park) parque m
infantil; ~**group** n jardín m de niños; ~**ing
card** n naipe m, carta; ~**ing field** n campo
de deportes; ~**mate** n compañero/a de
juego; ~-**off** n (SPORT) (partido de)
desempate m; ~**pen** n corral m; ~**thing** n
juguete m; ~**time** n (SCOL) recreo; ~**wright**
n dramaturgo/a
plc abbr (= public limited company) ≈ S.A.
plea [pliː] n súplica, petición f; (LAW) alegato,
defensa; ~ **bargaining** n (LAW) acuerdo entre
fiscal y defensor para agilizar los trámites
judiciales
plead [pliːd] vt (LAW): **to ~ sb's case** defender
a uno; (give as excuse) poner como pretexto
♦ vi (LAW) declararse; (beg): **to ~ with sb**
suplicar or rogar a uno
pleasant ['plɛznt] adj agradable; ~**ries** npl
cortesías fpl
please [pliːz] excl ¡por favor! ♦ vt (give
pleasure to) dar gusto a, agradar ♦ vi (think
fit): **do as you ~** haz lo que quieras;
~ **yourself!** (inf) ¡haz lo que quieras!, ¡como
quieras!; ~**d** adj (happy) alegre, contento;
~**d** (with) satisfecho (de); ~**d to meet you**
¡encantado!, ¡tanto gusto!; **pleasing** adj
agradable, grato
pleasure ['plɛʒə*] n placer m, gusto; "**it's a
~**" "el gusto es mío"
pleat [pliːt] n pliegue m

pledge [plɛdʒ] n (promise) promesa, voto
♦ vt prometer
plentiful ['plɛntɪful] adj copioso, abundante
plenty ['plɛntɪ] n: ~ **of** mucho(s)/a(s)
pliable ['plaɪəbl] adj flexible
pliers ['plaɪəz] npl alicates mpl, tenazas fpl
plight [plaɪt] n situación f difícil
plimsolls ['plɪmsɔlz] (BRIT) npl zapatos mpl
de tenis
plinth [plɪnθ] n plinto
plod [plɔd] vi caminar con paso pesado; (fig)
trabajar laboriosamente
plonk [plɔŋk] (inf) n (BRIT: wine) vino peleón
♦ vt: **to ~ sth down** dejar caer algo
plot [plɔt] n (scheme) complot m, conjura; (of
story, play) argumento; (of land) terreno, lote
m (AM) ♦ vt (mark out) trazar; (conspire)
tramar, urdir ♦ vi conspirar
plough [plau] (US **plow**) n arado ♦ vt (earth)
arar; **to ~ money into** invertir dinero en;
~ **through** vt fus (crowd) abrirse paso por la
fuerza por; ~**man's lunch** (BRIT) n almuerzo
de pub a base de pan, queso y encurtidos
pluck [plʌk] vt (fruit) coger (SP), recoger
(AM); (musical instrument) puntear; (bird)
desplumar; (eyebrows) depilar; **to ~ up
courage** hacer de tripas corazón
plug [plʌg] n tapón m; (ELEC) enchufe m,
clavija; (AUT: also: spark(ing) ~) bujía ♦ vt
(hole) tapar; (inf: advertise) dar publicidad a;
~ **in** vt (ELEC) enchufar
plum [plʌm] n (fruit) ciruela
plumb [plʌm] vt: **to ~ the depths of** alcanzar
los mayores extremos de
plumber ['plʌmə*] n fontanero/a (SP),
plomero/a (AM)
plumbing ['plʌmɪŋ] n (trade) fontanería,
plomería; (piping) cañería
plummet ['plʌmɪt] vi: **to ~ (down)** caer a
plomo
plump [plʌmp] adj rechoncho, rollizo ♦ vi: **to
~ for** (inf: choose) optar por; ~ **up** vt mullir
plunder ['plʌndə*] vt pillar, saquear
plunge [plʌndʒ] n zambullida ♦ vt sumergir,
hundir ♦ vi (fall) caer; (dive) saltar; (person)
arrojarse; **to take the ~** lanzarse; **plunging**
adj: **plunging neckline** escote m pronunciado
pluperfect [pluː'pəːfɪkt] n pluscuamperfecto
plural ['pluərl] adj plural ♦ n plural m
plus [plʌs] n (also: ~ **sign**) signo más ♦ prep
más, y, además de; **ten/twenty ~** más de
diez/veinte
plush [plʌʃ] adj lujoso
plutonium [pluː'təunɪəm] n plutonio
ply [plaɪ] vt (a trade) ejercer ♦ vi (ship) ir y
venir ♦ n (of wool, rope) cabo; **to ~ sb with
drink** insistir en ofrecer a uno muchas copas;
~**wood** n madera contrachapada
P.M. n abbr = **Prime Minister**

p.m. *adv abbr* (= *post meridiem*) de la tarde or noche

pneumatic [nju:'mætık] *adj* neumático; **~ drill** *n* martillo neumático

pneumonia [nju:'məʊnɪə] *n* pulmonía

poach [pəʊtʃ] *vt* (*cook*) escalfar; (*steal*) cazar (or pescar) en vedado ♦ *vi* cazar (or pescar) en vedado; **~ed** *adj* escalfado; **~er** *n* cazador(a) *m/f* furtivo/a

P.O. Box *n abbr* = **Post Office Box**

pocket ['pɔkɪt] *n* bolsillo; (*fig: small area*) bolsa ♦ *vt* meter en el bolsillo; (*steal*) embolsar; **to be out of ~** (*BRIT*) salir perdiendo; **~book** (*US*) *n* cartera; **~ calculator** *n* calculadora de bolsillo; **~ knife** *n* navaja; **~ money** *n* asignación *f*

pod [pɔd] *n* vaina

podgy ['pɔdʒı] *adj* gordinflón/ona

podiatrist [pɔ'di:ətrıst] (*US*) *n* pedicuro/a

poem ['pəʊɪm] *n* poema *m*

poet ['pəʊɪt] *n* poeta *m/f*; **~ic** [-'etık] *adj* poético; **~ry** *n* poesía

poignant ['pɔɪnjənt] *adj* conmovedor(a)

point [pɔɪnt] *n* punto; (*tip*) punta; (*purpose*) fin *m*, propósito; (*use*) utilidad *f*; (*significant part*) lo significativo; (*moment*) momento; (*ELEC*) toma (de corriente); (*also: decimal ~*): **2 ~ 3 (2.3)** dos coma tres (2,3) ♦ *vt* señalar; (*gun etc*): **to ~ sth at sb** apuntar algo a uno ♦ *vi*: **to ~ at** señalar; **~s** *npl* (*AUT*) contactos *mpl*; (*RAIL*) agujas *fpl*; **to be on the ~ of doing sth** estar a punto de hacer algo; **to make a ~ of** poner empeño en; **to get/miss the ~** comprender/no comprender; **to come to the ~ ir al meollo; there's no ~ (in doing)** no tiene sentido (hacer); **~ out** *vt* señalar; **~ to** *vt fus* (*fig*) indicar, señalar; **~-blank** *adv* (*say, refuse*) sin más hablar; (*also: at ~-blank range*) a quemarropa; **~ed** *adj* (*shape*) puntiagudo, afilado; (*remark*) intencionado; **~edly** *adv* intencionadamente; **~er** *n* (*needle*) aguja, indicador *m*; **~less** *adj* sin sentido; **~ of view** *n* punto de vista

poise [pɔɪz] *n* aplomo, elegancia

poison ['pɔɪzn] *n* veneno ♦ *vt* envenenar; **~ing** *n* envenenamiento; **~ous** *adj* venenoso; (*fumes etc*) tóxico

poke [pəʊk] *vt* (*jab with finger, stick etc*) empujar; (*put*): **to ~ sth in(to)** introducir algo en; **~ about** *vi* fisgonear

poker ['pəʊkə*] *n* atizador *m*; (*CARDS*) póker *m*

poky ['pəʊkı] *adj* estrecho

Poland ['pəʊlənd] *n* Polonia

polar ['pəʊlə*] *adj* polar; **~ bear** *n* oso polar

Pole [pəʊl] *n* polaco/a

pole [pəʊl] *n* palo; (*fixed*) poste *m*; (*GEO*) polo; **~ bean** (*US*) *n* ≈ judía verde; **~ vault** *n* salto con pértiga

police [pə'li:s] *n* policía ♦ *vt* vigilar; **~ car** *n* coche patrulla *m*; **~man** (*irreg*) *n* policía *m*, guardia *m*; **~ state** *n* estado policial; **~ station** *n* comisaría; **~woman** (*irreg*) *n* mujer *f* policía

policy ['pɔlısı] *n* política; (*also: insurance ~*) póliza

polio ['pəʊlɪəʊ] *n* polio *f*

Polish ['pəʊlıʃ] *adj* polaco ♦ *n* (*LING*) polaco

polish ['pɔlıʃ] *n* (*for shoes*) betún *m*; (*for floor*) cera (de lustrar); (*shine*) brillo, lustre *m*; (*fig: refinement*) educación *f* ♦ *vt* (*shoes*) limpiar; (*make shiny*) pulir, sacar brillo a; **~ off** *vt* (*food*) despachar; **~ed** *adj* (*fig: person*) elegante

polite [pə'laɪt] *adj* cortés, atento; **~ness** *n* cortesía

political [pə'lıtıkl] *adj* político; **~ly** *adv* políticamente; **~ly correct** políticamente correcto

politician [pɔlı'tıʃən] *n* político/a

politics ['pɔlıtıks] *n* política

poll [pəʊl] *n* (*election*) votación *f*; (*also: opinion ~*) sondeo, encuesta ♦ *vt* encuestar; (*votes*) obtener

pollen ['pɔlən] *n* polen *m*

polling day ['pəʊlɪŋ-] *n* día *m* de elecciones

polling station *n* centro electoral

pollute [pə'lu:t] *vt* contaminar

pollution [pə'lu:ʃən] *n* polución *f*, contaminación *f* del medio ambiente

polo ['pəʊləʊ] *n* (*sport*) polo; **~-necked** *adj* de cuello vuelto; **~ shirt** *n* polo, niqui *m*

polyester [pɔlı'estə*] *n* poliéster *m*

polystyrene [pɔlı'staıri:n] *n* poliestireno

polythene ['pɔlıθi:n] (*BRIT*) *n* politeno

pomegranate ['pɔmıgrænıt] *n* granada

pomp [pɔmp] *n* pompa

pompous ['pɔmpəs] *adj* pomposo

pond [pɔnd] *n* (*natural*) charca; (*artificial*) estanque *m*

ponder ['pɔndə*] *vt* meditar

ponderous ['pɔndərəs] *adj* pesado

pong [pɔŋ] (*BRIT: inf*) *n* hedor *m*

pony ['pəʊnı] *n* poney *m*, jaca, potro (*AM*); **~tail** *n* cola de caballo; **~ trekking** (*BRIT*) *n* excursión *f* a caballo

poodle ['pu:dl] *n* caniche *m*

pool [pu:l] *n* (*natural*) charca; (*also: swimming ~*) piscina (*SP*), alberca (*AM*); (*fig: of light etc*) charco; (*SPORT*) chapolín *m* ♦ *vt* juntar; **~s** *npl* (*football ~s*) quinielas *fpl*; **typing ~** servicio de mecanografía

poor [pʊə*] *adj* pobre; (*bad*) de mala calidad ♦ *npl*: **the ~** los pobres; **~ly** *adj* mal, enfermo ♦ *adv* mal

pop [pɔp] *n* (*sound*) ruido seco; (*MUS*) (música) pop *m*; (*inf: father*) papá *m*; (*drink*) gaseosa ♦ *vt* (*put quickly*) meter (de prisa)

♦ vi reventar; (cork) saltar; ~ **in/out** vi
entrar/salir un momento; ~ **up** vi aparecer
inesperadamente; **~corn** n palomitas fpl
pope [pəup] n papa m
poplar ['pɔplə*] n álamo
popper ['pɔpə*] (BRIT) n automático
poppy ['pɔpɪ] n amapola
Popsicle ® ['pɔpsɪkl] (US) n polo
pop star n estrella del pop
populace ['pɔpjuləs] n pueblo, plebe f
popular ['pɔpjulə*] adj popular
population [pɔpju'leɪʃən] n población f
porcelain ['pɔːslɪn] n porcelana
porch [pɔːtʃ] n pórtico, entrada; (US) veranda
porcupine ['pɔːkjupaɪn] n puerco m espín
pore [pɔː*] n poro ♦ vi: **to ~ over** engolfarse
en
pork [pɔːk] n carne f de cerdo (SP) or chancho
(AM)
pornography [pɔː'nɔgrəfɪ] n pornografía
porpoise ['pɔːpəs] n marsopa
porridge ['pɔrɪdʒ] n gachas fpl de avena
port [pɔːt] n puerto; (NAUT: left side) babor m;
(wine) vino de Oporto; ~ **of call** puerto de
escala
portable ['pɔːtəbl] adj portátil
porter ['pɔːtə*] n (for luggage) maletero;
(doorkeeper) portero/a, conserje m/f
portfolio [pɔːt'fəulɪəu] n cartera
porthole ['pɔːthəul] n portilla
portion ['pɔːʃən] n porción f; (of food) ración
f
portrait ['pɔːtreɪt] n retrato
portray [pɔː'treɪ] vt retratar; (subj: actor)
representar
Portugal ['pɔːtjugl] n Portugal m
Portuguese [pɔːtju'giːz] adj portugués/esa
♦ n inv portugués/esa m/f; (LING) portugués
m
pose [pəuz] n postura, actitud f ♦ vi
(pretend): **to ~ as** hacerse pasar por ♦ vt
(question) plantear; **to ~ for** posar para
posh [pɔʃ] (inf) adj elegante, de lujo
position [pə'zɪʃən] n posición f; (job) puesto;
(situation) situación f ♦ vt colocar
positive ['pɔzɪtɪv] adj positivo; (certain)
seguro; (definite) definitivo
possess [pə'zɛs] vt poseer; **~ion** [pə'zɛʃən] n
posesión f; **~ions** npl (belongings)
pertenencias fpl
possibility [pɔsɪ'bɪlɪtɪ] n posibilidad f
possible ['pɔsɪbl] adj posible; **as big as ~** lo
más grande posible; **possibly** adv
posiblemente; **I cannot possibly come** me es
imposible venir
post [pəust] n (BRIT: system) correos mpl;
(BRIT: letters, delivery) correo; (job, situation)
puesto; (pole) poste m ♦ vt (BRIT: send by
post) echar al correo; (BRIT: appoint): **to ~ to**

enviar a; **~age** n porte m, franqueo; **~age
stamp** n sello de correos; **~al** adj postal, de
correos; **~al order** n giro postal; **~box** (BRIT)
n buzón m; **~card** n tarjeta postal; **~code**
(BRIT) n código postal
postdate [pəust'deɪt] vt (cheque) poner
fecha adelantada a
poster ['pəustə*] n cartel m
poste restante [pəust'rɛstɔ̃t] (BRIT) n lista
de correos
postgraduate ['pəust'grædjuət] n
posgraduado/a
posthumous ['pɔstjuməs] adj póstumo
postman ['pəustmən] (irreg) n cartero
postmark ['pəustmɑːk] n matasellos m inv
post-mortem [-'mɔːtəm] n autopsia
post office n (building) (oficina de) correos
m; (organization): **the Post Office**
Administración f General de Correos; **Post
Office Box** n apartado postal (SP), casilla de
correos (AM)
postpone [pəs'pəun] vt aplazar
postscript ['pəustskrɪpt] n posdata
posture ['pɔstjə*] n postura, actitud f
postwar [pəust'wɔː*] adj de la posguerra
posy ['pəuzɪ] n ramillete m (de flores)
pot [pɔt] n (for cooking) olla; (tea~) tetera;
(coffee~) cafetera; (for flowers) maceta; (for
jam) tarro, pote m; (inf: marijuana) chocolate
m ♦ vt (plant) poner en tiesto; **to go to ~**
(inf) irse al traste
potato [pə'teɪtəu] (pl **~es**) n patata (SP), papa
(AM); ~ **peeler** n pelapatatas m inv
potent ['pəutnt] adj potente, poderoso;
(drink) fuerte
potential [pə'tɛnʃl] adj potencial, posible ♦ n
potencial m; **~ly** adv en potencia
pothole ['pɔthəul] n (in road) bache m;
(BRIT: underground) gruta; **potholing** (BRIT)
n: **to go potholing** dedicarse a la espeleología
potluck [pɔt'lʌk] n: **to take ~** tomar lo que
haya
potted ['pɔtɪd] adj (food) en conserva;
(plant) en tiesto or maceta; (shortened)
resumido
potter ['pɔtə*] n alfarero/a ♦ vi: **to ~ around,
~ about** (BRIT) hacer trabajitos; **~y** n
cerámica; (factory) alfarería
potty ['pɔtɪ] n orinal m de niño
pouch [pautʃ] n (ZOOL) bolsa; (for tobacco)
petaca
poultry ['pəultrɪ] n aves fpl de corral; (meat)
pollo
pounce [pauns] vi: **to ~ on** precipitarse sobre
pound [paund] n libra (weight = 453g or
16oz; money = 100 pence) ♦ vt (beat)
golpear; (crush) machacar ♦ vi (heart) latir;
~ **sterling** n libra esterlina
pour [pɔː*] vt echar; (tea etc) servir ♦ vi

correr, fluir; **to ~ sb a drink** servirle a uno una copa; **~ away** or **off** vt vaciar, verter; **~ in** vi (people) entrar en tropel; **~ out** vi salir en tropel ♦ vt (drink) echar, servir; (fig): **to ~ out one's feelings** desahogarse; **~ing** adj: **~ing rain** lluvia torrencial

pout [paut] vi hacer pucheros

poverty ['pɔvətɪ] n pobreza, miseria; **~-stricken** adj necesitado

powder ['paudə*] n polvo; (face ~) polvos mpl ♦ vt polvorear; **to ~ one's face** empolvarse la cara; **~ compact** n polvera; **~ed milk** n leche f en polvo; **~ room** n aseos mpl

power ['pauə*] n poder m; (strength) fuerza; (nation, TECH) potencia; (drive) empuje m; (ELEC) fuerza, energía ♦ vt impulsar; **to be in ~** (POL) estar en el poder; **~ cut** (BRIT) n apagón m; **~ed** adj: **~ed by** impulsado por; **~ failure** n = **~ cut**; **~ful** adj poderoso; (engine) potente; (speech etc) convincente; **~less** adj: **~less (to do)** incapaz (de hacer); **~ point** (BRIT) n enchufe m; **~ station** n central f eléctrica

p.p. abbr (= per procurationem): **~ J. Smith** p.p. (por poder de) J. Smith; (= pages) págs

PR n abbr = **public relations**

practical ['præktɪkl] adj práctico; **~ity** [-'kælɪtɪ] n factibilidad f; **~ joke** n broma pesada; **~ly** adv (almost) casi

practice ['præktɪs] n (habit) costumbre f; (exercise) práctica, ejercicio; (training) adiestramiento; (MED: of profession) práctica, ejercicio; (MED, LAW: business) consulta ♦ vt, vi (US) = **practise**; **in ~** (in reality) en la práctica; **out of ~** desentrenado

practise ['præktɪs] (US **practice**) vt (carry out) practicar; (profession) ejercer; (train at) practicar ♦ vi ejercer; (train) practicar; **practising** adj (Christian etc) practicante; (lawyer) en ejercicio

practitioner [præk'tɪʃənə*] n (MED) médico/a

prairie ['preərɪ] n pampa

praise [preɪz] n alabanza(s) f(pl), elogio(s) m(pl) ♦ vt alabar, elogiar; **~worthy** adj loable

pram [præm] (BRIT) n cochecito de niño

prank [præŋk] n travesura

prawn [prɔːn] n gamba; **~ cocktail** n cóctel m de gambas

pray [preɪ] vi rezar

prayer [preə*] n oración f, rezo; (entreaty) ruego, súplica

preach [priːtʃ] vi (also fig) predicar; **~er** n predicador(a) m/f

precaution [prɪ'kɔːʃən] n precaución f

precede [prɪ'siːd] vt, vi preceder

precedent ['presɪdənt] n precedente m

preceding [prɪ'siːdɪŋ] adj anterior

precinct ['priːsɪŋkt] n recinto; **~s** npl contornos mpl; **pedestrian ~** (BRIT) zona peatonal; **shopping ~** (BRIT) centro comercial

precious ['preʃəs] adj precioso

precipitate [prɪ'sɪpɪteɪt] vt precipitar

precise [prɪ'saɪs] adj preciso, exacto; **~ly** adv precisamente, exactamente

precocious [prɪ'kəuʃəs] adj precoz

precondition [priːkən'dɪʃən] n condición f previa

predecessor ['priːdɪsesə*] n antecesor(a) m/f

predicament [prɪ'dɪkəmənt] n apuro

predict [prɪ'dɪkt] vt pronosticar; **~able** adj previsible; **~ion** [-'dɪkʃən] n predicción f

predominantly [prɪ'dɔmɪnəntlɪ] adv en su mayoría

pre-empt [priː'emt] vt adelantarse a

preen [priːn] vt: **to ~ itself** (bird) limpiarse (las plumas); **to ~ o.s.** pavonearse

preface ['prefəs] n prefacio

prefect ['priːfekt] (BRIT) n (in school) monitor(a) m/f

prefer [prɪ'fɜː*] vt preferir; **to ~ doing** or **to do** preferir hacer; **~able** ['prefrəbl] adj preferible; **~ably** ['prefrəblɪ] adv de preferencia; **~ence** ['prefrəns] n preferencia; (priority) prioridad f; **~ential** [prefə'renʃəl] adj preferente

prefix ['priːfɪks] n prefijo

pregnancy ['pregnənsɪ] n (of woman) embarazo; (of animal) preñez f

pregnant ['pregnənt] adj (woman) embarazada; (animal) preñada

prehistoric ['priːhɪs'tɔrɪk] adj prehistórico

prejudice ['predʒudɪs] n prejuicio; **~d** adj (person) predispuesto

premarital ['priː'mærɪtl] adj premarital

premature ['premətʃuə*] adj prematuro

premier ['premɪə*] adj primero, principal ♦ n (POL) primer(a) ministro/a

première ['premɪeə*] n estreno

premise ['premɪs] n premisa; **~s** npl (of business etc) local m; **on the ~s** en el lugar mismo

premium ['priːmɪəm] n premio; (insurance) prima; **to be at a ~** ser muy solicitado; **~ bond** (BRIT) n bono del estado que participa en una lotería nacional

premonition [premə'nɪʃən] n presentimiento

preoccupied [priː'ɔkjupaɪd] adj ensimismado

prep [prep] n (SCOL: study) deberes mpl

prepaid [priː'peɪd] adj porte pagado

preparation [prepə'reɪʃən] n preparación f; **~s** npl preparativos mpl

preparatory [prɪ'pærətərɪ] adj preparatorio,

preliminar; **~ school** n escuela preparatoria
prepare [prɪ'pɛə*] vt preparar, disponer;
(CULIN) preparar ♦ vi: **to ~ for** (action)
prepararse or disponerse para; (event) hacer
preparativos para; **~d to** dispuesto a; **~d for**
listo para
preposition [prɛpə'zɪʃən] n preposición f
preposterous [prɪ'pɔstərəs] adj absurdo,
ridículo
prep school n = **preparatory school**
prerequisite [priː'rɛkwɪzɪt] n requisito
Presbyterian [prɛzbɪ'tɪərɪən] adj, n
presbiteriano/a m/f
preschool ['priː'skuːl] adj preescolar
prescribe [prɪ'skraɪb] vt (MED) recetar
prescription [prɪ'skrɪpʃən] n (MED) receta
presence ['prɛzns] n presencia; **in sb's ~** en
presencia de uno; **~ of mind** aplomo
present [adj, n 'prɛznt, vb prɪ'zɛnt] adj (in
attendance) presente; (current) actual ♦ n
(gift) regalo; (actuality): **the ~** la actualidad,
el presente ♦ vt (introduce, describe)
presentar; (expound) exponer; (give)
presentar, dar, ofrecer; (THEATRE) representar;
to give sb a ~ regalar algo a uno; **at ~**
actualmente; **~able** [prɪ'zɛntəbl] adj: **to**
make o.s. ~able arreglarse; **~ation** [-'teɪʃən] n
presentación f; (of present etc) exposición f;
(formal ceremony) entrega de un regalo; **~-**
day adj actual; **~er** [prɪ'zɛntə*] n (RADIO, TV)
locutor(a) m/f; **~ly** adv (soon) dentro de
poco; (now) ahora
preservative [prɪ'zɜːvətɪv] n conservante m
preserve [prɪ'zɜːv] vt (keep safe) preservar,
proteger; (maintain) mantener; (food)
conservar ♦ n (for game) coto, vedado; (often
pl: jam) conserva, confitura
president ['prɛzɪdənt] n presidente m/f; **~ial**
[-'dɛnʃl] adj presidencial
press [prɛs] n (newspapers): **the P~** la prensa;
(printer's) imprenta; (of button) pulsación f
♦ vt empujar; (button etc) apretar; (clothes:
iron) planchar; (put pressure on: person)
presionar; (insist): **to ~ sth on sb** insistir en
que uno acepte algo ♦ vi (squeeze) apretar;
(pressurize): **to ~ for** presionar por; **we are**
~ed for time/money estamos apurados de
tiempo/dinero; **~ on** vi avanzar; (hurry)
apretar el paso; **~ agency** n agencia de
prensa; **~ conference** n rueda de prensa;
~ing adj apremiante; **~ stud** (BRIT) n botón
m de presión; **~-up** (BRIT) n plancha
pressure ['prɛʃə*] n presión f; **to put ~ on sb**
presionar a uno; **~ cooker** n olla a presión;
~ gauge n manómetro; **~ group** n grupo
de presión; **pressurized** adj (container) a
presión
prestige [prɛs'tiːʒ] n prestigio
presumably [prɪ'zjuːməblɪ] adv es de

suponer que, cabe presumir que
presume [prɪ'zjuːm] vt: **to ~ (that)** presumir
(que), suponer (que)
pretence [prɪ'tɛns] (US **pretense**) n
fingimiento; **under false ~s** con engaños
pretend [prɪ'tɛnd] vt, vi (feign) fingir
pretentious [prɪ'tɛnʃəs] adj presumido;
(ostentatious) ostentoso, aparatoso
pretext ['priːtɛkst] n pretexto
pretty ['prɪtɪ] adj bonito (SP), lindo (AM)
♦ adv bastante
prevail [prɪ'veɪl] vi (gain mastery) prevalecer;
(be current) predominar; **~ing** adj (dominant)
predominante
prevalent ['prɛvələnt] adj (widespread)
extendido
prevent [prɪ'vɛnt] vt: **to ~ sb from doing sth**
impedir a uno hacer algo; **to ~ sth from**
happening evitar que ocurra algo; **~ative** adj
= **preventive**; **~ive** adj preventivo
preview ['priːvjuː] n (of film) preestreno
previous ['priːvɪəs] adj previo, anterior; **~ly**
adv antes
prewar [priː'wɔː*] adj de antes de la guerra
prey [preɪ] n presa ♦ vi: **to ~ on** (feed on)
alimentarse de; **it was ~ing on his mind** le
preocupaba, le obsesionaba
price [praɪs] n precio ♦ vt (goods) fijar el
precio de; **~less** adj que no tiene precio;
~ list n tarifa
prick [prɪk] n (sting) picadura ♦ vt pinchar;
(hurt) picar; **to ~ up one's ears** aguzar el oído
prickle ['prɪkl] n (sensation) picor m; (BOT)
espina; **prickly** adj espinoso; (fig: person)
enojadizo; **prickly heat** n sarpullido causado
por exceso de calor
pride [praɪd] n orgullo; (pej) soberbia ♦ vt: **to**
~ o.s. on enorgullecerse de
priest [priːst] n sacerdote m; **~hood** n
sacerdocio
prim [prɪm] adj (demure) remilgado; (prudish)
gazmoño
primarily ['praɪmərɪlɪ] adv ante todo
primary ['praɪmərɪ] adj (first in importance)
principal ♦ n (US: POL) (elección f) primaria;
~ school (BRIT) n escuela primaria
prime [praɪm] adj primero, principal;
(excellent) selecto, de primera clase ♦ n: **in**
the ~ of life en la flor de la vida ♦ vt (wood,
fig) preparar; **~ example** ejemplo típico;
P~ Minister n primer(a) ministro/a
primeval [praɪ'miːvəl] adj primitivo
primitive ['prɪmɪtɪv] adj primitivo; (crude)
rudimentario
primrose ['prɪmrəuz] n primavera, prímula
Primus (stove) ® ['praɪməs-] (BRIT) n
hornillo de camping
prince [prɪns] n príncipe m
princess [prɪn'sɛs] n princesa

principal ['prɪnsɪpl] *adj* principal, mayor ♦ *n* director(a) *m/f*; ~**ity** [-'pælɪtɪ] *n* principado

principle ['prɪnsɪpl] *n* principio; **in ~** en principio; **on ~** por principio

print [prɪnt] *n* (*foot~*) huella, (*finger~*) huella dactilar; (*letters*) letra de molde; (*fabric*) estampado; (*ART*) grabado; (*PHOT*) impresión *f* ♦ *vt* imprimir, (*cloth*) estampar, (*write in capitals*) escribir en letras de molde; **out of ~** agotado; ~**ed matter** *n* impresos *mpl*; ~**er** *n* (*person*) impresor(a) *m/f*; (*machine*) impresora; ~**ing** *n* (*art*) imprenta; (*act*) impresión *f*; ~**out** *n* (*COMPUT*) impresión *f*

prior ['praɪə*] *adj* anterior, previo; (*more important*) más importante; ~ **to** antes de

priority [praɪ'ɔrɪtɪ] *n* prioridad *f*; **to have ~ (over)** tener prioridad (sobre)

prison ['prɪzn] *n* cárcel *f*, prisión *f* ♦ *cpd* carcelario; ~**er** *n* (*in prison*) preso/a; (*captured person*) prisionero; ~**er-of-war** *n* prisionero de guerra

privacy ['prɪvəsɪ] *n* intimidad *f*

private ['praɪvɪt] *adj* (*personal*) particular; (*property, industry, discussion etc*) privado; (*person*) reservado; (*place*) tranquilo ♦ *n* soldado raso; "~" (*on envelope*) "confidencial"; (*on door*) "prohibido el paso"; **in ~** en privado; ~ **enterprise** *n* empresa privada; ~ **eye** *n* detective *m/f* privado/a; ~ **property** *n* propiedad *f* privada; ~ **school** *n* colegio particular

privet ['prɪvɪt] *n* alheña

privilege ['prɪvɪlɪdʒ] *n* privilegio; (*prerogative*) prerrogativa

privy ['prɪvɪ] *adj*: **to be ~ to** estar enterado de

prize [praɪz] *n* premio ♦ *adj* de primera clase ♦ *vt* apreciar, estimar; ~**-giving** *n* distribución *f* de premios; ~**winner** *n* premiado/a

pro [prəʊ] *n* (*SPORT*) profesional *m/f* ♦ *prep* a favor de; **the ~s and cons** los pros y los contras

probability [prɔbə'bɪlɪtɪ] *n* probabilidad *f*; **in all ~** con toda probabilidad

probable ['prɔbəbl] *adj* probable

probably ['prɔbəblɪ] *adv* probablemente

probation [prə'beɪʃən] *n*: **on ~** (*employee*) a prueba; (*LAW*) en libertad condicional

probe [prəʊb] *n* (*MED, SPACE*) sonda; (*enquiry*) encuesta, investigación *f* ♦ *vt* sondar; (*investigate*) investigar

problem ['prɔbləm] *n* problema *m*

procedure [prə'si:dʒə*] *n* procedimiento; (*bureaucratic*) trámites *mpl*

proceed [prə'si:d] *vi* (*do afterwards*): **to ~ to do sth** proceder a hacer algo; (*continue*): **to ~ (with)** continuar *or* seguir (con); ~**ings** *npl* acto(s) (*pl*); (*LAW*) proceso; ~**s** ['prəʊsi:dz] *npl* (*money*) ganancias *fpl*, ingresos *mpl*

process ['prəʊses] *n* proceso ♦ *vt* tratar, elaborar; ~**ing** *n* tratamiento, elaboración *f*; (*PHOT*) revelado

procession [prə'seʃən] *n* desfile *m*; **funeral ~** cortejo fúnebre

pro-choice [prəʊ'tʃɔɪs] *adj* en favor del derecho a elegir de la madre

proclaim [prə'kleɪm] *vt* (*announce*) anunciar

procrastinate [prəʊ'kræstɪneɪt] *vi* demorarse

procure [prə'kjʊə*] *vt* conseguir

prod [prɔd] *vt* empujar ♦ *n* empujón *m*

prodigy ['prɔdɪdʒɪ] *n* prodigio

produce [*n* 'prɔdju:s, *vt* prə'dju:s] *n* (*AGR*) productos *mpl* agrícolas ♦ *vt* producir; (*play, film, programme*) presentar; ~**r** *n* productor(a) *m/f*; (*of film, programme*) director(a) *m/f*; (*of record*) productor(a) *m/f*

product ['prɔdʌkt] *n* producto

production [prə'dʌkʃən] *n* producción *f*; (*THEATRE*) presentación *f*; ~ **line** *n* línea de producción

productivity [prɔdʌk'tɪvɪtɪ] *n* productividad *f*

profession [prə'feʃən] *n* profesión *f*; ~**al** *adj* profesional ♦ *n* profesional *m/f*; (*skilled person*) perito

professor [prə'fesə*] *n* (*BRIT*) catedrático/a; (*US, Canada*) profesor(a) *m/f*

proficient [prə'fɪʃənt] *adj* experto, hábil

profile ['prəʊfaɪl] *n* perfil *m*

profit ['prɔfɪt] *n* (*COMM*) ganancia ♦ *vi*: **to ~ by** *or* **from** aprovechar *or* sacar provecho de; ~**ability** [-ə'bɪlɪtɪ] *n* rentabilidad *f*; ~**able** *adj* (*ECON*) rentable

profound [prə'faʊnd] *adj* profundo

profusely [prə'fju:slɪ] *adv* profusamente

programme ['prəʊgræm] (*US* program) *n* programa *m* ♦ *vt* programar; ~**r** (*US* programer) *n* programador(a) *m/f*; ~**ming** (*US* programing) *n* programación *f*

progress [*n* 'prəʊgres, *vi* prə'gres] *n* progreso; (*development*) desarrollo ♦ *vi* progresar, avanzar; **in ~** en curso; ~**ive** [-'gresɪv] *adj* progresivo; (*person*) progresista

prohibit [prə'hɪbɪt] *vt* prohibir; **to ~ sb from doing sth** prohibir a uno hacer algo; ~**ion** [-'bɪʃn] *n* prohibición *f*; (*US*): **P~ion** Ley *f* Seca

project [*n* 'prɔdʒekt, *vb* prə'dʒekt] *n* proyecto ♦ *vt* proyectar ♦ *vi* (*stick out*) salir, sobresalir; ~**ion** [prə'dʒekʃən] *n* proyección *f*; (*overhang*) saliente *m*; ~**or** [prə'dʒektə*] *n* proyector *m*

pro-life [prəʊ'laɪf] *adj* pro-vida

prolong [prə'lɒŋ] *vt* prolongar, extender

prom [prɒm] *n abbr* = **promenade**; (*US: ball*) baile *m* de gala

promenade [prɒmə'nɑ:d] *n* (*by sea*) paseo

marítimo; **~ concert** (*BRIT*) n concierto (en
que parte del público permanece de pie)
prominence ['prɒmɪnəns] n importancia
prominent ['prɒmɪnənt] adj (*standing out*)
saliente; (*important*) eminente, importante
promiscuous [prə'mɪskjuəs] adj (*sexually*)
promiscuo
promise ['prɒmɪs] n promesa ♦ vt, vi
prometer; **promising** adj prometedor(a)
promote [prə'məut] vt (*employee*) ascender;
(*product, pop star*) hacer propaganda por;
(*ideas*) fomentar; **~r** n (*of event*) promotor(a)
m/f; (*of cause etc*) impulsor(a) m/f; **promotion** [-'məuʃən] n (*advertising campaign*)
campaña de promoción f; (*in rank*) ascenso
prompt [prɒmpt] adj rápido ♦ adv: **at 6
o'clock ~** a las seis en punto ♦ n (*COMPUT*)
aviso ♦ vt (*urge*) mover, incitar; (*when
talking*) instar; (*THEATRE*) apuntar; **to ~ sb to
do sth** instar a uno a hacer algo; **~ly** adv
rápidamente; (*exactly*) puntualmente
prone [prəun] adj (*lying*) postrado; **~ to**
propenso a
prong [prɒŋ] n diente m. punta
pronoun ['prəunaun] n pronombre m
pronounce [prə'nauns] vt pronunciar; **~d**
adj (*marked*) marcado
pronunciation [prənʌnsɪ'eɪʃən] n
pronunciación f
proof [pru:f] n prueba ♦ adj: **~ against** a
prueba de
prop [prɒp] n apoyo; (*fig*) sostén m ♦ vt
(*also: ~ up*) apoyar; (*lean*): **to ~ sth against**
apoyar algo contra
propaganda [prɒpə'gændə] n propaganda
propel [prə'pɛl] vt impulsar, propulsar; **~ler**
n hélice f
propensity [prə'pɛnsɪtɪ] n propensión f
proper ['prɒpə*] adj (*suited, right*) propio;
(*exact*) justo; (*seemly*) correcto, decente;
(*authentic*) verdadero; (*referring to place*):
the village ~ el pueblo mismo; **~ly** adv
(*adequately*) correctamente; (*decently*)
decentemente; **~ noun** n nombre m propio
property ['prɒpətɪ] n propiedad f; (*personal*)
bienes mpl muebles; **~ owner** n dueño/a de
propiedades
prophecy ['prɒfɪsɪ] n profecía
prophesy ['prɒfɪsaɪ] vt (*fig*) predecir
prophet ['prɒfɪt] n profeta m
proportion [prə'pɔːʃən] n proporción f;
(*share*) parte f; **~al** adj: **~al** (**to**) en
proporción (con); **~al representation** n
representación f proporcional; **~ate** adj: **~ate
(to)** en proporción (con)
proposal [prə'pəuzl] n (*offer of marriage*)
oferta de matrimonio; (*plan*) proyecto
propose [prə'pəuz] vt proponer ♦ vi

declararse; **to ~ to do** tener intención de
hacer
proposition [prɒpə'zɪʃən] n propuesta
proprietor [prə'praɪətə*] n propietario/a,
dueño/a
propriety [prə'praɪətɪ] n decoro
pro rata [-'rɑːtə] adv a prorrateo
prose [prəuz] n prosa
prosecute ['prɒsɪkjuːt] vt (*LAW*) procesar;
prosecution [-'kjuːʃən] n proceso, causa;
(*accusing side*) acusación f; **prosecutor** n
acusador(a) m/f; (*also: public prosecutor*)
fiscal m
prospect [n 'prɒspekt, vb prə'spekt] n
(*possibility*) posibilidad f; (*outlook*)
perspectiva ♦ vi: **to ~ for** buscar; **~s** npl (*for
work etc*) perspectivas fpl; **~ing** n prospección
f; **~ive** [prə'spektɪv] adj futuro
prospectus [prə'spektəs] n prospecto
prosper ['prɒspə*] vi prosperar; **~ity**
[-'spɛrɪtɪ] n prosperidad f; **~ous** adj próspero
prostitute ['prɒstɪtjuːt] n prostituta f; (*male*)
hombre que se dedica a la prostitución
protect [prə'tɛkt] vt proteger; **~ion** [-'tɛkʃən]
n protección f; **~ive** adj protector(a)
protein ['prəutiːn] n proteína
protest [n 'prəutɛst, vb prə'tɛst] n protesta
♦ vi: **to ~ about** or **at/against** protestar de/
contra ♦ vt (*insist*): **to ~ (that)** insistir en
(que)
Protestant ['prɒtɪstənt] adj, n protestante
m/f
protester [prə'tɛstə*] n manifestante m/f
protracted [prə'træktɪd] adj prolongado
protrude [prə'truːd] vi salir, sobresalir
proud [praud] adj orgulloso; (*pej*) soberbio,
altanero
prove [pruːv] vt probar; (*show*) demostrar
♦ vi: **to ~ (to be) correct** resultar correcto; **to
~ o.s.** probar su valía
proverb ['prɒvəːb] n refrán m
provide [prə'vaɪd] vt proporcionar, dar; **to
~ sb with sth** proveer a uno de algo; **~d
(that)** conj con tal de que, a condición de
que; **~ for** vt fus (*person*) mantener a;
(*problem etc*) tener en cuenta; **providing**
[prə'vaɪdɪŋ] conj: **providing (that)** a condición
de que, con tal de que
province ['prɒvɪns] n provincia; (*fig*) esfera;
provincial [prə'vɪnʃəl] adj provincial; (*pej*)
provinciano
provision [prə'vɪʒən] n (*supplying*)
suministro, abastecimiento; (*of contract etc*)
disposición f; **~s** npl (*food*) comestibles mpl;
~al adj provisional
proviso [prə'vaɪzəu] n condición f,
estipulación f
provocative [prə'vɒkətɪv] adj provocativo
provoke [prə'vəuk] vt (*cause*) provocar,

incitar; (*anger*) enojar
prowess ['prauis] *n* destreza
prowl [praul] *vi* (*also:* ~ *about*, ~ *around*)
merodear ♦ *n*: **on the ~** de merodeo; **~er**
n merodeador(a) *m/f*
proxy ['prɒksɪ] *n*: **by ~** por poderes
prudent ['pru:dənt] *adj* prudente
prune [pru:n] *n* ciruela pasa ♦ *vt* podar
pry [praɪ] *vi*: **to ~ (into)** entrometerse (en)
PS *n abbr* (= *postscript*) P.D.
psalm [sɑ:m] *n* salmo
pseudonym ['sju:dəunɪm] *n* seudónimo
psyche ['saɪkɪ] *n* psique *f*
psychiatric [saɪk'ætrɪk] *adj* psiquiátrico
psychiatrist [saɪ'kaɪətrɪst] *n* psiquiatra *m/f*
psychic ['saɪkɪk] *adj* (*also:* ~al) psíquico
psychoanalyse [saɪkəu'ænəlaɪz] *vt*
psicoanalizar; **psychoanalysis** [-ə'nælɪsɪs] *n*
psicoanálisis *m inv*
psychological [saɪkə'lɒdʒɪkl] *adj* psicológico
psychologist [saɪ'kɒlədʒɪst] *n* psicólogo/a
psychology [saɪ'kɒlədʒɪ] *n* psicología
PTO *abbr* (= *please turn over*) sigue
pub [pʌb] *n abbr* (= *public house*) pub *m*, bar
m
puberty ['pju:bətɪ] *n* pubertad *f*
public ['pʌblɪk] *adj* público ♦ *n*: **the ~** el
público; **in ~** en público; **to make ~** hacer
público; **~ address system** *n* megáfono
publican ['pʌblɪkən] *n* tabernero/a
publication [pʌblɪ'keɪʃən] *n* publicación *f*
public: ~ **company** *n* sociedad *f* anónima;
~ **convenience** (*BRIT*) *n* aseos *mpl* públicos
(*SP*), sanitarios *mpl* (*AM*); ~ **holiday** *n* día de
fiesta (*SP*), (día) feriado (*AM*); ~ **house** (*BRIT*)
n bar *m*, pub *m*
publicity [pʌb'lɪsɪtɪ] *n* publicidad *f*
publicize ['pʌblɪsaɪz] *vt* publicitar
publicly ['pʌblɪklɪ] *adv* públicamente, en
público
public: ~ **opinion** *n* opinión *f* pública;
~ **relations** *n* relaciones *fpl* públicas;
~ **school** *n* (*BRIT*) escuela privada; (*US*)
instituto; **~-spirited** *adj* que tiene sentido del
deber ciudadano; ~ **transport** *n* transporte
m público
publish ['pʌblɪʃ] *vt* publicar; **~er** *n* (*person*)
editor(a) *m/f*; (*firm*) editorial *f*; **~ing** *n*
(*industry*) industria del libro
pub lunch *n* almuerzo que se sirve en un pub;
to go for a ~ almorzar o comer en un pub
pucker ['pʌkə*] *vt* (*pleat*) arrugar; (*brow etc*)
fruncir
pudding ['pudɪŋ] *n* pudín *m*; (*BRIT*: *dessert*)
postre *m*; **black ~** morcilla
puddle ['pʌdl] *n* charco
puff [pʌf] *n* soplo; (*of smoke*, *air*) bocanada;
(*of breathing*) resoplido ♦ *vt*: **to ~ one's pipe**
chupar la pipa ♦ *vi* (*pant*) jadear; ~ **out** *vt*

hinchar; ~ **pastry** *n* hojaldre *m*; **~y** *adj*
hinchado
pull [pul] *n* (*tug*): **to give sth a ~** dar un tirón
a algo ♦ *vt* tirar de; (*press: trigger*) apretar;
(*haul*) tirar, arrastrar; (*close: curtain*) echar
♦ *vi* tirar; **to ~ to pieces** hacer pedazos; **to
not ~ one's punches** no andarse con bromas;
to ~ one's weight hacer su parte; **to ~ o.s.
together** sobreponerse; **to ~ sb's leg** tomar el
pelo a uno; ~ **apart** *vt* (*break*) romper;
~ **down** *vt* (*building*) derribar; ~ **in** *vi* (*car
etc*) parar (junto a la acera); (*train*) llegar a la
estación; ~ **off** *vt* (*deal etc*) cerrar; ~ **out** *vi*
(*car*, *train etc*) salir ♦ *vt* sacar, arrancar;
~ **over** *vi* (*AUT*) hacerse a un lado;
~ **through** *vi* (*MED*) reponerse; ~ **up** *vi*
(*stop*) parar ♦ *vt* (*raise*) levantar; (*uproot*)
arrancar, desarraigar
pulley ['pulɪ] *n* polea
pullover ['puləuvə*] *n* jersey *m*, suéter *m*
pulp [pʌlp] *n* (*of fruit*) pulpa
pulpit ['pulpɪt] *n* púlpito
pulsate [pʌl'seɪt] *vi* pulsar, latir
pulse [pʌls] *n* (*ANAT*) pulso; (*rhythm*)
pulsación *f*; (*BOT*) legumbre *f*
pump [pʌmp] *n* bomba; (*shoe*) zapatilla ♦ *vt*
sacar con una bomba; ~ **up** *vt* inflar
pumpkin ['pʌmpkɪn] *n* calabaza
pun [pʌn] *n* juego de palabras
punch [pʌntʃ] *n* (*blow*) golpe *m*, puñetazo;
(*tool*) punzón *m*; (*drink*) ponche *m* ♦ *vt*
(*hit*): **to ~ sb/sth** dar un puñetazo or golpear
a uno/algo; **~line** *n* palabras que rematan un
chiste; **~-up** (*BRIT*: *inf*) *n* riña
punctual ['pʌŋktjuəl] *adj* puntual
punctuation [pʌŋktju'eɪʃən] *n* puntuación *f*
puncture ['pʌŋktʃə*] (*BRIT*) *n* pinchazo ♦ *vt*
pinchar
pungent ['pʌndʒənt] *adj* acre
punish ['pʌnɪʃ] *vt* castigar; **~ment** *n* castigo
punk [pʌŋk] *n* (*also:* ~ *rocker*) punki *m/f*;
(*also:* ~ *rock*) música punk; (*US*: *inf*: *hoodlum*)
rufián *m*
punt [pʌnt] *n* (*boat*) batea
punter ['pʌntə*] (*BRIT*) *n* (*gambler*)
jugador(a) *m/f*; (*inf*) cliente *m/f*
puny ['pju:nɪ] *adj* débil
pup [pʌp] *n* cachorro
pupil ['pju:pl] *n* alumno/a; (*of eye*) pupila
puppet ['pʌpɪt] *n* títere *m*
puppy ['pʌpɪ] *n* cachorro, perrito
purchase ['pə:tʃɪs] *n* compra ♦ *vt* comprar;
~r *n* comprador(a) *m/f*
pure [pjuə*] *adj* puro
purée ['pjuəreɪ] *n* puré *m*
purely ['pjuəlɪ] *adv* puramente
purge [pə:dʒ] *n* (*MED*, *POL*) purga ♦ *vt* purgar
purify ['pjuərɪfaɪ] *vt* purificar, depurar
purple ['pə:pl] *adj* purpúreo; morado

purpose |'pə:pəs| n propósito; **on ~** a
propósito, adrede; **~ful** adj resuelto,
determinado

purr |pə:*| vi ronronear

purse |pə:s| n monedero; (US) bolsa (SP),
cartera (AM) ♦ vt fruncir

pursue |pə'sju:| vt seguir; **~r** n
perseguidor(a) m/f

pursuit |pə'sju:t| n (chase) caza; (occupation)
actividad f

push |puʃ| n empuje m, empujón m; (of
button) presión f; (drive) empuje m ♦ vt
empujar; (button) apretar; (promote)
promover ♦ vi empujar; (demand): **to ~ for**
luchar por; **~ aside** vt apartar con la mano;
~ off (inf) vi largarse; **~ on** vi seguir
adelante; **~ through** vi (crowd) abrirse paso
a empujones ♦ vt (measure) despachar; **~ up**
vt (total, prices) hacer subir; **~chair** (BRIT) n
sillita de ruedas; **~er** n (drug ~er) traficante
m/f de drogas; **~over** (inf) n: **it's a ~over**
está tirado; **~-up** (US) n plancha; **~y** (pej) adj
agresivo

puss |pus| (inf) n minino

pussy(-cat) |'pusɪ-| (inf) n = **puss**

put |put| (pt, pp **put**) vt (place) poner,
colocar; (~ into) meter; (say) expresar; (a
question) hacer; (estimate) estimar; **~ about**,
or **around** vt (rumour) diseminar; **~ across**
vt (ideas etc) comunicar; **~ away** vt (store)
guardar; **~ back** vt (replace) devolver a su
lugar; (postpone) aplazar; **~ by** vt (money)
guardar; **~ down** vt (on ground) poner en el
suelo; (animal) sacrificar; (in writing)
apuntar; (revolt etc) sofocar; (attribute): **to
~ sth down to** atribuir algo a; **~ forward** vt
(ideas) presentar, proponer; **~ in** vt
(complaint) presentar; (time) dedicar; **~ off**
vt (postpone) aplazar; (discourage) desanimar;
~ on vt ponerse; (light etc) encender; (play
etc) presentar; (gain): **to ~ on weight**
engordar; (brake) echar; (record, kettle etc)
poner; (assume) adoptar; **~ out** vt (fire,
light) apagar; (rubbish etc) sacar; (cat etc)
echar; (one's hand) alargar; (inf: person): **to
be ~ out** alterarse; **~ through** vt (TEL) poner;
(plan etc) hacer aprobar; **~ up** vt (raise)
levantar, alzar; (hang) colgar; (build)
construir; (increase) aumentar;
(accommodate) alojar; **~ up with** vt fus
aguantar

putt |pʌt| n putt m, golpe m corto; **~ing
green** n green m; minigolf m

putty |'pʌtɪ| n masilla

put-up |'putʌp| adj: **~ job** (BRIT) amaño

puzzle |'pʌzl| n rompecabezas m inv; (also:
crossword ~) crucigrama m; (mystery) misterio
♦ vt dejar perplejo, confundir ♦ vi: **to ~ over**
sth devanarse los sesos con algo; **puzzling**

adj misterioso, extraño

pyjamas |pɪ'dʒɑ:məz| (BRIT) npl pijama m

pylon |'paɪlən| n torre f de conducción
eléctrica

pyramid |'pɪrəmɪd| n pirámide f

Pyrenees |pɪrə'ni:z| npl: **the ~** los Pirineos

python |'paɪθən| n pitón m

Q, q

quack |kwæk| n graznido; (pej: doctor)
curandero/a

quad |kwɔd| n abbr = **quadrangle**; **quadruplet**

quadrangle |'kwɔdræŋgl| n patio

quadruple |kwɔ'drupl| vt, vi cuadruplicar

quadruplets |kwɔ'dru:plɪts| npl cuatrillizos/
as

quail |kweɪl| n codorniz f ♦ vi: **to ~ at** or
before amedrentarse ante

quaint |kweɪnt| adj extraño; (picturesque)
pintoresco

quake |kweɪk| vi temblar ♦ n abbr =
earthquake

Quaker |'kweɪkə*| n cuáquero/a

qualification |kwɔlɪfɪ'keɪʃən| n (ability)
capacidad f; (often pl: diploma etc) título;
(reservation) salvedad f

qualified |'kwɔlɪfaɪd| adj capacitado;
(professionally) titulado; (limited) limitado

qualify |'kwɔlɪfaɪ| vt (make competent)
capacitar; (modify) modificar ♦ vi (in
competition): **to ~ (for)** calificarse (para);
(pass examination(s)): **to ~ (as)** calificarse
(de), graduarse (en); (be eligible): **to ~ (for)**
reunir los requisitos (para)

quality |'kwɔlɪtɪ| n calidad f; (of person)
cualidad f; **~ time** n tiempo dedicado a la
familia y a los amigos

qualm |kwɑ:m| n escrúpulo

quandary |'kwɔndrɪ| n: **to be in a ~** tener
dudas

quantity |'kwɔntɪtɪ| n cantidad f; **in ~** en
grandes cantidades; **~ surveyor** n
aparejador(a) m/f

quarantine |'kwɔrəntiːn| n cuarentena

quarrel |'kwɔrl| n riña, pelea ♦ vi reñir,
pelearse

quarry |'kwɔrɪ| n cantera

quart |kwɔ:t| n = litro

quarter |'kwɔ:tə*| n cuarto, cuarta parte f;
(US: coin) moneda de 25 centavos; (of year)
trimestre m; (district) barrio ♦ vt dividir en
cuartos; (MIL: lodge) alojar; **~s** npl (barracks)
cuartel m; (living ~s) alojamiento; **a ~ of an
hour** un cuarto de hora; **~ final** n cuarto de
final; **~ly** adj trimestral ♦ adv cada 3 meses,
trimestralmente

quartet(te) |kwɔ:'tet| n cuarteto

quartz [kwɔ:ts] n cuarzo
quash [kwɒʃ] vt (verdict) anular
quaver ['kweɪvə*] (BRIT) n (MUS) corchea ♦ vi temblar
quay [ki:] n (also: ~side) muelle m
queasy ['kwi:zɪ] adj: **to feel ~** tener náuseas
queen [kwi:n] n reina; (CARDS etc) dama; **~ mother** n reina madre
queer [kwɪə*] adj raro, extraño ♦ n (inf: highly offensive) maricón m
quell [kwɛl] vt (feeling) calmar; (rebellion etc) sofocar
quench [kwɛntʃ] vt: **to ~ one's thirst** apagar la sed
query ['kwɪərɪ] n (question) pregunta ♦ vt dudar de
quest [kwɛst] n busca, búsqueda
question ['kwɛstʃən] n pregunta; (doubt) duda; (matter) asunto, cuestión f ♦ vt (doubt) dudar de; (interrogate) interrogar, hacer preguntas a; **beyond ~** fuera de toda duda; **out of the ~** imposible; ni hablar; **~able** adj dudoso; **~ mark** n punto de interrogación; **~naire** [-'nɛə*] n cuestionario
queue [kju:] (BRIT) n cola ♦ vi (also: ~ up) hacer cola
quibble ['kwɪbl] vi sutilizar
quick [kwɪk] adj rápido; (agile) ágil; (mind) listo ♦ n: **cut to the ~** (fig) herido en lo vivo; **be ~!** ¡date prisa!; **~en** vt apresurar ♦ vi apresurarse, darse prisa; **~ly** adv rápidamente, de prisa; **~sand** n arenas fpl movedizas; **~-witted** adj perspicaz
quid [kwɪd] (BRIT: inf) n inv libra
quiet ['kwaɪət] adj (voice, music etc) bajo; (person, place) tranquilo; (ceremony) íntimo ♦ n silencio; (calm) tranquilidad f ♦ vt, vi (US) = **~en**; **~en** (also: ~en down) vi calmarse; (grow silent) callarse ♦ vt calmar; hacer callar; **~ly** adv tranquilamente; (silently) silenciosamente; **~ness** n silencio; tranquilidad f
quilt [kwɪlt] n edredón m
quin [kwɪn] n abbr = **quintuplet**
quintet(te) [kwɪn'tɛt] n quinteto
quintuplets [kwɪn'tju:plɪts] npl quintillizos/as
quip [kwɪp] n pulla
quirk [kwə:k] n peculiaridad f; (accident) capricho
quit [kwɪt] (pt, pp **quit** or **quitted**) vt dejar, abandonar; (premises) desocupar ♦ vi (give up) renunciar; (resign) dimitir
quite [kwaɪt] adv (rather) bastante; (entirely) completamente; **that's not ~ big enough** no acaba de ser lo bastante grande; **a few of them** un buen número de ellos; **~ (so)!** ¡así es!, ¡exactamente!
quits [kwɪts] adj: **~ (with)** en paz (con); **let's**

call it ~ dejémoslo en tablas
quiver ['kwɪvə*] vi estremecerse
quiz [kwɪz] n concurso ♦ vt interrogar; **~zical** adj burlón(ona)
quota ['kwəʊtə] n cuota
quotation [kwəʊ'teɪʃən] n cita; (estimate) presupuesto; **~ marks** npl comillas fpl
quote [kwəʊt] n cita; (estimate) presupuesto ♦ vt citar; (price) cotizar ♦ vi: **to ~ from** citar de; **~s** npl (inverted commas) comillas fpl

R, r

rabbi ['ræbaɪ] n rabino
rabbit ['ræbɪt] n conejo; **~ hutch** n conejera
rabble ['ræbl] (pej) n chusma, populacho
rabies ['reɪbi:z] n rabia
RAC (BRIT) n abbr = **Royal Automobile Club**
rac(c)oon [rə'ku:n] n mapache m
race [reɪs] n carrera; (species) raza ♦ vt (horse) hacer correr; (engine) acelerar ♦ vi (compete) competir; (run) correr; (pulse) latir a ritmo acelerado; **~ car** (US) n = **racing car**; **~ car driver** (US) n = **racing driver**; **~course** n hipódromo; **~horse** n caballo de carreras; **~track** n pista; (for cars) autódromo
racial ['reɪʃl] adj racial
racing ['reɪsɪŋ] n carreras fpl; **~ car** (BRIT) n coche m de carreras; **~ driver** (BRIT) n corredor(a) m/f de coches
racism ['reɪsɪzəm] n racismo; **racist** [-sɪst] adj, n racista m/f
rack [ræk] n (also: luggage ~) rejilla; (shelf) estante m; (also: roof ~) baca, portaequipajes m inv; (dish ~) escurreplatos m inv; (clothes ~) percha ♦ vt atormentar; **to ~ one's brains** devanarse los sesos
racket ['rækɪt] n (for tennis) raqueta; (noise) ruido, estrépito; (swindle) estafa, timo
racquet ['rækɪt] n raqueta
racy ['reɪsɪ] adj picante, salado
radar ['reɪdɑ:*] n radar m
radiant ['reɪdɪənt] adj radiante (de felicidad)
radiate ['reɪdɪeɪt] vt (heat) radiar; (emotion) irradiar ♦ vi (lines) extenderse
radiation [reɪdɪ'eɪʃən] n radiación f
radiator ['reɪdɪeɪtə*] n radiador m
radical ['rædɪkl] adj radical
radii ['reɪdɪaɪ] npl of **radius**
radio ['reɪdɪəʊ] n radio f; **on the ~** por radio
radio... [reɪdɪəʊ] prefix: **~active** adj radioactivo; **~graphy** [reɪdɪ'ɒɡrəfɪ] n radiografía; **~logy** [reɪdɪ'ɒlədʒɪ] n radiología
radio station n emisora
radiotherapy [-'θerəpɪ] n radioterapia
radish ['rædɪʃ] n rábano
radius ['reɪdɪəs] n (pl **radii**) n radio
RAF n abbr = **Royal Air Force**

raffle |'ræfl| n rifa, sorteo
raft |rɑːft| n balsa; (also: life ~) balsa salvavidas
rafter |'rɑːftə*| n viga
rag |ræg| n (piece of cloth) trapo; (torn cloth) harapo; (pej: newspaper) periodicucho; (for charity) actividades estudiantiles benéficas; **~s** npl (torn clothes) harapos mpl; **~ doll** n muñeca de trapo
rage |reɪdʒ| n rabia, furor m ♦ vi (person) rabiar, estar furioso; (storm) bramar; **it's all the ~** (very fashionable) está muy de moda
ragged |'rægɪd| adj (edge) desigual, mellado; (appearance) andrajoso, harapiento
raid |reɪd| n (MIL) incursión f; (criminal) asalto; (by police) redada ♦ vt invadir, atacar; asaltar
rail |reɪl| n (on stair) barandilla, pasamanos m inv; (on bridge, balcony) pretil m; (of ship) barandilla; (also: towel ~) toallero; **~s** npl (RAIL) vía; **by ~** por ferrocarril; **~ing(s)** n(pl) vallado; **~road** (US) n = **~way**; **~way** (BRIT) n ferrocarril m, vía férrea; **~way line** (BRIT) n línea (de ferrocarril); **~wayman** (BRIT irreg) n ferroviario; **~way station** (BRIT) n estación f de ferrocarril
rain |reɪn| n lluvia ♦ vi llover; **in the ~** bajo la lluvia; **it's ~ing** llueve, está lloviendo; **~bow** n arco iris; **~coat** n impermeable m; **~drop** n gota de lluvia; **~fall** n lluvia; **~forest** n selvas fpl tropicales; **~y** adj lluvioso
raise |reɪz| n aumento ♦ vt levantar; (increase) aumentar; (improve: morale) subir; (: standards) mejorar; (doubts) suscitar; (a question) plantear; (cattle, family) criar; (crop) cultivar; (army) reclutar; (loan) obtener; **to ~ one's voice** alzar la voz
raisin |'reɪzn| n pasa de Corinto
rake |reɪk| n (tool) rastrillo; (person) libertino ♦ vt (garden) rastrillar
rally |'rælɪ| n (POL etc) reunión f, mitin m; (AUT) rallye m; (TENNIS) peloteo ♦ vt reunir ♦ vi recuperarse; **~ round** vt fus (fig) dar apoyo a
RAM |ræm| n abbr (= random access memory) RAM f
ram |ræm| n carnero; (also: battering ~) ariete m ♦ vt (crash into) dar contra, chocar con; (push: fist etc) empujar con fuerza
ramble |'ræmbl| n caminata, excursión f en el campo ♦ vi (pej: also: ~ on) divagar; **~r** n excursionista m/f; (BOT) trepadora; **rambling** adj (speech) inconexo; (house) laberíntico; (BOT) trepador(a)
ramp |ræmp| n rampa; **on/off ~** (US: AUT) vía de acceso/salida
rampage |ræm'peɪdʒ| n: **to be on the ~** desmandarse ♦ vi: **they went rampaging through the town** recorrieron la ciudad

armando alboroto
rampant |'ræmpənt| adj (disease etc): **to be ~** estar extendiéndose mucho
ram raid vt atracar (rompiendo el escaparate con un coche)
ramshackle |'ræmʃækl| adj destartalado
ran |ræn| pt of **run**
ranch |rɑːntʃ| n hacienda, estancia; **~er** n ganadero
rancid |'rænsɪd| adj rancio
rancour |'ræŋkə*| (US **rancor**) n rencor m
random |'rændəm| adj fortuito, sin orden; (COMPUT, MATH) aleatorio ♦ n: **at ~** al azar
randy |'rændɪ| (BRIT: inf) adj cachondo
rang |ræŋ| pt of **ring**
range |reɪndʒ| n (of mountains) cadena de montañas, cordillera; (of missile) alcance m; (of voice) registro; (series) serie f; (of products) surtido; (MIL: also: shooting ~) campo de tiro; (also: kitchen ~) fogón m ♦ vt (place) colocar; (arrange) arreglar ♦ vi: **to ~ over** (extend) extenderse por; **to ~ from ... to ...** oscilar entre ... y ...
ranger |'reɪndʒə*| n guardabosques m inv
rank |ræŋk| n (row) fila; (MIL) rango; (status) categoría; (BRIT: also: taxi ~) parada de taxis ♦ vi: **to ~ among** figurar entre ♦ adj fétido, rancio; **the ~ and file** (fig) la base
ransack |'rænsæk| vt (search) registrar; (plunder) saquear
ransom |'rænsəm| n rescate n; **to hold to ~** (fig) hacer chantaje a
rant |rænt| vi divagar, desvariar
rap |ræp| vt golpear, dar un golpecito en ♦ n (music) rap m
rape |reɪp| n violación f; (BOT) colza ♦ vt violar; **~ (seed) oil** n aceite m de colza
rapid |'ræpɪd| adj rápido; **~ity** |rə'pɪdɪtɪ| n rapidez f; **~s** npl (GEO) rápidos mpl
rapist |'reɪpɪst| n violador m
rapport |ræ'pɔː*| n simpatía
rapturous |'ræptʃərəs| adj extático
rare |reə*| adj raro, poco común; (CULIN: steak) poco hecho
rarely |'reəlɪ| adv pocas veces
raring |'reərɪŋ| adj: **to be ~ to go** (inf) tener muchas ganas de empezar
rascal |'rɑːskl| n pillo, pícaro
rash |ræʃ| adj imprudente, precipitado ♦ n (MED) sarpullido, erupción f (cutánea); (of events) serie f
rasher |'ræʃə*| n lonja
raspberry |'rɑːzbərɪ| n frambuesa
rasping |'rɑːspɪŋ| adj: **a ~ noise** un ruido áspero
rat |ræt| n rata
rate |reɪt| n (ratio) razón f; (price) precio; (: of hotel etc) tarifa; (of interest) tipo; (speed) velocidad f ♦ vt (value) tasar; (estimate)

estimar; **~s** npl (BRIT: *property tax*) impuesto municipal; (*fees*) tarifa; **to ~ sth/sb as** considerar algo/a uno como; **~able value** (BRIT) n valor m impuesto; **~payer** (BRIT) n contribuyente m/f

rather ['rɑ:ðə*] adv: **it's ~ expensive** es algo caro; (*too much*) es demasiado caro; (*to some extent*) más bien; **there's ~ a lot** hay bastante, **I would** or **I'd ~ go** preferiría ir; **or ~** mejor dicho

rating ['reɪtɪŋ] n tasación f; (*score*) índice m; (*of ship*) clase f; **~s** npl (RADIO, TV) niveles mpl de audiencia

ratio ['reɪʃɪəu] n razón f; **in the ~ of 100 to 1** a razón de 100 a 1

ration ['ræʃən] n ración f ♦ vt racionar; **~s** npl víveres mpl

rational ['ræʃənl] adj (*solution, reasoning*) lógico, razonable; (*person*) cuerdo, sensato; **~e** [-'nɑ:l] n razón f fundamental; **~ize** vt justificar

rat race n lucha incesante por la supervivencia

rattle ['rætl] n golpeteo; (*of train etc*) traqueteo; (*for baby*) sonaja, sonajero ♦ vi castañetear; (*car, bus*): **to ~ along** traquetear ♦ vt hacer sonar agitando; **~snake** n serpiente f de cascabel

raucous ['rɔ:kəs] adj estridente, ronco

ravage ['rævɪdʒ] vt hacer estragos en, destrozar; **~s** npl estragos mpl

rave [reɪv] vi (*in anger*) encolerizarse; (*with enthusiasm*) entusiasmarse; (MED) delirar, desvariar ♦ n (*inf: party*) rave m

raven ['reɪvən] n cuervo

ravenous ['rævənəs] adj hambriento

ravine [rə'vi:n] n barranco

raving ['reɪvɪŋ] adj: **~ lunatic** loco/a de atar

ravishing ['rævɪʃɪŋ] adj encantador(a)

raw [rɔ:] adj crudo; (*not processed*) bruto; (*sore*) vivo; (*inexperienced*) novato, inexperto; **~ deal** (inf) n injusticia; **~ material** n materia prima

ray [reɪ] n rayo; **~ of hope** (rayo de esperanza)

raze [reɪz] vt arrasar

razor ['reɪzə*] n (*open*) navaja, (*safety ~*) máquina de afeitar; (*electric ~*) máquina (eléctrica) de afeitar; **~ blade** n hoja de afeitar

Rd abbr = **road**

re [ri:] prep con referencia a

reach [ri:tʃ] n alcance m; (*of river etc*) extensión f entre dos recodos ♦ vt alcanzar, llegar a; (*achieve*) lograr ♦ vi extenderse; **within ~** al alcance (de la mano); **out of ~** fuera del alcance; **~ out** vt (*hand*) tender ♦ vi: **to ~ out for** alargar or tender la mano para tomar algo

react [ri:'ækt] vi reaccionar; **~ion** [-'ækʃən] n reacción f

reactor [ri:'æktə*] n (*also: nuclear ~*) reactor m (nuclear)

read [ri:d, pt, pp red] (pt, pp **read**) vi leer ♦ vt leer; (*understand*) entender; (*study*) estudiar; **~ out** vt leer en alta voz; **~able** adj (*writing*) legible; (*book*) leíble; **~er** n lector(a) m/f; (BRIT: *at university*) profesor(a) m/f adjunto/a; **~ership** n (*of paper etc*) (número de) lectores mpl

readily ['redɪlɪ] adv (*willingly*) de buena gana; (*easily*) fácilmente; (*quickly*) en seguida

readiness ['redɪnɪs] n buena voluntad f; (*preparedness*) preparación f; **in ~** (*prepared*) listo, preparado

reading ['ri:dɪŋ] n lectura; (*on instrument*) indicación f

ready ['redɪ] adj listo, preparado; (*willing*) dispuesto; (*available*) disponible ♦ adv: **~-cooked** listo para comer ♦ n: **at the ~** (MIL) listo para tirar; **to get ~** vi prepararse ♦ vt preparar; **~-made** adj confeccionado; **~-to-wear** adj confeccionado

real [rɪəl] adj verdadero, auténtico; **in ~ terms** en términos reales; **~ estate** n bienes mpl raíces; **~istic** [-'lɪstɪk] adj realista

reality [ri:'ælɪtɪ] n realidad f

realization [rɪəlaɪ'zeɪʃən] n comprensión f; (*fulfilment, COMM*) realización f

realize ['rɪəlaɪz] vt (*understand*) darse cuenta de

really ['rɪəlɪ] adv realmente; (*for emphasis*) verdaderamente; (*actually*): **what ~ happened** lo que pasó en realidad; **~? ¿de veras?; ~!** (*annoyance*) ¡vamos!, ¡por favor!

realm [relm] n reino; (*fig*) esfera

realtor ® ['rɪəltɔ:*] n (US) n corredor(a) m/f de bienes raíces

reap [ri:p] vt segar; (*fig*) cosechar, recoger

reappear [ri:ə'pɪə*] vi reaparecer

rear [rɪə*] adj trasero ♦ n parte f trasera ♦ vt (*cattle, family*) criar ♦ vi (*also: ~ up*) (*animal*) encabritarse; **~guard** n retaguardia

rearmament [ri:'ɑ:məmənt] n rearme m

rearrange [ri:ə'reɪndʒ] vt ordenar or arreglar de nuevo

rear-view mirror n (AUT) (*espejo*) retrovisor m

reason ['ri:zn] n razón f ♦ vi: **to ~ with sb** tratar de que uno entre en razón; **it stands to ~ that** es lógico que; **~able** adj razonable; (*sensible*) sensato; **~ably** adv razonablemente; **~ing** n razonamiento, argumentos mpl

reassurance [ri:ə'ʃuərəns] n consuelo

reassure [ri:ə'ʃuə*] vt tranquilizar, alentar; **to ~ sb that** tranquilizar a uno asegurando que

rebate ['ri:beɪt] n (*on tax etc*) desgravación f

rebel [n 'rebl, vi ri'bel] n rebelde m/f ♦ vi rebelarse, sublevarse; **~lious** [rɪ'beljəs] adj rebelde; (*child*) revoltoso

rebirth [ˈriːbəːθ] *n* renacimiento

rebound [*vi* rɪˈbaund, *n* ˈriːbaund] *vi* (*ball*) rebotar ♦ *n* rebote *m*; **on the ~** (*also fig*) de rebote

rebuff [rɪˈbʌf] *n* desaire *m*, rechazo

rebuild [riːˈbɪld] (*irreg*) *vt* reconstruir

rebuke [rɪˈbjuːk] *n* reprimenda ♦ *vt* reprender

rebut [rɪˈbʌt] *vt* rebatir

recall [*vb* rɪˈkɔːl, *n* ˈriːkɔl] *vt* (*remember*) recordar; (*ambassador etc*) retirar ♦ *n* recuerdo; retirada

recap [ˈriːkæp], **recapitulate** [riːkəˈpɪtjuleɪt] *vt*, *vi* recapitular

rec'd *abbr* (= *received*) rbdo

recede [rɪˈsiːd] *vi* (*memory*) ir borrándose; (*hair*) retroceder; **receding** *adj* (*forehead, chin*) huidizo; **to have a receding hairline** tener entradas

receipt [rɪˈsiːt] *n* (*document*) recibo; (*for parcel etc*) acuse *m* de recibo; (*for receiving*) recepción *f*; **~s** *npl* (*COMM*) ingresos *mpl*

receive [rɪˈsiːv] *vt* recibir; (*guest*) acoger; (*wound*) sufrir; **~r** *n* (*TEL*) auricular *m*; (*RADIO*) receptor *m*; (*of stolen goods*) perista *m/f*; (*COMM*) administrador *m* jurídico

recent [ˈriːsnt] *adj* reciente; **~ly** *adv* recientemente; **~ly arrived** recién llegado

receptacle [rɪˈseptɪkl] *n* receptáculo

reception [rɪˈsepʃən] *n* recepción *f*; (*welcome*) acogida; **~ desk** *n* recepción *f*; **~ist** *n* recepcionista *m/f*

recess [rɪˈses] *n* (*in room*) hueco; (*for bed*) nicho; (*secret place*) escondrijo; (*POL etc: holiday*) clausura

recession [rɪˈseʃən] *n* recesión *f*

recipe [ˈresɪpɪ] *n* receta; (*for disaster, success*) fórmula

recipient [rɪˈsɪpɪənt] *n* recibidor(a) *m/f*; (*of letter*) destinatario/a

recital [rɪˈsaɪtl] *n* recital *m*

recite [rɪˈsaɪt] *vt* (*poem*) recitar

reckless [ˈrekləs] *adj* temerario, imprudente; (*driving, driver*) peligroso; **~ly** *adv* imprudentemente; **de modo peligroso**

reckon [ˈrekən] *vt* calcular; (*consider*) considerar; (*think*): **I ~ that ...** me parece que ...; **~ on** *vt fus* contar con; **~ing** *n* cálculo

reclaim [rɪˈkleɪm] *vt* (*land, waste*) recuperar; (*land: from sea*) rescatar; (*demand back*) reclamar

reclamation [rekləˈmeɪʃən] *n* (*of land*) acondicionamiento de tierras

recline [rɪˈklaɪn] *vi* reclinarse; **reclining** *adj* (*seat*) reclinable

recluse [rɪˈkluːs] *n* recluso/a

recognition [rekəgˈnɪʃən] *n* reconocimiento; **transformed beyond ~** irreconocible

recognizable [ˈrekəgnaɪzəbl] *adj*: **~ (by)** reconocible (por)

recognize [ˈrekəgnaɪz] *vt*: **to ~ (by/as)** reconocer (por/como)

recoil [*vi* rɪˈkɔɪl, *n* ˈriːkɔɪl] *vi* (*person*): **to ~ from doing sth** retraerse de hacer algo ♦ *n* (*of gun*) retroceso

recollect [rekəˈlekt] *vt* recordar, acordarse de; **~ion** [-ˈlekʃən] *n* recuerdo

recommend [rekəˈmend] *vt* recomendar

reconcile [ˈrekənsaɪl] *vt* (*two people*) reconciliar; (*two facts*) compaginar; **to ~ o.s. to sth** conformarse a algo

recondition [riːkənˈdɪʃən] *vt* (*machine*) reacondicionar

reconnoitre [rekəˈnɔɪtə*] (*US* **reconnoiter**) *vt*, *vi* (*MIL*) reconocer

reconsider [riːkənˈsɪdə*] *vt* repensar

reconstruct [riːkənˈstrʌkt] *vt* reconstruir

record [*n* ˈrekɔːd, *vt* rɪˈkɔːd] *n* (*MUS*) disco; (*of meeting etc*) acta; (*register*) registro, partida; (*file*) archivo; (*also: criminal: ~*) antecedentes *mpl*; (*written*) expediente *m*; (*SPORT, COMPUT*) récord *m* ♦ *vt* registrar; (*MUS: song etc*) grabar; **in ~ time** en un tiempo récord; **off the ~** *adj* no oficial ♦ *adv* confidencialmente; **~ card** *n* (*in file*) ficha; **~ed delivery** (*BRIT*) *n* (*POST*) entrega con acuse de recibo; **~er** *n* (*MUS*) flauta de pico; **~ holder** *n* (*SPORT*) actual poseedor(a) *m/f* del récord; **~ing** *n* (*MUS*) grabación *f*; **~ player** *n* tocadiscos *m* *inv*

recount [rɪˈkaunt] *vt* contar

re-count [ˈriːkaunt] *n* (*POL: of votes*) segundo escrutinio

recoup [rɪˈkuːp] *vt*: **to ~ one's losses** recuperar las pérdidas

recourse [rɪˈkɔːs] *n*: **to have ~ to** recurrir a

recover [rɪˈkʌvə*] *vt* recuperar ♦ *vi* (*from illness, shock*) recuperarse; **~y** *n* recuperación *f*

recreation [rekrɪˈeɪʃən] *n* recreo; **~al** *adj* de recreo; **~al drug** droga recreativa

recruit [rɪˈkruːt] *n* recluta *m/f* ♦ *vt* reclutar; (*staff*) contratar

rectangle [ˈrektæŋgl] *n* rectángulo; **rectangular** [-ˈtæŋgjulə*] *adj* rectangular

rectify [ˈrektɪfaɪ] *vt* rectificar

rector [ˈrektə*] *n* (*REL*) párroco; **~y** *n* casa del párroco

recuperate [rɪˈkuːpəreɪt] *vi* reponerse, restablecerse

recur [rɪˈkəː*] *vi* repetirse; (*pain, illness*) producirse de nuevo; **~rence** [rɪˈkʌrəns] *n* repetición *f*; **~rent** [rɪˈkʌrənt] *adj* repetido

recycle [riːˈsaɪkl] *vt* reciclar

red [red] *n* rojo ♦ *adj* rojo; (*hair*) pelirrojo; (*wine*) tinto; **to be in the ~** (*account*) estar en números rojos; (*business*) tener un saldo

negativo; **to give sb the ~ carpet treatment**
recibir a uno con todos los honores;
R~ Cross n Cruz f Roja; **~currant** n grosella
roja; **~den** vt enrojecer ♦ vi enrojecerse
redeem [rɪ'diːm] vt redimir; (*promises*)
cumplir; (*sth in pawn*) desempeñar; (*fig, also*
REL) rescatar; **~ing** adj: **~ing feature** rasgo
bueno *or* favorable
redeploy [riːdɪ'plɔɪ] vt (*resources*) reorganizar
red: **~-haired** adj pelirrojo; **~-handed** adj: **to**
be caught ~-handed cogerse (*SP*) *or* pillarse
(*AM*) con las manos en la masa; **~head** n
pelirrojo/a; **~ herring** n (*fig*) pista falsa; **~-**
hot adj candente
redirect [riːdaɪ'rekt] vt (*mail*) reexpedir
red light n: **to go through a ~** (*AUT*) pasar la
luz roja; **red-light district** n barrio chino
redo [riː'duː] (*irreg*) vt rehacer
redress [rɪ'dres] vt reparar
Red Sea n: **the ~** el mar Rojo
redskin ['redskɪn] n piel roja m/f
red tape n (*fig*) trámites mpl
reduce [rɪ'djuːs] vt reducir; **to ~ sb to tears**
hacer llorar a uno; **to be ~d to begging** no
quedarle a uno otro remedio que mendigar;
"**~ speed now**" (*AUT*) "reduzca la
velocidad"; **at a ~d price** (*of goods*) (a precio)
rebajado; **reduction** [rɪ'dʌkʃən] n reducción
f; (*of price*) rebaja; (*discount*) descuento;
(*smaller-scale copy*) copia reducida
redundancy [rɪ'dʌndənsɪ] n (*dismissal*)
despido; (*unemployment*) desempleo
redundant [rɪ'dʌndnt] adj (*BRIT: worker*)
parado, sin trabajo; (*detail, object*) superfluo;
to be made ~ quedar(se) sin trabajo
reed [riːd] n (*BOT*) junco, caña; (*MUS*)
lengüeta
reef [riːf] n (*at sea*) arrecife m
reek [riːk] vi: **to ~ (of)** apestar (a)
reel [riːl] n carrete m, bobina; (*of film*) rollo;
(*dance*) baile m escocés ♦ vt (*also: ~ up*)
devanar; (*also: ~ in*) sacar ♦ vi (*sway*)
tambalear(se)
ref [ref] (*inf*) n abbr = **referee**
refectory [rɪ'fektərɪ] n comedor m
refer [rɪ'fəː*] vt (*send: patient*) referir;
(: *matter*) remitir ♦ vi: **to ~ to** (*allude to*)
referirse a, aludir a; (*apply to*) relacionarse
con; (*consult*) consultar
referee [refə'riː] n árbitro; (*BRIT: for job*
application): **to be a ~ for sb** proporcionar
referencias a uno ♦ vt (*match*) arbitrar en
reference ['refrəns] n referencia; (*for job*
application: letter) carta de recomendación;
with ~ to (*COMM: in letter*) me remito a;
~ book n libro de consulta; **~ number** n
número de referencia
refill [vt riː'fɪl, n 'riːfɪl] vt rellenar ♦ n
repuesto, recambio

refine [rɪ'faɪn] vt refinar; **~d** adj (*person*) fino;
~ment n cultura, educación f; (*of system*)
refinamiento
reflect [rɪ'flekt] vt reflejar ♦ vi (*think*)
reflexionar, pensar; **it ~s badly/well on him** le
perjudica/le hace honor; **~ion** [-'flekʃən] n
(*act*) reflexión f; (*image*) reflejo; (*criticism*)
crítica; **on ~ion** pensándolo bien; **~or** n (*AUT*)
captafaros m inv; (*of light, heat*) reflector m
reflex ['riːfleks] adj, n reflejo; **~ive** [rɪ'fleksɪv]
adj (*LING*) reflexivo
reform [rɪ'fɔːm] n reforma ♦ vt reformar;
~atory (*US*) n reformatorio
refrain [rɪ'freɪn] vi: **to ~ from doing**
abstenerse de hacer ♦ n estribillo
refresh [rɪ'freʃ] vt refrescar; **~er course**
(*BRIT*) n curso de repaso; **~ing** adj
refrescante; **~ments** npl refrescos mpl
refrigerator [rɪ'frɪdʒəreɪtə*] n nevera (*SP*),
refrigeradora (*AM*)
refuel [riː'fjuəl] vi repostar (*combustible*)
refuge ['refjuːdʒ] n refugio, asilo; **to take ~ in**
refugiarse en
refugee [refju'dʒiː] n refugiado/a
refund [n 'riːfʌnd, vb rɪ'fʌnd] n reembolso
♦ vt devolver, reembolsar
refurbish [riː'fəːbɪʃ] vt restaurar, renovar
refusal [rɪ'fjuːzəl] n negativa; **to have first**
~ on tener la primera opción a
refuse[1] ['refjuːs] n basura; **~ collection** n
recolección f de basuras
refuse[2] [rɪ'fjuːz] vt rechazar; (*invitation*)
declinar; (*permission*) denegar ♦ vi: **to ~ to**
do sth negarse a hacer algo; (*horse*) rehusar
regain [rɪ'geɪn] vt recobrar, recuperar
regal ['riːgl] adj regio, real
regard [rɪ'gɑːd] n mirada; (*esteem*) respeto;
(*attention*) consideración f ♦ vt (*consider*)
considerar; **to give one's ~s to** saludar de su
parte a; "**with kindest ~s**" "con muchos
recuerdos"; **~ing, as ~s, with ~ to** con
respecto a, en cuanto a; **~less** adv a pesar de
todo; **~less of** sin reparar en
régime [reɪ'ʒiːm] n régimen m
regiment ['redʒɪmənt] n regimiento; **~al**
[-'mentl] adj militar
region ['riːdʒən] n región f; **in the ~ of** (*fig*)
alrededor de; **~al** adj regional
register ['redʒɪstə*] n registro ♦ vt registrar;
(*birth*) declarar; (*car*) matricular; (*letter*)
certificar; (*subj: instrument*) marcar, indicar
♦ vi (*at hotel*) registrarse; (*as student*)
matricularse; (*make impression*) producir
impresión; **~ed** adj (*letter, parcel*) certificado;
~ed trademark n marca registrada
registrar ['redʒɪstrɑː*] n secretario/a (del
registro civil)
registration [redʒɪs'treɪʃən] n (*act*)
declaración f; (*AUT: also: ~ number*) matrícula

registry ['rɛdʒɪstrɪ] n registro; ~ **office** (BRIT) n registro civil; **to get married in a ~ office** casarse por lo civil

regret [rɪ'grɛt] n sentimiento, pesar m ♦ vt sentir, lamentar; **~fully** adv con pesar; **~table** adj lamentable

regular ['rɛgjulə*] adj regular; (soldier) profesional; (usual) habitual; (: doctor) de cabecera ♦ n (client etc) cliente/a m/f habitual; **~ly** adv con regularidad; (often) repetidas veces

regulate ['rɛgjuleɪt] vt controlar; **regulation** [-'leɪʃən] n (rule) regla, reglamento

rehearsal [rɪ'hə:səl] n ensayo

rehearse [rɪ'hə:s] vt ensayar

reign [reɪn] n reinado; (fig) predominio ♦ vi reinar; (fig) imperar

reimburse [ri:ɪm'bə:s] vt reembolsar

rein [reɪn] n (for horse) rienda

reindeer ['reɪndɪə*] n.inv reno

reinforce [ri:ɪn'fɔ:s] vt reforzar; **~d concrete** n hormigón m armado; **~ments** npl (MIL) refuerzos mpl

reinstate [ri:ɪn'steɪt] vt reintegrar; (tax, law) reinstaurar

reiterate [ri:'ɪtəreɪt] vt reiterar, repetir

reject [n 'ri:dʒɛkt, vb rɪ'dʒɛkt] n (thing) desecho ♦ vt rechazar; (suggestion) descartar; (coin) expulsar; **~ion** [rɪ'dʒɛkʃən] n rechazo

rejoice [rɪ'dʒɔɪs] vi: **to ~ at** or **over** regocijarse or alegrarse de

rejuvenate [rɪ'dʒu:vəneɪt] vt rejuvenecer

relapse [rɪ'læps] n recaída

relate [rɪ'leɪt] vt (tell) contar, relatar; (connect) relacionar ♦ vi relacionarse; **~d** adj afín; (person) emparentado; **~d to** (subject) relacionado con; **relating to** prep referente a

relation [rɪ'leɪʃən] n (person) familiar m/f, pariente/a m/f; (link) relación f; **~s** npl (relatives) familiares mpl; **~ship** n relación f; (personal) relaciones fpl; (also: family **~ship**) parentesco

relative ['rɛlətɪv] n pariente/a m/f, familiar m/f ♦ adj relativo; **~ly** adv (comparatively) relativamente

relax [rɪ'læks] vi descansar; (unwind) relajarse ♦ vt (one's grip) soltar, aflojar; (control) relajar; (mind, person) descansar; **~ation** [ri:læk'seɪʃən] n descanso; (of rule, control) relajamiento; (entertainment) diversión f; **~ed** adj relajado; (tranquil) tranquilo; **~ing** adj relajante

relay ['ri:leɪ] n (race) carrera de relevos ♦ vt (RADIO, TV) retransmitir

release [rɪ'li:s] n (liberation) liberación f; (from prison) puesta en libertad; (of gas etc) escape m; (of film etc) estreno; (of record) lanzamiento ♦ vt (prisoner) poner en libertad; (gas) despedir, arrojar; (from wreckage)

soltar; (catch, spring etc) desenganchar; (film) estrenar; (book) publicar; (news) difundir

relegate ['rɛləgeɪt] vt relegar; (BRIT: SPORT): **to be ~d to** bajar a

relent [rɪ'lɛnt] vi ablandarse; **~less** adj implacable

relevant ['rɛləvənt] adj (fact) pertinente; **~ to** relacionado con

reliable [rɪ'laɪəbl] adj (person, firm) de confianza, de fiar; (method, machine) seguro; (source) fidedigno; **reliably** adv: **to be reliably informed that ...** saber de fuente fidedigna que ...

reliance [rɪ'laɪəns] n: **~ (on)** dependencia (de)

relic ['rɛlɪk] n (REL) reliquia; (of the past) vestigio

relief [rɪ'li:f] n (from pain, anxiety) alivio; (help, supplies) socorro, ayuda; (ART, GEO) relieve m

relieve [rɪ'li:v] vt (pain) aliviar; (bring help to) ayudar, socorrer; (take over from) sustituir; (: guard) relevar; **to ~ sb of sth** quitar algo a uno; **to ~ o.s.** hacer sus necesidades

religion [rɪ'lɪdʒən] n religión f; **religious** adj religioso

relinquish [rɪ'lɪŋkwɪʃ] vt abandonar; (plan, habit) renunciar a

relish ['rɛlɪʃ] n (CULIN) salsa; (enjoyment) entusiasmo ♦ vt (food etc) saborear; (enjoy): **to ~ sth** hacerle mucha ilusión a uno algo

relocate [ri:ləu'keɪt] vt cambiar de lugar, mudar ♦ vi mudarse

reluctance [rɪ'lʌktəns] n renuencia

reluctant [rɪ'lʌktənt] adj renuente; **~ly** adv de mala gana

rely on [rɪ'laɪ-] vt fus depender de; (trust) contar con

remain [rɪ'meɪn] vi (survive) quedar; (be left) sobrar; (continue) quedar(se), permanecer; **~der** n resto; **~ing** adj que queda(n); (surviving) restante(s); **~s** npl restos mpl

remand [rɪ'mɑ:nd] n: **on ~** detenido (bajo custodia) ♦ vt: **to be ~ed in custody** quedar detenido bajo custodia; **~ home** (BRIT) n reformatorio

remark [rɪ'mɑ:k] n comentario ♦ vt comentar; **~able** adj (outstanding) extraordinario

remarry [ri:'mærɪ] vi volver a casarse

remedial [rɪ'mi:dɪəl] adj de recuperación

remedy ['rɛmədɪ] n remedio ♦ vt remediar, curar

remember [rɪ'mɛmbə*] vt recordar, acordarse de; (bear in mind) tener presente; (send greetings to): **~ me to him** dale recuerdos de mi parte; **remembrance** n recuerdo; **R~ Day** n ≈ día en el que se recuerda a los caídos en las dos guerras

remind → reproach

mundiales

remind [rɪ'maɪnd] vt: **to ~ sb to do sth**
recordar a uno que haga algo; **to ~ sb of sth**
(of fact) recordar algo a uno; **she ~s me of
her mother** me recuerda a su madre; **~er** n
notificación f; (memento) recuerdo

reminisce [rɛmɪ'nɪs] vi recordar (viejas
historias); **reminiscent** adj: **to be
reminiscent of sth** recordar algo

remiss [rɪ'mɪs] adj descuidado; **it was ~ of
him** fue un descuido de su parte

remission [rɪ'mɪʃən] n remisión f; (of prison
sentence) disminución f de pena; (REL) perdón
m

remit [rɪ'mɪt] vt (send: money) remitir, enviar;
~tance n remesa, envío

remnant ['rɛmnənt] n resto; (of cloth) retal
m; **~s** npl (COMM) restos mpl de serie

remorse [rɪ'mɔːs] n remordimientos mpl;
~ful adj arrepentido; **~less** adj (fig)
implacable, inexorable

remote [rɪ'məut] adj (distant) lejano;
(person) distante; **~ control** n telecontrol m;
~ly adv remotamente; (slightly) levemente

remould ['riːməuld] (BRIT) n (tyre) neumático
or llanta (AM) recauchutado/a

removable [rɪ'muːvəbl] adj (detachable)
separable

removal [rɪ'muːvəl] n (taking away) el quitar;
(BRIT: from house) mudanza; (from office:
dismissal) destitución f; (MED) extirpación f;
~ van (BRIT) n camión m de mudanzas

remove [rɪ'muːv] vt quitar; (employee)
destituir; (name: from list) tachar, borrar;
(doubt) disipar; (abuse) suprimir, acabar con;
(MED) extirpar

Renaissance [rɪ'neɪsɑ̃s] n: **the ~** el
Renacimiento

render ['rɛndə*] vt (thanks) dar; (aid)
proporcionar, prestar; (make): **to ~ sth
useless** hacer algo inútil; **~ing** n (MUS etc)
interpretación f

rendezvous ['rɒndɪvuː] n cita

renew [rɪ'njuː] vt renovar; (resume) reanudar;
(loan etc) prorrogar; **~able** adj renovable;
~al n reanudación f; prórroga

renounce [rɪ'nauns] vt renunciar a; (right,
inheritance) renunciar

renovate ['rɛnəveɪt] vt renovar

renown [rɪ'naun] n renombre m; **~ed** adj
renombrado

rent [rɛnt] n (for house) arriendo, renta ♦ vt
alquilar; **~al** n (for television, car) alquiler m

rep [rɛp] n abbr = **representative**; **repertory**

repair [rɪ'pɛə*] n reparación f, compostura
♦ vt reparar, componer; (shoes) remendar;
in good/bad ~ en buen/mal estado; **~ kit** n
caja de herramientas

repatriate [riː'pætrɪeɪt] vt repatriar

repay [riː'peɪ] (irreg) vt (money) devolver,
reembolsar; (person) pagar; (debt) liquidar;
(sb's efforts) devolver, corresponder a;
~ment n reembolso, devolución f; (sum of
money) recompensa

repeal [rɪ'piːl] n revocación f ♦ vt revocar

repeat [rɪ'piːt] n (RADIO, TV) reposición f ♦ vt
repetir ♦ vi repetirse; **~edly** adv repetidas
veces

repel [rɪ'pɛl] vt (drive away) rechazar;
(disgust) repugnar; **~lent** adj repugnante
♦ n: **insect ~lent** crema (or loción f) anti-
insectos

repent [rɪ'pɛnt] vi: **to ~ (of)** arrepentirse (de);
~ance n arrepentimiento

repercussions [riːpə'kʌʃənz] npl
consecuencias fpl

repertory ['rɛpətərɪ] n (also: ~ theatre) teatro
de repertorio

repetition [rɛpɪ'tɪʃən] n repetición f

repetitive [rɪ'pɛtɪtɪv] adj repetitivo

replace [rɪ'pleɪs] vt (put back) devolver a su
sitio; (take the place of) reemplazar, sustituir;
~ment n (act) reposición f; (thing)
recambio; (person) suplente m/f

replay ['riːpleɪ] n (SPORT) desempate m; (of
tape, film) repetición f

replenish [rɪ'plɛnɪʃ] vt rellenar; (stock etc)
reponer

replica ['rɛplɪkə] n copia, reproducción f
(exacta)

reply [rɪ'plaɪ] n respuesta, contestación f ♦ vi
contestar, responder

report [rɪ'pɔːt] n informe m; (PRESS etc)
reportaje m; (BRIT: also: school ~) boletín m
escolar; (of gun) estallido ♦ vt informar de;
(PRESS etc) hacer un reportaje sobre; (notify:
accident, culprit) denunciar ♦ vi (make a
report) presentar un informe; (present o.s.):
to ~ (to sb) presentarse (ante uno); **~ card** n
(US, Scottish) cartilla escolar; **~edly** adv
según se dice; **~er** n periodista m/f

repose [rɪ'pəuz] n: **in ~** (face, mouth) en
reposo

reprehensible [rɛprɪ'hɛnsɪbl] adj
reprensible, censurable

represent [rɛprɪ'zɛnt] vt representar; (COMM)
ser agente de; (describe): **to ~ sth as** describir
algo como; **~ation** [-'teɪʃən] n representación
f; **~ations** npl (protest) quejas fpl; **~ative** n
representante m/f; (US: POL) diputado/a m/f
♦ adj representativo

repress [rɪ'prɛs] vt reprimir; **~ion** [-'prɛʃən] n
represión f

reprieve [rɪ'priːv] n (LAW) indulto; (fig) alivio

reprisals [rɪ'praɪzlz] npl represalias fpl

reproach [rɪ'prəutʃ] n reproche m ♦ vt: **to
~ sb for sth** reprochar algo a uno; **~ful** adj de
reproche, de acusación

reproduce [ri:prə'dju:s] vt reproducir ♦ vi reproducirse; **reproduction** [-'dʌkʃən] n reproducción f

reprove [rɪ'pru:v] vt: **to ~ sb for sth** reprochar algo a uno

reptile ['reptaɪl] n reptil m

republic [rɪ'pʌblɪk] n república; **~an** adj, n republicano/a m/f

repudiate [rɪ'pju:dɪeɪt] vt rechazar; (violence etc) repudiar

repulsive [rɪ'pʌlsɪv] adj repulsivo

reputable ['repjutəbl] adj (make etc) de renombre

reputation [repju'teɪʃən] n reputación f

reputed [rɪ'pju:tɪd] adj supuesto; **~ly** adv según dicen or se dice

request [rɪ'kwest] n petición f; (formal) solicitud f ♦ vt: **to ~ sth of** or **from sb** solicitar algo a uno; **~ stop** (BRIT) n parada discrecional

require [rɪ'kwaɪə*] vt (need: subj: person) necesitar, tener necesidad de; (: thing, situation) exigir; (want) pedir; **to ~ sb to do sth** pedir a uno que haga algo; **~ment** n requisito; (need) necesidad f

requisition [rekwɪ'zɪʃən] n: **~ (for)** solicitud f (de) ♦ vt (MIL) requisar

rescue ['reskju:] n rescate m ♦ vt rescatar; **~ party** n expedición f de salvamento; **~r** n salvador(a) m/f

research [rɪ'sɜ:tʃ] n investigaciones fpl ♦ vt investigar; **~er** n investigador(a) m/f

resemblance [rɪ'zembləns] n parecido

resemble [rɪ'zembl] vt parecerse a

resent [rɪ'zent] vt tomar a mal; **~ful** adj resentido; **~ment** n resentimiento

reservation [rezə'veɪʃən] n reserva

reserve [rɪ'zɜ:v] n reserva; (SPORT) suplente m/f ♦ vt (seats etc) reservar; **~s** npl (MIL) reserva; **in ~** de reserva; **~d** adj reservado

reshuffle [ri:'ʃʌfl] n: **Cabinet ~** (POL) remodelación f del gabinete

residence ['rezɪdəns] n (formal: home) domicilio; (length of stay) permanencia; **~ permit** (BRIT) n permiso de permanencia

resident ['rezɪdənt] n (of area) vecino/a; (in hotel) huésped(a) m/f ♦ adj (population) permanente; (doctor) residente; **~ial** [-'denʃəl] adj residencial

residue ['rezɪdju:] n resto

resign [rɪ'zaɪn] vt renunciar a ♦ vi dimitir; **to ~ o.s. to** (situation) resignarse a; **~ation** [rezɪg'neɪʃən] n dimisión f; (state of mind) resignación f; **~ed** adj resignado

resilient [rɪ'zɪlɪənt] adj (material) elástico; (person) resistente

resist [rɪ'zɪst] vt resistir, oponerse a; **~ance** n resistencia

resolute ['rezəlu:t] adj resuelto; (refusal) tajante

resolution [rezə'lu:ʃən] n (gen) resolución f

resolve [rɪ'zɔlv] n resolución f ♦ vt resolver ♦ vi: **to ~ to do** resolver hacer; **~d** adj resuelto

resort [rɪ'zɔ:t] n (town) centro turístico; (recourse) recurso ♦ vi: **to ~ to** recurrir a; **in the last ~** como último recurso

resounding [rɪ'zaundɪŋ] adj sonoro, (fig) clamoroso

resource [rɪ'sɔ:s] n recurso; **~s** npl recursos mpl; **~ful** adj despabilado, ingenioso

respect [rɪs'pekt] n respeto ♦ vt respetar; **~s** npl recuerdos mpl, saludos mpl; **with ~ to** con respecto a; **in this ~** en cuanto a eso; **~able** adj respetable; (large: amount) apreciable; (passable) tolerable; **~ful** adj respetuoso

respective [rɪs'pektɪv] adj respectivo; **~ly** adv respectivamente

respite ['respaɪt] n respiro

respond [rɪs'pɔnd] vi responder; (react) reaccionar; **response** [-'pɔns] n respuesta; reacción f

responsibility [rɪspɔnsɪ'bɪlɪtɪ] n responsabilidad f

responsible [rɪs'pɔnsɪbl] adj (character) serio, formal; (job) de confianza; (liable): **~ (for)** responsable (de)

responsive [rɪs'pɔnsɪv] adj sensible

rest [rest] n descanso, reposo; (MUS: pause) pausa, silencio; (support) apoyo; (remainder) resto ♦ vi descansar; (be supported): **to ~ on** descansar sobre ♦ vt (lean): **to ~ sth on/ against** apoyar algo en or sobre/contra; **the ~ of them** (people, objects) los demás; **it ~s with him to ...** depende de él el que ...

restaurant ['restərɒŋ] n restaurante m; **~ car** (BRIT) n (RAIL) coche-comedor m

restful ['restful] adj descansado, tranquilo

rest home n residencia para jubilados

restive ['restɪv] adj inquieto; (horse) rebelón(ona)

restless ['restlɪs] adj inquieto

restoration [restə'reɪʃən] n restauración f; devolución f

restore [rɪ'stɔ:*] vt (building) restaurar; (sth stolen) devolver; (health) restablecer; (to power) volver a poner a

restrain [rɪs'treɪn] vt (feeling) contener, refrenar; (person): **to ~ (from doing)** disuadir (de hacer); **~ed** adj reservado; **~t** n (restriction) restricción f; (moderation) moderación f; (of manner) reserva

restrict [rɪs'trɪkt] vt restringir, limitar; **~ion** [-kʃən] n restricción f, limitación f; **~ive** adj restrictivo

rest room (US) n aseos mpl

result [rɪ'zʌlt] n resultado ♦ vi: **to ~ in** terminar en, tener por resultado; **as a ~ of a**

consecuencia de

resume [rɪˈzjuːm] vt reanudar ♦ vi comenzar de nuevo

résumé [ˈreɪzjuːmeɪ] n resumen m; (US) currículum m

resumption [rɪˈzʌmpʃən] n reanudación f

resurgence [rɪˈsəːdʒəns] n resurgimiento

resurrection [rezəˈrekʃən] n resurrección f

resuscitate [rɪˈsʌsɪteɪt] vt (MED) resucitar

retail [ˈriːteɪl] adj, adv al por menor; **~er** n detallista m/f; **~ price** n precio de venta al público

retain [rɪˈteɪn] vt (keep) retener, conservar; **~er** n (fee) anticipo

retaliate [rɪˈtælɪeɪt] vi: to **~ (against)** tomar represalias (contra); **retaliation** [-ˈeɪʃən] n represalias fpl

retarded [rɪˈtɑːdɪd] adj retrasado

retch [retʃ] vi dársele a uno arcadas

retentive [rɪˈtentɪv] adj (memory) retentivo

retire [rɪˈtaɪə*] vi (give up work) jubilarse; (withdraw) retirarse; (go to bed) acostarse; **~d** adj (person) jubilado; **~ment** n (giving up work: state) retiro; (: act) jubilación f; **retiring** adj (leaving) saliente; (shy) retraído

retort [rɪˈtɔːt] vi contestar

retrace [riːˈtreɪs] vt: to **~ one's steps** volver sobre sus pasos, desandar lo andado

retract [rɪˈtrækt] vt (statement) retirar; (claws) retraer; (undercarriage, aerial) replegar

retrain [riːˈtreɪn] vt reciclar; **~ing** n readaptación f profesional

retread [ˈriːtred] n neumático (SP) or llanta (AM) recauchutado/a

retreat [rɪˈtriːt] n (place) retiro; (MIL) retirada ♦ vi retirarse

retribution [retrɪˈbjuːʃən] n desquite m

retrieval [rɪˈtriːvəl] n recuperación f

retrieve [rɪˈtriːv] vt recobrar; (situation, honour) salvar; (COMPUT) recuperar; (error) reparar; **~r** n perro cobrador

retrospect [ˈretrəspekt] n: in **~** retrospectivamente; **~ive** [-ˈspektɪv] adj retrospectivo; (law) retroactivo

return [rɪˈtəːn] n (going or coming back) vuelta, regreso; (of sth stolen etc) devolución f; (FINANCE: from land, shares) ganancia, ingresos mpl ♦ cpd (journey) de regreso; (BRIT: ticket) de ida y vuelta; (match) de vuelta ♦ vi (person etc: come or go back) volver, regresar; (symptoms etc) reaparecer; (regain): to **~ to** recuperar ♦ vt devolver; (favour, love etc) corresponder a; (verdict) pronunciar; (POL: candidate) elegir; **~s** npl (COMM) ingresos mpl; in **~ (for)** a cambio (de); **by ~ of post** a vuelta de correo; **many happy ~s (of the day)!** ¡feliz cumpleaños!

reunion [riːˈjuːnɪən] n (of family) reunión f; (of two people, school) reencuentro

reunite [riːjuːˈnaɪt] vt reunir; (reconcile) reconciliar

rev [rev] (AUT) n abbr (= revolution) revolución f ♦ vt (also: **~ up**) acelerar

reveal [rɪˈviːl] vt revelar; **~ing** adj revelador(a)

revel [ˈrevl] vi: to **~ in sth/in doing sth** gozar de algo/con hacer algo

revenge [rɪˈvendʒ] n venganza; **to take ~ on** vengarse de

revenue [ˈrevənjuː] n ingresos mpl, rentas fpl

reverberate [rɪˈvəːbəreɪt] vi (sound) resonar, retumbar; (fig: shock) repercutir

reverence [ˈrevərəns] n reverencia

Reverend [ˈrevərənd] adj (in titles): the **~ John Smith** (Anglican) el Reverendo John Smith; (Catholic) el Padre John Smith; (Protestant) el Pastor John Smith

reversal [rɪˈvəːsl] n (of order) inversión f; (of direction, policy) cambio; (of decision) revocación f

reverse [rɪˈvəːs] n (opposite) contrario, lo contrario; (back: of cloth) revés m; (: of coin) reverso; (: of paper) dorso; (AUT: also: **~ gear**) marcha atrás; (setback) revés m ♦ adj (order) inverso; (direction) contrario, opuesto ♦ vt (decision, AUT) dar marcha atrás a; (position, function) invertir ♦ vi (BRIT: AUT) dar marcha atrás; **~-charge call** (BRIT) n llamada a cobro revertido; **reversing lights** (BRIT) npl (AUT) luces fpl de retroceso

revert [rɪˈvəːt] vi: to **~ to** volver a

review [rɪˈvjuː] n (magazine, MIL) revista; (of book, film) reseña; (US: examination) repaso, examen m ♦ vt repasar, examinar; (MIL) pasar revista a; (book, film) reseñar; **~er** n crítico/a

revise [rɪˈvaɪz] vt (manuscript) corregir; (opinion) modificar; (price, procedure) revisar ♦ vi (study) repasar; **revision** [rɪˈvɪʒən] n corrección f; modificación f; (for exam) repaso

revival [rɪˈvaɪvəl] n (recovery) reanimación f; (of interest) renacimiento; (THEATRE) reestreno; (of faith) despertar m

revive [rɪˈvaɪv] vt resucitar; (custom) restablecer; (hope) despertar; (play) reestrenar ♦ vi (person) volver en sí; (business) reactivar

revolt [rɪˈvəult] n rebelión f ♦ vi rebelarse, sublevarse ♦ vt dar asco a, repugnar; **~ing** adj asqueroso, repugnante

revolution [revəˈluːʃən] n revolución f; **~ary** adj, n revolucionario/a m/f; **~ize** vt revolucionar

revolve [rɪˈvɔlv] vi dar vueltas, girar; (life, discussion): to **~ (a)round** girar en torno a

revolver [rɪˈvɔlvə*] n revólver m

revolving [rɪˈvɔlvɪŋ] adj (chair, door etc) giratorio

revue [rɪ'vju:] n (THEATRE) revista

revulsion [rɪ'vʌlʃən] n asco, repugnancia

reward [rɪ'wɔ:d] n premio, recompensa ♦ vt: **to ~ (for)** recompensar or premiar (por); **~ing** adj (fig) valioso

rewind [ri:'waɪnd] (irreg) vt rebobinar

rewire [ri:'waɪə*] vt (house) renovar la instalación eléctrica de

rheumatism ['ru:mətɪzəm] n reumatismo, reúma m

Rhine [raɪn] n: **the ~** el (río) Rin

rhinoceros [raɪ'nɔsərəs] n rinoceronte m

rhododendron [rəudə'dendrɪn] n rododendro

Rhone [rəun] n: **the ~** el (río) Ródano

rhubarb ['ru:bɑ:b] n ruibarbo

rhyme [raɪm] n rima; (verse) poesía

rhythm ['rɪðm] n ritmo

rib [rɪb] n (ANAT) costilla ♦ vt (mock) tomar el pelo a

ribbon ['rɪbən] n cinta; **in ~s** (torn) hecho trizas

rice [raɪs] n arroz m; **~ pudding** n arroz m con leche

rich [rɪtʃ] adj rico; (soil) fértil; (food) pesado; (: sweet) empalagoso; (abundant): **~ in** (minerals etc) rico en; **the ~** npl los ricos; **~es** npl riqueza; **~ly** adv ricamente; (deserved, earned) bien

rickets ['rɪkɪts] n raquitismo

rid [rɪd] (pt, pp rid) vt: **to ~ sb of sth** librar a uno de algo; **to get ~ of** deshacerse or desembarazarse de

ridden ['rɪdn] pp of ride

riddle ['rɪdl] n (puzzle) acertijo; (mystery) enigma m, misterio ♦ vt: **to be ~d with** ser lleno or plagado de

ride [raɪd] (pt rode, pp ridden) n paseo; (distance covered) viaje m, recorrido ♦ vi (as sport) montar; (go somewhere: on horse, bicycle) dar un paseo, pasearse; (travel: on bicycle, motorcycle, bus) viajar ♦ vt (a horse) montar a; (a bicycle, motorcycle) andar en; (distance) recorrer; **to take sb for a ~** (fig) engañar a uno; **~r** n (on horse) jinete/a m/f; (on bicycle) ciclista m/f; (on motorcycle) motociclista m/f

ridge [rɪdʒ] n (of hill) cresta; (of roof) caballete m; (wrinkle) arruga

ridicule ['rɪdɪkju:l] n irrisión f, burla ♦ vt poner en ridículo, burlarse de; **ridiculous** [-'dɪkjuləs] adj ridículo

riding ['raɪdɪŋ] n equitación f; **I like ~** me gusta montar a caballo; **~ school** n escuela de equitación

rife [raɪf] adj: **to be ~** ser muy común; **to be ~ with** abundar en

riffraff ['rɪfræf] n gentuza

rifle ['raɪfl] n rifle m, fusil m ♦ vt saquear;

~ through vt (papers) registrar; **~ range** n campo de tiro; (at fair) tiro al blanco

rift [rɪft] n (in clouds) claro; (fig: disagreement) desavenencia

rig [rɪg] n (also: oil ~: at sea) plataforma petrolera ♦ vt (election etc) amañar; **~ out** (BRIT) vt disfrazar; **~ up** vt improvisar; **~ging** n (NAUT) aparejo

right [raɪt] adj (correct) correcto, exacto; (suitable) indicado, debido; (just) justo; (morally good) bueno; (not left) derecho ♦ n bueno; (title, claim) derecho; (not left) derecha ♦ adv bien, correctamente; (not left) a la derecha; (exactly): **~ now** ahora mismo ♦ vt enderezar; (correct) corregir ♦ excl ¡bueno!, ¡está bien!; **to be ~** (person) tener razón; (answer) ser correcto; **is that the ~ time?** (of clock) ¿es esa la hora buena?; **by ~s** en justicia; **on the ~** a la derecha; **to be in the ~** tener razón; **~ away** en seguida; **~ in the middle** exactamente en el centro; **~ angle** n ángulo recto; **~eous** ['raɪtʃəs] adj justado, honrado; (anger) justificado; **~ful** adj legítimo; **~-handed** adj diestro; **~-hand man** n brazo derecho; **~-hand side** n derecha; **~ly** adv correctamente, debidamente; (with reason) con razón; **~ of way** n (on path etc) derecho de paso; (AUT) prioridad f; **~-wing** adj (POL) derechista

rigid ['rɪdʒɪd] adj rígido; (person, ideas) inflexible

rigmarole ['rɪgmərəul] n galimatías m inv

rigorous ['rɪgərəs] adj riguroso

rile [raɪl] vt irritar

rim [rɪm] n borde m; (of spectacles) aro; (of wheel) llanta

rind [raɪnd] n (of bacon) corteza; (of lemon etc) cáscara; (of cheese) costra

ring [rɪŋ] (pt rang, pp rung) n (of metal) aro; (on finger) anillo; (of people) corro; (of objects) círculo; (gang) banda; (for boxing) cuadrilátero; (of circus) pista; (bull ~) ruedo, plaza; (sound of bell) toque m ♦ vi (on telephone) llamar por teléfono; (bell) repicar; (doorbell, phone) sonar; (also: ~ out) sonar; (ears) zumbar ♦ vt (BRIT: TEL) llamar, telefonear; (bell etc) hacer sonar; (doorbell) tocar; **to give sb a ~** (BRIT: TEL) llamar or telefonear a alguien; **~ back** (BRIT) vt, vi (TEL) devolver la llamada; **~ off** (BRIT) vi (TEL) colgar, cortar la comunicación; **~ up** (BRIT) vt (TEL) llamar, telefonear; **~ing** n (of bell) repique m; (of phone) señal f; (in ears) zumbido; **~ing tone** n (TEL) tono de llamada; **~leader** n (of gang) cabecilla m; **~lets** ['rɪŋlɪts] npl rizos mpl, bucles mpl; **~ road** n (BRIT) carretera periférica or de circunvalación

rink |rɪŋk| n (also: ice ~) pista de hielo

rinse |rɪns| n aclarado; (dye) tinte m ♦ vt aclarar; (mouth) enjuagar

riot |'raɪət| n motín m, disturbio ♦ vi amotinarse; **to run ~** desmandarse; **~ous** adj alborotado; (party) bullicioso

rip |rɪp| n rasgón m, rasgadura ♦ vt rasgar, desgarrar ♦ vi rasgarse, desgarrarse; **~cord** n cabo de desgarre

ripe |raɪp| adj maduro; **~n** vt madurar; (cheese) curar ♦ vi madurar

ripple |'rɪpl| n onda, rizo; (sound) murmullo ♦ vi rizarse

rise |raɪz| (pt **rose**, pp **risen**) n (slope) cuesta, pendiente f; (hill) altura; (BRIT: in wages) aumento; (in prices, temperature) subida; (fig: to power etc) ascenso ♦ vi subir; (waters) crecer; (sun, moon) salir; (person: from bed etc) levantarse; (also: ~ up: rebel) sublevarse; (in rank) ascender; **to give ~ to** dar lugar o origen a; **to ~ to the occasion** ponerse a la altura de las circunstancias; **risen** |'rɪzn| pp of **rise**; **rising** adj (increasing: number) creciente; (: prices) en aumento or alza; (tide) creciente; (sun, moon) naciente

risk |rɪsk| n riesgo, peligro ♦ vt arriesgar; (run the ~ of) exponerse a; **to take** or **run the ~ of doing** correr el riesgo de hacer; **at ~** en peligro; **at one's own ~** bajo su propia responsabilidad; **~y** adj arriesgado, peligroso

rissole |'rɪsəʊl| n croqueta

rite |raɪt| n rito; **last ~s** exequias fpl

ritual |'rɪtjʊəl| adj ritual ♦ n ritual m, rito

rival |'raɪvl| n rival m/f; (in business) competidor(a) m/f ♦ adj rival, opuesto ♦ vt competir con; **~ry** n competencia

river |'rɪvə*| n río ♦ cpd (port) de río; (traffic) fluvial; **up/down ~** río arriba/abajo; **~bank** n orilla (del río); **~bed** n lecho, cauce m

rivet |'rɪvɪt| n roblón m, remache m ♦ vt (fig) captar

Riviera |rɪvɪ'eərə| n: **the (French) ~** la Costa Azul (francesa)

road |rəʊd| n camino; (motorway etc) carretera; (in town) calle f ♦ cpd (accident) de tráfico; **major/minor ~** carretera principal/ secundaria; **~ accident** n accidente m de tráfico; **~block** n barricada; **~hog** n loco/a del volante; **~ map** n mapa m de carreteras; **~ rage** n agresividad en la carretera; **~ safe-ty** n seguridad f vial; **~side** n borde m (del camino); **~sign** n señal f de tráfico; **~ user** n usuario/a de la vía pública; **~way** n calzada; **~works** npl obras fpl; **~worthy** adj (car) en buen estado para circular

roam |rəʊm| vi vagar

roar |rɔː*| n rugido; (of vehicle, storm) estruendo; (of laughter) carcajada ♦ vi rugir; hacer estruendo; **to ~ with laughter** reírse a carcajadas; **to do a ~ing trade** hacer buen negocio

roast |rəʊst| n carne f asada, asado ♦ vt asar; (coffee) tostar; **~ beef** n rosbif m

rob |rɒb| vt robar; **to ~ sb of sth** robar algo a uno; (fig: deprive) quitar algo a uno; **~ber** n ladrón/ona m/f; **~bery** n robo

robe |rəʊb| n (for ceremony etc) toga; (also: bath~, US) albornoz m

robin |'rɒbɪn| n petirrojo

robot |'rəʊbɒt| n robot m

robust |rəʊ'bʌst| adj robusto, fuerte

rock |rɒk| n roca; (boulder) peña, peñasco; (US: small stone) piedrecita; (BRIT: sweet) ≈ pirulí ♦ vt (swing gently: cradle) balancear, mecer; (: child) arrullar; (shake) sacudir ♦ vi mecerse, balancearse; sacudirse; **on the ~s** (drink) con hielo; (marriage etc) en ruinas; **~ and roll** n rocanrol m; **~-bottom** n (fig) punto más bajo; **~ery** n cuadro alpino

rocket |'rɒkɪt| n cohete m

rocking |'rɒkɪŋ|: **~ chair** n mecedora; **~ horse** n caballo de balancín

rocky |'rɒkɪ| adj rocoso

rod |rɒd| n vara, varilla; (also: fishing ~) caña

rode |rəʊd| pt of **ride**

rodent |'rəʊdnt| n roedor m

roe |rəʊ| n (species: also: ~ deer) corzo; (of fish): **hard/soft ~** hueva/lecha

rogue |rəʊg| n pícaro, pillo

role |rəʊl| n papel m

roll |rəʊl| n rollo; (of bank notes) fajo; (also: bread ~) panecillo; (register, list) lista, nómina; (sound: of drums etc) redoble m ♦ vt hacer rodar; (also: ~ up: string) enrollar; (: sleeves) arremangar; (cigarette) liar; (also: ~ out: pastry) aplanar; (flatten: road, lawn) apisonar ♦ vi rodar; (drum) redoblar; (ship) balancearse; **~ about** or **around** vi (person) revolcarse; (object) rodar (por); **~ by** vi (time) pasar; **~ over** vi dar una vuelta; **~ up** vi (inf: arrive) aparecer ♦ vt (carpet) arrollar; **~ call** n: **to take a ~ call** pasar lista; **~er** n rodillo; (wheel) rueda; (for road) apisonadora; (for hair) rulo; **~erblade** n patín m (en línea); **~er coaster** n montaña rusa; **~er skates** npl patines mpl de rueda

rolling |'rəʊlɪŋ| adj (landscape) ondulado; **~ pin** n rodillo (de cocina); **~ stock** n (RAIL) material m rodante

ROM |rɒm| n abbr (COMPUT: = read only memory) ROM f

Roman |'rəʊmən| adj romano/a; **~ Catholic** adj, n católico/a m/f (romano/a)

romance |rə'mæns| n (love affair) amor m; (charm) lo romántico; (novel) novela de amor

Romania |ru:'meɪnɪə| n = **Rumania**

Roman numeral n número romano

romantic [rə'mæntık] *adj* romántico
Rome [rəum] *n* Roma
romp [rɔmp] *n* retozo, juego ♦ *vi* (*also:*
~ *about*) jugar, brincar
rompers ['rɔmpəz] *npl* pelele *m*
roof [ru:f] (*pl* ~s) *n* (*gen*) techo; (*of house*)
techo, tejado ♦ *vt* techar, poner techo a; the
~ **of the mouth** el paladar; ~**ing** *n* techumbre
f; ~ **rack** *n* (*AUT*) baca, portaequipajes *m inv*
rook [ruk] *n* (*bird*) graja; (*CHESS*) torre *f*
room [ru:m] *n* cuarto, habitación *f*, pieza (*esp
AM*); (*also: bed~*) dormitorio; (*in school etc*)
sala; (*space, scope*) sitio, cabida; ~**s** *npl*
(*lodging*) alojamiento; "~**s to let**", "~**s for
rent**" (*US*) "se alquilan cuartos"; **single/
double** ~ habitación individual/doble *or* para
dos personas; ~**ing house** (*US*) *n* pensión *f*;
~**mate** *n* compañero/a de cuarto; ~ **service**
n servicio de habitaciones; ~**y** *adj* espacioso;
(*garment*) amplio
roost [ru:st] *vi* pasar la noche
rooster ['ru:stə*] *n* gallo
root [ru:t] *n* raíz *f* ♦ *vi* arraigarse; ~ **about** *vi*
(*fig*) buscar y rebuscar; ~ **for** *vt fus* (*support*)
apoyar a; ~ **out** *vt* desarraigar
rope [rəup] *n* cuerda; (*NAUT*) cable *m* ♦ *vt*
(*tie*) atar *or* amarrar con (una) cuerda; (*climbers: also:* ~ *together*) encordarse; (*an
area: also:* ~ *off*) acordonar; **to know the** ~**s**
(*fig*) conocer los trucos (del oficio); ~ **in** *vt*
(*fig*): **to** ~ **sb in** persuadir a uno a tomar parte
rosary ['rəuzərı] *n* rosario
rose [rəuz] *pt of* **rise** ♦ *n* rosa; (*shrub*) rosal *m*;
(*on watering can*) roseta
rosé ['rəuzeı] *n* vino rosado
rosebud ['rəuzbʌd] *n* capullo de rosa
rosebush ['rəuzbuʃ] *n* rosal *m*
rosemary ['rəuzmərı] *n* romero
roster ['rɔstə*] *n*: **duty** ~ lista de deberes
rostrum ['rɔstrəm] *n* tribuna
rosy ['rəuzı] *adj* rosado, sonrosado; **a** ~ **future**
un futuro prometedor
rot [rɔt] *n* podredumbre *f*; (*fig: pej*) tonterías
fpl ♦ *vt* pudrir ♦ *vi* pudrirse
rota ['rəutə] *n* (sistema *m* de) turnos *mpl*
rotary ['rəutərı] *adj* rotativo
rotate [rəu'teıt] *vt* (*revolve*) hacer girar, dar
vueltas a; (*jobs*) alternar ♦ *vi* girar, dar
vueltas; **rotating** *adj* rotativo; **rotation**
[-'teıʃən] *n* rotación *f*
rotten ['rɔtn] *adj* podrido; (*dishonest*)
corrompido; (*inf: bad*) pocho; **to feel** ~ (*ill*)
sentirse fatal
rotund [rəu'tʌnd] *adj* regordete
rouble ['ru:bl] (*US* **ruble**) *n* rublo
rough [rʌf] *adj* (*skin, surface*) áspero; (*terrain*)
quebrado; (*road*) desigual; (*voice*) bronco;
(*person, manner*) tosco, grosero; (*weather*)
borrascoso; (*treatment*) brutal; (*sea*) picado;

(*town, area*) peligroso; (*cloth*) basto; (*plan*)
preliminar; (*guess*) aproximado ♦ *n* (*GOLF*): **in
the** ~ en las hierbas altas; **to** ~ **it** vivir sin
comodidades; **to sleep** ~ (*BRIT*) pasar la noche
al raso; ~**age** *n* fibra(*s*) *f(pl*); ~**-and-ready**
adj improvisado; ~ **copy** *n* borrador *m*;
~ **draft** *n* = ~ **copy**; ~**ly** *adv* (*handle*)
torpemente; (*make*) toscamente; (*speak*)
groseramente; (*approximately*)
aproximadamente; ~**ness** *n* (*of surface*)
aspereza; (*of person*) rudeza
roulette [ru:'let] *n* ruleta
Roumania [ru:'meɪnɪə] *n* = **Rumania**
round [raund] *adj* redondo ♦ *n* círculo; (*BRIT:
of toast*) rebanada; (*of policeman*) ronda; (*of
milkman*) recorrido; (*of doctor*) visitas *fpl*;
(*game: of cards, in competition*) partida; (*of
ammunition*) cartucho; (*BOXING*) asalto; (*of
talks*) ronda ♦ *vt* (*corner*) doblar ♦ *prep*
alrededor de; (*surrounding*): ~ **his neck/the
table** en su cuello/alrededor de la mesa; (*in a
circular movement*): **to move** ~ **the room/sail**
~ **the world** dar una vuelta a la habitación/
circunnavigar el mundo; (*in various
directions*): **to move** ~ **a room/house** moverse
por toda la habitación/casa; (*approximately*)
alrededor de ♦ *adv*: **all** ~ por todos lados; **the
long way** ~ por el camino menos directo; **all
the year** ~ durante todo el año; **it's just** ~ **the
corner** (*fig*) está a la vuelta de la esquina;
~ **the clock** *adv* las 24 horas; **to go** ~ **to sb's
(house)** ir a casa de uno; **to go** ~ **the back**
pasar por atrás; **enough to go** ~ bastante
(para todos); **a** ~ **of applause** una salva de
aplausos; **a** ~ **of drinks/sandwiches** una ronda
de bebidas/bocadillos; ~ **off** *vt* (*speech etc*)
acabar, poner término a; ~ **up** *vt* (*cattle*)
acorralar; (*people*) reunir; (*price*) redondear;
~**about** (*BRIT*) *n* (*AUT*) isleta; (*at fair*) tiovivo
♦ *adj* (*route, means*) indirecto; ~**ers** *n*
(*game*) juego similar al béisbol; ~**ly** *adv* (*fig*)
rotundamente; ~ **trip** *n* viaje *m* de ida y
vuelta; ~**up** *n* rodeo; (*of criminals*) redada;
(*of news*) resumen *m*
rouse [rauz] *vt* (*wake up*) despertar; (*stir up*)
suscitar; **rousing** *adj* (*cheer, welcome*)
caluroso
route [ru:t] *n* ruta, camino; (*of bus*) recorrido;
(*of shipping*) derrota
routine [ru:'ti:n] *adj* rutinario ♦ *n* rutina;
(*THEATRE*) número
rove [rəuv] *vt* vagar *or* errar por
row[1] [rəu] *n* (*line*) fila, hilera; (*KNITTING*)
pasada ♦ *vi* (*in boat*) remar ♦ *vt* conducir
remando; **4 days in a** ~ 4 días seguidos
row[2] [rau] *n* (*racket*) escándalo; (*dispute*)
bronca, pelea; (*scolding*) regaño ♦ *vi*
pelear(se)
rowboat ['rəubəut] (*US*) *n* bote *m* de remos

rowdy ['raudi] *adj* (*person: noisy*) ruidoso; (*occasion*) alborotado

rowing ['rəuɪŋ] *n* remo; **~ boat** (*BRIT*) *n* bote *m* de remos

royal ['rɔɪəl] *adj* real; **R~ Air Force** *n* Fuerzas *fpl* Aéreas Británicas; **~ty** *n* (*~ persons*) familia real; (*payment to author*) derechos *mpl* de autor

rpm *abbr* (= *revs per minute*) r.p.m.

R.S.V.P. *abbr* (= *répondez s'il vous plaît*) SRC

Rt. Hon. *abbr* (*BRIT*: = *Right Honourable*) título honorífico de diputado

rub [rʌb] *vt* frotar; (*scrub*) restregar ♦ *n*: **to give sth a ~** frotar algo; **to ~ sb up** *or* **~ sb** (*US*) **the wrong way** entrarle uno por mal ojo; **~ off** *vi* borrarse; **~ off on** *vt fus* influir en; **~ out** *vt* borrar

rubber ['rʌbə*] *n* caucho, goma; (*BRIT: eraser*) goma de borrar; **~ band** *n* goma, gomita; **~ plant** *n* ficus *m*

rubbish ['rʌbɪʃ] *n* basura; (*waste*) desperdicios *mpl*; (*fig: pej*) tonterías *fpl*; (*junk*) pacotilla; **~ bin** (*BRIT*) *n* cubo (*SP*) *or* bote *m* (*AM*) de la basura; **~ dump** *n* vertedero, basurero

rubble ['rʌbl] *n* escombros *mpl*

ruble ['ruːbl] (*US*) *n* = **rouble**

ruby ['ruːbɪ] *n* rubí *m*

rucksack ['rʌksæk] *n* mochila

rudder ['rʌdə*] *n* timón *m*

ruddy ['rʌdɪ] *adj* (*face*) rubicundo; (*inf: damned*) condenado

rude [ruːd] *adj* (*impolite: person*) mal educado; (*: word, manners*) grosero; (*crude*) crudo; (*indecent*) indecente; **~ness** *n* descortesía

ruffle ['rʌfl] *vt* (*hair*) despeinar; (*clothes*) arrugar; **to get ~d** (*fig: person*) alterarse

rug [rʌg] *n* alfombra; (*BRIT: blanket*) manta

rugby ['rʌgbɪ] *n* (*also:* ~ **football**) rugby *m*

rugged ['rʌgɪd] *adj* (*landscape*) accidentado; (*features*) robusto

ruin ['ruːɪn] *n* ruina ♦ *vt* arruinar; (*spoil*) estropear; **~s** *npl* ruinas *fpl*, restos *mpl*

rule [ruːl] *n* (*norm*) norma, costumbre *f*; (*regulation, ruler*) regla; (*government*) dominio ♦ *vt* (*country, person*) gobernar ♦ *vi* gobernar; (*LAW*) fallar; **as a ~** por regla general; **~ out** *vt* excluir; **~d** *adj* (*paper*) rayado; **~r** *n* (*sovereign*) soberano; (*for measuring*) regla; **ruling** *adj* (*party*) gobernante; (*class*) dirigente ♦ *n* (*LAW*) fallo, decisión *f*

rum [rʌm] *n* ron *m*

Rumania [ruːˈmeɪnɪə] *n* Rumanía; **~n** *adj* rumano/a ♦ *n* rumano/a *m/f*; (*LING*) rumano

rumble ['rʌmbl] *n* (*noise*) ruido sordo ♦ *vi* retumbar, hacer un ruido sordo; (*stomach, pipe*) sonar

rummage ['rʌmɪdʒ] *vi* (*search*) hurgar

rumour ['ruːmə*] (*US* **rumor**) *n* rumor *m* ♦ *vt*: **it is ~ed that ...** se rumorea que ...

rump [rʌmp] *n* (*of animal*) ancas *fpl*, grupa; **~ steak** *n* filete *m* de lomo

rumpus ['rʌmpəs] *n* lío, jaleo

run [rʌn] (*pt* **ran**, *pp* **run**) *n* (*fast pace*): **at a ~** corriendo, (*SPORT, in tights*) carrera, (*outing*) paseo, excursión *f*; (*distance travelled*) trayecto; (*series*) serie *f*; (*THEATRE*) temporada; (*SKI*) pista ♦ *vt* correr; (*operate: business*) dirigir; (*: competition, course*) organizar; (*: hotel, house*) administrar, llevar; (*COMPUT*) ejecutar; (*pass: hand*) pasar; (*PRESS: feature*) publicar ♦ *vi* correr; (*work: machine*) funcionar, marchar; (*bus, train: operate*) circular, ir; (*: travel*) ir; (*continue: play*) seguir; (*: contract*) ser válido; (*flow: river*) fluir; (*colours, washing*) desteñirse; (*in election*) ser candidato; **there was a ~ on** (*meat, tickets*) hubo mucha demanda de; **in the long ~** a la larga; **on the ~** en fuga; **I'll ~ you to the station** te llevaré a la estación (en coche); **to ~ a risk** correr un riesgo; **to ~ a bath** llenar la bañera; **~ about** *or* **around** *vi* (*children*) correr por todos lados; **~ across** *vt fus* (*find*) dar or topar con; **~ away** *vi* huir; **~ down** *vt* (*production*) ir reduciendo; (*factory*) ir restringiendo la producción en; (*subj: car*) atropellar; (*criticize*) criticar; **to be ~ down** (*person: tired*) estar debilitado; **~ in** (*BRIT*) *vt* (*car*) rodar; **~ into** *vt fus* (*meet: person, trouble*) tropezar con; (*collide with*) chocar con; **~ off** *vt* (*water*) dejar correr; (*copies*) sacar ♦ *vi* huir corriendo; **~ out** *vi* (*person*) salir corriendo; (*liquid*) irse; (*lease*) caducar, vencer; (*money etc*) acabarse; **~ out of** *vt fus* quedar sin; **~ over** *vt* (*AUT*) atropellar ♦ *vt fus* (*revise*) repasar; **~ through** *vt fus* (*instructions*) repasar; **~ up** *vt* (*debt*) contraer; **to ~ up against** (*difficulties*) tropezar con; **~away** *adj* (*horse*) desbocado; (*truck*) sin frenos; (*child*) escapado de casa

rung [rʌŋ] *pp of* **ring** ♦ *n* (*of ladder*) escalón *m*, peldaño

runner ['rʌnə*] *n* (*in race: person*) corredor(a) *m/f*; (*: horse*) caballo; (*on sledge*) patín *m*; **~ bean** (*BRIT*) *n* ≈ judía verde; **~-up** *n* subcampeón/ona *m/f*

running ['rʌnɪŋ] *n* (*sport*) atletismo; (*business*) administración *f* ♦ *adj* (*water, costs*) corriente; (*commentary*) continuo; **to be in/out of the ~ for sth** tener/no tener posibilidades de ganar algo; **6 days ~** 6 días seguidos; **~ commentary** *n* (*TV, RADIO*) comentario en directo; (*on guided tour etc*) comentario detallado; **~ costs** *npl* gastos *mpl* corrientes

runny ['rʌnɪ] adj fluido; (nose, eyes) gastante

run-of-the-mill adj común y corriente

runt [rʌnt] n (also pej) redrojo, enano

run-up n: ~ **to** (election etc) período previo a

runway ['rʌnweɪ] n (AVIAT) pista de aterrizaje

rural ['ruərl] adj rural

rush [rʌʃ] n ímpetu m; (hurry) prisa; (COMM) demanda repentina; (current) corriente f fuerte; (of feeling) torrente; (BOT) junco ♦ vt apresurar; (work) hacer de prisa ♦ vi correr, precipitarse; **~ hour** n horas fpl punta

rusk [rʌsk] n bizcocho tostado

Russia ['rʌʃə] n Rusia; **~n** adj ruso/a ♦ n ruso/a m/f; (LING) ruso

rust [rʌst] n herrumbre f, moho ♦ vi oxidarse

rustic ['rʌstɪk] adj rústico

rustle ['rʌsl] vi susurrar ♦ vt (paper) hacer crujir

rustproof ['rʌstpruːf] adj inoxidable

rusty ['rʌstɪ] adj oxidado

rut [rʌt] n surco; (ZOOL) celo; **to be in a ~** ser esclavo de la rutina

ruthless ['ruːθlɪs] adj despiadado

rye [raɪ] n centeno

S, s

Sabbath ['sæbəθ] n domingo; (Jewish) sábado

sabotage ['sæbətɑːʒ] n sabotaje m ♦ vt sabotear

saccharin(e) ['sækərɪn] n sacarina

sachet ['sæʃeɪ] n sobrecito

sack [sæk] n (bag) saco, costal m ♦ vt (dismiss) despedir; (plunder) saquear; **to get the ~** ser despedido; **~ing** n despido; (material) arpillera

sacred ['seɪkrɪd] adj sagrado, santo

sacrifice ['sækrɪfaɪs] n sacrificio ♦ vt sacrificar

sad [sæd] adj (unhappy) triste; (deplorable) lamentable

saddle ['sædl] n silla (de montar); (of cycle) sillín m ♦ vt (horse) ensillar; **to be ~d with sth** (inf) quedar cargado con algo; **~bag** n alforja

sadistic [sə'dɪstɪk] adj sádico

sadly ['sædlɪ] adv lamentablemente; **to be ~ lacking in** estar por desgracia carente de

sadness ['sædnɪs] n tristeza

s.a.e. abbr (= stamped addressed envelope) sobre con las propias señas de uno y con sello

safari [sə'fɑːrɪ] n safari m

safe [seɪf] adj (out of danger) fuera de peligro; (not dangerous, sure) seguro; (unharmed) ileso ♦ n caja de caudales, caja fuerte; **~ and sound** sano y salvo; **(just) to be on the ~ side** para mayor seguridad; **~-conduct** n salvoconducto; **~-deposit** n (vault) cámara

acorazada; (box) caja de seguridad; **~guard** n protección f, garantía ♦ vt proteger, defender; **~keeping** n custodia; **~ly** adv seguramente, con seguridad; **to arrive ~ly** llegar bien; **~ sex** n sexo seguro or sin riesgo

safety ['seɪftɪ] n seguridad f; **~ belt** n cinturón m (de seguridad); **~ pin** n imperdible m (SP), seguro (AM); **~ valve** n válvula de seguridad

saffron ['sæfrən] n azafrán m

sag [sæg] vi aflojarse

sage [seɪdʒ] n (herb) salvia; (man) sabio

Sagittarius [sædʒɪ'tɛərɪəs] n Sagitario

Sahara [sə'hɑːrə] n: **the ~ (Desert)** el (desierto del) Sáhara

said [sed] pt, pp of **say**

sail [seɪl] n (on boat) vela; (trip): **to go for a ~** dar un paseo en barco ♦ vt (boat) gobernar ♦ vi (travel: ship) navegar; (SPORT) hacer vela; (begin voyage) salir; **they ~ed into Copenhagen** arribaron a Copenhague; **~ through** vt fus (exam) aprobar sin ningún problema; **~boat** (US) n velero, barco de vela; **~ing** n (SPORT) vela; **to go ~ing** hacer vela; **~ing boat** n barco de vela; **~ing ship** n velero; **~or** n marinero, marino

saint [seɪnt] n santo; **~ly** adj santo

sake [seɪk] n: **for the ~ of** por

salad ['sæləd] n ensalada; **~ bowl** n ensaladera; **~ cream** (BRIT) n (especie f de) mayonesa; **~ dressing** n aliño

salary ['sælərɪ] n sueldo

sale [seɪl] n venta; (at reduced prices) liquidación f, saldo; (auction) subasta; **~s** npl (total amount sold) ventas fpl, facturación f; **"for ~"** "se vende"; **on ~** en venta; **on ~ or return** (goods) venta por reposición; **~room** n sala de subastas; **~s assistant** (US **~s clerk**) n dependiente/a m/f; **salesman/woman** (irreg) n (in shop) dependiente/a m/f; (representative) viajante m/f

salmon ['sæmən] n inv salmón m

salon ['sælɔn] n (hairdressing ~) peluquería; (beauty ~) salón m de belleza

saloon [sə'luːn] n (US) bar m, taberna; (BRIT: AUT) (coche m de) turismo; (ship's lounge) cámara, salón m

salt [sɔːlt] n sal f ♦ vt salar; (put ~ on) poner sal en; **~ cellar** n salero; **~water** adj de agua salada; **~y** adj salado

salute [sə'luːt] n saludo; (of guns) salva ♦ vt saludar

salvage ['sælvɪdʒ] n (saving) salvamento, recuperación f; (things saved) objetos mpl salvados ♦ vt salvar

salvation [sæl'veɪʃən] n salvación f; **S~ Army** n Ejército de Salvación

same [seɪm] adj mismo ♦ pron: **the ~** el/la mismo/a, los/las mismos/as; **the ~ book as** el mismo libro que; **at the ~ time** (*at the ~ moment*) al mismo tiempo; (*yet*) sin embargo; **all** *or* **just the ~** sin embargo, aun así; **to do the ~ (as sb)** hacer lo mismo (que uno); **the ~ to you!** ¡igualmente!

sample ['sɑ:mpl] *n* muestra ♦ *vt* (*food*) probar; (*wine*) catar

sanction ['sæŋkʃən] *n* aprobación *f* ♦ *vt* sancionar; aprobar; **~s** *npl* (*POL*) sanciones *fpl*

sanctity ['sæŋktɪtɪ] *n* santidad *f*; (*inviolability*) inviolabilidad *f*

sanctuary ['sæŋktjuərɪ] *n* santuario *f*; (*refuge*) asilo, refugio; (*for wildlife*) reserva

sand [sænd] *n* arena; (*beach*) playa ♦ *vt* (*also: ~ down*) lijar

sandal ['sændl] *n* sandalia

sand: ~box (*US*) *n* = **~pit**; **~castle** *n* castillo de arena; **~ dune** *n* duna; **~paper** *n* papel *m* de lija; **~pit** *n* (*for children*) cajón *m* de arena; **~stone** *n* piedra arenisca

sandwich ['sændwɪtʃ] *n* bocadillo (*SP*), sandwich *m*, emparedado (*AM*) ♦ *vt* intercalar; **~ed between** apretujado entre; **cheese/ham ~** sandwich de queso/jamón; **~ course** (*BRIT*) *n* curso de medio tiempo

sandy ['sændɪ] *adj* arenoso; (*colour*) rojizo

sane [seɪn] *adj* cuerdo; (*sensible*) sensato

sang [sæŋ] *pt of* **sing**

sanitary ['sænɪtərɪ] *adj* sanitario; (*clean*) higiénico; **~ towel** (*US* **~ napkin**) *n* paño higiénico, compresa

sanitation [sænɪ'teɪʃən] *n* (*in house*) servicios *mpl* higiénicos; (*in town*) servicio de desinfección; **~ department** (*US*) *n* departamento de limpieza y recogida de basuras

sanity ['sænɪtɪ] *n* cordura; (*of judgment*) sensatez *f*

sank [sæŋk] *pt of* **sink**

Santa Claus [sæntə'klɔ:z] *n* San Nicolás, Papá Noel

sap [sæp] *n* (*of plants*) savia ♦ *vt* (*strength*) minar, agotar

sapling ['sæplɪŋ] *n* árbol nuevo *or* joven

sapphire ['sæfaɪə*] *n* zafiro

sarcasm ['sɑ:kæzm] *n* sarcasmo

sardine [sɑ:'di:n] *n* sardina

Sardinia [sɑ:'dɪnɪə] *n* Cerdeña

sash [sæʃ] *n* faja

sat [sæt] *pt, pp of* **sit**

Satan ['seɪtn] *n* Satanás *m*

satchel ['sætʃl] *n* (*child's*) cartera (*SP*), mochila (*AM*)

satellite ['sætəlaɪt] *n* satélite *m*; **~ dish** *n* antena de televisión por satélite; **~ television** *n* televisión *f* vía satélite

satin ['sætɪn] *n* raso ♦ *adj* de raso

satire ['sætaɪə*] *n* sátira

satisfaction [sætɪs'fækʃən] *n* satisfacción *f*

satisfactory [sætɪs'fæktərɪ] *adj* satisfactorio

satisfy ['sætɪsfaɪ] *vt* satisfacer; (*convince*) convencer; **~ing** *adj* satisfactorio

Saturday ['sætədɪ] *n* sábado

sauce [sɔ:s] *n* salsa; (*sweet*) crema; jarabe *m*; **~pan** *n* cacerola, olla

saucer ['sɔ:sə*] *n* platillo

Saudi ['saudɪ]: **~ Arabia** *n* Arabia Saudí *or* Saudita; **~ (Arabian)** *adj*, *n* saudí *m/f*, saudita *m/f*

sauna ['sɔ:nə] *n* sauna

saunter ['sɔ:ntə*] *vi*: **to ~ in/out** entrar/salir sin prisa

sausage ['sɔsɪdʒ] *n* salchicha; **~ roll** *n* empanadita de salchicha

sauté ['səuteɪ] *adj* salteado

savage ['sævɪdʒ] *adj* (*cruel, fierce*) feroz, furioso; (*primitive*) salvaje ♦ *n* salvaje *m/f* ♦ *vt* (*attack*) embestir

save [seɪv] *vt* (*rescue*) salvar, rescatar; (*money, time*) ahorrar; (*put by, keep: seat*) guardar; (*COMPUT*) salvar (*y* guardar); (*avoid: trouble*) evitar; (*SPORT*) parar ♦ *vi* (*also: ~ up*) ahorrar ♦ *n* (*SPORT*) parada ♦ *prep* salvo, excepto

saving ['seɪvɪŋ] *n* (*on price etc*) economía ♦ *adj*: **the ~ grace of** el único mérito de; **~s** *npl* ahorros *mpl*; **~s account** *n* cuenta de ahorros; **~s bank** *n* caja de ahorros

saviour ['seɪvjə*] (*US* **savior**) *n* salvador(a) *m/f*

savour ['seɪvə*] (*US* **savor**) *vt* saborear; **~y** *adj* sabroso; (*dish: not sweet*) salado

saw [sɔ:] (*pt* **sawed**, *pp* **sawed** *or* **sawn**) *pt of* **see** ♦ *n* (*tool*) sierra ♦ *vt* serrar; **~dust** *n* (a)serrín *m*; **~mill** *n* aserradero; **~n-off shotgun** *n* escopeta de cañones recortados

saxophone ['sæksəfəun] *n* saxófono

say [seɪ] (*pt, pp* **said**) *n*: **to have one's ~** expresar su opinión ♦ *vt* decir; **to have a** *or* **some ~ in sth** tener voz *or* tener que ver en algo; **to ~ yes/no** decir que sí/no; **could you ~ that again?** ¿podría repetir eso?; **that is to ~** es decir; **that goes without ~ing** ni que decir tiene; **~ing** *n* dicho, refrán *m*

scab [skæb] *n* costra; (*pej*) esquirol *m*

scaffold ['skæfəuld] *n* cadalso; **~ing** *npl* andamio, andamiaje *m*

scald [skɔ:ld] *n* escaldadura ♦ *vt* escaldar

scale [skeɪl] *n* (*gen, MUS*) escala; (*of fish*) escama; (*of salaries, fees etc*) escalafón *m* ♦ *vt* (*mountain*) escalar; (*tree*) trepar; **~s** *npl* (*for weighing: small*) balanza; (*: large*) báscula; **on a large ~** en gran escala; **~ of charges** tarifa, lista de precios; **~ down** *vt* reducir a escala

scallop ['skɔləp] *n* (*ZOOL*) venera; (*SEWING*) festón *m*

scalp [skælp] *n* cabellera ♦ *vt* escalpar

scampi ['skæmpɪ] *npl* gambas *fpl*

scan [skæn] *vt* (*examine*) escudriñar; (*glance*

at quickly) dar un vistazo a; (TV, RADAR)
explorar, registrar ♦ n (MED): **to have a ~**
pasar por el escáner

scandal ['skændl] n escándalo; (gossip)
chismes mpl

Scandinavia [skændɪ'neɪvɪə] n Escandinavia;
~n adj, n escandinavo/a m/f

scant [skænt] adj escaso; **~y** adj (meal)
insuficiente; (clothes) ligero

scapegoat ['skeɪpgəʊt] n cabeza de turco,
chivo expiatorio

scar [skɑ:] n cicatriz f; (fig) señal f ♦ vt dejar
señales en

scarce [skɛəs] adj escaso; **to make o.s. ~** (inf)
esfumarse; **~ly** adv apenas; **scarcity** n
escasez f

scare [skɛə*] n susto, sobresalto; (panic)
pánico ♦ vt asustar, espantar; **to ~ sb stiff** dar
a uno un susto de muerte; **bomb ~** amenaza
de bomba; **~ off** or **away** vt ahuyentar;
~crow n espantapájaros m inv; **~d** adj: **to be**
~d estar asustado

scarf [skɑ:f] (pl **~s** or **scarves**) n (long)
bufanda; (square) pañuelo

scarlet ['skɑ:lɪt] adj escarlata; **~ fever** n
escarlatina

scarves [skɑ:vz] npl of **scarf**

scary ['skɛərɪ] (inf) adj espeluznante

scathing ['skeɪðɪŋ] adj mordaz

scatter ['skætə*] vt (spread) esparcir,
desparramar; (put to flight) dispersar ♦ vi
desparramarse; dispersarse; **~brained** adj
ligero de cascos

scavenger ['skævəndʒə*] n (person)
basurero/a

scenario [sɪ'nɑ:rɪəʊ] n (THEATRE) argumento;
(CINEMA) guión m, (fig) escenario

scene [si:n] n (THEATRE, fig etc) escena; (of
crime etc) escenario; (view) panorama m;
(fuss) escándalo; **~ry** n (THEATRE) decorado;
(landscape) paisaje m; **scenic** adj pintoresco

scent [sɛnt] n perfume m, olor m; (fig: track)
rastro, pista

sceptic ['skɛptɪk] (US **skeptic**) n escéptico/a;
~al adj escéptico

sceptre ['sɛptə*] (US **scepter**) n cetro

schedule ['ʃɛdju:l, (US) 'skɛdju:l] n
(timetable) horario; (of events) programa m;
(list) lista ♦ vt (visit) fijar la hora de; **to arrive**
on ~ llegar a la hora debida; **to be ahead of/**
behind ~ estar adelantado/en retraso; **~d**
flight n vuelo regular

scheme [ski:m] n (plan) plan m, proyecto;
(plot) intriga; (arrangement) disposición f;
(pension ~ etc) sistema m ♦ vi (intrigue)
intrigar; **scheming** adj intrigante ♦ n intrigas
fpl

schizophrenic [skɪtsə'frɛnɪk] adj
esquizofrénico

scholar ['skɒlə*] n (pupil) alumno/a; (learned
person) sabio/a, erudito/a; **~ship** n erudición
f; (grant) beca

school [sku:l] n escuela, colegio; (in university) facultad f ♦ cpd escolar; **~ age** n
edad f escolar; **~book** n libro de texto; **~boy**
n alumno; **~ children** npl alumnos mpl;
~girl n alumna; **~ing** n enseñanza;
~master/mistress n (primary) maestro/a;
(secondary) profesor(a) m/f; **~teacher** n
(primary) maestro/a; (secondary) profesor(a)
m/f

schooner ['sku:nə*] n (ship) goleta

sciatica [saɪ'ætɪkə] n ciática

science ['saɪəns] n ciencia; **~ fiction** n
ciencia-ficción f; **scientific** [-'tɪfɪk] adj
científico; **scientist** n científico/a

scissors ['sɪzəz] npl tijeras fpl; **a pair of ~** unas
tijeras

scoff [skɒf] vt (BRIT: inf: eat) engullir ♦ vi: **to**
~ (at) (mock) mofarse (de)

scold [skəʊld] vt regañar

scone [skɒn] n pastel de pan

scoop [sku:p] n (for flour etc) pala; (PRESS)
exclusiva; **~ out** vt excavar; **~ up** vt recoger

scooter ['sku:tə*] n moto f; (toy) patinete m

scope [skəʊp] n (of plan) ámbito; (of person)
competencia; (opportunity) libertad f (de
acción)

scorch [skɔ:tʃ] vt (clothes) chamuscar; (earth,
grass) quemar, secar

score [skɔ:*] n (points etc) puntuación f;
(MUS) partitura; (twenty) veintena ♦ vt (goal,
point) ganar; (mark) rayar; (achieve: success)
conseguir ♦ vi marcar un tanto; (FOOTBALL)
marcar (un) gol; (keep score) llevar el tanteo;
~s of (very many) decenas de; **on that ~** en lo
que se refiere a eso; **to ~ 6 out of 10** obtener
una puntuación de 6 sobre 10; **~ out** vt
tachar; **~ over** vt fus obtener una victoria
sobre; **~board** n marcador m

scorn [skɔ:n] n desprecio; **~ful** adj
desdeñoso, despreciativo

Scorpio ['skɔ:pɪəʊ] n Escorpión m

scorpion ['skɔ:pɪən] n alacrán m

Scot [skɒt] n escocés/esa m/f

Scotch [skɒtʃ] n whisky m escocés

Scotland ['skɒtlənd] n Escocia

Scots [skɒts] adj escocés/esa; **~man/woman**
(irreg) n escocés/esa m/f; **Scottish** ['skɒtɪʃ]
adj escocés/esa; **Scottish Parliament** n
Parlamento escocés

scoundrel ['skaʊndrəl] n canalla m/f,
sinvergüenza m/f

scout [skaʊt] n (MIL, also: boy ~) explorador
m; **girl ~** (US) niña exploradora; **~ around** vi
reconocer el terreno

scowl [skaʊl] vi fruncir el ceño; **to ~ at sb**
mirar con ceño a uno

scrabble ['skræbl] vi (claw): **to ~ (at)** arañar; (also: **to ~ around**: search) revolver todo buscando ♦ n: **S~** ® Scrabble ® m

scraggy ['skrægɪ] adj descarnado

scram [skræm] (inf) vi largarse

scramble ['skræmbl] n (climb) subida (difícil); (struggle) pelea ♦ vi: **to ~ through/out** abrirse paso/salir con dificultad; **to ~ for** pelear por; **~d eggs** npl huevos mpl revueltos

scrap [skræp] n (bit) pedacito; (fig) pizca; (fight) riña, bronca; (also: **~ iron**) chatarra, hierro viejo ♦ vt (discard) desechar, descartar ♦ vi reñir, armar (una) bronca; **~s** npl (waste) sobras fpl, desperdicios mpl; **~book** n álbum m de recortes; **~ dealer** n chatarrero/a

scrape [skreɪp] n: **to get into a ~** meterse en un lío ♦ vt raspar; (skin etc) rasguñar; (~ against) rozar ♦ vi: **to ~ through** (exam) aprobar por los pelos; **~ together** vt (money) arañar, juntar

scrap: ~ heap n (fig): **to be on the ~ heap** estar acabado; **~ merchant** (BRIT) n chatarrero/a; **~ paper** n pedazos mpl de papel

scratch [skrætʃ] n rasguño; (from claw) arañazo ♦ cpd: **~ team** equipo improvisado ♦ vt (paint, car) rayar; (with claw, nail) rasguñar, arañar; (rub: nose etc) rascarse ♦ vi rascarse; **to start from ~** partir de cero; **to be up to ~** cumplir con los requisitos

scrawl [skrɔːl] n garabatos mpl ♦ vi hacer garabatos

scrawny ['skrɔːnɪ] adj flaco

scream [skriːm] n chillido ♦ vi chillar

screech [skriːtʃ] vi chirriar

screen [skriːn] n (CINEMA, TV) pantalla; (movable barrier) biombo ♦ vt (conceal) tapar; (from the wind etc) proteger; (film) proyectar; (candidates etc) investigar a; **~ing** n (MED) investigación f médica; **~play** n guión m

screw [skruː] n tornillo ♦ vt (also: **~ in**) atornillar; **~ up** vt (paper etc) arrugar; **to ~ up one's eyes** arrugar el entrecejo; **~driver** n destornillador m

scribble ['skrɪbl] n garabatos mpl ♦ vt, vi garabatear

script [skrɪpt] n (CINEMA etc) guión m; (writing) escritura, letra

Scripture(s) ['skrɪptʃə*(z)] n(pl) Sagrada Escritura

scroll [skrəʊl] n rollo

scrounge [skraʊndʒ] (inf) vt: **to ~ sth off or from sb** obtener algo de uno de gorra ♦ n: **on the ~** de gorra; **~r** n gorrón/ona m/f

scrub [skrʌb] n (land) maleza ♦ vt fregar, restregar; (inf: reject) cancelar, anular

scruff [skrʌf] n: **by the ~ of the neck** por el pescuezo

scruffy ['skrʌfɪ] adj desaliñado, piojoso

scrum(mage) ['skrʌm(mɪdʒ)] n (RUGBY) melée f

scruple ['skruːpl] n (gen pl) escrúpulo

scrutinize ['skruːtɪnaɪz] vt escudriñar; (votes) escrutar; **scrutiny** ['skruːtɪnɪ] n escrutinio, examen m

scuff [skʌf] vt (shoes, floor) rayar

scuffle ['skʌfl] n refriega

sculptor ['skʌlptə*] n escultor(a) m/f

sculpture ['skʌlptʃə*] n escultura

scum [skʌm] n (on liquid) espuma; (pej: people) escoria

scurry ['skʌrɪ] vi correr; **to ~ off** escabullirse

scuttle ['skʌtl] n (also: **coal ~**) cubo, carbonera ♦ vt (ship) barrenar ♦ vi (scamper): **to ~ away**, **~ off** escabullirse

scythe [saɪð] n guadaña

SDP (BRIT) n abbr = **Social Democratic Party**

sea [siː] n mar m ♦ cpd de mar, marítimo; **by ~** (travel) en barco; **on the ~** (boat) en el mar; (town) junto al mar; **to be all at ~** (fig) estar despistado; **out to ~**, **at ~** en alta mar; **~board** n litoral m; **~food** n mariscos mpl; **~ front** n paseo marítimo; **~-going** adj de altura; **~gull** n gaviota

seal [siːl] n (animal) foca; (stamp) sello ♦ vt (close) cerrar; **~ off** vt (area) acordonar

sea level n nivel m del mar

sea lion n león m marino

seam [siːm] n (of material) costura; (of metal) juntura; (of coal) veta, filón m

seaman ['siːmən] (irreg) n marinero

seance ['seɪɒns] n sesión f de espiritismo

seaplane ['siːpleɪn] n hidroavión m

seaport ['siːpɔːt] n puerto de mar

search [sɜːtʃ] n (for person, thing) busca, búsqueda; (COMPUT) búsqueda; (inspection: of sb's home) registro ♦ vt (look in) buscar en; (examine) examinar; (person, place) registrar ♦ vi: **to ~ for** buscar; **in ~ of** en busca de; **~ through** vt fus registrar; **~ing** adj penetrante; **~light** n reflector m; **~ party** n pelotón m de salvamento; **~ warrant** n mandamiento (judicial)

sea: ~shore n playa, orilla del mar; **~sick** adj mareado; **~side** n playa, orilla del mar; **~side resort** n centro turístico costero

season ['siːzn] n (of year) estación f; (sporting etc) temporada; (of films etc) ciclo ♦ vt (food) sazonar; **in/out of ~** en sazón/fuera de temporada; **~al** adj estacional; **~ed** adj (fig) experimentado; **~ing** n condimento, aderezo; **~ ticket** n abono

seat [siːt] n (in bus, train) asiento; (chair) silla; (PARLIAMENT) escaño n; (buttocks) culo, trasero; (of trousers) culera ♦ vt sentar; (have room for) tener cabida para; **to be ~ed** sentarse; **~ belt** n cinturón m de seguridad

sea: ~ **water** n agua del mar; ~**weed** n alga marina; ~**worthy** adj en condiciones de navegar

sec. abbr = **second(s)**

secluded [sɪ'klu:dɪd] adj retirado

seclusion [sɪ'klu:ʒən] n reclusión f

second ['sekənd] adj segundo ♦ adv en segundo lugar ♦ n segundo; (AUT: also: ~ gear) segunda; (COMM) artículo con algún desperfecto; (BRIT: SCOL: degree) título de licenciado con calificación de notable ♦ vt (motion) apoyar; ~**ary** adj secundario; ~**ary school** n escuela secundaria; ~-**class** adj de segunda clase ♦ adv (RAIL) en segunda; ~**hand** adj de segunda mano, usado; ~ **hand** n (on clock) segundero; ~**ly** adv en segundo lugar; ~**ment** [sɪ'kɔndmənt] (BRIT) n traslado temporal; ~-**rate** adj de segunda categoría; ~ **thoughts** npl: **to have** ~ **thoughts** cambiar de opinión; **on** ~ **thoughts** or **thought** (US) pensándolo bien

secrecy ['si:krəsɪ] n secreto

secret ['si:krɪt] adj, n secreto; **in** ~ en secreto

secretarial [sekrɪ'teərɪəl] adj de secretario; (course, staff) de secretariado

secretary ['sekrətərɪ] n secretario/a; **S~ of State (for)** (BRIT: POL) Ministro (de)

secretive ['si:krətɪv] adj reservado, sigiloso

secretly ['si:krɪtlɪ] adv en secreto

sect [sekt] n secta; ~**arian** [-'teərɪən] adj sectario

section ['sekʃən] n sección f; (part) parte f; (of document) artículo; (of opinion) sector m; (cross-~) corte m transversal

sector ['sektə*] n sector m

secular ['sekjulə*] adj secular, seglar

secure [sɪ'kjuə*] adj seguro; (firmly fixed) firme, fijo ♦ vt (fix) asegurar, afianzar; (get) conseguir

security [sɪ'kjuərɪtɪ] n seguridad f; (for loan) fianza; (: object) prenda

sedate [sɪ'deɪt] adj tranquilo ♦ vt tratar con sedantes

sedation [sɪ'deɪʃən] n (MED) sedación f

sedative ['sedɪtɪv] n sedante m, sedativo

seduce [sɪ'dju:s] vt seducir; **seduction** [-'dʌkʃən] n seducción f; **seductive** [-'dʌktɪv] adj seductor(a)

see [si:] (pt **saw**, pp **seen**) vt ver; (accompany): **to** ~ **sb to the door** acompañar a uno a la puerta; (understand) ver, comprender ♦ vi ver ♦ n (arz)obispado; **to** ~ **that** (ensure) asegurar que; ~ **you soon!** ¡hasta pronto!; ~ **about** vt fus atender a, encargarse de; ~ **off** vt despedir; ~ **through** vt fus (fig) calar ♦ vt (plan) llevar a cabo; ~ **to** vt fus atender a, encargarse de

seed [si:d] n semilla; (in fruit) pepita; (fig: gen pl) germen m; (TENNIS etc) preseleccionado/

a; **to go to** ~ (plant) granar; (fig) descuidarse; ~**ling** n planta de semillero; ~**y** adj (shabby) desaseado, raído

seeing ['si:ɪŋ] conj: ~ (**that**) visto que, en vista de que

seek [si:k] (pt, pp **sought**) vt buscar; (post) solicitar

seem [si:m] vi parecer; **there** ~**s to be ...** parece que hay ...; ~**ingly** adv aparentemente, según parece

seen [si:n] pp of **see**

seep [si:p] vi filtrarse

seesaw ['si:sɔ:] n subibaja

seethe [si:ð] vi hervir; **to** ~ **with anger** estar furioso

see-through adj transparente

segment ['segmənt] n (part) sección f; (of orange) gajo

segregate ['segrɪgeɪt] vt segregar

seize [si:z] vt (grasp) agarrar, asir; (take possession of) secuestrar; (: territory) apoderarse de; (opportunity) aprovecharse de; ~ (**up)on** vt fus aprovechar; ~ **up** vi (TECH) agarrotarse

seizure ['si:ʒə*] n (MED) ataque m; (LAW, of power) incautación f

seldom ['seldəm] adv rara vez

select [sɪ'lekt] adj selecto, escogido ♦ vt escoger, elegir; (SPORT) seleccionar; ~**ion** [-'lekʃən] n selección f, elección f; (COMM) surtido

self [self] (pl **selves**) n uno mismo; **the** ~ el yo ♦ prefix auto...; ~-**assured** adj seguro de sí mismo; ~-**catering** (BRIT) adj (flat etc) con cocina; ~-**centred** (US ~-**centered**) adj egocéntrico; ~-**confidence** n confianza en sí mismo; ~-**conscious** adj cohibido; ~-**contained** (BRIT) adj (flat) con entrada particular; ~-**control** n autodominio; ~-**defence** (US ~-**defense**) n defensa propia; ~-**discipline** n autodisciplina; ~-**employed** adj que trabaja por cuenta propia; ~-**evident** adj patente; ~-**governing** adj autónomo; ~-**indulgent** adj autocomplaciente; ~-**interest** n egoísmo; ~**ish** adj egoísta; ~**ishness** n egoísmo; ~**less** adj desinteresado; ~-**made** adj: ~-**made man** hombre m que se ha hecho a sí mismo; ~-**pity** n lástima de sí mismo; ~-**portrait** n autorretrato; ~-**possessed** adj sereno, dueño de sí mismo; ~-**preservation** n propia conservación f; ~-**respect** n amor m propio; ~-**righteous** adj santurrón/ona; ~-**sacrifice** n abnegación f; ~-**satisfied** adj satisfecho de sí mismo; ~-**service** adj de autoservicio; ~-**sufficient** adj autosuficiente; ~-**taught** adj autodidacta

sell [sel] (pt, pp **sold**) vt vender ♦ vi venderse; **to** ~ **at** or **for £10** venderse a 10 libras; ~ **off** vt liquidar; ~ **out** vi: **to** ~ **out of tickets/milk**

vender todas las entradas/toda la leche; **~-by date** n fecha de caducidad; **~er** n vendedor(a) m/f; **~ing price** n precio de venta

Sellotape ® ['sɛləʊteɪp] (*BRIT*) n cinta adhesiva, celo (*SP*), scotch m (*AM*)

selves [sɛlvz] npl of **self**

semblance ['sɛmbləns] n apariencia

semen ['siːmən] n semen m

semester [sɪ'mɛstə*] (*US*) n semestre m

semi... [sɛmɪ] prefix semi..., medio...; **~circle** n semicírculo; **~colon** n punto y coma; **~conductor** n semiconductor m; **~detached (house)** n (casa) semiseparada; **~-final** n semi-final m

seminar ['sɛmɪnɑː*] n seminario

seminary ['sɛmɪnərɪ] n (*REL*) seminario

semiskilled ['sɛmɪskɪld] adj (*work, worker*) semi-cualificado

semi-skimmed (milk) n leche semidesnatada

senate ['sɛnɪt] n senado; **senator** n senador(a) m/f

send [sɛnd] (*pt, pp* **sent**) vt mandar, enviar; (*signal*) transmitir; **~ away** vt despachar; **~ away for** vt fus pedir; **~ back** vt devolver; **~ for** vt fus mandar traer; **~ off** vt (*goods*) despachar; (*BRIT: SPORT: player*) expulsar; **~ out** vt (*invitation*) mandar; (*signal*) emitir; **~ up** vt (*person, price*) hacer subir; (*BRIT: parody*) parodiar; **~er** n remitente m/f; **~-off** n: **a good ~-off** una buena despedida

senior ['siːnɪə*] adj (*older*) mayor, más viejo; (: *on staff*) de más antigüedad; (*of higher rank*) superior; **~ citizen** n persona de la tercera edad; **~ity** [-'ɔrɪtɪ] n antigüedad f

sensation [sɛn'seɪʃən] n sensación f; **~al** adj sensacional

sense [sɛns] n (*faculty, meaning*) sentido; (*feeling*) sensación f; (*good* ~) sentido común, juicio ♦ vt sentir, percibir; **it makes ~** tiene sentido; **~less** adj estúpido, insensato; (*unconscious*) sin conocimiento; **~ of humour** n sentido del humor

sensible ['sɛnsɪbl] adj sensato; (*reasonable*) razonable, lógico

sensitive ['sɛnsɪtɪv] adj sensible; (*touchy*) susceptible

sensual ['sɛnsjuəl] adj sensual

sensuous ['sɛnsjuəs] adj sensual

sent [sɛnt] pt, pp of **send**

sentence ['sɛntns] n (*LING*) oración f; (*LAW*) sentencia, fallo ♦ vt: **to ~ sb to death/to 5 years (in prison)** condenar a uno a muerte/a 5 años de cárcel

sentiment ['sɛntɪmənt] n sentimiento; (*opinion*) opinión f; **~al** [-'mɛntl] adj sentimental

sentry ['sɛntrɪ] n centinela m

separate [adj 'sɛprɪt, vb 'sɛpəreɪt] adj separado; (*distinct*) distinto ♦ vt separar; (*part*) dividir ♦ vi separarse; **~s** npl (*clothes*) coordinados mpl; **~ly** adv por separado; **separation** [-'reɪʃən] n separación f

September [sɛp'tɛmbə*] n se(p)tiembre m

septic ['sɛptɪk] adj séptico; **~ tank** n fosa séptica

sequel ['siːkwl] n consecuencia, resultado; (*of story*) continuación f

sequence ['siːkwəns] n sucesión f, serie f; (*CINEMA*) secuencia

sequin ['siːkwɪn] n lentejuela

serene [sɪ'riːn] adj sereno, tranquilo

sergeant ['sɑːdʒənt] n sargento

serial ['sɪərɪəl] n (*TV*) telenovela, serie f televisiva; (*BOOK*) serie f; **~ize** vt emitir como serial; **~ killer** n asesino/a múltiple; **~ number** n número de serie

series ['sɪəriːz] n inv serie f

serious ['sɪərɪəs] adj serio; (*grave*) grave; **~ly** adv en serio; (*ill, wounded etc*) gravemente

sermon ['sɑːmən] n sermón m

serrated [sɪ'reɪtɪd] adj serrado, dentellado

serum ['sɪərəm] n suero

servant ['sɑːvənt] n servidor(a) m/f; (*house* ~) criado/a

serve [sɑːv] vt servir; (*customer*) atender; (: *subj: train*) pasar por; (*apprenticeship*) hacer; (*prison term*) cumplir ♦ vi (*at table*) servir; (*TENNIS*) sacar; **to ~ as/for/to do** servir de/para/para hacer ♦ n (*TENNIS*) saque m; **it ~s him right** se lo tiene merecido; **~ out** vt (*food*) servir; **~ up** vt = **~ out**

service ['sɑːvɪs] n servicio; (*REL*) misa; (*AUT*) mantenimiento; (*dishes etc*) juego ♦ vt (*car etc*) revisar; (: *repair*) reparar; **the S~s** npl las fuerzas armadas; **to be of ~ to sb** ser útil a uno; **~ included/not included** servicio incluído/no incluído; **~able** adj servible, utilizable; **~ area** n (*on motorway*) area de servicio; **~ charge** (*BRIT*) n servicio; **~man** n militar m; **~ station** n estación f de servicio

serviette [sɑːvɪ'ɛt] (*BRIT*) n servilleta

session ['sɛʃən] n sesión f; **to be in ~** estar en sesión

set [sɛt] (*pt, pp* **set**) n juego; (*RADIO*) aparato; (*TV*) televisor m; (*of utensils*) batería; (*of cutlery*) cubierto; (*of books*) colección f; (*TENNIS*) set m; (*group of people*) grupo; (*CINEMA*) plató m; (*THEATRE*) decorado; (*HAIRDRESSING*) marcado ♦ adj (*fixed*) fijo; (*ready*) listo ♦ vt (*place*) poner, colocar; (*fix*) fijar; (*adjust*) ajustar, arreglar; (*decide: rules etc*) establecer, decidir ♦ vi (*sun*) ponerse; (*jam, jelly*) cuajarse; (*concrete*) fraguar; **to be ~ on doing sth** estar empeñado en hacer algo; **to ~ to music** poner música a; **to ~ on fire** incendiar, poner fuego a; **to ~ free** poner en libertad; **to ~ sth going** poner algo en marcha; **to ~ sail** zarpar, hacerse a la vela; **~ about** vt fus ponerse a; **~ aside** vt poner aparte, dejar de lado; (money, time) reservar; **~ back** vt (cost): **to ~ sb back £5** costar a uno cinco libras; (: in time): **to ~ back (by)** retrasar (por); **~ off** vi partir ♦ vt (bomb) hacer estallar; (events) poner en marcha; (show up well) hacer resaltar; **~ out** vi partir ♦ vt (arrange) disponer; (state) exponer; **to ~ out to do sth** proponerse hacer algo; **~ up** vt establecer; **~back** n revés m, contratiempo; **~ menu** n menú m

settee [se'ti:] n sofá m

setting ['setɪŋ] n (scenery) marco; (position) disposición f; (of sun) puesta; (of jewel) engaste m, montadura

settle ['setl] vt (argument) resolver; (accounts) ajustar, liquidar; (MED: calm) calmar, sosegar ♦ vi (dust etc) depositarse; (weather) serenarse; (also: ~ down) instalarse; tranquilizarse; **to ~ for sth** convenir en aceptar algo; **to ~ on sth** decidirse por algo; **~ in** vi instalarse; **~ up** vi: **to ~ up with sb** ajustar cuentas con uno; **~ment** n (payment) liquidación f; (agreement) acuerdo, convenio; (village etc) pueblo; **~r** n colono/a, colonizador(a) m/f

setup ['setʌp] n sistema m; (situation) situación f

seven ['sevn] num siete; **~teen** num diez y siete, diecisiete; **~th** num séptimo; **~ty** num setenta

sever ['sevə*] vt cortar; (relations) romper

several ['sevərl] adj, pron varios/as m/fpl, algunos/as m/fpl; **~ of us** varios de nosotros

severance ['sevərəns] n (of relations) ruptura; **~ pay** n indemnización f por despido

severe [sɪ'vɪə*] adj severo; (serious) grave; (hard) duro; (pain) intenso; **severity** [sɪ'verɪtɪ] n severidad f; gravedad f; intensidad f

sew [səu] (pt sewed, pp sewn) vt, vi coser; **~ up** vt coser, zurcir

sewage ['su:ɪdʒ] n aguas fpl residuales

sewer ['su:ə*] n alcantarilla, cloaca

sewing ['səuɪŋ] n costura; **~ machine** n máquina de coser

sewn [səun] pp of sew

sex [seks] n sexo; (lovemaking): **to have ~** hacer el amor; **~ist** adj, n sexista m/f; **~ual** ['seksjuəl] adj sexual; **~y** adj sexy

shabby ['ʃæbɪ] adj (person) desharrapado; (clothes) raído, gastado; (behaviour) ruin inv

shack [ʃæk] n choza, chabola

shackles ['ʃæklz] npl grillos mpl, grilletes mpl

shade [ʃeɪd] n sombra; (for lamp) pantalla; (for eyes) visera; (of colour) matiz m, tonalidad f; (small quantity): **a ~ (too big/more)** un poquitín (grande/más) ♦ vt dar sombra a; (eyes) proteger del sol; **in the ~** en la sombra

shadow ['ʃædəu] n sombra ♦ vt (follow) seguir y vigilar; **~ cabinet** (BRIT) n (POL) gabinete paralelo formado por el partido de oposición; **~y** adj sombreado; (dim) indistinto

shady ['ʃeɪdɪ] adj sombreado; (fig: dishonest) sospechoso; (: deal) turbio

shaft [ʃɑːft] n (of arrow, spear) astil m; (AUT, TECH) eje m, árbol m; (of mine) pozo; (of lift) hueco, caja; (of light) rayo

shaggy ['ʃægɪ] adj peludo

shake [ʃeɪk] (pt shook, pp shaken) vt sacudir; (building) hacer temblar; (bottle, cocktail) agitar ♦ vi (tremble) temblar; **to ~ one's head** (in refusal) negar con la cabeza; (in dismay) mover or menear la cabeza, incrédulo; **to ~ hands with sb** estrechar la mano a uno; **~ off** vt sacudirse; (fig) deshacerse de; **~ up** vt agitar; (fig) reorganizar; **shaky** adj (hand, voice) trémulo; (building) inestable

shall [ʃæl] aux vb: **~ I help you?** ¿quieres que te ayude?; **I'll buy three, ~ I?** compro tres, ¿no te parece?

shallow ['ʃæləu] adj poco profundo; (fig) superficial

sham [ʃæm] n fraude m, engaño ♦ vt fingir, simular

shambles ['ʃæmblz] n confusión f

shame [ʃeɪm] n vergüenza ♦ vt avergonzar; **it is a ~ that/to do** es una lástima que/hacer; **what a ~!** ¡qué lástima!; **~ful** adj vergonzoso; **~less** adj desvergonzado

shampoo [ʃæm'pu:] n champú m ♦ vt lavar con champú; **~ and set** n lavado y marcado

shamrock ['ʃæmrɔk] n trébol m (emblema nacional irlandés)

shandy ['ʃændɪ] n mezcla de cerveza con gaseosa

shan't [ʃɑ:nt] = shall not

shantytown ['ʃæntɪtaun] n barrio de chabolas

shape [ʃeɪp] n forma ♦ vt formar, dar forma a; (sb's ideas) formar; (sb's life) determinar; **to take ~** tomar forma; **~ up** vi (events) desarrollarse; (person) formarse; **~d** suffix: **heart-~d** en forma de corazón; **~less** adj informe, sin forma definida; **~ly** adj (body etc) esbelto

share [ʃeə*] n (part) parte f, porción f; (contribution) cuota; (COMM) acción f ♦ vt dividir; (have in common) compartir; **to ~ out** (among or between) repartir (entre); **~holder** (BRIT) n accionista m/f

shark [ʃɑːk] n tiburón m

sharp [ʃɑːp] adj (blade, nose) afilado; (point)

puntiagudo; (*outline*) definido; (*pain*) intenso; (*MUS*) desafinado; (*contrast*) marcado; (*voice*) agudo; (*person: quick-witted*) astuto; (: *dishonest*) poco escrupuloso ♦ n (*MUS*) sostenido ♦ adv: **at 2 o'clock ~ a** las 2 en punto; **~en** vt afilar; (*pencil*) sacar punta a; (*fig*) aqudizar; **~ener** n (*also: pencil ~ener*) sacapuntas m inv; **~-eyed** adj de vista aguda; **~ly** adv (*turn, stop*) bruscamente; (*stand out, contrast*) claramente; (*criticize, retort*) severamente

shatter ['ʃætə*] vt hacer añicos or pedazos; (*fig: ruin*) destruir, acabar con ♦ vi hacerse añicos

shave [ʃeɪv] vt afeitar, rasurar ♦ vi afeitarse, rasurarse ♦ n: **to have a ~** afeitarse; **~r** n (*also: electric ~r*) máquina de afeitar (eléctrica)

shaving ['ʃeɪvɪŋ] n (*action*) el afeitarse, rasurado; **~s** npl (*of wood etc*) virutas fpl; **~ brush** n brocha (de afeitar); **~ cream** n crema de afeitar; **~ foam** n espuma de afeitar

shawl [ʃɔːl] n chal m

she [ʃiː] pron ella; **~-cat** n gata

sheaf [ʃiːf] (pl **sheaves**) n (*of corn*) gavilla; (*of papers*) fajo

shear [ʃɪə*] (pt **sheared**, pp **sheared** or **shorn**) vt esquilar, trasquilar; **~s** npl (*for hedge*) tijeras fpl de jardín

sheath [ʃiːθ] n vaina; (*contraceptive*) preservativo

sheaves [ʃiːvz] npl of **sheaf**

shed [ʃed] (pt, pp **shed**) n cobertizo ♦ vt (*skin*) mudar; (*tears, blood*) derramar; (*load*) derramar; (*workers*) despedir

she'd [ʃiːd] = **she had; she would**

sheen [ʃiːn] n brillo, lustre m

sheep [ʃiːp] n inv oveja; **~dog** n perro pastor; **~skin** n piel f de carnero

sheer [ʃɪə*] adj (*utter*) puro, completo; (*steep*) escarpado; (*material*) diáfano ♦ adv verticalmente

sheet [ʃiːt] n (*on bed*) sábana; (*of paper*) hoja; (*of glass, metal*) lámina; (*of ice*) capa

sheik(h) [ʃeɪk] n jeque m

shelf [ʃelf] (pl **shelves**) n estante m

shell [ʃel] n (*on beach*) concha; (*of egg, nut etc*) cáscara; (*explosive*) proyectil m, obús m; (*of building*) armazón f ♦ vt (*peas*) desenvainar; (*MIL*) bombardear

she'll [ʃiːl] = **she will; she shall**

shellfish ['ʃelfɪʃ] n inv crustáceo; (*as food*) mariscos mpl

shell suit n chándal m de calle

shelter ['ʃeltə*] n abrigo, refugio ♦ vt (*aid*) amparar, proteger; (*give lodging to*) abrigar ♦ vi abrigarse, refugiarse; **~ed** adj (*life*) protegido; (*spot*) abrigado; **~ed housing** n

viviendas vigiladas para ancianos y minusválidos

shelve [ʃelv] vt (*fig*) aplazar; **~s** npl of **shelf**

shepherd ['ʃepəd] n pastor m ♦ vt (*guide*) guiar, conducir; **~'s pie** (*BRIT*) n pastel de carne y patatas

sherry ['ʃerɪ] n jerez m

she's [ʃiːz] = **she is; she has**

Shetland ['ʃetlənd] n (*also: the ~s, the ~ Isles*) las Islas de Zetlandia

shield [ʃiːld] n escudo; (*protection*) blindaje m ♦ vt: **to ~ (from)** proteger (de)

shift [ʃɪft] n (*change*) cambio; (*at work*) turno ♦ vt trasladar; (*remove*) quitar ♦ vi moverse; **~ work** n trabajo a turnos; **~y** adj tramposo; (*eyes*) furtivo

shimmer ['ʃɪmə*] n reflejo trémulo

shin [ʃɪn] n espinilla

shine [ʃaɪn] (pt, pp **shone**) n brillo, lustre m ♦ vi brillar, relucir ♦ vt (*shoes*) lustrar, sacar brillo a; **to ~ a torch on sth** dirigir una linterna hacia algo

shingle ['ʃɪŋgl] n (*on beach*) guijarros mpl; **~s** n (*MED*) herpes mpl or fpl

shiny ['ʃaɪnɪ] adj brillante, lustroso

ship [ʃɪp] n buque m, barco ♦ vt (*goods*) embarcar; (*send*) transportar or enviar por vía marítima; **~building** n construcción f de buques; **~ment** n (*goods*) envío; **~ping** n (*act*) embarque m; (*traffic*) buques mpl; **~wreck** n naufragio ♦ vt: **to be ~wrecked** naufragar; **~yard** n astillero

shire ['ʃaɪə*] (*BRIT*) n condado

shirt [ʃɜːt] n camisa; **in (one's) ~ sleeves** en mangas de camisa

shit [ʃɪt] (*inf!*) excl ¡mierda! (!)

shiver ['ʃɪvə*] n escalofrío ♦ vi temblar, estremecerse; (*with cold*) tiritar

shoal [ʃəʊl] n (*of fish*) banco; (*fig: also: ~s*) tropel m

shock [ʃɒk] n (*impact*) choque m; (*ELEC*) descarga (eléctrica); (*emotional*) conmoción f; (*start*) sobresalto, susto; (*MED*) postración f nerviosa ♦ vt dar un susto a; (*offend*) escandalizar; **~ absorber** n amortiguador m; **~ing** adj (*awful*) espantoso; (*outrageous*) escandaloso

shoddy ['ʃɒdɪ] adj de pacotilla

shoe [ʃuː] (pt, pp **shod**) n zapato; (*for horse*) herradura ♦ vt (*horse*) herrar; **~brush** n cepillo para zapatos; **~lace** n cordón m; **~ polish** n betún m; **~shop** n zapatería; **~string** n (*fig*): **on a ~string** con muy poco dinero

shone [ʃɒn] pt, pp of **shine**

shook [ʃʊk] pt of **shake**

shoot [ʃuːt] (pt, pp **shot**) n (*on branch, seedling*) retoño, vástago ♦ vt disparar; (*kill*) matar a tiros; (*wound*) pegar un tiro;

(*execute*) fusilar; (*film*) rodar, filmar ♦ *vi*
(*FOOTBALL*) chutar; **~ down** *vt* (*plane*)
derribar; **~ in/out** *vi* entrar corriendo/salir
disparado; **~ up** *vi* (*prices*) dispararse; **~ing** *n*
(*shots*) tiros *mpl*; (*HUNTING*) caza con
escopeta; **~ing star** *n* estrella fugaz

shop [ʃɔp] *n* tienda; (*workshop*) taller *m* ♦ *vi*
(*also: go ~ping*) ir de compras; **~ assistant**
(*BRIT*) *n* dependiente/a *m/f*; **~ floor** (*BRIT*) *n*
(*fig*) taller *m*, fábrica; **~keeper** *n* tendero/a;
~lifting *n* mechería; **~per** *n* comprador(a)
m/f; **~ping** *n* (*goods*) compras *fpl*; **~ping
bag** *n* bolsa (de compras); **~ping centre**
(*US* **~ping center**) *n* centro comercial; **~-
soiled** *adj* deteriorado; **~ steward** (*BRIT*) *n*
(*INDUSTRY*) enlace *m* sindical; **~ window** *n*
escaparate *m* (*SP*), vidriera (*AM*)

shore [ʃɔː*] *n* orilla ♦ *vt*: **to ~ (up)** reforzar; **on
~** en tierra

shorn [ʃɔːn] *pp of* **shear**

short [ʃɔːt] *adj* corto; (*in time*) breve, de corta
duración; (*person*) bajo; (*curt*) brusco, seco;
(*insufficient*) insuficiente; **(a pair of) ~s** (unos)
pantalones *mpl* cortos; **to be ~ of sth** estar
falto de algo; **in ~** en pocas palabras; **~ of
doing ...** fuera de hacer ...; **it is ~ for** es la
forma abreviada de; **to cut ~** (*speech, visit*)
interrumpir, terminar inesperadamente;
everything ~ of ... todo menos ...; **to fall ~ of**
no alcanzar; **to run ~** quedarle a uno poco;
to stop ~ parar en seco; **to stop ~ of**
detenerse antes de; **~age** *n* escasez, falta de;
~bread *n* especie de mantecada; **~-
change** *vt* no dar el cambio completo a; **~-
circuit** *n* cortocircuito; **~coming** *n* defecto,
deficiencia; **~(crust) pastry** (*BRIT*) *n* pasta
quebradiza; **~cut** *n* atajo; **~en** *vt* acortar;
(*visit*) interrumpir; **~fall** *n* déficit *m*; **~hand**
(*BRIT*) *n* taquigrafía; **~hand typist** (*BRIT*) *n*
taquimecanógrafo/a; **~ list** (*BRIT*) *n* (*for job*)
lista de candidatos escogidos; **~-lived** *adj*
efímero; **~ly** *adv* en breve, dentro de poco;
~-sighted (*BRIT*) *adj* miope; (*fig*) imprudente; **~-staffed** *adj*: **to be ~-staffed** estar
falto de personal; **~ story** *n* cuento; **~-
tempered** *adj* enojadizo; **~-term** *adj* (*effect*)
a corto plazo; **~wave** *n* (*RADIO*) onda corta

shot [ʃɔt] *pt, pp of* **shoot** ♦ *n* (*sound*) tiro,
disparo; (*try*) tentativa; (*injection*) inyección
f; (*PHOT*) toma, fotografía; **to be a good/poor
~** (*person*) tener buena/mala puntería; **like a ~**
(*without any delay*) como un rayo; **~gun** *n*
escopeta

should [ʃud] *aux vb*: **I ~ go now** debo irme
ahora; **he ~ be there now** debe de haber
llegado (ya); **I ~ go if I were you** yo en tu
lugar me iría; **I ~ like to** me gustaría

shoulder ['ʃəuldə*] *n* hombro ♦ *vt* (*fig*)
cargar con; **~ bag** *n* cartera de bandolera;

~ blade *n* omóplato

shouldn't ['ʃudnt] = **should not**

shout [ʃaut] *n* grito ♦ *vt* gritar ♦ *vi* gritar, dar
voces; **~ down** *vt* acallar a gritos; **~ing** *n*
griterío

shove [ʃʌv] *n* empujón *m* ♦ *vt* empujar; (*inf:
put*): **to ~ sth in** meter algo a empellones;
~ off (*inf*) *vi* largarse

shovel ['ʃʌvl] *n* pala; (*mechanical*)
excavadora ♦ *vt* mover con pala

show [ʃəu] (*pt* **showed**, *pp* **shown**) *n* (*of
emotion*) demostración *f*; (*semblance*)
apariencia; (*exhibition*) exposición *f*; (*THEATRE*)
función *f*, espectáculo; (*TV*) show *m* ♦ *vt*
mostrar, enseñar; (*courage etc*) mostrar,
manifestar; (*exhibit*) exponer; (*film*) proyectar
♦ *vi* mostrarse; (*appear*) aparecer; **for ~** para
impresionar; **on ~** (*exhibits etc*) expuesto;
~ in *vt* (*person*) hacer pasar; **~ off** (*pej*) *vi*
presumir ♦ *vt* (*display*) lucir; **~ out** *vt*: **to
~ sb out** acompañar a uno a la puerta; **~ up**
vi (*stand out*) destacar; (*inf: turn up*) aparecer
♦ *vt* (*unmask*) desenmascarar; **~ business** *n*
mundo del espectáculo; **~down** *n*
enfrentamiento (final)

shower ['ʃauə*] *n* (*rain*) chaparrón *m*,
chubasco; (*of stones etc*) lluvia; (*for bathing*)
ducha (*SP*), regadera (*AM*) ♦ *vi* llover ♦ *vt*
(*fig*): **to ~ sb with sth** colmar a uno de algo;
to have a ~ ducharse; **~proof** *adj*
impermeable

showing ['ʃəuɪŋ] *n* (*of film*) proyección *f*

show jumping *n* hípica

shown [ʃəun] *pp of* **show**

show: **~-off** (*inf*) *n* (*person*) presumido/a;
~piece *n* (*of exhibition etc*) objeto cumbre;
~room *n* sala de muestras

shrank [ʃræŋk] *pt of* **shrink**

shrapnel ['ʃræpnl] *n* metralla

shred [ʃred] *n* (*gen pl*) triza, jirón *m* ♦ *vt*
hacer trizas; (*CULIN*) desmenuzar; **~der** *n*
(*vegetable ~der*) picadora; (*document ~der*)
trituradora (de papel)

shrewd [ʃruːd] *adj* astuto

shriek [ʃriːk] *n* chillido ♦ *vi* chillar

shrill [ʃrɪl] *adj* agudo, estridente

shrimp [ʃrɪmp] *n* camarón *m*

shrine [ʃraɪn] *n* santuario, sepulcro

shrink [ʃrɪŋk] (*pt* **shrank**, *pp* **shrunk**) *vi*
encogerse; (*be reduced*) reducirse; (*also:
~ away*) retroceder ♦ *n* (*inf:
pej*) loquero/a; **to ~ from (doing) sth** no
atreverse a hacer algo; **~wrap** *vt* embalar
con película de plástico

shrivel ['ʃrɪvl] (*also: ~ up*) *vt* (*dry*) secar ♦ *vi*
secarse

shroud [ʃraud] *n* sudario ♦ *vt*: **~ed in mystery**
envuelto en el misterio

Shrove Tuesday ['ʃrəuv-] *n* martes *m* de

carnaval

shrub [ʃrʌb] n arbusto; **~bery** n arbustos mpl

shrug [ʃrʌg] n encogimiento de hombros ♦ vt, vi: **to ~ (one's shoulders)** encogerse de hombros; **~ off** vt negar importancia a

shrunk [ʃrʌŋk] pp of **shrink**

shudder ['ʃʌdə*] n estremecimiento, escalofrío ♦ vi estremecerse

shuffle ['ʃʌfl] vt (cards) barajar ♦ vi: **to ~ (one's feet)** arrastrar los pies

shun [ʃʌn] vt rehuir, esquivar

shunt [ʃʌnt] vt (train) maniobrar; (object) empujar

shut [ʃʌt] (pt, pp **shut**) vt cerrar ♦ vi cerrarse; **~ down** vt, vi cerrar; **~ off** vt (supply etc) cortar; **~ up** vi (inf: keep quiet) callarse ♦ vt (close) cerrar; (silence) hacer callar; **~ter** n contraventana; (PHOT) obturador m

shuttle ['ʃʌtl] n lanzadera; (also: ~ service) servicio rápido y continuo entre dos puntos: (: AVIAT) puente m aéreo; **~cock** n volante m; **~ diplomacy** n viajes mpl diplomáticos

shy [ʃaɪ] adj tímido; **~ness** n timidez f

Sicily ['sɪsɪlɪ] n Sicilia

sick [sɪk] adj (ill) enfermo; (nauseated) mareado; (humour) negro; (vomiting): **to be ~** (BRIT) vomitar; **to feel ~** tener náuseas; **to be ~ of** (fig) estar harto de; **~ bay** n enfermería; **~en** vt dar asco a; **~ening** adj (fig) asqueroso

sickle ['sɪkl] n hoz f

sick~ **leave** n baja por enfermedad; **~ly** adj enfermizo; (smell) nauseabundo; **~ness** n enfermedad f, mal m; (vomiting) náuseas fpl; **~ pay** n subsidio de enfermedad

side [saɪd] n (gen) lado; (of body) costado; (of lake) orilla; (of hill) ladera; (team) equipo; ♦ adj (door, entrance) lateral ♦ vi: **to ~ with sb** tomar el partido de uno; **by the ~ of** al lado de; **~ by ~** juntos/as; **from ~ to ~** de un lado para otro; **from all ~s** de todos lados; **to take ~s (with)** tomar partido (con); **~board** n aparador m; **~boards** (BRIT) npl = **~burns**; **~burns** npl patillas fpl; **~ drum** n tambor m; **~ effect** n efecto secundario; **~light** n (AUT) luz f lateral; **~line** n (SPORT) línea de banda; (fig) empleo suplementario; **~long** adj de soslayo; **~ order** n plato de acompañamiento; **~ show** n (stall) caseta; **~step** vt (fig) esquivar; **~ street** n calle f lateral; **~track** vt (fig) desviar (de su propósito); **~walk** (US) n acera; **~ways** adv de lado

siding ['saɪdɪŋ] n (RAIL) apartadero, vía muerta

siege [siːdʒ] n cerco, sitio

sieve [sɪv] n colador m ♦ vt cribar

sift [sɪft] vt cribar; (fig: information) escudriñar

sigh [saɪ] n suspiro ♦ vi suspirar

sight [saɪt] n (faculty) vista; (spectacle)

espectáculo; (on gun) mira, alza ♦ vt divisar; **in ~** a la vista; **out of ~** fuera de (la) vista; **on ~** (shoot) sin previo aviso; **~seeing** n excursionismo, turismo; **to go ~seeing** hacer turismo

sign [saɪn] n (with hand) señal f, seña; (trace) huella, rastro; (notice) letrero; (written) signo ♦ vt firmar; (SPORT) fichar; **to ~ sth over to sb** firmar el traspaso de algo a uno; **~ on** vi (BRIT: as unemployed) registrarse como desempleado; (for course) inscribirse ♦ vt (MIL) alistar; (employee) contratar; **~ up** vi (MIL) alistarse; (for course) inscribirse ♦ vt (player) fichar

signal ['sɪgnl] n señal f ♦ vi señalizar ♦ vt (person) hacer señas a; (message) comunicar por señales; **~man** (irreg) n (RAIL) guardavía m

signature ['sɪgnətʃə*] n firma; **~ tune** n sintonía de apertura de un programa

signet ring ['sɪgnət-] n anillo de sello

significance [sɪg'nɪfɪkəns] n (importance) trascendencia

significant [sɪg'nɪfɪkənt] adj significativo; (important) trascendente

signify ['sɪgnɪfaɪ] vt significar

sign language n lenguaje m para sordomudos

signpost ['saɪnpəʊst] n indicador m

silence ['saɪlns] n silencio ♦ vt acallar; (guns) reducir al silencio; **~r** n (on gun, BRIT: AUT) silenciador m

silent ['saɪlnt] adj silencioso; (not speaking) callado; (film) mudo; **to remain ~** guardar silencio; **~ partner** n (COMM) socio/a comanditario/a

silhouette [sɪluː'et] n silueta

silicon chip ['sɪlɪkən-] n plaqueta de silicio

silk [sɪlk] n seda ♦ adj de seda; **~y** adj sedoso

silly ['sɪlɪ] adj (person) tonto; (idea) absurdo

silt [sɪlt] n sedimento

silver ['sɪlvə*] n plata; (money) moneda suelta ♦ adj de plata; (colour) plateado; **~ paper** (BRIT) n papel m de plata; **~-plated** adj plateado; **~smith** n platero/a; **~ware** n plata; **~y** adj argentino

similar ['sɪmɪlə*] adj: **~ (to)** parecido o semejante (a); **~ity** [-'lærɪtɪ] n semejanza; **~ly** adv del mismo modo

simmer ['sɪmə*] vi hervir a fuego lento

simple ['sɪmpl] adj (easy) sencillo; (foolish, COMM: interest) simple; **simplicity** [-'plɪsɪtɪ] n sencillez f; **simplify** ['sɪmplɪfaɪ] vt simplificar

simply ['sɪmplɪ] adv (live, talk) sencillamente; (just, merely) sólo

simulate ['sɪmjuleɪt] vt fingir, simular; **~d** adj simulado; (fur) de imitación

simultaneous [sɪmǝl'teɪnɪəs] adj simultáneo; **~ly** adv simultáneamente

sin [sɪn] n pecado ♦ vi pecar
since [sɪns] adv desde entonces, después ♦ prep desde ♦ conj (time) desde que; (because) ya que, puesto que; **~ then, ever ~** desde entonces
sincere [sɪn'sɪə*] adj sincero; **~ly** adv: **yours ~ly** (in letters) le saluda atentamente; **sincerity** [-'serɪtɪ] n sinceridad f
sinew ['sɪnjuː] n tendón m
sing [sɪŋ] (pt **sang**, pp **sung**) vt, vi cantar
Singapore [sɪŋə'pɔː*] n Singapur m
singe [sɪndʒ] vt chamuscar
singer ['sɪŋə*] n cantante m/f
singing ['sɪŋɪŋ] n canto
single ['sɪŋgl] adj único, solo; (unmarried) soltero; (not double) simple, sencillo ♦ n (BRIT: also: **~ ticket**) billete m sencillo; (record) sencillo, single m; **~s** npl (TENNIS) individual m; **~ out** vt (choose) escoger; **~ bed** cama individual; **~-breasted** adj recto; **~ file** n: **in ~ file** en fila de uno; **~-handed** adv sin ayuda; **~-minded** adj resuelto, firme; **~ parent** n padre m soltero, madre f soltera (o divorciado etc); **~ parent family** familia monoparental; **~ room** n cuarto individual
singly ['sɪŋglɪ] adv uno por uno
singular ['sɪŋgjulə*] adj (odd) raro, extraño; (outstanding) excepcional ♦ n (LING) singular m
sinister ['sɪnɪstə*] adj siniestro
sink [sɪŋk] (pt **sank**, pp **sunk**) n fregadero ♦ vt (ship) hundir, echar a pique; (foundations) excavar ♦ vi (gen) hundirse; **to ~ sth into** hundir algo en; **~ in** vi (fig) penetrar, calar
sinner ['sɪnə*] n pecador(a) m/f
sinus ['saɪnəs] n (ANAT) seno
sip [sɪp] n sorbo ♦ vt sorber, beber a sorbitos
siphon ['saɪfən] n sifón m; **~ off** vt desviar
sir [sə*] n señor m; **S~ John Smith** Sir John Smith; **yes ~** sí, señor
siren ['saɪərn] n sirena
sirloin ['səːlɔɪn] n (also: **~ steak**) solomillo
sister ['sɪstə*] n hermana; (BRIT: nurse) enfermera jefe; **~-in-law** n cuñada
sit [sɪt] (pt, pp **sat**) vi sentarse; (be sitting) estar sentado; (assembly) reunirse; (for painter) posar ♦ vt (exam) presentarse a; **~ down** vi sentarse; **~ in on** vt fus asistir a; **~ up** vi incorporarse; (not go to bed) velar
sitcom ['sɪtkɔm] n abbr (= situation comedy) comedia de situación
site [saɪt] n sitio; (also: building **~**) solar m ♦ vt situar
sit-in n (demonstration) sentada
sitting ['sɪtɪŋ] n (of assembly etc) sesión f; (in canteen) turno; **~ room** n sala de estar
situated ['sɪtjueɪtɪd] adj situado
situation [sɪtju'eɪʃən] n situación f; **"~s vacant"** (BRIT) "ofrecen trabajo"

six [sɪks] num seis; **~teen** num diez y seis, dieciséis; **~th** num sexto; **~ty** num sesenta
size [saɪz] n tamaño; (extent) extensión f; (of clothing) talla; (of shoes) número; **~ up** vt formarse una idea de; **~able** adj importante, considerable
sizzle ['sɪzl] vi crepitar
skate [skeɪt] n patín m; (fish: pl inv) raya ♦ vi patinar; **~board** n monopatín m; **~boarding** n monopatín m; **~r** n patinador(a) m/f; **skating** n patinaje m; **skating rink** n pista de patinaje
skeleton ['skelɪtn] n esqueleto; (TECH) armazón f; (outline) esquema m; **~ staff** n personal m reducido
skeptic etc ['skeptɪk] (US) = **sceptic**
sketch [sketʃ] n (drawing) dibujo; (outline) esbozo, bosquejo; (THEATRE) sketch m ♦ vt dibujar; (plan etc: also: **~ out**) esbozar; **~ book** n libro de dibujos; **~y** adj incompleto
skewer ['skjuː*] n broqueta
ski [skiː] n esquí m ♦ vi esquiar; **~ boot** n bota de esquí
skid [skɪd] n patinazo ♦ vi patinar
ski: ~er n esquiador(a) m/f; **~ing** n esquí m; **~ jump** n salto con esquís
skilful ['skɪlful] (BRIT) adj diestro, experto
ski lift n telesilla m, telesquí m
skill [skɪl] n destreza, pericia, técnica; **~ed** adj hábil, diestro; (worker) cualificado; **~full** (US) adj = **skilful**
skim [skɪm] vt (milk) desnatar; (glide over) rozar, rasar ♦ vi: **to ~ through** (book) hojear; **~med milk** n leche f desnatada
skimp [skɪmp] vt (also: **~ on**: work) chapucear; (cloth etc) escatimar; **~y** adj escaso; (skirt) muy corto
skin [skɪn] n piel f; (complexion) cutis m ♦ vt (fruit etc) pelar; (animal) despellejar; **~ cancer** n cáncer m de piel; **~-deep** adj superficial; **~ diving** n buceo; **~ny** adj flaco; **~tight** adj (dress etc) muy ajustado
skip [skɪp] n brinco, salto; (BRIT: container) contenedor m ♦ vi brincar; (with rope) saltar a la comba ♦ vt saltarse
ski: ~ pass n forfait m (de esquí); **~ pole** n bastón m de esquiar
skipper ['skɪpə*] n (NAUT, SPORT) capitán m
skipping rope ['skɪpɪŋ-] (BRIT) n comba
skirmish ['skəːmɪʃ] n escaramuza
skirt [skəːt] n falda (SP), pollera (AM) ♦ vt (go round) ladear; **~ing board** (BRIT) n rodapié m
ski slope n pista de esquí
ski suit n traje m de esquiar
ski tow n remonte m
skittle ['skɪtl] n bolo; **~s** n (game) boliche m
skive [skaɪv] (BRIT: inf) vi gandulear

skull [skʌl] n calavera; (ANAT) cráneo

skunk [skʌŋk] n mofeta

sky [skaɪ] n cielo; **~light** n tragaluz m, claraboya; **~scraper** n rascacielos m inv

slab [slæb] n (stone) bloque m; (flat) losa; (of cake) trozo

slack [slæk] adj (loose) flojo; (slow) de poca actividad; (careless) descuidado; **~s** npl pantalones mpl; **~en** (also: **~en off**) vi aflojarse ♦ vt aflojar; (speed) disminuir

slag heap ['slæg-] n escorial m, escombrera

slag off (BRIT: inf) vt poner como un trapo

slam [slæm] vt (throw) arrojar (violentamente); (criticize) criticar duramente ♦ vi (door) cerrarse de golpe; **to ~ the door** dar un portazo

slander ['slɑːndə*] n calumnia, difamación f

slang [slæŋ] n argot m; (jargon) jerga

slant [slɑːnt] n sesgo, inclinación f; (fig) interpretación f; **~ed** adj (fig) parcial; **~ing** adj inclinado; (eyes) rasgado

slap [slæp] n palmada; (in face) bofetada ♦ vt dar una palmada o bofetada a; (paint etc): **to ~ sth on sth** embadurnar algo con algo ♦ adv (directly) exactamente, directamente; **~dash** adj descuidado; **~stick** n comedia de golpe y porrazo; **~-up** adj: **a ~up meal** (BRIT) un banquetazo, una comilona

slash [slæʃ] vt acuchillar; (fig: prices) fulminar

slat [slæt] n tablilla, listón m

slate [sleɪt] n pizarra ♦ vt (fig: criticize) criticar duramente

slaughter ['slɔːtə*] n (of animals) matanza; (of people) carnicería ♦ vt matar; **~house** n matadero

Slav [slɑːv] adj eslavo

slave [sleɪv] n esclavo/a ♦ vi (also: **~ away**) sudar tinta; **~ry** n esclavitud f

slay [sleɪ] (pt **slew**, pp **slain**) vt matar

sleazy ['sliːzɪ] adj de mala fama

sledge [sledʒ] n trineo; **~hammer** n mazo

sleek [sliːk] adj (shiny) lustroso; (car etc) elegante

sleep [sliːp] (pt, pp **slept**) n sueño ♦ vi dormir; **to go to ~** quedarse dormido; **~ around** vi acostarse con cualquiera; **~ in** vi (oversleep) quedarse dormido; **~er** n (person) durmiente m/f; (BRIT: RAIL: on track) traviesa; (: train) coche-cama m; **~ing bag** n saco de dormir; **~ing car** n coche-cama m; **~ing partner** (BRIT) n (COMM) socio comanditario; **~ing pill** n somnífero; **~less** adj: **a ~less night** una noche en blanco; **~walker** n sonámbulo/a; **~y** adj soñoliento; (place) soporífero

sleet [sliːt] n aguanieve f

sleeve [sliːv] n manga; (TECH) manguito; (of record) portada; **~less** adj sin mangas

sleigh [sleɪ] n trineo

sleight [slaɪt] n: **~ of hand** escamoteo

slender ['slendə*] adj delgado; (means) escaso

slept [slept] pt, pp of **sleep**

slew [sluː] pt of **slay** ♦ vi (BRIT: veer) torcerse

slice [slaɪs] n (of meat) tajada; (of bread) rebanada; (of lemon) rodaja; (utensil) pala ♦ vt cortar (en tajos); rebanar

slick [slɪk] adj (skilful) hábil, diestro; (clever) astuto ♦ n (also: oil ~) marea negra

slide [slaɪd] (pt, pp **slid**) n (movement) descenso, desprendimiento; (in playground) tobogán m; (PHOT) diapositiva; (BRIT: also: hair ~) pasador m ♦ vt correr, deslizar ♦ vi (slip) resbalarse; (glide) deslizarse; **sliding** adj (door) corredizo; **sliding scale** n escala móvil

slight [slaɪt] adj (slim) delgado; (frail) delicado; (pain etc) leve; (trivial) insignificante; (small) pequeño ♦ n desaire m ♦ vt (insult) ofender, desairar; **not in the ~est** en absoluto; **~ly** adv ligeramente, un poco

slim [slɪm] adj delgado, esbelto; (fig: chance) remoto ♦ vi adelgazar

slime [slaɪm] n limo, cieno

slimming ['slɪmɪŋ] n adelgazamiento

slimy ['slaɪmɪ] adj cenagoso

sling [slɪŋ] (pt, pp **slung**) n (MED) cabestrillo; (weapon) honda ♦ vt tirar, arrojar

slip [slɪp] n (slide) resbalón m; (mistake) descuido; (underskirt) combinación f; (of paper) papelito ♦ vt (slide) deslizar ♦ vi deslizarse; (stumble) resbalar(se); (decline) decaer; (move smoothly): **to ~ into/out of** (room etc) introducirse en/salirse de; **to give sb the ~** eludir a uno; **a ~ of the tongue** un lapsus; **to ~ sth on/off** ponerse/quitarse algo; **~ away** vi escabullirse; **~ in** vt meter ♦ vi meterse; **~ out** vi (go out) salir (un momento); **~ up** vi (make mistake) equivocarse; meter la pata; **~ped disc** n vértebra dislocada

slipper ['slɪpə*] n zapatilla, pantufla

slippery ['slɪpərɪ] adj resbaladizo

slip: **~ road** (BRIT) n carretera de acceso; **~-up** n (error) desliz m; **~way** n grada, gradas fpl

slit [slɪt] (pt, pp **slit**) n raja; (cut) corte m ♦ vt rajar; cortar

slither ['slɪðə*] vi deslizarse

sliver ['slɪvə*] n (of glass, wood) astilla; (of cheese etc) raja

slob [slɒb] n (inf) abandonado/a

slog [slɒg] (BRIT) vi sudar tinta; **it was a ~** costó trabajo (hacerlo)

slogan ['sləʊgən] n eslogan m, lema m

slope [sləʊp] n (up) cuesta, pendiente f; (down) declive m; (side of mountain) falda, vertiente m ♦ vi: **to ~ down** estar en declive;

to ~ up inclinarse; **sloping** *adj* en pendiente; en declive; (*writing*) inclinado

sloppy ['slɔpɪ] *adj* (*work*) descuidado; (*appearance*) desaliñado

slot [slɔt] *n* ranura ♦ *vt*: **to ~ into** encajar en

slot machine *n* (*BRIT: vending machine*) distribuidor *m* automático; (*for gambling*) tragaperras *m inv*

slouch [slautʃ] *vi* andar *etc* con los hombros caídos

Slovenia [sləu'vi:nɪə] *n* Eslovenia

slovenly ['slʌvənlɪ] *adj* desaliñado, desaseado; (*careless*) descuidado

slow [sləu] *adj* lento; (*not clever*) lerdo; (*watch*): **to be ~** atrasar ♦ *adv* lentamente, despacio ♦ *vt*, *vi* (*also: ~ down, ~ up*) retardar; **"~"** (*road sign*) "disminuir velocidad"; **~down** (*US*) *n* huelga de manos caídas; **~ly** *adv* lentamente, despacio; **~ motion** *n*: **in ~ motion** a cámara lenta

sludge [slʌdʒ] *n* lodo, fango

slug [slʌg] *n* babosa; (*bullet*) posta; **~gish** *adj* lento; (*person*) perezoso

sluice [slu:s] *n* (*gate*) esclusa; (*channel*) canal *m*

slum [slʌm] *n* casucha

slump [slʌmp] *n* (*economic*) depresión *f* ♦ *vi* hundirse; (*prices*) caer en picado

slung [slʌŋ] *pt*, *pp* de **sling**

slur [slɜ:*] *n*: **to cast a ~ on** insultar ♦ *vt* (*speech*) pronunciar mal

slush [slʌʃ] *n* nieve *f* a medio derretir

slut [slʌt] *n* putona

sly [slaɪ] *adj* astuto; (*smile*) taimado

smack [smæk] *n* bofetada ♦ *vt* dar con la mano a; (*child, on face*) abofetear ♦ *vi*: **to ~ of** saber a, oler a

small [smɔ:l] *adj* pequeño; (*also: ~-up*) choque *m*; **~ ads** (*BRIT*) *npl* anuncios *mpl* por palabras; **~ change** *n* suelto, cambio; **~holder** (*BRIT*) *n* granjero/a, parcelero/a; **~ hours** *npl*: **in the ~ hours** a las altas horas (de la noche); **~pox** *n* viruela; **~ talk** *n* cháchara

smart [smɑ:t] *adj* elegante; (*clever*) listo, inteligente; (*quick*) rápido, vivo ♦ *vi* escocer, picar; **~en up** *vi* arreglarse ♦ *vt* arreglar

smash [smæʃ] *n* (*also: ~-up*) choque *m*; (*MUS*) exitazo ♦ *vt* (*break*) hacer pedazos; (*car etc*) estrellar; (*SPORT: record*) batir ♦ *vi* hacerse pedazos; (*against wall etc*) estrellarse; **~ing** (*inf*) *adj* estupendo

smattering ['smætərɪŋ] *n*: **a ~ of** algo de

smear [smɪə*] *n* mancha; (*MED*) frotis *m inv* ♦ *vt* untar; **~ campaign** *n* campaña de desprestigio

smell [smel] (*pt*, *pp* **smelt** or **smelled**) *n* olor *m*; (*sense*) olfato ♦ *vt*, *vi* oler; **~y** *adj* maloliente

smile [smaɪl] *n* sonrisa ♦ *vi* sonreír

smirk [smɜ:k] *n* sonrisa falsa or afectada

smith [smɪθ] *n* herrero; **~y** ['smɪðɪ] *n* herrería

smog [smɔg] *n* esmog *m*

smoke [sməuk] *n* humo ♦ *vi* fumar; (*chimney*) echar humo ♦ *vt* (*cigarettes*) fumar; **~d** *adj* (*bacon, glass*) ahumado; **~r** *n* fumador(a) *m/f*; (*RAIL*) coche *m* fumador; **~ screen** *n* cortina de humo; **~ shop** (*US*) *n* estanco (*SP*), tabaquería (*AM*); **smoking** *n*: **"no smoking"** "prohibido fumar"; **smoky** *adj* (*room*) lleno de humo; (*taste*) ahumado

smolder ['sməuldə*] (*US*) *vi* = **smoulder**

smooth [smu:ð] *adj* liso; (*sea*) tranquilo; (*flavour, movement*) suave; (*sauce*) fino; (*person: pej*) meloso ♦ *vt* (*also: ~ out*) alisar; (*creases, difficulties*) allanar

smother ['smʌðə*] *vt* sofocar; (*repress*) contener

smoulder ['sməuldə*] (*US* **smolder**) *vi* arder sin llama

smudge [smʌdʒ] *n* mancha ♦ *vt* manchar

smug [smʌg] *adj* presumido; orondo

smuggle ['smʌgl] *vt* pasar de contrabando; **~r** *n* contrabandista *m/f*; **smuggling** *n* contrabando

smutty ['smʌtɪ] *adj* (*fig*) verde, obsceno

snack [snæk] *n* bocado; **~ bar** *n* cafetería

snag [snæg] *n* problema *m*

snail [sneɪl] *n* caracol *m*

snake [sneɪk] *n* serpiente *f*

snap [snæp] *n* (*sound*) chasquido; (*photograph*) foto *f* ♦ *adj* (*decision*) instantáneo ♦ *vt* (*break*) quebrar; (*fingers*) castañetear ♦ *vi* quebrarse; (*fig: speak sharply*) contestar bruscamente; **to ~ shut** cerrarse de golpe; **~ at** *vt fus* (*subj: dog*) intentar morder; **~ off** *vi* partirse; **~ up** *vt* agarrar; **~ fastener** (*US*) *n* botón *m* de presión; **~py** (*inf*) *adj* (*answer*) instantáneo; (*slogan*) conciso; **make it ~py!** (*hurry up*) ¡date prisa!; **~shot** *n* foto *f* (instantánea)

snare [snɛə*] *n* trampa

snarl [snɑ:l] *vi* gruñir

snatch [snætʃ] *n* (*small piece*) fragmento ♦ *vt* (*~ away*) arrebatar; (*fig*) agarrar; **to ~ some sleep** encontrar tiempo para dormir

sneak [sni:k] (*pt* (*US*) **snuck**) *vi*: **to ~ in/out** entrar/salir a hurtadillas ♦ *n* (*inf*) soplón/ona *m/f*; **to ~ up on sb** aparecérsele de improviso a uno; **~ers** *npl* zapatos *mpl* de lona; **~y** *adj* furtivo

sneer [snɪə*] *vi* reír con sarcasmo; (*mock*): **to ~ at** burlarse de

sneeze [sni:z] *vi* estornudar

sniff [snɪf] *vi* sollozar ♦ *vt* husmear, oler; (*drugs*) esnifar

snigger ['snɪgə*] *vi* reírse con disimulo

snip [snɪp] *n* tijeretazo; (*BRIT: inf: bargain*) ganga ♦ *vt* tijeretear

sniper ['snaɪpə*] n francotirador(a) m/f
snippet ['snɪpɪt] n retazo
snob [snɔb] n (e)snob m/f; **~bery** n (e)snobismo; **~bish** adj (e)snob
snooker ['snu:kə*] n especie de billar
snoop [snu:p] vi: **to ~ about** fisgonear
snooze [snu:z] n siesta ♦ vi echar una siesta
snore [snɔ:*] n ronquido ♦ vi roncar
snorkel ['snɔ:kl] n (tubo) respirador m
snort [snɔ:t] n bufido ♦ vi bufar
snout [snaut] n hocico, morro
snow [snəu] n nieve f ♦ vi nevar; **~ball** n bola de nieve ♦ vi (fig) agrandirse, ampliarse; **~bound** adj bloqueado por la nieve; **~drift** n ventisquero; **~drop** n campanilla; **~fall** n nevada; **~flake** n copo de nieve; **~man** (irreg) n figura de nieve; **~plough** (US **~plow**) n quitanieves m inv; **~shoe** n raqueta (de nieve); **~storm** n nevada, nevasca
snub [snʌb] vt (person) desairar ♦ n desaire m, repulsa; **~nosed** adj chato
snuff [snʌf] n rapé m
snug [snʌg] adj (cosy) cómodo; (fitted) ajustado
snuggle ['snʌgl] vi: **to ~ up to sb** arrimarse a uno

KEYWORD

so [səu] adv **1** (thus, likewise) así, de este modo; **if ~** de ser así; **I like swimming — ~ do I** a mí me gusta nadar — a mí también; **I've got work to do — ~ has Paul** tengo trabajo que hacer — Paul también; **it's 5 o'clock — ~ it is!** son las cinco — ¡pues es verdad!; **I hope/think ~** espero/creo que sí; **~ far** hasta ahora; (in past) hasta este momento
2 (in comparisons etc: to such a degree) tan; **~ quickly (that)** tan rápido (que); **~ big (that)** tan grande (que); **she's not ~ clever as her brother** no es tan lista como su hermano; **we were ~ worried** estábamos preocupadísimos
3: **~ much** adj, adv tanto; **~ many** tantos/as
4 (phrases): **10 or ~** unos 10, 10 o así; **~ long!** (inf: goodbye) ¡hasta luego!
♦ conj **1** (expressing purpose): **~ as to do** para hacer; **~ (that)** para que + sub
2 (expressing result) así que; **~ you see, I could have gone** así que ya ves, (yo) podría haber ido

----

soak [səuk] vt (drench) empapar; (steep in water) remojar ♦ vi remojarse, estar a remojo; **~ in** vi penetrar; **~ up** vt absorber
soap [səup] n jabón m; **~flakes** npl escamas fpl de jabón; **~ opera** n telenovela; **~ powder** n jabón m en polvo; **~y** adj jabonoso
soar [sɔ:*] vi (on wings) remontarse; (rocket, prices) dispararse; (building etc) elevarse

sob [sɔb] n sollozo ♦ vi sollozar
sober ['səubə*] adj (serious) serio; (not drunk) sobrio; (colour, style) discreto; **~ up** vt quitar la borrachera
so-called adj así llamado
soccer ['sɔkə*] n fútbol m
social ['səuʃl] adj social ♦ n velada, fiesta; **~ club** n club m; **~ism** n socialismo; **~ist** adj, n socialista m/f; **~ize** vi: **to ~ize (with)** alternar (con); **~ly** adv socialmente; **~ security** n seguridad f social; **~ work** n asistencia social; **~ worker** n asistente/a m/f social
society [sə'saɪətɪ] n sociedad f; (club) asociación f; (also: high ~) alta sociedad
sociology [səusɪ'ɔlədʒɪ] n sociología
sock [sɔk] n calcetín m (SP), media (AM)
socket ['sɔkɪt] n cavidad f; (BRIT: ELEC) enchufe m
sod [sɔd] n (of earth) césped m; (BRIT: inf!) cabrón/ona m/f (!)
soda ['səudə] n (CHEM) sosa; (also: ~ water) soda; (US: also: ~ pop) gaseosa
sofa ['səufə] n sofá m
soft [sɔft] adj (lenient, not hard) blando; (gentle, not bright) suave; **~ drink** n bebida no alcohólica; **~en** ['sɔfn] vt ablandar; suavizar; (effect) amortiguar ♦ vi ablandarse; suavizarse; **~ly** adv suavemente; (gently) delicadamente, con delicadeza; **~ness** n blandura; suavidad f; **~ware** n (COMPUT) software m
soggy ['sɔgɪ] adj empapado
soil [sɔɪl] n (earth) tierra, suelo ♦ vt ensuciar; **~ed** adj sucio
solar ['səulə*] adj: **~ energy** n energía solar; **~ panel** n panel m solar
sold [səuld] pt, pp of **sell**; **~ out** adj (COMM) agotado
solder ['səuldə*] vt soldar ♦ n soldadura
soldier ['səuldʒə*] n soldado; (army man) militar m
sole [səul] n (of foot) planta; (of shoe) suela; (fish: pl inv) lenguado ♦ adj único
solemn ['sɔləm] adj solemne
sole trader n (COMM) comerciante m exclusivo
solicit [sə'lɪsɪt] vt (request) solicitar ♦ vi (prostitute) importunar
solicitor [sə'lɪsɪtə*] (BRIT) n (for wills etc) ≈ notario/a; (in court) ≈ abogado/a
solid ['sɔlɪd] adj sólido; (gold etc) macizo ♦ n sólido; **~s** npl (food) alimentos mpl sólidos
solidarity [sɔlɪ'dærɪtɪ] n solidaridad f
solitary ['sɔlɪtərɪ] adj solitario, solo; **~ confinement** n incomunicación f
solo ['səuləu] n solo ♦ adv (fly) en solitario; **~ist** n solista m/f
soluble ['sɔljubl] adj soluble

solution [sə'lu:ʃən] n solución f
solve [sɔlv] vt resolver, solucionar
solvent ['sɔlvənt] adj (COMM) solvente ♦ n (CHEM) solvente m

KEYWORD

some [sʌm] adj 1 (a certain amount or number of): ~ **tea/water/biscuits** té/agua/(unas) galletas; **there's ~ milk in the fridge** hay leche en el frigo; **there were ~ people outside** había algunas personas fuera; **I've got ~ money, but not much** tengo algo de dinero, pero no mucho
2 (certain: in contrasts) algunos/as; ~ **people say that ...** hay quien dice que ...; ~ **films were excellent, but most were mediocre** hubo películas excelentes, pero la mayoría fueron mediocres
3 (unspecified): ~ **woman was asking for you** una mujer estuvo preguntando por ti; **he was asking for ~ book (or other)** pedía un libro; ~ **day** algún día; ~ **day next week** un día de la semana que viene
♦ pron 1 (a certain number): **I've got ~** (books etc) tengo algunos/as
2 (a certain amount) algo; **I've got ~** (money, milk) tengo algo; **could I have ~ of that cheese?** ¿me puede dar un poco de ese queso?; **I've read ~ of the book** he leído parte del libro
♦ adv: ~ **10 people** unas 10 personas, una decena de personas

some: ~**body** ['sʌmbədɪ] pron = **someone**; ~**how** adv de alguna manera; (for some reason) por una u otra razón; ~**one** pron alguien; ~**place** (US) adv = **somewhere**
somersault ['sʌməsɔ:lt] n (deliberate) salto mortal; (accidental) vuelco ♦ vi dar un salto mortal; dar vuelcos
some: ~**thing** pron algo; **would you like** ~**thing to eat/drink?** ¿te gustaría cenar/tomar algo?; ~**time** adv (in future) algún día, en algún momento; (in past): ~**time last month** durante el mes pasado; ~**times** adv a veces; ~**what** adv algo; ~**where** adv (be) en alguna parte; (go) a alguna parte; ~**where else** (be) en otra parte; (go) a otra parte
son [sʌn] n hijo
song [sɔŋ] n canción f
son-in-law n yerno
soon [su:n] adv pronto, dentro de poco; ~ **afterwards** poco después; see also **as**; ~**er** adv (time) antes, más temprano; (preference): **I would ~er do that** preferiría hacer eso; ~**er or later** tarde o temprano
soot [sut] n hollín m
soothe [su:ð] vt tranquilizar; (pain) aliviar
sophisticated [sə'fɪstɪkeɪtɪd] adj sofisticado

sophomore ['sɔfəmɔ:*] (US) n estudiante m/f de segundo año
sopping ['sɔpɪŋ] adj: ~ (**wet**) empapado
soppy ['sɔpɪ] (pej) adj tonto
soprano [sə'prɑ:nəu] n soprano f
sorcerer ['sɔ:sərə*] n hechicero
sore [sɔ:*] adj (painful) doloroso, que duele ♦ n llaga; ~**ly** adv: **I am ~ly tempted to** estoy muy tentado a
sorrow ['sɔrəu] n pena, dolor m; ~**s** npl pesares mpl; ~**ful** adj triste
sorry ['sɔrɪ] adj (regretful) arrepentido; (condition, excuse) lastimoso; ~! ¡perdón!, ¡perdone!; ~? ¿cómo?; **to feel ~ for sb** tener lástima a uno; **I feel ~ for him** me da lástima
sort [sɔ:t] n clase f, género, tipo ♦ vt (also: ~ **out**: papers) clasificar; (: problems) arreglar, solucionar; ~**ing office** n sala de batalla
SOS n SOS m
so-so adv regular, así así
soufflé ['su:fleɪ] n suflé m
sought [sɔ:t] pt, pp of **seek**
soul [səul] n alma; ~**ful** adj lleno de sentimiento
sound [saund] n (noise) sonido, ruido; (volume: on TV etc) volumen m; (GEO) estrecho ♦ adj (healthy) sano; (safe, not damaged) en buen estado; (reliable: person) digno de confianza; (sensible) sensato, razonable; (secure: investment) seguro ♦ adv: ~ **asleep** profundamente dormido ♦ vt (alarm) sonar ♦ vi sonar, resonar; (fig: seem) parecer; **to ~ like** sonar a; ~ **out** vt sondear; ~ **barrier** n barrera del sonido; ~**bite** n cita jugosa; ~ **effects** npl efectos mpl sonoros; ~**ly** adv (sleep) profundamente; (defeated) completamente; ~**proof** adj insonorizado; ~**track** n (of film) banda sonora
soup [su:p] n (thick) sopa; (thin) caldo; ~ **plate** n plato sopero; ~**spoon** n cuchara sopera
sour ['sauə*] adj agrio; (milk) cortado; **it's ~ grapes** (fig) están verdes
source [sɔ:s] n fuente f
south [sauθ] n sur m ♦ adj del sur, sureño ♦ adv al sur, hacia el sur; **S~ Africa** n África del Sur; **S~ African** adj, n sudafricano/a m/f; **S~ America** n América del Sur, Sudamérica; **S~ American** adj, n sudamericano/a m/f; ~**-east** n sudeste m; ~**erly** ['sʌðəlɪ] adj sur; (from the ~) del sur; ~**ern** ['sʌðən] adj del sur, meridional; **S~ Pole** n Polo Sur; ~**ward(s)** adv hacia el sur; ~**-west** n suroeste m
souvenir [su:və'nɪə*] n recuerdo
sovereign ['sɔvrɪn] adj, n soberano/a m/f; ~**ty** n soberanía
soviet ['səuvɪət] adj soviético; **the S~ Union** la Unión Soviética

sow¹ [səu] (*pt* **sowed**, *pp* **sown**) *vt* sembrar

sow² [sau] *n* cerda (*SP*), puerca (*SP*), chancha (*AM*)

soy [sɔɪ] (*US*) *n* = **soya**

soya [ˈsɔɪə] (*BRIT*) *n* soja; **~ bean** *n* haba de soja; **~ sauce** *n* salsa de soja

spa [spɑː] *n* balneario

space [speɪs] *n* espacio; (*room*) sitio ♦ *cpd* espacial ♦ *vt* (*also*: **~ out**) espaciar; **~craft** *n* nave *f* espacial; **~man/woman** (*irreg*) *n* astronauta *m/f*, cosmonauta *m/f*; **~ship** *n* = **~craft**; **spacing** *n* espaciado

spacious [ˈspeɪʃəs] *adj* amplio

spade [speɪd] *n* (*tool*) pala, laya; **~s** *npl* (*CARDS*: *British*) picas *fpl*; (: *Spanish*) espadas *fpl*

spaghetti [spəˈgɛtɪ] *n* espaguetis *mpl*, fideos *mpl*

Spain [speɪn] *n* España

span [spæn] *n* (*of bird, plane*) envergadura; (*of arch*) luz *f*; (*in time*) lapso ♦ *vt* extenderse sobre, cruzar; (*fig*) abarcar

Spaniard [ˈspænjəd] *n* español(a) *m/f*

spaniel [ˈspænjəl] *n* perro de aguas

Spanish [ˈspænɪʃ] *adj* español(a) ♦ *n* (*LING*) español *m*, castellano; **the ~** *npl* los españoles

spank [spæŋk] *vt* zurrar

spanner [ˈspænə*] (*BRIT*) *n* llave *f* (inglesa)

spare [speə*] *adj* de reserva; (*surplus*) sobrante, de más ♦ *n* = **part** ♦ *vt* (*do without*) pasarse sin; (*refrain from hurting*) perdonar; **to ~** (*surplus*) sobrante, de sobra; **~ part** *n* pieza de repuesto; **~ time** *n* tiempo libre; **~ wheel** *n* (*AUT*) rueda de recambio

sparingly [ˈspeərɪŋlɪ] *adv* con moderación

spark [spɑːk] *n* chispa; (*fig*) chispazo; **~(ing) plug** *n* bujía

sparkle [ˈspɑːkl] *n* centelleo, destello ♦ *vi* (*shine*) relucir, brillar; **sparkling** *adj* (*eyes, conversation*) brillante; (*wine*) espumoso; (*mineral water*) con gas

sparrow [ˈspærəu] *n* gorrión *m*

sparse [spɑːs] *adj* esparcido, escaso

spartan [ˈspɑːtən] *adj* (*fig*) espartano

spasm [ˈspæzəm] *n* (*MED*) espasmo

spastic [ˈspæstɪk] *n* espástico/a

spat [spæt] *pt, pp of* **spit**

spate [speɪt] *n* (*fig*): **a ~ of** un torrente de

spawn [spɔːn] *vi* desovar, frezar ♦ *n* huevas *fpl*

speak [spiːk] (*pt* **spoke**, *pp* **spoken**) *vt* (*language*) hablar; (*truth*) decir ♦ *vi* hablar; (*make a speech*) intervenir; **to ~ to sb/of or about sth** hablar con uno/de or sobre algo; **~ up!** ¡habla fuerte!; **~er** *n* (*in public*) orador(a) *m/f*; (*also*: **loud~er**) altavoz *m*; (*for stereo etc*) bafle *m*; (*POL*): **the S~er** (*BRIT*) el Presidente de la Cámara de los Comunes; (*US*) el Presidente del Congreso

spear [spɪə*] *n* lanza ♦ *vt* alancear; **~head** *vt* (*attack etc*) encabezar

spec [spɛk] (*inf*) *n*: **on ~** como especulación

special [ˈspɛʃl] *adj* especial; (*edition etc*) extraordinario; (*delivery*) urgente; **~ist** *n* especialista *m/f*; **~ity** [spɛʃɪˈælɪtɪ] (*BRIT*) *n* especialidad *f*, **~ize** *vi*: **to ~ize (in)** especializarse (en); **~ly** *adv* sobre todo, en particular; **~ty** (*US*) *n* = **~ity**

species [ˈspiːʃiːz] *n inv* especie *f*

specific [spəˈsɪfɪk] *adj* específico; **~ally** *adv* específicamente

specify [ˈspɛsɪfaɪ] *vt, vi* especificar, precisar

specimen [ˈspɛsɪmən] *n* ejemplar *m*; (*MED*: *of urine*) espécimen *m*; (: *of blood*) muestra

speck [spɛk] *n* grano, mota

speckled [ˈspɛkld] *adj* moteado

specs [spɛks] (*inf*) *npl* gafas *fpl* (*SP*), anteojos *mpl*

spectacle [ˈspɛktəkl] *n* espectáculo; **~s** *npl* (*BRIT*: *glasses*) gafas *fpl* (*SP*), anteojos *mpl*; **spectacular** [-ˈtækjulə*] *adj* espectacular; (*success*) impresionante

spectator [spɛkˈteɪtə*] *n* espectador(a) *m/f*

spectrum [ˈspɛktrəm] (*pl* **spectra**) *n* espectro

speculate [ˈspɛkjuleɪt] *vi*: **to ~ (on)** especular (en); **speculation** [spɛkjuˈleɪʃən] *n* especulación *f*

speech [spiːtʃ] *n* (*faculty*) habla; (*formal talk*) discurso; (*spoken language*) lenguaje *m*; **~less** *adj* mudo, estupefacto; **~ therapist** *n* especialista que corrige defectos de pronunciación en los niños

speed [spiːd] *n* velocidad *f*; (*haste*) prisa; (*promptness*) rapidez *f*; **at full or top ~ a** máxima velocidad; **~ up** *vi* acelerarse ♦ *vt* acelerar; **~boat** *n* lancha motora; **~ily** *adv* rápido, rápidamente; **~ing** *n* (*AUT*) exceso de velocidad; **~ limit** *n* límite *m* de velocidad, velocidad *f* máxima; **~ometer** [spɪˈdɔmɪtə*] *n* velocímetro; **~way** *n* (*sport*) pista de carrera; **~y** *adj* (*fast*) veloz, rápido; (*prompt*) pronto

spell [spɛl] (*pt, pp* **spelt** (*BRIT*) or **spelled**) *n* (*also*: *magic* ~) encanto, hechizo; (*period of time*) rato, período ♦ *vt* deletrear; (*fig*) anunciar, presagiar; **to cast a ~ on sb** hechizar a uno; **he can't ~** pone faltas de ortografía; **~bound** *adj* embelesado, hechizado; **~ing** *n* ortografía

spend [spɛnd] (*pt, pp* **spent**) *vt* (*money*) gastar; (*time*) pasar; (*life*) dedicar; **~thrift** *n* derrochador(a) *m/f*, pródigo/a

sperm [spəːm] *n* esperma

sphere [sfɪə*] *n* esfera

sphinx [sfɪŋks] *n* esfinge *f*

spice [spaɪs] *n* especia ♦ *vt* condimentar

spicy [ˈspaɪsɪ] *adj* picante

spider ['spaɪdə*] n araña

spike [spaɪk] n (point) punta; (BOT) espiga

spill [spɪl] (pt, pp spilt or spilled) vt derramar, verter ♦ vi derramarse; **to ~ over** desbordarse

spin [spɪn] (pt, pp spun) n (AVIAT) barrena; (trip in car) paseo (en coche); (on ball) efecto ♦ vt (wool etc) hilar; (ball etc) hacer girar ♦ vi girar, dar vueltas

spinach ['spɪnɪtʃ] n espinaca; (as food) espinacas fpl

spinal ['spaɪnl] adj espinal; **~ cord** n columna vertebral

spin doctor n informador(a) parcial al servicio de un partido político etc

spin-dryer (BRIT) n secador m centrífugo

spine [spaɪn] n espinazo, columna vertebral; (thorn) espina; **~less** adj (fig) débil, pusilánime

spinning ['spɪnɪŋ] n hilandería; **~ top** n peonza

spin-off n derivado, producto secundario

spinster ['spɪnstə*] n solterona

spiral ['spaɪərl] n espiral f ♦ vi (fig: prices) subir desorbitadamente; **~ staircase** n escalera de caracol

spire ['spaɪə*] n aguja, chapitel m

spirit ['spɪrɪt] n (soul) alma f; (ghost) fantasma m; (attitude, sense) espíritu m; (courage) valor m, ánimo; **~s** npl (drink) licor(es) m(pl); **in good ~s** alegre, de buen ánimo; **~ed** adj enérgico, vigoroso

spiritual ['spɪrɪtjuəl] adj espiritual ♦ n espiritual m

spit [spɪt] (pt, pp spat) n (for roasting) asador m, espetón m; (saliva) saliva ♦ vi escupir; (sound) chisporrotear; (rain) lloviznar

spite [spaɪt] n rencor m, ojeriza ♦ vt causar pena a, mortificar; **in ~ of** a pesar de, pese a; **~ful** adj rencoroso, malévolo

spittle ['spɪtl] n saliva, baba

splash [splæʃ] n (sound) chapoteo; (of colour) mancha ♦ vt salpicar ♦ vi (also: ~ about) chapotear

spleen [spliːn] n (ANAT) bazo

splendid ['splendɪd] adj espléndido

splint [splɪnt] n tablilla

splinter ['splɪntə*] n (of wood etc) astilla; (in finger) espigón m ♦ vi astillarse, hacer astillas

split [splɪt] (pt, pp split) n hendedura, raja; (fig) división f; (POL) escisión f ♦ vt partir, rajar; (party) dividir; (share) repartir ♦ vi dividirse, escindirse; **~ up** vi (couple) separarse; (meeting) acabarse

spoil [spɔɪl] (pt, pp spoilt or spoiled) vt (damage) dañar; (mar) estropear; (child) mimar, consentir; **~s** npl despojo, botín m; **~sport** n aguafiestas m inv

spoke [spəʊk] pt of speak ♦ n rayo, radio

spoken ['spəʊkn] pp of speak

spokesman ['spəʊksmən] (irreg) n portavoz m; **spokeswoman** ['spəʊkswʊmən] (irreg) n portavoz f

sponge [spʌndʒ] n esponja; (also: ~ cake) bizcocho ♦ vt (wash) lavar con esponja ♦ vi: **to ~ off** or **on sb** vivir a costa de uno; **~ bag** (BRIT) n esponjera

sponsor ['spɒnsə*] n patrocinador(a) m/f ♦ vt (applicant, proposal etc) proponer; **~ship** n patrocinio

spontaneous [spɒn'teɪnɪəs] adj espontáneo

spooky ['spuːkɪ] (inf) adj espeluznante, horripilante

spool [spuːl] n carrete m

spoon [spuːn] n cuchara; **~-feed** vt dar de comer con cuchara a; (fig) tratar como a un niño a; **~ful** n cucharada

sport [spɔːt] n deporte m; (person): **to be a good ~** ser muy majo ♦ vt (wear) lucir, ostentar; **~ing** adj deportivo; (generous) caballeroso; **to give sb a ~ing chance** darle a uno una (buena) oportunidad; **~ jacket** (US) n = **~s jacket**; **~s car** n coche m deportivo; **~s jacket** (BRIT) n chaqueta deportiva; **~sman** (irreg) n deportista m; **~smanship** n deportividad f; **~swear** n trajes mpl de deporte or sport; **~swoman** (irreg) n deportista y

spot [spɒt] n sitio, lugar m; (dot: on pattern) punto, mancha; (pimple) grano; (RADIO) cuña publicitaria; (TV) espacio publicitario; (small amount): **a ~ of** un poquito de ♦ vt (notice) notar, observar; **on the ~** allí mismo; **~ check** n reconocimiento rápido; **~less** adj perfectamente limpio; **~light** n foco, reflector m; (AUT) faro auxiliar; **~ted** adj (pattern) de puntos; **~ty** adj (face) con granos

spouse [spauz] n cónyuge m/f

spout [spaut] n (of jug) pico; (of pipe) caño ♦ vi salir en chorro

sprain [spreɪn] n torcedura ♦ vt: **to ~ one's ankle/wrist** torcerse el tobillo/la muñeca

sprang [spræŋ] pt of spring

sprawl [sprɔːl] vi tumbarse

spray [spreɪ] n rociada; (of sea) espuma; (container) atomizador m; (for paint etc) pistola rociadora; (of flowers) ramita ♦ vt rociar; (crops) regar

spread [spred] (pt, pp spread) n extensión f; (for bread etc) pasta para untar; (inf: food) comilona ♦ vt extender; (butter) untar; (wings, sails) desplegar; (work, wealth) repartir; (scatter) esparcir ♦ vi (also: ~ out: stain) extenderse; (news) diseminarse; **~ out** vi (move apart) separarse; **~-eagled** adj a pata tendida; **~sheet** n hoja electrónica or de cálculo

spree [spriː] n: **to go on a ~** ir de juerga

sprightly ['spraɪtlɪ] adj vivo, enérgico

spring [sprɪŋ] (pt **sprang**, pp **sprung**) n (season) primavera; (leap) salto, brinco; (coiled metal) resorte m; (of water) fuente f, manantial m ♦ vi saltar, brincar; ~ **up** vi (thing: appear) aparecer; (problem) surgir; ~**board** n trampolín m; ~**clean(ing)** n limpieza general; ~**time** n primavera

sprinkle ['sprɪŋkl] vt (pour: liquid) rociar; (: salt, sugar) espolvorear; **to** ~ **water etc on**, ~ **with water etc** rociar or salpicar de agua etc; ~**r** n (for lawn) rociadera; (to put out fire) aparato de rociadura automática

sprint [sprɪnt] n esprint m ♦ vi esprintar

sprout [spraut] vi brotar, retoñar; **(Brussels)** ~**s** npl coles fpl de Bruselas

spruce [spruːs] n inv (BOT) pícea ♦ adj aseado, pulcro

sprung [sprʌŋ] pp of **spring**

spun [spʌn] pt, pp of **spin**

spur [spəː*] n espuela; (fig) estímulo, aguijón m ♦ vt (also: ~ **on**) estimular, incitar; **on the** ~ **of the moment** de improviso

spurious ['spjuəriəs] adj falso

spurn [spəːn] vt desdeñar, rechazar

spurt [spəːt] n chorro; (of energy) arrebato ♦ vi chorrear

spy [spaɪ] n espía m/f ♦ vi: **to** ~ **on** espiar a ♦ vt (see) divisar, lograr ver; ~**ing** n espionaje m

sq. abbr = **square**

squabble ['skwɔbl] vi reñir, pelear

squad [skwɔd] n (MIL) pelotón m; (POLICE) brigada; (SPORT) equipo

squadron ['skwɔdrən] n (MIL) escuadrón m; (AVIAT, NAUT) escuadra

squalid ['skwɔlɪd] adj vil; (fig: sordid) sórdido

squall [skwɔːl] n (storm) chubasco; (wind) ráfaga

squalor ['skwɔlə*] n miseria

squander ['skwɔndə*] vt (money) derrochar, despilfarrar; (chances) desperdiciar

square [skwɛə*] n cuadro, plaza; (in town) plaza; (inf: person) carca m/f ♦ adj cuadrado; (inf: ideas, tastes) trasnochado ♦ vt (arrange) arreglar; (MATH) cuadrar; (reconcile) compaginar; **all** ~ igual(es); **to have a** ~ **meal** comer caliente; **2 metres** ~ 2 metros en cuadro; **2** ~ **metres** 2 metros cuadrados; ~**ly** adv de lleno

squash [skwɔʃ] n (BRIT: drink): **lemon/orange** ~ zumo (SP) or jugo (AM) de limón/naranja; (US: BOT) calabacín m; (SPORT) squash m, frontenis m ♦ vt aplastar

squat [skwɔt] adj achaparrado ♦ vi (also: ~ **down**) agacharse, sentarse en cuclillas; ~**ter** n persona que ocupa ilegalmente una casa

squeak [skwiːk] vi (hinge) chirriar, rechinar; (mouse) chillar

squeal [skwiːl] vi chillar, dar gritos agudos

squeamish ['skwiːmɪʃ] adj delicado, remilgado

squeeze [skwiːz] n presión f; (of hand) apretón m; (COMM) restricción f ♦ vt (hand, arm) apretar; ~ **out** vt exprimir

squelch [skweltʃ] vi chapotear

squid [skwɪd] n inv calamar m; (CULIN) calamares mpl

squiggle ['skwɪgl] n garabato

squint [skwɪnt] vi bizquear, ser bizco ♦ n (MED) estrabismo

squirm [skwəːm] vi retorcerse, revolverse

squirrel ['skwɪrəl] n ardilla

squirt [skwəːt] vi salir a chorros ♦ vt chiscar

Sr abbr = **senior**

St abbr = **saint; street**

stab [stæb] n (with knife) puñalada; (of pain) pinchazo; (inf: try): **to have a** ~ **at (doing) sth** intentar (hacer) algo ♦ vt apuñalar

stable ['steɪbl] adj estable ♦ n cuadra, caballeriza

stack [stæk] n montón m, pila ♦ vt amontonar, apilar

stadium ['steɪdɪəm] n estadio

staff [stɑːf] n (work force) personal m, plantilla; (BRIT: SCOL) cuerpo docente ♦ vt proveer de personal

stag [stæg] n ciervo, venado

stage [steɪdʒ] n escena; (point) etapa; (platform) plataforma; (profession): **the** ~ el teatro ♦ vt (play) poner en escena, representar; (organize) montar, organizar; **in** ~**s** por etapas; ~**coach** n diligencia; ~ **manager** n director(a) m/f de escena

stagger ['stægə*] vi tambalearse ♦ vt (amaze) asombrar; (hours, holidays) escalonar; ~**ing** adj asombroso

stagnant ['stægnənt] adj estancado

stag party n despedida de soltero

staid [steɪd] adj serio, formal

stain [steɪn] n mancha; (colouring) tintura ♦ vt manchar; (wood) teñir; ~**ed glass window** n vidriera de colores; ~**less steel** n acero inoxidable; ~ **remover** n quitamanchas m inv

stair [stɛə*] n (step) peldaño, escalón m; ~**s** npl escaleras fpl; ~**case** n = ~**way**; ~**way** n escalera

stake [steɪk] n estaca, poste m; (COMM) interés m; (BETTING) apuesta ♦ vt (money) apostar; (life) arriesgar; (reputation) poner en juego; (claim) presentar una reclamación; **to be at** ~ estar en juego

stale [steɪl] adj (bread) duro; (food) pasado; (smell) rancio; (beer) agrio

stalemate ['steɪlmeɪt] n tablas fpl (por ahogado); (fig) estancamiento

stalk [stɔːk] n tallo, caña ♦ vt acechar, cazar al acecho; ~ **off** vi irse airado

stall [stɔ:l] n (in market) puesto; (in stable) casilla (de establo) ♦ vt (AUT) calar; (fig) dar largas a ♦ vi (AUT) calarse; (fig) andarse con rodeos; ~s npl (BRIT: in cinema, theatre) butacas fpl

stallion [ˈstæliən] n semental m

stamina [ˈstæminə] n resistencia

stammer [ˈstæmə*] n tartamudeo ♦ vi tartamudear

stamp [stæmp] n sello (SP), estampilla (AM); (mark, also fig) marca, huella; (on document) timbre m ♦ vi (also: ~ one's foot) patear ♦ vt (mark) marcar; (letter) poner sellos or estampillas en; (with rubber ~) sellar; ~ **album** n álbum m para sellos or estampillas; ~ **collecting** n filatelia

stampede [stæmˈpiːd] n estampida

stance [stæns] n postura

stand [stænd] (pt, pp stood) n (position) posición f, postura; (for taxis) parada; (hall ~) perchero; (music ~) atril m; (SPORT) tribuna; (at exhibition) stand m ♦ vi (be) estar, encontrarse; (be on foot) estar de pie; (rise) levantarse; (remain) quedar en pie; (in election) presentar candidatura ♦ vt (place) poner, colocar; (withstand) aguantar, soportar; (invite to) invitar; **to make a ~** (fig) mantener una postura firme; **to ~ for parliament** (BRIT) presentarse (como candidato) a las elecciones; ~ **by** vi (be ready) estar listo ♦ vt fus (opinion) aferrarse a; (person) apoyar; ~ **down** vi (withdraw) ceder el puesto; ~ **for** vt fus (signify) significar; (tolerate) aguantar, permitir; ~ **in for** vt fus suplir a; ~ **out** vi destacarse; ~ **up** vi levantarse, ponerse de pie; ~ **up for** vt fus defender; ~ **up to** vt fus hacer frente a

standard [ˈstændəd] n patrón m, norma; (level) nivel m; (flag) estandarte m ♦ adj (size etc) normal, corriente; (text) básico; ~s npl (morals) valores mpl morales; ~ **lamp** (BRIT) n lámpara de pie; ~ **of living** n nivel m de vida

stand-by [ˈstændbai] n (reserve) recurso seguro; **to be on ~** estar sobre aviso; ~ **ticket** n (AVIAT) (billete m) standby m

stand-in [ˈstændin] n suplente m/f

standing [ˈstændiŋ] adj (on foot) de pie, en pie; (permanent) permanente ♦ n reputación f; **of many years' ~** que lleva muchos años; ~ **joke** n broma permanente; ~ **order** (BRIT) n (at bank) orden f de pago permanente; ~ **room** n sitio para estar de pie

stand- ~**point** n punto de vista; ~**still** n: **at a** ~**still** (industry, traffic) paralizado; (car) parado; **to come to a** ~**still** quedar paralizado; pararse

stank [stæŋk] pt of stink

staple [ˈsteipl] n (for papers) grapa ♦ adj (food etc) básico ♦ vt grapar; ~**r** n grapadora

star [stɑː*] n estrella; (celebrity) estrella, astro ♦ vt (THEATRE, CINEMA) ser el/la protagonista de; **the ~s** npl (ASTROLOGY) el horóscopo

starboard [ˈstɑːbəd] n estribor m

stareh [stɑːtʃ] n almidón m

stardom [ˈstɑːdəm] n estrellato

stare [steə*] n mirada fija ♦ vi: **to ~ at** mirar fijo

starfish [ˈstɑːfiʃ] n estrella de mar

stark [stɑːk] adj (bleak) severo, escueto ♦ adv: ~ **naked** en cueros

starling [ˈstɑːliŋ] n estornino

starry [ˈstɑːri] adj estrellado; ~**-eyed** adj (innocent) inocentón/ona, ingenuo

start [stɑːt] n principio, comienzo; (departure) salida; (sudden movement) salto, sobresalto; (advantage) ventaja ♦ vt empezar, comenzar; (cause) causar; (found) fundar; (engine) poner en marcha ♦ vi comenzar, empezar; (with fright) asustarse, sobresaltarse; (train etc) salir; **to ~ doing** or **to do sth** empezar a hacer algo; ~ **off** vi empezar, comenzar; (leave) salir, ponerse en camino; ~ **up** vi comenzar; (car) ponerse en marcha ♦ vt comenzar; poner en marcha; ~**er** n (AUT) botón m de arranque; (SPORT: official) juez m/f de salida; (BRIT: CULIN) entrada; ~**ing point** n punto de partida

startle [ˈstɑːtl] vt asustar, sobrecoger; **startling** adj alarmante

starvation [stɑːˈveiʃən] n hambre f

starve [stɑːv] vi tener mucha hambre; (to death) morir de hambre ♦ vt hacer pasar hambre

state [steit] n estado ♦ vt (say, declare) afirmar; **the S~s** los Estados Unidos; **to be in a ~** estar agitado; ~**ly** adj majestuoso, imponente; ~**ly home** n casa señorial, casa solariega; ~**ment** n afirmación f; ~**sman** (irreg) n estadista m

static [ˈstætik] n (RADIO) parásitos mpl ♦ adj estático; ~ **electricity** n estática

station [ˈsteiʃən] n (gen) estación f; (RADIO) emisora; (rank) posición f social ♦ vt colocar, situar; (MIL) apostar

stationary [ˈsteiʃnəri] adj estacionario, fijo

stationer [ˈsteiʃənə*] n papelero/a; ~**'s (shop)** (BRIT) n papelería; ~**y** [-nəri] n papel m de escribir, artículos mpl de escritorio

station master n (RAIL) jefe m de estación

station wagon (US) n ranchera

statistic [stəˈtistik] n estadística; ~**s** n (science) estadística

statue [ˈstætjuː] n estatua

status [ˈsteitəs] n estado; (reputation) estatus m; ~ **symbol** n símbolo de prestigio

statute [ˈstætjuːt] n estatuto, ley f; **statutory** adj estatutario

staunch [stɔːntʃ] *adj* leal, incondicional

stay [steɪ] *n* estancia ♦ *vi* quedar(se); (*as guest*) hospedarse; **to ~ put** seguir en el mismo sitio; **to ~ the night/5 days** pasar la noche/estar 5 días; **~ behind** *vi* quedar atrás; **~ in** *vi* quedarse en casa; **~ on** *vi* quedarse; **~ out** *vi* (*of house*) no volver a casa; (*on strike*) permanecer en huelga; **~ up** *vi* (*at night*) velar, no acostarse; **~ing power** *n* aguante *m*

stead [sted] *n*: **in sb's ~** en lugar de uno; **to stand sb in good ~** ser muy útil a uno

steadfast ['stedfɑːst] *adj* firme, resuelto

steadily ['stedɪlɪ] *adv* constantemente; (*firmly*) firmemente; (*work, walk*) sin parar; (*gaze*) fijamente

steady ['stedɪ] *adj* (*firm*) firme; (*regular*) regular; (*person, character*) sensato, juicioso; (*boyfriend*) formal; (*look, voice*) tranquilo ♦ *vt* (*stabilize*) estabilizar; (*nerves*) calmar

steak [steɪk] *n* (*gen*) filete *m*; (*beef*) bistec *m*

steal [stiːl] (*pt* **stole**, *pp* **stolen**) *vt* robar ♦ *vi* robar; (*move secretly*) andar a hurtadillas

stealth [stelθ] *n*: **by ~** a escondidas, sigilosamente; **~y** *adj* cauteloso, sigiloso

steam [stiːm] *n* vapor *m*; (*mist*) vaho, humo ♦ *vt* (*CULIN*) cocer al vapor ♦ *vi* echar vapor; **~ engine** *n* máquina de vapor; **~er** *n* (*buque de de*) vapor *m*; **~roller** *n* apisonadora; **~ship** *n* = **~er**; **~y** *adj* (*room*) lleno de vapor; (*window*) empañado; (*heat, atmosphere*) bochornoso

steel [stiːl] *n* acero ♦ *adj* de acero; **~works** *n* acería

steep [stiːp] *adj* escarpado, abrupto; (*stair*) empinado; (*price*) exorbitante, excesivo ♦ *vt* empapar, remojar

steeple ['stiːpl] *n* aguja; **~chase** *n* carrera de obstáculos

steer [stɪə*] *vt* (*car*) conducir (*SP*), manejar (*AM*); (*person*) dirigir ♦ *vi* conducir, manejar; **~ing** *n* (*AUT*) dirección *f*; **~ing wheel** *n* volante *m*

stem [stem] *n* (*of plant*) tallo; (*of glass*) pie *m* ♦ *vt* detener; (*blood*) restañar; **~ from** *vt fus* ser consecuencia de

stench [stentʃ] *n* hedor *m*

stencil ['stensl] *n* (*pattern*) plantilla ♦ *vt* hacer un cliché de

stenographer [ste'nɔgrəfə*] (*US*) *n* taquígrafo/a

step [step] *n* paso; (*on stair*) peldaño, escalón *m* ♦ *vi*: **to ~ forward/back** dar un paso adelante/hacia atrás; **~s** *npl* (*BRIT*) = **~ladder**; **in/out of ~** (**with**) acorde/en disonancia (con); **~ down** *vi* (*fig*) retirarse; **~ on** *vt fus* pisar; **~ up** *vt* (*increase*) aumentar; **~brother** *n* hermanastro; **~daughter** *n* hijastra; **~father** *n* padrastro; **~ladder** *n* escalera

doble *or* de tijera; **~mother** *n* madrastra; **~ping stone** *n* pasadera; **~sister** *n* hermanastra; **~son** *n* hijastro

stereo ['steriəu] *n* estéreo ♦ *adj* (*also*: **~phonic**) estéreo, estereofónico

sterile ['sterail] *adj* estéril; **sterilize** ['sterilaiz] *vt* esterilizar

sterling ['stɜːlɪŋ] *adj* (*silver*) de ley ♦ *n* (*ECON*) (libras *fpl*) esterlinas *fpl*; **one pound ~** una libra esterlina

stern [stɜːn] *adj* severo, austero ♦ *n* (*NAUT*) popa

stew [stjuː] *n* cocido (*SP*), estofado (*SP*), guisado (*AM*) ♦ *vt* estofar, guisar; (*fruit*) cocer

steward ['stjuːəd] *n* camarero; **~ess** *n* (*esp on plane*) azafata

stick [stik] (*pt, pp* **stuck**) *n* palo; (*of dynamite*) barreno; (*as weapon*) porra; (*walking ~*) bastón *m* ♦ *vt* (*glue*) pegar; (*inf: put*) meter; (: *tolerate*) aguantar, soportar; (*thrust*): **to ~ sth into** clavar *or* hincar algo en ♦ *vi* pegarse; (*be unmoveable*) quedarse parado; (*in mind*) quedarse grabado; **~ out** *vi* sobresalir; **~ up** *vi* sobresalir; **~ up for** *vt fus* defender; **~er** *n* (*label*) etiqueta engomada; (*with slogan*) pegatina; **~ing plaster** *n* esparadrapo

stick-up ['stikʌp] (*inf*) *n* asalto, atraco

sticky ['stiki] *adj* pegajoso; (*label*) engomado; (*fig*) difícil

stiff [stif] *adj* rígido, tieso; (*hard*) duro; (*manner*) estirado; (*difficult*) difícil; (*person*) inflexible; (*price*) exorbitante ♦ *adv*: **scared/bored ~** muerto de miedo/aburrimiento; **~en** *vi* (*muscles etc*) agarrotarse; **~ neck** *n* torticolis *m inv*; **~ness** *n* rigidez *f*, tiesura

stifle ['staifl] *vt* ahogar, sofocar; **stifling** *adj* (*heat*) sofocante, bochornoso

stigma ['stigmə] *n* (*fig*) estigma *m*

stile [stail] *n* portillo, portilla

stiletto [sti'letəu] (*BRIT*) *n* (*also*: **~ heel**) tacón *m* de aguja

still [stil] *adj* inmóvil, quieto ♦ *adv* todavía; (*even*) aun; (*nonetheless*) sin embargo, aun así; **~born** *adj* nacido muerto; **~ life** *n* naturaleza muerta

stilt [stilt] *n* zanco; (*pile*) pilar *m*, soporte *m*

stilted ['stiltid] *adj* afectado

stimulate ['stimjuleit] *vt* estimular

stimulus ['stimjuləs] (*pl* **stimuli**) *n* estímulo, incentivo

sting [stiŋ] (*pt, pp* **stung**) *n* picadura; (*pain*) escozor *m*, picazón *f*; (*organ*) aguijón *m* ♦ *vt, vi* picar

stingy ['stindʒi] *adj* tacaño

stink [stiŋk] (*pt* **stank**, *pp* **stunk**) *n* hedor *m*, tufo ♦ *vi* heder, apestar; **~ing** *adj* hediondo, fétido; (*fig: inf*) horrible

stint [stint] *n* tarea, trabajo ♦ *vi*: **to ~ on**

escatimar

stir [stəːʳ] n (fig: agitation) conmoción f ♦ vt (tea etc) remover; (fig: emotions) provocar ♦ vi moverse; ~ **up** vt (trouble) fomentar

stirrup ['stɪrəp] n estribo

stitch [stɪtʃ] n (SEWING) puntada; (KNITTING) punto; (MED) punto (de sutura); (pain) punzada ♦ vt coser; (MED) suturar

stoat [stəut] n armiño

stock [stɔk] n (COMM: reserves) existencias fpl, stock m; (: selection) surtido; (AGR) ganado, ganadería; (CULIN) caldo; (descent) raza, estirpe f; (FINANCE) capital m ♦ adj (fig: reply etc) clásico ♦ vt (have in ~) tener existencias de; ~**s and shares** acciones y valores; **in ~** en existencia or almacén; **out of ~** agotado; to **take ~ of** (fig) asesorar, examinar; ~ **up with** vt fus abastecerse de; ~**broker** ['stɔkbrəukəʳ] n agente m/f or corredor(a) m/f de bolsa; ~ **cube** (BRIT) n pastilla de caldo; ~ **exchange** n bolsa

stocking ['stɔkɪŋ] n media

stock: ~ **market** n bolsa (de valores); ~**pile** n reserva ♦ vt acumular, almacenar; ~**taking** (BRIT) n (COMM) inventario

stocky ['stɔkɪ] adj (strong) robusto; (short) achaparrado

stodgy ['stɔdʒɪ] adj indigesto, pesado

stoke [stəuk] vt atizar

stole [stəul] pt of **steal** ♦ n estola

stolen ['stəuln] pp of **steal**

stomach ['stʌmək] n (ANAT) estómago; (belly) vientre m ♦ vt tragar, aguantar; ~**ache** n dolor m de estómago

stone [stəun] n piedra; (in fruit) hueso; = 6.348 kg; 14 libras ♦ adj de piedra ♦ vt apedrear; (fruit) deshuesar; ~-**cold** adj helado; ~-**deaf** adj sordo como una tapia; ~**work** n (art) cantería; **stony** adj pedregoso; (fig) frío

stood [stud] pt, pp of **stand**

stool [stuːl] n taburete m

stoop [stuːp] vi (also: ~ **down**) doblarse, agacharse; (also: **have a ~**) ser cargado de espaldas

stop [stɔp] n parada; (in punctuation) punto ♦ vt parar, detener; (break off) suspender; (block: pay) suspender; (: cheque) invalidar; (also: **put a ~ to**) poner término a ♦ vi pararse, detenerse; (end) acabarse; to ~ **doing sth** dejar de hacer algo; ~ **dead** vi pararse en seco; ~ **off** vi interrumpir el viaje; ~ **up** vt (hole) tapar; ~**gap** n (person) interino/a; (thing) recurso provisional; ~**over** n parada; (AVIAT) escala

stoppage ['stɔpɪdʒ] n (strike) paro; (blockage) obstrucción f

stopper ['stɔpəʳ] n tapón m

stop press n noticias fpl de última hora

stopwatch ['stɔpwɔtʃ] n cronómetro

storage ['stɔːrɪdʒ] n almacenaje m; ~ **heater** n acumulador m

store [stɔːʳ] n (stock) provisión f; (depot: BRIT: large shop) almacén m; (US) tienda; (reserve) reserva, repuesto ♦ vt almacenar; ~**s** npl víveres mpl; **in** ~ (fig): **to be in** ~ **for sb** esperarle a uno; ~ **up** vt acumular; ~**room** n despensa

storey ['stɔːrɪ] (US **story**) n piso

stork [stɔːk] n cigüeña

storm [stɔːm] n tormenta; (fig: of applause) salva; (: of criticism) nube f ♦ vi (fig) rabiar ♦ vt tomar por asalto; ~**y** adj tempestuoso

story ['stɔːrɪ] n historia; (lie) mentira; (US) = **storey**; ~**book** n libro de cuentos

stout [staut] adj (strong) sólido; (fat) gordo, corpulento; (resolute) resuelto ♦ n cerveza negra

stove [stəuv] n (for cooking) cocina; (for heating) estufa

stow [stəu] vt (also: ~ **away**) meter, poner; (NAUT) estibar; ~**away** n polizón/ona m/f

straggle ['strægl] vi (houses etc) extenderse; (lag behind) rezagarse

straight [streɪt] adj recto, derecho; (frank) franco, directo; (simple) sencillo ♦ adv derecho, directamente; (drink) sin mezcla; to **put** or **get sth** ~ dejar algo en claro; ~ **away**, ~ **off** en seguida; ~**en** vt (also: ~**en out**) enderezar, poner derecho; ~-**faced** adj serio; ~**forward** adj (simple) sencillo; (honest) honrado, franco

strain [streɪn] n tensión f; (TECH) presión f; (MED) torcedura; (breed) tipo, variedad f ♦ vt (back etc) torcerse; (resources) agotar; (stretch) estirar; (food, tea) colar; ~**s** npl (MUS) son m; ~**ed** adj (muscle) torcido; (laugh) forzado; (relations) tenso; ~**er** n colador m

strait [streɪt] n (GEO) estrecho; **to be in dire** ~**s** pasar grandes apuros; ~-**jacket** n camisa de fuerza; ~-**laced** adj mojigato, gazmoño

strand [strænd] n (of thread) hebra; (of hair) trenza; (of rope) ramal m

stranded ['strændɪd] adj (person: without money) desamparado; (: without transport) colgado

strange [streɪndʒ] adj (not known) desconocido; (odd) extraño, raro; ~**ly** adv de un modo raro; see also **enough**; ~**r** n desconocido/a; (from another area) forastero/a

strangle ['stræŋgl] vt estrangular; ~**hold** n (fig) dominio completo

strap [stræp] n correa; (of slip, dress) tirante m

strategic [strəˈtiːdʒɪk] adj estratégico

strategy ['strætɪdʒɪ] n estrategia

straw [strɔː] n paja; (drinking ~) caña, pajita;

that's the last ~! ¡eso es el colmo!

strawberry ['strɔːbərɪ] n fresa (SP), frutilla (AM)

stray [streɪ] adj (animal) extraviado; (bullet) perdido; (scattered) disperso ♦ vi extraviarse, perderse

streak [striːk] n raya; (in hair) raya ♦ vt rayar ♦ vi: **to ~ past** pasar como un rayo

stream [striːm] n riachuelo, arroyo; (of people, vehicles) riada, caravana; (of smoke, insults etc) chorro ♦ vt (SCOL) dividir en grupos por habilidad ♦ vi correr, fluir; **to ~ in/out** (people) entrar/salir en tropel

streamer ['striːmə*] n serpentina

streamlined ['striːmlaɪnd] adj aerodinámico

street [striːt] n calle f; **~car** (US) n tranvía m; **~ lamp** n farol m; **~ plan** n plano; **~wise** (inf) adj que tiene mucha calle

strength [streŋθ] n fuerza; (of girder, knot etc) resistencia; (fig: power) poder m; **~en** vt fortalecer, reforzar

strenuous ['strenjuəs] adj (energetic, determined) enérgico

stress [stres] n presión f; (mental strain) estrés m; (accent) acento ♦ vt subrayar, recalcar; (syllable) acentuar

stretch [stretʃ] n (of sand etc) trecho ♦ vi estirarse; (extend): **to ~ to** or **as far as** extenderse hasta ♦ vt extender, estirar; (make demands of) exigir el máximo esfuerzo a; **~ out** vi tenderse ♦ vt (arm etc) extender; (spread) estirar

stretcher ['stretʃə*] n camilla

strewn [struːn] adj: **~ with** cubierto or sembrado de

stricken ['strɪkən] adj (person) herido; (city, industry etc) condenado; **~ with** (disease) afectado por

strict [strɪkt] adj severo; (exact) estricto; **~ly** adv severamente; estrictamente

stride [straɪd] (pt **strode**, pp **stridden**) n zancada, tranco ♦ vi dar zancadas, andar a trancos

strife [straɪf] n lucha

strike [straɪk] (pt, pp **struck**) n huelga; (of oil etc) descubrimiento; (attack) ataque m ♦ vt golpear, pegar; (oil etc) descubrir; (bargain, deal) cerrar ♦ vi declarar la huelga; (attack) atacar; (clock) dar la hora; **on ~** (workers) en huelga; **to ~ a match** encender un fósforo; **~ down** vt derribar; **~ up** vt (MUS) empezar a tocar; (conversation) entablar; (friendship) trabar; **~r** n huelguista m/f; (SPORT) delantero; **striking** adj llamativo

string [strɪŋ] (pt, pp **strung**) n (gen) cuerda; (row) hilera ♦ vt: **to ~ together** ensartar; **to ~ out** extenderse; **the ~s** npl (MUS) los instrumentos de cuerda; **to pull ~s** (fig) mover palancas; **~ bean** n judía verde,

habichuela; **~(ed) instrument** n (MUS) instrumento de cuerda

stringent ['strɪndʒənt] adj riguroso, severo

strip [strɪp] n tira; (of land) franja; (of metal) cinta, lámina ♦ vt desnudar; (paint) quitar; (also: ~ **down**: machine) desmontar ♦ vi desnudarse; **~ cartoon** n tira cómica (SP), historieta (AM)

stripe [straɪp] n raya; (MIL) galón m; **~d** adj a rayas, rayado

strip lighting n alumbrado fluorescente

stripper ['strɪpə*] n artista m/f de striptease

strive [straɪv] (pt **strove**, pp **striven**) vi: **to ~ for sth/to do sth** luchar por conseguir/hacer algo

strode [strəud] pt of **stride**

stroke [strəuk] n (blow) golpe m; (SWIMMING) brazada; (MED) apoplejía; (of paintbrush) toque m ♦ vt acariciar; **at a ~** de un solo golpe

stroll [strəul] n paseo, vuelta ♦ vi dar un paseo or una vuelta; **~er** (US) n (for child) sillita de ruedas

strong [strɔŋ] adj fuerte; **they are 50 ~** son 50; **~hold** n fortaleza; (fig) baluarte m; **~ly** adv fuertemente, con fuerza; (believe) firmemente; **~room** n cámara acorazada

strove [strəuv] pt of **strive**

struck [strʌk] pt, pp of **strike**

structure ['strʌktʃə*] n estructura; (building) construcción f

struggle ['strʌɡl] n lucha ♦ vi luchar

strum [strʌm] vt (guitar) rasguear

strung [strʌŋ] pt, pp of **string**

strut [strʌt] n puntal m ♦ vi pavonearse

stub [stʌb] n (of ticket etc) talón m; (of cigarette) colilla; **to ~ one's toe on sth** dar con el dedo (del pie) contra algo; **~ out** vt apagar

stubble ['stʌbl] n rastrojo; (on chin) barba (incipiente)

stubborn ['stʌbən] adj terco, testarudo

stuck [stʌk] pt, pp of **stick** ♦ adj (jammed) atascado; **~-up** adj engreído, presumido

stud [stʌd] n (shirt ~) corchete m; (of boot) taco; (earring) pendiente m (de bolita); (also: ~ **farm**) caballeriza; (also: ~ **horse**) caballo semental ♦ vt (fig): **~ded with** salpicado de

student ['stjuːdənt] n estudiante m/f ♦ adj estudiantil; **~ driver** (US) n aprendiz(a) m/f

studio ['stjuːdɪəu] n estudio; (artist's) taller m; **~ flat** (US **~ apartment**) n estudio

studious ['stjuːdɪəs] adj estudioso; (studied) calculado; **~ly** adv (carefully) con esmero

study ['stʌdɪ] n estudio ♦ vt estudiar; (examine) examinar, investigar ♦ vi estudiar

stuff [stʌf] n materia; (substance) material m, sustancia; (things) cosas fpl ♦ vt llenar;

(*CULIN*) rellenar; (*animals*) disecar; (*inf: push*) meter; **~ing** n relleno; **~y** adj (*room*) mal ventilado; (*person*) de miras estrechas

stumble ['stʌmbl] vi tropezar, dar un traspié; **to ~ across, ~ on** (*fig*) tropezar con; **stumbling block** n tropiezo, obstáculo

stump [stʌmp] n (*of tree*) tocón m; (*of limb*) muñón m ♦ vt: **to be ~ed for an answer** no saber qué contestar

stun [stʌn] vt dejar sin sentido

stung [stʌŋ] pt, pp of **sting**

stunk [stʌŋk] pp of **stink**

stunning ['stʌnɪŋ] adj (*fig: news*) pasmoso; (*: outfit etc*) sensacional

stunt [stʌnt] n (*in film*) escena peligrosa; (*publicity ~*) truco publicitario; **~man** (*irreg*) n doble m

stupid ['stjuːpɪd] adj estúpido, tonto; **~ity** [-'pɪdɪtɪ] n estupidez f

sturdy ['stɜːdɪ] adj robusto, fuerte

stutter ['stʌtə*] n tartamudeo ♦ vi tartamudear

sty [staɪ] n (*for pigs*) pocilga

stye [staɪ] n (*MED*) orzuelo

style [staɪl] n estilo; **stylish** adj elegante, a la moda

stylus ['staɪləs] n aguja

suave [swɑːv] adj cortés

sub... [sʌb] prefix sub...; **~conscious** adj subconsciente; **~contract** vt subcontratar; **~divide** vt subdividir

subdue [səb'djuː] vt sojuzgar; (*passions*) dominar; **~d** adj (*light*) tenue; (*person*) sumiso, manso

subject [n 'sʌbdʒɪkt, vb səb'dʒɛkt] n súbdito; (*SCOL*) asignatura; (*matter*) tema m; (*GRAMMAR*) sujeto ♦ vt: **to ~ sb to sth** someter a uno a algo; **to be ~ to** (*law*) estar sujeto a; (*subj: person*) ser propenso a; **~ive** [-'dʒɛktɪv] adj subjetivo; **~ matter** n (*content*) contenido

sublet [sʌb'lɛt] vt subarrendar

submarine [sʌbmə'riːn] n submarino

submerge [səb'mɜːdʒ] vt sumergir ♦ vi sumergirse

submissive [səb'mɪsɪv] adj sumiso

submit [səb'mɪt] vt someter ♦ vi: **to ~ to sth** someterse a algo

subnormal [sʌb'nɔːməl] adj anormal

subordinate [sə'bɔːdɪnət] adj, n subordinado/a m/f

subpoena [səb'piːnə] n (*LAW*) citación f

subscribe [səb'skraɪb] vi suscribir; **to ~ to** (*opinion, fund*) suscribir, aprobar; (*newspaper*) suscribirse a; **~r** n (*to periodical*) subscriptor(a) m/f; (*to telephone*) abonado/a

subscription [səb'skrɪpʃən] n abono; (*to magazine*) subscripción f

subsequent ['sʌbsɪkwənt] adj subsiguiente,

posterior; **~ly** adv posteriormente, más tarde

subside [səb'saɪd] vi hundirse; (*flood*) bajar; (*wind*) amainar; **subsidence** [-'saɪdns] n hundimiento; (*in road*) socavón m

subsidiary [səb'sɪdɪərɪ] adj secundario ♦ n sucursal f, filial f

subsidize ['sʌbsɪdaɪz] vt subvencionar

subsidy ['sʌbsɪdɪ] n subvención f

subsistence [səb'sɪstəns] n subsistencia; **~ allowance** n salario mínimo

substance ['sʌbstəns] n sustancia

substantial [səb'stænʃl] adj sustancial, sustancioso; (*fig*) importante

substantiate [səb'stænʃɪeɪt] vt comprobar

substitute ['sʌbstɪtjuːt] n (*person*) suplente m/f; (*thing*) sustituto ♦ vt: **to ~ A for B** sustituir A por B, reemplazar B por A

subtitle ['sʌbtaɪtl] n subtítulo

subtle ['sʌtl] adj sutil; **~ty** n sutileza

subtotal [sʌb'təutl] n total m parcial

subtract [səb'trækt] vt restar, sustraer; **~ion** [-'trækʃən] n resta, sustracción f

suburb ['sʌbɜːb] n barrio residencial; **the ~s** las afueras (de la ciudad); **~an** [sə'bɜːbən] adj suburbano; (*train etc*) de cercanías; **~ia** [sə'bɜːbɪə] n barrios mpl residenciales

subway ['sʌbweɪ] n (*BRIT*) paso subterráneo or inferior; (*US*) metro

succeed [sək'siːd] vi (*person*) tener éxito; (*plan*) salir bien ♦ vt suceder a; **to ~ in doing** lograr hacer; **~ing** adj (*following*) sucesivo

success [sək'sɛs] n éxito; **~ful** adj exitoso; (*business*) próspero; **to be ~ful (in doing)** lograr (hacer); **~fully** adv con éxito

succession [sək'sɛʃən] n sucesión f, serie f

successive [sək'sɛsɪv] adj sucesivo, consecutivo

succinct [sək'sɪŋkt] adj sucinto

such [sʌtʃ] adj tal, semejante; (*of that kind*): **~ a book** tal libro; (*so much*): **~ courage** tanto valor ♦ adv tan; **~ a long trip** un viaje tan largo; **~ a lot of** tanto(s)/a(s); **~ as** (*like*) tal como; **as ~** como tal; **~-and-~** adj tal o cual

suck [sʌk] vt chupar; (*bottle*) sorber; (*breast*) mamar; **~er** n (*ZOOL*) ventosa; (*inf*) bobo, primo

suction ['sʌkʃən] n succión f

Sudan [su'dæn] n Sudán m

sudden ['sʌdn] adj (*rapid*) repentino, súbito; (*unexpected*) imprevisto; **all of a ~** de repente; **~ly** adv de repente

suds [sʌdz] npl espuma de jabón

sue [suː] vt demandar

suede [sweɪd] n ante m (*SP*), gamuza (*AM*)

suet ['suɪt] n sebo

Suez ['suːɪz] n: **the ~ Canal** el Canal de Suez

suffer ['sʌfə*] vt sufrir, padecer; (*tolerate*) aguantar, soportar ♦ vi sufrir; **to ~ from** (*illness etc*) padecer; **~er** n víctima; (*MED*) enfermo/a; **~ing** n sufrimiento

sufficient [sə'fɪʃənt] adj suficiente, bastante; **~ly** ad suficientemente, bastante

suffocate ['sʌfəkeɪt] vi ahogarse, asfixiarse; **suffocation** [-'keɪʃən] n asfixia

sugar ['ʃugə*] n azúcar m ♦ vt echar azúcar a, azucarar; **~ beet** n remolacha; **~ cane** n caña de azúcar

suggest [sə'dʒɛst] vt sugerir; **~ion** [-'dʒɛstʃən] n sugerencia; **~ive** (pej) adj indecente

suicide ['suɪsaɪd] n suicidio; (person) suicida m/f; see also **commit**

suit [su:t] n (man's) traje m; (woman's) conjunto; (LAW) pleito; (CARDS) palo ♦ vt convenir; (clothes) sentar a, ir bien a; (adapt): **to ~ sth to** adaptar or ajustar algo a; **well ~ed** (well matched: couple) hecho el uno para el otro; **~able** adj conveniente; (apt) indicado; **~ably** adv convenientemente; (impressed) apropiadamente

suitcase ['su:tkeɪs] n maleta (SP), valija (AM)

suite [swi:t] n (of rooms, MUS) suite f; (furniture): **bedroom/dining room ~** (juego de) dormitorio/comedor

suitor ['su:tə*] n pretendiente m

sulfur ['sʌlfə*] (US) n = **sulphur**

sulk [sʌlk] vi estar de mal humor; **~y** adj malhumorado

sullen ['sʌlən] adj hosco, malhumorado

sulphur ['sʌlfə*] (US **sulfur**) n azufre m

sultana [sʌl'tɑːnə] n (fruit) pasa de Esmirna

sultry ['sʌltrɪ] adj (weather) bochornoso

sum [sʌm] n suma; (total) total m; **~ up** vt resumir ♦ vi hacer un resumen

summarize ['sʌməraɪz] vt resumir

summary ['sʌmərɪ] n resumen m ♦ adj (justice) sumario

summer ['sʌmə*] n verano ♦ cpd de verano; **in ~** en verano; **~ holidays** npl vacaciones fpl de verano; **~house** n (in garden) cenador m, glorieta; **~time** n (season) verano; **~ time** (by clock) hora de verano

summit ['sʌmɪt] n cima, cumbre f; (also: ~ conference, ~ meeting) (conferencia) cumbre f

summon ['sʌmən] vt (person) llamar; (meeting) convocar; (LAW) citar; **~ up** vt (courage) armarse de; **~s** n llamamiento, llamada ♦ vt (LAW) citar

sump [sʌmp] (BRIT) n (AUT) cárter m

sumptuous ['sʌmptjuəs] adj suntuoso

sun [sʌn] n sol m; **~bathe** vi tomar el sol; **~block** n filtro solar; **~burn** n (painful) quemadura; (tan) bronceado; **~burnt** adj quemado por el sol

Sunday ['sʌndɪ] n domingo; **~ school** n catequesis f dominical

sundial ['sʌndaɪəl] n reloj m de sol

sundown ['sʌndaun] n anochecer m

sundry ['sʌndrɪ] adj varios/as, diversos/as; **all and ~** todos sin excepción; **sundries** npl géneros mpl diversos

sunflower ['sʌnflauə*] n girasol m

sung [sʌŋ] pp of **sing**

sunglasses ['sʌnglɑːsɪz] npl gafas fpl (SP) or anteojos mpl de sol

sunk [sʌŋk] pp of **sink**

sun: ~light n luz f del sol; **~lit** adj iluminado por el sol; **~ny** adj soleado; (day) de sol; (fig) alegre; **~rise** n salida del sol; **~ roof** n (AUT) techo corredizo; **~screen** n protector m solar; **~set** n puesta del sol; **~shade** n (over table) sombrilla; **~shine** n sol m; **~stroke** n insolación f; **~tan** n bronceado; **~tan oil** n aceite m bronceador

super ['su:pə*] (inf) adj genial

superannuation [su:pərænjʊ'eɪʃən] n cuota de jubilación

superb [su:'pə:b] adj magnífico, espléndido

supercilious [su:pə'sɪlɪəs] adj altanero

superfluous [su:'pə:fluəs] adj superfluo, de sobra

superhuman [su:pə'hju:mən] adj sobrehumano

superimpose ['su:pərɪm'pəuz] vt sobreponer

superintendent [su:pərɪn'tɛndənt] n director(a) m/f; (POLICE) subjefe/a m/f

superior [su'pɪərɪə*] adj superior; (smug) desdeñoso ♦ n superior m; **~ity** [-'ɔrɪtɪ] n superioridad f

superlative [su'pə:lətɪv] n superlativo

superman [su'pəmæn] (irreg) n superhombre m

supermarket ['su:pəmɑ:kɪt] n supermercado

supernatural [su:pə'nætʃərəl] adj sobrenatural ♦ n: **the ~** lo sobrenatural

superpower ['su:pəpauə*] n (POL) superpotencia

supersede [su:pə'si:d] vt suplantar

superstar ['su:pəstɑ:*] n gran estrella

superstitious [su:pə'stɪʃəs] adj supersticioso

supertanker ['su:pətæŋkə*] n superpetrolero

supervise ['su:pəvaɪz] vt supervisar; **supervision** [-'vɪʒən] n supervisión f; **supervisor** n supervisor(a) m/f

supper ['sʌpə*] n cena

supple ['sʌpl] adj flexible

supplement [n 'sʌplɪmənt, vb sʌplɪ'mɛnt] n suplemento ♦ vt suplir; **~ary** [-'mɛntərɪ] adj suplementario; **~ary benefit** (BRIT) n subsidio suplementario de la seguridad social

supplier [sə'plaɪə*] n (COMM) distribuidor(a) m/f

supply [sə'plaɪ] vt (provide) suministrar; (equip): **to ~ (with)** proveer (de) ♦ n provisión f; (gas, water etc) suministro; **supplies** npl (food) víveres mpl; (MIL) pertrechos mpl; **~ teacher** n profesor(a) m/f suplente

support [sə'pɔːt] n apoyo; (TECH) soporte m ♦ vt apoyar; (financially) mantener; (uphold, TECH) sostener; **~er** n (POL etc) partidario/a; (SPORT) aficionado/a

suppose [sə'pəuz] vt suponer; (imagine) imaginarse; (duty): **to be ~d to do sth** deber hacer algo; **~dly** [sə'pəuzɪdlɪ] adv según cabe suponer; **supposing** conj en caso de que

suppress [sə'prɛs] vt suprimir; (yawn) ahogar

supreme [su'priːm] adj supremo

surcharge ['səːtʃɑːdʒ] n sobretasa, recargo

sure [ʃuə*] adj seguro; (definite, convinced) cierto; **to make ~ of sth/that** asegurarse de algo/asegurar que; **~!** (of course) ¡claro!, ¡por supuesto!; **~ enough** efectivamente; **~ly** adv (certainly) seguramente

surf [səːf] n olas fpl

surface ['səːfɪs] n superficie f ♦ vt (road) revestir ♦ vi (also fig) salir a la superficie; **by ~ mail** por vía terrestre

surfboard ['səːfbɔːd] n tabla (de surf)

surfeit ['səːfɪt] n: **a ~ of** un exceso de

surfing ['səːfɪŋ] n surf m

surge [səːdʒ] n oleada, oleaje m ♦ vi (wave) romper; (people) avanzar en tropel

surgeon ['səːdʒən] n cirujano/a

surgery ['səːdʒərɪ] n cirugía; (BRIT: room) consultorio; **~ hours** (BRIT) npl horas fpl de consulta

surgical ['səːdʒɪkl] adj quirúrgico; **~ spirit** (BRIT) n alcohol m de 90°

surname ['səːneɪm] n apellido

surpass [səː'pɑːs] vt superar, exceder

surplus ['səːpləs] n excedente m; (COMM) superávit m ♦ adj excedente, sobrante

surprise [sə'praɪz] n sorpresa ♦ vt sorprender; **surprising** adj sorprendente; **surprisingly** adv: **it was surprisingly easy** me sorprendió lo fácil que fue

surrender [sə'rɛndə*] n rendición f, entrega ♦ vi rendirse, entregarse

surreptitious [sʌrəp'tɪʃəs] adj subrepticio

surrogate ['sʌrəgɪt] n sucedáneo; **~ mother** n madre f portadora

surround [sə'raund] vt rodear, circundar; (MIL etc) cercar; **~ing** adj circundante; **~ings** npl alrededores mpl, cercanías fpl

surveillance [səː'veɪləns] n vigilancia

survey [n 'səːveɪ, vb səː'veɪ] n inspección f, reconocimiento; (inquiry) encuesta ♦ vt examinar, inspeccionar; (look at) mirar, contemplar; **~or** n agrimensor(a) m/f

survival [sə'vaɪvl] n supervivencia

survive [sə'vaɪv] vi sobrevivir; (custom etc)

perdurar ♦ vt sobrevivir a; **survivor** n superviviente m/f

susceptible [sə'sɛptəbl] adj: **~ (to)** (disease) susceptible (a); (flattery) sensible (a)

suspect [adj, n 'sʌspɛkt, vb səs'pɛkt] adj, n sospechoso/a m/f ♦ vt (person) sospechar de; (think) sospechar

suspend [səs'pɛnd] vt suspender; **~ed sentence** n (LAW) libertad f condicional; **~er belt** n portaligas m inv; **~ers** npl (BRIT) ligas fpl; (US) tirantes mpl

suspense [səs'pɛns] n incertidumbre f, duda; (in film etc) suspense m; **to keep sb in ~** mantener a uno en suspense

suspension [səs'pɛnʃən] n (gen, AUT) suspensión f; (of driving licence) privación f; **~ bridge** n puente m colgante

suspicion [səs'pɪʃən] n sospecha; (distrust) recelo; **suspicious** [-ʃəs] adj receloso; (causing suspicion) sospechoso

sustain [səs'teɪn] vt sostener, apoyar; (suffer) sufrir, padecer; **~able** adj sostenible; **~ed** adj (effort) sostenido

sustenance ['sʌstɪnəns] n sustento

swab [swɔb] n (MED) algodón m

swagger ['swægə*] vi pavonearse

swallow ['swɔləu] n (bird) golondrina ♦ vt tragar; (fig, pride) tragarse; **~ up** vt (savings etc) consumir

swam [swæm] pt of swim

swamp [swɔmp] n pantano, ciénaga ♦ vt (with water etc) inundar; (fig) abrumar, agobiar; **~y** adj pantanoso

swan [swɔn] n cisne m

swap [swɔp] n canje m, intercambio ♦ vt: **to ~ (for)** cambiar (por)

swarm [swɔːm] n (of bees) enjambre m; (fig) multitud f ♦ vi (bees) formar un enjambre; (people) pulular; **to be ~ing with** ser un hervidero de

swastika ['swɔstɪkə] n esvástica

swat [swɔt] vt aplastar

sway [sweɪ] vi mecerse, balancearse ♦ vt (influence) mover, influir en

swear [swεə*] (pt swore, pp sworn) vi (curse) maldecir; (promise) jurar ♦ vt jurar; **~word** n taco, palabrota

sweat [swɛt] n sudor m ♦ vi sudar

sweater ['swɛtə*] n suéter m

sweatshirt ['swɛtʃəːt] n suéter m

sweaty ['swɛtɪ] adj sudoroso

Swede [swiːd] n sueco/a

swede [swiːd] (BRIT) n nabo

Sweden ['swiːdn] n Suecia; **Swedish** ['swiːdɪʃ] adj sueco ♦ n (LING) sueco

sweep [swiːp] (pt, pp swept) n (act) barrido; (also: chimney ~) deshollinador(a) m/f ♦ vt barrer; (with arm) empujar; (subj: current) arrastrar ♦ vi barrer; (arm etc) moverse

rápidamente; (wind) soplar con violencia;
~ **away** vt barrer; ~ **past** vi pasar
majestuosamente; ~ **up** vi barrer; ~**ing** adj
(gesture) dramático; (generalized: statement)
generalizado

sweet |swiːt| n (candy) dulce m, caramelo;
(BRIT: pudding) postre m ♦ adj dulce; (fig:
kind) dulce, amable; (: attractive) mono;
~**corn** n maíz m; ~**en** vt (add sugar to)
poner azúcar a; (person) endulzar; ~**heart** n
novio/a; ~**ness** n dulzura; ~ **pea** n guisante
m de olor

swell |swel| (pt **swelled**, pp **swollen** or
swelled) n (of sea) marejada, oleaje m ♦ adj
(US: inf: excellent) estupendo, fenomenal ♦ vt
hinchar, inflar ♦ vi (also: ~ up) hincharse;
(numbers) aumentar; (sound, feeling) ir
aumentando; ~**ing** n (MED) hinchazón f

sweltering ['sweltərɪŋ] adj sofocante, de
mucho calor

swept [swept] pt, pp of **sweep**

swerve [swɜːv] vi desviarse bruscamente

swift [swɪft] n (bird) vencejo ♦ adj rápido,
veloz; ~**ly** adv rápidamente

swig [swɪg] (inf) n (drink) trago

swill [swɪl] vt (also: ~ out, ~ down) lavar,
limpiar con agua

swim |swɪm| (pt **swam**, pp **swum**) n: to go
for a ~ ir a nadar or a bañarse ♦ vi nadar;
(head, room) dar vueltas ♦ vt nadar; (the
Channel etc) cruzar a nado; ~**mer** n
nadador(a) m/f; ~**ming** n natación f; ~**ming
cap** n gorro de baño; ~**ming costume**
(BRIT) n bañador m, traje m de baño; ~**ming
pool** n piscina (SP), alberca (AM); ~**ming
trunks** n bañador m (de hombre); ~**suit** n
= ~**ming costume**

swindle ['swɪndl] n estafa ♦ vt estafar

swine [swaɪn] (inf!) canalla (!)

swing [swɪŋ] (pt, pp **swung**) n (in playground) columpio; (movement) balanceo,
vaivén m; (change of direction) viraje m;
(rhythm) ritmo ♦ vt balancear; (also:
~ round) voltear, girar ♦ vi balancearse,
columpiarse; (also: ~ round) dar media
vuelta; to be in full ~ estar en plena marcha;
~ **bridge** n puente m giratorio; ~ **door** (US
~**ing door**) n puerta giratoria

swingeing ['swɪndʒɪŋ] (BRIT) adj (cuts) atroz

swipe [swaɪp] vt (hit) golpear fuerte; (inf:
steal) guindar

swirl [swɜːl] vi arremolinarse

Swiss |swɪs| adj, n inv suizo/a m/f

switch [swɪtʃ] n (for light etc) interruptor m;
(change) cambio ♦ vt (change) cambiar de;
~ **off** vt apagar; (engine) parar; ~ **on** vt
encender (SP), prender (AM); (engine,
machine) arrancar; ~**board** n (TEL) centralita
(de teléfonos) (SP), conmutador m (AM)

Switzerland ['swɪtsələnd] n Suiza

swivel ['swɪvl] vi (also: ~ round) girar

swollen ['swəʊlən] pp of **swell**

swoon [swuːn] vi desmayarse

swoop [swuːp] n (by police etc) redada ♦ vi
(also: ~ down) calarse

swop [swɒp] = **swap**

sword [sɔːd] n espada; ~**fish** n pez m espada

swore [swɔː*] pt of **swear**

sworn [swɔːn] pp of **swear** ♦ adj (statement)
bajo juramento; (enemy) implacable

swot [swɒt] (BRIT) vt, vi empollar

swum [swʌm] pp of **swim**

swung [swʌŋ] pt, pp of **swing**

sycamore ['sɪkəmɔː*] n sicomoro

syllable ['sɪləbl] n sílaba

syllabus ['sɪləbəs] n programa m de estudios

symbol ['sɪmbl] n símbolo

symmetry ['sɪmɪtrɪ] n simetría

sympathetic [sɪmpə'θetɪk] adj
(understanding) comprensivo; (likeable)
simpático; (showing support): ~ **to**(**wards**)
bien dispuesto hacia

sympathize ['sɪmpəθaɪz] vi: to ~ **with**
(person) compadecerse de; (feelings)
comprender; (cause) apoyar; ~**r** n (POL)
simpatizante m/f

sympathy ['sɪmpəθɪ] n (pity) compasión f;
sympathies npl (tendencies) tendencias fpl;
with our deepest ~ nuestro más sentido
pésame; **in** ~ en solidaridad

symphony ['sɪmfənɪ] n sinfonía

symptom ['sɪmptəm] n síntoma m, indicio

synagogue ['sɪnəgɒg] n sinagoga

syndicate ['sɪndɪkɪt] n (gen) sindicato; (of
newspapers) agencia (de noticias)

syndrome ['sɪndrəʊm] n síndrome m

synopsis [sɪ'nɒpsɪs] (pl **synopses**) n sinopsis f
inv

synthesis ['sɪnθəsɪs] (pl **syntheses**) n síntesis
f inv

synthetic [sɪn'θetɪk] adj sintético

syphilis ['sɪfɪlɪs] n sífilis f

syphon ['saɪfən] = **siphon**

Syria ['sɪrɪə] n Siria; ~**n** adj, n sirio/a

syringe [sɪ'rɪndʒ] n jeringa

syrup ['sɪrəp] n jarabe m; (also: golden ~)
almíbar m

system ['sɪstəm] n sistema m; (ANAT)
organismo; ~**atic** [-'mætɪk] adj sistemático,
metódico; ~ **disk** n (COMPUT) disco del
sistema; ~**s analyst** n analista m/f de
sistemas

T, t

ta [tɑː] (BRIT: inf) excl ¡gracias!

tab [tæb] n lengüeta; (label) etiqueta; **to keep**

~s on (fig) vigilar
tabby ['tæbɪ] n (also: ~ cat) gato atigrado
table ['teɪbl] n mesa; (of statistics etc) cuadro,
tabla ♦ vt (BRIT: motion etc) presentar; **to lay**
or **set the ~** poner la mesa; **~cloth** n mantel
m; **~ of contents** n índice m de materias;
~ d'hôte [taːblˈdəʊt] adj del menú; **~ lamp**
n lámpara de mesa; **~mat** n (for plate)
posaplatos m inv; (for hot dish) salvamantel
m; **~spoon** n cuchara de servir; (also:
~spoonful: as measurement) cucharada
tablet ['tæblɪt] n (MED) pastilla, comprimido;
(of stone) lápida
table tennis n ping-pong m, tenis m de
mesa
table wine n vino de mesa
tabloid ['tæblɔɪd] n periódico popular
sensacionalista
tack [tæk] n (nail) tachuela; (fig) rumbo ♦ vt
(nail) clavar con tachuelas; (stitch) hilvanar
♦ vi virar
tackle ['tækl] n (fishing ~) aparejo (de
pescar); (for lifting) aparejo ♦ vt (difficulty)
enfrentarse con; (challenge: person) hacer
frente a; (grapple with) agarrar; (FOOTBALL)
cargar; (RUGBY) placar
tacky ['tækɪ] adj pegajoso; (pej) cutre
tact [tækt] n tacto, discreción f; **~ful** adj
discreto, diplomático
tactics ['tæktɪks] n, npl táctica
tactless ['tæktlɪs] adj indiscreto
tadpole ['tædpəʊl] n renacuajo
tag [tæg] n (label) etiqueta; **~ along** vi ir (or
venir) también
tail [teɪl] n cola; (of shirt, coat) faldón m ♦ vt
(follow) vigilar a; **~s** npl (formal suit) levita;
~ away vi (in size, quality etc) ir
disminuyendo; **~ off** vi = **~ away**; **~back**
(BRIT) n (AUT) cola; **~ end** n cola, parte f
final; **~gate** n (AUT) puerta trasera
tailor ['teɪlə*] n sastre m; **~ing** n (cut) corte
m; (craft) sastrería; **~-made** adj (also fig)
hecho a la medida
tailwind ['teɪlwɪnd] n viento de cola
tainted ['teɪntɪd] adj (food) pasado; (water,
air) contaminado; (fig) manchado
take [teɪk] (pt **took**, pp **taken**) vt tomar;
(grab) coger (SP), agarrar (AM); (gain: prize)
ganar; (require: effort, courage) exigir;
(tolerate: pain etc) aguantar; (hold:
passengers etc) tener cabida para;
(accompany, bring, carry) llevar; (exam)
presentarse a; **to ~ sth from** (drawer etc) sacar
algo de; (person) quitar algo a; **I ~ it that ...**
supongo que ...; **~ after** vt fus parecerse a;
~ apart vt desmontar; **~ away** vt (remove)
quitar; (carry off) llevar; (MATH) restar;
~ back vt (return) devolver; (one's words)
retractarse de; **~ down** vt (building) derribar;

(letter etc) apuntar; **~ in** vt (deceive)
engañar; (understand) entender; (include)
abarcar; (lodger) acoger, recibir; **~ off** vi
(AVIAT) despegar ♦ vt (remove) quitar; **~ on**
vt (work) aceptar; (employee) contratar;
(opponent) desafiar; **~ out** vt sacar; **~ over**
vt (business) tomar posesión de; (country)
tomar el poder ♦ vi: **to ~ over from sb**
reemplazar a uno; **~ to** vt fus (person) coger
cariño a, encariñarse con; (activity)
aficionarse a; **~ up** vt (a dress) acortar;
(occupy: time, space) ocupar; (engage in:
hobby etc) dedicarse a; (accept): **to ~ sb up
on** aceptar; **~away** (BRIT) adj (food) para
llevar ♦ n tienda (or restaurante m) de
comida para llevar; **~off** n (AVIAT) despegue
m; **~out** (US) n = **~away**; **~over** n (COMM)
absorción f
takings ['teɪkɪŋz] npl (COMM) ingresos mpl
talc [tælk] n (also: ~um powder) (polvos de)
talco
tale [teɪl] n (story) cuento; (account) relación
f; **to tell ~s** (fig) chivarse
talent ['tælnt] n talento; **~ed** adj de talento
talk [tɔːk] n charla; (conversation)
conversación f; (gossip) habladurías fpl,
chismes mpl ♦ vi hablar; **~s** npl (POL etc)
conversaciones fpl; **to ~ about** hablar de; **to
~ sb into doing sth** convencer a uno para que
haga algo; **to ~ sb out of doing sth** disuadir a
uno de que haga algo; **to ~ shop** hablar del
trabajo; **~ over** vt discutir; **~ative** adj
hablador(a); **~ show** n programa m de
entrevistas
tall [tɔːl] adj alto; (object) grande; **to be 6 feet
~** (person) ≈ medir 1 metro 80
tally ['tælɪ] n cuenta ♦ vi: **to ~ (with)**
corresponder (con)
talon ['tælən] n garra
tambourine [tæmbəˈriːn] n pandereta
tame [teɪm] adj domesticado; (fig) mediocre
tamper ['tæmpə*] vi: **to ~ with** tocar, andar
con
tampon ['tæmpən] n tampón m
tan [tæn] n (also: sun~) bronceado ♦ vi
ponerse moreno ♦ adj (colour) marrón
tang [tæŋ] n sabor m fuerte
tangent ['tændʒənt] n (MATH) tangente f; **to
go off at a ~** (fig) salirse por la tangente
tangerine [tændʒəˈriːn] n mandarina
tangle ['tæŋgl] n enredo; **to get in(to) a ~**
enredarse
tank [tæŋk] n (water ~) depósito, tanque m;
(for fish) acuario; (MIL) tanque m
tanker ['tæŋkə*] n (ship) buque m cisterna;
(truck) camión m cisterna
tanned [tænd] adj (skin) moreno
tantalizing ['tæntəlaɪzɪŋ] adj tentador(a)
tantamount ['tæntəmaunt] adj: **~ to**

equivalente a

tantrum ['tæntrəm] *n* rabieta

tap [tæp] *n* (*BRIT: on sink etc*) grifo (*SP*), canilla (*AM*); (*gas* ~) llave *f*; (*gentle blow*) golpecito ♦ *vt* (*hit gently*) dar golpecitos en; (*resources*) utilizar, explotar; (*telephone*) intervenir; **on** ~ (*fig: resources*) a mano; ~ **dancing** *n* claqué *m*

tape [teɪp] *n* (*also: magnetic* ~) cinta magnética; (*cassette*) cassette *f*, cinta; (*sticky* ~) cinta adhesiva; (*for tying*) cinta ♦ *vt* (*record*) grabar (en cinta); (*stick with* ~) pegar con cinta adhesiva; ~ **deck** *n* grabadora; ~ **measure** *n* cinta métrica, metro

taper ['teɪpə*] *n* cirio ♦ *vi* afilarse

tape recorder *n* grabadora

tapestry ['tæpɪstrɪ] *n* (*object*) tapiz *m*; (*art*) tapicería

tar [tɑː] *n* alquitrán *m*, brea

target ['tɑːgɪt] *n* (*gen*) blanco

tariff ['tærɪf] *n* (*on goods*) arancel *m*; (*BRIT: in hotels etc*) tarifa

tarmac ['tɑːmæk] *n* (*BRIT: on road*) asfaltado; (*AVIAT*) pista (de aterrizaje)

tarnish ['tɑːnɪʃ] *vt* deslustrar

tarpaulin [tɑː'pɔːlɪn] *n* lona imper- meabilizada

tarragon ['tærəgən] *n* estragón *m*

tart [tɑːt] *n* (*CULIN*) tarta; (*BRIT: inf: prostitute*) puta ♦ *adj* agrio, ácido; ~ **up** (*BRIT: inf*) *vt* (*building*) remozar; **to** ~ **o.s. up** acicalarse

tartan ['tɑːtn] *n* tejido escocés *m*

tartar ['tɑːtə*] *n* (*on teeth*) sarro, ~(**e**) **sauce** *n* salsa tártara

task [tɑːsk] *n* tarea; **to take to** ~ reprender; ~ **force** *n* (*MIL, POLICE*) grupo de operaciones

taste [teɪst] *n* (*sense*) gusto; (*flavour*) sabor *m*; (*also: after*~) sabor *m*, dejo; (*sample*): **have a** ~**!** ¡prueba un poquito!; (*fig*) muestra, idea ♦ *vt* (*also fig*) probar ♦ *vi*: **to** ~ **of** *or* **like** (*fish, garlic etc*) saber a; **you can** ~ **the garlic (in it)** se nota el sabor a ajo; **in good/bad** ~ de buen/mal gusto; ~**ful** *adj* de buen gusto; ~**less** *adj* (*food*) soso; (*remark etc*) de mal gusto; **tasty** *adj* sabroso, rico

tatters ['tætəz] *npl*: **in** ~ hecho jirones

tattoo [tə'tuː] *n* tatuaje *m*; (*spectacle*) espectáculo militar ♦ *vt* tatuar

tatty ['tætɪ] (*BRIT: inf*) *adj* cochambroso

taught [tɔːt] *pt, pp* of **teach**

taunt [tɔːnt] *n* burla ♦ *vt* burlarse de

Taurus ['tɔːrəs] *n* Tauro

taut [tɔːt] *adj* tirante, tenso

tax [tæks] *n* impuesto ♦ *vt* gravar (con un impuesto); (*fig: memory*) poner a prueba (*: patience*) agotar; ~**able** *adj* (*income*) gravable; ~**ation** [-'seɪʃən] *n* impuestos *mpl*; ~ **avoidance** *n* evasión *f* de impuestos;

~ **disc** (*BRIT*) *n* (*AUT*) pegatina del impuesto de circulación; ~ **evasion** *n* evasión *f* fiscal; ~**free** *adj* libre de impuestos

taxi ['tæksɪ] *n* taxi *m* ♦ *vi* (*AVIAT*) rodar por la pista; ~ **driver** *n* taxista *m/f*; ~ **rank** (*BRIT*) *n* = ~ **stand**; ~ **stand** *n* parada de taxis

tax: ~ **payer** *n* contribuyente *m/f*; ~ **relief** *n* desgravación *f* fiscal; ~ **return** *n* declaración *f* de ingresos

TB *n abbr* = **tuberculosis**

tea [tiː] *n* té *m*; (*BRIT: meal*) ≈ merienda (*SP*); cena; **high** ~ (*BRIT*) merienda-cena (*SP*); ~ **bag** *n* bolsita de té; ~ **break** (*BRIT*) *n* descanso para el té

teach [tiːtʃ] (*pt, pp* **taught**) *vt*: **to** ~ **sb sth,** ~ **sth to sb** enseñar algo a uno ♦ *vi* (*be a teacher*) ser profesor(a), enseñar; ~**er** *n* (*in secondary school*) profesor(a) *m/f*; (*in primary school*) maestro/a, profesor(a) de EGB; ~**ing** *n* enseñanza

tea cosy *n* cubretetera *m*

teacup ['tiːkʌp] *n* taza para el té

teak [tiːk] *n* (madera de) teca

team [tiːm] *n* equipo; (*of horses*) tiro; ~**work** *n* trabajo en equipo

teapot ['tiːpɔt] *n* tetera

tear¹ [tɪə*] *n* lágrima; **in** ~**s** llorando

tear² [tɛə*] (*pt* **tore**, *pp* **torn**) *n* rasgón *m*, desgarrón *m* ♦ *vt* romper, rasgar ♦ *vi* rasgarse; ~ **along** *vi* (*rush*) precipitarse; ~ **up** *vt* (*sheet of paper etc*) romper

tearful ['tɪəfəl] *adj* lloroso

tear gas ['tɪə-] *n* gas *m* lacrimógeno

tearoom ['tiːruːm] *n* salón *m* de té

tease [tiːz] *vt* tomar el pelo a

tea set *n* servicio de té

teaspoon *n* cucharita; (*also:* ~**ful:** *as measurement*) cucharadita

teat [tiːt] *n* (*of bottle*) tetina

teatime ['tiːtaɪm] *n* hora del té

tea towel (*BRIT*) *n* paño de cocina

technical ['tɛknɪkl] *adj* técnico; ~ **college** (*BRIT*) *n* ≈ escuela de artes y oficios (*SP*); ~**ity** [-'kælɪtɪ] *n* (*point of law*) formalismo; (*detail*) detalle *m* técnico; ~**ly** *adv* en teoría; (*regarding technique*) técnicamente

technician [tɛk'nɪʃn] *n* técnico/a

technique [tɛk'niːk] *n* técnica

technological [tɛknə'lɔdʒɪkl] *adj* tecnológico

technology [tɛk'nɔlədʒɪ] *n* tecnología

teddy (bear) ['tɛdɪ-] *n* osito de felpa

tedious ['tiːdɪəs] *adj* pesado, aburrido

teem [tiːm] *vi*: **to** ~ **with** rebosar de; **it is** ~**ing (with rain)** llueve a cántaros

teenage ['tiːneɪdʒ] *adj* (*fashions etc*) juvenil; (*children*) quinceañero; ~**r** *n* quinceañero/a

teens [tiːnz] *npl*: **to be in one's** ~ ser adolescente

tee-shirt ['tiːʃəːt] n = T-shirt

teeter ['tiːtə*] vi balancearse; (fig): **to ~ on the edge of ...** estar al borde de ...

teeth [tiːθ] npl of **tooth**

teethe [tiːð] vi echar los dientes

teething ['tiːðɪŋ]: **~ ring** n mordedor m; **~ troubles** npl (fig) dificultades fpl iniciales

teetotal ['tiː'təutl] adj abstemio

telegram ['telɪgræm] n telegrama m

telegraph ['telɪgrɑːf] n telégrafo; **~ pole** n poste m telegráfico

telepathy [tə'lepəθɪ] n telepatía

telephone ['telɪfəun] n teléfono ♦ vt llamar por teléfono, telefonear; (message) dar por teléfono; **to be on the ~** (talking) hablar por teléfono; (possessing ~) tener teléfono; **~ booth** n cabina telefónica; **~ box** (BRIT) n = **~ booth**; **~ call** n llamada (telefónica); **~ directory** n guía (telefónica); **~ number** n número de teléfono; **telephonist** [tə'lefənɪst] (BRIT) n telefonista m/f

telesales ['telɪseɪlz] npl televenta(s) f(pl)

telescope ['telɪskəup] n telescopio

television ['telɪvɪʒən] n televisión f; **on ~** en la televisión; **~ set** n televisor m

tell [tel] (pt, pp **told**) vt decir; (relate: story) contar; (distinguish): **to ~ sth from** distinguir algo de ♦ vi (talk): **to ~ (of)** contar; (have effect) tener efecto; **to ~ sb to do sth** mandar a uno hacer algo; **~ off** vt: **to ~ sb off** regañar a uno; **~er** n (in bank) cajero/a; **~ing** adj (remark, detail) revelador(a); **~tale** adj (sign) indicador(a)

telly ['telɪ] (BRIT: inf) n abbr (= television) tele f

temp [temp] n abbr (BRIT: = temporary) temporero/a

temper ['tempə*] n (nature) carácter m; (mood) humor m; (bad ~) (mal) genio; (fit of anger) acceso de ira ♦ vt (moderate) moderar; **to be in a ~** estar furioso; **to lose one's ~** enfadarse, enojarse

temperament ['temprəmənt] n (nature) temperamento

temperate ['temprət] adj (climate etc) templado

temperature ['temprətʃə*] n temperatura; **to have or run a ~** tener fiebre

temple ['templ] n (building) templo; (ANAT) sien f

tempo ['tempəu] (pl **tempos** or **tempi**) n (MUS) tempo, tiempo; (fig) ritmo

temporarily ['tempərərɪlɪ] adv temporalmente

temporary ['tempərərɪ] adj provisional; (passing) transitorio; (worker) temporero; (job) temporal

tempt [tempt] vt tentar; **to ~ sb into doing sth** tentar or inducir a uno a hacer algo; **~ation** [-'teɪʃən] n tentación f; **~ing** adj

tentador(a); (food) apetitoso/a

ten [ten] num diez

tenacity [tə'næsɪtɪ] n tenacidad f

tenancy ['tenənsɪ] n arrendamiento, alquiler m

tenant ['tenənt] n inquilino/a

tend [tend] vt cuidar ♦ vi: **to ~ to do sth** tener tendencia a hacer algo

tendency ['tendənsɪ] n tendencia

tender ['tendə*] adj (person, care) tierno, cariñoso; (meat) tierno; (sore) sensible ♦ n (COMM: offer) oferta; (money): **legal ~** moneda de curso legal ♦ vt ofrecer; **~ness** n ternura; (of meat) blandura

tenement ['tenəmənt] n casa de pisos (SP)

tennis ['tenɪs] n tenis m; **~ ball** n pelota de tenis; **~ court** n cancha de tenis; **~ player** n tenista m/f; **~ racket** n raqueta de tenis

tenor ['tenə*] n (MUS) tenor m

tenpin bowling ['tenpɪn-] n (juego de los) bolos

tense [tens] adj (person) nervioso; (moment, atmosphere) tenso; (muscle) tenso, en tensión ♦ n (LING) tiempo

tension ['tenʃən] n tensión f

tent [tent] n tienda (de campaña) (SP), carpa (AM)

tentative ['tentətɪv] adj (person, smile) indeciso; (conclusion, plans) provisional

tenterhooks ['tentəhuks] npl: **on ~** sobre ascuas

tenth [tenθ] num décimo

tent peg n clavija, estaca

tent pole n mástil m

tenuous ['tenjuəs] adj tenue

tenure ['tenjuə*] n (of land etc) tenencia; (of office) ejercicio

tepid ['tepɪd] adj tibio

term [təːm] n (word) término; (period) período; (SCOL) trimestre m ♦ vt llamar; **~s** npl (conditions, COMM) condiciones fpl; **in the short/long ~ a** corto/largo plazo; **to be on good ~s with sb** llevarse bien con uno; **to come to ~s with** (problem) aceptar

terminal ['təːmɪnl] adj (disease) mortal; (patient) terminal ♦ n (ELEC) borne m; (COMPUT) terminal m; (also: air ~) terminal f; (BRIT: also: coach ~) (estación f) terminal f

terminate ['təːmɪneɪt] vt terminar

terminus ['təːmɪnəs] (pl **termini**) n término, (estación f) terminal f

terrace ['terəs] n terraza; (BRIT: row of houses) hilera de casas adosadas; **the ~s** (BRIT: SPORT) las gradas fpl; **~d** adj (garden) en terrazas; (house) adosado

terrain [te'reɪn] n terreno

terrible ['terɪbl] adj terrible, horrible; (inf) atroz; **terribly** adv terriblemente; (very badly) malísimamente

terrier ['terɪə*] n terrier m

terrific [tə'rɪfɪk] adj (very great) tremendo; (wonderful) fantástico, fenomenal

terrify ['terɪfaɪ] vt aterrorizar

territory ['terɪtərɪ] n (also fig) territorio

terror ['terə*] n terror m; **~ism** n terrorismo; **~ist** n terrorista m/f

test [test] n (gen, CHEM) prueba; (MED) examen m; (SCOL) examen m, test m; (also: driving ~) examen de conducir ♦ vt probar, poner a prueba; (MED, SCOL) examinar

testament ['testəmənt] n testamento; the Old/New T~ el Antiguo/Nuevo Testamento

testicle ['testɪkl] n testículo

testify ['testɪfaɪ] vi (LAW) prestar declaración; to ~ to sth atestiguar algo

testimony ['testɪmənɪ] n (LAW) testimonio

test: ~ match n (CRICKET, RUGBY) partido internacional; **~ tube** n probeta

tetanus ['tetənəs] n tétano

tether ['teðə*] vt atar (con una cuerda) ♦ n: to be at the end of one's ~ no aguantar más

text [tekst] n texto; **~book** n libro de texto

textiles ['tekstaɪlz] npl textiles mpl; (textile industry) industria textil

texture ['tekstʃə*] n textura

Thailand ['taɪlænd] n Tailandia

Thames [temz] n: the ~ el (río) Támesis

than [ðæn] conj (in comparisons): more ~ 10/ once más de 10/una vez; I have more/less ~ you/Paul tengo más/menos que tú/Paul; she is older ~ you think es mayor de lo que piensas

thank [θæŋk] vt dar las gracias a, agradecer; ~ you (very much) muchas gracias; ~ God! ¡gracias a Dios!; **~s** npl gracias fpl ♦ excl (also: many ~s, ~s a lot) ¡gracias!; **~s to** prep gracias a; **~ful** adj: **~ful (for)** agradecido (por); **~less** adj ingrato; **T~sgiving (Day)** n día m de Acción de Gracias

that [ðæt] (pl those) adj (demonstrative) ese/a, pl esos/as; (more remote) aquel/aquella, pl aquellos/as; leave those books on the table deja esos libros sobre la mesa; ~ one ése/ésa; (more remote) aquél/aquélla; ~ one over there ése/ésa de ahí; aquél/aquélla de allí
♦ pron 1 (demonstrative) ése/a, pl ésos/as; (neuter) eso; (more remote) aquél/aquélla, pl aquéllos/as; (neuter) aquello; what's ~? ¿qué es eso (or aquello)?; who's ~? ¿quién es ése/a (or aquél/aquélla)?; is ~ you? ¿eres tú?; will you eat all ~? ¿vas a comer todo eso?; ~'s my house ésa es mi casa; ~'s what he said eso es lo que dijo; ~ is (to say) es decir
2 (relative: subject, object) que; (with preposition) (el/la) que etc, el/la cual etc; the book (~) I read el libro que leí; the books

~ are in the library los libros que están en la biblioteca; all (~) I have todo lo que tengo; the box (~) I put it in la caja en la que or donde lo puse; the people (~) I spoke to la gente con la que hablé
3 (relative: of time) que; the day (~) he came el día (en) que vino
♦ conj que; he thought ~ I was ill creyó que yo estaba enfermo
♦ adv (demonstrative): I can't work ~ much no puedo trabajar tanto; I didn't realise it was ~ bad no creí que fuera tan malo; ~ high así de alto

thatched [θætʃt] adj (roof) de paja; (cottage) con tejado de paja

thaw [θɔ:] n deshielo ♦ vi (ice) derretirse; (food) descongelarse ♦ vt (food) descongelar

the [ði:, ðə] def art 1 (gen) el, f la, pl los, fpl las (NB = el immediately before f n beginning with stressed (h)a; a+ el = al; de+ el = del); ~ boy/girl el chico/la chica; ~ books/flowers los libros/las flores; to ~ postman/from ~ drawer al cartero/del cajón; I haven't ~ time/money no tengo tiempo/dinero
2 (+ adj to form n) los; lo; ~ rich and ~ poor los ricos y los pobres; to attempt ~ impossible intentar lo imposible
3 (in titles): Elizabeth ~ First Isabel primera; Peter ~ Great Pedro el Grande
4 (in comparisons): ~ more he works ~ more he earns cuanto más trabaja más gana

theatre ['θɪətə*] (US **theater**) n teatro; (also: lecture ~) aula; (MED: also: operating ~) quirófano; **~-goer** n aficionado/a al teatro

theatrical [θɪ'ætrɪkl] adj teatral

theft [θeft] n robo

their [ðeə*] adj su; **~s** pron (el) suyo/(la) suya etc; see also **my**; **mine¹**

them [ðem, ðəm] pron (direct) los/las; (indirect) les; (stressed, after prep) ellos/ellas; see also **me**

theme [θi:m] n tema m; ~ **park** n parque de atracciones (en torno a un tema central); ~ **song** n tema m (musical)

themselves [ðəm'selvz] pl pron (subject) ellos mismos/ellas mismas; (complement) se; (after prep) sí (mismos/as); see also **oneself**

then [ðen] adv (at that time) entonces; (next) después; (later) luego, después; (and also) además ♦ conj (therefore) en ese caso, entonces ♦ adj: the ~ president el entonces presidente; by ~ para entonces; from ~ on desde entonces

theology [θɪ'ɔlədʒɪ] n teología

theory ['θɪərɪ] n teoría

therapist ['θerəpɪst] n terapeuta m/f
therapy ['θerəpɪ] n terapia

┌─────────────────┐
│ KEYWORD │
└─────────────────┘

there ['ðeə*] adv 1: ~ **is**, ~ **are** hay; ~ **is** no-one **here/no bread left** no hay nadie aquí/no queda pan; ~ **has been an accident** ha habido un accidente

2 (referring to place) ahí; (distant) allí; **it's** ~ está ahí; **put it in/on/up/down** ~ ponlo ahí dentro/encima/arriba/abajo; **I want that book** ~ quiero ese libro de ahí; ~ **he is!** ¡ahí está!

3: ~, ~ (esp to child) ea, ea

there: **~abouts** adv por ahí; **~after** adv después; **~by** adv así, de ese modo; **~fore** adv por lo tanto; **~'s** = there is; there has

thermal ['θə:ml] adj termal; (paper) térmico
thermometer [θə'mɔmɪtə*] n termómetro
Thermos ® ['θə:məs] n (also: ~ **flask**) termo
thermostat ['θə:məustæt] n termostato
thesaurus [θɪ'sɔ:rəs] n tesoro
these [ði:z] pl adj estos/as ♦ pl pron éstos/as
thesis ['θi:sɪs] (pl **theses**) n tesis f inv
they [ðeɪ] pl pron ellos/ellas; (stressed) ellos (mismos)/ellas (mismas); ~ **say that** ... (it is said that) se dice que ...; **~'d** = they had; they would; **~'ll** = they shall; they will; **~'re** = they are; **~'ve** = they have

thick [θɪk] adj (in consistency) espeso; (in size) grueso; (stupid) torpe ♦ n: **in the** ~ **of the battle** en lo más reñido de la batalla; **it's 20 cm** ~ tiene 20 cm de espesor; **~en** vi espesarse ♦ vt (sauce etc) espesar; **~ness** n espesor m; grueso; **~set** adj fornido
thief [θi:f] (pl **thieves**) n ladrón/ona m/f
thigh [θaɪ] n muslo
thimble ['θɪmbl] n dedal m
thin [θɪn] adj (person, animal) flaco; (in size) delgado; (in consistency) poco espeso; (hair, crowd) escaso ♦ vt: **to** ~ (**down**) diluir
thing [θɪŋ] n cosa; (object) objeto, artículo; (matter) asunto; (mania): **to have a** ~ **about sb/sth** estar obsesionado con uno/algo; **~s** npl (belongings) efectos mpl (personales); **the best** ~ **would be to** ... lo mejor sería ...; **how are ~s?** ¿qué tal?
think [θɪŋk] (pt, pp **thought**) vi pensar ♦ vt pensar, creer; **what did you** ~ **of them?** ¿qué te parecieron?; **to** ~ **about sth/sb** pensar en algo/uno; **I'll** ~ **about it** lo pensaré; **to** ~ **of doing sth** pensar en hacer algo; **I** ~ **so/not** creo que sí/no; **to** ~ **well of sb** tener buen concepto de uno; ~ **over** vt reflexionar sobre, meditar; ~ **up** vt (plan etc) idear; ~ **tank** n gabinete m de estrategia
thinly ['θɪnlɪ] adv (cut) fino; (spread) ligeramente
third [θə:d] adj (before n) tercer(a); (following

n) tercero/a ♦ n tercero/a; (fraction) tercio; (BRIT: SCOL: degree) título de licenciado con calificación de aprobado; **~ly** adv en tercer lugar; ~ **party insurance** (BRIT) n seguro contra terceros; **~-rate** adj (de calidad) mediocre; **T~ World** n Tercer Mundo
thirst [θə:st] n sed f; **~y** adj (person, animal) sediento; (work) que da sed; **to be ~y** tener sed
thirteen ['θə:'ti:n] num trece
thirty ['θə:tɪ] num treinta

┌─────────────────┐
│ KEYWORD │
└─────────────────┘

this [ðɪs] (pl **these**) adj (demonstrative) este/a; pl estos/as; (neuter) esto; ~ **man/woman** este hombre/esta mujer; **these children/flowers** estos chicos/estas flores; ~ **one** (here) éste/a, esto (de aquí)

♦ pron (demonstrative) éste/a; pl éstos/as; (neuter) esto; **who is ~?** ¿quién es éste/ésta?; **what is ~?** ¿qué es esto?; ~ **is where I live** aquí vivo; ~ **is what he said** esto es lo que dijo; ~ **is Mr Brown** (in introductions) le presento al Sr. Brown; (photo) éste es el Sr. Brown; (on telephone) habla el Sr. Brown

♦ adv (demonstrative): ~ **high/long** etc así de alto/largo etc; ~ **far** hasta aquí

thistle ['θɪsl] n cardo
thorn [θɔ:n] n espina
thorough ['θʌrə] adj (search) minucioso; (wash) a fondo; (knowledge, research) profundo; (person) meticuloso; **~bred** adj (horse) de pura sangre; (cattle) f; **"no ~fare"** "prohibido el paso"; **~ly** adv (search) minuciosamente; (study) profundamente; (wash) a fondo; (utterly: bad, wet etc) completamente, totalmente
those [ðəuz] pl adj esos/esas; (more remote) aquellos/as
though [ðəu] conj aunque ♦ adv sin embargo
thought [θɔ:t] pt, pp of **think** ♦ n pensamiento; (opinion) opinión f; **~ful** adj pensativo; (serious) serio; (considerate) atento; **~less** adj desconsiderado
thousand ['θauzənd] num mil; **two** ~ dos mil; **~s of** miles de; **~th** num milésimo
thrash [θræʃ] vt azotar; (defeat) derrotar; ~ **about** or **around** vi debatirse; ~ **out** vt discutir a fondo
thread [θred] n hilo; (of screw) rosca ♦ vt (needle) enhebrar; **~bare** adj raído
threat [θret] n amenaza; **~en** vi amenazar ♦ vt: **to ~en sb with/to do** amenazar a uno con/con hacer
three [θri:] num tres; **~-dimensional** adj tridimensional; **~-piece suit** n traje m de tres piezas; **~-piece suite** n tresillo; **~-ply** adj (wool) de tres cabos

threshold ['θrɛʃhəuld] n umbral m

threw [θruː] pt of **throw**

thrifty ['θrɪftɪ] adj económico

thrill [θrɪl] n (excitement) emoción f; (shudder) estremecimiento ♦ vt emocionar; **to be ~ed** (with gift etc) estar encantado; **~er** n novela (or obra or película) de suspense; **~ing** adj emocionante

thrive [θraɪv] (pt, pp **thrived**) vi (grow) crecer; (do well): **to ~ on sth** sentarle muy bien a uno algo; **thriving** adj próspero

throat [θrəut] n garganta; **to have a sore ~** tener dolor de garganta

throb [θrɔb] vi latir; dar punzadas; vibrar

throes [θrəuz] npl: **in the ~ of** en medio de

throne [θrəun] n trono

throng [θrɔŋ] n multitud f, muchedumbre f ♦ vt agolparse en

throttle ['θrɔtl] n (AUT) acelerador m ♦ vt estrangular

through [θruː] prep por, a través de; (time) durante; (by means of) por medio de, mediante; (owing to) gracias a ♦ adj (ticket, train) directo ♦ adv completamente, de parte a parte; de principio a fin; **to put sb ~ to sb** (TEL) poner or pasar a uno con uno; **to be ~** (TEL) tener comunicación; (have finished) haber terminado; **"no ~ road"** (BRIT) "calle sin salida"; **~out** prep (place) por todas partes de, por todo; (time) durante todo ♦ adv por or en todas partes

throw [θrəu] (pt **threw**, pp **thrown**) n tiro; (SPORT) lanzamiento ♦ vt tirar, echar; (SPORT) lanzar; (rider) derribar; (fig) desconcertar; **to ~ a party** dar una fiesta; **~ away** vt tirar; (money) derrochar; **~ off** vt deshacerse de; **~ out** vt tirar; (person) echar; expulsar; **~ up** vi vomitar; **~away** adj para tirar, desechable; (remark) hecho de paso; **~-in** n (SPORT) saque m

thru [θruː] (US) = **through**

thrush [θrʌʃ] n zorzal m, tordo

thrust [θrʌst] (pt, pp **thrust**) vt empujar (con fuerza)

thud [θʌd] n golpe m sordo

thug [θʌg] n gamberro/a

thumb [θʌm] n (ANAT) pulgar m; **to ~ a lift** hacer autostop; **~ through** vt fus (book) hojear; **~tack** (US) n chincheta (SP)

thump [θʌmp] n golpe m; (sound) ruido seco or sordo ♦ vt golpear ♦ vi (heart etc) palpitar

thunder ['θʌndə*] n trueno ♦ vi tronar; (train etc): **to ~ past** pasar como un trueno; **~bolt** n rayo; **~clap** n trueno; **~storm** n tormenta; **~y** adj tormentoso

Thursday ['θəːzdɪ] n jueves m inv

thus [ðʌs] adv así, de este modo

thyme [taɪm] n tomillo

thyroid ['θaɪrɔɪd] n (also: ~ gland) tiroides m

inv

tic [tɪk] n tic m

tick [tɪk] n (sound: of clock) tictac m; (mark) palomita; (ZOOL) garrapata; (BRIT: inf): **in a ~** en un instante ♦ vi hacer tictac ♦ vt marcar; **~ off** vt marcar; (person) reñir; **~ over** vi (engine) girar en marcha lenta; (fig) ir tirando

ticket ['tɪkɪt] n billete m (SP), tíquet m, boleto (AM); (for cinema etc) entrada (SP), boleto (AM); (in shop: on goods) etiqueta; (for raffle) papeleta; (for library) tarjeta; (parking ~) multa por estacionamiento ilegal; **~ collector** n revisor(a) m/f; **~ office** n (THEATRE) taquilla (SP), boletería (AM); (RAIL) despacho de billetes (SP) or boletos (AM)

tickle ['tɪkl] vt hacer cosquillas a ♦ vi hacer cosquillas; **ticklish** adj (person) cosquilloso; (problem) delicado

tidal ['taɪdl] adj de marea; **~ wave** n maremoto

tidbit ['tɪdbɪt] (US) n = **titbit**

tiddlywinks ['tɪdlɪwɪŋks] n juego infantil con fichas de plástico

tide [taɪd] n marea; (fig: of events etc) curso, marcha; **~ over** vt (help out) ayudar a salir del apuro

tidy ['taɪdɪ] adj (room etc) ordenado; (dress, work) limpio; (person) (bien) arreglado ♦ vt (also: ~ up) poner en orden

tie [taɪ] n (string etc) atadura; (BRIT: also: neck~) corbata; (fig: link) vínculo, lazo; (SPORT etc: draw) empate m ♦ vt atar ♦ vi (SPORT etc) empatar; **to ~ in a bow** atar con un lazo; **to ~ a knot in sth** hacer un nudo en algo; **~ down** vt (fig: person: restrict) atar; (: to price, date etc) obligar a; **~ up** vt (parcel) envolver; (dog, person) atar; (arrangements) concluir; **to be ~d up** (busy) estar ocupado

tier [tɪə*] n grada; (of cake) piso

tiger ['taɪgə*] n tigre m

tight [taɪt] adj (rope) tirante; (money) escaso; (clothes) ajustado; (bend) cerrado; (shoes, schedule) apretado; (budget) ajustado; (security) estricto; (inf: drunk) borracho ♦ adv (squeeze) muy fuerte; (shut) bien; **~en** vt (rope) estirar; (screw, grip) apretar; (security) reforzar ♦ vi estirarse; apretarse; **~-fisted** adj tacaño; **~ly** adv (grasp) muy fuerte; **~rope** n cuerda floja; **~s** (BRIT) npl panti mpl

tile [taɪl] n (on roof) teja; (on floor) baldosa; (on wall) azulejo; **~d** adj de tejas; embaldosado; (wall) alicatado

till [tɪl] n caja (registradora) ♦ vt (land) cultivar ♦ prep, conj = **until**

tilt [tɪlt] vt inclinar ♦ vi inclinarse

timber ['tɪmbə*] n (material) madera

time [taɪm] n tiempo; (epoch: often pl) época; (by clock) hora; (moment) momento; (occasion) vez f; (MUS) compás m ♦ vt calcular or medir el tiempo de; (*race*) cronometrar; (*remark, visit etc*) elegir el momento para; **a long ~** mucho tiempo; **4 at a ~ de** 4 en 4; 4 a la vez; **for the ~ being** de momento, por ahora; **from ~ to ~** de vez en cuando; **at ~s** a veces; **in ~** (*soon enough*) a tiempo; (*after some time*) con el tiempo; (*MUS*) al compás; in a week's ~ dentro de una semana; **in no ~** en un abrir y cerrar de ojos; **any ~** cuando sea; **on ~** a la hora; **5 ~s** 5 5 por 5; **what ~ is it?** ¿qué hora es?; **to have a good ~** pasarlo bien, divertirse; **~ bomb** *n* bomba de efecto retardado; **~less** *adj* eterno; **~ limit** *n* plazo; **~ly** *adj* oportuno; **~ off** *n* tiempo libre; **~r** *n* (*in kitchen etc*) programador *m* horario; **~ scale** (*BRIT*) *n* escala de tiempo; **~-share** *n* apartamento (*or* casa) a tiempo compartido; **~ switch** (*BRIT*) *n* interruptor *m* (horario); **~table** *n* horario; **~ zone** *n* huso horario

timid ['tɪmɪd] *adj* tímido

timing ['taɪmɪŋ] *n* (*SPORT*) cronometraje *m*; **the ~ of his resignation** el momento que eligió para dimitir

tin [tɪn] *n* estaño; (*also: ~ plate*) hojalata; (*BRIT: can*) lata; **~foil** *n* papel *m* de estaño

tinge [tɪndʒ] *n* matiz *m* ♦ *vt*: **~d with** teñido de

tingle ['tɪŋgl] *vi* (*person*): **to ~ (with)** estremecerse (de); (*hands etc*) hormiguear

tinker ['tɪŋkə*] : **~ with** *vt fus* jugar con, tocar

tinned [tɪnd] (*BRIT*) *adj* (*food*) en lata, en conserva

tin opener [-əupnə*] (*BRIT*) *n* abrelatas *m inv*

tinsel ['tɪnsl] *n* (guirnalda de) espumillón *m*

tint [tɪnt] *n* matiz *m*; (*for hair*) tinte *m*; **~ed** *adj* (*hair*) teñido; (*glass, spectacles*) ahumado

tiny ['taɪnɪ] *adj* minúsculo, pequeñito

tip [tɪp] *n* (*end*) punta; (*gratuity*) propina; (*BRIT: for rubbish*) vertedero; (*advice*) consejo ♦ *vt* (*waiter*) dar una propina a; (*tilt*) inclinar; (*empty: also: ~ out*) vaciar, echar; (*overturn: also: ~ over*) volcar; **~-off** *n* (*hint*) advertencia; **~ped** (*BRIT*) *adj* (*cigarette*) con filtro

Tipp-Ex ® ['tɪpɛks] *n* Tipp-Ex ® *m*

tipsy ['tɪpsɪ] (*inf*) *adj* alegre, mareado

tiptoe ['tɪptəu] *n*: **on ~** de puntillas

tire ['taɪə*] *n* (*US*) = **tyre** ♦ *vt* cansar ♦ *vi* (*gen*) cansarse; (*become bored*) aburrirse; **~d** *adj* cansado; **to be ~d of sth** estar harto de algo; **~less** *adj* incansable; **~some** *adj* aburrido; **tiring** *adj* cansado

tissue ['tɪʃuː] *n* tejido; (*paper handkerchief*) pañuelo de papel, kleenex ® *m*; **~ paper** *n* papel *m* de seda

tit [tɪt] *n* (*bird*) herrerillo común; **to give ~ for tat** dar ojo por ojo

titbit ['tɪtbɪt] (*US* **tidbit**) *n* (*food*) golosina;

(*news*) noticia sabrosa

title ['taɪtl] *n* título; **~ deed** *n* (*LAW*) título de propiedad; **~ role** *n* papel *m* principal

TM *abbr* = **trademark**

to [tuː, tə] *prep* **1** (*direction*) a; **to go ~ France/ London/school/the station** ir a Francia/ Londres/al colegio/a la estación; **to go ~ Claude's/the doctor's** ir a casa de Claude/al médico; **the road ~ Edinburgh** la carretera de Edimburgo

2 (*as far as*) hasta, a; **from here ~ London** de aquí a *or* hasta Londres; **to count ~ 10** contar hasta 10; **from 40 ~ 50 people** entre 40 y 50 personas

3 (*with expressions of time*): **a quarter/twenty ~ 5** las 5 menos cuarto/veinte

4 (*for, of*): **the key ~ the front door** la llave de la puerta principal; **she is secretary ~ the director** es la secretaría del director; **a letter ~ his wife** una carta a *o* para su mujer

5 (*expressing indirect object*) a; **to give sth ~ sb** darle algo a alguien; **to talk ~ sb** hablar con alguien; **to be a danger ~ sb** ser un peligro para alguien; **to carry out repairs ~ sth** hacer reparaciones en algo

6 (*in relation to*): **3 goals ~ 2** 3 goles a 2; **30 miles ~ the gallon** ≈ 9,4 litros a los cien (kms)

7 (*purpose, result*): **to come ~ sb's aid** venir en auxilio *or* ayuda de alguien; **to sentence sb ~ death** condenar a uno a muerte; **~ my great surprise** con gran sorpresa mía

♦ *with vb* **1** (*simple infin*): **~ go/eat** ir/comer

2 (*following another vb*): **to want/try/start ~ do** querer/intentar/empezar a hacer; *see also relevant vb*

3 (*with vb omitted*): **I don't want ~** no quiero

4 (*purpose, result*) para; **I did it ~ help you** lo hice para ayudarte; **he came ~ see you** vino a verte

5 (*equivalent to relative clause*): **I have things ~ do** tengo cosas que hacer; **the main thing is ~ try** lo principal es intentarlo

6 (*after adj etc*): **ready ~ go** listo para irse; **too old ~ ...** demasiado viejo (como) para ...

♦ *adv*: **pull/push the door ~** tirar de/empujar la puerta

toad [təud] *n* sapo; **~stool** *n* hongo venenoso

toast [təust] *n* (*CULIN*) tostada; (*drink, speech*) brindis *m* ♦ *vt* (*CULIN*) tostar; (*drink to*) brindar por; **~er** *n* tostador *m*

tobacco [tə'bækəu] *n* tabaco; **~nist** *n* estanquero/a (*SP*), tabaquero/a (*AM*); **~nist's (shop)** (*BRIT*) *n* estanco (*SP*), tabaquería (*AM*)

toboggan [tə'bɔgən] *n* tobogán *m*

today [tə'deɪ] *adv, n (also fig)* hoy *m*

toddler ['tɔdlə*] *n* niño/a (que empieza a andar)

toe [təu] *n* dedo (del pie); *(of shoe)* punta; **to ~ the line** *(fig)* conformarse; **~nail** *n* uña del pie

toffee ['tɔfɪ] *n* toffee *m*; **~ apple** *(BRIT) n* manzana acaramelada

together [tə'geðə*] *adv* juntos; *(at same time)* al mismo tiempo, a la vez; **~ with** junto con

toil [tɔɪl] *n* trabajo duro, labor *f* ♦ *vi* trabajar duramente

toilet ['tɔɪlət] *n* retrete *m*; *(BRIT: room)* servicios *mpl (SP)*, wáter *m (SP)*, sanitario *(AM)* ♦ *cpd (soap etc)* de aseo; **~ paper** *n* papel *m* higiénico; **~ries** *npl* artículos *mpl* de tocador; **~ roll** *n* rollo de papel higiénico

token ['təukən] *n (sign)* señal *f*, muestra; *(souvenir)* recuerdo; *(disc)* ficha ♦ *adj (strike, payment etc)* simbólico; **book/record ~** *(BRIT)* vale *m* para comprar libros/discos; **gift ~** *(BRIT)* vale-regalo

Tokyo ['təukjəu] *n* Tokio, Tókio

told [təuld] *pt, pp of* **tell**

tolerable ['tɔlərəbl] *adj (bearable)* soportable; *(fairly good)* pasable

tolerant ['tɔlərnt] *adj*: **~ of** tolerante con

tolerate ['tɔləreɪt] *vt* tolerar

toll [təul] *n (of casualties)* número de víctimas; *(tax, charge)* peaje *m* ♦ *vi (bell)* doblar

tomato [tə'mɑːtəu] *(pl ~es) n* tomate *m*

tomb [tuːm] *n* tumba

tomboy ['tɔmbɔɪ] *n* marimacho

tombstone ['tuːmstəun] *n* lápida

tomcat ['tɔmkæt] *n* gato (macho)

tomorrow [tə'mɔrəu] *adv, n (also: fig)* mañana; **the day after ~** pasado mañana; **~ morning** mañana por la mañana

ton [tʌn] *n* tonelada *(BRIT = 1016 kg; US = 907 kg)*; *(metric ~)* tonelada métrica; **~s of** *(inf)* montones de

tone [təun] *n* tono ♦ *vi (also: ~ in)* armonizar; **~ down** *vt (criticism)* suavizar; *(colour)* atenuar; **~ up** *vt (muscles)* tonificar; **~-deaf** *adj* con mal oído

tongs [tɔŋz] *npl (for coal)* tenazas *fpl*; *(curling ~)* tenacillas *fpl*

tongue [tʌŋ] *n* lengua; **~ in cheek** irónicamente; **~-tied** *adj (fig)* mudo; **~-twister** *n* trabalenguas *m inv*

tonic ['tɔnɪk] *n (MED, also fig)* tónico; *(also: ~ water)* (agua) tónica

tonight [tə'naɪt] *adv, n* esta noche; esta tarde

tonsil ['tɔnsl] *n* amígdala; **~litis** [-'laɪtɪs] *n* amigdalitis *f*

too [tuː] *adv (excessively)* demasiado; *(also)* también; **~ much** demasiado; **~ many** demasiados/as

took [tuk] *pt of* **take**

tool [tuːl] *n* herramienta; **~ box** *n* caja de herramientas

toot [tuːt] *n* pitido ♦ *vi* tocar el pito

tooth [tuːθ] *(pl teeth) n (ANAT, TECH)* diente *m*; *(molar)* muela; **~ache** *n* dolor *m* de muelas; **~brush** *n* cepillo de dientes; **~paste** *n* pasta de dientes; **~pick** *n* palillo

top [tɔp] *n (of mountain)* cumbre *f*, cima; *(of tree)* copa; *(of head)* coronilla; *(of ladder, page)* lo alto; *(of table)* superficie *f*; *(of cupboard)* parte *f* de arriba; *(lid: of box)* tapa; *(: of bottle, jar)* tapón *m*; *(of list etc)* cabeza; *(toy)* peonza; *(garment)* blusa, camiseta ♦ *adj* de arriba; *(in rank)* principal, primero; *(best)* mejor ♦ *vt (exceed)* exceder; *(be first in)* encabezar; **on ~ of** *(above)* sobre, encima de; *(in addition to)* además de; **from ~ to bottom** de pies a cabeza; **~ off** *(US)* **vt = ~ up**; **~ up** *vt* llenar; **~ floor** *n* último piso; **~ hat** *n* sombrero de copa; **~-heavy** *adj (object)* mal equilibrado

topic ['tɔpɪk] *n* tema *m*; **~al** *adj* actual

top: **~less** *adj (bather, bikini)* topless *inv*; **~-level** *adj (talks)* al más alto nivel; **~most** *adj* más alto

topple ['tɔpl] *vt* derribar ♦ *vi* caerse

top-secret *adj* de alto secreto

topsy-turvy ['tɔpsɪ'tɜːvɪ] *adj* al revés ♦ *adv* patas arriba

torch [tɔːtʃ] *n* antorcha; *(BRIT: electric)* linterna

tore [tɔː*] *pt of* **tear²**

torment [*n* 'tɔːment, *vt* tɔː'ment] *n* tormento ♦ *vt* atormentar; *(fig: annoy)* fastidiar

torn [tɔːn] *pp of* **tear²**

torrent ['tɔrnt] *n* torrente *m*

tortoise ['tɔːtəs] *n* tortuga; **~shell** ['tɔːtəʃel] *adj* de carey

torture ['tɔːtʃə*] *n* tortura ♦ *vt* torturar; *(fig)* atormentar

Tory ['tɔːrɪ] *(BRIT) adj, n (POL)* conservador(a) *m/f*

toss [tɔs] *vt* tirar, echar; *(one's head)* sacudir; **to ~ a coin** echar a cara o cruz; **to ~ up for sth** jugar a cara o cruz algo; **to ~ and turn** *(in bed)* dar vueltas

tot [tɔt] *n (BRIT: drink)* copita; *(child)* nene/a *m/f*

total ['təutl] *adj* total, entero; *(emphatic: failure etc)* completo, total ♦ *n* total *m*, suma ♦ *vt (add up)* sumar; *(amount to)* ascender a; **~ly** *adv* totalmente

touch [tʌtʃ] *n* tacto; *(contact)* contacto ♦ *vt* tocar; *(emotionally)* conmover; **a ~ of** *(fig)* un poquito de; **to get in ~ with sb** ponerse en contacto con uno; **to lose ~** *(friends)* perder contacto; **~ on** *vt fus (topic)* aludir (brevemente) a; **~ up** *vt (paint)* retocar; **~-and-go** *adj* arriesgado; **~down** *n* aterrizaje

m; (*on sea*) amerizaje *m*; (*US: FOOTBALL*)
ensayo; **~ed** *adj* (*moved*) conmovido; **~ing**
adj (*moving*) conmovedor(a); **~line** *n* (*SPORT*)
línea de banda; **~y** *adj* (*person*) quisquilloso

tough [tʌf] *adj* (*material*) resistente; (*meat*)
duro; (*problem etc*) difícil; (*policy, stance*)
inflexible; (*person*) fuerte; **~en** *vt* endurecer

toupée ['tuːpeɪ] *n* peluca

tour ['tuə*] *n* viaje *m*, vuelta; (*also: package ~*)
viaje *m* todo comprendido; (*of town,
museum*) visita; (*by band etc*) gira ♦ *vt*
recorrer, visitar; **~ guide** *n* guía *m* turístico,
guía *f* turística

tourism ['tuərɪzm] *n* turismo

tourist ['tuərɪst] *n* turista *m/f* ♦ *cpd* turístico;
~ office *n* oficina de turismo

tousled ['tauzld] *adj* (*hair*) despeinado

tout [taut] *vi*: **to ~ for business** solicitar
clientes ♦ *n* (*also: ticket ~*) revendedor(a) *m/f*

tow [təu] *vt* remolcar; **"on** or **in** (*US*) **~"** (*AUT*)
"a remolque"

toward(s) [tə'wɔːd(z)] *prep* hacia; (*attitude*)
respecto a, con; (*purpose*) para

towel ['tauəl] *n* toalla; **~ling** *n* (*fabric*) felpa;
~ rail (*US* = **rack**) *n* toallero

tower ['tauə*] *n* torre *f*; **~ block** (*BRIT*) *n*
torre *f* (de pisos); **~ing** *adj* muy alto,
imponente

town [taun] *n* ciudad *f*; **to go to ~** ir a la
ciudad; (*fig*) echar la casa por la ventana;
~ centre *n* centro de la ciudad; **~ council** *n*
ayuntamiento, consejo municipal; **~ hall** *n*
ayuntamiento; **~ plan** *n* plano de la ciudad;
~ planning *n* urbanismo

towrope ['təurəup] *n* cable *m* de remolque

tow truck (*US*) *n* camión *m* grúa

toy [tɔɪ] *n* juguete *m*; **~ with** *vt fus* jugar con;
(*idea*) acariciar; **~shop** *n* juguetería

trace [treɪs] *n* rastro ♦ *vt* (*draw*) trazar,
delinear; (*locate*) encontrar; (*follow*) seguir la
pista de; **tracing paper** *n* papel *m* de calco

track [træk] *n* (*mark*) huella, pista; (*path:
gen*) camino, senda; (*: of bullet etc*)
trayectoria; (*: of suspect, animal*) pista, rastro;
(*RAIL*) vía; (*SPORT*) pista; (*on tape, record*)
canción *f* ♦ *vt* seguir la pista de; **to keep ~
of** mantenerse al tanto de, seguir; **~ down** *vt*
(*prey*) seguir el rastro de; (*sth lost*) encontrar;
~suit *n* chandal *m*

tract [trækt] *n* (*GEO*) región *f*

traction ['trækʃən] *n* (*power*) tracción *f*; **in ~**
(*MED*) en tracción

tractor ['træktə*] *n* tractor *m*

trade [treɪd] *n* comercio; (*skill, job*) oficio ♦ *vi*
negociar, comerciar ♦ *vt* (*exchange*): **to ~ sth
(for sth)** cambiar algo (por algo); **~ in** *vt* (*old
car etc*) ofrecer como parte del pago; **~ fair**
n feria comercial; **~mark** *n* marca de fábrica;
~ name *n* marca registrada; **~r** *n*

comerciante *m/f*; **~sman** (*irreg*) *n*
(*shopkeeper*) tendero; **~ union** *n* sindicato;
~ unionist *n* sindicalista *m/f*

tradition [trə'dɪʃən] *n* tradición *f*; **~al** *adj*
tradicional

traffic ['træfɪk] *n* (*gen, AUT*) tráfico, circulación
f, tránsito (*AM*) ♦ *vi*: **to ~ in** (*pej: liquor,
drugs*) traficar en; **~ circle** (*US*) *n* isleta;
~ jam *n* embotellamiento; **~ lights** *npl*
semáforo; **~ warden** *n* guardia *m/f* de tráfico

tragedy ['trædʒədɪ] *n* tragedia

tragic ['trædʒɪk] *adj* trágico

trail [treɪl] *n* (*tracks*) rastro, pista; (*path*)
camino, sendero; (*dust, smoke*) estela ♦ *vt*
(*drag*) arrastrar; (*follow*) seguir la pista de
♦ *vi* arrastrar; (*in contest etc*) ir perdiendo;
~ behind *vi* quedar a la zaga; **~er** *n* (*AUT*)
remolque *m*; (*caravan*) caravana; (*CINEMA*)
trailer *m*, avance *m*; **~er truck** (*US*) *n* trailer
m

train [treɪn] *n* tren *m*; (*of dress*) cola; (*series*)
serie *f* ♦ *vt* (*educate, teach skills to*) formar;
(*sportsman*) entrenar; (*dog*) adiestrar; (*point:
gun etc*): **to ~ on** apuntar a ♦ *vi* (*SPORT*)
entrenarse; (*learn a skill*): **to ~ as a teacher
etc** estudiar para profesor *etc*; **one's ~ of
thought** el razonamiento de uno; **~ed** *adj*
(*worker*) cualificado; (*animal*) amaestrado;
~ee [treɪ'niː] *n* aprendiz/a *m/f*; **~er** *n*
(*SPORT: coach*) entrenador(a) *m/f*; (*: shoe*):
~ers zapatillas *fpl* (de deporte); (*of animals*)
domador(a) *m/f*; **~ing** *n* formación *f*;
entrenamiento; **to be in ~ing** (*SPORT*) estar
entrenando; **~ing college** *n* (*gen*) colegio
de formación profesional; (*for teachers*)
escuela de formación del profesorado; **~ing
shoes** *npl* zapatillas *fpl* (de deporte)

trait [treɪt] *n* rasgo

traitor ['treɪtə*] *n* traidor(a) *m/f*

tram [træm] (*BRIT*) *n* (*also: ~car*) tranvía *m*

tramp [træmp] *n* (*person*) vagabundo/a; (*inf:
pej: woman*) puta

trample ['træmpl] *vt*: **to ~ (underfoot)**
pisotear

trampoline ['træmpəliːn] *n* trampolín *m*

tranquil ['træŋkwɪl] *adj* tranquilo; **~lizer** *n*
(*MED*) tranquilizante *m*

transact [træn'zækt] *vt* (*business*) despachar;
~ion [-'zækʃən] *n* transacción *f*, operación *f*

transfer [*n* 'trænsfə:*, *vb* træns'fə:*] *n* (*of
employees*) traslado; (*of money, power*)
transferencia; (*SPORT*) traspaso; (*picture,
design*) calcomanía ♦ *vt* trasladar; transferir;
to ~ the charges (*BRIT: TEL*) llamar a cobro
revertido

transform [træns'fɔːm] *vt* transformar

transfusion [træns'fjuːʒən] *n* transfusión *f*

transient ['trænzɪənt] *adj* transitorio

transistor [træn'zɪstə*] *n* (*ELEC*) transistor *m*;

~ radio n transistor m
transit ['trænzɪt] n: **in ~** en tránsito
transitive ['trænzɪtɪv] adj (LING) transitivo
transit lounge n sala de tránsito
translate [trænz'leɪt] vt traducir; **translation** [-'leɪʃən] n traducción f; **translator** n traductor(a) m/f
transmit [trænz'mɪt] vt transmitir; **~ter** n transmisor m
transparency [træns'pɛərnsɪ] n transparencia; (BRIT: PHOT) diapositiva
transparent [træns'pærnt] adj transparente
transpire [træns'paɪə*] vi (turn out) resultar; (happen) ocurrir, suceder; **it ~d that ...** se supo que ...
transplant ['trænsplɑːnt] n (MED) transplante m
transport [n 'trænspɔːt, vt træns'pɔːt] n transporte m; (car) coche m (SP), carro (AM), automóvil m ♦ vt transportar; **~ation** [-'teɪʃən] n transporte m; **~ café** (BRIT) n bar-restaurant m de carretera
transvestite [trænz'vestaɪt] n travestí m/f
trap [træp] n (snare, trick) trampa; (carriage) cabriolé m ♦ vt coger (SP) or agarrar (AM) en una trampa; (trick) engañar; (confine) atrapar; **~ door** n escotilla
trapeze [trə'piːz] n trapecio
trappings ['træpɪŋz] npl adornos mpl
trash [træʃ] n (rubbish) basura; (pej): **the book/film is ~** el libro/la película no vale nada; (nonsense) tonterías fpl; **~ can** (US) n cubo (SP) or balde (AM) de la basura
travel ['trævl] n el viajar ♦ vi viajar ♦ vt (distance) recorrer; **~s** npl (journeys) viajes mpl; **~ agent** n agente m/f de viajes; **~ler** (US **~er**) n viajero/a; **~ler's cheque** (US **~er's check**) n cheque m de viajero; **~ling** (US **~ing**) n los viajes, el viajar; **~ sickness** n mareo
trawler ['trɔːlə*] n pesquero de arrastre
tray [treɪ] n bandeja; (on desk) cajón m
treacherous ['tretʃərəs] adj traidor, traicionero; (dangerous) peligroso
treacle ['triːkl] (BRIT) n melaza
tread [tred] (pt **trod**, pp **trodden**) n (step) paso, pisada; (sound) ruido de pasos; (of stair) escalón m; (of tyre) banda de rodadura ♦ vi pisar; **~ on** vt fus pisar
treason ['triːzn] n traición f
treasure ['treʒə*] n (also fig) tesoro ♦ vt (value: object, friendship) apreciar; (: memory) guardar
treasurer ['treʒərə*] n tesorero/a
treasury ['treʒərɪ] n: **the T~** el Ministerio de Hacienda
treat [triːt] n (present) regalo ♦ vt tratar; **to ~ sb to sth** invitar a uno a algo
treatment ['triːtmənt] n tratamiento

treaty ['triːtɪ] n tratado
treble ['trebl] adj triple ♦ vt triplicar ♦ vi triplicarse; **~ clef** n (MUS) clave f de sol
tree [triː] n árbol m; **~ trunk** tronco (de árbol)
trek [trek] n (long journey) viaje m largo y difícil; (tiring walk) caminata
trellis ['trelɪs] n enrejado
tremble ['trembl] vi temblar
tremendous [trɪ'mendəs] adj tremendo, enorme; (excellent) estupendo
tremor ['tremə*] n temblor m; (also: **earth ~**) temblor m de tierra
trench [trentʃ] n zanja
trend [trend] n (tendency) tendencia; (of events) curso; (fashion) moda; **~y** adj de moda
trespass ['trespəs] vi: **to ~ on** entrar sin permiso en; **"no ~ing"** "prohibido el paso"
trestle ['tresl] n caballete m
trial ['traɪəl] n (LAW) juicio, proceso; (test: of machine etc) prueba; (hardship) **~s** npl dificultades fpl; **by ~ and error** a fuerza de probar
triangle ['traɪæŋgl] n (MATH, MUS) triángulo
tribe [traɪb] n tribu f
tribunal [traɪ'bjuːnl] n tribunal m
tributary ['trɪbjutərɪ] n (river) afluente m
tribute ['trɪbjuːt] n homenaje m, tributo; **to pay ~ to** rendir homenaje a
trick [trɪk] n (skill, knack) tino, truco; (conjuring ~) truco; (joke) broma; (CARDS) baza ♦ vt engañar; **to play a ~ on sb** gastar una broma a uno; **that should do the ~** a ver si funciona así; **~ery** n engaño
trickle ['trɪkl] n (of water etc) goteo ♦ vi gotear
tricky ['trɪkɪ] adj difícil; delicado
tricycle ['traɪsɪkl] n triciclo
trifle ['traɪfl] n bagatela; (CULIN) dulce de bizcocho borracho, gelatina, fruta y natillas ♦ adv: **a ~ long** un poquito largo; **trifling** adj insignificante
trigger ['trɪgə*] n (of gun) gatillo; **~ off** vt desencadenar
trim [trɪm] adj (house, garden) en buen estado; (person, figure) esbelto ♦ n (haircut etc) recorte m; (on car) guarnición f ♦ vt (neaten) arreglar; (cut) recortar; (decorate) adornar; (NAUT: a sail) orientar; **~mings** npl (CULIN) guarnición f
trip [trɪp] n viaje m; (excursion) excursión f; (stumble) traspié m ♦ vi (stumble) tropezar; (go lightly) andar a paso ligero; **on a ~** de viaje; **~ up** vi tropezar, caerse ♦ vt hacer tropezar or caer
tripe [traɪp] n (CULIN) callos mpl
triple ['trɪpl] adj triple; **triplets** ['trɪplɪts] npl trillizos/as mpl/fpl; **triplicate** ['trɪplɪkət] n: **in triplicate** por triplicado

trite [traɪt] adj trillado

triumph ['traɪəmf] n triunfo ♦ vi: to ~ (over) vencer; ~ant [traɪ'ʌmfənt] adj (team etc) vencedor(a); (wave, return) triunfal

trivia ['trɪvɪə] npl trivialidades fpl

trivial ['trɪvɪəl] adj insignificante; (commonplace) banal

trod [trɒd] pt of tread

trodden ['trɒdn] pp of tread

trolley ['trɒlɪ] n carrito; (also: ~ bus) trolebús m

trombone [trɒm'bəʊn] n trombón m

troop [tru:p] n grupo, banda; ~s npl (MIL) tropas fpl; ~ in/out vi entrar/salir en tropel; ~ing the colour n (ceremony) presentación f de la bandera

trophy ['trəʊfɪ] n trofeo

tropical ['trɒpɪkl] adj tropical

trot [trɒt] n trote m ♦ vi trotar; on the ~ (BRIT: fig) seguidos/as

trouble ['trʌbl] n problema m, dificultad f; (worry) preocupación f; (bother, effort) molestia, esfuerzo; (unrest) inquietud f; (MED): stomach etc ~ problemas mpl gástricos etc ♦ vt (disturb) molestar; (worry) preocupar, inquietar ♦ vi: to ~ to do sth molestarse en hacer algo; ~s npl (POL etc) conflictos mpl; (personal) problemas mpl; to be in ~ estar en un apuro; it's no ~! ¡no es molestia (ninguna)!; what's the ~? (with broken TV etc) ¿cuál es el problema?; (doctor to patient) ¿qué pasa?; ~d adj (person) preocupado; (country, epoch, life) agitado; ~maker n agitador/a m/f; (child) alborotador m; ~shooter n (in conflict) conciliador(a) m/f; ~some adj molesto

trough [trɒf] n (also: drinking ~) abrevadero; (also: feeding ~) comedero; (depression) depresión f

troupe [tru:p] n grupo

trousers ['traʊzəz] npl pantalones mpl; short ~ pantalones mpl cortos

trousseau ['tru:səʊ] (pl ~x or ~s) n ajuar m

trout [traʊt] n inv trucha

trowel ['traʊəl] n (of gardener) palita; (of builder) paleta

truant ['truənt] n: to play ~ (BRIT) hacer novillos

truce [tru:s] n tregua

truck [trʌk] n (lorry) camión m; (RAIL) vagón m; ~ driver n camionero; ~ farm (US) n huerto

true [tru:] adj verdadero; (accurate) exacto; (genuine) auténtico; (faithful) fiel; to come ~ realizarse

truffle ['trʌfl] n trufa

truly ['tru:lɪ] adv (really) realmente; (truthfully) verdaderamente; (faithfully): yours ~ (in letter) le saluda atentamente

trump [trʌmp] n triunfo

trumpet ['trʌmpɪt] n trompeta

truncheon ['trʌntʃən] n porra

trundle ['trʌndl] vi: to ~ along ir sin prisas

trunk [trʌŋk] n (of tree, person) tronco; (of elephant) trompa; (case) baúl m; (US: AUT) maletero; ~s npl (also: swimming ~s) bañador m (de hombre)

truss [trʌs] vt: ~ (up) atar

trust [trʌst] n confianza; (responsibility) responsabilidad f; (LAW) fideicomiso ♦ vt (rely on) tener confianza en; (hope) esperar; (entrust): to ~ sth to sb confiar algo a uno; to take sth on ~ aceptar algo a ojos cerrados; ~ed adj de confianza; ~ee [trʌs'ti:] n (LAW) fideicomisario; (of school) administrador m; ~ful adj confiado; ~ing adj confiado; ~worthy adj digno de confianza

truth [tru:θ, pl tru:ðz] n verdad f; ~ful adj veraz

try [traɪ] n tentativa, intento; (RUGBY) ensayo ♦ vt (attempt) intentar; (test: also: ~ out) probar, someter a prueba; (LAW) juzgar, procesar; (strain: patience) hacer perder ♦ vi probar; to have a ~ probar suerte; to ~ to do sth intentar hacer algo; ~ again! ¡vuelve a probar!; ~ harder! ¡esfuérzate más!; well, I tried al menos lo intenté; ~ on vt (clothes) probarse; ~ing adj (experience) cansado; (person) pesado

T-shirt ['ti:ʃə:t] n camiseta

T-square n regla en T

tub [tʌb] n cubo (SP), balde m (AM); (bath) tina, bañera

tube [tju:b] n tubo; (BRIT: underground) metro; (for tyre) cámara de aire

tuberculosis [tjubə:kju'ləʊsɪs] n tuberculosis f inv

tube station (BRIT) n estación f de metro

tubular ['tju:bjʊlə*] adj tubular

TUC (BRIT) n abbr (= Trades Union Congress) federación nacional de sindicatos

tuck [tʌk] vt (put) poner; ~ away vt (money) guardar; (building): to be ~ed away esconderse, ocultarse; ~ in vt meter dentro; (child) arropar ♦ vi (eat) comer con apetito; ~ up vt (child) arropar; ~ shop n (SCOL) tienda; ≈ bar m (del colegio) (SP)

Tuesday ['tju:zdɪ] n martes m inv

tuft [tʌft] n mechón m; (of grass etc) manojo

tug [tʌg] n (ship) remolcador m ♦ vt tirar de; ~-of-war n lucha de tiro de cuerda; (fig) tira y afloja m

tuition [tju:'ɪʃən] n (BRIT) enseñanza; (: private ~) clases fpl particulares; (US: school fees) matrícula

tulip ['tju:lɪp] n tulipán m

tumble ['tʌmbl] n (fall) caída ♦ vi caer; to ~ to sth (inf) caer en la cuenta de algo;

~down adj destartalado; **~ dryer** (BRIT) n secadora

tumbler ['tʌmblə*] n (glass) vaso

tummy ['tʌmi] (inf) n barriga, tripa

tumour ['tju:mə*] (US **tumor**) n tumor m

tuna ['tju:nə] n inv (also: **~ fish**) atún m

tune [tju:n] n melodía ♦ vt (MUS) afinar; (RADIO, TV, AUT) sintonizar; **to be in/out of** (instrument) estar afinado/desafinado; (singer) cantar afinadamente/desafinar; **to be in/out of ~ with** (fig) estar de acuerdo/en desacuerdo con; **~ in** vi: **to ~ in (to)** (RADIO, TV) sintonizar (con); **~ up** vi (musician) afinar (su instrumento); **~ful** adj melodioso; **~r** n: **piano ~r** afinador(a) m/f de pianos

tunic ['tju:nɪk] n túnica

Tunisia [tju:'nɪzɪə] n Túnez m

tunnel ['tʌnl] n túnel m; (in mine) galería ♦ vi construir un túnel/una galería

turban ['tə:bən] n turbante m

turbulent ['tə:bjulənt] adj turbulento

tureen [tə'ri:n] n sopera

turf [tə:f] n césped m; (clod) tepe m ♦ vt cubrir con césped; **~ out** (inf) vt echar a la calle

Turk [tə:k] n turco/a

Turkey ['tə:kɪ] n Turquía

turkey ['tə:kɪ] n pavo

Turkish ['tə:kɪʃ] adj, n turco

turmoil ['tə:mɔɪl] n: **in ~** revuelto

turn [tə:n] n turno; (in road) curva; (of mind, events) rumbo; (THEATRE) número; (MED) ataque m ♦ vt girar, volver; (collar, steak) dar la vuelta a; (page) pasar; (change): **to ~ sth into** convertir algo en ♦ vi volver; (person: look back) volverse; (reverse direction) dar la vuelta; (milk) cortarse; (become): **to ~ nasty/ forty** ponerse feo/cumplir los cuarenta; **a good ~** un favor; **it gave me quite a ~** me dio un susto; **"no left ~"** (AUT) "prohibido girar a la izquierda"; **it's your ~** te toca a ti; **in ~** por turnos; **to take ~s (at)** turnarse (en); **~ away** vi apartar la vista ♦ vt rechazar; **~ back** vi volverse atrás ♦ vt hacer retroceder; (clock) retrasar; **~ down** vt (refuse) rechazar; (reduce) bajar; (fold) doblar; **~ in** vi (inf: go to bed) acostarse ♦ vt (fold) doblar hacia dentro; **~ off** vi (from road) desviarse ♦ vt (light, radio etc) apagar; (tap) cerrar; (engine) parar; **~ on** vt (light, radio etc) encender (SP), prender (AM); (tap) abrir; (engine) poner en marcha; **~ out** vt (light, gas) apagar; (produce) producir ♦ vi (voters) concurrir; **to ~ out to be ...** resultar ser ...; **~ over** vi (person) volverse ♦ vt (object) dar la vuelta a; (page) volver; **~ round** vi volverse; (rotate) girar; **~ up** vi (person) llegar, presentarse; (lost object) aparecer ♦ vt (gen) subir; **~ing** n (in road)

vuelta; **~ing point** n (fig) momento decisivo

turnip ['tə:nɪp] n nabo

turn: **~out** n concurrencia; **~over** n (COMM: amount of money) volumen m de ventas; (: of goods) movimiento; **~pike** (US) n autopista de peaje; **~stile** n torniquete m; **~table** n plato; **~up** (BRIT) n (on trousers) vuelta

turpentine ['tə:pəntaɪn] n (also: **turps**) trementina

turquoise ['tə:kwɔɪz] n (stone) turquesa ♦ adj color turquesa

turret ['tʌrɪt] n torreón m

turtle ['tə:tl] n galápago; **~neck (sweater)** n jersey m de cuello vuelto

tusk [tʌsk] n colmillo

tutor ['tju:tə*] n profesor(a) m/f; **~ial** [-'tɔ:rɪəl] n (SCOL) seminario

tuxedo [tʌk'si:dəu] (US) n smóking m, esmoquin m

TV [ti:'vi:] n abbr (= television) tele f

twang [twæŋ] n (of instrument) punteado; (of voice) timbre m nasal

tweezers ['twi:zəz] npl pinzas fpl (de depilar)

twelfth [twelfθ] num duodécimo

twelve [twelv] num doce; **at ~ o'clock** (midday) a mediodía; (midnight) a medianoche

twentieth ['twentɪɪθ] adj vigésimo

twenty ['twentɪ] num veinte

twice [twaɪs] adv dos veces; **~ as much** dos veces más

twiddle ['twɪdl] vi: **to ~ (with) sth** dar vueltas a algo; **to ~ one's thumbs** (fig) estar mano sobre mano

twig [twɪg] n ramita

twilight ['twaɪlaɪt] n crepúsculo

twin [twɪn] adj, n gemelo a m/f ♦ vt hermanar; **~-bedded room** n habitación f doble

twine [twaɪn] n bramante m ♦ vi (plant) enroscarse

twinge [twɪndʒ] n (of pain) punzada; (of conscience) remordimiento

twinkle ['twɪŋkl] vi centellear; (eyes) brillar

twirl [twə:l] vt dar vueltas a ♦ vi dar vueltas

twist [twɪst] n (action) torsión f; (in road, coil) vuelta; (in wire, flex) doblez f; (in story) giro ♦ vt torcer; (weave) trenzar; (roll around) enrollar; (fig) deformar ♦ vi serpentear

twit [twɪt] (inf) n tonto

twitch [twɪtʃ] n (pull) tirón m; (nervous) tic m ♦ vi crisparse

two [tu:] num dos; **to put ~ and ~ together** (fig) atar cabos; **~-door** adj (AUT) de dos puertas; **~-faced** adj (pej: person) falso; **~-fold** adv: **to increase ~fold** doblarse; **~-piece (suit)** n traje m de dos piezas; **~-piece (swimsuit)** n dos piezas m inv, bikini m; **~some** n (people) pareja; **~-way** adj: **~-**

way traffic circulación f de dos sentidos
tycoon [taɪ'kuːn] n: (business) ~ magnate m
type [taɪp] n (category) tipo, género; (model) tipo; (TYP) tipo, letra ♦ vt (letter etc) escribir a máquina; ~**cast** adj (actor) encasillado; ~**face** n letra; ~**script** n texto mecanografiado; ~**writer** n máquina de escribir; ~**written** adj mecanografiado
typhoid ['taɪfɔɪd] n tifoidea
typical ['tɪpɪkl] adj típico
typing ['taɪpɪŋ] n mecanografía
typist ['taɪpɪst] n mecanógrafo/a
tyrant ['taɪərnt] n tirano/a
tyre ['taɪə*] (US **tire**) n neumático (SP), llanta (AM); ~ **pressure** n presión f de los neumáticos

U, u

U-bend ['juː'bend] n (AUT, in pipe) recodo
udder ['ʌdə*] n ubre f
UFO ['juːfəʊ] n abbr = (unidentified flying object) OVNI m
ugh [əːh] excl ¡uf!
ugly ['ʌglɪ] adj feo; (dangerous) peligroso
UHT abbr: ~ **milk** leche f UHT, leche f uperizada
UK n abbr = United Kingdom
ulcer ['ʌlsə*] n úlcera; (mouth ~) llaga
Ulster ['ʌlstə*] n Ulster m
ulterior [ʌl'tɪərɪə*] adj: ~ **motive** segundas intenciones fpl
ultimate ['ʌltɪmət] adj último, final; (greatest) máximo; ~**ly** adv (in the end) por último, al final; (fundamentally) a or en fin de cuentas
umbilical cord [ʌm'bɪlɪkl-] n cordón m umbilical
umbrella [ʌm'brelə] n paraguas m inv; (for sun) sombrilla
umpire ['ʌmpaɪə*] n árbitro
umpteen [ʌmp'tiːn] adj enésimos/as; ~**th** adj: for the ~**th time** por enésima vez
UN n abbr (= United Nations) NN. UU.
unable [ʌn'eɪbl] adj: to be ~ to do sth no poder hacer algo
unaccompanied [ʌnə'kʌmpənɪd] adj no acompaña; (song) sin acompañamiento
unaccustomed [ʌnə'kʌstəmd] adj: to be ~ to no estar acostumbrado a
unanimous [juː'nænɪməs] adj unánime
unarmed [ʌn'ɑːmd] adj (defenceless) inerme; (without weapon) desarmado
unattached [ʌnə'tætʃt] adj (person) soltero y sin compromiso; (part etc) suelto
unattended [ʌnə'tendɪd] adj desatendido
unattractive [ʌnə'træktɪv] adj poco atractivo

unauthorized [ʌn'ɔːθəraɪzd] adj no autorizado
unavoidable [ʌnə'vɔɪdəbl] adj inevitable
unaware [ʌnə'weə*] adj: to be ~ of ignorar; ~**s** adv de improviso
unbalanced [ʌn'bælənst] adj (report) poco objetivo; (mentally) trastornado
unbearable [ʌn'beərəbl] adj insoportable
unbeatable [ʌn'biːtəbl] adj (team) invencible; (price) inmejorable; (quality) insuperable
unbelievable [ʌnbɪ'liːvəbl] adj increíble
unbend [ʌn'bend] (irreg) vi (relax) relajarse ♦ vt (wire) enderezar
unbiased [ʌn'baɪəst] adj imparcial
unborn [ʌn'bɔːn] adj que va a nacer
unbroken [ʌn'brəʊkən] adj (seal) intacto; (series) continuo; (record) no batido; (spirit) indómito
unbutton [ʌn'bʌtn] vt desabrochar
uncalled-for [ʌn'kɔːldfɔː*] adj gratuito, inmerecido
uncanny [ʌn'kænɪ] adj extraño
unceremonious ['ʌnserɪ'məʊnɪəs] adj (abrupt, rude) brusco, hosco
uncertain [ʌn'səːtn] adj incierto; (indecisive) indeciso
unchanged [ʌn'tʃeɪndʒd] adj igual, sin cambios
uncivilized [ʌn'sɪvɪlaɪzd] adj inculto; (fig: behaviour etc) bárbaro; (hour) inoportuno
uncle ['ʌŋkl] n tío
uncomfortable [ʌn'kʌmfətəbl] adj incómodo; (uneasy) inquieto
uncommon [ʌn'kɔmən] adj poco común, raro
uncompromising [ʌn'kɔmprəmaɪzɪŋ] adj intransigente
unconcerned [ʌnkən'səːnd] adj indiferente, despreocupado
unconditional [ʌnkən'dɪʃənl] adj incondicional
unconscious [ʌn'kɔnʃəs] adj sin sentido; (unaware): to be ~ of no darse cuenta de ♦ n: the ~ el inconsciente
uncontrollable [ʌnkən'trəʊləbl] adj (child etc) incontrolable; (temper) indomable; (laughter) incontenible
unconventional [ʌnkən'venʃənl] adj poco convencional
uncouth [ʌn'kuːθ] adj grosero, inculto
uncover [ʌn'kʌvə*] vt descubrir; (take lid off) destapar
undecided [ʌndɪ'saɪdɪd] adj (character) indeciso; (question) no resuelto
under ['ʌndə*] prep debajo de; (less than) menos de; (according to) según, de acuerdo con; (sb's leadership) bajo ♦ adv debajo, abajo; ~ **there** allí abajo; ~ **repair** en

reparación

under... |'ʌndə*| *prefix* sub; **~age** *adj* menor de edad; (*drinking etc*) de los menores de edad; **~carriage** (*BRIT*) *n* (*AVIAT*) tren *m* de aterrizaje; **~charge** *vt* cobrar menos de la cuenta; **~clothes** *npl* ropa interior (*SP*) or íntima (*AM*); **~coat** *n* (*paint*) primera mano; **~cover** *adj* clandestino; **~current** *n* (*fig*) corriente *f* oculta; **~cut** *vt irreg* vender más barato que; **~developed** *adj* subdes-arrollado; **~dog** *n* desvalido/a; **~done** *adj* (*CULIN*) poco hecho; **~estimate** *vt* subestimar; **~exposed** *adj* (*PHOT*) subexpuesto; **~fed** *adj* subalimentado; **~foot** *adv* con los pies; **~go** *vt irreg* sufrir; (*treatment*) recibir; **~graduate** *n* estudiante *m/f*; **~ground** *n* (*BRIT: railway*) metro; (*POL*) movimiento clandestino ♦ *adj* (*car park*) subterráneo ♦ *adv* (*work*) en la clan-destinidad; **~growth** *n* maleza; **~hand(ed)** *adj* (*fig*) socarrón; **~lie** *vt irreg* (*fig*) ser la razón fundamental de; **~line** *vt* subrayar; **~mine** *vt* socavar, minar; **~neath** |ʌndə'niːθ| *adv* debajo ♦ *prep* debajo de, bajo; **~paid** *adj* mal pagado; **~pants** *npl* calzoncillos *mpl*; **~pass** (*BRIT*) *n* paso subterráneo; **~privileged** *adj* desposeído; **~rate** *vt* menospreciar, subestimar; **~shirt** (*US*) *n* camiseta; **~shorts** (*US*) *npl* calzoncillos *mpl*; **~side** *n* parte *f* inferior; **~skirt** (*BRIT*) *n* enaguas *fpl*

understand |ʌndə'stænd| (*irreg*) *vt, vi* entender, comprender; (*assume*) tener entendido; **~able** *adj* comprensible; **~ing** *adj* comprensivo ♦ *n* comprensión *f*, entendimiento; (*agreement*) acuerdo

understatement |'ʌndəsteitmənt| *n* modestia (excesiva); **that's an ~!** ¡eso es decir poco!

understood |ʌndə'stud| *pt, pp of* **understand** ♦ *adj* (*agreed*) acordado; (*implied*): **it is ~** that se sobreentiende que

understudy |'ʌndəstʌdɪ| *n* suplente *m/f*

undertake |ʌndə'teɪk| (*irreg*) *vt* emprender; **to ~ to do sth** comprometerse a hacer algo

undertaker |'ʌndəteɪkə*| *n* director(a) *m/f* de pompas fúnebres

undertaking |'ʌndəteɪkɪŋ| *n* empresa; (*promise*) promesa

under: **~tone** *n*: **in an ~tone** en voz baja; **~water** *adv* bajo el agua ♦ *adj* submarino; **~wear** *n* ropa interior (*SP*) or íntima (*AM*); **~world** *n* (*of crime*) hampa, inframundo; **~writer** *n* (*INSURANCE*) asegurador(a) *m/f*

undesirable |ʌndɪ'zaɪərəbl| *adj* (*person*) indeseable; (*thing*) poco aconsejable

undo |ʌn'duː| *vt* (*irreg*) *vt* (*laces*) desatar; (*button etc*) desabrochar; (*spoil*) deshacer; **~ing** *n* ruina, perdición *f*

undoubted |ʌn'dautɪd| *adj* indudable

undress |ʌn'dres| *vi* desnudarse

undulating |'ʌndjuleɪtɪŋ| *adj* ondulante

unduly |ʌn'djuːlɪ| *adv* excesivamente, demasiado

unearth |ʌn'əːθ| *vt* desenterrar

unearthly |ʌn'əːθlɪ| *adj* (*hour*) inverosímil

uneasy |ʌn'iːzɪ| *adj* intranquilo, preocupado; (*feeling*) desagradable; (*peace*) inseguro

uneducated |ʌn'edjukeɪtɪd| *adj* ignorante, inculto

unemployed |ʌnɪm'plɔɪd| *adj* parado, sin trabajo ♦ *npl*: **the ~** los parados

unemployment |ʌnɪm'plɔɪmənt| *n* paro, desempleo

unending |ʌn'endɪŋ| *adj* interminable

unerring |ʌn'əːrɪŋ| *adj* infalible

uneven |ʌn'iːvn| *adj* desigual; (*road etc*) lleno de baches

unexpected |ʌnɪk'spektɪd| *adj* inesperado; **~ly** *adv* inesperadamente

unfailing |ʌn'feɪlɪŋ| *adj* (*support*) indefectible; (*energy*) inagotable

unfair |ʌn'feə*| *adj*: **~ (to sb)** injusto (con uno)

unfaithful |ʌn'feɪθful| *adj* infiel

unfamiliar |ʌnfə'mɪlɪə*| *adj* extraño, desconocido; **to be ~ with** desconocer

unfashionable |ʌn'fæʃnəbl| *adj* pasado or fuera de moda

unfasten |ʌn'fɑːsn| *vt* (*knot*) desatar; (*dress*) desabrochar; (*open*) abrir

unfavourable |ʌn'feɪvərəbl| (*US* **unfavorable**) *adj* desfavorable

unfeeling |ʌn'fiːlɪŋ| *adj* insensible

unfinished |ʌn'fɪnɪʃt| *adj* inacabado, sin terminar

unfit |ʌn'fɪt| *adj* bajo de forma; (*incompetent*): **~ (for)** incapaz (de); **~ for work** no apto para trabajar

unfold |ʌn'fəuld| *vt* desdoblar ♦ *vi* abrirse

unforeseen |'ʌnfɔː'siːn| *adj* imprevisto

unforgettable |ʌnfə'getəbl| *adj* inolvidable

unfortunate |ʌn'fɔːtʃnət| *adj* desgraciado; (*event, remark*) inoportuno; **~ly** *adv* desgraciadamente

unfounded |ʌn'faundɪd| *adj* infundado

unfriendly |ʌn'frendlɪ| *adj* antipático; (*behaviour, remark*) hostil, poco amigable

ungainly |ʌn'geɪnlɪ| *adj* desgarbado

ungodly |ʌn'gɔdlɪ| *adj*: **at an ~ hour** a una hora inverosímil

ungrateful |ʌn'greɪtful| *adj* ingrato

unhappiness |ʌn'hæpɪnɪs| *n* tristeza, desdicha

unhappy |ʌn'hæpɪ| *adj* (*sad*) triste; (*unfortunate*) desgraciado; (*childhood*) infeliz; **~ about/with** (*arrangements etc*) poco contento con, descontento de

unharmed [ʌnˈhɑːmd] *adj* ileso
unhealthy [ʌnˈhelθɪ] *adj* (*place*) malsano; (*person*) enfermizo; (*fig*: *interest*) morboso
unheard-of *adj* inaudito, sin precedente
unhurt [ʌnˈhɜːt] *adj* ileso
unidentified [ʌnaɪˈdentɪfaɪd] *adj* no identificado, sin identificar; *see also* **UFO**
uniform [ˈjuːnɪfɔːm] *n* uniforme *m* ♦ *adj* uniforme
unify [ˈjuːnɪfaɪ] *vt* unificar, unir
uninhabited [ʌnɪnˈhæbɪtɪd] *adj* desierto
unintentional [ʌnɪnˈtenʃənəl] *adj* involuntario
union [ˈjuːnɪən] *n* unión *f*; (*also*: *trade ~*) sindicato ♦ *cpd* sindical; **U~ Jack** *n* bandera del Reino Unido
unique [juːˈniːk] *adj* único
unison [ˈjuːnɪsn] *n*: **in ~** (*speak, reply, sing*) al unísono
unit [ˈjuːnɪt] *n* unidad *f*; (*section*: *of furniture etc*) elemento; (*team*) grupo; **kitchen ~** módulo de cocina
unite [juːˈnaɪt] *vt* unir ♦ *vi* unirse; **~d** *adj* unido; (*effort*) conjunto; **U~d Kingdom** *n* Reino Unido; **U~d Nations (Organization)** *n* Naciones *fpl* Unidas; **U~d States (of America)** *n* Estados *mpl* Unidos
unit trust (*BRIT*) *n* bono fiduciario
unity [ˈjuːnɪtɪ] *n* unidad *f*
universe [ˈjuːnɪvɜːs] *n* universo
university [juːnɪˈvɜːsɪtɪ] *n* universidad *f*
unjust [ʌnˈdʒʌst] *adj* injusto
unkempt [ʌnˈkempt] *adj* (*appearance*) descuidado; (*hair*) despeinado
unkind [ʌnˈkaɪnd] *adj* poco amable; (*behaviour, comment*) cruel
unknown [ʌnˈnəʊn] *adj* desconocido
unlawful [ʌnˈlɔːful] *adj* ilegal, ilícito
unleaded [ʌnˈledɪd] *adj* (*petrol, fuel*) sin plombo
unless [ʌnˈles] *conj* a menos que; **~ he comes** a menos que venga; **~ otherwise stated** salvo indicación contraria
unlike [ʌnˈlaɪk] *adj* (*not alike*) distinto de *or* a; (*not like*) poco propio de ♦ *prep* a diferencia de
unlikely [ʌnˈlaɪklɪ] *adj* improbable; (*unexpected*) inverosímil
unlimited [ʌnˈlɪmɪtɪd] *adj* ilimitado
unlisted [ʌnˈlɪstɪd] (*US*) *adj* (*TEL*) que no consta en la guía
unload [ʌnˈləʊd] *vt* descargar
unlock [ʌnˈlɔk] *vt* abrir (con llave)
unlucky [ʌnˈlʌkɪ] *adj* desgraciado; (*object, number*) que da mala suerte; **to be ~** tener mala suerte
unmarried [ʌnˈmærɪd] *adj* soltero
unmistak(e)able [ʌnmɪsˈteɪkəbl] *adj* inconfundible

unnatural [ʌnˈnætʃrəl] *adj* (*gen*) antinatural; (*manner*) afectado; (*habit*) perverso
unnecessary [ʌnˈnesəsərɪ] *adj* innecesario, inútil
unnoticed [ʌnˈnəʊtɪst] *adj*: **to go** *or* **pass ~** pasar desapercibido
UNO [ˈjuːnəʊ] *n abbr* (= *United Nations Organization*) ONU *f*
unobtainable [ʌnəbˈteɪnəbl] *adj* inconseguible; (*TEL*) inexistente
unobtrusive [ʌnəbˈtruːsɪv] *adj* discreto
unofficial [ʌnəˈfɪʃl] *adj* no oficial; (*news*) sin confirmar
unorthodox [ʌnˈɔːθədɔks] *adj* poco ortodoxo; (*REL*) heterodoxo
unpack [ʌnˈpæk] *vi* deshacer las maletas ♦ *vt* deshacer
unpalatable [ʌnˈpælətəbl] *adj* incomible; (*truth*) desagradable
unparalleled [ʌnˈpærəleld] *adj* (*unequalled*) incomparable
unpleasant [ʌnˈpleznt] *adj* (*disagreeable*) desagradable; (*person, manner*) antipático
unplug [ʌnˈplʌg] *vt* desenchufar, desconectar
unpopular [ʌnˈpɔpjulə*] *adj* impopular, poco popular
unprecedented [ʌnˈpresɪdəntɪd] *adj* sin precedentes
unpredictable [ʌnprɪˈdɪktəbl] *adj* imprevisible
unprofessional [ʌnprəˈfeʃənl] *adj* (*attitude, conduct*) poco ético
unqualified [ʌnˈkwɔlɪfaɪd] *adj* sin título, no cualificado; (*success*) total
unquestionably [ʌnˈkwestʃənəblɪ] *adv* indiscutiblemente
unreal [ʌnˈrɪəl] *adj* irreal; (*extraordinary*) increíble
unrealistic [ʌnrɪəˈlɪstɪk] *adj* poco realista
unreasonable [ʌnˈriːznəbl] *adj* irrazonable; (*demand*) excesivo
unrelated [ʌnrɪˈleɪtɪd] *adj* sin relación; (*family*) no emparentado
unreliable [ʌnrɪˈlaɪəbl] *adj* (*person*) informal; (*machine*) poco fiable
unremitting [ʌnrɪˈmɪtɪŋ] *adj* constante
unreservedly [ʌnrɪˈzɜːvɪdlɪ] *adv* sin reserva
unrest [ʌnˈrest] *n* inquietud *f*, malestar *m*; (*POL*) disturbios *mpl*
unroll [ʌnˈrəʊl] *vt* desenrollar
unruly [ʌnˈruːlɪ] *adj* indisciplinado
unsafe [ʌnˈseɪf] *adj* peligroso
unsaid [ʌnˈsed] *adj*: **to leave sth ~** dejar algo sin decir
unsatisfactory [ˈʌnsætɪsˈfæktərɪ] *adj* poco satisfactorio
unsavoury [ʌnˈseɪvərɪ] (*US* **unsavory**) *adj* (*fig*) repugnante
unscrew [ʌnˈskruː] *vt* destornillar

unscrupulous [ʌnˈskruːpjuləs] *adj* sin
escrúpulos

unsettled [ʌnˈsetld] *adj* inquieto, intranquilo;
(*weather*) variable

unshaven [ʌnˈʃeɪvn] *adj* sin afeitar

unsightly [ʌnˈsaɪtlɪ] *adj* feo

unskilled [ʌnˈskɪld] *adj* (*work*) no
especializado; (*worker*) no cualificado

unspeakable [ʌnˈspiːkəbl] *adj* indecible;
(*awful*) incalificable

unstable [ʌnˈsteɪbl] *adj* inestable

unsteady [ʌnˈstedɪ] *adj* inestable

unstuck [ʌnˈstʌk] *adj*: **to come ~** despegarse;
(*fig*) fracasar

unsuccessful [ʌnsəkˈsesful] *adj* (*attempt*)
infructuoso; (*writer, proposal*) sin éxito; **to be
~** (*in attempting sth*) no tener éxito, fracasar;
~ly *adv* en vano, sin éxito

unsuitable [ʌnˈsuːtəbl] *adj* inapropiado;
(*time*) inoportuno

unsure [ʌnˈʃuəʳ] *adj* inseguro, poco seguro

unsuspecting [ˈʌnsəsˈpektɪŋ] *adj*
desprevenido

unsympathetic [ʌnsɪmpəˈθetɪk] *adj* poco
comprensivo; (*unlikeable*) antipático

unthinkable [ʌnˈθɪŋkəbl] *adj* inconcebible,
impensable

untidy [ʌnˈtaɪdɪ] *adj* (*room*) desordenado;
(*appearance*) desaliñado

untie [ʌnˈtaɪ] *vt* desatar

until [ənˈtɪl] *prep* hasta ♦ *conj* hasta que; **~ he
comes** hasta que venga; **~ now** hasta ahora;
~ then hasta entonces

untimely [ʌnˈtaɪmlɪ] *adj* inoportuno; (*death*)
prematuro

untold [ʌnˈtəuld] *adj* (*story*) nunca contado;
(*suffering*) indecible; (*wealth*) incalculable

untoward [ʌntəˈwɔːd] *adj* adverso

unused [ʌnˈjuːzd] *adj* sin usar

unusual [ʌnˈjuːʒuəl] *adj* insólito, poco
común; (*exceptional*) inusitado

unveil [ʌnˈveɪl] *vt* (*statue*) descubrir

unwanted [ʌnˈwɔntɪd] *adj* (*clothing*) viejo;
(*pregnancy*) no deseado

unwelcome [ʌnˈwelkəm] *adj* inoportuno;
(*news*) desagradable

unwell [ʌnˈwel] *adj*: **to be/feel ~** estar
indispuesto/sentirse mal

unwieldy [ʌnˈwiːldɪ] *adj* difícil de manejar

unwilling [ʌnˈwɪlɪŋ] *adj*: **to be ~ to do sth**
estar poco dispuesto a hacer algo; **~ly** *adv* de
mala gana

unwind [ʌnˈwaɪnd] (*irreg: like* wind²) *vt*
desenvolver ♦ *vi* (*relax*) relajarse

unwise [ʌnˈwaɪz] *adj* imprudente

unwitting [ʌnˈwɪtɪŋ] *adj* inconsciente

unworthy [ʌnˈwəːðɪ] *adj* indigno

unwrap [ʌnˈræp] *vt* desenvolver

unwritten [ʌnˈrɪtn] *adj* (*agreement*) tácito;

(*rules, law*) no escrito

KEYWORD

up [ʌp] *prep*: **to go/be ~ sth** subir/estar subido
en algo; **he went ~ the stairs/the hill** subió las
escaleras/la colina; **we walked/climbed ~ the
hill** subimos la colina; **they live further ~ the
street** viven más arriba en la calle; **go ~ that
road and turn left** sigue por esa calle y gira a
la izquierda

♦ *adv* **1** (*upwards, higher*) más arriba; **~ in
the mountains** en lo alto (de la montaña);
put it a bit higher ~ ponlo un poco más arriba
or alto; **~ there** ahí or allí arriba; **~ above** en
lo alto, por encima, arriba

2: **to be ~** (*out of bed*) estar levantado;
(*prices, level*) haber subido

3: **~ to** (*as far as*) hasta; **~ to now** hasta
ahora or la fecha

4: **to be ~ to** (*depending on*): **it's ~ to you**
depende de ti; **he's not ~ to it** (*job, task etc*)
no es capaz de hacerlo; **his work is not ~ to
the required standard** su trabajo no da la
talla; (*inf: be doing*): **what is he ~ to?** ¿que
estará tramando?

♦ *n*: **~s and downs** altibajos *mpl*

---

upbringing [ˈʌpbrɪŋɪŋ] *n* educación *f*

update [ʌpˈdeɪt] *vt* poner al día

upgrade [ʌpˈgreɪd] *vt* (*house*) modernizar;
(*employee*) ascender

upheaval [ʌpˈhiːvl] *n* trastornos *mpl*; (*POL*)
agitación *f*

uphill [ʌpˈhɪl] *adj* cuesta arriba; (*fig: task*)
penoso, difícil ♦ *adv*: **to go ~** ir cuesta arriba

uphold [ʌpˈhəuld] (*irreg*) *vt* defender

upholstery [ʌpˈhəulstərɪ] *n* tapicería

upkeep [ˈʌpkiːp] *n* mantenimiento

upon [əˈpɔn] *prep* sobre

upper [ˈʌpəʳ] *adj* superior, de arriba ♦ *n* (*of
shoe: also: ~s*) empeine *m*; **~-class** *adj* de
clase alta; **~ hand** *n*: **to have the ~ hand**
tener la sartén por el mango; **~most** *adj* el
más alto; **what was ~most in my mind** lo que
me preocupaba más

upright [ˈʌpraɪt] *adj* derecho; (*vertical*)
vertical; (*fig*) honrado

uprising [ˈʌpraɪzɪŋ] *n* sublevación *f*

uproar [ˈʌprɔːʳ] *n* escándalo

uproot [ʌpˈruːt] *vt* (*also fig*) desarraigar

upset [*n* ˈʌpset, *vb, adj* ʌpˈset] *n* (*to plan etc*)
revés *m*, contratiempo; (*MED*) trastorno
♦ (*irreg*) *vt* (*glass etc*) volcar; (*plan*) alterar;
(*person*) molestar, disgustar ♦ *adj* molesto,
disgustado; (*stomach*) revuelto

upshot [ˈʌpʃɔt] *n* resultado

upside-down *adv* al revés; **to turn a place ~**
(*fig*) revolverlo todo

upstairs [ʌpˈsteəz] *adv* arriba ♦ *adj* (*room*) de

arriba ♦ *n* el piso superior
upstart ['ʌpstɑːt] *n* advenedizo/a
upstream [ʌp'striːm] *adv* río arriba
uptake ['ʌpteɪk] *n*: **to be quick/slow on the ~** ser muy listo/torpe
uptight [ʌp'taɪt] *adj* tenso, nervioso
up-to-date *adj* al día
upturn ['ʌptəːn] *n* (*in luck*) mejora; (*COMM: in market*) resurgimiento económico
upward ['ʌpwəd] *adj* ascendente; **~(s)** *adv* hacia arriba; (*more than*): **~(s) of** más de
urban ['əːbən] *adj* urbano
urchin ['əːtʃɪn] *n* pilluelo, golfillo
urge [əːdʒ] *n* (*desire*) deseo ♦ *vt*: **to ~ sb to do sth** animar a uno a hacer algo
urgent ['əːdʒənt] *adj* urgente; (*voice*) perentorio
urinate ['juərɪneɪt] *vi* orinar
urine ['juərɪn] *n* orina, orines *mpl*
urn [əːn] *n* urna; (*also: tea ~*) cacharro metálico grande para hacer té
Uruguay ['juərəgwaɪ] *n* (el) Uruguay; **~an** [-'gwaɪən] *adj, n* uruguayo/a *m/f*
US *n abbr* (= *United States*) EE. UU.
us [ʌs] *pron* nos; (*after prep*) nosotros/as; *see also* **me**
USA *n abbr* (= *United States* (*of America*)) EE. UU.
usage ['juːzɪdʒ] *n* (*LING*) uso
use [*n* juːs, *vb* juːz] *n* uso, empleo; (*usefulness*) utilidad *f* ♦ *vt* usar, emplear; **she ~d to do it** (ella) solía *or* acostumbraba hacerlo; **in ~** en uso; **out of ~** en desuso; **to be of ~** servir; **it's no ~** (*pointless*) es inútil; (*not useful*) no sirve; **to be ~d to** estar acostumbrado a, acostumbrar; **~ up** *vt* (*food*) consumir; (*money*) gastar; **~d** *adj* (*car*) usado; **~ful** *adj* útil; **~fulness** *n* utilidad *f*; **~less** *adj* (*unusable*) inservible; (*pointless*) inútil; (*person*) inepto; **~r** *n* usuario/a; **~r-friendly** *adj* (*computer*) amistoso
usher ['ʌʃə*] *n* (*at wedding*) ujier *m*; **~ette** [-'rɛt] *n* (*in cinema*) acomodadora
USSR *n* (*HIST*): **the ~** la URSS
usual ['juːʒuəl] *adj* normal, corriente; **as ~** como de costumbre; **~ly** *adv* normalmente
utensil [juː'tɛnsl] *n* utensilio; **kitchen ~s** batería de cocina
uterus ['juːtərəs] *n* útero
utility [juː'tɪlɪtɪ] *n* utilidad *f*; (*public ~*) (empresa de) servicio público; **~ room** *n* ofis *m*
utilize ['juːtɪlaɪz] *vt* utilizar
utmost ['ʌtməust] *adj* mayor ♦ *n*: **to do one's ~** hacer todo lo posible
utter ['ʌtə*] *adj* total, completo ♦ *vt* pronunciar, proferir; **~ly** *adv* completamente, totalmente
U-turn ['juː'təːn] *n* viraje *m* en redondo

V, v

v. *abbr* = **verse**; **versus**; (= *volt*) v; (= *vide*) véase
vacancy ['veɪkənsɪ] *n* (*BRIT: job*) vacante *f*; (*room*) habitación *f* libre; **"no vacancies"** "completo"
vacant ['veɪkənt] *adj* desocupado, libre; (*expression*) distraído
vacate [və'keɪt] *vt* (*house, room*) desocupar; (*job*) dejar (vacante)
vacation [və'keɪʃən] *n* vacaciones *fpl*
vaccinate ['væksɪneɪt] *vt* vacunar
vaccine ['væksiːn] *n* vacuna
vacuum ['vækjum] *n* vacío; **~ cleaner** *n* aspiradora; **~flask** (*BRIT*) *n* termo; **~-packed** *adj* empaquetado al vacío
vagina [və'dʒaɪnə] *n* vagina
vagrant ['veɪgrnt] *n* vagabundo/a
vague [veɪg] *adj* vago; (*memory*) borroso; (*ambiguous*) impreciso; (*person: absent-minded*) distraído; (: *evasive*): **to be ~** no decir las cosas claramente; **~ly** *adv* vagamente; distraídamente; con evasivas
vain [veɪn] *adj* (*conceited*) presumido; (*useless*) vano, inútil; **in ~** en vano
valentine ['væləntaɪn] *n* (*also: ~ card*) tarjeta del Día de los Enamorados
valet ['væleɪ] *n* ayuda *m* de cámara
valid ['vælɪd] *adj* válido; (*ticket*) valedero; (*law*) vigente
valley ['vælɪ] *n* valle *m*
valuable ['væljuəbl] *adj* (*jewel*) de valor; (*time*) valioso; (*judgement of quality*) valioso; **~s** *npl* objetos *mpl* de valor
valuation [vælju'eɪʃən] *n* tasación *f*, valuación *f*; (*judgement of quality*) valoración *f*
value ['væljuː] *n* valor *m*; (*importance*) importancia ♦ *vt* (*fix price of*) tasar, valorar; (*esteem*) apreciar; **~s** *npl* (*principles*) principios *mpl*; **~ added tax** (*BRIT*) *n* impuesto sobre el valor añadido; **~d** *adj* (*appreciated*) apreciado
valve [vælv] *n* válvula
van [væn] *n* (*AUT*) furgoneta (*SP*), camioneta (*AM*)
vandal ['vændl] *n* vándalo/a; **~ism** *n* vandalismo; **~ize** *vt* dañar, destruir
vanilla [və'nɪlə] *n* vainilla
vanish ['vænɪʃ] *vi* desaparecer
vanity ['vænɪtɪ] *n* vanidad *f*
vantage point ['vɑːntɪdʒ-] *n* (*for views*) punto panorámico
vapour ['veɪpə*] (*US* **vapor**) *n* vapor *m*; (*on breath, window*) vaho
variable ['vɛərɪəbl] *adj* variable
variation [vɛərɪ'eɪʃən] *n* variación *f*
varicose ['værɪkəus] *adj*: **~ veins** varices *fpl*

varied ['vɛərɪd] *adj* variado

variety [vəˈraɪətɪ] *n* (*diversity*) diversidad *f*; (*type*) variedad *f*; ~ **show** *n* espectáculo de variedades

various ['vɛərɪəs] *adj* (*several: people*) varios/as; (*reasons*) diversos/as

varnish ['vɑːnɪʃ] *n* barniz *m·* (*nail ~*) esmalte *m* ♦ *vt* barnizar; (*nails*) pintar (con esmalte)

vary ['vɛərɪ] *vt* variar; (*change*) cambiar ♦ *vi* variar

vase [vɑːz] *n* florero

Vaseline ® ['væsɪliːn] *n* vaselina ®

vast [vɑːst] *adj* enorme

VAT [væt] *n abbr* (= value added tax) IVA *m*

vat [væt] *n* tina, tinaja

Vatican ['vætɪkən] *n*: **the ~** el Vaticano

vault [vɔːlt] *n* (*of roof*) bóveda; (*tomb*) panteón *m*; (*in bank*) cámara acorazada ♦ *vt* (*also:* ~ *over*) saltar (por encima de)

vaunted ['vɔːntɪd] *adj*: **much ~** cacareado, alardeado

VCR *n abbr* = **video cassette recorder**

VD *n abbr* = **venereal disease**

VDU *n abbr* (= visual display unit) UPV *f*

veal [viːl] *n* ternera

veer [vɪə*] *vi* (*vehicle*) virar; (*wind*) girar

vegan ['viːgən] *n* vegetariano/a estricto/a, vegetaliano/a

vegeburger ['vɛdʒɪbəːgə*] *n* hamburguesa vegetal

vegetable ['vɛdʒtəbl] *n* (*BOT*) vegetal *m*; (*edible plant*) legumbre *f*, hortaliza ♦ *adj* vegetal; **~s** *npl* (*cooked*) verduras *fpl*

vegetarian [vɛdʒɪˈtɛərɪən] *adj*, *n* vegetariano/a *m/f*

vehement ['viːɪmənt] *adj* vehemente, apasionado

vehicle ['viːɪkl] *n* vehículo; (*fig*) medio

veil [veɪl] *n* velo ♦ *vt* velar; **~ed** *adj* (*fig*) velado

vein [veɪn] *n* vena; (*of ore etc*) veta

velocity [vɪˈlɔsɪtɪ] *n* velocidad *f*

velvet ['vɛlvɪt] *n* terciopelo

vending machine ['vɛndɪŋ-] *n* distribuidor *m* automático

veneer [vəˈnɪə*] *n* chapa, enchapado; (*fig*) barniz *m*

venereal disease [vɪˈnɪərɪəl-] *n* enfermedad *f* venérea

Venetian blind [vɪˈniːʃən-] *n* persiana

Venezuela [vɛnɪˈzweɪlə] *n* Venezuela; **~n** *adj*, *n* venezolano/a *m/f*

vengeance ['vɛndʒəns] *n* venganza; **with a ~** (*fig*) con creces

venison ['vɛnɪsn] *n* carne *f* de venado

venom ['vɛnəm] *n* veneno; (*bitterness*) odio; **~ous** *adj* venenoso; lleno de odio

vent [vɛnt] *n* (*in jacket*) respiradero; (*in wall*)

rejilla (de ventilación) ♦ *vt* (*fig: feelings*) desahogar

ventilator ['vɛntɪleɪtə*] *n* ventilador *m*

venture ['vɛntʃə*] *n* empresa ♦ *vt* (*opinion*) ofrecer ♦ *vi* arriesgarse, lanzarse; **business ~** empresa comercial

venue ['vɛnjuːl] *n* lugar *m*

veranda(h) [vəˈrændə] *n* terraza

verb [vɜːb] *n* verbo; **~al** *adj* verbal

verbatim [vɜːˈbeɪtɪm] *adj*, *adv* palabra por palabra

verdict ['vɜːdɪkt] *n* veredicto, fallo; (*fig*) opinión *f*, juicio

verge [vɜːdʒ] (*BRIT*) *n* borde *m*; **"soft ~s"** (*AUT*) "arcén *m* no asfaltado"; **to be on the ~ of doing sth** estar a punto de hacer algo; **~ on** *vt fus* rayar en

verify ['vɛrɪfaɪ] *vt* comprobar, verificar

vermin ['vɜːmɪn] *npl* (*animals*) alimañas *fpl*; (*insects, fig*) parásitos *mpl*

vermouth ['vɜːməθ] *n* vermut *m*

versatile ['vɜːsətaɪl] *adj* (*person*) polifacético; (*machine, tool etc*) versátil

verse [vɜːs] *n* poesía; (*stanza*) estrofa; (*in bible*) versículo

version ['vɜːʃən] *n* versión *f*

versus ['vɜːsəs] *prep* contra

vertebra ['vɜːtɪbrə] (*pl* **~e**) *n* vértebra

vertical ['vɜːtɪkl] *adj* vertical

verve [vɜːv] *n* brío

very ['vɛrɪ] *adv* muy ♦ *adj*: **the ~ book which** el mismo libro que; **the ~ last** el último de todos; **at the ~ least** al menos; **~ much** muchísimo

vessel ['vɛsl] *n* (*ship*) barco; (*container*) vasija; *see* **blood**

vest [vɛst] *n* (*BRIT*) camiseta; (*US: waistcoat*) chaleco; **~ed interests** *npl* (*COMM*) intereses *mpl* creados

vet [vɛt] *vt* (*candidate*) investigar ♦ *n abbr* (*BRIT*) = **veterinary surgeon**

veteran ['vɛtərn] *n* veterano

veterinary surgeon ['vɛtrɪnərɪ] (*US* **veterinarian**) *n* veterinario/a *m/f*

veto ['viːtəu] (*pl* **~es**) *n* veto ♦ *vt* prohibir, poner el veto a

vex [vɛks] *vt* fastidiar; **~ed** *adj* (*question*) controvertido

VHF *abbr* (= very high frequency) muy alta frecuencia

via ['vaɪə] *prep* por, por medio de

vibrant ['vaɪbrənt] *adj* (*lively*) animado; (*bright*) vivo; (*voice*) vibrante

vibrate [vaɪˈbreɪt] *vi* vibrar

vicar ['vɪkə*] *n* párroco (de la Iglesia Anglicana); **~age** *n* parroquia

vice [vaɪs] *n* (*evil*) vicio; (*TECH*) torno de banco

vice- [vaɪs] *prefix* vice-; **~-chairman** *n*

vicepresidente m
vice squad n brigada antivicio
vice versa ['vaɪsɪ'vəːsə] adv viceversa
vicinity [vɪ'sɪnɪtɪ] n: **in the ~ (of)** cercano (a)
vicious ['vɪʃəs] adj (attack) violento; (words)
cruel; (horse, dog) resabido; **~ circle** n
círculo vicioso
victim ['vɪktɪm] n víctima
victor ['vɪktə*] n vencedor(a) m/f
victory ['vɪktərɪ] n victoria
video ['vɪdɪəu] cpd video ♦ n (~ film)
videofilm m; (also: ~ cassette) videocassette f;
(also: ~ cassette recorder) magnetoscopio;
~ game n videojuego; **~ tape** n cinta de
video
vie [vaɪ] vi: **to ~ (with sb for sth)** competir
(con uno por algo)
Vienna [vɪ'enə] n Viena
Vietnam [vjet'næm] n Vietnam m; **~ese**
[-nə'miːz] n inv, adj vietnamita m/f
view [vjuː] n vista; (outlook) perspectiva;
(opinion) opinión f, criterio ♦ vt (look at)
mirar; (fig) considerar; **on ~** (in museum etc)
expuesto; **in full ~ (of)** en plena vista (de); **in
~ of the weather/the fact that** en vista del
tiempo/del hecho de que; **in my ~** en mi
opinión; **~er** n espectador(a) m/f; (TV)
telespectador(a) m/f; **~finder** n visor m de
imagen; **~point** n (attitude) punto de vista;
(place) mirador m
vigour ['vɪgə*] (US **vigor**) n energía, vigor m
vile [vaɪl] adj vil, infame; (smell) asqueroso;
(temper) endemoniado
villa ['vɪlə] n (country house) casa de campo;
(suburban house) chalet m
village ['vɪlɪdʒ] n aldea; **~r** n aldeano/a
villain ['vɪlən] n (scoundrel) malvado/a; (in
novel) malo; (BRIT: criminal) maleante m/f
vindicate ['vɪndɪkeɪt] vt vindicar, justificar
vindictive [vɪn'dɪktɪv] adj vengativo
vine [vaɪn] n vid f
vinegar ['vɪnɪgə*] n vinagre m
vineyard ['vɪnjɑːd] n viña, viñedo
vintage ['vɪntɪdʒ] n (year) vendimia, cosecha
♦ cpd de época; **~ wine** n vino añejo
vinyl ['vaɪnl] n vinilo
viola [vɪ'əulə] n (MUS) viola
violate ['vaɪəleɪt] vt violar
violence ['vaɪələns] n violencia
violent ['vaɪələnt] adj violento; (intense)
intenso
violet ['vaɪələt] adj violado, violeta ♦ n (plant)
violeta
violin [vaɪə'lɪn] n violín m; **~ist** n violinista m/f
VIP n abbr (= very important person) VIP m
virgin ['vəːdʒɪn] n virgen f
Virgo ['vəːgəu] n Virgo
virtually ['vəːtjuəlɪ] adv prácticamente
virtual reality ['vəːtjuəl-] n (COMPUT)

mundo or realidad f virtual
virtue ['vəːtjuː] n virtud f; (advantage)
ventaja; **by ~ of** en virtud de
virtuous ['vəːtjuəs] adj virtuoso
virus ['vaɪərəs] n (also: COMPUT) virus m
visa ['viːzə] n visado (SP), visa (AM)
visible ['vɪzəbl] adj visible
vision ['vɪʒən] n (sight) vista; (foresight, in
dream) visión f
visit ['vɪzɪt] n visita ♦ vt (person: US: also:
~ with) visitar, hacer una visita a; (place) ir a,
(ir a) conocer; **~ing hours** npl (in hospital
etc) horas fpl de visita; **~or** n (in museum)
visitante m/f; (invited to house) visita; (tourist)
turista m/f
visor ['vaɪzə*] n visera
visual ['vɪzjuəl] adj visual; **~ aid** n medio
visual; **~ display unit** n unidad f de
presentación visual; **~ize** vt imaginarse
vital ['vaɪtl] adj (essential) esencial,
imprescindible; (dynamic) dinámico; (organ)
vital; **~ly** adv: **~ly important** de primera
importancia; **~ statistics** npl (fig) medidas
fpl vitales
vitamin ['vɪtəmɪn] n vitamina
vivacious [vɪ'veɪʃəs] adj vivaz, alegre
vivid ['vɪvɪd] adj (account) gráfico; (light)
intenso; (imagination, memory) vivo; **~ly** adv
gráficamente; (remember) como si fuera hoy
V-neck ['viːnek] n cuello de pico
vocabulary [vəu'kæbjulərɪ] n vocabulario
vocal ['vəukl] adj vocal; (articulate)
elocuente; **~ cords** npl cuerdas fpl vocales
vocation [vəu'keɪʃən] n vocación f; **~al** adj
profesional
vodka ['vɔdkə] n vodka m
vogue [vəug] n: **in ~** en boga, de moda
voice [vɔɪs] n voz f ♦ vt expresar; **~ mail** n
fonobuzón m
void [vɔɪd] n vacío; (hole) hueco ♦ adj
(invalid) nulo, inválido; (empty): **~ of** carente
or desprovisto de
volatile ['vɔlətaɪl] adj (situation) inestable;
(person) voluble; (liquid) volátil
volcano [vɔl'keɪnəu] (pl **~es**) n volcán m
volition [və'lɪʃən] n: **of one's own ~** de su
propia voluntad
volley ['vɔlɪ] n (of gunfire) descarga; (of
stones etc) lluvia; (fig) torrente m; (TENNIS
etc) volea; **~ball** n vol(e)ibol m
volt [vəult] n voltio; **~age** n voltaje m
volume ['vɔljuːm] n (gen) volumen m;
(book) tomo
voluntary ['vɔləntərɪ] adj voluntario
volunteer [vɔlən'tɪə*] n voluntario/a ♦ vt
(information) ofrecer ♦ vi ofrecerse (de
voluntario); **to ~ to do** ofrecerse a hacer
vomit ['vɔmɪt] n vómito ♦ vt, vi vomitar
vote [vəut] n voto; (votes cast) votación f;

(*right to* ~) derecho de votar; (*franchise*) sufragio ♦ vt (*chairman*) elegir; (*propose*): **to ~ that** proponer que ♦ vi votar, ir a votar; **~ of thanks** voto de gracias; **~r** n votante m/f; **voting** n votación f

vouch [vautʃ]: **to ~ for** vt fus garantizar, responder de

voucher ['vautʃə*] n (*for meal, petrol*) vale m

vow [vau] n voto ♦ vt: **to ~ to do/that** jurar hacer/que

vowel ['vauəl] n vocal f

voyage ['vɔɪɪdʒ] n viaje m

vulgar ['vʌlgə*] adj (*rude*) ordinario, grosero; (*in bad taste*) de mal gusto; **~ity** [-'gærɪtɪ] n grosería; mal gusto

vulnerable ['vʌlnərəbl] adj vulnerable

vulture ['vʌltʃə*] n buitre m

W, w

wad [wɔd] n bolita; (*of banknotes etc*) fajo

waddle ['wɔdl] vi anadear

wade [weɪd] vi: **to ~ through** (*water*) vadear; (*fig: book*) leer con dificultad; **wading pool** (US) n piscina para niños

wafer ['weɪfə*] n galleta, barquillo

waffle ['wɔfl] n (CULIN) gofre m ♦ vi dar el rollo

waft [wɔft] vt llevar por el aire ♦ vi flotar

wag [wæg] vt menear, agitar ♦ vi moverse, menearse

wage [weɪdʒ] n (*also:* ~s) sueldo, salario ♦ vt: **to ~ war** hacer la guerra; **~ earner** n asalariado/a; **~ packet** n sobre m de paga

wager ['weɪdʒə*] n apuesta

wag(g)on ['wægən] n (*horse-drawn*) carro; (*BRIT: RAIL*) vagón m

wail [weɪl] n gemido ♦ vi gemir

waist [weɪst] n cintura, talle m; **~coat** (BRIT) n chaleco; **~line** n talle m

wait [weɪt] n (*interval*) pausa ♦ vi esperar; **to lie in ~ for** acechar a; **I can't ~ to** (*fig*) estoy deseando; **to ~ for** esperar (a); **~ behind** vi quedarse; **~ on** vt fus servir a; **~er** n camarero; **~ing** n: "**no ~ing**" (BRIT: AUT) "prohibido estacionarse"; **~ing list** n lista de espera; **~ing room** n sala de espera; **~ress** n camarera

waive [weɪv] vt suspender

wake [weɪk] (pt **woke** or **waked**, pp **woken** or **waked**) vt (*also:* ~ up) despertar ♦ vi (*also:* ~ up) despertarse ♦ n (*for dead person*) vela, velatorio; (NAUT) estela; **waken** vt, vi = **wake**

Wales [weɪlz] n País m de Gales; **the Prince of ~** el príncipe de Gales

walk [wɔːk] n (*stroll*) paseo; (*hike*) excursión f a pie, caminata; (*gait*) paso, andar m; (*in*

park etc) paseo, alameda ♦ vi andar, caminar; (*for pleasure, exercise*) pasear ♦ vt (*distance*) recorrer a pie, andar; (*dog*) pasear; **10 minutes' ~ from here** a 10 minutos de aquí andando; **people from all ~s of life** gente de todas las esferas; **~ out** vi (*audience*) salir; (*workers*) declararse en huelga; **~ out on** (*inf*) vt fus abandonar; **~er** n (*person*) paseante m/f, caminante m/f; **~ie-talkie** ['wɔːkɪ'tɔːkɪ] n walkie-talkie m; **~ing** n el andar; **~ing shoes** npl zapatos mpl para andar; **~ing stick** n bastón m; **W~man** ® ['wɔːkmæn] n Walkman ® m; **~out** n huelga; **~over** (*inf*) n: **it was a ~over** fue pan comido; **~way** n paseo

wall [wɔːl] n pared f; (*exterior*) muro; (*city ~ etc*) muralla; **~ed** adj amurallado; (*garden*) con tapia

wallet ['wɔlɪt] n cartera (SP), billetera (AM)

wallflower ['wɔːlflauə*] n alhelí m; **to be a ~** (*fig*) comer pavo

wallow ['wɔləu] vi revolcarse

wallpaper ['wɔːlpeɪpə*] n papel m pintado ♦ vt empapelar

walnut ['wɔːlnʌt] n nuez f; (*tree*) nogal m

walrus ['wɔːlrəs] (pl ~ or ~es) n morsa

waltz [wɔːlts] n vals m ♦ vi bailar el vals

wand [wɔnd] n (*also: magic ~*) varita (mágica)

wander ['wɔndə*] vi (*person*) vagar; deambular; (*thoughts*) divagar ♦ vt recorrer, vagar por

wane [weɪn] vi menguar

wangle ['wæŋgl] (BRIT: inf) vt agenciarse

want [wɔnt] vt querer, desear; (*need*) necesitar ♦ n: **for ~ of** por falta de; **~s** npl (*needs*) necesidades fpl; **to ~ to do** querer hacer; **to ~ sb to do sth** querer que uno haga algo; **~ed** adj (*criminal*) buscado; "**~ed**" (*in advertisements*) "se busca"; **~ing** adj: **to be found ~ing** no estar a la altura de las circunstancias

war [wɔː*] n guerra; **to make ~** (**on**) (*also fig*) declarar la guerra (a)

ward [wɔːd] n (*in hospital*) sala; (POL) distrito electoral; (LAW: child: also: ~ **of court**) pupilo/a; **~ off** vt (*blow*) desviar, parar; (*attack*) rechazar

warden ['wɔːdn] n (BRIT: of institution) director(a) m/f; (*of park, game reserve*) guardián/ana m/f; (BRIT: also: traffic ~) guardia m/f

warder ['wɔːdə*] (BRIT) n guardián/ana m/f, carcelero/a

wardrobe ['wɔːdrəub] n armario, guardarropa, ropero (*esp AM*)

warehouse ['wɛəhaus] n almacén m, depósito

wares [wɛəz] npl mercancías fpl

warfare ['wɔːfeə'] n guerra
warhead ['wɔːhed] n cabeza armada
warily ['weərɪlɪ] adv con cautela, cautelosamente
warm [wɔːm] adj caliente; (thanks) efusivo; (clothes etc) abrigado; (welcome, day) caluroso; **it's ~** hace calor; **I'm ~** tengo calor; **~ up** vi (room) calentarse; (person) entrar en calor; (athlete) hacer ejercicios de calentamiento ♦ vt calentar; **~-hearted** adj afectuoso; **~ly** adv afectuosamente; **~th** n calor m
warn [wɔːn] vt avisar, advertir; **~ing** n aviso, advertencia; **~ing light** n luz f de advertencia; **~ing triangle** n (AUT) triángulo señalizador
warp [wɔːp] vi (wood) combarse ♦ vt combar; (mind) pervertir
warrant ['wɔrənt] n autorización f; (LAW: to arrest) orden f de detención; (: to search) mandamiento de registro
warranty ['wɔrəntɪ] n garantía
warren ['wɔrən] n (of rabbits) madriguera; (fig) laberinto
warrior ['wɔrɪə'] n guerrero/a
Warsaw ['wɔːsɔː] n Varsovia
warship ['wɔːʃɪp] n buque m o barco de guerra
wart [wɔːt] n verruga
wartime ['wɔːtaɪm] n: **in ~** en tiempos de guerra, en la guerra
wary ['weərɪ] adj cauteloso
was [wɔz] pt of **be**
wash [wɔʃ] vt lavar ♦ vi lavarse; (sea etc): **to ~ against/over sth** llegar hasta/cubrir algo ♦ n (clothes etc) lavado; (of ship) estela; **to have a ~** lavarse; **~ away** vt (stain) quitar lavando; (subj: river etc) llevarse; **~ off** vi quitarse (al lavar); **~ up** vi (BRIT) fregar los platos; (US) lavarse; **~able** adj lavable; **~basin** (US **~bowl**) n lavabo; **~ cloth** (US) n manopla; **~er** n (TECH) arandela; **~ing** n (dirty) ropa sucia; (clean) colada; **~ing machine** n lavadora; **~ing powder** (BRIT) n detergente m (en polvo)
Washington ['wɔʃɪŋtən] n Washington m
wash: ~ing-up (BRIT) n fregado, platos mpl (para fregar); **~ing-up liquid** (BRIT) n líquido lavavajillas; **~-out** (inf) n fracaso; **~room** (US) n servicios mpl
wasn't ['wɔznt] = **was not**
wasp [wɔsp] n avispa
wastage ['weɪstɪdʒ] n desgaste m; (loss) pérdida
waste [weɪst] n derroche m, despilfarro; (of time) pérdida; (food) sobras fpl; (rubbish) basura, desperdicios mpl ♦ adj (material) de desecho; (left over) sobrante; (land) baldío, descampado ♦ vt malgastar, derrochar;

(time) perder; (opportunity) desperdiciar; **~s** npl (area of land) tierras fpl baldías; **~ away** vi consumirse; **~ disposal unit** (BRIT) n triturador m de basura; **~ful** adj derrochador(a); (process) antieconómico; **~ ground** (BRIT) n terreno baldío; **~paper basket** n papelera; **~ pipe** n tubo de desagüe
watch [wɔtʃ] n (also: wrist ~) reloj m; (MIL: group of guards) centinela m; (act) vigilancia; (NAUT: spell of duty) guardia ♦ vt (look at) mirar, observar; (: match, programme) ver; (spy on, guard) vigilar; (be careful of) cuidarse de, tener cuidado de ♦ vi ver, mirar; (keep guard) montar guardia; **~ out** vi cuidarse, tener cuidado; **~dog** n perro guardián; (fig) persona u organismo encargado de asegurarse de que las empresas actúan dentro de la legalidad; **~ful** adj vigilante, sobre aviso; **~maker** n relojero/a; **~man** (irreg) n see **night**; **~ strap** n pulsera (de reloj)
water ['wɔːtə'] n agua ♦ vt (plant) regar ♦ vi (eyes) llorar; (mouth) hacerse la boca agua; **~ down** vt (milk etc) aguar; (fig: story) dulcificar, diluir; **~ closet** n wáter m; **~colour** n acuarela; **~cress** n berro; **~fall** n cascada, salto de agua; **~ heater** n calentador m de agua; **~ing can** n regadera; **~ lily** n nenúfar m; **~line** n (NAUT) línea de flotación; **~logged** adj (ground) inundado; **~ main** n cañería del agua; **~melon** n sandía; **~proof** adj impermeable; **~shed** n (GEO) cuenca; (fig) momento crítico; **~-skiing** n esquí m acuático; **~tight** adj hermético; **~way** n vía fluvial or navegable; **~works** n central f depuradora; **~y** adj (coffee etc) aguado; (eyes) lloroso
watt [wɔt] n vatio
wave [weɪv] n (of hand) señal f con la mano; (on water) ola; (RADIO, in hair) onda; (fig) oleada ♦ vi agitar la mano; (flag etc) ondear ♦ vt (handkerchief, gun) agitar; **~length** n longitud f de onda
waver ['weɪvə'] vi (voice, love etc) flaquear; (person) vacilar
wavy ['weɪvɪ] adj ondulado
wax [wæks] n cera ♦ vt encerar ♦ vi (moon) crecer; **~ paper** (US) n papel m apergaminado; **~works** n museo de cera ♦ npl figuras fpl de cera
way [weɪ] n camino; (distance) trayecto, recorrido; (direction) dirección f, sentido; (manner) modo, manera; (habit) costumbre f; **which ~?** — **this ~** ¿por dónde?, ¿en qué dirección? — por aquí; **on the ~** (en route) en (el) camino; **to be on one's ~** estar en camino; **to be in the ~** bloquear el camino; (fig) estorbar; **to go out of one's ~ to do sth**

desvivirse por hacer algo; **under ~** en marcha; **to lose one's ~** extraviarse; **in a ~** en cierto modo o sentido; **no ~!** (inf) ¡de eso nada!; **by the ~** ... a propósito ...; **"~ in"** (BRIT) "entrada"; **"~ out"** (BRIT) "salida"; **the ~ back** el camino de vuelta; **"give ~"** (BRIT: AUT) "ceda el paso"

waylay ['weɪleɪ] (irreg) vt salir al paso a

wayward ['weɪwəd] adj díscolo

W.C. n (BRIT) wáter m

we |wiː| pl pron nosotros/as

weak [wiːk] adj débil, flojo; (tea etc) claro; **~en** vi debilitarse; (give way) ceder ♦ vt debilitar; **~ling** n debilucho/a; (morally) persona de poco carácter; **~ness** n debilidad f; (fault) punto débil; **to have a ~ness for** tener debilidad por

wealth [wɛlθ] n riqueza; (of details) abundancia; **~y** adj rico

wean [wiːn] vt destetar

weapon ['wɛpən] n arma

wear [wɛə*] (pt **wore**, pp **worn**) n (use) uso; (deterioration through use) desgaste m; (clothing): **sports/baby~** ropa de deportes/de niños ♦ vt (clothes) llevar; (shoes) calzar; (damage: through use) gastar, usar ♦ vi (last) durar; (rub through etc) desgastarse; **evening ~** ropa de etiqueta; **~ away** vt gastar ♦ vi desgastarse; **~ down** vt gastar; (strength) agotar; **~ off** vi (pain etc) pasar, desaparecer; **~ out** vt desgastar; (person, strength) agotar; **~ and tear** n desgaste m

weary ['wɪərɪ] adj cansado; (dispirited) abatido ♦ vi: **to ~ of** cansarse de

weasel ['wiːzl] n (ZOOL) comadreja

weather ['wɛðə*] n tiempo ♦ vt (storm, crisis) hacer frente a; **under the ~** (fig: ill) indispuesto, pachucho; **~-beaten** adj (skin) curtido; (building) deteriorado por la intemperie; **~cock** n veleta; **~ forecast** n boletín m meteorológico; **~man** (irreg: inf) n hombre m del tiempo; **~ vane** n = **~cock**

weave [wiːv] (pt **wove**, pp **woven**) vt (cloth) tejer; (fig) entretejer; **~r** n tejedor(a) m/f; **weaving** n tejeduría

web [wɛb] n (of spider) telaraña; (on duck's foot) membrana; (network) red; f; **the (World Wide) W~** el o la Web

website ['wɛbsaɪt] n espacio Web

wed [wɛd] (pt, pp **wedded**) vt casar ♦ vi casarse

we'd [wiːd] = **we had; we would**

wedding ['wɛdɪŋ] n boda, casamiento; **silver/golden ~** (anniversary) bodas fpl de plata/de oro; **~ day** n día m de la boda; **~ dress** n traje m de novia; **~ present** n regalo de boda; **~ ring** n alianza

wedge [wɛdʒ] n (of wood etc) cuña; (of cake) trozo ♦ vt acuñar; (push) apretar

Wednesday ['wɛnzdɪ] n miércoles m inv

wee [wiː] (Scottish) adj pequeñito

weed [wiːd] n mala hierba, maleza ♦ vt escardar, desherbar; **~killer** n herbicida m; **~y** adj (person) mequetréfico

week [wiːk] n semana; **a ~ today/on Friday** de hoy/del viernes en ocho días; **~day** n día m laborable; **~end** n fin m de semana; **~ly** adv semanalmente, cada semana ♦ adj semanal ♦ n semanario

weep [wiːp] (pt, pp **wept**) vi, vt llorar; **~ing willow** n sauce m llorón

weigh [weɪ] vt, vi pesar; **to ~ anchor** levar anclas; **~ down** vt sobrecargar; (fig: with worry) agobiar; **~ up** vt sopesar

weight [weɪt] n peso; (metal~) pesa; **to lose/put on ~** adelgazar/engordar; **~ing** n (allowance): **(London) ~ing** dietas (por residir en Londres); **~lifter** n levantador m de pesas; **~y** adj pesado; (matters) de relevancia o peso

weir |wɪə*| n presa

weird [wɪəd] adj raro, extraño

welcome ['wɛlkəm] adj bienvenido ♦ n bienvenida ♦ vt dar la bienvenida a; (be glad of) alegrarse de; **thank you — you're ~** gracias — de nada

weld [wɛld] n soldadura ♦ vt soldar

welfare ['wɛlfɛə*] n bienestar m; (social aid) asistencia social; **~ state** n estado del bienestar

well [wɛl] n fuente f, pozo ♦ adv bien ♦ adj: **to be ~** estar bien (de salud) ♦ excl ¡vaya!, ¡bueno!; **as ~** también; **as ~ as** además de; **~ done!** ¡bien hecho!; **get ~ soon!** ¡que te mejores pronto!; **to do ~** (business) ir bien; (person) tener éxito; **~ up** vi (tears) saltar

we'll [wiːl] = **we will; we shall**

well: ~-behaved adj bueno; **~-being** n bienestar m; **~-built** adj (person) fornido; **~-deserved** adj merecido; **~-dressed** adj bien vestido; **~-groomed** adj de buena presencia; **~-heeled** (inf) adj (wealthy) rico

wellingtons ['wɛlɪŋtənz] npl (also: **wellington boots**) botas fpl de goma

well: ~-known adj (person) conocido; **~-mannered** adj educado; **~-meaning** adj bienintencionado; **~-off** adj acomodado; **~-read** adj leído; **~-to-do** adj acomodado; **~-wisher** n admirador(a) m/f

Welsh [wɛlʃ] adj galés/esa ♦ n (LING) galés m; **the ~** npl los galeses; **the ~ Assembly** el Parlamento galés; **~man** (irreg) n galés m; **~ rarebit** n pan m con queso tostado; **~woman** (irreg) n galesa

went [wɛnt] pt of **go**

wept [wɛpt] pt, pp of **weep**

were [wə:*] pt of **be**

we're [wɪə*] = **we are**

weren't [wə:nt] = **were not**

west [wɛst] n oeste m ♦ adj occidental, del

oeste ♦ adv al o hacia el oeste; **the W~** el Oeste, el Occidente; **W~ Country** (BRIT) n: **the W~ Country** el suroeste de Inglaterra; **~erly** adj occidental; (wind) del oeste; **~ern** adj occidental ♦ n (CINEMA) película del oeste; **W~ Germany** n Alemania Occidental; **W~ Indian** adj, n antillano/a m/f; **W~ Indies** npl Antillas fpl; **~ward(s)** adv hacia el oeste

wet [wɛt] adj (damp) húmedo; (~ through) mojado; (rainy) lluvioso ♦ (BRIT) n (POL) conservador(a) m/f moderado/a; **to get ~** mojarse; **"~ paint"** "recién pintado"; **~suit** n traje m térmico

we've [wi:v] = **we have**

whack [wæk] vt dar un buen golpe a

whale [weɪl] n (ZOOL) ballena

wharf [wɔ:f](pl **wharves**) n muelle m

KEYWORD

what [wɔt] adj **1** (in direct/indirect questions) qué; **~ size is he?** ¿qué talla usa?; **~ colour/ shape is it?** ¿de qué color/forma es?
2 (in exclamations): **~ a mess!** ¡qué desastre!; **~ a fool I am!** ¡qué tonto soy!
♦ pron **1** (interrogative) qué; **~ are you doing?** ¿qué haces o estás haciendo?; **~ is happening?** ¿qué pasa o está pasando?; **~ is it called?** ¿cómo se llama?; **~ about me?** ¿y yo qué?; **~ about doing ...?** ¿qué tal si hacemos ...?
2 (relative) lo que; **I saw ~ you did/was on the table** vi lo que hiciste/había en la mesa
♦ excl (disbelieving) ¡cómo!; **~, no coffee!** ¡que no hay café!

whatever [wɔt'ɛvə*] adj: **~ book you choose** cualquier libro que elijas ♦ pron: **do ~ is necessary** haga lo que sea necesario; **~ happens** pase lo que pase; **no reason ~ or whatsoever** ninguna razón a la que sea; **nothing ~** nada en absoluto

whatsoever [wɔtsəu'ɛvə*] adj see **whatever**

wheat [wi:t] n trigo

wheedle ['wi:dl] vt: **to ~ sb into doing sth** engatusar a uno para que haga algo; **to ~ sth out of sb** sonsacar algo a uno

wheel [wi:l] n rueda; (AUT: also: steering ~) volante m; (NAUT) timón m ♦ vt (pram etc) empujar ♦ vi (also: ~ round) dar la vuelta, girar; **~barrow** n carretilla; **~chair** n silla de ruedas; **~ clamp** n (AUT) cepo

wheeze [wi:z] vi resollar

KEYWORD

when [wɛn] adv cuando; **~ did it happen?** ¿cuándo ocurrió?; **I know ~ it happened** sé cuándo ocurrió
♦ conj **1** (at, during, after the time that) cuando; **be careful ~ you cross the road** ten cuidado al cruzar la calle; **that was ~ I needed you** fue entonces que te necesité
2 (on, at which): **on the day ~ I met him** el día en qué lo conocí
3 (whereas) cuando

whenever [wɛn'ɛvə*] conj cuando; (every time that) cada vez que ♦ adv cuando sea

where [wɛə*] adv dónde ♦ conj donde; **this is ~** aquí es donde; **~abouts** adv dónde ♦ n: **nobody knows his ~abouts** nadie conoce su paradero; **~as** conj visto que, mientras; **~by** pron por lo cual; **wherever** [-'ɛvə*] conj dondequiera que; (interrogative) dónde; **~withal** n recursos mpl

whether ['wɛðə*] conj si; **I don't know ~ to accept or not** no sé si aceptar o no; **~ you go or not** vayas o no vayas

KEYWORD

which [wɪtʃ] adj **1** (interrogative: direct, indirect) qué; **~ picture(s) do you want?** ¿qué cuadro(s) quieres?; **~ one?** ¿cuál?
2: in ~ case en cuyo caso; **we got there at 8 pm, by ~ time the cinema was full** llegamos allí a las 8, cuando el cine estaba lleno
♦ pron **1** (interrogative) cual; **I don't mind ~** el/la que sea
2 (relative: replacing noun) que; (: replacing clause) lo que; (: after preposition) (el/la) que etc, el/la cual etc; **the apple ~ you ate/~ is on the table** la manzana que comiste/que está en la mesa; **the chair on ~ you are sitting** la silla en la que estás sentado; **he said he knew, ~ is true/I feared** dijo que lo sabía, lo cual or lo que es cierto/me temía

whichever [wɪtʃ'ɛvə*] adj: **take ~ book you prefer** coja (SP) el libro que prefiera; **~ book you take** cualquier libro que coja

while [waɪl] n rato, momento ♦ conj mientras; (although) aunque; **for a ~** durante algún tiempo; **~ away** vt pasar

whim [wɪm] n capricho

whimper ['wɪmpə*] n sollozo ♦ vi lloriquear

whimsical ['wɪmzɪkl] adj (person) caprichoso; (look) juguetón/ona

whine [waɪn] n (of pain) gemido; (of engine) zumbido; (of siren) aullido ♦ vi gemir; zumbar; (fig: complain) gimotear

whip [wɪp] n látigo; (POL: person) encargado de la disciplina partidaria en el parlamento ♦ vt azotar; (CULIN) batir; (move quickly): **to ~ sth out/off** sacar/quitar algo de un tirón; **~ped cream** n nata or crema montada; **~-round** (BRIT) n colecta

whirl [wə:l] vt hacer girar, dar vueltas a ♦ vi girar, dar vueltas; (leaves etc) arremolinarse;

~pool n remolino; **~wind** n torbellino
whirr [wə:*] vi zumbar
whisk [wɪsk] n (CULIN) batidor m ♦ vt (CULIN) batir; **to ~ sb away** or **off** llevar volando a uno
whiskers ['wɪskəz] npl (of animal) bigotes mpl; (of man) patillas fpl
whiskey ['wɪskɪ] (US, Ireland) n = **whisky**
whisky ['wɪskɪ] n whisky m
whisper ['wɪspə*] n susurro ♦ vi, vt susurrar
whistle ['wɪsl] n (sound) silbido; (object) silbato ♦ vi silbar
white [waɪt] adj blanco; (pale) pálido ♦ n blanco; (of egg) clara; **~ coffee** (BRIT) n café m con leche; **~-collar worker** n oficinista m/f; **~ elephant** n (fig) maula; **~ lie** n mentirilla; **~ness** n blancura; **~ noise** n sonido blanco; **~ paper** n (POL) libro rojo; **~wash** n (paint) jalbegue m, cal f ♦ vt (also fig) blanquear
whiting ['waɪtɪŋ] n inv (fish) pescadilla
Whitsun ['wɪtsn] n pentecostés m
whizz [wɪz] vi: **to ~ past** or **by** pasar a toda velocidad; **~ kid** (inf) n prodigio

who [hu:] pron **1** (interrogative) quién; **~ is it?, ~'s there?** ¿quién es?; **~ are you looking for?** ¿a quién buscas?; **I told her ~ I was** le dije quién era yo
2 (relative) que; **the man/woman ~ spoke to me** el hombre/la mujer que habló conmigo; **those ~ can swim** los que saben or sepan nadar

whodun(n)it [hu:'dʌnɪt] (inf) n novela policíaca
whoever [hu:'evə*] pron: **~ finds it** cualquiera or quienquiera que lo encuentre; **ask ~ you like** pregunta a quien quieras; **~ he marries** no importa con quién se case
whole [həul] adj (entire) todo, entero; (not broken) intacto ♦ n todo; (all): **the ~ of the town** toda la ciudad, la ciudad entera ♦ n (total) total m; (sum) conjunto; **on the ~, as a ~** en general; **~food(s)** n(pl) alimento(s) m(pl) integral(es); **~hearted** adj sincero, cordial; **~meal** adj integral; **~sale** n venta el por mayor ♦ adj al por mayor; (fig: destruction) sistemático; **~saler** n mayorista m/f; **~some** adj sano; **~wheat** adj = **~meal**; **wholly** adv totalmente, enteramente

whom [hu:m] pron **1** (interrogative): **~ did you see?** ¿a quién viste?; **to ~ did you give it?** ¿a quién se lo diste?; **tell me from ~ you received it** dígame de quién lo recibió
2 (relative) que; **to ~** a quien(es); **of ~** de quien(es), del/de la que etc; **the man ~ I**

saw/to ~ **I wrote** el hombre que vi/a quien escribí; **the lady about/with ~ I was talking** la señora de (la) que/con quien or (la) que hablaba

whooping cough ['hu:pɪŋ-] n tos f ferina
whore [hɔ:*] (inf: pej) n puta

whose [hu:z] adj **1** (possessive: interrogative): **~ book is this?, ~ is this book?** ¿de quién es este libro?; **~ pencil have you taken?** ¿de quién es el lápiz que has cogido?; **~ daughter are you?** ¿de quién eres hija?
2 (possessive: relative) cuyo/a, pl cuyos/as; **the man ~ son you rescued** el hombre cuyo hijo rescataste; **those ~ passports I have** aquellas personas cuyos pasaportes tengo; **the woman ~ car was stolen** la mujer a quien le robaron el coche
♦ pron de quién; **~ is this?** ¿de quién es esto?; **I know ~ it is** sé de quién es

why [waɪ] adv por qué; **~ not?** ¿por qué no?; **~ not do it now?** ¿por qué no lo haces (or hacemos etc) ahora?
♦ conj: **I wonder ~ he said that** me pregunto por qué dijo eso; **that's not ~ I'm here** no es por eso (por lo) que estoy aquí; **the reason ~** la razón por la que
♦ excl (expressing surprise, shock, annoyance) ¡hombre!, ¡vaya! (explaining): **~, it's you!** ¡hombre, eres tú!; **~, that's impossible** ¡pero sí eso es imposible!

wicked ['wɪkɪd] adj malvado, cruel
wicket ['wɪkɪt] n (CRICKET: stumps) palos mpl; (: grass area) terreno de juego
wide [waɪd] adj ancho; (area, knowledge) vasto, grande; (choice) amplio ♦ adv: **to open ~** abrir de par en par; **to shoot ~** errar el tiro; **~-angle lens** n objetivo de gran angular; **~-awake** adj bien despierto; **~ly** adv (travelled) mucho; (spaced) muy; **it is ~ly believed/known that ...** mucha gente piensa/ sabe que ...; **~n** vt ensanchar; (experience) ampliar ♦ vi ensancharse; **~ open** adj abierto de par en par; **~spread** adj extendido, general
widow ['wɪdəu] n viuda; **~ed** adj viudo; **~er** n viudo
width [wɪdθ] n anchura; (of cloth) ancho
wield [wi:ld] vt (sword) blandir; (power) ejercer
wife [waɪf] (pl wives) n mujer f, esposa
wig [wɪg] n peluca
wiggle ['wɪgl] vt menear

wild [waɪld] adj (animal) salvaje; (plant) silvestre; (person) furioso, violento; (idea) descabellado; (rough: sea) bravo; (: land) agreste; (: weather) muy revuelto; **~s** npl regiones fpl salvajes, tierras fpl vírgenes; **~erness** ['wɪldənɪs] n desierto; **~life** n fauna; **~ly** adv (behave) locamente; (lash out) a diestro y siniestro; (guess) a lo loco; (happy) a más no poder

wilful ['wɪlful] (US willful) adj (action) deliberado; (obstinate) testarudo

---
KEYWORD
---

will [wɪl] aux vb **1** (forming future tense): I **~ finish it tomorrow** lo terminaré or voy a terminar mañana; I **~ have finished it by tomorrow** lo habré terminado para mañana; **~ you do it? — yes I ~/no I won't** ¿lo harás? — sí/no

2 (in conjectures, predictions): **he ~ or he'll be there by now** ya habrá or debe (de) haber llegado; **that ~ be the postman** será or debe ser el cartero

3 (in commands, requests, offers): **~ you be quiet!** ¿quieres callarte?; **~ you help me?** ¿quieres ayudarme?; **~ you have a cup of tea?** ¿te apetece un té?; **I won't put up with it!** ¡no lo soporto!

♦ vt (pt, pp **willed**): **to ~ sb to do sth** desear que alguien haga algo; **he ~ed himself to go on** con gran fuerza de voluntad, continuó
♦ n voluntad f; (testament) testamento

---

willing ['wɪlɪŋ] adj (with goodwill) de buena voluntad; (enthusiastic) entusiasta; **he's ~ to do it** está dispuesto a hacerlo; **~ly** adv con mucho gusto; **~ness** n buena voluntad

willow ['wɪləu] n sauce m

willpower ['wɪlpauə*] n fuerza de voluntad

willy-nilly [wɪlɪ'nɪlɪ] adv quiérase o no

wilt [wɪlt] vi marchitarse

win [wɪn] (pt, pp **won**) n victoria, triunfo ♦ vt ganar; (obtain) conseguir, lograr ♦ vi ganar; **~ over** vt convencer a; **~ round** (BRIT) vt = **~ over**

wince [wɪns] vi encogerse

winch [wɪntʃ] n torno

wind¹ [wɪnd] n viento; (MED) gases mpl ♦ vt (take breath away from) dejar sin aliento a

wind² [waɪnd] (pt, pp **wound**) vt enrollar; (wrap) envolver; (clock, toy) dar cuerda a ♦ vi (road, river) serpentear; **~ up** vt (clock) dar cuerda a; (debate, meeting) concluir, terminar

windfall ['wɪndfɔːl] n golpe m de suerte

winding ['waɪndɪŋ] adj (road) tortuoso; (staircase) de caracol

wind instrument [wɪnd-] n (MUS) instrumento de viento

windmill ['wɪndmɪl] n molino de viento

window ['wɪndəu] n ventana; (in car, train) ventanilla; (in shop etc) escaparate m (SP), vitrina (AM); **~ box** n jardinera de ventana; **~ cleaner** n (person) limpiador m de cristales; **~ ledge** n alféizar m, repisa; **~ pane** n cristal m; **~ seat** n asiento junto a la ventana; **~-shopping** n: **to go ~-shopping** ir de escaparates; **~sill** n alféizar m, repisa

windpipe ['wɪndpaɪp] n tráquea

wind power n energía eólica

windscreen ['wɪndskriːn] (US **windshield**) n parabrisas m inv; **~ washer** n lavaparabrisas m inv; **~ wiper** n limpiaparabrisas m inv

windswept ['wɪndswept] adj azotado por el viento

windy ['wɪndɪ] adj de mucho viento; **it's ~** hace viento

wine [waɪn] n vino; **~ bar** n enoteca; **~ cellar** n bodega; **~ glass** n copa (para vino); **~ list** n lista de vinos; **~ waiter** n escanciador m

wing [wɪŋ] n ala; (AUT) aleta; **~s** npl (THEATRE) bastidores mpl; **~er** n (SPORT) extremo

wink [wɪŋk] n guiño, pestañeo ♦ vi guiñar, pestañear

winner ['wɪnə*] n ganador(a) m/f

winning ['wɪnɪŋ] adj (team) ganador(a); (goal) decisivo; (smile) encantador(a); **~s** npl ganancias fpl

winter ['wɪntə*] n invierno ♦ vi invernar; **wintry** ['wɪntrɪ] adj invernal

wipe [waɪp] n: **to give sth a ~** pasar un trapo sobre algo ♦ vt limpiar; (tape) borrar; **~ off** vt limpiar con un trapo; (remove) quitar; **~ out** vt (debt) liquidar; (memory) borrar; (destroy) destruir; **~ up** vt limpiar

wire [waɪə*] n alambre m; (ELEC) cable m (eléctrico); (TEL) telegrama m ♦ vt (house) poner la instalación eléctrica en; (also: **~ up**) conectar; (person: telegram) telegrafiar

wireless ['waɪəlɪs] (BRIT) n radio f

wiring ['waɪərɪŋ] n instalación f eléctrica

wiry ['waɪərɪ] adj (person) enjuto y fuerte; (hair) crespo

wisdom ['wɪzdəm] n sabiduría, saber m; (good sense) cordura; **~ tooth** n muela del juicio

wise [waɪz] adj sabio; (sensible) juicioso

...wise [waɪz] suffix: **time~** en cuanto a or respecto al tiempo

wish [wɪʃ] n deseo ♦ vt querer; **best ~es** (on birthday etc) felicidades fpl; **with best ~es** (in letter) saludos mpl, recuerdos mpl; **he ~ed me well** me deseó mucha suerte; **to ~ to do/sb to do sth** querer hacer/que alguien haga algo; **to ~ for** desear; **~ful** adj: **it's ~ful thinking** eso sería soñar

wisp [wɪsp] n mechón m; (of smoke) voluta

wistful ['wɪstful] adj pensativo
wit [wɪt] n ingenio, gracia; (also: ~s)
inteligencia; (person) chistoso/a
witch [wɪtʃ] n bruja; ~craft n brujería; ~
hunt n (fig) caza de brujas

KEYWORD

with [wɪð, wɪθ] prep 1 (accompanying, in the
company of) con (con+ mí, tí, sí = conmigo,
contigo, consigo); I was ~ him estaba con él;
we stayed ~ friends nos quedamos en casa de
unos amigos; I'm (not) ~ you (understand)
(no) te entiendo; to be ~ it (inf: person: up-
to-date) estar al tanto; (: alert) ser despabilado
2 (descriptive, indicating manner etc) con; de;
a room ~ a view una habitación con vistas;
the man ~ the grey hat/blue eyes el hombre
del sombrero gris/de los ojos azules; red
~ anger rojo de ira; to shake ~ fear temblar
de miedo; to fill sth ~ water llenar algo de
agua

withdraw [wɪð'drɔː] (irreg) vt retirar, sacar
♦ vi retirarse; to ~ money (from the bank)
retirar fondos (del banco); ~al n retirada; (of
money) reintegro; ~al symptoms npl (MED)
síndrome m de abstinencia; ~n adj (person)
reservado, introvertido
wither ['wɪðə*] vi marchitarse
withhold [wɪθ'həuld] (irreg) vt (money)
retener; (decision) aplazar; (permission)
negar; (information) ocultar
within [wɪð'ɪn] prep dentro de ♦ adv dentro;
~ reach (of) al alcance (de); ~ sight (of) a la
vista (de); ~ the week antes de acabar la
semana; ~ a mile (of) a menos de una milla
(de)
without [wɪð'aut] prep sin; to go ~ sth pasar
sin algo
withstand [wɪθ'stænd] (irreg) vt resistir a
witness ['wɪtnɪs] n testigo m/f ♦ vt (event)
presenciar; (document) atestiguar la veracidad
de; to bear ~ to (fig) ser testimonio de;
~ box n tribuna de los testigos; ~ stand
(US) n = ~ box
witty ['wɪtɪ] adj ingenioso
wives [waɪvz] npl of wife
wk abbr = week
wobble ['wɒbl] vi temblar; (chair) cojear
woe [wəu] n desgracia
woke [wəuk] pt of wake
woken ['wəukən] pp of wake
wolf [wulf] n lobo; **wolves** [wulvz] npl of
wolf
woman ['wumən] (pl women) n mujer f;
~ doctor n médica; women's lib (inf: pej)
n liberación f de la mujer; ~ly adj femenino
womb [wuːm] n matriz f, útero

women ['wɪmɪn] npl of woman
won [wʌn] pt, pp of win
wonder ['wʌndə*] n maravilla, prodigio;
(feeling) asombro ♦ vi: to ~ whether/why
preguntarse si/por qué; to ~ at asombrarse
de; to ~ about pensar sobre or en; it's no
~ (that) no es de extrañarse (que + subjun);
~ful adj maravilloso
won't [wəunt] = will not
wood [wud] n (timber) madera; (forest)
bosque m; ~ carving n (act) tallado en
madera; (object) talla en madera; ~ed adj
arbolado; ~en adj de madera; (fig)
inexpresivo; ~pecker n pájaro carpintero;
~wind n (MUS) instrumentos mpl de viento
de madera; ~work n carpintería; ~worm n
carcoma
wool [wul] n lana; to pull the ~ over sb's eyes
(fig) engatusar a uno; ~en (US) adj = ~len;
~len adj de lana; ~lens npl géneros mpl de
lana; ~ly adj lanudo, de lana; (fig: ideas)
confuso; ~y (US) adj = ~ly
word [wəːd] n palabra; (news) noticia;
(promise) palabra (de honor) ♦ vt redactar;
in other ~s en otras palabras; to break/keep
one's ~ faltar a la palabra/cumplir la promesa;
to have ~s with sb reñir con uno; ~ing n
redacción f; ~ processing n proceso de
textos; ~ processor n procesador m de
textos
wore [wɔː*] pt of wear
work [wəːk] n trabajo; (job) empleo, trabajo;
(ART, LITERATURE) obra ♦ vi trabajar;
(mechanism) funcionar, marchar; (medicine)
ser eficaz, surtir efecto ♦ vt (shape) trabajar;
(stone etc) tallar; (mine etc) explotar;
(machine) manejar, hacer funcionar; ~s n
(BRIT: factory) fábrica ♦ npl (of clock, machine)
mecanismo; to be out of ~ estar parado, no
tener trabajo; to ~ loose (part) desprenderse;
(knot) aflojarse; ~ on vt fus trabajar en,
dedicarse a; (principle) basarse en; ~ out vi
(plans etc) salir bien, funcionar ♦ vt (problem)
resolver; (plan) elaborar; it ~s out at £100
suma 100 libras; ~ up vt: to get ~ed up
excitarse; ~able adj (solution) práctico,
factible; ~aholic [wəːkə'hɒlɪk] n
trabajador(a) obsesivo/a m/f; ~er n
trabajador(a) m/f, obrero/a; ~force n mano f
de obra; ~ing class n clase f obrera; ~ing-
class adj obrero; ~ing order n: in ~ing
order en funcionamiento; ~man (irreg) n
obrero; ~manship n habilidad f, trabajo;
~sheet n hoja de trabajo; ~shop n taller m;
~ station n puesto or estación f de trabajo;
~-to-rule (BRIT) n huelga de celo
world [wəːld] n mundo ♦ cpd (champion) del
mundo; (power, war) mundial; to think the
~ of sb (fig) tener un concepto muy alto de

uno; **~ly** adj mundano; **~-wide** adj mundial, universal; **W~-Wide Web** n: the **W~-Wide Web** el World Wide Web

worm [wɜːm] n (also: earth~) lombriz f

worn [wɔːn] pp of wear ♦ adj usado; **~-out** adj (object) gastado; (person) rendido, agotado

worried ['wʌrɪd] adj preocupado

worry ['wʌrɪ] n preocupación f ♦ vt preocupar, inquietar ♦ vi preocuparse; **~ing** adj inquietante

worse [wɜːs] adj, adv peor ♦ n lo peor; a change for the **~** un empeoramiento; **~n** vt, vi empeorar; **~ off** adj (financially): to be **~ off** tener menos dinero; (fig): you'll be **~ off this way** de esta forma estarás peor que nunca

worship ['wɜːʃɪp] n adoración f ♦ vt adorar; Your W~ (BRIT: to mayor) señor alcalde; (: to judge) señor juez

worst [wɜːst] adj, adv peor ♦ n lo peor; **at ~** en lo peor de los casos

worth [wɜːθ] n valor m ♦ adj: to be **~** valer; it's **~** it vale or merece la pena; to be **~** one's while (to do) merecer la pena (hacer); **~less** adj sin valor; (useless) inútil; **~while** adj (activity) que merece la pena; (cause) loable

worthy ['wɜːðɪ] adj respetable; (motive) honesto; **~ of** digno de

---

KEYWORD

---

would [wʊd] aux vb **1** (conditional tense): if you asked him he **~** do it si se lo pidieras, lo haría; if you had asked him he **~** have done it si se lo hubieras pedido, lo habría or hubiera hecho

2 (in offers, invitations, requests): **~** you like a biscuit? ¿quieres una galleta?; (formal) ¿querría una galleta?; **~** you ask him to come in? ¿quiere hacerle pasar?; **~** you open the window please? ¿quiere or podría abrir la ventana, por favor?

3 (in indirect speech): I said I **~** do it dije que lo haría

4 (emphatic): it WOULD have to snow today! ¡tenía que nevar precisamente hoy!

5 (insistence): she **~n't** behave no quiso comportarse bien

6 (conjecture): it **~** have been midnight sería medianoche; it **~** seem so** parece ser que sí

7 (indicating habit): he **~** go there on Mondays iba allí los lunes

---

would-be (pej) adj presunto

wouldn't ['wʊdnt] = would not

wound¹ [wuːnd] n herida ♦ vt herir

wound² [waʊnd] pt, pp of wind

wove [wəʊv] pt of weave

woven ['wəʊvən] pp of weave

wrap [ræp] vt (also: **~** up) envolver; **~per** n (on chocolate) papel m; (BRIT: of book) sobrecubierta; **~ping paper** n papel m de envolver; (fancy) papel m de regalo

wreak [riːk] vt: to **~** havoc (on) hacer estragos (en); to **~** vengeance (on) vengarse (de)

wreath [riːθ, pl riːðz] n (funeral **~**) corona

wreck [rɛk] n (ship: destruction) naufragio; (: remains) restos mpl del barco; (pej: person) ruina ♦ vt (car etc) destrozar; (chances) arruinar; **~age** n restos mpl; (of building) escombros mpl

wren [rɛn] n (ZOOL) reyezuelo

wrench [rɛntʃ] n (TECH) llave f inglesa; (tug) tirón m; (fig) dolor m ♦ vt arrancar; to **~** sth from sb arrebatar algo violentamente a uno

wrestle ['rɛsl] vi: to **~** (with sb) luchar (con or contra uno); **~r** n luchador(a) m/f (de lucha libre); **wrestling** n lucha libre

wretched ['rɛtʃɪd] adj miserable

wriggle ['rɪgl] vi (also: **~** about) menearse, retorcerse

wring [rɪŋ] (pt, pp wrung) vt retorcer; (wet clothes) escurrir; (fig): to **~** sth out of sb sacar algo por la fuerza a uno

wrinkle ['rɪŋkl] n arruga ♦ vt arrugar ♦ vi arrugarse

wrist [rɪst] n muñeca; **~watch** n reloj m de pulsera

writ [rɪt] n mandato judicial

write [raɪt] (pt wrote, pp written) vt escribir; (cheque) extender ♦ vi escribir; **~** down vt escribir; (note) apuntar; **~** off vt (debt) borrar (como incobrable); (fig) desechar por inútil; **~** out vt escribir; **~** up vt redactar; **~-off** n siniestro total; **~r** n escritor(a) m/f

writhe [raɪð] vi retorcerse

writing ['raɪtɪŋ] n escritura; (hand-**~**) letra; (of author) obras fpl; in **~** por escrito; **~ paper** n papel m de escribir

written ['rɪtn] pp of write

wrong [rɒŋ] adj (wicked) malo; (unfair) injusto; (incorrect) equivocado, incorrecto; (not suitable) inoportuno, inconveniente; (reverse) del revés ♦ adv equivocadamente ♦ n injusticia ♦ vt ser injusto con; you are **~** to do it haces mal en hacerlo; you are **~** about that, you've got it **~** en eso estás equivocado; to be in the **~** no tener razón, tener la culpa; what's **~**? ¿qué pasa?; to go **~** (person) equivocarse; (plan) salir mal; (machine) estropearse; **~ful** adj injusto; **~ly** adv mal, incorrectamente; (by mistake) por error; **~ number** n (TEL): you've got the **~ number** se ha equivocado de número

wrote [rəʊt] pt of write

wrought iron [rɔːt-] n hierro forjado

wrung [rʌŋ] pt, pp of wring

wt. abbr = weight

WWW n abbr (= World Wide Web) WWW m

X, x

Xmas ['eksməs] *n abbr* = **Christmas**
X-ray ['eksreɪ] *n* radiografía ♦ *vt* radiografiar, sacar radiografías de
xylophone ['zaɪləfəʊn] *n* xilófono

Y, y

Y2K *abbr* (= *Year 2000*): **the ~ problem** el efecto 2000
yacht [jɔt] *n* yate *m*; **~ing** *n* (*sport*) balandrismo; **~sman/woman** (*irreg*) *n* balandrista *m/f*
Yank [jæŋk] (*pej*) *n* yanqui *m/f*
Yankee ['jæŋkɪ] (*pej*) *n* = **Yank**
yap [jæp] *vi* (*dog*) aullar
yard [jɑːd] *n* patio; (*measure*) yarda; **~stick** *n* (*fig*) criterio, norma
yarn [jɑːn] *n* hilo; (*tale*) cuento, historia
yawn [jɔːn] *n* bostezo ♦ *vi* bostezar; **~ing** *adj* (*gap*) muy abierto
yd(s). *abbr* = **yard(s)**
yeah [jɛə] (*inf*) *adv* sí
year [jɪə*] *n* año; **to be 8 ~s old** tener 8 años; **an eight-~-old child** un niño de ocho años (de edad); **~ly** *adj* anual ♦ *adv* anualmente, cada año
yearn [jɜːn] *vi*: **to ~ for sth** añorar algo, suspirar por algo
yeast [jiːst] *n* levadura
yell [jɛl] *n* grito, alarido ♦ *vi* gritar
yellow ['jɛləʊ] *adj* amarillo
yelp [jɛlp] *n* aullido ♦ *vi* aullar
yes [jɛs] *adv* sí ♦ *n* sí *m*; **to say/answer ~** decir/contestar que sí
yesterday ['jɛstədɪ] *adv* ayer ♦ *n* ayer *m*; **~ morning/evening** ayer por la mañana/tarde; **all day ~** todo el día de ayer
yet [jɛt] *adv* ya; (*negative*) todavía ♦ *conj* sin embargo, a pesar de todo; **it is not finished ~** todavía no está acabado; **the best ~** el/la mejor hasta ahora; **as ~** hasta ahora, todavía
yew [juː] *n* tejo
yield [jiːld] *n* (*AGR*) cosecha; (*COMM*) rendimiento ♦ *vt* ceder; (*results*) producir, dar; (*profit*) rendir ♦ *vi* rendirse, ceder; (*US: AUT*) ceder el paso
YMCA *n abbr* (= *Young Men's Christian Association*) Asociación *f* de Jóvenes Cristianos
yog(h)ourt ['jəʊgət] *n* yogur *m*
yog(h)urt ['jəʊgət] *n* = **yog(h)ourt**
yoke [jəʊk] *n* yugo
yolk [jəʊk] *n* yema (de huevo)

KEYWORD

you [juː] *pron* **1** (*subject: familiar*) tú, *pl* vosotros/as (*SP*), ustedes (*AM*); (*polite*) usted, *pl* ustedes; **~ are very kind** eres/es *etc* muy amable; **~ Spanish enjoy your food** a vosotros (*or* ustedes) los españoles os (*or* les) gusta la comida; **~ and I will go** iremos tú y yo
2 (*object: direct: familiar*) te, *pl* os (*SP*), les (*AM*); (*polite*) le, *pl* les, *f* la, *pl* las; **I know ~** te/le *etc* conozco
3 (*object: indirect: familiar*) te, *pl* os (*SP*), les (*AM*); (*polite*) le, *pl* les; **I gave the letter to ~ yesterday** te/os *etc* di la carta ayer
4 (*stressed*): **I told YOU to do it** te dije a ti que lo hicieras, a ti a quien dije que lo hicieras; *see also* **3, 5**
5 (*after prep*: NB: con+ ~ = contigo: *familiar*) ti, *pl* vosotros/as (*SP*), ustedes (*AM*); (: *polite*) usted, *pl* ustedes; **it's for ~** es para ti/vosotros *etc*
6 (*comparisons: familiar*) tú, *pl* vosotros/as (*SP*), ustedes (*AM*); (: *polite*) usted, *pl* ustedes; **she's younger than ~** es más joven que tú/ vosotros *etc*
7 (*impersonal: one*): **fresh air does ~ good** el aire puro (te) hace bien; **~ never know** nunca se sabe; **~ can't do that!** ¡eso no se hace!

---

you'd [juːd] = **you had**; **you would**
you'll [juːl] = **you will**; **you shall**
young [jʌŋ] *adj* joven ♦ *npl* (*of animal*) cría; (*people*): **the ~** los jóvenes, la juventud; **~er** *adj* (*brother etc*) menor; **~ster** *n* joven *m/f*
your [jɔː*] *adj* tu; (*pl*) vuestro; (*formal*) su; *see also* **my**
you're [juə*] = **you are**
yours [jɔːz] *pron* tuyo; (*pl*) vuestro; (*formal*) suyo; *see also* **faithfully; mine**[1]; **sincerely**
yourself [jɔːˈsɛlf] *pron* tú mismo; (*complement*) te; (*after prep*) ti (mismo); (*formal*) usted mismo; (: *complement*) se; (: *after prep*) sí (mismo); **yourselves** *pl pron* vosotros mismos; (*after prep*) vosotros (mismos); (*formal*) ustedes (mismos); (: *complement*) se; (: *after prep*) sí mismos; *see also* **oneself**
youth [juːθ, *pl* juːðz] *n* juventud *f*; (*young man*) joven *m*; **~ club** *n* club *m* juvenil; **~ful** *adj* juvenil; **~ hostel** *n* albergue *m* de juventud
you've [juːv] = **you have**
Yugoslav ['juːgəʊslɑːv] *adj, n* yugo(e)slavo/a *m/f*
Yugoslavia [juːgəʊˈslɑːvɪə] *n* Yugoslavia
yuppie ['jʌpɪ] (*inf*) *adj, n* yupi *m/f*, yupy *m/f*
YWCA *n abbr* (= *Young Women's Christian Association*) Asociación *f* de Jóvenes Cristianas

Z, z

zany ['zeɪnɪ] *adj* estrafalario

zap [zæp] *vt* (*COMPUT*) borrar

zeal [ziːl] *n* celo, entusiasmo; **~ous** ['zeləs] *adj* celoso, entusiasta

zebra ['ziːbrə] *n* cebra; **~ crossing** (*BRIT*) *n* paso de peatones

zero ['zɪərəu] *n* cero

zest [zest] *n* ánimo, vivacidad *f*; (*of orange*) piel *f*

zigzag ['zɪgzæg] *n* zigzag *m* ♦ *vi* zigzaguear, hacer eses

zinc [zɪŋk] *n* cinc *m*, zinc *m*

zip [zɪp] *n* (*also*: ~ **fastener**, (*US*) ~**per**) cremallera (*SP*), cierre *m* (*AM*) ♦ *vt* (*also*: ~ **up**) cerrar la cremallera de; **~ code** (*US*) *n* código postal

zodiac ['zəudɪæk] *n* zodíaco

zone [zəun] *n* zona

zoo [zuː] *n* (jardín *m*) zoo *m*

zoology [zuːˈɔlədʒɪ] *n* zoología

zoom [zuːm] *vi*: **to ~ past** pasar zumbando; **~ lens** *n* zoom *m*

zucchini [zuːˈkiːnɪ] (*US*) *n*(*pl*) calabacín(ines) *m*(*pl*)

SPANISH VERB TABLES

1 Gerund. **2** Imperative. **3** Present. **4** Preterite. **5** Future. **6** Present subjunctive. **7** Imperfect subjunctive. **8** Past participle. **9** Imperfect. *Etc* indicates that the irregular root is used for all persons of the tense, *e.g.* **oír: 6** oiga, oigas, oigamos, oigáis, oigan.

agradecer 3 agradezco **6** agradezca *etc*

aprobar 2 aprueba **3** apruebo, apruebas, aprueba, aprueban **6** apruebe, apruebes, apruebe, aprueben

atravesar 2 atraviesa **3** atravieso, atraviesas, atraviesa, atraviesan **6** atraviese, atravieses, atraviese, atraviesen

caber 3 quepo **4** cupe, cupiste, cupo, cupimos, cupisteis, cupieron **5** cabré *etc* **6** quepa *etc* **7** cupiera *etc*

caer 1 cayendo **3** caigo **4** cayó, cayeron **6** caiga *etc* **7** cayera *etc*

cerrar 2 cierra **3** cierro, cierras, cierra, cierran **6** cierre, cierres, cierre, cierren

COMER 1 comiendo **2** come, comed **3** como, comes, come comemos, coméis, comen **4** comí, comiste, comió, comimos, comisteis, comieron **5** comeré, comerás, comerá, comeremos, comeréis, comerán **6** coma, comas, coma, comamos, comáis, coman **7** comiera, comieras, comiera, comiéramos, comierais, comieran **8** comido **9** comía, comías, comía, comíamos comíais, comían

conocer 3 conozco **6** conozca *etc*

contar 2 cuenta **3** cuento, cuentas, cuenta, cuentan **6** cuente, cuentes, cuente, cuenten

dar 3 doy **4** di, diste, dio, dimos, disteis, dieron **7** diera *etc*

decir 2 di **3** digo **4** dije, dijiste, dijo, dijimos, dijisteis, dijeron **5** diré *etc* **6** diga *etc* **7** dijera *etc* **8** dicho

despertar 2 despierta **3** despierto, despiertas, despierta, despiertan **6** despierte, despiertes, despierte, despierten

divertir 1 divirtiendo **2** divierte **3** divierto, diviertes, divierte, divierten **4** divirtió, divirtieren **6** divierta, diviertas, divierta, divirtamos, divirtáis, diviertan **7** divirtiera *etc*

dormir 1 durmiendo **2** duerme **3** duermo, duermes, duerme, duermen **4** durmió, durmieron **6** duerma, duermas, duerma, durmamos, durmáis, duerman **7** durmiera *etc*

empezar 2 empieza **3** empiezo, empiezas, empieza, empiezan **4** empecé **6** empiece, empieces, empiece, empecemos, empecéis, empiecen

entender 2 entiende **3** entiendo, entiendes, entiende, entienden **6** entienda, entiendas, entienda, entiendan

ESTAR 2 está **3** estoy, estás, está, están **4** estuve, estuviste, estuvo, estuvimos, estuvisteis, estuvieron **6** esté, estés, esté, estén **7** estuviera *etc*

HABER 3 he, has, ha, hemos, han **4** hube, hubiste, hubo, hubimos, hubisteis, hubieron **5** habré *etc* **6** haya *etc* **7** hubiera *etc*

HABLAR 1 hablando **2** habla, hablad **3** hablo, hablas, habla, hablamos, habláis, hablan **4** hablé, hablaste, habló, hablamos, hablasteis, hablaron **5** hablaré, hablarás, hablará, hablaremos, hablaréis, hablarán **6** hable, hables, hable, hablemos, habléis, hablen **7** hablara, hablaras, hablara, habláramos, hablarais, hablaran **8** hablado **9** hablaba, hablabas, hablaba, hablábamos, hablabais, hablaban

hacer 2 haz **3** hago **4** hice, hiciste, hizo, hicimos, hicisteis, hicieron **5** haré *etc* **6** haga *etc* **7** hiciera *etc* **8** hecho

instruir 1 instruyendo **2** instruye **3** instruyo, instruyes, instruye, instruyen **4** instruyó, instruyeron **6** instruya *etc* **7** instruyera *etc*

ir 1 yendo **2** ve **3** voy, vas, va, vamos, vais, van **4** fui, fuiste, fue, fuimos, fuisteis, fueron **6** vaya, vayas, vaya, vayamos, vayáis, vayan **7** fuera *etc* **9** iba, ibas, iba, íbamos, ibais, iban

jugar 2 juega **3** juego, juegas, juega, juegan **4** jugué **6** juegue *etc*

leer 1 leyendo **4** leyó, leyeron **7** leyera *etc*

morir 1 muriendo **2** muere **3** muero, mueres, muere, mueren **4** murió, murieron **6** muera, mueras, muera, muramos, muráis, mueran **7** muriera *etc* **8** muerto

mover 2 mueve **3** muevo, mueves, mueve, mueven **6** mueva, muevas, mueva, muevan

negar 2 niega **3** niego, niegas, niega, niegan **4** negué **6** niegue, niegues, niegue, neguemos, neguéis, nieguen

ofrecer 3 ofrezco **6** ofrezca *etc*

oír 1 oyendo **2** oye **3** oigo, oyes, oye, oyen **4** oyó, oyeron **6** oiga *etc* **7** oyera *etc*

oler 2 huele **3** huelo, hueles, huele, huelen **6** huela, huelas, huela, huelan

parecer 3 parezco **6** parezca *etc*

pedir 1 pidiendo **2** pide **3** pido, pides, pide, piden **4** pidió, pidieron **6** pida *etc* **7** pidiera *etc*

pensar 2 piensa **3** pienso, piensas, piensa, piensan **6** piense, pienses, piense, piensen

perder 2 pierde **3** pierdo, pierdes, pierde, pierden **6** pierda, pierdas, pierda, pierdan

poder 1 pudiendo **2** puede **3** puedo, puedes, puede, pueden **4** pude, pudiste, pudo, pudimos, pudisteis, pudieron **5** podré *etc* **6** pueda, puedas, pueda, puedan **7** pudiera *etc*

poner 2 pon **3** pongo **4** puse, pusiste, puso, pusimos, pusisteis, pusieron **5** pondré *etc* **6** ponga *etc* **7** pusiera *etc* **8** puesto

preferir 1 prefiriendo **2** prefiere **3** prefiero, prefieres, prefiere, prefieren **4** prefirió, prefirieron **6** prefiera, prefieras, prefiera, prefiramos, prefiráis, prefieran **7** prefiriera *etc*

querer 2 quiere **3** quiero, quieres, quiere, quieren **4** quise, quisiste, quiso, quisimos, quisisteis, quisieron **5** querré *etc* **6** quiera, quieras, quiera, quieran **7** quisiera *etc*

reír 2 rie **3** río, ríes, ríe, ríen **4** rio, rieron **6** ría, rías, ría, riamos, riáis, rían **7** riera *etc*

repetir 1 repitiendo **2** repite **3** repito, repites, repite, repiten **4** repitió, repitieron **6** repita *etc* **7** repitiera *etc*

rogar 2 ruega **3** ruego, ruegas, ruega, ruegan **4** rogué **6** ruegue, ruegues, ruegue, roguemos, roguéis, rueguen

saber 3 sé **4** supe, supiste, supo, supimos, supisteis, supieron **5** sabré *etc* **6** sepa *etc* **7** supiera *etc*

salir 2 sal **3** salgo **5** saldré *etc* **6** salga *etc*

seguir 1 siguiendo **2** sigue **3** sigo, sigues, sigue, siguen **4** siguió, siguieron **6** siga *etc* **7** siguiera *etc*

sentar 2 sienta **3** siento, sientas, sienta, sientan **6** siente, sientes, siente, sienten

sentir 1 sintiendo **2** siente **3** siento, sientes, siente, sienten **4** sintió, sintieron **6** sienta, sientas, sienta, sintamos, sintáis, sientan **7** sintiera *etc*

SER 2 sé **3** soy, eres, es, somos, sois, son **4** fui, fuiste, fue, fuimos, fuisteis, fueron **6** sea *etc* **7** fuera *etc* **9** era, eras, era, éramos, erais, eran

servir 1 sirviendo **2** sirve **3** sirvo, sirves, sirve, sirven **4** sirvió, sirvieron **6** sirva *etc* **7** sirviera *etc*

soñar 2 sueña **3** sueño, sueñas, sueña, sueñan **6** sueñe, sueñes, sueñe, sueñen

tener 2 ten **3** tengo, tienes, tiene, tienen **4** tuve, tuviste, tuvo, tuvimos, tuvisteis, tuvieron **5** tendré *etc* **6** tenga *etc* **7** tuviera *etc*

traer 1 trayendo **3** traigo **4** traje, trajiste, trajo, trajimos, trajisteis, trajeron **6** traiga *etc* **7** trajera *etc*

valer 2 val **3** valgo **5** valdré *etc* **6** valga *etc*

venir 2 ven **3** vengo, vienes, viene, vienen **4** vine, viniste, vino, vinimos, vinisteis, vinieron **5** vendré *etc* **6** venga *etc* **7** viniera *etc*

ver 3 veo **6** vea *etc* **8** visto **9** veía *etc*

vestir 1 vistiendo **2** viste **3** visto, vistes, viste, visten **4** vistió, vistieron **6** vista *etc* **7** vistiera *etc*

VIVIR 1 viviendo **2** vive, vivid **3** vivo, vives, vive, vivimos, vivís, viven **4** viví, viviste, vivió, vivimos, vivisteis, vivieron **5** viviré, vivirás, vivirá, viviremos, viviréis, vivirán **6** viva, vivas, viva, vivamos, viváis, vivan **7** viviera, vivieras, viviera, viviéramos, vivierais, vivieran **8** vivido **9** vivía, vivías, vivía, vivíamos, vivías, vivían

volver 2 vuelve **3** vuelvo, vuelves, vuelve, vuelven **6** vuelva, vuelvas, vuelva, vuelvan **8** vuelto

VERBOS IRREGULARES EN INGLÉS

present	pt	pp	present	pt	pp
arise	arose	arisen	dream	dreamed,	dreamed,
awake	awoke	awaked		dreamt	dreamt
be (am,	was,	been	drink	drank	drunk
is, are;	were		drive	drove	driven
being)			dwell	dwelt	dwelt
bear	bore	born(e)	eat	ate	eaten
beat	beat	beaten	fall	fell	fallen
become	became	become	feed	fed	fed
begin	began	begun	feel	felt	felt
behold	beheld	beheld	fight	fought	fought
bend	bent	bent	find	found	found
beset	beset	beset	flee	fled	fled
bet	bet,	bet,	fling	flung	flung
	betted	betted	fly (flies)	flew	flown
bid	bid,	bid,	forbid	forbade	forbidden
	bade	bidden	forecast	forecast	forecast
bind	bound	bound	forget	forgot	forgotten
bite	bit	bitten	forgive	forgave	forgiven
bleed	bled	bled	forsake	forsook	forsaken
blow	blew	blown	freeze	froze	frozen
break	broke	broken	get	got	got, (US)
breed	bred	bred			gotten
bring	brought	brought	give	gave	given
build	built	built	go	went	gone
burn	burnt,	burnt,	(goes)		
	burned	burned	grind	ground	ground
burst	burst	burst	grow	grew	grown
buy	bought	bought	hang	hung,	hung,
can	could	(been		hanged	hanged
		able)	have	had	had
cast	cast	cast	(has;		
catch	caught	caught	having)		
choose	chose	chosen	hear	heard	heard
cling	clung	clung	hide	hid	hidden
come	came	come	hit	hit	hit
cost	cost	cost	hold	held	held
creep	crept	crept	hurt	hurt	hurt
cut	cut	cut	keep	kept	kept
deal	dealt	dealt	kneel	knelt,	knelt,
dig	dug	dug		kneeled	kneeled
do (3rd	did	done	know	knew	known
person;			lay	laid	laid
he/she/			lead	led	led
it/does)			lean	leant,	leant,
draw	drew	drawn		leaned	leaned

present	pt	pp	present	pt	pp
leap	leapt, leaped	leapt, leaped	sink	sank	sunk
learn	learnt, learned	learnt, learned	sit	sat	sat
			slay	slew	slain
leave	left	left	sleep	slept	slept
lend	lent	lent	slide	slid	slid
let	let	let	sling	slung	slung
lie (lying)	lay	lain	slit	slit	slit
light	lit, lighted	lit, lighted	smell	smelt, smelled	smelt, smelled
lose	lost	lost	sow	sowed	sown, sowed
make	made	made	speak	spoke	spoken
may	might	—	speed	sped, speeded	sped, speeded
mean	meant	meant			
meet	met	met	spell	spelt, spelled	spelt, spelled
mistake	mistook	mistaken	spend	spent	spent
mow	mowed	mown, mowed	spill	spilt, spilled	spilt, spilled
must	(had to)	(had to)	spin	spun	spun
pay	paid	paid	spit	spat	spat
put	put	put	split	split	split
quit	quit, quitted	quit, quitted	spoil	spoiled, spoilt	spoiled, spoilt
read	read	read	spread	spread	spread
rid	rid	rid	spring	sprang	sprung
ride	rode	ridden	stand	stood	stood
ring	rang	rung	steal	stole	stolen
rise	rose	risen	stick	stuck	stuck
run	ran	run	sting	stung	stung
saw	sawed	sawn	stink	stank	stunk
say	said	said	stride	strode	stridden
see	saw	seen	strike	struck	struck, stricken
seek	sought	sought			
sell	sold	sold	strive	strove	striven
send	sent	sent	swear	swore	sworn
set	set	set	sweep	swept	swept
shake	shook	shaken	swell	swelled	swollen, swelled
shall	should	—			
shear	sheared	shorn, sheared	swim	swam	swum
shed	shed	shed	swing	swung	swung
shine	shone	shone	take	took	taken
shoot	shot	shot	teach	taught	taught
show	showed	shown	tear	tore	torn
shrink	shrank	shrunk	tell	told	told
shut	shut	shut	think	thought	thought
sing	sang	sung	throw	threw	thrown

present	pt	pp	present	pt	pp
thrust	thrust	thrust	**wed**	wedded,	wedded,
tread	trod	trodden		wed	wed
wake	woke,	woken,	**weep**	wept	wept
	waked	waked	**win**	won	won
wear	wore	worn	**wind**	wound	wound
weave	wove,	woven,	**wring**	wrung	wrung
	weaved	weaved	**write**	wrote	written

LOS NÚMEROS

NUMBERS

un, uno(a)	1	one
dos	2	two
tres	3	three
cuatro	4	four
cinco	5	five
seis	6	six
siete	7	seven
ocho	8	eight
nueve	9	nine
diez	10	ten
once	11	eleven
doce	12	twelve
trece	13	thirteen
catorce	14	fourteen
quince	15	fifteen
dieciséis	16	sixteen
diecisiete	17	seventeen
dieciocho	18	eighteen
diecinueve	19	nineteen
veinte	20	twenty
veintiuno	21	twenty-one
veintidós	22	twenty-two
treinta	30	thirty
treinta y uno(a)	31	thirty-one
treinta y dos	32	thirty-two
cuarenta	40	forty
cincuenta	50	fifty
sesenta	60	sixty
setenta	70	seventy
ochenta	80	eighty
noventa	90	ninety
cien, ciento	100	a hundred, one hundred
ciento uno(a)	101	a hundred and one
doscientos(as)	200	two hundred
doscientos(as) uno(a)	201	two hundred and one
trescientos(as)	300	three hundred
cuatrocientos(as)	400	four hundred
quinientos(as)	500	five hundred
seiscientos(as)	600	six hundred
setecientos(as)	700	seven hundred
ochocientos(as)	800	eight hundred
novecientos(as)	900	nine hundred
mil	1 000	a thousand
mil dos	1 002	a thousand and two
cinco mil	5 000	five thousand
un millón	1 000 000	a million

LOS NÚMEROS

NUMBERS

primer, primero(a), 1º, 1er (1ª, 1era)	first, 1st
segundo(a) 2º (2ª)	second, 2nd
tercer, tercero(a), 3º (3ª)	third, 3rd
cuarto(a), 4º (4ª)	fourth, 4th
quinto(a), 5º (5ª)	fifth, 5th
sexto(a), 6º (6ª)	sixth, 6th
séptimo(a)	seventh
octavo(a)	eighth
noveno(a)	ninth
décimo(a)	tenth
undécimo(a)	eleventh
duodécimo(a)	twelfth
decimotercio(a)	thirteenth
decimocuarto(a)	fourteenth
decimoquinto(a)	fifteenth
decimosexto(a)	sixteenth
vigésimo(a)	twentieth
vigésimo(a) primero(a)	twenty-first
trigésimo(a)	thirtieth
centésimo(a)	hundredth
centésimo(a) primero(a)	hundred-and-first
milésimo(a)	thousandth

Números Quebrados *etc*

Fractions *etc*

un medio	a half
un tercio	a third
un cuarto	a quarter
un quinto	a fifth
cero coma cinco, 0,5	(nought) point five, 0.5
diez por cien(to)	ten per cent

N.B. In Spanish the ordinal numbers from 1 to 10 are commonly used; from 11 to 20 rather less; above 21 they are rarely written and almost never heard in speech. The custom is to replace the forms for 21 and above by the cardinal number.

LA HORA	THE TIME
¿qué hora es?	*what time is it?*
es/son	*it's* o *it is*
medianoche, las doce (de la noche)	midnight, twelve p.m.
la una (de la madrugada)	one o'clock (in the morning), one (a.m.)
la una y cinco	five past one
la una y diez	ten past one
la una y cuarto *or* quince	a quarter past one, one fifteen
la una y veinticinco	twenty-five past one, one twenty-five
la una y media *or* treinta	half-past one, one thirty
las dos menos veinticinco, la una treinta y cinco	twenty-five to two, one thirty-five
las dos menos veinte, la una cuarenta	twenty to two, one forty
las dos menos cuarto, la una cuarenta y cinco	a quarter to two, one forty-five
las dos menos diez, la una cincuenta	ten to two, one fifty
mediodía, las doce (de la tarde)	twelve o'clock, midday, noon
la una (de la tarde)	one o'clock (in the afternoon), one (p.m.)
las siete (de la tarde)	seven o'clock (in the evening), seven (p.m.)
¿a qué hora?	*(at) what time?*
a medianoche	at midnight
a las siete	at seven o'clock
en veinte minutos	in twenty minutes
hace quince minutos	fifteen minutes ago

LA FECHA	DATES
hoy	today
todos los días	every day
ayer	yesterday
esta mañana	this morning
mañana por la noche	tomorrow night
anteanoche; antes de ayer por la noche	the night before last
antes de ayer; anteayer	the day before yesterday
anoche	last night
hace dos días/seis años	2 days/six years ago
mañana por la tarde	tomorrow afternoon
pasado mañana	the day after tomorrow
todos los jueves, el jueves	every Thursday, on Thursday
va los viernes	he goes on Fridays
"miércoles cerrado"	"closed on Wednesdays"
de lunes a viernes	from Monday to Friday
para el jueves	by Thursday
un sábado de marzo	one Saturday in March
dentro de una semana	in a week's time
dentro de dos martes	a week next/on Tuesday/Tuesday week
el domingo que viene	next Sunday
esta semana/la semana que viene/la semana pasada	this/next/last week
dentro de dos semanas	in 2 weeks or a fortnight
dentro de tres lunes	two weeks on Monday
el primer/último viernes del mes	the first/last Friday of the month
el mes que viene	next month
el año pasado	last year
el uno de junio, el primero de junio (LAM)	the 1st of June, June first
el dos de octubre	the 2nd of October, October 2nd
nací en 1987	I was born in 1987
su cumpleaños es el 6 de junio	his birthday is on June 6th (BRIT) or 6th June (US)
el 18 de agosto	on 18th August (BRIT) or August 18th (US)
en el 96	in '96
en la primavera del 94	in the Spring of '94
del 19 al 3	from the 19th to the 3rd
¿qué fecha es hoy?, ¿a cuanto estamos?	what's the date?, what date is it today?
hoy es 15, estamos a quince	today's date is the 15th, today is the 15th
mil novecientos ochenta y ocho	1988 - nineteen (hundred and) eighty-eight
hoy hace 10 años	10 years to the day
a final de mes	at the end of the month
a final de mes	at the month end (ACCOUNTS)

LA FECHA

diariamente/semanalmente/
 mensualmente
anualmente
dos veces a la semana/dos veces
 al mes/dos veces al año
dos veces al mes
en el año 2006 (dos mil seis)
4 a. de C.
79 d. de C.
en el siglo XIII
en *o* durante los (años) 80
a mediados de la década de los 70
en mil novecientos noventa y
 tantos

HEADINGS OF LETTERS

9 de octubre de 1995

DATES

daily/weekly/monthly

annually
twice a week/month/year

bi-monthly
in the year 2006
4 B.C., B.C. 4
79 A.D., A.D. 79
in the 13th century
in *or* during the 1980s
in the mid seventies
in 1990 something

9th October 1995 *or* 9 October
 1995

PESOS YE MEDIDAS
CONVERSION CHARTS

In the weight and length charts the middle figure can be either metric or imperial. Thus 3.3 feet = 1 metre, 1 foot = 0.3 metres, and so on.

feet		metres	inches		cm	lbs		kg
3.3	1	0.3	0.39	1	2.54	2.2	1	0.45
6.6	2	0.61	0.79	2	5.08	4.4	2	0.91
9.9	3	0.91	1.18	3	7.62	6.6	3	1.4
13.1	4	1.22	1.57	4	10.6	8.8	4	1.8
16.4	5	1.52	1.97	5	12.7	11.0	5	2.2
19.7	6	1.83	2.36	6	15.2	13.2	6	2.7
23.0	7	2.13	2.76	7	17.8	15.4	7	3.2
26.2	8	2.44	3.15	8	20.3	17.6	8	3.6
29.5	9	2.74	3.54	9	22.9	19.8	9	4.1
32.9	10	3.05	3.9	10	25.4	22.0	10	4.5
			4.3	11	27.9			
			4.7	12	30.1			

°C	0	5	10	15	17	20	22	24	26	28	30	35	37	38	40	50	100
°F	32	41	50	59	63	68	72	75	79	82	86	95	98.4	100	104	122	212

Km	10	20	30	40	50	60	70	80	90	100	110	120
Miles	6.2	12.4	18.6	24.9	31.0	37.3	43.5	49.7	56.0	62.0	68.3	74.6

Liquids

gallons	1.1	2.2	3.3	4.4	5.5	pints	0.44	0.88	1.76
litres	5	10	15	20	25	litres	0.25	0.5	1